SECOND EDITION

GENDER, RACE, AND CLASS IN MEDIA

SECOND EDITION

GENDER, RACE, AND CLASS IN MEDIA

A TEXT-READER

GAIL DINES
Wheelock College

JEAN M. HUMEZ
University of Massachusetts, Boston

EDITORS

SAGE Publications
International Educational and Professional Publisher
Thousand Oaks ▪ London ▪ New Delhi

For information:

Sage Publications, Inc.
2455 Teller Road
Thousand Oaks, California 91320
E-mail: order@sagepub.com

Sage Publications Ltd.
6 Bonhill Street
London EC2A 4PU
United Kingdom

Sage Publications India Pvt. Ltd.
M-32 Market
Greater Kailash I
New Delhi 110 048 India

Printed in the United States of America

Library of Congress Cataloging-in-Publication Data

Gender, race, and class in media : a text-reader / Gail Dines and Jean
M. Humez, editors.— 2nd ed.
    p. cm.
Includes bibliographical references and index.
  ISBN 0-7619-2260-1 (c) — ISBN 0-7619-2261-X (p)
 1. Mass media and culture—United States. 2. Mass media and
sex—United States. 3. Mass media and race relations—United States.
4. Social classes in mass media. 5. Mass media—Social aspects—United
States. 6. Popular culture—United States. 7. United States—Social
conditions—1980- I. Dines, Gail. II. Humez, Jean McMahon, 1944-
 P94.65.U6 G46 2002
  302.23′0973—dc21

                              2002005203

02 03 04 05 10 9 8 7 6 5 4 3 2 1

Acquiring Editor:	Margaret H. Seawell
Editorial Assistant:	Alicia Carter
Production Editor:	Claudia A. Hoffman
Copy Editor:	Kate Peterson
Typesetter:	C&M Digitals (P) Ltd.
Indexer:	Molly Hall
Cover Designer:	Michelle Lee

CONTENTS

PART II. MARKETING
A CONSUMER CULTURE

PART III. ADVERTISING AND IDENTITIES

PART IV. THE VIOLENCE DEBATES

PART VI. TV BY NIGHT

PART VII. THE INTERNET

PREFACE

In this new edition, our overall goal remains the same: to introduce undergraduate students to some of the richness, sophistication, and diversity that characterizes contemporary media scholarship in a way that is accessible and builds on students' own media experiences and interests. We intend to help demystify the nature of mass media entertainment culture by examining its industrial production, analyzing some of the most pervasive forms or genres, and exploring the processes by which audiences make meaning out of media imagery or texts—meaning that helps shape our personal, social, and political worlds.

We, the editors, are both teachers: in college-level media studies, sociology, American studies, and women's studies courses. We have designed this as a volume to help teachers (a) introduce the most powerful theoretical concepts in contemporary media studies, (b) survey some of the most influential and interesting genres of contemporary media, and (c) focus on issues of gender and sexuality, class, and race from a critical perspective. Most of the readings in this book thus take an explicitly critical or progressive political perspective. They assume, as we do, that industrialized and high-tech societies such as the United States, Western European countries, and Japan are stratified along lines of race, class, and gender; that everyone living in such a society "has" race, class, and gender, as well as other aspects of social identity that help structure our experience; and that economic and other resources, advantages, and privileges are distributed inequitably in part because of power dynamics involving these categories of experience (as well as others such as age, ethnicity, ability, or disability). We believe that a critical education should enable people to conceptualize social justice clearly and to work toward it more effectively. For us, greater social justice would mean beginning with a fairer distribution of our society's cultural and economic resources.

When we started working on the first edition of *Gender, Race, and Class in Media* in the early 1990s, cultural studies was a relatively new academic field in this country, although it had been popular for some time in England (where it originated at Birmingham University). At that time, U.S. media studies was still dominated by a social scientific, positivist approach, which tended to focus on laboratory research studies on media "effects"— measurable changes in attitudes and behavior hypothetically "caused" by exposure of experimental subjects to media texts of various kinds. This "effects" research paradigm has increasingly been challenged as overly simplistic (see Part IV for examples), and the cultural studies approach has now become dominant in U.S. media studies. Several other interdisciplinary fields concerned with social issues, such as American studies and women's studies, have also increasingly been influenced by what British cultural critic Raymond Williams has called the "baggy monster" of cultural studies.

Cultural studies is actually a multidisciplinary field, drawing from history, literary studies, philosophy, sociology, and psychology. Because of its progressive politics and because it offers a much broader and apparently more democratic definition of culture than was used in humanistic studies such as literary criticism in the past, many scholars and students who are particularly interested in race, gender, and class have been attracted to it. (For a more extended discussion of the development of multiculturalism and cultural studies in the last decades of the 20th century, see Douglas Kellner's lead chapter in Part I.)

In this second edition, we continue to emphasize, with Kellner, the three discreet but interconnected areas of analysis in a cultural studies approach to mass media entertainment: *political economy, textual analysis,* and *audience reception.* For Kellner, it is crucial to link all three areas of analysis to provide an understanding of the communication "chain" from production to consumption. Political economy looks at the ways in which texts are produced within a society marked by class, gender, and racial inequality. Questions such as who owns and controls the media, who makes the decisions about content, how financing impacts on the range of texts produced, and the ways in which the profit motive drives production are central to an understanding of what eventually gets produced and circulated in the media. Textual analysis, be it quantitative or qualitative (the latter being more popular in cultural studies) provides us with insights into how texts are structured and how to analyze their ideological significance—since media representations are never just simple "reflections of reality." However, no matter how sophisticated our textual analysis, we can never know for certain how audiences interpret, make sense of, understand and use the text. One's gender, race, ethnicity, class, sexuality, political beliefs, and age are important factors to take into account when exploring what audiences take away from an advertisement, movie, sitcom, and so on. It is only by studying all three components of media representations that we come to a better understanding of how such texts can and do strengthen or perhaps undermine or subvert systems of gender, race, and class inequality.

We have maintained our thematic focus on gender, race, and class because we believe that media studies need to address issues of social inequality that continue to plague our society and undermine its democratic potential. However, we have worked to expand the concept of race in ways that would move our thinking beyond the black-white dualism of U.S. civil rights-era history. Many of the chapters in this book that look at race necessarily include an analysis of gender and/or class. It is now widely understood that to speak of women as a unitary category or to suggest that all Chinese Americans occupy the same social location is to ignore the complexity of our experiences of social and cultural identity. We have attempted to select chapters that give voice to the multiple levels of analysis needed to make media studies a truly multicultural endeavor.

The 1990s saw the development of sophisticated studies in "critical race theory" and "postcolonial theory" that critiqued Western European and U.S. historical narratives of "progress" and "civilization" and assimilation, narratives in which the politically and culturally dominant (white) group defined the terms and projected simplicity, closeness to Nature, and a host of other less desirable characteristics upon the racial "Other." Such studies help us understand the role of "race" ideas in U.S. culture more globally, and in relation to international politics.

Similarly, the term *gender* has acquired a whole new range of associations in light of the developing field of "queer studies" in the 1990s. Much of the more recent work on gays and lesbians in the media is due to the development of queer theory that grew out of activist politics and postmodern scholarship. Queer theory questions the traditional ideas of normal and deviant by arguing against the taken-for-granted notion that there are only two genders, male and female. In queer theory, gender, sexuality, and desire are ambiguous, shifting, unstable, and too complex to fit neatly into a binary system. Drag, cross-dressing, and transgendered people illustrate how limited, and often useless, our attempts are to neatly categorize humans as male/female, gay/straight. Queer theory has thus given us a new way of thinking about gender and sexuality, and some of the chapters in this book illustrate how things that were once clear, are now queer.[1]

For the second edition, we located, read, and discussed many new journal articles and book chapters. We consulted with colleagues who teach media courses and spoke to students to see what they found compelling. More than two thirds of the readings in this second edition are new. This reflects both the rapid evolution of the field and our desire to provide analysis of relatively recent current media texts that would be familiar to students. The chapters we reprint from the first edition were instrumental in developing the field and/or offer important and clearly articulated theoretical insights into media analysis. We also include several new essays commissioned especially for this book. In our editing of published articles and newly written essays, we sought to make the often difficult analytical language of cultural studies as accessible as possible for undergraduates, while retaining the challenging ideas. We welcome comments by users of this book about our selections, about what worked well in the classroom and what did not. And we especially invite suggested articles for future editions.

For teachers who may have used the first edition, three changes in emphasis deserve a brief explanation. First, we now have two sections devoted to consumerism, marketing, and advertising (Parts II and III). This reflects our own strong convictions that a key element of critical media literacy for contemporary U.S. students is an understanding of mass media culture's commercial imperatives.

Second, we have reconfigured our treatment of sexual representation and added a new section, Part IV, which we are called "The Violence Debates." We expanded the former pornography section to deal with representations of violence in the media in general. Pornography is still featured in this section, but it is discussed as one of many types of media texts around which debate and "moral panic" cluster.

Since publication of the first edition, there have been a number of dreadful school shootings and this has reignited the violence debate. Although much of the discussion is still framed within a positivist mode, cultural studies theorists have begun to turn their attention to the effects of violence. As the chapters in Part IV show, however, there is still strong disagreement regarding the nature of media effects. We have included a range of views in order to introduce students to this debate and to illustrate the complexity involved in studying the impact of living in a society where so many mass-mediated images of mayhem and destruction may be so readily consumed by all and sundry.

Third, we have added a section on the Internet (Part VII). The Internet has changed the way we communicate, do business, buy products (including the sexual services of real and virtual women), conduct academic research, form and sustain "communities," link with like-minded people, and organize against oppressive systems. We feel, however, that within the academic community, there tends to be an overly optimistic view of the democratic potential of the Internet. One reason for this is that much of the work tends to ignore the economics of the Internet and instead focuses on the development of Internet communities.

No single collection of essays can be comprehensive in its coverage of the massive field—or more accurately, group of fields—of media studies. We have been unable to include many important areas covered in media studies courses, such as film theory and history, journalism and the news business, and popular music. But we hope that teachers and students will find the themes and genres represented in this collection provocative, stimulating, and an invitation to further thinking, research, and perhaps even media activism. We have provided a sample list of the many media activist organizations easily located on the Internet for those who, inspired by the egalitarian ideals espoused by many of the writers in this collection, would like to explore this kind of grassroots citizens' activism on behalf of a more democratic media culture in the future.

Note ◆

1. See the title of the influential book in film studies, Alexander Doty's *Making Things Perfectly Queer: Interpreting Mass Culture* (Minneapolis: University of Minnesota Press, 1993).

PART I

A CULTURAL STUDIES APPROACH TO GENDER, RACE, AND CLASS IN MEDIA

In this book, we offer a selection of critical discussions of mass media entertainment culture.[1] These discussions exemplify a powerful method of analysis that you will be able to apply on your own to other examples. In this way, we hope to promote and support media literacy.

We have divided our introductory section into two separate but connected areas, Media Theory and Gender, Race, and Class. We begin with media theory because we think students will find it useful to have a good grasp of several central concepts, introduced here, before going on to tackle later readings in which an understanding of these concepts is presumed. In the Media Theory section, we highlight especially the central concepts and terms of the field of *cultural studies* as applied to mass media: *political economy* (including global transformations in media production in relation to changing technology), *ideology*, *hegemony*, *textual analysis*, and *audience reception*. As in all the other sections in this book, there are many ways in which the collected chapters in this Part I introduction are in dialogue with one another. In these opening comments, we give only one possible reading of the ways in which their main themes connect.

◆ Media Theory

We open our Media Theory section with "Cultural Studies, Multiculturalism, and Media Culture," by Douglas Kellner (Chapter 1). This sets out the three-part approach to cultural studies (political economy/production, textual analysis, and audience reception) that informs this book. With Kellner, we believe that to understand fully a media product such as a TV show or advertising image or romance novel, one ideally needs to be able to understand the socioeconomic context in which it is created (political economy/production), analyze its constructed meaning(s) through careful attention to its particular visual/verbal/auditory languages or "codes" (textual analysis), and determine through ethnographic research what its real-world audiences contribute to the meaning-making process (audience reception). In addition, Kellner points to the importance of better integrating considerations of gender, race, and class as categories of social analysis in cultural studies work in the future.

We begin with political economy because above all, commercial entertainment is profit-oriented business, largely controlled by giant corporations. When talking about political economy, we need to foreground some crucial recent changes in global media industries, including, according to David Croteau and William Hoynes in "The New Media Giants" (Chapter 2)

1. *Growth.* Mergers and buyouts have made media corporations bigger than ever.

2. *Integration.* The new media giants have integrated either horizontally by moving into multiple forms of media, such as film, publishing, radio, and so on, or vertically by owning different stages or production and distribution, or both.

3. *Globalization.* To varying degrees, the major media conglomerates have become global entities, marketing their wares worldwide.

4. *Concentration of ownership.* As major players acquire more media holdings, the ownership of mainstream media has become increasingly concentrated.

These authors explore how developments in the wider economy in the industrialized West in recent years have affected the media industry (and vice versa). A similar point was made by George Lipsitz when looking at an earlier period, immediately after World War II through the 1950s. In "The Meaning of Memory" (Chapter 3), Lipsitz shows how the needs of the postwar U.S. economy facilitated the development of mass television production. He explores how the increase in the sale of televisions and the development of a group of situation comedies (sitcoms) were used to transform a traditional, ethnic immigrant ideology, which stressed values of community, thrift, and commitment to labor unions, into an American Dream ideology, which stressed individualism, consumerism, and suburban domesticity—values consistent with the needs of the expanding postwar capitalist economy.

Capitalist economies by definition require an ever-increasing level of consumption of goods and services, and new media technologies play a crucial role both in increasing overall consumption of media products and in changing the conditions under which consumption takes place—often helping to "domesticate" the entertainment, as in Lipsitz's example of TV sitcoms. More recently, as videotape and the VCR brought the movies into the consumer's living room, this new technology played a role in the "mainstreaming" of the formerly outlaw entertainment industry *pornography*, and this process continues today as consumer appetite for pornography has helped fuel the early growth of the Internet. At the same time, as Frank Rich argues in "Naked Capitalists" (Chapter 4), through diversification of their entertainment holdings, major companies such as Marriott Hotels are now among the purveyors of X-rated movies.

What does the rapid expansion of media technologies and products mean at a political and cultural level? One way of understanding this is provided by the neo-Marxist theory of hegemony developed by theorists such as Antonio Gramsci, Louis Althusser, and Stuart Hall, who have been highly influential in contemporary media studies. Drawing on the thought of these theorists, James Lull defines *hegemony* as "the power or dominance that one social group holds over others" (Chapter 5). As Lull points out,

> Owners and managers of media industries can produce and reproduce the content, inflections, and tones of ideas favorable to them far more easily than other social groups because they manage key socializing institutions, thereby guaranteeing that their points of view are constantly and attractively cast into the public arena.

As Douglas Kellner argues, however, even though dominant ideas held by economic and social elites are "encoded" within media texts such as sitcoms or advertisements, we cannot simply assume we know how consumers of media texts actually *decode* (construct meaning from) a given text. For that piece of the equation, we must turn to audience reception studies, such as Janice Radway's and Robin Coleman's.

Consumers of the media should not be conceptualized as mere passive pawns of media imagery controlled by the dominant culture, according to the influential concept of oppositional readings, first proposed by Stuart Hall (also discussed by Kellner in Chapter 1). The meaning of media texts cannot simply be established by one critic's decoding of the text—no matter how subtle and full—because all texts are to some degree "open" (*polysemic*, or capable of multiple meanings). Therefore, we must also seek to know how different audiences (often subcultural communities), bringing different experiences and identities to the process of reading/viewing, actually understand these texts. Specific audiences can either accept those meanings that are *preferred* by the text or produce *negotiated* or even *oppositional readings* of their own.

Janice Radway's *ethnographic* research into the audience reception of romance novels, in "Women Read the Romance" (Chapter 6), begins to add this dimension, bringing forward women's own interpretations of the role or romance reading in their lives as wives and mothers. Radway shows how one specific group of white lower-income women negotiate with the genre, both in terms of the books they select and in terms of the ways they actually read the text and appropriate its meanings. Radway acknowledges that "romance reading . . . can function as a kind of training for the all-too-common task of reinterpreting a spouse's unsettling actions as the signs of passion, devotion, and love." Yet she sees in their selection of certain books as favorites, and rejection of others, their active tendency to critique certain patriarchal masculine behaviors, substituting an ideal of the "nurturing" male that may be missing in their own family lives. Through the act of reading itself, this group of women romance readers escaped temporarily from familial demands on their time, and Radway interprets this action as potential resistance to the patriarchal restrictions of their lives. While encouraging respect for women's own experiences as cultural consumers, however, Radway warns against confusing modes of resistance that reside in textual consumption with a more real-world resistance, which might take the form of organized protest against the patriarchal abuses women meet in real life.

A more recent example of audience reception research is Coleman's study of how black audiences actually respond to black sitcoms (Chapter 7). She highlights the range of different responses, alerting us to the complexity of how audiences actually make meaning. This study reveals how the diversity and multiplicity of experience and identity within the African American community produces divergent readings of media texts. Although it might have been predicted that black viewers would "shun the characterizations, seeing absolutely no congruence between these funny men and women and their own self-image," Coleman found the actual range of reactions to be more complex. In her sample of participants, women viewers in particular were able to identify "some compatibility between the lived experiences of African Americans and that which is represented on television."

Some media theorists have begun to warn (as Kellner does) of the dangers of overemphasizing the power of media audiences to resist the ideologies encoded in dominant media texts. We would agree that audience resistance alone cannot serve as a counterbalance, nor substitute for political efforts, both to get mainstream producers to change imagery and ultimately to achieve a more democratic system of media ownership and access. But as long-term battles are being waged on the political fronts, we would also advocate taking a view of ourselves as media audiences, which is grounded in respect for our own *agency*, values, and intelligence.

◆ Gender, Race, and Class

The articles in this section apply many of the theoretical concepts isolated above to the analysis of gender, race, and class in media production, text construction, and consumption. Some media scholars tend to focus almost exclusively on theory, relegating social and political concerns to the background. However, over the years there has been a shift toward an approach that insists on the need to develop theory within an understanding of how media texts may either contribute to or undermine the inequalities that exist in postindustrialized societies like our own. The linkage of media theory and politics is particularly true within cultural studies, which is concerned with the lived experience of socially subordinate groups, and the ways in which media industries contribute to the continuation of inequalities.

Central to the project of cultural studies as it relates to analysis of gender, race, and class representations, therefore, is the concept of ideology, defined briefly in Stuart Hall's chapter, "The Whites of Their Eyes" (Chapter 8), as "those images, concepts and premises . . . through which we represent, interpret, understand and 'make sense' of some aspect of social existence." For critical media theorists, the study of ideology is intimately connected to the study of media texts, because these play a major role in producing and reproducing ideologies.

What do we mean when we say that we view gender (and sexuality), race, and class as "social constructs"? To take this approach means to reduce the explanatory role of biology or "nature" in our social arrangements and to shift our attention to the social, economic, and political forces that shape and reshape these conceptual categories over time and place. Many examples can be offered of the "instability" or artificial and shifting nature of these concepts, even from recent U.S. history.

One of the major accomplishments of late-20th-century feminism(s) has been the widespread recognition that women are "not born but made"—that the process of taking on "feminine" gender attributes begins at birth and requires intensive socialization—and that a given culture's idea of the "perfect woman" (its gender norms) can shift dramatically in response to changing economic and social conditions. (The "Rosie the Riveter" propaganda campaign during World War II, succeeded by the "just a housewife" propaganda of the postwar period and the 1950s, is one well-known example.) Even what seems the most biologically fixed of the three categories, then, gender, has had to be reconceptualized, first by *feminists* and more recently by *queer theorists*, as both unstable and multidimensional (rather than fixed by nature and binary).

Queer theory, which grew out of activist politics and *postmodern* scholarship, questions the traditional ideas of "normal" and "deviant" in the realms of gender and sexuality. Historians of sexuality have pointed out that even the words for the concepts of heterosexuality and homosexuality are only about a century old, and are the products of a "medicalized" *discourse*—a discussion produced by the new professional health fields of psychology and sexology, beginning at the end of the 19th century (D'Emilio & Freedman, 1988; Katz, 1996). Making use of this and many other new insights produced in gay and lesbian studies, queer theory argues against the taken-for-granted notion that there are only two genders, corresponding to biological maleness and biological femaleness. In queer theory, both gender and sexuality (desire) are ambiguous, shifting, unstable, and too complex to fit neatly into an either/or (binary) model. Some theorists propose locating both gender and sexuality on a continuum, like that used by the early sexologist Alfred Kinsey, to distinguish different degrees of "homosexuality" and "heterosexuality" (Schwartz & Rutter, 1998). The influential theorist Judith Butler (1999) has likened gender to a theatrical performance—a matter of role-playing, with no necessary correlation to one's biological sex. Drag, cross-dressing, and other types of transgender activities, behavior, and identities in 21st-century urban culture illustrate how limited, and often useless, are

attempts to maintain the traditionally *binary* categories masculine/feminine, gay/straight, and even male/female (Nanda, 2000; Schwartz & Rutter, 1998).

Queer theory has thus given us a new, certainly unsettling but also exciting and potentially liberating way of thinking about gender representations in popular culture (Doty, 1993). For example, from a queer theory perspective, the Barbie doll, which we usually think of as such a hyper-heterosexual feminine icon, can quite easily be read as a drag queen, as Mary Rogers does in "Hetero Barbie?" (Chapter 9). In "Popular Culture and Queer Representation" (Chapter 10), Diane Raymond offers an introductory discussion of queer theory, as well as an analysis of the limits placed on queer representation of gays and lesbians in recent TV fiction.

Hall's classic essay "The Whites of Their Eyes" (Chapter 8) brings Western *race ideologies* to the foreground by examining the role of media in constructing the meaning of "blackness." *Critical race theory* in recent years has aimed to reveal the social nature of our racial ideas—in particular by focusing on how the idea of "whiteness" evolved and functioned in the context of European and American political history. For example, in "White Negroes" (Chapter 11), Jan Pieterse reminds us that the 19th-century Irish were conceptualized as "black" by the Anglo-American elite and that the first Chinese immigrants to America were also stereotyped according to a conceptual template already worked out for African Americans. Although not denying the different histories of different peoples classified as "nonwhite," he emphasizes the similarities of their representation as inferior through dominant (white supremacist) racial ideology.

When it comes to our ideas about social *class*, we are similarly likely to presume a "natural" basis for media representations that clearly help preserve the status quo. As Richard Butsch shows in a study on television representations of the male working-class buffoon (Part VI), viewers are offered the idea that people in the "lower class" (working low-income people) are not succeeding in becoming rich because they are laughably stupid, rather than because they confront an economic and educational structure that limits class mobility. Butsch (1992) also alerts us to the possibility that "class is symbolically coded in gender terms" when working-class males are devalued in television sitcoms through being characterized with stereotypically "feminine" attributes.

As the last example suggests, cultural critics have begun to agree that gender, race, and class are most usefully understood not as discrete categories but as intertwined in complex ways. In the early days of feminist media discussions, gender analysis did not sufficiently acknowledge race and class differences among women, and it tended to generalize from the experiences of white middle- and upper-class women—other "femininities" and most "masculinities" were frequently missing from the discussion. Thankfully, media studies as a field now has a more sophisticated understanding of the interrelationships among gender, race, and class. Many of the readings in this book will acknowledge these interrelationships, discussing the way gender is "inflected by" (influenced by) race, or class by gender. In this introductory section, we include two chapters that demonstrate the ways in which gender analysis can usefully be informed by particularities of class and race.

In "Inventing the Cosmo Girl" (Chapter 12), Laurie Ouellette shows how Helen Gurley Brown, author of the best-selling *Sex and the Single Girl*, and later the editor who made *Cosmopolitan* magazine such a major success in the 1960s and 1970s, took on the cultural mission of showing working-class white women the path to upward mobility. For these white working-class women in the prefeminist 1960s, learning to fake a middle-class version of femininity was the key to real class mobility, through ensnaring a well-off man.

Even a half century later, we note, many media texts, including sitcoms, continue to reproduce this gender/class ideology. Kristal Brent Zook's "*Living Single* and the 'Fight for Mr. Right'" (Chapter 13) argues that the "desperation theme"—"the premise that the world is teeming with black women who'll do just about anything to land a single, and preferably rich, man"—is one of several "contradictory ideological forces at work in *Living Single*." Side by side with the socially conservative desperation theme, Zook identifies a highly contrasting "radical womanism" theme, embodied in "the fictional, presentational, and documentary personas of Queen Latifah."

Living Single was created by Yvette Lee Bowser, "the first African American women to create a successful prime-time series for network television," and herself a believer in a "moderate feminism," according to Zook. This ambiguous television text is a good example of the dilemmas creatively encountered by artists from nonelite backgrounds who work within media production industries still controlled by elite interests and attempt to create in these contexts "authentic" representations of the experiences of racial and sexual minorities, women, and the working poor. Imani Perry offers yet another case study, that of contemporary women hip-hop artists, in her chapter, "Who(se) Am I? The Identity and Image of Women in Hip-Hop" (Chapter 14).

Cyberspace (Internet-facilitated communication) appears to offer a new arena where nonelites can exercise some control over cultural representations of gender, race, and class. Chris Berry and Fran Martin's "Queer 'n'Asian on—and off—the Net" (Chapter 15) reports on an ethnographic study of Internet use by nonnormative sexual communities in two Asian locations. The authors explore the impact of the Internet on community building, and they argue that "the net is neither a substitute for nor an escape from real life, . . . and in the emergent queer cultures of Taiwan and South Korea, it is a particularly substantial and dynamic component."

The issues related to gender, sexuality, race, and class ideology in media culture that have been highlighted here in the Part I introduction will be important to bear in mind throughout subsequent chapters, where a wide array of media cultural forms are examined in more depth.

◆ Note

1. For many people, the term *media* makes them think immediately of the (TV) news. We do not include analysis of journalism or the news industries in this book. We are very much aware of the impact of the news industries on our cultural, political, and social lives, but we have chosen to focus this volume on media products that do not claim to play a serious role in informing or educating the public. Even in this area of pop culture mass entertainment we do not aim to be comprehensive. We do not attempt to represent film studies, for example, and we only nod at such areas as commercial pop music, sports entertainment media, and many others. Many other books amply cover areas we have had to omit.

References ◆

Butler, J. (1999). *Gender trouble: Feminism and the subversion of identity* (2nd ed.). New York: Routledge.

Butsch, R. (1992). Class and gender in four decades of television situation comedy: Plus ça change. . . . *Critical Studies in Mass Communication, 9,* 387-399.

Doty, A. (1993). *Making things perfectly queer: Interpreting mass culture.* Minneapolis: University of Minnesota Press.

D'Emilio, J., & Freedman, E. (1988). *Intimate matters: A history of sexuality in America.* New York: Harper and Row.

Katz, J. N. (1996). *The invention of heterosexuality.* New York: Plume.

Nanda, S. (2000). *Gender diversity: Cross-cultural variations.* Prospect Heights, IL: Waveland.

Schwartz, P., & Rutter, V. (1998). *The gender of sexuality.* Thousand Oaks, CA: Pine Forge.

CULTURAL STUDIES, MULTICULTURALISM, AND MEDIA CULTURE

◆ Douglas Kellner

Radio, television, film, and the other products of media culture provide materials out of which we forge our very identities; our sense of selfhood; our notion of what it means to be male or female; our sense of class, of ethnicity and race, of nationality, of sexuality; and of "us" and "them." Media images help shape our view of the world and our deepest values: what we consider good or bad, positive or negative, moral or evil. Media stories provide the symbols, myths, and resources through which we constitute a common culture and through the appropriation of which we insert ourselves into this culture. Media spectacles demonstrate who has power and who is powerless, who is allowed to exercise force and violence, and who is not. They dramatize and legitimate the power of the forces that be and show the powerless that they must stay in their places or be oppressed.

We are immersed from cradle to grave in a media and consumer society and thus it is important to learn how to understand, interpret, and criticize its meanings and messages. The media are a profound and often misperceived source of cultural pedagogy: They contribute to educating us how to behave and what to think, feel, believe, fear, and desire—and what not to. The media are forms of pedagogy that teach us how to be men and women. They show us how to dress, look, and consume; how to react to members of different social groups; how to be popular and successful and how to avoid failure; and how to conform to the dominant system of norms, values, practices, and institutions. Consequently, the gaining of critical media literacy is an important resource for individuals and citizens in learning how to cope with a seductive cultural environment. Learning how to read, criticize, and resist socio-cultural manipulation can help empower oneself in relation to dominant forms of media and culture. It can enhance individual sovereignty vis-à-vis media culture and give people more power over their cultural environment.

In this chapter, I will discuss the potential contributions of a cultural studies perspective to media critique and literacy. In recent years, cultural studies has emerged as a set of approaches to the study of culture and society. The project was inaugurated by the University of Birmingham Centre for Contemporary Cultural Studies, which developed a variety of critical methods for the analysis, interpretation, and criticism of cultural artifacts.[1] Through a set of internal debates, and responding to social struggles and movements of the 1960s and the 1970s, the Birmingham group came to focus on the interplay of representations and ideologies of class, gender, race, ethnicity, and nationality in cultural texts, including media culture. They were among the first to study the effects of newspapers, radio, television, film, and other popular cultural forms on audiences. They also focused on how various audiences interpreted and used media culture differently, analyzing the factors that made different audiences respond in contrasting ways to various media texts.

Through studies of youth subcultures, British cultural studies demonstrated how culture came to constitute distinct forms of identity and group membership. For cultural studies, media culture provides the materials for constructing views of the world, behavior, and even identities. Those who uncritically follow the dictates of media culture tend to "mainstream" themselves, conforming to the dominant fashion, values, and behavior. Yet cultural studies is also interested in how subcultural groups and individuals resist dominant forms of culture and identity, creating their own style and identities. Those who obey ruling dress and fashion codes, behavior, and political ideologies thus produce their identities within the mainstream group, as members of specific social groupings (such as white, middle-class conservative Americans). Persons who identify with subcultures, like punk culture, or black nationalist subcultures, look and act differently from those in the mainstream, and thus create oppositional identities, defining themselves against standard models.

Cultural studies insists that culture must be studied within the social relations and system through which it is produced and consumed and that thus study of culture is intimately bound up with the study of society, politics, and economics. Cultural studies shows how media culture articulates the dominant values, political ideologies, and social developments and novelties of the era. It conceives of U.S. culture and society as a contested terrain with various groups and ideologies struggling for dominance (Kellner, 1995). Television, film, music, and other popular cultural forms are thus often liberal or conservative, although they occasionally articulate more radical or oppositional positions and are often ideologically ambiguous, combining various political positions.

Cultural studies is valuable because it provides some tools that enable one to read and interpret one's culture critically. It also subverts distinctions between "high" and "low" culture by considering a wide continuum of cultural artifacts ranging from novels to television and by refusing to erect any specific cultural hierarchies or canons. Previous approaches to culture tended to be primarily literary and elitist, dismissing media culture as banal, trashy, and not worthy of serious attention. The project of cultural studies, by contrast, avoids cutting the field of culture into high and low, or popular against elite. Such distinctions are difficult to maintain and generally serve as a front for normative aesthetic valuations and, often, a political program (i.e., either dismissing mass culture for high culture, or celebrating what is deemed "popular" while scorning "elitist" high culture).

Cultural studies allows us to examine and critically scrutinize the whole range of culture without prior prejudices toward one or another sort of cultural text, institution, or practice. It also opens the way toward more differentiated political, rather than aesthetic, valuations of cultural artifacts in which one attempts to distinguish critical and oppositional from conformist and conservative moments in a cultural artifact. For instance, studies of Hollywood film show how key 1960s films promoted the views of radicals and the counterculture and how film in the 1970s was a battleground between liberal and conservative positions; late 1970s films, however, tended toward conservative positions that helped elect Ronald Reagan as president (see Kellner & Ryan, 1988).

There is an intrinsically critical and political dimension to the project of cultural studies that distinguishes it from objectivist and apolitical academic approaches to the study of culture and society. British cultural studies, for example, analyzed culture historically in the context of its societal origins and effects. It situated culture within a theory of social production and reproduction, specifying the ways that cultural forms served either to further social domination or to enable people to resist and struggle against domination. It analyzed society as a hierarchical and antagonistic set of social relations characterized by the oppression of subordinate class, gender, race, ethnic, and national strata. Employing Gramsci's (1971) model of hegemony and counterhegemony, it sought to analyze "hegemonic," or ruling, social and cultural forces of domination and to seek "counterhegemonic" forces of resistance and struggle. The project was aimed at social transformation and attempted to specify forces of domination and resistance in order to aid the process of political struggle and emancipation from oppression and domination.

For cultural studies, the concept of ideology is of central importance, for dominant ideologies serve to reproduce social relations of domination and subordination.[2] Ideologies of class, for instance, celebrate upper-class life and denigrate the working class. Ideologies of gender promote sexist representations of women and ideologies of race utilize racist representations of people of color and various minority groups. Ideologies make inequalities and subordination appear natural and just, and thus induce consent to relations of domination. Contemporary societies are structured by opposing groups who have different political ideologies (liberal, conservative, radical, etc.) and cultural studies specifies what, if any, ideologies are operative in a given cultural artifact (which could involve, of course, the specification of ideological contradictions). In the course of this study, I will provide some examples of how different ideologies are operative in media cultural texts and will accordingly provide examples of ideological analysis and critique.

Because of its focus on representations of race, gender, and class, and its critique of ideologies that promote various forms of oppression, cultural studies lends itself to a multiculturalist program that demonstrates how culture reproduces certain forms of racism, sexism, and biases against members of subordinate classes, social groups, or alternative lifestyles. Multiculturalism affirms the worth of different types of culture and cultural groups, claiming, for instance, that black, Latino, Asian, Native American, gay and lesbian, and other oppressed and marginal voices have their own validity and importance. An insurgent multiculturalism attempts to show how various people's voices and experiences are silenced and omitted from mainstream culture and struggles to aid in the articulation of diverse views, experiences, and cultural forms, from groups excluded from the mainstream. This makes it a target of conservative forces who wish to preserve the existing canons of white male, Eurocentric privilege and thus attack multiculturalism in cultural wars raging from the 1960s to the present over education, the arts, and the limits of free expression.

Cultural studies thus promotes a multiculturalist politics and media pedagogy that aims to make people sensitive to how relations of power and domination are "encoded" in cultural texts, such as those of television or film. But it also specifies how people can resist the dominant encoded meanings and produce their own critical and alternative readings. Cultural studies can show how media culture manipulates and indoctrinates us, and thus can empower individuals to resist the dominant meanings in media cultural products and to produce their own meanings. It can also point to moments of resistance and criticism within media culture and thus help promote development of more critical consciousness.

A critical cultural studies—embodied in many of the chapters collected in this reader—thus develops concepts and analyses that will enable readers to analytically dissect the artifacts of contemporary media culture and to gain power over their cultural environment. By exposing the entire field of culture to knowledgeable scrutiny, cultural studies provides a broad, comprehensive framework to undertake studies of culture, politics, and society for the purposes of individual empowerment and social and political struggle and transformation. In the following pages, I will therefore indicate some of the chief components of the type of cultural studies that I find most useful.

◆ Components of a Critical Cultural Studies

At its strongest, cultural studies contains a threefold project of analyzing the production and political economy of culture, cultural texts, and the audience reception of those texts and their effects. This comprehensive approach avoids too narrowly focusing on one dimension of the project to the exclusion of others. To avoid such limitations, I would thus propose a multiperspectival approach that (a) discusses production and political economy, (b) engages in textual analysis, and (c) studies the reception and use of cultural texts.[3]

PRODUCTION AND POLITICAL ECONOMY

Because it has been neglected in many modes of recent cultural studies, it is important to stress the importance of analyzing cultural texts within their system of production and distribution, often referred to as the political economy of culture.[4] Inserting texts into the system of culture within which they are produced and distributed can help elucidate features and effects of the texts that textual analysis alone might miss or downplay. Rather than being antithetical approaches to culture, political economy can actually contribute to textual analysis and critique. The system of production often determines what sort of artifacts will be produced, what structural limits there will be as to what can and cannot be said and shown, and what sort of audience effects the text may generate.

Study of the codes of television, film, or popular music, for instance, is enhanced by studying the formulas and conventions of production. These cultural forms are structured by well-defined rules and conventions, and the study of the production of culture can help elucidate the codes actually in play. Because of the demands of the format of radio or music television, for instance, most popular songs are three to five minutes, fitting into the frames of the distribution system. Because of their control by giant corporations oriented primarily toward profit, film and television production in the United States is dominated by specific genres such as talk and game shows, soap operas, situation comedies, action/adventure series, reality TV, and so on. This economic factor explains why there are cycles of certain genres and sub-genres, sequelmania in the film industry, crossovers of popular films into television series, and a certain homogeneity in products constituted within systems of production marked by rigid generic codes, formulaic conventions, and well-defined ideological boundaries.

Likewise, study of political economy can help determine the limits and range of political and ideological discourses and effects. My study of television in the United States, for instance, disclosed that takeover of the television networks by major transnational corporations and communications conglomerates was part of a "right turn" within U.S. society in the 1980s whereby powerful corporate groups won control of the state and the mainstream media (Kellner, 1990). For example, during the 1980s all three networks were taken over by major corporate conglomerates: ABC was bought out in 1985 by Capital Cities, NBC was absorbed by GE, and CBS was purchased by the Tisch Financial Group. Both ABC and NBC sought corporate mergers and this motivation, along with other benefits derived from Reaganism, might well have influenced them to downplay criticisms of Reagan and to generally support his conservative programs, military adventures, and simulated presidency.

Corporate conglomeratization has intensified further and today AOL and Time Warner, Disney, and other global media conglomerates control ever more domains of the production and distribution of culture (McChesney, 2000). In this global context, one cannot really analyze the role of the media in the Gulf war, for instance, without analyzing the production and political economy of news and information, as well as the actual text of the Gulf war and its reception by its audience (see Kellner, 1992). Likewise, the ownership by conservative corporations of dominant media corporations helps explain mainstream media support of the Bush administration and their policies, such as the 2000 U.S. presidential election (Kellner, 2001).

Looking toward entertainment, one cannot fully grasp the Madonna phenomenon without analyzing her marketing strategies, her political environment, her cultural artifacts, and their effects (Kellner, 1995). In a similar fashion, younger female pop music stars and groups such as Mariah Carey, Britney Spears, Jennifer Lopez, or N'Sync also deploy the tools of the glamour industry and media spectacle to make certain stars the icons of fashion, beauty, style, and sexuality, as well as purveyors of music. And in appraising the full social impact of pornography, one needs to be aware of the sex industry and the production process of, say, pornographic films, and not just dwell on the texts themselves and their effects on audiences.

Furthermore, in an era of globalization, one must be aware of the global networks that produce and distribute media culture in the interests of profit and corporate hegemony. Yet political economy alone does not hold the key to cultural studies and important as it is, it has limitations as a single approach. Some political economy analyses reduce the meanings and effects of texts to rather circumscribed and reductive ideological functions, arguing that media culture merely reflects the ideology of the ruling economic elite that controls the culture industries and is nothing more than a vehicle for capitalist ideology. It is true that media culture overwhelmingly supports capitalist values, but it is also a site of intense struggle between different races, classes, gender, and social groups. Thus, in order to fully grasp the nature and effects of media culture, one needs to develop methods to analyze the full range of its meanings and effects.

TEXTUAL ANALYSIS

The products of media culture require multidimensional close textual readings to analyze their various forms of discourses, ideological positions, narrative strategies, image construction, and effects. There have been a wide range of types of textual criticism of media culture, ranging from quantitative content analysis that dissects the number of, say, episodes of violence in a text, to qualitative study that examines images of women, blacks, or other groups, or that applies various critical theories to unpack the meanings of the texts or to explicate how texts function to produce meaning. Traditionally, the qualitative analysis of texts has been the task of formalist literary criticism, which explicates the central meanings, values, symbols, and ideologies in cultural artifacts by attending to the formal properties of imaginative literature texts—such as style, verbal imagery, characterization, narrative structure and point of view, and other formal elements of the artifact. From the 1960s on, however, literary-formalist textual analysis has been enhanced by methods derived from semiotics, a critical approach for investigating the creation of meaning not only in written languages but also in other, nonverbal codes, such as the visual and auditory languages of film and TV.

Semiotics analyzes how linguistic and nonlinguistic cultural "signs" form systems of meanings, as when giving someone a rose is interpreted as a sign of love, or getting an A on a college paper is a sign of mastery of the rules of the specific assignment. Semiotic analysis can be connected with genre criticism (the study of conventions governing established types of cultural forms, such as soap operas) to reveal how the codes and forms of particular genres follow certain meanings. Situation comedies, for instance, classically follow a conflict/resolution model that demonstrates how to solve certain social problems by correct actions and values, and thus provide morality tales of proper and improper behavior. Soap operas, by contrast, proliferate problems and provide messages concerning the endurance and suffering needed to get through life's endless miseries, while

generating positive and negative models of social behavior. And advertising shows how commodity solutions solve problems of popularity, acceptance, success, and the like.

A semiotic and genre analysis of the film *Rambo* (1982) for instance, would show how it follows the conventions of the Hollywood genre of the war film that dramatizes conflicts between the United States and its "enemies" (see Kellner, 1995). Semiotics describes how the images of the villains are constructed according to the codes of World War II movies and how the resolution of the conflict and happy ending follows the traditional Hollywood classical cinema, which portrays the victory of good over evil. Semiotic analysis would also include study of the strictly cinematic and formal elements of a film like *Rambo*, dissecting the ways that camera angles present Rambo as a god, or slow-motion images of him gliding through the jungle code him as a force of nature. Semiotic analysis of the 2001 film *Vanilla Sky* could engage how Cameron Crowe's film presents a remake of a 1997 Spanish film, and how the use of celebrity stars Tom Cruise and Penelope Cruz, involved in a real-life romance, provides a spectacle of modern icons of beauty, desire, sexuality, and power. The science fiction theme and images present semiotic depictions of a future in which technoscience can make everyone beautiful and we can live out our culture's dreams and nightmares.

The textual analysis of cultural studies thus combines formalist analysis with critique of how cultural meanings convey specific ideologies of gender, race, class, sexuality, nation, and other ideological dimensions. Ideological textual analysis should deploy a wide range of methods to fully explicate each dimension and to show how they fit into textual systems. Each critical method focuses on certain features of a text from a specific perspective: The perspective spotlights some features of a text while ignoring others. Marxist methods tend to focus on class, for instance, while feminist approaches will highlight gender, critical race theory spotlights race and ethnicity, and gay and lesbian theories explicate sexuality.

More sophisticated critical Marxism, feminisms, or semiotics articulate their own method with the other approaches to develop multiperspectivist positions. Yet each critical methods on its own has its particular strengths and limitations, with specific optics and blindspots. Traditionally, Marxian ideology critiques have been strong on class and historical contextualization and weak on formal analysis, while some versions are highly "reductionist," reducing textual analysis to denunciation of ruling class ideology. Feminism excels in gender analysis and in some versions is formally sophisticated, drawing on such methods as psychoanalysis and semiotics, although some versions are reductive and early feminism often limited itself to analysis of images of gender. Psychoanalysis in turn calls for the interpretation of unconscious contents and meaning, which can articulate latent meanings in a text, as when Alfred Hitchcock's dream sequences in films like *Spellbound* (1945) or *Vertigo* (1958) project cinematic symbols that illuminate his characters' dilemmas, or when the image of the female character in *Bonnie and Clyde* (1967) framed against the bars of her bed suggests her sexual frustration, imprisonment in lower-middle-class family life, and need for revolt.

Of course, each reading of a text is only one possible reading from one critic's subject position, no matter how multiperspectival, and may or may not be the reading preferred by audiences (which themselves will be significantly different according to their class, race, gender, ethnicity, ideologies, and so on). Because there is a split between textual encoding and audience decoding, there is always the possibility of a multiplicity of readings of any text of media culture (Hall, 1980b). There are limits to the openness or polysemic nature of any text, of course, and textual analysis can explicate the parameters of possible readings and delineate perspectives that aim at illuminating the text and its cultural and ideological effects. Such analysis also provides the materials for criticizing misreadings, or readings that are one-sided and incomplete. Yet to further carry through a cultural studies analysis, one must also examine how diverse audiences actually read media texts, and attempt to determine what effects they have on audience thought and behavior.

Audience Reception ◆ and Use of Media Culture

All texts are subject to multiple readings depending on the perspectives and subject positions of the reader. Members of distinct genders, classes, races, nations, regions, sexual preferences, and political ideologies are going to read texts differently, and cultural studies can illuminate why diverse audiences interpret texts in various, sometimes conflicting, ways. It is indeed one of the merits of cultural studies to have focused on audience reception in recent years and this focus provides one of its major contributions, though there are also some limitations and problems with the standard cultural studies approaches to the audience.[5]

A standard way to discover how audiences read texts is to engage in ethnographic research, in an attempt to determine how texts affect audiences and shape their beliefs and behavior. Ethnographic cultural studies have indicated some of the various ways that audiences use and appropriate texts, often to empower themselves. Radway's (1983; see also her chapter in this volume) study of women's use of Harlequin novels, for example, shows how these books provide escapism for women and could be understood as reproducing traditional women's roles, behavior, and attitudes. Yet they can also empower women by promoting fantasies of a different life and may thus inspire revolt against male domination. Or they may enforce, in other audiences, female submission to male domination and trap women in ideologies of romance, in which submission to Prince Charming is seen as the alpha and omega of happiness for women.

Media culture provides materials for individuals to create identities and meanings and cultural studies detects specific ways that individuals use cultural forms. Teenagers use video games and music television as an escape from the demands of a disciplinary society. Males use sports as a terrain of fantasy identification, in which they feel empowered as "their" team or star triumphs. Such sports events also generate a form of community, currently being lost in the privatized media and consumer culture of our time. Indeed, fandoms of all sorts, ranging from *Star Trek* fans ("Trekkies") to devotees of *Buffy the Vampire Slayer*, or various soap operas, also form communities that enable people to relate to others who share their interests and hobbies. Some fans, in fact, actively recreate their favorite cultural forms, such as rewriting the scripts of preferred shows, sometimes in the forms of "slash," which redefine characters' sexuality, or in the forms of music poaching or remaking such as "filking" (see examples in Lewis, 1992, and Jenkins, 1992).

This emphasis on audience reception and appropriation helps cultural studies overcome the previous one-sided textualist orientations to culture. It also directs focus on the actual political effects that texts have and how audiences use texts. In fact, sometimes audiences subvert the intentions of the producers or managers of the cultural industries that supply them, as when astute young media users laugh at obvious attempts to hype certain characters, shows, or products (see de Certeau, 1984, for more examples of audiences constructing meaning and engaging in practices in critical and subversive ways). Audience research can reveal how people are actually using cultural texts and what sort of effects they are having on everyday life. Combining quantitative and qualitative research, new reception studies, including some of the essays in this reader, are providing important contributions into how audiences actually interact with cultural texts (see the studies in Lewis, 1992, and Ang, 1996, and Lee and Cho in this volume for further elaboration of decoding and audience reception).

Yet there are several problems that I see with reception studies as they have been constituted within cultural studies, particularly in the United States. First, there is a danger that class will be downplayed as a significant variable that structures audience decoding and use of cultural texts. Cultural studies in England were particularly sensitive to class differences—as well as subcultural differences—in the use and reception of cultural texts, but I have noted many dissertations, books, and articles in cultural studies in the United States where attention to class has been downplayed or is missing altogether. This is not surprising as a neglect of class as a constitutive feature of culture and society is an endemic deficiency in the American academy in most disciplines.

There is also the reverse danger, however, of exaggerating the constitutive force of class, and downplaying, or ignoring, such other variables as gender or ethnicity. Staiger (1992) notes that Fiske (1989a, 1989b), building on Hartley, lists seven "subjectivity positions" that are important in cultural reception, "self, gender, age-group, family, class, nation, ethnicity," and proposes adding sexual orientation. All of these factors, and no doubt more, interact in shaping how audiences receive and use texts and must be taken into account in studying cultural reception, for audiences decode and use texts according to the specific constituents of their class, race or ethnicity, gender, sexual preferences, and so on.

Furthermore, I would warn against a tendency to romanticize the "active audience," by claiming that all audiences produce their own meanings and denying that media culture may have powerful manipulative effects. Some individuals who do cultural studies (tradition of) reception research distinguish between dominant and oppositional readings (Hall, 1980b), a dichotomy that structures much of Fiske's work. "Dominant" readings are those in which audiences appropriate texts in line with the interests of the hegemonic culture and the ideological intentions of a text, as when audiences feel pleasure in the restoration of male power, law and order, and social stability at the end of a film like *Die Hard*, after the hero and representatives of authority eliminate the terrorists who had taken over a high-rise corporate headquarters. An "oppositional" reading, by contrast, celebrates the resistance to this reading in audience appropriation of a text; for example, Fiske (1993) observes resistance to dominant readings when homeless individuals in a shelter cheered the destruction of police and authority figures, during repeated viewings of a videotape of *Die Hard*.

Although this can be a useful distinction, there is a tendency in cultural studies to celebrate resistance per se without distinguishing between types and forms of resistance (a similar problem resides with indiscriminate celebration of audience pleasure in certain reception studies). For example, resistance to social authority by the homeless evidenced in their viewing of *Die Hard* could serve to strengthen brutal masculist behavior and encourage manifestations of physical violence to solve social problems. Jean-Paul Sartre, Frantz Fanon, and Herbert Marcuse, among others, have argued that violence can be either emancipatory, when directed at forces of oppression, or reactionary, when directed at popular forces struggling against oppression. Many feminists, by contrast, or those in the Gandhian tradition, see all violence as forms of brute masculist behavior and many people see it as a problematical form of conflict resolution. Resistance and pleasure cannot therefore be valorized per se as progressive elements of the appropriation of cultural texts, but difficult discriminations must be made as to whether the resistance,

oppositional reading, or pleasure in a given experience is progressive or reactionary, emancipatory or destructive.

Thus, while emphasis on the audience and reception was an excellent correction to the one-sidedness of purely textual analysis, I believe that in recent years cultural studies has overemphasized reception and textual analysis, while underemphasizing the production of culture and its political economy. This type of cultural studies fetishizes audience reception studies and neglects both production and textual analysis, thus producing populist celebrations of the text and audience pleasure in its use of cultural artifacts. This approach, taken to an extreme, would lose its critical perspective and would lead to a positive gloss on audience experience of whatever is being studied. Such studies also might lose sight of the manipulative and conservative effects of certain types of media culture and thus serve the interests of the cultural industries as they are presently constituted.

A new way, in fact, to research media effects is to use the databases that collect media texts such as Nexis/Lexis, or search engines like Google, and to trace the effects of media artifacts like *The X-Files*, *Buffy the Vampire Slayer*, or advertising corporations like Nike and McDonald's, through analysis of references to them in the media. Likewise, there is a new terrain of Internet audience research that studies how fans act in chat rooms devoted to their favorite artifacts of media culture, create their own fansites, or construct artifacts that disclose how they are living out the fantasies and scripts of the culture industries. Previous studies of the audience and the reception of media privileged ethnographic studies that selected slices of the vast media audiences, usually from the site where researchers themselves lived. Such studies are invariably limited and broader effects research can indicate how the most popular artifacts of media culture have a wide range of effects. In my book *Media Culture* (1995), I studied some examples of popular cultural artifacts that clearly influenced behavior in audiences throughout the globe. Examples include groups of kids and adults who imitated Rambo in various forms of asocial behavior, or fans of *Beavis and Butt-Head* who started fires or tortured animals in the modes practiced by the popular MTV cartoon characters. Media effects are complex and controversial and it is the merit of cultural studies to make their study an important part of its agenda.

◆ Toward a Cultural Studies Approach That Is Critical, Multicultural, and Multiperspectival

To avoid the one-sidedness of textual analysis approaches, or audience and reception studies, I propose that cultural studies itself be multiperspectival, getting at culture from the perspectives of political economy, text analysis, and audience reception, as outlined above. Textual analysis should utilize a multiplicity of perspectives and critical methods, and audience reception studies should delineate the wide range of subject positions, or perspectives, through which audiences appropriate culture. This requires a multicultural approach that sees the importance of analyzing the dimensions of class, race and ethnicity, and gender and sexual preference within the texts of media culture, while studying as well their impact on how audiences read and interpret media culture.

In addition, a critical cultural studies attacks sexism, racism, or bias against specific social groups (i.e., gays, intellectuals, and so on), and criticizes texts that promote any kind of domination or oppression. As an example of how considerations of production, textual analysis, and audience readings can fruitfully intersect in cultural studies, let us reflect on the Madonna phenomenon. Madonna first appeared in the moment of Reaganism and embodied the materialistic and consumer-oriented ethos of the 1980s ("Material Girl"). She also appeared in a time of dramatic image proliferation, associated with MTV, fashion fever, and intense marketing of products. Madonna was one of the first MTV music video superstars who consciously crafted images to attract a mass audience. Her early music videos were aimed at teenage girls (the Madonna wanna-be's), but she soon incorporated black, Hispanic, and minority audiences with her images of interracial sex and multicultural "family" in her concerts. Madonna also appealed to gay and lesbian audiences, as well as to feminist and academic audiences, as her videos became more complex and political (i.e., "Like a Prayer," "Express Yourself," "Vogue," and so on).

Thus, Madonna's popularity was in large part a function of her marketing strategies and her production of music videos and images that appealed to diverse audiences. To conceptualize the meanings and effects in her music, films, concerts, and public relations stunts requires that her artifacts be interpreted within the context of their production and reception, which involves discussion of MTV, the music industry, concerts, marketing, and the production of images (see Kellner, 1995). Understanding Madonna's popularity also requires focus on audiences, not just as individuals but as members of specific groups, such as teenage girls, who were empowered in their struggles for individual identity by Madonna, or gays, who were also empowered by her incorporation of alternative images of sexuality within popular mainstream cultural artifacts. Yet appraising the politics and effects of Madonna also requires analysis of how her work might merely reproduce a consumer culture that defines identity in terms of images and consumption. It would make an interesting project to examine how former Madonna fans view the evolution and recent incarnations of the superstar, such as her second marriage and 2001 Drowned World tour, as well as to examine how contemporary fans view Madonna in an age that embraces younger teen pop singers like Britney Spears or Mariah Carey.

In short, a cultural studies that is critical and multicultural provides comprehensive approaches to culture that can be applied to a wide variety of artifacts from pornography to Madonna, from MTV to TV news, or to specific events like the 2000 U.S. presidential election (Kellner, 2001), or media representations of the 2001 terrorist attacks on the United States and the U.S. response. Its comprehensive perspectives encompass political economy, textual analysis, and audience research and provide critical and political perspectives that enable individuals to dissect the meanings, messages, and effects of dominant cultural forms. Cultural studies is thus part of a critical media pedagogy that enables individuals to resist media manipulation and to increase their freedom and individuality. It can empower people to gain sovereignty over their culture and to be able to struggle for alternative cultures and political change. Cultural studies is thus not just another academic fad, but can be part of a struggle for a better society and a better life.

◆ Notes

1. For more information on British cultural studies, see Hall (1980b), Hall et al. (1980), Johnson (1986/1987), Fiske (1986), O'Conner (1989), Turner (1990), Grossberg (1989), Agger (1992), and the articles collected in Grossberg, Nelson, and Triechler (1992), During (1992, 1998), and Durham and Kellner (2000). I might note that the Frankfurt school also provided much material for a critical cultural studies in their works on mass culture from the 1930s through the present; on the relation between the Frankfurt school and British cultural studies, see Kellner (1997).

2. On the concept of ideology, see Kellner (1978, 1979), Centre for Contemporary Cultural Studies (1980), Kellner and Ryan (1988), and Thompson (1990).

3. This model was adumbrated in Hall (1980a) and Johnson (1986/1987) and guided much of the early Birmingham work. Around the mid-1980s, however, the Birmingham group began to increasingly neglect the production and political economy of culture (some believe that this was always a problem with their work) and much of their studies became more academic, cut off from political struggle. I am thus trying to recapture the spirit of the early Birmingham project, reconstructed for our contemporary moment. For a fuller development of my conception of cultural studies, see Kellner (1992, 1995, 2001).

4. The term *political economy* calls attention to the fact that the production and distribution of culture take place within a specific economic system, constituted by relations between the state and economy. For instance, in the United States a capitalist economy dictates that cultural production is governed by laws of the market, but the democratic imperatives of the system mean that there is some regulation of culture by the state. There are often tensions within a given society concerning how many activities should be governed by the imperatives of the market, or economics, alone and how much state regulation or intervention is desirable, to assure a wider diversity of broadcast programming, for instance, or the prohibition of phenomena agreed to be harmful, such as cigarette advertising or pornography (see Kellner, 1990).

5. Cultural studies that have focused on audience reception include Brunsdon and Morley (1978), Radway (1983), Ang (1985, 1996), Morley (1986), Fiske (1989a, 1989b), Jenkins (1992), and Lewis (1992).

References ◆

Agger, B. (1992). *Cultural studies*. London: Falmer.

Ang, I. (1985). *Watching* Dallas. New York: Methuen.

Ang, I. (1996). *Living room wars: Rethinking media audiences for a postmodern world*. London and New York: Routledge.

Brunsdon, C., & Morley, D. (1978). *Everyday television: "Nationwide."* London: British Film Institute.

Centre for Contemporary Cultural Studies. (1980). *On ideology.* London: Hutchinson.

de Certeau, M. (1984). *The practice of everyday life.* Berkeley: University of California Press.

Durham, M. G., & Kellner, D. (Eds.). (2001). *Media and cultural studies: Keyworks.* Malden, MA, and Oxford, UK: Basil Blackwell.

During, S. (1992). *Cultural studies.* London and New York: Routledge.

During, S. (1998). *Cultural studies* (2nd ed.). London and New York: Routledge.

Fiske, J. (1986). British cultural studies and television. In R. C. Allen (Ed.), *Channels of discourse* (pp. 254-289). Chapel Hill: University of North Carolina Press.

Fiske, J. (1987). *Television culture.* New York and London: Routledge.

Fiske, J. (1989a). *Reading the popular.* Boston: Unwin Hyman.

Fiske, J. (1989b). *Understanding popular culture.* Boston: Unwin Hyman.

Fiske, J. (1993). *Power plays, power works.* London: Verso.

Gramsci, A. (1971). *Selections from the prison notebooks.* New York: International.

Grossberg, L. (1989). The formations of cultural studies: An American in Birmingham. *Strategies, 22,* 114-149.

Grossberg, L., Nelson, C., & Treichler, P. (1992). *Cultural studies.* New York: Routledge.

Hall, S. (1980a). Cultural studies and the Centre: Some problematics and problems. In S. Hall et al., *Culture, media, language* (pp. 15-47). London: Hutchinson.

Hall, S. (1980b). Encoding/decoding. In S. Hall et al., *Culture, media, language* (pp. 128-138). London: Hutchinson.

Hall, S. et al. (1980). *Culture, media, language.* London: Hutchinson.

Jenkins, H. (1992). *Textual poachers.* New York: Routledge.

Johnson, R. (1986/1987). What is cultural studies anyway? *Social Text, 16,* 38-80.

Kellner, D. (1978, November-December). Ideology, Marxism, and advanced capitalism. *Socialist Review, 42,* 37-65.

Kellner, D. (1979, May-June). TV, ideology, and emancipatory popular culture. *Socialist Review, 45,* 13-53.

Kellner, D. (1990). *Television and the crisis of democracy.* Boulder, CO: Westview.

Kellner, D. (1992). *The Persian Gulf TV war.* Boulder, CO: Westview.

Kellner, D. (1995). *Media culture. Cultural studies, identity, and politics between the modern and the postmodern.* London and New York: Routledge.

Kellner, D. (1997). Critical theory and British cultural studies: The missed articulation. In J. McGuigan (Ed.), *Cultural methodologies* (pp. 12-41). London: Sage.

Kellner, D. (2001). *Grand theft 2000.* Lanham, MD: Rowman & Littlefield.

Kellner, D., & Ryan, M. (1988). *Camera politica: The politics and ideology of contemporary Hollywood film.* Bloomington: Indiana University Press.

Lewis, L. A. (1992). *Adoring audience: Fan culture and popular media.* New York: Routledge.

McChesney, R. (2000). *Rich media, poor democracy: Communications politics in dubious times.* New York: New Press.

Morley, D. (1986). *Family television.* London: Comedia.

O'Connor, A. (1989, December). The problem of American cultural studies. *Critical Studies in Mass Communication,* pp. 405-413.

Radway, J. (1983). *Reading the romance.* Chapel Hill: University of North Carolina Press.

Staiger, J. (1992). Film, reception, and cultural studies. *Centennial Review, 26*(1), 89-104.

Thompson, J. (1990). *Ideology and modern culture.* Cambridge, UK, and Stanford, CA: Polity Press and Stanford University Press.

Turner, G. (1990). *British cultural studies: An introduction.* New York: Unwin Hyman.

THE NEW MEDIA GIANTS

Changing Industry Structure

◆ David Croteau and William Hoynes

In September of 1999, Viacom announced its merger with CBS.[1] The huge deal combined CBS's television network, its 15 TV stations, more than 160 radio stations, and several Internet sites with Viacom's well-known cable channels (e.g., MTV, Nickelodeon, Showtime, TNN), 19 television stations, movie and television production (Paramount Pictures, UPN), publishing (Simon & Schuster), theme parks, and more. The $38 billion merger was bigger than any previous deal between two media companies. In fact, it was almost double the size of the previous record. The 1995 record-setting deal in which Disney acquired Capital Cities/ABC had been worth $19 billion [$21.2 billion].

While the size of the Viacom/CBS deal was unprecedented, the basic dynamic underlying the merger was not. Since the mid-1980s, major media companies had been engaged in a feeding frenzy, swallowing up other media firms to form ever-larger conglomerates. Including the Viacom/CBS merger, the 1990s alone saw well over $300 billion in major media deals. So rather than being unique, the Viacom/CBS announcement was just

NOTE: From *The Business of Media: Corporate Media and the Public Interest* (pp. 71-107), by David Croteau and William Hoynes, 2001, Thousand Oaks, CA: Pine Forge. Copyright 2001. Reprinted by permission of Sage Publications, Inc.

another example—and certainly not the last—of the mergers that transformed the industry toward the end of the 20th century.

These deals not only changed the media industry playing field but also sometimes made it difficult to figure out who, exactly, were the players. While media mergers and acquisitions had been mostly between media companies, there were also non-media companies who ventured into the lucrative media market. In 1985, manufacturing giant General Electric bought RCA—owners of the NBC broadcast network. Westinghouse—producer of everything from household appliances to components for nuclear reactors—bought CBS in 1995. Three years later, the combined company dropped the Westinghouse name in favor of CBS Corporation and then proceeded to sell off the manufacturing parts of the conglomerate—in essence splitting back into two companies. Seagram's, best known for its alcoholic drinks and Tropicana orange juice, became a major media company, buying MCA in 1995 (now Universal Studios), Polygram records in 1998, and others. Microsoft, the software behemoth, also began investing in traditional media companies such as the cable company Comcast, as well as Internet sites, and entering into a vast number of other media deals. Most important, traditional telecommunications firms also became central media players. In fact, at the time of the Viacom/CBS merger, the only media deals that had been larger were the ones in which phone company giant AT&T acquired two cable companies, TCI (for $48 billion in 1998) and MediaOne (for $54 billion in 1999); a sign of the coming integration of telephony, cable television, and Internet access.

◆ Making Sense of Mergers

At various points in history antimonopoly concerns have resulted in the dismantling of media conglomerates. In more recent years, facilitated by an increasingly lax regulatory environment, major media companies have been buying and merging with other companies to create ever-larger media conglomerates, all of which are now global in their activities. A decade and a half of such mergers have rapidly transformed the organizational structure and ownership pattern of the media industry. In the process, the dilemmas associated with the market and public sphere models of media have been dramatically highlighted.

From a market perspective, industry changes such as the Viacom/CBS deal can be understood as the rational actions of media corporations attempting to maximize sales, create efficiencies in production, and position themselves strategically to face potential competitors. Despite the growth in media conglomerates, many observers believe the profusion of media outlets made possible by recent technological developments—especially cable and the Internet—makes the threat of monopolistic misbehavior by these media giants highly unlikely. How can we talk about monopolies, they ask, when we have moved from a system of three television networks to one that will soon boast 500+ channels? How can a handful of companies monopolize the decentralized Internet? The media industry as a whole has grown, they also note, and the larger media companies simply reflect the expansion of this field.

But the public sphere perspective directs us to a different set of concerns. Growth in the number of media outlets, for example, does not necessarily ensure content that serves the public interest. Centralized corporate ownership of vast media holdings raises the possibility of stifling diverse expression and raises important questions about the powerful role of media in a democratic society. Even with new media outlets, it is still a handful of media giants who dominate what we see, hear, and read. The expansion of new media technologies has only strengthened, not undermined, the power and influence of new media conglomerates. . . .

◆ Structural Trends in the Media Industry

The basic structural trends in the media industry have been characterized in recent years by four broad developments.

1. *Growth.* Mergers and buyouts have made media corporations bigger than ever.

2. *Integration.* The new media giants have integrated either horizontally by moving into multiple forms of media such as film, publishing, radio, and so on, or vertically by owning different stages of production and distribution, or both.

3. *Globalization.* To varying degrees, the major media conglomerates have become global entities, marketing their wares worldwide.

4. *Concentration of ownership.* As major players acquire more media holdings, the ownership of mainstream media has become increasingly concentrated.

Some of these phenomena are overlapping or interrelated developments. However, to describe the specifics of these developments, we examine each separately.

GROWTH

The last decades of the 20th century will be remembered as ones of expansive media growth. Not only was the number of media outlets available to the public via cable, satellite, and the Internet greater than ever, but the media companies themselves were growing at an unprecedented pace. In 1983, the largest media merger to date had been when the Gannett newspaper chain bought Combined Communications corporation—owner of billboards, newspapers, and broadcast stations—for $340 million [$581 million]. Even when the value of that deal is adjusted for inflation, 1999's $38 billion Viacom-CBS deal was more than 65 times as big.

This enormous growth in conglomeration was largely fueled by a belief in the various benefits to be had from being big. Larger size meant more available capital to finance increasingly expensive media projects and size was also associated with efficiencies of scale. But most important, integrated media conglomerates can exploit the "synergy" created by having many outlets in multiple media. *Synergy* refers to the dynamic where components of a company work together to produce benefits that would be impossible for a single, separately operated unit of the company. In the corporate dreams of media giants, synergy occurs when, for example, a magazine writes about an author, whose book is converted into a movie (whose CD soundtrack is played on radio stations), which becomes the basis of a television series, which has its own Web site and computer games. Packaging a single idea across all these various media allows corporations to generate multiple revenue streams from a single concept. To do this, however, media companies had to expand to unprecedented size.

Ironically, as the scale of corporate growth increased, concern with regulating potential media monopolies virtually disappeared from mainstream political discourse. As a result, the big media players have—with sometimes stunning frequency—been merging with or buying out other big media players. (See Exhibit 2.1.) To better understand these mergers and acquisitions, it is informative to take a closer look at one example, the Viacom/CBS deal mentioned earlier.

The Viacom/CBS Merger

CBS was created in 1928 and has long been a major broadcaster with a strong radio and television presence. Through much of its history, it was popularly associated with its news programming, especially with Edward R. Murrow and Walter Cronkite, who were among the preeminent

(Text continues on page 28)

Exhibit 2.1   Select Media Mergers and Acquisitions of $1 Billion (current) or More
(1984-2000)

Year	The Deal	Value (in billions $)	
		Current Dollars	Constant 2000 Dollars
1985	Rupert Murdoch's News Corp. (newspapers, television in Australia, Britain, U.S.) buys Metromedia (six television stations) as the launching pad for his new Fox network	$1.6	$2.5
	Turner Broadcasting buys MGM/United Artists (keeping MGM's library of 3,000 films but selling off the rest for $.8 billion)	1.5	2.4
	General Electric buys RCA (owners of NBC network)	6.4	10.1
	Capital Cities (backed by investor Warren Buffett) buys the much larger ABC television network	3.5	5.5
1986	National Amusements (movie theaters) buys Viacom	3.4	5.3
1987	Sony buys CBS Records	2	3
1989	Time Inc. merges with Warner Communications	14.1	19.4
	Sony acquires control of Columbia Pictures and TriStar movie studios	4.8	6.6
1990	Matsushita Electric Industrial Co. buys MCA (Universal Studios, Geffen Records, Motown)	6.6	8.6
1993	US West buys a quarter share of Time Warner	2.5	2.9
	Viacom buys Paramount Communications (Universal Studios, Geffen Records, New York Knicks, publishing)	8.3	9.8
	Viacom buys Blockbuster	4.9	5.8

Year	The Deal	Value (in billions $)	
		Current Dollars	Constant 2000 Dollars
	TCI re-purchases Liberty Media, which it has spun-off earlier (in prelude to failed Bell Atlantic takeover)	3.5	4.1
1994	Cox Cable buys Times Mirror Cable	2.3	2.6
	US West buys Wometco and Georgia Cable TV	1.2	1.4
1995	Telecommunications Act of 1996 introduced in Congress		
	Gannett buys Multimedia Inc.	2.3	2.6
	Time Warner buys Houston Industries	2.5	2.8
	Time Warner buys Cablevision Industries	2.7	3
	Seagram's (beverages) buys 80% of MCA from Matsushita, renames it Universal Studios	5.7	6.4
	MCI buys 10% share of News Corp	2	2.2
	Westinghouse Corporation buys CBS (three years later, Westinghouse changes the company name to CBS Corporation)	5.4	6
	Walt Disney Co. buys Capital Cities/ABC	19	21.2
	Time Warner buys Turner Communications	8.5	9.5
	TCI buys Viacom's cable TV system	2.3	2.6
1996	Telecommunications Act of 1996 passed		
	Westinghouse (CBS) buys Infinity Broadcasting (radio stations)	4.9	5.3

(Continued)

Exhibit 2.1 continued

Year	The Deal	Value (in billions $)	
		Current Dollars	Constant 2000 Dollars
	News Corp. buys New World Communications Group, Inc.	3.6	3.9
	US West buys controlling interest in Continental Cablevision	10.8	11.7
	A. H. Belo Corporation buys Providence Journal Company (16 TV stations plus major newspapers)	1.5	1.6
	Tribune Company buys Renaissance Communications (TV stations)	1.1	1.2
1997	Microsoft buys an 11.5% stake in Comcast Corp	1	1.1
	Reed Elsevier and Wolters Kluwer merge (print/electronic publishing/databases; Lexis/Nexis)	7.8	8.3
	News Corp buys international Family Entertainment (Family Channel and MTM Entertainment TV production)	1.9	2
	TCI buys one-third of Cablevision Systems	1.1	1.2
	Westinghouse-CBS buys American Radio Systems	2.6	2.8
	Westinghouse-CBS acquires Gaylord, owners of Country Music TV and The Nashville Network	1.6	1.7
1998	AT&T buys TCI (Tele-Communications, Inc)	53.6	56
	Bertelsmann buys Random House/Alfred a. Knopf/Crown Publishing	1.3	1.4
	AOL (America Online) buys Netscape (Internet browser)	4.2	4.4
	Seagram buys Polygram (music)	15.1	15.8

		Value (in billions $)	
Year	The Deal	Current Dollars	Constant 2000 Dollars
1999	DirectTV (Hughes Electronics) buys PrimeStar	1.8	1.8
	Charter Communications buys Bresnan Communications (cable)	3.1	3.2
	AT&T buys MediaOne	54	55.2
	@Home Corp. buys Excite (Internet company)	6.7	6.8
	Columbia House (owned by Time Warner and Sony) merges with online retailer CDNow	2	2
	CBS buys King World (syndicated television programs)	2.5	2.6
	Yahoo! buys GeoCities Inc. (Internet company)	4.7	4.8
	Yahoo! buys broadcast.com	5.7	5.8
	VNU (Dutch publisher) acquires Nielsen Media Research	2.7	2.8
	CBS (via subsidiary, Infinity Broadcasting) buys Outdoor Systems (billboards)	6.5	6.6
	Viacom announces merger with CBS	38	38.9
	Cox Communications buys cable assets of Gannett Co.	2.7	2.8
	Cox Communications buys TCA Cable TV Inc.	3.3	3.4
	Cox Communications buys Media General Inc.	1.4	1.4
	Clear Channel Communications buys AMFM Inc.	23	23.5

(Continued)

Exhibit 2.1 continued

Year	The Deal	Value (in billions $)	
		Current Dollars	Constant 2000 Dollars
2000+	America Online (AOL) acquires Time Warner in biggest media deal to date	166	166
	Tribune Company buys Times Mirror Company	6.5	6.5
	Telefonica of Spain acquires Lycos, the Internet portal; as part of deal, Telefonica establishes a partnership with Bertelsmann	12.5	12.5
	Gannett acquires Central Newspapers, owners of six dailies, including the *Arizona Republic* and the *Indianapolis Star*	2.6	2.6
	Vivendi, a French pay-TV and telecommunication company, buys Seagram (Universal, Polygram)	34	34
	News Corp (Fox) buys 10 television stations from Chris-Craft Industries	5.4	5.4

SOURCE: Media accounts.

NOTE: Most dates refer to the announcement of the deal. Many deals were not finalized until the following year. Constant dollar adjustments are based on the Bureau of Labor Statistics' Consumer Price Index and were developed using the American Institute for Economic Research's online cost-of-living calculator (www.aier.org/cgi-aier/colcalculator.cgi). Constant dollar values should be considered approximate.

journalists of their day. CBS dominated network broadcasting through much of the 1960s. In 1963, CBS owned nine of the top ten prime-time shows, and all ten of the top ten daytime shows. In its heyday, it was known as the "Tiffany Network" because of what was seen as its quality programming. In the mid-1980s, the network went into decline after being taken over by Loew's, which instituted cuts in the CBS news division as one way to increase profits. Ten years after the Loew's takeover, CBS was sold again, this time to the Westinghouse Corporation, an electrical hardware manufacturer that changed its name to CBS Corporation.

Viacom is a much younger company. In 1970, the FCC introduced new regulations requiring networks to purchase their programs from independent producers. The rules meant that networks could not own their new programs and could not sell the right to air reruns of their old programs—a process known as "syndication." The goal, according to the FCC, was "to limit network control over television programming and thereby encourage the development of a diversity of programs through diverse sources of program services."[2] This became known as the "financial interest and syndication" rules," or "fin-syn" for short. Viacom was created in 1971 as a spin-off of

CBS to comply with these new FCC regulations. In order to sell the syndication rights to its old programs, such as *I Love Lucy* and *The Andy Griffith Show*, CBS was required to create a new corporate entity, separate from the network. Thus, Viacom was born.

In 1986, National Amusements, a movie theater chain headed by Sumner Redstone, purchased Viacom for $3.4 billion [$5.3 billion], keeping the name for the new company. Viacom grew quickly, purchasing other media enterprises. Most notably, in 1993, it bought Paramount for $8.3 billion [$9.8 billion] and Blockbuster Video for $4.9 billion [$5.8 billion]. From a stepchild of CBS, Viacom had become a media giant in its own right. In 1999, the circle was completed as Viacom returned to purchase its former parent, CBS, for $38 billion, creating a new Viacom that was estimated to be worth over $70 billion.

So what happened? Why was a much smaller media company being broken up in 1971 under the fear of monopoly, while a much larger company was allowed to keep growing in 1999? The equation was something like this: technology + politics = deregulation. It was the combination of changing communications technology, coupled with a conservative shift in national politics, that led to major deregulation of the media industry. This deregulation, in turn, allowed media corporations to expand rapidly.

Changing Technology

New technology is one key element facilitating industry changes. When CBS was forced to spin off Viacom in 1971, television viewer options were usually limited to three national broadcast networks (ABC, CBS, and NBC), public television, and perhaps one or two local independent stations. By the end of the century, there were six national broadcast networks of varying size (including Fox, WB, UPN), a virtually countless number of cable channels, and "direct TV" satellite options. Media corporations argued that many ownership regulations were no longer needed in this world of proliferating media outlets.

If television offered abundant choices, critics of regulation contended, then the Internet was virtually limitless in its offerings. In its early days, especially, the Internet was seen even by many critics of mainstream media as an antidote to big media. Because of the apparently low cost of entry and virtually no-cost distribution, it was thought to be a way to level the playing field between large media conglomerates and smaller independent producers. This, too, was a part of the argument against regulation of big media.

But while technology has undoubtedly changed the face of mass media, some of the changes amount to less than they first appear. For example, while changes in television technology are ushering in the era of the 500-channel universe, these new options—unlike traditional broadcast television—are expensive alternatives that many Americans cannot afford. At the end of the century, nearly a third of American households had no cable service at all and another third had only basic cable. Expensive premium channels, pay-per-view selections, and other options remain unaffordable to most families.

Also, more channels have not necessarily meant more diversity. Instead, many of the cable options simply air either reruns of broadcast programs or provide a certain type of previously existing programming (sports, music videos, etc.) 24 hours a day. *More* content does not necessarily mean *different* content.

The Internet, too, has shown signs of becoming dominated by major media giants. For a short period of time, many major media companies were not heavily involved in Internet ventures. As a result, there was a brief window of opportunity for new companies to get established. However, as this first stage of the industry passed, a second stage of consolidation took place.

Two major types of players were driving this consolidation stage. First, as successful new Internet companies saw the value of their stock rise, they often tried to solidify that value by buying something tangible with the money—often other media firms.

That way, when stock prices on overvalued Internet companies fell—as they inevitably did—these companies still had valuable, if more traditional, media assets. Second, after small ventures began showing how the Internet might be used for commerce, major media players stepped in either buying up smaller companies or forcing them to merge in order to stay alive. Thus, established companies used their resources to buy their way into the expanding Internet market. In the first half of 1999 alone, there were over 650 Internet mergers and acquisitions valued at over $37 billion.[3] This was more than three times the number of deals made in the first six months of 1998.

The large-scale companies make it difficult for new companies to compete independently. The once relatively low startup costs of running a significant World Wide Web site—once touted as a central reason for the Internet's revolutionary character—now routinely exceeds $1 million.[4] As a result, media companies with major capital to invest now dominate the most popular sites on the World Wide Web.[5]

The Politics of Deregulation

If technology provided the tracks upon which deregulation was able to ride, then conservative pro-business politics was the engine that propelled it along. The relaxation of key regulations was absolutely central to the rapid expansion of media conglomerates. . . .

In 1993, a U.S. District Court ruled that broadcast networks should no longer be subject to many of the fin-syn regulations. Previously, television networks acquired programming from outside producers who continued to own the programs. However, with the elimination of "fin-syn" rules, networks were now free to air their own programming. Increased vertical integration of production and exhibition resulted. For example, in the summer of 1999, Disney formalized its vertical integration in television by merging its television production studios with its ABC network operations. The shift was aimed at controlling costs by

encouraging the in-house development and production of programs by Disney/ABC for broadcast on the ABC network.[6] Such integration would have been impossible without the change in fin-syn regulations. . . .

The anti-regulatory sentiment in government that had escalated with the Republican Reagan and Bush administrations continued into Democrat Bill Clinton's administration. Nowhere was this more clear than in the passage of the wide-ranging 1996 Telecommunications Act. The act had been heavily promoted by the media and telecommunications industries, leading even the *New York Times* to editorialize, "Forty million dollars' worth of lobbying bought telecommunications companies a piece of Senate legislation they could relish. But consumers have less to celebrate." The *Times* went on to argue that the bill's "anti-regulatory zeal goes too far, endangering the very competition the bill is supposed to create."[7]

But antiregulation ruled the day and among the many provisions of the act were those that relaxed the regulations on the number of media outlets a single company may own. (See Exhibit 2.2.) While the Telecommunications Act was promoted using a market approach that emphasized more competition, the changes actually helped to fuel a new wave of media mergers and acquisitions.

Patricia Aufderheide notes that "in the months following the act, mergers and buyouts multiplied. In 1997 alone, $154 billion [$163 billion] in media and telecommunication deals was recorded in the following categories, according to Paul Kagan Associates research, telephone, $90 [b]illion; radio, $8.3 billion; TV station deals, $9.3 billion; and entertainment and media networks, $22 billion."[8]

One of the act's provisions called for a review of certain ownership restrictions and, as a result, the FCC announced another round of deregulation in the summer of 1999. This time the FCC eased restrictions on the number of local radio and television stations a single company can own. The FCC eliminated regulations

Exhibit 2.2 Select Ownership Rules Changes in the 1996 Telecommunications Act

The 1996 Telecommunications Act eased restrictions on media ownership, leading to larger media companies and more concentration of ownership.

Previous Rules	*New Rule Changes*
National television	

A single entity:
Can own up to 12 stations
    nationwide or
Can own stations reaching up to
    25% of U.S. TV households
	No limit on number of stations
	Station reach increased to 35% of
	    U.S. TV households

Local television	

A single entity:
Can own only one station in a market
	Telecom Act called for review
	In 1999, FCC announced it would
	    allow multiple station ownership in
	    a single market under certain
	    circumstances

National radio	
A single entity: Can own up to 20 FM and 20 AM stations	No limit on station ownership
Local radio	

A single entity:
Cannot own, operate, or control more
    than 2 AM and 2 FM stations
    in a market
Audience share of co-owned
    stations cannot exceed 25%
	Ownership adjusted by market size:
	In markets with 45+ stations, a single
	    entity cannot own more than
	    8 stations total and no more than 5 in
	    the same service (AM or FM)
	. . . with 30-44 stations; 7 total,
	    5 same service
	. . . with 15-29 stations; 6 total,
	    3 same service (but no more than
	    50% of the stations in the market)
	. . . with 14 or fewer; 5 total, 3 same
	    service (but no more than 50% of
	    the stations in the market)
	Limits may be waived if the FCC rules
	    it will increase the total number of
	    stations in operation.

restricting companies to one local TV station in a market. Now companies are allowed to own two stations, as long as at least eight other competitors are in the same market and one of the company's two stations is not among the market's top four. Other conditions too, such as a failing station, can be used to justify multiple station ownership. In a reflection of the convergence of media forms, another regulatory change now allows for a single company to own two TV stations and six radio stations in a market as long as there are at least 20 competitors among all media—cable, newspapers, and other broadcast stations.[9]

Consumer advocates bemoaned the changes, arguing that they once again would lead to more media outlets in fewer hands. But media executives once again had something to cheer about. Lowell "Bud" Paxon, owner of PAX TV, greeted the changes by saying, "I can't wait to have a glass of champagne and toast the FCC!" Barry Diller, chairman and CEO of USA Networks, observed, "This is a real significant step. . . . This is going to change things."[10]

He was right. Less than a month after these new FCC regulatory changes, Viacom and CBS announced their plans to merge—a deal that would have been impossible before the relaxation of FCC regulations. Even with the new rules, the new Viacom would violate existing regulations. For example, its television stations could reach into 41% of American households, but the FCC cap was 35%. In addition, it owned both the CBS network and had a 50% stake in the UPN network, but FCC regulations prevent a network owner from having an ownership interest in another network. Finally, Viacom's ownership of numerous radio and television stations violated ownership limitation rules in a half dozen markets. Upon approval of the deal, the FCC gave Viacom time to comply with such regulations.[11] Some observers, though, believed that the FCC might change some of these limits by the time the compliance period expired.

So the growth in media conglomerates has been fueled, in part, by the changing regulatory environment. In the years when public interest concerns about monopolies were preeminent, media companies were constrained in their ability to grow unchecked. However, with the rise of more media outlets via new technology, the conservative shift toward business deregulation since the Reagan era, and the growth in the media industry's lobbying clout, media corporations have been relatively unencumbered in their desire to grow.

Thus, as the 20th century came to a close, a loose regulatory environment allowed Viacom and CBS to create a new media giant. As announced, the 1999 merger created a Viacom that

◆ was the nation's largest owner of TV stations,

◆ was the nation's largest owner of radio stations,

◆ controlled the nation's largest cable network group,

◆ controlled the nation's largest billboard company,

◆ was the world's largest seller of advertising with estimated sales of $11 billion— nearly twice that of second-place News Corp ($5.8 billion), and more than double its next two competitors (Disney's $5.1 billion and Time Warner's $3.8 billion).

In an earlier era, such concentrated market power would likely have been met by regulatory roadblocks. In this new era of deregulation, it is likely that the deal will be followed in the coming years by further industry consolidation and even larger deals. . . .

INTEGRATION

Horizontal Integration

A media corporation that is horizontally integrated owns many different types of media products. Viacom is clearly a horizontally integrated conglomerate because it owns, among other things, properties in broadcast and cable television, film, radio, and the Internet—all different types of media. . . .

With the transformation of text, audio, and visual media into digital data, the technological platforms that underlie different media forms have begun to converge, blurring the lines between once-distinct media.

One visible symbol of convergence is the compact disk. This single digital data storage device can be used for text, audio, video, or all three simultaneously. Its introduction—along with other types of digital data storage devices—has changed the nature of media. The personal computer is another symbol of change. It can be used to create and read text documents; show static and animated graphics; listen to audio CDs or digital music files; play CD computer games that combine audio, video, and text; watch digital videos; access and print photos taken with a digital camera; and surf the Internet, among other things. All this is possible because of the common digital foundation for various media.

But the significance of digital data extends way beyond CDs and computers. Now, the digital platform encompasses all forms of media. Television and radio broadcast signals are being digitized and analog signals phased out. Newspapers exist in digital form on the Internet, and their paper versions are often printed in plants that download the paper's content in digital form from satellites. This allows for simultaneous publication in many cities of national papers such as *USA Today*. Filmless digital movie theaters are beginning to appear, where movies, that were digitally downloaded via the Internet, are shown with a sophisticated computerized projector.

The convergence of media products has meant that media businesses have also converged. The common digital foundation to contemporary media has made it easier for companies to create products in different media. For example, it was a relatively small step for newspapers—with content already produced on computers in digital form—to developed online World Wide Web sites and upload newspaper articles to it. Thus, newspaper publishers have become Internet companies. In fact, many media have embraced the Internet as a close digital cousin of what they already do. The music industry, to use another example, has responded to the proliferation of bootlegged digital music files (MP3, Napster, etc.) by developing its own systems to deliver music via the Web to consumers—for a fee, of course.

Furthermore, convergence has eroded the walls between what used to be three distinct industries: media, telecommunications, and computers. Recently, major cable TV companies began entering the phone service business and offering cabled-based Internet access. "Baby Bells" and long-distance phone companies are getting involved in video delivery and Internet access. Computer software firms are teaming up with cable companies to create various "smart boxes" that facilitate delivery of cable-based media and communications services. Integration, therefore, involves even companies outside of the traditional media industry, making it more difficult than ever to mark clear boundaries.

Vertical Integration

While horizontal integration involves owning and offering different types of media products, vertical integration involves owning assets that are involved in the different steps in the production, distribution, exhibition, and sale of a single type of media product. In the media industry, vertical integration tends to be more limited than horizontal integration, but it can still play a significant role. For some time, there has been a widespread belief that "content is king." That is, the rise of the Internet and cable television in particular has led to an explosion in outlets available to deliver media products. Consequently, owning the media content that is to be distributed via these channels is widely believed to be more valuable than owning the channels themselves. However, with the elimination of most fin-syn rules, interest in vertical integration has resurfaced, enabling broadcast networks to once again produce and exhibit their own programs.

Viacom's vertical integration can be seen, for example, in the fact that it owns film production and distribution companies (e.g., Paramount Pictures) and multiple venues to exhibit these films. These venues include theater chains to show first-run films (e.g., Famous Players and United Cinemas International theater chains) and a video store chain to distribute the movie once it is available on videotape for rental (Blockbuster Video). Viacom also owns premium cable channels (e.g., Showtime, The Movie Channel), basic cable channels (e.g., Comedy Central), and a broadcast network (CBS), all to air a film after its rental life is over. Thus, when Viacom produces a movie, it is assured of multiple venues for exhibition.

. . . The numerous mergers that have left an industry dominated by larger companies have also produced an industry where the major players are highly integrated.

At first glance, the average person may be unaware of these trends that have reshaped the media industry. It is usually difficult to discern that apparently diverse media products are, in fact, all owned by a single company. Take television, for example. If you surf the television universe, you might come across a local CBS affiliate, MTV, Comedy Central, Nickelodeon, Showtime, a UPN affiliate, VH-1, The Movie Channel, The Nashville Network, and your local team on Home Team Sports. It is virtually impossible for the casual viewer to realize that all of these are actually owned—all or in part—by Viacom. It is even less likely that they will connect the owners of all these stations with the owner of their local theme park, movie theater, and radio stations. But again, one company could own them all: Viacom. However, Viacom is not unique in this regard. The same phenomenon is true of other collections of disparate media outlets that are owned by the other media giants.

GLOBALIZATION

Growth in the size and integration of companies has been accompanied by another development: the globalization of media conglomerates. More and more, major media players are targeting the global marketplace for the sale of their products.

There are three basic reasons for this strategy. First, domestic markets are saturated with media products so many media companies see international markets as the key to future growth. Media corporations want to be well positioned to tap these developing markets.

Second, media giants are often in a position to effectively compete with—and even dominate—the local media in other countries. These corporations can draw on their enormous capital resources to produce expensive media products, such as Hollywood blockbuster movies, that are beyond the capability of local media. Media giants can also adapt already successful products for new markets, again reaping the rewards of expanding markets in these areas.

Third, by distributing existing media products to foreign markets, media companies are able to tap a lucrative source of revenue at virtually no additional cost. For example, a movie shown in just one country costs the same to make as a movie distributed globally. Once the tens of millions of dollars involved in producing a major motion picture are spent, successful foreign distribution of the resulting film can spell the difference between profit and loss. As a result, current decision making as to whether a script becomes a major film routinely includes considerations of its potential for success in foreign markets. Action and adventure films translate well, for example, because they have limited dialogue, simple plots, and rely heavily on special effects and action sequences. Sexy stars, explosions, and violence travel easily to other cultures. Comedies, however, are often risky because humor does not always translate well across cultural boundaries.

We can see examples of globalization strategies in the case of Viacom. . . . For example, MTV is a popular Viacom cable channel reaching over 70 million U.S. households.[12] It originated as a venue for record companies to show music videos to advertise their artists' latest releases. Over time, MTV has added a stable of regular series (e.g., *The Real World*, *Road Rules*, *Beavis and Butthead*), specials (e.g., *MTV's House of Style*), and events (e.g., *MTV Video Music Awards*, *MTV's Spring Break*), all aimed at the lucrative teen and young adult market.

MTV describes itself in publicity material as having an environment that is "unpredictable and irreverent, reflecting the cutting edge spirit of rock n' roll that is the heart of its programming." In reality, MTV is a well-developed commercial formula that Viacom has exported globally, by making small adjustments to account for local tastes. In fact, MTV is really a global collection of MTV's. Together, these MTV channels are available in over 300 million households in 82 territories that, Viacom says, makes MTV the most widely distributed network in the world. Over three-quarters of households that receive MTV are *outside* of the United States.

Viacom's global ventures do not end with MTV. Virtually every aspect of its media business has a global component. Examples include the following specifics.

◆ Major motion pictures are routinely distributed internationally and many, such as Paramount's *Forrest Gump* and *Mission Impossible*, earn more money for Viacom internationally than they do in the United States.

◆ Famous Players Theatres Canada operates more than 660 screens in more than 100 locations. United Cinemas International—a joint venture with Universal—operates more than 90 theaters in Asia, Europe, and South America.

◆ Paramount International Television distributes more than 2,600 series and movies internationally.

◆ Blockbuster Video operates 6,000 stores in 27 different countries.

◆ Publisher Simon & Schuster has international operations in both the United Kingdom and Australia and sells books in dozens of countries.

◆ Nickelodeon distributes its children's programming in more than 100 countries and, much like MTV, operates its own cable channels across the globe. These include Nickelodeon Latin America, Nickelodeon in the Nordic Region, Nickelodeon Turkey, Nickelodeon U.K., Nickelodeon Australia, and the Nickelodeon Global Network. Nickelodeon even has theme parks in Australia and other locations.

◆ Viacom's production companies license and coproduce programs based on U.S. hits to be sold in international markets. These include *Entertainment Tonight/ China*, a 50-minute Mandarin-language series produced in cooperation with the Chinese government, and other national versions of the *Entertainment Tonight* series that appear in the United Kingdom, Germany, and other countries.

International revenues are making up an increasingly large percentage of the income of such companies as Viacom, Disney, Time Warner, and News Corp. As a result, all major media conglomerates are now global players, representing a major shift in industry structure.

CONCENTRATION OF OWNERSHIP

While individual media companies grow, integrate, and pursue global strategies, ownership in the media industry as a whole becomes more concentrated in the hands of these new media giants. There is considerable debate about the significance of this trend but the trend itself has been clear. . . .

Ben Bagdikian is a researcher whose work on the ownership of media has revealed increased concentration. In the various editions of his *The Media Monopoly*, Bagdikian has tracked the number of firms that control the majority of all media products. This number has been declining dramatically in the last 15 years. He notes that in recent years, "a small number of the country's largest industrial corporations has acquired more public communications power—including ownership of the news—than any private businesses have ever before possessed in world history." [13] In the fifth edition of his book, he reports that in 1996, just 10 media companies dominated the entire mass communication industry. With recent high-profile mergers, this figure continues to decline.

Within each sector of the industry, a few large companies dominate smaller competitors.

◆ Two companies—Borders/Walden and Barnes & Noble—make a third of all U.S. retail book sales.[14]

◆ Five movie companies—Disney's Buena Vista, News Corporation's Fox, Time Warner's Warner Bros., Viacom's Paramount, and Sony—dominate that industry, accounting for more than 75% of the domestic box office in the summer of 1998.[15]

◆ Five companies—Seagram's Universal, Sony, Time Warner, Bertelsmann, and EMI—distribute 95% of all music carried by record stores in the United States.

◆ Television continues to be dominated by four major networks—Disney's ABC, Viacom's CBS, News Corporation's Fox, and General Electric's NBC. Several new fledgling networks have entered the field but are not yet major competitors—WB (Time Warner), UPN (Viacom), USA, and PAX. . . .

◆ Interpreting Structural Changes

The media industry, then, has been undergoing significant changes in recent decades as companies have grown, integrated, and become global players. There is little debate about these basic trends. However, the significance of these trends is a subject of intense debate. Market advocates see these structural changes as the normal evolution of a growing and maturing industry. But the public sphere framework reminds us that media cannot be treated simply as any other industry. Furthermore, it raises serious questions about what these structural changes mean for diversity and independence in content and for the power of newly emerging media corporations.

THE MARKET PERSPECTIVE

From the perspective of the market model, the media industry is one that has enjoyed enormous growth in recent years. With that growth has come a repositioning of major players, the introduction of some significant new players, and an evolution in the basic terrain of the industry. This perspective tends to see the growth of larger media companies as the logical outcome of an industry that has become more integrated across media and more global in scope. To operate effectively in such a new environment, media corporations must develop new business strategies and draw on the larger capital resources available only to major global corporations. The structural changes of growth, integration, and globalization are merely the signs of companies positioning themselves to operate in this new media world. The concentration of media ownership, on the other hand, is the natural by-product of a maturing industry, as young start-ups and older, underperforming firms are consolidated into the business plans of mature but innovative companies.

The rapid growth in media outlets, the constant shifts in consumer tastes, and the ever-changing terrain of the industry itself make any apparent domination of the industry by a few companies an illusion. No one can control such a vast and constantly evolving industry. Companies such as America Online (AOL), who have become major players in the industry, did not exist a few years ago, while old media standards, such as ABC, were long ago incorporated into newly consolidated media companies. Change is built into the market and no company can really dominate the marketplace.

Market advocates note that we should not be nostalgic about the media era gone by. In reality, as recently as the mid-1970s, the media landscape was much more sparsely populated than it is today and consumers had far fewer choices, on the whole. Compared with this earlier period, market advocates point out, we have a cornucopia of media outlets and products available to us.

It is true that more communities had competing daily newspapers than there are today, but often the quality of those smaller local papers was mediocre at best. In contrast, today's papers may be local monopolies and part of larger chains, but by drawing on the resources of their owners, they are able to produce a higher-quality product. Also, consumers have many more options for news—especially cable television and the Internet—than they ever did in the days of more competing daily papers, making local newspaper monopolies less significant.

In the 1970s, many communities had only small local bookstores with very limited inventory and choice. Today, more and more communities have "superstore" booksellers with thousands of diverse selections of books and magazines. Rather than killing the old print medium, the Internet has been a shot in the arm for book sales as online retailers such as Amazon.com offer hundreds of thousands of titles for sale at the click of a mouse. This has made books and other media products more widely available than ever.

In the 1970s, local movie theaters were beginning to feature more multiscreen offerings, but these were limited compared to what is available today. Video rentals were not readily available because VCRs were still primitive in those days. Today, more multiplex theaters bring more options to moviegoers, while VCRs are in 85% of homes and a wide array of videos is readily available for low-cost renting.

DVDs, too, have entered the media landscape.

Radio was admittedly more diverse in terms of regional preferences, but it is not clear whether a broader range of music was readily available to listeners. Today, radio has become largely a chain-owned affair with new standards of professionalism and high production values. In addition, online streaming offers the potential of greater musical variety to listeners.

Most striking, 90% of the prime-time television audience in the mid-1970s was watching just three television networks. Cable television was not really an alternative because it was still largely used to transmit the "big three" broadcast networks to homes where reception was difficult. Satellite television, of course, was unheard of. Today, three new broadcast networks have joined the older "big three." Nearly three-quarters of U.S. homes have cable, delivering an average of almost 60 channels. Satellite television, with hundreds of channels, is expanding and by 2000, was in more than 10% of homes.

Finally, the vast universe of the Internet is becoming available to more and more people at work and home, opening up unprecedented avenues for news, entertainment, and commerce via the printed word or streaming audio-video.

In light of these rapid changes, as we have seen, market advocates have called for more deregulation of the industry in order to spur increased competition. Because of digitization, companies in fields that were previously separate can now compete with each other if regulations are lifted. On the delivery side, telephone companies, for example, can now offer Internet access as well, while cable companies can enter the telephone and Internet business. On the content side, companies that had traditionally been focused in one medium can now branch out to work in films, television, print, Internet, and other media. All of this, market advocates contended, means more choices and better media for the consumer; a regulatory system created in a far different era is obsolete in this new dynamic media environment.

QUESTIONING THE MARKET: REVISITING THE PUBLIC SPHERE APPROACH

Although the market approach may celebrate the new media environment, there are questions that this focus on markets and profits effectively obscures. The public sphere perspective suggests that the technological change and growth in the number of media outlets should not be accepted as an unequivocal benefit, especially if these outlets are linked to a growing concentration in media ownership.

The introduction of new media has never ensured quality content. History has shown that the great potential of new media forms has often been subverted for purely commercial purposes. Both radio and television, at various points, were touted as having profound educational and civic potential. That potential was never reached. Cable television has, in many ways, simply reproduced the formats and formulas of broadcast television. Because it is not covered by the same content rules that regulate broadcast television, cable has had more leeway to air raunchy, violent, and sensationalistic entertainment. This type of entertainment could be seen in everything from adult-oriented cable movies to the funny, but foul-mouthed, animated pre-pubescent offerings of *South Park*. Cable's vast wasteland was perhaps epitomized by its most highly rated programs in the late 1990s: professional wrestling. The popularity of such cable programming pressured broadcast television to seek increasingly wild and aggressive programs, leading many parents to despair about the lack of appropriate entertainment and educational television for their children.

More wasted potential seems to have plagued the growth of the Internet. Early discussion of the "information superhighway" was quickly supplanted by a focus on e-commerce. Here, too, adult-oriented sites proved to be very popular. While there may be more media outlets, we need to examine what these channels are delivering.

A concern for the health of the public sphere leads us to argue that media outlets are only truly beneficial if they serve the public interest by delivering content that is genuinely diverse and substantive. Early indications were that, to the contrary, much of cable television was delivering more of the same commercial fare that characterized broadcast television. Why couldn't some of these many channels be used to deliver innovative, diverse, and inclusive public affairs programming? Or alternative visions from independent filmmakers and other artists? Or programming that specifically spoke to the common challenges we face as a society? Instead, the fragmentary nature of the cable television world might even be exacerbating cultural divisions in the society, as segregated programming targeted separate demographic groups based on age, gender, class, and race. The Internet, too, has been used by major media companies primarily to sell products to consumers and to promote other media ventures, little of which added significantly to a vibrant public sphere.

Finally, the blurring of boundaries between media coupled with calls for deregulation raise the specter of fully integrated, multinational media giants that can simultaneously dominate multiple media. Old monopoly criteria seem incapable of dealing with this new market reality. Despite the fact that it was promoted as a means of increasing competition, the 1996 Telecommunications Act has resulted in renewed consolidation in the media industry. Despite this continuing consolidation, market advocates continue to talk about the new "competition," and policymakers seem unwilling to examine the significance of an emerging media monopoly by a few giant firms. . . .

On the content side, market theory promised diversity from an unregulated market, but the reality seems to be quite different, as the same old media content is being sold in new packaging and underserved communities continue to be marginalized. Little that is fresh or independent seems to come from the new media giants. This, coupled with the growth in the sheer size of these corporations, raises the disturbing specter of concentrated corporate power capable of stifling diverse expression and exerting significant political power. . . .

◆ *Notes*

1. Details of the Viacom/CBS deal used throughout this chapter were obtained from company press releases and media accounts, including the following: Paul Farhi, "Viacom to Buy CBS, Uniting Multimedia Heavyweights, " *Washington Post* (September 8, 1999): A1; Sallie Hofmeister, "Viacom, CBS to Merge in Record $37-Billion Deal," *Los Angeles Times* (September 8, 1999), online at: www.latimes. com, accessed September 9, 1999; Brian Lowry; "What Effect? Only Prime Time Will Tell," *Los Angeles Times* (September 8, 1999), online at: www.latimes.com, accessed September 9, 1999; Lawrie Mifflin, "Viacom Set to Acquire CBS in Biggest Media Merger Ever," *New York Times* (September 8, 1999), online at: www.nytimes. com, accessed September 9, 1999; Lisa de Moraes, "Can Fledgling UPN Fly to New Viacom Nest?," *Washington Post* (September 8, 1999): C1; Judy Sarasohn, "Special Interests: A Silence That May Not Be Golden," *Washington Post* (September 9, 1999): A19; John Schwartz and Paul Farhi, "Mel Karmazin's Signal Achievement," *Washington Post* (September 8, 1999): E1.

2. Federal Communications Commission. "Comments Sought on November 1995 Expiration of Fin-Syn Rules," New Report No. DC95-54, April 5, 1995, online at: www.fcc.gov, accessed October 12, 1999.

3. Noelle Knox, "Internet Mergers Up Sharply," *Richmond Times Dispatch* (July 17, 1999): C1.

4. Maryann Jones Thompson, "Got a Million Bucks? Get a Web Site," *The Industry Standard*, online at: www.thestandard.com/ metrics/display/0,1283,899,00.html, accessed June 16, 1999; www.thestandard.com/research/ display/0,2799,9845,00.html, accessed August 29, 2000.

5. See, for example, the latest list of popular sites at: www.100hot.com. This particular service tracks a sample of more than 100,000 user to develop its listing. Other services, using different methodologies, will have slightly different results. See, for example, the "Top Rankings" list at: www.mediametrix.com/home.jsp? language=us, or the top sites listed by PC Data Online at: www.pcdataonline.com/reports/tm SitesSingleFree.asp.

6. Kyle Pope, "Disney to Merge Television Studio With ABC Network," *Wall Street Journal* (July 9, 1999): B4.

7. "A Flawed Communications Bill," *New York Times* (June 20, 1995): A14.

8. Patricia Aufderheide, *Communications Policy and the Public Interest* (New York: Guilford Press, 1999), p. 89.

9. Bill Carter, "FCC Will Permit Owning Stations in Big TV Markets," *New York Times* (August 6, 1999): A1.

10. John Schwartz, "FCC Opens Up Big TV Markets," *Washington Post* (August 6, 1999): E3.

11. Federal Communications Commission, "FCC Approves Transfer of CBS to Viacom; Gives Combined Company Time to Comply With Ownership Rules" (May 3, 2000 press release), online at: www.fcc.gov, accessed May 8, 2000.

12. MTV descriptive information is from the Web sites of Viacom (www.viacom.com) and MTV (www.mtv.com), and from Viacom's "1998 Annual Report."

13. Ben Bagdikian, *The Media Monopoly*, 5th ed. (Boston: Beacon, 1997), p. ix.

14. Ben Bagdikian, *The Media Monopoly*, 5th ed. (Boston: Beacon, 1997), p. xxix.

15. "Summer Market Share," *Variety* (September 14, 1998).

3

THE MEANING OF MEMORY

Family, Class, and Ethnicity
in Early Network Television

George Lipsitz

◆ *The Meaning of Memory*

. . . In the midst of extraordinary social change, television emerged as the most important discursive medium in American culture. As such, it was charged with special responsibilities for making new economic and social relations credible and legitimate to audiences haunted by ghosts from the past. Urban, ethnic, working-class comedies provided one means of addressing the anxieties and contradictions emanating from the clash between the consumer present of the 1950s and collective memory about the 1930s and 1940s.

The consumer consciousness generated by economic and social change in postwar America conflicted with the lessons of historical experience for many middle- and working-class American families. The Great Depression of the 1930s had not only damaged the economy, it had also undercut the political and cultural legitimacy of American capitalism. Herbert Hoover had been a national hero in the 1920s, with his credo of "rugged

NOTE: Reproduced by permission of the American Anthropological Association from *Cultural Anthropology* 1(4). Not for sale or further reproduction.

individualism" forming the basis for a widely shared cultural ideal. But the Depression discredited Hoover's philosophy and made him a symbol of yesterday's blasted hopes to millions of Americans. In the 1930s, cultural ideals based on mutuality and collectivity eclipsed the previous decade's individualism, and helped propel massive union organizingdrives, anti-eviction movements, and general strikes. President Roosevelt's New Deal attempted to harness and co-opt that grass-roots mass activity in its efforts to restore social order and recapture credibility and legitimacy for the capitalist system.[1] The social welfare legislation of the "Second New Deal" in 1935 went far beyond any measures previously favored by Roosevelt and most of his advisors, but radical action proved necessary if the administration was to contain the upsurge of activism that characterized the decade. Even in the private sector, industrial corporations conceded more to workers than naked power realities necessitated because they feared the political consequences of mass disillusionment with the system.[2]

World War II ended the Depression and brought prosperity, but it did so on a basis even more collective than the New Deal of the 1930s. Government intervention in the wartime economy reached unprecedented levels, bringing material reward and shared purpose to a generation raised on the deprivation and sacrifice of the Depression. In the postwar years, the largest and most disruptive strike wave in American history won major improvements in the standard of living for the average worker, through both wage increases and government commitments to support full employment, decent housing, and expanded educational opportunities. Grass-roots militancy and working-class direct action wrested concessions from a reluctant business and government elite—mostly because the public at large viewed workers' demands as more legitimate than the desires of capital.[3]

Yet the collective nature of working-class mass activity in the postwar era posed severe problems for capital. In sympathy strikes and secondary boycotts, workers placed the interests of their class ahead of their own individual material aspirations. Strikes over safety and job control far outnumbered wage strikes, revealing aspirations to control the process of production that conflicted with the imperatives of capitalist labor-management relations. Mass demonstrations demanding government employment and housing programs indicated a collective political response to problems previously adjudicated on a personal level. Radical challenges to the authority of capital (like the United Auto Workers' 1946 demand during the General Motors strike that wage increases come out of corporate profits rather than from price hikes passed on to consumers) demonstrated a social responsibility and a commitment toward redistributing wealth rare in the history of American labor.[4]

Capital attempted to regain the initiative in the postwar years by making qualified concessions to working-class pressures for redistribution of wealth and power. Rather than paying wage increases out of corporate profits, business leaders instead worked to expand the economy through increases in government spending, foreign trade, and consumer debt. Such expansion could meet the demands of workers and consumers without undermining capital's dominant role in the economy. On the presumption that "a rising tide lifts all boats," business leaders sought to connect working-class aspirations for a better life to policies that ensured a commensurate rise in corporate profits, thereby leaving the distribution of wealth unaffected. Federal defense spending, highway construction programs, and home-loan policies expanded the economy at home in a manner conducive to the interests of capital, while the Truman Doctrine and Marshall Plan provided models for enhanced access to foreign markets and raw materials for American corporations. The Taft-Hartley Act of 1947 banned the class-conscious collective activities most threatening to capital (mass strikes, sympathy strikes, secondary boycotts): the leaders of labor, government, and business accepted as necessary the practice of paying wage hikes for organized workers out of the pockets of consumers and unorganized workers in the form of higher prices.[5]

Commercial network television played an important role in this emerging economy, functioning as a significant new object of consumer purchases as well as an important marketing medium. Sales of sets jumped from three million during the entire decade of the 1940s to over five million *a year* during the 1950s.[6] But television's most important economic function came from its role as an instrument of legitimation for transformations in values initiated by the new economic imperatives of postwar America. For Americans to accept the new world of 1950s consumerism, they had to make a break with the past. The Depression years had helped generate fears about installment buying and excessive materialism, while the New Deal and wartime mobilization had provoked suspicions about individual acquisitiveness and upward mobility. Depression era and wartime scarcities of consumer goods had led workers to internalize discipline and frugality while nurturing networks of mutual support through family, ethnic, and class associations. Government policies after the war encouraged an atomized acquisitive consumerism at odds with the lessons of the past. At the same time, federal home-loan policies stimulated migrations to the suburbs from urban, ethnic, working-class neighborhoods. The entry of television into the American home disrupted previous patterns of family life and encouraged fragmentation of the family into separate segments of the consumer market.[7] The priority of consumerism in the economy at large and on television may have seemed organic and unplanned, but conscious policy decisions by officials from both private and public sectors shaped the contours of the consumer economy and television's role within it.

Commercial Television ◆ and Economic Change

Government policies during and after World War II shaped the basic contours of home television as an advertising medium. Government-sponsored research and development during the war perfected the technology of home television while federal tax policies solidified its economic base. The government allowed corporations to deduct the costs of advertising from their taxable incomes during the war, despite the fact that rationing and defense production left businesses with few products to market. Consequently, manufacturers kept the names of their products before the public while lowering their tax obligations on high wartime profits. Their advertising expenditures supplied radio networks and advertising agencies with the capital reserves and business infrastructure that enabled them to dominate the television industry in the postwar era. After the war, federal antitrust action against the motion-picture studios broke up the "network" system in movies, while the FCC sanctioned the network system in television. In addition, FCC decisions to allocate stations on the narrow VHF band, to grant the networks ownership and operation rights over stations in prime markets, and to place a freeze on the licensing of new stations during the important years between 1948 and 1952 all combined to guarantee that advertising-oriented programming based on the model of radio would triumph over theater TV, educational TV, or any other form.[8] Government decisions, not market forces, established the dominance of commercial television, but these decisions reflected a view of the American economy and its needs which had become so well accepted at the top levels of business and government that it had virtually become the official state economic policy.

Fearing both renewed Depression and awakened militancy among workers, influential corporate and business leaders considered increases in consumer spending—of 30% to 50%—to be necessary to perpetuate prosperity in the postwar era.[9] Defense spending for the Cold War and the Korean conflict had complemented an aggressive trade policy to improve the state of the economy, but it appeared that the hope for an ever-expanding economy rested on increased consumer spending fueled by an expansion of credit.[10] Here, too, government policies led the way, especially with regard to stimulating credit purchases of homes and automobiles. During World War II, the marginal tax rate for most wage earners jumped from 4% to 25%, making the home ownership deduction more desirable. Federal housing-loan policies favored construction of new single-family, detached suburban houses over renovation or construction of central-city multi-family units. Debt-encumbered home ownership in accord with these policies stimulated construction of 30 million new housing units in just twenty years, bringing the percentage of homeowning Americans from below 40% in 1940 to more than 60% by 1960. Mortgage policies encouraging long-term debt and low down payments freed capital for other consumer purchases, while government highway building policies undermined mass-transit systems and contributed to increased demand for automobiles. Partly as a result of these policies, consumer spending on private cars averaged $7.5 billion per year in the 1930s and 1940s, but grew to $22 billion per year in 1950 and almost $30 billion by 1955.[11]

Business leaders understood the connection between suburban growth and increased consumer spending. A 1953 article in *Fortune* celebrated the "lush new suburban market" which "has centered its customs and conventions on the needs of children and geared its buying habits to them."[12] For the first time in U.S. history, middle-class and working-class families could routinely expect to own homes or buy new cars every few years. Between 1946 and 1965, residential mortgage debt rose three times as fast as the gross national product and disposable income. Mortgage debt accounted for just under 18% of disposable income in 1946, but it grew to almost 55% by 1965.[13] To ensure the eventual payment of current debts, the economy had to generate tremendous growth and expansion, further stimulating the need to increase consumer spending. Manufacturers had to find ways of motivating consumers to buy ever-increasing amounts of commodities. Television provided an important means of accomplishing that end.

Television advertised individual products, but it also provided a relentless flow of information and persuasion that placed acts of consumption at the core of everyday life. The physical fragmentation of suburban growth and subsequent declines in motion-picture attendance created an audience more likely to stay at home and to receive entertainment there than ever before. But television also provided a forum for redefining American ethnic, class, and family identities into consumer identities. To accomplish this task effectively, television programs had to address some of the psychic, moral, and political obstacles to consumption among the public at large.

The television and advertising industries knew they had to overcome consumer resistance. Marketing expert and motivational specialist Ernest Dichter observed that "one of the basic problems of this prosperity is to give people that sanction and justification to enjoy it and to demonstrate that the hedonistic approach to life is a moral one, not an immoral one."[14] Dichter later noted the many barriers inhibiting consumer acceptance of unrestrained hedonism, and he called on advertisers "to train the average citizen to accept growth of his country and its economy as *his* growth rather than as a strange and frightening event."[15] One method of encouraging that acceptance, according to Dichter, consisted of identifying new products and styles of consumption with traditional, historically sanctioned practices and behaviors. He noted that such an approach held particular relevance in addressing consumers who had only recently acquired the means to spend freely and who might harbor a lingering conservatism about spending based on their previous experiences.[16] . . .

◆ *Family Formation and the Economy— The Television View*

Advertisers incorporated their messages into urban, ethnic, working-class comedies through direct and indirect means. Tensions developed in the programs often found indirect resolutions in commercials. Thus Jeannie MacClennan's search for an American sweetheart in one episode of *Hey Jeannie* set up commercials proclaiming the virtues of Drene shampoo for keeping one prepared to accept last-minute ideas and of Crest toothpaste for producing an attractive smile.[17] Conversations about shopping for new furniture in an episode of *The Goldbergs* directed viewers' attention to furnishings in the Goldberg home provided for the show by Macy's department store in exchange for a commercial acknowledgment.[18]

The content of the shows themselves offered even more direct emphasis on consumer spending. In one episode of *The Goldbergs*, Molly expresses disapproval of her future daughter-in-law's plan to buy a washing machine on the installment plan. "I know Papa and me never bought anything unless we had the money to pay for it," she intones with logic familiar to a generation with memories of the Great Depression. Her son, Sammy, confronts this "deviance" by saying, "Listen, Ma, almost everybody in this country lives above their means—and everybody enjoys it." Doubtful at first, Molly eventually learns from her children and announces her conversion to the legitimacy of installment buying, proposing that the family buy two cars in order to "live above our means—the American way."[19] In a subsequent episode, Molly's daughter, Rosalie, assumes the role

of ideological tutor to her mother. When planning a move out of their Bronx apartment to a new house in the suburbs, Molly ruminates about where to place her old furniture in her new home. "You don't mean we're going to take all this junk with us into a brand new house?" asks an exasperated Rosalie. With traditionalist sentiment Molly answers, "Junk? My furniture's junk? My furniture that I lived with and loved for twenty years is junk?" But by the end of the episode she accepts Rosalie's argument—even selling off all her old furniture to help meet the down payment on the new house and deciding to buy all new furniture on the installment plan.[20]

Chester A. Riley confronts similar choices about family and commodities in *The Life of Riley*. His wife complains that he only takes her out to the neighborhood bowling alley and restaurant, not to "interesting places." Riley searches for ways to impress her and discovers from a friend that a waiter at the fancy Club Morambo will let them eat first and pay later, for a cost of a dollar per week plus 10% interest. "Ain't that dishonest?" asks Riley. "No, it's usury," his friend replies. Riley does not borrow the money, but he impresses his wife anyway by taking the family out to dinner on the proceeds of a prize that he receives for being the one thousandth customer in a local flower shop. Though we eventually learn that Peg Riley only wanted attention and not an expensive meal, the happy ending of the episode hinges on Riley's restored prestige once he demonstrates his ability to provide a luxury outing for the family.[21]

The same episode of *The Life of Riley* reveals another consumerist element common to this subgenre. When Riley protests that he lacks the money needed to fulfill Peg's desires, she answers that he would have plenty of cash if he didn't spend so much on "needless gadgets." His shortage of funds becomes personal failure caused by incompetent behavior as a consumer. Nowhere do we hear about the size of his paycheck, relations between his union and his employer, or, for that matter, of the relationship between the value of his labor and the wages paid to him by the Stevenson Aircraft Company. Like Uncle David in *The Goldbergs* (who buys a statue of Hamlet shaking hands with Shakespeare and an elk's tooth with the Gettysburg address carved on it), Riley's comic character stems in part from a flaw which might be more justly applied to the entire consumer economy: a preoccupation with "needless gadgets." By contrast, Peg Riley's desire for an evening out is portrayed as reasonable and modest, as reparations due her for the inevitable tedium of housework. The solution to her unhappiness comes from an evening out, rather than from a change in her work circumstance. Even within the home, television elevates consumption over production· production is assumed to be a constant, only consumption can be varied. But more than enjoyment is at stake. Unless Riley can provide Peg with the desired night on the town, he will fail in his obligations as a husband and father.[22] . . .

. . . "Mama's Birthday," broadcast in 1954, delineated the tensions between family loyalty and consumer desire endemic to modern capitalist society. The show begins with Mama teaching Katrin to make Norwegian meatballs, which she used long ago to "catch" Papa. Unimpressed by that accomplishment, Katrin changes the subject and asks Mama what she wants for her birthday. In an answer that locates Mama within the gender roles of the 1950s, she replies, "Well, I think a fine new job for your Papa. You and Dagmar to marry nice young men and have a lot of wonderful children—just like I have. And Nels, well, Nels to become president of the United States."[23] In one sentence Mama sums up the dominant culture's version of legitimate female expectations: success at work for her husband, marriage and childrearing for her daughters, the presidency for her son—and nothing for herself.

But we learn that Mama does have some needs, although we do not hear it from her lips. Her sister, Jenny, asks Mama to attend a fashion show, but Mama cannot leave the house because she has to cook a roast for a guest whom Papa has invited to dinner. Jenny comments that Mama never seems to get out of the kitchen, adding that "it's a shame that a married woman can't have some time to herself." The complaint is a valid one, and we can imagine how it might have resonated for women in the 1950s. The increased availability of household appliances and the use of synthetic fibers and commercially processed food should have decreased the amount of time women spent in housework, but surveys showed that homemakers spent the same number of hours per week (between 51 and 56) doing housework as had been the norm in the 1920s. Advertising and marketing strategies undermined the labor-saving potential of technological changes because they upgraded standards of cleanliness in the home and expanded desires for more varied wardrobes and menus for the average family.[24] In that context, Aunt Jenny would have been justified in launching into a tirade about the division of labor within the Hansen household or about the possibilities for cooperative housework, but network television specializes in less social and more commodified dialogues about problems like housework. Aunt Jenny suggests that her sister's family buy Mama a "fireless cooker," a cast-iron stove, for her birthday. "They're wonderful," she tells them in language borrowed from the rhetoric of advertising. "You just put your dinner inside them, close 'em up, and go wherever you please. When you come back your dinner is all cooked." Papa protests that Mama likes to cook on her woodburning stove, but Jenny dismisses that objection with an insinuation about his motives when she replies, "Well I suppose it *would* cost a little more than you could afford, Hansen."[25]

By identifying a commodity as the solution to Mama's problem, Aunt Jenny unites the inner voice of Mama with the outer voice of the television sponsor. . . . Prodded by their aunt, the Hansen children go shopping and purchase the fireless cooker from a storekeeper who calls the product "the new Emancipation Proclamation—setting housewives free from their old kitchen range."[26] Our exposure to advertising hyperbole should not lead us to miss the analogy here: housework is compared to slavery and the commercial product takes on the aura of Abraham Lincoln. The shopkeeper's appeal convinces the children to pool their resources and buy the stove for Mama. But we soon learn that Papa plans to make a fireless cooker for Mama with his tools. When Mama discovers Papa's intentions, she persuades the children to buy her another gift. Even Papa admits that his stove will not be as efficient as one made in a factory, but Mama nobly affirms that she will like his better because he made it himself. The children use their money to buy dishes for Mama (a gift hardly likely to leave her with less work), and Katrin remembers the episode as Mama's happiest birthday ever.

The stated resolution of "Mama's Birthday" favors traditional values. Mama prefers to protect Papa's pride instead of having a better stove. The product built by a family member has more value than the one sold as a commodity. Yet as was so often the case in these urban, ethnic, working-class comedies, the entire development of the plot leads in the opposite direction. The "fireless cooker" is the star of the episode, setting in motion all the other characters, and it has an unquestioned value, even in the face of Jenny's meddlesome brashness, Papa's insensitivity, and Mama's old-fashioned ideals. Buying a product appears as the true means of changing the unpleasant realities and low status of women's work in the home.

This resolution of the conflict between consumer desires and family roles reflected television's social role as mediator between the family and the economy. . . . The television industry recognized and promoted its privileged place within families in advertisements like the one in *The New York Times* in 1950 that claimed, "Youngsters today need television for their morale as much as they need fresh air and sunshine for their health."[27] Like previous communications media, television sets occupied honored places in family living rooms and helped structure family time, but unlike other previous communications media, television displayed available commodities in a way that transformed home entertainment into a glorified shopping catalog. . . .

Notes

1. See Romasco (1965) and Bernstein (1968).

2. Berger (1982).

3. Lipsitz (1981).

4. Lipsitz (1981).

5. Lipsitz (1981).

6. *TV Facts* (1980, p. 141).

7. Nielsen ratings epitomize television's view of the family as separate market segments to be addressed independently.

8. Boddy (1986); Allen (1983).

9. Lipsitz (1981, pp. 120-121).

10. Moore and Klein (1962); Jezer (1982).

11. Hartmann (1982, pp. 165-168); Mollenkopf (1983, p. 111).

12. "The Lush New Suburban Market" (1953, p. 128).

13. Stone (1983, p. 122).

14. Quoted in Jezer (1982, p. 127).

15. Dichter (1960, p. 210).

16. Dichter (1960, p. 209).

17. "The Rock and Roll Kid," *Hey, Jeannie*, Academy of Television Arts Collection, University of California, Los Angeles.

18. "The In-Laws," *The Goldbergs (Molly)*, Academy of Television Arts Collection, University of California, Los Angeles.

19. "The In-Laws," *The Goldbergs (Molly)*.

20. "Moving Day," *The Goldbergs (Molly)*, Academy of Television Arts Collection, University of California, Los Angeles.

21. "R228," *Life of Riley*, Academy of Television Arts Collection, University of California, Los Angeles.

22. "R228," *Life of Riley*; "Bad Companions," *The Goldbergs (Molly)*, Academy of

Television Arts Collection, University of California, Los Angeles.

23. Elizabeth Meehan and Bradford Ropes, "Mama's Birthday," Theater Arts Collection, University Research Library. University of California, Los Angeles.

24. Hartmann (1982, p. 168).

25. Elizabeth Meehan and Bradford Ropes, "Mama's Birthday."

26. Elizabeth Meehan and Bradford Ropes, "Mama's Birthday."

27. Wolfenstein (1951).

◆ References

Allen, J. (1983). The social matrix of television: Invention in the United States. In E. A. Kaplan (Ed.), *Regarding television* (pp. 109-119). Los Angeles: University Publications of America.

Berger, H. (1982, March 12). *Social protest in St. Louis.* Paper presented at a Missouri Committee for the Humanities Forum, St. Louis, MO.

Bernstein, B. (1968). The conservative achievements of New Deal reform. In B. Bernstein (Ed.), *Towards a new past.* New York: Vintage.

Boddy, W. (1986). The studios move into prime time: Hollywood and the television industry in the 1950s. *Cinema Journal, 12*(4), 23-27.

Dichter, E. (1960). *The strategy of desire.* Garden City, NY: Doubleday.

Hartmann, S. (1982). *The home front and beyond.* Boston: Twayne.

Jezer, M. (1982). *The dark ages.* Boston: South End.

Lipsitz, G. (1981). *Class and culture in cold war America.* Westport, CT: Greenwood.

The lush new suburban market. (1953, November). *Fortune.*

Mollenkopf, J. (1983). *The contested city.* Princeton, NJ: Princeton University Press.

Moore, G., & Klein, P. (1976). *The quality of consumer installment credit.* Washington, DC: National Bureau of Economics Research.

Romasco, A. U. (1965). *The poverty of attendance.* New York: Oxford University Press.

Stone, M. (1983). Housing: The economic crisis. In C. Hartman (Ed.), *America's housing crisis: What is to be done?* New York: Routledge & Kegan Paul.

TV facts. (1980). New York: Facts on File.

Wolfenstein, M. (1951). The emergence of fun morality. *Journal of Social Issues, 7*(4), 15-25.

4

NAKED CAPITALISTS

◆ Frank Rich

The men and women in the San Fernando Valley who produce "adult" videos are not the gold-chained creeps of your fantasies. They're as American as consumerism, presiding over a $10 billion business that gives millions of viewers exactly what they want.

In late January 1998, during the same week that America first heard the ribald tale of the president and the intern, Variety tucked onto Page 5 a business story that caused no stir whatsoever. Under a Hollywood dateline, the show-biz trade paper reported that the adult-video business "saw record revenues last year" of some $4.2 billion in rentals and sales.

It soon became clear to me that these bicoastal stories, one from the nation's political capital and the other from its entertainment capital, were in some essential way the same story.

In the weeks that followed, Washington commentators repeatedly predicted that the public would be scandalized by the nonmissionary-position sex acts performed illicitly in the White House. But just as repeatedly voters kept telling pollsters that they weren't blushing as brightly as, say, Cokie Roberts. The Variety story, I realized, may have in part explained why. An unseemly large percentage of Americans was routinely

NOTE: From *New York Times Magazine*, May 20, 2001, Section 6. Copyright © 2001, the New York Times. Used by permission.

seeking out stories resembling that of the president and the intern—and raunchier ones—as daily entertainment fare.

The $4 billion that Americans spend on video pornography is larger than the annual revenue accrued by either the N.F.L., the N.B.A. or Major League Baseball. But that's literally not the half of it: the porn business is estimated to total between $10 billion and $14 billion annually in the United States when you toss in porn networks and pay-per-view movies on cable and satellite, Internet Web sites, in-room hotel movies, phone sex, sex toys and that archaic medium of my own occasionally misspent youth, magazines. Take even the low-end $10 billion estimate (from a 1998 study by Forrester Research in Cambridge, Mass.), and pornography is a bigger business than professional football, basketball and baseball put together. People pay more money for pornography in America in a year than they do on movie tickets, more than they do on all the performing arts combined. As one of the porn people I met in the industry's epicenter, the San Fernando Valley, put it, "We realized that when there are 700 million porn rentals a year, it can't just be a million perverts renting 700 videos each."

Yet in a culture where every movie gross and Nielsen rating is assessed ad infinitum in the media, the enormous branch of show business euphemistically called "adult" is covered as a backwater, not as the major industry it is. Often what coverage there is fixates disproportionately on Internet porn, which may well be the only Web business that keeps expanding after the dot-com collapse but still accounts for barely a fifth of American porn consumption. Occasionally a tony author—David Foster Wallace, George Plimpton and Martin Amis, most recently—will go slumming at a porn awards ceremony or visit a porn set to score easy laughs and even easier moral points. During sweeps weeks, local news broadcasts "investigate" adult businesses, mainly so they can display hard bodies in the guise of hard news. And of course, there is no

shortage of academic literature and First Amendment debate about pornography, much of it snarled in the ideological divisions among feminists, from the antiporn absolutism of Catharine MacKinnon and Andrea Dworkin to the pro-porn revisionism of Sallie Tisdale and Susie Bright.

I'm a lifelong show-biz junkie, and what sparked my interest in the business was what I stumbled upon in Variety—its sheer hugeness. Size matters in the cultural marketplace. If the machinations of the mainstream TV, movie and music industries offer snapshots of the American character, doesn't this closeted entertainment behemoth tell us something as well? At $10 billion, porn is no longer a sideshow to the mainstream like, say, the $600 million Broadway theater industry—it *is* the mainstream.

And so I went to the San Fernando Valley, aka Silicone Valley, on the other side of the Hollywood Hills, to talk with the suits of the adult business. I did not see any porn scenes being shot. I did not talk to any antiporn crusaders or their civil-libertarian adversaries. I did not go to construct a moral brief. I wanted to find out how some of the top players conduct their business and how they viewed the Americans who gorge on their products.

Among other things, I learned that the adult industry is in many ways a mirror image of Hollywood. Porn movies come not only in all sexual flavors but also in all genres, from period costume dramas to sci-fi to comedy. (One series is modeled on the old Hope-Crosby "Road" pictures.) Adult has a fabled frontier past about which its veterans wax sentimental—the "Boogie Nights" '70s, when porn was still shot only on film and seen in adult movie theaters. (The arrival of home video revolutionized porn much as sound did Hollywood.) Adult also has its own Variety (Adult Video News), its own starmaking machinery (the "girls" at Vivid and Wicked are promoted like bygone MGM contract players), its own prima donnas and cineastes. It has (often silent) business partners in high places: two of the country's more prominent porn purveyors, Marriott (through in-room X-rated movies) and General Motors (through its ownership of the satellite giant DirecTV, now probably to be sold to Rupert Murdoch), were also major sponsors of the Bush-Cheney Inaugural. Porn even has its own Matt Drudge— a not-always-accurate Web industry gossip named Luke Ford, who shares his prototype's political conservatism and salacious obsessiveness yet is also, go figure, a rigorously devout convert to Judaism.

I didn't find any porn titans in gold chains, but I did meet Samantha Lewis, former real-estate saleswoman and current vice president of Digital Playground, whose best-selling "Virtual Sex" DVDs are, she says, "the Rolexes and Mercedeses of this business." I talked with Bill Asher, 38, the head of Vivid, who is an alumnus of Dartmouth and U.S.C. (for his M.B.A.) and Lawry's (the restaurant chain). I listened to the story of John Stagliano, who was once a U.C.L.A. economics major with plans "to teach at the college level" but who instead followed his particular erotic obsession and became Buttman, the creator of hugely popular improvisational *cinema-verite* porn videos that have been nicknamed "gonzo" in honor of the freewheeling literary spirit of Hunter S. Thompson. A political libertarian, Stagliano was for a while a big-time contributor to the Cato Institute.

If the people who make and sell pornography are this "normal"—and varied— might not the audience be, too? It can't be merely the uneducated and unemployed who shell out the $10 billion. And it isn't. Porn moguls describe a market as diverse as America. There's a college-age crowd that favors tattooed and pierced porn performers; there's an older, suburban audience that goes for "sweeter, nicer, cuter girls," as Bill Asher of Vivid Pictures puts it. There is geriatric porn (one fave is called "Century Sex"), and there's a popular video called "Fatter, Balder, Uglier." Oral sex sells particularly well in the Northeast, ethnic and interracial videos sell in cities (especially in

the South), and the Sun Belt likes to see outdoor sex set by beaches and pools.

Yet such demographics are anecdotally, not scientifically, obtained. So few Americans fess up when asked if they are watching adult product, says Asher, "that you'd think there is no business." But in truth, there's no business like porn business. Porn is the one show that no one watches but that, miraculously, never closes.

"Porn doesn't have a demographic—it goes across all demographics," says Paul Fishbein, 42, the compact and intense man who founded Adult Video News. "There were 11,000 adult titles last year versus 400 releases in Hollywood. There are so many outlets that even if you spend just $15,000 two days—and put in some plot and good-looking people and decent sex—you can get satellite and cable sales. There are so many companies, and they rarely go out of business. You have to be really stupid or greedy to fail."

He points me toward the larger producers whose videos top AVN's charts and have the widest TV distribution. There are many successful companies, but some of them cater to niche markets (like gay men) that as of yet haven't cracked the national mass market of TV, where pay-per-view pornographic movies, though priced two or three times higher and not promoted, often outsell the Hollywood hits competing head to head. In a business with no barrier to entry—anyone with a video camera can be a director or star—there are also countless bottom feeders selling nasty loops on used tape. Whatever the quality or origin of a product, it can at the very least be exhibited on one of the 70,000 adult pay Web sites, about a quarter of which are owned by a few privately held companies that slice and dice the same content under different brands.

Fishbein has a staff of 62 to track it all. He seems smart, sensible and mercurial—in other words, just like any other successful editor. And like almost everyone else I met in porn, he says he fell into it by accident. While a journalism student at Temple University in his hometown, Philadelphia, he managed a video store and found that customers kept asking him how to differentiate one adult tape from another. It was the early '80s, and the VCR was starting to conquer America, its popularity in large part driven (as the Internet's would be later) by the easier and more anonymous access it offered to porn. Prior to home video, pornography had a far smaller audience, limited mainly to men willing to venture into the muck of a Pussycat Cinema—the "raincoaters," as the trade refers to that dying breed of paleo-consumer. The VCR took porn into America's bedrooms and living rooms—and, by happenstance, did so at the same time that the spread of AIDS began to give sexual adventurers a reason to stay home. There is no safer sex than porn.

As adult titles on tape proliferated, Fishbein started a newsletter to rate them. Other video-store owners, uncertain about which porn films to stock, took a look. Now, some 18 years later. Fishbein runs an empire that includes 10 Web sites and spin-off journals like AVN Online. He also stages trade shows and presents the AVN Awards in Vegas in January. An issue of AVN can run in excess of 350 slick pages, much of it advertising, in which a daunting number of reviews (some 400 a month) jostle for space with sober reportage like "For Adult, Ashcroft Signals Circle the Wagons Time." Fishbein has a soft spot for porn veterans like Al Goldstein, the 65-year-old paterfamilias of Screw magazine who writes a column for Fishbein's main Web site, AVN.com, in which Goldstein sometimes rails against the new corporate generation of pornographers who have no memory of the daring and sacrifice of their elders. "Al Goldstein took 19 arrests for this business." Fishbein says reverently.

Though he embodies the corporatization of porn, Fishbein exudes a certain swagger. "I'm here by accident, and now that I'm here, I'm proud of what I do," he says. "My

mother sits at my awards table each year when girls accept awards for oral sex. Sex sells and it drives the media, and it always has. Billboards, movies, ads, commercials. It's what we're thinking about at all times of the day. We're told it's bad, and it manifests itself as political debates."

Fishbein assures me that he has no "naked girls running through the office," and alas, he is right—though a staff member does wander in with a photo to ask, "Was that the naked sushi party?" But there's a pleasant buzz and bustle about the place—one I associate with journalism. "This could be a magazine about pens and pencils," Fishbein says. Maybe.

The browsers on the two computers behind his desk are kept on CNN.com and AVN.com, which is modeled on CNN's as a (porn) news portal. The decor of his large, meticulous office is mostly movie memorabilia. A film buff as well as a news junkie. Fishbein is a particular fan of the high-end comedies of Woody Allen, Albert Brooks and Preston Sturges, and he could be a highly articulate, slightly neurotic leading man out of one of them. He speaks glowingly of having just taken his 12-year-old stepdaughter to "Yi Yi." Does he watch the movies that AVN reviews? He flinches. "I haven't watched an adult movie without fast-forwarding since I saw one in a theater at 18. I watch them for business reasons. My wife and I don't watch them for entertainment. It is hard for me to look at it as more than product."

Many of the top porn producers are within blocks of Fishbein's office in the utterly anonymous town of Chatsworth—an unhurried, nondescript sprawl of faded strip malls, housing developments and low-slung (and usually unmarked) business complexes that look more like suburban orthodontic offices than porn factories. Everyone in the business seems to know one another. "There's a certain camaraderie among those who are on the fringe of society, a similarity to outlaws," Fishbein says. Yet he seems like anything but an outlaw; he was about to fly off to the

Super Bowl and then a skiing vacation. I ask if organized crime is a factor in today's porn world. "When I got here, I heard there were mob companies," he answers. "But I've never even been approached by a criminal element. I've never been threatened or bribed. So if it ever existed, it's part of the history of the business." He almost sounds disappointed.

Russell Hampshire, who owns one of the biggest companies, VCA Pictures, did do time in jail—nine months in 1988 for shipping obscene videotapes across state lines to federal agents in Alabama. Somewhat more prosaically, he is also a graduate of McDonald's Hamburger U., which he attended while running McDonald's franchises in El Paso in the '70s. It's business training that came in handy in the porn biz. "I learned about inventory, buying the proper insurance, doing everything by the book, not taking shortcuts," he says.

Hampshire, who runs VCA with his wife of 10 years, Betty, has an Oscar Madison look—Hawaiian shirts, gym shorts and a baseball cap. I wouldn't want to get on his bad side. He's big and leathery and sounds like Lee Marvin as written by Damon Runyon. Asked why the sign outside says "Trac Tech" instead of VCA, he says he wants to stay "as innocuous as possible."

He has been in the business since 1978 and waxes nostalgic for the early video days, when you could transfer a prevideo Marilyn Chambers classic to cassette and sell it wholesale for up to a hundred bucks. Now his top movies wholesale for $18 or $19, sometimes lower. "There used to be only 10 to 12 titles to choose from in a video store," he says. "Now there are thousands of titles." A typical release may sell only 2,000 units or less—7,500 would be a modest hit—but thanks to TV and international sales, Hampshire says he makes money "on every title." Though the total income from a hit is pocket money by Hollywood standards, Hollywood should only have such profit margins. An adult film that brings in $250,000 may cost only $50,000 to make—five times the original investment. Production locations are often rented homes, shooting schedules run less than a week, and most projects are not shot on the costly medium of film. There are no unions or residuals. Marketing costs are tiny, since quote ads run in AVN and skin magazines, not in national publications or on TV. Most economically of all, porn movies don't carry the huge expense of theatrical distribution: video killed off adult movie theaters far more effectively than it did regular movie theaters.

Still, Hampshire resents the lower overhead of porn's newcomers: "I have 80 employees. I have a 100 percent medical plan for everyone's family—dental and vision care too. Some of my guys have been working here 17 or 18 years. And I'm up against amateurs with $800 Handicams." He also grouses about the new administration in Washington, as many in the industry do, fearing there could be a replay of the war on porn during the Reagan years, when Attorney General Edwin Meese called for restrictions on live sex shows and the dissemination of pornographic materials. "I like the rest of Bush's cabinet—just not Ashcroft," Hampshire says.

With the company's in-house press rep, a former preschool teacher named Mischa Allen, in tow, Hampshire takes me on a tour of VCA's 40,000-square-foot operation, proudly showing off the state-of-the-art video-editing bays, the room containing 3,000 video-duplication decks (churning out 400,000 tapes a month) and the prop room in which I spot a neon sign for "Bada Boom" from the set of the recent "Sopornos 2." The mechanized assembly line on which the tapes are boxed and shrink-wrapped is as efficient as that for bottling Coke.

But more than anything, VCA resembles the corporate headquarters of a sports franchise. Only on close inspection do I realize that a towering glass case full of what look like trophies in the reception area in fact contains awards such as the 1996 Best

Group Sex Scene, bestowed upon the "Staircase Orgy" from "New Wave Hookers 4." Hampshire, an avid golfer and bowler, has lined VCA's corridors with his collection of autographed sports jerseys, the latest from Tiger Woods. On one wall are plaques of appreciation from the Hampshires' philanthropic beneficiaries, including a local school to which they donate video equipment and free yearbook printing.

Hampshire's own office is spacious, outfitted with leather furniture, but—characteristically for the business—looks like a bunker. Above his desk is a console of TV screens tuned into the feeds from security cameras. Incongruously, this inner sanctum's walls are festooned with another variety of pompously framed "collectibles"—autographed letters and photographs from Anwar Sadat, Menachem Begin, Jimmy Carter and Richard Nixon. Hampshire says they're all copies, but he points to a melted-looking clock and says, "I've got Salvador Dalis all over the place—*authentic* Salvador Dalis." He also shows off a vintage group photo of Murder Inc.

But Hampshire describes his existence as considerably more mundane than Bugsy Siegel's. He almost never goes to a set, where the hurry-up-and-wait pace makes it as "boring as Hollywood." He ticks off his duties: "Dealing with distributors and OSHA rules and regulations. I have to write reviews of all my department heads and decide raises."

As I leave his office I notice still another framed artifact: a Bronze Star for "exceptionally valorous action on 12/8/67" while serving as a Company C rifleman in combat in Vietnam. The citation says that Hampshire "continually exposed himself to hostile fire" while saving the lives of his fellow soldiers.

It's the only thing that seems to embarrass him. "I buried it for so long," he says. "When I first came out here. I was ashamed to say anything because people might say I'm a bad person."

Almost every adult company is pursuing innovative media, preparing for Internet broadband and interactive hotel-room TV. At Wicked Pictures' newly revamped Web site, for instance, a visitor can cross-index a particular porn star with a sexual activity, then watch (and pay for) just those scenes that match. Digital Playground's "Virtual Sex" DVDs resemble video games in how they allow the user to control and inject himself into the "action."

As in nonadult video, DVD is cutting into videocassette sales—even more so in adult, perhaps, because DVDs have the added virtue of being more easily camouflaged on a shelf than cassettes. Hampshire is particularly proud of VCA's DVD technology. With his vast catalog, he is following the model of Hollywood studios by rereleasing classics—"The Devil in Miss Jones 2," "The Opening of Misty Beethoven"—in "Collectors Editions," replete with aural commentaries from original stars like Jamie Gillis. As with Hollywood's DVD rereleases, they are pitched at nostalgic consumers in the "boomer-retro" market. "These aren't 'adult'—they're pop culture now," says Mischa Allen.

But VCA aims far higher than merely recycling golden oldies. In a windowless VCA office, I meet Wit Maverick, the head of its DVD production unit. He is 37, and with his blue Oxford shirt, goatee and glasses, he could be a professor somewhere—perhaps at Cal Arts, where he got a master's in film directing. He ended up at VCA, he says, because it was "the best opportunity to push the envelope of technology."

Maverick knocks mainstream studios for providing only a linear cinematic experience on their DVDs. "There's a great hubris in Hollywood," he says. "They think the way the director made the film is the only way the story can be told. We have a lot more humility. If a viewer wants something different, we give it to him." As an example he cites "Being With Juli Ashton," VCA's take on "Being John Malkovich." The viewer, Maverick says, "can go inside the head of the person having sex with Juli Ashton, male or female. He can choose which character to follow. He can re-edit the movie. Would James Cameron let anyone do that with 'Titanic'?

"I feel like filmmakers 100 years ago," Maverick continues. "It's a great technology, but we still don't know what to do with it. A hundred years from now I want grad students to read what I've done on DVD the way I read about D. W. Griffith."

Wit Maverick collaborates on his DVDs at VCA with Veronica Hart, 44, one of the business's most prominent female executives and, before that, a leading porn star of the late '70s and early '80s.

Universally known as Janie—her real name is Jane Hamilton—she is typical of the mostly likeable people I met in the porn world. She combines hardheaded show-biz savvy and humor with an utter lack of pretension and even some actual candor—a combination unheard of on the other side of the hills.

"The difference between us and Hollywood," she elaborates, "is money and ego. We deal with thousands of dollars, not millions. In mainstream, people are more cutthroat and pumped up about themselves. We're just like regular people—it has to do with exposing yourself. If you show something this intimate, there isn't a lot you can hide behind. You're a little more down to earth. We're not curing cancer. We're providing entertainment."

Hart studied theater at the University of Nevada in her hometown, Las Vegas. After acting leads in plays by Pinter and Garcia Lorca—as far east as Kennedy Center's annual college theater festival—she passed through the music business in England and worked as a secretary at Psychology Today magazine in New York before ending up in movies like "Wanda Whips Wall Street." While we are talking in her office she looks up Veronica Hart's 100-plus performing credits on the Internet, including

some non-hard-core B movies with faded mainstream actors like Farley Granger and Linda Blair. "In this one I played a stripper," she says while scrolling down the list. "*That* was a real stretch."

She pulls back from the computer screen and sums up her career: "I was lucky enough to be a performer in the golden age of porn cinema. I'm no raving beauty, and I don't have the best body in the world, but I look approachable. And I've always really enjoyed sex." More recently, she played a cameo as a judge in "Boogie Nights," but she disputes that movie's historical accuracy about porn's prevideo age. "We never shot in L.A. back then, only in New York and San Francisco," she says. Indeed, adult exactly mimicked movie-industry history—beginning in New York, then moving west.

In 1982, at the top of her career, Hart fell in love and left the business. "AIDS had just started up, and I lost every gay person I knew," she says, listing close friends who worked on the production side of the straight-porn business. She had two sons and helped support her family in part by stripping. Though not intending to re-enter porn, eventually she did, as a producer and director.

Hart has been in adult longer than anyone I met and has done "everything" in it, she jokes, "including windows." She warns me that "any blanket statement about the business is meaningless" because it's so big that "every conceivable type of person" can be found in it. "You'll find someone who's into it to provide spiritual uplift and educational self-help," she says. "And if you want to find rotten, vicious, misogynistic bastards—you'll find them. You'll find everyone who fits the stereotype and everyone who goes against the stereotype. In the loop and disposable-porno section of our business, you'll find the carnival freak-show mentality. There has to be a geek show somewhere in our society. What ticks me off is that all of adult is classified according to the lowest that's out there. We've always been legal. Child molestation has never been in mainstream adult. We've always policed ourselves. There's no coerced sex. But there are little pipsqueaks who get their disgusting little videos out there. There's a trend in misogynistic porn, and it's upsetting. I've been in the business for more than 20 years, and I helped make it possible for these guys to make these kinds of movies. I don't believe that's what America wants to see."

As for her own movies, Hart, like many of her peers, is preoccupied with the industry's biggest growth market—women and couples. The female audience was thought to be nearly nil when consuming pornography required a visit to a theater, an adult bookstore or the curtained adult section of a video store. But now hard core is available at chains like Tower (though not Blockbuster), through elaborate Web sites like Adultdvdempire that parallel Amazon and by clicking a pay-per-view movie on a TV menu (where the bill won't specify that an adult title was chosen).

The Valley's conventional wisdom has it that women prefer more romance, foreplay and story, as well as strong female characters who, says Bill Asher of Vivid, "are not only in charge of the sex but the rest of the plot." Hart isn't sure. "Just because women like romance doesn't mean we want soft sex," she says. "We want hot and dirty sex just like anybody else. For instance, many women love the fantasy of being taken—but how do you portray it without sending a message to some guys to abduct?"

Hart, who thought of herself as a sexual pioneer when she was a porn performer, finds that there is no shortage of women who want to appear in adult now. She never has to search for new talent; willing performers call her "from all over the country." The men? "They're props."

Today's porn stars can be as temperamental as their Hollywood counterparts, or more so. "I assume Sarah Jessica Parker and Kim Cattrall show up on the set on time," said Paul Fishbein rather tartly when I asked

about Jenna Jameson, the industry's reigning It girl of recent years. Though he was trying to give her a free vacation as thanks for her work as host of the recent AVN awards, Jameson wasn't returning his calls. "In adult, they don't show up and don't care," Fishbein says. "Lots of girls in this business—and guys, too—are dysfunctional. The girls get here at 18 and aren't mature. They do it because they're rebels or exhibitionists or need money. They think they're making real movies and get really upset when they don't win awards or get good reviews."

Some porn directors have similar pretensions. They can receive grandiose billing— "A Brad Armstrong Motion Picture"—and are sometimes grudgingly indulged with a "big budget" project ($250,000 tops) made on film, even though sex scenes are far harder to shoot on film (with its trickier lighting and shot setups) than on video— and even though adult films are almost never projected on screens. "We have our own Brad Pitts wanting to make 'Seven Days in Tibet,'" said one executive. Performers are paid at fairly standardized rates—by the day or sex scene, as much as $1,000 per day for women, as little as $200 for men. The contract girls at Vivid and Wicked sign for $100,000 and up a year, in exchange for which they might make nine movies, with two sex scenes each, over that time, along with any number of brand-boosting promotional appearances at consumer conventions and video stores. The top stars double or triple that figure by running their own subscription Web sites, marketing autographs (along with less innocent mementos) and most lucratively, dancing in the nation's large circuit of strip clubs at fees that can top $10,000 a week.

But porn stars have an even shorter shelf life than Hollywood's female stars and fare worse in love. Though HIV and drug testing, as well as condom use, are rigorous at the top adult companies, one producer asks rhetorically, "Who wants to date a woman who's had sex with 60 people in two months?"

Since I've rarely found actors to be the most insightful observers of the movie business, I wasn't eager to sample the wisdom of porn stars. But I did seek out Sydnee Steele, a newly signed Wicked contract girl who is by many accounts a rarity in the business—she's happily married. Her husband is Michael Raven, 36, a top adult director. They met in Dallas in the early '90s, when she was a jewelry saleswoman in a shopping mall and he was a car salesman who sold her a mariner blue Miata. Eventually they drifted into the local swingers' scene. (One porn worker would later tell me, "Texas, Florida and Arizona are where all the swingers and strippers come from, though no one knows why.")

"The industry looks up to our relationship," Raven says when I meet the couple, now married nine years, at Sin City, another production company in Chatsworth. Avid porn fans in Texas, they migrated to the Valley to turn their avocation into a livelihood. Like many of the directors and male performers in the business, Raven is a somewhat lumpy everyman, heading toward baldness and sporting a meticulous goatee. A Kandinsky poster decorates the Sin City office. "I've gotten jealous on occasion," Raven allows. "I'm not jealous of her because of sex in movies; I'm jealous when her work takes her away from me. I get lonely if she's gone two weeks on the road."

"Sometimes I'm too tired for my husband," Steele says. "We love what we do, but it's hard work—lots of 12-hour days." By now, I've watched some of what she does and find it hard to square the rapacious star of "Hell on Heels" with the woman before me, who is softer-spoken, prettier and considerably less animated than her screen persona. Maybe she *can* act.

The daughter of a college professor, Steele comes from what she calls a "'Leave It to Beaver' nuclear family," Raven from a religious one. "I've leaned toward the right in my politics," he says, "but I'm bothered by the Republicans' association with the religious right. I know from my experience of religious people that those who protest and scream the loudest usually have the biggest collection of adult under their bed." He wishes they'd protest violent entertainment instead: "In video games, you're supposed to destroy, maim and dismember an opponent. But if one person is giving pleasure to another in adult, that's evil. Sex on TV is more destructive than hard core. You can depict a rape on TV—we don't touch that subject."

Like his wife, Raven is increasingly recognized by strangers—largely because "Behind the Scenes" documentaries about his movies appear on DVDs and on cable erotic networks, much like Backstory features on American Movie Classics. But Raven no longer stays in contact with his own family. And Steele's parents, she says, "don't totally know what I'm doing and don't ask. We don't lie, but they've never really been told."

The secrecy among porn people is so prevalent that it's a running, if bittersweet, gag in a made-for-the-Internet TV series called "The Money Shot" that Paul Fishbein of AVN is producing as a lark. If you care to sample only one product of the adult industry, this is it—and the episodes can be seen free in streaming video on a nonporn site, moneyshot-theseries.com. But be warned, its rating clocks in at about PG-13. "The Money Shot" is a roman à clef comedy, much in the spirit of HBO's classic "Larry Sanders Show," about daily life in the adult biz, as it filters into the offices of an AVN-like publication called "Blue Movie Guide." In a rather poignant episode titled "The Parents Show," one character dolefully concludes, "Nobody in this business tells their folks nothing."

Bryn Pryor, 33, is the director and a writer of "The Money Shot." He's an AVN staff member who arrived in the Valley after nine years in the theater, much of it children's theater, in Arizona. "The Money Shot" hits his friends where they live. "Porn is legal now, but it has the mentality of other businesses, like prostitution and gambling, that started with organized-crime connections," he says. "People approach it as if they've done something wrong. If our customers project shame, then you must be doing something wrong. Everyone at AVN writes under a pseudonym. We have people here who don't want anyone to know their real name." Variations on this theme were visible everywhere I went in the Valley. Receptionists at porn companies tend to answer the phone generically: "Production Company" or "Corporate Office."

Typifying this ambivalence is Steve Orenstein, 38, the owner of Wicked Pictures. He made his accidental entrance into the porn business through his mother—who got him a part-time job when she worked as a bookkeeper at an adult-book distributor and he was 18. But he does not seem eager to reveal his calling to his 9-year-old stepdaughter.

"Being in the business you walk that line all the time—do you say what you do or not?" he says. Orenstein has revealed his true profession to only a handful of people whom he and his wife have met on the PTA circuit. "I'm comfortable with what I do," he says, "but I don't want parents of our child's friends saying their kids can't play with her because of it." His stepdaughter has noticed the Wicked logo on his shirt. "She knows I make something only adults can see."

The Orensteins have spoken to a therapist about the inevitable day of reckoning with their child. "The counselors say don't tell her yet," he says, "don't overexplain." But surely she'll guess by adolescence? Orenstein, a slight, nervous man with a reputation as a worrier, merely shrugs. For the moment, he's more concerned about protecting the child from prime-time television, citing a recent episode of the sitcom "The King of Queens" on CBS. He recalls: "The guy's rolling off his wife, and my 9-year-old asks, 'What do they mean by that?' Should I be letting her watch it?"

Russell Hampshire's gambit is to tell strangers he's in "the video-duplication business." Allen Gold, a VCA executive with daughters ages 1 and 3, says he's "in the DVD business." Paul Fishbein doesn't bring either AVN or adult product into his house. Michael Raven and Sydnee Steele have decided for now not to have children.

I ask Veronica Hart, whose two teenage sons are at magnet schools for the highly gifted, what they have made of the career. "It's horrible for them," she says. "I'm their loving mommy, and nobody likes to think of their parents having sex and being famous for it. I'm not ashamed of what I do. I take responsibility for who I am. I chose. From the time they were kids, my stripping gear was washed and hanging in the bathtub. At the same time I apologize to my kids for how the choices in my life have affected them. They're well adjusted and can joke with me about it: 'I know I'm going to spend the rest of my life on the couch.'"

No wonder the porn industry has its finger on the pulse of American tastes. Not only do its players have a lifestyle more middle class than that of their Beverly Hills counterparts, but in their desire to keep their porn careers camouflaged in a plain brown wrapper, they connect directly with their audience's shame and guilt. Still, the next generation of porn consumers and producers alike may break with that puritan mind-set. The teenagers who grew up with cable and the VCR "come to the table already saturated with sex," says Bryn Pryor. "They've never known a time without Calvin Klein ads and MTV. By the time they see porn, they've already seen so many naked people they're pre-jaded."

This may explain why Americans are clamoring for over more explicit fare. In mainstream TV, sex is no longer sequestered on late-night public access shows like "Robin Byrd." At HBO, Sheila Nevins, the highly regarded executive in charge of its nonfiction programming, has been stunned by the success of sexual documentaries like "Real Sex," now in its

11th year, and "Taxicab Confessions." Focus groups complain to HBO that another hit series, "G-String Divas," doesn't go far enough. "They know what really happens in a strip club," Nevins says, and find HBO's version "too R-rated." Though HBO, known for its heavy promotions of "The Sopranos" and "Sex and the City," spends nothing to advertise its sex series, they always are among the network's most watched. "I can do all the shows I want about poverty in the Mississippi Delta," Nevins says, "but this is what hard-working Americans want to see. At first we were embarrassed by the sex shows, and producers didn't want their names on them. Now we have Academy Award producers, and their names can't be big enough."

At Playboy, Jim English, the head of its TV division, and his boss, Christie Hefner, have felt the heat. Its Playboy and Spice channels have been squeezed from both sides in the cable-satellite marketplace. The softer, if X-rated, cuts of hard-core movies that it runs are no longer much more explicit than regular cable programming at HBO, Showtime ("Queer as Folk") and MTV ("Spring Break"). Even the Learning Channel (with "Bra Wars" and "Wild Weddings") and the History Channel (with its four-part "Sex in the 20th Century") are testing the waters. Meanwhile, erotic networks like Hot and Ecstasy, which run XX films, are cannibalizing Playboy's audience from the other end of the erotic spectrum. The result: This summer Playboy plans to start "Spice Platinum Live," which edges toward XXX. (I'll leave the codified yet minute clinical distinctions separating X, XX and:to your imagination.)

Even in an economic downturn, everything's coming up porn. Newly unemployed dot-com techies who can't find jobs in Silicon Valley are heading to Silicone Valley, where the work force is expanding, not contracting. "Vivid overall has doubled, tripled revenues and profits in the past couple of years," says Bill Asher. While he says there's no such thing as a Hollywood-style "home run" in porn—unless another celebrity like Pamela Anderson turns up in a sex video, intentionally or not—he sees potentially "a tenfold jump" in profits as distribution increases through broadband and video-on-demand. (Porn executives are no less fuzzy than Hollywood's as to when this might be.) "There are opportunities here that Paramount will never have in terms of growth," Asher says. "Our product travels well internationally and is evergreen. Five-year-old product is still interesting to someone; it's not yesterday's news like a five-year-old Hollywood blockbuster. Our costs are relatively fixed. As there's more distribution, 90 cents of a dollar hits the bottom line." The absence of adult retail stores in conservative pockets of the country is no longer a barrier. "You can get a dish relatively anywhere," Asher says, "and get whatever you want."

When Vivid took over and expanded the Hot Network in 1999, Asher says, "there was no outcry. We got thank-you letters and sales boomed. We put up two more channels in months. Cable companies were begging for them. It doesn't take a genius to do this. Literally the customers say, I like what you've got—give me some more of it." Entertainment-industry executives not directly involved in the adult business confirm its sunny future. Satellite and cable companies have found that the more explicit the offerings, the more the market grows. AVN reports that TV porn may actually be increasing video-store sales and rentals rather than cannibalizing them—by introducing new customers to the product. Though some cable companies say they don't want adult, only one of the country's eight major cable providers, Adelphia, forbids it. The others are too addicted to the cash flow to say no. The organized uproar that recently persuaded a teetering Yahoo to drop its adult Web store—but not its gateways into other adult sites—is the exception, not the rule.

And despite a rumor that one porn mogul keeps a Cessna waiting at Van Nuys airport to escape to Brazil if there's a government crackdown, the odds of that look slim. Too many Fortune 500 corporations with Washington clout, from AT&T to AOL Time Warner, make too much money on porn—whether through phone sex, chat rooms or adult video. At the local level, the Supreme Court's 1973 "community standard" for obscenity may be a non sequitur now that there's a XX national standard disseminated everywhere by satellite and the Web. A busted local video retailer in a conservative community can plead that his product is consistent with what the neighbors are watching on pay-per-view—as one such owner successfully did in Utah last fall.

Should John Ashcroft's Justice Department go after porn, smart betting has him pursuing shadowy purveyors of extreme porn on the Internet (though it's not clear that the actionable stuff originates in the United States) and child pornography, all of which is condemned by the professional adult industry. "No one in this business will complain if Ashcroft goes for the kid angle," Fishbein says.

Jim English of Playboy suggests that one way to meet the typical American porn audience en masse is to accompany him to a live broadcast of a hit Playboy show called "Night Calls 411." Fittingly, "Night Calls" is televised from a studio in Hollywood, right by the old Gower Gulch, where low-budget studios long ago churned out early features in bulk much as the adult business does now.

Two underclad hostesses, Crystal Knight and Flower, intersperse wisecracks and sex tips with viewers' phone calls. Though only a few callers get on the air, as many as 100,000 try to get through, with still more deluging the show with "Miss Lonelyhearts" e-mail.

It's not "Larry King Live," but in some ways it could be an adult version of the "Today" show, whose fans cross the country with the hope of being in view as the camera pans Rockefeller Center. The "Night Calls" devotees go further: many of them are engaging in sex when they call. "Having sex is not enough of a turn-on in America—you have to be on TV too," jokes English. The callers often ask that the hosts talk them through to what The Starr Report called completion, and the women oblige—hoping for slam-bam speed so they can move on to the next caller. I'm struck by how much the male and female callers alike mimic porn performers, with their clichéd sex talk and over-the-top orgasmic shrieks. The adult audience apes its entertainers as slavishly as teenagers do rock idols.

By now, I've become intimately familiar with the conventions of adult entertainment, having asked those I met in the business to steer me to their best products. I've watched Wicked's "Double Feature," a multiple winner of AVN awards, among them Best Comedy, and found it full of erudite cinematic references, including a campy spoof of Ed Wood films. I've seen Vivid's new "Artemesia," a costume drama set in 16th-century Italy and given AVN's highest rating; it is laced with high-flown ruminations on the meaning of art, somewhat compromised by the tattoos on the performers. From Video Team, a company specializing in interracial porn, there is a thriller called "Westside" with a social conscience reminiscent of "West Side Story," a soundtrack that features music by Aaron Copland and a take on the drug wars that wouldn't be out of place in "Traffic."

It's no wonder, though, that Stagliano's gonzo, in which the performers just get it on, has such a following. All the plot and costuming and set decoration and arty cinematography—why bother? The acting—who needs it? (In "Flashpoint," Jenna Jameson, cast as a female firefighter, sounds the same when sobbing over a colleague's death as she does in coital ecstasy.) The films are tedious, and I'm as tempted to fast-forward through the sex scenes as the nonsex scenes. No matter what the period or setting, no matter what the genre, every video comes to the same dead halt as the performers drop whatever characters they're supposed to be assuming and repeat the same sex acts, in almost exactly the same way, at the same intervals, in every film. At a certain point, the Kabuki-like ritualization of these sequences becomes unintentionally farcical, like the musical numbers in a '30s Hollywood musical or the stylized acrobatics in a martial-arts film. Farcical, but not exactly funny. All the artful mise en scène in the world cannot, for me anyway, make merchandised sex entertaining or erotic.

I tell Bryn Pryor of AVN and "The Money Shot" my reaction. He's a professional porn critic. Is this the best that adult has to offer?

"The top of the heap in porn is the bottom in mainstream," he says. "The sad fact is that while consumers are more aware than they've ever been, nobody cares if it's a good movie, and we all know that. They care if it's hot in whatever subjective way it's hot to them. Most porn directors don't even watch the sex; they just direct the dialogue. They tell the camera people they want three positions and then go off and eat."

He continues: "Porn is not a creative medium. Everyone in the porn industry says he's on the way to something else, like waiters and bartenders, but it may be that most of us belong here. If we were really good, we'd be doing something else."

Pryor envisions a day when adult and Hollywood will converge, but in a sense that's already the case. If much of porn ranges from silly to degrading, what's the alternative offered on the other side of the hills? The viewer who isn't watching a mediocre porn product is watching—what? "Temptation Island"? W.W.F.?

Moralists like to see in pornography a decline in our standards, but in truth it's an all-too-ringing affirmation of them. Porn is no more or less imaginative than much of the junk in the entertainment mainstream—though unlike much of that junk, it does have an undeniable practical use. In that regard, anyway, there may be no other product in the entire cultural marketplace that is more explicitly American.

5

HEGEMONY

James Lull

Hegemony is the power or dominance that one social group holds over others. This can refer to the "asymmetrical interdependence" of political-economic-cultural relations between and among nation-states (Straubhaar, 1991) or differences between and among social classes within a nation. Hegemony is "dominance and subordination in the field of relations structured by power" (Hall, 1985). But hegemony is more than social power itself; it is a method for gaining and maintaining power.

Classical Marxist theory, of course, stresses economic position as the strongest predictor of social differences. Today, more than a century after Karl Marx and Friedrich Engels wrote their treatises about capitalist exploitation of the working class, economic disparities still underlie and help reproduce social inequalities in industrialized societies. In that important, basic sense, Marxism and Marxist critical theory, which have been so badly maligned in the rhetoric surrounding the recent political transformation of communist nations, remain fundamentally on target. Technological developments in the twentieth century, however, have made the manner of social domination much more complex than before. Social class differences in today's world are not determined solely or directly by economic factors. Ideological influence is crucial now in the exercise of social power.

The Italian intellectual Antonio Gramsci—to whom the term hegemony is attributed—broadened materialist Marxist theory into the realm of ideology. Persecuted by his country's then fascist government (and writing from prison), Gramsci emphasized society's "super structure," its ideology-producing institutions, in struggles over meaning and power (1971, 1973, 1978; see also Boggs, 1976; Sassoon, 1980; and Simon, 1982). A shift in critical theory thus was made away from a preoccupation with capitalist society's "base" (its economic foundation) and towards its dominant dispensaries of ideas. Attention was given to the structuring of authority and dependence in symbolic environments that correspond to, but are not the same as, economically determined class-based structures and processes of industrial production. Such a theoretical turn seems a natural and necessary development in an era when communications technology is such a pervasive and potent ideological medium. According to Gramsci's theory of ideological hegemony, mass media are tools that ruling elites use to "perpetuate their power, wealth, and status [by popularizing] their own philosophy, culture and morality" (Boggs, 1976: 39). The mass media uniquely "introduce elements into individual consciousness that would not otherwise appear there, but will not be rejected by consciousness because they are so commonly shared in the cultural community" (Nordenstreng, 1977: 276). Owners and managers of media industries can produce and reproduce the content, inflections, and tones of ideas favorable to them far more easily than other social groups because they manage key socializing institutions, thereby guaranteeing that their points of view are constantly and attractively cast into the public arena.

Mass-mediated ideologies are corroborated and strengthened by an interlocking system of efficacious information-distributing agencies and taken-for-granted social practices that permeate every aspect social and cultural reality. Messages supportive of the status quo emanating from schools, businesses, political organizations, trade unions, religious groups, the military, and the mass media all dovetail together ideologically. This inter-articulating, mutually reinforcing process of ideological influence is the essence of hegemony. Society's most entrenched and powerful institutions—which all depend in one way or another on the same sources for economic support—fundamentally agree with each other ideologically.

Hegemony is not a *direct* stimulation of thought or action, but, according to Stuart Hall, is a "framing [of] all competing definitions of reality within [the dominant class's] range, bringing all alternatives within their horizons of thought. [The dominant class] sets the limits—mental and structural—within which subordinate classes 'live' and make sense of their subordination in such a way as to sustain the dominance of those ruling over them" (1977: 333). British social theorist Philip Elliott suggested similarly that the most potent effect of mass media is how they subtly influence their audiences to perceive social roles and routine personal activities. The controlling economic forces in society use the mass media to provide a "rhetoric [through] which these [concepts] are labeled, evaluated, and explained" (1974: 262). Television commercials, for example, encourage audiences to think of themselves as "markets rather than as a public, as consumers rather than citizens" (Gitlin, 1979: 255).

But hegemony does not mature strictly from ideological articulation. Dominant ideological streams must be subsequently reproduced in the activities of our most basic social units—families, workplace networks, and friendship groups in the many sites and undertakings of everyday life. Gramsci's theory of hegemony, therefore, connects ideological representation to culture. Hegemony requires that ideological assertions become self-evident cultural assumptions. Its effectiveness depends on subordinated peoples accepting the dominant ideology as "normal reality or common sense . . . in active forms of experience and consciousness" (Williams, 1976: 145). Because information and entertainment technology is so thoroughly integrated into the everyday realities of modern societies, mass media's social influence is not always recognized, discussed, or criticized, particularly in societies where the overall standard of living is relatively high. Hegemony, therefore, can easily go undetected (Bausinger, 1984).

Hegemony implies a willing agreement by people to be governed by principles, rules, and laws they believe operate in their best interests, even though in actual practice they may not. Social consent can be a more effective means of control than coercion or force. Again, Raymond Williams: "The idea of hegemony, in its wide sense, is . . . especially important in societies [where] electoral politics and public opinion are significant factors, and in which social practice is seen to depend on consent to certain dominant ideas which in fact express the needs of a dominant class" (1976: 145). Thus, in the words of Colombian communication theorist Jesús Martín-Barbero, "one class exercises hegemony to the extent that the dominating class has interests which the subaltern classes recognize as being in some degree their interests too" (1993: 74).

Relationships between and among the major information-diffusing, socializing agencies of a society and the interacting, cumulative, socially accepted ideological orientations they create and sustain is the essence of hegemony. The American television industry, for instance, connects with other large industries, especially advertising companies but also national and multinational corporations that produce, distribute, and market a wide range of commodities. So, for example, commercial TV networks no longer buy original children's television shows. Network executives only want new

program ideas associated with successful retail products already marketed to children. By late 1990 more than 20 toy-based TV shows appeared on American commercial TV weekly. Television also has the ability to absorb other major social institutions—organized religion, for instance—and turn them into popular culture. The TV industry also connects with government institutions, including especially the federal agencies that are supposed to regulate telecommunications. The development of American commercial broadcasting is a vivid example of how capitalist economic forces assert their power. Evacuation of the legislatively mandated public service ideal could only have taken place because the Federal Communications Commission stepped aside while commercial interests amassed power and expanded their influence. Symptomatic of the problem is the fact that government regulators typically are recruited from, and return to, the very industries they are supposed to monitor.

Transmedia and transgenre integrations with mutually reinforcing ideological consequences are also commonplace. Popular radio and video songs, for example, can also be commercials. . . . Commercial logos become products themselves and are reproduced on tee-shirts, posters, beach towels, and other informal media. The rhetoric of TV commercials and programs is recycled in the lyrics of rap music and in the routines of stand-up comedians performing live and on television. . . . There are films made for television, magazines published about television, and television news magazines. The most well-known national newspaper in the United States, *USA Today*, is sold nationwide in vending boxes that resemble TV sets. Television commercial appear on Channel One, an educational news channel shown to students in American elementary school classrooms. Logos that advertise only national gasoline, food, and motel chains appear on government highway signs, advising travelers of their availability at upcoming freeway exits. Expensive public relations campaigns of major corporations distribute "informational" supplementary textbooks to elementary and secondary school systems. Major business organizations send digests of their annual reports and other promotional materials to college instructors, hoping this biased information will be incorporated into teaching and research. Similar materials are sent to political and religious leaders so they will pass the information along to their constituencies and congregations.

In the United States, advocacy of alternative political ideologies, parties, and candidates, or suggestions of viable consumer alternatives to the commercial frenzy stimulated and reinforced by advertising and other marketing techniques, are rarely seen on the popular media. Radical ideas typically appear only on underfinanced, noncommercial radio and TV stations and in low-budget print media. These media have tiny public followings compared to commercial television and video outlets, metropolitan daily newspapers, and national magazines. When genuinely divergent views appear on mainstream media, the information is frequently shown in an unfavorable light or is modified and co-opted to surrender to the embrace of mainstream thought. . . . The mass media help create an impression that even society's roughest edges ultimately must conform to the conventional contours of dominant ideologies.

Hegemony has been central to the management of ideology in communist nations too, though it develops differently. Central ideological planning and the creation of propaganda to advise "the people" represent the same intention—to protect the interests of ruling elites. . . .

The collapse of political authority in Eastern and Central Europe and the former Soviet Union was a breakdown in communist ideological hegemony. Conflict between culture producers and young audiences in East Germany and Hungary is typical of what happened in the Soviet bloc (Wicke, 1992; Szemere, 1985). Young rock musicians and their enthusiastic audiences led a cultural and political struggle against the repressive institutions and the ideology behind them. Trying to contain and control rebellious youth, the former communist governments attempted in sinister ways to defuse the politically charged musical and cultural activity of youth by incorporating and sponsoring them. Young people and other dissenters saw through the strategy, however, challenged the hegemony, and stimulated policy changes that later contributed to the dramatic downfall of the European communist governments. In China, the extraordinary student and worker uprising in 1989 is but the most visible sign of widespread resistance among that country's disaffected urban population.[1] Recent popular revolutions in communist countries developed from widespread discontent with an interacting spectrum of economic, political, and cultural conditions. Ironically, the workers' uprising that Marx and Engels theorized would take place in repressive, class-based capitalist economies developed instead in communist nations which had proven in many respects to be even more repressive.

Hegemony as an Incomplete Process ◆

Two of our leading critical theorists, Raymond Williams and Stuart Hall, remind us that hegemony in any political context is indeed fragile. It requires renewal and modification through the assertion and reassertion of power. Hall suggests that "it is crucial to the concept that hegemony is not a 'given' and permanent state of affairs, but it has to be actively won and secured; it can also be lost" (1977: 333). Ideological work is the winning and securing of hegemony over time. . . . Ideology is composed of "texts that are not closed" according to Hall, who also notes that ideological "counter-tendencies" regularly appear in the seams and cracks of dominant forms (Hall, 1985). Mediated communications ranging from popular television shows to rap and rock music, even graffiti scrawled over surfaces of public spaces, all inscribe messages that challenge central political positions and cultural assumptions.

Counter-hegemonic tendencies do not inhere solely in texts. They are formulated in processes of communication—in the interpretations, social circulation, and uses of media content. As with the American soldiers' use of military gas masks as inhaling devices to heighten the effect of marijuana smoke, or the homeless's transformation of supermarket shopping carts into personal storage vehicles, ideological resistance and appropriation frequently involve reinventing institutional messages for purposes that differ greatly from their creators' intentions. Expressions of the dominant ideology are sometimes reformulated to assert alternative, often completely resistant or contradictory messages. . . .

Furthermore, resistance to hegemony is not initiated solely by media consumers. Texts themselves are implicated. Ideology can never be stated purely and simply. Ways of thinking are always reflexive and embedded in a complex, sometimes contradictory, ideological regress. . . .

Audience interpretations and uses of media imagery also eat away at hegemony. Hegemony fails when dominant ideology is weaker than social resistance. Gay subcultures, feminist organizations, environmental groups, radical political parties, music-based formations such as punks, B-boys, Rastafarians, and metal heads all use media and their social networks to endorse counter-hegemonic values and lifestyles. Indeed, we have only just begun to examine the complex relationship between ideological representation and social action.

Note ◆

1. It's important to realize that the military suppression of the student-worker uprising in Beijing in 1989 did not stop the Chinese revolutionary movement. It made possible the dramatic and far-reaching (if less visually spectacular) economic and cultural changes that characterize the People's Republic today.

References ◆

Bausinger, H. (1984). Media, technology, and everyday life. *Media, Culture & Society*, 6, 340-52.

Boggs, C. (1976). *Gramsci's Marxism*. London: Pluto.

Elliott, P. (1974). Uses and gratifications research: A critique and a sociological alternative. In J. G. Blumler and E. Katz (eds.), *The Uses of Mass Communications: Current Perspectives on Gratifications Research*. Beverly Hills, CA: Sage.

Gitlin, T. (1979). Prime-time ideology: the hegemonic process in television entertainment. *Social Problems*, 26, 251-66.

Gramsci, A. (1971). *Selections from the Prison Notebooks*. New York: International.

Gramsci, A. (1973). *Letters from Prison*. New York: Harper and Row.

Gramsci, A. (1978). *Selections from Cultural Writings*. Cambridge, MA: Harvard University Press.

Hall, S. (1977). Culture, media, and the "ideological effect." In J. Curran, M. Gurevitch, and J. Woollacott (eds.), *Mass Communication and Society*. London: Edward Arnold.

Hall, S. (1985). Master's session. International Communication Association. Honolulu, Hawaii.

Martín-Barbero, J. (1993). *Communication, Culture and Hegemony*. Newbury Park, CA: Sage.

Nordenstreng, K. (1977). From mass media to mass consciousness. In G. Gerbner (ed.),

Mass Media Policies in Changing Cultures. New York: Wiley.

Sassoon, A. S. (1980). *Gramsci's Politics.* New York: St. Martin's.

Simon, R. (1982). *Gramsci's Political Thought.* London: Lawrence and Wishart.

Straubhaar, J. (1991). Beyond media imperialism: asymmetrical interdependence and cultural proximity. *Critical Studies in Mass Communication*, 8, 39-59.

Szemere, A. (1985). Pop music in Hungary. *Communication Research*, 12, 401-11.

Wicke, P. (1992). The role of rock music in the political disintegration of East Germany. In J. Lull (ed.), *Popular Music and Communication.* Newbury Park, CA: Sage.

Williams, R. (1976). *Key Words: A Vocabulary of Culture and Society.* New York: Oxford University Press.

6

WOMEN READ THE ROMANCE
The Interaction of Text and Context

♦ Janice A. Radway

. . . The interpretation of the romance's cultural significance offered here
has been developed from a series of extensive ethnographic-like interviews
with a group of compulsive romance readers in a predominantly urban,
central midwestern state among the nation's top twenty in total population.[1] I discovered my principal informant and her customers with the aid
of a senior editor at Doubleday whom I had been interviewing about the
publication of romances. Sally Arteseros told me of a bookstore employee
who had developed a regular clientele of fifty to seventy-five regular
romance readers who relied on her for advice about the best romances to
buy and those to avoid. When I wrote to Dot Evans, as I will now call her,
to ask whether I might question her about how she interpreted, categorized, and evaluated romantic fiction, I had no idea that she had also begun
to write a newsletter designed to enable bookstores to advise their
customers about the quality of the romances published monthly. She has
since copyrighted this newsletter and incorporated it as a business. Dot
is so successful at serving the women who patronize her chain outlet

NOTE: From Janice A. Radway, "Women Read the Romance: The Interaction
of Text and Context." This chapter was originally published in *Feminist Studies*,
Volume 9, Number 1 (Spring 1983): 53-78, by permission of the publisher,
Feminist Studies, Inc.

that the central office of this major chain occasionally relies on her sales predictions to gauge romance distribution throughout the system. Her success has also brought her to the attention of both editors and writers for whom she now reads manuscripts and galleys.

My knowledge of Dot and her readers is based on roughly sixty hours of interviews conducted in June 1980, and February 1981. I have talked extensively with Dot about romances, reading, and her advising activities as well as observed her inter-actions with her customers at the bookstore. I have also conducted both group and indi-vidual interviews with sixteen of her regular customers and administered a lengthy ques-tionnaire to forty-two of these women. Although not representative of all women who read romances, the group appears to be demographically similar to a sizable seg-ment of that audience as it has been mapped by several rather secretive publish-ing houses.

Dorothy Evans lives and works in the community of Smithton, as do most of her regular customers. A city of about 112,000 inhabitants, Smithton is located five miles due east of the state's second largest city, in a metropolitan area with a total population of over 1 million. Dot was forty-eight years old at the time of the survey, the wife of a journeyman plumber, and the mother of three children in their twenties. She is extremely bright and articulate and, while not a proclaimed feminist, holds some beliefs about women that might be labeled as such. Although she did not work outside the home when her children were young and does not now believe that a woman needs a career to be fulfilled, she feels women should have the opportunity to work and be paid equally with men. Dot also believes that women should have the right to abortion, though she admits that her deep religious convictions would pre-vent her from seeking one herself. She is not disturbed by the Equal Rights Amendment and can and does converse eloquently about the oppression women have endured

for years at the hands of men. Despite her opinions, however, she believes implicitly in the value of true romance and thoroughly enjoys discovering again and again that women can find men who will love them as they wish to be loved. Although most of her regular customers are more conservative than Dot in the sense that they do not advo-cate political measures to redress past griev-ances, they are quite aware that men commonly think themselves superior to women and often mistreat them as a result.

In general, Dot's customers are married, middle-class mothers with at least a high school education.[2] More than 60 percent of the women were between the ages of twenty-five and forty-four at the time of the study, a fact that duplicates fairly closely Harlequin's finding that the majority of its readers is between twenty-five and forty-nine.[3] Silhouette Books has also recently reported that 65 percent of the romance market is below the age of 40.[4] Exactly 50 percent of the Smithton women have high school diplomas, while 32 percent report completing at least some college work. Again, this seems to suggest that the inter-view group is fairly representative, for Silhouette also indicates that 45 percent of the romance market has attended at least some college. The employment status and family income of Dot's customers also seem to duplicate those of the audience mapped by the publishing houses. Forty-two percent of the Smithton women, for instance, work part-time outside the home. Harlequin claims that 49 percent of its audience is sim-ilarly employed. The Smithton women report slightly higher incomes than those of the average Harlequin reader (43 percent of the Smithton women have incomes of $15,000 to $24,999, 33 percent have incomes of $25,000 to $49,999—the aver-age income of the Harlequin reader is $15,000 to $20,000), but the difference is not enough to change the general sociologi-cal status of the group. . . .

When asked why they read romances, the Smithton women overwhelmingly cite escape or relaxation as their goal. They use the word "escape," however, both literally and figuratively. On the one hand, they value their romances highly because the act of reading them literally draws the women away from their present surroundings. Because they must produce the meaning of the story by attending closely to the words on the page, they find that their attention is withdrawn from concerns that plague them in reality. One woman remarked with a note of triumph in her voice: "My body may be in that room, but I'm not!" She and her sister readers see their romance reading as a legitimate way of denying a present reality that occasionally becomes too onerous to bear. This particular means of escape is better than television viewing for these women, because the cultural value attached to books permits them to overcome the guilt they feel about avoiding their responsibilities. They believe that reading of any kind is, by nature, educational.[5] They insist accordingly that they also read to learn.[6]

On the other hand, the Smithton readers are quite willing to acknowledge that the romances which so preoccupy them are little more than fantasies or fairy tales that always end happily. They readily admit in fact that the characters and events discovered in the pages of the typical romance do not resemble the people and occurrences they must deal with in their daily lives. On the basis of the following comments, made in response to a question about what romances "do" better than other novels available today, one can conclude that it is precisely the unreal, fantastic shape of the story that makes their literal escape even more complete and gratifying. Although these are only a few of the remarks given in response to the undirected question, they are representative of the group's general sentiment.

Romances hold my interest and do not leave me depressed or up in the air at the end like many modern day books tend to do. Romances also just make me feel good reading them as I identify with the heroines.

The kind of books I mainly read are very different from everyday living. That's why I read them. Newspapers, etc., I find boring because all you read is sad news. I can get enough of that on TV news. I like stories that take your mind off everyday matters.

Different than everyday life.

Everyone is always under so much pressure. They like books that let them escape.

Because it is an escape and we can dream. And pretend that it is our life.

I'm able to escape the harsh world a few hours a day.

It is a way of escaping from everyday living.

They always seem an escape and they usually turn out the way you wish life really was.

I enjoy reading because it offers me a small vacation from everyday life and an interesting and amusing way to pass the time.

These few comments all hint at a certain sadness that many of the Smithton women seem to share because life has not given them all that it once promised. A deep-seated sense of betrayal also lurks behind their deceptively simple expressions of a need to believe in a fairy tale. Although they have not elaborated in these comments, many of the women explained in the interviews that despite their disappointments, they feel refreshed and strengthened by their vicarious participation in a fantasy relationship where the heroine is frequently treated as they themselves would most like to be loved.

This conception of romance reading as an escape that is both literal and figurative implies flight from some situation in the real world which is either stifling or overwhelming, as well as a metaphoric transfer to another, more desirable universe where events are happily resolved. Unashamed to admit that they like to indulge in temporary escape, the Smithton women are also surprisingly candid about the circumstances that necessitate their desire. When asked to specify what they are fleeing from, they invariably mention the "pressures" and "tensions" they experience as wives and mothers. Although none of the women can cite the voluminous feminist literature about the psychological toll exacted by the constant demand to physically and emotionally nurture others, they are nonetheless eloquent about how draining and unrewarding their duties can be.[7] When first asked why women find it necessary to escape, Dot gave the following answer without once pausing to rest:

> As a mother, I have run 'em to the orthodontist, I have run 'em to the swimming pool. I have run 'em to baton twirling lessons. I have run up to school because they forgot their lunch. You know, I mean really. And you do it. And it isn't that you begrudge it. That isn't it. Then my husband would walk in the door and he'd say, "Well, what did you do today?" You know, it was like, "Well, tell me how you spent the last eight hours, because I've been out working." And I finally got to the point where I would say, "Well, I read four books, and I did the wash and got the meal on the table and the beds are all made and the house is tidy." And I would get defensive like, "So what do you call all this? Why should I have to tell you because I certainly don't ask you what you did for eight hours, step by step."
>
> But their husbands do do that. We've compared notes. They hit the house and it's like "Well, all right, I've been out earning a living. Now what have you been doin' with your time?" And you begin to be feeling, "Now, really, why is he questioning me?"

Romance reading, as Dot herself puts it, constitutes a temporary "declaration of independence" from the social roles of wife and mother. By placing the barrier of the book between themselves and their families, these women reserve a special space and time for themselves alone. As a consequence, they momentarily allow themselves to abandon the attitude of total self-abnegation in the interest of family welfare which they have so dutifully learned is the proper stance for a good wife and mother. Romance reading is both an assertion of deeply felt psychological needs and a means for satisfying those needs. Simply put, these needs arise because no other member of the family, as it is presently constituted in this still-patriarchal society, is yet charged with the affective and emotional reconstitution of a wife and mother. If she is depleted by her efforts to care for others, she is nonetheless expected to restore and sustain herself as well. As one of Dot's customers put it, "You always have to be a Mary Poppins. You can't be sad, you can't be mad, you have to keep everything bottled up inside."

Nancy Chodorow has recently discussed this structural peculiarity of the modern family and its impact on the emotional lives of women in her influential book, *The Reproduction of Mothering*,[8] a complex reformulation of the Freudian theory of female personality development. Chodorow maintains that women often continue to experience a desire for intense affective nurturance and relationality well into adulthood as a result of an unresolved separation from their primary caretaker. It is highly significant, she argues, that in patriarchal society this caretaker is almost inevitably a woman. The felt similarity between mother and daughter creates an unusually intimate connection between them which later makes it exceedingly difficult for the daughter to establish autonomy and independence. Chodorow maintains, on the other hand, that because male children are also reared by women, they tend to separate more completely from their mothers by suppressing their own emotionality and capacities for tenderness which they associate with mothers and femininity. The resulting asymmetry in human personality, she concludes, leads to a situation where men typically cannot fulfill all of a woman's emotional needs. As a consequence, women turn to the act of mothering as a way of vicariously recovering that lost relationality and intensity.

My findings about Dot Evans and her customers suggest that the vicarious pleasure a woman receives through the nurturance of others may not be completely satisfying, because the act of caring for them also makes tremendous demands on a woman and can deplete her sense of self. In that case, she may well turn to romance reading in an effort to construct a fantasy-world where she is attended, as the heroine is, by a man who reassures her of her special status and unique identity.

The value of the romance may have something to do, then, with the fact that women find it especially difficult to indulge in the restorative experience of visceral regression to an infantile state where the self is cared for perfectly by another. This regression is so difficult precisely because women have been taught to believe that men must be their sole source of pleasure. Although there is nothing biologically lacking in men to make this ideal pleasure unattainable, as Chodorow's theories tell us, their engendering and socialization by the patriarchal family traditionally masks the very traits that would permit them to nurture women in this way. Because they are encouraged to be aggressive, competitive, self-sufficient, and unemotional, men often find sustained attention to the emotional needs of others both unfamiliar and difficult. While the Smithton women only minimally discussed their husbands' abilities to take care of them as they would like, when they commented on their favorite romantic heroes they made it clear that they enjoy imagining themselves being tenderly cared for and solicitously protected by a fictive character who inevitably proves to be spectacularly masculine and unusually nurturant as well.[9]

Indeed, this theme of pleasure recurred constantly in the discussions with the Smithton women. They insisted repeatedly that when they are reading a romance, they feel happy and content. Several commented that they particularly relish moments when they are home alone and can relax in a hot tub or in a favorite chair with a good book. Others admitted that they most like to read in a warm bed late at night. Their association of romances with contentment, pleasure, and good feelings is apparently not unique, for in conducting a market research study, Fawcett discovered that when asked to draw a woman reading a romance, romance readers inevitably depict someone who is exaggeratedly happy.[10]

The Smithton group's insistence that they turn to romances because the experience of reading the novels gives them hope, provides pleasure, and causes contentment raises the unavoidable question of what aspects of the romantic narrative itself could possibly give rise to feelings such as these. How are we to explain, furthermore, the obvious contradiction between this reader emphasis on pleasure and hope, achieved through vicarious appreciation of the ministrations of a tender hero, and the observations of the earlier critics of romances that such books are dominated by men who at least temporarily abuse and hurt the women they purportedly love? In large part, the contradiction arises because the two groups are not reading according to the same interpretive strategies, neither are they reading nor commenting on the same books. Textual analyses like those offered by Douglas, Modleski, and Snitow are based on the common assumption that because romances are formulaic and therefore essentially identical, analysis of a randomly chosen sample will reveal the meaning unfailingly communicated by every example of the genre. This methodological procedure is based on the further assumption that category readers do not themselves perceive variations within the genre, nor do they select their books in a manner significantly different from the random choice of the analyst.

In fact, the Smithton readers do not believe the books are identical, nor do they approve of all the romances they read. They have elaborated a complex distinction between "good" and "bad" romances and they have accordingly experimented with various techniques that they hoped would enable them to identify bad romances before they paid for a book that would only offend them. Some tried to decode titles and cover blurbs by looking for key words serving as clues to the book's tone; others refused to buy romances by authors they didn't recognize; still others read several pages *including the ending* before they bought the book. Now, however, most of the people in the Smithton group have been freed from the need to rely on these inexact predictions because Dot Evans shares their perceptions and evaluations of the category and can alert them to unusually successful romantic fantasies while steering them away from those they call "disgusting perversions."

When the Smithton readers' comments about good and bad romances are combined with the conclusions drawn from an analysis of twenty of their favorite books and an equal number of those they classify as particularly inadequate, an illuminating picture of the fantasy fueling the romance-reading experience develops.[11] To begin with, Dot and her readers will not tolerate any story in which the heroine is seriously abused by men. They find multiple rapes especially distressing and dislike books in which a woman is brutally hurt by a man only to fall desperately in love with him in the last four pages. The Smithton women are also offended by explicit sexual description and scrupulously avoid the work of authors like Rosemary Rogers and Judith Krantz who deal in what they call "perversions" and "promiscuity." They also do not like romances that overtly perpetuate the double standard by excusing the hero's simultaneous involvement with several women. They insist, one reader commented, on "one woman—one man." They also seem to dislike any kind of detailed description of male genitalia, although the women enjoy suggestive descriptions of how the hero is emotionally aroused to an overpowering desire for the heroine. Their preferences seem to confirm Beatrice Faust's argument in *Women, Sex, and Pornography* that women are not interested in the visual display characteristic of male pornography, but prefer process-oriented materials detailing the development of deep emotional connection between two individuals.[12]

According to Dot and her customers, the quality of the *ideal* romantic fantasy is directly dependent on the character of the heroine and the manner in which the hero treats her. The plot, of course, must always focus on a series of obstacles to the final declaration of love between the two principals. However, a good romance involves an unusually bright and determined woman and a man who is spectacularly masculine, but at the same time capable of remarkable empathy and tenderness. Although they enjoy the usual chronicle of misunderstandings and mistakes which inevitably leads to the heroine's belief that the hero intends to harm her, the Smithton readers prefer stories that combine a much-understated version of this continuing antagonism with a picture of a gradually developing love. They most wish to participate in the slow process by which two people become acquainted, explore each other's foibles, wonder about the other's feelings, and eventually "discover" that they are loved by the other.

In conducting an analysis of the plots of the twenty romances listed as "ideal" by the Smithton readers, I was struck by their remarkable similarities in narrative structure. In fact, all twenty of these romances are very tightly organized around the evolving relationship between a single couple composed of a beautiful, defiant, and sexually immature woman and a brooding, handsome man who is also curiously capable of soft, gentle gestures. Although minor foil figures are used in these romances, none of the ideal stories seriously involves either hero or heroine with one of the rival characters.[13] They are employed mainly as contrasts to the more likable and proper central pair or as purely temporary obstacles to the pair's delayed union because one or the other mistakenly suspects the partner of having an affair with the rival. However, because the reader is never permitted to share this mistaken assumption in the ideal romance, she knows all along that the relationship is not as precarious as its participants think it to be. The rest of the narrative in the twenty romances chronicles the gradual crumbling of barriers between these two individuals who are fearful of being used by the other. As their defenses against emotional response fall away and their sexual passion rises inexorably, the typical narrative plunges on until the climactic point at which the hero treats the heroine to some supreme act of tenderness, and she realizes that his apparent emotional indifference was only the mark of his hesitancy about revealing the extent of his love for and dependence upon her.

The Smithton women especially like romances that commence with the early marriage of the hero and heroine for reasons of convenience. Apparently, they do so because they delight in the subsequent, necessary chronicle of the pair's growing awareness that what each took to be indifference or hate is, in reality, unexpressed love and suppressed passion. In such favorite romances as *The Flame and the Flower*, *The Black Lyon*, *Shanna*, and *Made For Each Other* the heroine begins marriage thinking that she detests and is detested by her spouse. She is thrown into a quandary, however, because her partner's behavior vacillates from indifference, occasional brusqueness, and even cruelty to tenderness and passion. Consequently, the heroine spends most of her time in these romances, as well as in the others comprising this sample, trying to read the hero's behavior as a set of signs expressing his true feelings toward her. The final outcome of the story turns upon a fundamental process of reinterpretation, whereby she suddenly and clearly sees that the behavior she feared

was actually the product of deeply felt passion and a previous hurt. Once she learns to reread his past behavior and thus to excuse him for the suffering he has caused her, she is free to respond warmly to his occasional acts of tenderness. Her response inevitably encourages him to believe in her and finally to treat her as she wishes to be treated. When this reinterpretation process is completed in the twenty ideal romances, the heroine is always tenderly enfolded in the hero's embrace and the reader is permitted to identify with her as she is gently caressed, carefully protected, and verbally praised with words of love.[14] At the climactic moment (pp. 201-202) of *The Sea Treasure*, for example, when the hero tells the heroine to put her arms around him, the reader is informed of his gentleness in the following way:

> She put her cold face against his in an attitude of surrender that moved him to unutterable tenderness. He swung her clear of the encroaching water and eased his way up to the next level, with painful slowness. . . . When at last he had finished, he pulled her into his arms and held her against his heart for a moment. . . . Tenderly he lifted her. Carefully he negotiated the last of the treacherous slippery rungs to the mine entrance. Once there, he swung her up into his arms, and walked out into the starlit night.
>
> The cold air revived her, and she stirred in his arms.
> "Dominic?" she whispered.
> He bent his head and kissed her.
> "Sea Treasure," he whispered.

Passivity, it seems, is at the heart of the romance-reading experience in the sense that the final goal of the most valued romances is the creation of perfect union in which the ideal male, who is masculine and strong, yet nurturant, finally admits his recognition of the intrinsic worth of the heroine. Thereafter, she is required to do nothing more than exist as the center of this paragon's attention. Romantic escape is a temporary but literal denial of the demands these women recognize as an integral part of their roles as nurturing wives and mothers. But it is also a figurative journey to a utopian state of total receptiveness in which the reader, as a consequence of her identification with the heroine, feels herself the passive *object* of someone else's attention and solicitude. The romance reader in effect is permitted the experience of feeling cared for, the sense of having been affectively reconstituted, even if both are lived only vicariously.

Although the ideal romance may thus enable a woman to satisfy vicariously those psychological needs created in her by a patriarchal culture unable to fulfill them, the very centrality of the rhetoric of reinterpretation to the romance suggests also that the reading experience may indeed have some of the unfortunate consequences pointed to by earlier romance critics.[15] Not only is the dynamic of reinterpretation an essential component of the plot of the ideal romance, but it also characterizes the very process of constructing its meaning because the reader is inevitably given more information about the hero's motives than is the heroine herself. Hence, when Ranulf temporarily abuses his young bride in *The Black Lyon* the reader understands that what appears as inexplicable cruelty to Lyonene, the heroine, is an irrational desire to hurt her because of what his first wife did to him.[16] It is possible that in reinterpreting the hero's behavior before Lyonene does, the Smithton women may be practicing a procedure which is valuable to them precisely because it enables them to reinterpret their own spouse's similar emotional coldness and likely preoccupation with work or sports. In rereading this category of behavior, they reassure themselves that it does not necessarily mean that a woman is not loved. Romance reading, it would seem, can function as a kind of training for the all-too-common task of reinterpreting a spouse's unsettling actions as the signs of passion, devotion, and love.

If the Smithton women are indeed learning reading behaviors that help them to dismiss or justify their husbands' affective distance, this procedure is probably carried out on an unconscious level. In any form of cultural or anthropological analysis in which the subjects of the study cannot reveal all the complexity or covert significance of their behavior, a certain amount of speculation is necessary. The analyst, however, can and should take account of any other observable evidence that might reveal the motives and meanings she is seeking. In this case, the Smithton readers' comments about bad romances are particularly helpful.

In general, bad romances are characterized by one of two things: an unusually cruel hero who subjects the heroine to various kinds of verbal and physical abuse, or a diffuse plot that permits the hero to become involved with other women before he settles upon the heroine. Since the Smithton readers will tolerate complicated subplots in some romances if the hero and heroine continue to function as a pair, clearly it is the involvement with others rather than the plot complexity that distresses them. When asked why they disliked these books despite the fact that they all ended happily with the hero converted into the heroine's attentive lover, Dot and her customers replied again and again that they rejected the books precisely because they found them unbelievable. In elaborating, they insisted indignantly that *they* could never forgive the hero's early transgressions and they see no reason why they should be asked to believe that the heroine can. What they are suggesting, then, is that certain kinds of male behavior associated with the stereotype of male machismo can never be forgiven or reread as the signs of love. They are thus not interested *only* in the romance's happy ending. They want to involve themselves in a story that will permit them to enjoy the hero's tenderness *and* to reinterpret his momentary blindness and cool indifference as the marks of a love so intense that he is wary of admitting it. Their delight in both these aspects of the process of romance reading and their deliberate attempt to select books that will include "a gentle hero" and "a slight misunderstanding" suggest that deeply felt needs are the source of their interest in both components of the genre. On the one hand, they long for emotional attention and tender care; on the other, they wish to rehearse the discovery that a man's distance can be explained and excused as his way of expressing love.

It is easy to condemn this latter aspect of romance reading as a reactionary force that reconciles women to a social situation which denies them full development, even as it refuses to accord them the emotional sustenance they require. Yet to identify romances with this conservative moment alone is to miss those other benefits associated with the act of reading as a restorative pastime whose impact on a beleaguered woman is not so simply dismissed. If we are serious about feminist politics and committed to reformulating not only our own lives but those of others, we would do well not to condescend to romance readers as hopeless traditionalists who are recalcitrant in their refusal to acknowledge the emotional costs of patriarchy. We must begin to recognize that romance reading is fueled by dissatisfaction and disaffection, not by perfect contentment with woman's lot. Moreover, we must also understand that some romance readers' experiences are not strictly congruent with the set of ideological propositions that typically legitimate patriarchal marriage. They are characterized, rather, by a sense of longing caused by patriarchal marriage's failure to address all their needs.

In recognizing both the yearning and the fact that its resolution is only a vicarious one not so easily achieved in a real situation, we may find it possible to identify more precisely the very limits of patriarchal ideology's success. Endowed thus with a better understanding of what women want, but often fail to get from the traditional arrangements they consciously support, we may provide ourselves with that very issue whose discussion would reach many more women and potentially raise their consciousnesses about the particular dangers and failures of patriarchal institutions. By helping romance readers to see why they long for relationality and tenderness and are unlikely to get either in the form they desire if current gender arrangements are continued, we may help to convert their amorphous longing into a focused desire for specific change. . . .

Notes ◆

1. All information about the community has been taken from the 1970 U.S. Census of the Population *Characteristics of the Population*, U.S. Department of Commerce, Social and Economic Statistics Administration, Bureau of the Census, May 1972. I have rounded off some of the statistics to disguise the identity of the town.

2. See Table 6.1.

3. Quoted by Brotman (1980). All other details about the Harlequin audience have been taken from Brotman's article. Similar information was also given by Harlequin to Margaret Jensen (1980), whose dissertation, *Women and Romantic Fiction: A Case Study of Harlequin Enterprises, Romances, and Readers*, is the only other study I know of to attempt an investigation of romance readers. Because Jensen encountered the same problems in trying to assemble a representative sample, she relied on interviews with randomly selected readers at a used bookstore. However, the similarity of her findings to those in my study indicates that the lack of statistical representativeness in the case of real readers does not necessarily preclude applying those readers' attitudes and opinions more generally to a large portion of the audience for romantic fiction.

4. See Brotman (1980). All other details about the Silhouette audience have been drawn from Brotman's article. The similarity of the Smithton readers to other segments of the romance audience is explored in greater depth in my book (Radway, 1984). However, the only other available study of romance readers which

Table 6.1   Select Demographic Data: Customers of Dorothy Evans

Category	Responses	Number	%
Age	(42) Less than 25	2	5
	25-44	26	62
	45-54	12	28
	55 and older	2	5
Marital Status	(40) Single	3	8
	Married	33	82
	Widowed / separated	4	10
Parental Status	(40) Children	35	88
	No children	4	12
Age at Marriage	Mean-19.9		
	Median-19.2		
Educational Level	(40) High school diploma	21	53
	1-3 years of college	1	25
	College degree	8	20
Work Status	(40) Full or part time	18	45
	Child or home care	17	43
Family Income	(38) $14,999 or below	2	5
	15,000-24,999	18	47
	25,000-49,999	14	37
	50,000 +	4	11
Church Attendance	(40) Once or more a week	15	38
	1-3 times per month	8	20
	A few times per year	9	22
	Not in two (2) years	8	20

NOTE: (40) indicates the number of responses per questionnaire category. A total of 42 responses per category is the maximum possible. Percent calculations are all rounded to the nearest whole number.

includes some statistics, Peter H. Mann's (1969) *The Romantic Novel: A Survey of Reading Habits*, indicates that the British audience for such fiction has included in the past more older women as well as younger, unmarried readers than are represented in my sample. However, Mann's survey raises suspicions because it was sponsored by the company that markets the novels and because its findings are represented in such a polemical form. For an analysis of Mann's work, see Jensen (1980, pp. 389-392).

5.   The Smithton readers are not avid television watchers. Ten of the women, for instance, claimed to watch television less than three hours per week. Fourteen indicated that they watch four to seven hours a week, while eleven claimed

eight to fourteen hours of weekly viewing. Only four said they watch an average of fifteen to twenty hours a week, while only one admitted viewing twenty-one or more hours a week. When asked how often they watch soap operas, twenty-four of the Smithton women checked "never," five selected "rarely," seven chose "sometimes," and four checked "often." Two refused to answer the questions.

6.   The Smithton readers' constant emphasis on the educational value of romances was one of the most interesting aspects of our conversations, and chapter 3 of *Reading the Romance* (Radway, 1984) discusses it in depth. Although their citation of the instructional value of romances to a college professor interviewer may

well be a form of self-justification, the women also provided ample evidence that they do in fact learn and remember facts about geography, historical customs, and dress from the books they read. Their emphasis on this aspect of their reading, I might add, seems to betoken a profound curiosity and longing to know more about the exciting world beyond their suburban homes.

7. For material on housewives' attitudes toward domestic work and their duties as family counselors, see Oakley (1975a, 1975b); see also Komorovsky (1967) and Lopata (1971).

8. Chodorow (1978). I would like to express my thanks to Sharon O'Brien for first bringing Chodorow's work to my attention and for all those innumerable discussions in which we debated the merits of her theory and its applicability to women's lives, including our own.

9. After developing my argument that the Smithton women are seeking ideal romances which depict the generally tender treatment of the heroine, I discovered Beatrice Faust's (1981) *Women, Sex, and Pornography: A Controversial Study* in which Faust points out that certain kinds of historical romances tend to portray their heroes as masculine, but emotionally expressive. Although I think Faust's overall argument has many problems, not the least of which is her heavy reliance on hormonal differences to explain variations in female and male sexual preferences, I do agree that some women prefer the detailed description of romantic love and tenderness to the careful anatomical representations characteristic of male pornography.

10. Maryles (1979, p. 69).

11. Ten of the twenty books in the sample for the ideal romance were drawn from the Smithton group's answers to requests that they list their three favorite romances and authors. . . . Because I did not include a formal query in the questionnaire about particularly bad romances, I drew the twenty titles from oral interviews and from Dot's newsletter reviews. . . .

12. See Faust (1981), passim.

13. There are two exceptions to this assertion. Both *The Proud Breed* by Celeste DeBlasis and *The Fulfillment* by LaVyrle Spencer detail the involvement of the principal characters with other individuals. Their treatment of the subject, however, is decidedly different from that typically found in the bad romances. Both of these books are highly unusual in that they begin by detailing the extraordinary depth of the love shared by hero and heroine, who marry early in the story. The rest of each book chronicles the misunderstandings that arise between heroine and hero. In both books the third person narrative always indicates very clearly to the reader that the two are still deeply in love with each other and are acting out of anger, distrust, and insecurity.

14. In the romances considered awful by the Smithton readers, the reinterpretation takes place much later in the story than in the ideal romances. In addition, the behavior that is explained away is more violent, aggressively cruel, and obviously vicious. Although the hero is suddenly transformed by the heroine's reinterpretation of his motives, his tenderness, gentleness, and care are not emphasized in the "failed romances" as they are in their ideal counterparts.

15. Modleski (1980) has also argued that "the mystery of male motives" is a crucial concern in all romantic fiction (p. 439). Although she suggests, as I will here, that the process through which male misbehavior is reinterpreted in a more favorable light is a justification or legitimation of such action, she does not specifically connect its centrality in the plot to a reader's need to use such a strategy in her own marriage. While there are similarities between Modleski's analysis and that presented here, she emphasizes the negative, disturbing effects of romance reading on readers. In fact, she claims, the novels "end up actually intensifying conflicts for the reader" (p. 445) and cause women to "reemerge feeling . . . more guilty than ever" (p. 447). While I would admit that romance reading might create unconscious guilt, I think it absolutely essential that any explanation of such behavior take into account the substantial amount of evidence indicating that women not only *enjoy* romance reading, but feel replenished and reconstituted by it as well.

16. Deveraux (1980, p. 66).

◆ *References*

Brotman, B. (1980, June 2). Ah, romance! Harlequin has an affair for its readers. *Chicago Tribune.*

Chodorow, N. (1978). *The reproduction of mothering: Psychoanalysis and the sociology of gender.* Berkeley: University of California Press.

Deveraux, J. (1980). *The black lyon.* New York: Avon.

Faust, B. (1981). *Women, sex and pornography: A controversial study.* New York: Macmillan.

Jensen, M. (1980). *Women and romantic fiction: A case study of Harlequin Enterprises, romances, and readers.* Unpublished doctoral dissertation, McMaster University, Ontario.

Komorovsky, M. (1967). *Blue collar marriage.* New York: Vintage.

Lopata, H. Z. (1971). *Occupation: Housewife.* New York: Oxford University Press.

Mann, P. H. (1969). *The romantic novel: A survey of reading habits.* London: Mills & Boon.

Maryles, D. (1979, September 3). Fawcett launches romance imprint with brand marketing techniques. *Publishers Weekly,* pp. 69-70.

Modleski, T. (1980). The disappearing act: A study of Harlequin romances. *Signs, 5,* 435-448.

Oakley, A. (1975a). *The sociology of housework.* New York: Pantheon.

Oakley, A. (1975b). *Woman's work: The housewife, past and present.* New York: Pantheon.

Radway, J. (1984). *Reading the romance: Women, patriarchy and popular literature.* Chapel Hill: University of North Carolina Press.

7

BLACK SITCOM PORTRAYALS

Robin R. Means Coleman

◆ *Class Depictions*

Through television, race has frequently been linked to the underclass, more specifically the working poor. Beulah of *Beulah* and Nell of *Gimme a Break* may have worked as maids in fine middle-class households, but we were not led to believe that *they* were middle class. Instead they appeared fully reliant upon their White families for not only a paycheck, but a place to live, eat, and sleep—in essence, their very survival. Fred of *Sanford and Son* was an entrepreneur who lived in his junkyard, much like Roc of the series *Roc* who lived with the junk he collected on his garbage route. Therefore, the inferiority assigned to the race is also often linked to class failures, that is, the lack of upward mobility. And while depictions of the poor/working class, such as *Good Times*, have garnered some praise, when African Americans are presented as breaking economic boundaries that is typically reserved for White portrayals, the portrayals draw intense scrutiny as we see with *The Jeffersons*. While the participants struggled to offer a genre-wide assessment of what favorable traits the comedies held, a number of them found it easier to provide specific examples, within single programs, that are evidence of the elusive positive. Freddie and J. C. credited *The Jeffersons* for presenting economic achievement within the Black community.

For Freddie, who does not share the economic status depicted on *The Jeffersons*, the series becomes important because it assigns a higher class status, and in turn elevates the race, which is often seen as not self-sufficient, or failing to be economically contributory to society.

F. D.: "Here's a guy [George Jefferson], got a little money from a loan to open up the cleaning business, and he's able to expand and move up. But it's good to show, yes. . . . [It shows] we can hire Black people . . . in the community."

J. C., too, was not part of the economic class as seen in *The Jeffersons*, and thus the series was positive, not because he shared an identification with the characters' socioeconomic level, but because it offered a unique image of rich African Americans.

J. C. B.: "Yeah, I think it's important to see because too many of our Blacks that achieve, the community for the most part tends to shun them and call them names, [such as] tryin' to be White and all this stuff like that. And I think it's positive to have more people that are showing advancement in life."

So here, Freddie lends importance to not only self-sufficiency, but also maintaining contact with the lower and working class in the Black community. This contact seems key, as J. C. reveals, because wealth can be misconstrued as Whiteness, as seen in the assimilation controversy that haunted *Julia* and *The Cosby Show*. Again, then, we are reminded how bound Blackness and economic deprivation is on television, and in turn, in the minds of viewers.

Fresh Prince of Bel Air also received a favorable nod from some participants for depictions of poor, ghetto-dwelling African Americans and wealthy, suburban ones still being able to interact. Lonette cited this single series for handling the two classes in an exemplary manner.

L. E.: "Well, it's still clean comedy. It shows how a brother from the 'hood has relatives that are very wealthy and they are different, and the same; how they help each other. The uncle, . . . Phil treats the Fresh Prince just like a son. He doesn't treat him as if he has made it out of the ghetto, and 'here I have this nephew from the ghetto and he is this big problem for me.' He is very loving and he treats him exactly like a son. I like the way they blend the two different communities together. I really enjoy that."

Class, as Lonette, J. C., and Freddie are negotiating it, is not about material worth, but rather is an often overlooked cultural yardstick for Blackness. With a growing Black middle class in American society, African Americans are no longer economically, geographically, or educationally restricted. As Henry Louis Gates, Jr. (1998), detailed in his PBS documentary *The Two Nations of Black America*, Martha's Vineyard is now a popular African American vacation spot; Blacks have their own exclusive restaurants complete with doorman and valet parking; and what W. E. B. Du Bois would call the "talented tenth" are assembling think tanks in the most prestigious ivy leagues. Gates ponders over this newly created socioeconomic gap between the Black working class and the upper echelon as the middle and upper classes continue to grow.

These three participants seem to hold similar concerns, yet find solace in representations such as *The Jeffersons* and *Fresh Prince of Bel Air*, where having "arrived" is not depicted as leaving behind cultural connectedness such as music, dance, art, dress, religion, food, and history, along with concerns over how race relations and racism still impacts their much enriched lives.

Race and class consciousness appear to be an unwieldy conundrum for the participants (as it is for Gates) who, on the one hand, argue that television has failed to represent the full economic spectrum of African Americans. Yet they also seem to believe that (a) all economically ascended Blacks have their immediate roots in the underclass and/or ghetto, and (b) "real" Blacks never forget or sever themselves from this underclass.

J. C. thought *The Jeffersons* made an important contribution to Black imagery by presenting what he called economic achievement. He again works to identify a single, exemplar attribute in a series, this time in *Fresh Prince of Bel Air*. J. C. acknowledged that this series too depicted Black wealth; however, he was most struck by one character's moralistic representation. As a devout Christian, J. C. sees a void in television where morally sound behaviors are rarely depicted, yet the wayward and inappropriate are privileged. He saw one character, *Fresh Prince's* Carlton, as finally breaking the deviance mold.

J. C. B.:   "There are some good, like the Carlton character on *The Fresh Prince*. He's a good kid. I don't like the fact that when they have him dealing with other Blacks they negative him so much, you know. If I had a son, and I had a choice of my son being like this kid, or being like, say Martin or somebody, I would prefer this kid [Carlton] over here."

For J. C., Carlton is a "good kid" because the character possesses values such as good behavior, honesty, a love for education, and a respect for his parents that is rarely seen in depictions of young Black males. Few, if any of these values are presented as being prized in Carlton's counterpart on the series, Will. J. C.'s lament is that when such positive portrayals, such as Carlton's, do appear, they are the source for ridicule by the other Black characters, and hence, "they negative him so much."

FAMILIAL RELATIONSHIPS

... Several participants, whether they considered the programs positive or negative, believe that the depiction of the Black family is a notable strength of the genre. Lonette shares her opinion of *Good Times*.

L. E.:   "*Good Times*. It was funny. It was about the dozens kinda. They did play the dozens in every episode. [Yet] I think that particular show targeted a lower-class Black family trying to struggle to make it, yet they stuck together as a family, they showed how hard it is to be poor and try to make it. But they had, there was a lot of love in that family. Although they were poor, there was a lot of love there."

In my conversations with Gale, a devout Christian, she emphasized and reemphasized that she views herself as a strong, independent woman. This assertion is important because she also believes that men should be leaders in the church and the heads of households. Her beliefs are rooted, she says, in Bible Scripture, and it is her biblically based values that also moves her to support her husband's participation in the Promise Keepers movement. Also politically conscious, Gale advances her belief that men, especially Black men, should be seen as "head man" or authority because African American men are the least respected and accepted by (White) America. Ever deemed threatening to non-African Americans, Gale believes the Black male is dismissed by a society who finds African American women as less threatening. Thus, Black women, more than Black men, have an increasing number of opportunities available to them (e.g., access to higher education and employment). Gale argues that once Black men are viewed as leaders in society, their sense of self-worth and self-esteem can be restored.

Insight into Gale's values and belief system helps us to understand her praise for *Good Times*, the first Black sitcom to feature an intact traditional family. In reading her remarks, keep in mind the series' star Esther Rolle had to *demand* that the father character be written into the series.

G. E.: "Well, I liked Esther Rolle. I felt she played a good, strong Black woman figure. And I liked her husband too, James. Because he was always in control. Because nothing got past James and he was actually functioning as the head of the household. They didn't make him look like a buffoon, an idiot. And they didn't let him be a welcome mat where they could walk all over him. So he still had control of the family. Even though the son, J. J., he had a tendency to waver. But somebody always brought him back in line.... That's important to see because we need role models. We need good, positive role models—standing up, being the father figure, the mother figure."

Gale was just one of several participants who hailed the presence of two, loving parents in a household. The *Make Room for Daddys*, the *Leave It to Beavers*, and the more contemporary *Roseannes* and (albeit, trashy) *Married ... With Childrens* all naturally, and almost automatically featured a husband and wife team. Most family-oriented Black sitcoms, however, seemed to have a spouse missing. Just consider a few comedies: *Julia, Sanford and Son, That's My Mama, What's Happening!, The Gregory Hines Show, Me and the Boys, Sinbad, Thea, South Central, Out All Night*, and *Amen*.

Robert, who was raised by both parents (today his mother is a widow), is particularly cognizant of the single-parent trend. Like Gale, he prefers series that portray an intact family. For him, *Roc* was exemplary, even more so, because it also depicted an extended-family bond.

R. P.: "He [Roc] tried to portray more of a father image than in any other Black comedy that I've seen. Him and his wife were together, which was important to me. It was a Black man and a Black woman. He was also helping out his family as far as his brother was concerned and his father was living with him."

Some participants acknowledged that certain series are now featuring praise-worthy Black men (e.g., *Sinbad, Me and the Boys, The Gregory Hines Show*). When positive, responsible father figures are depicted, such portrayals do not go unnoticed. Dana, a newlywed raised in a single-parent home, is particularly sensitive to familial representations. She identifies *Me and the Boys* for what was its exceptional representation of a role-model father. She also likes that this comedy was very funny.

D. A.: "It is just *so* funny. His character, he is light-hearted, he's a good father. His children are real children. They're not like good all the time. They're real kids, they get into some things. The fact that his mother-in-law's there and supporting him. And he talks about his wife even though she's passed on. He talks about her very favorably. And then he has his sister. Um, very positive role models in it.... Not everybody is the same carbon copy of one another. It's refreshing, it's a refreshing show. I like that."

NEGATIVE/STEREOTYPICAL

. . . J. C. did not explicitly cite the comedies for depicting African Americans as being oversexed as Billie had. He did, however, note that the Black females are frequently portrayed as partnerless, yet ever-hungry jezebel characterizations. J. C. also offers that on television such women often choose good looks over substance. Such a selection, J. C. believes, is rarely communicated as a poor choice for women, or as one that can backfire. He observes that the comedies often depict a deficient woman in love with a deficient man, and that somehow this is an acceptable relationship.

J. C. B.: "The woman who can't find a steady man, the Jackeé character [from *227*], the *Thea* character, the *That's My Mama* character. There's always that one sister that can't find a man. And if she does find a man, he is the good looking suave guy who is so screwed up."

J. C. continues that the African American male is not only depicted as deficient in love, but also in family life. J. C. noted the presence of what I call "White savior" sitcoms (e.g., *Diff'rent Strokes*; *Webster*). In these comedies, Black children are rescued from their dysfunctional families or communities by Whites. If it is not Whites depicted as coming to the rescue, then others in the Black community are called upon to intervene in negligent familial situations. These troubled families are presented as deviant due to the absence of the Black father. J. C. believes, that be it the "White savior," or the Black intervener scenario, the message is the same: Black men are largely failures. . . .

For the participants, female images are plentiful, but are as troubling as the imagistic mistreatment of Black men. Billie and Claire take great offense at the portrayal of women and the misogynistic abuse

directed toward them. Billie shares what most upsets her about the depiction of women. She draws on *Martin* to illustrate what is most wrong with the comedies.

B. B.: ". . . they're always puttin' women down and talking about their butts, even when it's a decent little comedy or something, they make fun of each other so bad, and I hate that. Nothing ever positive about each other. Every show just about, you know what's gonna happen. They're gonna talk about each other. They're gonna put each other down. The men are gonna talk about the women. The women are gonna make strong statements against the men. Same old thing. . . . Martin's gonna make fun of one of the women on the show, even his girlfriend or talk about her butt. I just hate that negativity."

Claire too cites *Martin* as blameworthy for its garish, offensive depictions. Her dismay over the gross exaggerations and self-deprecating ridicule depicted on this series is congruent to the term "hyper-racial."

C. R.: "For instance, like Martin's show, he exaggerates some of the characters, especially the women characters. He exaggerates them. . . . A lot of them are exaggerated. But he exaggerated the character of his mother! He exaggerates the character of Sheneneh. His characters are not complimentary at all. I cannot see how someone could not be offended by that. For some reason, they have to push it to the point of buffoonery. I know a lot of the people are offended by some of the things he does, but I still like the show. To a degree, I still like the show."

Claire began to explore what troubles her about the depictions of women, and ended up making what was, even to her, a surprising confession—she truly likes the comedies, even those like the controversial *Martin.* Although she qualifies her remarks by saying, "to a degree, I still like the show," she feels compelled to make sense of her reception. Aloud she inventoried her thoughts, stating that she finds the lead character in *Martin* a despicable presentation, but, at the same time, his physical, slapstick humor is genuinely funny. In the end, Claire surmises, she can occasionally overlook or tolerate the negative portrayals ("exaggerations" as she called them) because she loves comedies. Her only alternative is to give up Black portrayals, and not watch. . . .

There is one other issue that several participants said plagued them—Hollywood's preference for lighter-skinned African Americans. A new twist on "White is right," the participants saw television communicating that African Americans with White features are better. Gale believes it all began with *Julia,* a series blasted for shedding its Blackness opting for assimilationist Whiteness.

G. E.: I didn't like *Julia.* Because they took Diahann Carroll. She portrayed a nurse. First of all, to me, she doesn't look like a Black woman. She has the features of a European. They were trying to push this European looking Black woman off as a Black woman. . . . I never cared for Julia."

Jennifer states that she could never see the character Julia as being a representative Black woman. Her fairer skin complexion, long and straight hair, and glamorous look was not the average Black female. More, Jennifer feels few Black women could have lived up to Julia's standard of beauty. Speaking of herself, Jennifer laments:

J. F.: "I'm not a pretty Black woman that's a nurse like on *Julia.* That's

very refined, very pretty, very sophisticated, you know."

. . . Robert, a darker-skinned male, intimates that he feels rejected by television's erasure of those who look like him. He uses *The Cosby Show* to lay bare the intraracial harm he believes people who look like him can experience.

R. P.: "And everyone in the [Huxtable] family was high yellow. . . . And that is not the norm for the Black family. That's not reality. In all families there's all shades of color. What it really comes down to is, ah, even as a child with my dark complexion I was segregated within my own race because of the complexion of my skin. I grew up like that. For years and years and years, until I was mature enough to understand what was going on. The real problem with that, as I see it, is we're bringing up children doing the same thing we were doing 30 years ago. The lighter you are, the better you are."

African American ◆ Culture/Communities

In this final subtheme, some of the participants related that Black situation comedies present characters and situations that are so dissimilar from Blackness, that is, African American culture and communities, that they find the images, and the inherent messages, incongruent to their lived experiences, beliefs, and values. . . .

Several participants wanted to emphasize their dissatisfaction with the absence of the Black church, a prominent part of the culture's infrastructure, in Black situation comedies. Billie, who is not even a regular church-goer, still sees the importance of featuring the church.

B. B.: "You never see a situation on TV where the family goes to church. I'd like to see a good Christian family portrayed."

Calvin, a church leader, also finds this omission striking. To him, it makes African Americans look morally sloven when viewers do not have an opportunity to see Blacks engaged in worship.

C. E.: "They don't never go to church, they don't say nothing about God."

The core group of participants were provided the opportunity to address the issue of the depiction of Black church during the second round of interviews. Some found the topic relevant and supported the constructions of Billie and Calvin.

Billie elaborates on her original point.

B. B.: "[The Black church is seen] only in a derogatory way. Just jumpin' around, dancin'. Black people's roots are in the church, but they never see us as Catholics or Presbyterians. Just [as] rockin' and dancin' and jumpin' up and down."

J. C. and Jennifer, who are actively involved with their churches, argue that all religions are either overlooked completely, or when included, they are portrayed negatively. J. C. begins:

J. C.: "I don't know they show [the positive] about the White church either. I guess it's the church in general they don't show."

Jennifer agreed:

J. F.: "I don't think that the church is ever portrayed in a positive light, period. Whether it's the Black church, the White church. There just seems to be a disdain for the church and

everybody is portrayed as crazy. Even in drama, they're completely insane. If they're really a homicidal maniac they've had some religious influence, um . . . [the film] *Cape Fear*. So it's not just the Black church, it's universal."

. . . Finally, we hear from Jennifer, who notes that sometimes the comedies attempt to "probe" (as Benjamin called it) too much into Black struggles, settling singularly on issues of racism. . . .

J. F.: "Well see, I have a problem with watching TV where it deals with social issues and racism because I have to deal with it too much in real life, and I don't want to watch it for entertainment. And I usually pretty much avoid shows, if they're going to get into race, I pretty much don't watch it. Because, um, who wants to deal with something as entertainment that is too close to reality. I don't want to think about it all the time.
"If I'm on my job I have to wonder, um, am I being overlooked for this because of my race? Am I going to have to act different because of my race? Um, is the sales clerk in the store dealing with me like this because of my race? Am I not being waited on because of my race? Ok. Then I have to deal with, how do I vote because of my race. Um, how's this politician going to affect me because he's a White politician? How does he regard race? So, I have to deal with it every day, I don't want to deal with it when I'm sitting down relaxing, you know. And then when you deal with it on TV, you have to see the full scope of it. You have to see the issue, you have to see how it affected them, you have to see how it hurt them and then, you have to see that they don't have any more solution than you

do. And then, so you're frustrated about your own life, and then you're going to be frustrated about some TV character's life too. And you don't want to deal with that. I don't want to be frustrated about some fictional situation on TV that has no solution, and then you have to think about that, and then with it in your own life too. So when they start getting into that I stop watching the show. So I stopped watching *Roc* when they started getting into all that."

◆ Black Like Me? Identity and Self-Image

How do African Americans regard themselves in relation to the characters appearing in Black situation comedies? We may *think* we know the answer based on some previously detailed sharp criticisms of the genre. These Black viewers will probably shun the characterizations, seeing absolutely no congruence between these funny men and women and their own self-image.

Well, this vantage point is only half correct. Indeed, the participants did find the portrayals dissimilar to their self-image—their personal, internal definition of Blackness. However, some also commented on how akin the comedic images really are to their personal situations. . . .

SIMILAR

Some participants were able to identify similarities between themselves, their experiences, or Black culture, and the depictions of Blackness in Black situation comedies. Robyn, Lonette, and Jennifer each identified some compatibility between the lived experiences of African Americans and that which is represented on television.

Robyn shared with me the trials she faced in starting her own (successful) business, finding a mate who could tolerate her independent spirit, and challenging the "unprofessional professional" myth associated with those like her who are deemed "minority contracts" in the White business world. She maintains that real-life scenarios of struggle like these inform the comedies' content.

R. F.: "Well, when I'm watching a show and it's talking about the struggle that we were going through or some of the prejudice we run up against, I've experienced most of that stuff or know someone who has, so it's pretty much true. I think when . . . a comedy is made, it's based on some real stuff, that's what makes it funny. So I think it's pretty close to real life, I think that's where it comes from. Yeah."

Part of the Black situation comedy definition is that this genre of programming often makes a point of attending to Black issues: the racial, economic, political, and social, as they pertain to the Black community. Robyn clearly has picked up on this unique feature of the programming, since she has identified its ability to address racial discrimination and other trials.

Likewise, Lonette describes the comedies as also capturing the personal and the social of the Black experience.

L. E.: "I would say that they resemble various people in life. I would say that it's not totally unrealistic. There are, as a Black person who has experienced relationships, or have relationships, or has some kind of contact with other Black people on all social levels, I would say that these shows represent the variety of Black people and their personal and social lives."

. . . Rose and Jasmine also praised the comedies' ability to capture the nuances of familial relationships. Each was able to correlate her family experiences to those presented in the comedies.

Rose, who was raised with both parents present, believes *The Cosby Show* depicted a relationship between parent and child that closely resembled the interactions she had with her parents when she was a youth.

R. K.: "It [*The Cosby Show*] was funny because, um, a lot of it I can relate to. The way they dealt with their kids, the same way my parents dealt with me."

Jasmine and her siblings were reared by her widower father. She relates that although her family structure was a bit different, she still could identify with the family situations in the Black comedies.

J. F.: "Just like some of the relationships with the children. You know, the way they, the way they talk to each other and stuff. I can just see my brothers and sisters when we were little doing stuff or teasing each other or getting away with stuff. Or telling on each other. So, that way, I guess in the children's portrayals, yeah. Um, the way the husband and the wife relate. I can relate to that, but I can't say that I saw that in my family."

Valerie, Lonette, and Jasmine each cited similarities between their self-image as independent Black women and the portrayals of what they described as strong African American women.

Valerie sees herself as a bit of a fighter and most certainly a survivor. A few years ago, she recovered from a very serious accident that left her critically ill. Today she has taken on the difficult task of caring for an ailing parent, a parent who is extremely angry about experiencing deteriorating health. More, during my contact with Valerie, she revealed that the father of her child is ever-threatening a custody battle

(a battle that has yet to come to fruition). Valerie identifies only with the strongest and the most independent women in Black situation comedy—the women of *Living Single*. "As long as they portray . . . a positive, strong Black woman," she remarked, she would continue to identify with this group of single entrepreneurs, who are self-sufficient.

Lonette, a college senior, too expresses an ability to see herself in the characters presented on *Living Single*. For her, the characters' friendships, independence, and entrepreneurial spirit struck a chord of familiarity.

L. E.: "Yeah, I would say *Living Single*, being independent, young women. Um, the role that Queen Latifah plays as an entrepreneur, I was an entrepreneur once. I see myself aspiring to achieve other goals. So I would say that her character and some of the other characters on that show resemble the lifestyle that I've led and [am] trying to lead again. . . . Because I can identify with those particular young women being women of the 90s, single, independent, interdependent young women who rely on each other as sisters. It's a bond of sisterhood. They have their differences, however, the middle ground is that 'hey we're sisters, we're in this together.' It's a really for-real show, and how good friends work out different situations. They are successful Black women. It's a very, very encouraging show. I would say the different personalities, you could see one of your friends being one of those characters."

I encouraged the participants to consider whether they could see themselves in any of the comedy portrayals, or whether any specific character resembled their experiences. Jasmine was hesitant to liken herself to anything she essentially viewed as being negative. Like Valerie, she did concede that she saw herself in some of the stronger African American females. She remarks that she is particularly attracted to women who do not put up with troublesome nonsense, but who are disciplinarians in their households, not just with their children, but in most situations encountered.

J. F.: "Um, not all of them, but, the Black woman role. I was just thinking like *Thea*, if you ever watched that show. And then, like on *Roc*, Eleanor, like even though a lot of things happen, when she got mad you knew it was 'time' [that she was angry and everyone should straighten up]. And then like even on *The Cosby Show* with Claire, when she said, 'That is it!,' that was it! So I think that, I think, um, the strong Black woman role, yeah."

. . . There were a few images identified as congruent to a select group of viewers' self-image. I found it fascinating that African American women talked about how well the comedies captured their spirit of strength and independence. The characters cited as positive, realistic images of Black women were those that seemed to have little in common with each other. The Thea character of the same-titled series was a poor single parent; Eleanor of *Roc* was married and working class; Claire Huxtable of *The Cosby Show* was an upper-middle-class attorney with a host of children; and the women of *Living Single* were variously employed and educated, but all were self-sufficient and moderately successful. The tie that seems to bind all these female characters together is their depicted interaction with men. These characters held equal status to their male counterparts. They were as self-sufficient, as capable, as smart, and as hard working. They were not reliant upon men for validation or worth; rather, they were self-possessed, never submissive, and appeared to have high self-esteem. These women, it was argued, were more like real Black women.

These characters (e.g., Eleanor; Claire) resisted the stereotypes that so often encumber other female depictions. Absent from this list of congruent images is the sexual predator jezebel, the ever-ready to fight Sheneneh, or the loud-mouth Sapphire/mammy characterizations. The participants are both choosy and savvy (who would say I am Aunt Esther of *Sanford and Son*?) in their selection of more dignified roles to dub as similar to themselves. Thus we see the participants reject distorted characters who possess some deficiency—the socially powerless—opting instead to accept only the powerful part of the images. This means, the positive, at times, must be carved out of imagery of exaggeration and ridicule.

8

THE WHITES OF THEIR EYES
Racist Ideologies and the Media

◆ Stuart Hall

. . . We begin by defining some of the terms of the argument. "Racism and the media" touches directly the problem of *ideology*, since the media's main sphere of operations is the production and transformation of ideologies. An intervention in the media's construction of race is an intervention in the *ideological* terrain of struggle. Much murky water has flowed under the bridge provided by this concept of ideology in recent years; and this is not the place to develop the theoretical argument. I am using the term to refer to those images, concepts and premises which provide the frameworks through which we represent, interpret, understand, and "make sense" of some aspect of social existence. Language and ideology are not the same—since the same linguistic term ("democracy," for example, or "freedom") can be deployed within different ideological discourses. But language, broadly conceived, is by definition the principal medium in which we find different ideological discourses elaborated.

Three important things need to be said about ideology in order to make what follows intelligible. First, ideologies do not consist of isolated and separate concepts, but in the articulation of different elements into a distinctive set or chain of meanings. In liberal ideology, "freedom" is

NOTE: From *Silver Linings: Some Strategies for the Eighties*, edited by G. Bridges and R. Brunt, 1981, London: Lawrence and Wishart Ltd. Reprinted by permission.

◆ 89

connected (articulated) with individualism and the free market; in socialist ideology, "freedom" is a collective condition, dependent on, not counterposed to, "equality of condition," as it is in liberal ideology. The same concept is differently positioned within the logic of different ideological discourses. One of the ways in which ideological struggle takes place and ideologies are transformed is by articulating the elements differently, thereby producing a different meaning: breaking the chain in which they are currently fixed (e.g., "democratic" = the "Free" West) and establishing a new articulation (e.g., "democratic" = deepening the democratic content of political life). This "breaking of the chain" is not, of course, confined to the head: it takes place through social practice and political struggle.

Second, ideological statements are made by individuals: but ideologies are not the product of individual consciousness or intention. Rather we formulate our intentions *within ideology*. They pre-date individuals, and form part of the determinate social formations and conditions in which individuals are born. We have to "speak through" the ideologies which are active in our society and which provide us with the means of "making sense" of social relations and our place in them. The transformation of ideologies is thus a collective process and practice, not an individual one. Largely, the processes work *unconsciously*, rather than by conscious intention. Ideologies produce different forms of social consciousness, rather than being produced by them. They work most effectively when we are not aware that how we formulate and construct a statement about the world is underpinned by ideological premises; when our formations seem to be simply descriptive statements about how things are (i.e., must be), or of what we can "take-for-granted." "Little boys like playing rough games; little girls, however, are full of sugar and spice" is predicated on a whole set of ideological premises, though it seems to be an aphorism which is grounded, not in how

masculinity and femininity have been historically and culturally constructed in society, but in Nature itself. Ideologies tend to disappear from view into the taken-for-granted "naturalised" world of common sense. Since (like gender) race appears to be "given" by Nature, racism is one of the most profoundly "naturalised" of existing ideologies.

Third, ideologies "work" by constructing for their subjects (individual and collective) positions of identification and knowledge which allow them to "utter" ideological truths as if they were their authentic authors. This is not because they emanate from our innermost, authentic, and unified experience, but because we find ourselves mirrored in the positions at the centre of the discourses from which the statements we formulate "make sense." Thus the same "subjects" (e.g., economic classes or ethnic groups) can be differently constructed in different ideologies. . . .

Let us look, then, a little more closely at the apparatuses which generate and circulate ideologies. In modern societies, the different media are especially important sites for the production, reproduction, and transformation of ideologies. Ideologies are, of course, worked on in many places in society, and not only in the head. . . . But institutions like the media are peculiarly central to the matter since they are, by definition, part of the dominant means of *ideological* production. What they "produce" is, precisely, representations of the social world, images, descriptions, explanations and frames for understanding how the world is and why it works as it is said and shown to work. And, amongst other kinds of ideological labour, the media construct for us a definition of what *race* is, what meaning the imagery of race carries, and what the "problem of race" is understood to be. They help to classify out the world in terms of the categories of race.

The media are not only a powerful source of ideas about race. They are also one place where these ideas are articulated, worked on, transformed, and elaborated. We have said "ideas" and "ideologies" in the plural. For it would be wrong and misleading to see the media as uniformly and conspiratorially harnessed to a single, racist conception of the world. Liberal and humane ideas about "good relations" between the races, based on open-mindedness and tolerance, operate inside the world of the media. . . . .

It would be simple and convenient if all the media were simply the ventriloquists of a unified and racist "ruling class" conception of the world. But neither a unifiedly conspiratorial media nor indeed a unified racist "ruling class" exist in anything like that simple way. I don't insist on complexity for its own sake. But if critics of the media subscribe to too simple or reductive a view of their operations, this inevitably lacks credibility and weakens the case they are making because the theories and critiques don't square with reality. . . .

Another important distinction is between what we might call "overt" racism and "inferential" racism. By *overt* racism, I mean those many occasions when open and favourable coverage is given to arguments, positions and spokespersons who are in the business of elaborating an openly racist argument or advancing a racist policy or view. . . .

By *inferential* racism I mean those apparently naturalised representations of events and situations relating to race, whether "factual" or "fictional," which have racist premises and propositions inscribed in them as a set of *unquestioned assumptions*. These enable racist statements to be formulated without ever bringing into awareness the racist predicates on which the statements are grounded. . . .

An example of *this* type of racist ideology is the sort of television programme which deals with some "problem" in race relations. It is probably made by a good and honest liberal broadcaster, who hopes to do some good in the world for "race relations" and who maintains a scrupulous balance and neutrality when questioning people interviewed for the programme. The programme will end with a homily on how, if only the "extremists" on *either* side would go away, "normal blacks and whites" would be better able to get on with learning to live in harmony together. Yet every word and image of such programmes are impregnated with unconscious racism because they are all predicated on the unstated and unrecognized assumption that the *blacks* are the *source of the problem*. Yet virtually the whole of "social problem" television about race and immigration—often made, no doubt, by well-intentioned and liberal-minded broadcasters—is precisely predicated on racist premises of this kind. . . .

. . . Recent critics of the literature of imperialism have argued that, if we simply extend our definition of nineteenth-century fiction from one branch of "serious fiction" to embrace popular literature, we will find a second, powerful strand of the English literary imagination to set beside the *domestic* novel: the male-dominated world of imperial adventure, which takes *empire*, rather than *Middlemarch*, as its microcosm. . . . In this period, the very idea of *adventure* became synonymous with the demonstration of the moral, social and physical mastery of the colonisers over the colonised.

Later, this concept of "adventure"—one of the principal categories of modern *entertainment*—moved straight off the printed page into the literature of crime and espionage, children's books, the great Hollywood extravaganzas and comics. There, with recurring persistence, they still remain. Many of these older versions have had their edge somewhat blunted by time. They have been distanced from us, apparently, by our superior wisdom and liberalism. But they still reappear on the television screen, especially in the form of "old movies" (some "old movies," of course, continue to be made). But we can grasp their recurring resonance better if we identify some of the base-images of the "grammar of race."

There is, for example, the familiar *slave-figure*: dependable, loving in a simple, childlike way—the devoted "Mammy" with the rolling eyes, or the faithful fieldhand or retainer, attached and devoted to "his" Master. The best-known extravaganza of all—*Gone With the Wind*—contains rich variants of both. The "slave-figure" is by no means limited to films and programmes *about* slavery. Some "Injuns" and many Asians have come on to the screen in this disguise. A deep and unconscious ambivalence pervades this stereotype. Devoted and childlike, the "slave" is also unreliable, unpredictable and undependable—capable of "turning nasty," or of plotting in a treacherous way, secretive, cunning, cut-throat once his or her Master's or Mistress's back is turned: and inexplicably given to running way into the bush at the slightest opportunity. The whites can never be sure that this childish simpleton—"Sambo"—is not mocking his master's white manners behind his hand even when giving an exaggerated caricature of white refinement.

Another base-image is that of the "native." The good side of this figure is portrayed in a certain primitive nobility and simple dignity. The bad side is portrayed in terms of cheating and cunning, and, further out, savagery and barbarism. Popular culture is still full today of countless savage and restless "natives," and sound-tracks constantly repeat the threatening sound of drumming in the night, the hint of primitive rites and cults. Cannibals, whirling dervishes, Indian tribesmen, garishly got up, are constantly threatening to over-run the screen. They are likely to appear at any moment out of the darkness to decapitate the beautiful heroine, kidnap the children, burn the encampment or threatening to boil, cook and eat the innocent explorer or colonial administrator and his lady-wife. These "natives" always move as an anonymous collective mass—in tribes or hordes. And against them is always counterposed the isolated white figure, alone "out there," confronting his Destiny or shouldering his Burden in the "heart of darkness," displaying coolness under fire and an unshakeable authority—exerting mastery over the rebellious natives or quelling the threatened uprising with a single glance of his steel-blue eyes.

A third variant is that of the "clown" or "entertainer." This captures the "innate" humour, as well as the physical grace of the licensed entertainer—putting on a show for The Others. It is never quite clear whether we are laughing with or at this figure: admiring the physical and rhythmic grace, the open expressivity and emotionality of the "entertainer," or put off by the "clown's" stupidity.

One noticeable fact about all these images is their deep *ambivalence*—the double vision of the white eye through which they are seen. The primitive nobility of the aging tribesman or chief, and the native's rhythmic grace, always contain both a nostalgia for an innocence lost forever to the civilised, and the threat of civilisation being over-run or undermined by the recurrence of savagery, which is always lurking just below the surface; or by an untutored sexuality, threatening to "break out." Both are aspects—the good and the bad sides—of *primitivism*. In these images, "primitivism" is defined by the fixed proximity of such people to Nature.

Is all this so far away as we sometimes suppose from the representation of race which fill the screens today? These *particular* versions may have faded. But their *traces* are still to be observed, reworked in many of the modern and up-dated images. And though they may appear to carry a different meaning, they are often still constructed on a very ancient grammar. Today's restless native hordes are still alive and well and living, as guerilla armies and freedom fighters in the Angola, Zimbabwe, or Namibian "bush." Blacks are still the most frightening, cunning, and glamorous crooks (and policemen) in New York cop series. They are the fleet-footed, crazy-talking under-men who connect Starsky and Hutch to the drug-saturated ghetto. The scheming villains and their giant-sized bully boys in the world of James Bond and his progeny are still, unusually, recruited from "out there" in Jamaica, where savagery lingers on. The sexually-available "slave girl" is alive and kicking, smouldering away on some exotic TV set or on the covers of paperbacks, though she is now the centre of a special admiration, covered in a sequinned gown and supported by a white chorus line. Primitivism, savagery, guile and unreliability—all "just below the surface"—can still be identified in the faces of black political leaders around the world, cunningly plotting the overthrow of "civilisation." . . .

9

HETERO BARBIE?

◆ Mary F. Rogers

As they enter their teenage years, if not before, most heterosexual females begin putting a boy or young man at the center of their lives. Moving through puberty toward adulthood, girls and young women find that their popularity at school, their feminine credibility, and much else hinge on their attractiveness to boys and their relationship with one particular boy.[1] As they get heterosexualized, then, girls and young women face pressures to give boys and dating a lot of priority. In turn, they pay increasing attention to the size and shape of their bodies, the range and contents of their wardrobes, the styling of their hair, and the making up of their faces. Barbie epitomizes, even exaggerates, these families mandates. She gives girls endless opportunities to costume her, brush and style her hair, and position her in settings like aerobics class, a school dance, or the shopping mall.

Yet Barbie escapes the typical outcomes of such activities. In the end she seems not to have her heart in her relationship with Ken, who in no way monopolizes her attention. Barbie exudes an independence that deviates from the codes of mainstream femininity. That she is insistently single and perpetually childless means that hers is no "normal" femininity. Again, one comes up short by looking for an explanation in Barbie's teenage status, for she is no teenager when it comes to occupations, travel, and other aspects of her lifestyle. The facts of Barbie's having neither a husband

NOTE: From *Barbie Culture*, by Mary F. Rogers, 1999, London: Sage Publications Ltd. Copyright © 1999. Reprinted by permission of Sage Publications Ltd.

nor a child do not speak for themselves, then. Instead, these circumstances leave Barbie open to multiple, conflicting interpretations. They enlarge this icon's field of meanings and thus the range of consumers she can attract.

Within that field of cultural meanings stands the possibility that Barbie may not be heterosexual. Indeed, she may not even be a woman. Barbie may be a drag queen. Much in the tradition made widely visible by stars like RuPaul, Barbie may be the ultrafeminine presence that drag queens personify. Her long, long legs and flat hips suggest this possibility. So does her wardrobe, especially her shimmering evening gowns, high heels, heavyhanded makeup, and brilliant tiaras and other headpieces. Barbie's is a bright, glittery femininity never visibly defiled by a Lady Schick or Kotex. This exceptionally, emphatically feminine icon has some appeal among gay men.

That appeal shows up in diverse ways. I have no interest in whether or not this designer or that, this collector or that, this event or that is gay, however. My concern is with the *gay-themed* character of what one comes across in some corners of Barbie's far-reaching world. In many cultural worlds heterocentrism and heterosexism prevail in no uncertain terms. In the world of "Father Knows Best" or the feminine mystique, attention to gender and family center on heterosexuality strongly enough to snuff out alternative readings whereby "transgressive" sexualities such as lesbianism or bisexuality can enter the picture. Commonly intertwined with such heterocentrism are values celebrating heterosexuality as normal and natural while condemning or at least rejecting lesbigay sexualities. The world of Barbie is *relatively* free of such heterocentrism and heterosexism and thus holds *relative* appeal for nonheterosexual people, especially gay men. Lesbians, particularly those inclined toward feminism, are more likely to reject some of the central features of Barbie's world, as are bisexuals who might find her

apparent monosexuality unappealing. In any case, Barbie's world allows for non-straight readings, just as many other "straight" cultural products do.[2] I tap such possibilities here by treating Barbie's sexual identity as less than certain while arguing that her sweeping appeal revolves around such ambiguities.

As an icon of drag, Barbie illustrates what feminists and culture critics have been saying for some years. In no uncertain terms Barbie demonstrates that femininity is a manufactured reality. It entails a lot of artifice, a lot of clothes, a lot of props such as cuddly poodles and shopping bags, and a lot of effort, however satisfying at times.[3] If Barbie can join drag queens as an exemplar of the constructed character of femininity, she can also be an icon of nonheterosexual femininity. In the extreme Barbie might be a lipstick lesbian, a lesbian fem, or a lesbian closeted more tightly than most who choose not to "come out." She might be a bisexual woman who once cared about and pursued a relationship with Ken but now prefers her "best friend" Midge. Most radically of all, Barbie might be asexual. She might be sexy without being sexual, attractive without being attracted. . . .

Not surprisingly, RuPaul sometimes shows up in Barbie's world. Scott Arend (1995) reports Ivan Burton, who designs artist dolls, has done a "one-of-a-kind RuPaul." Jim Washburn (1994) says that Michael Osborne, a Barbie doll collector, wants to be buried with what he calls his "Ru-Paul Barbie, or Ru-Barbie for short." Osborne's favorite doll is made from a My Size Barbie, the 18-inch version of the doll, and has "brown skin, blue eyes and platinum hair."

The feature story on Osborne, which appeared in the *Los Angeles Times*, illustrates how a gay-themed text fits into a mainstream publication, that is, how a gay reading of a supposedly straight text involves little stretch of the non-heterosexual imagination. Twenty-four-year-old Osborne, who has been collecting Barbie dolls since he was thirteen, has nearly 300 of them and makes no attempt to hide his "love" for them. Osborne says he has friends employed by Mattel who help him acquire some of his more unusual dolls such as a hairless Skipper, Barbie's little sister. Like other collectors, Osborne keeps a lot of his dolls in their original packaging. (NRFB, or Never Removed From Box, enhances the market value of a doll.) Osborne, however, has "play-with dolls, whose outfits he changes monthly." He also shampoos his dolls' hair and gives them permanents. Also, Osborne once dressed as Barbie at Halloween and claims to have "looked pretty darn snappy." Asked about the possibility that his sizable Barbie collection could be an obstacle to "finding a mate," Osborne responds in terms of "friends who have had rocky relationships with *people* because they did not really like Barbie." Washburn poses the more difficult question: What "if it came down to a choice between giving up the Barbies or the *person*?" Osborne answers, "It depends on the *person*, but probably the *person*."

Where a heterocentrist text would talk about finding a wife or a woman, this one refers only to mates and people and persons. In view of its subject matter this text readily passes as gay-themed. Along those lines Osborne reports, "I had always liked fashion, always liked doing hair. When people asked what I wanted to be when I grew up, I said I wanted to be a hairdresser and president of Mattel." Osborne's interest in being a hairdresser expresses an interest in what queer theorists, who theorize about nonheterosexual or "transgressive" sexualities, call *non-normative occupations*. Such lines of work are those that attract disproportionate numbers of lesbigay people and are widely considered inappropriate for people of a given gender. The ballet and hairdressing for men and the military and auto mechanics for women are examples. In any event Osborne's interest in a non-normative occupation bespeaks a

gay-themed text, as does his claim that "the best times of his life have been Barbie times." . . .

More generally, *Barbie Bazaar* often offers gay-themed fare for those attuned to it. Like most such material, it does not leap out to most readers as lesbigay even while leaving room for "queer" interpretations. . . . Often, too, gay-themed material shows up in comments about or articles on doll artists, most of whom appear to be men often working in conjunction with male "partners" to refashion Barbie in designs of their own. In one *Barbie Bazaar* article Pattie Jones (1995), for instance, mentions Jim Faraone, who once designed jewelry for Anne Klein but now "designs hand-beaded Barbie doll outfits." Faraone began collecting in 1986 and now has a thousand Barbie dolls. Two of his artist dolls are pictured in Janine Fennick's *The Collectible Barbie Doll* (1996). One is AIDS Awareness Barbie where the AIDS-awareness red ribbon runs around the back of Barbie's neck, across her breasts, and then crosses at her waist. Also showing up in *Barbie Bazaar* are references to Mattel's participation with collectors and other Barbie fans in AIDS fundraisers, often targeting children with AIDS as beneficiaries. . . .

Barbie thus points to what Jesse Berrett (1996) sees as "mass culture's power to define, commodify, and mutate sexual identity." Put more queerly in terms used in *Out* magazine:

> RuPaul's larger-than-life, gayer-than-gay presence on runways, VH1, and New York radio and everywhere else . . . suggests that the mall of America has embraced him not as a novelty but as a genuine homo star. But it doesn't take a drag queen to have an impact. (1997: 96)

Mattel can unintentionally sponsor the same impact, it seems. . . .

◆ *Notes*

1. For insights into this state of affairs, see Eder with Evans and Parker (1995), Fine (1992), and Walkerdine (1990).

2. See, for example, Valerie Traub, "The Ambiguities of 'Lesbian' Viewing Pleasure: The (Dis)Articulation of *Black Widow*," in Julia Epstein and Kristina Straub (eds.), *Body Guards: The Cultural Politics of Gender Ambiguity* (New York, Routledge, 1991), pp. 304-9; Bonnie Zimmerman, "Seeing, Reading, Knowing: The Lesbian Appropriation of Literature," in Joan E. Hartman and Ellen Messer-Davidow (eds.), *(En)Gendering Knowledge: Feminists in Academe* (Knoxville, University of Tennessee Press, 1991), pp. 92-7.

3. Dorothy E. Smith is one of the best commentators on how pleasurable some of the projects of femininity can be. She talks, for example, about the pleasures of female community built up around such feminine pastimes as clothes shopping. See *Texts, Facts, and Femininity: Exploring the Relations of Ruling* (London and New York: Routledge, 1990), p. 199.

References ◆

Arend, S. (1994). Review of mondo Barbie. *Barbie Bazaar, 6,* 51.

Berrett, J. (1996). The sex revolts: Reading gender and identity in mass culture. *Radical History Review, 66,* 210-219.

Eder, D., with Evans, C., & Parker, P. (1995). *School talk: Gender and adolescent culture.* New Brunswick, NJ: Rutgers University Press.

Fennick, J. (1996). *The collectable Barbie doll: An Illustrated guide to her dreamy world.* Philadelphia: Courage Books.

Fine, M. (1992). *Disruptive voices: The possibilities of feminist research.* Ann Arbor: University of Michigan Press.

Jones, P. (1995). Viva la Barbie. *Barbie Bazaar, 7,* 63-7.

Walkerdine, V. (1990). *Schoolgirl fictions.* London and New York: Verso.

Washburn, J. (1994). The man who would be Ken. *Los Angeles Times,* 2 August: 1: Life & Style Section.

10

POPULAR CULTURE AND QUEER REPRESENTATION

A Critical Perspective

◆ Diane Raymond

"Queer" is a category in flux. Once a term of homophobic abuse, recently the term has been reappropriated as a marker for some gay, lesbian, bisexual, transgender (glbt), and other marginalized sexual identities. In addition, "queer theory" has emerged in academic scholarship to identify a body of knowledge connected to but not identical with lesbian/gay studies. The term is itself open-ended, and its advocates argue that its fluidity is to be embraced rather than "fixed." Though there is no consensus on the term's meaning (and who is included and who excluded), there is general agreement that the "queer" is politically radical, rejects binary categories (like heterosexual/homosexual), embraces more fluid categories, and tends to be "universalizing" rather than "minoritizing," to use literary theorist Eve Kosofsky Sedgwick's (1990) distinction. That is, queer theory reads queerness throughout the culture and not simply as a fixed, clearly demarcated category. Further, queer theory problematizes certain sorts of questions that have been standard in gay and lesbian theory. Queer theory, for example, tends to be interested less in whether homosexuality is a result of nature or nurture and more in what function the question of causation serves in the culture and in ideology.

Queer theory emerged as one of the many oppositional discourses of the 1960s and 1970s, including postcolonial, feminist, and multicultural theory. Unlike their earlier theoretical forebears like Marxism and feminism that demanded exclusive theoretical allegiance or hegemony, these theoretical positions remained open to multiple ways of combining perspectives and subverting monocausal explanations for oppression. Indeed, in queer theory and a number of others, hyphenations became common and hybrid theories borrowing from a variety of views promised rich opportunities for analysis. Regardless of their specific differences, these marginalized views sought to move the "margins" to the "center": "This way of seeing affirmed otherness and difference, and the importance of attending to marginalized, minority, and oppositional groups and voices previously excluded from the cultural dialogue" (Kellner, 1995, p. 24). In addition, these theoretical perspectives tended, unlike earlier theoretical approaches to culture like the Frankfurt School, to reject any strict dichotomy between high and low culture and to reject any vision of popular culture that constructed it as monolithic and viewers as passive dupes. The relationship between viewers and cultural artifacts, including popular media, was, according to these postmodern views, more complex, culturally mediated, and open to a mix of possible "readings."

A number of queer theorists have used these foundational principles to analyze media from a queer or non-dominant perspective. Alexander Doty's 1993 book, *Making Things Perfectly Queer*, for example, used queer theory to offer new ways to read mainstream television. There he argued that "ghosts," to use his term, inhabited cultural texts and that those ghosts ought to be driven out of their closets. Like Sedgwick, Doty suggested that cultural texts offer the potential for queer readings that focus on connotative rather than denotative meaning, that is, that seek to find credible readings hidden in a text that a culture of homophobia and heterosexism bars us from seeing. Though some texts certainly contain explicit themes or characters marked as queer, Doty's concern

was to look at "queerness" in acts of production or acts of reception. *Making Things Perfectly Queer* looks especially at same-sex relationships—between Lucy and Ethel, Jack Benny and Rochester, and Laverne and Shirley, to name a few—as offering to viewers a buried, yet undeniable, queer pleasure.

This chapter takes a somewhat different approach from that of Doty. Though I agree with Doty that there is no unambiguous meaning in a cultural text and that the reception positions that audience members occupy are culturally and historically grounded, I want to look at denotation rather than connotation. At the time that Doty wrote his analysis, connotation was about all that queer viewers had available as a source of pleasurable viewing. But today, as the section below points out, prime-time television is rife with gay and lesbian (if not bisexual and transgender) characters offering the potential for new sorts of analysis; that change is significant and has occurred since Doty's work appeared. I want to suggest that this new cultural phenomenon should not be uncritically valorized as an unambiguous symptom of heightened cultural tolerance and inclusion. Rather, while I do not wish to minimize the benefits of such shifts in cultural consciousness, I want in addition to offer somewhat more suspicious readings of these themes and trends.

More specifically, I want to look at three recurring patterns or tropes that I have identified in situation comedies. The first pattern—the increased appearance of glbt major or supporting characters—acknowledges the very real changes that have occurred in the constitution of the characters populating television's worlds. The remaining two tropes—that of the "gay pretender" and that of the "straight-mistaken-for-gay"—have less to do with the actual diversity of characters we see and more with how gayness itself is understood and metaphorized. All three offer the potential for subverting heterosexist norms and assumptions. I shall argue, however, that how these shows resolve tensions often results in a "reinscription" of heterosexuality and a "containment" of queer sexuality, that is, that the resolution these programs offer enables viewers to distance themselves from the queer and thereby to return to their comfortable positions as part of the dominant culture. Such a dynamic enables power to mask itself, making it all the harder to pin down and question. Thus, where Doty attempts to "queer the straight," my approach suggests how what might seem to be "queer" can come to be normalized in mainstream culture.

In making this argument, I shall rely mostly on feminist and queer theory, and the second section of the essay will outline briefly the conceptual underpinnings of those views on which my analysis depends. It is important to distinguish queer theory as an academic field from the glbt "community" and to acknowledge in this context that gays and lesbians are not a homogeneous group with a singular, uncomplicated sense of identity. The search for identity always occurs on contested terrain and the struggle to find a voice takes place in a dynamic relationship with the dominant culture where signs and signifiers can be appropriated and reappropriated in an endless chain of interpretation. Thus, meaning is rarely predictable and never fixed. Further, queer viewers and readers, however much they resist dominant messages about sexuality, the family, and love, nonetheless are constituted by dominant ideology's messages about these practices. Such readers, then, are neither completely autonomous beings severed from social relations who invent their own readings of texts nor are they completely submerged in social structures, blindly responsive to group norms. As feminist theorist Jacqueline Rose (1986) has noted, "The relationship between viewer and scene is always one of fracture, partial identification, pleasure and distrust" (p. 227). Finally, debates within the glbt community remind us that gender, race, class, age, and other variables of identity undermine the homogeneity of any group, including this one.

Given my own theoretical overview, I must insist here that my conclusions can be tentative at best and are meant to suggest more complex ways of reading rather than determinative readings themselves. Thus, I am not suggesting here that I have discovered or deciphered any truth residing below the surface of these popular texts. Indeed, this essay will be successful if it enriches my readers' abilities to create meanings different from my own suggested ones in the popular cultural texts they read. Further, given the truism that no social group is homogeneous and that even a single individual occupies multiple subject positions, I in no way mean to imply that my readings here are "queer," generalizable to any particular group or sort of person, or noncontroversial. To put the point more simply, there is no "correct" queer reading, no one queer reading, and no unchanging queer perspective.

This chapter does not take issue with the claim that the increasing visibility of gays and lesbians in the media has important direct and indirect positive effects, not least of which has been the new availability of role models and cultural icons for younger glbt people, the attention to homophobia and hate crime, the growing recognition of demands for civil rights for glbt people, and the public's seeming greater comfort with "out" glbt celebrities. Having acknowledged such changes, I want move beyond them here to complexify the issue of representation, more specifically the representation of glbt people in a period in which gays and lesbians (if not bisexuals and transgendered individuals) seem to be everywhere in the media—situation comedies, dramas, *People* magazine, *MTV*, even the hit reality show *Survivor*.

Despite the occasional mention of a drama, my focus here is on comedy, the arena where images of glbt people appear most frequently. To attempt to explain in any persuasive way why such is the case would take me far from my topic. But

I might briefly conjecture two possible explanations. First, as traditional family comedies—along with the traditional family—began to disappear, space opened up for "alternative" sorts of narratives, including those of nontraditional "families" (e.g., *Friends, Designing Women,* and the vast number of workplace comedies whose origins lie in *The Mary Tyler Moore Show*); even so-called "family" shows like, for example, *Party of Five* diverge from the traditional model. With the gradual disappearance of the traditional family sitcom, even heterosexual characters began to occupy nonnormative narrative positions. For example, the oldest son in *Party of Five* becomes a surrogate father *and* mother to his younger siblings; married characters on popular shows like *Mary Tyler Moore* get divorced; in some cases married characters are never seen with their spouses; and holidays like Thanksgiving, traditionally constructed as times for "family," get reconstructed on shows like *Friends*. These shifts in roles and viewer expectations clearly allowed for the appearance of nonheterosexual characters in major and supporting roles; cultural shifts linked to an increasingly visible gay and lesbian movement no doubt helped to buttress such changes. Finally, situation comedies—however "realistic" they might be—do not claim, like dramas, to be offering us "real life." That lack of seriousness may allow these programs to play with themes under cover of humor where those themes might be too volatile or even too didactic for another sort of audience. Such play and flexibility may also help to account for what may be a wider variety of possible readings. I want now to turn to an overview of those representations.

◆ *The Queering of Television*

Until very recently, it was not unusual for glbt activists and scholars to bemoan their virtual absence in popular media, particularly television. For example, in 1995, Larry Gross used the term "symbolic annihilation" (p. 62) to describe the invisibility of gays and lesbians in mass media; if, as Gross suggested, representation attaches to power, then that invisibility evidences the powerlessness of the queer community. Even media studies sensitive to portrayals of "minorities in the media" (e.g., Greenberg, 1986) tended to focus mostly on ethnic and racial minorities and to ignore sexual orientation as a defining aspect of identity. According to Gross, gays and lesbians tend to be even more isolated and invisible than members of racial and ethnic minorities and are therefore "probably the least permitted to speak for ourselves in the mass media" (p. 63).

Finally, media critics pointed out that those rare depictions of glbt people tended both to dichotomize anyone glbt as victim or villain and to reinforce demeaning stereotypes and caricatures: gay men as effeminate and lesbians as unattractive man-haters, for example. According to Gross (1995), "Hardly ever shown in the media are just plain gay folks, used in roles which do not center on their deviance as a threat to the moral order which must be countered through ridicule or physical violence" (p. 65). An underlying assumption of such an apparently commonsensical critique is not only that more images of marginalized peoples will effect social transformation but also that the notion of a "positive" image—"just plain gay folks"—is uncontroversial and transparent.

Today's even casual television viewers, however, would find such critiques oddly out-of-date. Network programs are now full of gay/queer characters; indeed, the more-than-occasional prime-time television viewer would likely be mystified by Gross's (1995) claim that the rare continuing gay character "tend[s] to be so subtle as to be readily misunderstood by the innocent" (p. 66). Forty-two million people watched the coming-out episode on *Ellen* on April 30, 1997, making it the highest-ranked show on television that year except for the Academy Awards. Though some argue that Ellen DeGeneres's sexuality led to the cancellation of her show in 1998, the queering of prime-time television since that time is without dispute.[1]

A recent *Boston Globe* article notes there are at least two dozen gay television characters scattered throughout prime-time shows (Rothaus, 2000). Where once soap operas floated gay characters only to have them die of AIDS or leave town mysteriously, *All My Children* has introduced a new plot line in which a character who has grown up on the show comes out as a lesbian. According to the actress who plays the character, the story-line—about how an almost obsessively heterosexual mother deals with her daughter's lesbianism—is meant to be "accessible to everyone" (Rothaus, 2000) and, though allegedly not didactic, makes a "concerted effort to show that a gay relationship is just like any other" (Rothaus, 2000).[2] *Will and Grace*, two of whose four major characters are openly gay, is one of the most popular shows on television. Indeed, one might argue that television is light years ahead of mainstream film, whose "gay" characters still seem to be confined to psychopathic murderers (e.g., *Basic Instinct*, *The Talented Mr. Ripley*, *Silence of the Lambs*, *Braveheart*, *JFK*, *American Beauty*, etc.) or lonely, asexual best friends (e.g., *Silkwood*, *As Good as it Gets*, etc.);[3] for the most part, one needs to turn to independent films to see the "just plain gay folks" Gross seeks.

Where once glbt characters were the "exemplar of degeneracy" (Mohr, 1997, p. 331), today's gay characters are "queer as folk," to borrow the title of one continuing cable television program. Given that the majority viewing audience is heterosexual, programming sympathetic to glbt communities must appeal to mainstream liberal viewers who today most likely know someone gay in the workplace, the family, or among friends.[4] Thus, where once glbt viewers had to resort to oppositional or subversive readings like Doty's in order to

find viewing pleasure—are Cagney and Lacey really lovers? Can one find a queer resonance in the films of Rock Hudson? and so forth—such readings seem quaint and tame by today's television standards when gayness is much discussed, gay sexual practices are the subject of comedic banter, and a range of appealing characters are openly gay or lesbian.

Albeit somewhat one-dimensional, these gay or lesbian television characters are attractive and professional—Will Truman is a lawyer, and the lesbians on *Friends* and the now-defunct but highly popular *Mad About You* are doctors, accountants, and mothers. They include younger characters—*Buffy the Vampire Slayer* has featured two teenaged girls in a budding lesbian relationship, and *Dawson's Creek* featured a main character's coming out in its story line. They are occasionally people of color—*Spin City* includes an African American gay man as part of the political team. Viewers have seen lesbian weddings, lesbian and gay parenting arrangements, gay therapists, gay seniors, and the angst and humor of coming out. Such "mainstreaming" seems likely to change popular perceptions and misperceptions about homosexuality. As Mohr points out, "Without demonization, it is hard, perhaps impossible, to conceptualize homosexuality as a vampire-like corruptive contagion, a disease that spreads itself to the pure and innocent by mere proximity" (p. 333).

Though there is no question that the majority of the viewing audience for these shows is heterosexual, these portrayals engage with viewers who see themselves as hip, nonjudgmental, mostly urban, and gay-friendly. *Will and Grace* is full of campy in-jokes (many referring back to popular culture itself) and sexual innuendo, and as viewers we are asked to feel superior to Jack's mother who fails to realize that he is gay. *Saturday Night Live* pokes fun at a Batman-and-Robin-like team of superheroes, the Ambiguously Gay Duo, in animated sketches full of phallic imagery and less-than-subtle references to anal intercourse. Smithers is clearly smitten with (and even has erotic dreams about) Mr. Burns in *The Simpsons* and in one episode gay director John Waters is the voice of an antique dealer Homer idolizes until he discovers that the dealer is gay. We are amused that Jaimie's impossible-to-please mother-in-law in *Mad About You* prefers her lesbian daughter's lover to Jaimie. The stars of *Xena* discuss without defensiveness in mainstream periodicals the "lesbian subtext" of that long-running series. It is now homophobes, not gays and lesbians, who are vilified or ignored, and often the test of a character (e.g., the gay plotline in *Dawson's Creek*) comes down to how well he or she deals with a friend or family member's coming out.

This "queering" of television goes well beyond the presence of glbt characters. A recent *New York Times* article references the growing number of gay television writers who are influencing shows even where there are no gay characters. The article suggests that "a gay sensibility has infiltrated American comedy, even when flying beneath the radar in an ostensibly heterosexual situation" (Kirby, 2001, p. 23). This phenomenon—sometimes termed "gay winking" or "gay vague"—allows for multiple readings of a character or situation, those readings dependent on the subject position of the viewer. Thus, *Frasier*'s two brothers, but for the fact that they sleep with women, are stereotypically gay in their tastes and preferences; knowing more about Puccini than basketball, these brothers evidence a gay sensibility striking to all but the most naïve. Indeed, much of the humor emerges from their macho-cop father's vain attempts to make his sons more "butch." Further, Niles and Frasier's shared memories of the childhood trauma they experienced as a result of being fussy, intelligent, artistic, and averse to athletics resonate with the experiences of many glbt people who did not as youths conform to the dominant culture's gender codes.

These more subtle gestures may, as Danae Clark (1993) suggests in her discussion of advertising campaigns, serve a dual function: They avoid alienating gay audiences at the same time that they mask the gay content and retain majority viewers. Finally, in a number of cases, actors playing heterosexual characters are known to viewing audiences to be gay, lesbian, or bisexual. For example, David Hyde Pierce, who plays Frasier's brother Niles Crane, is openly gay; knowledgeable viewers, then, can play with multiple levels of reading performances such as Pierce's, even where the ostensible plot line involves, for example, his long-term obsession with Daphne, his father's live-in physical therapist.

Thus, queer images, themes, and tropes are now in circulation in a way that marks this particular period as distinct from earlier eras where homosexuality could only be hinted at or, if explicit, pathologized. Now that, as Mohr puts it, queer folks "are no longer something monstrous, repulsive, unthinkably abject" (p. 333), how do these new images function in popular discourse? Though cultural studies critics have tended to look for so-called subversive moments in television and film as opportunities for resistant readings, my approach here adopts a different orientation to suggest how moments of apparently subversive potential are undermined and ultimately contained. Recent queer and feminist theory offers new ways of thinking about such dynamics.

Queering Theory ◆ *and Representation*

Ideology, as cultural studies theorists have persuasively argued, constructs viewing positions and identities. Sexuality, at least in modern times, is one component of that ideology, a component whose regulation occurs both formally and informally. In a culture grounded in what Adrienne Rich (1980) has termed "compulsory heterosexuality," popular culture will tend to portray heterosexuality as if it were natural and inevitable and to position alternative forms of sexuality as "other." Compulsory heterosexuality (or what some have called "heteronormativity") functions to underline the fact that heterosexuality is an institution, a practice, with its own set of expectations, norms, and principles of conduct. If, however, heterosexuality is not a naturalized, innate state of being, then its existence is more fragile than is obvious at first glance. Given that fragility, heterosexuality cannot be taken as a given or presumed; in a culture framed by homophobia and heterosexism, institutions both formal and informal; police behavior, boundaries, expectations, and values; a dynamic blend of incentives and disincentives function to channel desire in "appropriate" ways and to make invisible those practices falling outside its discursive domain.

Heterosexuality and homophobia organize the structures in which we are immersed, structures so pervasive as to become almost invisible. Sociologist Pierre Bourdieu (1990) has employed the notion of *habitus* to describe how what is constructed can come to seem inevitable and natural. Like the fish that does not feel the weight of the water, human beings live in a world of "social games embodied and turned into second nature" (p. 63). Indeed, the very fact that our culture organizes itself around sexuality and that sexuality is defined in terms of the sex of one's object of desire is noteworthy. As Sedgwick (1990) conjectures, one can, with a bit of imagination, conceive any number of ways to organize sexual identity, including "preference[s] for certain acts, certain zones or sensations, certain physical types, a certain frequency, certain symbolic investments, certain relations of age or power, a certain species, a certain number of participants, etc. etc. etc." (p. 8). Finally, the cultural energy involved in disciplining gender and sexuality suggests how fragile those institutions actually are; if Butler and Foucault are right that gender and sexuality are *achievements* rather than givens, then sexual identity is complex, incomplete, and unstable.

The mechanisms that serve to construct and regulate sexuality may not be obvious or even intentional; indeed, as Foucault (1990) puts it, "Power is tolerable only on condition that it mask a substantial part of itself. Its success is proportional to its ability to hide its own mechanisms" (p. 86). If ideology generally effaces itself, then even the very producers of popular culture—whatever their explicit political leanings, sexuality, or agenda—are immersed in that ideology. Further, power's ability to mask itself may mean that, ironically, the mechanisms of power produce pleasure. We don't have to go far to find such examples—Gothic romances, pornography, certain clothing styles, exercise regimens, gendered toys for children, and so forth—all function to produce pleasure as they disguise the ways that they reinforce norms relating to sexuality and sexuality and, less obviously, race, age, and class. The question becomes, then, not whether queer (or straight) viewers find pleasure in the proliferation of these television images (they would not endure if they did not produce pleasure) but rather how one might read and understand such pleasure. Pleasure itself is never innocent or neutral and there is a danger in valorizing pleasure without looking at its context. Given that, I want to ask how the new representations of gays and lesbians circulate in culture.

If the homo/hetero schema is "written into the cultural organization of Western societies" (Epstein, 1987, p. 133), then the question of the homosexual/heterosexual matrix rather than the question of personal identity becomes primary. Such a perspective would suggest that what is at stake is less the question how many gay/queer characters populate television or even how sympathetically they are portrayed but rather about the ways desire and meaning are structured, even in the absence of such images. Thus, identity must be thought of as always in relation, never fixed or stable. As Fuss, Sedgwick, Butler, and others have noted, heterosexuality is a parasitic notion, dependent on that-what-it-is-not, namely, homosexuality. "Each is haunted by the other" (Fuss, 1991, p. 4), and the homosexual comes to represent the "terrifying [sexual] other" of the heterosexual. Yet popular television programming seems to belie this theoretical claim, bombarding us with images of gayness and far less threatening homosexuals who suggest the possibility of new normative understandings of sexual difference.

First, one should note that the appearance of *difference* per se is not necessarily subversive. As bell hooks (1999) points out in her essay "Eating the Other," the commodification of difference can have the effect of silencing resistance and transforming resistance to consumption. Without a mutual recognition of the role that homophobia plays in these dynamics, "boundaries [ ] remain intact" (p. 186). That heterosexuals now can, like tourists, visit glbt culture does not in itself guarantee social change. Further, capitalist systems need difference to create desire and to sell commodities. Kellner (1995) notes:

> Difference sells. Capitalism must constantly multiply markets, styles, fads, and artifacts to keep absorbing consumers into its practices and lifestyles. The mere valorization of "difference" as a mark of opposition can simply help market new styles and artifacts if the difference in question and its effects are not adequately appraised. (p. 40)

Stuart and Elizabeth Ewen (1992) are right that "novelty and disposability make up the backbone of the market" (p. 193), then the static is the enemy of popular media. Difference can also serve to provide one with a sense of uniqueness or individuality. As Jonathan Rutherford has quipped, "It's no longer about keeping up with the Joneses, it's about being different from them" (quoted in hooks, 1995, p. 157). Further, the promotion of gayness as a "lifestyle" tends to attach it to commodities rather than practices as an expression of the self. *Will and Grace*'s bitchy attention to

fashion, weight, career, and popular media is exemplary in this respect.[5]

In addition, Torres (1993) points to the ways visits from "real lesbians" may help to deflect the viewer's attention from the possibility that ongoing characters may harbor same-sex feelings. Especially in shows that feature all, or mostly, female troupes like *Kate and Allie*, *Designing Women*, *Cagney and Lacey*, and *Golden Girls*, for example, the introduction of lesbian and gay characters may serve to reassure viewers that the same-sex groupings are purely platonic. Cultural unease with lesbianism may be tied to cultural unease with feminism, but it may also emerge from lesbianism's own murky boundaries. Obviously, my case would be much easier to make if these characters reflected negative or insulting stereotypes; yet, I have already suggested that the characters we see exhibit a range of personality types, interests, values, and flaws. But I want to look more closely for a moment at a dynamic in *Will and Grace* that may help to clarify how the subversive potential in these images is ultimately policed and contained.

IT'S NOT JUST THE NUMBERS . . .

The dynamic I want to explore pervades this show, and its repetition suggests a certain ambivalence over sexuality, queer sexuality in particular. To illustrate this phenomenon more concretely, let's look at the montage that opens the show. In these brief scenes, we see the show's four main characters in a variety of poses and places. Yet, strikingly, we never see the two gay men together and the only times we see the women together occur when they are with at least one of the men. Instead, we are treated to a number of opposite-sex couplings. We see, in the first clip, Will and Grace dancing a tango, a dance which has come to epitomize sexual heat and romance. We see Jack and Karen frequently together in other scenes, including one where they bounce off each other's chests and another where they hug. In episodes of the show, we frequently see Will and Grace in bed together and, though Grace recently had and lost a boyfriend, Will's relationships are rare and end almost as soon as they begin. Will and Grace's behavior mirrors that of a traditional heterosexual husband and wife, and Karen is quick to point to Grace's neurotic attachment to Will (indeed, she often refers to Will as Grace's gay husband). Grace becomes the supremely neurotic fag hag par excellence who identifies with gay culture, surrounds herself with gay men, and is never guilty of even the mildest expression of homophobia. Will and Grace are comfortable physically with one another, they finish each other's sentences, and, though they briefly lived apart (across the hall from one another!), they soon came back together as roommates. Do we, like Grace, hope someday that the two will be united, that Will can be converted to the heterosexual partner that Grace desperately wants? Further, Jack's flamboyance and his stereotypical nature may suggest that Will is somehow less gay and therefore recuperable to heterosexuality.

As already noted, there is no question that the new glbt characters we see on television are an attractive group both morally and physically. In some cases, for example, *ER* and *Buffy*, shows allow a long-standing character to play with a same-sex attraction, even if the feelings/relationships are temporary. The famous "kisses"—one thinks back to the *Roseanne* show for one of the first—and the more recent kisses on *Friends* and *Ally McBeal*—occur during sweeps weeks and are unabashed strategies to increase the viewing audience. The fact that these episodes earn viewer warnings is noteworthy in itself. But even more noteworthy, it seems to me, is the fact that these episodes result in no change in diegesis or character evolution. These kisses come and go as if they were a dream; they are never incorporated into a character's understanding of his/her identity and sexuality, and the possibility of bisexuality,

a more fluid sexual identity, or even a recurrence is rarely if ever entertained.

Indeed, fluidity seems to pose such a threat that its possibility is rarely if ever acknowledged. Thus, when "real" gay or lesbian characters tell their stories, their narratives tend almost always to reinscribe gayness as innate, and those who are gay as having no choice. Thus, we hear that Will has always loved Grace, but that he has never had any sexual feelings of any kind for her. When she is devastated to learn that he has had sex with another woman, he insists that it was merely to have the experience and that he had no real interest in the woman. The idea that Will's best friend Jack might have been attracted to a woman is so obviously ludicrous that the very idea earns a huge laugh. The noteworthy absence of bisexuals in these comedies suggests that the fluidity of a bisexual sexual identity may be too disruptive for such programming. In that sense, bisexuals may be television's abject subjects, in the Butlerian sense that they are unthinkable and/or unnameable, not even subjects in discourse (1993). To be explicitly prohibited permits the possibility of a "reverse discourse," but to be "implicitly proscribed is not even to qualify as an object of prohibition" (p. 312). Finally, these deterministic narratives also tend to privilege gay men's perspectives who, far more than lesbians, tend to recount their sexual histories as inevitable, predetermined, and innate (Whisman, 1996). One possible exception is Ross's ex-wife Susan, who falls in love with a woman and leaves Ross for her. Yet the show's narrative consistently teases Ross for having married a lesbian, thus occluding the possibility that Susan is *either* bisexual or that she was heterosexual while married and later chose or became a lesbian.

Finally, an important strategy for learning to read popular texts like television sitcoms is to look for those moments where a moral voice seems to speak. Because these shows, as mentioned earlier, are meant to be light and entertaining, they cannot afford to be overly didactic. But there is no question that moral ideology permeates these shows. In some cases, it is certain characters who seem to represent the voice of moral authority. In *Will and Grace* that character seems to be Grace, who, despite her ditziness, often seems to be the moral voice of the show. As mentioned above, Grace's total absence of any vestiges of homophobia makes her a kind of model for the heterosexual viewer. Karen, though also heterosexual, is far too over-the-edge and campy for viewers to identify with. In contrast, Grace is a dependable friend, a creative and dedicated professional, and enemy of oppression. In one episode, Grace is horrified to discover that Jack is not out to his mother. She urges him to come out and emphasizes the importance of being honest about his identity. In another episode, for example, Grace refuses to speak to Will because he is willing to date someone who is in the closet. Grace repeatedly pushes on this issue and accuses Will of hypocrisy and self-loathing. The fact that the heterosexual woman on the show is the one to insist on being openly gay is itself worth noting. Even more striking, however, is the fact that the narrative vilifies those glbt people who, for a variety of powerful reasons, decide not to come out. Never acknowledging any costs to being openly gay, the moral message seems to be that all secrets are bad and the decision to stay in the closet is just another secret that one is never justified in keeping. Questions of power and subordination are thereby erased in the effort to homogenize all lies and secrets. Indeed, once Jack does tell his mother that he is gay, she immediately responds, "I have a secret too." The momentum switches away from Jack's confession and its possible implications to her announcement that the man Jack's biological father is not who he thinks he is.

PRETENDING TO BE GAY . . .

My second theme, the trope of the gay pretender, has been a staple of situation comedies ever since Jack Tripper in *Three's Company* posed as gay so that his uptight landlord would let him live with two attractive women. While it may not have been the *modus operandi* of an entire show (as in *Three's Company*), it has been used repeatedly. Martin, Frasier's dad, poses as gay in order to avoid having to date a woman he's not interested in. Kate and Allie in that long-defunct series, pose as lesbians in order to curry favor (and a new lease) from their lesbian landladies. In *Three Sisters*, one sister's ex-husband convinced her that he was gay in order to get a quickie divorce. Klinger in *M.A.S.H.* was, we assume as viewers, a heterosexual man posing as gay or transvestite in order to secure a release from the military. Finally, and most recently, the soap opera *Days of Our Lives* introduced a new plotline where Jack "outs" himself to Greta so as not to hurt her feelings and confess that he is not attracted to her.

Readers no doubt will be able to come up with examples of their own, and the ease with which we are able to produce these examples suggests how common this trope is. How might one explain its recurrence? On the one hand, one reading suggests that these examples of gender and sexuality play may be consistent with a progressive queer agenda that suggests either that we're all queer or that there's a little queer in each of us. Sedgwick labels this approach to sexuality a "universalizing discourse," meaning that it views queerness/sexuality as nonbinary and more amorphous than is traditionally believed. Though one might read the gay pretender trope along these lines, such a reading, I suggest, is possible yet unpersuasive. What makes for the humor in these situations is, at least partly, the fact that the viewers knows that the character 's heterosexuality is never in doubt. Such certainty enables these characters to play with gay stereotypes without seeming to be homophobic—in *Frasier*, for example, Martin suddenly becomes limp-wristed, interested in décor, and able to express his emotions. Certain mannerisms come to be coded as gay even though the character expressing them is not. The character we "know" is straight is positioned against the character we "know" is gay (interestingly, this trope seems to be rarely used with female characters; does this suggest that lesbians have fewer identifiable mannerisms?) and the comedy of errors and misreadings ensues.

Yet there is never any suggestion whatsoever of any temptation or questioning on the part of the "straight" character; that firmness of resolve serves once again not only to reinforce a strict binary of gay/straight but also to suggest that solid and impermeable boundaries frame one's sexuality. Thus, potentially oppositional discourses are subverted by naturalizing them within terms that make sense in the context of the dominant perspective.

In addition, the "gay pretender" trope implicitly creates a fantasy world where not only do gays and lesbians not experience cultural ostracism and legal discrimination; they also enjoy *more* power than hetero-sexuals. In addition, it is striking that sex and sexuality seem to be foregrounded in these dynamics. They are landlords who favor "their own kind"; they are released from the burdens of heterosexual dating and romance (and, indeed from having to tell the truth!); they do not have to serve in the military; and they are simply able to have more fun, as Karen in *Will and Grace* discovers, when posing as a lesbian enables her to offer make-up tips and kiss cute women. This inversion results in humor and unanticipated consequences but it may also serve to mask the ways that power operates and to make the mechanisms of power even more covert.

I'M NOT GAY BUT MY BOYFRIEND IS . . .

Finally, the "straight-mistaken-for-gay" trope is common throughout comedy. This trope represents an almost total inversion of the tendency in earlier television

audiences to ignore telltale signs of gayness if a television character or actor. To the less naïve viewer today, the flamboyance and campiness of a Liberace, Flip Wilson, or PeeWee Herman suggest a gay sensibility too obvious to be overlooked. But today's situation comedies manipulate signs of gayness to create humor and playfulness. For example, in a now-classic *Seinfeld* episode, Jerry and George are mistakenly identified as a gay couple by a college reporter who then outs them in her school newspaper. The refrain "not that there's anything wrong with it" serves in part to mock standard liberal attitudes toward homosexuality. Even when Jerry finally ends up dating the reporter, she continues to have doubts about his sexuality. This particular episode also borrows from the gay pretender trope, as George, desperately wanting to break up with a woman he's seeing, finally decides to use this misunderstanding as an opportunity to extract himself from the relationship. In *Third Rock From the Sun*, John Lithgow attempts to "come out" as an alien and is instead assumed to be coming out as gay. *Friends* often hints at the ways Chandler's affect positions him as gay. Again, this trope might serve to undermine essentialist notions of a clear boundary between hetero- and homosexual identity. Indeed, part of the humor in these episodes is that the heterosexual character's mannerisms come to be recoded as queer. Further, this trope suggests the ways that virtually any behavior can be reread as gay once the viewer's perspective is framed by that lens.

The "straight-mistaken-for-gay" trope, like the gay pretender, derives much of its humor from the audience's knowledge that the character(s) in question is/are *not* in fact gay. Such an epistemological advantage sets the audience member apart from the mistaken character and provides the audience member not only with a certain degree of distance but also with reinscribed boundaries between the gay and the straight. If we ever wondered, for example, whether Jerry and George were even vaguely attracted to each other, our identification with them and not with the mistaken reporter ensures that we leave with no doubt whatsoever. In this context, it is perhaps significant that Chandler in *Friends* is the first character to "truly" fall in love and marry. Further, viewers are explicitly told that his "cold feet" prior to the marriage result directly from his fear of commitment and not from any vestiges of bi- or homosexuality. *Third Rock*'s mistaken-gay episode teaches everyone that there is a little alien in each of us but not that the character himself might be gay.

Further, both the gay pretender and the mistaken gay tropes seem to give these programs permission to play with sex and sexuality more explicitly than they might with a heterosexual characters. The use of double entendre in these scenes of misunderstanding is one strategy that opens up and foregrounds the sexual aspects of homosexuality. So, for example, a scene from *Days of Our Lives* allows its generally more buttoned-down characters to joke obliquely about penis size: Harold, who *is* gay, is coming on to Jack, who is pretending but is not gay. Greta, their mutual friend, accuses Harold of having a big ego. Jack, innocently, says, "It's not how big your ego is. It's what you do with it." Harold, who assumes that Jack is playing with him, finds this banter incredibly erotic. Moments later, Jack returns to this theme when he informs them both (still referring, he believes, back to "ego") that "size doesn't matter." Harold is totally charmed, but two conversations and not one have taken place. Such dialogue is all the more significant when one remembers that the character of Jack is one that has been part of the show off-and-on for over twenty years. It is only when he is "playing gay" that we have access to an erotic side of him that the culture links with gay male sexuality.

Queer theory embraces a kind of intellectual tension: where, on the one hand, the viewer insists that sexuality and the domain of the sexual are cultural inventions and not essential, on the other hand, it deploys

sexuality as a (if not *the*) significant determinant of cultural and individual identity. If Doty (1993) is right that queerness should "challenge and confuse our understanding and uses of sexual and gender categories" (p. xvii), then the sorts of examples I've been describing and analyzing here represent failures.

Marginalized identities are not just oppressed by power; they are also, as Foucault points out, constructed by those very same power relations. Thus, there is no doubt that these new representations of glbt characters and of heterosexuality will give birth to new meanings and new signifiers attached to queer sexuality. But we must wait for that next episode.

Notes

1. Indeed, fall 2001 premiered a new show starring DeGeneres, who plays an out lesbian who returns to her hometown. Unlike her earlier show, where it took years and much publicity for her to out herself, in this new show she is already out in the first episode and her sexuality is treated casually by her family and those she meets.

2. I cannot help but wonder about this phenomenon in light of the increasing *in*visibility of race in popular media. Timothy Simone (1989) has noted the "increasingly clandestine" (p. 10) presence of race concepts. As the language of popular culture is increasingly "cleansed of overt racial reference" (p. 17), queer folks have become the latest "other."

3. Unless the film deals explicitly with "gay issues" like AIDS *(Philadelphia, Long Time Companion,* etc.) or homophobic violence (e.g., *Boys Don't Cry*).

4. Gross (1995) suggests that misinformation and homophobic stereotyping in the media are connected to most heterosexual people's lack of first-hand knowledge of gays and lesbians. I'm not sure that was true ten years ago, but it certainly seems not to be the case today.

5. Note too how this dynamic functions to efface the element of class. Thus, it is not surprising that Rosario, Karen's third-world main, serves as the butt of much of the show's humor.

◆ References

Bourdieu, P. (1990). *In other words: Essays towards a reflexive sociology.* Cambridge, UK: Polity.

Butler, J. (1990). *Gender trouble: Feminism and the subversion of identity.* New York: Routledge.

Butler, J. (1993). Imitation and gender subordination. In H. Abelove, M. Aina Barale, & D. M. Halperin (Eds.), *The lesbian and gay studies reader* (pp. 307-320). New York: Routledge.

Clark, D. (1993). Commodity lesbianism. In H. Abelove, M. Aina Barale, & D. M. Haperin (Eds.), *The lesbian and gay studies reader* (pp. 186-201). New York: Routledge.

Doty, A. (1993). *Making things perfectly queer: Interpreting mass culture.* Minneapolis: University of Minnesota Press.

Epstein, S. G. (1987). Gay politics, ethnic identity: The limits of social constructionism. *Socialist Review, 93/94.*

Ewen, S., & Ewen, E. (1992). *Channels of desire: Mass images and the shaping of American consciousness.* Minneapolis: University of Minnesota Press.

Foucault, M. (1990). *The history of sexuality* (Vol. 1, R. Hurley, Trans.). New York: Vintage Books.

Fuss, D. (1991). *Inside/out: Lesbian theories, gay theories.* New York: Routledge.

Greenberg, B. S. (1986). Minorities and the mass media. In J. Bryant & D. Zillmann (Eds.), *Perspectives on media effects* (pp. 165-188). Hillsdale, NJ: Lawrence Erlbaum.

Gross, L. (1995). Out of the mainstream: Sexual minorities and the mass media. In G. Dines & J. M. Humez (Eds.), *Gender, race and class in media: A text-reader* (pp. 61-69). Thousand Oaks, CA: Sage.

hooks, b. (1999). Eating the other. In S. Hesse-Biber, C. Gilmartin, & R. Lydenberg (Eds.), *Feminist approaches to theory and methodology.* New York: Oxford University Press.

hooks, b. (1995) *Killing rage: Ending racism.* New York: Henry Holt.

Kellner, D. (1995). *Media culture: Cultural studies, identity, and politics between the modern and the postmodern.* London: Routledge.

Kirby, D. (2001, June 17). The boys in the writers' room. *New York Times,* pp. 23, 33.

Mohr, R. (1997). A gay and straight agenda. In J. Corvino (Ed.), *Same sex: Debating the ethics, science, and culture of homosexuality* (pp. 331-344). Lanham, MD: Rowman & Littlefield.

Rich, A. (1980, Summer). Compulsory heterosexuality and lesbian existence. *Signs, 5*(4), 631-660.

Rose, J. (1986). *Sexuality in the field of vision.* London: Verso.

Rothaus, S. (2000, December 30). Better reception for gay TV characters. *Boston Globe,* p. D26.

Sedgwick, E. K. (1990). *Epistemology of the closet.* Berkeley: University of California Press.

Simone, T. M. (1989). *About face: Race in postmodern America.* Brooklyn, NY: Autonomedia.

Torres, S. (1993). Television/feminism: *Heartbeat* and prime time lesbianism. In H. Abelove, M. Aina Barale, & D. M. Halperin (Eds.), *The lesbian and gay studies reader* (pp. 176-185). New York: Routledge.

Whisman, V. (1996). *Queer by choice: Lesbians, gay men, and the politics of identity.* New York: Routledge.

11

WHITE NEGROES

♦ Jan Nederveen Pieterse

. . . The interplay of race, class, and gender, the main systems of domination, . . . is a well-established theme, but most discussions concern the way these systems intersect rather than the way they interact. Comparisons are rare between racism, classism, and sexism in terms of their histories, ideologies, imageries, and underlying logic; we are offered a wealth of vignettes but systematic explorations are lacking. However brief an excursion into a large and difficult area, the focus here on images and stereotypes may shed new light. . . .

♦ *Situations: Irishmen, Chinese, Jews*

Statements in which comparisons are made between blacks and other groups, without a reason why being given, seem to be relatively simple; presumably the comparison is in terms of status, treatment, or appearance. Thus Chamfort, in the eighteenth century: "The poor are the negroes of Europe." The British in India often referred to Indians as "niggers," mostly on the basis of skin colour. Of a similar nature is the statement . . . by the Belgian socialist leader Emiel Vandervelde, who compared the way the working class was treated with the treatment of negroes.[1] John Lennon said, "Women are the niggers of the world." A little more complex is a statement by Francisco Cabral, superior of the Portuguese Jesuit mission in Japan (1570-81), about the Japanese: "After all, they are Niggers, and their customs are barbarous."[2] So to the pious Portuguese, after a hundred years of Portuguese experience in Africa, the Japanese were put in the same category as Africans.

In some cases comparison of blacks with other groups goes much further. In 1880 the Belgian essayist Gustave de Molinari noted, in a series of articles about Ireland, that England's most important newspapers and magazines "allow no occasion to escape them of treating the Irish as a kind of inferior race—as a kind of white negroes—and a glance in *Punch* is sufficient to show the difference between the plump and robust personification of John Bull and the wretched figure of lean and bony Pat."[3]

English views of Ireland display an interesting zigzag pattern. In the early Middle Ages Ireland was famed as a centre of Christian civilization: several English kings went there to be educated. Ireland's reputation declined, however, as England's interest in conquering and colonizing it increased. In the wake of the Anglo-Norman invasion and after the classic description of Ireland by Gerald of Wales in the twelfth century, which set the tone for later descriptions, Ireland was considered savage and barbarous. Down to the present this notion of the "wilde Irish" has hardly changed, although there have been marked shifts of emphasis. The distinction between Celtic and Anglo-Saxon "races" in the British Isles is one of long standing, but from the mid-nineteenth century onward the British image of the Irish was recast in biological racial terms.[4] In addition, from about 1840, the standard image of the good-natured Irish peasant was revised, becoming that of a repulsive ape-like creature.

In cartoons and caricatures as well as prose, Paddy began to resemble increasingly the chimpanzee, the orangutan, and, finally, the gorilla. The transformation of peasant Paddy into ape-man or simianized Caliban was completed by the 1860s and 1870s, when for various reasons it became necessary for a number of Victorians to assign Irishmen to a place closer to the apes than the angels.[5]

Irishmen were depicted with low foreheads, prognathous features and an apelike gait by cartoonists such as Sir John Tenniel of *Punch*. In 1862 a satire in *Punch* attacked Irish immigration under the title "The Missing Link": "A creature manifestly between the Gorilla and the Negro is to be met with in some of the lowest districts of London and Liverpool by adventurous explorers. It comes from Ireland, whence it has contrived to migrate; it belongs in fact to a tribe of Irish savages: the lowest species of Irish Yahoo."[6]

What prompted the metamorphosis of Paddy the peasant to Paddy the ape was the stream of Irish immigrants, in the wake of the famines of the 1840s, along with the mounting Irish resistance to British domination. The "Fenian outrages" of the 1860s involved anti-English acts of sabotage and subversion. Thus, English images of the Irish hardened in the context of colonialism, migration, and resistance. About this time the first apes were brought to Europe (the first live adult gorilla arrived at the London Zoo in 1860), and as they made their first appearance in zoos, they began to appear in cartoons and as a new metaphor in popular imagery. . . .

. . . What is striking is how consistent the colonizer's cultural politics are, regardless of geography or ethnicity. Like Africans and blacks, the Irish have been referred to as "savages" and likened to "apes," to "women." and to "children," just as the Celts were often described as a "feminine" race, by contrast with the "masculine" Anglo-Saxons. . . .

Cartoons in periodicals such as *Harper's Weekly (A Journal of Civilization)* made the hostile equation of Irishmen with blacks a routine part of American culture.[7]

These comparisons, in England between Irish people and Africans, and in the United States between the Irish and blacks, were made under the heading of race, but this only serves as a reminder that, until fairly recently, the terms "race" and "nation" (or "people") were synonymous. The peoples of Europe, within regions as well as within countries, were viewed as much as rungs on the racial "ladder" as were peoples or "races" outside Europe. Indeed, virtually all the images and stereotypes projected outside Europe in the age of empire had been used first within Europe. However, when they were *re-used* within Europe the repertoire was infused with the imagery of empire, with other, wider logics of exclusion, of which the imperial construction of "race" was one. Thus in 1885 the English physician John Beddoe devised an "index of nigrescence," a formula for identifying a people's racial components. "He concluded that the Irish were darker than the people of eastern and central England, and were closer to the aborigines of the British Isles, who in turn had traces of 'negro' ancestry in their appearances. The British upper classes also regarded their own working class as almost a race apart, and claimed that they had darker skin and hair than themselves."[8]

This profile could be extended to other minorities. An example is the Chinese who entered the western United States in the nineteenth century as a cheap labour force, following in the footsteps of blacks. Imported on a contract basis to work on the railroads, the "coolie" had in common with the black slave that both were perceived as enemies of free labour and republicanism; what ensued has been termed the "Negroization" of the Chinese.

Racial qualities that had been assigned to blacks became Chinese characteristics. Calling for Chinese exclusion, the editor of the *San Francisco Alta* claimed the Chinese had most of the vices of the African: "Every reason that exists against the toleration of free blacks in Illinois may be argued against that of the Chinese here." Heathen, morally inferior, savage, and childlike, the Chinese were also viewed as lustful and sensual. Chinese women were condemned as a "depraved class" and their depravity was associated with their almost African-like physical appearance. While their complexions approached "fair," one writer observed, their whole physiognomy indicated "but a slight removal from the African race." Chinese men were denounced as threats to white women. . . .[9]

Thus virtually the whole repertoire of anti-black prejudice was transferred to the Chinese: projected on to a different ethnic group which did, however, occupy a similar position in the labour market and in society. The profile of the new minority was constructed on the model of the already existing minority.

Americans often drew comparisons between national minorities (blacks or Native Americans) and peoples overseas. When the U.S. annexed or colonized Hawaii, the Philippines, Puerto Rico and Cuba at the turn of the century, the American popular press characterized the native populations by analogy with either "red Injuns" or blacks. The *Literary Digest* of August 1898 spoke casually of "Uncle Sam's New-Caught Anthropoids."[10] On the American conquest of the Philippines, Rudyard Kipling, the bard of imperialism, characterized the native inhabitants as "half devil and half child." The American press regularly presented Filipinos and other peoples *as* blacks—images which suggest graphically that the sensation of power and supremacy was the same, whether on the American continent or overseas, and was being expressed through the same metaphors. Again, it is not ethnicity, or "race" that governs imagery and discourse, but rather, the nature of the *political relationship* between peoples which causes a people to be viewed in a particular light.

A similar dynamic was at work during the Vietnam war. A common expression among American GIs in Vietnam was "The only good gook is a dead gook," with "gook" (the term of abuse for Vietnamese) replacing "nigger" or Indian ("Injun") in the existing formula.[11] The underlying logic of dehumanizing the enemy by means of stereotyping is the same. These examples of dehumanization and victimization illustrate what Ron Dellums has called, in a phrase, the "niggering process."[12] . . .

. . . What racism, classism, sexism all have in common is social inequality: the key to all the social relations discussed above is the pathos of hierarchy. While the common denominator is power—the power that arises from a hierarchical situation and the power required to maintain that situation—it is also a matter of the anxiety that comes with power and privilege. Existing differences and inequalities are magnified for fear they will diminish. Stereotypes are reconstructed and reasserted precisely when existing hierarchies are being challenged and inequalities are or may be lessening. Accordingly, stereotyping tends to be not merely a matter of domination, but above all, of humiliation. Different and subordinate groups are not merely described, they are *debased*, degraded. Perceptions are manipulated in order to enhance and to magnify social distance. The rhetoric and the imagery of domination and humiliation permeate society. They concern processes in which we all take part, as receivers and senders, in the everyday rituals of impression management, in so far as taking part in society means taking part in some kind of status-ranking.

As the negative of the denigrating images sketched above, there emerges the top-dog position, whose profile is approximately as follows: white, western, civilized, male, adult, urban, middle-class, heterosexual, and so on. It is this profile that has monopolized the definition of humanity in mainstream western imagery. It is a programme of fear for the rest of the world population.

Notes ◆

1. Quoted in Vints (1984, p. 26).
2. Boxer (1978, p. 23).
3. Quoted in Curtis (1971, p. 1).
4. A classic source is J. Beddoe, *The Races of Britain* (1885). See MacDougall (1982) and Rich (1986, pp. 13-20).
5. Curtis (1971, p. 2).
6. Curtis (1971, p. 100). See cartoons by Tenniel and others (pp. 55, 56, 57, 58, 59, 60, 62).
7. During a visit to America in 1881, the English historian Edward Freeman wrote: "This would be a great land if only every Irishman would kill a Negro, and be hanged for it. I find this sentiment generally approved—sometimes with the qualification that they want Irish and negroes for servants, not being able to get any other" (Curtis, 1984, p. 58).
8. Curtis (1984, p. 55) and Beddoe (1885).
9. Takaki (1980, pp. 217-218). "The 'Negroization' of the Chinese reached a high point when a magazine cartoon depicted [one of] them as a bloodsucking vampire with slanted eyes, a pigtail, dark skin, and thick lips. White workers made the identification even more explicit when they referred to the Chinese as 'nagurs.'" One may add that there were also differences between the stereotypes of Chinese and blacks.
10. See Drinnon (1980, pp. 276-277) and Jacobs and Landau (1971).
11. Lifton (1973/1985, p. 204).
12. Dellums (1978).

References ◆

Beddoe, J. (1885). *The races of Britain*. London.

Boxer, C. R. (1978). *The church militant and Iberian expansion, 1440-1770*. Ann Arbor, MI: Books on Demand.

Curtis, L. P., Jr. (1971). *Apes and angels: The Irishman in Victorian caricature*. London: Newton Abbot.

Curtis, L. (1984). *Nothing but the same old story: The roots of anti-Irish racism*. London.

Dellums, R. V. (1978). *The link between struggles for human rights in the United States and Third World*. Washington, DC.

Drinnon, R. (1980). *Facing west: The metaphysics of Indian-hating and Empire-building*. New York: Schocken.

Jacobs, P., & Landau, S. (1971). *To serve the devil* (2 vols.). New York.

Lifton, R. J. (1985). *Home from the war: Vietnam veterans—Neither victims nor executioners*. Boston: Beacon. (Original work published 1973)

MacDougall, H. A. (1982). *Racial myth in English history*. Montreal: Hannover.

Rich, P. B. (1986). *Race and empire in British politics*. Cambridge.

Takaki, R. T. (1980). *Iron cages: Race and culture in nineteenth-century America*. London: Oxford University Press.

Vints, L. (1984). *Kongo: Made in Belgium*. Leuven, Belgium.

12

INVENTING THE COSMO GIRL
Class Identity and Girl-Style American Dreams

◆ Laurie Ouellette

I am a materialist, and it is a materialistic world.

—Helen Gurley Brown[1]

In February 1997, a former secretary named Helen Gurley Brown stepped down from her position as the editor-in-chief of *Cosmopolita*n, the hugely successful consumer magazine she developed for the "single girl" market in the mid-1960s. Still an American cultural icon, Brown was suddenly back in the media spotlight, espousing her credo on topics ranging from sex and the workplace to the Cosmo Girl, the fictionalized woman she invented to characterize the magazine's imagined 18- to 34-year-old female reader. Just as feminist historians have recognized Brown's role in partly subverting patriarchal sexual ideologies (Douglas, 1994; Ehrenreich et al., 1986), media commentators framed the departure by casting Brown as the feminine piper of the sexual revolution.[2] What cannot be explained by a singular focus on sexual politics, however, are the class-specific dimensions of Brown's message and popular appeal.

NOTE: Reprinted by permission of Sage Publications Ltd. from Laurie Ouellette, "Inventing the Cosmo Girl: Class Identity and Girl-Style American Dreams," *Media, Culture & Society*, 21, 359-383. Copyright © 1999 Sage Publications Ltd.

This article analyzes Helen Gurley Brown's early advice to women as a cultural discourse that managed some of the social and economic tensions of the 1960s and early 1970s, while also offering certain women the symbolic material to enable them to think about themselves as historical subjects in new ways. John Fiske's understanding of discourse is especially helpful for making sense of Brown's position as a capitalist media maven and an immensely popular spokeswoman for everygirl. As Fiske argues, discourse is a "system of representation that has developed socially in order to make and circulate a coherent set of meanings about an important topic area" (1987: 14). Discourses are ideological insofar as their "meanings serve the interests of that section of society within which the discourse originates and which works ideologically to naturalize those meanings into common sense," but they are not conspiratorial or "produced" by individual authors or speakers (1987: 14). Rather, discourses are socially produced and often institutionalized ways of making sense of a certain topic that "preexist their use in any one discursive practice," and that construct "a sense, or social identity, of us" as we speak them (Fiske, 1987: 14-15).

. . . I wish to show how Brown's advice spoke to major changes in women's economic and sexual roles, while also constructing a suggested social identity for her "working girl" readers. . . . The cultural discourse Brown articulated legitimated sexism and the capitalist exploitation of women's labor, while simultaneously expressing hardships and desires in a voice that spoke with credibility to an expanding class of pink-collar women.

Based on my examination of *Cosmopolitan* magazine (1965-75) as well as Brown's books, recordings and interviews during this period, I am suggesting that she articulated a girl-style American Dream that promised transcendence from class roles as well as sexual ones. Brown was one of the first mainstream figures to free women from the guilt of premarital sex by advising

them to disregard the patriarchal double standard. But she was also concerned with shaping and transforming the class position of the Cosmo Girl through a combination of self-management strategies, performative tactics, sexuality, and upwardly mobile romance.[3] At a time when the term often seems in danger of slipping from the critical vocabulary, Brown's advice to women offers a case study in the cultural construction of class—not as an economic category or even a relationship in the Marxist sense—but as a fragmented and sexualized identity. As Brown explained,

> There are girls who . . . don't want to be that driven, to have that many affairs; they don't want more than one man or one dress at a time. They don't care about jewelry and they don't want a sable coat or Paris for the weekend. . . . But "my girl" wants it. She is on the make. Her nose is pressed to the glass and she does get my message. These girls are like my children all over the country. Oh, I have so much advice for them. . . . (Quoted in *Guardian Weekly*, 1968)

Inventing the Cosmo Girl ◆

In 1962, at the age of 42, Brown wrote the bestseller *Sex and the Single Girl* (1962) and became an overnight celebrity. According to Brown, the book was an unabashed self-help credo for "the girl who doesn't have anything going for her . . . who's not pretty, who maybe didn't go to college and who may not even have a decent family background" (quoted in Didion, 1965: 35). Drawing partly from Brown's experience as a woman who held 18 secretarial jobs before she was promoted to an advertising copywriter and then married at the age of 37, the book offered step-by-step advice on personal appearance, budget apartment dwelling, working, and, above all, flirting. Brown guided women through encounters with men who were not their husbands, instructing them how to attract the best ones, date them, cajole dinners and presents out of them, have affairs, and eventually marry the most eligible man available. In a year when "married people on television slept in twin beds" (Douglas, 1994: 68) and the sexual revolution remained the prerogative of men and student counterculture types, *Sex and the Single Girl* suggested that ordinary women could lead fully sexual lives outside marriage (Brown, 1962: 11). Brown critiqued mandatory motherhood, advised birth control, condoned divorce, encouraged women to work outside the home, and recommended sexual and financial independence within boundaries. However, the book was by no means anti-marriage: As Brown explained, it was a response to the "man shortage," a guide to attracting desirable men while remaining "single in superlative style" ("A Proposal for *Cosmopolitan*," n.d.).

Sex and the Single Girl was mocked by intellectuals, reviewed, as one journalist observed, "only to provide a fixed target for reviewers eager to point up (amid considerable merriment) the superiority of their own perceptions over those of Mrs. Brown" (Didion, 1965: 36). But the book appealed to hundreds of thousands of women who were living out a growing gap between "girlhood and marriage" made possible by shifting urban migration patterns and the expanding pink-collar labor force (Ehrenreich et al., 1986: 54). *Single Girl* sold more than two million copies in three weeks, due to extensive publicity and Brown's rigorous efforts to get in touch with the kind of women critics derided as "subliterate and culturally deprived" (Didion, 1965: 36). Following the book's initial success, Brown was interviewed extensively in the press, appeared as a frequent guest on radio and television talk shows, and sold the motion-picture rights to *Single Girl* to Hollywood. She wrote a series of follow-up books, including *Sex and the Office* (1964) and *Sex and the New Single Girl* (1970a), recorded best-selling

lectures with names like *Lessons in Love* (1963), and wrote a syndicated newspaper column called "Woman Alone." While early feminist leaders like Betty Friedan found Brown's message "obscene and horrible," few could deny that she had developed an "astonishing rapport with America's single-girldom" (quoted in Welles, 1965: 65).

In 1965, Brown took her credo and her phenomenal sales figures to Hearst Publications, owners of *Cosmopolitan* magazine, and became the magazine's new editor-in-chief. With close monitoring by Hearst, she transformed *Cosmopolitan* from a fledgling intellectual publication into a "compendium of everything I know about how to get through the emotional, social and business shoals that confront a girl and have a better life" (Brown, 1970a: 7). Brown maintained such strict control over the magazine that critics began to ridicule the singular, gushy voice that permeated article after article, but the editorial formula she devised drew new readers (Brown, 1965a). Circulation rose by more than 100,000 the first year alone, advertising sales grew 43 percent (*Newsweek*, 1966: 60), and a series of self-help books distributed through the *Cosmopolitan* Book-of-the-Month Club were equally successful. By the mid-1970s, *Cosmopolitan* was reaching more than two million readers, advertising sales were still soaring, 12 foreign-language editions had been launched and Brown was a celebrity who claimed to embody much of the advice she distributed through her media enterprise.[4] Due to Brown's characterizations and the "I'm that Cosmopolitan Girl" advertising campaign, which she helped write, the fictionalized Cosmo Girl had entered the cultural lexicon as a sexualized symbol of pink-collar femininity. Before elaborating on her construction, it is useful to sketch out the historical context during which she arose.

As the economist Julie Matthaei has shown, the growth of the service sector has been "central in the absorption of female labor" (1982: 282). In the 1960s, as the U.S.A. moved rapidly toward a post-Fordist economy, women entered the paid workforce in greater numbers, and began to stay there for longer periods of time, earning approximately 59 cents on the male dollar (Howe, 1977: 3). According to the U.S. Department of Labor, between 1962 and 1974, the number of employed women rose by 10 million, or 45 percent. Some women entered the male-dominated professions, but the majority entered "feminine" pink-collar jobs, and the largest gain occurred in secretarial and clerical occupations that often required no college education (Howe, 1977: 10-11). Women were already the mainstay of these occupational fields, but the capitalist expansion of the service sector was a new development, as was the growing number of women working for prolonged periods of time to support themselves (and families) in these positions.[5] *Sex and the Single Girl* spoke directly to unmarried working women, and *Cosmopolitan* was the first consumer magazine to target single "girls with jobs" with feature articles, advice columns, budget fashions and advertisements for mainly "feminine" consumer items, such as cosmetics, personal care products, lingerie, and clothing.[6] The magazine also featured advertisements for temporary employment agencies, training centers and correspondence schools where women could learn stenography, typing, and dictation and similar clerical skills. Hearst's interest in hiring Brown to address self-sufficient working women was thus linked to their emergence as a consumer market capable of purchasing certain goods and services with their own wages.[7]

Cosmopolitan's pink-collar orientation and economic base is especially clear when compared to that of its nearest competitor, *Ms.* magazine. Critics have observed that when *Ms.* debuted in 1972 as a voice of the women's movement, it tended to emphasize the goals and aspirations of liberal feminism and college-educated women. Editorial material aimed at pink-collar women was less typical, and the female consumer hailed by "dress-for-success" fashions and durable consumer goods differed from the one hailed by *Cosmopolitan* (McCracken, 1993: 278-80; Valverde, 1986: 81). Both magazines claimed to serve independent working women, but market research found *Ms.* readers had higher incomes and were more than twice as likely to have attended college. More than a third of *Ms.* readers (as opposed to virtually no *Cosmopolitan* readers) also held advanced degrees (Harrington, 1974). Critics, however, downplayed the social and economic basis of the skew and blamed Brown for the "Two Faces of the Same Eve," explaining that intelligent women with graduate degrees were not apt to be called "little Cosmo Girl" or buy a magazine whose editor insists that ideas be made "baby simple" (Harrington, 1974: 12). With considerable scorn, Brown was characterized as the "working girl's Simone de Beauvoir" of her era (*Newsweek*, 1966: 60).

In the U.S.A., women's mass entry into the workforce is often attributed to the second wave of the women's movement. However, when we consider the stratification within the female labor force, Barbara Ehrenreich's thesis that "male revolt" from the traditional breadwinning role was an earlier and more significant catalyst seems highly plausible. Breadwinning, according to Ehrenreich, was an informal economic contract rooted in the family wage system, and as such it was dependent upon the voluntary cooperation of men:

> Men are favored in the labor market, both by the kinds of occupations open to them and by informal discrimination within occupations, so that they earn, on the average, 40 percent more than women do. Yet nothing compels them to spread the wealth to those—women and children—who are excluded from work or less generously rewarded for it. Men cannot be forced to marry; once married, they cannot be forced to bring home their paychecks, to be reliable job holders, or, of course, to remain married. In fact, considering the absence of legal

coercion, the surprising thing is that men have for so long, and, on the whole, so reliably, adhered to what might be called the "breadwinner" ethic. (1983: 11)

Once held together by popular culture, expert opinion and religious expectations, the breadwinning ethic began to unravel around the time the Beats, with their flagrant celebration of male freedom, appeared on the scene, says Ehrenreich (1983: 12; 52). When *Playboy* magazine debuted in 1953, she argues, "male revolt" was expressed in a broader context. While *Playboy* is often associated with the mainstreaming of soft-core pornography, it also promoted a "Dale Carnegie-style credo of male success" rooted in free enterprise, a strong work ethic and materialistic consumption. The only difference between conventional success mythology and Hugh Hefner's message was that men were not encouraged to share their money, says Ehrenreich. Wives and single women were depicted as shrews and "gold-diggers," while bachelors were advised to pursue sex on a casual basis to avoid getting snared in a "long term contract" (1983: 46). By the 1970s, alimony reductions and no-fault divorce laws—however progressive in the feminist sense—had legitimated male revolt at the official level of the state. For the first time in U.S. history, observed sociologist Jane Mansbridge, "society was beginning to condone a man leaving his family on the sole grounds that living with them and providing for them made him unhappy" (1986: 108).

Brown's advice spoke to the social and economic flux generated by these shifts by offering a modified sexual contract, and by presenting certain women, who may no longer have recognized their place in male-oriented American Dream mythology, with the discursive material to envision themselves as upwardly mobile sexual agents. Brown was clear in her wish for women to see themselves in the fictionalized persona of the Cosmo Girl. "A guy reading *Playboy* can say, 'Hey, That's me.' I want my girl to

be able to say the same thing," she explained (quoted in *Providence Journal*, 1965). While her advice was often antagonistic, the social structure that was the cause of the dilemma was never challenged. . . .

The Beautiful Phony ◆

. . . Brown's credo required an understanding of identity as something that could always be reworked, improved upon, and even dramatically changed. *Sex and the Single Girl* promised every girl the chance to acquire a stylish and attractive aura by copying fashion models and wealthy women (Brown, 1962: 189-94). Expenditures on clothing, cosmetics, and accessories were presented as necessary investments in the construction of a desirable (and thus saleable) self. *Cosmopolitan* columns with names like "So You're Bored to Death with the Same Old You" (1972) extended these possibilities by offering women the ability to construct a "whole new identity," " defined in terms of fashion and style. According to the column, "A new lipstick will really not work a sudden transformation, but have you considered going further? Perhaps even to the point of changing everything (hair, makeup, clothes, manner), in short, changing your type?" (*Cosmopolitan*, 1972: 172). Other articles with names like "Yes, You Can Change Your Image" (De Santis, 1969) stressed the fluidity of female subjectivity, encouraging readers to make themselves over and even construct multiple selves, often to meet the demands and opportunities of prolonged courtship.

To "get into the position to sink a man" it was not necessary that a woman be beautiful, but she had to know how to create "an illusion of beauty" (Brown, 1962: 204). Phoniness was often celebrated as a form of trickery—a way to create a prettier, sexier, and more desirable self beyond one's allotted means. Even the *Cosmopolitan* cover girl was exposed as a "fake," her breasts made to appear more alluring with masking tape and Vaseline (Kent, 1972; Reisig, 1973). According to another column called the "The Beautiful Phony" (*Cosmopolitan*, 1966a), "naturalness" was an imposed value that destroyed the possibility of such illusions. Taking sides with the imagined reader, it opened with the advice:

> They're always telling you to be the most natural girl in the world and you want to cooperate but, well, they just ought to see you in your natural state. Pale, lashless, lusterless, bustless and occasionally, after a grinding day at the typewriter, almost fingernail-less! Darling, not another apology! (1966a: 104)

Instead, "new looks" created with wigs, false eyelashes, tinted contact lenses, fake beauty spots, false toenails, false fingernails, nose surgery, padded bras, false derrieres, and fake jewelry were recommended. Another article explaining "Why I Wear My False Eyelashes to Bed" (Cunningham, 1968) presented the problem of a shower with a lover, a situation where the investments of a highly produced femininity (and hence its material rewards) might be erased. Recommending hurling soap suds in his eyes so "he won't be able to see how you look" (Cunningham, 1968: 18), it got to the core of Brown's advice by linking femininity to the modified sexual contract she espoused.

The aspirations of the Cosmo Girl were white, heterosexual, and upper-middle class. "Other" women were sometimes acknowledged in *Cosmopolitan* articles like "What It Means to Be a Negro Girl" (Guy, 1966), but they were not presented as models for emulation, primarily because Brown's mobility credo forbade it. White working-class culture appeared more often, but as a reference point for makeover and improvement. Similar to femininity, class was presented as a malleable identity that could be easily changed through performative

tactics, covert strategies, and cultural consumption.

Unlike her feminist contemporaries who believed in the possibilities of a female sex class (Firestone, 1970; Millett, 1970), Brown was especially concerned with improving the lot of women stuck lower on the economic ladder. While her most radical suggestion may have been to carry Karl Marx's *Das Kapital* as a way to meet potential eligibles (1962: 63), the Cosmo Girl was often addressed as a have-not, and was offered instructions to remedy the situation. Instead of critiquing the capitalist distribution of resources or the politics of wage labor, reworking one's identity was presented as an individual route to mobility. The extent to which these narratives constructed a feminine version of American Dream mythology is revealed by Brown's own version of the Horatio Alger story:

> We have two Mercedes-Benzes, one hundred acres of virgin forest near San Francisco, a Mediterranean house overlooking the Pacific, a full-time maid and a good life. I am not beautiful, or even pretty . . . I didn't go to college. My family was, and is, desperately poor and I have always helped support them. . . . But I don't think it's a miracle that I married my husband. I think I deserved him! For seventeen years I worked hard to become the kind of woman who might interest him. (Brown, 1962: 4-5)

Drawing from John Berger (1972), Ellen McCracken has shown how commercial women's magazines trade on female insecurities by offering a temporary "window to a future self" rooted in male visions of idealized femininity and consumer solutions (1993: 13). Jackie Stacey discusses something similar in her analysis of women and film stars, but proposes that the perpetual gap between "self and ideal" is the subjective space where female identities are negotiated (1993: 206). In *Sex and the Single Girl*, Brown extended these processes by constructing an idealized but never fully realized class subjectivity for her readers, which then manifested in the fragmented identity of the fictionalized Cosmo Girl. Although rooted in upper-class reverence and materialistic desires, her advice is difficult to dismiss as entirely co-optive or advertising-driven, because it was presented as a guide to overcoming the gendered class barriers Brown encountered. Her path to success stressed the conventional motto of hard work and conspicuous consumption, but it also required covert strategies and performative behaviors on the part of the Cosmo Girl. As I see it, the tenuous sense of agency Brown's advice offered is central to the tension between class fluidity and class consciousness in the politicized sense.

Women were essentially advised to "pass" as members of the bourgeoisie by studying and copying its presumably superior tastes, knowledges, and cultural competencies. This performative strategy was rooted in the unauthorized acquisition of what Pierre Bourdieu (1984) calls "cultural capital," or the symbolic resources that signify and legitimate class dominance in capitalist democracies. In the U.S.A., the myth of equality of opportunity proposes that anyone can gain access to economic capital (what wealth buys) through individual effort and talent, while the cultural capital that breeds success is inherited via "proper" family socialization or acquired through extended years of schooling (Jhally and Lewis, 1992: 69). Brown subverted these intersecting mythologies in a roundabout way by revealing pink-collar barriers to the American Dream, and partly subverting the uneven distribution of cultural capital. According to Brown's girl-style American Dream, anyone—even the Cosmo Girl— could appropriate the surface markers of cultural capital. Once acquired, these surface markers of class position could be traded for economic capital (or access to it) on the dating and marriage market.

The credibility of this advice was rooted in the fact that women who may have married directly into the lower classes were spending longer periods of time working as office workers. Under the ambiguous label "pink collar," they encountered men with more education, money, and resources. Brown's advice encouraged women to exploit these opportunities and prepared them to do so by offering a basic introduction to upper-class customs and cultural traditions. "Some girls have it . . . some don't. But that elusive little quality separating the haves from the [have-]nots is within everyone's grasp," claimed one *Cosmopolitan* article (Geng, 1970: 92).

Since the advice was always tempered to the experience of the Cosmo Girl, the reader was allowed to participate in two class cultures simultaneously, which encouraged a fragmented class subjectivity. However, the point of the lessons was to conceal one's working-class lineage. Thus, *The Cosmo Girl's Guide to the New Etiquette* warned women about common phrases that were "instant lower-class betrayals" (Brown, 1970b: 55). Similarly, *Cosmopolitan* articles with names like "Poor Girl Paintings," (*Cosmopolitan*, 1966c), "If You Don't Know Your Crepes From Your Coquilles" (Matlin, 1969), "Go Ahead, Pretend You're Rich" (Barnes and Downey, 1968), "Good Taste" (Johnson, 1974), and "Live Beyond Your Means" (de Dubovay, 1975) presented lessons on the ways of the educated, wealthy, and culturally sophisticated.

This advice often involved appropriating cultural signifiers of class, particularly European cuisine, art, foreign languages, and good books. One especially vivid example here was "A Handbook of Elegant Starvation," a *Cosmopolitan* guide to maintaining a "desirable image" while pursuing the arts and getting by on unemployment insurance (Dowling, 1966). According to the article, which offered detailed instructions for serving "Bogus Beef Bourguignon" to a male dinner guest, "The clue to faking it on $12.50 a week is a front. You've got to keep up a front—an aura of prosperity—at all times" (1966: 30). Another article proposed that an ordinary secretary who "would probably expire from malnutrition if she didn't have a dinner date at least two nights a week" could easily pass as a member of the New York "jet set" or a corporation president's daughter (Tornabene, 1966: 43). By extending the aura of cultural capital to the female masses, this discourse subverted myth that class is inevitable or natural. However, it also upheld the class pyramid and reproduced social and cultural hierarchies. . . .

◆ *Pink-Collar Sexuality*

Feminist historians have suggested that what was potentially transforming about *Cosmopolitan* magazine was the emphasis placed on female sexuality (Douglas, 1994; Ehrenreich et al., 1986).[8] Features on female orgasm, birth control, masturbation, casual sex, and sexual experimentation appeared under Brown's editorship, while quizzes with names like "How Sexy Are You?" (*Cosmopolitan*, 1969) invited ordinary women into the sexual revolution and the *Cosmopolitan Love Book* (Brown, 1972) offered them instructions on the new sexual protocol. At the close of the 1970s, Brown hired a sociologist to survey the sexual practices of *Cosmopolitan* readers and they were found to be the most experienced group in western history (Wolfe, 1981). However, what a focus on sexual politics cannot fully explain are the class dimensions of Brown's discourse on female sexuality, as epitomized by her credo "Poor girls are not sexy!" (1962: 108).

. . . Sexual fantasies presented in *Cosmopolitan* fiction excerpts and in *Cosmopolitan's Love Book* encouraged women to identify with female heroines whose male sexual partners (or desired partners) were above them socially and economically. . . . Female desire was linked to what the male object represented socially and economically. As Brown explained in *Sex and the Single Girl*, a woman is "more favorably disposed toward a man who is solvent and

successful than someone without status. She prefers a tycoon to a truck driver no matter how sexy the latter looks peering down at her from the cab of his chrome chariot" (1962: 227).

Cosmopolitan's "Bachelor of the Month" column was similarly constructed. This sought-after eligible was always solvent and socially established, as were the men presented as desirable in articles like "It's Just as Easy to Love a Rich Man" (Lilly, 1965), "How Much Will He Earn?" (Sloane, 1966), "The Big Catch" (Blyth, 1972), and "Used Men: A Definitive Guide for the Selective Shopper" (Price, 1972). When acknowledged, working-class men were almost always presented as undesirable, as epitomized by the juxtaposition in February 1966 of two *Cosmopolitan* profiles, one featuring "Six Current (But Perennial) Fascinators" (1966d), the other featuring "10 Most Wanted Men (by the FBI)" (Reed, 1966). While the first roster was comprised of men characterized as rich, famous, successful, charming, and attractive, the second opened with the warning "You've seen the most fascinating men, now read about the most feared" (Reed, 1966: 72). Police mug shots were accompanied by one-liners detailing the physical characteristics of the men as well as their occupations, which included clerk, dishwasher, hospital orderly, tractor driver, and mason's helper.

While female sexual desire was linked to upward mobility through men, the construction of female sexual desirability in *Cosmopolitan* was linked to the cultural codes of the working-class prostitute. Indeed, sexually explicit representations of women were the only places readers were encouraged to forge positive identifications with working-class traditions. Bourgeois tastes were transgressed by these images, especially on the cover, where the desirability of the model was constructed through class-coded signifiers such as exposed cleavage, teased hair, heavy make-up, and flamboyant and suggestive costumes.[9] The sexualized Cosmo Girl was not the wholesome middle-class sex object of the era, and she appeared to contradict Brown's discreet schemes for mobility. However, the sexualized imagery also offered an entry point into the modified sexual contract Brown espoused.

In the 1960s, when college-educated women were beginning to demand and sometimes secure equality in the professional workplace, most pink-collar office workers were not so fortunate. Brown articulated an alternative way to get men to part with their disproportionate share of power and resources. She subverted the moral shame surrounding sex and reframed the sexual code as an individual ethic and a commodity exchange. In this sense, her advice was rooted in the history of working-class women's sexual practices. Kathy Peiss, for example, has shown how a turn-of-the-century system of "treating" allowed young, unmarried workers to trade "sexual favors" ranging from flirting and kissing to sexual intercourse for small presents, meals, and admissions to amusement parks, which they could not otherwise afford (1983: 78). Some "charity girls" appropriated the look of a prostitute, using "high-heeled shoes, fancy dresses, costume jewelry, elaborate pompadours and cosmetics" to attract male attention (1983: 78). The system of treating was also present in the workplace, says Peiss, where sexual harassment was rampant (1983: 78-9). Brown's advice articulated an updated sexual barter system by encouraging the Cosmo Girl to never go dutch, but to instead coax gifts, dinners, vacations, groceries, and cash presents from male dates, bosses, colleagues, and partners. Her revised sexual contract promoted women's sexual freedom and financial independence, while also encouraging the exchange of sexual "favors" for material comforts and luxuries. Perhaps the most significant difference between the system Peiss describes and what Brown articulated is that the Cosmo Girl was encouraged to pursue men who may have been off limits in earlier eras. . . .

While the mainstream women's movement strove for equality in the workplace,

Brown often framed sexual activity in terms of work and achievement. "Sex is a powerful weapon for a single woman in getting what she wants from life," she explained to an interviewer (quoted in *San Francisco*, 1962). A similar message was conveyed in her memoir, where Brown described the ability to bring a man to orgasm as a "specialty" every upwardly mobile girl should acquire (1982: 212). Occasionally, *Cosmopolitan* explained the advantages of being "kept" and "slightly kept" girls (Baumgold, 1970; Condos, 1974), and articles glamorizing upscale prostitution were not uncommon. However, these explicit cases of sexual trading were not nearly as prevalent as the sexualization of the office, especially the relationship between male superiors and female secretaries. Again, this pattern drew from and reworked historical assumptions about the role of women in offices. . . .

By the 1960s, office work was a rapidly growing occupational field, and women were an expanding part of the labor force. By the time *Sex and the Single Girl* appeared, almost one of every three employed women worked in clerical and secretarial jobs (Matthaei, 1982: 282), and by 1974 women held four out of five jobs in this category (Howe, 1977: 10). The capitalist expansion of the service sector opened the field to women outside the middle class, while women with college degrees were struggling to move into male-dominated professions. What remained was the middle-class respectability of office work compared to factory work and other working-class wage labor (Matthaei, 1982: 282). Despite the low pay and dead-end nature of most pink-collar jobs, this made it easier for women to see themselves as upwardly mobile. . . .

Cosmopolitan elevated the sexual worth of the secretary by suggesting that "a secretary is not necessarily rich, beautiful or brilliant, but she is the most sought-after female since King Kong chased Fay Wray" (Lewis, 1969: 133). Likewise, the rewards for working for women were defined through the types of men one encountered. In *Sex and the Single Girl*, Brown promoted secretarial jobs because they were "all-time great spots" for meeting men (1962: 37). *Cosmopolitan* articles with titles like "Secretaries Who've Made Very, Very Good" (James, 1969), "Be a 9-to-5 Show Off" (Fisher, 1970), and "Hollywood Secretaries" *(Cosmopolitan*, 1975a) also glamorized secretarial jobs as excellent places to meet well-connected bosses, dreamy executives, and traveling salesmen with expense accounts. One article even recommended "A Different Job Every Day" (Fahey, 1966), contracted through temporary employment agencies, as a chance to meet dozens of eligible men in a single week. The low pay, insecurity, and lack of benefits offered by the growing temporary workforce were obscured. . . .

Brown clearly understood women's subordination in the office, but she did not directly challenge it because "in an ideal world, we might move onward and upward by using only our brains and talent, but since this is an imperfect world a certain amount of listening, giggling, wriggling, smiling, winking, flirting and fainting is required in our rise from the mailroom" (1964: 3). . . .

There were exceptions to these patterns, especially after 1970, when Brown proclaimed herself a friend of women's lib and *Cosmopolitan* began to negotiate feminist discourse, however haltingly. Several feminist articles were published, including an excerpt in November 1970 from Kate Millett's book *Sexual Politics* (1970) critiquing the gendered aspects of economic inequality and the ideology of heterosexual romance. As was typical, however, it was shockingly out of place, juxtaposed with a fashion spread proclaiming "Be His Fortune Cookie in Our Gala Gypsy Dress" (*Cosmopolitan*, 1970). Liberal feminist demands for professional equality had a more lasting impact on Brown's thinking, and on the partial incorporation of conventional success mythology in *Cosmopolitan*. While she continued to value street smarts

over a college degree and promote the sensational opportunities offered by secretarial work, Brown modified her credo to suggest that the Cosmo Girl might be both a sex object and a "high powered" executive (Brown, 1982: 19-20).

Girl-Style ◆ American Dreams

Many pink-collar women may have found the Cosmo Girl's fragmented identity as an upwardly mobile sexual agent more attractive and even more feasible than what the mainstream women's movement offered. Brown's advice offered a gendered success myth to women who found themselves taking on new roles as breadwinners, but who lacked the wages, education, professional skills, and social opportunities to recognize themselves in more conventional, male-oriented upward-mobility narratives. She articulated, in feminine terms, the materialistic desires that so often underpin popular structures of feeling in a consumer-oriented nation where the class structure is officially denied. Brown's reworking of American Dream mythology involved the construction and reconstruction of a desirable self, the presentation of identity as self-made, the valorization of femininity as a creative production, the partial subversion of natural class distinctions, the refusal of Victorian sexual norms, and the expression of multiple hardships and frustrations—all within a framework that legitimated capitalism, consumerism, and patriarchal privilege. However, to dismiss the fragmented, sexualized class identity she promoted as wholly co-optive or less than "real' would be to lose touch with the way social beings construct a sense of self.

As Stuart Hall suggests with his theory of articulation, there is no necessary link between economics and class. Class awareness is a social construct, produced in a political sense only when individual experiences are articulated as a "political force," enabling subjects to enter the stage as historical agents (Hall, 1986: 55). Brown's advice encouraged women to rework their identities on the basis of upper-class ideals, and to assess their current situations and future possibilities on the basis of those constructions. One of the consequences of the discourse may have been the way it positioned women as individual competitors in the quest for mobility, rather than part of a growing female labor force with many differences, to be sure, but with collective interests and bargaining power. Characterizing her own self-transformation, for example, Brown explained that "early on you have to separate yourself in the head from those people (friends, family, colleagues) you don't want to be like . . . be one of the girls, but also don't be one of the girls" (1982: 38).

Helen Gurley Brown's historical resonance as the "working girl's Simone de Beauvoir" suggests the need to take the cultural construction of class seriously. . . .

◆ Notes

1. Quoted in *Time* (1965a: 60).

2. See, for example, Brown's appearance, 25 January 1997, on CNN's *Larry King Live*.

3. Mariana Valverde (1986) also observed the promotion of mobility in *Cosmopolitan*, arguing that what both the Cosmo Girl and the Ms woman of the 1980s wanted, despite their different paths to achievement (e.g., getting a man vs. merit) was to be white, upper-middle class, and heterosexual. While she sees both magazines imposing unified capitalist and patriarchal ideologies on women (a view similar to early feminist Marxist criticism), I see Brown's advice in poststructuralist terms, as a contradictory, historically specific and productive discourse that constructed a social identity for pink-collar women.

4. Harrington, 1974. *Cosmopolitan* now has a U.S. circulation of 2.5 million, resulting in $156 million in estimated annual advertising revenue (Pogrebin, 1997).

5. In 1940, about one-third of employed Americans were in white-collar occupations, while in 1959 nearly half were due to the expanding service economy and the growing number of women who joined the "white-collar ranks." However, many of these jobs were "essentially manual" in that they were routine, repetitive, and sometimes minimally skilled. They paid less than the professions and often less than skilled blue-collar work, but were "rated" above traditional working-class wage labor because they were perceived as "cleaner" and more "dignified" (Packard, 1959: 25-6). Advertisers played on the social ambiguity, promising status through consumer goods. In this [chapter] I refer to non-professional white-collar jobs taken up predominantly by women as pink-collar. For more on the post-Fordist economy see Harvey (1990: 121-97).

6. Brown envisioned the "untapped" market for *Cosmopolitan* as single women, divorcees, and widows, separated, and "otherwise neglected wives" who worked outside the home. Working married women who were (because of their independent attitude) "women on their own" were considered a secondary market ("A Proposal for *Cosmopolitan*," n.d.; "Statement for Advertisers," n.d.). Early marketing discourse inflated the spending power of the magazine's readers, describing them as well educated, high income, and "working in top occupations" despite statistic that contradicted these generalizations. Thus, there was overlap between the class performativity Brown encouraged and the strategies used to court advertisers. While the Cosmo Girl was constructed as single and sexually free, a high percentage of readers were married. This would suggest that they too were drawn to the magazine's guide to changing sexual and economic roles.

7. Products and services said to be bought by *Cosmopolitan* readers included cosmetics, perfumes, fashion and personal products, wines and liquors, travel, miscellaneous, and mail order *(Cosmopolitan* Advertising Kit, 1965). The first three categories comprised most of the advertising according to my research.

8. Ehrenreich et al. note that Brown championed independence and guiltless sex at a time when few women "could imagine options other

than marriage and full-time motherhood" (1986: 56). Susan Douglas (1994) also cites Brown as a key figure in the transformation of female sexuality.

9.   As McCracken argues, "If the *Cosmopolitan* cover photo presents women with an ideal image of their future selves, it is an image at the other end of the social spectrum from that of the affluent *Vogue* or *Bazaar* cover" (1993: 158). While she sees this image as an invitation to male fantasy and sexual voyeurism, I see it rooted in the class dimensions of Brown's revised sexual code.

◆ References

"A Proposal for *Cosmopolitan* from Helen Gurley Brown" (n.d.) Helen Gurley Brown papers, Sophia Smith Collection, Smith College, Northampton, MA (hereafter HGB papers), Box 14, Folder 4.

Barnes, J. and M. Downey (1968) "Go Ahead— Pretend You're Rich," *Cosmopolitan* (July): 54-5.

Baumgold, J. (1970) "The Slightly Kept Girl," *Cosmopolitan* (Sept.): 154.

Berger, J. (1972) *Ways of Seeing*. London: Penguin Books.

Blyth, M. (1972) "The Big Catch," *Cosmopolitan* (Jan.): 128-36.

Bourdieu, P. (1984) *Distinction: A Social Critique of the Judgment of Taste*. Cambridge, MA: Harvard University Press.

Brown, H. G. (1962) *Sex and the Single Girl*. New York: Bernard Geis Associates.

Brown, H. G. (1963) *Lessons in Love*. New York: Crescendo Records.

Brown, H. G. (1964) *Sex and the Office*. New York: Bernard Geis Associates.

Brown, H. G. (1965a) "New Directions for *Cosmopolitan*," *The Writer* (July): 20.

Brown, H. G. (1970a) *Sex and the New Single Girl*. New York: Bernard Geis Associates.

Brown, H. G. (ed.). (1970b) *The Cosmo Girl's Guide to the New Etiquette*. New York: Cosmopolitan Books.

Brown, H. G. (ed.). (1972) *Cosmopolitan's Love Book: A Guide to Ecstasy in Bed*. New York: Cosmopolitan Books.

CNN Television. (1997) Interview with Helen Gurley Brown, *Larry King Live* (25 Jan.).

Condos, B. (1974) "I Was Kept," *Cosmopolitan* (May): 60, 66-74.

Cosmopolitan Advertising Kit, July 1965, HGB papers, Box 8, Folder 12.

Cosmopolitan (1966a) "The Beautiful Phony" (March): 104-7.

Cosmopolitan (1966b) "*Cosmopolitan* Interviews Hugh M. Hefner" (May): 76-81.

Cosmopolitan (1966c) "Poor Girl Paintings" (Aug.): 88.

Cosmopolitan (1966d) "Six Current (But Perennial) Fascinators" (Feb.): 66-71.

Cosmopolitan (1969) "How Sexy Are You?" (April): 54-6.

Cosmopolitan (1970) "Be His Fortune Cookie in Our Gala Gypsy Dress" (Nov.): 104.

Cosmopolitan (1975a) "Hollywood Secretaries" (Aug.): 36.

Cosmopolitan (1975b) "How to Sink into a Man" (Nov.): 48-9.

Cunningham, L. (1968) "Why I Wear My False Eyelashes to Bed," *Cosmopolitan* (Oct.): 46-51.

de Dubovay, D. (1975) "Live Beyond Your Means," *Cosmopolitan* (Aug.): 132-4.

De Santis, M. (1969) "Yes, You Can Change Your Image," *Cosmopolitan* (April). 91-3.

Didion, J. (1965) "Bosses Make Lousy Lovers," *Saturday Evening Post* (30 Jan.): 34-8.

Douglas, S. (1994) *Where the Girls Are: Growing Up Female with the Mass Media*. New York: Time Books.

Dowling, C. (1966) "A Handbook of Elegant Starvation," *Cosmopolitan* (Oct.): 30-2.

Ehrenreich, B. (1983) *The Hearts of Men*. New York: Anchor Books.

Ehrenreich, B. et al. (1986) *Re-Making Love: The Feminization of Sex*. New York: Anchor Books.

Fahey, P. (1966) "A Different Job Every Day," *Cosmopolitan* (Oct.): 128-31.

Ferguson, M. (1983) *Forever Feminine: Women's Magazines and the Cult of Femininity*. London: Heinemann.

Firestone, S. (1970) *The Dialectic of Sex*. New York: Quill Press (repr. 1993).

Fisher, K. (1970) "Be a 9-to-5 Showoff," *Cosmopolitan* (Nov.): 150-1.

Fiske, J. (1987) *Television Culture*. New York: Routledge.

Geng, V. (1970) "A Little Bit of Class," *Cosmopolitan* (Oct.): 92-7.

Greller, J. (1966) "Night School Isn't All Education," *Cosmopolitan* (July): 87-8.

Guardian Weekly (1968) newspaper clipping (12 Nov.) HGB papers, Box 7, Folder 3.

Guy, R. (1966) "What It Means to Be a Negro Girl," *Cosmopolitan* (July): 76-81.

Hall, S. (1986) "On Postmodernism and Articulation: An Interview," *Journal of Communication Inquiry* 10(2): 45-60.

Harrington, S. (1974) "Two Faces of the Same Eve: *Ms.* Versus *Cosmo*," *New York Times Magazine* (11 Aug.): 10-11, 36, 74-6.

Harvey, D. (1990) *The Condition of Postmodernity*. London: Blackwell.

Hennessy, R. (1993) *Materialist Feminism and the Politics of Discourse*. New York: Routledge.

Howe, L. (1977) *Pink Collar Workers*. New York: G. P. Putnam's Sons.

James, T. (1969) "4 Secretaries Who've Made Very, Very Good," *Cosmopolitan* (June): 134-5.

Jhally, S. and J. Lewis (1992) *Enlightened Racism:* The Cosby Show, *Audiences and the Myth of the American Dream*. Boulder, CO: Westview.

Johnson, N. (1974) "Good Taste!" *Cosmopolitan* (Feb.) 122-31.

Joyce, P. (ed.) (1995) *Class*. New York: Oxford University Press.

Kent, R. (1972) "Cover Girl: Behind the Scenes," *Cosmopolitan* (Aug.): 94-117.

Lewis, B. (1969) "Today's Secretary—Wow!" *Cosmopolitan* (June): 133.

Lilly, D. (1965) "It's Just as Easy to Love a Rich Man," *Cosmopolitan* (July): 66-9.

McCracken, E. (1993) *Decoding Women's Magazines*. New York: St Martin's.

Mansbridge, J. (1986) *Why We Lost the ERA*. Chicago: University of Chicago Press.

Matlin, P. (1969) "If You Don't Know Your Crepes From Your Coquilles, Or How to Order From a French Restaurant," *Cosmopolitan* (April): 96-9.

Matthaei, J. (1982) *An Economic History of Women in America*. New York: Schocken.

Millett, K. (1970) *Sexual Politics*. Garden City, NY: Doubleday.

Newsweek (1966) "Down with "Pippypoo" (18 July): 60.

Packard, V. (1959) *The Status Seekers: An Exploration of Class Behavior in America*. New York: David McKay.

Peiss, K. (1983) "'Charity Girls' and City Pleasures: Historical Notes on Working-Class Sexuality, 1880-1920," pp. 74-87 in Ann Snitow et al. *Powers of Desire*. New York: Monthly Review Press.

Pogrebin, R. (1997) "Changing of Guard at Cosmo," *New York Times* (13 Jan.): D1.

Price, R. (1972) "Used Men: A Definitive Guide for the Selective Shopper," *Cosmopolitan* (Aug.): 68-73.

Providence Journal (1965) newspaper clipping (1 July) HGB papers, Box 8, Folder 1.

Reed, R. (1966) "10 Most Wanted Men (by the FBI)," *Cosmopolitan* (Feb.): 72-81.

Reisig, R. (1973) "The Feminine Plastique," *Ramparts* (March): 25-9, 53-5.

San Francisco News Call Bulletin (1962) "Single Gal's Quandary" (6 July). HGB papers, Box 8, Folder 3.

Sloane, L. (1966) "How Much Will He Earn?" *Cosmopolitan* (Feb.): 30-7.

Stacey, J. (1993) *Star Gazing: Hollywood Cinema and Female Spectatorship*. London: Routledge.

"Statement from Helen Gurley Brown for Advertisers" (n.d.) HGB papers, Box 14, Folder 3.

Time (1965a) "Big Sister' (9 Feb.): 60.

Tornabene, L. (1966) "How to Live Beautifully on $100 a Week," *Cosmopolitan* (Aug.): 42-7.

Valverde, M. (1986) "The Class Struggles of the Cosmo Girl and the Ms. Woman," *Heresies* 18: 78-82.

Welles, C. (1965) "Soaring Success of the Iron Butterfly," *Life* (19 Nov.): 65-6.

Wolfe, L. (1981) *The Cosmo Report*. New York: Arbor House.

13

LIVING SINGLE AND THE "FIGHT FOR MR. RIGHT"

Latifah Don't Play

◆ Kristal Brent Zook

There is an episode of *Martin* in which Lawrence's character is prompted by his "boys" to prove a point. While working out at the gym, Martin removes his wedding ring to show his best friends, Tommy and Cole, that he can still get "da honeys." Sure enough, writhing girl-toys flock to his side mere seconds after the gold band disappears. This scene illustrates why it was appropriate that *Martin* served as the lead-in for *Living Single*: Both shared the premise that the world is teeming with black women who'll do just about anything to land a single, and preferably rich, man.[1]

In this chapter, I want to highlight three contradictory ideological forces at work in *Living Single*. The first is what I call the "desperation theme," which is based on the market-driven theory that black audiences appreciate regressive representations of women and which was touted by network executives riding the wave of Terry McMillan's best-selling 1992 novel *Waiting to Exhale*. The second is a moderate feminism inspired by the autobiographical vision of *Living Single's* creator, Yvette Lee Bowser. And the third is a radical womanism presented, more unconsciously than not, through the fictional, presentational, and documentary personas of Queen Latifah.

In an interview with *Ebony* magazine, Bowser said that she wanted to write and produce a show about her own life experiences, her girlfriends, and "the ups and downs of being twenty-something."[2] Because Bowser is a successful, independent woman, relatively sympathetic to feminist aims, her characters reflected this sensibility.

According to Bowser, these *Living Single* characters were extensions of different parts of herself: Regine (Kim Fields) is a materialistic fashion horse; Khadijah James (Queen Latifah) is a self-made entrepreneur who publishes her own magazine, *Flavor*; Synclaire James (Kim Coles) is Khadijah's dimwitted but adorable cousin; and Maxine Shaw (Erika Alexander), the ever-present neighbor, is a ruthless attorney who thrives on large quantities of food and sex. In addition, Kyle Barker (T. C. Carson), another neighbor, is a direct play on Kyle Bowser, then director of creative affairs at HBO Independent Productions and the man who would become Bowser's husband.

In television, of course, there is no such thing as absolute creative power—black, female, or otherwise. So Bowser's *conscious* intention to represent black female desire did not always succeed. In this case, there were other forces involved in the production and reception of *Living Single* that interacted with and, at times, overshadowed her autobiographical vision. One was the popular narrative of the desperate black woman; another was the radical womanism inspired by Queen Latifah.[3]

I begin with a brief history of the show. A comedy about four girlfriends sharing a New York brownstone, *Living Single* was born, like most network series, of pragmatic concerns: The production company, Warner Brothers, had what is known as a "holding deal" with both Kim Fields and Queen Latifah, and it needed to find a television pilot to showcase their talents. Because Fields and Latifah urged the studio to meet with at least one black woman writer (a not unreasonable request given that the show to be created was about black women), television history was made: Yvette Lee Bowser (who had worked previously on *A Different World* and *Hangin' With Mr. Cooper*) became the first African American woman to create a successful prime-time series for network television.

We might speak then of black female authorship as something of an executive "accident" in the case of *Living Single*. While neither Warner Brothers nor Fox intentionally set out to create a feminist-minded narrative, the mere act of hiring an African American woman effectively created a space within which collective black female autobiography could potentially thrive.[4] *Living Single*, in other words, presented an unprecedented opportunity to experiment with black female subjectivity on a weekly basis.

At the same time, however, the tension between Bowser's autobiographical impulse and market-driven sensibilities was evident from the start. For example, a revealing bit of *Living Single* trivia involves the battle over the show's title. Initially dubbed *My Girls* by Bowser, the name was changed to *Living Single* by network executives in order to avoid what they feared would amount to male alienation. With the change came a whole host of narrative shifts. Contrary to Bowser's intentions, the show went from being a slice-of-life comedy about girlfriends to a narrative about the "male quest," or the "Fight for Mr. Right" as one two-part episode was dubbed. From its inception, *Living Single* charged head-on, at Fox's urging, toward the imagined *Waiting to Exhale* audience.

Indeed, Bowser admits that the initial impulse behind *Living Single* was in response to Fox's request for something "along the lines" of McMillan's novel. And *Waiting to Exhale* is essentially—as the jacket cover reminds us—a story about "four black women waiting for the men who will finally make things right." As Bowser told *Ebony*: "*Exhale* was definitely an inspiration for the networks to realize that there was a voice out there that people wanted to hear, a black female voice in particular. The popularity of the book helped pave the way for this show."[5] Almost immediately, *Living Single* skyrocketed to the number one spot among African American viewers.

As the following sampling of story lines reveals, a number of episodes from the show's first year portrayed the women as hopelessly obsessed with men: (1) Regine's new man, Brad, is married; (2) Regine's new man, Patrick, has a daughter; (3) Max dates the man Regine has just broken up with; (4) Max, who is twenty-six, is embarrassed to admit that she has been seeing a handsome eighteen-year-old student; (5) a photographer who works with Khadijah is depressed because she broke up with her boyfriend and hasn't done "the wild thing" in a long time. Basically Fox executives chose to focus on male-oriented episodes the first season, as Bowser told me, because they felt these were "stronger."

In this chapter, I propose that the radical womanist persona of Latifah provided an implicit challenge to both *Martin's* mythical black macho and the regressive politics of female desperation evident in so many episodes of *Living Single*. It was no coincidence, for example, that the only three episodes of the show's first season that did *not* center around men featured Latifah's character, Khadijah James, as an independent entrepreneur: (1) Khadijah asks her lawyer friend, Maxine, to represent her in court; (2) Maxine loans Khadijah money; (3) Synclaire, Khadijah's cousin and employee, feels unappreciated at work and quits.

In order to explore this implicit womanism evoked by Latifah's persona, I borrow from film theorist Christina Lane's 1995 essay "The Liminal Iconography of Jodie Foster," which was published in *The Journal of Popular Film and Television*.

In her essay, Lane argues that there is "a strategic sexual liminality" surrounding Jodie Foster. Inherent in this liminality, says Lane, is a refusal to submit to polarized notions of gay-straight or masculine-feminine, a refusal that also works to destabilize fixed gender identities in Foster's films.[6] I find Lane's thesis enormously useful in that it allows us to "read" Foster in a dynamic, intertextual manner—as do viewers.

Like Foster, Latifah has also been associated with nontraditional representations of femininity, sexuality, and power. Because of her own brand of "sexual liminality," she too has entered (whether willingly or not) into a discourse around both feminism and lesbianism. And like Foster, both Latifah's public and private personas reveal an "ability to slide up and down the registers of masculine and feminine."

I certainly do *not* mean to suggest here that Latifah is a lesbian. I neither know nor seek the answer to that question. It is not even necessarily relevant that Latifah does not wish to characterize herself as a feminist. As she has explained: "I'm inclined to show women in as positive a light as I can. . . . A lot of people call me a feminist because of that, but I prefer the term common-sensist."[7]

Rather, I'm interested here in Latifah's refusal of monolithic definitions of "female" experience and desire. This refusal, I would say, plays an important role in shaping gender representation (and reception) in *Living Single*. In the next part of this chapter, then, I want to look closely at Latifah's pre-*Living Single* productions, both as a rapper and as a feature film actor.

Beginning with *All Hail the Queen*, her 1989 debut album, we find what cultural theorist Tricia Rose describes as a strong statement for "black female unity, independence, and power."[8]

As a rapper, Latifah was part of a network of female performers (including MC Lyte, Monie Love, and Yo-Yo) who addressed both male chauvinism and racism in their personal lives as well as in their music. In fact, the political activism of

Yo-Yo (who later landed a recurrent role on *Martin*) led to the founding of what she called the Intelligent Black Women's Coalition, a support network "for sisters of all races" dedicated to "increasing the status and self-esteem of all women."[9] It is important to note that Latifah was strongly associated with the collective work of black women rappers and activists.

Next we come to Latifah's feature role in the 1991 film *House Party* 2. Here the actor plays Zora, a dashiki-wearing feminist activist and African American studies major named after 1930s author and anthropologist Zora Neale Hurston. In a delightful twist of intertextuality, Latifah's character becomes both roommate and mentor to a starry-eyed young student named Sydney, played by an extremely young-looking Tisha Campbell.

If Khadijah James of *Living Single* could have rapped to Gina Waters of *Martin*, their conversation might have resembled Sydney and Zora's first meeting. Settling into her new dorm room, Sydney holds up a bit of lingerie and asks: "Isn't it cute?" Zora's reply is icy. "When I first got here," she warns, "I had a drawer *full* of little boy-toy frou-frous just like that. . . . But I grew up and let my consciousness evolve. And when I left all that male materialism behind, I began to see things in a more politically correct light."

"You *do* like boys, don't you?" demands Sydney, her eyes suddenly growing wide. "I like men," replies Zora. "But I don't need one to define me. And any woman who wants to define herself . . . has to free herself of all that tired, lame male bullshit" ("bullshit" being the frou-frou lingerie). With that, Sydney's boyfriend, played by the rapper Kid, appears armed with a rainbow strip of condoms. "Pick a color," he urges Sydney. "Male bullshit," adds Zora, exiting in a huff.

Thanks to Zora's influence, Sydney undergoes dramatic changes during her first year at college. She begins to wear headscarfs and kente cloth and, much to Kid's dismay, even replaces a course entitled

Afro-American Consciousness of the Sixties (which examines James Baldwin, Ralph Ellison, Richard Wright, and the theme of growing up as a black male in America) with one recommended by Zora—Male Mythology: A Feminist Perspective.

A particularly interesting scene takes place at a rally against ethnic studies cutbacks. At the protest, Zora the activist makes a rousing speech and, in a fascinating insertion of Latifah, inspires her cohorts with a song. What's intriguing about this performance is the lyrics. Although the setting is an ethnic studies rally and not a specifically feminist one, Zora's song focuses on sexual harassment on the job, which she then refers to, oddly enough, as "racism."

This unlikely confluence—of ethnic studies, racism, and sexual harassment—is indicative of the profound subtextual tension embodied in Latifah's persona: that is, the tension between race and gender, and the struggle to reconcile feminist and nationalist desires.[10] In Spike Lee's 1991 *Jungle Fever*, for example, Latifah plays a regally clad waitress hostile to the notion of interracial dating. The nationalist aesthetics of *Living Single* also expressed a certain racial pride, symbolized by books such as *African Americans: Voices of Triumph* and *I Dream A World*, strewn across the coffee table, Africanesque statues placed throughout the living room, kente fabrics hanging from a coatrack, and baseball caps reading "Negro League." This aesthetic was not presented *in opposition* to feminist desire; rather, the two coexisted.

Returning to the conclusion of *House Party 2*, Zora takes an unconventionally "masculine" stance. When an abusive suitor attempts to woo Sydney, Zora inserts her own body to prevent them from touching. And although it is Kid who eventually rescues Sydney from sexual assault, Zora has a hand in saving the day by delivering a right jab to the con artist who stole Kid's scholarship funds (played by supermodel Iman).

In *Living Single*, it becomes clear that Latifah brings these extratextual personas with her. In one storyline, for example, a male acquaintance refers to Regine as a "bitch." At the end of the episode, there is a music video tag scene in which Latifah performs her 1994 testament against sexism, "U.N.I.T.Y." As she told a reporter when her single went gold: "I'm clearly not the only one tired of hearing black women being referred to as bitches and ho's."[11]

In the tag scene, Naughty By Nature's Treach (Anthony Criss) physically assaults Latifah by grabbing her ass as she walks down the street. In response, Latifah spins around to confront him—"Who you calling a bitch?"—just before throwing a punch. This tag scene performs a unique ideological function within the *Living Single* episode, effectively recruiting the feminist persona of Latifah (donning dark shades and black leather, no less) to respond to the fictional Regine's objectification.

Finally, I want to look at Latifah's most controversial and critically acclaimed role: as Cleo in F. Gary Gray's 1996 feature film *Set It Off*. In the action drama, Latifah plays a hot-blooded, tequila-drinking, ganja-smoking woman from the 'hood who decides, with three of her girlfriends, to rob a bank. Cleo, as Latifah explains, is "a straight-up dyke . . . men's drawers, the whole nine."[12] In one particularly memorable scene, Cleo shares her loot with her svelte, blond-Afroed girlfriend, Ursula (Samantha MacLachlan). As the scantily clad Ursula dances seductively above her, Cleo caresses and kisses her thigh. Latifah acknowledged the role was a daring one—not only because she tongue-kisses a woman on camera, but because, as *Vibe* writer Danyel Smith noted, "she does it so well."

And yet, more than two years after the release of *Set It Off*, the nation's most venerated rap magazine, *The Source*, continued to entertain the question—"Wassup with dat gay stuff anyway?" as writer Amy Linden put it—in a lengthy six-page cover story on Latifah.[13] The fuel for this most recent fire was provided by the rapper's own 1998 CD, *Order In the Court*, or rather, by two missing songs found only on an underground mix tape sampler. "Nigga get off my dick," she raps, "and tell your bitch to come here."

When asked about the lyrics by *The Source*, Latifah spends a great deal of time discussing intimate details of her sexual past, likes and dislikes, and yet she refuses to address directly the question of lesbianism. This is precisely what Christina Lane means, I think, when she refers to the "space of unknowing" that serves to disalign Foster, and in this case Latifah, from static definitions of female sexuality. "I wanted to drop something hard," notes the rapper, "something hot. I wanted to rhyme without worrying about what I said."

"Latifah knows there are people who question her own sexuality," writes Smith. "Folks make a parlor game of trying to find homoerotic subtexts in the heterocentric *Living Single*." But *Set It Off* director F. Gary Gray is dismissive of the is-she-or-isn't-she question that swirls around Latifah. "Latifah is different from Cleo; Cleo is different from Khadijah; Khadijah is different from Dana [Owens, Latifah's given name]."

In looking at Latifah's various on-screen roles, then, we see that her feminist and lesbian characterizations represent an integral part of her overall persona as a popular icon among African American audiences. Moreover, because she is situated within a community of hip-hop artists, a whole body of narrative possibilities is linked to her characterizations—possibilities that both challenge patriarchal contexts and affirm a kind of womanist Africanity. Latifah's sexual liminality is present not only in fictional television and film but also in her documentary or real-life persona.

In a 1991 interview for *Essence* magazine, writer Deborah Gregory gushes over Latifah's newfound attraction to eyeliner, lipstick, and acrylic nail tips, concluding that Latifah proves "female rappers can look like real women too." In contrast, Latifah squashes that angle by saying that despite her "feminine additions," she will never become "the ultrafem kind of girl who's scared of knocking one hair out of place."[14]

In another 1993 interview, this time for *Ebony*, Latifah's "masculine" look is again noted, as writer Aldore Collier describes her appearance in overalls, hiking boots, and a sweatshirt. After the workday is over, notes Collier, Latifah "grabs a helmet, tosses her sandy hair, jumps on her motorcycle and zooms off." When Collier asks the actor about the matter of her dress, Latifah responds with this: "Some girls would not wear this at all. They would feel boyish. I feel comfortable and I wear what I like. Some people place femininity on the exterior, but it's inside."[15]

In conclusion, I propose that black female autobiography and authorship, as well as strong feminist (even lesbian) tendencies, are evident throughout *Living Single*. This comes about not only through the powerful fictional, presentational, and documentary personas of Latifah, but also through the show's overt story lines. For example, one episode depicts a lesbian marriage between an old college roommate of Max's and her lover. Interestingly, Regine, Synclaire, and Maxine all react to news of the wedding in ways that are either inappropriate or hostile. Khadijah, however, manages to stroll through the proceedings unperturbed.

We might say that this popular icon, this Dana-Latifah-Zora-Cleo-Khadijah figure, serves as a meeting ground upon which gender and sexual battles can be negotiated. As Danyel Smith wrote of Latifah's *Set It Off* character: "Cleo is not some boilerplate bulldagger. She's a full-blown human with issues that have roots in the black part, the poor part, the woman part, and the provincial part." Now that's more like it: a woman of intrigue, whose sexuality represents only part of her total black, womanist self.

Notes ◆

1. During the 1996-97 season, Khadijah is so bedazzled by an $8,000 diamond engagement ring that she blindly accepts a marriage proposal, only to back out later. Meanwhile, Regine kicks herself for having rejected a wealthy entrepreneur before learning of his assets.

2. Collier, February 1996.

3. This is Alice Walker's term, who offers this definition: "Womanist is to feminist as purple to lavender." See Walker 1983.

4. Autobiographical content is often subtle, but definitely present in Bowser's productions. For example, the writer-producer is biracial. In *Living Single*, Synclaire is also depicted as the biracial daughter of a white mother and a black father, as is Karyn Parsons's character, Margot, in *Lush Life*, a pilot also created by Bowser.

5. Collier 1996.

6. Lane.

7. Gregory.

8. Rose. Permission to reprint these and other Latifah lyrics was denied by the rapper, due to a possible "conflict of interest" with her own forthcoming book.

9. Lynell George.

10. I'm enormously indebted to Elliott Butler-Evans here, whose *Race, Gender and Desire* was the first to highlight this tension in the literary works of Toni Cade Bambara, Alice Walker, and Toni Morrison.

11. Alan Carter.

12. Danyel Smith.

13. Linden.

14. Gregory, 60.

15. Collier 1993, 116.

References ◆

WORKS CONSULTED

Butler-Evans, Elliott. *Race, Gender and Desire: Narrative Strategies in the Fiction of Toni Cade Bambara, Toni Morrison, and Alice*

Walker. Philadelphia: Temple University Press, 1989.

Carter, Alan. "Single Minded." *Entertainment Weekly*, May 13, 1994: 31-33.

___. "Behind the Scenes of *Living Single*." *Ebony*, February 1996: 26-34.

George, Lynell. "This One's for the Ladies." In *No Crystal Stair: African Americans in the City of Angels*. London and New York: Verso, 1992.

Gregory, Deborah. "Rapping Back." *Essence*, August 1991: 57-60.

Lane, Christina. "The Liminal Iconography of Jodie Foster." *Journal of Popular Film and Television* 22, no. 4 (Winter 1995): 149-153.

Linden, Amy. "Queen Latifah" From Here to Royalty." *The Source*, August 1998: 154-60.

___. "Heads Ain't Ready for Queen Latifah's Next Move." *Vibe*, December 1996-January 1997: 99-102.

___. *In Search of Our Mothers' Gardens: Womanist Prose*. San Diego, CA: Harcourt Brace Jovanovich, 1983.

PERSONAL INTERVIEWS AND TELEVISION PROGRAMS

[EDITORS' NOTE: See *Color by Fox*, pp. 137ff, for a full list of personal interviews and television programs.]

14

WHO(SE) AM I?

The Identity and Image of Women in Hip-Hop

◆ Imani Perry

This is an argument for media literacy with regards to gender politics in contemporary hip-hop. Specifically, it is concerned with the interplay of the visual and linguistic texts, the image and words. I begin by analyzing the recent trend of objectifying and subjugating black women in hip-hop music videos, and their potentially damaging social impact. Next, I consider how feminist recording artists respond to this dynamic. I argue that although we find some clearly gender liberatory images and arguments we also find abundant examples in which the feminist message in certain songs is neutralized by an objectifying visual image of the artists singing those songs. This image is often consistent with or supportive of the larger sexist trend in music videos. I compare two versions of the song "Lady Marmalade" to demonstrate how contemporary women recording artists are objectified, and how contemporary musical texts derive some of their meaning from the visual images of the singers. Next, I argue that the tensions between feminism and female subjugation often reflect the tensions between artistic creation and record company image making and the artist as creator versus the artist as commodity. In concluding the chapter, I contemplate manners in which artists might use their property in their words to subvert the power of the image. I also encourage critical media literacy among viewers and listeners as a means of understanding the operation of race and gender in this complex landscape.

◆ Black Women's Bodies in Hip-Hop Videos

In the last few years of the 20th century, the visual image of black women in hip-hop rapidly deteriorated into one of widespread sexual objectification and degradation. For years before, hip-hop had been accused of misogyny—critics often citing the references to women as bitches and "hoes." But it is also true that hip-hop was often scapegoated, being no more misogynistic than American popular culture in general although perhaps peppered with less polite language. But in the late years of the 20th century, hip-hop took a particularly pernicious turn, which is not only full of sexist assertions but threatens patriarchal impact.

It seemed to happen suddenly. Every time you turned on BET or MTV there was a disturbing music video. Black men rapped surrounded by dozens of black and Latina women dressed in swimsuits, or scantily clad in some other fashion. Video after video was the same, each one more objectifying than the next. Some were in strip clubs, some at the pool, beach, hotel rooms, but the recurrent theme was dozens of half-naked women.

This was a complex kind of sexist message as well. Its attack on black female identity was multifaceted. First, and most obviously, the women are commodified. They appear in the videos quite explicitly as property, not unlike the luxury cars, Rolex watches, and platinum and diamond medallions that were also featured. The male stars of the videos do not get these legions of women because of charisma or sexual prowess. Rather, they are able to buy them because they are wealthy. The message is not, "I am a Don Juan," but instead, "I am rich and these are my spoils." Not only are the women commodified, but so is sex as a whole.

Moreover, the women are often presented as vacuous, doing nothing but swaying around seductively. Their eyes are averted from the camera, thereby allowing the viewer to have a voyeuristic relationship to them. Or they look at the camera, eyes fixed in seductive invitation, mouth slightly open. Extremely rare are any signs of thought, humor, irony, intelligence, anger, or any other emotion.

Even the manner in which the women dance is a signal of cultural destruction. Black American dance is "discursive" (in that sexuality is usually combined with humor and the body is used to converse with other moving bodies). The women who appear in these videos are usually dancing in a two-dimensional fashion, a derivative but unintellectual version of black dance, more reminiscent of symbols of pornographic male sexual fantasy than of the ritual, conversational, and sexual traditions of black dance. Despite all the gyrations of the video models, their uninterested wet-lipped languor stands in sharp contrast to (for example) the highly sexualized "boodie dancing" of the Deep South (which features polyrhythmic rear end movement, innuendo, and sexual bravado).

This use of black women in the music videos of male hip-hop artists often makes very clear reference to the culture of strip clubs and pornography. Women dance around poles; porn actresses and exotic dancers are often featured in the videos and they bring the movement-based symbols of their trades with them. The introduction of porn symbols into music videos is consistent with a larger movement that began in the late 1990s, in which pornographic imagery, discourses, and themes began to enter American popular culture. Powerful examples may be found in the *Howard Stern Show*, E! Entertainment television, and daytime talk shows. Stars of pornographic films attain mainstream celebrity, exotic dancers are routine talk show guests, and the public face of lesbianism becomes not a matter of the sexual preference of women, but the sexual consumption and fantasy life of men. The videos are an appropriate companion piece to this wider trend. Although the music videos are male centered in that they assume a heterosexual male viewer who will appreciate the images of sexually available young women, it is clear that young women watch them as well. The messages such videos send to young women are instructions on how to be sexy and how to look in order to capture the attention of men with wealth and charisma. Magazines geared toward young women have given such instructions on how women should participate in their own objectification for decades. However, never before has a genre completely centralized black women in this process.[1]

The beauty ideal for black women presented in these videos is as impossible to achieve as the waif-thin models in *Vogue* magazine are for white women. There is a preference for lighter-complexioned women of color, with long and straight or loosely curled hair. Hair that hangs slick against the head when wet as the model emerges out of a swimming pool (a common video image) is at a premium too. Neither natural tightly curled hair nor most coarse relaxed hair becomes slick, shining, and smooth when wet. It is a beauty ideal that contrasts sharply to the real hair of most black women. When brown-skinned or dark-skinned women appear in the videos, they always have hair that falls well below shoulder length, despite the fact that the average length of black women's natural hair in the United States today is 4 to 6 inches, according to renowned black hairstylist John Atchison.

The types of bodies that the camera shots linger on are specific. The videos have assimilated the African American ideal of a large rotund behind, but the video ideal also features a very small waist, large breasts, and slim shapely legs and arms. Often while the camera features the faces of lighter-complexioned women it will linger on the behinds of darker women, implying the same thing as the early 1990s refrain from Sir Mix a Lot's "Baby Got Back" that lauded the face of a woman from Los Angeles and the behind of a woman from Oakland. That is, the ideal is a high-status face combined with a highly sexualized body (which is often coded as the body of a poor or working-class woman).[2] Color is aligned with class and women are "created" (i.e., through weaves, pale makeup, and camera filters) and valued by how many fantasy elements have been pieced together in their bodies.

The Impact of the Image ◆

Although one might argue that the celebration of the rotund behind signals an appreciation of black women's bodies, the image taken as a whole indicates how difficult a beauty ideal this is to attain for anyone. A small percentage of women, even black women, have such "Jessica Rabbit" (the voluptuous cartoon character from the 1990s film *Who Framed Roger Rabbit?*) proportions. As journalist Tomika Anderson wrote for *Essence* magazine, "In movies, rap songs and on television, we're told that the attractive, desirable and sexy ladies are the ones with 'junk in their trunks.' And even though this might seem ridiculous, some of us actually listen to (and care about) these obviously misogynistic subliminal messages—just as we are affected by racialized issues like hair texture and skin tone."[3]

Americans have reacted with surprise to abundant social scientific data that show that black girls are the social group who score highest on self-esteem assessments and tend to have much better body images than white girls. Although these differences in esteem and body image are to a large extent attributable to cultural differences, with black girls having been socialized to see beauty in strong personality characteristics and grooming rather than in particular body types, I believe the media play a role as well. White girls are inundated with images of beauty that are impossible for most to attain: sheets of blond hair, waif-thin bodies, large breasts, no cellulite, small but round features, high cheekbones. Over the years, black women have been relatively absent from public images of beauty, an exclusion that may have saved black girls from aspiring to impossible ideals. But with the recent explosion of objectified and highly idealized images of black women in music videos, it is quite possible that the body images and even self-esteem of black girls will begin to drop, particularly as they move into adolescence and their bodies come under scrutiny. Many of the music videos feature neighborhood scenes, which include children. In them, little black girls are beautiful. They laugh, smile, play Double Dutch, and more. They are full of personality, and they are a cultural celebration. Their hair is plaited, twisted or curled, and adorned with colorful ribbons that match their outfits in characteristic black girl grooming style. And yet the adult women are generally two dimensional and robbed of personality. Is this what puberty is supposed to hold for these girls?

◆ *A Feminist Response?*

In such troubling moments, we should all look for a gender critical voice, in the world, in ourselves. Where do we find a response to this phenomenon that will compellingly argue against such characterizations of black women, a hip-hop feminism? There has been a feminist presence in hip-hop since the 1980s. From Salt n Pepa to Queen Latifah to MC Lyte and others, there is a feminist legacy in hip-hop and hip-hop feminism continues to exist despite the widespread objectification of black female bodies. We can find numerous examples of feminist and antisexist songs in hip-hop and hip-hop soul. Mary J. Blige, Lauryn Hill, Destiny's Child, Missy Elliot, Erykah Badu, and others all have their individual manners of representing black female identity and self-definition.

Missy transgresses gender categories with her man-tailored suits and her frequent presence as narrator of the action in the music videos of male hip-hop artists, an extremely rare location for a woman. Missy is a large woman who presents a glamorous and stylish image but never is presented in an objectifying manner. She uses bizarreness to entice rather than being a sexpot (appearing in one video in an outfit that resembled a silver balloon before a fun-house mirror). Although Missy Elliot may not be distinctive for brilliant rhyming, she has a noteworthy acumen for making hit songs as a producer and rapper, and she consistently maintains her personal dignity.

Alicia Keys, one of the crop of new singer songwriters who fit into the hip-hop nation, also presents an image that contrasts sharply with the video models. The classically trained pianist, who has claimed Biggie Smalls and Jay Z among her music influences, appeared in her first music video for the song "Fallin" in a manner that was stylish and sexy but decidedly not self-exploiting. Her hair in cornrows, wearing a leather jacket and fedora, she sings with visible bluesy emotion. She describes repeatedly falling in love with a man who is not good for her. In the music video, Keys travels by bus to visit the man in prison. This element is an important signifier of hip-hop sensibilities, as it is the one art form that consistently engages with the crisis of black imprisonment and considers imprisoned people as part of its community. As she rides in the bus, she gazes at women prisoners working in a field outside the window. They sing the refrain to the song, "I keep on fallin' in and out, of love with you. I never loved someone the way I love you."[4] The women on the bus riding to visit men in prison mirror the women outside of the bus, who are prison laborers. This visual duality is a commentary on the problem of black female imprisonment, a problem that is often overlooked in discussions about the rise of American imprisonment and black imprisonment in particular. It makes reference both to the fact that many black women are the mates of men who are imprisoned and to the reality that many black women wind up in prison because of being unwittingly or naively involved with men who participate in illegal activities.[5] These social ills are poignantly alluded to in the video by a close-up of a stone-faced woman in prison clothing with a single tear rolling down her cheek.

Another critical example of a black feminist space in the hip-hop world is found in singer songwriter India.Arie. A young brown-skinned and dreadlocked woman, she burst upon the music scene with her song and companion music video "Video," which is a critique of the image of women in videos. In the refrain, Arie tells listeners that she's not the type of woman who appears in music videos, that her body type is not that of a supermodel but nevertheless she loves herself without hesitation.

Similar lyrics assert that value is found in intelligence and integrity rather than expensive clothes, liquor, and firearms. The video celebrates Arie, who smiles and dances and pokes fun at the process of selecting girls for music videos. She rides her bicycle into the sunshine with her guitar strapped across her shoulder. Arie refuses to condemn artists who present a sexy image but has stated that she will not wear a skirt above calf length on stage and that she will do nothing that will embarrass her family. Musically, although her sound is folksy soul, she does understand her work as being related to hip-hop. "I'm trying to blend acoustic and hip-hop elements," India explains. "I used the most acoustic-sounding drum samples, to have something loud enough to compete with other records, but to keep the realistic, softer feel."[6]

More than the compositional elements, Arie understands her work as inflected with hip-hop sensibilities. She says:

> I don't define hip-hop the way a record company would. The thread that runs though both my music and hip-hop is that it's a very precise expression of my way of life. It's like blues; it's very real and honest output of emotion into a song. Because of that legacy, my generation now has an opportunity to candidly state our opinions. That's what my album is about. I just wanna be me.[7]

Arie's definition of hip-hop as honest self-expression is true to the ideology that was at the heart of hip-hop at its beginnings and that continues to be a concept professed to by multitudes of hip-hop artists. However, that element of hip-hop is in tension with the process of celebrity creation. The "honest" words in hip-hop exist in a swamp of image making. It is not enough to examine the clear and simple feminist presences in hip-hop; we must consider the murkier ones as well. When it comes to feminist messages, often the words and language of a hip-hop song may have feminist content but the visual image may be implicated in the subjugation of black women. Unlike the individualistic and expressive visuals we have of Arie, Keys, or Elliot, other artists are often marketed in a manner that is quite similar to the way in which objectified video models are presented.

Tensions Between Texts ◆

Women hip-hop artists who are self-consciously "sexy" in their appearance, style, and words have a much more difficult road in carving out a feminist space in hip-hop than performers such as Elliot, Keys, and Arie. This is because the language of sexiness is also the language of sexism in American popular culture in general, and in hip-hop videos in particular.

In the first edition of this book, I published a chapter titled "It's My Thang and I'll Swing It the Way That I Feel! Sexuality and Black Women Rappers." In it I argued that a feminist space existed in hip-hop where women articulated sexual subjectivity and desire. I do still believe this is possible. However, when the women who articulate subjectivity are increasingly presented in visual media as objects rather than subjects, as they are now, then their statement to the world is ambiguous at best, and at worst the feminist message of their work is undermined.

The space a musical artist occupies in popular culture is multitextual. Lyrics, interviews, music, and videos together create a collage, often finely planned, out of which we are supposed to form impressions. But the texts may be in conflict with one another. Lil Kim, the much discussed, critiqued, and condemned nasty-talking bad girl of hip-hop, is a master of shock appeal. Her outfits often expose her breasts, her nipples covered by sequined pasties that are color coordinated with the rest of her attire. Despite Kim's visual and lyrical vulgarity, many of her critics admit to finding her endearing. She is known by her interviewers to be sweet-natured and generous. But Lil Kim is a contradiction because although she interviews as vulnerable and sweet, she raps with a hardness adored by her fans. She has an impressive aggressive sexual presence, and she has often articulated through words a sexual subjectivity along with an in-your-face camera presence. However, as Kim has developed as an entertainer it is clear that her image is complicit in the oppressive language of American cinematography with regards to women's sexuality. She has adopted a "Pamela Anderson in brown skin" aesthetic, calling on pornographic tropes, but losing the subversiveness that was sometimes apparent in her early career. Andre Leon Talley of *Vogue* magazine noted her transformation from an "around-the-way girl" with a flat chest, big behind, and jet black (or green, or blue) hair weave, to the celebrity Kim who shows off breast implants and shakes her long blond hair. In her videos, the camera angles exploit her sexuality. In the video for the song "How Many Licks," she appears as a Barbie-type doll, her body parts welded together in a factory. The video is an apt metaphor for her self-commodification and use of white female beauty ideals. The video closes off its own possibilities. The doll factory image might have operated as a tongue-in-cheek criticism of image making or white female beauty standards, but instead it is a serious vehicle for Kim to be constructed as beautiful

and seductive with blond hair and blue eyes. To be a doll is to be perfect, and as many times as she is replicated, that many male fantasies will be satisfied. Over several years, Kim has become defined more by her participation in codes of pornographic descriptions of woman than by her challenge of concepts of respectability or her explicit sexuality.

It is a delicate balance, but it is important to distinguish between sexual explicitness and internalized sexism. Although many who have debated the image of female sexuality have put "explicit" and "self-objectifying" on one side, and "respectable" and "covered-up" on the other, that is a flawed means of categorization. The nature of sexual explicitness is important to consider, and will be increasingly important as more nuanced images will present themselves. There is a creative possibility for explicitness to be liberatory because it may expand the confines of what women are allowed to say and do. We just need to refer to the history of blues music, which is full of raunchy, irreverent, and transgressive women artists, for examples. However, the overwhelming prevalence of the Madonna/whore dichotomy in American culture means that any woman who uses explicit language or images in her creative expression is in danger of being symbolically cast into the role of whore regardless of what liberatory intentions she may have, particularly if she doesn't have complete control over her image.

Let us turn to other examples to further explore the tensions between text and visual image in women's hip-hop. Eve is one of the strongest feminist voices in hip-hop today. She rhymes against domestic violence and for women's self-definition and self-reliance. She encourages women to hold men in their lives accountable for behavior that is disrespectful or less than loving. Yet the politics of Eve's image are conflicted. She has appeared in music videos for songs on which she has collaborated with male hip-hop artists. Those videos are filled with the stock legions of objectified video models. Eve is dressed provocatively and therefore validates the idea of attractiveness exemplified by the models. But she is distinguished from these women because she is the star. She is dignified and expressive while they are not. Her distinction from the other women supports their objectification. She is the exception that makes the rule, and it is her exceptionalism that allows her to have a voice. Similar dynamics have appeared in videos in which hip-hop singer Lil' Mo has been featured. In fact, a number of women hip-hop artists, who claim to be the only woman in their crews, to be the one who can hang with the fellas, are making arguments through their exceptionalization that justify the subjugation of other women, even the majority of women.

Moreover, both Eve and Lil Kim often speak of the sexual power they have as being derived from their physical attractiveness to men. It is therefore a power granted by male desire, rather than a statement of the power of female sexual desire. Although neither artist has completely abandoned the language of empowering female subjectivity in her music, any emphasis on power granted through being attractive in conventional ways in this media language limits the feminist potential of their music. In one of the songs in which Eve most explicitly expresses desire, "Gotta Man," it is a desire for a man that is rooted in his ability to be dominant. She describes him as "the only thug in the hood who is wild enough to tame me"[8] and therefore she is "The Shrew," willingly stripped of her defiant power by a sexual union. Instead of using her aggressive tongue to challenge prevailing sexist sexual paradigms, she affirms them by saying that she simply needs a man who is stronger than most, stronger than she is, to bring everything back to normal.

The tensions present in hip-hop through the interplay of the visual and the linguistic, and the intertextuality of each medium, are various. Even Lauryn Hill, often seen as the redeemer of hip-hop due to her dignified, intellectually challenging, and spiritual

lyricism, has a complicated image. As a member of the Fugees, she was often dressed casually, in baggy yet interesting clothes, thoroughly rooted in hip-hop style. It seems to be no accident that Lauryn Hill became a celebrity, gracing the covers of *British GQ*, *Harper's Bazaar*, and numerous other magazines, only when her sartorial presentation changed. Her skirts got shorter and tighter, her cleavage more pronounced, and her dreadlocks longer. When she began to sport an alternative style that nevertheless had mainstream acceptability, she was courted by high-end designers such as Armani. As Lauryn's image became more easily absorbable into the language of American beauty culture, her celebrity grew. She even appeared on the cover of *Sophisticates Black Hair Styles and Care Guide*, a black beauty magazine in which natural hair is at best relegated to a couple of small pictures of women with curly afros or afro weaves, while the vast majority of photos are of women with long straight weaves and relaxers. She was certainly one of the few *Sophisticates* cover models ever to have natural hair and the only with locks. (Interestingly, the silhouette of the locks was molded into the shape of shoulder-length relaxed hair.) In the issue of *British GQ* that featured Lauryn as a cover model, journalist Sanjiv writes, "She could be every woman in a way Chaka Khan could only sing about—the decade's biggest new soul arrival with the looks of a supermodel and Hollywood knocking at her door."[9]

In September 1999, Lauryn appeared on the cover of *Harper's Bazaar*. The article inside discussed her community service projects, and the cover celebrated her model-like beauty. There was of course something subversive about the cover. Dark-skinned and kinky-haired Lauryn Hill was beautiful, and the image was ironic. Her locks were styled into the shape of a Farrah Fawcett flip, a tongue-in-cheek hybridization that at once referenced the 1970s heyday of unprocessed afro hair and that era's symbol of white female beauty,

Farrah Fawcett. The hybrid cover is analogous to the diverse elements used in the creation of the new in hip-hop. Nevertheless, it is important to note that Lauryn became widely attractive when her silhouette, thin body and big hair, matched that of mainstream beauty. So even as Lauryn has been treated as the symbol of black women's dignity and intelligence in hip-hop (and rightfully so given her brilliant lyricism), she too was pulled into the sexist world of image making. Although she has made some public appearances since cutting off her long hair, getting rid of the make-up, and returning to baggy clothes, publicity about her has noticeably dropped.[10]

In contrast to the image making of Lauryn Hill, Erykah Badu has been unapologetically committed to the drama of her neo-Afrocentric stylings and therefore has been able to achieve only limited mainstream beauty acceptance. After she shaved her head and doffed her enormous head wrap, and wore a dress that was shaped like a ballgown (although in reality it was a deconstructed, rough textured "warrior princess," as she referred to it, work of art), Joan Rivers named her the best dressed at the 2000 Grammys. However she also said, and I paraphrase, that this was the best Badu had ever looked and that Erykah Badu was such a beautiful woman (rather than complimenting the dress or her style). It seemed then to be an insinuation that she was getting the recognition for coming closer to looking "as beautiful as she really is," not for truly being the best dressed. In a 2001 *Vogue* magazine, Badu was discussed in an article about how ugliness could be beautiful and the fine line between the two, making reference to her unusual attire, again a sign of how disturbing the beauty industry finds her unwillingness to fit into standard paradigms of female presentation, even as her large hazel eyes and high cheekbones are undeniably appealing to individuals in that industry.

I used the examples of Lil Kim, Eve, Lauryn Hill, and Erykah Badu, all very distinct artists, to draw attention to the kinds of tensions that might exist between a feminist content in hip-hop lyrics and the visual image of that artist. To further illustrate this point, let us now turn to a comparison that offers a dramatic example of the relationship between visual images and the message of musical texts.

Comparative Readings of ◆ the Creole Prostitute

In 2001, a remake of the 1975 LaBelle classic "Lady Marmalade" hit the airwaves. Twenty-six years after it was first recorded, it once again became a hit. The 2001 version was performed by a quartet of successful young female artists, pop sensation Christina Aguilera, R&B singers Pink and Mya, and rapper Lil Kim. Recorded for the soundtrack of the movie *Moulin Rouge*, a postmodern rendering of the famous Parisian cabaret circa 1899, the song served as a fantastic commercial for the film. And with all those popular songstresses, it was a surefire moneymaker. The cultural impact of the most recent version of "Lady Marmalade," however, was quite distinct from that of the original.

The original version of the song was sung by a trio of young black women who had recently shed their super sweet name "The Bluebells," a fourth member, their bouffant hairdos, and their chiffon gowns for a more radical image as LaBelle. Patti LaBelle sang the lead on the song penned by Kenny Nolan and produced by Allen Toussaint. She told a fable about a Creole prostitute in New Orleans, Lady Marmalade. Through the rhythm of her voice, Patti was able to transmit Lady Marmalade's strut and attitude. Marmalade turned her conservative john's world upside down, and thereby robbed her exploiter of some of his power. The song, with the racy lyrics Voulez vous couchez avec moi, ce soir?" was provocative and yet melancholy. And despite the fact that LaBelle's members purportedly didn't know the meaning of the

French lyrics when they recorded the song, the song had a feminist sensibility about it. This was due to Patti's vocal interpretation and the visual presentation of all of LaBelle. They were telling a story of the past in which a woman found a little subversive power, but the storytellers themselves were contemporary women, futuristic even. Bizarrely adorned, wearing "silver lame space suits and studded breastplates" they signaled "the death of the traditional three girl three gown group."[11] LaBelle were rock glam stars and they stood outside of standard paradigms of female sexuality and objectification. They were somehow women's movement women, black power women, and transgressive women at once.

Patti brought the listener of the song to a corner in Storyville, the historic sex district in New Orleans. She told the story of a sister there, and made that listener feel the energy and melancholy of the Creole prostitute, sympathize with her, recognize her power. Yet Patti escaped being cast into Marmalade's position herself. In 2001, the singers of the song "Lady Marmalade" did not tell Marmalade's legendary story—rather, they became her. That process of embodying the Creole prostitute occurred largely through the visual representation of the song in the music video, which received a huge amount of airplay on MTV and BET, and one live performance.

In the video, the four women are attired in vintage style elaborate lingerie and dance about in rooms that look like the images of bordello boudoirs we have seen in film before. This embodiment had no subversive elements but instead was a glamorization of a turn-of-the-century image of prostitution. Moreover, the diversity and hybridity of the artists are exploited for the sake of the sexual fantasy. There is Christina, blond and blue eyed, Latina and Irish, who sings with the trills and moans of black gospel tradition. There is Mya, whose café au lait skin and long curling hair remind us of the song's description of Lady Marmalade's appearance. There is Pink, a white woman with the whiskey voice of a black blues singer, and Lil Kim, the brown-skinned rapper with the blond wig and blue contact lenses. Their hybridity is used for no more interesting purpose than the reification of the well-worn and generations-old image of the whore at the racial crossroads, the lascivious and tragic mulatto who is defined by her sexuality. Lil Kim is the one of the group who ultimately reveals that these women are embodiments of Lady Marmalade. She raps the story in the first person rather than the third. She tells listeners that she and her "sisters" are about the business of using their sexualities in exchange for material goods from men.

The racial and gender politics of the video are supportive of historic racist imagery of women of color. *Moulin Rouge* is filled with white stars, yet "Lady Marmalade," the song that introduces the movie, is racialized as black, being a hip-hop and R&B creation. The song advertises the film but its blackness is not central to the film's imagination. While the singers reflect the status of the movie's star as a courtesan, dancer, and singer, the politics of race and sex automatically locate them in a lower-status position than that of the star of the film. The degradation of black female space simultaneously with the use of black discourses to define mainstream sexuality is nothing new in American culture. The film is not alone in playing that game. But that this version hearkens so closely to the fate of the Creole woman in relationship to white women in Louisiana history, socially defined as prostitute rather than lady, through everything from antimiscegenation laws and quadroon balls to cultures of concubinage, is particularly troubling. It claims to be, and symbolically is, 1899 all over again.

Ironically, the earlier version of the song was produced by a man, and the later version was produced by a black woman, hip-hop phenom Missy Elliot, discussed earlier. Despite her own feminist presentation, she participates in this subjugating image, in a manner analogous to the way in which Eve participates in the subjugation of other women in music videos in which she appears. Elliot's image in the video as narrator/madam in the video is free from objectification, but supports the objectification of her fellow artists. Moreover, Elliot's own arguably feminist presence is trumped by the subjugated presence of the others.

◆ The Colonizer and Colonized

Novelist and cultural critic Toni Cade Bambara had great insight into the race and gender politics of American media. She reminded us in her essay "Language and the Writer" that

> the creative imagination has been colonized. The global screen has been colonized. And the audience—readers and viewers—is in bondage to an industry. It has the money, the will, the muscle, and the propaganda machine oiled up to keep us all locked up in a delusional system—as to even what America is.[12]

Musical artists are cultural actors, but those backed by record labels are hardly independent actors. In music videos and photo layouts they exist within what Bambara has described as colonized space, particularly around race and gender. In a context in which a short tight dress, and a camera rolling up the body, lingering on behinds and breasts, has particular very charged meanings with regard to gender and personal value, we must ask, How powerful are words that intend to contradict such objectification? How subversive are revolutionary words in a colonized visual world full of traditional gender messages?

In the same essay, Bambara directs us to consider the use of metaphors, themes, and other ritualized structures to create meaning in American film. She writes:

> There is the conventional cinema that masks its ideological imperatives as entertainment and normalizes its hegemony with the term "convention," that is to say the cinematic practices—of editing, particular uses of narrative structure, the development of genres, the language of spatial relationships, particular performatory styles of acting—are called conventions because they are represented somehow to be transcendent or universal, when in fact these practices are based on a history of imperialism and violence.[13]

Bambara is speaking specifically of movies, but her observation about the normalization and universalization of conventions that guide interpretation and that are part of sexist and racist hegemonic structures is applicable to this discussion. Often, language, even aggressive liberatory language, becomes nearly powerless in the face of the powerful discourse of the visual within the texts of music videos.

So then we ask, How should we read these artists who have feminist voices and sexist images? If they are linguistic proponents of women's power, subjectivity, and black feminism, why do they participate in creating such conflicting visual textual representations? First, it is important to acknowledge that in a society with such strong hegemonies of race, class, gender, and sexuality, virtually all of us, regardless of how committed we are to social justice and critical thinking, are conflicted beings. We want to be considered attractive even though we understand how attractiveness is racialized, gendered, and classed in our society, and how the designation often affirms structures of power and domination. Separating out healthy desires to be deemed attractive from those desires for attractiveness that are complicit in our oppression is challenging. Similarly, we want to be successful, but success is often tied to race, class, gender, and body politics that implicitly affirm the oppression of others. We support the status quo in order to succeed within it, despite our better judgment.

These tensions exist within the artist as much as within the average citizen, and we should therefore be cautious in our judgment of the artists. However, even if we were insensitive to these internal conflicts as they might exist in famous hip-hop artists, the artists still should not be considered solely responsible for the tensions between their words and image. The reality is that the "realness" in popular hip-hop and R&B stars is as much an illusion as it is real. Their public images are constructed by teams more often than by themselves. The conflicted images we see from some "feminist talking, sexpot walking" hip-hop artists may be as much a sign of a conflict between their agendas and those of the record companies, stylists, video directors, and so forth, as a sign of internal conflict. Each artist is a corporate creation—pun intended.[14]

◆ *Property and Subversive Potential*

As a college student, I met the black woman filmmaker Julie Dash. I had recently seen her short film *Illusions* and her landmark feature *Daughters of the Dust*. Excited by her work and thrilled to meet her, I gushed about how I wanted to "do what she did." She warned me that if I wrote a screenplay I'd better direct the movie myself if I wanted the substance to be intact once it was completed. In giving me this warning she was testifying as to the degrees of ownership of art, the interaction between words and image, and the importance of black female self-articulation in a colonized media.

Despite the powerful hand of corporate interests in hip-hop, it is a music that has sustained a revolutionary current with respect to consumer culture, albeit one that is increasingly fragile. This revolutionary current exists in the underground communities of unsigned artists (rappers, or MCs, as well as poets or "spoken word" artists) who push forward creative development

without corporate involvement. They are cultural workers and artists in the organic sense, and proprietors of their own images. Analogous to independent filmmakers, local underground artists are a good source when we seek feminist and other politically progressive messages in hip-hop. However, most of the contemporary hip-hop audience has little access to underground artists. It is now overwhelmingly, albeit not exclusively, a recorded art form. Therefore, as cultural readers we should consider what the scope of power is for artists who are signed to record labels.

One clear location of authorial power exists in their ownership of their copyrighted lyrics. The owned lyrics are an asserted property right that competes with the concept that the artist herself is a "property."[15] For women artists who have written and copyrighted their own lyrics, the lyrics might be one of their only areas of control, and it may be where we can best find their intended political messages. Looking to the distinction between the copyrighted material owned by artists and the music videos owned by the record companies, we have some indication of what particular political tensions face a given artist.

Conclusion: ◆ *Possibilities for Dissent*

We know that the politics of the artist are often neutralized by the image made by the record company. Although a famous person has a legally cognizable property interest in his or her public image as a whole, when she consents to making a music video, she grants the record company the use of her image. She allows for the creation of a product that features her as a product and that in turn encourages the sale of her words and music. Perhaps there is a clue in that web to how artists might regain subversive power through language. If their words were not simply liberatory and progressive but also critically engaged, mocked, or challenged the very images that made the artist into a celebrity, the words of the artist might not be dwarfed by the image. Instead they might latch onto the image, shift its meaning, and bring it closer to being owned by the artist. Imagine an artist looking lustily into the camera while critiquing the gaze she is giving you, or discussing the sexism implicit in the sexy dress she is wearing. Although this strategy might simply give rise to further conflicted images, there is the possibility that it would force the listener to critically read the image. Certainly, in earlier periods of hip-hop groups such as a Tribe Called Quest and De La Soul often embedded in their music strong critiques of the music industry to which they understood themselves to be "enslaved" as commodities. Such critiques played a role in their success at being popular, political, and authentic groups, and they provide a useful model for a feminist voice in hip-hop.

There are surely a number of other strategies as well that might be employed by women hip-hop artists who seek innovative modes of feminist articulation and self-definition in an arena dominated by corporate interests and sexism. Hip-hop is an art form that has consistently been engaged in innovation, improvisation, and reinterpretation. It is therefore neither unreasonable nor naive to anticipate a new generation of feminist voices in hip-hop that will respond in increasingly sophisticated and complex ways to a sexist and racist society.

◆ *Notes*

1. The most prominent black women's magazines, *Essence* and *Honey*, as well as *Girl*, which is geared toward a multicultural audience of adolescent girls, all have an explicitly feminist agenda. Readers of these magazines are not offered articles about how to seduce men or appear sexy, which frequently appear in publications such as *Cosmopolitan*, *YM*, and *Glamour*.

2. There are a many hip-hop lyrics that identify the voluptuous body with women who live in housing projects or from the 'hood. As well, the assumption of lighter-complexioned black women being of higher socioeconomic status or greater sexual desirability is a longstanding aspect of black American culture. Although this cultural phenomenon was challenged in the late civil rights era, it flourishes in the images that appear in many television shows, movies, and books and in the tendency of black male movie stars musicians and athletes to choose very light complexioned spouses if they marry black women.

3. Tomika Anderson, "Nothing Butt the Truth" *Essence*, November 2001, 116.

4. Words and music by Alicia Keys. © 2001 EMI April Music Inc. and Lellow Productions. All rights controlled and administered by EMI April Music Inc. All rights reserved. International copyright secured. Used by permission.

5. President Clinton pardoned Kendra Smith, the most famous representative of this population, who spent years in prison as a result of the crimes of her boyfriend.

6. India.Arie interview, http://www.mtv.com.

7. India.Arie interview, http://www.mtv.com.

8. Eve, "Gotta Man," Ruffryders Interscope Records (2000).

9. Sanjiv, "Queen of the Hill: Lauryn Fugee Finds Her Voice," *British GQ*, October 1998, 188.

10. At the time of the publication of this chapter, I have found no interviews or articles that address the reason for Lauryn Hill's second transformation but it will be interesting to see if she understands it as a rejection of the way in which she was styled in order to be palatable to a widespread audience.

11. "The Music Portfolio," *Vanity Fair*, November 2001, 299.

12. Toni Cade Bambara. "Language and the Writer," *Deep Sightings and Rescue Missions: Fiction, Essays and Conversations*, ed. by Toni Morrison (New York: Pantheon, 1996), 140.

13. Toni Cade Bambara. "Language and the Writer," *in Deep Sightings and Rescue Missions: Fiction, Essays and Conversations* ed. By Toni Morrison. (New York: Pantheon, 1996) 140.

14. Although there are some artists who are able to maintain a good deal of creative control

(often those labeled "alternative"), record companies are even aware of the extent to which there is a consumer market for the "alternative" and "iconoclast" so they will allow for that space to exist to some extent within the boundaries of their control.

15. The description of recording artists as "products" in the music industry articulates the sense in which they (as public images) are seen as a kind of property to be purchased by consumers.

15

QUEER 'N' ASIAN ON— AND OFF—THE NET

The Role of Cyberspace in Queer Taiwan and Korea

◆ Chris Berry and Fran Martin

Writing about community and internet communications back in 1995, Nancy Baym bemoaned a general lack of empirical field research (1995: 139). This situation still prevails regarding published research on lesbian, gay, and bisexual internet use, even though queer people are among the net's most enthusiastic users (McLean and Schubert, 1995; Shaw, 1997). . . . Our research based on field trips between August 1997 and January 1998 in South Korea and Taiwan helps to address this lack of data by examining the uses of net communication in lesbian, gay, and queer communities there.[1] (To save space, we'll use the term "queer" throughout this chapter to denote lesbian, gay, and bisexual identities.)

. . . Earlier studies start out from a focus on particular net groups or users as though they were autonomous and separate from "daily reality." In contrast, our study starts from individuals and communities in the context of real life to look at their particular uses of the net. We find that in Taiwan and Korea queer communities and subjects use computer-mediated communication to construct their identities and communities on and off the net in a dialectical and mutually informing manner.

Furthermore, queer subjects have a particular investment in retaining and further developing the connection between their on- and off-net lives. As people who usually have to make a conscious decision to form and maintain public identities and communities offline, the net can be an important tool in that ongoing struggle. Similarly, Marj Kibby notes that far from hiding their gender or their bodies, women on the net often use photographs that emphasize these in their homepages. In this way, she brings down to earth rapture-like fantasies of leaving the body behind as "meat" while one ascends into cyberspace. She notes that "the creator of the electronic persona is the self at the keyboard, the embodied self," and "while this new medium allows the possibility of creating a new genderless self, the tools of creation are still those of gendered society" (1997: 41-42). She also quotes transgender activist and cyber enthusiast Allucquere Roseanne Stone's astute comment that "forgetting about the body is an old Cartesian trick, one that has unpleasant consequences for those bodies whose speech is silenced by the act of forgetting . . . usually women and minorities" (1991: 100).

. . . We were drawn to Taiwan and Korea as spaces where the emergence of public queer communities has been more or less contemporaneous with the availability of the net.[2] In these circumstances, instead of simply fitting into and extending pre-existing identities and communities, there is the possibility that the net might inform the character of the queer identities and communities that were being constructed (on and off the net) from their inception.[3]

Taiwan and South Korea have enough in common to provide a suitable comparative context for studies of sexuality and net use. Neither state has specific legal prohibitions on homosexuality.[4] However, kinship conventions emphasize heterosexual reproduction in both states, and until recently both were ruled by right-wing regimes under which the populations were strongly disciplined and the development of popular initiatives was harshly restrained (Wachman, 1994; Cumings, 1997). Now, those right-wing regimes have been replaced by democratic systems with pluralistic policies. Combined with economic growth that has made youth less reliant upon family, this has produced preconditions for the emergence of both public queer cultures and widespread internet use.

Discrete queer subcultures invisible to the general public existed in both states prior to more recent developments (Berry, 1996). However, a public culture emerged earlier in Taiwan than in South Korea. In Taiwan the first openly homosexual group was established in 1990, and by the mid-1990s there was a steady output of queer novels, films, and magazines, whereas in South Korea, groups only began to be formed in the mid-1990s, and the first glossy magazine appeared in 1998. Various differences may account for this. First, whereas Taiwanese queer activists draw upon a long history of same-sex cultural activities and representations, this is currently not so in South Korea (see Hinsch, 1990; Pai, 1995; Chao, 1996; Rutt, 1969). Second, fundamentalist Christianity is far more influential in South Korea than in Taiwan (Song, 1990: 47-50; Palmer, 1986; Jordan, 1994). Third, while the dismantling of military rule began in Taiwan in the early 1980s, this period remained one of severe repression in Korea. Taiwan's desire to appear internationally as a modern democratic society has produced attempts at liberalization in many areas, including sexual politics (Patton, 1998). Political reform in Korea, meanwhile, has not extended to policy on sexuality.

Traditional family values continue to be officially endorsed.

. . . We found that the participants in the publicly visible queer cultures of Taiwan and South Korea are young, highly educated and, in many cases, still students. A total of 90 percent of Korean survey respondents were tertiary educated, 60 percent were in the 23- to 28-year-old age bracket, and almost three-quarters were men.[5] The most significant general demographic difference concerns domestic situation. Fully 64 percent of Korean survey respondents were living with their parents. Taiwan interview responses indicate that many more queer-identified people live away from their families. Student dormitories are more common there, and deposits on rental apartments are prohibitively high in South Korea.

. . . When asked, "What lesbian, gay or queer computer activities do you engage in?" the most popular response was "Visiting chatrooms to meet lesbian, gay or queer people" (82 percent within Korea, 17 percent overseas), followed by "Visiting internet sites for activist information" (63 percent within Korea, and 26 percent overseas). E-mailing friends was popular, and more than one in five said they e-mailed friends to spread activist information. The internet was also used for other kinds of conversation, information sharing, and for reading queer fiction. Only 12 percent said they visited chatrooms for cybersex. Interviews indicate that all these activities were popular, to similar degrees, in Taiwan. One of the most significant findings was the low use of overseas queer sites, despite high levels of foreign language proficiency. Taiwan data indicated that this even applied to overseas sites in Chinese. This data makes sense in the light of our data on the most popular activities, namely extensions of the socializing activities you might find in bars, followed by information seeking. Interview responses in Korea indicated a desire to meet people on the net as a prelude to possible meetings in real space. Of course, local sites are best for this.

. . . Amongst this wide range and high level of activity, two particular patterns interested us. First, much of the activity in both Taiwan and Korea is focused on sites where high levels of interaction are possible. We believe this creates sizable and substantial social formations within Taiwan and Korea's emergent queer cultures that we would call "online discursive communities."

In Taiwan, the most popular sites are university-based bulletin board systems (BBSs) known as MOTSS (members of the same sex) sites, of which there are now around 80. In Korea, university administrators seem less accommodating, and the most popular sites are at the Web homepages of major commercial ISPs. Chollian's *Queernet*, Nownuri's *Rainbow*, and Hitel's *Dosamo* are huge text-based sites incorporating multiple chatrooms, message boards, and other subgroups. One interviewee estimated that one site gets up to 5,000 hits a day. Comparative lack of interactivity has made other Web pages less popular in both Taiwan and Korea.[6]

Several interviewees pointed out that many queer net users have no access to other aspects of queer culture. They may be too young or too poor to attend bars, or remote from the queer cultures of Taipei and Seoul. However, the range of activities pursued in these online discursive communities also indicates frequent integration with offline life.

The most common activities are social. As well as searching for partners, interviewees specified counseling and information exchange as particularly popular. "When I was that age, we had to keep it to ourselves. We had no one to tell," one Taipei woman explained about relationship break-ups. "You'd just go and play basketball or whatever till you felt better. The kids today have it so good." A Korean interviewee drew attention to a discussion thread, which "warns about people who exploit young gays. They fall in love quickly, and those guys borrow money and then leave." Interviewees also emphasized that many topics were discussed that had no direct relation to sexuality. A Taiwanese interviewee suggested this could be explained as a desire to speak freely on all topics safe in the knowledge that everyone chatting was queer.

These online discursive communities are not only integrated with existing offline activities but often also stimulate new offline connections. One interviewee in Taiwan cited birthday parties held by MOTSS members to which the condition of entry was membership of a particular MOTSS. Similarly, a Korean interviewee had posted a message when living in a small college town asking if there was anyone else online from the same town. After online exchanges, the group met to see a movie and began more regular social activities. Another Korean interviewee reported that a similar process had facilitated the rapid recent development of queer student groups across the whole country.

Queer online discursive communities also engage in the publication and dissemination of queer cyberfiction. Although no star writers have emerged yet in Korea, in Taiwan there is now a series of books composed of material that originated on the net.[7]

Finally, online discursive communities have proved important tools for queer activists. They use message boards to distribute information about activities and stimulate debate. A Korean activist explained, "I set up a sub-group in Nownuri's *Rainbow* called Tank Girls and Tank Boys. My intention was to fight against stereotyped identities in the gay and lesbian community through discussion of popular culture." This group met both on and off the net.

As examples of direct action, a petition was widely posted in 1997 protesting the Taipei Municipal Government's decision to outlaw prostitution, with the result of mobilizing an influential campaign of public protest. And while we were carrying out our survey, the First Seoul Queer Film and Video Festival was banned. News and petitions were circulated by fax, e-mail, snail mail, and by hand. E-mail proved particularly effective internationally. A year later, a festival worker laughed, "Now we are more famous overseas than the Pusan International Film Festival"—Korea's largest mainstream event.[8]

The second pattern that caught our interest related to the formation of identities. Mantovani has argued that instead of being used to escape from offline selves, the net may function as a testing ground for "possible selves" that can then inform offline identity (1996: 123-27). In the case of queer subjects, who face very serious obstacles in the construction of offline identities, this may be particularly true.

In Taiwan, a common response to questions about the role of internet technology in shaping users' experience of their queer identities emphasizes how BBS boards allow queer subjects the rare opportunity to assert their sexual politics in the face of the homophobia of broader society. Bruce relates:

> To me, "queer politics" means something very progressive, active, positive, and proud. It's saying to people "Yes, I'm here. . . . I don't want your sympathy. I don't want your acceptance. What I want is *to be here*. That's my right. It you don't give it to me, I'll take it anyway." Because of the net's anonymity and its speed, . . . that kind of queer attitude has developed easily there . . . as compared with other media or with "real life." Actually, I think I've learned my own queer politics and queer attitude from the net.[9]

Bruce's response goes beyond simply celebrating the freedoms of cyberspace, suggesting that his very sense of himself as identifying with the outspoken, anti-assimilationist politics of "queer" arises from his experience as a net user.

. . . A woman net user in Taiwan has an interesting point to make about how the net affects lesbians' experience of themselves as gendered according to the categories "T" and "*po*," comparable to the English "butch" and "femme." She says:

To a girl, her name is very important, because the name she has grown up with was given to her by her father. On the net . . . people are free to play language games with their real names and mix up the roles. . . . A T may have a very "feminine" name in real life, but on the net she can use a name she chooses herself . . . taking on the role she prefers.[10]

This comment implies that for Taiwan's lesbians, the net enables an extension of the gendered relations of the "T bar" (lesbian bar). In T bars, it is common practice for women to introduce themselves using fictitious nicknames—in the case of Ts, these names are often androgynous or masculine, symbolizing their rejection of traditional "feminine" style (Chao, 1996). This woman's observation suggests that the net offers further possibilities for reworking feminine gender norms, enabling Ts actively to rename themselves, shaping new identities defined by their assertion of a specifically "T" lesbian gender.

In conclusion, we would argue that our findings on online discursive communities and possible selves in queer net use in Taiwan and South Korea underline the need to rethink the ways in which we conceptualize internet communications. In the cases we have studied, the net is neither a substitute for nor an escape from real life. Nor is it simply an extension of existing offline communities and identities. Instead, it is part of live culture, informed by and informing other parts of users' lives. And in the emergent queer cultures of Taiwan and South Korea, it is a particularly substantial and dynamic component.

◆ *Notes*

1. We would like to thank Lee Chung-Woo, Seo Dong-Jin, and the staff members of the Seoul Queer Film and Video Festival for distributing and collecting survey forms. They also helped translate the questionnaires together with Kim Hyun-Sook, who also helped with the design. We would also like to thank the respondents in both Korea and Taiwan. Thanks also to National Taiwan Central University's Center for the Study of Sexuality and Difference, as well as Grace, Bruce Chen, Davy Chi, and Josette Tang in Taiwan, all of whom helped with the Taiwan research.

2. In speaking of "queer subjects and communities" in the Taiwan and South Korean situations, we refer to the appearance of recognizable, public identities such as "lesbian," "gay," "queer," or "homosexual," in distinction to older, subcultural, and less generally visible traditions around sexually non-normative behaviour.

3. Although it is not our main focus here, these issues also raise debates around what has been called "global queering," for example by Dennis Altman in *The Australian Humanities Review*, No. 2, July-September 1996 (www.lib. latrobe.edu.au/AHR/home.html). The net is often linked explicitly with strongly homogenizing arguments about cultural globalization. So it might be expected that our project would align itself either in terms of the ways in which the net helps bring about the "westernization" of homosexual identifications in these East Asian states or else in terms of "indigenous" resistances to this process. Instead, as already indicated, the information we have gathered to date suggests a view more akin to Appadurai's "heterogenizing" view of cultural globalization as a moment in which all forces involved are mutually (if unequally) transformed by it (see Appadurai, 1990). For a more extended discussion of the data presented here in relation to global queering, see Martin and Berry, 1998).

4. Same-sex sexual behavior, however, has had scant public recognition in either place. And those who engage in it are liable to prosecution under laws regulating "public obscenity" or "hooliganism."

5. In both places, the transgender scene is relatively separate, explaining the few transgender respondents.

6. For an example of a more sophisticated and interactive Taiwanese Web page, see Dingo's lesbian pages and online pub at www.to-get-her.org/. There is also a list of links at www.

dakini.org. For a list of Korean links see www.geocities.com/WestHollywood Stonewall /6460.

7. "Ask," *Xiao Mo* (Hong Kong: Huasheng Shudian, 1996), "Garrido," *Meimei Wan'an* (Hong Kong: Huasheng Shudian, 1996).

8. For a report on the Second Seoul Queer Film and Video Festival, which was not banned, see Chris Berry, "My Queer Korea" at http://www sshe.murdoch.edu.au/hum/as/intersections/ current2/Berry.html.

9. Interview with Bruce, 20 January 1998, Chungli. "Bruce" (Bu-lu-si) is the name his friends call him both on and off the net, but he also uses his birth name when necessary in pursuing his "queer" activist politics.

10. Paper presented by "Waiter" to National Central University's December 1997 mini-conference on lesbian/gay/queer internet activism.

◆ References

Appadurai, A., 1996: *Modernity at Large: Cultural Dimensions of Globalization*. Minneapolis: University of Minnesota Press.

Baym, N. K., 1995b: "The emergence of community in computer-mediated communication," in Jones, S. G. (ed.), *CyberSociety: Computer-Mediated Communication and Community*. Thousand Oaks, CA: Sage, 138-63.

Berry, C., 1996: "Seoul man: A night on the town with Korea's first gay activist," *Outrage* 159, August, 38-40.

Chao, A., 1996: "The Performative Context of the T Bar" in *Embodying the Invisible: Body Politics in Constructing Contemporary Taiwanese Lesbian Identities*, Ph.D. dissertation, Cornell University.

Cumings, B., 1997: *Korea's Place in the Sun: A Modern History*. New York: W. W. Norton.

Hinsch, B., 1990: *Passions of the Cut Sleeve: the Male Homosexual Tradition in China*. Berkeley: University of California Press.

Jordan, D. K., 1994: "Changes in postwar Taiwan and their impact on the popular practice or religion" in Harrell, S. and Chün-chieh, H. (eds.), *Cultural Change in Postwar Taiwan*. Taipei: SMC Publishing.

Kibby, M., 1997: "Babes on the Web: Sex identity and the home page," *Media Information Australia* 84.

McLean, R. and Schubert, R., 1995: "Queers and the internet," *Media Information Australia* 78.

Mantovani, G., 1996: *New Communication Environments: From Everyday to Virtual*. London: Taylor and Francis.

Martin, F. and Berry, C., 1998: "Queer 'n' Asian on the net: Syncretic sexualities in Taiwan and Korean cyberspaces," *Critical InQueeries* 2:1, 67-93.

Pai, H.-Y., 1995 (first published 1983): *Crystal Boys* (trans. Howard Goldblatt). San Francisco: Gay Sunshine Press.

Palmer, S. J., 1986: *Korea and Christianity*. Seoul: Seoul Computer Press.

Patton, C., 1998: "Stealth bombers of desire: The globalisation of "alterity" in emerging democracies," unpublished manuscript.

Rutt, R., 1969: "The Flower Boys of Silla (Hwarang): Notes on the sources," *Transactions of the Korea Branch of the Royal Asiatic Society* 38, 1-66.

Shaw, D. F., 1997: "Gay men and computer communication: A discourse of sex and identity in cyberspace" in Jones, S. G. (ed.), *CyberSociety: Computer-Mediated Communication and Community*. Thousand Oaks, CA: Sage.

Song, B. N., 1990: *The Rise of the Korean Economy*. Hong Kong: Oxford University Press.

Stone, A. R., 1991: "Will the real body please stand up? Boundary stories about virtual cultures" in Benedikt, M. (ed.), *Cyberspace: First Steps*. Cambridge, MA: MIT Press, 81-118.

Wachman, A. M., 1994: *Taiwan: National Identity and Democratization*. Armonk, NY: M. E. Sharpe.

PART II

MARKETING A CONSUMER CULTURE

The central theme of the chapters in this section is the role of the media industries in the production and maintenance of an overwhelmingly consumption-oriented cultural environment in postindustrial economies like our own. Critics of such a culture point to a long list of social and political costs related to unchecked consumption of world resources, including environmental degradation, the dangerously increasing gap between rich and poor nations, erosion of political democracy, and even global warming—but the multinational corporate drive to increase levels of product consumption seems largely unaffected by these warnings.

Media industries, like other corporations, continually seek out new ways of addressing new audiences in new locations. Marketing strategies developed to target new consumers frequently play a complex role in creating or reinforcing cultural images of gender, sexuality, race, and class. Often what appears on the surface to be "progressive" marketing to formerly underserved groups, through the use of "positive" social messages, should be examined more closely, with an awareness of economic and social realities that lie behind the window dressing.

We begin this section with two chapters that call our attention to the invasion of spaces formerly considered "public" by the marketing of media corporations for commercial purposes. In "Space Jam: Media

Conglomerates Build the Entertainment City" (Chapter 16), Susan Davis shows us how entertainment mega-companies such as the Disney Company "are in the process of creating public spaces defined by marketing criteria and shaped to the most profitable audiences." Using their experiences with building theme parks, such companies are partnering with real estate developers and city planners to create public "location-based entertainment projects" designed to lure potential consumers out of their "private" worlds of home entertainment.

> The explosion of experimentation with the built environment is evidence that the mass media corporations are joining the suburb builders, urban redevelopers, and shopping mall magnates in sculpting the physical world we move about in and the social space we share with neighbors and fellow citizens.

Such projects offer "a sense of place" as one of the "products" they are selling. To do this successfully, as Davis points out, they must "shape and manage spaces to appeal to the most economically desirable customers, making sure to exclude the undesirables through price, marketing, or explicit policy."

Henry Giroux joins Davis in warning that corporations are commercializing areas of public space necessary to the development of civic culture. In "Kids for Sale: Corporate Culture and the Challenge of Public Schooling" (Chapter 17), Giroux describes how cash-poor public schools "have had to lease out space in their hallways, buses, rest rooms, monthly lunch menus, and school cafeterias, transforming such spaces into glittering billboards for the highest corporate bidder." In one notorious case, some school systems struck a bargain with the Channel One company to allow commercials to be broadcast along with "free" news and current events, in exchange for gifts of electronic equipment to the schools. Giroux points out that such practices leave students "subject to the

whims and practices of marketers whose agenda has nothing to do with critical learning and a great deal to do with restructuring civic life in the image of market culture." From such market-oriented school lessons, is it surprising that some students define democracy as "the freedom to buy and consume whatever they wish, without government restriction"?

Commercial television has accustomed us to the commodification of every aspect of life and to the interpenetration of marketing campaigns over a whole range of media, because "nearly everything on television is an advertisement for some form of entertainment or product available in another medium," as George Lipsitz argues in "The Greatest Story Ever Sold: Marketing and the O. J. Simpson Trial" (Chapter 18). In this provocative reading of the O. J. Simpson trial as a marketing triumph, Lipsitz shows how

> If it was something less than the trial of the century in terms of legal significance, it was certainly the "sale" of the century in terms of its ability to bring together the various apparatuses of advertising, publicity, spectator sports, motion pictures, television, and marketing into a unified totality generating money-making opportunities at every turn.

Fueled by all-pervasive marketing by corporations, current sky-high levels of consumption in wealthy Western nations threaten the erosion of our quality of life and the destruction of the environment, and exacerbate tensions between the postindustrial and industrializing countries. In "The New Politics of Consumption" (Chapter 19), economist Juliet Schor points to the "upscaling of lifestyle norms" that characterizes "the new consumerism." Schor argues that after a decade of economic boom times in the United States, "luxury, rather than mere comfort, is a widespread aspiration." She shows the role of television, in particular, in contributing to the "upscaling of lifestyle norms."

Because television shows are so heavily skewed to the "lifestyles of the rich and upper middle-class," they inflate the viewer's perceptions of what others have, and by extension what is worth acquiring—what one must have in order to avoid being "out of it."

A form of "upscale emulation" was encouraged among the urban teenagers targeted by intense advertising during fierce "sneaker wars" between Nike and Reebok for market share in the early 1990s. In "Nike, Social Responsibility, and the Hidden Abode of Production" (Chapter 20), Carol Stabile recounts the way in which Nike's aggressive marketing campaign using "disciplined African American bodies" to sell its basketball sneakers threatened to backfire when "a spate of publicity in 1989 suggested that children were killing each other over athletic shoes . . . specifically for Air Jordans." Analyzing the undercurrent of "implicit racism" that informs even apparently antiracist representations of African American "positive role models" within the advertising texts, she also calls our attention to the generally "invisible" conditions of production that lie behind the highly visible marketing campaigns—contradictions that undermine Nike's promotion of itself for its liberal and upscale market as a "socially responsible" corporation.

The concept of "target marketing" is central to understanding how corporations such as Nike or Reebok hope to motivate specific groups of consumers to choose one brand over another. As Sean Griffin tells us in "'You've Never Had a Friend Like Me': Target Marketing Disney to a Gay Community" (Chapter 21),

Disney was . . . one of the first to capitalize on the concept of target audiences, a key development in the eventual attempt to woo the homosexual customer. . . . By moving from advertising the benefits of the product itself to advertising the benefits of belonging to a certain audience

segment which used the product, segmenting moved to increasingly isolate specific groups . . . hopefully including those groups which had spending power but had not been addressed effectively in marketing heretofore.

As media corporations target ever more specific demographic groups and attempt to reach multiple market segments with different versions of their campaigns, they may resort to covert techniques for appealing to one group without offending another. The classic example is "gay window advertising." Griffin shows how the Walt Disney Company, once known for its social conservatism and "family values," discovered the gay and lesbian market segment and in the 1990s developed sly strategies for reaching this market without offending its more conservative traditional consumers.

Ever since the discovery of the upscale gay male market niche by national advertisers in the 1970s, national and local magazines and newspapers have been able to court advertising dollars by selling this desirable demographic. As Fred Fejes points out in "Advertising and the Political Economy of Lesbian/Gay Identity" (Chapter 22), there are many tradeoffs when commercial cultural visibility (through advertising images) is embraced as a route to social equality. Only that part of the gay and lesbian community that fits the attractive demographic profile gains greater visibility—those without high incomes continue to be marginalized, even in the gay community's own media institutions, which once contained a greater diversity of images.

Despite their need to capitalize on every possible market segment, advertisers are not always eager to be the first to embrace new groups of consumers. Recounting her experience seeking advertisers to support *Ms.* magazine in its early days, Gloria Steinem shows us, in "Sex, Lies and Advertising" (Chapter 23), how advertisers targeting women as consumers subscribed to very limited notions of what constitutes femininity (i.e., dependency, concern with beauty, fixation on family and nurturance, fear of technology), and consequently "feminine" buying patterns. Feminist efforts to redefine gender ideals for advertisers in the 1970s and 1980s met with disbelief, resistance, and downright hostility. Steinem's chapter reveals the extent to which advertisers also assumed the right to control editorial content of the media—citing, among other practices, efforts to censor feature stories that might conflict with the interests of advertisers.

Because of the way 20th-century gender ideology assigned (middle-class) women the role of shoppers for families, marketing to male consumers has been more of a challenge than marketing to females. Kenon Breazeale examines the history of *Esquire* magazine (Chapter 24), focusing on its Depression-era creation of an early version of consumerist masculinity that we tend to associate with *Playboy* magazine. The strategy was very much about turning men into consumers and thus locating them in the female defined domestic arena, but to do so, it had to "displace all the women-identified associations so firmly lodged at the center of America's commodified domestic environment."

16

SPACE JAM

Media Conglomerates
Build the Entertainment City

◆ Susan G. Davis

For more than a decade, architects, geographers, and cultural critics have explored the privatization of public space, describing a speculative and spectacular postmodern city built on foundations of grinding inequality. This is, in Michael Sorkin's phrase, the city as theme park, where corporately built public spaces have helped kill the street and cash out democracy (Sorkin, 1991; see also Schiller, 1989: especially 89-110).

The notion of the city as theme park makes rough metaphorical sense of scores of urban transformations and suburban projects, but in this discussion an important question has been overlooked. The urban reshapers are increasingly, and literally, the theme park builders, the conglomerate media corporations that now lead the international economy (Herman and McChesney, 1997). The Walt Disney Company's central role at "ground zero" of the redevelopment of 42nd Street and Broadway in Manhattan is the obvious example, but Time-Warner, Viacom, Seagram's Universal Studios, and Sony are also commissioning, designing, and financing massive real estate projects. So the neglected question: Why are these mega media conglomerates moving beyond the construction of literal theme parks and helping to rebuild city centres, reshaping shopping malls and

NOTE: From *European Journal of Communication*, Vol. 14, No. 4, 1999. Copyright © 1999. Reprinted with permission of Sage Publications Ltd.

suburbs, and even designing residential and work communities? The same media behemoths that have brought the world a revolutionary and supposedly placeless electronic transnational culture are demonstrating a powerful interest in the problem of space and place. But why, and with what implications for collective and cultural life? . . .

In the first half of the 20th century, the entertainment conglomerates were central in creating a nearly all-penetrating national and international mass culture, first through film and later through animation, popular music, and televised sports. In the second half of the century, they have brought this largely American mass culture thoroughly and extensively into the home, to hundreds of millions of people. At the cusp of the 21st century, they are poised to weave the private realm together with the collective through the creation of dramatic and focused media-filled spaces. In the process, as they further displace smaller businesses and older, heterogeneous uses of the streets, the media conglomerates are changing the relationships between public and private experience. They are in the process of creating public spaces defined by marketing criteria and shaped to the most profitable audiences. These spaces will be devoted to the circulation of well-tested and "safe" media content and will exclude experimental imagery or oppositional ideas. Privately produced collective spaces based on and filled with familiar mass media content can create a kind of seamless world, one in which the home—currently devoted to extensive consumption of conglomerate culture—is tightly knit to and continuous with the outside. The city (or at least certain districts of the city), seen as dangerous in its diverse unpredictability, is being made safe imagistically as well as physically.

◆ *The Scale of the Boom*

"Entertainment is the hottest topic in real estate circles," as many economic analysts

have noted, but the reverse is just as true: real estate is now indispensable to an entertainment company's portfolio, its growth, and promotional strategies (Phillips, 1995; *The Economist*, 1994; Hartnett, 1993). While they worry about how the Internet will change their fundamental businesses, the media conglomerates are elevating their corporate vice presidents for real estate and development. These strategists are less visible publicly than executives in charge of film, television, and multimedia, but they are charged with doing more than building offices. They speak of the old-fashioned ideas of place and community as growth opportunities for their companies.[1]

No recent statistics are able to summarize the extent of location-based entertainment projects, but they are ubiquitous (see, for example, Hannigan, 1998). In today's rebuilt city centres, they are important conceptual, architectural, and speculative interventions. In Philadelphia, Denver, Baltimore, Atlanta, New Orleans, Cleveland, San Francisco, and Washington, D.C., these new projects have been born out of the political clout of the developers using state and federal redevelopment funds, the skills of prestigious architects, and tourism promotion policies (Boyer, 1991; on Atlanta see Rutheiser, 1996; Levine, 1997; Smith, 1996). At their core are buildings that integrate product, most predominantly media product, into space more fully than ever before, using architecture to synthesize marketing goals with the creation of awe and personal identification.

As usual, Manhattan provides striking examples. On the East Side, within the few blocks between East 57th and 55th Streets is a cluster of entertainment retail projects. The Warner Bros. Store features 75,000 square feet of licensed merchandise, 24 video screens, "a giant zoetrope in a moving picture cafe" (Gragg, 1997: 84), and hands-on interactive animation stations. Nearby, NikeTown features a museum of Olympic medals and trophies; films of U.S. hockey, World Cup soccer, Michigan football; and a three-storey screen that descends from the ceiling every 30 minutes to show an inspirational sports film. NikeTown alone claims 10,000 visitors daily, evenly split between tri-state residents and tourists. A Disney Store is just a few blocks south on 55th Street, again filled with giant video, interactive toys, merchandise, and a travel and ticket agency to help customers connect with other Disney products, such as theme parks, cruises, and Broadway shows (*The Architectural Review*, 1997; Gragg, 1997). At Times Square the Disney Company has anchored the area's "rebirth" as a film, theatre, and "interactive entertainment" district. Forty-Second Street is now a showcase for Disney's endless array of family-friendly products, and the New Amsterdam Theatre is not only the stage for Disney's new live theatrical enterprises but also a celebration of the company's vast international cultural power (Pulley, 1995; Roman and Evans, 1996; Berman, 1995). . . .

The same phenomenon of the interjection of media content into shared social space can be seen repeated in many places on a smaller scale. Immediate causes and particular corporate actors may vary, particular projects succeed or fail, but the penetration of public space by media content is decisive. For example, shopping and regional speciality malls around the United States are clustering new media venues and mini theatres near the familiar multiplex to try to create life, light, and a kind of busy, heterogeneous street of activity (Phillips, 1995; Hartnett, 1993). "We are trying to take the best attractions out of the theme park and put them in the cities," says Vito Sanzone, the chief executive of Iwerks, the specialty theatre and film company. . . .

Sega, the mammoth video game company, is engaged in very diverse large- and small-scale location-based projects. Its interactive sites in Yokohama and Osaka are small theme parks that try to "make full use of [Sega's] newest and most advanced technology" (O'Brien, 1996b), that is, they take the Sega game out of the home and transform it into pay-to-enter urban recreation (O'Brien, 1994b; Katayama,

1994). In 1994, after launching a 90,000-square-foot flagship game park in Tokyo, Sega announced that it would build 50 more virtual-reality and video-game parks across Japan. A huge SegaWorld unveiled at Piccadilly Circus in London accommodates thousands of simultaneous, interactive players. Described as "a hybrid between a giant video arcade and a small theme park," SegaWorld arranges the latest proprietary high-tech rides and games across themed zones spread over seven floors in four buildings (O'Brien, 1996b).

Sega is firing up Gameworks, an international software ride-game development in a collaboration with the media theme park conglomerate Universal/Seagram and Stephen Spielberg's Dreamworks SKG studio. Starting in Seattle, Las Vegas, and southern California, Gameworks plans to build a string of as many as one hundred play sites in the United States and to team up with the Toronto-based Playdium Entertainment to build 40 Sega Cities across Canada. The first Sega City, outside Ontario, is a Can$17 million sports and film-themed entertainment complex with "more than 180 video simulators and interactive games" (Zoltak, 1996c: 31-2). On another track, Gameworks is at work with Cineplex Odeon on a project called Cinescape, which will combine Sega game centres with movie theatres and restaurants, again in major retail outlets (*Wall Street Journal*, 1996; Zoltak, 1996a). . . .

At the lower end of the retail market, the media penetration of shared space is just as advanced, though it looks different. For example, *Advertising Age* reports that "marketers increasingly are realizing the potential of in-store entertainment fixtures, such as walls of TV screens, scattered TV monitors, or audio systems" (Cuneo, 1997). Polaroid, for example, recently screened a commercial inside almost 2,000 mass merchandise malls around the United States. In autumn 1998, country singer Garth Brooks debuted a new album via a live concert broadcast exclusively into hundreds of American Wal-Marts. Retailers have discovered that they can sell video or audio time in their own stores, and national mall management chains are currently negotiating similar deals with television networks, as well as local television and radio stations. For example, Wells Park Group, a national mall manager, will offer "media partner[s] space in common areas or in stores in exchange for on-air promotions" (Cuneo, 1997). In such common commercial space, parents and children will take a shopping break to watch commercial television.

Also at the less affluent end of the spectrum are examples of the emerging pattern of turning local public services over to entertainment companies under the guise of partnered community development. To the extent that it is successfully promoted as providing social amelioration—jobs, education, community centres, ways to keep children off the streets—the entertainment-media-retail model of the city is reworking the fragments of an older public sphere.[2] In 1996, Austin, Texas, became the first municipality in the United States to build a publicly owned Family Entertainment Center, "to aid the [largely Chicano East Austin] community in its search to give youth a safe place to hang out" (Waddell, 1996: 24). With city-purchased land, and a federal Department of Housing and Urban Development loan, the facility was constructed by the city but planned and run for a fee and incentives by a major leisure management company. Instead of an old-fashioned public recreation centre, the Central City Entertainment Center is "all entertainment" for a profit, geared to generate the maximum amount of revenue for the concessionaires and the managing company.

Similarly, the Battle Creek, Michigan, Parks and Recreation Department sponsored the Full Tilt Entertainment Mall as part of a city centre revitalization project. With a single admission price, Full Tilt contains a small water park, a video arcade, a food court, a gym franchise, a laser tag arena, and a teenage club, among other attractions. Described by its general

manager as a "very aggressive private enterprise sort of thing," Full Tilt will operate on its own without city funding (O'Brien, 1997b). A scheme called tax-increment financing, widely used to support private interests in urban redevelopment around the United States, means that taxes on Full Tilt's revenues do not return to the city's general fund for education and services. Revenues are funnelled into a special district account to help expand similar redevelopment projects.

Both the Austin and Battle Creek projects aim to attract and serve young people and families by modelling themselves on the corporately produced theme park, including its concessionaires, leases, and, perhaps later, its pricing structures and promotional and sponsorship arrangements. The main difference is that each has been built almost entirely with public money, rather than by the usual public-private financing blend. Nonetheless, the main effect is to privilege private profit-making.

The Rationale for the ◆ Entertainment-Retail Boom

There are several powerful and intersecting reasons for the entertainment-retail building boom. Real estate developers are partnering with entertainment corporations in part because retail and office space were overbuilt in the 1980s and remain so today as speculation runs far ahead of demand. Traditional shopping centres and malls, and even Jon Jerde's elaborate pseudo-cities, are facing tremendous competitive pressure as American incomes "remain flat and retail space per capita increases" (Phillips, 1995; see also Pacelle, 1997). In addition to retail saturation, the development of new shopping media and ways of selling to people in the home via catalogues, cable, infomercials, and Internet shopping is also forcing traditional retailers to be ever more inventive to reach the older, affluent though slower consuming segment of the population. At the same time, these consumers are better understood than ever before—they have been subject to more than a generation of traditional and now computerized electronic and video information gathering. Market researchers now speak of knowing most of the consuming population as niches, each with its particular tastes, habits, and preferences (Gladwell, 1996).

Entertainment retail is a strategy to get people out of the house. From the point of view of landlords, retailers, and especially the vast coalitions of institutional real estate speculators called REITs (real estate investment trusts, essentially mutual funds specializing in real estate), the injection of entertainment content into commercial spaces is a coordinated way to differentiate one retail space from another, to bring people out to shop, and, in metropolitan locations, to capture the important tourists. In this effort, media conglomerates like Disney, Sony, MCA, and Time-Warner—which own the widely familiar film, television, and sports imagery—have a long head start. In the risky and overbuilt retail sector, the already tested media content bolsters investor confidence as do Hollywood's corporate deep pockets. Here Pocahontas, Daffy Duck, and the Tasmanian Devil provide a kind of insurance that the customers will keep coming. Indeed, they provide sure ways to locate and appeal to important groups within the broad population of customers. . . .

Like developers, media conglomerates and theatre chains have a range of good reasons to support entertainment retail experiments. Theatrical film exhibitors feel pressure to get people out of the house, to break down the cocoon of television, cable, home video, computer and video games, and the Internet. The video-game industry sees the problem similarly. One manager of a Seattle virtual-reality centre put it this way: "What we're doing, and what everyone else is experimenting with, is 'What

does it take to get people out of the house to spend time with other people?' What is the right mix? In a sense this is an R&D project" (quoted in Goldberg, 1997).

New technologies are an important differentiating draw for the game arcades and specialty theatres. The special-format film producers, for example, speak in terms of increasing the difference between their products and both movie going and staying home with a video by intensifying the film experience through technology. As a number of film critics have noticed, the promoters of IMAX and the new mini-ride theatres are trying to recreate filmed entertainment as a kinetic, sensory, aural, and even olfactory experience, and so they are resurrecting the claim to "total cinema," the cinema of advanced and perfected perception, engaging all the senses with complete realism (Arthur, 1996). Special-format film's promoters speak of "total immersion." According to Iwerks's Vito Sanzone: "The core attraction [of the big screen simulator theatre] is that it's a totally immersive, visual and audio experience. . . . You're battered and flabbergasted for five minutes," in a way that breaks through the "inundation" of the rest of everyday life (quoted in Johnson, 1995). So too do the new video and virtual-reality products from Sega and Gameworks claim to offer more intense experiences based on technologies that engulf the player's body and immerse him or her in a whole environment. Here the inundation of everyday life, which must be shattered, means not only the routines of suburb, freeway, and workplace, but also the rest of the media world: video, television, advertising, radio, and print.

Yet, from the media conglomerates' perspective it is not just a question of breaking through the "cocoon" of home entertainment. Oddly—or perhaps not—what is being used to get people out of the house is the material that has been invading it for 40 years. The largest media conglomerates have realized that they need what Disney chief executive Michael Eisner has called an "inside/outside" strategy, encompassing both the inside (media consumption in private and domestic spaces) *and* the outside (traditional and new forms of media consumption in public). The two spheres must work together and be mutually supportive. Eisner "wants to keep luring people out of their homes to see Disney's movies and visit its theme parks, while giving them an increasing number of products to entertain and inform themselves [with] when they do stay home."[3] But now the inside and outside of entertainment culture are interdependent, as, for example, when a successful film's box office drives home video sales, or ABC sports enhances interest in the ESPN Zone restaurants. These companies not only can work on both the inside and the outside; they must. Finding new ways to occupy space gives the conglomerates a new grounding for their mobile cultural products.

◆ *Aesthetic Strategies*

From an aesthetic point of view, location-based entertainment projects face a central and perhaps paradoxical problem. Inserted into standardized and relentlessly exploited commercial spaces, they must create—out of thin air—a sense of place. Place is the product on offer, built up out of the design strategies learned in the theme park industry. The key theme park lessons applied to retail-entertainment are, first, shape and manage spaces to appeal to the most economically desirable customers, making sure to exclude the undesirables through price, marketing, or explicit policy. Because so much retail-entertainment space is entirely privately owned, in shopping malls and theme parks, screening of visitors can be subtle but intense. Most retail-entertainment spaces have developed careful entrance and exit control; set back from the street, they are effectively gated, since visitors enter through a hotel, from a freeway off-ramp or from huge parking garages (for commentary on this see Straight, 1997). They have also

developed architectural and security techniques to discourage undesirables—the homeless, who may beg, or teenagers, who will spend little money, for example (Goss, 1993). At the same time, surprisingly detailed information gathered by covert surveillance cameras is fed back into the pool of retail and market research data, to help further refine the design and control of space.[4]

The same spatial control can be accomplished and supported by "themeing," which when successful, applies strong narratives to spaces while eliminating undesirable or conflicting images, ideas, or experiences. Themes themselves—preexisting and well-understood narratives—can help control these spaces by drawing in and confirming the identities of the desired customers. Themed space carefully coordinates design elements, from the shape of open areas and the forms of buildings, to paint, lighting, sound, signs, and sometimes costume, all referring to a cultural story. In addition to creating an attraction, the point of themeing is to achieve as much experiential coherence as possible, even if the theme itself is one of heterogeneity, carnival, or even chaos. So Universal CityWalk's theme is "city," a collage and repackaging of pieces of Los Angeles's mass cultural image, occasionally even including references to grit and danger. This compressed, selected Hollywood gives eating, shopping, and people-watching a charge; they become theatrical experiences, performances in themselves (Goss, 1996; cf. Gottdeiner, 1997). Again, media companies have a long headstart in building themed space; they have spent decades specializing in narratives and the icons that compress narratives. Indeed, they own outright huge banks of these images and stories.

At the heart of the location-based entertainment projects is this paradox: within the context of themed space, they aim to reproduce a sense of authentic space, and this means evoking the diversity and unpredictability of the older city using carefully calibrated recipes. The projects aim to reproduce a life and liveliness that looks like the older commercial town centre, but in order to do this profitably, in order to turn out the right sort of crowd, they must control mixing and reduce real unpredictability. The appeal of Gameworks, Disney Stores, Rain-forest Cafes, and ESPN Zones for mall developers is not just the increased rents and sales per square foot. It is that, when successful, these venues create visible sociability—noise, movement, and the dense presence of people—inside and outside their doors. Whether they are installed in regional specialty malls, shoe-horned into redeveloped town centres, or added to the mix of mega-destinations, like Orlando and Las Vegas, developers and investors hope that by combining upholstered lounges, Internet cafes, movie theatres, and restaurants with interactive media content, location-based entertainment can pull in the "destination audience." These are people, 25 years and older, especially couples, "looking for an evening that will combine food, going to a Virtual World, a nightclub, a movie" (Zoltak, 1996a). Destination audiences can be persuaded to open their wallets at more than one attraction, and crowds, the sense of the mixed and heterogeneous city, are part of the attraction. Heavy mall traffic itself, like the crowd at the county fair or theme park, can loosen restraints on spending and overcome the sameness of the suburbs and the dispersal of the automotive city. The recipe results in small and large spaces that are close relatives of the theme park's ideal city, a closed city free from the uncertainty, poverty, and potential crime of the real streets (Goss, 1996). . . .

◆ *Materializing Media*

The most important example of themeing is, of course, the focus on media product as the central story of the retail space. Like the use of high-impact film and game technologies, the integration of Hollywood and television

narratives aims to push new energy into a familiar experience and to bring people out. By all accounts the Walt Disney Company has been most far-sighted and aggressive in finding endless three-dimensional and spatial forms for its media products. As is well known, Disney was the first to really undertake (and understand the possibilities of) the meshing of mass media content, merchandising, and promotion in his 1950s theme park. At Disneyland, films and animated cartoons became three-dimensional in the landscape. Robots and rides were media images that customers could touch, just as the park's live performances, parades, and theatre could touch customers. . . .

Making media content three-dimensional and locating it in space has a variety of uses for the entertainment conglomerates. Entertainment merchandise stores—Disney has 700 worldwide and more than 450 in the United States—have become widely familiar in the last decade. They supplement the all-important licensed merchandise sales tied to box office hits (White, 1997).[5] In these stores, media content in the form of merchandise is a profit stream in its own right, contributing enormously to the bottom lines of the licensing and "creative content" divisions, which, in the case of Disney, has contributed more than a third of annual gross revenue in recent years. Just as important, themed merchandise in the form of clothing, books, toys, and collectible knick-knacks gives an added promotional boost to the latest film, television show, or video game. . . .

The stores offer visitors a kind of journey through its world of brand-name concepts; the very concept of Disney (and the power of conglomerate media ownership) is celebrated through products and product histories. These spaces are dedicated to corporate identification. As one Warner's executive put it, the stores create "a presence in the community"—and by this he meant a marketing presence—the more effective because it is so much fun.[6]

Location-based entertainment projects have multiple and overlapping uses for media conglomerates: they help cross-promote media content, intensifying profits and adding new profit streams, even if these streams may also flood the market. They "bomb the brand" and act as walk-through public relations; they provide a place to test new products and gather information about the customers. But beyond this, material-ized mass media content paradoxically creates a sense of the local. As the most familiar cultural material of all, transna-tional media content (originating largely in the United States) not only serves to give spaces stories, it adds in a powerful sense of history, a sense of a shared past that links the family past to the shared social past. And its ability to pull familiar media con-tent into collective space helps spaces com-municate authenticity—an all too fragile commodity in standardized, controlled, and centrally designed spaces.

Media content in collective space is also helping to create new commodities. The feeling of the authentic, the connected, and the local is extraordinarily useful in leading the way into underexplored markets. The Walt Disney Company's new chain of branded children's centres, Club Disney, pro-vides an excellent example of how the mar-keter's exploration of the social importance of space can help uncover a new set of profit nodes. The Club Disney chain represents the absorption of an older world of children's cheap amusements into a standardized con-glomerate project, and its adaptation to broad, unmet social needs. On the one hand, Club Disney is a small-scale spin-off of the theme park concept, marketed to con-sumers who might not be able to afford the time and money for an Orlando or Anaheim holiday. On the other, Club Disney is a canny assessment of the shortage, indeed, the crisis of safe recreational space and activities for American children.

The old kiddy land and its successor, the family entertainment centre, were often modest family businesses or small fran-chises, featuring a mix of miniature golf courses, games arcades and redemption games, a playground, a snack bar, a go-kart track, and perhaps some small carnival rides. In the last decade, fun parks have been absorbed into national companies; more recently they are being pulled into (or displaced by) much more elaborate chains of pay-to-enter indoor playgrounds.[7] The Discovery Zone franchise, which aims at families with small children in a resident market, is the best-known intermediate development. Founded in 1989 by a Missouri gymnastics coach "who figured harried parents—particularly on rainy days—would happily pay for a clean, safe, indoor play area filled with games, mazes, and climbing areas" (Gubernick, 1996: 66; Miller, 1993), Discovery Zone sells safety and insulation from tough playgrounds and dangerous streets, a real appeal in many places. "We offer a safe secure environ-ment," said Chuck Gelman, vice president of marketing for Discovery Zone. "Let's face it, you can't go to an outdoor play-ground in a lot of areas. It's a treat for the kids, and it's a hell of a value. Think about the price of mom taking her three kids to the movie" (quoted in Miller, 1993: 19). Discovery Zone admissions are about US$6-7 per child, and adults go free.

In the late 1990s, Discovery Zone and its competitors [branched] out, seeking sites near anchor stores in regional malls, for example, and offering a new product. The pay-to-play-grounds are doubling as com-mercial baby-sitting centres for parents in need of time to shop. There is some mass media content in these zones. Movies, videos, computers, and computer games are available to divert the children, and Discov-ery Zone claims it is looking ahead to offer educational and social services as "music, dance, and computer classes at the centres; hosting parties for Christmas, Halloween, and other holidays; even sponsoring parent groups" (Davids, 1996: 20-1). Tests are under way to see if older children and pre-teens will use Discovery Zone centres at weekends. "We see ourselves in the future as a paid for community center," says Donna Moore, the company's president and chief executive (Davids, 1996). Again, these location-based products are designed to draw the right customers. Retail developers consider playgrounds, family entertainment centres, drop-off baby-sitting, and chain day care centres "desirable because they attract a coveted market," help these customers stay longer at the shopping centre, and can occupy large, difficult to lease spaces, such as former supermarkets (Phillips, 1995). Many of these chains are providing personal services once performed in the home, usually by women. These include help with homework, haircuts for children, frozen dinner selections, birthday cake ordering, dry-cleaning drop-off and pick-up, chauffeuring, and loans of car seats and pagers (Caminiti, 1993; *Advertising Age*, 1992).[8] Clearly, Discovery Zone and its competitors are showing that the potential for businesses to fill in the gaps in the sagging familial and social support systems is enormous, although their focus is on upper-income groups.

Discovery Zone had a partnership with Blockbuster Video in the early 1990s, and although this venture fell apart, it suggested the potential of tying in neighbourhood-level commercial space for children with branded mass media content. The Walt Disney Company, always alert to make connections between families, media, and merchandising, apparently watched Discovery Zone carefully. In 1997, Disney entered the children's recreation arena with its own ambitious prototype. Its first 24,500-square-foot Club Disney premiered in Thousand Oaks, California, in the spring of 1997 (O'Brien, 1996c; Martin, 1996). The Club contains "more than a dozen play areas in four intensively themed sections based on Disney characters." It is geared for "parental interaction with children ranging in age from infants to 10-year-olds," around such features as a mirror maze filled with stuffed Dalmatians, a "Goofy golf" course, gear to climb the walls, painting, and costumed play acting (Martin, 1996). The Club has differently gauged activity areas, ranging from active play, to creative play, to interactive play.

With its nearly universal name recognition and its middle-class, family-oriented brand identity, Disney profits wildly from parental anxieties about sex and violence in mass media content. With Club Disney, the company will also profit from parents' fear about public space. Fear, rather than real danger, is the emphasis here: so far, the Clubs are being built only in affluent suburbs. As usual, Disney is also offering added value, incorporating self-improvement, education, and new technology into its safe media spaces. Disney understands that parents can be efficiently reached if their children's recreation is themed "educational" and its clubs are themed to look much more rational than the traditional video arcade or go-kart park could ever hope to appear. Its centres will offer "multimedia and science workshops and parent-child art classes" (Rasulo, quoted in O'Brien, 1996c: 19).[9] The Clubs also feature "banks of computers for Internet surfing and CD-ROM game playing" connected to (and, doubtless, testing) Disney's growing multimedia and cyberspace products.

In addition to being educational, Club Disney is cast as therapeutic. Disney spokespersons assert that "Club Disney will set a new standard for family entertainment" (Rasulo, quoted in Martin, 1996: 2) as its interactive structure goes beyond parents watching kids jump in rooms full of plastic balls to "nurture the bond within families." Indeed, "children will learn and the bonding within family elements will be rewarding for all" (Rasulo, quoted in O'Brien, 1996c: 19). This mawkish public relations talk signals that the Disney touch adds value to time spent with the children, thus producing that much sought-after American commodity, quality time. . . .

Conclusions ◆

We have seen how energetically the entertainment space designers are moving beyond architecture and decoration to discover ways that desirable persons can be encouraged to enter and participate in products, undesirables kept out, and, generally, how every niche of space can be turned to promotional or marketing purposes. . . . The explosion of experimentation with the built environment is evidence that the mass media corporations are joining the suburb builders, urban redevelopers, and shopping mall magnates in sculpting the physical world we move about in and the social space we share with neighbours and fellow citizens.

If entertainment-retail projects were only monumental, like CityWalk, NikeTown, or 42nd Street, these reconstructions of space would still be evidence of a deep, continual reworking of experience. After all, in the past, monumental architecture has celebrated national identity, historical events, memories of suffering, narratives of loyalty, and sacrifice. Now the most striking architectural points of pilgrimage cultivate awe for the brand and the magic of belonging through the corporation. Like the old-fashioned monuments and memorials, they are sites where people connect with core cultural ideas and stories. But in these new spaces, the core cultural ideas are not only embodied by products, they *are* products. Citizens are collapsed into consumers, and loyalty is a technique that expands the bottom line. . . .

◆ Notes

1. Strategic thinking about the location of entertainment is nothing new, as the history of 42nd Street illustrates. There, between the end of the 19th century and the Great Depression, entertainment entrepreneurs helped create an extraordinary district that embodied American commercial culture's world dominance. Broadway was a space that promoted, tied in, and cross-promoted the plays, musicals, sheet music, celebrities, and films of the entertainment industries; it also was shaped into an extraordinarily liberated space for sexual minorities and sex workers of all kinds, and so both moved and marked the boundaries of respectability (see Agnew, 1991). On real estate forces creating Times Square, see Blackmar (1991) and Hammack (1991); on sexuality and space, see Chauncey (1991) and Senelick (1991).

2. The developers and promoters of the entertainment-retail projects rely heavily on financial and political help from state and local governments. As is well known, city governments, redevelopment authorities, planning commissions, state and local tax codes, tax abatements, and zoning ordinances all play an important role in smoothing the way for large-scale commercial real estate projects, and so they actively promote the high-consumption, and now retail-entertainment, redefinition of social space, as they have for less flamboyant real estate developers for decades. In California, current state law makes it much easier to issue public debt to build a shopping centre than to build a new school, a massive privileging of the interests of private speculation over the provision of public education, goods, and services (Lipsitz, 1998). As Thomas Hanchett (1966) has shown, since the late 1950s, vast tracts of today's hyper-consumption landscape have been built in part with public financing and public subsidies in the form of tax subsidies, and often at the expense of projects that would meet basic housing, schooling, and open space needs for a broad public.

3. For Disney, Internet-based cyber-entertainment will shortly join the ESPNs and Disney channels, increasing its in-home presence (Orwall, 1998).

4. Paco Underhill's research firm, Envirosell, has pioneered the research uses of video cameras in stores (Gladwell, 1996; Underhill, 1994).

5. Licensed merchandise sales now account for more of the profits from a blockbuster film than do box office ticket sales.

6. Similarly, NikeTown on 57th St., New York, was designed to be a "brand bomb," "the face of the brand," "to educate consumers about product design, research and sports in general," by "exploding Nike's image in the hottest retail district in the world" (Gragg, 1997: 84).

7. Family entertainment centres are divided into product for several different niches or special markets. They are hard to count, since their overlap with other amusement industries (like game arcades) is extensive, but they number in the thousands nationwide (O'Brien, 1997a).

8. On the commercialization of formerly domestic functions, cf. Hochschild (1997).

9. Jay Rasulo is vice president of Disney Regional Entertainment.

◆ References

Advertising Age (1992) "Extra Frills Pay Dividend for Child Centers," 63(30): 28-30.

Agnew, Jean Christophe (1991) "Times Square: Secularization and Sacralization," pp. 2-15 in William R. Taylor (ed.) *Inventing Times Square: Commerce and Culture at the Crossroads of the World*. New York: Russell Sage Foundation.

Arthur, Paul (1996) "In the Realm of the Senses: IMAX 3-D and the Myth of Total Cinema," *Film Comment* 322(1): 78-81.

Berman, Marshall (1995) "Signs Square: Times Square," *Village Voice* 18 July: 23-6.

Blackmar, Elizabeth (1991) "Uptown Real Estate and the Creation of Times Square," pp. 51-65 in William R. Taylor (ed.) *Inventing Times Square: Commerce and Culture at the Crossroads of the World*. New York: Russell Sage Foundation.

Boyer, M. Christine (1991) "Cities for Sale: Merchandising History at South Street Seaport," pp. 181-204 in Michael Sorkin (ed.) *Variations on a Theme Park: The New American City and the End of Public Space*. New York: Hill and Wang.

Caminiti, Susan (1993) "Kindercare Learning Centers: New Lessons in Company Service," *Fortune* 128(6): 79-80.

Chauncey, George, Jr. (1991) "The Policed: Gay Men's Strategies of Everyday Resistance," pp. 315-28 in William R. Taylor (ed.) *Inventing Times Square: Commerce and Culture at the Crossroads of the World*. New York: Russell Sage Foundation.

Cuneo, Alice Z. (1997) "Marketers Drawn to In-Store Entertainment: Polaroid Latest Using Video to Reach Consumers While They're Shopping," *Advertising Age* 28 April: 20.

Davids, Meryl (1996) "Tunnel Vision," *Chief Executive* 116 (September): 20-1.

Gladwell, Malcolm (1996) "The Science of Shopping," *The New Yorker* 4 November: 66-75.

Goldberg, Carey (1997) "Game Centers Lure Computer Loners to High-Tech Team Activities," *New York Times* (California edition) 4 August: A7.

Goss, Jon (1993) "The 'Magic of the Mall': An Analysis of Form, Function and Meaning in the Contemporary Retail Built Environment," *Annals of the Association of American Geographers* 83(1): 18-47.

Goss, Jon (1996) "Disquiet on the Waterfront: Reflections on Nostalgia and Utopia in the Urban Archetypes of the Festival Marketplaces," *Urban Geography* 17(3): 221-47.

Gottdeiner, Mark (1997) *The Themeing of America: Dreams, Visions, and Commercial Space*. Boulder, CO: Westview.

Gragg, Randy (1997) "Domination by Design," *Metropolis* June: 62-7, 83-5.

Grover, Ron (1994) "Where Buying a Ticket Puts You Right in the Action," *Business Week* 3361(7 March): 73-6.

Gubernick, Lisa (1996) "Disaster Zone?" *Forbes* 157(12): 66-75.

Hammack, David C. (1991) "Developing for Commercial Culture," pp. 36-50 in William R. Taylor (ed.) *Inventing Times Square: Commerce and Culture at the Crossroads of the World*. New York: Russell Sage Foundation.

Hanchett, Thomas W. (1966) "U.S. Tax Policy and the Shopping Center Booms of the 1950s and 1960s," *American Historical Review* October: 1082-110.

Hannigan, John (1998) *Fantasy City: Pleasure and Profit in the Postmodern Metropolis*. London and New York: Routledge.

Hartnett, Michael (1993) "Fun and Games," *Stores* 75(10): 62-6.

Herman, Edward S. and Robert W. McChesney (1997) *The Global Media: The New Missionaries of Corporate Capitalism*. London and Washington, DC: Cassell.

Hochschild, Arlie Russell (1997) *The Time Bind: When Work Becomes Home and Home Becomes Work*. New York: Metropolitan Books.

Johnson, David (1995) "Iwerks Entertainment," *TCI* 29(1): 22-3.

Katayama, O. (1994) "The Aim of the Game," *Look Japan* July: 18-19.

Levine, Joshua (1997) "Zap-Proof Advertising," *Forbes* 22 September: 146-50.

Lipsitz, George (1998) "Consumer Spending as State Project: Yesterday's Solutions and Today's Problems," pp. 127-47 in Susan Strasser, Charles McGovern, and Matthias Judt (eds.) *Getting and Spending: European and American Consumer Societies in the Twentieth Century*. Cambridge and New York: Cambridge University Press.

Martin, Richard (1996) "Disney Returns to Foodservice [*sic*] with its Club Disney Prototype," *Nation's Restaurant News* 30(47): 1, 2, 81.

Miller, Cyndee (1993) "'Health Clubs' for Kids Target Guilty Parents," *Marketing News* 27(18): 1, 19.

O'Brien, Tim (1994a) "MCA Announces Plans for Japan Studio Attraction," *Amusement Business* 17-23 January: 28.

O'Brien, Tim (1994b) "Sega's New Joypolis Expands on High-Tech Theme Park Concept," *Amusement Business* 1-7 August: 3, 54.

O'Brien, Tim (1996b) "SegaWorld Expects 1.7 Mil First-Year Attendance," *Amusement Business* 16-22 September: 1, 34.

O'Brien, Tim (1996c) "Club Disney Debuts Soon," *Amusement Business* 18-24 November: 19.

O'Brien, Tim (1997a) "IAFEC Survey Results: Growth in 1996 Slowed Some, But FECs Still Thriving," *Amusement Business* 3 February: 19, 22.

O'Brien, Tim (1997b) "City of Battle Creek to Build Family Entertainment Mall," *Amusement Business* 7 April: 1, 18.

Orwall, Bruce (1998) "Disney Cuts Costs, Plans Growth in Cyberspace," *Wall Street Journal* (national edition) 24 September: B-1.

Pacelle, Mitchell (1997) "Simon DeBartolo Group to Invite Wide Variety of Firms into Malls," *Wall Street Journal* 29 August: B-3.

Phillips, Patrick (1995) "Merging Entertainment and Retail," *Economic Development Review* 13(2): 13-15 (online version, *Abstracts of Business Information*, online pages 1-3).

Pulley, Brett (1995) "Disney's Deal: A Mix of Glamour and Hardball Won Disney a Piece of 42nd Street," *New York Times* 29 July: A1, A9.

Roman, Monica and Greg Evans (1996) "Mouse in Manhattan: Beauty or Beast?" *Variety* 1-14 July: 1, 50.

Rutheiser, Charles (1996) *Imagineering Atlanta: The Politics of Place in the City of Dreams*. London: Verso.

Schiller, Herbert I. (1989) *Culture Inc.: The Corporate Takeover of Public Expression*. New York and Oxford, UK: Oxford University Press.

Senelick, Laurence (1991) "Private Parts in Public Places," pp. 329-55 in William R. Taylor (ed.) *Inventing Times Square: Commerce and Culture at the Crossroads of the World*. New York: Russell Sage Foundation.

Smith, Neil (1996) *The New Urban Frontier: Gentrification and the Revanchist City*. New York and London: Routledge.

Sorkin, Michael (ed.) (1991) *Variations on a Theme Park: The New American City and the End of Public Space*. New York: Hill and Wang.

Straight, Susan (1997) "Safe Indoors," *Hungry Mind Review* 41(Spring): 9, 50.

The Architectural Review (1997) "NikeTown USA," 201(1203): 95.

The Economist (1994) "Theme Parks: Feeling the Future," 330(7851): 74-9.

Underhill, Paco (1994) "Kids in Stores," *American Demographics* June: 23-6.

Waddell, Ray (1996) "Austin Backing Multi-Million Dollar FEC; LMI Negotiating Mgmt. Deal," *Amusement Business* 18 November: 24.

Wall Street Journal (western edition) (1996) "Cineplex Odeon New Division," 2 May: B4.

White, George (1997) "New Theme Player," *Los Angeles Times* 16 September: D-1, D-20.

Zoltak, James (1996a) "Destination-Locations Prime Spots for Virtual World Attractions," *Amusement Business* 8-14 January: 24.

Zoltak, James (1996c) "First Sega City Playdium Under Way Near Toronto," *Amusement Business* 24-30 June: 31-2.

17

KIDS FOR SALE

Corporate Culture and the
Challenge of Public Schooling

◆ Henry A. Giroux

◆ *Commercialization in Schools*

Corporate culture can be seen not only in the placement of public schools in the control of corporate contractors. It is also visible in the growing commercialization of school space and curricula. Strapped for money, many public schools have had to lease out space in their hallways, buses, rest rooms, monthly lunch menus, and school cafeterias, transforming such spaces into glittering billboards for the highest corporate bidder.[1] School notices, classroom displays, and student artwork have been replaced by advertisements for Coca-Cola, Pepsi, Nike, Hollywood films, and a litany of other products. Invaded by candy manufacturers, breakfast cereal makers, sneaker companies, and fast food chains, schools increasingly offer the not-so-subtle message to students that everything is for sale including student identities, desires, and values. Seduced by the lure of free

NOTE: From *Stealing Innocence: Youth, Corporate Power, and the Politics of Culture*, by Henry A. Giroux, 2000, New York: Palgrave. Copyright © 2000 by Henry A. Giroux. Reprinted by permission of Macmillan, Ltd.

equipment and money, schools all too readily make the transition from advertising to offering commercial merchandise in the form of curricula materials designed to build brand loyalty and markets among a captive public school audience. Although schools may reap small financial benefit from such school-business transactions, the real profits go to the corporations that spend millions on advertising to reach a market of an estimated 43 million children in school "with spending power of over $108 billion per year and the power to influence parental spending."[2]

The commercial logic that fuels this market-based reform movement is also evident in the way in which corporate culture targets schools not simply as investments for substantial profits but also as training grounds for educating students to define themselves as consumer rather than as multifaceted social actors. As schools struggle to raise money for texts, curricula, and extracurricular activities, they engage in partnerships with businesses that are all too willing to provide free curriculum packages; as in the case of companies such as Channel One that provide each school with $50,000 in "free" electronic equipment, including VCRs, televisions, and satellite dishes, on the condition that the schools agree to broadcast a ten-minute program of current events and news material along with two minutes of commercials.[3] A number of companies want to capitalize on cash-poor schools in order to gain a foothold to promote learning as a way to create "consumers in training." For example, ZapMe, a Silicon Valley company, "gives schools free personal computers and Internet access in exchange for the right to display a constant stream of on-screen advertisements. Participating schools must also promise that the system will be in use for at least four hours per school day."[4]

The marriage of commercialism and education often takes place in schools with too few resources to critically monitor how learning is structured or to recognize the sleight-of-hand that appears to be a generous offer on the part of corporations. A few examples will suffice. In a recent cover story, *Business Week* magazine reported on the adoption of a McDonald's-sponsored curriculum package by the Pembroke Lakes elementary school in Broward County, Florida. Commenting on what one ten-year-old learned from the curricula, *Business Week* claimed that "Travis Licate recently learned how to design a McDonald's restaurant, how a McDonald's works, and how to apply and interview for a job at McDonald's thanks to [the] seven-week company-sponsored class intended to teach kids about the work world."[5] When Travis was asked if the curriculum was worthwhile, he responded: "If you want to work in a McDonald's when you grow up, you already know what to do. . . . Also, McDonald's is better than Burger King."[6] According to the Center for Commercial-Free Public Education, Exxon developed a curriculum that teaches young students that the Valdez oil spill was an example of environmental protection. The center also cites a Nike-sponsored curriculum that teaches students to learn how a Nike shoe is created but fails to address "the sweatshop portion of the manufacturing process."[7] McGraw-Hill recently published an elementary-school math textbook full of advertisements for products such as Nike, Gatorade, and Sony PlayStations. Another company offers a math exercise book that "purports to teach third-graders math by having them count Tootsie Rolls."[8]

. . . Many school systems not only accept corporate-sponsored curricula, they also lease out space in their hallways, on their buses, and even on book covers. Cover Concepts Marketing Services, Inc., for example, provides schools with free book covers strategically designed to promote brand-name products that include Nike, Gitano, FootLocker, Starburst, Nestle, and Pepsi. The covers are distributed to over 8,000 public schools and reach an audience of over 6 million high school, junior high, and elementary school students.[9] In Colorado Springs, Colorado, Palmer High

School allows Burger King and Sprite to advertise on the sides of its school buses. In Salt Lake City, Youthtalk Advertising Agency places acrylic-faced advertising billboards in school rest rooms and cafeterias. It is estimated by the company that over "80,000 students are exposed to the ads while standing at urinals and sitting in toilet stalls."[10]

A number of public and private schools are also allowing corporations to harness students as captive audiences for market research during the school day. Trading student time for industry resources, many schools forge partnerships with corporations in which students become the objects of market-based group research. Corporations give the schools money, equipment, or curricula for the right to use students to take taste tests, experiment with different products, or answer opinion polls in which they are asked questions that range from "where they got their news [to] what television shows they like."[11] Some educators eager to justify such blatant acts of commercialism argue that these practices constitute a genuine learning experience for students; in doing so they often appear to be merely echoing the words of research consultants who claim that such market-based approaches are actually empowering for kids. For example, Martha Marie Pooler, the principal of Our Lady of Assumption elementary school in Lynnfield, Massachusetts, agreed to accept $600 for her school in exchange for a corporation using students in a cereal taste test. She justified this type of corporate intrusion by claiming that the test had educational benefits in that it was similar "to conducting a science-class experiment."[12] ... The National Association of State Boards of Education recently argued that schools that offer captive audiences of children in classrooms as fodder for commercial profit are engaging in practices that constitute both an act of "exploitation and a violation of the public trust."[13] Such violations of the public trust present a major challenge to those educators, parents, and concerned

citizens who want to protect children from corporate intrusion into their lives.

Schools are being transformed into commercial rather than public spheres as students become subject to the whims and practices of marketers whose agenda has nothing to do with critical learning and a great deal to do with restructuring civic life in the image of market culture.[14] Civic courage—upholding the most basic noncommercial principles of democracy—as a defining principle of society is devalued as corporate power transforms school knowledge so that students are taught to recognize brand names or learn the appropriate attitudes for future work in low-skilled, low-paying jobs. They are no longer taught how to connect the meaning of work to the imperatives of a strong democracy. What links Channel One, Nike, Pepsi, the Campbell Soup Company, the McDonald Corporation, and a host of others is that they substitute corporate propaganda for real learning, upset the requisite balance between the public and the private, and in doing so treat schools like any other business.

Underlying the attempt to redefine the meaning and purpose of schooling as part of a market economy rather than a fundamental feature of substantive democracy is a model of society in which "consumer accountability [is] mediated by a relationship with an educational market [rather than] a democratic accountability mediated by a relationship with the whole community of citizens."[15] Most disturbing about the market approach to schooling is that it contains no special consideration for the vocabulary of ethics and values. British educator Gerald Grace insightfully argues that when public education becomes a venue for making a profit, delivering a product, or constructing consuming subjects, education reneges on its responsibilities for creating a democracy of citizens by shifting its focus to producing a democracy of consumers.[16]

Growing up corporate has become a way of life for American youth. This is evident as corporate mergers consolidate control of assets and markets, particularly as they extend their influence over the media and its management of public opinion. But it is also apparent in the accelerated commercialism in all aspects of everyday life, including the "commercialization of public schools, the renaming of public streets for commercial sponsors, Janis Joplin's Mercedes pitch, restroom advertising, and [even the marketing] of an official commercial bottled water for a papal visit."[17] Although it is largely recognized that market culture exercises a powerful educational role in mobilizing desires and shaping identities, it still comes as a shock when an increasing number of pollsters report that young people, when asked to provide a definition for democracy, answered by referring to "the freedom to buy and consume whatever they wish, without government restriction."[18] . . .

As market culture permeates the social order, it threatens to diminish the tension between market values and democratic values, such as justice; freedom; equality; respect for children; and the rights of citizens as equal, free human beings. Without such values, children are relegated to the role of economic calculating machines, and the growing disregard for public life that appears to be gaining ground in the United States is left unchecked. . . .

Educational critic Alex Molnar rightfully cautions educators that the market does not provide "guidance on matters of justice and fairness that are at the heart of a democratic civil society."[19] The power of corporate culture, when left to its own devices, respects few boundaries and even fewer basic social needs, such as the need for uncontaminated food, decent health care, and safe forms of transportation. This was made clear, for example, in recent revelations about the failure of tobacco companies to reveal evidence about the addictive nature of nicotine. In direct violation of broader health considerations, these corporations effectively promoted the addiction of young smokers to increase sales and profits. Moreover, as multinational corporations increase their control over the circulation of information in the media, little is mentioned about how they undermine the principles of justice and freedom that should be at the center of our most vital civic institutions. Developing a vocabulary that affirms non-market values such as love, trust, and compassion is particularly important for the public schools, whose function, in part, is to teach students about the importance of critical dialogue, debate, and decision making in a participatory democracy.

One recent incident at a public school in Evans, Georgia, provides an example of how corporate culture actually can be used to punish students who challenge the corporate approach to learning. Greenbrier High School decided to participate in an Education Day as part of a larger district-wide contest sponsored by Coca-Cola executives. Each school that entered the contest sponsored rallies, heard speeches from Coke executives, analyzed the sugar content of Coke in chemistry classes, and gathered for "an aerial photograph of the student's bodies dressed in red and white and forming the word 'coke.' The reward for winning the district-wide contest—five hundred dollars."[20] Two students decided to disrupt the photo shoot by removing their shirts to reveal Pepsi logos. Both students were suspended on the grounds that they were rude. What students learned as a result is that the individual right to dissent, to freely express their opinions and ideas, and to challenge authority, when addressed within the context of commercial culture, is a punishable offense. Choice in this context is about choosing the right soft drink, not about the right to question whether schools should be turned into advertising billboards for corporate interests.

Notes ◆

1. Consumer Union Education Services, *Captive Kids: A Report on Commercial Pressures on Kids at Schools* (Yonkers, NY: Consumer Union Education Services, 1998).

2. Phyllis Sides. "Captive Kids: Teaching Students to Be Consumers," in *Selling Out Our Schools: Vouchers, Markets, and the Future of Public Education* (Milwaukee: Rethinking Schools Publication, 1996), p. 36.

3. For an extensive analysis of Channel One, see Henry A. Giroux, *Disturbing Pleasures: Learning Popular Culture* (New York: Routledge, 1994), esp. chap. 3, pp. 47-67.

4. Steven Manning. "Classrooms for Sale," *New York Times,* March 4, 1999, p. A27; see also Steven Manning "Zapped," *The Nation*, September 27, 1999, p. 9.

5. Cover story. "This Lesson Is Brought to You By," *Business Week*, June 30, 1997, p. 69.

6. Ibid.

7. Cited in Editors, "Reading, Writing . . . and Purchasing," *Educational Leadership* 56:2 (1998), p. 16.

8. Manning, "Classrooms for Sale," p. A27.

9. Consumer Union, *Captive Kids*, p. 9.

10. Ibid., p. 26.

11. Mary B. W. Tabor, "School Profit From Offering Pupils for Market Research," *New York Times*, April 5, 1999, pp. A1, A16.

12. Ibid., p. A16.

13. Tabor, "Schools Profit From Offering Pupils for Market Research," p. A16.

14. This issue is taken up in great detail in Alex Molnar, *Giving Kids the Business* (Boulder, CO: Westview, 1996). For a more general analysis of the relationship between corporate culture and schooling, see Joe Kincheloe and Shirley Steinberg, eds., *Kinder Culture: The Corporate Construction of Childhood* (Boulder, CO: Westview, 1997).

15. Gerald Grace, "Politics, Markets, and Democratic Schools: On the Transformation of School Leadership," in A. H. Halsey, Hugh Lauder, Phillip Brown, and Amy Stuart Wells, eds., *Education: Culture, Economy, Society* (New York: Oxford, 1997), p. 314.

16. Ibid., p. 315.

17. R. George Wright, *Selling Words: Free Speech in a Commercial Culture* (New York: New York University Press, 1997), p. 181.

18. Ibid., p. 182.

19. Molnar, *Giving Kids the Business*, p. 17.

20. This issue is explored in Ken Saltman, "Collateral Damage: Public School Privatization and the Threat to Democracy," Ph.D. diss., Pennsylvania State University, May 1999, p. 92.

18

THE GREATEST STORY EVER SOLD

Marketing and the O. J. Simpson Trial

◆ George Lipsitz

When you have this kind of public awareness and preconditioning, the long-term cash-in has got to be enormous.

—Jack Myers, President, Myers Communications[1]

The public hates itself for its fascination with O. J. Simpson.

—David Bartlett, President, Radio-Television
News Directors Association[2]

In publicizing the O. J. Simpson case, media conglomerates publicized themselves and the world in which they work. The "salability" of this story stemmed from its smooth fit with the long history of sales that

NOTE: From *Birth of a Nation'hood: Gaze, Script, and Spectacle in the O. J. Simpson Case*, edited by Toni Morrison and Claudia Brodsky Lacour, 1987, New York: Pantheon. Copyright © 1997 by Toni Morrison and Claudia Brodsky Lacour. Used by permission of Pantheon Books, a division of Random House, Inc.

preceded it—sales of individual celebrity images, cross-marketing campaigns aimed at connecting fame to commercial endorsements, and the general dramatization of wealth and material goods that forms the subtext of so many television commercials, Hollywood films, and even news broadcasts. The O. J. Simpson case was about an entertainment figure, but it also was entertainment. The reach and scope of media interest in the trial bears a close relation to the financial benefits that media outlets derived from selling the kind of story that fits neatly into their preexisting categories. The Simpson story made huge amounts of money for cable and broadcast television networks, for tabloid newspapers and magazines, and for the merchandisers whose videotapes and books have only just begun to reach the market. But beyond its utility as a means for capital accumulation, the Simpson trial also enables us to ask and answer questions about the power of publicity, the meaning of money, and the interpenetration of public and private concerns in our culture. Why did this story take on the proportions that it did? What were its uses and effects? What can we say about a society that spends so much of its time and resources on a story like this one?

Cultural theorist Arthur Kroker claims that nothing happens in our society unless it happens on television. Of course we know that this is not quite correct, that one of the problems with television programs is that they do so little to reflect the realities that people confront every day. Kroker's overstatement is perhaps a deliberate provocation designed to get our attention, to emphasize the central role played by commercial culture in framing public events and private concerns. But even if Kroker's formulation is flawed, the obverse of it is certainly true: If something happens over and over again on television, then it certainly "happens" to all of us. Television played the key role in the Simpson case in many ways. The trial was telecast live, and its details were aired endlessly on news and entertainment programs. The case opened up whole new television markets with gavel-to-gavel coverage on cable and broadcast outlets. It helped spur the development of new programs and the creation of new celebrities through specialized discussions on cable channels. It provided a constant frame of reference for late-night comedians, talk shows, and news features, and even served as the source of a new line of Halloween masks featuring the case's central "characters."

Simpson's status as an already-famous celebrity gave his case a particularly significant meaning to television programming not just because he has appeared often in the medium as an athlete, broadcaster, film star, and spokesperson famous for his commercial endorsements but rather his prominence in diverse areas of entertainment gave him the kind of visibility that television loves to recycle and repackage. His segueing from athletics to entertainment to news simply augmented that capacity, or rather, to be more precise, brought the news where news directors, advertisers, and public relations firms deeply desire it to be—squarely within the realm of entertainment. Commercial television in the United States has long rested on intertextual engagement with other media—television presents motion pictures, sporting events, and concerts; it mixes celebrities from different realms of endeavor on talk and game shows; it engages in relentless cross-programming, plugging purchases of other kinds of entertainment by placing television at the nexus of publishing, broadcasting, filmmaking, music recording, and shopping. Television stars make films that enable them to appear on talk shows to prepare audiences for their best-selling books, which give them name recognition valuable for product endorsements, etc. As Daniel Czitrom noted years ago, nearly everything on television is an advertisement for some form of entertainment or product available in another medium; the "infomercial" or program-length commercial that dominates late-night programming on cable is simply a refinement of what the medium does more crudely elsewhere.

The Simpson trial became a story that was easy to sell, in part, because it seemed to replicate so perfectly the world of commercial television and its generic conventions. The athlete/actor/celebrity defendant charged with murder could have come out of *Murder, She Wrote* or *Columbo* while the details about his residence and vehicles might fit easily into segments of *Dallas, Dynasty*, or *Life Styles of the Rich and Famous*. For experienced television viewers, courtroom confrontations enacted half-remembered episodes of L.A. *Law, Perry Mason*, and *Quincy*, while the history of unheeded claims of spousal abuse evoked the concerns and conflicts often aired in the movie-of-the-week. The search for justice by grieving relatives and the short, glamorous lives of the victims sparked associations with daily soap operas or weekly serial dramas, Indeed, one source of public dissatisfaction with the trial, with its participants and its outcome, seems to stem from the failure of the trial to fit the frame that television established for it, to come to a "happy ending" in the form of an unambiguous verdict of guilty—which certainly would have been the case had this been simply a television melodrama. But instead of following the clearly defined character roles and unambiguous narrative closures offered by television programs, the trial and its participants instead reflected the ambiguities, uncertainties, and contradictions of everyday life and its complex social relations, giving the entire enterprise the look of being out of control in comparison to the other stories that television tells and sells.

From start to finish, the O. J. Simpson story demonstrated an eerie engagement with, and an unusual affinity for, the money-making mechanisms within commercial culture.

If it was something less than the trial of the century in terms of legal significance, it was certainly the "sale" of the century in terms of its ability to bring together the various apparatuses of advertising, publicity, spectator sports, motion pictures, television, and marketing into a unified totality generating money-making opportunities at every turn. A major Los Angeles radio station gave defense witness Brian "Kato" Kaelin his own talk show because of the trial. One outside "expert" frequently employed by television networks during the trial, attorney Gerry Spence, parlayed his guest commentaries on the Simpson case on a variety of programs into his own televised talk show on CNBC. The William Morris Agency won a hotly contested battle to serve as theatrical and public relations representative for lead prosecutor Marcia Clark.[3] Edward Billet Productions purportedly offered Judge Lance Ito $1 million to star in a new version of the television program *The People's Court*.[4] Industry experts confided to *Advertising Age* reporters that "Simpson-related marketing could produce as much as $1 billion in media and merchandising sales." During the trial, Simpson had his lawyers take out patent protection for his full name as well as for his nicknames "O. J." and "The Juice," and had them file more than fifty lawsuits against merchandisers marketing items bearing his name. In addition, Simpson negotiated deals for a video, a book, pay-per-view interviews, and other projects that might eventually net as much as $18 million.[5]

During the trial, jurors were dismissed for allegedly keeping notes designed to aid them in writing books about their experiences. One dismissed juror published a book that came out before the trial ended. After the verdict, some jurors asked television producers and magazine editors for as much as $100,000 for interviews; one agreed to pose nude for *Playboy*.[6] Prosecutor Christopher Darden and chief defense lawyer Robert Shapiro produced highly publicized and broadly marketed books that appeared some six months after the trial. In his book, Darden accused a member of Simpson's defense team of drafting a book on a laptop computer even while the trial was taking place. Journalist Brent Staples speculated in the *New York Times* that Shapiro hired Alan Dershowitz as part of the defense team not for his potential contributions to the actual case but mainly to prevent Dershowitz from serving as a television analyst and making comments that might embarrass Shapiro.[7] Proof of Mark Fuhrman's perjury did not emerge through vigorous cross-examination but rather from remarks he made to an aspiring screenwriter in the hope that he could have his real and imagined deeds as a member of the Los Angeles Police Department immortalized and publicized in a Hollywood film.[8]

The story of O. J. Simpson on trial sold well. CNN (the Cable News Network) presented 631 hours of direct televised coverage of the Simpson trial, attracting an average of 2.2 million viewers at any given time. This content increased the channel's ratings and revenues by close to fifty percent.[9] On the day of the verdict, an unusually large number of daytime viewers—representing forty-two percent of the nation's television homes and more than ninety percent of the sets actually in use—were tuned to channels covering the case. For the entire week leading up to the verdict, Simpson programming gave CNN fourteen of the fifteen most-watched basic cable programs. Court TV, available in only about twenty-four million homes, nonetheless accounted for three of the most-watched shows on cable during the fall 1995 ratings period.[10] Industry officials attributed much of cable television's collective twenty-five percent jump in ratings between 1994 and 1995 to the Simpson case.[11] Tabloid television shows featuring the Simpson story registered dramatic gains as well. During the week when the verdict was announced, *Entertainment Tonight* secured an audience that was thirty-nine percent larger than the previous week's. *Inside Edition* increased its viewership by twenty-four percent over the same time period the previous year, while *American Journal* attracted double its average audience for that season.[12]

Mass circulation magazines devoted fifty-four cover stories to the Simpson case during the last half of 1994, and ninety cover stories to it during 1995—almost three times the attention they gave to their second favorite cover story personality, television talk-show host Oprah Winfrey.[13] More than one million Internet users visited CNN's O. J. Simpson Web site in the first six hours after the trial verdict, an average of 3,800 per minute.[14] A live interview with O. J. Simpson in January 1996 enabled Black Entertainment Television (BET) to reach three million households and secure the highest ratings in the channel's sixteen-year history, easily surpassing the previous high of 1.2 million households, much less its average viewership of 300,000 homes in prime time. The network did not pay Simpson for this interview as he initially requested, but they did allow him to purchase time before and after the program to advertise his mail-order video available for purchase at $29.95 apiece.[15]

Stories about the O. J. Simpson trial enjoyed a powerful presence in the market, in part because they could draw on the main themes that organize television discourse in the United States: the primacy of products as the center of social life, the stimulation and management of appetites, and alarm about the family in jeopardy. A story linking any two of these categories will always make the news (i.e., a news event that resembles a popular motion picture—"a real-life *Home Alone* right here in your town," the existence of a new product that can affect your appetite for another product—"Will a new exercise machine help you quit smoking?" "Are you eating fat-free foods and still gaining weight? Find out why at eleven."). A story that links all three is even better—i.e., "Could your child be receiving sexually explicit images on the Internet?" One reason why the O. J. Simpson trial became so prominent in the media is because it contained all these elements necessary for televisual representation: it was a story about products, appetites, and the family in jeopardy.

O. J. Simpson's identity immediately raises associations with products. Over the years, he has done commercials as a spokesperson for Hertz Rent A Car, Chevrolet, Wilson Sporting Goods, and Royal Crown Cola. He has been visible as a commodity himself, as a football player, as an announcer for ABC television's *Monday Night Football* games, as an actor in motion pictures, including the *Naked Gun* series, as a motivational speaker at corporate events, and as a personality on exercise videos. In addition, he has become wealthy from these endeavors and lives a visibly affluent life. Each part of his career has served as a form of advertising for the other parts: his fame as a football player gave him an edge as an actor; his visibility as both an actor and athlete made him more desirable for commercial endorsements. His sources of fame are mutually reinforcing, and this history makes him quite desirable as the object of news or feature stories on television. Audiences will recognize him; their attention will translate into future commodity purchases. O. J. replicates the kinds of cross-marketing fundamental to television's relationship to other media. . . .

Media coverage of the Simpson trial drew upon and reinforced the connection between Simpson and commodities. Coincidentally, the key pieces of material evidence in the trial were almost all commodities: the white Bronco and the Rolls Royce, the mysterious knife and the expensive Italian shoes, the unusual pair of designer leather gloves, some missing luggage, a golf bag, and even O. J.'s socks. Like testimony about the swimming pool, guest house, or video equipment on Simpson's property, the prominence of these items allowed journalists to report the news and talk about shopping at the same time. "News" reports on the trial paid close attention to Robert Shapiro's ties and Marcia Clark's hairstyles. Perhaps that preoccupation with appearances helps explain a recurrent preoccupation in Christopher Darden's book on the trial—what reviewer Adam Hochschild describes as Darden's "suitomania"—a compulsion to comment on other attorney's "expensive suits," Simpson's "thousand-dollar suit," and Johnnie Cochran's off-white linen suit."[16]

The priority given to products in televisual discourse makes the issue of appetites crucially important. Commercials promote desire by projecting images of plenitude and fulfillment through commodity accumulation, but they also raise anxieties about desires that get out of control. Some commercials profess to monitor consumption by describing the dangers of reckless or foolish indulgences, for which they sell remedies ranging from indigestion medicine to diet pills to rehabilitation from drug, alcohol, or gambling addictions. In a similar way, television programs often work the same way, to inflame our desires but make us fear excess at the same time. In the Simpson case, the same things that made O. J. a symbol of fulfilled desires also made him a focal point for rumination about uncurbed appetites, cocaine use, indiscriminate sex, and unrestrained violence. John Fiske points out the ways in which tabloid newspaper accounts particularly emphasized these connections with stories like "Sex Secrets That Drove O. J. Crazy" and "Shocking Truth About Nicole's 911 Call, O. J. Caught Her Making Love While Kids Slept in the Next Room."[17] The talents that brought him wealth may have led him to use drugs. The good looks that made him a movie star may have enabled him to engage in obsessive extramarital sexual escapades. The physical strength that made him a successful athlete may have enabled him to murder two people brutally.

Finally, there is the issue of the family in jeopardy. This is a major theme of television drama, comedy, and news as well as a central preoccupation of commercials. As literary scholars Nancy Armstrong and Roddy Reid remind us, it is an old theme, one that dates back to the mid-nineteenth century, when domestic fiction first became a profitable market item. They argue that the theme emerged less because families actually experienced new threats from the world at large but instead because the best way to constitute the middle-class family as a consumption unit organized around the acquisition of household products was to create fearful images of the outside world and then "sell" the family as a defense against them.[18] To this day, the family is described in the media largely in terms of affection, intimacy, and its role as "a haven in a heartless world," with little open acknowledgment of its central role as a site for consumption, as an economic unit that transfers wealth and property across generations, and as an entity coveted by marketers who divide each family into separate market segments. . . .

The Simpson trial revolved around narratives of family closure and rupture. One tabloid ran a picture of O. J., Nicole, and their first child with the caption: "How this dream family portrait turned into a murderous nightmare."[19] Was Nicole Brown's marriage to a wealthy and handsome celebrity the fulfillment of the dreams of an Orange Country suburban girl, or was it a cruel deception that trapped her in a tempestuous relationship with a jealous, violent, and philandering husband? Did O. J. love Nicole and their children as evidenced by his presence at the recital the day that Nicole was murdered, or was his attention merely a device to control others while allowing himself unbridled liberty? Both sides used family solidarity as an emblem of what was at stake for their side; the Goldman family's public weeping and timely press conferences served the prosecution in the same way that the tight family circle of sisters and O. J.'s mother presented "proof" of Simpson's virtue in the eyes of the defense. Hints of a sexual relationship between Nicole Brown Simpson and Ron Goldman or between Nicole and Kato Kaelin had to be quashed by the prosecution, while O. J.'s romantic and sexual entanglements with other women had to be narrativized as irrelevant to his devotion to Nicole. From an entertainment perspective, the issue was not so much character or motivation for murder but rather exposure of the close relationship between foundational narratives of family fidelity and the lived experiences that revealed them as

fictions. As in the daytime soap opera or nighttime serial drama, family ties become invoked all the more passionately in the abstract as they disintegrate in actual practice. Affirmation of the family as the center of the social world is required, but that affirmation can exist easily alongside practices that contradict it.

The primacy of property, appetites, and the family in jeopardy in television discourse made the Simpson trial unusually susceptible to media exposure. In any art form, it is easy to go with the conventions and core grammar of the form and difficult to go against it. The Simpson trial was a story that could be told easily on television because television had long been involved in preparing the audience for stories like this one. Just as the Western films of John Ford seemed immediately credible to audiences accustomed to previous representations of the region in the paintings of Remington and Russell, on the covers of Western novels, and through performances of the Wild West Show, the O. J. Simpson trial could be immediately comprehended as "true" by viewers accustomed to television and its conventions.[20] In this context, there is no danger of overexposure; even disgust at the media attention devoted to the Simpson trial can be easily incorporated into the narrative—simply another aspect of the Simpson case that can be marketed on its own as a topic for discussion on talk shows or as the subject of magazine articles. . . .

Notes ◆

1. Joe Mandrese and Jeff Jensen, "'Trial of a Century,' Break of a Lifetime," *Advertising Age*, October 9, 1995, p. 1.

2. Christopher Stern, "Cameras in Courts Take a Hit," *Broadcasting & Cable*, October 9, 1995, p. 10.

3. Rich Brown, "The Juice Powers Some Players," *Broadcasting & Cable*, October 9, 1995, p. 10.

4. Mandrese and Jensen, "Trial of a Century,' Break of a Lifetime," p. 41.

5. Ibid., p. 1; Michael Wilke, "O. J. verdict; 'Hero' days are over," *Advertising Age*, October 2, 1995, p. 8.

6. Cynthia Littleton, "Verdict Propels Tabloid Ratings," *Broadcasting & Cable*, October 9, 1995, p. 7.

7. Brent Staples, "Millions for Defense," *New York Times Book Review*, April 28, 1996, p. 15; Adam Hochschild, "Closing Argument," *New York Times Book Review*, April 28, 1996, p. 15.

8. Hochschild, "Closing Argument," p. 15.

9. Steve McClellan, "All Eyes on O. J.," *Broadcasting & Cable*, October 9, 1995, p. 6; Mandrese and Jensen, "Trial of a Century,' Break of a Lifetime," p. 1.

10. Joe Mandrese and Thomas Tyler, "Simpson Shakes New TV Season," *Advertising Age*, October 16, 1995, p. 48.

11. Ibid.; Jim McConville, "Down Is Up for Cable Networks," *Broadcasting & Cable*, October 30, 1995, p. 51.

12. Littleton, "Verdict Propels Tabloid Ratings," p. 7.

13. Julie Johnson, "O. J. Scores Again on '95 Covers," *Advertising Age*, January 1, 1996, p. 4.

14. Mark Berniker, "CNN Web Site Flooded With O. J. Interest," *Broadcasting & Cable*, October 9, 1995, p. 71.

15. J. M., "O. J. Simpson Interview Scores Big for BET," *Broadcasting & Cable*, January 29, 1996, p. 7.

16. Hochschild, "Closing Argument," p. 14.

17. John Fiske, *Media Matters: Everyday Culture and Political Change* (Minneapolis: University of Minnesota Press, 1994), p. xix.

18. Nancy Armstrong, *Desire in Domestic Fiction* (New York: Oxford, 1985); Roddy Reid, *Families in Jeopardy* (Stanford, CA: Stanford University Press, 1994).

19. Fiske, *Media Matters*, p. xix.

20. William Howze, "John Ford's Celluloid Canvas," *Southwest Media Review* 3 (1985).

THE NEW POLITICS
OF CONSUMPTION

*Why Americans Want So Much More
Than They Need*

◆ Juliet Schor

In contemporary American culture, consuming is as authentic as it gets.
Advertisements, getting a bargain, garage sales, and credit cards are
firmly entrenched pillars of our way of life. We shop on our lunch hours,
patronize outlet malls on vacation, and satisfy our latest desires with a late-
night click of the mouse.[1]

Yet for all its popularity, the shopping mania provokes considerable
dis-ease: many Americans worry about our preoccupation with getting and
spending. They fear we are losing touch with more worthwhile values and
ways of living. But the discomfort rarely goes much further than that; it
never coheres into a persuasive, well-articulated critique of consumerism.
By contrast, in the 1960s and early 1970s, a far-reaching critique of consumer culture was a part of our political discourse. Elements of the New
Left, influenced by the Frankfurt school, as well as by John Kenneth
Galbraith and others, put forward a scathing indictment. They argued that
Americans had been manipulated into participating in a dumbed-down,
artificial consumer culture, which yielded few true human satisfactions.

NOTE: Reprinted by permission of Juliet Schor.

For reasons that are not hard to imagine, this particular approach was short-lived, even among critics of American society and culture. It seemed too patronizing to talk about manipulation or the "true needs" of average Americans. In its stead, critics adopted a more liberal point of view and deferred to individuals on consumer issues. Social critics again emphasized the distribution of resources, with the more economistic goal of maximizing the incomes of working people. The good life, they suggested, could be achieved by attaining a comfortable, middle-class standard of living. This outlook was particularly prevalent in economics, where even radical economists have long believed that income is the key to well-being. While radical political economy, as it came to be called, retained a powerful critique of alienation in production and the distribution of property, it abandoned the nascent intellectual project of analyzing the consumer sphere. Few economists now think about how we consume, and whether it reproduces class inequality, alienation, or power. "Stuff" is the part of the equation that the system is thought to have gotten nearly right.

Of course, many Americans retained a critical stance toward our consumer culture. They embody that stance in their daily lives—in the ways they live and raise their kids. But the rejection of consumerism, if you will, has taken place principally at an individual level. It is not associated with a widely accepted intellectual analysis, and an associated *critical politics of consumption*.

But such a politics has become an urgent need. The average American now finds it harder to achieve a satisfying standard of living than 25 years ago. Work requires longer hours, jobs are less secure, and pressures to spend more intense. Consumption-induced environmental damage remains pervasive, and we are in the midst of widespread failures of public pre vision. While the current economic boom has allayed consumers' fears for the moment, many Americans have long-term worries about their ability to meet basic needs, ensure a decent standard of living for their children, and keep up with an ever-escalating consumption norm.

In response to these developments, social critics continue to focus on income. In his impressive analysis of the problems of contemporary American capitalism, *Fat and Mean*, economist David Gordon emphasized income *adequacy*. The "vast majority of U.S. households," he argues, "can barely make ends meet. . . . Meager livelihoods are a *typical* condition, an *average* circumstance." Meanwhile, the Economic Policy Institute focuses on the distribution of income and wealth, arguing that the gains of the top 20 percent have jeopardized the well-being of the bottom 80 percent. Incomes have stagnated and the robust 3 percent growth rates of the 1950s and 1960s are long gone. If we have a consumption problem, this view implicitly states, we can solve it by getting more income into more people's hands. The goals are redistribution and growth.

It is difficult to take exception to this view. It combines a deep respect for individual choice (the liberal part) with a commitment to justice and equality (the egalitarian part). I held it myself for many years. But I now believe that by failing to look deeper—to examine the very nature of consumption—it has become too limiting. In short, I do not think that the "income solution" addresses some of the most profound failures of the current consumption regime.

Why not? First, consuming is part of the problem. Income (the solution) leads to consumption practices that exacerbate and reproduce class and social inequalities, resulting in—and perhaps even worsening—an unequal distribution of income. Second, the system is structured such that an *adequate* income is an elusive goal. That is because adequacy is relative defined by reference to the incomes of others. Without an analysis of consumer desire and need, and a different framework for understanding what is adequate, we are likely to find ourselves, twenty years from now, arguing that a median income of $100,000—rather than half that—is adequate. These arguments underscore the social context of consumption: the ways in which our sense of social standing and belonging comes from what we consume. If true, they suggest that attempts to achieve equality or adequacy of individual incomes without changing consumption patterns will be self-defeating.

Finally, it is difficult to make an ethical argument that people in the world's richest country need more when the global income gap is so wide, the disparity in world resource use so enormous, and the possibility that we are already consuming beyond the Earth's ecological carrying capacity so likely. This third critique will get less attention in this essay—because it is more familiar, not because it is less important—but I will return to it in the conclusion.

I agree that justice requires a vastly more equal society, in terms of income and wealth. The question is whether we should also aim for a society in which our relationship to consuming changes, a society in which we consume *differently*. I argue here for such a perspective: for a critique of consumer culture and practices. Somebody needs to be for quality of life, not just quantity of stuff. And to do so requires an approach that does not trivialize consumption, but accords it the respect and centrality it deserves.

◆ The New Consumerism

A new politics of consumption should begin with daily life, and recent developments in the sphere of consumption. I describe these developments as "the new consumerism," by which I mean an upscaling of lifestyle norms; the pervasiveness of conspicuous, status goods and of competition for acquiring them; and the growing disconnect between consumer desires and incomes.

Social comparison and its dynamic manifestation—the need to "keep up"—have

long been part of American culture. My term is "competitive consumption," the idea that spending is in large part driven by a comparative or competitive process in which individuals try to keep up with the norms of the social group with which they identify—a "reference group." Although the term is new, the idea is not.

Thorstein Veblen, James Duesenberry, Fred Hirsch, and Robert Frank have all written about the importance of relative position as a dominant spending motive. What's new is the redefinition of reference groups: today's comparisons are less likely to take place between or among households of similar means. Instead, the lifestyles of the upper middle class and the rich have become a more salient point of reference for people throughout the income distribution. Luxury, rather than mere comfort, is a widespread aspiration.

One reason for this shift to "upscale emulation" is the decline of the neighborhood as a focus of comparison. Economically speaking, neighborhoods are relatively homogeneous groupings. In the 1950s and 1960s, when Americans were keeping up with the Joneses down the street, they typically compared themselves to other households of similar incomes. Because of this focus on neighbors, the gap between aspirations and means tended to be moderate.

But as married women entered the workforce in larger numbers—particularly in white-collar jobs—they were exposed to a more economically diverse group of people, and became more likely to gaze upward. Neighborhood contacts correspondingly declined, and the workplace became a more prominent point of reference. Moreover, as people spent less time with neighbors and friends, and more time on the family-room couch, television became more important as a source of consumer cues and information. Because television shows are so heavily skewed to the "lifestyles of the rich and upper middle class," they inflate the viewer's perceptions of what others have, and by extension what is worth acquiring—what one must have in order to avoid being "out of it."

Trends in inequality also helped to create the new consumerism. Since the 1970s, the distribution of income and wealth has shifted decisively in the direction of the top 20 percent. The share of after-tax family income going to the top 20 percent rose from 41.4 percent in 1979 to 46.8 percent in 1996. The share of wealth controlled by the top 20 percent rose from 81.3 percent in 1983 to 84.3 percent in 1997. This windfall resulted in a surge in conspicuous spending at the top. Remember the 1980s—the decade of greed and excess? Beginning with the super-rich, whose gains have been disproportionately higher, and trickling down to the merely affluent, visible status spending was the order of the day. Slowed down temporarily by the recession during the early 1990s, conspicuous luxury consumption has intensified during the current boom. Trophy homes, diamonds of a carat or more, granite countertops, and sport utility vehicles are the primary consumer symbols of the late 1990s. Television, as well as films, magazines, and newspapers, ensure that the remaining 80 percent of the nation is aware of the status purchasing that has swept the upper echelons.

In the meantime, upscale emulation had become well established. Researchers Susan Fournier and Michael Guiry found that 35 percent of their sample aspired to reach the top 6 percent of the income distribution, and another 49 percent aspired to the next 12 percent. Only 15 percent reported that they would be satisfied with "living a comfortable life"—that is, being middle class. But 85 percent of the population cannot earn the six-figure incomes necessary to support upper-middle-class lifestyles. The result is a growing aspirational gap: with desires persistently outrunning incomes, many consumers find themselves frustrated. One survey of U.S. households found that the level of income needed to fulfill one's dreams doubled between 1986 and 1994 and is currently more than twice the median household income.

The rapid escalation of desire and need, relative to income, also may help to explain the precipitous decline in the savings rate—from roughly 8 percent in 1980, to 4 percent in the early 1990s, to the current level of zero. (The stock market boom may also be inducing households not to save, but financial assets are still highly concentrated, with half of all households at net worths of $10,000 or less, including the value of their homes.) About two-thirds of American households do not save in a typical year. Credit card debt has skyrocketed, with unpaid balances now averaging about $7,000 and the typical household paying $1,000 each year in interest and penalties. These are not just low-income households. Bankruptcy rates continue to set new records, rising from 200,000 a year in 1980 to 1.4 million in 1998.

The new consumerism, with its growing aspirational gap, has begun to jeopardize the quality of American life. Within the middle class—and even the upper middle class—many families experience an almost threatening pressure to keep up, both for themselves and their children. They are deeply concerned about the rigors of the global economy, and the need to have their children attend "good" schools. This means living in a community with relatively high housing costs. For some households this also means providing their children with advantages purchased on the private market (computers, lessons, extra-curriculars, private schooling). Keeping two adults in the labor market—as so many families do, to earn the incomes to stay middle class—is expensive, not only because of the second car, child-care costs, and career wardrobe. It also creates the need for time-saving, but costly, commodities and services, such as take-out food and dry cleaning, as well as stress-relieving experiences. Finally, the financial tightrope that so many households walk—high expenses, low savings—is a constant source of stress and worry. While precise estimates are difficult to come by, one can argue that somewhere between a quarter and half of all households live paycheck-to-paycheck.

These problems are magnified for low-income households. Their sources of income have become increasingly erratic and inadequate, on account of employment instability, the proliferation of part-time jobs, and restrictions on welfare payments. Yet most low-income households remain firmly integrated within consumerism. They are targets for credit card companies, who find them an easy mark. They watch more television, and are more exposed to its desire—creating properties. Low-income children are more likely to be exposed to commercials at school, as well as home. The growing prominence of the values of the market, materialism, and economic success make financial failure more consequential and painful.

These are the effects at the household level. The new consumerism has also set in motion another dynamic: it siphons off resources that could be used for alternatives to private consumption. We use our income in four basic ways: private consumption, public consumption, private savings, and leisure. When consumption standards can be met easily out of current income, there is greater willingness to support public goods, save privately, and cut back on time spent at work (in other words, to "buy leisure"). Conversely, when lifestyle norms are upscaled more rapidly than income, private consumption "crowds out" alternative uses of income. That is arguably what happened in the 1980s and 1990s: resources shifting into private consumption, and away from free time, the public sector, and saving. Hours of work have risen dramatically; saving rates have plummeted; and public funds for education, recreation, and the arts have fallen in the wake of a grassroots tax revolt. The timing suggests a strong coincidence between these developments and the intensification of competitive consumption— though I would have to do more systematic research before arguing causality. Indeed, this scenario makes good sense of an otherwise surprising finding: that indicators of "social health" or "genuine progress" (i.e., basic quality-of-life measures) began to diverge from GDP in the mid-1970s, after

moving in tandem for decades. Can it be that consuming and prospering are no longer compatible states?

To be sure, other social critics have noted some of these trends. But they often draw radically different conclusions. For example, there is now a conservative jeremiad that points to the recent tremendous increases in consumption and concludes that Americans just don't realize how good they have it, that they have become overly entitled and spoiled. Reduced expectations, they say, will cure our discontents. A second, related perspective suggests that the solution lies in an act of psychological independence—individuals can just ignore the upward shift in consumption norms, remaining perfectly content to descend in the social hierarchy.

These perspectives miss the essence of consumption dynamics. Americans did not suddenly become greedy. The aspirational gap has been created by structural changes— such as the decline of community and social connection, the intensification of inequality, the growing role of mass media, and heightened penalties for failing in the labor market. Upscaling is mainly defensive, and has both psychological and practical dimsions.

Similarly, the profoundly social nature of consumption ensures that these issues cannot be resolved by pure acts of will. Our notions of what is adequate, necessary, or luxurious are shaped by the larger social context. Most of us are deeply tied into our particular class and other group identities, and our spending patterns help reproduce them.

Thus, a collective, not just an individual, response is necessary. Someone needs to address the larger question of the consumer culture itself. But doing so risks complaints about being intrusive, patronizing, or elitist. We need to understand better the ideas that fuel those complaints.

Consumer Knows Best ◆

The current consumer boom rests on growth in incomes, wealth, and credit. But it also rests on something more intangible: social attitudes toward consumer decision making and choices. Ours is an ideology of noninterference—the view that one should be able to buy what one likes, where one likes, and as much as one likes, with nary a glance from the government, neighbors, ministers, or political parties. Consumption is perhaps the clearest example of an individual behavior that our society takes to be almost wholly personal, completely outside the purview of social concern and policy. The consumer is king. And queen.

This view has much to recommend it. After all, who would relish the idea of sumptuary legislation, rationing, or government controls on what can be produced or purchased? The liberal approach to consumption combines a deep respect for the consumer's ability to act in her own best interest and an emphasis on the efficiency gains of unregulated consumer markets: a commitment to liberty and the general welfare.

Cogent as it is, however, this view is vulnerable on a number of grounds. Structural biases and market failures in the operation of consumer markets undermine its general validity; consumer markets are neither so free nor so efficient as the conventional story suggests. The basis of a new consumer policy should be an understanding of the presence of structural distortions in consumers' choices, the importance of social inequalities and power in consumption practices, a more sophisticated understanding of consumer motivations, and serious analysis of the processes that form our preferences. To appreciate the force of these criticisms, we need a sharper statement of the position they reject.

THE CONVENTIONAL VIEW

The liberal view on markets for consumer goods has adherents in many disciplines, but its core analytic argument comes from standard economic theory, which begins from some well-known assumptions about consumers and the markets in which they operate.

1. *Consumers are rational.* They act to maximize their own well-being. They know what they prefer, and make decisions accordingly. Their "preferences" are taken as given, as relatively unchanging, and as unproblematic in a normative sense. They do not act capriciously, impulsively, or self-destructively.

2. *Consumers are well-informed.* They have perfect information about the products offered in the market. They know about all relevant (to the consumer) characteristics pertaining to the production and use of the product.

3. *Consumer preferences are consistent (both at a point in time and over time).* Consistency at a point in time means transitivity: If A is preferred to B and B to C, then A will be preferred to C. (In other words, if roast beef is preferred to hamburgers and hamburgers to hot dogs, then roast beef is preferred to hot dogs.) Consistency over time can be thought of as a "no regrets" assumption. If the consumer is faced with a choice of a product that yields satisfaction in the present, but has adverse consequences in the future—eat chocolate today and feel great, but gain five unwanted pounds by next week—and the consumer chooses that product today, he or she will not regret the choice when the future arrives. (This does not mean the extra pounds are welcomed, only that the pleasure of the chocolate continues to outweigh the pain of the pounds.)

4. *Each consumer's preferences are independent of other consumers' preferences.* We are self-contained in a social sense. If I want a sport utility vehicle, it is because I like them, not because my neighbor does. The trendiness of a product does not affect my desire to have it, either positively or negatively.

5. *The production and consumption of coods have no "external" effects.* There are

no consequences for the welfare of others that are unreflected in product prices. (A well-known example of external effects is pollution, which imposes costs on others that are not reflected in the price of the good that produces the pollution.)

6. *There are complete and competitive markets in aternatives to consumption.* Alternatives to consumption include savings, public goods, and the "purchase" of leisure. Unless these alternatives are available, the choice of consumption—over other uses of economic resources—may not be the optimal outcome.

Taken together, and combined with conditions of free entry and exit of firms providing consumer goods, these assumptions imply that no consumer policy is the best consumer policy. Individual consumers know best and will act in their own interest. Firms will provide what the consumers want; those that don't will not survive a competitive marketplace. Competition and rationality together ensure that consumers will be sovereign—that is, that their interests will "rule." And the results will be better than any we could achieve through government regulation or political action.

To be sure, conventional theory and policy have always admitted some deviations from these highly idealized conditions. In some areas interventionist policy has been long-standing. First, some consumers are not considered to be fully rational—for example, children or, in an earlier era, women. Because kids are not thought to be capable of acting in their own interest, the state justifies protective policies, such as the restricting advertising aimed at them. Second, the state has traditionally regulated highly addictive or harmful commodities, such as drugs, alcohol, and explosives. (As the debates surrounding the legalization of drugs make clear, the analytical basis for this policy is by no means universally accepted.) A third class of highly regulated commodities involve sex: pornography, contraceptives, sexual paraphernalia, and

so forth. Here the rationale is more puritanical. American society has always been uncomfortable about sex and willing to override its bias against consumer regulation because of that. Finally, the government has for much of this century—though less forcefully since the Reagan administration—attempted to ensure minimum standards of product safety and quality.

These exceptions aside, the standard model holds strongly to the idea that unfettered markets yield the optimal outcomes, a conclusion that follows logically and inexorably from the initial assumptions. Obviously, the assumptions of the standard model are extreme, and the real world deviates from them. On that everyone agrees. The question is, by how much, how often, and under what conditions? Is the world sufficiently different from this model that its conclusions are misguided?

Serious empirical investigations suggest that these assumptions do not adequately describe a wide range of consumer behaviors. The simple rational-economic model is reasonable for predicting some fraction of choice behavior for some class of goods—apples versus oranges, milk versus orange juice—but it is inadequate when we are led to more consequential issues: consumption versus leisure, products with high symbolic content, fashion, consumer credit, and so on. In particular, it exaggerates how rational, informed, and consistent people are. It overstates their independence. And it fails to address the pressures that consumerism imposes on individuals with respect to available choices and the consequences of various consumption decisions. Understand those pressures, and you may well arrive at very different conclusions about politics and policy.

Rational, Deliberative, and in Control?

The economic model presents the typical consumer as deliberative and highly forward-looking, not subject to impulsive behavior. Shopping is seen as an information-gathering exercise in which the buyer looks for the best possible deal for product she has decided to purchase. Consumption choices represent optimizing within an environment of deliberation, control, and long-term planning.

Were such a picture accurate it would be news (and news of a very bad sort) to a whole industry of advertisers, marketers, and consultants whose research on consumer behavior tells a very different story. Indeed, their findings are difficult to reconcile with the picture of the consumer as highly deliberative and purposive.

Consider some of the stylized facts of modern marketing. For example, the "law of the invariant right": shoppers overwhelmingly turn right, rather than left, upon entering a store. This is only consistent with the rational search model if products are disproportionately to be found on the right side of the aisle. Or consider the fact that products placed in the so-called "decompression zone" at the entrance to a store are 30 percent less likely to be purchased than those placed beyond it. Or that the number of feet into a store the customer walks is correlated with the number of items purchased. It's far harder to square these findings with "rational" behavior than with an unplanned and contingent action. Finally, the standard model has a very hard time explaining the fact that if, while shopping, a woman is accidentally brushed from behind, her propensity to purchase falls precipitously.

Credit cards present another set of anomalies for the reigning assumptions. Surveys suggest that most people who acquire credit cards say that they do not intend to borrow on them, yet roughly two-thirds do. The use of credit cards leads to higher expenditures. Psychological research suggests that even the visual cue of a credit card logo spurs spending. Survey data shows that many people are in denial about the level of credit card debt that they hold, on average underestimating by a factor of two. And the explosion of personal bankruptcies, now running at roughly 1.5 million a year, can be taken as evidence of a lack of foresight, planning, and control for at least some consumers.

More generally, credit card habits are one example of what economists call "hyperbolic discounting," that is, an extreme tendency to discount the future. Such a perspective calls into question the idea of time consistency—the ability of individuals to plan spending optimally throughout their lifetimes, to save enough for the future, or to delay gratification. If people are constitutionally inclined to be hyperbolic discounters, as some are now arguing, then forced-saving programs such as Social Security and government-sponsored retirement accounts, restriction on access to credit, waiting periods for major purchases, and a variety of other approaches might improve well-being. Compulsive buying, as well as the milder and far more pervasive control problems that many consumers manifest, can also be incorporated into this framework.

The model of deliberative and informed rationality is also ill-adapted to account for the phenomenon of brand preference, perhaps the backbone of the modern consumer market. As any beginning student of advertising knows, much of what advertising does is take functionally identical or similar goods and differentiate them on the basis of a variety of nonoperational traits. The consumer is urged to buy Pepsi because it represents the future, or Reebok shoes because the company stands for strong women. The consumer develops a brand preference, and believes that his brand is superior in quality. The difficulty for the standard model arises because, absent the labels, consumers are often unable to distinguish among brands, or fail to choose their favorites. From the famous beer taste test of the 1960s (brand loyalists misidentified their beers), to cosmetics, garments, and other tests of more recent vintage, it seems that we love our brands, but we often can't tell which brands are which.

What can we conclude from consumers' inability to tell one washing powder, lipstick, sweater, or toothpaste from another?

Not necessarily that they are foolishly paying a brand premium for goods. (Although there are some consumers who do fall into this category—they wouldn't pay the brand premium, as distinct from a true quality premium, if they knew it existed.) What is more generally true, I believe, is that many consumers do not understand why they prefer one brand over another, or desire particular products. This is because there is a significant dimension of consumer desire that operates at the nonrational level. Consumers *believe* their brand loyalties are driven by functional dimensions, but a whole host of other motivators are at work—for example, social meanings as constructed by advertisers; personal fantasies projected onto goods; competitive pressures. While this behavior is not properly termed "irrational," neither is it conscious, deliberative, and narrowly purposive. Consumers are not deluded, duped, or completely manipulated. But neither do they act like profit-maximizing entrepreneurs or scientific management experts. The realm of consumption, as a rich historical literature has taught us, has long been a "dream world," where fantasy, play, inner desire, escape, and emotion loom large. This is a significant part of what draws us to it.

CONSUMPTION IS SOCIAL

Within economics, the major alternative to the assumption that individuals' preferences are independent—that people do not want things because others want them—is the "relative" income, positional, or "competitive consumption" perspective noted above. In this model, a person's well-being depends on his or her relative consumption—how it compares to some selected group of others. Such positioning is one of the hallmarks of the new consumerism.

Of course, social comparison predates the 1980s. In 1984, French sociologist Pierre Bourdieu explored the social patterning of consumption and taste in *Distinction: A Social Critique of the Judgment of Taste*. Bourdieu found that family socialization processes and educational experiences are the primary determinants of taste for a wide range of cultural goods, including food, dress, and home decor. In contrast to the liberal approach, in which consumption choices are both personal and trivialized—that is, socially inconsequential—Bourdieu argues that class status is gained, lost, and reproduced in part through everyday acts of consumer behavior. Being dressed incorrectly or displaying "vulgar" manners can cost a person a management or professional job. Conversely, one can gain entry into social circles, or build lucrative business contacts, by revealing appropriate tastes, manners, and culture. Thus, consumption practices become important in maintaining the basic structures of power and inequality that characterize our world. Such a perspective helps to illuminate why we invest so much meaning in consumer goods—for the middle class its very existence is at stake. And it suggests that people who care about inequality should talk explicitly about the stratification of consumption practices.

If we accept that what we buy is deeply implicated in the structures of social inequality, then the idea that unregulated consumption promotes the general welfare collapses. When people care only about relative position, then general increases in income and consumption do not yield gains in well-being. If my ultimate consumer goal is to maintain parity with my sister, or my neighbor, or Frasier, and our consumption moves in tandem, my well-being is not improved. I am on a "positional treadmill." Indeed, because consuming has costs (in terms of time, effort, and natural resources), positional treadmills can have serious negative effects on well-being. The "working harder to stay in place" mantra of the early 1990s expresses some of this sentiment. In a pure reversal of the standard prescription, collective interventions that stabilize norms, through government policy or other mechanisms, *raise* rather than lower welfare. People should welcome initiatives that reduce the pressure to keep up with a rising standard.

Free and Structurally Unbiased?

The dynamic of positionally driven spending suggests that Americans are "overconsuming" at least those private goods that figure in our consumption comparisons. There is another reason we may be overconsuming, which has to do with the problems in markets for alternatives to status or positional goods. In particular, I am referring to nonpositional private consumption, household savings, public goods, and leisure. Generally speaking, if the markets for these alternatives are incomplete, noncompetitive, or do not fully account for social benefits and costs, then overconsumption with respect to *private consumption* may result. I do not believe this is the case with household savings: financial markets are highly competitive and offer households a wide range of ways to save. (The deceptive and aggressive tactics of consumer credit companies might be reckoned a distortion in this market, but I'll leave that aside.) Similarly, I do not argue that the markets for private consumer goods that we tend not to compete about are terribly flawed. Still, there are two markets in which the standard assumptions do not apply: the market for public goods and the market for time. Here I believe the deviations from the assumptions are large, and extremely significant.

In the case of public goods, there are at least two big problems. The first is the underproduction of a clean environment. Because environmental damage is typically not included in the price of the product that causes it (e.g., cars, toxic chemicals, pesticides), we overconsume environmentally damaging commodities. Indeed, because all production has an impact on the environment, we overconsume virtually all commodities. This means that we consume too much *in toto*, in comparison to non-environmentally damaging human activities.

The second problem arises from the fact that business interests—the interests of the producers of private goods—have privileged access to the government and disproportionately influence policy. Because they are typically opposed to public provision, the "market" for public goods is structurally biased against provision. In comparison to what a truly democratic state might provide, we find that a business-dominated government skews outcomes in the direction of private production. We don't get enough, or good enough, education, arts, recreation, mass transport, and other conventional public goods. We get too many cars, too many clothes, too many collectibles.

For those public goods that are complementary with private spending (roads and cars versus bicycle lanes and bicycles), this bias constrains the choices available to individuals. Without the bicycle lanes or mass transport, private cars are unavoidable. Because so much of our consumption *is* linked to larger collective decisions, the individual consumer is always operating under particular constraints. Once we move to HDTV, our current televisions will become obsolete. As public telephone booths disappear, mobile phones become more necessary. Without adequate public libraries, I need to purchase more books.

We also underproduce "leisure." That's because employers make it difficult to choose free time, rather than long hours and higher incomes. To use the economist's jargon, the labor market offerings are incomplete with respect to trade-offs of time and money. Employers can exact severe penalties when individuals want to work part-time or forgo raises in favor of more vacations or days off. In some jobs, the options are just not available; in others the sacrifices in terms of career mobility and benefits are disproportionate to any productivity costs to the employer.

This is not a minor point. The standard model assumes that employees are free to vary their hours and that whatever combination of hours and income results represents the preferences of employees. But if employees lack the opportunity to vary their working hours, or to use improvements in productivity to reduce their worktime, then we can in no way assume that the trajectory of consumption reflects people's preferences. There may well be a path for the economy that involves less work and less stuff and is preferred by people to the high-work/high-consumption track. But if that option is blocked, then the fact that we buy a lot can no longer be taken *ipso facto* as proof of our inherent consumer desires. We may merely be doing what is on offer. Because free time is now a strongly desired alternative to income for large numbers of employees, this argument is more than a theoretical possibility. It has become one of the most pressing failures of the current moment.

◆ *A Politics of Consumption*

The idea that consumption is private should not, then, be a conversation-stopper. But what should a politics of consumption look like? To start the discussion—not to provide final answers—I suggest seven basic elements:

1. *A right to a decent standard of living.* This familiar idea is especially important now because it points us to a fundamental distinction between what people need and what they want. In the not very distant past, this dichotomy was not only well understood, but the basis of data collection and social policy. Need was a social concept with real force. All that's left now is an economy of desire. This is reflected in polling data. Just over 40 percent of adults earning $50,000 to $100,000 a year, and 27 percent of those earning more than $100,000, agree that "I cannot afford to buy everything I really need." One third and 19 percent, respectively, agree that "I spend nearly all of my money on the basic necessities of life." I believe that our politics would profit from reviving a discourse of need, in which we talk about the material requirements for every person and household to participate fully in society. Of course, there are many ways in which such a right might be enforced: government

income transfers or vouchers, direct provision of basic needs, employment guarantees, and the like. For reasons of space, I leave that discussion aside; the main point is to revive the distinction between needs and desires.

2. *Quality of life rather than quantity of stuff.* Twenty-five years ago quality-of-life indicators began moving in an opposite direction from our measures of income, or gross domestic product, a striking divergence from historic trends. Moreover, the accumulating evidence on well-being, at least its subjective measures (and to some extent objective measures, such as health), suggests that above the poverty line, income is relatively unimportant in affecting well-being. This may be because what people care about is relative, not absolute income. Or it may be because increases in output undermine precisely those factors that *do* yield welfare. Here I have in mind the growing worktime requirements of the market economy, and the concomitant decline in family, leisure, and community time; the adverse impacts of growth on the natural environment; and the potential link between growth and social capital.

This argument that consumption is not the same as well-being has great potential to resonate with millions of Americans. Large majorities hold ambivalent views about consumerism. They struggle with ongoing conflicts between materialism and an alternative set of values stressing family, religion, community, social commitment, equity, and personal meaning. We should be articulating an alternative vision of a quality of life, rather than a quantity of stuff. That is a basis on which to argue for a restructuring of the labor market to allow people to choose for time, or to penalize companies that require excessive hours for employees. It is also a basis for creating alternative indicators to the GNP, positive policies to encourage civic engagement, support for parents, and so forth.

3. *Ecologically sustainable consumption.* Current consumption patterns are wreaking

havoc on the planetary ecology. Global warming is perhaps the best known, but many other consumption habits have major environmental impacts. Sport utility vehicles, air conditioning, and foreign travel are all energy-intensive and contribute to global warming. Larger homes use more energy and building resources, destroy open space, and increase the use of toxic chemicals. All those granite countertops being installed in American kitchens were carved out of mountains around the world, leaving in their wake a blighted landscape. Our daily newspaper and coffee are contributing to deforestation and loss of species diversity. Something as simple as a T-shirt plays its part, since cotton cultivation accounts for a significant fraction of world pesticide use. Consumers know far less about the environmental impacts of their daily consumption habits than they should. And while the solution lies in greater part with corporate and governmental practices, people who are concerned about equality should be joining forces with environmentalists who are trying to educate, mobilize, and change practices at the neighborhood and household levels.

4. *Democratize consumption practices.* One of the central arguments I have made is that consumption practices reflect and perpetuate structures of inequality and power. This is particularly true in the "new consumerism," with its emphasis on luxury, expensiveness, exclusivity, rarity, uniqueness, and distinction. These are the values that consumer markets are plying, to the middle and lower middle class. (That is what Martha Stewart is doing at Kmart.)

But who needs to accept these values? Why not stand for consumption that is democratic, egalitarian, and available to all? How about making "access," rather than exclusivity, cool, by exposing the industries such as fashion, home decor, or tourism, which are pushing the upscaling of desire? This point speaks to the need for both cultural change and policies that might facilitate it. Why not tax high-end "status"

versions of products while allowing the low-end models to be sold tax-free?

5. *A politics of retailing and the "cultural environment."* The new consumerism has been associated with the homogenization of retail environments and a pervasive shift toward the commercialization of culture. The same mega-stores can be found everywhere, creating a blandness in the cultural environment. Advertising and marketing are also pervading hitherto relatively protected spaces, such as schools, doctors' offices, media programming (rather than commercial time), and so on. In my local mall, the main restaurant offers a book-like menu comprising advertisements for unrelated products. The daily paper looks more like a consumer's guide to food, wine, computer electronics, and tourism and less like a purveyor of news. We should be talking about these issues, and the ways in which corporations are remaking our public institutions and space. Do we value diversity in retailing? Do we want to preserve small retail outlets? How about ad-free zones? Commercial-free public education? Here too public policy can play a role by outlawing certain advertising in certain places and institutions, by financing publicly controlled media, and enacting zoning regulations that take diversity as a positive value.

6. *Expose commodity "fetishism."* everything we consume has been produced. So a new politics of consumption must take into account the labor, environmental, and other conditions under which products are made, and argue for high standards. This argument has been of great political importance in recent years, with public exposure of the so-called global sweatshop in the apparel, footwear, and fashion industries. Companies fear their public images, and consumers appear willing to pay a little more for products when they know they have been produced responsibly. There are fruitful and essential linkages between production, consumption, and the environment that we should be making.

7. *A consumer movement and governmental policy.* Much of what I have been arguing for could occur as a result of a consumer's movement. Indeed, the revitalization of the labor movement calls out for an analogous revitalization of long dormant consumers. We need independent organizations of consumers to pressure companies, influence the political agenda, provide objective product information, and articulate a vision of an appealing and humane consumer sphere. We also need a consumer movement to pressure the state to enact the kinds of policies that the foregoing analysis suggests are needed. These include taxes on luxury and status consumption, green taxes and subsidies, new policies toward advertising, more sophisticated regulations on consumer credit, international labor and environmental standards, revamping of zoning regulations to favor retail diversity, and the preservation of open space. There is a vast consumer policy agenda that has been mainly off the table. It's time to put it back on.

Note ◆

1. Sources for much of the data cited in this [chapter] can be found in the notes to *The Overspent American: Why We Want What We Don't Need* (HarperPerennial, 1999) or by contacting the author.

20

NIKE, SOCIAL RESPONSIBILITY, AND THE HIDDEN ABODE OF PRODUCTION

◆ Carol A. Stabile

In June 1996, responding to journalist Bob Herbert's scathing critique of Nike's promotional rhetoric of social responsibility (1996b, p. A19), Chairman and CEO Philip Knight reiterated Nike's alleged commitment to humanity. Nike, he avowed, has long "been concerned with developing safe and healthy work environments wherever it has worked with contractors in emerging market societies," it provides "free meals, housing and health care and transportation subsidies," and "we do our best to insure that labor abuses do not occur." In a concluding flourish, Knight wrote, "add to this the 200,000 people employed by our contractors at the factory level and you have a company that began in my basement and today creates wealth where none existed before" (p. A18).

Nike irrefutably has created wealth for its owners and shareholders (when the corporation went public in 1980, for example, at least six of its shareholders became multimillionaires), but its rhetoric of social responsibility—its self-presentation of the corporation as a now global

NOTE: From *Critical Studies in Media Consumption*, Vol. 17, No. 2, June 2000, pp. 186-204. Copyright © 2000. Used by permission of the National Communication Association.

citizen—constitutes a more dubious claim. Of course, Nike is not alone in engaging in such marketing discourse, but the corporation has long been in the vanguard of innovations in both production and marketing and therefore offers an instructive case study of how multinational corporations produce and manage their public images. . . .

◆ *Sneaker Wars*

"What too many people who live in other places don't understand is that there's a part of America where a Big Mac is a celebration. . . . Most of the people in this store, their lives are shit; their homes in the projects are shit—and it's not like they don't know it. There's no drop-in center around here anymore, and no local place to go that they can think of as their own. So they come to my store. They buy these shoes just like other kinds of Americans buy fancy cars and new suits. It's all about trying to find some status in the world."—Steven Roth, owner, Essex House of Fashion, Newark, N.J. (in Katz, 1994, p. 271)

One of the first high-profile controversies Nike encountered involved an association that emerged between sneakers and the media's representations of inner-city violence. These "sneaker wars" had their origins—ironically enough—in competition between Nike and Reebok over market share. In 1991, Nike and Reebok went head-to-head in a television advertising campaign known as "the sneaker wars."[1] Spending at least $130 million each, their dueling commercials featured NBA players who implied that their respective brand of sneakers gave them a competitive edge. Nike's own edge over Reebok (by January 1992, Nike had 40 percent of the market, while Reebok had only 16 percent) and the increased visibility of its Air Jordans eventually provoked a public relations crisis

when the sneaker wars merged with news coverage of inner-city violence (Rifkin, 1992, p. 10).

A spate of publicity in 1989 suggested that children were killing each other over athletic shoes and, in 1990, *Sports Illustrated* reported that inner-city youths were committing homicides specifically for Air Jordans. In August 1991, economic and racial tensions turned violent in the Crown Heights neighborhood of Brooklyn. In the months that followed the turmoil, a significant amount of print media coverage was devoted to the looting of a store in Crown Heights called Sneaker King, owned by a Korean family. The brand name "Nike" featured prominently in the coverage (Barron, 1991, p. 3; Faison, 1991, p. 25). In March 1992, a fifteen-year-old in Philadelphia reportedly was killed during the theft of his Air Jordans; in April 1992, South Central L.A. erupted, with looting and brand name sneakers again splashed across pages and screens; and in July 1992, KP Original Sporting Goods in Harlem was robbed. According to the *New York Times*, in Harlem "10,000 pairs of Nike, Reebok and other highpriced sneakers" were stolen in a "frenzy of looting and violence" that was "explained by two words: 'greed and sneakers'" (Fritsch, 1992, p. 25). The suburbs also became implicated in apparently sneaker-motivated criminal behavior. Fairfield, Connecticut's First Selectman, Jacquelyn C. Durrell, described "situations in town where youngsters not only had their bicycles stolen but their sneakers—their Michael Jordan Air Pumps—right off them" (Lomuscio, 1991, p. 1).

As the sneakers at issue became associated with the Nike brand (as inevitably they would given Nike's prominence in the market and its use of African American spokespersons), the corporation was confronted with both a problem and the opportunity for some free, albeit dual-edged, publicity. As Katz notes, "Magic had accrued to the most carefully made shoes, and this perception was clearly the result of a hundred intricate cultural signals—many of which had indeed been manufactured as a way to manipulate the shape of popular desire" (1994, p. 269). The problem Nike subsequently confronted had two main aspects. On one hand, the sneaker wars threatened to become a critique of the very consumerist desires Nike had so successfully manipulated. Had Nike been too successful in manipulating "popular desire"; so successful, in fact, that those without the wherewithal to purchase the shoes were willing to resort to violence to acquire a pair? From the perspective of an advertising-supported media industry, this line of questioning is especially dangerous since it threatens to cast doubt on the very practices that generate vast profits. Teen-agers, for example, currently spend $57 billion of their own money and $36 billion of their families' money each year (Conover, 1998, p. 13). Over the past forty years, communication research has invested enormous resources in analyzing the effects of media violence on viewers, while scant critical attention has been devoted to the effects of advertising's ability to stimulate desires for products and lifestyles outside viewers' economic grasp and related increases not in violence per se but in crimes like burglary and theft.[2] Since the articulation of sneakers and greed followed on the heels of the highly visible "sneaker wars" advertising campaign, the possibility that Nike's aggressive marketing campaign could have spurred such greed wasn't much of a stretch. Given the pervasiveness of media effects theory in popular culture, if children were killing one another over sneakers, blaming the media and Nike's advertising practices might not be far behind.[3]

On the other hand, since Nike's ads rely in large part on the positivism of the contrast between the disciplined African American bodies it uses to sell products and the criminalized African American bodies that abound in the media, when the contrast threatened to dissolve, the issue had to be carefully managed. If Nike sneakers became linked to gangs and inner-city violence—if the magic that had accrued to them became tainted—consumption might be affected, particularly if suburbanites feared that their Nike-shod children were at risk.[4]

Understanding the problem as a potential moral panic, Nike launched a crisis management campaign.[5] In 1992, Nike ran a number of antiracist ads by Spike Lee, and in November of that year, Nike and Michael Jordan jointly donated $200,000 to Chicago Public Schools. By 1993, Nike was a key supporter of "midnight basketball programs," and in 1994, during the intensified coverage of crime that heralded Clinton's Crime Bill, Nike formally launched PLAY (Participate in the Lives of America's Youth). With promotional moves that cost them very little in the end (one need only compare the $130 million dollars Nike spent on advertising during the sneaker wars with the corporation's paltry donation of $100,000 to Chicago schools), Nike managed not only to publicize a commitment to social responsibility, but to suggest that the corporation was part of the solution rather than part of the problem.

PLAY in particular enabled Nike to restore its veneer of social responsibility by implying that the solution to inner-city deterioration was through the discipline of sport and its promise of upward mobility. In so doing, the program relied on a logic of inferential racism:

> There's a crisis in America right now. Kids' sports and fitness programs are being axed from schools and the country's playgrounds aren't safe anymore. Access to play should be a kid's inalienable right. Nike wants to lead the charge to guarantee that these rights to America's children are preserved. (in Cole, 1996, pp. 7-8)

Framed in this way, the crisis locates the problem as reductions in spending to athletic programs thus implying that the central problem in inner-city schools is that poor children do not have access to the formal discipline of athletics. Despite the references to "America" and "America's children," the crisis clearly emanates from the inner city, where crime runs rampant and "playgrounds aren't safe anymore." Without sports programs, inner-city youths have no hope for the future. As one PLAY ad puts it, "If you couldn't dream of touchdowns, what would you dream?" The undermining of educational curricula in inner-city schools through federal and state reductions does not generate the same kind of marketing opportunities or moral outrage—a fact that underscores the self-interested nature of the campaign, as well as its inferential racism. This is a racist common sense that prioritizes (at least rhetorically) athletic programs for African American children while systematically and simultaneously attacking and eroding economic and educational programs. . . .

◆ *"There Is No Finish Line": Nike's Pitch to the Consumerist Caste*

. . . The "success" of Nike's ads and products has depended on the corporation's ability to reach a target audience of middle-class consumers through appeals to the values and belief systems of that audience. This does not mean that audiences who do not fit this demographic profile are untouched by Nike's advertising campaigns in particular or the commodity fetishism it promotes in general. It does mean, however, that Nike pitches its ads not to some fictive mass audience, but to those consumers most likely to be able to buy their products.

The specificity of Nike's address to this consumerist caste (not to mention the specificity of its product line) is evident in its television ads from the late 1970s when the corporation was gaining ascendancy. Capitalizing on the running fad among the demographic known as baby boomers, the early ads incorporated certain watered-down ideals from the 1960s with

the counterculture now firmly articulated to a particular consumer lifestyle. These advertisements repeatedly featured white men, loping through sylvan landscapes—sneaker-clad versions of Thoreau's rugged woodsman—while the voice-over equated the individualism of the runner with the individualized craftsmanship and technology of the nascent Nike corporation. Another ad established Nike's now familiar rhetoric of revolution. Set to the strains of the *1812 Overture*, Nike proclaimed a "revolution" in running-shoe technology, with the corporation positioned in the "vanguard" of such revolutionary change. The corporation's later use of the Beatle's "Revolution" in 1987 and Gil Scott Heron's "The Revolution Will Not Be Televised" in 1995 testify to the continued success of this countercultural theme. As Katz observes, "Somehow 'Just Do It' managed to evoke countless previously impeded visions of personal responsibility. The phrase entered popular discourse like some consumer-age variation on the old revolutionary interrogative, 'What is to be done?'" (1994, p. 146). These early advertisements contain a reasonably straightforward address. Representing itself as a small entrepreneurial venture long after it had become a multi-million dollar enterprise, Nike initially appealed to white male consumers on the basis of its craftsmanship, commitment to excellence, and social responsibility—all attractive characteristics to its audience. Its outdoor, naturally lit scenes and narrative focus on individuals spoke to the experiential framework of white, middle-class consumers for whom fitness was an increasingly important leisure activity.

Such a niche market of runners had its economic limitations, however, and in 1977, Nike executives discerned a shift in their consumers from "running geeks" to "yuppies"—an "emerging consumer [who] was shallow and had little sense of history" (Strasser & Becklund, 1991, p. 268). Nike had been diversifying its product line for some time: tennis shoes were introduced in

1972, the move into basketball shoes began in late 1974, the "Senorita Cortez" women's running shoe was introduced in 1976, and a clothing line in 1979. When the corporation went public in 1980, Nike began its aggressive advertising campaign. In 1982, Nike hired Chiat/Day, the firm that went on to produce Nike's city campaigns as well as many of its successful television commercials.

As Amy Hribar and Cheryl Cole point out, Nike achieved its most widespread publicity through basketball (1995, p. 349) and its marketing of African American celebrities like Michael Jordan and Spike Lee. This strategy has allowed Nike to capitalize on cutting-edge fashions that originate in inner cities and among urban minorities. Advertising industry experts claim that this emphasis on "inner-city chic" permits advertisers to "jazz up their sales pitches" (Tyson, 1996, p. 8) or, as in the case of ad agency DDB Needham's hiring of Spike Lee in 1996, to revitalize a company's "stodgy, lily white image" (Hirschfield, 1997, p. 36). Experts also assert that advertisers' growing emphasis on city fashion reflects the importance of the "urban market," which Ken Smikle, publisher of *Target Market News*, says "has become one of those phrases that can be used comfortably by those who don't want to say black or African-American" (Tyson, p. 8). Advertisers also admit that they use the term "urban market" so as not to alienate white consumers by openly casting a trend or product as African American or Hispanic.

Nike's move into basketball also coincided with a boom in the marketing of multicultural texts across the media, especially in the area of book publishing. The boom in multicultural images had specific ideological effects insofar as it helped to maintain the illusion that consumption reflected or was identical to political practice. First, multicultural images appeared to provide an antidote to the media's reliance on overtly racist stereotypes as well as an alternative to the criminalized images of African Americans that proliferate on the nightly news. By providing "positive" images, or role models, corporations (including the media) could represent themselves as being socially responsible to people of color and link this to the products being sold. The consumerist caste could participate in a feeling of social responsibility by consuming multicultural images that provided a simulacrum of racial integration. The representation of a very few successful African Americans further reinforced Nike's trademark of individual and individualized excellence, thereby denying the obstacles that institutionalized racism places in the paths of African Americans (indeed, to acknowledge the existence of this would be to contradict its very slogan—"Just Do It"). . . . Framed within the poles of "positive" and "negative" role models, Nike's use of African American men in its ad campaigns relied upon what Stuart Hall has described as a logic of inferential racism, a logic with a lengthy history and one that is all too frequently invisible to white consumers (1990, p. 13). Where sport for white athletes is equated with leisure (however competitive), sport has more gravity when connected to African Americans. After all, in a white supremacist culture, professional sport provides one of the few entry-points into the Horatio Alger myth for African Americans, with the traditional entertainment industry being another. And basketball, more than any other sport, has been inextricably articulated to urban spaces and African American athletes. Thus basketball, in a white imaginary, confirms that the American Dream is within the grasp of African Americans, if only they would pull themselves up by their Nike laces and "Just Do It." The implication of such narratives is that African Americans possess bodily capital rather than the entrepreneurial cunning of an Andrew Carnegie or Ted Turner. Their impulsiveness, or excess energy, must find an appropriate *physical* outlet—it must be disciplined—or else it runs the risk of turning into senseless, undisciplined violence. Even "successful" African Americans are represented as being dogged by this problem as the media attention to Michael Jordan's gambling illustrates.[6]

Although Nike has long cultivated "bad boy" endorsers for its products, the "bad boy" image functions quite differently for white athletes like Ilie Nastase and John McEnroe. In the case of African American spokespersons, crime implicitly and explicitly haunts Nike's commodification of African American athletes. Again, these ads take their meaning from and must be situated within a constant flow of television images that largely serve to criminalize African Americans and demonize inner-city communities. Nike's grainy black-and-white images of basketball courts stand in stark relief against nightly local and network coverage of urban carnage; the disciplined choreography of the court and athletic culture posed as the alternative to the ruthless anarchy of the streets, while organized sports offer an antidote to the criminal behavior of gangs. Given the levels of segregation that exist in the United States, many white Americans (and certainly a large percentage of the consumerist caste) have their perception of people of color structured around such mass-mediated poles.

◆ *"Dirty, Dangerous, and Difficult": Nike and the Mode of Production*[7]

. . . Certainly, the marketing of social responsibility works mainly for those more distant from economic necessity—those more likely to buy into the ideology of the corporation as global citizen. For those who recognize that "positive" role models do not pay the bills and that economic and political justice will not proceed from revarnished corporate images, Nike's veneer of social responsibility is less than persuasive.

Nike's commercial image, like many such corporate images, absolutely depends on maintaining the invisibility of real contradictions for the consumerist caste. For example, female consumers of Nike products can only find Nike's ads progressive insofar as its largely female labor force (not to mention its masculinist corporate culture) remains out of sight.[8] For instance, one can believe that Nike's "If you let me play sports" ad signifies a commitment to women's liberation and empowerment, as long as the Vietnamese women who make Nike shoes, working 12-hour days for a wage of between \$2.10 and \$2.40 a day, are kept off the screen. Similarly, middle-class consumers may very well believe that Nike's use of African American spokespersons indicates its commitment to people of color as long as nothing in the field of the media contradicts such a belief, or perhaps as long as journalists avoid mentioning that Michael Jordan's salary may well be greater than the combined annual payroll of the six Indonesian factories that make Nike shoes (Lipsyte, 1996, p. 2). For the consumerist caste, the PLAY campaign can appear as a signifier for Nike's commitment to "social responsibility" because the contradiction between corporate production and employment practices and chronic unemployment in African American communities remains outside the screen or printed page.[9]

To an extent, recent controversies involving Kathie Lee Gifford, Wal-Mart, and Nike have made visible some of these real contradictions. The targeting of Gifford, Wal-Mart, Nike, J.C. Penney, and the Disney Store by labor activists like the National Labor Committee, journalists like Bob Herbert, and activists like the Pittsburgh Labor Action Network for the Americas (PLANTA) is a strategic move that works to make visible some of the very contradictions discussed. Their purpose is not to boycott Air Jordans or Disney's popular Pocahontas doll (made by Haitian workers for eleven cents an hour—half of Haiti's already pitiful minimum wage) because such a boycott would only encourage consumers to buy other products likely to have been made under similarly exploitative conditions. Rather, their purpose has been to bring such relations of production into consumers' range of vision by singling out those corporations who sell their products on the basis of social responsibility, decent family values, and other nonsense, while at the same time engaging in labor practices that give the lie to their public propaganda. In a similar spirit, campus activists throughout the country have been protesting their schools' contracts with Nike. Some schools have now adopted anti-sweatshop codes as a result of this activism.

. . . Those who study the media and popular culture often spend a great deal of time analyzing what multinational corporations make visible in the form of advertising and corporate propaganda. In so doing, we only direct attention to what these corporations want us to see. Unless our goal as critics is to contribute to their market research and to add further sophistication to their advertising techniques, it might be more useful and politically effective for us to concentrate on making visible those practices and realities that are routinely kept out of sight.

◆ Notes

1. Actually, the "war" had begun earlier, in 1985, with Nike's "Guns of August" campaign, which was a marketing push to win back retail floor space from Reebok. "Guns of August," however, was unsuccessful: in 1986, Reebok had a 30 percent market share, while Nike had only 21 percent (Strasser & Becklund, 1991, p. 591).

2. For a suggestive analysis of television's impact on "instrumental crime," or "that aimed at acquiring money or property," see Hennigan et al. (1982).

3. It is worth noting that media effects theories that focus on amorphous categories of violence are among the few critiques that media institutions are willing to make of themselves, although generally in the shape of criticizing entertainment programming rather than news or, especially, advertising (the single exception to this last being very mild critiques of children's

programming and advertisements). In contrast to critiques of monopoly ownership of the media, media effects theory provides a simple explanation for social problems (i.e., "Kojak made me do it"), a quick and convenient fix (self-regulation), and an opportunity for some corporate promotion.

4. That the fear so central to the ideology of the suburbs is based on class interests rather than race was made clear in a *Washington Post* article on the African American suburb of Perrywood in Prince George's County (a suburb where homes sell for between $180,000 and $300,000). The Perrywood Community Association decided to hire policemen to make sure that those using the basketball court could "prove that they 'belong in the area.'" As one resident candidly put it, "People have a tendency to stick together because they want to maintain their property values, their homes—class issues. . . . We're just strong working people who want something nice. Race never entered the picture" (Saulny, 1996, p. A7).

5. Donald Katz is clear on the fact that Nike understood the sneaker wars as a "moral panic" in the sociological sense.

6. Cheryl Cole's "PLAY, Nike, and Michael Jordan" (1996) provides a detailed reading of this and related aspects.

7. T. H. Lee, a Nike employee who has worked in Portland, the Philippines, and South Korea, described shoe manufacturing as "dirty, dangerous, and difficult. Making shoes on a production line is something people do only because they see it as an important and lucrative job. Nobody who could do something else for the same wage would be here" (in Katz, p. 161).

8. For an example of a feminist argument about Nike's "progressive" ad campaigns, see Linda Scott's "Fresh Lipstick—Rethinking Images of Women in Advertising." For some unintentionally hilarious descriptions of Nike-style capitalists as puking frat boys, see Strasser and Becklund's numerous anecdotes in *Swoosh*.

9. In the city where I live, for example, unemployment among young black men is 37 percent as opposed to 13 percent for white men. Only corporate apologists and certain consumers can afford to believe that any amount of midnight basketball or PLAY can remedy this situation.

◆ References

Barron, J. (1991, August 22). Tension in Brooklyn. *New York Times*, p. 3.

Cole, C. (1996). *PLAY, Nike, and Michael Jordan: National fantasy and racialization of crime and punishment*. Memphis, TN: Working papers in sport and leisure commerce.

Cole, C., & Hribar, A. (1995). Celebrity feminism: Nike style, post-Fordism, transcendence, and consumer power. *Sociology of Sport Journal*, 12, 347-369.

Cole, C., & Andrews, D. (1996). Look—it's NBA show time! Visions of race in the popular imaginary. *Cultural Studies*, 1, 141-181.

Conover, K. A. (1998, February 10). Why Johnny has to have those sneakers. *Christian Science Monitor*, p. 13.

Faison, S. (1991, October 20). Looted Crown Heights store reopens. *New York Times*, p. 25.

Fritsch, J. (1992, July 18). Looters booty: A dream. *New York Times*, p. 25.

Hall, S. (1990). The whites of their eyes: Racist ideologies and the media. In M. Alvarado and J. O. Thompson (Eds.), *The media reader* (pp. 7-23). London: British Film Institute.

Hennigan, K. et al. (1982). Impact of the introduction of television on crime in the United States: Empirical findings and theoretical implications. *Journal of Personality and Social Psychology* 42(3), 461-477.

Herbert, B. (1996b, June 10). Nike's pyramid scheme. *New York Times*, p. A19.

Hirschfield, L. (1997, April 20). Spike Lee's 30 seconds. *New York Times Magazine*, p. 36.

Katz, D. (1994). Just do it: *The Nike spirit in the corporate world*. New York: Random House.

Katz, M. (Ed). (1993). *The "underclass" debate: Views from history*. Princeton, NJ: Princeton University Press.

Lipsyte, R. (1996, July 21). Pay for play: Jordan vs. old-timers. *New York Times*, Section 4, 2.

Lomuscio, J. (1991, October 6). Fairfield City suburbs. *New York Times*, Connecticut Weekly Desk, p. 1.

Rifkin, G. (1992, January 5). All about basketball shoes. *New York Times*, Section 3, 10.

Saulny, S. (1996, July 8). On the inside and looking out: Black suburb rebuffs uninvited black visitors. *Washington Post*, p. A1.

Scott, L. (1993). Fresh lipstick—Rethinking images of women in advertising. *Media Studies* 7(17), 141-155.

Strasser, J. B., & Becklund, L. (1991). *Swoosh: The unauthorized story of Nike and the men who played there*. New York: Harcourt Brace Jovanovich.

Tyson, J. L. (1996, December 27). Ad agencies walk fine line in tapping inner-city trends. *Christian Science Monitor*, p. 8.

21

"YOU'VE NEVER HAD A FRIEND LIKE ME"

Target Marketing Disney to a Gay Community

◆ Sean Griffin

◆ *Marketing the Mouse: A Short History of Disney Advertising and Publicity*

. . . Historians have noted that modern mass production made it necessary to create mass consumption and that this was primarily accomplished through advertising. In the mass production of 1930s Hollywood film-making, Walt Disney learned quickly how to differentiate his shorts from the rest of the pack through the use of merchandise as a form of advertising. Walt's first major contract with a Hollywood distributor was animating Oswald, the Lucky Rabbit. Oswald's success spawned product tie-ins such as a chocolate-coated marshmallow bar, buttons, and a stencil set.[1] Charles Mintz, who distributed the cartoons through a contract with Universal

Pictures, owned the rights to Oswald, so Disney did not share in the monies received from this merchandising. Yet, when Walt and his brother Roy broke from Mintz and started their own studio with their new character Mickey Mouse, the popularity of the Oswald items (as well as their impact on box-office revenues) was not forgotten.

In January of 1930, Mickey began appearing in his own nationally syndicated comic strip, and, in February, Roy signed a contract with Geo. Borgfeldt and Company, which would license manufacturers (both domestic and foreign) to produce specified Disney character products, import and distribute them, and then share the profits with Disney. The enormous success of Mickey Mouse cartoons resulted in a landslide of licensing contracts that helped keep the studio financially afloat. As Walt continually pushed for better "quality" in the cartoons, the budgets often ballooned beyond what most short subjects could expect to make at the box office. Consequently, the company needed the merchandise profits to stay in the black.

. . . Disney moved boldly into television when major studios were still wary, seeing the new medium's cross-promotional advantages. The series *Disneyland* (1954-58) won an Emmy its first season for a program that was basically an hour-long advertisement for the new feature *20,000 Leagues Under the Sea* (1954). Disney agreed to produce the program for ABC only when the network agreed to help finance the building of Disneyland, the theme park. Although the series promoted the park relentlessly, the studio did not look on television simply as an advertising medium. Now each division mutually supported the other. The success of "Davy Crockett" on TV, for example, spurred the selling of merchandise, promoted the "Frontierland" section of the new park, and was eventually released as a live-action feature, but also spurred further television production by the studio. . . .

Although Disney led this trend in the 1950s, other studios surpassed Disney's "synergetic" abilities during the stagnant years after Walt's death. Eisner, coming from Paramount, and Wells, having worked at Warners, took the corporate lessons they learned and updated Disney's older concepts. Taking advantage of the instant recognition of the Disney name and characters, all aspects of the corporation aggressively sold each other in a hyperefficient model that became the envy of the industry. For example, the popularity of the theatrical feature *Aladdin* was tied to a number of other related areas: miniature action figures of the film's characters; tie-ins with Burger King, which put images of the characters on plastic soft drink cups; the score from the film released on CD, as well as a children's album narrating the story; the release of the feature on home video, and eventually on the Disney Channel; a new show/restaurant in the "Adventureland" section of the theme parks, as well as "Aladdin" parades down Main Street; Little Golden Books' picture book of the story; an animated TV series based on the characters; the selling of original cel work done for the feature; and a CD-ROM based on the film. A more recent example of Disney's continued strategy of synergy between various corporate arms was the acquisition of the American Broadcasting Company (ABC) in 1996. Almost immediately, a number of the families of different ABC series made pilgrimages to Walt Disney World. *Roseanne, Step by Step*, and *Second Noah* all created "special" episodes that hoped to attract more viewers by their trips to the park but also effectively worked to advertise the place as well. ABC's daytime series *All My Children* publicized a "Cinderella"-themed wedding in May of 1996 to increase its audience but also made explicit reference to the Disney film version, which just happened to have been released on video the month before.

Disney was also one of the first to capitalize on the concept of target audiences, a key development in the eventual attempt to woo the homosexual customer. . . . After World War II, target marketing was developed by advertisers as an implicit admission that some potential customers were not "getting the message" that their clients were communicating. W. R. Smith introduced the idea of "target research" to marketing in 1956, which was defined as a shift from product differentiation (the "attempt to bend demand to the will of supply") to consumer differentiation ("bend[ing] supply to demand by identifying lucrative segments of the market and developing products to specifically fit those segments").[2] By moving from advertising the benefits of the product itself to advertising the benefits of belonging to a certain audience segment which used the product, segmenting moved to increasingly isolate specific groups from this ill-defined mass, hopefully including those groups which had spending power but had not been addressed effectively in marketing heretofore.

Disney had already proven the viability of Smith's ideas two years earlier. With the broadcast of the weekly *Disneyland* series, and especially the daily afternoon episodes of *The Mickey Mouse Club* (1955-58), the studio helped to create a culture of "children's television" and dominated what became an increasingly lucrative children's market.[3] These Disney TV shows promoted the theme parks and the new film releases, as well as a plenitude of tie-in products, by aiming their discourse directly at the child consumer. This trend continues in the present, as the success of the syndicated "Disney Afternoon" attests. Eisner began his career in children's programming for ABC and, immediately upon taking over at Disney, moved to create children's series. The phenomenal response to such syndicated series as *DuckTales* (1986-92) and *Chip 'n' Dale's Rescue Rangers* (1989-93) proved the company's ability to target and capture the younger consumer.[4]

In the Eisner era, such target research has gone beyond simply breaking up the audience into children and adults. Some ads for the film *Pretty Woman*, for example, were created to sell men on a "woman's" picture, and special ads for *Dead Poets Society* were made to air on David Letterman's late-night talk show, specifically aimed at the person that audience research said watched the program. Since the mid-1980s, the studio has regularly created campaigns for its theatrical releases that feature separate ads written specifically towards a different demographic group. For example, amongst the titles of different ads for the *Aladdin* campaign are "Young Boys/Good vs. Evil," "Kids Imagine," "Young Girls/Jasmine's Dream," "Moms," and "Adult Sneak Preview." Each TV spot attempts to create a reading of *Aladdin* that the studio figures will appeal to the specific group that it is addressing. "Young Boys" emphasizes the action sequences in the film, while "Young Girls" tries to make the film look as if Princess Jasmine is the lead character and Aladdin only a supporting character.[5] Such a strategy is also used now by the company to sell its video releases and to promote theme park attendance, with different commercials for kids, teenagers, young single adults, and parents. One of the strongest ad campaigns Disney came up with in the late 1980s focused directly on addressing the heterosexual adult male. In a number of TV spots, various sports celebrities were filmed just after a major victory (an Olympic win, the Super Bowl, the World Series) to announce that now they were "going to Disneyland!" . . .

The increased focus of the company on audience segmentation had to make Disney at least aware of the "gay market," a concept that arose by the early 1980s. Furthermore, at a point when the studio was attempting to get customers by any means necessary, it is unlikely that they would have completely ignored the possibilities of marketing to this segment. As well shall see, there are indications that they did not ignore it.

Be Our Guest: ◆ Disney Marketing to Homosexual Consumers

In 1986 . . . the Walt Disney Company, in conjunction with AIDS organizations in

Orange County, held a benefit at the park to raise funds for AIDS Project Los Angeles (APLA). Not only was the event sponsored directly by the company, but Disney pledged to match the money raised by ticket sales with an equal donation from corporate coffers. The ticket prices for this benefit (and subsequent benefits for the next few years) were higher than normal, thus attracting a "higher-income" crowd, but the success of these benefits started a trend at both Disneyland and Walt Disney World. In the 1990s, the Odyssey Tours travel agency began renting out the park one night a year (usually during the early winter, traditionally a slow period for the park) to hold "Gay Nights" at the park. Although never specifically advertised with such a phrase, the flyers and print ads announced that portions of the proceeds would go to the Aid for AIDS charity, and, judging by the crowds these nights attracted, most people "got the hint." Similarly, a number of organizations worked together to promote such an event at Walt Disney World but without any pretense; they simply announced it as "Gay & Lesbian Day at the Magical Kingdom That Walt Built." Before long, the annual event had become an entire weekend of activities in and around the Disney complex: a day at the Magic Kingdom, a reception and party at Pleasure Island, and even a buffet brunch with various Disney characters. . . .

Many might be surprised to find Disney reaching out to gay audiences. Yet, a number of factors make such a development in the company's business strategy understandable. First, the influx of openly lesbian and gay employees to the company would obviously have its effect on attempting to attract homosexual customers. Ronald Marchand, in his analysis of 1920s and '30s American advertising, noticed that those working in advertising agencies often assumed that their own wants and desires mirrored the rest of the populace, and hence often inadvertently created ads that appealed to their own specific outlook on life.[6] While not necessarily having a

"gay agenda" (as paranoid religious conservatives might see it), lesbians or gay men working for Disney marketing might tend to create campaigns that they themselves find appealing (and hence possibly appealing to gay or lesbian customers as well). Also, the close friendship that Jeffrey Katzenberg built with Howard Ashman had a profound effect on the executive according to many who worked at Disney during Ashman's illness, and thus, Katzenberg himself seemed more attuned to gay issues and causes than most Hollywood executives of the time.

Most important, when Eisner, Wells, and Katzenberg took over the company, they were eager to expand the profit margin to stave off future hostile takeover attempts. While one of the major methods was creating new venues for their product and consolidating control of those venues for maximum profit, the company also worked conscientiously on creating new audiences to consume the product in these new venues. . . .

Of course, companies such as Disney have to proceed carefully when addressing any "gay market," for fear of alienating their larger customer base of traditional heterosexual families. It is thus imperative to find a method of appealing to homosexual customers that will not disturb other consumers. The AIDS benefits previously described exemplify one such method, with the company not specifically championing "gay pride" but raising money for a disease that can strike anyone. Lesbians and gay men could also read this as much needed support for the number of homosexuals with AIDS, but Disney could promote this as larger than the scope of a homosexual audience. When these special nights and weekends were sponsored by various gay-oriented companies, Disney could absolve itself from culpability by claiming that they had just rented the use of the park out to an independent travel agency, and whom that agency brought to the park was none of Disney's responsibility.

Another effective method used to mask marketing to homosexual audiences is the relatively recent concept of "gay window advertising." . . . This new marketing approach addressed the gay consumer slyly and without offending the straight consumer (or even letting the straight consumer know that the gay consumer was being addressed). By "breaking through" the ad's surface, a gay consumer could find the "hidden message" aimed at the homosexual reader. As an example, Stabiner's article displays a Time Square ad for Calvin Klein jeans featuring a handsome, bare-chested male model staring seductively out of the viewer. The caption in the article points out another advantage to such a marketing strategy—deniability: "The ad agency denies that this billboard was aimed primarily at homosexual, adding, 'But you don't want to alienate them.'"[7] In other words, if any straight consumer "caught on," the company could deny any intentions of "gay address."

As the Calvin Klein jeans billboard reveals, "gay window advertising" has become relatively common practice in clothing, cologne, and liquor ads since the early 1980s. One could find coded gay messages in such diverse campaigns as Paco Rabanne's Pour Homme cologne print ads showing a man speaking to his gender-unspecified lover over the phone; Tanqueray Gin's overly cultured fictional spokesperson Mr. Jenkins; as well as the objectified male bodies displayed on Calvin Klein underwear billboards and in Levi's Loose Jeans TV spots. By the late 1980s, an aware viewer of Disney's TV ads could also find these subtle "gay windows." While Disney commonly labels its ads with titles like "Moms" or "Young Boys," there has never been (to my knowledge) an individual commercial in a campaign labeled "Gay Men/Lesbian Women." But there have been ads that, when watched, do produce a double-take reaction. A perfect example is the TV spot for *Aladdin* entitled "All Genie-B," which was produced by Disney by Craig Murray Productions and New Wave Productions. The spot begins with the narration, "When Aladdin discovered the lamp,

he found a genie who gave him everything he wanted—and more than he could handle." In between this narration, the Genie emerges from the lamp to exclaim, "It's good to be *out of there*!" Immediately after the narration finishes, the commercial presents the Genie acting as the "swishy tailor." This is the longest clip in the whole spot, emphasizing the Genie as a "queer figure." Immediately following this clip is a shot of the Genie in the lamp showing Aladdin how to rub the lamp right where his crotch would be, and the next shot shows the Genie transforming into a huge pair of lips, the better to kiss Aladdin with. All through the ad, the song "You've Never Had a Friend Like Me" plays in the background. Indeed. This ad might not be labeled "Gay Men," but it sure reads like it could have been.

Although this particular ad is possibly the strongest example of such "gay window advertising" in Disney's TV spots, one can find an equally strong example in Disney's print ads. During the initial theatrical release of *The Lion King*, Disney took out newspaper ads showing various characters speaking lines from the film that seemed to advise customers to see the film. Two of them stand out from a gay perspective. In one, Scar with a fey smile and a raised pinkie in his claw announces that the film is "to die for!" In another, the meerkat Timon pleads, "What do you want me to do, dress in drag and do the hula?!" The obviousness of this address almost pushes the boundaries of the coded nature of "gay window advertising."[8]

. . . Another overt appeal to possible gay customers can be found in the number of interviews given by openly homosexual employees of Disney to various gay publications. In journals such as *The Advocate*, *Out*, and *Frontiers*, reporters have done interviews with animator Andreas Deja, Hollywood Pictures executive Lauren Lloyd, and animation executive Tom Schumacher. Of course, employees do not need company approval to be interviewed, but these journals do need permission from the Walt Disney Company to publish the film stills that often accompany the articles. Also, not so coincidentally, the interviews are usually published just as one of the studio's films is about to be released to theatres. With the release of *Aladdin*, interviews with Deja appeared in both *The Advocate* and *Frontiers*. In these interviews, Deja "points proudly to . . . examples of gayish humor in *Aladdin*," such as agreeing that "Jafar might be gay."[9] Tom Schumacher's interview with *The Advocate* began by describing the supportive environment at Disney for gay and lesbian employees," but more exciting to Schumacher . . . is this month's theatrical launch of *The Lion King*."[10] Even with this more direct address, the studio can still keep from disturbing its family market. While these interviews . . . are more directly geared towards a homosexual subject, all of these are presented in forums far from the eyes of mainstream heterosexual culture. . . . Interviews with gay employees like Deja and Schumacher or ads for the "Gay Nights" at the theme parks are only in gay newspapers and periodicals—publications that the public at large have neither access to nor (for the most part) knowledge of.

By the 1990s, Disney seemed to be growing gradually more comfortable with speaking openly to a gay market. Three months before Schumacher's interview had appeared in *The Advocate*, the company allowed clips from *The Lion King* to be shown during Barbara Walters interview with Elton John (who had co-written the songs for the picture). During this interview, John revised the assertion he had made earlier in his career that he was bisexual, now announcing that he was homosexual. Since this interview was broadcast just before or just after the annual Oscar ceremony (depending on the area of the country), millions of people now knew that an open homosexual had worked on a Disney animated feature. Possibly the most famous and overt instance of marketing a Disney film towards a gay audience involved

Howard Ashman. As mentioned before, Ashman was posthumously posited by the studio's publicity material for *Beauty and the Beast* as the guiding force of the project. Almost all of the articles written about the film spent much of their time mourning the loss of Ashman, and they all prominently displayed the fact that Ashman was a gay man who had died as a result of the AIDS virus. This coverage was not isolated to the gay press. Stories in *Premiere* magazine, reviews in the *Los Angeles Times*, the *New York Times, Variety*, and *Newsweek* magazines, all mainstream publications, were part of the phenomenon.[11] With such widespread visibility, it would be impossible *not* to see the place of a gay constituency in the mass audience that *Beauty and the Beast* was appealing to.

. . . During a season when ABC was running low in the ratings, the Disney-owned network used the coming-out episode of *Ellen* as a way to spike viewership during the May sweeps period. To heighten ratings during this period, the network extended Diane Sawyer's interview with Ellen DeGeneres on *PrimeTime Live* over two nights. During the episode, Disney advertised many of its big summer movies, as well as promoted other ABC shows. Furthermore, within the show itself, Disney found a way to do some "product placement." When Ellen Morgan's therapist (played by Oprah Winfrey) asks her what she's going to do now that she's come out as a lesbian, Ellen parodies Disney's famous and campaign and announces "I'm going to Disneyland!" Yet, the network refused to allow the Human Rights Campaign (HRC), a homosexual rights organization, to buy time for a public service advertisement during the episode. ABC informed the HRC that the network held "a policy against issue ads."[12] Since ABC has had no trouble in the past airing ads about solving illiteracy, putting "Children First," or curing illegal drug use, this statement seems disingenuous. While ABC and Disney trumpeted the "issues" of Ellen Morgan's lesbianism to boost ratings and profits, political statements were not welcome. Furthermore, the network seemed to be antagonistic towards anyone else making a profit off lesbianism with *Ellen*, since the network not only turned down an ad by the HRC but also one by Olivia Cruises, a vacation company aimed at lesbians. Both organizations eventually bought ad time with local affiliates in certain cities (Atlanta, San Francisco, Los Angeles, Washington, Phoenix, Detroit), but only viewers in these areas saw these TV spots.

Sometimes, "the gay market" is not as cooperative as companies often envision. As capitalism tries to regulate sexual identity, inevitably some rebel against such strictures. In 1995, the lesbian and gay circles of Southern California by and large turned away from the annual "Gay Night" at Disneyland. While not a systemized boycott, word spread throughout the area that Odyssey Tours, who organized the event, was making only token donations of the proceeds to the Aid for AIDS charity—even though the publicity prominently described itself as a charity event. Conceiving of the "Gay Night" as a "con job" on lesbian and gay customers, attendance dropped precipitously. Yet, capitalism learns and adapts to such resistance, creating newer and more nuanced strategies instead of simply admitting defeat. The following year, Odyssey Tours decided not to donate proceeds to any charity and dropped mention of any such charity in their ads for the event. Because many somehow felt that the boycott had worked and made Odyssey more honest, attendance climbed for 1996's Disneyland "Gay Night"—even though now Aid for AIDS was not even getting a token payment. Examples such as these point out that the relationship between homosexuality and capitalism is a constant interplay between autonomy and exploitation, and that gay community and culture have historically been supported by businesses for profit and not for the advancement of homosexual causes.

Notes ◆

1. Cecil Munsey, *Disneyana: Walt Disney Collectibles* (New York: Hawthorn Books, 1974), 1. Unless otherwise noted, all other data from the Walt Disney era of the studio on merchandising are from this text.

2. James E. Grunig, "Publics, Audiences and Market Segments: Segmentation Principles for Campaigns," *Information Campaigns: Balancing Social Values and Social Change*, Charles T. Salmon, ed. (Newbury Park, CA: Sage, 1989), 201.

3. Amongst those who have analyzed Mickey Mouse Club and marketing towards children have been Kline, 166-167; and Lynn Spigel, "Seducing the Innocent: Childhood and Television in Postwar America," *Ruthless Criticism: New Perspectives in U.S. Communications History*, William S. Solomon and Robert W. McChesney, eds. (Minneapolis: University of Minnesota Press, 1993), 280-281.

4. An analysis of the company's specific marketing strategies towards children with the "Disney Afternoon" can be found in Pamela C. O'Brien, "Everybody's Busy Bringing You a Disney Afternoon: The Creation of a Consumption Community," paper presented at the Seventh Annual Society of Animation Studies Conference, University of North Carolina at Greensboro, 1995.

5. Kline's work on TV marketing towards children also discusses how commercials for children are often bifurcated into specific gender reception.

6. Roland Marchand, *Advertising the American Dream* (Berkeley: University of California Press, 1985), xxi.

7. Stabiner, Karen, 76.

8. Calvin Klein has also pushed up against the limits of coding with its 1996 underwear campaign. Featuring models that looked just under the "age of consent," the TV spots were a pastiche of low-budget "nudie loops." Although the campaign also featured female models, the ads mainly showed young men recreating scenes from the super-8 films sold by the Athletic Models Guild in the 1950s and 1960s that were targeted at homosexual men. Apparently, a

number of straight viewers caught what was going on, and recognition of the appropriation of pornographic *mise-en-scène* led to talk of legal action against the company for a few months.

9. Steve Warren, "Deja View," *Frontiers* 11:20 (Jan. 29, 1992): 48. Isherwood, 85.

10. Tom Provenzano, "The Lion in Summer," *The Advocate* (June 28, 1994): 66.

11. Ansen et al.; Fox; Janet Maslin, Review of *Beauty and the Beast*; Review of *Beauty and the Beast, Variety*.

12. "Rights Group Buys Air Time on 'Ellen,'" *New York Times* (Mar. 20, 1997): C6.

◆ References

Ansen, David, et al. "Just the Way Walt Made 'Em," *Newsweek* (Nov. 18, 1991): 74-80.

Grunig, James E. "Publics, Audiences and Market Segments: Segmentation Principles for Campaigns," in *Information Campaigns: Balancing Social Values and Social Change*, Charles T. Salmon, ed. (Newbury Park, CA: Sage, 1989), 199-228.

Kline, Stephen. *Out of the Garden: Toys and Children's Culture in the Age of TV Marketing.* (London: Verso, 1993).

Marchand, Roland. *Advertising the American Dream.* (Berkeley: University of California Press, 1985).

Maslin, Janet. Review of *Beauty and the Beast, New York Times* (Nov. 13, 1991): C17.

Munsey, Cecil. *Disneyana: Walt Disney Collectibles.* (New York: Hawthorn Books, 1974).

O'Brien, Pamela C. "Everybody's Busy Bringing You a Disney Afternoon: The Creation of a Consumption Community." Paper presented at the Seventh Annual Society of Animation Studies Conference, University of North Carolina at Greensboro, 1995.

Provenzano, Tom. "The Lion in Summer," *The Advocate* (June 28, 1994): 64-70.

"Rights Group Buys Air Time on 'Ellen,'" *New York Times* (Mar. 20, 1997): C6.

Spigel, Lynn. "Seducing the Innocent: Childhood and Television in Postwar America," *Ruthless Criticism: New Perspectives in U.S. Communications History*, William S. Solomon and Robert W. McChesney, eds. (Minneapolis: University of Minnesota Press, 1993), 280-281.

Stabiner, Karen. "Tapping the Homosexual Market," *New York Times Magazine* (May 2, 1982): 34-36, 74-85.

Warren, Steve. "Deja View," *Frontiers* 11:20 (Jan. 29, 1992): 48-49.

22

ADVERTISING AND THE POLITICAL ECONOMY OF LESBIAN/GAY IDENTITY

◆ Fred Fejes

Homosexuality is *"a pathetic little second-rate substitute for reality, a pitiable flight from life. As such it deserves fairness, compassion, understanding, and when possible, treatment. But it deserves no encouragement, no glamorization, no rationalization, no fake status as a minority group, no sophistry about simple differences in taste—and, above all, no pretense that it is anything but a pernicious sickness."*

—"The Homosexual in America," *Time,* 21 January 1966

IBM, DKNY, American Express, Waterford, Dockers, Tattinger, Nieman Marcus, Circuit City, Virgin Atlantic, Smirnoff, Movado, Rockport, Bacardi, Versace, New York Times, Air New Zealand, Calvin Klein, Hennessy, Camel, Grand Marnier, British Airways, Eyeworks, Chivas Regal, Armani, Stolichnaya, Parliament Lights, Doc Martens, Finlandia, Seiko, Freixnet, Lindermann's Graham's Port,

NOTE: From *Sex & Money: Feminism and Political Economy in the Media*, edited by Eileen R. Meehan and Ellen Riordan, 2001, Minneapolis and London: University of Minnesota Press, pp. 196-208. Copyright © 2001.

Beaulieu Vineyards, Clos Du Bois, Coors, Life Fitness, Verge, Creative Jewelers, Noa Jewelers, Tzabaco, Southern Comfort, Lucky Strike, Absolut, Kitchen Company, Prado, Tommy Hilfiger, Nautica, Hugo Boss, Diesel Denim, Tanqueray, Wilke-Rodriguez, Andrew Fezza, Dolce & Gabbana, Skyy Vodka, Moschino, Sauzo Tequila, Barneys, Solgar, Remy Martin, Aussie Hair, Kata Eyewear, Neptune Records, John Fluevog Shoes, Beverly Hills Institute of Aesthetic and Reconstructive Surgery, Bud Light, Propecia, Wilson Leather, Freshave, Metroman, Alize, Miller Light, Louis Vuitton, Baccarat, Gaultier, Benson and Hedges, Gianfranco Ferre, Bombay Sapphire, Nature's Recipe, Merit, Tropica

—Companies with full-page advertisements in the fall 1998 issued of *Out*, a national lesbian and gay magazine

If the struggle for legal and social equality for lesbians and gay males is still being fiercely fought (and often lost), the struggle to treat them as full and equal citizens in the republic of postscarcity, postmodern hyperconsumption is all over but the shouting. The good guys (and some of the girls) won. While it is typical to think of lesbians and gay males in terms of their sexual identities, with their emergence in recent years as economic subjects—self-conscious identities produced within the structure of commodity relationships—they have achieved an equality far greater than that found in the political or social realm. Indeed it seems the acceptance of lesbians and gay males as sexual/political subjects is predicated on their acceptance and importance as consuming subjects. While in the past other marginalized groups have attained political power through the marshaling of economic resources, for lesbians and gay males it is not in their role as producers or controllers of capital, but in their role as consumers, particularly as a defined market niche attractive to advertisers, that they are offered the surest route to equality. Perhaps in the history of social movements this represents a pioneering strategy in which pulling out the American Express Card has replaced the raised fist. An additional irony is that even while the commodification of lesbian/gay identity represents a pioneering

political strategy, in many ways it reproduces the same old gender disparities. Lesbians and gay males may have achieved equality, but because of their more attractive income profile, advertisers decided early in the game that gay males are more equal than lesbians. Even in the Republic of Hyperconsumption governed by advertisers and marketeers the iron law of politics still applies: *plus ça change, plus ça rest le même.*

Although at the birth of the gay liberation movement in 1969 homosexuals were perhaps one of the most marginalized, stigmatized minorities in the United States, it did not take long for advertisers to ask about the potential of selling to the homosexual market. Mindful of the stereotypic image of gay men as upscale, high-spending consumers interested in the latest in fashion (then as now, lesbians figured very little in these discussions), *Advertising Age* in the early 1970s began running periodic reports about the possibilities of marketing to gays. The first report in 1972 was not very hopeful. Noting that most advertisers were reluctant to have their product identified with a gay market, many media outlets would not use the word "gay" in an advertisement, and in any event most gay men were very closeted (Baltera 1972). Three years later *Advertising Age* reported that advertisers were becoming more aware of gay men as a separate market niche, yet, fearing a backlash from heterosexual consumers, they still were very reluctant to have their product identified as a "gay product." Moreover, they argued that they could reach the gay consumer through the regular advertising aimed at the straight market (Baltera 1975).

A more practical reason why advertisers and marketing companies were hesitant to take the gay market seriously was lack of reliable marketing data about gay men. If gay media were serious about attracting mainstream advertising dollars, they first had to construct a statistical picture of the gay consumer. The first marketing survey of gay men was conducted in 1977 when the *Advocate*, at that time the only gay publication with a national audience, hired an independent marketing research firm to conduct a survey of its readers in an attempt to attract major national advertisers. According to results, the typical *Advocate* readers were gay professional men between the ages of twenty and forty with above-average incomes. Free of the financial burden of supporting a family, they could afford to spend their large incomes on themselves, particularly on high-priced liquors, clothes, and travel. According to the magazine's publisher, gay men were not merely trying to prove that we can "live as well as the Joneses, (but) we live a damn sight better" (Stabiner 1982). By picturing the gay market as one composed of upscale gay men with high-priced habits of consumption, the survey seemed to confirm what was thought about the gay market, and by extension, the gay community. By 1980 *Advertising Age* noted that national advertisers such as Seagrams, Simon and Schuster, and the major film companies were beginning to place ads in national publications like the *Advocate* and in local gay newspapers (Pendleton 1980). Advertisers were also becoming aware of how, particularly in urban areas, the consumption habits and fashion tastes of gay men were being imitated by straight men, particularly in clothing designs that emphasized a

highly eroticized masculinity. Rather than being an isolated marginalized niche, gay men were seen as both hyperconsumers and powerful trendsetters for new designs and products (Stabiner 1982).

Yet reaching the gay market was problematic. In the early 1980s there was as yet no slick glossy publication that explicitly targeted gay men. Publications that did exist, such as the *Advocate* and local gay newspapers and magazines, did not have the high production quality required by major national advertisers, particularly fashion advertisers, and their content—heavy with photos of half-dressed or nude handsome young men and advertisements for erotic, pornographic videos and sexual services—was too explicitly sexual for most mainstream advertisers. Moreover, many advertisers, particularly fashion advertisers, were still reluctant to have their products too closely associated with the gay market. Some fashion designer advertisers such as Paco Rabanne, Marlboro, Levi Strauss, and Calvin Klein got around this problem by utilizing the "gay window advertising" approach, constructing ads with homosexual subtexts very obvious to gay readers but unnoticed by straight readers and then placing these ads in mainstream men's fashion magazines (Stabiner 1982; Holland 1977; Merret 1988; see also Sender 1999).

In order to attract national advertisers, gay publications like the *Advocate* in the late 1980s and early 1990s upgraded their production quality and changed their format and editorial focus. The *Advocate*, for example, cordoned off its classified and other sexually explicit material into a separate publication—"We wanted the magazine to be something gay men could leave on the coffee table when their mothers came over" noted the publisher (Pogrebin 1996)—and redesigned itself as a news magazine with a focus on national events of interest to the gay community and cultural and feature stories about art and entertainment. Its strategy was successful and its ad revenue doubled from $1.9 million to $3.8 million between 1990 and 1992 (C. Miller

1992). In the early 1990s a number of new gay national magazines, including *Out, Genre, 10 Percent, QW,* and *Deneuve,* appeared. With the exception of the lesbian magazine *Deneuve* (which later changed its name to *Curve*), these publications were aimed at gay males. In an effort to attract national advertisers, particularly fashion advertisers, they all had the similar strategy of printing on high-grade glossy paper and emphasizing "lifestyle" content of general feature stories about fashion, celebrities, travel, and current events to target the upper-income segment of their markets. As these new publications were competing among themselves, and with the *Advocate,* for national advertising dollars, most had short lives. Among these new lifestyle entrants, *Out* emerged as the clear victor and by 1996 was the leading gay magazine with its 119,000 circulation topping the *Advocate*'s 74,000 (Wilke 1996).

With the explicit sexual material gone and market-survey data about gay consumers beginning to appear, by the mid-1990s most advertisers had overcome any reluctance about advertising in gay publications. As *Advertising Age* reported in bold headlines on its front page in 1997, "Big advertisers join move to embrace gay market" (Wilke 1997b). As the head of Rivendell Marketing, a gay and lesbian media placement company, noted, "Ten years ago we had a tough time getting an appointment at any agency. Now everybody will see us" (Pogrebin 1996). In addition to fashion designers such as Gucci, Versace, and Yves St. Laurent, traditional major advertisers like Aetna Life and Casualty, General Motors, Chase Manhattan Corporation, Johnson and Johnson, United Airlines, Merrill Lynch, and American Express began to take pages in gay publications. More recently even advertisers like Chesebrough-Pond's (Mentadent toothpaste), Bristol-Myers Squibb (Excedrin), and McNeil Consumer Products (Motrin) began advertising in gay media (Wilke 1998).

Moreover, many local and regional gay periodicals, noting the success of the

Advocate and *Out,* have undertaken a similar strategy of getting rid of sexually explicit material, improving production quality, and using market research to produce a statistical profile of their readership in an effort to attract nongay local and regional advertisers. For example, to improve their marketability to nongay advertisers, the ten major gay newspapers of the National Gay Newspaper Guild commissioned Simmons Market Research Bureau in 1991 to undertake a major market study of their readership. Data were produced about the gay readership in Miami, Los Angeles, Boston, San Francisco, Philadelphia, Washington, D.C., Dallas, New York, Houston, and Chicago that matched the results of the studies done for the national gay publications (Fejes and Lennon 2000).

There is little mystery as to why advertisers are very interested in the gay market. As the advertising director of *Out* explained, "Imagine going to an advertiser and saying 'above average income, highly educated, travels a lot, buys all the new electronic toys and gadgets'" (Rosen 1994). In 1994 the major marketing research company Yankelovich Partners conducted what was at that time the most sophisticated study of the gay and lesbian market. In contrast to previous studies, which were based on the readers of various periodicals who voluntarily responded to mail-in questionnaires, this study was based on a random sample of the general population, taking from that sample those who had voluntarily identified themselves as lesbian or gay. Interestingly, this study did not find lesbian and gay consumers to have incomes significantly greater than the general population. However, what was significant was the way the income was spent. The study, which received attention on the front page of the business section of the *New York Times* and the results of which were incorporated later in a book on how to reach the gay consumer, showed gay males and lesbians to be more educated, more technologically oriented, and more likely to be self-employed than the average heterosexual consumer. As a group they were seen as far more "cutting edge," more likely to spend their money on new products. To advertisers, they were a very desirable group of innovative consumers (Elliott 1994; Lukenbill 1995). But while advertisers and marketers talked of a "lesbian and gay" market and lifestyle, the picture generally called to mind was that of a gay male. In advertising the results of its readership study to advertisers, the National Gay Newspaper Guild used the photo of a young white man in a business suit (Fejes and Lennon 2000). For a moment in the early 1990s it seemed that a "lesbian chic" was achieving a mainstream currency, that in terms of style and fashion lesbians would perform the same function for heterosexual women that gay men do for heterosexual men, and that lesbians would be "broken out" as a separate market category (Clark 1991). Yet that moment quickly passed as the advertisers decided that lesbians were not an attractive, identifiable market niche and could moreover be reached through ads aimed at women generally.

Trying to reach a "gay" market is not easy. The effort to construct a market profile of lesbians and gays is fraught with a number of major problems. As with all surveys, the construction and size of the sample determine how representative the results are of the population being measured. The one survey that used a randomly selected sample had a sample size of less than 150 (Wilke 1996). Many of the studies that utilized larger sample sizes obtained their respondents from subscription lists of gay periodicals and direct-mail lists. As a result of this process of self-selection, the samples were highly skewed. A good example of this was the 1991 Simmons study of the readership of major lesbian and gay newspapers. The sample was predominantly male (9:1) and predominantly white-Anglo: in Miami, with a 50 percent Hispanic/Latino population, only 5 percent of the gay readership identified themselves as Hispanic/Latino; and in Washington, D.C.,

with a 66 percent African American population, again only 5 percent of the readers identified themselves as African American (Fejes and Lennon 2000). In contrast, in what is the most comprehensive study of sexual behavior in America, the sociologist Edwin Laumann and his colleagues found that the ratio of gay males to lesbians was 2:1 (Laumann et al. 1994, 303-05) and that more African American males engaged in same-sex behavior and more Hispanics/Latinos identified themselves as homo- or bisexual than Anglos. (Comparable data for females were not given.)

Beyond these technical problems, a basic conceptual problems is involved in these surveys. There is no established method or standard for defining a lesbian or gay person. For example, Laumann and his colleagues found it necessary to break down the category of homosexuality into three dimensions: desire, behavior, and identity, each yielding a different number of homosexuals (Laumann et al. 1994, 292-97). Generally the most common method of categorization is self-identification—it is also the most conservative one. According to Laumann, only 2.8 percent of the men and 1.4 percent of the women identified themselves as homosexual or bisexual. Given the fact that same-sex acts are still outlawed in most states and open disclosure of one's homosexuality can often lead to job loss and other harmful consequences, many lesbians and gay males are reluctant to respond to questions about sexual orientation posed by a census questionnaire, telephone marketing survey, or interviewer. Perhaps it is no surprise that marketing and consumer surveys often show lesbians and gay males as having higher incomes, being self-employed, having higher levels of education, and living in major urban areas. These individuals most likely enjoy a greater sense of personal, professional, and economic security and are thus more willing to be open about their sexual orientation. Finally, the terms "gay" and "lesbian" themselves are not without ambiguity. To many of the pre-Stonewall (pre-1969) generation, the preferred term is "homosexual"; to some of the younger generation, the term is "queer." Furthermore, such studies totally ignore emerging bisexual and transgendered identities.

Nonetheless, in spite of these difficulties, studies of the lesbian and gay consumer continue, as advertisers, marketers, and gay media try to get an accurate picture of what they are dealing with. In the process, advertisers construct identities for lesbians and gay men. As can be discerned, the results of the various studies provide odd and often conflicting information. Studies based on the readership of lesbian/gay periodicals that generally set the pattern have produced a picture of the lesbian/gay market as one consisting of affluent, well-educated individuals with upscale consumption patterns. For example, a 1996 study done by Simmons Market Research Bureau utilizing a sample of almost 4,000 respondents found that 28.6 percent had annual incomes exceeding $50,000 and 21 percent of the households had incomes above $100,000. Close to 60 percent of the respondents held management positions, 48 percent were college educated, and 61 percent had taken a foreign trip in the twelve months preceding the study (Wilke 1997b). However, the sample was drawn from subscription lists of gay periodicals and direct-mail lists. The studies based on samples other than subscription lists for lesbian/gay periodicals, such as the 1994 Yankelovich study and a 1998 study by the New York marketing consultants Spare Parts, tend to show lesbians and gays as having only marginally higher incomes than heterosexuals (Wilke 1998). The two scholarly studies of income among lesbians and gay males—the first using data from the 1990 census, which counted households with unmarried partners of the same sex, and the second using data from the General Social Survey of the National Opinion Research Center—both found that lesbians and gay males actually made less money than their heterosexual counterparts, even when the sample was controlled for profession, education, and region (Klawitter and Flatt 1998; Badgett 1995).

In spite of the problematic aspects of these studies, one can argue that they still represent a marketing process that culminates in more media representations of lesbians and gay males. To lesbians and gay males, after decades of invisibility and marginality and stigmatization, being aggressively courted by advertisers and the media can be a sign of progress. Rather than being portrayed as pathetic, mentally ill sex perverts and child molesters who are threats to religion, home, family, and the state, they are now portrayed as young, healthy, fun to be with, and having a lot of disposable income. Although this marketing campaign is not explicitly political, it fits very well into the broader "assimilationist" strategy advocated by major mainstream lesbian and gay political organizations such as the Human Rights Campaign. Indeed, gay writers about media and marketing—for example, Marshall Kirk and Hunter Madsen, authors of *After the Ball: How America Will Conquer Its Fear and Hatred of Gays in the '90s* (1989), and Grant Lukenbill, author of *Untold Millions: Positioning Your Business for the Gay and Lesbian Consumer Revolution* (1995)—see the proliferation of "positive" (read young, healthy, attractive, mainstream, affluent) gay and lesbian images in the media, be they on television shows or in advertising, as the surest route to political equality and power.

Yet the political benefits of this marketing attention are not all that clear. As Urvashi Vaid noted in her critical study of the problematic nature of the assimilation strategy, *Virtual Equality: The Mainstreaming of Gay and Lesbian Liberation* (1995), being highly valued by marketers means nothing politically unless there is also a strong political movement that presses for political rights and equality. In the 1970s and 1980s the single woman with her own income and life became a standard image in advertising and the media. Yet this did nothing to abate the growth of a strong conservative religious movement demanding that women be "restored" to their traditional role as subservient to their husbands. Racist media images are for the most part a thing of the past, and the inclusion of images of African Americans, Asians, and other people of color in advertising and media products is so common as to be unnoticed. Yet the efforts to scale back affirmative action programs and deny social benefits to immigrants are just one example of how racism is still very much a part of American life. For lesbians and gay males, all the attention that advertisers began to accord them in the late 1980s did little to temper the virulence of the opposition to giving lesbians and gays the right either to serve in the military or to have their relationships legally sanctioned.

Indeed, one can argue that the marketing studies and subsequent advertising and media attention have hurt the lesbian and gay community politically. While these marketing studies do not present a realistic or representative portrayal of the lesbian/gay community, what they have done—lacking any comprehensive demographic information—is to present a picture of the lesbian and gay community that has become very much part of the political discourse about that community. Indeed, in the various political debates about the political and legal status of lesbians and gays that form part of the ongoing "culture wars," the information provided by these marketing studies is often used as an objective description of lesbians and gay males. The professional, affluent image of lesbians and gays created by market research conforms well with the notion that the "homosexual lifestyle" is a choice made mostly by white, well-educated, middle-class males. More important, a claim frequently made by religious and conservative opponents of measures to ban discrimination on the basis of sexual orientation is that lesbians and gay males are not victims of discrimination; rather, if anything, they represent a privileged minority, particularly in terms of income and education (see Concerned Women of America 1991; Knight 1994). In the Supreme Court deliberations in *Romer v. Evans*, over the constitutionality of a Colorado state constitutional provision banning any laws protecting lesbians and gays against discrimination, Justice Antonin Scalia used this argument in voting to uphold the Colorado law ("Excerpts" 1996).

If the political consequences of marketing and advertising to the lesbian and gay community are problematic, so too are the consequences for the lesbian and gay community itself. It has been frequently noted that lesbians and gays often take advertising directed at their community as a sign of validation and legitimation (Penaloza 1996). If they have not yet achieved the status of citizens with full and equal rights, they at least have achieved the status of desirable consumers. For lesbians and gay males, consumption is often an act with political overtones (Kates 1998). They are aware of those companies that advertise in lesbian and gay media and that have lesbian/gay affirmative policies and benefits, and they tend to be loyal to those companies. Conversely, companies that have a reputation for being homophobic are avoided or even actively boycotted.

More significantly, media images and consumption play a more important role in the construction of a definition of the lesbian and gay community and lesbian and gay identity than they do in the process of identity formation of individuals in other groups. In contrast to people of color and other marginalized groups, youths and young adults with primarily same-sex desires and orientation have little or no help in understanding or defining themselves as gay or lesbian. Sexual orientation is fixed early in life, if not at birth, but a lesbian or a gay male develops, or "comes out," in an environment offering little information or role models (Savin-Williams 1990; Herdt 1989). Although the negative stigma attached to homosexuality is reinforced through interpersonal contact, persons who are coming out search both the interpersonal and media environment for clues to understanding their feelings and sense of difference. Thus media images, whether in advertising or other media products, become very powerful in helping one to develop a sense of identity.

In the past the images available to lesbians and gay males in the mainstream media were highly negative. Since the late 1960s, however, the lesbian and gay community began to develop its own community media, which presented alternate and affirmative images (Streitmatter 1995). The pages of these community media tended to be open to a diversity of viewpoints and experiences. For young lesbians and gay males coming out and beginning to define themselves both individually and as members of a community, the community media were very important in providing information and images that they used to construct their identities. However, in the 1980s this community-based nature of the media began to change as various publications decided to pursue the advertising dollars of mainstream advertisers. The publications became more professional and their focus became less the expression of the community's diversity than the shaping of a readership that would attract advertisers.

Today, if a gay male who is coming out turns to the gay media, most likely what he will find is that to be a homosexual in today's society is to be a masculine young white male, with a well-muscled body and handsome face, a good education, and a professional job. Moreover, he will learn, all the members of the gay community are alike. There may be a few African Americans or Asians, albeit with very Caucasian features, and a few women, but aside from their race or gender, there is very little difference. They all live in a gay-friendly environment where there is no sexism, racism, homophobia, or poverty. To be "gay" in this sense the gay male needs an annual income of at least $50,000 so that he can drink top-brand liquors, wear designer clothes, vacation in exotic places, go to the

gym, and ride in an SUV. Whereas in the past coming out was chiefly about sex, today it is as much about consumption.

For a young women coming out, the situation is even more problematic. While the major national magazines like *Out* and the *Advocate* define themselves as serving the entire lesbian and gay male community, in practice the gay male market is their target audience, and thus women are marginalized, if not made invisible. This was made clear in late 1997 when the female editor and cofounder of *Out* magazine was dismissed; the major complaint was directed at her strategy of taking the magazine in a "multifaceted direction . . . which [was] very inclusive of both gay and lesbian issues . . . [but was] not working in the eyes of money people." The new editor was expected to steer "the magazine toward gay men's issues at the expense of coverage of lesbians," as the men have higher incomes (Pogrebin 1997b). Because of their smaller readership, the few publications geared primarily toward lesbians, like *Curve* (formerly known as *Deneuve*), have to try even harder to attract an upscale audience in order to attract mainstream advertisers. These magazines also experienced the need to move away from sexually explicit and political subject matter. The West Coast magazine *Girlfriends* did away with its centerfold and began to concentrate on stories dealing with parenting and breast cancer. The erotic lesbian magazine *On Our Backs*, which symbolized a rebellious assertion of female sexuality, went out of business (Pogrebin 1996). And as is true with the other gay magazines, the concerns and images of the white, upper-middle-class Anglo woman strongly shape the construction of lesbian sexuality.

Social and sexual identities that do not match the desired audience profile are minimized or made totally invisible in these publications. With improvements in printing technology making the publication of small magazines relatively easy, and now with the proliferation of specialized web pages, marginalized desires and identities are allowed some exposure. There is, for example, a magazine for people—primarily gay males—with AIDS (*POZ*); a magazine for African American gay males (*BLK*); *Transgender Tapestry* for transvestites and transsexuals; and numerous magazines for the different sexual communities existing within the lesbian and gay male community, such as the leather and S/M community. Yet the existence of these other publications also reflects the fact that these identities have little place in the dominant gay and lesbian publications. The centuries-old underground gay and lesbian culture—in which people with strongly stigmatized identities blurred class and race boundaries and risked much to affirm their own desires—has been repackaged with its "rough edges" trimmed away. The commodification of gay and lesbian identity has resulted in the construction of a "straight" gay/lesbian identity. As Sarah Schulman notes, "A fake homosexuality has been constructed to facilitate a double marketing strategy: selling products to gay consumers that address their emotional need to be accepted while selling a palatable image of homosexuality to heterosexual consumers that meets their need to have their dominance obscured" (1998, 146). Updating Foucault, it would seem that today the consumer-based media, and not the state, the church, or the scientific professions, are the far more effective creators and regulators of identities and desires.

Furthermore, the consequences of such narrow representation in ads can go beyond the issue of images and identities. With the introduction in the 1990s of protease inhibitors, which significantly slow the progress of the AIDS virus in the body, pharmaceutical companies marketing these new drug therapies became big advertisers in magazines with large gay male readership. Typically their ads showed young, healthy, handsome, affluent, mostly white males engaged in strenuous physical sports or activities like mountain climbing or cross-country biking and encouraged readers with the HIV virus to talk to their

doctors about trying the advertised drug. According to drug companies, ads that put such a healthy and happy face on AIDS "motivat(ed) patients to talk to their doctors about treatment options." What the ads did not show was that the drug therapies did not work for all patients and that, for people for whom the drugs did work, there were often significant side effects, such as liver damage, increased cholesterol, reshaped facial structure, and redistribution of body fat, resulting in bulging stomachs and necks and fatless legs and arms. In reality very few people taking the drugs resembled the men in the ads. Such ads minimized the consequences of AIDS, according to a spring 2001 survey by the University of California, San Francisco, of gay men in health clinics. The overwhelming majority of those surveyed thought the ads promoted unsafe sex. Following the study's release, the U.S. Food and Drug Administration ordered the pharmaceutical companies to change their ads to reflect more accurately the consequences of contracting the AIDS virus (Kirby 2001).

In spite of advertising's open welcome to lesbians and gays, the "gays in the military" and "gay marriage" political firestorms of recent years show how tenuous is the political position of lesbians and gay males. Virulent homophobia is still very much a part of today's landscape, as witnessed by the October 1998 murder of Matthew Shepard, the young gay college student in Wyoming who was ferociously beaten, his skull literally cracked, and then tied to a fence, in a manner similar to ranchers displaying slain wolves, as a warning to others of his kind. Or as witnessed by the February 1999 murder of Billy Jack Gaither, a thirty-nine-year-old rural Alabama gay man who was lured to a deserted spot by two men who bludgeoned him to death with an axe handle and then set his body afire on top of a pyre of old tires. The charred remains of Gaither and the crucified figure of Shepard stand in stark contrast to the images of happy and healthy gay men and lesbians found in heavily ad-saturated magazines like *Out* and the *Advocate*. Homosexuality ignores class, race, ethnic, and regional boundaries; most lesbians and gay men are not twenty-six years old and do not live charmed, pro-tected, and carefree lives in trendy urban centers, earning high incomes in glamorous white-collar professions, going to the gym daily, wearing the latest fashions. The situ-ation of typical lesbians and gay males is much closer to that of Matthew Shepard or Billy Jack Gaither—living in an environ-ment quietly antagonistic at best or at worst openly hostile to their existence, being care-ful as to whom they disclose their sexual identity, and often at risk in the expression of their sexual desire. To these people, the advertising-filled magazines now filling the lesbian/gay magazine sections of chain bookstores like Borders and Barnes & Noble represent a reality in which their lives and experience are once again invisible.

◆ **References**

Badgett, M. V. L. 1995. "The Wage Effects of Sexual Orientation Discrimination." *Indus-trial and Labor Relations Review* 48(4): 726-739.

Baltera, L. 1972, August 28. "No Gay Market Yet, Admen, Gays Agree." *Advertising Age*: 3.

Baltera, L. 1975, July 7. "Marketers Still in Closet Over Gays." *Advertising Age*: 3.

Clark, D. 1991. "Commodity Lesbianism." *Camera Obscura*: 181-196.

Concerned Women for America. 1991. *The Homosexual Deception: Making Sin a Civil Right*. Washington, DC: Concerned Women for America.

Elliott, E. 1994, June 9. "A Sharper View of Gay Consumers." *New York Times*: D1.

"Excerpts from the Courts' Decision on Colorado's Provision for Homosexuals." 1996, May 21. *New York Times*: 20.

Fejes, F., and Lennon, R., 2000. "The Lesbian/ Gay Community? Market Research and the Lesbian/Gay Press." *Journal of Homo-sexuality*: 39(1).

Herdt, G. (Ed.). 1989. *Gay and Lesbian Youth*. Binghamton, NY: Haworth.

Holland, P. 1977, January. "How Straight Is Madison Avenue." *Christopher Street*: 26-29.

Kates, S. 1998. *Twenty Million New Customers: Understanding Gay Men's Consumer Behavior*. New York: Haworth.

Kirby, B. 2001, June 15. "Truth in Advertising." *Advocate*: 15.

Kirk, M., and Madsen, H. 1989. *After the Ball: How America Will Conquer Its Fear and Hatred of Gays in the '90s*. New York: Doubleday.

Klawitter, M. M., and Flatt, V. 1998. "The Effects of State and Local Anti-discrimination Policies for Sexual Orientation." *Journal of Policy Analysis and Management*. 14(4): 658-686.

Knight, Robert H., Family Research Council, Testimony. 1994. *Employment Non-Discrimination Act of 1994: Hearings Before the Committee on Labor and Human Resources*. 103rd Cong., 2d Sess. 29: 92-96.

Merret, M. 1988, December 5. "A Gay Look at Advertising." *Advocate*: 42-45.

Laumann, E. O., Gagnon, J. H., Michael, R. T., and Michaels, S. 1994. *The Social Organi-zation of Sexuality: Sexual Practices in the United States*. Chicago: University of Chicago Press.

Lukenbill, G. 1995. *Untold Millions: Position-ing Your Business for the Gay and Lesbian Consumer Revolution*. New York: Harper-Collins

Miller, C. 1992, July 20. "Mainstream Mar-keters Decide Time Is Right to Target Gays." *Marketing News*: 8.

Pendleton, J. 1980, October 6. "National Mar-keters Beginning to Recognize Gays." *Advertising Age*: 84-85.

Pogrebin, R 1996, December 23. "Lesbian Pub-lications Struggle for Survival in a Market Dominated by Gay Males." *New York Times*: D7.

Penaloza, L. 1996. "We're Here, We're Queer and We're Going Shopping: A Critical Per-spective on the Accommodation of Gays and Lesbians in the U.S. Marketplace." *Journal of Homosexuality* 31(1/2): 9-41.

Pogrebin, R. 1997, December 8. "Ousted Editor Sees Bias at Gay-Lesbian Monthly." *New York Times*: D12.

Rosen, J. 1994, March 7. "*Out* Magazine's National Reach." *New York Times*: D6.

Savin-Williams, R. C. 1990. *Gay and Lesbian Youth: Expressions of Identity*. New York: Hemisphere.

Schulman, S. 1998. *Stage Struck: Theater, AIDS and the Marketing of Gay America*. Durham, NC: Duke University Press.

Sender, K. 1999. "Selling Subjectivities: Audiences Respond to Gay Window Advertising." *Critical Studies in Mass Communication* 16: 172-196.

Stabiner, K. 1982, May 2. "Tapping the Homosexual Market." *New York Times Magazine*: 34.

Vaid, U. 1995. *Virtual Equality: The Mainstreaming of Gay and Lesbian Liberation*. New York: Anchor Books.

Wilke, M. 1996, February 19. "Simmons Plans a Definitive Survey of Gay Consumers" *Advertising Age*: 39.

Wilke, M. 1997a, February 3. "Data Shows Affluence of Gay Market." *Advertising Age*: 58.

Wilke, M. 1997b, August 4. "Big Advertisers Join Move to Embrace Gay Market." *Advertising Age*: 1.

Wilke, M. 1998, October 19. "Fewer Gays Are Wealthy, Data Says." *Advertising Age*: 58.

23

SEX, LIES AND ADVERTISING

◆ Gloria Steinem

... When *Ms.* began, we didn't consider *not* taking ads. The most important reason was keeping the price of a feminist magazine low enough for most women to afford. But the second and almost equal reason was providing a forum where women and advertisers could talk to each other and improve advertising itself. After all, it was (and still is) as potent a source of information in this country as news or TV and movie dramas.

We decided to proceed in two stages. First, we would convince makers of "people products" used by both men and women but advertised mostly to men—cars, credit cards, insurance, sound equipment, financial services, and the like—that their ads should be placed in a women's magazine. Since they were accustomed to the division between editorial and advertising in news and general interest magazines, this would allow our editorial content to be free and diverse. Second, we would add the best ads for whatever traditional "women's products" (clothes, shampoo, fragrance, food, and so on) that surveys showed *Ms.* readers used. But we would ask them to come in *without* the usual quid pro quo of "complementary copy."

We knew the second step might be harder. Food advertisers have always demanded that women's magazines publish recipes and articles on entertaining (preferably ones that name their products) in return for their ads: clothing advertisers expect to be surrounded by fashion spreads

NOTE: Excerpts reprinted from *Ms.*, July/August 1990, by permission of Gloria Steinem.

(especially ones that credit their designers); and shampoo, fragrance, and beauty products in general usually insist on positive editorial coverage of beauty subjects, plus photo credits besides. That's why women's magazines look the way they do. But if we could break this link between ads and editorial content, then we wanted good ads for "women's products," too. . . .

I thought then that our main problem would be the imagery in ads themselves. Carmakers were still draping blondes in evening gowns over the hoods like ornaments. Authority figures were almost always male, even in ads for products that only women used. Sadistic, he-man campaigns even won industry praise. (For instance, *Advertising Age* had hailed the infamous Silva Thin cigarette theme. "How to Get a Woman's Attention: Ignore Her," as "brilliant.") Even in medical journals, tranquilizer ads showed depressed housewives standing beside piles of dirty dishes and promised to get them back to work.

Obviously, *Ms.* would have to avoid such ads and seek out the best ones—but this didn't seem impossible. *The New Yorker* had been selecting ads for aesthetic reasons for years, a practice that only seemed to make advertisers more eager to be in its pages. *Ebony* and *Essence* were asking for ads with positive black images, and though their struggle was hard, they weren't being called unreasonable. . . .

. . . The fact that *Ms.* was asking companies to do business in a different way meant our saleswomen had to make many times the usual number of calls—first to convince agencies and then client companies besides—and to present endless amounts of research. I was often asked to do a final ad presentation, or see some higher decision maker, or speak to women employees so executives could see the interest of women they worked with. That's why I spent more time persuading advertisers than editing or writing for *Ms.* and why I ended up with an unsentimental education in the seamy underside of publishing that few writers see (and even fewer magazines can publish).

Let me take you with us through some experiences, just as they happened:

◆ Cheered on by early support from Volkswagen and one or two other car companies, we scrape together time and money to put on a major reception in Detroit. We know U.S. carmakers firmly believe that women choose the upholstery, not the car, but we are armed with statistics and reader mail to prove the contrary: a car is an important purchase for women, one that symbolizes mobility and freedom.

But almost nobody comes. We are left with many pounds of shrimp on the table, and quite a lot of egg on our face. We blame ourselves for not guessing that there would be a baseball pennant play-off on the same day, but executives go out of their way to explain they wouldn't have come anyway. Thus begins ten years of knocking on hostile doors, presenting endless documentation, and hiring a full-time saleswoman in Detroit: all necessary before *Ms.* gets any real results.

This long saga has a semihappy ending: foreign and, later, domestic carmakers eventually provided *Ms.* with enough advertising to make cars one of our top sources of ad revenue. Slowly, Detroit began to take the women's market seriously enough to put car ads in other women's magazines, too, thus freeing a few pages from the hothouse of fashion-beauty-food ads.

But long after figures showed a third, even a half, of many car models being bought by women, U.S. makers continued to be uncomfortable addressing women. Unlike foreign carmakers, Detroit never quite learned the secret of creating intelligent ads that exclude no one, and then placing them in women's magazines to overcome past exclusion. (*Ms.* readers were so grateful for a routine Honda ad featuring rack and pinion steering, for instance, that they sent fan mail.) Even now, Detroit continues to ask, "Should we make special ads for women?" Perhaps that's why some foreign cars still have a disproportionate share of the U.S. women's market.

◆ In the *Ms.* Gazette, we do a brief report on a congressional hearing into chemicals used in hair dyes that are absorbed through the skin and may be carcinogenic. Newspapers report this too, but Clairol, a Bristol-Myers subsidiary that makes dozens of products—a few of which have just begun to advertise in *Ms.*—is outraged. Not at newspapers or newsmagazines, just at us. It's bad enough that *Ms.* is the only women's magazine refusing to provide the usual "complementary" articles and beauty photos, but to criticize one of their categories—*that* is going too far.

We offer to publish a letter from Clairol telling its side of the story. In an excess of solicitousness, we even put this letter in the Gazette, not in Letters to the Editors where it belongs. Nonetheless—and in spite of surveys that show *Ms.* readers are active women who use more of almost everything Clairol makes than do the readers of any other women's magazine—*Ms.* gets almost none of these ads for the rest of its natural life.

Meanwhile, Clairol changes its hair coloring formula, apparently in response to the hearings we reported.

◆ Our saleswomen set out early to attract ads for consumer electronics: sound equipment, calculators, computers, VCRs, and the like. We know that our readers are determined to be included in the technological revolution. We know from reader surveys that *Ms.* readers are buying this stuff in numbers as high as those of magazines like *Playboy*, or "men 18 to 34," the prime targets of the consumer electronics industry. Moreover, unlike traditional women's products that our readers buy but don't need to read articles about, these are subjects they want covered in our pages. There actually *is* a supportive editorial atmosphere.

"But women don't understand technology," say executives at the end of ad presentations. "Maybe not," we respond, "but neither do men—and we all buy it."

"If women *do* buy it," say the decision makers, "they're asking their husbands and boyfriends what to buy first." We produce letters from *Ms.* readers saying how turned off they are when salesmen say things like "Let me know when your husband can come in."

After several years of this, we get a few ads for compact sound systems. Some of them come from JVC, whose vice president, Harry Elias, is trying to convince his Japanese bosses that there is something called a women's market. At his invitation, I find myself speaking at huge trade shows in Chicago and Las Vegas, trying to persuade JVC dealers that showrooms don't have to be locker rooms where women are made to feel unwelcome. But as it turns out, the shows themselves are part of the problem. In Las Vegas, the only women around the technology displays are seminude models serving champagne. In Chicago, the big attraction is Marilyn Chambers, who followed Linda Lovelace of *Deep Throat* fame as Chuck Traynor's captive and/or employee. VCRs are being demonstrated with her porn videos.

In the end, we get ads for a car stereo now and then, but no VCRs; some IBM personal computers, but no Apple or Japanese ones. We notice that office magazines like *Working Woman* and *Savvy* don't benefit as much as they should from office equipment ads either. In the electronics world, women and technology seem mutually exclusive. It remains a decade behind even Detroit.

◆ Because we get letters from little girls who love toy trains, and who ask our help in changing ads and box-top photos that feature little boys only, we try to get toy-train ads from Lionel. It turns out that Lionel executives *have* been concerned about little girls. They made a pink train, and were surprised when it didn't sell.

Lionel bows to consumer pressure with a photograph of a boy *and* a girl—but only on some of their boxes. They fear that, if trains are associated with girls, they will be devalued in the minds of boys. Needless to say, *Ms.* gets no train ads, and little girls remain a mostly unexplored market. By 1986, Lionel is put up for sale.

But for different reasons, we haven't had much luck with other kinds of toys either. In spite of many articles on child-rearing: an annual listing of nonsexist, multiracial toys by Letty Cottin Pogrebin; Stories for Free Children, a regular feature also edited by Letty; and other prizewinning features for or about children, we get virtually no toy ads. Generations of *Ms.* saleswomen explain to toy manufacturers that a larger proportion of *Ms.* readers have preschool children than do the readers of other women's magazines, but this industry can't believe feminists have or care about children.

◆ When *Ms.* begins, the staff decides not to accept ads for feminine hygiene sprays or cigarettes: they are damaging and carry no appropriate health warnings. Though we don't think we should tell our readers what to do, we do think we should provide facts so they can decide for themselves. Since the antismoking lobby has been pressing for health warnings on cigarette ads, we decide to take them only as they comply.

Philip Morris is among the first to do so. One of its brands, Virginia Slims, is also sponsoring women's tennis and the first national polls of women's opinions. On the other hand, the Virginia Slims theme, "You've come a long way, baby," has more than a "baby" problem. It makes smoking a symbol of progress for women.

We explain to Philip Morris that this slogan won't do well in our pages, but they are convinced its success with some women means it will work with *all* women. Finally, we agree to publish an ad for a Virginia Slims calendar as a test. The letters from readers are critical—and smart. For instance: Would you show a black man picking cotton, the same man in a Cardin suit, and symbolize the antislavery and civil rights movements by smoking? Of course not. But instead of honoring the test results,

the Philip Morris people seem angry to be proven wrong. They take away ads for *all* their many brands.

This costs *Ms.* about $250,000 the first year. After five years, we can no longer keep track. Occasionally, a new set of executives listens to *Ms.* saleswomen, but because we won't take Virginia Slims, not one Philip Morris product returns to our pages for the next 16 years.

Gradually, we also realize our naiveté, in thinking we *could* decide against taking cigarette ads. They became a disproportionate support of magazines the moment they were banned on television, and few magazines could compete and survive without them: certainly not *Ms.*, which lacks so many other categories. By the time statistics in the 1980s showed that women's rate of lung cancer was approaching men's, the necessity of taking cigarette ads has become a kind of prison.

◆ General Mills, Pillsbury, Carnation, Del Monte, Dole, Kraft, Stouffer, Hormel, Nabisco: you name the food giant, we try it. But no matter how desirable the *Ms.* readership, our lack of recipes is lethal.

We explain to them that placing food ads *only* next to recipes associates food with work. For many women, it is a negative that works *against* the ads. Why not place food ads in diverse media without recipes (thus reaching more men, who are now a third of the shoppers in supermarkets anyway), and leave the recipes to specialty magazines like *Gourmet* (a third of whose readers are also men)?

These arguments elicit interest, but except for an occasional ad for a convenience food, instant coffee, diet drinks, yogurt, or such extras as avocados and almonds, this mainstay of the publishing industry stays closed to us. Period.

◆ Traditionally, wines and liquors didn't advertise to women: men were thought to make the brand decisions, even if women did the buying. But after endless presentations, we begin to make a dent in this category. Thanks to the unconventional Michel Roux of Carillon Importers (distributors of Grand Marnier, Absolut Vodka, and others), who assumes that food and drink have no gender, some ads are leaving their men's club.

Beermakers are still selling masculinity. It takes *Ms.* fully eight years to get its first beer ad (Michelob). In general, however, liquor ads are less stereotyped in their imagery—and far less controlling of the editorial content around them—than are women's products. But given the underrepresentation of other categories, these very facts tend to create a disproportionate number of alcohol ads in the pages of *Ms.* This in turn dismays readers worried about women and alcoholism.

◆ We hear in 1980 that women in the Soviet Union have been producing feminist *samizdat* (underground, self-published books) and circulating them throughout the country. As punishment, four of the leaders have been exiled. Though we are operating on our usual shoestring, we solicit individual contributions to send Robin Morgan to interview these women in Vienna.

The result is an exclusive cover story that includes the first news of a populist peace movement against the Afghanistan occupation, a prediction of *glasnost* to come, and a grass-roots, intimate view of Soviet women's lives. From the popular press to women's studies courses, the response is great. The story wins a Front Page award.

Nonetheless, this journalistic coup undoes years of efforts to get an ad schedule from Revlon. Why? Because the Soviet women on our cover *are not wearing makeup.*

◆ Four years of research and presentations go into convincing airlines that women now make travel choices and business trips. United, the first airline to advertise in *Ms.*, is so impressed with the response from our readers that one of its executives appears in a film for our ad presentations. As usual, good ads get great results.

But we have problems unrelated to such results. For instance: because American Airlines flight attendants include among their labor demands the stipulation that they could choose to have their last names preceded by "Ms." on their name tags—in a long-delayed revolt against the standard, "I am your pilot, Captain Rothgart, and this is your flight attendant, Cindy Sue"—American officials seem to hold the magazine responsible. We get no ads.

There is still a different problem at Eastern. A vice president cancels subscriptions for thousands of copies on Eastern flights. Why? Because he is offended by ads for lesbian poetry journals in the *Ms.* Classified. A "family airline," as he explains to me coldly on the phone, has to "draw the line somewhere."

It's obvious that *Ms.* can't exclude lesbians and serve women. We've been trying to make that point ever since our first issue included an article by and about lesbians, and both Suzanne Levine, our managing editor, and I were lectured by such heavy hitters as Ed Kosner, then editor of *Newsweek* (and now of *New York Magazine*), who insisted that *Ms.* should "position" itself *against* lesbians. But our advertisers have paid to reach a guaranteed number of readers, and soliciting new subscriptions to compensate for Eastern would cost $150,000, plus rebating money in the meantime.

Like almost everything ad-related, this presents an elaborate organizing problem. After days of searching for sympathetic members of the Eastern board, Frank Thomas, president of the Ford Foundation, kindly offers to call Roswell Gilpatrick, a director of Eastern. I talk with Mr. Gilpatrick, who calls Frank Borman, then the president of Eastern. Frank Borman calls me to say that his airline is not in the business of censoring magazines: *Ms.* will be returned to Eastern flights. . . .

◆ Women of color read *Ms.* in disproportionate numbers. This is a source of pride to *Ms.* staffers, who are also more racially representative than the editors of other women's magazines. But this reality is obscured by ads filled with enough white women to make a reader snowblind.

Pat Carbine remembers mostly "astonishment" when she requested African American, Hispanic, Asian, and other diverse images. Marcia Ann Gillespie, a *Ms.* editor who was previously the editor in chief of *Essence*, witnesses ad bias a second time: having tried for *Essence* to get white advertisers to use black images (Revlon did so eventually, but L'Oréal, Lauder, Chanel, and other companies never did), she sees similar problems getting integrated ads for an integrated magazine. Indeed, the ad world often creates black and Hispanic ads only for black and Hispanic media. In an exact parallel of the fear that marketing a product to women will endanger its appeal to men, the response is usually, "But your [white] readers won't identify."

In fact, those we are able to get—for instance, a Max Factor ad made for *Essence* that Linda Wachner gives us after she becomes president—is praised by white readers, too. But there are pathetically few such images.

◆ By the end of 1986, production and mailing costs have risen astronomically, ad income is flat, and competition for ads is stiffer than ever. The 60/40 preponderance of edit over ads that we promised to readers becomes 50/50; children's stories, most poetry, and some fiction are casualties of less space: in order to get variety into limited pages, the length (and sometimes the depth) of articles suffers; and, though we do refuse most of the ads that would look like a parody in our pages, we get so worn down that some slip through. . . . Still, readers perform miracles. Though we haven't been able to afford a subscription mailing in two years, they maintain our guaranteed circulation of 450,000.

Nonetheless, media reports on *Ms.* often insist that our unprofitability must be due to reader disinterest. The myth that advertisers simply follow readers is very strong. Not one reporter notes that other comparable magazines our size (say, *Vanity Fair* or *The Atlantic*) have been losing more money in one year than *Ms.* has lost in 16 years. No matter how much never-to-be-recovered cash is poured into starting a magazine or keeping one going, appearances seem to be all that matter. (Which is why we haven't been able to explain our fragile state in public. Nothing causes ad-flight like the smell of nonsuccess.)

My healthy response is anger. My not-so-healthy response is constant worry. Also an obsession with finding one more rescue. There is hardly a night when I don't wake up with sweaty palms and pounding heart, scared that we won't be able to pay the printer or the post office; scared most of all that closing our doors will hurt the women's movement.

Out of chutzpah and desperation, I arrange a lunch with Leonard Lauder, president of Estée Lauder. With the exception of Clinique (the brainchild of Carol Phillips), none of Lauder's hundreds of products has been advertised in *Ms.* A year's schedule of ads for just three or four of them could save us. Indeed, as the scion of a family-owned company whose ad practices are followed by the beauty industry, he is one of the few men who could liberate many pages in all women's magazines just by changing his mind about "complementary copy."

Over a lunch that costs more than we can pay for some articles, I explain the need for his leadership. I also lay out the record of *Ms.*: more literary and journalistic prizes won, more new issues introduced into the mainstream, new writers discovered, and impact on society than any other magazine: more articles that became books, stories that became movies, ideas that became television series, and newly advertised products that became profitable: and, most important for him, a place for his ads to reach women who aren't reachable through any other women's magazine. Indeed, if there is one constant characteristic of the ever-changing *Ms.* readership, it is their impact as leaders. Whether it's waiting until later to have first babies, or pioneering PABA as sun protection in cosmetics, *whatever* they are doing today, a third to a half of American women will be doing three to five years from now. It's never failed.

But, he says, *Ms.* readers are not *our* women. They're not interested in things like fragrance and blush-on. If they were, *Ms.* would write articles about them.

On the contrary, I explain, surveys show they are more likely to buy such things than the readers of, say, *Cosmopolitan* or *Vogue.* They're good customers because they're out in the world enough to need several sets of everything: home, work, purse, travel, gym, and so on. They just don't need to read articles about these things. Would he ask a men's magazine to publish monthly columns on how to shave before he advertised Aramis products (his line for men)?

He concedes that beauty features are often concocted more for advertisers than readers. But *Ms.* isn't appropriate for his ads anyway, he explains. Why? Because Estée Lauder is selling "a kept-woman mentality."

I can't quite believe this. Sixty percent of the users of his products are salaried, and generally resemble *Ms.* readers. Besides, his company has the appeal of having been started by a creative and hardworking woman, his mother, Estée Lauder.

That doesn't matter, he says. He knows his customers, and they would *like* to be kept women. That's why he will never advertise in *Ms.*

In November 1987, by vote of the Ms. Foundation for Education and Communication (*Ms.*'s owner and publisher, the media subsidiary of the Ms. Foundation for Women), *Ms.* was sold to a company whose officers, Australian feminists Sandra Yates

and Anne Summers, raised the investment money in their country that *Ms.* couldn't find in its own. They also started *Sassy* for teenage women.

In their two-year tenure, circulation was raised to 550,000 by investment in circulation mailings, and, to the dismay of some readers, editorial features on clothes and new products made a more traditional bid for ads. Nonetheless, ad pages fell below previous levels. In addition, *Sassy*, whose fresh voice and sexual frankness were an unprecedented success with young readers, was targeted by two mothers from Indiana who began, as one of them put it, "calling every Christian organization I could think of." In response to this controversy, several crucial advertisers pulled out.

Such links between ads and editorial content was a problem in Australia, too, but to a lesser degree. "Our readers pay two times more for their magazines," Anne explained, "so advertisers have less power to threaten a magazine's viability."

"I was shocked," said Sandra Yates with characteristic directness. "In Australia, we think you have freedom of the press—but you don't."

Since Anne and Sandra had not met their budget's projections for ad revenue, their investors forced a sale. In October 1989, *Ms.* and *Sassy* were bought by Dale Lang, owner of *Working Mother, Working Woman*, and one of the few independent publishing companies left among the conglomerates. In response to a request from the original *Ms.* staff—as well as to reader letters urging that *Ms.* continue, plus his own belief that *Ms.* would benefit his other magazines by blazing a trail—he agreed to try the ad-free, reader-supported *Ms.* you hold now and to give us complete editorial control. . . .

24

IN SPITE OF WOMEN

Esquire *Magazine and the Construction of the Male Consumer*

◆ Kenon Breazeale

The proper study of mankind is man ... but the proper study of markets is woman.

—Ad in *Printer's Ink* 1929

Much of what the modern world deems appropriate sex roles is embedded in a nutshell dichotomy—men produce and women shop. For years, this stereotype has been attracting feminist scholarly attention. From Betty Friedan's *The Feminine Mystique* (1963) to the upsurge of publication on the subject during the last decade, feminist scholars have asserted that the encoding of modern female identity has everything to do with attempts to construct women as consumers.[1] In this [chapter] I want to expand the discussion by offering a refocused premise—that precisely because consumption has been viewed as an

NOTE: From "In Spite of Women," by Kenon Breazeale, in *Signs*, Vol. 20, No. 1, 1994, pp. 1-22. Copyright © 1994 by University of Chicago Press.

attribute of middle-class femininity, some of our era's most aggressively one-dimensional representations of women have resulted from attempts to court men as consumers. Specifically, I want to examine *Esquire* magazine, which I would argue was the first thoroughgoing, conscious attempt to organize a consuming male audience. From the magazine's origin in 1933 until the 1946 departure of its influential founding editor, Arnold Gingrich, *Esquire*'s editorial staff sought to constitute consumption as a new arena for masculine privilege by launching in text and image what amounted to an oppositional meta-commentary on female identity. In other words, this "magazine for men" was to a great extent a magazine about women. . . .

Two recent social histories of image making and design, *All Consuming Images* (Ewen 1988) and *Making the Modern* (Smith 1993), persuasively argue that modern American commercial culture came into being during the 1930s. Driven by the felt necessity of reviving market demand, corporate and governmental attention shifted from production to the consumer, encouraging the marketing industry to new levels of influence and new subtleties of theory. Economists and industrial engineers collaborated with admen to originate a new pseudo-science: "consumption engineering." They evolved the logic (still in place today) that real profits lie in constantly organizing taste in new ways (Meikle 1979, 68-70). Only by sophisticated methods of manipulating and reconceptualizing consumer audiences, they posited, could corporate America revive and prosper.[2] *Esquire*, I will show, was one of the first and clearest sites of this consciousness at work.

Depression-bred anxiety about the impact of devastating economic change on traditional bourgeois sex roles provided the specific inspiration for *Esquire*'s creation. Lois Scharf and others have documented that twenties-formed habits of consumption collided during the early thirties with massive unemployment to push a cohort of middle-class married women into the workforce (Scharf 1980, chap. 7). Surely not by coincidence, social commentators rapidly developed a discourse that highlighted diminished male self-esteem as an outgrowth of the Depression. Pundits of Eleanor Roosevelt's stature argued that losing one's job, whether real or feared, and the possibility of seeing one's wife forced to become a breadwinner was resulting in a dislocating loss of masculine self-respect (Roosevelt 1933, 20). The opportunity seized by *Esquire* was recognizing that this multivalent "loss" could be refigured into the site of a marketable new male identity. Key to such sleight of hand was the notion of "leisure," a buzzword among Roosevelt braintrusters who hoped that commodifying the free time attendant on a reduced work week would lead to more consumer spending.[3] In deluxe promotional booklets meant to alert ad agency directors to his magazine's first issue, Gingrich appropriated the term, suggesting: "Men have had leisure thrust upon them. Now they've got it, they must spend it somehow. . . . What more opportune occasion for the appearance of a new magazine—a new kind of magazine—one that will answer the question of What to do? What to eat, what to drink, what to wear, how to play, what to read—in short a magazine dedicated to the improvement of the new leisure" (Gingrich 1971, 102). . . .

As the ad industry of the twenties sought to professionalize itself, it generated a body of theory and research on marketing. No aspect of this lore made more of an impact than the "finding" that selling meant selling to women (Ewen 1976, 167). Articles touting women as the crucial market ran regularly in the advertising tradepaper *Printer's Ink*; and two influential books, Christine Frederick's *Selling Mrs. Consumer* (1929) and Carl Naether's *Advertising to Women* (1928), piled on statistics that demonstrated women's "buying power." The first line of Naether's introduction claimed, "Women are indeed the shoppers of the world." . . .

Widespread acceptance of not only the avalanche of statistics but also the mythology that accompanied it profoundly affected the publishing business. Women's magazines willing to organize editorial content around the presumption of "educated shopping" as a sign of responsible femininity benefited from an advertising bonanza (Matthews 1987, chap. 7). Both such values in and of themselves and the girlishly condescending style in which they were purveyed provided a ripe target for satire. Not surprisingly, some in the journalism fraternity began identifying the feminine with gullible vulnerability to consumerism's trashy faddishness. Throughout the 1920s a humorous discourse evolved that equated women's winning the vote with their gaining unbridled power as consumers. Male pundits (the best known being H. L. Mencken and Harold Nicholson) expressed a wide-ranging hostility toward women's (inferior) tastes and tendencies coming to dominate the cultural marketplace.[4]

Enter *Esquire*'s founders, David Smart and William Weintraub, partners whose backgrounds significantly lay in marketing rather than literature or journalism.[5] Both were in menswear, Smart as a producer of trade catalogs and Weintraub as an ad linage salesman. Their decision to found a magazine was inspired by *Fortune*, the surprise success story of early-thirties publishing. Henry Luce had taken the trade paper formula (i.e., business-to-business advertising) and repackaged it as an immensely stylish vehicle for the new corporate culture. What *Fortune* "proved" to Smart and Weintraub was that, with the right demographic, a male-identified magazine could arouse widespread interest among national advertisers. The partnership had expert knowledge of just such an audience. Customers of men's clothing stores were among the few reliably prosperous cohorts in U.S. society during the early thirties, and the partnership decided to launch a magazine that could serve as a vehicle for men's apparel ads.[6] Interestingly enough, the question of editorial content seems to have been a virtual afterthought. It was a young copywriter (soon to be editor)

in their employ, Arnold Gingrich, who conceived the new magazine's core concept. Shrewdly surveying the popular media landscape, he perceived real promise in the collision point between the success of formula women's magazines and masculine journalism's contempt for this phenomenon. In language that would have done Mencken proud, Gingrich simultaneously identified a readership and a cause, the "neglected" male: "It is our belief, in offering *Esquire* to the American male, that we are only getting around at last to a job that should have been done a long time ago—that of giving the masculine reader a break. The general magazines, in the mad scramble to increase the woman readership that seems to be so highly prized by national advertisers, have bent over backwards in catering to the special interests and tastes of the feminine audience. This has reached the point where the male reader is made to feel like an intruder on gynaecic mysteries" (*Esquire* 1933, 4).

Gingrich's rhetoric reveals in a nutshell what would become the crucial dynamic of his new magazine—simultaneous exploitation and denial of the feminine. Not that the young editor would have admitted it. He pointedly claimed as inspiration the *New Yorker* and *Vanity Fair* and hoped his magazine's reputation would derive from publishing fiction by the likes of Hemingway and Fitzgerald. But in truth *Esquire* appropriated the mix of contents that has characterized women's magazines from the 1920s on: a centerpiece of seductive "lifestyle" features whose job is to service advertisers by transforming reader into consumer, leavened with visuals and fiction. Like the *Ladies' Home Journal*, *Vogue*, and *Harper's Bazaar*, *Esquire*'s nonfiction core sought to create a comprehensive set of expectations about what constitutes a desirable upper-middle-class identity. But that very parallel offered up an enormous difficulty for the magazine. Most of the activities being touted—cooking, interior decoration, and so on—were by definition fatally associated with housewifery. Somehow

Esquire had to displace all the woman-identified associations so firmly lodged at the center of America's commodified domestic environment. The solution was a magazine replete with entire categories of nonfiction whose agenda, no matter what their surface content, was a thoroughgoing attempt to detach the imputation of femininity from that arena of domestic consumption *Esquire* planned to open for its male readers. From the beginning, a majority of its lifestyle articles were written to a formula, the tone arch but the point apocalyptic: American standards and taste are in decay, undermined by the pin-headed women who have come to dominate home and control pocketbook. In virtually every article on food, drink, home decor, gardening, etiquette, and the like published between 1933 and 1946, *Esquire* gave advice to counter the looming rhetorical prop of a woman who is doing things all wrong.

Article and columns on food—what and how to eat in home and restaurant, recipes, and cooking instructions—were a frequent locale for critiques of the appalling sway women's magazines and their "food disposition editors" supposedly maintained over the American housewife. In a 1936 article entitled "Dinner Bites Man," the author complained that "our table, once decorated by steaks, roasts and fowl . . . had been turned into a shambles of rosebud radishes and carrot teensie-weensies . . . our so-called dining room had taken on the aspect of a valentine store after an explosion" (Hough 1936, 46). . . . "Will anyone explain why women can't cook?" another author pleaded. "My private summing up is that women can't cook as well as men because pro primo, they are less generous, pro secondo, they have less imagination, and protertio, they just do not enjoy good food" (Pine 1939, 51).

In home decor women were also accused of overvaluing appearance, this time at the expense of comfort. In putting forth a notion of masculine taste, the author of a regular decorating column noted with approval "the passing of the vogue for cluttering up the home with antiques of the most unlivable type, so long an ardent passion with most women and always a posterior pain to most men" (Jackson 1935, 109). But certainly the most consistently cranky vision of feminine incompetence was evoked in matters of strong drink. A 1936 article instructing how to give a cocktail party cautioned, "Remember, we are well into Repeal, and people . . . expect good liquor—especially because you are a man. That's another reason women say they like men's parties better—you get better drinks" (Powell 1936, 118). Less generously, another author claimed that women can't tell good from bad and advised the thrifty bachelor to pass off "cheap native fizzy water" as imported champagne (Nathan 1945, 106). If left to their own devices, it is darkly hinted, women prefer "fluffy, multi-colored abominations," or worse, do not like to drink at all.

In such monthly columns, *Esquire*'s staff knit misogynistic cultural threads familiar for decades into a wide-ranging set of assertions about the gendered meaning of good and bad taste. Apologists for modernism since the late nineteenth century had linked their favored style with masculinity—clean, functional, machine-based design, indeed innovation itself, was virile. By contrast, ornamentation meant the mire of reflexive tradition meant the feminine, an opposition rooted in late-eighteenth-century reasoning that associated the corrupt excesses of the ancien régime with rococo as style and that, in turn, with illicit political influence à la Pompadour (Cheney and Cheney 1936, 48). A paradoxically reverse logic was contained in claims about women's attitudes toward food and drink. Here *Esquire* promoted a favorite canard: that women are deeply antisensual and, having no appreciation for the delights of the flesh, are given to irrational suspicion of all indulgence. Hence the female desire to interject irrelevant moral questions into areas of harmless pleasure and to call for controls where none are needed.

In concocting this take on femininity, *Esquire*'s writers drew on and powerfully reinforced a mythology basic to the twentieth century's "retelling" of nineteenth-century women's history. The temperance and social purity impulses were collapsed into the women's rights movement to create a one-dimensional historical cipher—a man-hating, prudish, censorious creature whose anti-alcohol obsession was a key to reimposing the worst aspects of Calvinist repression on the American psyche (Evans 1989, 175). Not coincidentally, such a caricature underwrote an agenda very important for the magazine. Repeal occurred in the year of *Esquire*'s founding, and reintroduction into the marketplace of a product strongly identified with masculinity was largely responsible for the magazine's initial success. Many periodicals disdained any connection with alcoholic beverages, so *Esquire*'s willingness to tout beer, wine, and liquor as adjuncts to the good life made those industries important early advertisers in its pages.[7] The magazine's equation of prohibitionist sentiments with powerful negative feminine stereotypes contributed a gender-loaded tilt to thirties arguments about public good and private enterprise. It identified support of economic opportunity with expressive individuality and linked both to tolerant, sophisticated masculinity.

. . . *Esquire*'s assertions about gender, taste, consumption, and social identity radically subverted not only assumptions about the meaning of femininity and masculinity implicit in women's magazines but also the very structure of the periodicals industry. From its beginnings the industry had cultivated a mode of address ("Dear Reader . . .") that endowed readers with a specifically gendered identity and by the mid-nineteenth century had evolved editorial genres tied to sex-categorized interests and activities (Shevelow 1989, 3). In fact an argument could be made that the widespread acceptance of separate social roles for bourgeois men and women was to some extent a product of magazine culture. Women's magazines of the twenties and thirties retained a strong echo of this worldview. They held that evident differences in masculine and feminine taste ultimately devolved from legitimately contrasting and mutually complementary biological and social roles. In embracing the women's magazine formula while trashing women, *Esquire* by definition confronted the popular periodical industry and its attendant arena of marketing culture with a very different premise—that women as women have no legitimate social role to play.

Taken as a whole, *Esquire*'s nonfiction of the thirties and forties added up to an ideological system, the project of which was remapping the territory on which difference was plotted. To recuperate successfully a female-identified role for men meant arguing against traditional sex-linked social roles. Yet claiming difference on some level was absolutely necessary to maintain male sex privilege. The magazine's lifestyle components—all of its advice and commentary modes—finessed this contradiction via a "postfeminist" argument. *Esquire*'s new domestic scenario was touted as "progress" for women as well as men, the enemy of both conceived of as some outmoded model of hyperdomestic femininity. Yet simultaneously the transformation of women's postsuffrage identity was read negatively. Modern womanhood, exploiting men's willingness to relinquish traditional modes of patriarchal dominance, was seen as out of control, a "problem" waiting to be "solved."[8] The solution was in essence proposed by the other body of contents in *Esquire* that sought to extensively represent women—its illustrations. As I will demonstrate below, *Esquire*'s pictorial contents offered its male audience what amounted to a system of compensatory control devised around the sexual gaze and specifically attuned to "modern" bourgeois sensibilities.

. . . As with its female-focused nonfiction, *Esquire*'s visual images of women originated in a kind of hysteria. Basic to my argument about *Esquire* is a contention that the magazine was compelled to represent women in order to negotiate its relationship to the feminine. Only with the question of femininity "settled" could a credible space be opened up wherein to construct the consuming male. Hence the project of the text was to displace that archetype of consuming femininity, the housewife. And hence the function of the visuals was to deny an even more dangerous association with femininity, homosexuality. From the moment of its inception, *Esquire*'s founders were fearful that their magazine's interest in apparel, food, decor, and so on might make it appear to be targeted at homosexuals (as Gingrich wrote, that "a whiff of lavender" might seem to perfume its pages [1971, 81]). It had to be made unequivocally clear that women were the natural objects of its readership's desire.[9] Thus it was taken as given that the magazine would prominently feature erotically coded representations of women. Much of the magazine's tone and character was determined by the means devised both to include such illustrations and to reassure its readership about consuming them. Implicit in all this was, I would suggest, one of modern popular culture's most influential attempts to embody represented femininity as a signifier for specifically hetero-sexual masculinity.

Featuring erotic spectacle in a mainstream publication was possible only because *Esquire* was founded at a moment when the function of illustration was being transformed. During the thirties, the visual contents of periodicals became detached from illustrational function, a move facilitated by improved color reproduction techniques and encouraged by the fragmenting fact of increased full-page advertising. (Two new magazines of the thirties, *Life* and *Look*, made the focus on visuals their founding premise.) For the first time, images were presented to be consumed on their own, creating a potential distance in production of meaning between textual and visual contents. Nowhere was this possibility more shrewdly exploited than in *Esquire*. There it became the means to negotiate around taboos that had heretofore limited the profitability of "male-oriented" periodicals.

Throughout the late nineteenth century and the early decades of the twentieth, a whole "for-men-only" publishing category of sexual provocation had existed (magazines with photographs of nude models intended for "artists," e.g.). But it remained only a modestly profitable endeavor segregated from the high-circulation market, where major advertisers catered to a "family" audience thought to be regulated by female sensibilities (Gabor 1972, 5). Once the decision had been made by *Esquire*'s founders to feature cheesecake, the challenge was to contrive a balance, or better put, a tension, between a sub rosa assertion that the magazine was enjoyably salacious and a more overt claim that it was absolutely respectable, belonging on the coffee table, not hidden upstairs in the sock drawer. Playing off the contrast between verbal and visual, an editorial structure was evolved wherein sexy visuals could be both exploited and rendered in a sense "invisible." Through editorial cues the magazine presented its identity as a set of overlapped contrasts—text versus visuals, male subject versus female object, writing virtually always by men versus running features with titles like "Legs and the Woman"—that coalesced into an overarching contrast of serious, verbal masculinity versus frivolous, mute femininity. The pictorial material was constituted as a kind of bimbo zone, unworthy of serious consideration and (hopefully) of serious complaint.[10]

. . . Lynda Nead, in her recently published *The Female Nude* (1992, 85), observes the vital distinctions Western culture has structured into the oppositional categories of fine arts versus pornography/obscenity. Her point is that nude images tend to be firmly contexualized into one or the other category. *Esquire*'s crucial innovation was to embrace both, creating a dyad that appeared in virtually every number, "framing" the magazine's representation of women.

"Fine arts" was signified in portfolio presentations of works by prominent artists such as Rockwell Kent, Salvador Dali, and Yasuo Kuniyoshi where generic art modes like landscape and still life legitimated the inclusion of nudes. At the other end of the register was the type of image that specifically signified prurient appeal—the pinup. Society takes the significant boundary between acceptable and pornographic images to be whether the audience is moved to contemplation or sexual activity. While a majority of *Esquire*'s images of women were meant to be provocative, it was the pinup that was explicitly coded as a masturbatory aide.

No doubt in an attempt to evoke associations with the Gibson Girl, *Esquire*'s pinups were called Petty Girls in tribute to their originator.[11] George Petty's drawings are exemplars of the fetishizing possibilities inherent in airbrush: bodies encased in a flawlessly taut sheath of skin that resembles inflated rubber. . . . The Petty Girl was both source and example of the generic anatomical formula used to depict women in a vast majority of *Esquire*'s illustrations. Prototypically blonde with large breasts, tiny waist, small buttocks, and long, slender legs, she is a specifically Caucasian archetype of erotic appeal. And reinforcing her "whiteness" is the emphasis airbrush perforce gives to depicted surface; the Petty Girl's most noticeable attribute is her flawlessly smooth, pale peach-colored skin.

With fine arts and pinups, *Esquire* associated itself with recognized ways of seeing: aesthetic contemplation and consuming desire. The former bore just the highbrow associations desirable for (if not necessarily desired by) a middle-classy readership. But the pinup was highly problematic, fraught with downscale (i.e., working-class) suggestions of deprivation and sweaty need. *Esquire* had to somehow reframe the conditions under which images deemed sexually provocative were consumed so as to create an aura of sophisticated recreation. Two other regular pictorial features—the covers and cartoons—worked to do just

that, socializing readers into a humorously presented vocabulary and point of view for sexual looking.

. . . By the 1920s, major magazines had refined cover art into a site wherein the demographically targeted reader was endowed with an identity and appealed to on that basis. After Norman Rockwell's covers for the *Saturday Evening Post*, *Esquire*'s covers were the most effectively recognizable in the industry. Under the magazine's logo appeared a photographed tableau of puppet figures starring Esky, the magazine's trademark. Esky (a cartoonish send-up of the *New Yorker*'s Edwardian dandy?) sported an upscale wardrobe, blonde walrus mustaches, and his most distinctive attribute, huge pop eyes with protruding button-like pupils that leered toward the complementary upthrust breasts of female companions who accompanied him in some seasonally themed scene. Repeated with minor variations for years, this cover design drove home *Esquire*'s basic proposition that heterosexual social life consists of a mutually agreeable dialogue between male consciousness and female anatomy.

Cartoons were the other locale in which *Esquire* promoted the normalcy of what Freud clinically termed *scopophilia*, that is, the voyeuristic gaze. "Adult" cartoons already had a track record as a popular illustrational form. During and after World War I racy cartoon books that capitalized on themes of sexual looking found a sizable audience. *Esquire* adopted the genre with two innovations: transforming the traditional format of cursory line drawings into full-page color "artworks" and reorienting what had been a fairly gender-neutral humor (about themes like nudism, e.g.) around a specifically masculine position. In an average of about five cartoons per issue, the magazine rang variations on stock situations in which men could conceivably encounter a naked woman. All emphasized a kind of looking in which the man is an initiate and the woman a more or less unsuspecting object. Women are surprised in the bathtub by window washers, burglars, and firefighters. Or there is the accidental loss of clothes, particularly bathing suit tops, to vagaries of wind, weather, outboard motors, sharks, etc. Doctor-patient jokes present a particularly unnerving riff on vulnerable nudity. (To an undressed woman surrounded by slobbering male medicos, "But surely Miss Lonsdale, you've heard of consultations?") But by far the single favorite theme was artist and model, where the joke is the lustful look concealed behind the artistic regard ("Why Mr. DeMunson, you're not painting me at all!"). Male gallery-goers, whose reaction to painted and sculpted nudes pointedly collapses the distance between art and life, form a variation on the theme ("$2,500 is rather high; I can get a live one for less than that!").[12]

Reinforcing *Esquire's* commitment to dichotomized sexualities was the concentrated attention cartoons gave to two comic female types—the gold digger and the black domestic. The gold digger constituted the perfect ideological foil for the male gaze, a Menckenesque persona all too willing to trade sex for money.[13] *Esquire* presented her in a variety of guises, from naive young working-class girl to the calculating sophisticate who is an expert at coaxing ever larger "gifts" out of befuddled elderly plutocrats. In what appeared to be studied contrast are the numerous cartoons that featured black maids and housekeepers. While the gold digger's anatomy was derived from the pinup and signifies sexual attractiveness, black women were imaged as fat or as simian and stringy. And while the gold digger's desires were taken to be purely acquisatory, black women were seen as quite sexual, that is, as promiscuous baby machines. (White employer meets black housekeeper with baby carriage on the street, "Why Maisie, I thought you were an old maid!" "Yassum, but I ain't a fussy old maid.")[14] *Esquire* endorsed a significant double-think about race and gender. With ostentatious liberal rhetoric the magazine featured the work of black author Langston

Hughes and illustrator Simms Campbell.[15] Yet in text as well as image *Esquire* constantly ridiculed black women. In addition to the cartoon features, the magazine published during the thirties a lengthy comic serial featuring one Mrs. Geranium Finn, a Harlem resident and the embodiment of every racist stereotype from nymphomania to illiteracy to comic social pretensions.

These monthly pictorial categories mapped the boundaries—art, sex, and ironic humor—within which women were to be represented and tutored the reader as to the position appropriate for him to assume when looking at women. But to my mind the most revealing *Esquire* visuals are the occasional features that deliberately put these elements into solution. With these features one can see clearly the ideological work—the veiling of contradiction—accomplished by *Esquire* during the thirties and forties that in turn made possible a postwar men's magazine industry predicated upon balancing titillation and reassurance.

Virtually all of *Esquire's* images of women attempted reference to the aesthetic, most obviously via use of a variety of art media and recognizably current art styles. Regularly included were oil, airbrush, and watercolor painting, pastels, sculpture, ceramics, collage, several printmaking media, and photography; stylistic codes ranged from cubism and fauvism to surrealism. (In sum, the virtual taxonomy of an art school curriculum.) Such arty manipulation was meant to transform not so much the woman in the image as the man looking at it—from voyeur to connoisseur. Certain pictorials pushed the signifier "fine arts" aggressively, hence fudging boundaries between high and low most obviously. A nicely literal example was a series created by Erwin Blumenthal in 1942. Semi-nude models were made-up, posed, accessorized, and sometimes trick-photographed "in the style of" famous artists such as Dürer, Renoir, and Picasso. In a more complex vein, the artistic eye as controlling presence was subtly figured in a series of glamour portraits of stars and starlets commissioned from Hollywood studio photographer George Hurrell during the late thirties. All are high-style black-and-white images wherein dramatic lighting seems literally to sculpt and paint the subject's face, transforming it into a fetishized mask. In one notable instance two photos of Simone Simon (entitled respectively "Sugar" and "Spice") were run back to back; "artistic" transformations in lighting, hairstyle, and expression make her appear to be two different people. A caption accompanying a self-portrait by Hurrell in another issue takes care to make the distinction between his art and mere photography: "The difference lies in the painter's eye, the painter's feel for form and composition, that brings black and white magic out of Hurrell's darkroom."[16]

Perhaps the single most revealing pictorial of these years was one entitled "Types of American Beauty" that ran for eight issues in 1940.[17] Here one sees the magazine ambitiously negotiating between regimes of meaning that had been the pretext for presenting provocative images of women in nineteenth- and early-twentieth-century illustration and the stripped-down fetishism that was to become the norm in *Esquire* during the forties and *Playboy* in the fifties. This feature was based on the notion of women as "types" apotheosizing some aspect of American culture, a staple of magazine illustration for decades.[18] The premise of the *Esquire* project is that each woman represents a physiological category and that not only her character and personality but really her whole past and future are determined by and readable through her appearance. . . . The images themselves reveal the ingenuity with which *Esquire* synthesized fine arts and cheesecake. Each month a specially commissioned sculpture of a nude woman was presented via gatefold photographs that combined an aura of artiness with the conventions of soft-core pornography—focus on breasts and buttocks. Typically the identities of the male "artists" involved, sculptor Frank Nagy

and photographer Andre de Dienes, were foregrounded, together with the author of analytical captions, pen name Nostradamus, "a prominent New York medical specialist." Here are samples of the descriptive text. Number One was Perdita, "Hips full but not fleshy, denoting the broad feminine pelvis. . . . This constitutional type is common among those of Scandinavian ancestry. ... She is a young woman who matured rather early and is in the first bloom of her active femininity. . . . Born on the wrong side of the tracks, crude sex is her ruin from the 6th Grade up. . . . If rescued into the haven of middle class domesticity, she promises to become the prize of the iceman." Number Two is Virginia, whose "breasts are on a broad base, their transversal diameter is greater than the vertical one. . . . The right date for a young man, good sport and no prude, but countenances petting only within strictly conventional limits. Will make a good wife and mother." In features such as these, the pleasures of sexual looking were annealed not only to aesthetic contemplation but also to the social scientific modes that employ inquiry via the visual. And if the highmindedness of the situation was not already sufficiently clear, *Esquire* typically took care to throw freedom of expression into the pot by publishing in the same issue a lengthy article on the history of censorship attempts against nudity in art.[19]

The captions accompanying "Types of American Beauty" are characteristic of *Esquire's* liminal content. It is from these informal enframing devices for occasional features that readers are most clearly appellated as subjects. Repeated, detailed guidance is given as to the attitudes "you," the *Esquire* Man, should bring to the illustrations and in turn take away from the magazine into your everyday reality.[20] Here is an excerpt from a whole paragraph hyping pinup calendars that suggests onanistic pleasures in a buzz of cute verbiage: "She restores your flagging sense of proportion, she is a tonic to your soul, a gladdener of the eye, a soft, sweet roustalont restorer of the old raison d'etre." Or this, from a pictorial featuring sketched models casually posed in studio settings that displaces the spectator's voyeuristic intent onto the woman herself: "While he was mixing his colors in preparation for the day's work, Mr. Smith the artist stole an amused glance at his model, noting the feline deliberation with which she preened herself for her portrait. . . . This cool creature remains like most models, as self-contained as a kitten—and as patently full of guile. . . . Her expressive eyes look thoughtful and faraway—well, at least as far as the mirror which hangs on the opposite wall."[21] And in case there was any doubt that sexual looking constituted a civilized recreational activity, in 1937 the magazine published a lengthy article that offered a history, philosophy, and guide to girl watching entitled "Essay on Jiggling":

> The jiggle . . . that champagne of movement which can only be accomplished by the human female . . . inspires more of the bubbly electric feeling of well-being for men than all the more publicized harbingers of spring. . . . It says in the language of the emotions . . . that it is not good for man to use all his energies in the grubby business of acquiring goods or to give all his thought to the injustices of society. . . . Everybody sees the girls walking along, and everybody is pleased. . . . And the remarkable part of it is that the girls have little to do with the cheer and good feeling they disseminate. . . . Young ladies are essentially serious creatures. They . . . worry enormously over the most trivial eventualities. It is only their bodies which are lively and irresponsible and keep them smiling and gay. (McNamara 1937, 43).

Here the frame of reference conceived for consuming images is effortlessly transferred into the world of lived experience.

Esquire's pictorial representations of women completed the logic premised by the text. If, as the text suggested, the relationship between the sexes is problematized by female waywardness, then here was the solution—"raw" femininity "cooked," so to speak, by the worldly wise *Esquire* Man's well-tutored gaze. And as with so much of *Esquire's* rhetoric, the pictorial content incorporated a smug liberality. Projected into a new zone beyond institutionalized oppression, masculine privilege was presented as something inherently benign. Men do not need the power to dominate women politically, the magazine implied (and, as evolved "modern" sorts, would not want it anyway), when they can exercise the pure control of fetishized pleasure over any woman who swims into their line of sight.

. . . It is not an exaggeration to say that the *Esquire* Man's model of urbane sophistication and cultivated sensuality constituted an enticing version of the American dream for a particular cohort of postwar masculinity. Certainly part of Hugh Hefner's self-evolved mythology was his early reverence for *Esquire* (he briefly worked in the magazine's circulation department during the late 1940s [Miller 1984, 27]). More to the point, when Hefner founded *Playboy* in 1953, it was very clearly a knock-off of the Gingrich version of *Esquire*—lifestyle articles and girlie visuals wrapped in a package of "serious" fiction and nonfiction. *Playboy* has been credited with first organizing and exploiting consuming masculine desire largely because its editors took for a starting premise the products of *Esquire's* ideological work. *Playboy* could present as unspoken givens certain assumptions about the legitimacy of catering to male desire that *Esquire* had labored to justify and put in place. Overall this meant that the new magazine was far less compelled to engage in rationalizing strategies regarding the feminine. Most notably, it indulged in relatively little of the housewife bashing that had structured and focused *Esquire's* lifestyle articles. The parent magazine had made the urban domestic scene safe for heterosexual men; a playboy could plunge right into "mixing up cocktails and an hors d'oeuvre or two" without having to denigrate woman as cook and drink—maker to justify his expertise.[22]

. . . *Esquire's* contribution to the ideology of consumerism was to propose both the territory of market relations and the landscape of desire as gender-identified, zero-sum battlegrounds. In effect the magazine argued that, by catering to female desire, commercial culture of the twenties had robbed men of their rightful privileges. Hence its effort to fabricate the male consumer had to involve "putting women in their place," In other words, whether by route of perception or invention, *Esquire's* editorial staff convinced itself that what men are truly "in the market" for is status achieved at the expense of women. It is not difficult to perceive this nugget of received wisdom at work in *Playboy,* or in any other male-oriented magazine for that matter, where women are usually represented as servicing men, not just on the sexual level but via markers of class as well. (The playboy is an upscale professional, whereas bunnies, playmates, and so on often are working class.)

Misogyny existed in popular culture long before *Esquire;* what *Esquire* demonstrated was that woman-trashing as such could be packaged and sold to a large, prosperous bourgeois audience. When Barbara Ehrenreich (1983) traces the history of sexist social attitudes from the forties through the sixties, what she is in part examining is cultural product fabricated for a male-identified market. And although she does not put it this way, what Susan Faludi documents in *Backlash* (1991) is how sexist biases were rationalized in marketplace terms during the eighties—the appearance of antifeminist opinion in books, magazines, TV commentary, and the like supposedly indicating a market for antifeminism that in turn justified the production of ever more antifeminist opinion. Now in the mid-nineties, sexism is proposed routinely as a disinterested demand of the market. Market research's most recent "discovery" is a male demographic

"neglected" because of the liberal media's supposed rush to service a politically correct feminist line. This time around the medium is radio—testosterone-saturated personas like Howard Stern cater to the eighteen- to thirty-four-year-old male market. But the mode of catering to that demographic—women, nothing but women, fantasized sexually and trashed socially— sounds all too familiar to anyone acquainted with *Esquire's* attempt to seduce and construct the male consumer.

Notes

1. Books published during the last decade that deal with female identity as inflected by consumerism include Bowlby 1985; Williamson 1985; Armstrong 1987; Winship 1987; Willis 1991; Spigel and Mann 1992; Radner 1994.

2. Different conclusions appear to have been reached by Strasser 1989, 125. She argues that, by 1900, producers of new products like likely safety razors and soft drinks had begun to consciously focus on the market from a consumer-based viewpoint. She does not demonstrate, however, that this perspective had created the elaborately manipulative consciousness that characterized the marketing industry after 1929.

3. The lead article in *Esquire's* first issue was an interview with Nicolas Murray Butler, then president of Columbia University, entitled "The New Leisure: What It Means in Terms of the Opportunity to Learn the Art of Living" (Butler 1933). Butler was a noted public figure during the early thirties who among other things argued for the economic benefits of Repeal. As we shall see, much of *Esquire's* earliest advertising revenue came from liquor and beer ads.

4. Mencken's definitively misogynistic social satire, *In Defense of Women* (1922), set a tone for ironic criticism of postsuffrage womanhood. Among others who capitalized on its arguments was Harold Nicholson, who functioned as a kind of in-house commentator on sex roles, marriage, and family for *Vanity Fair* from 1930 to 1933. In 1933 he authored a *Vanity Fair* article entitled "in Defense of the American

Man," which asserted that the American husband was forced to "cut himself away from all that makes life worth living in order to minister to the competitive instincts of his . . . wife [so that] she may have the opportunity to do the same silly and expensive things as other women" (12). Women's supposed receptivity to the manipulative tactics of merchandising was such a truism of the early thirties that Aldous Huxley employed it as an important trope in *Brave New World* (Bowlby 1993, 2).

5. Wilson, in his article on the advent of mass market magazine publishing during the 1880s and 1890s, points out the shift in standard background from literature to journalism (Wilson 1983, 47). During the twenties, experience in advertising became more common as a route to work in magazines. Even so, Smart and Weintraub were unusual in their lack of literature- or journalism-related experience.

6. Smart eventually became the magazine's sole publisher. He went on to parlay *Esquire* into a small publishing empire that included the slick art folio *Minotaur, Coronet* magazine and educational films, and a short-lived magazine of liberal commentary, *Ken.*

7. Early on, *Esquire* made a thorough commitment to glamorizing the consumption of alcohol. To illustrate an article entitled "Cocktail Hour around the World" (*Esquire* 1934), the magazine's editors commissioned from Margaret Bourke-White a full-page color photograph of artistically arranged wine and liquor bottles. The photographer was celebrated for her work in *Fortune* heroically visualizing the new "process" imagery of corporate capitalism. *Esquire* was obviously hoping she could provide a visual rhetoric as convincing for consumption as she had for production.

8. Dick Pine in "Women Can't Cook" (1939, 51) linked women's gaining suffrage with loss of domestic skills and blamed both on "male supineness."

9. *Esquire* put forward a negative commentary on homosexuality both overtly and covertly. In 1938 it published "Fashion Is a Fairy," an article on the supposedly "unhealthy" influence of homosexuals and lesbians in the design industries. And throughout the fashion features, good taste was defined in opposition to "effeteness."

10. While the strategy proved acceptable to readers and advertisers, contemporary media commentators complained about the hypocrisy of juxtaposing literature and cheesecake. One in *Scribner's* likened reading *Esquire* to listening to Mann, Dos Passos, or Hemingway "read aloud from his works in a burlesque house" (Pringle 1938, 33).

11. According to Gingrich's memoirs he discovered George Petty in the summer of 1933 while looking for visuals to fill out the magazine's first issue (Gingrich 1971, 100). Coming across posters that featured a girl "reminiscent of that line in T. S. Eliot about 'visions of pneumatic bliss,'" Gingrich was told they were by "an airbrush retoucher—you know does over photographs for catalogues . . . so they look like a bastard blend of photo and drawing—all smoothed out." Petty executed all of the pinups published during the thirties. Most from the forties are the work of Alberto Vargas.

12. These three cartoons appeared respectively in the issues of June 1938, 79; July 1940, 56; and November 1941, 83.

13. The term *gold digger* came into popular usage during the 1920s to refer to chorus girls who "mined" admirers for gifts and money. Movie musicals of the early thirties appropriated the term as a euphemism for party girls.

14. The cartoon appeared in the May 1934 issue, 142.

15. In its sixth issue *Esquire* published a story by Hughes that involved the theme of miscegenation (1934), having earlier exploited potential controversy by inviting its readership to comment on whether the magazine should carry such material by a Negro author. Simms Campbell was, as Gingrich puts it in his memoirs, "a fantastically talented colored kid" unable to get much work. Gingrich happily recounts how, due to his own racial tolerance, he was thus able to acquire an excellent illustrator for very little money (Gingrich 1971, 95).

16. The photos of Simone Simon appeared in the May 1937 issue, 33-34; the Hurrell self-portrait in the November 1936 issue, III.

17. The feature ran from April through December 1940. Number I (Perdita) appeared on 129-31 of the April issue; Number 2 (Virginia) was on 117-19 of the May issue.

18. Depicting women as "types" was an important mode of representation that evolved in art and literature throughout the nineteenth century. The immediate predecessor of *Esquire's* "Types of American Beauty" would have been the work of so-called girl illustrators like Gibson, Howard Chandler Christy, James M. Flagg, and Cole Phillips, who published variously in *Harper's, Scribner's, American Magazine,* and *Cosmopolitan* during the first three decades of the century (Banta 1987, chap. 9).

19. See Laing 1940. This lengthy article conflates allowable depiction of nudity with freedom of expression and works hard to demonstrate that the censor is invariably rendered history's fool. It was not the first article *Esquire* had published on the subject. In September 1936 the magazine's editors commissioned a piece from Havelock Ellis entitled "What Is Obscenity?" (Ellis's ready answer: "Obscenity is an idea born of ignorance and superstition" [48]). *Esquire* constantly engaged in an obfuscating discourse, usually carried on in editorial asides, about the provocative intentions of its content. The January 1937 "Salute to New Subscribers" says, "The publishers personally guarantee that its cartoons are as clean as the paper on which they are printed. They only refuse to be responsible for the state of your mind" (1937, 3). In 1942 the magazine went to court (and won) over the U.S. postmaster general's attempt to revoke its second-class mail permit because of the provocative cartoons.

20. *Esquire's* chummy mode of address was a quite conscious strategy. In *The Sixth New Year,* the most lavish of its promotional booklets produced for ad agencies, Gingrich trumpeted "the relationship between the magazine and its readers that makes *Esquire* by all odds the most intimate of magazines" (*Esquire* 1939, 3).

21. The calendar ad appeared in the November 1941 issue, 33; Smith's illustration (one of a regular feature called "Esquidorables") ran in December 1945, 84.

22. This tag comes from Hefner's introduction to his first issue, wherein he distinguishes *Playboy* from those magazines for men that "spend all their time out of doors—thrashing through thorny thickets or splashing about in fast flowing streams." In contrast, "we plan spending most of our time inside. We like our apartment. We enjoy mixing up cocktails and an hors d'oeuvre or two, putting a little mood music on the phonograph and inviting in a female for a quiet discussion of Picasso, Nietzsche, jazz and sex" (*Playboy:* 1953, 3).

References ◆

Armstrong, Nancy. 1987. *Desire and Domestic Fiction: A Political History of the Novel.* New York: Oxford University Press.

Banta, Martha. 1987. *Imaging American Women: Idea and Ideals in Cultural History.* New York: Columbia University Press.

Bowlby, Rachel. 1985. *Just Looking.* New York: Methuen.

———. 1993. *Shopping with Freud.* London: Routledge.

Brody, Iles. 1940. "Man the Kitchenette." *Esquire,* April, 105.

Butler, Nicolas Murray. 1933. "The New Leisure: What It Means in Terms of the Opportunity to Learn the Art of Living." *Esquire,* Autumn.

Cheney, Sheldon, and Martha Chandler Cheney. 1936. *Art and the Machine: An Account of Industrial Design in 20th Century America.* New York: Little, Brown.

Ehrenreich, Barbara. 1983. *The Hearts of Men: American Dreams and the Flight from Reality.* New York: Anchor.

Ellis, Havelock. 1936. "What Is Obscenity"? *Esquire,* September.

Esquire. 1933. "A Magazine for Men Only." *Esquire,* Autumn, 4.

———. 1934. "Cocktail Hour around the World." *Esquire,* January, 25-26.

———. 1937. "Salute to New Subscribers." *Esquire,* January, 5.

———. 1938. "Fashion Is a Fairy." *Esquire,* April, 35-36.

———. 1939. *The Sixth New Year.* Chicago: Esquire, Inc.

Evans, Sara M. 1989. *Born for Liberty: The History of Women in America.* New York: Free Press.

Ewen, Stuart. 1976. *Captains of Consciousness: Advertising and the Social Roots of Consumer Culture.* New York: McGraw-Hill.

———. 1988. *All Consuming Images: The Politics of Style in Contemporary Culture.* New York: Basic.

Faludi, Susan. 1991. *Backlash: The Undeclared War against American Women.* New York: Crown.

Frederick, Christine. 1929. *Selling Mrs. Consumer.* New York: Business Bourse.

Friedan, Betty. 1963. *The Feminine Mystique.* New York: Norton.

Gabor, Mark. 1972. *The Pinup: A Modest History.* New York: Bell.

Gingrich, Arnold. 1971. *Nothing but People.* New York: Crown.

Hough, Donald. 1936. "Dinner Bites Man." *Esquire,* October.

Hughes, Langston. 1934. "A Good Job Gone." *Esquire,* April.

Jackson, E. McKay. 1935. "The Bachelor at Home." *Esquire,* November.

Laing, Alexander. 1940. "The Struggle over Starko Barko." *Esquire,* April.

MacDougall, Michael, and John Kobler. 1939. "Ladies in Luck." *Esquire,* December.

McNamara, George. 1937. "Essay on Jiggling." *Esquire,* May.

Matthews, Glenna. 1987. *Just a Housewife: The Rise and Fall of Domesticity in America.* New York: Oxford University Press.

Meikle, Jeffrey. 1979. *Twentieth Century Limited: Industrial Design in America, 1925-1939.* Philadelphia: Temple University Press.

Mencken, H. L. 1922. *In Defense of Women.* New York: Knopf.

Miller, Russell. 1984. *Bunny: The Real Story of Playboy.* New York: Holt, Rinehart & Winston.

Naether, Carl. 1928. *Advertising to Women.* New York: Prentice Hall.

Nathan, George G. 1945. "First Nights and Passing Judgments." *Esquire,* April, 106-7.

Nead, Linda. 1992. *The Female Nude: Art, Obscenity and Sexuality.* London: Routledge.

Nicholson, Harold. 1933. "In Defense of the American Male." *Vanity Fair,* July, 12-14.

Pine, Dick. 1939. "Women Can't Cook." *Esquire,* September, 51.

Playboy. 1953. "From the Desk of the Publisher." *Playboy,* January, 5.

Pringle, Henry. 1938. "Sex, Esq." *Scribner's,* March, 33-45.

Printer's Ink. 1929. Ad for market research firm of Emerson B. Knight. *Printer's Ink,* November 7, 133.

Radner, Hillary. 1994. *Shopping Around.* London: Routledge.

Roosevelt, Eleanor. 1933. *It's Up to the Women.* New York: Frederick A. Stokes.

Scharf, Lois. 1980. *To Work and to Wed: Female Employment, Feminism and the Great Depression.* Westport, CT: Greenwood.

Shevelow, Kathryn. 1989. *Women and Print Culture: The Construction of Femininity in the Early Periodical.* London: Routledge.

Smith, Terry. 1993. *Making the Modern: Industry, Art and Design in America.* Chicago: University of Chicago Press.

Spigel, Lynn, and Denise Mann. 1992. *Private Screenings: Television and the Female Consumer.* Minneapolis: University of Minnesota Press.

Strasser, Susan. 1989. *Satisfaction Guaranteed: The Making of the American Mass Market.* New York: Pantheon.

Williamson, Judith. 1985. *Consuming Passions.* London: Boyars.

Willis, Susan. 1991. *A Primer for Daily Life.* London: Routledge.

Wilson, Christopher. 1983. "The Rhetoric of Consumption: Mass-Market Magazines and the Demise of the Gentle Reader." In *The Culture of Consumption: Critical Essays in American History,* 1880-1980, ed. Richard Wightman Fox and T. J. Jackson Lears, 40-64. New York: Pantheon.

Winship, Janet. 1987. *Inside Women's Magazines.* New York: Pandora.

PART III

ADVERTISING AND IDENTITIES

In our consumer culture, we live in a world saturated with advertising imagery urging us to buy and consume products as a path to future happiness and self-transformation. As Sut Jhally says in "Image-Based Culture" (Chapter 25), which introduces this section, "In the contemporary world, messages about goods are all pervasive—advertising has increasingly filled up the spaces of our daily existence . . . it is the air that we breathe as we live our daily lives." Any discussion of the role of media within a capitalist economy has to foreground the role of advertising, both as an industry in its own right and, in Jhally's words, as "a discourse through and about objects." Because advertising normalizes consumption as a way of life, it is critical to our ability to think for ourselves that we learn to analyze not just the meanings of advertising texts but also the place of the advertising industry in our society.

One of the main themes running through this chapter is the way in which our deepest sense of self may be distorted in a society where advertisements are ubiquitous. As Kellner argued (in Part I), we cannot help but construct notions of ourselves at least in part from the media images that surround us, and given that the advertiser uses idealized images of ourselves to sell us products, most of us will find ourselves woefully inadequate when we compare ourselves with such images.

Gender identity is a key aspect of our sense of self from an early age, and the pervasive "ideal body" imagery offered in contemporary advertising photography is one of the most powerful and universal cultural sources of gender ideology in our society. In "'The More You Subtract, the More

You Add': Cutting Girls Down to Size" (Chapter 26), media critic Jean Kilbourne calls such images of the currently ideal or "perfect" female body a type of national peer pressure that arguably contributes to the development of eating disorders and other unhealthy behavior in adolescent girls. Using a method for analyzing gender messages in ads that was first developed by the sociologist Erving Goffman, Kilbourne argues that the adolescent girl in particular is vulnerable to "the message that she should diminish herself, she should be *less* than she is."

Fashion advertising campaigns by Calvin Klein and others following in his footsteps have included male models as objects of desire for both heterosexual women and gay men, and in so doing have extended somewhat the range of *masculinities* visible in mainstream ads, as Susan Bordo has shown in *The Male Body* (1999). But most advertisers continue to work hard to ensure that only culturally dominant and *binary* (two diametrically opposed) versions of masculinity and femininity are produced and reproduced through advertising images and text. In "Cosmetics: A Clinique Case Study" (Chapter 27), Pat Kirkham and Alex Weller show provide a *textual analysis* of an advertising campaign that uses a variety of methods for *coding* masculine and feminine differently.

Gender representation in advertising becomes more complex when racial *difference* is to be represented as well, since male gender privilege is contradicted for "nonwhite" men by white supremacist history. For example, as Sanjukta Ghosh argues in "'Con-fusing' Exotica" (Chapter 28), when an "East Indian" male character is depicted in a magazine fashion spread, he is feminized by his clothes and heavy eye makeup, both of which code him as "inferior." Ghosh points out that within Western advertising scenarios, non-Western cultures are represented as unchanging and "'historyless,' as mysterious, sexually decadent and indolent, and steeped in traditions that kept them backward."

Western advertising images of "nonwhite" people can be more varied today than in the past, of course, in part because of political pressure to change the racist representations of the past, and in part because many companies have come to realize that it is in their economic self-interest to appeal to new target markets. In "Advertising and People of Color" (Chapter 29), Clint Wilson and Félix Gutiérrez provide important historical perspective on racialized representation in advertising texts. After years of neglect and/or demeaning stereotyping of blacks, Latinos, Native Americans, and Asian Americans in advertising aimed at white audiences, social protest (including boycotts) and target marketing brought significant changes to these historic practices. Especially in the case of blacks and Latinos, significant gains in visibility and in respectful representations in mass audience advertising occurred in the 1970s. Black and Latino consumers are now courted with "prestige imagery" of themselves, especially in media that target specific minority audiences (such as Spanish-language broadcasts or magazines and cable stations directed at African American viewers). Although the dollars generated by such advertising can be used by "owners of minority-formatted media . . . to better meet their social responsibility to their audience," the authors also remind us of potential community costs associated with this new kind of advertising imagery:

The slick, upscale lifestyle used by national advertisers is more a goal than a reality for most Blacks and Latinos. It is achieved through education, hard work, and equal opportunity. Yet advertisers promote consumption of their products as the short-cut to the good life, a quick fix for low-income consumers. The message to their low-income audience is clear: You may not be able to live in the best neighborhoods, wear the best clothes, or have the best job, but you can drink the same liquor, smoke the same cigarettes, and drive the same car as those who do.

Like nonwhite populations, people with disabilities have historically been invisible or distorted in advertising imagery. Beth Haller and Sue Ralph (Chapter 30) point to the crucial role of disability rights legislation (and the disability rights movement) in making businesses aware of another new market. Beginning in the 1980s, pioneering advertisers found that the disabled customer was highly appreciative of nonstigmatizing representations in ads, and many companies came to recognize the "profitability of including disabled people in their advertising and understanding the benefits of diverse images in advertising." Such advertising images continue to be shaped and limited by the fact that "advertising is a visual medium." This explains both the overrepresentation of wheelchair users in disability imagery in advertising as well as the more serious problem that "only 'pretty people' can become models."

So far, the chapters in this section have emphasized textual analysis, often in the context of the profit-driven production imperatives of corporate marketing. But how do different audiences actually read advertising images? Katherine Sender points out, in "Selling Sexual Subjectivities: Audiences Respond to Gay Window Advertising" (Chapter 31), that advertising research has "tended to privilege the text" as the site of meaning. Her own focus group research studied reactions of readers of different self-identified sexualities to a set of magazine advertisements she had selected, including some that offered the possibility of different readings for heterosexual and gay, lesbian, or bisexual viewers. Sender discovered that although bisexual, gay, and lesbian study participants were more likely to consider gay readings of the ads, "predictions of readings based upon sexual identification alone" were "unreliable, if not arbitrary."

Like Sender, Diana Crane (Chapter 32) applies *audience reception* research techniques to explore the way audiences make meaning out of fashion advertising. Reviewing the dramatic shift in the function of fashion photography in *Vogue* magazine in the last half of the 20th century, Crane shows us that "exhibiting the latest trends in appropriate clothing for women of means ceased to be the primary goal of the magazine; instead fashion photographs provide a kind of visual entertainment analogous to other forms of media culture, such as Hollywood films and music videos." Using focus groups to explore "the extent to which fashion photographs constitute a form of hegemonic femininity that is accepted as natural and incontestable by readers," she reads the focus groups' comments as suggesting "that they had internalized traditional norms of feminine demeanor and perceived these photographs as violating these norms" (especially when gender ambiguity or sexual assertiveness was suggested). On the other hand, her viewers did not appear to be intimidated by the beauty of the models. Nor did they apparently see fashion in the way the fashion magazine represented it: as a means of playing with identity in a *postmodern* manner. As with other audience response studies, Crane's helps us see the complexity of real people's interaction in specific social circumstances with specific media texts.

Reference ◆

Bordo, S. (1999). *The male body.* New York: Farrar, Straus and Giroux.

25

IMAGE-BASED CULTURE
Advertising and Popular Culture

◆   Sut Jhally

Because we live inside the consumer culture, and most of us have done so for most of our lives, it is sometimes difficult to locate the origins of our most cherished values and assumptions. They simply appear to be part of our natural world. It is a useful exercise, therefore, to examine how our culture has come to be defined and shaped in specific ways—to excavate the origins of our most celebrated rituals. For example, everyone in this culture knows a "diamond is forever." It is a meaning that is almost as "natural" as the link between roses and romantic love. However, diamonds (just like roses) did not always have this meaning. Before 1938 their value derived primarily from their worth as scarce stones (with the DeBeers cartel carefully controlling the market supply). In 1938 the New York advertising agency of N. W. Ayers was hired to change public attitudes toward diamonds—to transform them from a financial investment into a *symbol* of committed and everlasting love. In 1947 an Ayers advertising copywriter came up with the slogan "a diamond is forever" and the rest, as they say, is history. As an N. W. Ayers memorandum put it in 1959: "Since 1939 an entirely new generation of young people has grown to marriageable age. To the new generation, a diamond ring is considered a necessity for engagement to virtually everyone."[1]

This is a fairly dramatic example of how the institutional structure of the consumer society orients the culture (and its attitudes, values, and rituals) more and more toward the world of commodities. The marketplace (and its major ideological tool, advertising) is the major structuring institution of contemporary consumer society.

This of course was not always the case. In the agrarian-based society preceding industrial society, other institutions such as family, community, ethnicity, and religion were the dominant institutional mediators and creators of the cultural forms. Their influence waned in the transition to industrial society and then consumer society. The emerging institution of the marketplace occupied the cultural terrain left void by the evacuation of these older forms. Information about products seeped into public discourse. More specifically, public discourse soon became dominated by the "discourse through and about objects."[2]

At first, this discourse relied upon transmitting information about products alone, using the available means of textual communication offered by newspapers. As the possibility of more effective color illustration emerged and as magazines developed as competitors for advertising dollars, this "discourse" moved from being purely text-based. The further integration of first radio and then television into the advertising/media complex ensured that commercial communication would be characterized by the domination of *imagistic* modes of representation.

Again, because our world is so familiar, it is difficult to imagine the process through which the present conditions emerged. In this context, it is instructive to focus upon that period in our history that marks the transition point in the development of an image-saturated society—the 1920s. In that decade the advertising industry was faced with a curious problem—the need to sell increasing quantities of "nonessential"

goods in a competitive marketplace using the potentialities offered by printing and color photography. Whereas the initial period of national advertising (from approximately the 1880s to the 1920s) had focused largely in a celebratory manner on the products themselves and had used text for "reason why" advertising (even if making the most outrageous claims), the 1920s saw the progressive integration of people (via visual representation) into the messages. Interestingly, in this stage we do not see representations of "real" people in advertisements, but rather we see representations of people who "stand for" reigning social values such as family structure, status differentiation, and hierarchical authority.

While this period is instructive from the viewpoint of content, it is equally fascinating from the viewpoint of *form*; for while the possibilities of using visual imagery existed with the development of new technologies, there was no guarantee that the audience was sufficiently literate in visual imagery to properly decode the ever-more complex messages. Thus, the advertising industry had to educate as well as sell, and many of the ads of this period were a fascinating combination where the written (textual) material explained the visual material. The consumer society was literally being taught how to read the commercial messages. By the postwar period the education was complete and the function of written text moved away from explaining the visual and toward a more cryptic form where it appears as a "key" to the visual "puzzle."

In the contemporary world, messages about goods are all pervasive—advertising has increasingly filled up the spaces of our daily existence. Our media are dominated by advertising images, public space has been taken over by "information" about products, and most of our sporting and cultural events are accompanied by the name of a corporate sponsor. There is even an attempt to get television commercials into the nation's high schools under the pretense of "free" news programming. As we head toward the twenty-first century, advertising is ubiquitous—it is the air that we breathe as we live our daily lives.

◆ Advertising and the Good Life: Image and "Reality"

I have referred to advertising as being part of "a discourse through and about objects" because it does not merely tell us about things but of how things are connected to important domains of our lives. Fundamentally, advertising talks to us as individuals and addresses us about how we can become *happy*. The answers it provides are all oriented to the marketplace, through the purchase of goods or services. To understand the system of images that constitutes advertising we need to inquire into the definition of happiness and satisfaction in contemporary social life.

Quality of life surveys that ask people what they are seeking in life—what it is that makes them happy—report quite consistent results. The conditions that people are searching for—what they perceive will make them happy—are things such as having personal autonomy and control of one's life, self-esteem, a happy family life, loving relations, a relaxed, tension-free leisure time, and good friendships. The unifying theme of this list is that these things are not fundamentally connected to goods. It is primarily "social" life and not "material" life that seems to be the locus of perceived happiness. Commodities are only *weakly related* to these sources of satisfaction.[3]

A market society, however, is guided by the principle that satisfaction should be achieved via the marketplace, and through its institutions and structures it orients behavior in that direction. The data from the quality of life studies are not lost on advertisers. If goods themselves are not the locus of perceived happiness, then they need to be connected in some way with those things that are. Thus advertising promotes images of what the audience conceives of as "the good life": Beer can be connected with anything from eroticism to male fraternity to the purity of the old West; food can be tied up with family relations or health; investment advice offers early retirements in tropical settings. The marketplace cannot directly offer the real thing, but it can offer visions of it connected with the purchase of products.

Advertising thus does not work by creating values and attitudes out of nothing but by drawing upon and rechanneling concerns that the target audience (and the culture) already shares. As one advertising executive put it: "Advertising doesn't always mirror how people are acting but how they're *dreaming*. In a sense what we're doing is wrapping up your emotions and selling them back to you." Advertising absorbs and fuses a variety of symbolic practices and discourses, it appropriates and distills from an unbounded range of cultural references. In so doing, goods are knitted into the fabric of social life and cultural significance. As such, advertising is not simple manipulation, but what ad-maker Tony Schwartz calls "partipulation," with the audience participating in its own manipulation.

What are the consequences of such a system of images and goods? Given that the "real" sources of satisfaction cannot be provided by the purchase of commodities (merely the "image" of that source), it should not be surprising that happiness and contentment appear illusory in contemporary society. Recent social thinkers describe the contemporary scene as a "joyless economy,"[4] or as reflecting the "paradox of affluence."[5] It is not simply a matter of being "tricked" by the false blandishments of advertising. The problem is with the institutional structure of a market society that propels definition of satisfaction *through* the commodity/image system. The modern context, then, provides a curious satisfaction experience—one that William Leiss describes as "an ensemble of satisfactions and dissatisfactions" in which the consumption of commodities mediated by the image-system of advertising leads to consumer uncertainty and confusion.[6] The image-system of the marketplace reflects our desire and dreams, yet we have only the pleasure of the images to sustain us in our actual experience with goods.

The commodity image-system thus provides a particular vision of the world—a particular mode of self-validation that is integrally connected with what one *has* rather than what one *is*—a distinction often referred to as one between "having" and "being," with the latter now being defined through the former. As such, it constitutes a way of life that is defined and structured in quite specific political ways. Some commentators have even described advertising as part of a new *religious* system in which people construct their identities through the commodity form, and in which commodities are part of a supernatural magical world where anything is possible with the purchase of a product. The commodity as displayed in advertising plays a mixture of psychological, social, and physical roles in its relations with people. The object world interacts with the human world at the most basic and fundamental of levels, performing seemingly magical feats of enchantment and transformation, bringing instant happiness and gratification, capturing the forces of nature, and acting as a passport to hitherto untraveled domains and group relationships.[7]

In short, the advertising image-system constantly propels us toward things as means to satisfaction. In the sense that every ad says it is better to buy than not to buy, we can best regard advertising as a *propaganda* system for commodities. In the image-system as a whole, happiness lies at the end of a purchase. Moreover, this is not a minor propaganda system—it is all pervasive. It should not surprise us then to discover that the problem that it poses—how to get more things for everyone (as that is the root to happiness)—guides our political debates. The goal of *economic growth* (on which the commodity vision is based) is an unquestioned and sacred proposition of the political culture. As the environmental costs of the strategy of unbridled economic growth become more obvious, it is clear we must, as a society, engage in debate concerning the nature of future economic growth. However, as long as the commodity image-system maintains its ubiquitous presence and influence, the possibilities of opening such a debate are remote. At the very moment we most desperately need to pose new questions within the political culture, the commodity image-system propels us with even greater certainty and persuasion along a path that, unless checked, is destined to end in disaster.

Moreover, this problem will be exponentially compounded in the twenty-first century, as more and more nations (both Third World and "presently existing socialist") reach for the magic of the marketplace to provide the panacea for happiness. One of the most revealing images following the collapse of the Berlin Wall was the sight of thousands of East German citizens streaming into West Berlin on a Sunday (when the shops were closed) to simply stare in rapture and envy at the commodities in the windows. Transnational corporations are licking their lips at the new markets that Eastern Europe and China will provide for their products. Accompanying the products (indeed preceding them, preparing the way) will be the sophisticated messages of global advertising emerging from Madison Avenue. From a global perspective, again at the very moment that there needs to be informed debate about the direction and scope of industrial production, the commodity propaganda system is colonizing new areas and new media, and channeling debate into narrower confines.

The Spread of ◆ Image-Based Influence

While the commodity image-system is primarily about satisfaction, its influence and effect are not limited to that alone. I want to briefly consider four other areas in the contemporary world where the commodity system has its greatest impact. The first is in the area of gender identity. Many commercial messages use images and representations of men and women as central components of their strategy to both get attention and persuade. Of course, they do not use any gender images but images drawn from a narrow and quite concentrated pool. As Erving Goffman has shown, ads draw heavily upon the domain of gender display—not the way that men and women actually behave but the ways in which we think men and women behave.[8] It is because these conventions of gender display are so easily recognized by the audience that they figure so prominently in the image-system. Also, images having to do with gender strike at the core of individual identity; our understanding of ourselves as either male or female (socially defined within this society at this time) is central to our understanding of who we are. What better place to choose than an area of social life that can be communicated at a glance and that reaches into the core of individual identity.

However, we should not confuse these portrayals as true reflections of gender. In advertising, gender (especially for women) is defined almost exclusively along the lines of sexuality. The image-system thus distorts our perceptions and offers little that balances out the stress on sexuality. Advertisers, working within a "cluttered" environment in which there are more and more messages must have a way to break through the attendant noise. Sexuality provides a resource that can be used to get attention and communicate instantly. Within this sexuality is also a powerful component of gender that again lends itself even easier to imagistic representation.

If only one or two advertisers used this strategy, then the image-system would not have the present distorted features. The problem is that the vast majority do so. The iconography of the culture, perhaps more

than any previous society, seems to be obsessed with sexuality. The end result is that the commodity is part of an increasingly eroticized world—that we live in a culture that is more and more defined erotically through commodities.

Second, the image-system has spread its influence to the realm of electoral politics. Much has been written (mostly negatively) about the role that television advertising now plays within national electoral politics. The presidency seems most susceptible to "image-politics," as it is the office most reliant on television advertising. The social commentary on politics from this perspective has mostly concerned the manner in which the focus has shifted from discussion of real "issues" to a focus on symbolism and emotionally based imagery.

These debates are too important and complex to be discussed in any depth here, but there is a fundamental point to be made. The evidence suggests that George Bush won the 1988 presidential race because he ran a better ad and public relations campaign. Given the incredible swings in the polls over a relatively short period of time, when media information was the only thing that voters had to go on, it seems to be a conclusion with some substance. The implications of such a conclusion, though, have not really been explored the way they should. The fact that large numbers of people are changing their minds on who to vote for after seeing a thirty-second television commercial says a great deal about the nature of the political culture. It means that politics (for a significant portion of the electorate) is largely conducted on a symbolic realm and that a notion of politics that is based upon people having a coherent and deep vision of their relationship to the social world is no longer relevant. Politics is not about issues; it is about "feeling good" or "feeling bad" about a candidate—and all it takes to change this is a thirty-second commercial.

The grammar of these images, then, clearly is different to the grammar of verbal or written language. The intrusion of the image-system into the world of electoral politics has meant that the majority of committed voters are held ransom by those who are uncommitted (the undecided or swing votes) and that these groups are influenced differently—and have a different relationship to politics—than those who have an old style view of politics. These huge swings of opinion, based upon information provided by the image-system, suggest that the political culture is incredibly superficial and does not correspond to what we normally think of as "politics."

Third, the commodity image-system is now implicated, due to changes in the way that toys are marketed, in the very structure and experience of children's play. With both children's television programming and commercials oriented around the sale of toys, writers such as Stephen Kline argue that the context within which kids play is now structured around marketing considerations. In consequence, "Children's imaginative play has become the target of marketing strategy, allowing marketers to define the limits of children's imaginations. . . . Play in fact has become highly ritualized—less an exploration and solidification of personal experiences and developing conceptual schema than a rearticulation of the fantasy world provided by market designers. Imaginative play has shifted one degree closer to mere imitation and assimilation." Further, the segmentation of the child audience in terms of both age and gender has led to a situation where parents find it difficult to play with their children because they do not share the marketing fantasy world that toy advertisers have created and where there is a growing divide between boys and girls at play. "Since the marketing targets and features different emotional and narrative elements (action/conflict vs. emotional attachment and maintenance) boys and girls also experience difficulty in playing together with these toys."[9]

Fourth, the visual image-system has colonized areas of life that were previously largely defined (although not solely) by auditory perception and experience. The 1980s has seen a change in the way that popular music commodities (records, tapes, compact discs) are marketed, with a music video becoming an indispensable component of an overall strategy. These videos are produced as commercials for musical commodities by the advertising industry, using techniques learned from the marketing of products. Viewing these videos, there often seems to be little link between the song and the visuals. In the sense that they are commercials for records, there of course does not have to be. Video makers are in the same position as ad makers in terms of trying to get attention for their message and making it visually pleasurable. It is little wonder then that representations involving sexuality figure so prominently (as in the case of regular product advertising). The visuals are chosen for their ability to sell.

Many people report that listening to a song after watching the video strongly affects the interpretation they give to it—the visual images are replayed in the imagination. In that sense, the surrounding commodity image-system works to fix—or at least to limit—the scope of imaginative interpretation. The realm of listening becomes subordinated to the realm of seeing, to the influence of commercial images. There is also evidence suggesting that the composition of popular music is affected by the new video context. People write songs or lines with the vital marketing tool in mind.

Speed and Fragmentation: ◆ Toward a Twenty-First-Century Consciousness

In addition to issues connected with the colonization of the commodity image-system of other areas of social life (gender socialization, politics, children's play, popular cultural forms), there are also important broader issues connected with its relation to modes of perception and forms of consciousness within contemporary society. For instance, the commodity information-system has two basic characteristics: reliance on visual modes of representation and the increasing speed and rapidity of the images that constitute it. It is this second point that I wish to focus on here (I will return to the first point at the end of the [chapter]).

The visual images that dominate public space and public discourse are, in the video age, not static. They do not stand still for us to examine and linger over. They are here for a couple of seconds and then they are gone. Television advertising is the epitome of this speed-up. There is nothing mysterious in terms of how it arose. As commercial time slots declined from sixty seconds to thirty seconds (and recently to fifteen seconds and even shorter), advertisers responded by creating a new type of advertising—what is called the "vignette approach"—in which narrative and "reason-why" advertising are subsumed under a rapid succession of lifestyle images, meticulously timed with music, that directly sell feeling and emotion rather than products. As a commercial editor puts it of this new approach: "They're a wonderful way to pack in information: all those scenes and emotions—cut, cut, cut. Also they permit you a very freestyle approach—meaning that as long as you stay true to your basic vignette theme you can usually just drop one and shove in another. They're a dream to work with because the parts are sort of interchangeable."[10]

The speed-up is also a response by advertisers to two other factors: the increasing "clutter" of the commercial environment and the coming of age, in terms of disposable income, of a generation that grew up on television and commercials. The need for a commercial to stand out to a visually sophisticated audience drove the image-system to a greater frenzy of concentrated shorts. Again, sexuality became a key feature of the image-system within this.

The speed-up has two consequences. First, it has the effect of drawing the viewer into the message. One cannot watch these messages casually; they require undivided attention. Intensely pleasurable images, often sexual, are integrated into a flow of images. Watching has to be even more attentive to catch the brief shots of visual pleasure. The space "in between" the good parts can then be filled with other information, so that the commodity being advertised becomes a rich and complex sign.

Second, the speed-up has replaced narrative and rational response with images and emotional response. Speed and fragmentation are not particularly conducive to *thinking*. They induce *feeling*. The speed and fragmentation that characterize the commodity image-system may have a similar effect on the construction of consciousness. In one series of ads for MTV, a teenage boy or girl engages in a continuous monologue of events, characters, feelings, and emotions without any apparent connecting theme. As the video images mirror the fragmentation of thoughts, the ad ends with the plug: "Finally, a channel for the way you *think*." The generalization of this speed/fragmentation strategy to the entire domain of image culture may in fact mean that this is the form that thought increasingly is taking at the end of the twentieth century.

Political Implications: ◆ Education in an Image-Saturated Society

There really is not much to dispute in the analysis I have offered of the history, character, and consequences the commodity image-system may have. The real question concerning these issues has to do with the political implications that one may draw from this kind of approach. Put simply: Is there a problem with this situation, and if so what precisely is it? Further, what solutions may be offered?

In a provocative recent book, Stuart Ewen offers a clear evaluation of the contemporary image-system. He states it succinctly:

> The danger is this: as the world encourages us to accept the autonomy of images, "the given facts that appear" imply that substance is unimportant, not worth pursuing. Our own experiences are of little consequence, unless they are substantiated and validated by the world of style. In the midst of such charades, the chasm between surface and reality widens; we experience a growing sense of disorientation. . . . For meaningful alternatives to come into being, however, the dominance of surface over substance must be overcome. There must be a reconciliation of surface over substance, a reinvigoration of a politics of substance.[11]

Beneath his insightful analysis and his many examples from different domains, Ewen maintains a relatively simple division: There is a world of "substance" where real power rests and where people live their real lives (the "material" world of "essence") and there is a world of "style" and surface (the evanescent world of "appearances"). In the history of twentieth-century capitalism the world of substance has been hidden and given a false veil by the world of appearances. People have given up control of the real world and immersed themselves in the ultimately illusory world of appearances. Surface has triumphed over substance.

I am less sure than Ewen of the dichotomy that he works with—after all, appearance is the form in which essence reveals itself—but I am convinced that a modern cultural politics must be conducted on the terrain of the image-system. The question is, how is substance (reality) revealed? Given that our understanding of reality is always socially constructed (that "ideology" is present in any system or situation), visual images are the central mode through which the modern world understands itself. Images are the dominant language of the modern world. We are stuck with them. Further, we have to acknowledge the pleasure that such images provide. This is not simply trickery or manipulation—the pleasure is substantive.

I would focus a cultural politics on two related strategies. First, the struggle to reconstruct the existence and meaning of the world of substance has to take place on the terrain of the image-system. In some progressive cultural politics the very techniques associated with the image-system are part of the problem—that is, images themselves are seen as the problem. A struggle over definitions of reality (what else is cultural politics?) needs to use other mediums of communication. I believe such a strategy surrenders the very terrain on which the most effective battles can be fought—the language of the contemporary world.[12]

The second aspect of the strategy centers less on revealing matters of substance (the underlying reality) than on opening up further the analysis of the contemporary image-system, in particular, *democratizing* the image-system. At present the "discourse through and about objects" is profoundly authoritarian—it reflects only a few narrow (mostly corporate) interests. The institutions of the world of substance must be engaged to open up the public discourse to new and varied (and dissenting) voices.

The other set of concerns are connected to issues of *literacy* in an image-saturated society. As Raymond Williams has pointed out, in the early development of capitalism workers were taught to read but not to write. The skills of reading were all that were required to follow orders and to understand the Bible. Contemporary society is in a similar position. While we can read the images quite adequately (for the purposes of their creators) we do not know how to *produce* them. Such skills, or knowledge of the process, must be a prerequisite for functional literacy in the contemporary world. Basic course work in photography and video production should be required in all high schools. Moreover, while messages can be read adequately, most people do not understand *how* the language of images works. Just as knowledge of grammar is considered vital in learning foreign languages, so the grammar of images (how they work) needs to be integrated into the high school curriculum. "Visual literacy" courses should be taken right after the production courses.

Finally, information about the institutional context of the production and consumption of the image-system should be a prerequisite for literacy in the modern world. Advertisements, for example, are the only message forms that are not accompanied by credits in terms of who has produced them. In this sense, movies and television programs have a different status within the image-system in that at least *some* of their process of production is revealed. At minimum, we know that they are made by lots of people!

Ads, on the other hand, simply appear and disappear without any credits. A third set of courses could focus on the political economy of the media and advertising industries. Stripping away the veil of anonymity and mystery would by itself be of great value in demystifying the images that parade before our lives and through which we conceptualize the world and our role within it. As Noam Chomsky puts it (talking about the media in general) in his book *Necessary Illusions*: "Citizens of the democratic societies should undertake a course of intellectual self-defense to protect themselves from manipulation and control, and to lay the basis for meaningful democracy."[13] Such a course of action will not be easy, for the institutional structure of the image-system will work against it. However, the invigoration of democracy depends upon the struggle being engaged.

◆ Notes

1. See Epstein (1982).
2. This is discussed more fully in Leiss, Kline, and Jhally (1986).
3. See Hirsch (1976).
4. Scitovsky (1976).
5. Hirsch (1976).
6. Leiss (1976).
7. See Jhally (1987) and Kavanaugh (1981).
8. Goffman (1979).
9. Kline (1989, pp. 299, 315).
10. Quoted in Arlen (1981, p. 182).
11. Ewen (1988, p. 271).
12. For more on progressive cultural politics, see Angus and Jhally (1989, Introduction).
13. Chomsky (1989).

References ◆

Angus, I., & Jhally, S. (1989). *Cultural politics in contemporary America*. New York: Routledge.

Arlen, M. (1981). *Thirty seconds*. New York: Penguin.

Chomsky, N. (1989). *Necessary illusions: Thought control in democratic societies*. Boston: South End.

Epstein, E. (1982). *The rise and fall of diamonds*. New York: Simon & Schuster.

Ewen, S. (1988). *All consuming images: The politics of style in contemporary culture*. New York: Basic Books.

Goffman, E. (1979). *Gender advertisements*. New York: Harper & Row.

Hirsch, F. (1976). *Social limits to growth*. Cambridge, MA: Harvard University Press.

Jhally, S. (1987). *The codes of advertising*. New York: St. Martin's.

Kavanaugh, J. (1981). *Following Christ in a consumer society*. New York: Orbis.

Kline, S. (1989). Limits to the imagination: Marketing and children's culture. In I. Angus & S. Jhally (Eds.), *Cultural politics in contemporary America*. New York: Routledge.

Leiss, W. (1976). *The limits to satisfaction*. Toronto: Toronto University Press.

Leiss, W., Kline, S., & Jhally, S. (1986). *Social communication in advertising*. Toronto: Nelson.

Scitovsky, T. (1976). *The joyless economy*. New York: Oxford University Press.

26

"THE MORE YOU SUBTRACT, THE MORE YOU ADD"

Cutting Girls Down to Size

◆ Jean Kilbourne

. . . Adolescents are new and inexperienced consumers—and such prime targets. They are in the process of learning their values and roles and developing their self-concepts. Most teenagers are sensitive to peer pressure and find it difficult to resist or even to question the dominant cultural messages perpetuated and reinforced by the media. Mass communication has made possible a kind of national peer pressure that erodes private and individual values and standards, as well as community values and standards. As Margaret Mead once said, today our children are not brought up by parents, they are brought up by the mass media. [1]

Advertisers are aware of their role and do not hesitate to take advantage of the insecurities and anxieties of young people, usually in the guise of offering solutions. A cigarette provides a symbol of independence. A pair of designer jeans or sneakers conveys status. The right perfume or beer resolves doubts about femininity or masculinity. All young people are vulnerable to these messages and adolescence is a difficult time for most

NOTE: From *Can't Buy My Love: How Advertising Changes the Way We Think and Feel*, by Jean Kilbourne, 1999, a Touchstone Book published by Simon & Schuster. Copyright © 1999. Reprinted by permission.

people, perhaps especially these days. According to the Carnegie Corporation, "Nearly half of all American adolescents are at high or moderate risk of seriously damaging their life chances."[2] But there is a particular kind of suffering in our culture that afflicts girls.

As most of us know so well by now, when a girl enters adolescence, she faces a series of losses—loss of self-confidence, loss of a sense of efficacy and ambition, and the loss of her "voice," the sense of being a unique and powerful self that she had in childhood. Girls who were active, confident, feisty at the ages of eight and nine and ten often become hesitant, insecure, self-doubting at eleven. Their self-esteem plummets. As Carol Gilligan, Mary Pipher, and other social critics and psychologists have pointed out in recent years, adolescent girls in America are afflicted with a range of problems, including low self-esteem, eating disorders, binge drinking, date rape and other dating violence, teen pregnancy, and a rise in cigarette smoking.[3] Teenage women today are engaging in far riskier health behavior in greater numbers than any prior generation.[4]

The gap between boys and girls is closing, but this is not always for the best. According to a 1998 status report by a consortium of universities and research centers, girls have closed the gap with boys in math performance and are coming close in science.[5] But they are also now smoking, drinking, and using drugs as often as boys their own age. And, although girls are not nearly as violent as boys, they are committing more crimes than ever before and are far more often physically attacking each other.

It is important to understand that these problems go way beyond individual psychological development and pathology. Even girls who are raised in loving homes by supportive parents grow up in a toxic cultural environment, at risk for self-mutilation, eating disorders, and addictions. The culture, both reflected and reinforced by advertising, urges girls to adopt a false self, to bury alive their real selves, to become "feminine," which means to be nice and kind and sweet, to compete with other girls for the attention of boys, and to value romantic relationships with boys above all else. Girls are put into a terrible double bind. They are supposed to repress their power, their anger, their exuberance and be simply "nice," although they also eventually must compete with men in the business world and be successful. They must be overtly sexy and attractive but essentially passive and virginal. It is not surprising that most girls experience this time as painful and confusing, especially if they are unconscious of these conflicting demands.

Of course, it is impossible to speak accurately of girls as a monolithic group. The socialization that emphasizes passivity and compliance does not apply to many African American and Jewish girls, who are often encouraged to be assertive and outspoken, and working-class girls are usually not expected to be stars in the business world.[6] Far from protecting these girls from eating disorders and other problems, these differences more often mean that the problems remain hidden or undiagnosed and the girls are even less likely to get help. Eating problems affect girls from African American, Asian, Native American, Hispanic, and Latino families and from every socioeconomic background. The racism and classism that these girls experience exacerbate their problems. Sexism is by no means the only trauma they face.[7] . . .

Girls try to make sense of the contradictory expectations of themselves in a culture dominated by advertising. Advertising is one of the most potent messengers in a culture that can be toxic for girls' self-esteem. Indeed, if we looked only at advertising images, this would be a bleak world for females. Girls are extremely desirable to advertisers because they are new consumers, are beginning to have significant disposable income, and are developing brand loyalty that might last a lifetime. Teenage girls spend over $4 billion annually on cosmetics alone.[8]

Seventeen, a magazine aimed at girls about twelve to fifteen, sells these girls to advertisers in an ad that says, "She's the one you want. She's the one we've got." The copy continues, "She pursues beauty and fashion at every turn" and concludes with, "It's more than a magazine. It's her life." In another similar ad, *Seventeen* refers to itself as a girl's "Bible." Many girls read magazines like this and take the advice seriously. Regardless of the intent of the advertisers, what are the messages that girls are getting? What are they told?

Primarily girls are told by advertisers that what is most important about them is their perfume, their clothing, their bodies, their beauty. Their "essence" is their underwear. "He says the first thing he noticed about you is your great personality," says an ad featuring a very young woman in tight jeans. The copy continues, "He lies." "If this is your idea of a great catch," says an ad for a cosmetic kit from a teen magazine featuring a cute boy, "this is your tackle box." Even very little girls are offered makeup and toys like Special Night Barbie, which shows them how to dress up for a night out. Girls of all ages get the message that they must be flawlessly beautiful and, above all these days, they must be thin.

Even more destructively, they get the message that this is possible, that, with enough effort and self-sacrifice, they can achieve this ideal. Thus many girls spend enormous amounts of time and energy attempting to achieve something that is not only trivial but also completely unattainable. The glossy images of flawlessly beautiful and extremely thin women that surround us would not have the impact they do if we did not live in a culture that encourages us to believe we can and should remake our bodies into perfect commodities. These images play into the American belief of transformation and ever-new possibilities, no longer via hard work but via the purchase of the right products. As Anne Becker has pointed out, this belief is by no means universal. People in many other cultures may admire a particular body shape without seeking to emulate it. In the Western world, however, "the anxiety of nonrecognition ('I don't fit in') faced by the majority of spectators is more often translated into identifications ('I want to be like that') and attempts at self-alteration than into rage."[9]

Women are especially vulnerable because our bodies have been objectified and commodified for so long. And young women are the most vulnerable, especially those who have experienced early deprivation, sexual abuse, family violence, or other trauma. Cultivating a thinner body offers some hope of control and success to a young woman with a poor self-image and overwhelming personal problems that have no easy solutions.

Although troubled young women are especially vulnerable, these messages affect all girls. A researcher at Brigham and Women's Hospital in Boston found that the more frequently girls read magazines, the more likely they were to diet and to feel that magazines influence their ideal body shape.[10] Nearly half reported wanting to lose weight because of a magazine picture (but only 29 percent were actually overweight). Studies at Stanford University and the University of Massachusetts found that about 70 percent of college women say they feel worse about their own looks after reading women's magazines.[11] Another study, this one of 350 young men and women, found that a preoccupation with one's appearance takes a toll on mental health.[12] Women scored much higher than men on what the researchers called "self-objectification." This tendency to view one's body from the outside in—regarding physical attractiveness, sex appeal, measurements, and weight as more central to one's physical identity than health, strength, energy level, coordination, or fitness—has many harmful effects, including diminished mental performance, increased feelings of shame and anxiety, depression, sexual dysfunction, and the development of eating disorders. . . .

Adolescent girls are especially vulnerable to the obsession with thinness, for many reasons. One is the ominous peer pressure on young people. Adolescence is a time of such self-consciousness and terror of shame and humiliation. Boys are shamed for being too small, too "weak," too soft, too sensitive. And girls are shamed for being too sexual, too loud, too boisterous, too big (in any sense of the word), having too hearty an appetite. Many young women have told me that their boyfriends wanted them to lose weight. One said that her boyfriend had threatened to leave her if she didn't lose five pounds. "Why don't you leave him," I asked, "and lose 160?"

The situation is very different for men. The double standard is reflected in an ad for a low-fat pizza: "He eats a brownie . . . you eat a rice cake. He eats a juicy burger . . . you eat a low fat entree. He eats pizza . . . you eat pizza. Finally, life is fair." Although some men develop eating problems, the predominant cultural message remains that a hearty appetite and a large size are desirable in a man, but not so in a woman. . . .

Normal physiological changes during adolescence result in increased body fat for women. If these normal changes are considered undesirable by the culture (and by parents and peers), this can lead to chronic anxiety and concern about weight control in young women. A ten-year-old girl wrote to *New Moon*, a feminist magazine for girls, "I was at the beach and was in my bathing suit. I have kind of fat legs, and my uncle told me I had fat legs in front of all my cousins and my cousins' friends. I was so embarrassed, I went up to my room and shut the door. When I went downstairs again, everyone started teasing me."[13] Young women are even encouraged to worry about small fluctuations in their weight. "Sometimes what you wear to dinner may depend on what you eat for breakfast," says an ad for cereal that pictures a slinky black dress. In truth, daily and weekly and monthly fluctuations in weight are perfectly normal.

The obsession starts early. Some studies have found that from 40 to 80 percent of fourth-grade girls are dieting.[14] Today at least one-third of twelve- to thirteen-year-old girls are actively trying to lose weight, by dieting, vomiting, using laxatives, or taking diet pills.[15] One survey found that 63 percent of high school girls were on diets, compared with only 16 percent of men.[16] And a survey in Massachusetts found that the single largest group of high school students considering or attempting suicide are girls who feel they are overweight.[17] Imagine. Girls made to feel so terrible about themselves that they would rather be dead than fat. This wouldn't be happening, of course, if it weren't for our last "socially acceptable" prejudice—weightism.[18] Fat children are ostracized and ridiculed from the moment they enter school, and fat adults, women in particular, are subjected to public contempt and scorn. This strikes terror into the hearts of all women, many of whom, unfortunately, identify with the oppressor and become vicious to themselves and each other.

No wonder it is hard to find a woman, especially a young woman, in America today who has a truly healthy attitude toward her body and toward food. Just as the disease of alcoholism is the extreme end of a continuum that includes a wide range of alcohol use and abuse, so are bulimia and anorexia the extreme results of an obsession with eating and weight control that grips many young women with serious and potentially very dangerous results. Although eating problems are often thought to result from vanity, the truth is that they, like other addictions and compulsive behavior, usually have deeper roots—not only genetic predisposition and biochemical vulnerabilities but also childhood sexual abuse.[19]

Advertising doesn't cause eating problems, of course, any more than it causes alcoholism. Anorexia in particular is a disease with a complicated etiology, and media images probably don't play a major role. However, these images certainly contribute to the body-hatred so many young women feel and to some of the resulting eating problems, which range from bulimia to compulsive overeating to simply being obsessed with controlling one's appetite. Advertising does promote abusive and abnormal attitudes about eating, drinking, and thinness. It thus provides fertile soil for these obsessions to take root in and creates a climate of denial in which these diseases flourish.

The influence of the media is strikingly illustrated in a recent study that found a sharp rise in eating disorders among young women in Fiji soon after the introduction of television to the culture.[20] Before television was available, there was little talk of dieting in Fiji. "You've gained weight" was a traditional compliment and "going thin" the sign of a problem. In 1995 television came to the island. Within three years, the number of teenagers at risk for eating disorders more than doubled, 74 percent of the teens in the study said they felt "too big or too fat," and 62 percent said they had dieted in the past month. Of course, this doesn't prove a direct causal link between television and eating disorders. Fiji is a culture in transition in many ways. However, it seems more than coincidental that the Fiji girls who were heavy viewers of television were 50 percent more likely to describe themselves as fat and 30 percent more likely to diet than those girls who watched television less frequently. As Ellen Goodman says, "The big success story of our entertainment industry is our ability to export insecurity: We can make any woman anywhere feel perfectly rotten about her shape."[21] . . .

Not all of this is intentional on the part of the advertisers, of course. A great deal of it *is* based on research and *is* intended to arouse anxiety and affect women's self-esteem. But some of it reflects the unconscious attitudes and beliefs of the individual advertisers, as well as what Carl Jung referred to as the "collective unconscious." Advertisers are members of the culture too and have been as thoroughly conditioned as anyone else. The magazines and the ads deliberately *create* and intensify anxiety about weight because it is so profitable. On a deeper level, however, they *reflect* cultural concerns and conflicts about women's power. Real freedom for women would change the very basis of our male-dominated society. It is not surprising that many men (and women, to be sure) fear this.

"The more you subtract, the more you add," says an ad that ran in several women's and teen magazines in 1997. Surprisingly, it is an ad for clothing, not for a diet product. Overtly, it is a statement about minimalism in fashion. However, the fact that the girl in the ad is very young and very thin reinforces another message, a message that an adolescent girl constantly gets from advertising and throughout the popular culture, the message that she should diminish herself, she should be *less* than she is.

On the most obvious and familiar level, this refers to her body. However, the loss, the subtraction, the cutting down to size also refers to her sense of her self, her sexuality, her need for authentic connection, and her longing for power and freedom. I certainly don't think that the creators of this particular ad had all this in mind. They're simply selling expensive clothing in an unoriginal way, by using a very young and very thin woman—and an unfortunate tagline. It wouldn't be important at all were there not so many other ads that reinforce this message and did it not coincide with a cultural crisis taking place now for adolescent girls.

"We cut Judy down to size," says an ad for a health club. "Soon, you'll both be taking up less space," says an ad for a collapsible treadmill, referring both to the product and to the young woman exercising on it. *The obsession with thinness is most deeply about cutting girls and women down to size.* It is only a symbol, albeit a very powerful and destructive one, of tremendous fear of female power. Powerful women are seen by many people (women as well as men) as inherently destructive and dangerous. Some argue that it is men's awareness of just how powerful women can be that has created the attempts to keep women small.[22] Indeed, thinness as an ideal has always accompanied periods of greater freedom for women—as soon as we got the vote, boyish flapper bodies came into vogue. No wonder there is such pressure on young women today to be thin, to shrink, to be like little girls, not to take up too much space, literally or figuratively.

At the same time there is relentless pressure on women to be small, there is also pressure on us to succeed, to achieve, to "have it all." We can be successful as long as we stay "feminine" (i.e., powerless enough not to be truly threatening). One way to do this is to present an image of fragility, to look like a waif. This demonstrates that one is both in control and still very "feminine." One of the many double binds tormenting young women today is the need to be both sophisticated and accomplished, yet also delicate and child-like. Again, this applies mostly to middle- to upper-class white women.

The changing roles and greater opportunities for women promised by the women's movement are trivialized, reduced to the private search for the slimmest body. In one commercial, three skinny young women dance and sing about the "taste of freedom." They are feeling free because they can now eat bread, thanks to a low-calorie version. A commercial for a fast-food chain features a very slim young woman who announces, "I have a license to eat." The salad bar and lighter fare have given her freedom to eat (as if eating for women were a privilege rather than a need). "Free yourself," says ad after ad for diet products.

You can never be too rich or too thin, girls are told. This mass delusion sells a lot of products. It also causes enormous suffering, involving girls in false quests for power and control, while deflecting attention and energy from that which might really empower them. "A declaration of independence," proclaims an ad for perfume that features an emaciated model, but in fact the quest for a body as thin as the model's becomes a prison for many women and girls.

The quest for independence can be a problem too if it leads girls to deny the importance of and need for interpersonal relationships. Girls and young women today are encouraged by the culture to achieve a very "masculine" kind of autonomy and independence, one that excludes interdependence, mutuality, and connection with others. Catherine Steiner-Adair suggests that perhaps eating disorders emerge at adolescence because it is at this point that "females experience themselves to be at a crossroads in their lives where they must shift from a relational approach to life to an autonomous one, a shift that can represent an intolerable loss when independence is associated with isolation."[23] In this sense, she sees eating disorders as political statements, a kind of hunger strike: "Girls with eating disorders have a heightened, albeit confused, grasp of the dangerous imbalance of the culture's values, which they cannot articulate in the face of the culture's abject denial of their adolescent intuitive truth, so they tell their story with their bodies."

Most of us know by now about the damage done to girls by the tyranny of the ideal image, weightism, and the obsession with thinness. But girls get other messages too that "cut them down to size" more subtly. In ad after ad girls are urged to be "barely there"—beautiful but silent. Of course, girls are not just influenced by images of other girls. They are even more powerfully attuned to images of women, because they learn from these images what is expected of them, what they are to become. And they see these images again and again in the magazines they read, even those magazines designed for teenagers, and in the commercials they watch.

"Make a statement without saying a word," says an ad for perfume. And indeed this is one of the primary messages of the culture to adolescent girls. "The silence of a look can reveal more than words," says another perfume ad, this one featuring a woman lying on her back. "More than words can say," says yet another perfume ad, and a clothing ad says, "Classic is speaking your mind (without saying a word)." An ad for lipstick says, "Watch your mouth, young lady," while one for nail polish says, "Let your fingers do the talking," and one for hairspray promises "hair that speaks volumes." In another ad, a young woman's turtleneck is pulled over her mouth. And an ad for a movie soundtrack features a chilling image of a young woman with her lips sewn together.

It is not only the girls themselves who see these images, of course. Their parents and teachers and doctors see them and they influence their sense of how girls should be. A 1999 study done at the University of Michigan found that, beginning in preschool, girls are told to be quiet much more often than boys.[24] Although boys were much noisier than girls, the girls were told to speak softly or to use a "nicer" voice about three times more often. Girls were encouraged to be quiet, small, and physically constrained. The researcher concluded that one of the consequences of this socialization is that girls grow into women afraid to speak up for themselves or to use their voices to protect themselves from a variety of dangers.

A television commercial features a very young woman lying on a bed, giggling, silly.[25] Suddenly a male hand comes forward. His finger touches her lips and she becomes silent, her face blank. Another commercial features a very young woman, shot in black and white but with colored contact lenses.[26] She never speaks but she touches her face and her hair as a female voiceover says, "Your eyes don't just see, they also speak. . . . Your eyes can say a lot, but they don't have to shout. They can speak softly. Let your eyes be heard . . . without making a sound." The commercial ends with the young woman putting her finger in her mouth.

"Score high on nonverbal skills," says a clothing ad featuring a young African American woman, while an ad for mascara tells young women to "make up your own language." And an Italian ad features a very thin young woman in an elegant coat sitting on a window seat. The copy says, "This

woman is silent. This coat talks." Girls, seeing these images of women, are encouraged to be silent, mysterious, not to talk too much or too loudly. In many different ways, they are told "the more you subtract, the more you add." In this kind of climate, a Buffalo jeans ad featuring a young woman screaming, "I don't have to scream for attention but I do," can seem like an improvement—until we notice that she's really getting attention by unbuttoning her blouse to her navel. This is typical of the mixed messages so many ads and other forms of the media give girls. The young woman seems fierce and powerful, but she's really exposed, vulnerable.

The January 1998 cover of *Seventeen* highlights an article, "Do you talk too much?" On the back cover is an ad for Express mascara, which promises "high voltage volume instantly!" As if the way that girls can express themselves and turn up the volume is via their mascara. Is this harmless word-play, or is it a sophisticated and clever marketing ploy based on research about the silencing of girls, deliberately designed to attract them with the promise of at least some form of self-expression? Advertisers certainly spend a lot of money on psychological research and focus groups. I would expect these groups to reveal, among other things, that teenage girls are angry but reticent. Certainly the cumulative effect of these images and words urging girls to express themselves only through their bodies and through products is serious and harmful.

Many ads feature girls and young women in very passive poses, limp, doll-like, sometimes acting like little girls, playing with dolls and wearing bows in their hair. One ad uses a pacifier to sell lipstick and another the image of a baby to sell BabyDoll Blush Highlight. "Lolita seems to be a comeback kid," says a fashion layout featuring a woman wearing a ridiculous hairstyle and a baby-doll dress, standing with shoulders slumped and feet apart. In women's and teen magazines it is virtually impossible to tell the fashion layouts from the ads. Indeed, they exist to support each other.

As Erving Goffman pointed out in *Gender Advertisements*, we learn a great deal about the disparate power of males and females simply through the body language and poses of advertising.[27] . . .

In the ads in the March 1999 issues of *Child* and *Parents*, all of the boys are active and all of the girls are passive. In *Child*, a boy plays on the jungle gym in one ad, while in another, a girl stands quietly, looking down, holding some flowers. In *Parents*, a boy rides a bike, full of excitement, while a girl is happy about having put on lipstick. It's hard to believe that this is 1999 and not 1959. The more things change, the more they stay the same.

Girls are often shown as playful clowns in ads, perpetuating the attitude that girls and women are childish and cannot be taken seriously, whereas even very young men are generally portrayed as secure, powerful, and serious. People in control of their lives stand upright, alert, and ready to meet the world. In contrast, females often appear off-balance, insecure, and weak. Often our body parts are bent, conveying unpreparedness, submissiveness, and appeasement. We exhibit what Goffman terms "licensed withdrawal"—seeming to be psychologically removed, disoriented, defenseless, spaced out.

Females touch people and things delicately, we caress, whereas males grip, clench, and grasp. We cover our faces with our hair or our hands, conveying shame or embarrassment. And, no matter what happens, we keep on smiling.

◆ *Notes*

1. "As Margaret Mead": In a speech at Richland College in Dallas, Texas, on February 24, 1977.

2. "According to the Carnegie Corporation": Carnegie Corporation, 1995.

3. "As Carol Gilligan, Mary Pipher": Gilligan, 1982; Pipher, 1994; Sadker and Sadker, 1994.

4. "Teenage women today": Roan, 1993, 28.

5. "A 1998 status report": Vobejda and Perlstein, 1998, A3.

6. "The socialization that emphasizes passivity": Thompson, 1994.

7. "Eating problems affect girls from African American": Steiner-Adair and Purcell, 1996, 294.

8. "Teenage girls spend over $4 billion": Brown, Greenberg, and Buerkel-Rothfuss, 1993.

9. "Anne Becker": Becker and Burwell, 1999.

10. "A researcher at Brigham and Women's Hospital": Field, Cheung, Wolf, Herzog, Gortmaker, and Colditz, 1999, 36.

11. "Studies at Stanford University": Then, 1992. Also Richins, 1991, 71.

12. "This one of 350 young men and women": Fredrickson, 1998, 5.

13. "A ten-year-old girl wrote to New Moon": E-mail correspondence with Heather S. Henderson, editor-in-chief of *HUES Magazine*, New Moon Publishing, March 22, 1999.

14. "From 40 to 80 percent of fourth-grade girls": Stein, 1986, 1.

15. "One-third of twelve- to thirteen-year-old girls": Rodriguez, 1998, B9.

16. "63 percent of high school girls": Rothblum, 1994, 55.

17. "A survey in Massachusetts": Overlan, 1996, 15.

18. "Our last 'socially acceptable' prejudice—weightism": Steiner-Adair and Purcell, 1996, 294.

19. "Although eating problems are often thought to result": Smith, Fairburn, and Cowen, 1999, 171-76. Also Thompson, 1994. Also Krahn, 1991. Also Hsu, 1990. Also Jonas, 1989, 267-71.

20. "A recent study that found a sharp rise in eating disorders": Becker and Burwell, 1999.

21. "As Ellen Goodman says": Goodman, 1999, A23.

22. "Some argue that it is men's awareness": Faludi, 1991. Also Kilbourne, 1986.

23. "Catherine Steiner-Adair suggests": Steiner-Adair, 1986, 107, 110.

24. "A 1999 study done at the University of Michigan": Martin, 1998, 494-511.

25. "A very young woman lying on a bed": A commercial for Tresor perfume, broadcast on NBC on December 5, 1997.

26. "Colored contact lenses": Commercial for Focus Softcolors, broadcast on Fox during *Ally McBeal*, June 15, 1998.

27. "Erving Goffman": Goffman, 1978.

◆ References

Becker, A. E. and Burwell, R. A. (1999). *Acculturation and disordered eating in Fiji.* Poster presented at the American Psychiatric Association Annual Meeting, Washington, DC, May 19, 1999.

Brown, J. D., Greenberg, B. S., and Buerkel-Rothfuss, N. L. (1993). Mass media, sex and sexuality. In Strasburger, V. C. and Comstock, G. A., eds. *Adolescent medicine: adolescents and the media.* Philadelphia: Hanley & Belfus.

Carnegie Corporation (1995). *Great transitions: Preparing adolescents for a new century.* New York: Carnegie Corporation.

Faludi, S. (1991). *Backlash.* New York: Crown.

Field, A. E., Cheung, L., Wolf, A. M., Herzog, D. B., Gortmaker, S. L., and Colditz, G. A. (1999, March). Exposure to the mass media and weight concerns among girls. *Pediatrics,* vol. 103, no. 3, 36-41.

Fredrickson, B. L. (1998, Fall). *Journal of Personality and Social Psychology,* vol. 75, no. 1. Reported in Media Report to Women, 5.

Gilligan, C. (1982). *In a different voice.* Cambridge, MA: Harvard University Press.

Goffman, E. (1978). *Gender advertisements.* Cambridge, MA: Harvard University Press.

Goodman, E. (1999, May 27). The culture of thin bites Fiji teens. *Boston Globe,* A23.

Goodwin, R. N. (1997, February 5). The wreckage of politics. *Boston Globe,* A13.

Hsu, L. K. (1990). *Eating disorders.* New York: Guilford.

Jonas, J. M. (1989). Eating disorders and alcohol and other drug abuse. Is there an association? *Alcohol Health & Research World,* vol. 13, no. 3, 267-71.

Kilbourne, J. (1986). The child as sex object: Images of children in the media. In Nelson, M. and Clark, K., *The educator's guide to preventing child sexual abuse.* Santa Cruz, CA: Network Publications.

Krahn, D. D. (1991). Relationship of eating disorders and substance abuse. *Journal of Substance Abuse,* vol. 3, no. 2, 239-53.

Martin, K. A. (1998, August). Becoming a gendered body: Practices of preschools. *American Sociological Review,* vol. 63, no. 4, 494-511.

Overlan, L. (1996, July 2). "Overweight" girls at risk. *Newton Tab,* 15.

Pipher, M. (1994). *Reviving Ophelia: Saving the selves of adolescent girls.* New York: Putnam.

Richins, M. L. (1991). Social comparison and idealized images of advertising. *Journal of Consumer Research,* 18, 71-83.

Roan, S. (1993, June 8). Painting a bleak picture for teen girls. *Los Angeles Times,* 28.

Rodriguez, C. (1998, November 27). Even in middle school, girls are thinking thin. *Boston Globe,* B1, B9.

Rothblum, E. D. (1994). "I'll die for the revolution but don't ask me not to diet": *Feminism and the continuing stigmatization of obesity.* In Fallon, P., Katzman, M. A., and Wooley, S. C., *Feminist perspectives on eating disorders.* New York: Guilford, 53-76.

Sadker, M. and Sadker, D. (1994). *Failing at fairness: How our schools cheat girls.* New York: Simon & Schuster.

Smith, K. A., Fairburn, C. G., and Cowen, P. J. (1999). Symptomatic relapse in bulimia nervosa following acute tryptophan depletion. *Journal of the American Medical Association,* vol. 56, 171-76.

Stein, J. (1986, October 29). Why girls as young as 9 fear fat and go on diets to lose weight. *Los Angeles Times,* 1,10.

Steiner-Adair, C. (1986). The body politic: Normal female adolescent development and the development of eating disorders. *Journal of the American Academy of Psychoanalysis,* vol. 14, no. 1, 95-114.

Steiner-Adair, C. and Purcell, A. (1996, Winter). Approaches to mainstreaming eating disorders prevention. *Eating Disorders,* vol. 4, no. 4, 294-309.

Then, D. (1992, August). *Women's magazines: Messages they convey about looks, men and careers.* Paper presented at the annual convention of the American Psychological Association, Washington, DC.

Thompson, B. W. (1994). *A hunger so wide and so deep.* Minneapolis: University of Minnesota Press.

Vobejda, B. and Perlstein, L. (1998, June 17). Girls closing gap with boys, but not always for the best. *Boston Globe,* A3.

27

COSMETICS
A Clinique Case Study

♦ Pat Kirkham and Alex Weller

This chapter aims to examine the gendering of Clinique toiletry products for men and women, particularly the ways in which the advertising of those products differentially codes the "male" and "female" ones. The design requirements of product packaging and advertising include suggesting that certain qualities belong to a product. Within the worlds of advertising and marketing, the appearance and presentation of a product is at least as important as the product itself. Advertising conventions encourage the consumer to equate the quality of advertising with the quality of the product itself. At the same time, however, women, in particular, use their many and varied consumer skills to negotiate both advertisements and product packaging and arrive at informed choices, related to a variety of factors, from cost and appearance to smell and status. The meanings of an advertisement are dependent upon how its signs and "ideological" effects are organised internally (within the text) and externally (in relation to how it is read, produced, circulated, and consumed as well as other social, economic, and cultural factors, including gender relations).[1] Packaging is organised externally in much the same way and both translate statements about gendered objects into gendered statements about a variety of things including types of consumer behaviour and human relationships.

The differences between advertisements for male toiletries and those for female toiletries are marked and, to a certain degree, conform to certain binary oppositions which are generally accepted to relate to men and women. In this particular case, it needs to be acknowledged that in our society men are far less accustomed than women to purchasing and using a wide range of toiletries, especially those produced by a "select" company such as Clinique which has hitherto been associated with products for women. The 1994 advertisements for Clinique's "male" products, which were aimed not only at men but also at women buying for men, therefore needed to take account of this when promoting "masculine" products that, in some or many ways, had been regarded as "feminine."

An important factor in the different presentations of products for men and women is colour, a distinction by which gender stereotypes are reinforced. Cosmetic advertisements frequently use colour as an "objective correlation,"[2] that is, the colour of a product and its surroundings are used to link and enhance the qualities and style of that product. Not surprisingly, therefore, colour plays an important role in the gender differentiation of Clinique products. Those for men are mostly packaged in grey bottles or tubes, with the occasional muted blue. Those for women are often packaged in transparent bottles, through which one sees a range of pastel and soft colours, particularly pink, blue, cream, and yellow, while Clinique's opaque tubes and bottles are often a distinctive but soft green. The flat cake of "male" soap is ivory whereas the rounder, softer-shaped bar of "women's" soap is more yellow. Recent advertisements for the "male" products were produced in black and white whereas those promoting "female" products feature full-colour, pastel shades and soft tones.

Associated as it is with documentary "realism" and media reportage, the black-and-white photography is an essential element in the overall "rational" and "objective" tone of the "male" advertisements. There is a boldness in the strong contrast. By comparison, the pastel colours of the "female" advertisements signal softness, purity, gentleness, and innocence—features associated with babies and infants and which suggest the more delicate, passive, and soft sensibility associated with the more traditional representations of femininity. The products look as beautiful and feminine as the beauty and femininity they promise the beholder/purchaser.

The associations of seriousness and masculinity that underlie the black-and-white advertisements function to validate the male use of cosmetics and toiletries, products hitherto regarded as fundamentally "female." The references that black-and-white photography carries to the documentary mode of presentation and representation, and thus to realism, are crucial. The "factual" and "sensible" style of the advertisements indicates a desire to define the use of male cosmetics as a serious business, something that men should not be ashamed to acknowledge or take an interest in—as opposed to something reserved for women or effeminate men.

Another significant difference in the advertising is the amount of information supplied. The advertisements for male products carry significantly greater amounts of information about the product depicted. The inclusion of this informative text has a major influence upon the appearance and impact of the advertisements. It introduces new elements of "objective" factual reporting, reinforcing other references to documentary realism, and plays a major role in encouraging readers/potential purchasers that to buy and/or to use male cosmetics is not necessarily the first step on the road to abandoning one's masculinity. The inclusion of "factual" information in a direct style helps inform, initiate, and reassure men who are generally less experienced than women at buying toiletries, especially the variety offered by the up-market Clinique range which includes several gels and lotions for shaving alone. By providing a more exclusive, specialised, and expensive range, Clinique sets itself against more mainstream male toiletry brands such as Insignia or Gillette. The Clinique man has to *choose* the more suitable product rather than simply buying the only shaving cream produced by a particular brand, as is the case with more conventionally minded companies.

However, many women buy cosmetics and toiletries for men and they too have to negotiate the choice of "male" products. Despite bringing greater consumer skills to the process, the uncertainties experienced by the dozen women, aged 20-30 years, with whom we discussed this issue indicate that the process is not entirely unproblematic for women and that they too find reassurance in the information and factual mode of address. That reassurance goes beyond learning about the function of the product to accepting it as a necessary and desirable (by no means the same thing) element of the masculinity/ies of the man/men in their life. In other words, women as well as men find reassurance in the information given about the relatively new products—in content as well as form.

In terms of content, the written text draws on representations of traditional masculinities to help distance the products from the domain of female toiletries. The codes and conventions used include those of utilitarianism, science, rationalism, and efficiency, with words such as "convenient," "simple," "no fuss," and "unscented," working to this end—together with references to "experts" such as dermatologists including those who "favour aloe to avoid shaving discomfort." Some play is made with the language of business; the male face has "an important meeting" with a bar of soap. "Robust," "brisk," "feel fit," and "works quickly," suggest health, strength, and speed. Size, endurance, and reliability are also directly invoked; sexuality less directly so. Readers are informed that Clinique soap for men comes in a big brick-like bar that not only works quickly but lasts for months (they should be so lucky). The fact that the soap has no perfume is emphasised in the drive to get men to accept these new products as "no-nonsense" ones. At the same time, however, the sensuality and pleasure sought after by the "new man" users of these products and/or the women who buy them for them, are catered for; there is a reference to the "rich . . . lather that feels good on the face."

In general, the language upholds the over-determined masculinity evoked by the rest of the advertisement. By contrast, the over-determined femininity of female cosmetics and toiletries is so well established within our culture that Clinique feels confident enough to (by and large) omit the written word from their advertisements for women's products. The very opposite of much of what is there by *assertion* and *emphasis* in the advertisements for products for men, is there by *absence* in those for products for women. For example, in the "male" advertisements the emphasis on speed and convenience contrasts with the knowledge that the taking of time to cleanse and make-up are established points of the complex processes and rituals of being/becoming "feminine."

The "female" advertisements contain no information whatsoever, other than the names of the products. Young girls learn from teenage magazines, elder sisters, mothers, and friends about the benefits of cleansers, toners, and moisturisers as well as face masks and makeup. By the time they are old enough to afford Clinique products they do not need to be "educated" about the functions of them. However, only firms confident of the high standing of their product in the marketplace can afford to let the brand name stand for itself, and "sell" their products on aesthetics. The "classic" case in point is the famous Saatchi and Saatchi series of "Cut Silk" Silk Cut cigarette advertisements in the early 1980s. The lack of information within the "female" advertisements is testament to Clinique's reputation.

Some of the attributes of the "female" product are conveyed within the aesthetic quality of that product—within the packaging and the aesthetics of the advertisement itself. Gillian Dyer states that, in this sense, the *sign* (the product) goes beyond the "mere depiction of a . . . thing" and is used *indexically* "to indicate a further or additional meaning to the one immediately and obviously signified."[3] The product becomes the signifier of feelings through conventions such as colour, light, and water which evoke a series of affective responses including freshness and pleasure.

The visual pleasures of the advertisements evoke the pleasures involved in the application of cosmetics, not least because the images contain within them notions of the cosmetics having just been used or, perhaps, still being in use. There is a sense of identification—encouraged by a different type of realism to that used in the "male" advertisements, but, nevertheless, realism. The thumb-print on the foundation bottle, the opened lipstick, and the spilt blusher suggest not only the process of putting on makeup but that real people—messy ones who spill things—are doing it. These beautiful illustrations connect the reader/viewer to the process of self-beautification, to the making of the feminine. An understanding of the constructed nature of femininity informs not only the advertisements but also our readings of them. Associations and pleasures related to colour are added to those already evoked by the references to process and construction. The woman reader can equate the beauty, sexuality, or pleasure she will achieve with the aesthetics and attributes of the product; with the sexuality of the (beautifully photographed) full, red lipstick and with the softness of the baby-pink blusher. Although accepting that there are as many

readings of a text as there are readers (indeed more), we have been struck by the similarity of response of those male friends (mainly, but not exclusively, gay) who use makeup. Some of the more resolutely "hetero" men with whom we have discussed these advertisements and who would only buy "women's" cosmetics for women if at all (perfume, they said, "was a different matter"), also respond to the sexuality, softness, and deliberate aestheticisation of the images—but with no identification as user.

Absent here are images of or references to the impact of the product on another person, usually male. These Clinique advertisements do not directly imply "use this product and become more appealing to the opposite sex," as is the case with certain other cosmetic and perfume advertisements, but it needs to be remembered that they draw on and are read in the context of that notion which occupies a powerful position in our culture. In the case of toiletries, as opposed to makeup, references to freshness and purity prevail, the most common feature being jets of pure, clear water—with which the products are sprayed or in which they are submerged. The water symbolises the fresh cleanliness the product promises; it stands in for the acts of washing, cleansing, and purifying oneself but it is also sensual.

Two of the male advertisements also feature the cleansing aspect of beautification (far "safer" for men than using makeup). The soap sits in a flow of suds and the face scrub drips with water. The advertisements are gendered by the use of the male hand and hairy wrist (one of which wears another gendered object—a wristwatch) which occupy a large proportion of the image. Hands are large, hairy, and clearly defined as masculine. The hand surrounds the product, literally encapsulating it within the masculine and ensuring that we are in no doubt about whom this product is for and who is in control of it, in yet another attempt to break down the taboos standing between men and toiletries.

The naming and labelling of objects is an important element of their gender coding. The Clinique brand name is printed clearly on both the "male" and "female" products, the mix of clean "modern" form with more traditional serifs connoting the quality and status that is as important to male consumers as it is to female ones. However, when used on the "female" products the letter forms are made slightly taller, thinner, and more elegant and sophisticated, in contrast to the thicker, bolder, and somewhat squat form used on the "male" products.

Because the "female" products are well established, the label "Clinique" suffices but the company decided that this was not sufficient in the case of the men's range. To distance and differentiate the "male" products from the female world of cosmetics and toiletries, the subtitle of "Skin Supplies For Men" was added to the brand name. "Skin supplies" suggests a physical and commercial world rather than one of narcissism and pleasure. "Supplies" suggests an organised system of necessary feeding, even a health or life-giving activity. The whole term is "up-front" in that it openly acknowledges the connection with the skin but it shies off any references to the beautification of that skin that the use of the Clinique brand name carries through its association with women's cosmetics and toiletries. The new range is the one which has to be self-consciously gendered by the addition of a subtitle to the existing brand name; by contrast, the "female" products do not need to stipulate their gender with a subtitle; they are already culturally placed within the female sphere. In some cases the letter *M* is used to further emphasise that they are *Male* products. In addition, each product bears a further label, identifying it as "Cream Shave" or "Face Scrub." The coyness of avoiding the word "moisturiser" by referring to a face moisturising lotion as the "M Lotion" counteracts somewhat the "rationality" and apparent matter-of-factness of the advertisement which promotes it. When it comes to face

shaving—a more acceptable and highly masculine activity—however, a shaving gel can be called a shaving gel—or at least a "Clinique For Men M Shave Aloe Gel" (at Clinique prices one expects, and gets, a bit of class). Female products which are readily recognisable, such as lipsticks or blushers, are not given individual identifying labels but others are. For example, Clinique specifies "Wash-Away Gel Cleanser," "Rinse-Off Foaming Cleanser," and "Clarifying Lotion" (further graded by numbers), but none of them need to be labelled as "For Women."

Language undoubtedly plays an important role in the gender coding of Clinique products. Names such as "Cream Cleanser" and "Foaming Cleanser" are soft and sensual whilst playing upon notions of purity and cleanliness. By contrast, the names of the male products, such as "Face Scrub" or "Scruffing Lotion," incorporate more rough, tough, and vigorous qualities, in an attempt to validate the products within a range of masculinities acceptable to the type of purchaser (male and female) the firm wishes to attract.

In the "male" advertisements reference is continually made to "his," "him," or "this man," the use of the "third person" suggesting that the product is being sold to another person, as opposed to being sold directly to him. It is acknowledged by cosmetic and toiletry companies that the majority of their male products are bought by women for male partners, lovers, friends, or relatives—a gendered relationship of "giving" directly addressed in the "Merry Clinique" leaflet produced by Clinique for the Christmas season 1994. In that leaflet there are a variety of headings relating to "female" products, none of which refer to gender as they classify the gifts according to price (from under £20 to £55). The "male" products (which occupy one page as opposed to eight for the others) appear under the caption "His From Her: under £40."

In conclusion, it would appear that although the production and use of male toiletries are evidence of the blurring, if not breaking down, of what have been rigid gender boundaries in the "touchy" area of male cosmetics, the advertising and packaging practices which distinguish between Clinique's "male" and "female" products draw heavily on gender stereotypes based on binary oppositions. Indeed, the very breaking down of such well-entrenched boundaries and with them certain gender stereotypes ("real" men don't use aftershave, let alone use aloe shaving gel!) may well have been accelerated by the use of stereotypes in product promotion. The anxieties aroused by the adoption of what some have seen as quintessentially "feminine" products, i.e., cosmetics and toiletries, by men are real and complex and the advertisements discussed here offer ways for men—and women—to negotiate them. Products deemed to be in the female sphere need legitimating before entry into the male arena. The Clinique advertisements, through an astute combination of visual and literary devices, not only suitably distinguish the one gendered product range from the other but also suitably masculinise hitherto "feminine" products.

Notes

1. G. Dyer, *Advertising as Communication* (London: Methuen, 1982), p. 115.

2. Ibid., p. 120.

3. Ibid., p. 124.

28

"CON-FUSING" EXOTICA
Producing India in U.S. Advertising

◆ Sanjukta Ghosh

There is a long history in the United States of using race as a factor in establishing cultural, economic, and political membership in the country. Because mass media are a major arena where the struggle over national (racial) identity is played out, the lack of any or diverse images of minority groups in mainstream media is both significant and dangerous. Activist organizations such as the National Council of La Raz (NCLR), the National Association for the Advancement of Colored People (NAACP), and the Arab-American Anti-Discrimination Committee (ADC), along with numerous scholars, have documented the paucity of representations of African Americans, Latinos, and Native Americans in the media for decades. They have also complained that even when these groups are shown, their images remain narrow and clichéd. African Americans, for example, are shown as lazy and prone to criminal activity and violence (Dyson, 1996). Latinos are shown as cunning, ready to live by siphoning off of the system, and driven by primal urges. Native Americans, whose images are all too rare, are shown as primitive and simplistic (Kilpatrick, 1999), unaware of or unwilling to join "civilized" society. When confronted with these problems, media producers often point to the low ratio of these minority groups in the larger population and their lack of disposable income, which makes these groups irrelevant or marginally relevant to advertisers. Although this could, to some extent, explain the absolute absence of complex and multivalenced images or any images at all of African Americans, Native Americans, or Latinos, it does not even begin to give us answers as to why communities such as Indian Americans, who indeed have the desired disposable income, are ignored by the media.

Indians have been part of the American social and cultural landscape for centuries (Leonard, 1997; Prashad, 2000; Takaki, 1989). Yet they have been systematically written out, erased, silenced, and marginalized in any mainstream picture of America. In fact, absence, invisibility, and silence are the main tropes by which India and Indians in America are "re-presented." This chapter examines how media, in general, and advertising, in particular, produce a commodified and an Orientalist vision of India that simultaneously erases indigenous peoples out of the landscape or puts them in the background. It traces this erasure to the racist immigration policies of this country, which have redrawn ethnic and race lines continually to maintain some kind of "purity" for the country. The chapter also connects this visual racial cleansing to the monetarist policies of U.S. capitalist economy, which has needed South Asian labor but has never been able to come to terms with the presence of this community in the U.S. landscape. This has led to a situation where Indians in America, even if they have been naturalized citizens for generations, are treated as sojourners rather than as immigrants, people needed, as Vijay Prashad (2000) has said, for their labor, not their lives.

In his pivotal work *Orientalism*, Edward Said examines how the West has constructed the Orient through scholarly works in disciplines such as history, archaeology, philology, and philosophy; through artistic representations; and through travel literature. This construction, he says, is neither apolitical nor happenstance. Using French philosopher Michel Foucault's notion of "discourse" to explain the relationship between power and knowledge,[1] Said (1978) says the knowledge that was produced about the Orient was actually an ideological tool in the colonial ambitions and warfare of Europe. Because the chief function of Orientalism was "to control, manipulate, even incorporate what is manifestly a different world" (p. 12), he says Orientalist discourse about the East supported the enterprise of colonialism itself. Thus, analyzing the images produced by the Orientalist discourses is crucial to understanding how colonialism operates; it reveals more about the imperial ambitions of the West than any "essence" about the represented cultures.

In a variety of writings, Said and subsequent scholars investigating Orientalism have shown that Orientalist travel literature, scholarship, and art constructed non-Western cultures as unchanging and "historyless"; as mysterious, sexually decadent, and indolent; and steeped in traditions that kept them backward. This resulted in a dialectic between "self" and "other," between the familiar "us" and the peculiar "them." Because the study of the "orient" began with a fascination and desire for it in the first place, it gave rise to the exoticization of this "other." Representations about the Orient, in other words, worked to create clear and fixed demarcations between Europe and "others" and resulted in standards of inclusion and exclusion. They provided the foundational dichotomies of modern-premodern and primitive-civilized, which were crucial to Europe's own self-identity and the maintenance of its hegemony over the colonized.

Though Said's work examined the Orientalist literatures of the 19th century about the Middle East only,[2] the same regimes of representation continue to mark the images of other non-Western cultures being circulated even today. Scholars have found Orientalist imagery in contemporary Hollywood cinema (Shohat & Stam, 1994), in literature (Viswanathan, 1989), in fashion, and in news (Said, 1981). Though Orientalism in advertising has been common in the United States since the late 19th and early 20th centuries, little work has been done on examining representations of Indians or India that evoke Orientalist discourse either explicitly or implicitly.

This chapter contends that the most frequent representation of Indians in contemporary advertising is through absence. Far from being a simple omission in the linguistic and visual iconography of advertising, this is a significant strategy changing the nature of the image we do see and the way we read them. India and Indians are at one and the same time wiped out as subjects but reinserted as objects of Orientalist gaze so that ultimately they are defined within the parameters of "exotica" and the "otherness" that so often demarcates Orientalist discourse. This simultaneous absence-presence allows the representational apparatus to achieve several things at once. First, absence helps reinforce a group's already-held location in the power structure. Thus, although whiteness asserts its position in the social structure by its ability to remain unnamed,[3] the absence of South Asian Americans reinforces their absence in the power structure. In both cases, the group's image and identity relies on the already constructed regimes of powerful/powerless. Second, at a time when the processes of globalization have generated a sense of borderlessness and deterritorialization both economically and culturally, absence makes it possible for media empires to achieve a racially cleansed visual environment that reinforces the notion of who is "us" and who is "them," who is "in" and who is "out."[4] Third, absence also allows those in power to recode the cultural identities of minority groups such as Indians in a way so that they can be used in a war against other minority groups. Thus, at times Indian Americans are constructed as the "usurping hordes" and at other times as a "model minority." Both images serve to fan incendiary interminority community hatred and are used to keep all minorities in check. This changing image of the Indian American is very much in the tradition of the fluctuating

popular iconography of the non-European immigrant, and as scholars such as Lisa Lowe (1996) have pointed out, it has always reflected national anxieties.

In recent years, India, along with other Third World countries such as Pakistan and Taiwan, has been an easy source of cheap labor for the United States. Increasingly, U.S. companies have turned to these populations to keep their competitive edge. This has resulted in huge increases in the number of Indians and Indian Americans in the United States. According to the 2000 U.S. census, the Asian Indian population doubled in the past 10 years to 1.7 million, making it the third largest Asian American ethnic group in the United States and the nation's fastest-growing major immigrant group. The educational and income levels of this population are higher than other Asian American groups, whites, Hispanics, or blacks (1990 U.S. census figures). This makes the Indian community the most well educated and prosperous of all ethnic groups in the country. Close to 89% of Indians in the United States have completed high school, 65% have completed college, and 40% have master's or doctorate degrees. In addition, their spending habits rival that of the most credit-happy teenager (Moen, Dempster-McClain, & Walker, 1999).

Social historian Prashad (2000) notes that India entered the popular imaginary in the United States through vaudeville acts and spectacles organized by P. T. Barnum. Both fetishized India as a domain of spirituality and its people as ghastly and mysterious. In fact, Barnum's 1874 Congress of Nations, the 1884 Ethnological Congress, and all the post-1880s circuses paraded midgets from India as savage specimens representing a strange land (Prashad, 2000, pp. 30, 27). At the same time, India was also constructed as the domain of the spiritual and the transcendental both in the works of well-regarded thinkers such as Emerson and Thoreau and by agencies such as Barnum's circuses. This kind of popular Orientalism that reduces the multiplicity and heterogeneity of India and Indian

Americans into either an exoticized and commodified spiritual realm or the well-spring of primitivism is well and alive even today in advertising.

An example of this is a 14-page fashion advertising spread in the March 1997 issue of *Vogue* magazine. It seems to be telling the story of two people traveling along the famous Route 66—they get lost in the desert, they run out of gas, they have problems with their vehicle, but along the way, they also form a sexual bond. The two people represented here are a leggy, blonde female model and a highly feminized Sikh taxi driver.[5]

The first two pages show the cabbie sitting in the "lotus position" on the roof of his cab. His eyes are closed and the tilt of his head indicates that he is praying. He is wearing gaudy orange-bronze pants, a richly patterned paisley shirt in brown and yellow, and a bright red turban. In contrast, the woman, dressed in virginal white, is standing in front of the vehicle with her back to the cab. She has a map in her hand and is pointing in a direction away from where they are. Clearly, they are lost. But whereas she is sophisticated enough to look on a map and set them in the right direction, he is the simple "Third World native" who would rather get his directions from divine inspiration! His very reliance on impotent "traditional" methods rather than modern cartographic instruments such as maps signify him as incompetent and irrational and perhaps serve as a reminder of India's backward status.

When they are not seen as backward and simplistic, Indians are coded as inscrutable, difficult to read. Two photographs of the spread show the woman unwrapping the Sikh's turban. Although this could explain her libidinal attraction toward him—he is a package that needs to be unraveled—it also pointedly reveals the nature of the encounter between the West and the East. As with all Orientalist representations, these photographs inscribe within them the West's post-Enlightenment certitude of its own ability to investigate and know all.

Sex between the two is suggested in a number of photographs. In one, the woman is sitting on the man's lap, happily looking into the camera; he, on the other hand, looks worried and anxious. The cheap curtains behind suggest that they are in a motel room. In another photograph, both are atop the taxicab—he is lying on his stomach and she is sitting facing the camera. Both are eating out of a bucket marked KFC. His very stance and his pleasure at licking a piece of chicken leg fixes him as a childlike person, enjoying the simple pleasures of fast food. The final two photographs show the pair at a diner on Route 66 and later at a gas station. The famed highway, with its association of freedom in the popular imagination, is cleverly inverted here. Route 66 is, perhaps, relevant for the woman. Her quick road affair with a clearly unsuitable man (from a different class, religion, and ethnicity) is tantamount to freedom—freedom from the taboos of miscegenation that continue to exist even today, freedom from a tamed sexuality to wild abandon, and freedom to delve in the unknown and the forbidden. For the Sikh man, however, the folkloric baggage of Route 66 is just a mockery. Throughout the narrative, the power rests with the woman. She is the one in charge and his very happiness—both economical and emotional—rests in her hands. Any question of freedom is absolutely crushed. The "Indian" man is feminized by his clothes and heavy eye makeup, both of which code him as inferior. The ubiquitous taxicab is a pointed signifier of the man's class identity—he is merely a taxi driver. The binaries used in the fashion spread posit the Sikh as backward, unenlightened, lustful, irrational, driven by primal urges, left behind, both untouched by modernity and comically ill-equipped to handle modernity. By and large, he is a bumbling fool. Thus, thwarting the dominant "freedom" iconography of the famed highway, this pictorial reveals a parody of a roadtrip, and a parody of a relationship. Because of the inequality between the partners the spread is in no way a representation of a desert love story.

Although the *Vogue* pictorial is just one representation of an Indian man, it is still not merely a singular image. Because images gain meaning in relation to each other, this fashion spread becomes understandable only insofar as it invokes a whole host of similar images in history. Moreover, the paucity of any representations of Indians in the U.S. media multiplies the significance of this fashion spread. It reduces all Indian men to a homogeneous thing with neither complexity nor ability to change. It perpetuates the notion that Indian men are weak, primitive, and eager to please whites. It also manages to construct the "Third World native" as both desirable and forbidden, as both repugnant and appealing to some unconscious desires.

The more predominant trend of representing Indians in the United States is through their absence—as a spectral presence. In most cases, Indians are simply erased out of the picture, whereas their clothes, their homes, their cultural practices, and their artifacts are appropriated and used to sell a U.S.-identified product. This erasure conveniently creates the category of the "exotic" as an empty space that can be used to denote both the repulsive and the desired, the fearful and the fascinating, the fantastic and the phantasmatic. Thus, it inscribes within it both a fascination and desire for the exotic.

Ads in magazines such as *Harper's Bazaar*, *Esquire*, and *Vogue* show that couture designers often peddle as their own creations traditional products from certain regions of India. For example, an ad for Cole Haan footwear in *Bazaar* shows a pair of feet in leather slippers that bear intricate hand weaving. Clearly, the black-and-white photograph is meant to convey "exotica" as the woman is wearing a skirt with mirror embroidery and a toe ring. Yet there is no mention of the fact that these are the well-known *kohlapuri* slippers, indigenous to the Belgaum district of the southern India

state of Karnatak (SRUTI, 1995, p. 62). Though these slippers are trendy and used by urban Indians all over the country, largely they remain the stock footwear of rural folk because of their sturdy structure and flexibility. However, there is no acknowledgment of the footwear's history and regional origins.

Similarly, an ad for Tommy Hilfiger shows a Caucasian woman wearing a skirt in hues of deep red. Adorning the skirt is heavy embroidery work, and the small mirrors mark it as the famous mirrorwork embroidery of the Kutch region of Gujarat. In yet another ad, this time for Liz Claiborne, a Caucasian woman poses in a deep pink sarong made out of a silk sari. The gold border on the sari and the red *aalta* she wears on her feet all are indelible markers of Indian culture, yet any meaningful signification of India is absent. One final example is a storefront banner at the Body Shop, well-known as one of the biggest robbers of Third World peoples, announcing "Ayurverda: New Word in Healing." As Vaidyanathan (2000) points out, with remarkable gumption, the Body Shop wipes out centuries of history and tradition.

In ad after ad, Indian products are appropriated, even robbed, and then represented as works of haute couture designers whereas Indians are airbrushed or erased out of the picture. At the same time, their clothes (the kohlapuri slippers, the Kashmiri *pashmina* shawls, the Kutchi mirrorwork skirt, ritualistic adornments such as bindis and mehndi, touted as "henna tattoos") are appropriated and fetishized. It is a kind of an apolitical exoticism and uninformed ethnic chic that is both calculated and successful—after all, what better way of stripping people of their histories and their art of its oppositional or radical energy than co-opting them and transforming them into a First World consumer good. The couture designers draw their symbolic power and effectiveness precisely by masking and strategically revealing the origins of their products. The objects are of value so long as they expressly and overtly signify exotica—by stressing the exclusive use of hand labor (as opposed to mechanized labor) and by reiterating its unavailability in the West (such as wool from the severely endangered Pashmina goats of the Himalayas, which has made much-desired Pashmina shawls a banned commodity). It is a marker of sophistication, of taste, and of racial awareness. Yet these same objects, when in the hands of native artisans, become a signifier of primitiveness and backwardness. In other words, Indians are symbolically useful to these designers, so long as they remain symbols. In an effective way, thus, capitalism allows this kind of exploitation and even violence to masquerade as racial sensitivity.

A plethora of ads appropriating pro-ducts from India and other parts of the Third World shows that this robbing is both economical—it exploits artisans, who embroider, weave, and mold, and replaces them by replicating their art through machinery[6]—and cultural—it alienates artisans from their art, sundering the product from them, their histories, and their stories, which are woven into the very fabrics and the very clay of the artifacts. This dual act of reworking and rebranding of goods as "exotic objects" and conversely the erasure of cultural identities from other objects produces a generic commodified exoticism that knows no market boundaries; it is but one more tool aiding the globalization process.

Another representation frequently used in ads is the association of India, in specific, and the East, in general, with spirituality. The image of a saffron-robed, bearded guru can be seen in a variety of ads ranging from products such as Mementos candy to health insurance. The articulation of spirituality with women's cosmetics is also very common. Magazine ads for Covergirl and Maybelline cosmetics from 1999 and 2000 looked and read almost identical. Unveiling a new line of orange, pink, and fuchsia lipsticks, both ads invoked the idea of a transcendental spiritualism "from far and away." This produces a cultural distancing as the East is seen as the epitome of calmness that serves as a counterpoint to the dynamism and flux of the West.

The essence of exotic, spiritual India is also inscribed by an imaginative landscape that includes dark forests and animals. A Sunday newspaper flyer for JC Penney from 1988 announces "Expedition India" urging Americans to "share the spirit of India" by buying consumer goods. The 32-page advertisement promises a brief introduction to that "truly exotic land" through a new collection of clothes and handicrafts acquired "from the colorful native bazaars of Delhi." As usual, any "native" is written out or erased from the $8'' \times 11''$ photographs in the flyer. Foregrounded are white models in ethnic chic. Indians are usually shown in hordes and/or in ceremonial garb (a military parade, a classical dancer, polo players, a North Indian bride—mislabeled) as insets 1/12th the size of the foregrounded photograph. The two unmistakable signifiers of "exotica" and "primitivism"—a tiger and the Taj Mahal—are prominently featured. The exotic, as a trans-Atlantic commodity, is now extended from art and artifacts steeped in antiquity and tradition, to location and animals.

In this Orientalist/popular culture conceptualization, India is spectacularized as a unitary and fixed space—jungle-like, barbarous, remote, and dark. It is a vision of India as static, frozen in space and time, primordial, without a history—as opposed to the West, which is dynamic and a repository of history and change. It is also a space that is simultaneously dangerous and yet holds forbidden promise. It is worth noting here that the essence of India is seen as residing in some religious truth. Again and again, the "real" India is seen as the spirit, and sometimes India serves as a metaphor for the soul itself. This notion of the East (and therefore "India"), with its qualities of mystery, mysticism, and antiquity, what Prashad (2000) calls "a metaphor of spirituality in excelsis," is reinscribed in different forms in popular culture—in editorial copy, in film, in news reports, and in music videos (such as for Madonna's "Ray of Light" album). Interestingly, this selective appropriation of Indian culture constructs India solely as a mythologized, sanskritized Hindu India. The influence of Islam on India, home to the largest number of Muslims in the world, is completely ignored by the West. It is a representation of India that goes back to the Orientalist historiography of the colonial period. Ironically, absence/erasure of any Indians and their lived experiences allows the "real India" to be constructed as a cultural repository of religious values; after all, India is so well imbricated in popular imagination with the spiritual that it needs no overt mention.

These narrow constructions serve several purposes. First, they, of course, provide the token identity of Indianness. While it removes any sense of guilt about their absence in cultural representation, it also allows an atomized ethnic chic as I have discussed earlier. Second, it fuels white America's resentment against this "Other." Although most of the time this resentment remains in the realm of rhetoric, incidents of violence in cities such as New York in recent times and in New Jersey in the late 1980s are a constant reminder of how these fictive constructions play themselves out in the lived world. Finally, as Urmi Merchant (1998) has pointed out in her analysis of photographic art, these images also light up a curious desire for a return to their "homeland" by Indians who see themselves wiped out or reduced by America. Inadvertently, as Merchant says, such constructions reinforce nationalism within the South Asian diasporas because it strengthens a longing to be at "home."

Media need to stress the heterogeneity of Indians in America—their differences based on class, gender, age, sexuality, and religion—and an identity that is continually in flux, changing as the political and economic climate changes. They need to move away from pictures of a Hindu India

to a more complex, complicated vision of what India truly is—a poly-religious, polyglot amalgamation of principalities that only in recent years came to be known as a unified state. By politicizing issues of cultural representation through apparently benign practices such as advertising, one can challenge its appropriation and violent exploitation by the West in the name of universality.

Notes ◆

1. According to Foucault, knowledge is not neutral or innocent but implicated in the way power operates

2. The book never really makes it clear what Said means by the "Orient"; however, Malik (1996) suggests that Said seems to be referring mainly to the Middle East

3. Barthes (1979) uses the notion of "ex-nomination" to explain how the bourgeoisie maintains its power by remaining undefined itself and by defining others

4. Unfortunately, according to this analysis, the implication for social change seems limi-ted to erasing absence—that is, increasing and expanding more consciously and critically the images and discourses in order to introduce more dynamism (and resistance) in the cultural construction of race and ethnicity.

5. Interestingly, a Sikh man wearing a turban has become the most used iconic representation of "the male Indian." Examples can be seen in representations of Indians in Hollywood films, in television shows such as *Seinfeld*, and in numerous ads, like that for Zanadi jeans.

6. See Walter Benjamin's "The Work of Art in the Age of Mechanical Reproduction."

References ◆

Barthes, R. (1979). *Mythologies*. New York: Hill and Wang.

Benjamin, W. (1968). The work of art in the age of mechanical reproduction. In H. Arendt

(Ed.), *Illuminations*. New York: Schocken. (Original work published 1936)

Dyson, M. E. (1996). *Between God and gangsta rap: Bearing witness to black culture*. New York: Oxford University Press.

Kilpatrick, J. (1999). *Celluloid Indians: Native Americans and film*. Lincoln: University of Nebraska Press.

Leonard, K. I. (1997). *The South Asian Americans*. Westport, CT: Greenwood.

Lowe, L. (1996). *Immigrant acts*. Durham, NC: Duke University Press.

Malik, K. (1996). *The meaning of race*. Basingstoke: Macmillan.

Merchant, U. (1998). Picturing ourselves: South Asian identities within the image. *Cultural Studies From Birmingham, 2*(1).

Moen, P., Dempster-McClain, D., & Walker, H. A. (Eds.). (1999). *A nation divided: Diversity, inequality and community in American society*. Ithaca, NY: Cornell University Press.

Prashad, V. (2000). *The karma of brown folk*. Minneapolis: University of Minnesota Press.

Said, E. W. (1978). *Orientalism*. New York: Pantheon.

Said, E. W. (1981). *Covering Islam: How the media and the experts determine how we see the rest of the world*. New York: Pantheon.

Shohat, E., & Stam, R. (1994). *Unthinking Eurocentrism: Multiculturalism and the media*. New York: Routledge.

SRUTI. (1995). *India's artisans: Status report*. New Delhi: Excellent Publishing House.

Takaki, R. (1989). *Strangers from a different shore: A history of Asian Americans*. Boston: Little, Brown.

Vaidyanathan, S. (2000, June). Inside a "model minority": The complicated identity of South Asians. *Chronicle of Higher Education, 46*(42), B4.

Viswanathan, G. (1989). *Masks of conquest: Literary study and British rule in India*. New York: Columbia University Press.

Other Resources ◆

Gallini, C. (1996). Mass exoticisms. In I. Chambers & L. Curtis (Eds.) *The post-colonial question*. New York: Routledge.

Gilroy, P. (1993). *Small acts: Thoughts on the politics of black culture*. London: Serpent's Tail.

Gitlin, T. (1983). *Inside primetime*. New York: Pantheon.

Gotanda, N. (1995). Towards repeal of Asian exclusion: The Magnus Act of 1943, the Act of July 2, 1949, the Presidential Proclamation of July 4, 1946, the Act of August 9, 1949, and the Act of August 1, 1950. In H. C. Kim (Ed.), *Asian Americans in Congress: A documentary history*. Westport, CT: Greenwood.

Hall, C. (1996). Histories, empires and the post-colonial moment. In I. Chambers & L. Curtis (Eds.), *The post-colonial question*. New York: Routledge.

Hall, S. (1997). The local and the global: Globalization and ethnicity. In A. McClintock, A. Mufti, & E. Shohat (Eds.), *Dangerous liaisons: Gender, nation and postcolonial perspectives*. Minneapolis: University of Minnesota Press.

Herman, E. S., & Chomsky, N. (1988). *Manufacturing consent: The political economy of the mass media*. New York: Pantheon.

Jhally, S., & Livant, B. Watching as working: The valorization of audience consciousness. *Journal of Communication, 36*(3).

Mazumdar, S. (1989). Race and racism: South Asians in the United States. In G. M. Nomura et al. (Eds.), *Frontiers of Asian American studies: Writing, research, and commentary* (pp. 25-38). Pullman: Washington State University Press.

Mohanty, C. T. (1997). Under Western eyes: Feminist scholarship and colonial discourses. In A. McClintock, A. Mufti, & E. Shohat (Eds.), *Dangerous liaisons:*

Gender, nation and postcolonial perspectives. Minneapolis: University of Minnesota Press.

Rony, F. T. (1996). *The third eye: Race, cinema, and ethnographic spectacle*. Durham, NC: Duke University Press.

Schiller, H. I. (1989). Culture, Inc. In *The corporate takeover of public expression*. New York: Oxford University Press.

Smythe, D. (1981). *Dependency Road: Communications, capitalism, consciousness and Canada*. Norwood, NJ: Ablex.

van der Veer, P. (1995). *Nation and migration: The politics of space within the South Asian diaspora*. Philadelphia: University of Pennsylvania Press.

29

ADVERTISING AND PEOPLE OF COLOR

◆ Clint C. Wilson II and Félix Gutiérrez

... For years advertisers in the United States reflected the place of non-Whites in the social fabric of the nation either by ignoring them or, when they were included in advertisements for the mass audience, processing and presenting them in a way that would make them palatable salespersons for the products being advertised. These processed portrayals largely mirrored the stereotypic images of minorities in the entertainment media that, in turn, were designed to reflect the perceived values and norms of the White majority. In this way, non-White portrayals in advertising paralleled and reinforced their entertainment and journalistic images in the media.

The history of advertising in the United States is replete with characterizations that, like the Frito Bandito, responded to and reinforced the preconceived image that many White Americans apparently had of Blacks, Latinos, Asians, and Native Americans. Over the years advertisers have employed Latin spitfires like Chiquita Banana, Black mammies like Aunt

NOTE: From *Race, Multiculturalism, and the Media: From Mass to Class Communication*, 2nd ed., by Clint C. Wilson II and Félix Gutiérrez, 1995, Thousand Oaks, CA: Sage. Copyright © 1995 by Sage Publications, Inc. Reprinted by permission of Sage Publications, Inc.

Jemima, and noble savages like the Santa Fe Railroad's Super Chief to pitch their products to a predominantly White mass audience of consumers. In 1984 the Balch Institute for Ethnic Studies in Philadelphia sponsored an exhibit of more than 300 examples of racial and ethnic images used by corporations in magazines, posters, trade cards, and storyboards.

The advertising examples in the exhibit include positive White ethnic stereotypes, such as the wholesome and pure image of Quakers in an early Quaker Oats advertisement and the cleanliness of the Dutch in a turn-of-the-century advertisement for Colgate soaps. But they also featured a late-19th-century advertisement showing an Irish matron threatening to hit her husband over the head with a rolling pin because he didn't smoke the right brand of tobacco. Like Quaker Oats, some products even incorporated a stereotypical image on the package or product line being advertised.

"Lawsee! Folks sho' whoops with joy over AUNT JEMIMA PANCAKES," shouted a bandanna-wearing Black mammy in a magazine advertisement for Aunt Jemima pancake mix, which featured a plump Aunt Jemima on the box. Over the years, Aunt Jemima has lost some weight, but the stereotyped face of the Black servant continues to be featured on the box. Earlier advertisements for Cream of Wheat featured Rastus, the Black servant on the box, in a series of magazine cartoons with a group of cute but ill-dressed Black children. Some of the advertisements played on stereotypes ridiculing Blacks, such as an advertisement in which a Black schoolteacher, standing behind a makeshift lectern made out of a boldly lettered Cream of Wheat box, asks the class, "How do you spell 'Cream of Wheat?'" Others appeared to promote racial integration, such as a magazine advertisement captioned "Putting it down in Black and White," which showed Rastus serving bowls of the breakfast cereal to Black and White youngsters sitting at the same table.

Racial imagery was also integrated into the naming of trains by the Santa Fe railroad,

which named one of its passenger lines the Super Chief and featured highly detailed portraits of the noble Indian in promoting its service through the Southwestern United States. In another series of advertisements, the railroad used cartoons of Native American children to show the service and sights passengers could expect when they traveled the Santa Fe line.

These and other portrayals catered to the mass audience mentality by either neutralizing or making humor of the negative perceptions that many Whites may have had of racial minorities. The advertising images, rather than showing people of color as they really were, portrayed them as filtered through Anglo eyes. This presented an out-of-focus image of racial minorities, but one that was palatable, and even persuasive, to the White majority to which it was directed. In the mid-1960s Black civil rights groups targeted the advertising industry for special attention, protesting both the lack of integrated advertisements including Blacks and the stereotyped images that the advertisers continued to use. The effort, accompanied by support from federal officials, resulted in the overnight inclusion of Blacks as models in television advertising in 1967 and a downplaying of the images that many Blacks found objectionable.

"Black America is becoming visible in America's biggest national advertising medium," reported the *New York Times* in 1968. "Not in a big way yet, but it is a beginning and men in high places give assurances that there will be a lot more visibility."[1]

But the advertising industry did not generalize the concerns of Blacks, or the concessions made in response to them, to other groups. At the same time that some Black concerns were being addressed with integrated advertising, other groups were being ignored or singled out for continued stereotyped treatment in such commercials as those featuring the Frito Bandito.

Among the Latino advertising stereotypes cited in a 1969 article[2] by sociologist Tomás Martínez were commercials for

Granny Goose chips featuring fat gun-toting Mexicans, an advertisement for Arrid underarm deodorant showing a dusty Mexican bandito spraying his underarms after a hard ride as the announcer intones, "If it works for him it will work for you," and a magazine advertisement featuring a stereotypical Mexican sleeping under his sombrero as he leans against a Philco television set. Especially offensive to Martínez was a Liggett & Meyers commercial for L&M cigarettes that featured Paco, a lazy Latino who never "feenishes" anything, not even the revolution he is supposed to be fighting. In response to a letter complaining about the commercial, the director of public relations for the tobacco firm defended the commercial's use of Latino stereotypes.

"'Paco' is a warm, sympathetic and lovable character with whom most of us can identify because he has a little of all of us in him, that is, our tendency to procrastinate at times," wrote the Liggett & Meyers executive. "He seeks to escape the violence of war and to enjoy the pleasure of the moment, in this case, the good flavor of an L&M cigarette."[3] Although the company spokesman claimed that the character had been tested without negative reactions from Latinos (a similar claim was made by Frito-Lay regarding the Frito Bandito), Martínez roundly criticized the advertising images and contrasted them to what he saw as the gains Blacks were then making in the advertising field.

"Today, no major advertiser would attempt to display a black man or woman over the media in a prejudiced, stereotyped fashion," Martínez wrote.

> Complaints would be forthcoming from black associations and perhaps the FCC. Yet, these same advertisers, who dare not show "step'n fetch it" characters, uninhibitedly depict a Mexican counterpart, with additional traits of stinking and stealing. Perhaps the white hatred for blacks, which cannot find adequate expression in today's ads, is being transferred upon their brown brothers.[4]

In 1970 a Brown Position Paper prepared by Latino media activists Armando Rendón and Domingo Nick Reyes charged that the media had transferred the negative stereotypes it once reserved for Blacks to Latinos, who had become "the media's new nigger."[5] The protests of Latinos soon made the nation's advertisers more conscious of the portrayals that Latinos found offensive. But, as in the case of the Blacks, the advertising industry failed to apply the lessons learned from one group to other racial minorities.

Although national advertisers withdrew much of the advertising that negatively stereotyped Blacks and Latinos, sometimes replacing them with affluent, successful images that were as far removed from reality as the negative portrayals of the past, the advances made by those groups were not shared with Native Americans and Asians. Native Americans' names and images, no longer depicted either as the noble savage or as cute cartoon characters, have all but disappeared from broadcast commercials and print advertising. The major exceptions are advertising for automobiles and trucks that bear names such as Pontiac, Dakota, and Navajo and sports teams with racial nicknames such as the Kansas City Chiefs, Washington Redskins, Florida State University Seminoles, Atlanta Braves, and Cleveland Indians. Native Americans and others have protested these racial team names and images, as well as the pseudo-Native American pageantry and souvenirs that accompany many of them, but with no success in getting them changed.

Asians, particularly Japanese, continue to be dealt more than their share of commercials depicting them in stereotypes that cater to the fears and stereotypes of White America. As was the case with Blacks and Latinos, it took organized protests from Asian American groups to get the message across to the corporations and their advertising agencies. In the mid-1970s, a southern California supermarket chain agreed to remove a television campaign in which a young Asian karate-chopped his way down the store's aisles cutting prices. Nationally, several firms whose industries have been hard-hit by Japanese imports fought back through commercials, if not in the quality or prices of their products. One automobile company featured an Asian family carefully looking over a new car and commenting on its attributes in heavily accented English. Only after they bought it did they learn it was made in the United States, not Japan. Another automobile company that markets cars manufactured in Japan under an English-language name showed a parking lot attendant opening the doors of the car, only to find the car speaking to him in Japanese. For several years Sylvania television ran a commercial boasting that its television picture had repeatedly been selected over competing brands as an off-screen voice with a Japanese accent repeatedly asked, "What about Sony?" When the announcer responded that the Sylvania picture had also been selected over Sony's, the off-screen voice ran off shouting what sounded like a string of Japanese expletives. A 1982 *Newsweek* article observed that "attacking Japan has become something of a fashion in corporate ads" because of resentment over Japanese trade policies and sales of Japanese products in the United States, but quoted Motorola's advertising manager as saying, "We've been as careful as we can be" not to be racially offensive.[6]

But many of the television and print advertisements featuring Asians featured images that were racially insensitive, if not offensive. A commercial for a laundry product featured a Chinese family that used an "ancient Chinese laundry secret" to get their customers' clothes clean. Naturally, the Chinese secret turned out to be the packaged product paying for the advertisement. Companies pitching everything from pantyhose to airlines featured Asian women coiffed and costumed as seductive China dolls or exotic Polynesian natives to pitch and promote their products, some of them cast in Asian settings and others attentively caring for the needs of the Anglo men in the advertisement. One airline boasted that those who flew with it would be under the care of the Singapore Girl.

Asian women appearing in commercials were often featured as China dolls with the small, darkened eyes, straight hair with bangs, and a narrow, slit skirt. Another common portrayal featured the exotic, tropical Pacific Islands look, complete with flowers in the hair, a sarong or grass skirt, and shell ornament. Asian women hoping to become models sometimes found that they must conform to these stereotypes or lose assignments. Leslie Kawai, the 1981 Tournament of Roses Queen, was told to cut her hair with bangs by hairstylists when she auditioned for a beer advertisement. When she refused, the beer company decided to hire another model with shorter hair cut in bangs.[7]

The lack of a sizable Asian community, or market, in the United States was earlier cited as the reason that Asians are still stereotyped in advertising and, except for children's advertising, are rarely presented in integrated settings. The growth rate and income of Asians living in the United States in the 1980s and 1990s, however, reinforced the economic potential of Asian Americans to overcome the stereotyping and lack of visibility that Blacks and Latinos challenged with some success. By the mid-1980s there were a few signs that advertising was beginning to integrate Asian Americans into crossover advertisements that, like the Tostitos campaign, were designed to have a broad appeal. In one commercial, television actor Robert Ito was featured telling how he loves to call his relatives in Japan because the calls make them think that he is rich, as well as successful, in the United States. Of course, he adds, it is only because the rates of his long distance carrier were so low that he was able to call Japan so often.

In the 1970s mass audience advertising in the United States became more racially integrated than at any time in the nation's history. Blacks, and to a much lesser extent

Latinos and Asians, could be seen in television commercials spread across the broadcast week and in major magazines. In fact, the advertisements on network television often appeared to be more fully integrated than the television programs they supported. Like television, general circulation magazines also experienced an increase in the use of Blacks, although studies of both media showed that most of the percentage increase had come by the early 1970s. By the early 1970s the percentage of prime-time television commercials featuring Blacks had apparently leveled off at about 10%. Blacks were featured in between only 2% and 3% of magazine advertisements as late as 1978. That percentage, however small, was a sharp increase from the 0.06% of news magazine advertisements reported in 1960.[8]

The gains were also socially significant, because they demonstrated that Blacks could be integrated into advertisements without triggering a White backlash among potential customers in the White majority. Both sales figures and research conducted since the late 1960s have shown that the integration of Black models into television and print advertising does not adversely affect sales or the image of the product. Instead, a study by the American Newspaper Publishers Association showed, the most important influences on sales were the merchandise and the advertisement itself. In fact, while triggering no adverse affect among the majority of Whites, integrated advertisements were found to be useful in swaying Black consumers, who responded favorably to positive Black role models in print advertisements.[9] Studies conducted in the early 1970s also showed that White consumers did not respond negatively to advertising featuring Black models, although their response was more often neutral than positive.[10] One 1972 study examining White backlash, however, did show that an advertisement prominently featuring darker-skinned Blacks was less acceptable to Whites than those featuring lighter-skinned Blacks as background models.[11] Perhaps such findings help explain why research conducted later in the 1970s revealed that, for the most part, Blacks appearing in magazine and television advertisements were often featured as part of an integrated group.[12]

Although research findings have shown that integrated advertisements do not adversely affect sales, the percentage of Blacks and other minorities in general audience advertising did not increase significantly after the numerical gains made through the mid-1970s. Those minorities who did appear in advertisements were often depicted in upscale or integrated settings, an image that the Balch Institute's Stolarik criticized as taking advertising "too far in the other direction and created stereotypes of 'successful' ethnic group members that are as unrealistic as those of the past."[13] Equally unwise, from a business sense, was the low numbers of Blacks appearing in advertisements.

> Advertisers and their ad agencies must evaluate the direct economic consequences of alternative strategies on the firm. If it is believed that the presence of Black models in advertisements decreases the effectiveness of advertising messages, only token numbers of Black models will be used,

wrote marketing professor Lawrence Soley at the conclusion of a 1983 study.

> Previous studies have found that advertisements portraying Black models do not elicit negative affective or conative responses from consumers. . . . Given the consistency of the research findings, more Blacks should be portrayed in advertisements. If Blacks continue to be underrepresented in advertising portrayals, it can be said that this is an indication of prejudice on the part of the advertising industry, not consumers.[14]

◆ *Courtship of Spanish Gold and the Black Market*

Although Soley stopped short of accusing corporate executives of racial prejudice, he contended that a "counterpressure" to full integration of Blacks into mainstream media portrayals was that "advertising professionals are businessmen first and moralists second."[15] If so, then it was the business mentality of advertising and corporate professionals that led them into increasingly aggressive advertising and marketing campaigns to capture minority consumers, particularly Blacks and Latinos, in the 1970s and 1980s.

Long depicted as low-end consumers with little money to spend, Black and Latino customers became more important to national and regional advertisers of mainstream goods who took a closer look at the size, composition, and projected growth of those groups. Asian Americans, who experienced a sharp percentage growth in the 1970s and were generally more affluent than Blacks and Latinos, were not targeted to the same extent, probably because of their relatively small numbers and differences in national languages among the groups. And, except for regions in which they comprised a sizable portion of the population, Native Americans were largely ignored as potential consumers of mainstream products.

One part of the courtship of Blacks and Latinos grew out of the civil rights movements of the 1960s, in which both Blacks and Latinos effectively used consumer boycotts to push issues ranging from ending segregation to organizing farmworkers. Boycotts had long been threatened and used by minority consumers as economic leverage on social issues. But in the 1960s Black ministers organized the Philadelphia Selective Patronage Program in which Blacks did business with companies that supported their goals of more jobs for Blacks. This philosophy of repaying the corporations that invest in the minority communities through consumer purchases was replicated in other cities. It was followed by slick advertising campaigns directed at minority consumers. In 1984 the same line of thinking led to the brewers of Coors beer attempting to end disputes with Blacks and Latinos by signing controversial agreements with the National Association for the Advancement of Colored People (NAACP) and five national Latino groups that committed the brewery to increase its financial support of the activities of those organizations as Blacks and Latinos increased their drinking of Coors beer.

A second, and more influential, element of the courtship has been the hard-selling job of advertising agencies and media specializing in the Black and Spanish-speaking Latinos. Spurred by the thinking of Black advertising executive D. Parke Gibson in his 1968 book *The $30 Billion Negro* and a steady stream of articles on Black and Latino consumers in media trade publications, national advertisers became aware of the fact that minorities were potential consumers for a wide range of products. The advertisers also were persuaded that the inattention they had previously received from mainstream products made Blacks and Latinos respond more favorably and with greater loyalty to those products that courted them through advertisements on billboards and in the publications and broadcast stations used by Latinos and Blacks.

The third, and most far-reaching, element in the courtship was a fundamental change in the thinking of marketing and advertising executives that swayed them away from mass audience media. Witnessing the success they had in advertising on radio stations and magazines targeted to specific audience segments following the advent of television as the dominant mass medium in the 1950s, advertising agencies advised their clients to go after their potential customers identified with market segments, rather than the mass audience.

Advertisers found that differences in race, like differences in sex, residence, family status, and age, were easy to target through advertising appeals targeted to media whose content was designed to attract men or women, young or old, suburban or rural, Black or White, Spanish or English speaking. These media, in turn, produced audience surveys to show they were effective in reaching and delivering specific segments of the mass audience. By the mid-1980s, market and audience segmentation had become so important to advertisers that the term *mass media* was becoming an anachronism.

"It is a basic tenet of marketing that you go after markets with rifles, not shotguns. It is foolhardy—and idealistic in the worst way—to try to sell the same thing to everyone in the same way," wrote Caroline R. Jones, executive vice president of Mingo-Jones Advertising, in a 1984 article in the advertising trade magazine *Madison Avenue.*

> Good marketing involves breaking down potential markets into homogeneous segments; targeting the most desirable segments; and developing creative programs, tailored for each segment, that make your messages look different from your competitors'. All of that should be done with the guidance of thorough research on characteristics, beliefs and preferences of the people in the targeted markets.[16]

Like others who have pitched minority audiences to major corporations as ripe targets for slick advertisements, Jones advised advertising professionals reading the magazine to target advertising to Black consumers because *"there's money in it."* Among the factors she cited as making Blacks desirable customers was a reported disposable income of more than $150 million, a "high propensity for brand names and indulgence items," a high degree of "brand loyalty," a young and growing population, growing education and income, concentration in the nation's largest

25 cities, and "its own growing media network."[17]

Much the same approach has been used to sell Latinos to advertising agencies as a target too good to be passed up. A 1965 article on Latino consumers in the advertising trade magazine *Sponsor* was headlined "America's Spanish Treasure," a 1971 *Sales Management* article proclaimed "Brown Is Richer Than Black," and in 1972 *Television/Radio Age* advised readers, "The Spanish Market: Its Size, Income and Loyalties Make It a Rich Marketing Mine."[18] In addition to the characteristics that were cited as making Blacks an attractive market, Latinos have been depicted as being especially vulnerable to advertisements because their use of Spanish supposedly cuts them off from advertising in English-language media. Thus, advertisers are advised to use the language and culture that are familiar with their target audience to give their messages the greatest delivery and impact.

"U.S. Hispanics are most receptive to media content in the Spanish language," wrote Antonio Guernica in a 1982 book titled *Reaching the Hispanic Market Effectively.*[19] Guernica and others have counseled advertisers to package their commercial messages in settings that are reinforced by Latino culture and traditions. These appeals link the product being advertised with the language, heritage, and social system that Latinos are most comfortable with, thus creating the illusion that the product belongs in the Latino home.

"The language, the tradition, the kitchen utensils are different" (in a Latino home) said Shelly Perlman, media buyer for the Hispania division of the J. Walter Thompson advertising agency in a 1983 *Advertising Age* article.

> There are ads one can run in general media that appeal to everyone but that contain unmistakeable clues to Hispanics that they are being sought. It can be done with models, with scene and set design— a whole array of factors.[20]

Corporations seeking the Latino dollar also have been told to picture their products with Latino foods, celebrities, cultural events, community events, and family traditions. The goal has been to adapt the product to make it appear to be a part of the Latino lifestyle in the United States, which often requires being sensitive to the language, food, and musical differences among Latinos in different parts of the nation and from different countries in Latin America.

For both Blacks and Latinos the slick advertising approach often means selling high-priced, prestige products to low-income consumers who have not fully shared in the wealth of the country in which they live. But Blacks and Latinos, who have median family incomes well below national averages, have been nonetheless targeted as consumers for premium brand names in all product lines and particularly in liquor, beer, and cigarettes. In response, Black and Latino community groups and health organizations in the 1990s protested the targeting of alcohol and tobacco products to their communities and, in some cases, forced outdoor advertising companies to restrict the number of such billboards in these communities.

Through the 1990s, corporations making and marketing products ranging from beer to diapers tried to show Blacks and Latinos that consumption of their goods is part of the good life in America. It may not be a life that they knew when they grew up in the ghetto, barrio, or in another country. It may not even be a life that they or their children will ever achieve, but it is a lifestyle and happiness they can share by purchasing the same products used by the rich and famous. Prestige appeals are used in advertising to all audiences, not just minorities. But they have a special impact on those who are so far down on the socioeconomic scale that they are especially hungry for anything that will add status or happiness to their lives and help them show others that they are "making it." The advertisements promote conspicuous consumption, rather than hard work and savings, as the key to the good life. . . .

By recognizing elements of the Black or Latino experience that may have been ignored by White Americans, the advertisers also play on national or racial pride to boost sales of their products. In the 1970s, Anheuser-Busch commissioned a series of glossy advertisements commemorating the Great Kings of Africa, and Schlitz produced a Chicano history calendar. These and similar advertising campaigns provided long overdue recognition of Black and Latino heritage, but they also prominently displayed the corporate symbols of their sponsors and were designed to boost the sale of beer more than to recognize overlooked historical figures and events. . . .

The media targeted to non-Whites are eager to promote themselves as the most effective way to reach consumers of color. In 1974 one of New York's Black newspapers, the *Amsterdam News*, vigorously attacked the credibility of a New York *Daily News* audience survey that showed it reached more Black readers than the *Amsterdam News*. In a 1979 *Advertising Age* advertisement, *La Opinión*, Los Angeles's Spanish-language daily newspaper, promised advertisers it could show them how to "Wrap Up the Spanish-language Market." Advertising is the lifeblood of the print and broadcast media in the United States, and media that target people of color have been quick to promote themselves as the most effective vehicles for penetrating and persuading the people in their communities to purchase the products advertised on their airwaves and in their pages.

How Loud Is the Not-so- ◆ Silent Partner's Voice?

Minority-formatted publications and broadcasters depend on advertising to support their media. They have benefited from the increased emphasis on market segmentation by promoting the consumption patterns of the audiences they reach and their own effectiveness in delivering persuasive commercial messages to their readers, listeners, and viewers. But advertising is also a two-edged sword that expects to take more money out of a market segment than it invests in advertising to that segment. Black and Spanish-language media will benefit from the advertising dollars of national corporations only as long as dollars are the most cost-effective way for advertisers to persuade Blacks and Latinos to use their products. This places the minority-formatted media in an exploitative relationship with their audience, who because of language, educational, and economic differences sometimes are exposed to a narrower range of media than Whites. Advertisers support the media that deliver the audience with the best consumer profile at the lowest cost, not necessarily the media that best meet the information and entertainment needs of their audience.

The slick, upscale lifestyle used by national advertisers is more a goal than a reality for most Blacks and Latinos. It is achieved through education, hard work, and equal opportunity. Yet advertisers promote consumption of their products as the short-cut to the good life, a quick fix for low-income consumers. The message to their low-income audience is clear: You may not be able to live in the best neighborhoods, wear the best clothes, or have the best job, but you can drink the same liquor, smoke the same cigarettes, and drive the same car as those who do. At the same time, advertising appeals that play on the cultural or historical heritage of Blacks and Latinos make the products appear to be "at home" with minority consumers. Recognizing the importance of national holidays and the forgotten minority history, they have joined with Blacks and Latinos in commemorating dates, events, and persons. But they also piggy-back their commercial messages on the recognition of events, leaders, or heroes. Persons or events that in their time represented protest against slavery, oppression, or discrimination are now used to sell products.

Advertising, like mining, is an extractive industry. It enters the ghetto and barrio with a smiling face to convince all within its reach that they should purchase the products advertised and purchase them often. It has no goal other than to stimulate consumption of the product; the subsidization of the media is merely a by-product. But owners of minority-formatted media, having gained through the increased advertising investments of major corporations, now have greater opportunities to use those increased dollars to improve news and entertainment content and, thus, better meet their social responsibility to their audience. Unlike advertisers, who may support socially responsible activities for the purpose of promoting their own images, minority publishers and broadcasters have a long, though sometimes spotty, record of advocating the rights of the people they serve. Their growing dependence on major corporations and national advertising agencies should do nothing to blunt that edge as long as the audiences they serve continue to confront a system of inequality that keeps them below national norms in education, housing, income, health, and other social indicators.

Notes ◆

1. Cited in Philip H. Dougherty, "Frequency of Blacks in TV Ads," *New York Times*, May 27, 1982, p. D19.

2. Tomás Martínez, "How Advertisers Promote Racism," *Civil Rights Digest* (Fall 1969), p. 10.

3. Martínez, "How Advertisers Promote," p. 11.

4. Martínez, "How Advertisers Promote," pp. 9-10.

5. Domingo Nick Reyes and Armando Rendón, *Chicanos and the Mass Media* (Washington, DC: The National Mexican American Anti-Defamation Committee, 1971).

6. Joseph Treen, "Madison Ave. vs. Japan, Inc.," *Newsweek* (April 12, 1982), p. 69.

7. Ada Kan, *Asian Models in the Media*, Unpublished term paper, Journalism 466: Minority and the Media, University of Southern California, December 14, 1983, p. 5.

8. Studies on increase of Blacks in magazine and television commercials cited in James D. Culley and Rex Bennett, "Selling Blacks, Selling Women," *Journal of Communication* (Autumn 1976, Vol. 26, No. 4), pp. 160-174; Lawrence Soley, "The Effect of Black Models on Magazine Ad Readership," *Journalism Quarterly* (Winter 1983, Vol. 60, No. 4), p. 686; and Leonard N. Reid and Bruce G. Vanden Bergh, "Blacks in Introductory Ads," *Journalism Quarterly* (Autumn 1980, Vol. 57, No. 3), pp. 485-486.

9. Cited in D. Parke Gibson, *$70 Billion in the Black* (New York: Macmillan, 1979), pp. 83-84.

10. Laboratory studies on White reactions to Blacks in advertising cited in Soley, "The Effect of Black Models," pp. 585-587.

11. Carl E. Block, "White Backlash to Negro Ads: Fact or Fantasy?" *Journalism Quarterly* (Autumn 1980, Vol. 49, No. 2), pp. 258-262.

12. James D. Culley and Rex Bennett, "Selling Blacks, Selling Women."

13. "Using Ethnic Images," p. 9.

14. Soley, *The Effect of Black Models*, p. 690.

15. Soley, *The Effect of Black Models*, p. 690.

16. Caroline R. Jones, "Advertising in Black and White," *Madison Avenue* (May 1984), p. 53.

17. Jones, "Advertising in Black and White," p. 54.

18. Félix Frank Gutiérrez, *Spanish-language Radio and Chicano Internal Colonialism*, Doctoral Dissertation, Stanford University, 1976, pp. 312-314.

19. Antonio Guernica, *Reaching the Hispanic Market Effectively* (New York: McGraw-Hill, 1982), p. 5.

20. Theodore J. Gage, "How to Reach an Enthusiastic Market," *Advertising Age* (February 14, 1983), p. M-11.

30

CURRENT PERSPECTIVES ON ADVERTISING IMAGES OF DISABILITY

◆ Beth A. Haller and Sue Ralph

The disabled consumer is coming of age. Companies in the United States and Great Britain are seeing the profitability of including disabled people in their advertising. But what are the implications of the images produced in these advertisements? Are they moving away from the pity narratives of charity? Are they creating acceptance and integration of disabled people? . . .

Advocates for disabled people in United States have long known the importance of the "disabled consumer market." Carmen Jones of EKA Marketing (1997) says: "Few companies have enjoyed the profitability that results in targeting the consumer who happens to have a disability. . . . I believe if the business community were educated about the size and potential of the market, then advertising programs with the disabled consumer in mind would be created" (p. 4). In the new millennium, advertisers are realizing that disabled people buy soap, milk, socks, jewelry, makeup, home improvement goods, use travel services, live in houses, and enjoy nice home furnishings. There is some evidence that the disabled consumer is very much more brand loyal than other consumers

NOTE: From *Disabilities Studies Quarterly*, Spring 2001. Copyright © 2001. Reprinted with permission from the Society for Disability Studies.

(Quinn, 1995). For example, the hotel chain Embassy Suites found out that becoming sensitive to the needs of disabled people led to more business. And a study by the National Captioning Institute found that 73 percent of deaf people switched to a brand that had TV ad captioning (Quinn, 1995). . . .

However, some companies in both countries were slow to learn what accurate and non-stigmatizing advertising images were. For example, in 1990 a Fuji TV ad for film on British television that featured a man with learning disabilities being "improved" by a photograph of him smiling at the end was criticized by disabilities scholar Michael Oliver for its "medical model" approach (Deakin, 1996, Sept. 20, p. 37). The TV ad was interpreted as the Fuji film offering a type of "cosmetic surgery" on the disabled man through the advertisement. Ironically, the ad agency that created the Fuji ad consulted the British charity Mencap, but as Scott-Parker pointed out, "the perceptions and interests of a disability charity are not always synonymous with those of the disabled consumer" (Dourado, 1990, p. 27). Because of early faux pas like this, "disability is still an area in which few advertisers dare to deal" in Great Britain (Deakin, 1996, p. 37).

In both countries, new disability rights legislation (the U.S. Americans with Disability Act [ADA] and Work Incentives Improvement Act [WIIA] and the UK Disability Discrimination Act) has made the business community more aware of disabled consumers and that there are large numbers of them. These legislative acts have also given businesses an understanding that disabled people want to find more and better employment and in turn purchase more consumer goods. Some policy analysts actually called the ADA a mandate for marketers to begin to recognize the formerly invisible disabled market (Stephens & Bergman, 1995). In addition, WIIA would provide a $1,000 tax credit to help people with severe disabilities cover work-related expenses. President Clinton pushed for the act with an inclusive society perspective: "As anyone with a disability can tell you, it takes more than a job to enter the work force. Often, it takes successful transportation, specialized technology or personal assistance" (Clinton, 1999).

These types of legislative acts have made the U.S.A. and the UK more receptive to accommodating disabled people in terms of architecture and communication so more will have the ability to make purchases and become part of each society's "consumer culture." For example, in the United States, 48.5 million disabled people who are age 15 and over had an estimated total discretionary income of $175 billion (Prager, 1999, Dec. 15). In the UK, there are 6.5 million disabled people who represent a 33 billion pound market, which will increase (Deakin, 1996).

History of Advertising ◆ Use of Disabled People

A distinction must be made between community-specific advertising campaigns and general campaigns. For example, when the black community or the gay community advocates for better advertising representation, they are hoping for more accurate images in advertising to the general public, rather than to specialty group publications. The same is true of disabled people. Most disability-related magazines and other media already have numerous images; the advocacy currently is for more inclusion in advertising to the general population. This is where the disabled community hopes attitudes will be changed through inclusion.

Historically, most images of disability in advertising have been from charity organizations. . . . In the United States, charity advertising was a separate entity from commercial advertising and included programs such as telethons and promotional ads from "helping" societies such as Easter Seals, the Multiple Sclerosis Society, and Paralyzed

Veterans of America. American consumers seemed to more readily distinguish between the use of disabled people in charity advertising from commercial advertising; however, in the early days of commercial advertising's used of disabled models, there was concern about exploitation because disabled people had been associated with charity only. However, after numerous years of criticism by disability rights advocates, telethons have fallen in numbers and many stations have even dropped the most famous telethon—Jerry Lewis's MDA telethon—from their Labor Day line-up. And other charity organizations have retooled their promotions to be less stigmatizing, and one charity, Easter Seals, now makes it part of its mission to promote better media images through its EDI awards, which stands for Equality, Dignity, and Independence. . . .

In the United States, the business community began recognizing the disabled consumer in advertising images early in the 1980s. Early disability rights legislation such as the Rehabilitation Act of 1973, which required all federal programs and structures to be accessible and was finally being enforced by the early 1980s, began to build awareness of the disability community. Also, the disability rights movement began about this time in response to the lack of entitlements of the Rehab Act, when activists staged protests about it (Shapiro, 1993). In addition, the independent living movement, which gave disabled people educational and employment opportunities, also began in the early 1970s and gave disabled people more visibility in society (Shapiro, 1993). Longmore (1987) says that when TV ads with disabled people began, it illustrated that advertisers no longer feared that "nondisabled consumers will be distressed or offended" (p. 77). Finally, in 1980 closed captioning began on television, and the medium became more accessible to deaf people (Lipman, 1990, Feb. 28). All these factors converged to give businesses slightly more awareness of disabled people and their potential as consumers.

The first TV ad said to feature a disabled person was in a 1984 Levi's ad in which a wheelchair user popped a wheelie (Kaufman, 1999). . . . However, McDonald's claims to have been including wheelchair users in general shots of customers in TV ads since 1980. But its first TV ad to feature a disabled person was in 1986 when it depicted college-age deaf students discussing going to McDonald's in sign language (Dougherty, 1986). However, at this point in commercial advertising images, the company still thought ads with disabled people should be directed to other disabled people and that these types of ads built "good will." As the *New York Times* wrote: "Apparently aware of the notion that good deeds are best measured by the amount of publicity they amass, McDonald's Corporation is promoting a TV commercial for the deaf and starring the deaf" (Dougherty, 1986, p. D26). The TV also contained captioning, which was actually for the hearing viewers not the deaf viewers, because "regular hearing viewers get confused by the signs" (Dougherty, 1986). Deaf people became a popular disability group to depict in TV ads and by 1990 Crest, Citibank, and Levi's had all used deaf actors. In fact, AT&T capitalized on the Academy Award-winning actress Marlee Matlin's fame by using her in some ads. By 1990, the National Captioning Institute reported more than 200 advertisers were captioning their ads, resulting in 2,600 closed-captioned TV spots (Lipman, 1990, Feb. 28).

Wheelchair users became the other prominent category of disability in early U.S. commercial advertisements. After Levi's TV ad, companies such as Citicorp, Apple computers, Pacific Telesis, Nissan, and Target had all featured wheelchair users in TV or print ads by 1991. Target became somewhat of a pioneer in print ads using adults and children with disabilities in their sales circulars that went to 30 million households in 32 states (Sagon, 1991, Dec. 19). Target's vice president of marketing said their use of disabled people in their ads was so successful that they can actually point to specific products that sold much better because they were modeled by a disabled person (Goerne, 1992). In addition, the early campaign that depicted children with disabilities led to 1,000 supportive letters and "has been the single most successful consumer response we've ever gotten," according to the VP of marketing, Bob Thacker (Sagon, 1991, p. B10). Target then expanded its disability images past wheelchair use to children and teens with Down syndrome, leg braces, and artificial limbs.

However, Target's pioneering use of disability images was not easily implemented. Even Target's Bob Thacker, who has a daughter with a disability, worried that the store chain might get complaints that the company was exploiting disabled people (Rabinovitz, 1991, Sept. 23, p. D14). Target's public relations department reported that the company's suppliers were concerned: "Some buyers were worried that it would detract from the merchandise. Others felt it would look exploitative" (Sagon, 1991, p. B10.) But it had the opposite effect: "There isn't a single disabled person who will say they feel they're being exploited; they are thrilled and proud that they are being portrayed as just another member of society," according to the Target public relations vice president (Sagon, 1991, p. B10).

From the 1990s on, many of the advertisements featuring disabled peopled were accepted and considered nonstigmatizing. However, one major controversy arose in 1993, which illustrated how disabled and nondisabled people interpreted the images differently. Dow Chemical's Spray 'N Wash Stain Stick TV ad used a child with Down syndrome. The ad begins: "Halley has made my life very exciting. She's very affectionate, and she is very active. We use Stain Stick ... because the last place we need another challenge is the laundry room" (Goldman, 1993, Sept. 3, p. B8). The ad used no professional actors but a real mother and daughter from Atlanta,

Georgia, found through a connection to the National Down Syndrome Congress. The congress applauded the final ad, which made mention of Down's, and even gave it a media award. However, an *Advertising Age* writer called the ad exploitative, "appalling," and "the most crassly contrived slice-of-life in advertising history" (Goldman, 1993, Sept. 3, p. B8). Dow's toll-free telephone line contradicted this opinion with 700 calls, all positive except for seven calls.

But Burger King did not have such positive audience response when it ran a TV ad that featured a man with Down syndrome trying to memorize the company's slogan and being helped by his mother. The restaurant chain pulled the ad after some parents of children with Down syndrome complained. One mother called the image of a grown man being helped by his parent "insulting" (Goldman, 1993, Sept. 3, p. B8). In another case, the Alliance for the Mentally Ill in New York complained about an offensive ad from the discount clothing chain, Daffy's, which depicted a straightjacket in print and TV ads and indicated that someone was insane to pay more money for clothes (Case, 1992, May 2). . . .

Cultural Meaning ◆ of Disability Images in Advertising

Harlan Hahn (1987) wrote a seminal article about the role of advertising in culturally defining, or not defining, disabled people. His work creates the framework we will use for analyzing subsequent ads that include disabled people. . . .

Hahn argues generally that advertising's emphasis on beauty and bodily perfection has led to exclusion of disabled people in the images. In addition, the nondisabled audience members' fears of becoming disabled and viewing images of disability meant businesses were hesitant to used disabled people as models.

Apparently the common difficulty of disabled people in gaining acceptance as human beings even permitted the belief that a male seated in a wheelchair was not really a man. Advertising and other forms of mass imagery were not merely designed to increase sale of commodities; they also comprised a cultural force with an influence that has permeated all aspects of American life. From this perspective, issues of causation, such as whether advertising simply reflected widespread sentiments about disability or whether it contributed to implanting such feelings, become less critical than the assessment of contexts and effects. (Hahn, 1987, p. 562)

The context Hahn discusses is disabled people's "inability" to ever fit within a context of beautiful bodies and they are therefore rendered invisible. He points out that advertising promotes a specific "acceptable physical appearance" that it then reinforces itself. These advertising images tell society who is acceptable in terms of appearance and that transfers to who is acceptable to employ, associate with, communicate with, and value.

However, Hahn did see signs of hope in changing societal perceptions of disabled people through advertising and other forms of mass communication. He cites many historical examples in which physical appearances/attributes that were once prized were later seen as deviant or unattractive. Bogdan (1988) explained this phenomenon in his study of American freak shows, in which many disabled people were honored as celebrities; however, later people with the same disabilities were institutionalized.

In the modern understanding of diversity as a profitable undertaking for businesses, we argue that the cultural meaning of disability imagery in advertising is changing for the better. As Hahn predicted, some social attitudes are changing and advertising that features disabled people is being associated with profitability, both because

of the newfound power of the disabled consumer and general audience's desire to see "real life" in images. As discussed in the example of the Target advertising campaign, they received several thousand letters of positive feedback and sold products modeled by disabled people at a much higher rate. . . .

The positive cultural meanings of profitability and diversity in advertising images do not solve all potential problems with disability imagery. As with all advertising images, the beautiful and least disfigured disabled people are depicted. As mentioned, many early TV ads in the United States used primarily deaf people. Good-looking and sports-minded wheelchair users are another important visual category. But this does not truly represent the diversity within the disability community. As a disability publication editor said: "Not every person with a disability is young and beautiful and athletic, just like all women aren't size 10, and all African Americans don't have degrees from Harvard. . . . I know people with disabilities who aren't pretty. They drool. They scare the average person. So do we do more harm than good showing this cute little girl with CP?" (McLaughlin, 1993, Aug. 22, p. 31).

Some Current Disability ◆ Imagery in Advertising

TARGET

Target chain stores began a trend by including disabled children and teens in their print ad circulars in 1990. Though hesitant at first, the advertising was a rousing success and the corporate office received 2,000 letters of support early in the campaign.

First, the images are well used because of the way they naturalize disability rather than stigmatize it. In fact, many times it takes several looks at the circulars to actually find the disabled children, whose disabilities are visible, because they are part of scenes of groups of children or a number of images on one page. The way Target uses disabled people in its ads fits squarely within the cultural meaning of diversity in advertising imagery. In fact, in 1994 a circular ad depicted a Latina disabled girl in a wheelchair interacting with a nondisabled Caucasian girl to sell girls' pants sets. The ad is even more significant in that it depicts actual interaction between the children, rather than two girls staring at the camera. They are handing something to each other in a kitchen setting. This type of depiction sends several messages: That people of color have disabilities, too, and that interaction between disabled and nondisabled children is quite normal.

In another ad in 1994 for Target, a young blonde woman in a wheelchair is used to advertise women's T-shirts. Although she is alone in the picture and is a typical smiling, blond model with a peaches-and-cream complexion, the interesting aspect to this ad is that she is wearing jeans shorts, which show her legs. As a person with a mobility disability, her legs are not as muscular as a nondisabled person's might be and this is apparent in the photo. However, the image is not grotesque or disturbing. Once again, it just shows reality and the natural appearance of a wheelchair user's lower body.

In a 1995 Target ad, two teens are featured in an ad for women's cotton T-shirts. They are both smiling, fresh-faced blondes and one is a wheelchair user. The wheelchair is partially obscured by examples of the T-shirt embroidery at the bottom of the photo, so only a corner of a wheelchair peeks out. Again, this very subtle approach erases any stigma and makes the wheelchair-using teen the equal of her blonde counterpart in the ad. The nondisabled teen is bent down near to the disabled teen so there is less height difference between the standing and sitting teens.

Finally, Target's ad campaigns realized that wheelchair use is not the only disability, or even the most prevalent. In 1995, a circular depicted a boy with a walker in its ad for Power Ranger underwear sets. The walker, however, is placed behind him, possibly so the clothing was not covered in the picture. The boy stands up straight in his walker and is next to a girl modeling Power Ranger underwear for girls. The boy's tanned, smiling appearance is vigorous and healthy and really has little connection to a "medical model" depiction (Clogston, 1990), even with a walker in the scene. Another Target circular in Spanish advertised school uniform wear and featured a young model with a single crutch. She strikes a typical model pose with a sweater slung over her shoulder. She, too, has a healthy appearance and the illustration shows no misshapen extremities. In fact, her only "flaw" is one that normalizes her as a child—she is missing a front tooth. . . .

Nike's TV ads have a mixture of the incidental use of disabled models and one featured disabled athlete Craig Blanchette, who held two world records in wheelchair racing in 1989. The Blanchette spot is called "Cross Training With Craig Blanchette" and no scene or mention of his disability is made in the first 27 seconds of the 30-second commercial. He is referred to as a 1988 Olympic bronze medalist. The ad seethes with macho images, first of Blanchette lifting weights, then aggressively playing basketball and tennis. The scenes are intensely athletic, and Blanchette is seen reaching for and making difficult shots. Although he is the focus of the ad, he is not alone. Other male athletic types, both young and old, black and white, are depicted in the background of the weight room, and Blanchette smilingly tosses a basketball to another young man in one scene. Blanchette appears muscular with his massive arms and rugged with his scruffy beard. Only in the last few seconds is it revealed that Blanchette is a wheelchair athlete, when the camera pans down and he says: "So I never quit" and turns his back to the camera and races down the track in his sports wheelchair.

Nike officials said it was not relevant to them that Blanchette is a wheelchair-using double amputee. Their VP of marketing explained, "He's a great athlete, which ties to our usual strategy . . . and he's a really motivating guy to be around. The fact that he was handicapped was secondary" (Lipman, 1989, Sept. 7, p. 1). But profitability from disabled athletes or consumers was likely a strong motivation. As a *Wall Street Journal* article says, the Blanchette Nike ad is an example of commercial advertising becoming "increasingly enchanted with the disabled" (Lipman, 1989, Sept. 7, p. 1). Nike also illustrates general inclusiveness in two other TV ads, one of which, "Heritage U.S. Update" has an image of an African American wheelchair racer and concludes with a triumphant white wheelchair user winning a race with "There is no finish line" superimposed in the background. Another Nike ad called "Hope" focuses almost entirely on men and women athletes of color and includes two fast images of wheelchair races and then a concluding image of a wheelchair racer who pulls open his shirt to reveal the "Superman" emblem.

◆ *Conclusion and Discussion*

This analysis illustrates that companies in the United States and Great Britain are seeing the profitability of including disabled people in their advertising and understanding the benefits of diverse images in advertising. The implication of the images produced in these advertisements is that advertising not only includes disabled people for capitalistic reasons but realizes these must be accurate images to earn any profit from their use. This means companies have learned, due to their own desire for profits, to move away from the past pity narratives of charity. Our analyses illustrate that corporate America and Britain can create good

disability images in advertising that are sensitive and accurate and just represent disability as another slice of life.

However, we recognize that disability images in advertising are not perfect. There is almost total focus on two disabilities: wheelchair use and deafness. For example, McDonald's admitted early in advertising campaigns to taking the path of ease to show disabled people by just including wheelchair users in shots of "hordes of customers" (Dougherty, 1986, p. D26). Ironically, their "easy way out" actually became the best way to depict disability in ads—an incidental use of disability among a variety of people illustrates diversity in a very salient and accurate way. Although the incidence of wheelchair use is actually quite low when compared to other types of disabilities, it is also understood that advertising is a visual medium, which needs the equipment cues such as wheelchairs to denote disability as part of the diversity depicted. Disabled screenwriter Marc Moss explained that he was initially concerned about how wheelchair users were used in advertising as "proof of corporate soul." However, he does agree "that with varying degrees of finesse, they [advertisers] juggle two points: Their products or services are worthy, and so are people who can't walk" (Moss, 1992, June 19, p. A8).

Of course, as with all advertising, only "pretty people" can become models. This is the area in which many disabled people still have concern about the images of disability in advertising. "It would be nice to have a severely disabled person depicted instead of your superjock 'crip,'" says David Lewis, a quadriplegic, who is community relations coordinator for the Center for Independent Living, a nonprofit support group for the disabled based in Berkeley, California. "'Usually disabled people in commercials look like able bodied people in wheelchairs'" (Lipman, 1989, Sept. 7, p. 1). However, some disabled people applaud finally being visible in ads or being presented as anything other than a charity case. As one disabled actor said, "the Adonis in a wheelchair is better than the whimpering victim in a corner" (McLaughlin, 1993, Aug. 22, p. 31). Therefore, due to the nature of media effects, we believe that these disability advertising images, even if they tend to focus primarily on beautiful deaf people or wheelchair users, can enhance more acceptance and integration of disabled people into society. Several past studies of the potential for attitude changes toward disabled people through use of media images have confirmed this phenomenon (Farnall, 1996; Farnall & Smith, 1999; Panol & McBride, 1999).

Finally, the better and more prevalent use of disabled people in advertising, we believe, can be tied to important anti-discrimination legislation in the United States and the UK. The ADA kicked off a renewed awareness of disability rights, which can be seen in the growing number of disabled people in ads from 1990 on and a better understanding of the disabled consumer market. It can be hoped that the Disability Discrimination Act 1995 in the UK will lead to the same kind of inclusion of diverse disability in British advertising. . . .

Historically, this [chapter] has documented the changing cultural meanings of disability imagery in advertising. Currently, business concerns see profitability in disability imagery and have found diversity to be good business practice. This is quite a shift from the pre-Rehab Act and pre-ADA days. A National Easter Seals Society executive explained that in the mid-1970s she tried to persuade a Minneapolis company to use a disabled person in a promotional photo: "They were horrified at the idea. . . . They told me they would lose sales, it would scare people—they even used the word disgusting" (Sagon, 1991, Dec. 19, p. B10). By 1992, the same Easter Seals spokesperson praised companies like Kmart when they began a new TV ad campaign using a wheelchair-using actress to portray a customer. "Those of us in the nonprofit world have tried for years to change the way disabled people are perceived," Sandra

Gordon of Easter Seals said. "Now it seems the for-profit world is finally lending a hand" (Roberts & Miller, 1992, p. 40).

References ◆

Bogdan, R. (1988). *Freak show: Presenting human oddities for amusement and profit.* Chicago: University of Chicago Press

Case, T. (1992, May 2). Retail ad labelled offensive. *Editor & Publisher, 125* (18), 56.

Clinton, W. J. (1999, January 13). Remarks by the president on disability initiative. [White House press release].

Clogston, J. (1990). *Disability coverage in 16 newspapers.* Louisville: The Advocado Press.

Deakin, A. (1996, September 20). Body language. *Marketing Week, 19*(26), 37.

Dougherty, P. H. (1986, May 14). Advertising: TV spot for deaf viewers. *New York Times*, p. D26.

Dourado, P. (1990, August 16). Parity not charity. *Marketing*, pp. 26-27.

Farnall, O. (1996). *Positive images of the disabled in television advertising: Effects on attitude toward the disabled.* Paper presented at the annual meeting of the Association for Education in Journalism and Mass Communication, Anaheim, CA.

Farnall, O., & Smith, K. A. (1999). Reactions to people with disabilities: Personal contact versus viewing of specific media portrayals. *Journalism and Mass Communication Quarterly, 76*(4), 659-672.

Goerne, C. (1992, September 14). Marketing to the disabled: New workplace law stirs interest in largely untapped market. *Marketing News, 26*(19), 1, 32.

Goldman, K. (1993, September 3). Dow brands criticized and praised for ad featuring disabled child. *Wall Street Journal*, p. B8.

Hahn, H. (1987, March). Advertising the acceptably employable image: Disability and capitalism. *Policy Studies Journal, 15* (3), March, 551-570.

Jones, C. (1997). Disabled consumers. [Letter to the Editor]. *American Demographics*, *19*(11), 4.

Kaufman, L. (1999, December 3). Companies boost number of deaf actors appearing in commercials. *Los Angeles Times*, p. C1.

Lipman, J. (1989, September 7). Disabled people featured in more ads. *Wall Street Journal*, p. 1.

Lipman, J. (1990, February 28). Deaf consumers aren't ignored anymore. *Wall Street Journal*, p. B6.

Longmore, P. K. (1987). Screening stereotypes: Images of disabled people in television and motion pictures. In A. Garner & T. Joe (Eds.), *Images of the disabled* (pp. 65-78). New York: Praeger.

McLaughlin, P. (1993, August 22). Roll models. *Philadelphia Inquirer*, p. 31.

Moss, M. J. (1992, June 19). The disabled "discovered." *Wall Street Journal*, p. A8.

Panol, Z., & McBride, M. (1999). *Print advertising images of the disabled: Exploring the impact on nondisabled consumer attitudes*. Paper presented at the Association for Education in Journalism and Mass Communication annual conference, New Orleans, LA.

Prager, J. H. (1999, December 15). People with disabilities are next consumer niche—Companies see a market ripe for all-terrain wheelchairs, computers with "sticky keys." *Wall Street Journal*, pp. B1, 2.

Quinn, J. (1995). Able to buy. *Incentive*, *169*(9), 80.

Rabinovitz, J. (1991, September 23). The media business: Disabled people gain roles in ads and on TV. *New York Times*, p. D14.

Roberts, E., & Miller, A. (1992, February 24). This ad's for you. *Newsweek*, p. 40.

Sagon, C. (1991, December 19). Retailers reach to the disabled: Stores see profit in undeserved market. *Washington Post*, p. B10.

Shapiro, J. P. (1993). *No pity*. New York: Times Books.

Stephens, D. L., & Bergman, K. (1995, Spring). The Americans with Disabilities Act: A mandate for marketers. *Journal of Public Policy and Marketing*, *14*(1), 164-173.

31

SELLING SEXUAL SUBJECTIVITIES
Audiences Respond to
Gay Window Advertising

◆ Katherine Sender

In their study of shifts in advertising trends throughout the twentieth century, Leiss, Kline, and Jhally (1990) argue that advertisements constitute a system of cultural production offering meaning to a consumer society which is otherwise symbolically, mythically, or spiritually impoverished. Within this context, advertisements serve a two-fold function, to provide role models with whom we can identify and through whom we can aspire to appropriate constructions of ourselves as social beings, and to guide us towards what the marketplace considers to be desirable kinds and quantities of purchasing in an increasingly commodified social environment. In terms of the first of these aims, advertising has consistently reflected prevailing views of appropriate gender relations and heterosexual norms, both endorsing "proper" femininity and masculinity (Goffman, 1979; Jhally, 1989) and yoking these to the heterosexual dyad. These notions of appropriate gender and sexual behavior then become tied to "correct" purchasing decisions. However, an increasing acknowledgement

NOTE: From *Critical Studies in Mass Communication*, Vol. 16, pp. 172-196. Copyright by the National Communication Association, 1999. Reproduced by permission of the publisher.

by advertisers that lesbians, bisexuals, and gay men constitute a viable (i.e., profitable) market for the sale of goods and services has led to growing interest on the part of advertisers to court these populations (see the special reports in *Advertising Age*, January 18, 1993, and May 30, 1994, both titled "Marketing to Gays and Lesbians"). Advertising appeals can be made explicitly to lesbian, gay, and bisexual markets, as in the inclusion of a gay male couple in a 1994 Ikea television commercial, or implicitly, through the use of coded representations which can be interpreted as "gay" by bisexual, lesbian, and gay readers, a strategy known as "gay window advertising" (Bronski, 1984, p. 187).

I began this research with a series of questions about how audiences of differing sexual identifications understand representations of gender and sexual identification. Are lesbian, gay, or bisexual readings always and only available to lesbian, bisexual, and gay readers? How might we account for a relationship between cultural positions and texts if there *is* or, alternatively, *is not* a correspondence between sexual identification and readings? How might the concepts of polysemy and relevancy be useful in understanding audiences' interpretations of texts? Finally, what are the political implications of including consumers with non-dominant sexual identifications within the scope of the marketing gaze?

◆ Gay Window Advertising: Opportunities and Erasures

Explicit appeals using models coded as lesbian, gay, or bisexual remain rare in the mainstream press, although they do appear with increasing frequency in lesbian and gay publications, and not necessarily selling gay-specific products or services (Baker, 1997; Fejes & Lennon, 2000; Fejes & Petrich, 1993). *Advertising Age*'s feature on advertising to lesbians and gays emphasizes that this is a sensible *business* strategy; as a spokeswoman from the Miller Brewing Company said, "We market to gays and lesbians for business reasons, because we want to sell our product to consumers. It doesn't get more complicated than that" (Davis, 1994, p. S-1).

. . . While groups who identify with a non-dominant sexual subjectivity are gaining increasing interest from marketers, advertisers continue to be notoriously conservative, especially when it comes to potentially alienating a segment of their existing market. The result has been the phenomenon of gay window advertising, where images are coded with subtexts which are intended to be understood by lesbian, gay, and bisexual readers as "lesbian" and/or "gay" and/or "bisexual" texts, but which are assumed to remain innocuous to heterosexual readers. As Clark (1993) writes: "If heterosexual consumers do not notice these subtexts or subcultural codes, then advertisers are able to reach the homosexual market along with the heterosexual market without ever revealing their aim" (p. 188).

In her article for an advertising trade journal, *Print*, Kahn (1994) addresses gay window strategies employed to market to lesbian and gay audiences in both gay and straight-oriented media. She quotes Peter Fressola, Benetton's director of communications for North America, who says that "there's a joke in the gay community about 'gay-dar,'[1] . . . and I'm gay, so I can talk about this. There's a sensibility . . . that tips you off" (p. 24). Kahn goes on to outline some of the ways advertisers consciously appeal to lesbian, gay, and bisexual consumers, including using a single person instead of an opposite-sexed couple, showing "good-looking crowd scenes with no obvious different-sexed couples" (p. 24), having no people at all in an image, representing androgynous hands, showing rainbow flags and colors, AIDS awareness ribbons and pink triangles, and using lavender, pink, or purple type.

While explicit recognition of gay window marketing may be a relatively recent phenomenon, covert and semi-public representations of homosexuality are not new. . . . In his analysis of the construction of a "gay sensibility" and its relationship to the mainstream media, Bronski (1984) argues that coded homoerotic images of male models have been used in advertisements designed to appeal both to gay and to heterosexual audiences since at least as far back as the 1970s. While gay audiences recognize the codes as "gay" and can thus identify with these images, for heterosexual audiences "gay images imply distinction and nonconformity, granting straight consumers a longed-for placed outside of the humdrum mainstream" (p. 187).[2] Bronski claims that the hyper-masculine Marlboro man, at one end of the spectrum, and the effete, "European" Calvin Klein models on the other, both have a "unique sexual appeal, each with firm roots in the traditions of gay sensibility" (p. 186). Bronski is careful to note, however, that gay codings are appealing only insofar as they are veiled; ". . . blatant homosexuality does not have mass appeal, but the exotic implications of hidden homosexuality have huge sales potential" (p. 186). While Bronski's analysis of "gay sensibilities" is almost exclusively concerned with gay men, Haineault and Roy (1993) have similarly argued that lesbian images have been used to appeal to heterosexual women and men, through the titillating fantasy of lesbian sex (see also Clark, 1993).

Gluckman and Reed (1993) have argued that the inclusion of lesbians and gay men within marketing strategies is problematic, since through the hidden codes of gay window advertising the existence of lesbians and gays in all areas of society is erased. They argue that "the real contours of the multicultural, class stratified gay population are languishing in the closet, while images of white, upper-middle class lesbians and gay men become increasingly conspicuous" (p. 17).[3] Gay men in particular are represented as desirable models of consumption. Bronski (1998), Fejes and Petrich (1993), and Schulman (1998) note that the limited, heterosexist, inclusion of gay men and lesbians in the mass media and advertising has a "mainstreaming effect" (Fejes & Petrich, p. 408), where only those most "acceptable" to the masses—the lipstick lesbians and suitably masculine gay men—appear as representatives of gay communities.

Gluckman and Reed (1993) also suggest that positive images of lesbians and gays in advertising may be only "a limited victory" (p. 17), since by increasing our visibility, the image of wealth and power in advertising can easily be appropriated by the political right wing as an argument that homosexuals are not disadvantaged and therefore do not need action on issues of civil rights and discrimination. Badgett (1997) and Fejes and Lennon (2000) argue that while market research data are highly suspect, they have "come to function as an objective, empirical description of lesbians and gay males" (Fejes & Lennon). These authors found that the data have been used by groups such as the "Concerned Women For America" and opponents of the Employment Non-Discrimination Act (1994) to argue against affording gays and lesbians "special rights":

> Are homosexuals economically, educationally or culturally disadvantaged? Any homosexual claims to that effect seem clearly bogus in light of emerging marketing studies that show homosexuals to be enormously advantaged relative to the general population—and astronomically advantaged when compared to the truly disadvantaged minorities. ("Concerned Women For America," quoted in Fejes & Lennon, 2000)

. . . Gay window advertising, as the most conservative edge of the move towards gay marketing, can thus be seen as something of a double-edge sword. While offering lesbian, gay, and bisexual people images of ourselves as "legitimate consumers," these images are both narrow, in terms of who is "legitimate," and cynical, in their representations solely of *consumer* legitimacy to the exclusion of the social and political conditions of gay, bisexual, and lesbian lives.

◆ Advertising and Audiences: A Cultural Studies Approach

Advertising research within the academic domain has hitherto tended to privilege the text as the place to investigate "meaning" in advertising, despite considerable attention paid to producers and audiences of other media forms. . . . Textual analysis is problematic for three reasons. First, this approach positions the scholar as particularly qualified to decode the (absolute, unequivocal, true) meaning of the text under analysis; by virtue of training, experience, or special insight, she or he can read what the advertisement "says." Second, all text-based analyses of advertising messages make assumptions about how audiences respond to advertisements. Third, text-based research posits an "ideal" audience for advertising, an audience which tends, because it is hypothetical, to be homogenized both in its demographic make-up and in its interaction with ads.

As audience research within cultural studies has shown, the presumption of an inevitable relationship between text and audience in the creation of meaning and textual pleasures is problematic (see Fiske, 1987, 1988, 1989; Hall, 1980; Morley, 1980, 1986, 1992, 1993). One response to this has been the use of focus groups to supplement or replace textual analyses (see, e.g., Jhally & Lewis, 1992; Lewis, 1991; Morley, 1980; Press, 1991). . . .

Yet audience research itself is not without its own debates, in particular regarding the activity of the audience in the meaning-making process. . . .

Of particular relevance here is what readers might make of the intentional multiplicity of meanings in gay window advertising texts. Gay window advertising potentially disrupts the notion of a single "preferred" or dominant reading posited initially by Hall (1980), since here an advertiser intentionally codes a single text with at least two "preferred readings": one for bisexual, lesbian, and/or gay readers, and one for heterosexual readers. Gay window advertisements also challenge Fiske's notion of polysemy in two ways. On one hand, Fiske (1987) suggests that polysemy is always already available to audiences as a necessary part of the reading process, since all texts are open to a potentially infinite number of resistive readings. On the other, Fiske (1989) also suggests that producers intentionally *code* texts with more than one meaning to attract as wide a range of audiences as possible. Gay window advertising challenges Fiske's first use by suggesting that while audiences may resistively read texts in a number of different ways, they will be encouraged by the text's codes towards a particular interpretation which depends in part upon each audience member's sexual identification. Fiske's second meaning of polysemy seems closer to gay window strategies. . . .

Cultural studies scholars have been somewhat tardy in engaging with questions of how different sexual identifications may influence the reading of texts—questions of class and, more recently, race and gender have tended to dominate research agenda. In addition to the absence of cultural studies audience research in the field of advertising in general, it is also the scarcity of work on sexual identification as a relevant cultural position which I wish to redress here.

Method ◆

This research was based upon a focus group interview model of gathering data where groups were invited to discuss their interpretations of a number of magazine advertisements (see, e.g., Lunt & Livingstone, 1996;

Patton, 1990; Wimmer & Dominick, 1987).[4] . . .

I conducted five focus group interviews in March and April 1995, with between three and seven participants in each.[5] The participants were recruited through the Gay Lesbian and Bisexual Graduate Student Organization at the University of Massachusetts; were friends and colleagues of personal contacts; and/or were friends of undergraduates at the University of Massachusetts. . . .

Three groups were made up of mixed lesbian, gay, bisexual, and heterosexual participants (groups 1, 2 and 3); there was one lesbian, gay, and bisexual group (Group 4); and one heterosexual group (Group 5).[6] . . .

I selected nine advertisements for groups to discuss; these were chosen from a large number of possible examples in consultation with colleagues and supervisors. The advertisements were selected from recent issues of popular women's and men's magazines as well as other "interest" magazines such as sports and computer publications. I hoped to provide a spectrum of representations which reflected a range of gender and sexual representations; they were chosen not to represent an "objective" range of images, but rather to offer examples which would be productive for the focus groups to discuss. The ads were selected to suggest: a gay male subtext (Versace); a lesbian subtext (Dewar's); a more overt gay, lesbian, and bisexual text (cK one); two heavily coded heterosexual narratives (Brut Actif Blue and Jordache); a single woman (Tiffany) and single man (Zino); a same-sex group of women (Virginia Slims); and of men (Tommy Hilfiger).[7] . . .

◆ *Advertising, Audiences, and Sexual Address*

Because all the ads in this study were read in multiple ways by at least one group, questions regarding the extent of polysemy

available in these texts are concerned less with *whether* polysemy is possible in advertising texts, but rather with *why* some readings were made and not others, and why some texts were read as more "open" than others. . . . While it did appear that bisexual, gay, and lesbian participants were more likely to consider gay readings of the ads, this did not mean that all participants, or even all gay-, bisexual-, or lesbian-identified participants, inevitably read the texts as gay. A more complicated relationship prevailed among textual coding, the contexts of the ads, and the participants' identifications, making predictions of readings based upon sexual identification alone unreliable, if not arbitrary.

Brut Force: ◆
Heterosexual Masculinity

Some texts appeared to be constructed in such as way as to actively discourage a range of readings, particularly readings which might transgress normative standards of gender and sexuality. Many groups commented that a Brut Actif Blue ad with images of a male kayaker and an embracing heterosexual couple had particularly insistent representations of gender roles, both in terms of the images (the muscular, "virile" man, the passive, waiting woman) and in terms of the words "the essence of man," which naturalized a relationship between activity, courage, strength, and heterosexuality within the domain of idealized masculinity. A lesbian, Liz, and a heterosexual woman, Ellen, had the following exchange:

Liz: [. . .] he's just so *manly*, you know, he's huge, in terms of his build, he's heterosexual, clearly, and you know, he's involved in these very virile activities—

Ellen: he's got this muscular build, he's got the power and the strength to go stroking down this river [with his] arms raised—"I'm going down! "—and then you've got the lovely passive female who's just sitting there, waiting, and that's his reward at the end. . . . (Group 3)

The seeming transparency of the Brut ad may have been one reason that groups tended not to talk for long about its implied story. However, Group 5 produced three readings of this ad; the first of these corresponded to the preferred reading articulated by other groups, but the second and third were ironic readings, which appeared to resist the dominant narrative that active men inevitably "win" passive women. One participant suggested that the model carrying the kayak in the first panel and the model in the kayak are two different men, with amusing implications. Of the man in the first panel, Eva said:

Maybe he was supposed to be kayaking with his buddy here [second panel], in the kayak, [who] is alone and kayaking, and he [model in first panel] gets the girl, 'cause he didn't go kayaking! [laughter] (Group 5)

Thus the "active" man did not get the passive woman in this scenario, subverting the sexual inevitability of the implied gender equation.

This resistive reading, however, was not endorsed by the group as the ad's "true" meaning but rather one which allowed the group to disrupt what they apparently perceived as a stiflingly narrow narrative. In the case of this ad, as with others (such as a Jordache jeans ad), participants occasionally offered readings which appeared to subvert the implied narrative, but they were not able to articulate resistive readings which undermine the *heterosexual* insistence of these ads. In no group did participants play with the idea that, for example, the woman model in the Brut ad was keeping her brother company while his boyfriend was riding the rapids. This suggests that, despite

the appearance of a hyper-masculine man in the ad (that is, with a physique not dissimilar to the idealized gay man's body, Dyer, 1982), other codings in the text, such as the woman's leaning into the arms of her "boyfriend," strongly preferred a heterosexual narrative. Thus, at the level of gender representations in this ad, a couple of examples of resistive readings were made, but the possibilities of making specifically *gay* readings appeared to be more difficult.

"What It Is to ◆ Be a Woman": Heterosexual Femininity

All the women in the ads in this study were perceived to be heterosexual by most of the participants most of the time: the participants seemed confident in reading "femininity" from the codings of the ads. For example, of the Tiffany ad (a head shot of a young woman wearing pearls), one participant said, "This is a woman who is feminine, very basic: what it is to be a woman" (Group 3). It was interesting to observe, however, how discussions of the femininity of the female models were constructed very differently than were discussions of the masculinity of the male models, differences which seemed to create difficulties for participants in making specifically lesbian attributions. Codings of masculinity tended to be addressed in conjunction with complementary representations of femininity: for example, in both the Brut ad and the Jordache ad (male and female embracing) the masculinity of the male models was affirmed by their relations with the female models. This contrasted with discussions of feminine codings, where the female models were compared with *each other*, not with the codings of masculinity. Comparing the ad for Tiffany with that for Jordache, James made the following statement: "I am struck by the differences between the two women" to which Liz responded, "The Jordache one looks trampy now!" (Group 3). Jordache's image of a strong woman is also perceived to be sexually delinquent, having an "animal passion" and lacking in "class" when compared to the timeless sophistication of the wealthy Tiffany woman.

An ongoing concern in feminist theory is with how gender difference must be consistently socially constructed and enacted. Butler (1990), for example, outlines various feminist approaches to sexual difference, most of which analyze gender as established through differentiation from the other, that is, that femininity is constricted through its difference from masculinity, and vice versa. We understand femininity on the basis of how not-like masculinity it is, and masculinity on the basis of how not-like femininity it is. However, the responses by the groups in this research suggest an alternative—and at this stage—tentative understanding of gender construction: that while sufficiently masculine men appear to require a clear difference from femininity in order to affirm their adequacy, images of women are compared *with each other* in order to assess the style and adequacy of their femininity. Because women are compared with each other using the linked attributions of class and sexual propriety, rather than being compared with men, it is the *quality* of their femininity ("animal passion" versus "class") and not their apparent *difference from men* which is central to the appraisal of the models' womanhood.

◆ Gay Window Possibilities: Men

In many advertising texts, the heterosexuality of the scenario is suggested by representing physical intimacy between male and female models. In contrast, images of single men, in particular, were often available for gay readings. Yet as Dyer (1982) has observed, images of men have to work against the feminizing tendencies of "to-be-looked-at-ness" in order to construct a sufficiently masculine, sexual image. Dyer identifies a number of tropes commonly used to construct virile masculinity including a level or upward (rather than downcast) assertive gaze; the body as muscular, active, and taut (rather than passive); and the portrayal of men of color and "working class" coded men as hyper-masculine.

In this research, some readings of the ads as gay were possible because the image contravened at least some of the conventions Dyer identifies. The ad for Versace (a male model seated, with one leg over a chair arm), for example, was read as unambiguously gay by many group members. This ad portrays a single man wearing flamboyant apparel and appearing in opulent surroundings: here conventions most often associated with femininity in images of women are employed in the service of a gay coding. Indeed, the perceived effeminacy of the Versace model was seen as sufficient justification for one heterosexual man, Steve, to say, "This guy's a wanker, that's all I have to say—if Richard and I walked into that room . . . [Richard] would probably suggest kicking the shit out of that guy, just jump[ing] him" [Richard laughs] (Group 1). Two women discussed some of the conventions which they read as gay:

Ellen: It is very much a pose . . . if you look at some of the other ads where you see females draped and perched and slung over a couch or something, and they're not doing anything, they're not going anywhere, they are just there to be seen, to be watched passively.

Liz: I would think this was more geared towards gay men just because he is not set up like the typical, head-of-the-household, aggressive, straight man, as we were talking about before; he is more passive, and that is not something that is encouraged in an image like this one [for Brut]! [laughter] . . . (Group 3)

The Zino ad (a bare-chested man) was another example of the use of a single man to allow a gay reading. However, this ad emphasizes a muscular masculinity in order to allow both gay men's and heterosexual women's *desire*, as a response to the text, while not necessarily implying a gay *narrative*, as a property of the text. James, a gay man, said:

> I think that anybody looking at this ad, and I don't think it matters your gender or even your sexual orientation, is supposed to think, "Oh, this man is extremely desirable,"—by association, if you use this fragrance, you will be as desirable as this Grecian statue here, so that it appeals to, I think it is directed at men without regard to their orientation. . . . (Group 3)

One participant, Karen, admitted, "I actually ripped this out and put it on my wall once, I confess!" (Group 5). The Zino ad was thus perceived to be open to both gay and heterosexual interpretations through the elicitation of desire and through the lack of gender specificity of a fantasized, "invisible" sexual partner. This suggests that polysemy, the availability within a text for more than one reading, does not necessarily require the construction of multiple narratives, but may also allow for multiple kinds of desire, a point I will return to below.

Coding of the Tommy Hilfiger ad (four males, standing side by side) presented a different kind of polysemic problem for many of the groups. This ad tended to be read as a heterosexual narrative by heterosexual women and as either a heterosexual or a gay narrative by heterosexual men, as well as lesbians, bisexuals, and gay men.[8] Karen, a heterosexual woman, said: "Any ad with men bunched together like this, and all kind of chummy, makes me think of private boys school, a movie like 'Dead Poets' Society' or something. . . . They all look like they went to prep school together" (Group 5).

Somewhat surprisingly, gay men tended to consider and then distrust or discard gay readings of this ad. Here, although only men are represented in the ad, they were perceived by the groups as more "masculine" than the Versace model. The more emphatic masculinity of the Tommy Hilfiger models produced some intense debate over whether these models were supposed to be read as college buddies, fraternity brothers, or gay men. While some groups insisted that the style of dress together with the implied upper-class status of the models suggested the college theme, others took the absence of women and wedding rings, the physical intimacy of the models, and the presence of the "one way, do not enter" sign as symbols of homoerotic male bonding. However, one gay man reported that "'one way, do not enter' is something that people say they are going to tattoo on their butt . . ." (Group 1), that is, an extreme rejection of gay men's sexuality (perceived to be epitomized by anal sex) by hyper-heterosexually identified men.

In discussions of whether the Tommy Hilfiger ad represented fraternity brothers or gay men, the exclusively lesbian, gay, and bisexual group offered an interesting suggestion as to how to deal with this polarization:

Ina: These guys are walking that fine line, though, between gay boys and frat boys; you know, there's that fine line?

Jo: Once you get a few beers in the frat boys, they're hanging on to each other, just like the gay boys!

Nick: That wonderful concept of "drink til you're bi" [lots of laughter] . . . I've heard that applied to frat boys a lot, and like, men on athletic teams, and in high school: get a bunch of guys over, get some alcohol, they drink til they're bi, it's a wonderful time . . . (Group 4)

Thus, common knowledge suggests that the divide between acceptable fraternity culture and gay sexuality is not so wide, and is considerably narrowed by the disinhibitory (and pardonable) effects of drinking alcohol. Whereas the predominantly heterosexual groups tended to prefer a "buddy" reading which isolated gay sexuality in a separate sphere and prohibited any homoerotic possibilities in the Tommy Hilfiger image, such a comfortable distinction between frat boys and gay boys was eroded by participants in the predominantly lesbian, gay, and bisexual groups.

◆ Lesbian Windows: Shutters and Blinds

A Dewar's ad (two women, the text reading "Yeah, for some reason, 'What's your major?' just doesn't work anymore") was the only text I found in the popular magazines reviewed for this study which I thought suggested a lesbian window scenario.[9] However, this ad prompted only two lesbian readings from predominantly or exclusively lesbian, bisexual, and gay groups, and in both cases the groups' responses to a lesbian reading were ambivalent.[10] In Group 4, a lesbian participant, Mary, offered a gay reading of the Dewar's ad which was met with a mixture of both pleasure and suspicion, particularly by the lesbians in the group:

Mary: My initial take on this is that something's going on between [the two women]—that this is a pickup . . .

Ina: She's wearing a suit.

Mary: And [the blonde woman] has got this completely flirtatious look on her face.

Jo: That's funny, we didn't say anything about—it's always gay boys, but never can you say, "Oh, that's

appealing to lesbians, so dykes are really going to buy that."

Ina: But I don't even think that a pickup scene between these two women would be appealing to lesbians, I think they are appealing to straight men, because I think that any lesbian thing that would come into the mainstream is two very typically beautiful, thin women that men would find attractive, hooking up . . .

Ruth: So what do you think would be attractive to lesbians in advertising?

Mary: Well, firstly, I don't think people would advertise to lesbians, so . . .

Ruth: But even *Deneuve*, a lesbian magazine, all their models are very thin women, terribly fashionable, I mean it is so much like this kind of thing, only more naked. . . .

The apparent pleasure at recognizing what might be a lesbian text was immediately tempered by a consideration of the history of representations of women in general, and lesbians in particular. Thus the Dewar's ad could not be simply and pleasurably "recognized" as a lesbian text by the women in this group, without their simultaneously considering the implications of the appeal of this ad within a broader frame of representation.

Far more common readings of this ad by heterosexual, bisexual, lesbian, and gay participants inserted an unseen male romantic or potentially romantic figure into the text, either as the speaker or the subject of the statement "for some reason 'What's your major?' just doesn't work anymore." This reading strategy suggests how difficult it can be to reject the normativity of heterosexuality. Despite the physical proximity of the women, the suggestion that they are sharing some "private joke," the relative absence of male models, and the representation of one model as short-haired and suited, a lesbian reading was not easily made, even by lesbian participants who, I assume, would have the greatest investment in reading this ad as a lesbian text. This echoes Clark's (1993) assertion that the dominance of heterosexual representations means that "the 'straight' reading is never entirely erased or replaced" (p. 192), even for audiences who may be particularly motivated to "read gay," and suggests, further, that representations of women, in particular, are most difficult to read as gay.

The relative absence of lesbian readings can be understood, first, as a reflection of the relative lack of texts currently circulating in the mainstream which offer a lesbian reading, because lesbians are seen as a far less lucrative market than gay men (Johnson, 1993). Second, it may be easier to make gay attributions to male models because the stereotypes of gayness for men which can still be perceived as "attractive" are much easier to both code and read, while lesbians are stereotypically represented as far less attractive. In an *Advertising Age* special report on marketing to lesbians and gays, Johnson (1993) writes:

> Marketers have gone after gay men because the stereotype is so attractive: affluent, brand-conscious, interested in fashion and style, creating trends which straight men will follow. That's the marketing antithesis of the stereotypical lesbian who supposedly wears a lumberjack shirt, sandals and no makeup. (p. 34)

Despite the increasingly available image of "lipstick lesbians," gay men's appeal for advertisers suggests that they have a cultural currency that lesbians are only slowly beginning to accrue. Furthermore, the fact that men are far more likely to be perceived as sexually assertive means they can also be perceived to be sexual *between each other* in texts, while readers of texts representing women are more likely to presume an active male romantic figure, even when none is portrayed. Finally, it may have been more difficult to read the ads as lesbian because lesbian sexuality has historically been so much more submerged than either heterosexuality or male gayness.

Notes ◆

1. "Gay-dar" is derived from "gay radar," which ironically acknowledges the increased skill with which lesbians, bisexuals, and gays recognize other gay people on the basis of subcultural cues.

2. It is interesting to observe that where Clark takes the position that gay codings are invisible to heterosexuals, Bronski suggests that gay coding adds extra appeal to an advertising image for heterosexual audiences.

3. Figures published in the *New York Times* (Presley Noble, 1994) show that the average income of lesbians is lower than that of heterosexual women ($15,068 and $18,341 per year, respectively) and that both groups of women earn less than gay men ($26,321 per year), who, in turn, earn less than heterosexual men ($28,312 per year).

4. I chose magazine advertisements largely because magazines tend to have narrowly targeted audiences and therefore tend also to contain advertisements directed to a particular demographic and psychographic group. However, the use of magazine advertisements does not imply that conclusions drawn from these data can be unproblematically applied to other forms of advertising.

5. There were 14 women and 9 men, aged between 22 and 40, with a mean age of 27. One participant had a high school diploma, 8 participants had some college education, and 14 had some post-graduate education. One participant identified as mixed hispanic and caucasian, one identified as mixed native american and caucasian, all other participants identified as caucasian. The focus groups did not, therefore, reflect the racial and educational diversity of either the United States as a whole or western Massachusetts in particular: as a result, no conclusions can be reached here about the complexities of race, class, and sexual identification within cultural positions and the relative impacts

of these identifications on reading possibilities. All names are pseudonyms.

6. All identifications were self-chosen. I acknowledge the complications of identifying oneself as "lesbian," "bisexual," "gay," or "heterosexual": specifically, that these positions can be overly reductive, essentialist, or lend a false impression of stability.

7. The ads used in the study were taken from the following sources: Tiffany and Co. pearls, *The New Yorker*, Dec. 19, 1995; Brut Actif Blue cologne, *Sports Illustrated*, Sept. 17, 1995; Jordache jeans, *Cosmopolitan*, November 1994; Dewar's whisky, *Wired*, December 1994; Zino cologne, *Esquire Gentleman*, Fall Fashion Special, 1994; Versace men's couture, *Esquire Gentleman*, Fall Fashion Special, 1994; Tommy Hilfiger menswear, *Esquire Gentleman*, Fall Fashion Special, 1994; cK one cologne, *Cosmopolitan*, November 1994; Virginia Slims cigarettes, *Cosmopolitan*, November 1994. Photocopies of the ads are available from the author.

8. This ad was one of the few ads for which participants speculated over its source, perhaps *because of* its ambiguous coding. One heterosexual man said, "This isn't *Esquire*, this might be *Details*, which would make a lot of sense [since] *Details* is pretty friggin' closet homosexual. . . ."

9. However, advertisers for Guess jeans and other products have since brought out nauseatingly titillating campaigns of images of nubile "lesbian chicks."

10. It is possible that some group members are aware of an ongoing gender and sexual ambiguity in Dewar's advertising campaigns, as well as in Calvin Klein's ads, discussed below. What is interesting is that even if the participants had this intertextual awareness, lesbian window readings were still relatively uncommon.

◆ **References**

Badgett, M. V. L. (1997). Beyond biased samples: Challenging the myths on the economic status of lesbians and gay men. In A. Gluckman & B. Reed (Eds.), *Homo economics: Capitalism, community, and lesbian and gay life*. New York: Routledge, pp. 65-71.

Baker, D. (1997). A history in ads: The growth of the gay and lesbian market. In A. Gluckman & B. Reed (Eds.), *Homo economics: Capitalism, community, and lesbian and gay life*. New York: Routledge, pp. 11-20.

Bronski, M. (1984). *Culture clash: The making of gay sensibility*. Boston: South End.

Bronski, M. (1998). *The Pleasure Principle: Sex, backlash, and the struggle for gay freedom*. New York: St. Martin's.

Clark, D. (1993). Commodity lesbianism. In H. Abelove, M. A. Barale, & D. M. Halperin (Eds.), *The lesbian and gay studies reader*. New York: Routledge, pp. 186-201.

Davis, R. (1994, May 30). Marketers game for gay events. *Advertising Age*, p. S-1.

Dyer, R. (1982). Don't look now: The instability of the male pin-up. *Screen*, 23(3-4), 61-73.

Fejes, F., & Lennon, R. (2000). Defining the lesbian/gay community? Market research and the lesbian/gay press. *The Journal of Homosexuality*, 39(1), 28-42.

Fejes, F., & Petrich, K. (1993). Invisibility, homophobia and heterosexism: Lesbians, gays and the media. *Critical Studies in Mass Communication*, 10, 396-422.

Fiske, J. (1987). *Television culture*. London: Routledge.

Fiske, J. (1988). Critical responses: Meaningful moments. *Critical Studies in Mass Communication*, 5, 246-251.

Fiske, J. (1989). *Understanding popular culture*. Boston: Unwin Hyman.

Gluckman, A., & Reed, B. (1993, November/December). The gay marketing moment: leaving diversity in the dust. *Dollars and Sense*, pp. 16-19, 34-35.

Goffman, E. (1979). *Gender advertisements*. Cambridge, MA: Harvard University Press.

Haineault, D. L., & Roy, J. Y. (1993). *The unconscious for sale: Advertising, psychoanalysis and the public*. Minneapolis: University of Minnesota Press.

Hall, S. (1980). Encoding/decoding. In S. Hall, D. Hobson, A. Lowe, & P. Willis (Eds.), *Culture, media, language*. London: Hutchinson, pp. 128-136.

Jhally, S. (1989). Advertising, gender and sex: What's wrong with a little objectification? *Working Papers and Proceedings of the Center for Psychosocial Studies*. No. 29.

Jhally, S., & Lewis, J. (1992). *Enlightened racism:* The Cosby Show, *audiences and the myth of the American dream*. Boulder, CO: Westview.

Johnson, B. (1993, Jan. 18). Economics holds back the lesbian ad market. *Advertising Age*, pp. 34-37.

Leiss, W., Kline, S., & Jhally, S. (1990). *Social communication in advertising: Persons, products and images of well-being*. New York: Routledge.

Lewis, J. (1991). *The ideological octopus*. New York: Routledge.

Lunt, P., & Livingstone, S. (1996). Rethinking the focus group in media and communication research. *Journal of Communication*, 46(2), 79-98.

Morley, D. (1980). *The "nationwide" audience*. London: British Film Institute.

Morley, D. (1986). *Family television: Domestic leisure and cultural power*. London: Comedia.

Morley, D. (1992). *Television, audiences and cultural studies*. New York: Routledge.

Morley, D. (1993). Active audience theory: Pendulums and pitfalls. *Journal of Communication*, 43(4), 13-19.

Patton, M. Q. (1990). *Qualitative evaluation and research methods*. Newbury Park, CA: Sage.

Presley Noble, B. (1994, Dec. 4). Linking gay rights and unionism. *New York Times*, p. 25.

Press, A. (1991). *Women watching television: Gender, class and generation in the American television experience*. Philadelphia: University of Pennsylvania Press.

Schulman, S. (1998). Stagestruck: Theatre, AIDS, and the marketing of gay America. Durham, NC: Duke University Press.

Wimmer, R. D., & Dominick, J. R. (1987). *Mass media research* (2nd ed.). Belmont, CA: Wordsworth.

32

GENDER AND HEGEMONY IN FASHION MAGAZINES

Women's Interpretations of
Fashion Photographs

◆ Diana Crane

Fashion has generally been conceived as a form of hegemonic oppression, exerting an obligation to conform that weighs heavily on the female population (Wolf 1991). Robin T. Lakoff and Raquel L. Scherr (1984, p. 114) claim that fashion photographs generate enormous dissatisfaction among women because they create unrealistic expectations that most women are unable to meet. However, recent changes in the nature of fashion, the content of fashion magazines, and the ways women perceive fashion and fashion magazines raise questions concerning the accuracy of this interpretation. Few empirical studies exist that examine how women respond to these types of materials. The present study uses women's responses to fashion photographs elicited in the context of focus groups to examine these issues. . . .

Feminists argue that media images of women are always directed at men and that women are encouraged to look at themselves and other women the way men do (Davis 1997). They view hegemonic femininity as incorporating masculine standards for female appearance that emphasize physical attributes and sexuality. Images that express hegemonic femininity present women in sexualized and demeaning poses (Davis 1997). Media images are constructed for the male spectator's gaze and embody his expectations of women and of male-female relationships (Mulvey 1975-1976). The classic analysis of codes that are used to pose female subjects is Erving Goffman's (1979) study of "gender advertisements," in which he identifies characteristic poses in advertisements that present women as subordinate or inferior to men. According to Goffman, these poses are instantly understood by the public because they represent in an exaggerated manner stereotypical images of women that correspond to the ways in which women's roles are understood in American culture. One set of codes, "ritualization of subordination," relies on positions that subtly demean the female subject, such as showing the subject lying on her side or back, smiling in a ritualistically exaggerated manner, or assuming awkward stances with arms and legs thrust upward or to the side of the picture frame, sometimes in midair. Another stereotype is the female subject with a vacant gaze, seemingly directed at an unseen object inside the picture frame. Goffman interprets this gaze as "licensed withdrawal," implying that the subject is passive, alienated from, and not in control of the situation.

Recently, some authors have suggested that women in their teens and twenties view hegemonic femininity differently compared to middle-aged women and to the feminist interpretation of it (Winship 1985; Skeggs 1993). Younger women are said to view images identified with hegemonic femininity not as signs of weakness and passivity in women but as indications of being "in control" of their sexuality. Madonna's attitude toward her sexuality exemplifies this point of view.

In addition, traditional standards of feminine demeanor according to which women are expected to be constrained and passive,

but not sexually available, constitute a form of hegemony that might be characterized as "traditional" hegemonic femininity. Nancy M. Henley (1977) shows that norms for nonverbal behavior are different for each gender. Women, as a consequence of their inferior status, are expected to occupy less space than men and to exert greater control over their bodies and facial expressions. This is seen in the expectation that clothing should be neat and well put together and limbs placed in disciplined postures. Women's legs are supposed to be closed rather than apart and arms should be close to the sides of the body. Nudity and displays of breasts and genital areas are also defined as inappropriate.

Norms concerning eye contact proscribe staring on the part of women since staring is a gesture that indicates dominance. Women are expected to avert their eyes, particularly if the other person is male. They are expected to smile and to show pleasant emotions rather than indifference (Henley 1977, p. 194). Since gender is the primary factor determining how individuals relate to one another in social interaction, Henley (1977, p. 93) argues that gender ambiguity is highly disturbing for many people. The norm is that gender identification should be unambiguous. If traditional standards of feminine demeanor are still accepted by women, they are likely to respond negatively to images that do not conform to these standards.

These contrasting views challenge the usual claim that in contemporary culture there is a single dominant hegemony, whose definitions of reality, norms, and standards appear "natural" rather than contestable. Douglas Kellner (1990) suggests that contemporary American media and popular culture can more accurately be understood in terms of the concept of conflicted hegemony. Kellner argues that no single elite group dominates American society and that the media provide a site for conflicts, debates, and negotiations among different interpretations of the dominant culture. Fashion as a form of media culture can also be interpreted in terms of conflicted hegemony. In the nineties, there is no single fashion standard; the consumer chooses from different interpretations of fashion, depending on her social affiliations and ethnic background (Kaiser, Nagasawa, and Hutton 1991). In their analysis of women's images in fashion magazine advertising, Robert Goldman and his colleagues (1991, p. 71) argue that fashion advertisements are indications of an "internally contradictory hegemonic process—an ongoing dialectic between dominant and oppositional discourses." They conclude that advertisers have been forced to incorporate oppositional elements in order to hold the attention of increasingly sophisticated consumers. . . .

Susan B. Kaiser, Richard H. Nagasawa, and Sandra S. Hutton (1991) see postmodernism in fashion as liberating for women. Because a great variety of styles are fashionable at the same period of time, women are able to construct personal styles that are meaningful to them, using specific elements of fashionable styles, rather than merely "following" a new and well-defined style. Since the resulting styles are ambiguous and difficult to interpret, their meanings have to be negotiated through social interaction, leading to subsequent style changes. Anthony Freitas and his colleagues (1997), on the basis of a study of attitudes toward "least favorite" clothes, suggest that people tend to reject certain types of clothing that are associated with specific statuses (e.g., age, race, sexual orientation) as a way of indicating their lack of connections with specific groups. This may also occur when fashionable clothes suggest ambiguous or unconventional interpretations of identities. . . .

◆ Postmodernism, Feminism, and Fashion Magazines

Fashion, as represented in fashion magazines, has several diverse and contradictory social agendas. Fashion magazines must please both advertisers, who represent media culture, and consumers. The primary source of profit for these magazines is advertising; therefore, editorial content must supplement and reinforce advertising, while attempting to maintain or increase readership (McCracken 1993).

In the past decade, fashion photographers and editors have synchronized their themes and images with those that circulate in youth cultures and that are disseminated by the media, particularly rock music. This material frequently includes references to drugs, crime, violence, sexual orientations that are not widely accepted and negative attitudes toward women (Dowd 1997; Summer 1996). Fashion photography has incorporated blatantly sexual poses from pornographic publications (Myers 1987; Steele 1996) that include sexual cues, such as closed eyes, open mouth, legs spread to reveal the genital area, and nudity or seminudity, particularly in the areas of the breasts and genitals. A recent study of advertisements in fashion magazines covering the ten-year period 1985-1994 found a substantial increase in the extent to which parts of women's bodies were exposed and their bodies were shown in low-status, animal-like positions (Plous and Neptune 1997).

A second fashion agenda that appears in fashion magazines is a response to changes in the activities and goals of their readers. Women are portrayed as empowered and androgynous, capable of achieving goals and managing others (Davis 1992; Rabine 1994). These images show women wearing business suits and other costumes derived from masculine attire. A third agenda is to present women as creators of "heterogeneous and contradictory" identities when experimenting with clothes and products, such as perfume, that are deliberately designed to project different images of women (Partington 1996, p. 215; Rabine 1994).

As one of the leading fashion magazines throughout the twentieth century, *Vogue* exemplifies changes that have taken place in the representation of the fashionable woman and her clothing in photographs.[1] In 1947, the magazine's fashion photographs precisely documented an upper-middle-class world. Fashion photographs were taken in identifiable settings, such as city streets or beaches. Nude legs, thighs, or breasts were rare. There were no close-ups. Models rarely assumed demeaning or child-like poses. The camera was generally placed at eye level. The models were young women but not adolescents, as is frequently the case today. The center of attention in most of these photographs was the clothing rather than the model. This was a milieu viewed almost entirely from a feminine perspective. No men appeared in the fashion photographs. Women were almost invariably photographed alone.

By 1957, changes in certain aspects of *Vogue*'s fashion photography were beginning to be noticeable. More models were photographed looking directly at the camera, an indication of inferior status, according to some analysts (Lutz and Collins 1993). Few photographs were contextualized in urban or vacation settings. Many more women assumed contorted or exaggerated positions, typical of Goffman's (1979) "ritualization of subordination." There were occasional close-ups. However, there was still virtually no nudity, and men almost never appeared. The major focus of the photographs remained the clothing. By 1967, the magazine was showing close-ups of models in bathing suits. There was increasing emphasis on youth, youth cultures, and film stars as trendsetters (Lakoff and Scherr 1984, pp. 96-97). The supermodel rather than the society woman was becoming the role model.

By 1977, the character of the magazine had changed radically in comparison with its character in 1947. The proportion of advertising pages had doubled and, as a result, the visual impression of the magazine was conveyed more by advertising than by editorial content. The magazine's circulation had more than doubled since 1967.[2]

Both advertisements and editorial pages appeared to be oriented toward a male gaze (Rabine 1994, p. 65; Mulvey 1975-1976). Men were more likely to be included in the photographs, along with pairs or groups of women. Models generally looked directly at the camera and often assumed childlike or contorted positions. Most photographs were not contextualized. The vantage point of the camera was less likely to be at eye level and more likely to be looking down or looking up at its subject.

By 1987, the model's body was much more likely to be partially nude, either breasts or thighs, and more likely than the clothing to be the focus of the photographs. The camera's vantage point was frequently below its subject, emphasizing legs and thighs. Models wearing bathing suits were photographed in close-ups, resembling pinups. In many photographs, models looked directly at the camera without smiling and frequently assumed the exaggerated poses that characterize "ritualization of subordination." Models were expected "to look sexually provocative. . . . Modern beauty is deeply embedded in sexual politics—the woman acting out male fantasies engaging in purposeful provocation" (Lakoff and Scherr 1984, p. 106). Contextualization had virtually disappeared; most photographs were not located in any recognizable geographical space. These trends continued in the 1990s. In 1997, advertisements outnumbered editorial pages by more than three to one. Women in fashion layouts and clothing advertisements were frequently presented as sexually provocative, androgynous, or homoerotic.

Over time, the fashion photographs in the magazine appear to have changed their function. Exhibiting the latest trends in appropriate clothing for women of means ceased to be the primary goal of the magazine; instead fashion photographs provide a kind of visual entertainment analogous to other forms of media culture, such as Hollywood films and music videos.

◆ *Selection of*
Photographs and
Questions for Research

There are no previous studies of how women interpret representations of gender in fashion photographs.[3] The goal of this study was to examine responses to representations of gender in fashion photographs and clothing advertisements among young and middle-aged women representing diverse ethnicities and nationalities.[4] Eighteen photographs were selected from the February, March, and September 1997 issues of *Vogue* of which a subset of 6-9 photographs was shown to members of each focus group. The photographs were divided almost equally between fashion editorial photos and clothing advertisements. The clothing in these photographs had, in most cases, been produced by companies headed by leading American, French, and Italian designers. The photographs were selected to fit the following categories: (1) frontal gaze and eye contact, (2) side gaze: positive, (3) androgyny and gender ambiguity, (4) lesbianism, (5) ritualization of subordination, (6) licensed withdrawal, (7) sexuality/pornography, and (8) nudity. In addition to gender stereotypes, two of the photographs could be interpreted as representing racial stereotypes. Several photographs could be categorized as postmodern on the basis of ambiguities and contradictions in their imagery or in the nature of the clothing.

Focus group members were asked several questions designed to elicit their perceptions of these photographs and the extent to which they identified with the models in the photographs. Before the focus group began, they were asked to complete a short questionnaire that tapped their level of interest in fashion and their techniques for following fashion. . . .

The "Authority" ◆
of Fashion

Has fashion retained the "authority" that it appears to have exerted in the past? On the questionnaire, almost all (84 percent) of these women responded positively to the question: "Do you attempt to keep up with current fashion?"[5] When asked what aspects of fashion they particularly followed, the majority checked "specific styles" (65 percent) and "accessories" (55 percent). About one-quarter (24 percent) checked "brand names" and 18 percent noted "hemlines."

According to their responses on the questionnaires, these women relied on three different types of sources for information about fashion. The first type of source was their social milieu, broadly defined. This suggests that following fashion was motivated by a desire to be accepted by their peers. This category included "cool friends and relatives" (chosen by 53 percent) but also "what people are wearing on the street" (59 percent). Sixty-nine percent of the women relied on one or both of these sources. The second type of source for information about fashion was the media, including fashion magazines, television, and clothes worn by popular singers. Sixty-nine percent of the women relied on some form of media for information about fashion. The third type of source was also the most important: 76 percent relied on local stores for information about fashion.

Most of the women relied on more than one source for information about fashion (80 percent) and many relied on all three sources of information (43 percent). . . . Eighty-one percent of the women read fashion magazines at least occasionally but fashion magazines were a source of information about fashion for only 55 percent of the women. Magazines were apparently not considered sufficiently authoritative to be used as the individual's only source of information. Only 16 percent relied on fashion magazines without using other types of media, and just 4 percent relied only on fashion magazines (i.e., excluding all other sources of information).

These findings suggest a certain ambivalence about fashion magazines that was also expressed during the focus groups. Very rarely in the focus group discussions was there any suggestion that these women viewed fashion editors as authorities on fashion. Rather than viewing fashion editors as authoritative, some women questioned fashion editors' judgments about fashion. A black undergraduate said, "Like the image that they always set, that everyone is alike which everyone is not."

Some of these women doubted the capacity of fashion editors to understand or express the perspective of women:

> Even though the fashion editors in the magazines are usually women, I still think it's not really a woman's point of view. It's what a woman thinks a man wants to see or something like that. (white undergraduate)

Some white undergraduates perceived fashion as something remote from their own experience:

> These outfits remind me of the newer style that is coming out . . . bandish, faddish type stuff that I don't see around me that often. It is kind of removed from me is what I am trying to say.

Another young white woman asserted that the fashion standards set in these magazines were impossible for normal women to achieve:

> Anything in these magazines, especially high fashion, W and *Vogue* to a certain extent, nobody who is normal can wear any of those clothes. You cannot look good in those clothes. You just can't. (white college student)

. . . Some women suggested that fashion photographs should be viewed as a form of art and fantasy rather than as representations of fashion: "It's just like a dream because you know that 90 percent, probably 98 percent of the clothes, are unattainable."

Other women were able to distance themselves from these photographs by pointing out personal constraints that prevented them from being influenced by these images. A few mentioned financial constraints. Older women admitted that they were incapable of meeting the standards set by models in these photographs but attributed this failure to age differences rather than to personal failings. Almost half the middle-aged women said they did not attempt to follow fashion.

Almost half the African Americans also said they did not attempt to follow fashion. The comments of African American women suggested that they perceived fashionable styles as being created for white women and particularly for white bodies rather than black bodies.

> Interviewer: Would these clothes influence the way you dress at all?
>
> Black college student: This look is impossible for us to achieve. Genetically, that is not how we are mapped out and so if we are in the right frame of mind within ourselves, we know that it is going to be unlikely that we could achieve it through working out and what have you.

Only very occasionally did younger white women admit to being critical of themselves for not being able to meet the standards of beauty and physical perfection set by these photographs. A comment such as the following from a white undergraduate was rare: "I know I'll never never be able to look like her and it really pisses me off."

Some of these women may not have felt sufficiently comfortable in the social situation created in the focus groups to acknowledge their failure to meet these standards and to attribute this failure to their own inadequacies. Alternatively, some images in these photographs may have been too extreme to elicit identification on the part of the participants.

◆ The Fashion Magazine and Its Social Agendas: Images of Blatant and Marginal Sexuality

Several photographs presented women in a manner consistent with the representation of women in many aspects of rock music, including lyrics, album covers, and public appearances—in other words, in highly sexualized poses, suggesting that a woman's role is that of sex object (Signorielli, McLeod, and Healy 1994). Other photographs presented subjects whose sexuality was ambiguous—possibly lesbian or transvestite. To what extent did participants in the focus groups accept this agenda? If women subscribe to traditional norms of feminine demeanor (Henley 1977), one might expect them to reject images that depict overt sexuality, nudity, and sexual ambiguity.

One photograph that exemplified this agenda showed a woman wearing a very short, sleeveless, flesh-colored dress and very high-heeled shoes, with her body bent forward, leaning her buttocks against a wall. Many of these women, both young and middle-aged, did not identify with the level of sexuality expressed in the photograph, as suggested by the comments of two undergraduates.

Interviewer: What aspects of this photography do you like?

Tracee: Quite honestly, nothing, nothing. (black college student)

Nathalie: I would categorize it as an image of a slut or a prostitute or just not a good girl. (white college student)

Tracee: It's trying to be very seductive and I guess that's kind of what I associate with being a supermodel or just a model in general.

Nathalie: Like a negative sexy.

Another undergraduate expressed a somewhat more positive attitude toward this photograph:

Judy: She has a seductive feel. She gives off this aura. So like there are times when I'd want to feel like—going to a black-tie party you want to feel seductive or sexy, but, in my own way. Not like that.

A few younger white women associated the sexuality in this photograph with strength rather than weakness.

Sandy: There's something strong about her. I mean she doesn't look lost, you know. She's not the lost sex symbol. She's more like she wanted to be that way. It's not that she is the victim of something.

Helen: I think this photograph expresses a woman's point of view. She's ready to take on the world and she can "live-on-the-edge" kind of thing. Because it's sexy in a way that it's powerful—she's the one in control. It's not sexy like you know, she's lying on a bed half naked.

In a group of middle-aged women, participants objected to the emphasis on the body rather than the clothing in the photograph.

Christine: I don't like the way the model is posed. Because I think it's showing the body rather than the clothing. That's the first thing you see. The dress is barely there. Not that there's anything wrong, but it's the photograph itself that suggests that they're not showing the clothes; they're showing the woman's body. And without that, the clothing would be nothing.

Nina: She's selling herself. This woman's selling her body.

Dorothy: From a distance she could be naked. The dress almost blends into her body.

In keeping with norms of traditional feminine demeanor that sanction nudity, many of the women disliked nudity and transparent materials that revealed breasts and genital hair.

Anne: They're selling it to women. And we all have this body. We don't need to see her without a shirt on. Which I never understood. You know? That doesn't really excite me, being a girl, without her shirt on.

Their objections to transparent materials were not so much on the basis of modesty or prudishness but because they could not visualize themselves wearing such revealing clothes.

Interviewer: Would you like to look like this woman?

Tracee: No. Like she's going out of her way to be sexy and I tend to prefer things that are more. . . . You weren't trying to be sexy. . . . Whereas this almost seems as though they had to really work to make her look sexy, and so there's just something very negative about that.

Joan: I wouldn't ever wear something that let boobs show but I think for the image she's trying to convey, it's appropriate.

Another photograph showed an African American model, entirely nude except for costume jewelry, sitting on the floor. African American women disagreed in their evaluations of this photograph. Several of these participants did not like the fact that the model was nude. One woman in this group said: "I think the person who created this must be a man because he is just trying to expose her body and I doubt a woman would ever do this." Another African American woman had a different viewpoint:

Lisa: It's redefining nudity. It is not done in poor taste. I think that she is proud of her body and she is not afraid to—it is not really sexual—she is showing off the accessories.

A third photograph contained elements that could be interpreted as androgynous or homosexual. An advertisement for Chanel, it showed a woman wearing an unbuttoned suit jacket over a very pale, bare, flat torso with black jeans. The face was heavily made-up, particularly around the eyes, which were obscured by a shadow. The overall impression that participants received from this photograph was one of gender ambiguity. Most participants were puzzled, critical, and to some extent disturbed by it. The following comments by white undergraduates illustrate a desire to distance themselves from this image and particularly its connotations of marginality and gender ambiguity:

Ruth: It looks very androgynous. She doesn't have a chest at all. Like you see a glimpse of something. It's all pale and wiped out. Like a ghost. And her face looks very like a guy dressed in drag.

Nathalie: I would say scary, unnatural, and witch-like. And neither masculine nor feminine because this just seems so unnatural to me that it doesn't seem like it would appeal to any regular man or woman.

Older women also tended to attribute marginal connotations to the subject of this photograph. One woman commented on the model's expression, which connoted "licensed withdrawal" while another woman indicated she could not identify with her:

Dorothy: And that vacuous look she has— like she's almost dead. She looks like corpses I've seen.

Mary: I wouldn't want to look like her. There is something very harsh about her.

Another older woman was dismissive: "This isn't a serious fashion statement at all. They just want your attention."

A fourth photograph showed two women, wearing long transparent dresses and standing close together, one behind the other. The second woman's right hand was placed over the first woman's stomach. In keeping with Reina Lewis and Katrina Rolley's (1996) attribution of lesbian connotations to photographs showing two female models in the same photograph, some participants did in fact detect overtones of lesbianism in the photograph.

Nathalie: They look easy and maybe there is a hint of homosexuality. I just see where the hand is placed, and it doesn't look very friendly or sister-like; it looks like they are girlfriends. It's a hard image, like a heavy metal type of look, and it is just something that I don't aspire to.

A middle-aged participant had a different impression: "There's this fake sort of lesbianism in there too, the way the person had those two women pose. And I always associate that with men." Members of an African American focus group did not respond to any homosexual overtones in this photograph but interpreted it as representing a culture very removed from their own.

Tamara: Drug addict club models. I see them as being in a club.

Michelle: Rock star chicks.

Dina: I see this stereotypical, tall, skinny, anorexic-looking white female.

Discussions in the focus groups did not suggest that there were substantial differences between women in different generations in their conceptions of their gender identities. Younger participants were not more inclined than older women to accept as appropriate for themselves a wider range of sexual orientations. Most of these women tended to reject images that suggested bisexuality, lesbianism, and transvestism. Displays of nudity were generally sanctioned as inappropriate for their own lives. In general, their reactions were explicable on the basis of traditional norms of feminine demeanor, as described by Henley (1977). However, they were ambivalent toward a photograph of a woman in a very seductive pose. Some younger women admired her appearance of being in control, an interpretation that was consistent with recent changes in the ways expressions of sexuality by women are understood. Others interpreted her pose as demeaning.

The Fashion Magazine ◆ and Its Social Agendas: Images of Empowerment

Members of several focus groups were shown a Donna Karan advertisement that consisted of a black-and-white photograph of a woman in a pants suit staring directly at the camera. This woman's image could be interpreted as empowered, successful, and androgynous, another of the magazine's agendas. A male participant summed up what he viewed as the rationale underlying the way this model was being presented:

> Look, she's made it. It's not about her sexuality. It's not about her breasts. She's a working woman. Her clothes are about working woman's clothing. If you're successful and you're smart, I've got clothes for you. You don't have to put on tons of makeup. It's like you're the boss, darn it, and you can do what you want.

Most participants responded to this photograph on the basis of the model's personality, although their assessments of her personality varied. Some groups were repelled and others were attracted by the image the model appeared to convey. The model's stare violated a norm of appropriate female expressive behavior (Henley 1977), and this appeared to be a major factor in terms of their reactions to this image. The impact of the model's facial expression on the reactions of members of a focus group composed of white undergraduates is shown in the following discussion:

Interviewer: Are there any aspects of the photograph you don't like?

Ruth: The expression on her face.

Judy: I think she looks kind of aggressive. It's kind of portraying the attitude that the clothes are like, well, you know, I'm an elitist, like you can't touch me. I still like the clothes but the attitude the model is portraying . . .

Another undergraduate stated a preference for the type of expression that women have traditionally been expected to show:

"I like that she's powerful but I don't like . . . she's not smiling. She's not happy."

Asked whether on some occasions they might want to look like the model in this photograph, younger women found it difficult to identify with the woman in the Karan ad, as indicated by the comments from two focus groups.

Interviewer: Would you like to look like this woman?

Judy: This facial expression? No way.

Tracee: For me it's just like the whole image. I don't think I could ever be like that. . . . And I don't want to be like her.

Nathalie: I don't like her attitude. I think it's something that I don't relate to. I don't see myself as having that type of attitude in general. Although I do agree that there might be times in certain situations, certain office situations, where I might feel that it might be to my advantage to look a little bit more like her, to be strong, and to seem to have a sense of identity like that and confidence in myself.

One young woman doubted that she could convey an attitude of empowerment successfully by wearing those clothes.

> If I was wearing that, I wouldn't look like that. I'm not saying I wouldn't look good but I wouldn't feel like "Listen to me. I am woman. Hear me roar. I'm the boss."

In other words, adopting a type of clothing appropriate for the role would not necessarily allow her to perform the role convincingly. In contrast, a group of middle-aged women also interpreted the model's image as strong and confident but reacted more positively to it. One woman commented:

I wouldn't mind looking like that on a lot of occasions. Not just because she's beautiful but because of the message that she's giving . . . strong and don't contradict me.

◆ *The Fashion Magazine and Its Social Agendas: Postmodernist Role Playing*

In contrast to the fashion magazine, which proposed a postmodernist conception of multiple identities, women in the focus groups appeared to have a distinctly modernist outlook toward their identities and, consequently, toward fashionable clothing. They perceived the selection of suitable clothing as an expression of stable identities and as a task for which they possessed the requisite skills. They evaluated fashionable clothing in terms of its usefulness for the types of occasions in which they participated but not in terms of adopting a series of distinctly different roles. . . .

Consciously or unconsciously, these participants seemed to believe that clothes represent the self which they perceived as consistent and unchanging. This attitude underlies the following comment by an African American college student about an African American model:

I like the fact that she looks a lot like me. . . . So the question is not if I want to look like her but the fact that she looks like me, and that is what is appealing to me about her.

This was also seen in a phrase that was used many times, referring to an outfit:

It's not me. I just don't really like what she is wearing, the general style of it. . . . I guess also it is the attitude, the stance she is taking is not really me at all.

Or, referring to a model: "I think it's her."

One result of the variety of stylistic standards that postmodernist fashion proposes is that particular styles and costumes are likely to be difficult to interpret (Davis 1992; Kaiser et al. 1991). In some of the photographs, certain aspects of the model's clothing were considered puzzling or difficult to comprehend by focus group members. For example, participants commented on ambiguous qualities in the clothes portrayed in a photograph of a woman on a beach, such as the use of untied sneakers, combined with a very baggy man's suit, a necktie, and an untucked shirt, worn by a rather feminine woman.

Interviewer: What aspects of this photograph do you not like?

Tracee: The disorder, the shirt untucked. Kind of like, she was confused. What were they really trying to go for? Why is the shirt untucked? What's the point of the tie?

Ruth: When would you wear a suit with the shirt hanging out with sneakers?

Anne: I think the whole outfit is out of place. Like the shoes with the suit and the entire thing on the beach.

Interviewer: What meanings do you think the clothing in the photograph conveys?

Elena: Androgyny and professionalism because she's in a suit.

Joan: But she's in sneakers.

When the level of ambiguity in a model's appearance was very high, participants tended to reject it vehemently. One photograph showed a model with a highly toned, muscular body and very dark eyeshadow, wearing a very sheer, transparent dress of indeterminate color. The dress had connotations of fairy tales and fantasy for participants that seemed incongruous with the model's almost masculine body. Two older participants commented:

Catherine: The dress is soft and gauzy but she looks very hard. . . . It's kind of an aggressive pose and there's that little wispy dress on her.

Elizabeth: She looks a little grotesque.

Younger participants were particularly negative toward this photo:

Beth: She doesn't even look human.

Barbara: I wouldn't stay on that page for more than a second.

Evelyn: Her body's sick. Like she's so toned that it's disgusting.

Lucy: It looks like she got slimed.

Lauren: Distasteful.

Lucy: Prehistoric.

Evelyn: Out of touch.

Participants' conceptions of their own appearance appeared to be shaped by practical considerations and by conformity to traditional norms of feminine personal demeanor. These women were seeking comfortable, useful clothing and rejecting elements of ambiguity and subversion. They were not postmodernist role-players, manipulating visual codes to simulate different identities.

◆ The Model as Role Model

Rather than the clothes or fashion itself, the focus of attention in these photographs for most of the women in the focus groups was the model. Many of the women, particularly younger women, recognized well-known models and identified them by name. Almost invariably, the models elicited strong reactions on the part of these women, sometimes positive, often negative. The model as a physical presence and as a personality served both as the channel for the transmission of fashion ideals, along with whatever hegemony that might have entailed, and as the justification for rejecting these ideals, the latter on the grounds that the model projected a negative and undesirable image. Younger participants in the focus groups seemed to find it quite natural to make comparisons between themselves and the models in the photographs. They were inclined to identify with the models and seemed disappointed when they were unable to do so.

Participants discussed at length the models' physical attributes, their facial expressions, and their gender identifications. The models' bodies were analyzed in terms of body frame, height, weight, and skin. Body parts, such as feet, legs, arms, hands, waistlines, and bustlines, were examined, along with facial characteristics such as eyes, eyebrows, and expressions. Haircuts, makeup, and nail polish were also scrutinized. On the basis of physical characteristics and facial expressions, focus group members almost invariably drew inferences concerning the models' personalities (e.g., strong, aggressive, confident, aloof, carefree, fun-loving). They responded to the models as individuals, as people with distinct identities apart from the clothing they were wearing.

Facial expressions were a major factor that determined how participants reacted to the models and whether they appeared to identify with them. Only one woman (a white college student) said that for her the models' facial expressions were not important because "I know they're not real." Most women responded positively to one of the few models who was smiling and who appeared to be enjoying herself. A college student said:

Evelyn: She looks natural.

Interviewer: Why does she look natural to you?

Evelyn: She's smiling.

In keeping with norms concerning women's demeanor, the absence of positive facial expressions was perceived as disturbing. An older participant complained that two models in a photograph looked unhappy.

Interviewer: Do you think the fact that they look unhappy influences the way you respond to the photograph?

Louise: Yes, I do. It looks unnatural. The one on the left looks miserable.

Another older participant observed: "Her face is very cold. . . . That's why I don't like this photo. It's because of her face, not because of her clothes."

Some focus groups were shown an advertisement for Helmut Lang that was in black and white, depicting a very young model, head canted, shoulders slouched, wearing a sleeveless T-shirt. The young woman was not wearing any obvious makeup. The presence of small wrinkles around the mouth indicated that the photograph had not been airbrushed. Her shoulder-length blond hair was not parted and appeared to be uncombed. Although she was looking toward the camera, there were elements of "licensed withdrawal" in her serious, self-absorbed, alienated expression. Members of a group of white undergraduates close to the model's age described her as "mean," "upset," "unhappy," and "asexual." One middle-aged participant thought the model's body suggested drug addiction. A college student said: "I think she just looks like a heroin addict."

These comments reveal that the model's personality, as suggested by her facial expression, her personal demeanor as indicated by her stance, and the extent to which her image expressed sexuality or other aspects of gender, often had more impact on these participants than her clothes. Contrary to what is generally believed to be the impact of fashion images on women, these women were not intimidated by them. Models were not necessarily perceived as beautiful or as being exemplars of physical perfection. Their bodies were often criticized as being too thin, too muscular, or otherwise unappealing. Their clothes and their makeup were frequently described as bizarre, inappropriate, or unattractive. In spite of the fact that participants were as interested in the models as in their clothing and attempted to attribute distinct personalities and identities to the models on the basis of their physical appearance, these women did not often wish to emulate their appearance. When asked whether they would like to look like the models in these photographs on certain occasions, participants generally replied negatively. The images projected by these photographs were not ones these women wished to project themselves. These images were often incompatible with their attitudes and preferences. The image younger participants accepted most readily was that of the woman in a transparent dress leaning provocatively against a wall, in spite of the fact that many of them made critical remarks about the level of sexuality in her appearance. By contrast, the disheveled woman in a man's suit with sneakers was almost unanimously rejected.

These issues were particularly pertinent for African American women, as suggested by these comments from an African American focus group:

Interviewer: Does this photograph represent your point of view at all?

All: No.

Interviewer: Why not?

Tamara: She is blond-haired.

Kyla: I can't relate to her.

Interviewer: Why not?

Kyla: She is just different from me.

Tamara: She is six foot, very thin, pale.

By contrast, these women interpreted a photograph of an African model as clearly representing "the black woman's point of view." One of these women said: "I like her figure. It's an obvious African figure, the hips, butt, her arms. . . . She's an African woman. She's an elegant African woman."

◆ *The Visibility/Invisibility of the Pose*

Strongly implicated in the ways the models were perceived by participants were the kinds of poses in which they were placed and, in general, the various techniques underlying the social construction of the photographs. To what extent were these poses and techniques visible or invisible to these participants? These photographs, like many others in the issues of *Vogue* from which they were taken, relied on a small number of stereotypical poses that have been interpreted by social scientists as demeaning to women.

Members of the focus groups indicated their awareness of the social construction of these photographs through comments such as the following:

Nathalie: You can tell there's obviously a fan or wind machine blowing the hair.

Joan: I'm sure that they took a hundred pictures to get that and still her smile's not perfect. But like they tried hard to make it look natural.

Evelyn: It's intended to make you wonder if it's a man or a woman. It's meant to grab our attention. That's how they're going to get you into their ad.

Participants were clearly sensitive to the fact that these photographs were designed to sell clothing or at least the image of the designer or brand-name. At the same time, they expected these photographs to meet certain standards of realism, to match their conceptions of how young women actually behaved. The following comments are an example of this attitude:

Dorothy: It looks like a fashion photograph, whereas the other two photographs we just saw could be real.

Lucy: She looks like a mannequin. She doesn't really look real.

Members of the focus groups sometimes interpreted the "evidence" in these photographs in different ways. They varied in their sensitivity to the meanings of the stereotypical poses that appeared in certain photographs. Some photographs illustrated an aspect of what Goffman called "ritualization of subordination," the use of child-like, passive, awkward, or ridiculous body positions. In response to a photograph showing a model barefoot in midair with her arms outspread, one woman found the pose amusing: "I think the photograph is nice. It's kind of arresting—how they have her jumping. It looks kind of fun." Other participants who appeared to have a sense of the underlying connotations in the photograph said: "She looks like a marionette" and "She looks like Peter Pan because she's jumping."

If the stereotypical pose appeared to have sexual connotations or violated norms concerning bodily exposure, these participants were more likely to be critical of it. One of the photographs projected contradictory images. It showed a woman wearing a short black dress and lying supine on a chair. The upper part of the woman's body, her hair, and her face were neat, sleek, and well groomed. The lower part of the photograph showed her legs slightly open, revealing the inside of her right thigh, violating the norm against exposing this part of a woman's body (Henley 1977).

Participants responded differently, depending upon which part of the picture seemed most important to them:

Mark: She's pretty. Her face is the focal point.

Robin: You can totally see her crotch.

Laurie: You see her entire right thigh.

The following exchange of comments is generally favorable but reveals a slight ambivalence toward the pose.

Beth: She looks very pulled together and relaxed. She's obviously reclining but I like it.

Interviewer: Whose point of view does this photograph express?

Robin: I'd say a man's. . . . I don't know. I see her lying there.

Beth: Submissive.

Interviewer: Does this photograph express your point of view?

All: No.

Other participants were more critical of this pose:

Nathalie: It seems like she's giving herself away or something.

Tracee: I don't like the pose. . . . I just don't like the whole laid-back look, and it's almost as though her legs are gaped open and that's what really kind of offends me.

Another photo that illustrated Goffman's "ritualization of subordination" and that also had subtle sexual connotations showed the back of a young woman who was bent forward with her buttocks in the foreground of the picture. She was wearing a long dress in a colorful fabric. Again reactions to this photograph were mixed.

Interviewer: What adjectives would you use to describe the image of the woman?

Elena: I think she's sexual but it's not a very slutty sexual. . . . I think it's nice and I think it's feminine. (white undergraduate)

Another white participant was more critical of this pose:

Courtney: I don't like the pose. It's a sexualized pose.

Interviewer: Would you like to look like this woman on certain occasions?

Courtney: No. I don't care to be in that position.

African American students were also critical of the pose in this photograph:

Lisa: I don't like what she is doing. Why does her butt have to be in our faces?

Toyah: It's like she's an animal. She looks like a lizard.

One African American participant pointed to the racist aspects of a photograph that showed an African American model in a pose that also fit Goffman's "ritualization of subordination"—seated on the floor, wearing a long, elegant dress, smiling broadly, and holding a musical instrument:

I really like the dress and I think she is definitely very attractive. I guess mostly I have more negative feelings. I really don't like how she is sitting in this picture. It just looks really unnatural. . . . It just seems that there is a definite attempt to portray her as some kind of oddity. . . . I really don't like the expression on her face and I don't like the instrument in her hand because it brings up like a negative stereotype of a samba image, where they have the little pickaninny with a musical instrument or just with watermelon and it is to kind of make you think of that image. . . . If you were in a dress like this, you wouldn't be sitting on the floor in this kind of pose. You would be standing, you wouldn't actually be in that position.... It just seems so forced. It just seems like there could be a better picture to take of her and there is a definite attempt to make sure she looks kind of like this strange oddity of a person so that you can keep thinking she is different, she is not like the other models that you are going to see in a spread, or whatever.

In general, participants appeared to be more sensitive to the sexual or racist connotations of stereotypical poses than to connotations of childishness or passivity. Demeaning poses with sexual connotations were rejected unless the sexual aspects of the photograph were offset by elements in the photograph that had more positive implications for the participants.

◆ Conclusion

The findings from this study raise questions about the extent to which fashion photographs constitute a form of hegemonic femininity that is accepted as natural and uncontestable by readers. As exemplified by *Vogue*, the fashion magazine presents a wider range of social identities and "agendas" than was the case several decades ago. The overall effect is closer to conflicted hegemony than hegemonic femininity and probably facilitates the expression of negative attitudes toward these images. Judging from the responses of a racially and ethnically varied group of women of different ages, the authority of fashion magazines as arbiters of fashion is no greater than that of the television screen, the street, or local stores. Fashion editors were viewed as one source of information about fashion but not as being particularly authoritative.

The responses of most of the participants in the focus groups to images representing hegemonic femininity and feminine

empowerment suggest that they had internalized traditional norms of feminine demeanor and perceived these photographs as violating these norms. These taboos concerning appropriate gender behavior for women led them to reject exaggerated expressions of sexuality, both heterosexual and androgynous, and images that implied gender ambiguity. Images that conveyed feminine empowerment and dominance evoked ambivalent responses. On the one hand, they admired women who appeared to be strong, but expressions of strength that deviated from norms of feminine personal demeanor evoked negative responses. At times, they were insensitive to demeaning gender stereotypes that carried connotations of childishness but were more sensitive to stereotypes connoting sexual availability. African American participants were adept at decoding racial stereotypes and expressed explicitly their perception that these styles were not intended for women of color. Participants' attitudes toward the models were curiously ambivalent: they appeared to want to identify with them but they were not intimidated by their beauty, the perfection of their bodies, or their clothing.

Criticism of the images in these photographs came not just from women who, on the basis of age or ethnicity, might have perceived themselves as being outside the youthful audience for whom the clothing in the photographs was presumably intended, but also from young white college women. The often strident tone of their critiques may have resulted from an underlying emotional involvement in fashionable images and in the culturally prescribed requirement to look feminine and attractive (Thompson and Haytko 1997, p. 30). A group consisting of younger and less educated women might have responded differently to these photographs.[6]

This study suggests that women respond critically to the fashion press in part because these magazines express the tensions and contradictions of a conflicted hegemony and in part because traditional values and perceptions of personal demeanor (another form of hegemony) and modernist conceptions of social identity continue to shape women's perceptions of postmodern culture. These women did not appear likely to engage in postmodernist role-playing; they evaluated fashionable clothing with a strong sense of stable, personal identities. Instead of reveling in postmodernist ambiguity, they disliked outfits that appeared to convey conflicting messages. They examined clothes for their relevance to their personal lives and rejected a postmodernist confusion of styles and genders.

It is difficult to generalize these findings to women's clothing behavior in other contexts, such as shopping, where they are exposed directly to the clothing. Fashion photographs incorporate clothes into a complex gestalt of imagery that often overshadows the clothes themselves, so that participants respond as much to the setting in which the clothes are placed as to the clothes themselves. Seeing clothes in these unfamiliar contexts, they may be more likely to reject the identities associated with them than they would in a shopping mall. In other words, they may be responding to the ambiguities in the identities projected by these photographs by emphasizing their lack of connection with them (Freitas et al. 1997). Participants in the focus groups were sensitive to the ways in which their reactions to these photographs were affected by the fact that they were seeing them outside the covers of the magazine. Several participants commented that their responses would have been different if they had seen the photographs while flipping through the pages of the magazine, because they claimed they would have looked less carefully at certain photographs under those circumstances. The results of this study suggest the complexity of evaluating women's responses to visual representations in the media and the need for further research on this topic.

Notes ◆

1. *Vogue* was founded in 1893. For a brief history of *Vogue*, see Lakoff and Scherr (1984, pp. 69-114). This discussion is based on an analysis of the first three issues of the following years: 1947, 1957, 1967, 1977, 1987, and 1997.

2. *Vogue*'s circulation was 449,722 in 1968; 970,084 in 1978; and 1,126,193 in 1997 (the last date for which such figures are available) (*World Almanac and Book of Facts*, 1969, 1980, and 1999).

3. A different type of research on women's perceptions of advertisements in fashion magazines has attempted to ascertain the effects of ads showing images of highly attractive models on college women's perceived levels of satisfaction with their appearance (Richins 1991). McCracken (1988) showed fashion ads to college students and asked them to try to explain how they interpreted them.

4. Focus groups rather than interviews were used as a means of obtaining responses to fashion photographs because the task of commenting on photographs was unfamiliar to respondents. In developing their opinions, focus group members were stimulated by the comments of other respondents in the group setting. Focus group members were not obliged to participate to meet the requirements of a course. They varied in terms of age, racial background, and nationality: 83 percent were college age (the rest were middle-aged); 33 percent were African American, African, East and West Indian, Eurasian and Asian American (the remainder were Caucasian); and 13 percent were not American (Ghana, Indonesia, Iran, Lebanon, and Panama). Three of the respondents were male. Undergraduates were students in classes in sociology and communication. A total of forty-five people participated. The fifteen focus groups varied in size from 2 to 4 respondents and were conducted in college classrooms or private homes. They typically lasted for half an hour to an hour. As far as possible, each focus group was homogeneous in terms of age and racial background. Focus group leaders for groups of

college students were graduate students in most cases. An African American graduate student led the focus groups of African Americans. The other groups were led by the author. All focus groups were recorded and transcribed. All names used in the text are fictitious.

5. This figure is substantially higher than comparable figures obtained in American surveys (one-third and one-fifth, respectively) (Gutman and Mills 1982; Krafft 1991) and is probably due to the fact that the majority of the women who participated in the study were under age 25. It is also likely that most women who agreed to participate in the study had some interest in fashion.

6. Although the number of participants who were not U.S. citizens was small, it appeared that race was a more important influence than nationality on participants' responses to these images.

◆ References

Davis, Fred. 1992. *Fashion, Culture and Identity.* Chicago: University of Chicago Press.

Davis, Laurel R. 1997. *The Swimsuit Issue and Sport: Hegemonic Masculinity in Sports Illustrated.* Albany: State University of New York Press.

Dowd, Maureen. 1997. "Dressing for Contempt." *New York Times*, September 17, p. A31.

Freitas, Anthony, Susan Kaiser, Joan Chandler, Carol Hall, Jung-Won Kim, and Tania Hammidi. 1997. "Appearance Management as Border Construction: Least Favorite Clothing, Group Distancing, and Identity . . . Not!" *Sociological Inquiry* 67: 323-335.

Goffman, Erving. 1979. *Gender Advertisements.* Cambridge, MA: Harvard University Press.

Goldman, Robert, Deborah Heath, and Sharon L. Smith. 1991. "Commodity Feminism." *Critical Studies in Mass Communication* 8: 71-89.

Gutman, Jonathan, and Michael K. Mills. 1982. "Fashion Life Style, Self-Concept, Shopping Orientation, and Store Patronage: An Integrative Analysis." *Journal of Retailing* 58 (Summer): 64-68.

Henley, Nancy M. 1977. *Body Politics: Power, Sex and Nonverbal Communication.* Englewood Cliffs, NJ: Prentice Hall.

Kaiser, Susan B, Richard H. Nagasawa, and Sandra S. Hutton. 1991. "Fashion, Postmodernity and Personal Appearance: A Symbolic Interactionist Formulation." *Symbolic Interaction* 14: 165-185.

Kellner, Douglas. 1990. *Television and the Crisis of Democracy.* Boulder, CO: Westview.

Krafft, Susan. 1991. "Discounts Drive Clothes." *American Demographics* 13 (July): 11.

Lakoff, Robin T., and Raquel L. Scherr. 1984. *Face Value: The Politics of Beauty.* Boston: Routledge.

Lewis, Reina, and Katrina Rolley. 1996. "Ad(dressing) the Dyke: Lesbian Looks and Lesbian Looking." Pp. 178-189 in *Outlooks: Lesbian and Gay Sexualities and Visual Cultures*, edited by Peter Horne and Reina Lewis. London: Routledge.

Lutz, Catherine A., and Jane L. Collins. 1993. *Reading National Geographic.* Chicago: University of Chicago Press.

McCracken, Ellen. 1993. *Decoding Women's Magazines: From Mademoiselle to Ms.* New York: St. Martin's.

McCracken, Grant. 1988. *Culture and Consumption.* Bloomington: Indiana University Press.

Mulvey, Laura. 1975-1976. "Visual Pleasure and Narrative Cinema." *Screen* 16: 6-18.

Myers, Kathy. 1987. "Fashion 'n' Passion." Pp. 58-65 in *Looking On: Images of Femininity in the Visual Arts and Media*, edited by Rosemary Betterton. London: Pandora.

Partington, Angela. 1996. "Perfume: Pleasure, Packaging and Postmodernity." Pp. 204-218 in *The Gendered Object*, edited by Pat Kirkham. Manchester, UK: Manchester University Press.

Plous, S., and Dominique Neptune. 1997. "Racial and Gender Biases in Magazine

Advertising." *Psychology of Women Quarterly* 21: 627-644.

Rabine, Leslie. 1994. "A Woman's Two Bodies: Fashion Magazines, Consumerism, and Feminism." Pp. 59-75 in *On Fashion*, edited by Shari Benstock and Suzanne Ferris. New Brunswick, NJ: Rutgers University Press.

Richins, Marsha L.1991. "Social Comparison and the Idealized Images of Advertising." *Journal of Consumer Research* 18: 71-83.

Signorielli, Nancy, Douglas McLeod, and Elaine Healy. 1994. "Gender Stereotypes in MTV Commercials: The Beat Goes On." *Journal of Broadcasting and Electronic Media* 38: 91-101.

Skeggs, Beverly. 1993. "A Good Time for Women Only." Pp. 61-73 in *Deconstructing Madonna*, edited by Fran Lloyd. London: B. T. Batsford.

Steele, Valerie. 1996. *Fetish: Fashion, Sex and Power*. New York: Oxford University Press.

Summer, Christine C. 1996. "Tracking the Junkie Chic Look." *Psychology Today*, September/October, p. 14.

Thompson, Craig J., and Diana L. Haytko. 1997. "Speaking of Fashion: Consumers' Uses of Fashion Discourses and the Appropriation of Countervailing Cultural Meanings." *Journal of Consumer Research* 24 (June): 15-42.

Winship, Janice. 1985. "'A Girl Needs to Get Street-wise': Magazines for the 1980's." *Feminist Review* 21: 25-46.

Wolf, Naomi. 1991. *The Beauty Myth: How Images of Beauty Are Used Against Women*. New York: Anchor Books.

PART IV

THE VIOLENCE DEBATES

Do depictions of violence in the media cause or contribute to real-world violence? This question has been much debated by media theorists, psychologists, sociologists, child development experts, and the public. Common sense would seem to lead to the conclusion that there is some connection between apparently rising levels of interpersonal and social violence in the postindustrial world and the plethora of media images to which entertainment media consumers are exposed, featuring and glamorizing killings, combat, street fighting, domestic violence, car chases and explosions, torture, and other forms of physical aggression. But what kind of connection? Other factors are clearly implicated in rising rates of homicide and other violent crimes, and many media analysts argue that the meaning of the violent imagery varies tremendously with the individual consumer.

Empirical research on the effects of exposing people to media images of violence does not provide a clear answer to the question, despite thousands of published studies to date. One problem is that "laboratory" studies take place in artificial settings (very different from real-world consumption settings); another is that such studies are necessarily short term and cannot tell us about cumulative effects of exposure to imagery over time.

Our aim in this section is to provide some useful ways of thinking about the possible psychological and social effects of consumption of media images that depict and often glamorize or render pleasurable a variety of forms of interpersonal violence. The chapters in this section take a range of views. Some (such as Jenkins, Rose, Snitow, and Seiter) argue that public discussion of media violence is distorted thinking taking place in an atmosphere of "moral panic," in which certain "socially threatening" groups (such as adolescents in general, and young black men in particular) are targeted. Some of these analysts also point to a puritanical strain in the public outrage over media representations that seem to eroticize domination (Jenkins, Snitow). Others (Gerbner, Caputi, Dines, Levin and Carlsson-Paige) see media violence as one of the most important social issues of our time, and several use the example of pornography to make this case. Several chapters offer critical readings of the kind of research that has been done in the past and suggest new approaches to the exploration of the complex connections between media representations and social reality (Jensen, Seiter, Boyle).

George Gerbner, one of the leading media violence experts who believes that media violence is a serious social problem, argues in "Television Violence: At a Time of Turmoil and Terror" (Chapter 33) that the effects of televisual texts including representations of physical violence are long term and have implications for how we construct reality. In his longitudinal research comparing heavy and light TV viewers, Gerbner has found that the heavy viewers, bombarded with more images of violence than light viewers, become more fearful and scared and tend to see the world as a more dangerous place than it really is (overestimating their likelihood of being victimized by crime, for example). He argues that when we analyze the texts in which the violence is situated, we can find powerful messages regarding the nature of power in our society. From an empirical research base, his chapter nevertheless offers a complex analysis of how media violence should be studied and understood.

Gerbner emphasizes the role of TV violence in reinforcing viewers' perceptions of social "victimizers" as primarily poor and nonwhite, thus pointing to the racial and class dimensions of televisual representation. Jackson Katz, on the other hand, foregrounds the role of violence in helping us construct notions of gender, and in particular of white masculinity. In "Advertising and the Construction of Violent White Masculinity" (Chapter 34), Katz argues that "although there are significant differences between the various masculinities" associated with different social positions by race and class, "in patriarchal culture, violent behavior is typically gendered male." He calls for a more gender-conscious analysis of cultural areas "where violent masculinities are produced and legitimated: comic books, toys, the sports culture, professional wrestling, comedy, interactive video, music video, pornography." Only by attending to the links between "the construction of gender and the prevalence of violence," Katz argues, can we hope to pursue "effective antiviolence interventions."

Gerbner's call for informed public discussion of the impact of TV imagery on our culture and society is seconded by Diane Levin and Nancy Carlsson-Paige, who report on a study of the concerns of teachers working with small children with the children's TV show *Power Rangers* (Chapter 35). The teachers in this study almost unanimously felt that children who watched this show (in which five teenagers "morph" into superheroes to do battle with evildoers) were negatively affected in a variety of ways. Many believed "that the Power Rangers are desensitizing children to violence and undermining their conflict-resolution skills." Levin and Carlsson-Paige remind us that the deregulation of children's broadcasting in 1984 by the Federal Communications Commission allowed the entertainment corporations far more control over the content of children's TV than before, in effect giving the companies a role as "parents and teachers to children." They call for more public discussion and debate about "the change that deregulation has brought to children's lives."

In a careful ethnographic study of how social class affects teachers' views on the problem of media violence, Ellen Seiter shows in "Lay Theories of Media Effects: Power Rangers at Pre-school" (Chapter 36) that teachers have a range of beliefs, quite similar to the range expressed by media scholars. Seiter's interviews highlight how the class divisions between two teachers correlate with their views of popular culture On the one side we have Sara, the teacher of a Montessori school serving upper-middle-class students, who favors "high culture" products such as books and documentaries and expresses disdain for popular culture in the shape of TV entertainment shows for children. She tends to see TV as an all-powerful shaper of children's ideas—taking the more stimulus-response type approach that is characteristic of many psychologically based media studies. Jean, on the other hand, the teacher at a day care facility attached to a local hospital, sees popular culture as an important socializing agent for her children and thus she is more apt to allow them to watch shows like the *Power Rangers*. This teacher sounds more like the media scholars who argue for polysemic readings and the audience as active agents.

For Henry Jenkins, too, the focus of investigation should be on how viewers make sense of television violence rather than simply counting examples of car explosions in action films or using text analysis to argue for the damage media imagery may do to viewers. According to Jenkins, in "Lessons From Littleton" (Chapter 37),

> different consumers react to the same media content in fundamentally different ways as it is fit into their larger understanding of the world, and so universalizing claims are fundamentally inadequate for accounting for media's social and cultural impact.

Jenkins is writing in the aftermath of the school shootings in Columbine and Littleton that did indeed cause many different public constituencies to focus on the media

as the culprit, and he also calls for a more informed and less hasty public dialogue, as well as further exploration of the issues by educators. He points out the danger of mindlessly targeting "youth culture" during periods of "moral panic" such as those following high-profile media coverage of incidents of real-world violence that seem "inexplicable" because they involve white middle-class children.

As Jenkins notes, creating a moral panic works best when the targeted consumers of violent media imagery are widely feared as threats to the social order. Tricia Rose, in "Hidden Politics: Discursive and Institutional Policing of Rap Music" (Chapter 38), provides an excellent example of the way African American youth culture consumers have been viewed as "a dangerous internal element in urban America; an element that if allowed to roam about freely, will threaten the social order; an element that must be policed." In her description of attending a rap concert, she recounts the degrading treatment to which African American youth were subjected by both policing agents and the media. Hip-hop culture in general has created "moral panic" as a cultural force that threatens to disrupt the peace of white society. As Rose points out, African American hip-hop fans are seen as part of the "danger," while white fans of heavy metal music are constructed as "*victims* of its influence."

Although there are many other examples we might offer, we have chosen the case of pornography to explore in more depth in this section, because the question of whether pornography is implicated in violence against women has been one of the "hot" topics in feminism and has led to complex and troubling debates among feminists, as well as between feminists and civil libertarians—debates that have been termed the "porn wars." To simplify considerably, radical feminists (such as Andrea Dworkin, Catharine MacKinnon, Diana Russell, Laura Lederer) argued that heterosexual pornography harmed women in both in its production (exploiting the real, often impoverished women who participated as porn film or video actresses) and in its consumption (when male consumers learn to associate sexual pleasure with degrading or violent depictions of women). Liberal feminists took issue with the view that the representations in most pornography encouraged callous, domineering, and even violent male behavior toward women, and "pro-sex" feminists argued that antiporn feminists were reading "fantasy" as reality. They asserted that even representations of domination and violence within pornography constituted legitimate sexual expression not directly harmful to real women. Indeed, some pro-sex feminists produced and rationalized their own pornographic imagery containing sadomasochistic scenarios for consumption by women.

The chapters on pornography in this section have been chosen to situate the pornography question within the debate over the relationship of media violence to real-world violence.

We begin with two discussions of the problems of the effects research, as applied to the study of pornography's real-world effects. Karen Boyle, in "The Pornography Debates" (Chapter 39), and Robert Jensen, in "Pornography and the Limits of Experimental Research" (Chapter 40), are both critical of the scientific research on pornography that attempts to "prove" a clear relationship between pornography and violence against women. The problem with this model, as Jensen and Boyle point out, is that it fails to take into account the possible effects of real-world contexts in which pornography is actually used, and it cannot tell us what ideological impact long-term use of pornography has. This type of questioning has led to a movement away from overreliance on the experimental model. Both Jensen and Boyle call for a more ethnographic type of research, one that would include analysis of women's and men's testimony about its place in their lives.

Pornography, like other media genres, consists of codes and conventions that can be found in other various media forms. Indeed, two chapters in this section argue that elements of the pornographic can be located in romance novels and advertisements. With respect to the former, Ann Barr Snitow asks provocatively, in "Mass Market Romance" (Chapter 41), whether romance novels should be seen as a form of "pornography for women"—that is, a less explicit and visual text than that aimed at male consumers but one that still aims to eroticize male domination, for a specifically female audience. Many of the themes in romance novels (the domineering male, the passive female, the sexualization of female subordination) form the core of the pornographic mode of representation. Similarly, Jane Caputi, in "Everyday Pornography" (Chapter 42), by adopting feminist definitions of pornography, argues that many mainstream advertisements constitute what she calls everyday pornography.

In both romance novels and pornography, masculinity and femininity are constructed in conventional and oppositional ways. The relationships are depicted as unequal in that the male is stronger, bigger, and has the ability to hurt the woman. In romance novels, this violence is subtly suggested, whereas in pornography it is clearly depicted. The advertisements that Caputi explores fall in both categories. However, she goes on to argue that in the advertisements "it's not always so easy to recognize the oppressive character of pornography and its popular culture manifestations precisely because it is so normal." This normalization of violence against women is what most concerns radical feminists because much of what we think about femininity, masculinity, and heterosexual relationships are derived from media representations.

In pornography, as in all media representations, masculinity and femininity are not fixed entities, but rather are mediated by race and class. This is clearly demonstrated by Gail Dines in "King Kong and the White Woman" (Chapter 43), on the image of black men in *Hustler* magazine.

The caricatured black male as the spoiler of white womanhood, a staple of *Hustler* cartoons, is drawn from historical images that date back to slavery. These images, without a doubt, help to fuel the moral panic of blacks as dangerous that Rose so eloquently explains. If these images only appeared in *Hustler*, then maybe we could write them off as examples of racist cartoonists that work for a magazine with a dubious reputation. However, their very power lay in the wider ideological constructions of black men that have helped legitimize a range of racist practices that include lynching, racial-profiling, and police brutality. In this country, much of the debate on violence has been racially coded as when the media refer to "inner-city youths" or "drug dealers." This moral panic has, as Jenkins points out, short-circuited a thoughtful dialogue on the issue of media violence.

33

TELEVISION VIOLENCE
At a Time of Turmoil and Terror

◆ George Gerbner

Humankind may have had more bloodthirsty eras, but none as filled with images of violence as the present. Monitoring by the *Des Moines Register* found that of the six top stories on Des Moines evening newscasts during February 1994, 118 stories dealt with crime and violence, 27 featured business, 17 dealt with government, 15 reported on racial relations, and 2 discussed schools. A 1994 study of local news by the University of Miami found that time devoted to crime ranged from 23% to 50% (averaging 32%) while violent crime in the city remained constant, involving less that one tenth of 1% of the population.

Community leaders have often said that blacks, Hispanics, and now people of Middle Eastern appearance or Muslim religion are demonized by the choice of faces shown in crime stories. Evidence supports that charge. For example, a study for the Chicago Council on Urban Affairs found that "a high percentage of African-Americans and Latinos are shown as victimizers of society, and few as social helpers." This distorted portrayal, the council said, contributes to the notion that "the inner city is dominated by dangerous and irresponsible minorities." Similarly, the *Journalism Quarterly* reported that Chicago newspapers carried stories on only one of every three homicides in the city and that the slayings most likely to be selected were those in which the victims were white, contrary to actual crime statistics.

NOTE: This chapter originally appeared in the first edition and has been revised and updated.

We have studied local news on Philadelphia television stations since 1967 as part of the Cultural Indicators monitoring project. We found that crime and/or violence items usually lead newscast and preempt balanced coverage of the city. Furthermore, only 20% of crime and violence on local news were local to the city, only 40% were local to the region, and since the September 11, 2001, attacks on the World Trade Center and the Pentagon, that proportion shrank even further. As also found in other studies, whites are more likely to be reported as victims, and people of color as the perpetrators.

Crime and violence also play a prominent and pervasive role in TV entertainment. Scenes of violence occur an average 3 to 5 times per hour in prime-time dramatic fiction, and between 20 and 25 times per hour in cartoons. We are awash in a tide of violent representations such as the world has never seen. Images of expertly choreographed brutality at home and half a world of away drench our homes. There is no escape from the mass-produced mayhem pervading the life space of ever larger areas of the world.

The television overkill has clearly drifted out of democratic reach. Children all over the world are born into homes dominated by television's global monopoly of turmoil and terror. They are fully integrated into television's mean and violent world. The United States dominates that world, throwing its military weight around from Panama to Afghanistan. As Sam Smith, editor of the online Undernews, wrote: "Our leaders have failed us by creating a world so filled with hatred for our land."

TV's investment in mayhem was first reported by the National Association of Educational Broadcasters in 1951. The first Congressional hearings were held by Senator Estes Kefauver's Subcommittee on Juvenile Delinquency in 1954. Through several more rounds of hearings in the 1960s and 1970s, despite the accumulation of critical research results, despite condemnation by government commissions and virtually all medical, law enforcement, parents', educational, and other organizations, and in the face of international embarrassment, violence still saturates the airways (Gerbner, Gross, Morgan, & Signorielli, 1993).

Broadcasters are licensed by the Federal Communications Commission (FCC) to serve "the public interest, convenience, and necessity." But they are paid to deliver a receptive audience to their business sponsors. Few industries are as public relations-conscious as television. What compels them to endure public humiliation, risk the threat of repressive legislation, and invite charges of visions of violence undermines health, security, and the social order? The answer is not popularity.

The usual rationalization that television violence "gives the audience what it wants" is disingenuous. As the trade knows well, violence is not highly rated. But there is no free market or box office for television programs through which audiences could express their wants.

Unlike other media use, viewing is a ritual; people watch by the clock and not by the program. Ratings are determined more by the time of the program, the lead-in (previous program), and what else is competing for viewers at the same time than by their quality or other attractions. Ratings are important only because they set the price the advertiser pays for "buying" viewers available to the set at a certain time, but they have limited use as indicators of popularity.

Therefore, it is clear that something is wrong with the way the problem has been posed and addressed. Either the damage is not what it is commonly assumed to be, or television violence and global mayhem must have some driving force and utility other than popularity, or both. Indeed, it is both, and more.

The usual question—"Does television violence incite real-life violence?"—is itself a symptom of the problem. It obscures and, despite its alarming implications and intent, trivializes the issues involved. Television violence must be understood as a complex scenario and an indicator of social relationships. It has both utility and consequences other than those usually considered in media and public discussion. And it is driven by forces other than free expression and audience demand.

Whatever else it does, violence in drama and news demonstrates power. It portrays victims as well as victimizers. It intimidates more than it incites. It paralyzes more than triggers action. It defines majority might and minority risk. It shows one person's, country's, race's, or ethnic group's place in the "pecking order" that runs the world.

Violence and now war, no matter how distant, is but the tip of the iceberg of a massive underlying connection to television's role as universal story-teller and an industry dependent on global markets. These relationships have not yet been recognized and integrated into any theory or regulatory practice. Television has been seen as one medium among many rather than as the mainstream of the cultural environment in which most children grow up and learn. Traditional regulatory and public interest conceptions are based on the obsolete assumption that the number of media outlets determines freedom and diversity of content. Today, however, a handful of global conglomerates can own many outlets in all media, deny entry to new and alternative perspectives, and homogenize content. The common-carrier concept of access and protection applicable to a public utility such as the telephone also falls short when the issue is not so much the number of channels and individual access to them but the centralized mass production of the content of all the stories we grow on in common.

Let us, then, preview the task of broadening a discourse that has gone on too long in a narrow and shallow groove. Violence on television is an integral part of a system of global marketing. It dominates an increasing share of the world's screens despite its relative lack of popularity in any country. Its consequences go far beyond inciting aggression. The system inhibits the portrayal of diverse dramatic approaches to conflict. It depresses independent television production and thereby diversity of choicer, views, perspectives, and, not incidentally, political parties. No other country that calls itself democratic has such a monopoly on political expression and organization, lacking socialist, communist, religious, and regional parties, and therefore, alternative views on how society might be organized.

Television's socio-political-cultural monopoly deprives viewers of more popular choices, victimizes some and emboldens others, heightens general intimidation, and invites repressive measures that exploit the widespread insecurities it itself generates.

The First Amendment to the U.S. Constitution forbade the only censors its authors knew—government—from interfering with the freedom of their press. Since then, large conglomerates, virtual private governments, have imposed their formulas of overkill on media they own. Therefore, raising the issue of overkill directs attention to the controls that in fact abridge creative freedom, dominate markets, and constrain democratic cultural policy.

Behind the problem of television violence is the critical issue of who makes cultural policy on whose behalf in the electronic age. The debate about the current tidal wave of mayhem creates an opportunity to move the larger cultural policy issue to center stage, where it has been in other democracies for some time. The convergence of communication technologies concentrates control over the most widely shared messages and images. Despite all the technocratic fantasies about hundreds of channels, it is rare to encounter discussion of the basic issue of who makes cultural policy. In the absence of such discussion, cultural policy is made on private and limited grounds by an invisible corporate directorate whose members are unknown, unelected, and unaccountable to the public.

We need to ask the kinds of questions that can place the discussion of television violence as a cultural policy issue in a useful perspective. For example: What creative sources and resources will provide what mix of content moving on the "electronic superhighway" into every home? Who will tell the stories and for what underlying purpose? How can we ensure survival of alternative perspectives, regardless of profitability and selling power?

There are no clear answers to these questions because, for one thing, they have not yet been placed on the agenda of public discourse. It will take organization, deliberation, and exploration to develop an approach to answering them. What follows, then, is an attempt to draw from our research answers to some questions that can help develop such an approach. We will be asking: What is unique about television, and about violence on television? What systems of "casting" and "fate" dominate its representations of life? What conceptions of reality do these systems cultivate? Why does violence play such a prominent, pervasive, and persistent role in them? And, finally, how can we as a society deal with the overkill while, at the same time, enhancing rather then further curtailing cultural freedom and diversity?

◆ The New Cultural Environment

Nielsen figures show that an American child today is born into a home in which television is on an average of more than 7 hours a day. For the first time in human history, most of the stories about people, life, and values are told not by parents, schools, churches, or others in the community who have something to tell, but by a group of distant conglomerates that have something to sell.

Television, the mainstream of the new cultural environment, has brought about a radical change in the way children grow up, learn, and live in our society. Television is a relatively nonselectively used ritual; children are its captive audience. Most people watch by the clock and not by the program. The

television audience depends on the time of the day and the day of the week more than on the program. Other media require literacy, growing up, going out, and selection based on some previously acquired tastes, values, predispositions. Traditional media research assumed such selectivity. But there are no "previously acquired tastes, values, predispositions" with television. Viewing starts in infancy and continues throughout life.

Television helps to shape from the outset the predispositions and selections that govern the use of other media. Unlike other media, television requires little or no attention; its repetitive patterns are absorbed in the course of living. They become part and parcel of the family's style of life, but they neither stem from nor respond to its particular and selective needs and wants. It is television itself that cultivates the tastes, values, and predisposition that guide future selection of other media. That is why television had a major impact on what movies, magazines, newspapers, and books can be sold best in the new cultural environment.

The roles children grow into are no longer homemade, handcrafted, community-inspired. They are products of a complex, integrated, and globalized manufacturing and marketing system. Television violence, defined as overt physical action that hurts or kills (or threatens to do so), is an integral part of that system. A study titled *The Limits of Selective Viewing* (Sun, 1989) found that, on the whole, prime-time television presents a relatively small set of common themes, and violence pervades most of them.

Of course, representations of violence are not necessarily undesirable. There is blood in fairy tales, gore in mythology, murder in Shakespeare. Not all violence is alike. In some contexts, violence can be a legitimate and even necessary cultural expression. Individually crafted, historically inspired, sparingly and selectively used expressions of symbolic violence can indicate the tragic costs of deadly compulsions. However, such tragic sense of violence has been swamped by "happy violence" produced on the dramatic assembly line. This happy violence is cool, swift, painless, and often spectacular, even thrilling, but usually sanitized. It always leads to a happy ending. After all, it is designed to entertain and not to upset; it must deliver the audience to the next commercial in a receptive mood.

The majority of network viewers have little choice of thematic context or cast of character types, and virtually no chance of avoiding violence. Nor has the proliferation of channels led to greater diversity of actual viewing (see, e.g., Gerbner, 1993; Gerbner et al., 1993; Morgan & Shanahan, 1991). If anything, the dominant dramatic patterns penetrate more deeply into viewer choices through more outlets managed by fewer owners airing programs produced by fewer creative sources.

◆ Message System Analysis

My conclusions are based on the findings of our Cultural Indicators project (CI) that began in 1967.[1] CI is a cumulative database and an ongoing research project that relates recurrent features of the world of television to media policy and viewer conceptions of reality. Its computer archive contain observations on over 3,000 programs and 35,000 characters coded according to many thematic, demographic, and action categories.

CI is a three-pronged research effort. "Message system analysis" is the annual monitoring of television program content; "institutional policy analysis" looks at the economic and political bases of media decision making; "cultivation analysis" is an assessment of the long-range consequences of exposure to television's systems of messages.

Message system analysis is the study of the content of television programs. It includes every dramatic (fictional) program in each annual sample. It provides an unusual view of familiar territory. It is not a view of individual programs but an aggregate picture of the world of television, a bird's-eye view of what large communities of viewers absorb over long periods of time.

The role of violence in that world can be seen in our analysis of prime-time network programs and characters. Casting and fate, the demography of that world, are the important building blocks of the storytelling process. They have presented a stable pattern over the almost 30 years of monitoring network television drama and coding every speaking character in each year's sample. Middle-class white male characters dominate in numbers and power. Women play one out of three characters. Young people comprise one third and old one fifth of their actual proportions of the population. Most other minorities are even more underrepresented. That cast sets the stage for stories of conflict, violence, and the projection of white male prime-of-life power. Most of those who are underrepresented are also those who, when portrayed, suffer the worst fate.

The average viewer of prime-time television drama (serious as well as comedic) sees in a typical week an average of 21 criminals arrayed against an army of 41 public and private law enforcers. There are 14 doctors, 6 nurses, 6 lawyers, and 2 judges to handle them. An average of 150 acts of violence and about 15 murders entertain them and their children every week, and that does not count cartoons and the news. Those who watch more than 3 hours a day (more than half of all viewers) absorb much more.

About one out of three (31%) of all characters and more than half (52%) of major characters are involved in violence either as victims or as victimizers (or both) in any given week. The ratio of violence to victimization defines the price to be paid for committing violence. When one group can commit violence with relative impunity, the price it pays for violence is relatively low. When another group suffers more violence than it commits, the price is high.

In the total cast of prime-time characters, defined as all speaking parts regardless of the importance of the role, the average "risk ratio" (number of victims per 10 violents) is 12. Violence is an effective victimizer—and characterizer. Its distribution is not random; the calculus of risk is not evenly distributed. Women, children, poorer, and older people and some minorities pay a higher price for violence than do males in the prime of life. The price paid in victims for every 10 violents is 15 for boys, 16 for girls, 17 for young women, 18.5 for lower-class characters, and more than 20 for elderly characters.

Violence takes on an even more defining role for major characters. It involves more than half of all major characters (58% of men and 41% of women). Most likely to be involved either as perpetrators or victims, or both, are characters portrayed as mentally ill (84%), characters with mental or other disability (70%), young adult males (69%), and Latino/Hispanic Americans (64%). Children, lower class and mentally ill or otherwise disabled characters, pay the highest price—13 to 16 victims for every 10 perpetrators.

Lethal victimization further extends the pattern. About 5% of all characters and 10% of major characters are involved in killing (kill or get killed or both). Being Latino/Hispanic or lower class means bad trouble: they are the most likely to kill and be killed. Being poor, old, Hispanic, or a woman of color means double trouble, a disproportionate chance of being killed; they pay the highest relative price for taking another's life.

Among major characters, for every 10 "good" (positively valued) men who kill, about 4 are killed. But for every 10 "good" women who kill, 6 women are killed, and for every 10 women of color who kill, 17 women are killed. Older women characters get involved in violence only to be killed.

We calculated a violence "pecking order" by ranking the risk ratios of the different groups. Women, children, young people, lower class, disabled, and Asian Americans are at the bottom of the heap. When it comes to killing, older and

Latino/Hispanic characters also pay a higher than average price. In other words, hurting and killing by most majority groups extracts a tooth for a tooth. But minority groups tend to pay a higher price for their show of force. That imbalance of power is, in fact, what makes them minorities even when, as women, they are a numerical majority.

Cultivation Analysis: The ◆ "Lessons" of Television

What are the consequences? These representations are not the sole or necessarily even the main determinants of what people think or do. But they are the most pervasive, inescapable, and policy-directed common and stable cultural contributions to what large communities absorb over long periods of time. We use the term *cultivation* to distinguish the long-term cultivation of assumptions about life and values from short term "effects" that are usually assessed by measuring change as a consequence of exposure to certain messages. With television, one cannot take a measure before exposure and rarely without exposure. Television tends to cultivate and confirm stable conceptions about life.

Cultivation analysis measures these "lessons" as it explores whether those who spend more time with television are more likely than comparable groups of lighter viewers to perceive the real world in ways that reflect the most common and repetitive features of the television world. (See Morgan & Signorielli, 1990, for a detailed discussion of the theoretical assumptions and methodological procedures of cultivation analysis.)

The systemic patterns in television content that we observe through message system analysis provide the basis for formulating survey questions about people's conceptions of social reality. These questions form the basis of surveys administered to large and representative national samples of respondents. The surveys include questions about fear of crime, trusting other people, walking at night in one's own neighborhood, chances of victimization, inclination to aggression, and so on. Respondents in each sample are divided into those who watch the most television, those who watch a moderate amount, and those who watch the least. Cultivation is assessed by comparing patterns of responses in the three viewing groups (light, medium, and heavy) while controlling for important demographic and other characteristics such as education, age, income, gender, newspaper reading, neighborhood, and so forth.

These surveys indicate that long-term regular exposure to violence-laden television tends to make an independent contribution (i.e., in addition to all other factors) to the feeling of living in a mean and gloomy world. The "lessons" range from aggression to desensitization and to a sense of vulnerability and dependence.

The symbolic overkill takes its toll on all viewers. However, heavier viewers in every subgroup express a greater sense of apprehension than do light viewers in the same groups. They are more likely than comparable groups of light viewers to overestimate their chances of involvement in violence; to believe that their neighborhoods are unsafe; to state that fear of crime is a very serious personal problem and to assume that crime is rising, regardless of the facts of the case. Heavy viewers are also more likely to buy new locks, watchdogs, and guns "for protection." It makes no difference what they watch because only light viewers watch more selectively; heavy viewers watch more of everything that is on the air. Our studies show that they cannot escape watching violence (see, e.g., Gerbner et al., 1993; Sun, 1989).

Moreover, viewers who see members of their own group underrepresented but over-victimized seem to develop a greater sense of apprehension, mistrust, and alienation, what we call the "mean world syndrome."

Insecure, angry people may be prone to violence but are even more likely to be dependent on authority and susceptible to deceptively simple, strong, hard-line postures. They may accept and even welcome repressive measures such as more jails, capital punishment, harsher sentences—measures that have never reduced crime but never fail to get votes—if that promises to relieve their anxieties. That is the deeper dilemma of violence-laden television.

The Structural Basis of ◆ Television Violence

Formula-driven violence in entertainment and news is not an expression of freedom, viewer preference, or even crime statistics. The frequency of violence in the media seldom, if ever, reflects the actual occurrence of crime in a community. It is, rather, the product of a complex manufacturing and marketing machine.

Mergers, consolidation, conglomeratization, and globalization speed the machine. "Studios are clipping productions and consolidating operations, closing off gateways for newcomers," notes the trade paper *Variety* on the front page of its August 2, 1993, issue. The number of major studios declines while their share of domestic and global markets rises. Channels proliferate while investment in new talent drops, gateways close, and creative sources shrink.

Concentration brings denial of access to new entries and alternative perspectives. It places greater emphasis on dramatic ingredients most suitable for aggressive international promotion. Having fewer buyers for their products forces program producers into deficit financing. That means that most producers cannot break even on the license fees they receive for domestic airings. They are forced into syndication and foreign sales to make a profit. They need dramatic ingredients that require no translation, "speak action" in any language, and fit any culture. That ingredient is violence and mayhem. The events of September 11 were a striking example. (Sex is second but, ironically, it runs into more inhibitions and restrictions.)

Syndicators demand "action" (the code word for violence) because it "travels well around the world," said the producer of *Die Hard 2* (which killed 264 compared to 18 in *Die Hard 1*). "Everyone understands an action movie. If I tell a joke, you may not get it but if a bullet goes through the window, we all know how to hit the floor, no matter the language" (quoted in Auletta, 1993).

Our analysis shows that violence dominates U.S. exports. We compared 250 U.S. programs exported to 10 countries with 111 programs shown in the United States during the same year. Violence was the main theme of 40% of home-shown and 49% of exported programs. Crime/action series comprised 17% of home-shown and 46% of exported programs.

The rationalization for all that is that violence "sells." But what does it sell to whom, and at what price? There is no evidence that, other factors being equal, violence per se is giving most viewers, countries, and citizens "what they want." The most highly rated programs are usually not violent. The trade paper *Broadcasting & Cable* (Editorial, 1993) editorialized that "the most popular programming is hardly violent as anyone with a passing knowledge of Nielsen ratings will tell you." The editorial added that "action hours and movies have been the most popular exports for years"—that is, with the exporters, not the audiences. In other words, violence may help sell programs cheaply to broadcasters in many countries despite the dislike of their audiences. But television audiences do not buy programs, and advertisers, who do, pay for reaching the available audience at the least cost.

We compared data from more than 100 violent and the same number of nonviolent prime-time programs stored in the CI database. The average Nielsen rating of the violent sample was 11.1; the same for the nonviolent sample was 13.8. The share of viewing households in the violent and nonviolent samples was 18.9 and 22.5, respectively. The amount and consistency of violence in a series further increased the gap. Furthermore, the nonviolent sample was more highly rated than the violent sample for each of the five seasons studied.

However, despite their low average popularity, what violent programs lose on general domestic audiences they more than make up by grabbing younger viewers the advertisers want to reach and by extending their reach to the global market hungry for a cheap product. Even though these imports are typically also less popular abroad than quality shows produced at home, their extremely low cost, compared to local production, makes them attractive to the broadcasters who buy them.

Of course, some violent movies, videos, video games, and other spectacles do attract sizable audiences. But those audiences are small compared to the home audience for television. They are the selective retail buyers of what television dispenses wholesale. If only a small proportion of television viewers growing up with the violent overkill become addicted to it, they can make many movies and games spectacularly successful.

Public Response ◆ and Action

Most television viewers suffer the violence daily inflicted on them with diminishing tolerance. Organizations of creative workers in media, health professionals, law enforcement agencies, and virtually all other media-oriented professional and citizen groups have come out against "gratuitous" television violence. A March 1985 Harris survey showed that 78% disapprove of violence they see on television. A Gallup poll of October 1990 found 79% in favor of "regulating" objectionable content in television. A Times-Mirror national poll in 1993 showed that Americans who said they were "personally bothered" by violence in entertainment shows jumped to 59% from 44% in 1983. Furthermore, 80% said entertainment violence was "harmful" to society, compared with 64% in 1983.

Local broadcasters, legally responsible for what goes on the air, also oppose the overkill and complain about loss of control. *Electronic Media* reported on August 2, 1993, the results of its own survey of 100 general managers across all regions and in all market sizes. Three out of four said there is too much needless violence on television; 57% would like to have "more input on program content decisions."

The Hollywood Caucus of Producers, Writers and Directors, speaking for the creative community, said in a statement issued in August 1993: "We stand today at a point in time when the country's dissatisfaction with the quality of television is at an all-time high, while our own feelings of helplessness and lack of power, in not only choosing material that seeks to enrich, but also in our ability to execute to the best of our ability, is at an all-time low."

Far from reflecting creative freedom, the marketing of formula violence restricts freedom and chills originality. The violence formula is, in fact, a de facto censorship extending the dynamics of domination, intimidation, and repression domestically and globally. Much of the typical political and legislative response exploits the anxieties violence itself generates and offers remedies ranging from labeling and advisories to even more censorship.

There is a liberating alternative. It exists in various forms in most other democratic countries. It is public participation in making decisions about cultural investment and cultural policy. Independent grassroots citizen organization and action can provide the broad support needed for loosening the global marketing noose around the necks of producers, writers, directors, actors, and journalists.[2]

More freedom from violent and other inequitable and intimidating formulas, not more censorship, is the effective and acceptable way to increase diversity and reduce the dependence of program producers on the violence formula, and to reduce television violence to its legitimate role and proportion. The role of Congress, if any, is to turn its antitrust and civil rights oversight on the centralized and globalized industrial structures and marketing strategies that impose violence on creative people and foist it on the children and adults of the world. It is high time to develop a vision of the right of children to be born into a reasonably free, fair, diverse, and nonthreatening cultural environment. It is time for citizen involvement in cultural decisions that shape our lives and the lives of our children.

Notes

1. The study is conducted at the University of Pennsylvania's Annenberg School for Communication in collaboration with Michael Morgan at the University of Massachusetts at Amherst and Nancy Signorielli at the University of Delaware. Thanks for research assistance are due to Maria Elena Bartesaghi, Cynthia Kandra, Robin Kim, Brian Linson, Amy Nyman, and Nejat Ozyegin.

2. One such alternative is the Cultural Environment Movement (CEM). CEM is a nonprofit educational corporation, an umbrella coalition of independent media, professional, labor, religious, health-related, women's, and minority groups opposed to private corporate as well as government censorship. CEM is working for freedom from stereotyped formulas and for investing in a freer and more diverse cultural environment. It can be reached by writing to Cultural Environment Movement, P.O. Box 31847, Philadelphia, PA 19104.

◆ References

[Editorial]. (1993, September 20). *Broadcasting & Cable*, p. 66.

Auletta, K. (1993, May 17). What won't they do? *The New Yorker*, pp. 45-46.

Gerbner, G. (1993). "Miracles" of communication technology: Powerful audiences, diverse choices and other fairy tales. In J. Wasko (Ed.), *Illuminating the blind spots*. New York: Ablex.

Gerbner, G., Gross, L., Morgan, M., & Signorielli, N. (1993). Growing up with television: The cultivation perspective. In J. Bryant & D. Zillmann (Eds.), *Media effects: Advances in theory and research*. Hillsdale, NJ: Lawrence Erlbaum.

Morgan, M., & Shanahan, J. (1991). Do VCRs change the TV picture? VCRs and the cultivation process. *American Behavioral Scientist, 35*(2), 122-135.

Morgan, M., & Signorielli, N. (1990). Cultivation analysis: Conceptualization and methodology. In N. Signorielli & M. Morgan (Eds.), *Cultivation analysis: New directions in media effects research* (pp. 13-33). Newbury Park, CA: Sage.

Sun, L. (1989). *The limits of selective viewing: An analysis of "diversity" in dramatic programming*. Unpublished master's thesis, Annenberg School for Communication, University of Pennsylvania, Philadelphia.

34

ADVERTISING AND THE CONSTRUCTION OF VIOLENT WHITE MASCULINITY

From Eminem to Clinique for Men

◆ Jackson Katz

The terrorist attacks on the World Trade Center and the Pentagon on September 11, 2001, prompted an intense national conversation about violence and its consequences. Commentators in the print and broadcast media frequently observed that these extraordinary events were without precedent in American history. But although the scale of the carnage on September 11 was certainly unprecedented, horrific violence on American soil is hardly a new subject. In fact, long before 9/11, violence was one of the most pervasive and serious domestic problems in the United States.

In recent years, academics, community activists, and politicians have increasingly been paying attention to the role of the mass media in producing, reproducing, and legitimating this violence.[1] Unfortunately, however, much of the mainstream debate about the effects of media violence on violence in the "real" world fails to include an analysis of gender. Although, according to the Federal Bureau of Investigation (1999), approximately 86% of violent crime is committed by males, newspaper and magazine headline writers continue to use degendered language to talk about the perpetrators of violence (e.g., "kids killing kids"). It is unusual even to hear mention of "masculinity" or "manhood" in these discussions, much less a thorough deconstruction of the gender order and the way that cultural definitions of masculinity and femininity might be implicated. Under these conditions, a class-conscious discussion of masculine gender construction is even less likely.

In the past few years, there has been growing attention paid in media and cultural studies to the power of cultural images of masculinity. This focus is long overdue. But historically, an absence of a thorough body of research and inquiry into the construction of masculine imagery is consistent with the lack of attention paid to other dominant groups. Discussions about racial representation in media, for example, tend to focus on African Americans, Asians, or Hispanics, and not on Anglo Whites.[2] Writing about the representation of Whiteness as an ethnic category in mainstream film, Richard Dyer (1988) argues that "white power secures its dominance by seeming not to be anything in particular"; "Whiteness" is constructed as the norm against which nondominant groups are defined as "other." Robert Hanke (1992), in an article about hegemonic masculinity in transition, argues that masculinity, like Whiteness, "does not appear to be a cultural/historical category at all, thus rendering invisible the privileged position from which (white) men in general are able to articulate their interests to the exclusion of the interests of women, men and women of color, and children" (p. 186).

There has been some discussion, since the mid-1970s, of the ways in which cultural definitions of White manhood have been shaped by stereotypical representations in advertising. One area of research has looked at the creation of modern masculine archetypes such as the Marlboro Man. In the 21st century, it has become apparent that this research needs to be increasingly international in focus. Satellite telecommunications, the Internet, and other technological developments have rendered obsolete the notion of discreet national boundaries for advertising and other cultural imagery. And as Naomi Klein argues in her groundbreaking book *No Logo* (1999), it is crucial to understand not simply how advertisers create and sell images but how multinational corporations in the contemporary era essentially construct and sell brand identity and loyalty.

But in the midst of these historical developments, there has been little attention paid, in scholarship or antiviolence activism, to the relationship between the construction of violent masculinities in what Sut Jhally (1990) refers to as the "commodity image-system" of advertising and the pandemic of violence committed by boys and men in the homes and streets of the United States.

This chapter is an attempt to sketch out some of the ways in which hegemonic constructions of masculinity in mainstream magazine advertising normalize male violence. Theorists and researchers in profeminist sociology and men's studies have developed the concept of *masculinities,* as opposed to *masculinity,* to more adequately describe the complexities of male social position, identity, and experience. At any given time, the class structure and gender order produce numerous masculinities stratified by socioeconomic class, racial and ethnic difference, and sexual orientation. The central delineation is between the hegemonic, or dominant, masculinity (generally, White, heterosexual, and middle class) and the subordinated masculinities.

But although there are significant differences between the various masculinities, in patriarchal culture, violent behavior is typically gendered male. This doesn't mean that all men are violent but that violent behavior is considered masculine (as opposed to feminine) behavior. This masculine gendering of violence in part explains why the movie *Thelma and Louise* in the early 1990s touched such a chord and still resonates a decade later: Women had appropriated, however briefly, the male prerogative for, and identification with, violence.

One need not look very closely to see how pervasive is the cultural imagery linking various masculinities to the potential for violence. One key source of constructions of dominant masculinity is the movie industry, which has introduced into the culture a seemingly endless stream of violent male icons. Tens of millions of people, disproportionately male and young, flock to theaters and rent videocassettes of the "action-adventure" (a Hollywood euphemism for *violent)* films of White male icons such as Arnold Schwarzenegger, Sylvester Stallone, Jean-Claude Van Damme, Bruce Willis, et al.

These cultural heroes first rose to prominence in an era, the mid- to late 1970s into the 1980s, in which working-class White males had to contend with increasing economic instability and dislocation, the perception of gains by people of color at the expense of the White working class, and a women's movement that overtly challenged male hegemony. In the face of these pressures, then, it is not surprising that White men (especially but not exclusively working class) would latch onto big, muscular, violent men as cinematic heroes. For many males who were experiencing unsettling changes, one area of masculine power remained attainable: physical size and strength and the ability to use violence successfully.

Harry Brod (1987) and other theorists have argued that macro changes in postindustrial capitalism have created deep tensions in the various masculinities. For example, according to Brod,

> Persisting images of masculinity hold that "real men" are physically strong, aggressive, and in control of their work. Yet the structural dichotomy between manual and mental labor under capitalism means that no one's work fulfills all these conditions. Manual laborers work for others at the low end of the class spectrum, while management sits at a desk. Consequently, while the insecurities generated by these contradictions are personally dissatisfying to men, these insecurities also impel them to cling all

the more tightly to sources of masculine identity validation offered by the system. (p. 14)

One way that the system allows working-class men (of various races) the opportunity for what Brod refers to as "masculine identity validation" is through the use of their body as an instrument of power, dominance, and control. For working-class males, who have less access to more abstract forms of masculinity-validating power (economic power, workplace authority), the physical body and its potential for violence provide a concrete means of achieving and asserting "manhood."

At any given time, individual men as well as groups of men are engaged in an ongoing process of creating and maintaining their own masculine identities. Advertising, in a commodity-driven consumer culture, is an omnipresent and rich source of gender ideology. Contemporary ads contain numerous images of men who are positioned as sexy because they possess a certain aggressive "attitude." Men's magazines and mainstream newsweeklies are rife with ads featuring violent male icons, such as uniformed football players, big-fisted boxers, and leather-clad bikers. Sports magazines aimed at men, and televised sporting events, carry millions of dollars worth of military ads. In the past 20, there have been hundreds of ads for products designed to help men develop muscular physiques, such as weight training machines and nutritional supplements.

Historically, use of gender in advertising has stressed difference, implicitly and even explicitly reaffirming the "natural" dissimilarity of males and females. In early 21st century, U.S. culture, advertising that targets young White males (with the exception of fashion advertising, which often features more of an androgynous male look), has the difficult task of stressing gender difference in an era characterized by a loosening of rigid gender distinctions. Stressing gender difference in this context means defining masculinity in opposition to femininity.

This requires constantly reasserting what is masculine and what is feminine. One of the ways this is accomplished, in the image system, is to equate masculinity with violence, power, and control (and femininity with passivity).

The need to differentiate from the feminine by asserting masculinity in the form of power and aggression might at least partially account for the ubiquity of representations of male violence in contemporary advertising, as well as in video games, rap/rock music and video, children's toys, cartoons, professional wrestling, Hollywood film, and the sports culture.

By helping to differentiate masculinity from femininity, images of masculine aggression and violence—including violence against women—afford young males across class a degree of self-respect and security (however illusory) within the more socially valued masculine role.

◆ Violent White Masculinity in Advertising

The appeal of violent behavior for men, including its rewards, is coded into mainstream advertising in numerous ways: from violent male icons (such as particularly aggressive athletes or superheroes) overtly threatening consumers to buy products to ads that exploit men's feelings of not being big, strong, or violent enough by promising to provide them with products that will enhance those qualities. These codes are present in television and radio commercials as well, but this chapter focuses primarily on mainstream American magazine ads (*Newsweek, People, Sports Illustrated, GQ, Maxim, Rolling Stone, Spin,* etc.), from the mid-1990s through 2001.

Several recurring themes in magazine advertising targeting men help support the equation of White masculinity and violence. Among them are the following: The angry, aggressive, White working-class male as antiauthority rebel (21st-century version);

violence as genetically programmed male behavior; the use of military and sports symbolism to enhance the masculine identification and appeal of products; the association of muscularity with ideal masculinity; and the equation of heroic masculinity with violent masculinity. Let us now consider, briefly, each of these themes.

THE ANGRY, AGGRESSIVE, WHITE WORKING-CLASS MALE AS ANTIAUTHORITY REBEL (21ST-CENTURY VERSION)

The rock, heavy metal, and rap-metal cultures of recent decades have produced numerous male artists who perform a White, working-class "rebel" masculinity that embodies all sorts of violent angers and resentments and seeks validation in the defiance of middle-class manners and social conventions. Not surprisingly, advertisers have sought to use this young-White-man-with-an-attitude in their marketing of products to young males. In one characteristic example, a 2001 ad for JVC audio equipment features Nikki Sixx of the 1980s metal band Mötley Crüe with an angry expression on his face. Prominently placed in the foreground (visually "in your face") is a large speaker system and CD/cassette unit. The copy reads "Big, Mean, Loud."

The superstar White rap artist Eminem (nee Marshall Mathers) is the most well-known of the contemporary "angry White males" with attitude who have been skillfully marketed to young people—especially White boys—as antiauthority "rebels." The rage-rock group Limp Bizkit and the metal rapper Kid Rock are other notables in this genre. Compared to their "rebel" actor counterparts from the postwar era of Hollywood cinema (e.g., Marlon Brando, James Dean), these 21st-century artists affect a much more overtly violent and aggressive demeanor.

Eminem, for example, in ads for his music CDs and other projects, is almost always portrayed with scowls on his face or with looks of grim seriousness. But in the marketing of artists like Eminem, it is important to note that the line between advertisements and editorial copy is erased, because magazine covers and articles about him essentially function as ads for his music, as well as the products he is selling. Sometimes the process is blatant, as in the high-profile cover of the seventh anniversary issue of *Vibe* magazine, which features Eminem pictured next to his mentor, the misogynous African American gangsta rapper-producer Dr. Dre. Eminem is wearing a cap with the Nike swoosh logo prominently displayed—a decidedly unrebellious fashion statement.

In magazine layouts that function as de facto unpaid ads, Eminem is often portrayed in cartoonishly violent guises. In one 2000 layout in the hip-hop magazine *The Source*, he appeared in an old hockey goalie's mask (an homage to the serial murderer Jason from the film *Friday the 13th*), holding a chainsaw. The article was titled "American Psycho"; the page smeared with a bloodied handprint. People who are offended by these sorts of crude displays of violent male rage, including feminists and gay and lesbian civil rights activists who object to Eminem's blatant misogyny and gay-bashing lyrics and public pronouncements, are ridiculed by the rapper's defenders as "not getting it," or not having a sense of humor.

Judging by the number of violent poses struck by Eminem in similar magazine articles and other promotional materials (the tatoo on his stomach, featured prominently and repeatedly in photo layouts, reads "Kim rot in pieces"; Kim is his wife/ ex-wife), it is safe to say that violent posturing is central to Eminem's constructed identity as a rebellious White rapper who's "keepin' it real." But what exactly is a White rapper like Eminem rebelling *against*? Powerful women who oppress weak and vulnerable men? Omnipotent gays and lesbians who make life a living hell for straight people? Eminem's misogyny and homophobia, far from being rebellious,

are actually extremely traditional and conservative. But because his crude profanity offends a lot of parents, kids can "rebel" against their parents' wishes by listening to him, buying his CDs, and so on. The irony is that by buying into Eminem's clever "bad boy" act, they are being obedient, predictable consumers. ("If you want to express your rebellious side, we have just the right product for you! The Marshall Mathers LP! Come get your Slim Shady!") It's rebellion as a purchasable commodity.

Some admirers of Eminem, Limp Bizkit, and Kid Rock argue that their detractors don't respond well to the antisocial disdain and nihilism—found in parts of young, White, working-class male culture—that these now multimillionaires capture so skillfully in their personae and music. There might be some truth to this. But it is also true that advertisers for the music and movie industries are constantly developing marketing strategies to appeal to the lucrative markets of young consumers of all socioeconomic classes. In recent years, one of the most successful of these strategies involves praising young consumers for how media-savvy they are, especially in contrast with their parents and other older people. Then, as the young consumers absorb the props for their sophistication, they are sold CDs, movies, and myriad other products whose sensibilities supposedly prove how "savvy" their purchasers really are. This process would be laughable were it not for the fact that some of the products (e.g., Eminem) often simply reinforce or legitimate violent masculinity—and other cultural pathologies—as rebellious or "cool."

VIOLENCE AS GENETICALLY PROGRAMMED MALE BEHAVIOR

One way that advertisers demonstrate the "masculinity" of a product or service is through the use of violent male icons or types from popular history. This helps to associate the product with manly needs and pursuits that presumably have existed from time immemorial. It also furthers the ideological premise, disguised as common sense, that men have always been aggressive and brutal and that their dominance over women is biologically based. "Historical" proof for this is shown in a multitude of ways.

An ad for the Chicago Mercantile Exchange, an elite financial institution, depicts a medieval battlefield where muscle-bound toy figurines, accompanied by para-doxically muscular skeleton men, prepare to engage in a sword fight. They might wear formal suits and sit behind desks, the ad implies, but the men in high finance (and those whose money they manage) are actu-ally rugged warriors. Beneath the veneer of wealth and class privilege, all men are really brutes. The text reads "How the Masters of the Universe Overcame the Attack of the Deutschemarks."

An ad for Trojan condoms features a giant-sized Roman centurion, in full uni-form, muscles rippling, holding a package of condoms as he towers over the buildings of a modern city. Condom manufacturers know that the purchase and use of con-doms by men can be stressful, partially because penis size, in popular Western folk-lore, is supposedly linked to virility. One way to assuage the anxieties of male con-sumers is to link the product with a recog-nizably violent (read: masculine) male archetype. It is no coincidence that the two leading brands of condoms in the United States are named for ancient warriors and kings (Trojan and Ramses).

Sometimes products with no immedi-ately apparent connection to gender or violence nonetheless make the leap. A mid-1990s ad for Dell computers, for example, shows a painting of a group of White cow-boys on horseback shooting at mounted Indians who are chasing them. The copy reads "Being Able to Run Faster Could Come in Real Handy." The cowboys are foregrounded and the viewers are posi-tioned to identify with them against the Indian "other." The cowboys' violence is depicted as defensive, a construction that

was historically used to justify genocide. The ad explains that "you never know when somebody [read: Indians, Japanese business competitors] is going to come around the corner and surprise you." It thus masculinizes the White middle-class world of the computer business by using the violent historical metaphor of cowboys versus Indians.

An even more sinister use of historical representations involves portraying violence that would not be acceptable if shown in contemporary settings. Norwegian Cruise Line, for example, in an ad that ran in the 1990s in major newsweekly magazines, depicted a colorful painting of a scene on a ship's deck, set sometime in the pirate era, where men, swords drawn, appear simulta-neously to be fighting each other while a couple of them are carrying off women. The headline informs us that Norwegian is the "first cruise line whose entertainment doesn't revolve around the bar."

It is highly doubtful that the cruise line could have set what is clearly a rape or gang rape scenario on a modern ship. It would no doubt have prompted feminist protests about the company's glorification of the rape of women. Controversy is avoided by depicting the scene as historical.[3] But Norwegian Cruise Line, which calls itself "The Pleasure Ships," in this ad reinforces the idea that rape is a desirable male pastime. Whether intentional or not, the underlying message is that real men (pirates, swashbucklers) have always enjoyed it.

USE OF MILITARY AND SPORTS SYMBOLISM TO ENHANCE THE MASCULINE IDENTIFICATION AND APPEAL OF PRODUCTS

Well before the September 11, 2001, attacks prompted an upsurge in advertisers' use of martial displays of patriotic senti-ment, advertisers who wanted to demon-strate the unquestioned manliness of their products could do so by using one of the two key subsets in the symbolic image system of violent masculinity: the military and sports. Uniformed soldiers and players, as well as their weapons and gear, appear frequently in ads of all sorts. Advertisers can use these signifiers in numerous creative ways to make their products appear manly.

One ad, for *The Economist* magazine, manages explicitly to link the magazine with White heterosexual sexism, military masculinity, and imperialist aggression, all in one page. In the top left-hand corner is a photo of a classic (White) pinup girl from the 1940s at the beach in a bathing suit. The text reads "Sex Symbol." In the top right-hand corner is a picture of a U.S. fighter jet in flight. The text reads "Power Symbol." Front and center is a picture of the magazine's cover, with a distorted map of North America portrayed as towering over Central and South America; Africa and Asia are small and off to the side. The map is headlined "America's world" and features one-word designations of various geographical areas: "Surfin'" in the Pacific; "Huntin'" in northwest Canada; "Exploitin'" in Central America; "Fishin'" in the Caribbean; "Fightin'" in Africa and Asia. The bold text underneath says simply: "Status Symbol." It might as well say, "This magazine is for 'real' men, and real men are sexist and violent."

The now defunct Joe Camel cigarette ads, which also attracted controversy in the 1990s due to Camel's use of cartoon images to lure children and adolescents, featured numerous displays of submarines surfacing or fighter jets streaking by as Joe Camel stood confidently in the foreground. One ad featured Joe Camel himself wearing an air force bomber pilot's jacket. The message to the young boys and adolescent males targeted by the campaign was obvious: Violence (as signified by the military vehicles) is cool and suave. The sexy blond woman gazing provocatively at the James Bond-like camel provided female ratification of Joe's masculinity.

Ads for the military itself also show the linkage between masculinity and force. The U.S. military spends more than $100 million annually on advertising. Not surprisingly, armed services advertisements appear disproportionately on televised sporting events and in sports and so-called men's magazines. Military ads are characterized by exciting outdoor action scenes with accompanying text replete with references to "leadership," "respect," and "pride." Although these ads sometimes promote the educational and financial benefits of military service, what they're really selling to young working-class males is a vision of masculinity—adventurous, aggressive, and violent—that provides men of all classes with a standard of "real manhood" against which to judge themselves.

Boxers and football players appear in ads regularly, promoting products from underwear to deodorants. A black-and-white photo of a young White man in uncovered football shoulder pads adorns some Abercrombie and Fitch advertising layouts. In Abercrombie and Fitch mall stores, a dramatically enlarged version of this photo greets customers as they enter the store. Abercrombie and Fitch does not sell football equipment. Rather, the clothing company—which attracted attention and controversy in the 1990s for its risqué layouts of scantily clad teenagers—is presumably seeking to accentuate its appeal to adolescent males by creating brand identification with the archetypally masculine young man: the football player.

Sometimes athletes are positioned simply to sanction the masculinity of a suspect product. For example, a 1999 ad for a new cologne by Clinique depicts a clean-cut young White man in a football uniform, holding a football and running toward the camera. Standing beside him is a young White woman, in a white dress, holding a white frosted birthday cake with candles. The only copy says, in bold letters, "Clinique Happy. Now for Men." It seems reasonable to infer that the goal of this ad was to shore up the masculine image of a product whose name (Clinique) has feminine connotations. The uniformed football player, a signifier of violent masculinity, achieves this task by visually transmitting the message: Real men can wear Clinique. The birthday cake in the woman's arms, of course, sends a signal to women that this product is an acceptable present for their (masculine) boyfriends.

Advertisers know that using high-profile violent male athletes can help to sell products, such as yogurt and light beer, that have historically been gendered female. Because violence establishes masculinity, if these guys (athletes) use traditionally "female" products, they don't lose their masculinity. Rather, the masculinity of the product—and hence the size of the potential market—increases. Miller Brewing Company proved the efficacy of this approach in its long-running television ad campaign for Lite beer. The Miller Lite campaign, which first appeared in the early 1970s, helped bring Miller to the top of the burgeoning light beer market and is often referred to as the most successful TV ad campaign in history.

THE ASSOCIATION OF MUSCULARITY WITH IDEAL MASCULINITY

Men across socioeconomic class and race might feel insecure in their masculinity, relatively powerless or vulnerable in the economic sphere and uncertain about how to respond to the challenges of women in many areas of social relations. But, in general, males continue to have an advantage over females in the area of physical size and strength. Because one function of the image system is to legitimate and reinforce existing power relations, representations that equate masculinity with the qualities of size, strength, and violence thus become more prevalent.

The anthropologist Alan Klein (1993)[4] has looked at how the rise in popularity of bodybuilding is linked to male insecurity. "Muscles," he argues, "are about more than just the functional ability of men to defend home and hearth or perform heavy labor. Muscles are markers that separate men from each other and, most important perhaps, from women. And while he may not realize it, every man—every accountant, science nerd, clergyman, or cop—is engaged in a dialogue with muscles" (p. 16).

Advertising is one area of the popular culture that helps feed this "dialogue." Sports and other magazines with a large male readership are filled with ads offering men products and services to enhance their muscles. Often these ads explicitly equate muscles with violent power, as in an ad for a Marcy weight machine that tells men to "Arm Yourself" under a black-and-white photograph of a toned, muscular White man, biceps and forearms straining, in the middle of a weight lifting workout. The military, too, offers to help men enhance their bodily prowess. An ad for the Army National Guard shows three slender young men, Black and White, working out, over copy that reads "Get a Part-Time Job in Our Body Shop."

The discourse around muscles as signifiers of masculine power involves not only working-class men but also middle- and upper-class males. This is apparent in the male sports subculture, where size and strength are valued by men across class and racial boundaries. But muscularity as masculinity is also a theme in advertisements aimed at upper-income males. Many advertisers use images of physically rugged or muscular male bodies to masculinize products and services geared to elite male consumers. An ad for the business insurance firm Brewer and Lord uses a powerful male body as a metaphor for the more abstract form of (financial) power. The ad shows the torso of a muscular man curling a barbell, accompanied by a headline that reads "The benefits of muscle defined." The text states that "the slow building of strength and definition is no small feat. In fact, that training has shaped the authority that others see in you, as well."

Saab, targeting an upscale, educated market in the early 1990s, billed itself as "the most intelligent car ever built." But in one ad, they called their APC Turbo "the muscle car with a social conscience"— which signaled to wealthy men that by driving a Saab they could appropriate the working-class tough guy image associated with the concept of a "muscle car" while making clear their more privileged class position. In a more recent version of the same phenomenon, Chevy, in a 2001 ad for the expensive Avalanche SUV, shows a close-up photo of the big vehicle turning sharply on a dusty road. The text reads "Rarely do you get to see the words 'ingenious' and 'muscle-bound' in the same sentence."

THE EQUATION OF HEROIC MASCULINITY WITH VIOLENT MASCULINITY

The cultural power of Hollywood film in the construction of violent masculinity is not limited to the movies themselves. In fact, many more people see the advertising for a given film than see the film itself.

Advertising budgets for major Hollywood releases typically run in the millions of dollars. Larger-than-life billboards enhance the heroic stature of the icons. Movie ads appear frequently on prime-time TV and daily in newspapers and magazines. Not surprisingly, these ads highlight the movies' most violent and sexually titillating scenes.

Violence on-screen, like that in real life, is perpetrated overwhelmingly by males. Males constitute the majority of the audience for violent films, as well as violent sports such as football and hockey. It is important to note, then, that what is being sold is not just "violence," but rather a glamorized form of violent masculinity.

Guns are an important signifier of virility and power and hence are an important part of the way violent masculinity is constructed and then sold to audiences. In fact, the presence of guns in magazine and newspaper ads is crucial in communicating the extent of a movie's violent content. Because so many films contain explicit violence, images of gun-toting macho males (police detectives, old West gunslingers, futuristic killing machines) pervade the visual landscape.

Conclusion ◆

Research over the past decade in sociology, media, and cultural studies strongly suggests that we need to develop a much more sophisticated approach to understanding cultural constructions of masculinity. Feminists, who have been at the forefront in studying the social construction of gender, have, historically, focused on images and representations of women. Clearly, we need to continue with a similarly intensive examination of the representation of men— particularly in light of the ongoing crisis of men's violence in our society, and around the world.

This chapter focuses attention on constructions of violent White masculinity in mainstream magazine advertising. But we need also to examine critically a number of other areas where violent masculinities are produced and legitimated: comic books, toys, the sports culture, professional wrestling, comedy, interactive video, music video, pornography. This will help us to understand more fully the links between the construction of gender and the prevalence of violence, which might then lead to more effective antiviolence interventions.

Notes ◆

1. *Violence* refers to immediate or chronic situations that result in injury to the psychological, social, or physical well-being of individuals or groups. For the purpose of this chapter, I will use the American Psychological Association's (APA) more specific definition of interpersonal

violence. Although acknowledging the multi-dimensional nature of violence, the APA Commission on Violence and Youth defines interpersonal violence as "behavior by persons against persons that threatens, attempts, or completes intentional infliction of physical or psychological harm" (APA, 1993, p. 1).

2. Although hegemonic constructions of masculinity affect men of all races, there are important variables due to racial differences. Because it is not practical to do justice to these variables in a chapter of this length, and because the vast majority of images of men in mainstream magazine advertisements are of White men, for the purpose of this chapter, I will focus on the *constructions of* various White masculinities.

3. Some feminist groups did protest the ad, such as the Cambridge, Massachusetts-based group Challenging Media Images of Women. But the protests never reached a wide audience and had no discernible effect.

4. The article cited here was excerpted from Klein's book *Little Big Men: Bodybuilding Subculture and Gender Construction* (Albany: State University of New York Press, 1993).

References ◆

American Psychological Association. (1993). *Violence and youth: Psychology's response.* Washington, DC: Author.

Brod, H. (Ed.). (1987). *The making of masculinities: The new men's studies.* Boston: Allen and Unwin.

Dyer, R. (1988). White. *Screen, 29*(4), 44-65.

Federal Bureau of Investigation. (1999). *Uniform crime reports.* Washington, DC: Author.

Hanke, R. (1992). Redesigning men: Hegemonic masculinity in transition. In S. Craig (Ed.), *Men, masculinity and the media* (pp. 185-198). Newbury Park, CA: Sage.

Jhally, S. (1990, July). Image-based culture: Advertising and popular culture. *The World and I,* pp. 508-519.

Klein, A. (1993, January). Little big men. *Northeastern University Magazine,* pp. 14-19.

Klein, N. (1999). *No logo.* New York: Picador USA.

35

THE MIGHTY MORPHIN POWER RANGERS

Teachers Voice Concern

◆ Diane E. Levin and Nancy Carlsson-Paige

The Mighty Morphin Power Rangers have been in the spotlight of children's popular culture since the fall of 1993. Since that time they have been a presence to contend with in classrooms and a dilemma for many teachers, who ask how to respond to this media craze and its effects on the children they teach.

The creator and marketer of Power Rangers, Saban Productions, has been more successful in its marketing efforts than any of its predecessors (Pecora in press). By 1994 the Power Ranger toy line had reached the top of the best-selling toy charts, and retail sales of Power Ranger products surpassed one billion dollars, a record for the industry. The release of the Power Ranger movie in June 1995 promises to keep this theme in the forefront of children's minds for the foreseeable future.

Power Rangers is the latest in a long list of children's TV programs that have been successfully marketed to young children along with whole lines of toys and other licensed products—such as clothing, food, video games, and other media—since the deregulation of children's broadcasting by the

NOTE: From *Young Children*, September 1995. Copyright © 1995. Reprinted with permission from the National Association for the Education of Young Children.

Federal Communications Commission in 1984 (Carlsson-Paige & Levin 1990). The Power Rangers have replaced the Teenage Mutant Ninja Turtles (Carlsson-Paige & Levin 1991), which were at the top of the charts for many years. Before the Ninja Turtles were G.I. Joe, Transformers, and Masters of the Universe. All of these shows are based on similar themes, which pit good against evil in a world filled with gratuitous violence.

Each Power Ranger TV episode follows the same basic formula. Five teenagers (three boys and two girls) are doing normal, everyday activities when they are unexpectedly attacked by the henchmen of an intergalactic witch named Rita Repulsa (replaced in the fall 1994 season with Dr. Zed, her former boss) who are trying to take over the universe and can only be stopped by the Power Rangers. When the going gets rough, the five teenagers become Power Rangers by "morphing" (transforming through special effects) into costumed superheroes, each with a different designated color. They fight with karate chops and their special powers—enlisting the superpowers of giant, mechanical dinosaurs. The Power Rangers always win, return to everyday teenage life in high school, and wait for the next episode, which is essentially a repeat of the previous one.

But while the Power Ranger program has features similar to many other children's cartoon programs, it also has special features that distinguish it from its predecessors. First, there are more acts of violence per hour than on any previous show—averaging more than 200 acts of violence per hour (Lisosky 1995), compared with just under 100 for the Teenage Mutant Ninja Turtles. Second, the Power Ranger show intersperses footage of real-life actors and settings with special effects and animation footage (imported from a television program in Japan), so that children see real actors doing what up until now was carried out only by characters in animated cartoons.

Teachers Voice Concern ◆

Almost immediately after the show premiered on television, teachers began telling us their concerns about how the Power Rangers were affecting children in their classrooms. They reported seeing an increase in violence as children imitated what they had seen on the screen. They described concerns about children's play, as children tried to be Power Rangers and ended up hurting other children with their Power Ranger moves. They also mentioned children who were very confused over whether the Power Rangers were pretend or real.

Teacher concern about the effects of media violence on young children is not a new phenomenon (National Association for the Education of Young Children [NAEYC] 1990; Carlsson-Paige & Levin 1991). As soon as children's broadcasting was deregulated in 1984—which, for the first time, made it legal for manufacturers to make TV shows to sell program-linked toys—teachers began noting increased levels of violence among children in their classrooms and increases in repetitive, imitative, and violent play (Carlsson-Paige & Levin 1987).

The United States is the most violent country in the industrialized world, with homicide, rape, assault, and battery rates many times those of other countries. While the reasons for the violence epidemic in the United States are many and go to the very root of social and economic injustice, the mass media play a significant role in socializing young children into violence (Garbarino 1992; American Psychological Association 1993). Crime rates are increasing most rapidly among youth who were in their formative early years when children's TV was deregulated and violent programs and toys successfully deluged childhood culture.

Children ages 2 to 5 watch an average of four hours of television a day—that equals seven years of TV by high school graduation.

Much of this programming is very violent; by the time children complete elementary school they will have seen 8,000 killings and more than 100,000 other acts of violence (Diamant 1994). Beyond the actual numbers, much of what children see on television does not meet their developmental needs, thereby potentially undermining their healthy development (Levin & Carlsson-Paige 1994).

◆ *The Study*

The many concerns voiced by teachers about the Power Rangers led us to examine these concerns more closely. We wanted to collect information on what teachers are seeing, the nature of their concerns, and how widespread these concerns are. We also wanted to find out more about what teachers are doing to respond to the presence of the Power Rangers in their classrooms.

In the winter of 1994, we distributed a questionnaire on the Power Rangers[1] to interested teachers working with young children. This is a technique we have used effectively in the past to explore teachers' observations of how mass media affects children in their classrooms (Carlsson-Paige & Levin 1987, 1991).

WHAT TEACHERS SAID

Almost all respondents (97%) voiced at least one concern about the negative effects of the Power Rangers on children in their classrooms. Most of the concerns teachers expressed fell into two main areas:

◆ increase levels of violence among children; or

◆ violence, imitation, and lack of creativity in children's play.

Many concerns were also expressed about some children's

◆ confusion about fantasy and reality;

◆ obsessive involvement with the Power Rangers;

◆ use of the Power Rangers as role models for social behavior; and/or

◆ preoccupation with buying Power Rangers products.

Concerns about violence. The concern about Power Rangers most commonly expressed by teachers (98% of the teachers who voiced a concern) is related to seeing increased levels of violence and aggression among children. Teachers associate the Power Rangers with aggression in a wide range of children's school activities, including their overall interactions with one another; their play; their casual conversations throughout the day; their artwork, story "writing," and storytelling; and their free-time activities in the classroom and on the playground. Many teachers also believe that the Power Rangers are desensitizing children to violence and undermining their conflict-resolution skills. Following are typical comments teachers made:

◆ "The Power Rangers seem to be taking a good part of the children's energy and turning it into the negative behavior that is modeled for them on the show. Kids are getting hurt."

◆ "The playground became so violent that we have to tell children not to play Power Rangers at school."

◆ "One child is so consumed with the Power Rangers that all his play consists of is violence, and it scares me."

◆ "We have seen children actually push each other over and walk on someone who is in their way and then say they did it because they are Power Rangers."

◆ "When the boys draw Power Ranger pictures with blood dripping from faces or out of stomachs and laugh the whole time, I fear they are learning that pain and suffering are a joke."

◆ "The show says it is teaching about good versus evil, but all the children seem to remember is the fight."

◆ "Power Rangers seem to promote 'gang' behavior, in which children declare themselves the 'good Ranger' and then feel the right to hurt other children who are 'bad.'"

Concerns about play. The second-most frequent concern teachers express about the Power Rangers (58%) is how they are affecting children's play. The most common concerns are that children repeatedly imitate the fighting of the Power Rangers in their play; many conflicts erupt as children imitate Power Rangers; and Power Ranger play usually lacks creativity, imagination, or positive content. Here are some comments teachers made about Power Ranger play:

◆ "I feel they [the Power Rangers] encourage more violent play and have interfered with imaginative, cooperative play. I am concerned about the squelching of creativity in play. They are so much a single idea and do not lead into other plot lines."

◆ "When they [the children] play, they cannot 'get out' of the play, and it carries over to all other activities."

◆ "One boy was a real problem because he was obsessed with Power Ranger play. Then, he suddenly dropped them. We talked to his parents, who said they had put away their TV set."

Other concerns. Some teachers are worried about children's confusion over whether the Power Rangers are real or pretend. A few said that children's confusion seems greater with Power Rangers than with previous shows, such as the Teenage Mutant Ninja Turtles, because the show mixes footage of real actors with animation. They also believed that this mixture contributes to the influence of Power Rangers as role models. These are typical comments:

◆ "The fact that they [the Power Rangers] are not animated is one of my biggest concerns. At 4 and 5 years old, the children in my class do not have the cognitive skills to separate the fantasy from the reality of the show."

◆ "I am concerned that, once again, young children have fallen prey, through no fault of their own, to idealizing inappropriate heroes/heroines. They see the Power Rangers as real role models, and then, their role models use physical means—karate, kicking, hitting, etc.—as the way to solve all their problems."

Many teachers worried about the effects that the marketing of Power Ranger products has on children:

◆ "I am ashamed about the twisted values this program reflects about our country—the monetary profit often outweighs that is best for our children."

◆ "It is a thinly veiled direct marketing attempt which takes advantage of my children's need to feel powerful and their love of action and color."

INTERPRETING THE TEACHERS' OBSERVATIONS

The responses to this survey clearly show that teachers believe the Power Rangers are having far-reaching and negative effects on the children in their classrooms. Most of the teachers' concerns focus on three key areas: concerns about play, concerns about violence, and concerns about the extent to which the Power Rangers are serving as role models for children.

Power Rangers and play. Early childhood teachers understand that play is one of the most important resources children have for achieving emotional and intellectual equilibrium and growth. When children play they bring together their personal needs, experiences, and understanding in a creative process, which leads to new understandings and growth. For play to fulfill its role optimally, children must shape it themselves; no two children should play in exactly the same way (Carlsson-Paige & Levin 1987).

Children's television shows such as the Power Rangers present material that is removed from children's direct experience and understanding. Children who watch Power Rangers have difficulty integrating its content with their own experience and imagination, which makes it difficult for them to create meaningful play episodes from this material. Instead, they tend to imitate the shows, acting out what they are able to understand, primarily the kicking, fighting, and shooting they have seen (Boyatzis, Matillo, & Nesbitt in press).

Single-purpose toys marketed along with these shows further this tendency toward imitation. These realistic toys focus children's attention on a single violent action; they show children how to play and channel them into playing violently. As children imitate more and play less, they are at risk of losing a central avenue for making sense of experience and the feeling of mastery and equilibrium it can provide.

Power Rangers and violence. The early years are a time when children develop the foundation of attitudes and skills for interacting with others in the social world. During these years children can learn the many skills and values involved in relating positively to others; they can learn to control their aggressive impulses when they are angry, to use words instead of fists to express their feelings and needs, and to care about the needs and feelings of others. They build a repertoire of skills through a process of construction in which new learnings continually build on earlier ones. Children take what they have seen and try it out in their play and interactions with each other. If children see a lot of violence, it sets the course of learning in the direction of violence by contributing to the base on which new ideas are built (Carlsson-Paige & Levin 1992; DeVries & Zan 1994; Levin 1994).

Teachers' overwhelming response to the Power Rangers survey points to the fact that the Power Rangers are undermining children's positive social development.

Power Rangers as role models. Many teachers say that children seem to be identifying with Power Rangers to an extent not seen with other superheroes. They describe children who insist on being called by a particular Power Ranger name and will not answer to their own name; who take offense when adults suggest less violent ways to play Power Rangers, saying they "need to do just what the Power Rangers do."

The power of role models is affected by the personal characteristics of the model, whether what the model does is within the child's range of abilities, and whether the child's own situation is perceived to be similar to that of the role model (Slaby et al. 1995). Unlike with previous animated TV superheroes, such as the Ninja Turtles, the Power Rangers are "real people"; they are teenagers (actors) who go to real high school. Many children see them as being like the teenagers they know—like what they want to be now and when they are in high school. One teacher wrote, "Many of my children say they are going to grow up and be the black or red Ranger."

When the role models that children emulate demonstrate violent, antisocial behavior, it has serious effects on young children's social values and development. Because the Power Rangers are valued heroes who are rewarded for their violence, children's identification with them and their aggressive behavior is strengthened (Huesmann 1994).

Deciding What to Do ◆

Finding a classroom approach that deals with the influences of the Power Rangers is very difficult for most teachers (Carlsson-Paige & Levin 1995; Greenberg 1995;

Klemm 1995; Kuykendall 1995). There is a range of options from which teachers can choose (Carlsson-Paige & Levin 1987), but none of them is perfect. What seems most important is to be aware of the options and implications of each approach so that you can adapt and change your approach as you try to meet the needs of everyone in your classroom.

GENERAL GUIDELINES

Whichever option you choose to deal with the Power Ranger phenomenon, work to do the following:

◆ Keep a sense of safety in your classroom as your first guiding principle.

◆ Plan a total curriculum that also presents children with alternative stories that resonate with their deep developmental needs and inspire dramatic and artistic recreations. When teachers do this, they frequently report that media-related play diminishes as children get caught up with the more substantive content.

◆ Talk with children on a regular basis about whatever approach you are taking in the classroom—sharing your reasons, as a teacher, for your preferences; listening to children's thoughts and feelings and reasons for them. Such discussions will help children understand what is behind the classroom approach, will help them feel included in the decision making, and will help you find an approach that best meets the needs of everyone in your classroom community (Levin 1994).

◆ Reach out to parents to involve them in discussions on the issue. Through parent newsletters, meetings, and workshops, parents can also be part of shaping an approach. (NAEYC brochures and position statements on media violence in children's lives and violence in the lives of children [NAEYC 1994] are available to assist teachers with this effort.) As teachers communicate information about this topic to parents, it can influence how parents deal with the Power Rangers at home and can lead to parents and teachers working together to solve this disturbing problem.

Empowering Teachers, ◆ Parents, and Children

Until recent times, the major socializing agents in children's lives were parents and, to a lesser extent, teachers. But since the 1984 lifting of regulations governing children's broadcasting, corporations have increasingly become parents and teachers to children too, teaching them concepts and values and behavior. But these new teachers and parents are not motivated by what is best for children; they are interested in selling products and programs to maximize their profits. As we can see from the responses of the teachers in this study, their influence has been very negative.

There has been almost no public discussion or debate about the change that deregulation has brought to children's lives. What little discussion has occurred has been narrowly framed in terms of first amendment rights for corporations (Carlsson-Paige & Levin 1990; Gerbner 1994). While manufacturers have been protected by government in their unlimited right to market violent products to children and to realize enormous profits from doing so, no public discussion about protecting children and parents from the effects of marketed violence has taken place.

Over the decade since deregulation, teachers—who are trained to understand and nurture children's development and learning—have continually voiced concerns about the effects of these shows and marketing practices (Carlsson-Paige & Levin 1990, 1991). As the Power Rangers have entered the lives of children, families, and schools, we are seeing the voices of teachers continue to go unheeded. It is time to put the interests of children—and, ultimately, all of society—ahead of the drive for profits and to begin listening to teachers, whose expert knowledge should be a guiding force in government policies that affect children.

◆ *Note*

1. This questionnaire is similar to one distributed to teachers in the spring of 1994 for a smaller, preliminary study of the Power Rangers, which was reported in December 1994 (Pereira 1994). The findings reported here are very similar to those reported in the earlier study.

◆ *References*

American Psychological Association. 1993. *Violence and youth: Psychology's response.* Vol. 1, *Summary report of the APA Commission on Violence and Youth.* Washington, DC: American Psychological Association.

Boyatzis, C., G. Matillo, & K. Nesbitt. In press. Effects of the "Mighty Morphin Power Rangers" on children's aggression with peers. *Child Study Journal.*

Carlsson-Paige, N., & D. E. Levin. 1987. *The war play dilemma: Balancing needs and values in the early childhood classroom.* New York: Teachers College Press.

Carlsson-Paige, N., & D. E. Levin. 1990. *Who's calling the shots? How to respond effectively to children's fascination with war play and war toys.* Philadelphia: New Society Publishers.

Carlsson-Paige, N., & D. E. Levin. 1991. The subversion of healthy development and play: Teachers' reactions to the Teenage Mutant Ninja Turtles. *Day Care and Early Education* 19 (2): 14-20.

Carlsson-Paige, N., & D. E. Levin. 1992. Making peace in violent times: A constructivist approach to conflict resolution. *Young Children* 48 (1): 4-13.

Carlsson-Paige, N., & D. E. Levin. 1995. Viewpoint #4—Can teachers resolve the war-play dilemma? *Young Children* 50 (5): 62-63.

DeVries, R., & B. S. Zan. 1994. *Moral classrooms, moral children: Creating a constructivist atmosphere in early education.* New York: Teachers College Press.

Diamant, A. 1994. Special report: Media violence. *Parents Magazine* 69 (10): 40-41, 45.

Garbarino, J., N. Dubrow, K. Kostelny, & C. Parao. 1992. *Children in danger: Dealing with the effects of community violence.* San Francisco: Jossey-Bass.

Gerbner, G. 1994. Reclaiming our cultural mythology: Television's global marketing strategy creates a damaging and alienated window on the world. *In Context* 38: 40-42.

Greenberg, J. 1995. Various viewpoints on violence. Viewpoint #3—Making friends with the Power Rangers. *Young Children* 50 (5): 60-61.

Huesmann, L. R. 1994. Long-term effects of repeated exposure to media violence in childhood. In *Aggressive behavior: Current perspectives,* ed. L. R. Heusmann. New York: Plenum.

Klemm, B. 1995. Various viewpoints on violence. Viewpoint #1—Video-game violence. *Young Children* 50 (5): 53-55.

Kuykendall, J. 1995. Various viewpoints on violence. Viewpoint #2—Is gun play OK here??? *Young Children* 50 (5): 56-59.

Levin, D. E. 1994. *Teaching young children in violent times: Building a peaceable classroom.* Cambridge, MA: Educators for Social Responsibility.

Levin, D. E., & N. Carlsson-Paige. 1994. Developmentally appropriate television: Putting children first. *Young Children* 49 (5): 38-44.

Lisosky, J. M. 1995. *Battling standards worldwide—"Mighty Morphin Power Rangers" fight for their lives.* Paper presented at the World Summit for Children and Television, 12-16 March, in Melbourne, Australia.

National Association for the Education of Young Children. 1990. NAEYC position statement on media violence in children's lives. *Young Children* 45 (5): 18-21.

National Association for the Education of Young Children. 1994. *Position statement as of July 1994*. Washington, DC: Author.

Pecora, N. In press. *The business of entertainment*. New York: Guilford.

Pereira, J. 1994. Caution: "Morphing" may be hazardous to your teacher. *Wall Street Journal*, 7 December, 224 (111): 1, 8

Slaby, R., W. C. Roedell, D. Arezzo, & K. Hendrix. 1995. *Early violence prevention: Tools for teachers of young children*. Washington, DC: National Association for the Education of Young Children.

36

LAY THEORIES OF MEDIA EFFECTS

Power Rangers at Pre-school

◆ Ellen Seiter

◆ *Lay Theories*

In the case studies that follow I trace the variety of teachers' beliefs about media effects—an example of what social scientists call lay theories—and how these beliefs impact media use in the pre-school environment. My motivation in initiating this study was to compare the "weak" theory of media effects held by cultural studies academics, by many industry professionals, and proposed in my own work on children's television (Seiter 1993) with the theories of "strong" effects that were often implicit in conversations I had had with teachers and childcare professionals. Studying "lay theories" allows us to compare academic and lay theories, implicating both in a relationship of mutual influence and finding contradictions in both forms of theorizing.

Going into this study I was conscious of—indeed compelled to reconsider—inconsistencies in my own position as a parent and a teacher vis-à-vis the media. Attending film school in the 1970s, I had been greatly influenced by the ideological analysis of popular media. Yet, as a television audience researcher and later as a parent, I was equally influenced by academic work that celebrates popular pleasure and the possibilities for expressing social resistance through fandom (L. Lewis 1992). As a mother, I was predisposed to feel most sympathetic towards teachers in my study whose lay theories suggested weak media effects (and a permissive attitude towards children) but a race- or gender- or class-conscious critique of media representations.

In engaging in the interviews for this study, I was interested to hear what teachers with a vastly greater store of direct observation than mine thought about the media. It seemed important to note that so many people who dealt with children on a regular basis held a theory of stronger effects than the academics such as myself who had much less direct contact with children other than their own, or contact only with research subjects encountered for a short time.

As used within sociology and anthropology, "lay theories" seek to investigate the cultural determinants on people's common sense and worldview. This kind of study "looks specifically at the sort of information that people select and reject, and how they use this information to examine or test, various hypotheses that they may wish for or have been asked to verify" (Furnham 1988: 46). Social scientists have found that there is a tendency to rely on individual, psychological explanations rather than societal or structural ones. Additionally, "because they are rarely, if ever, presented formally, lay theories are frequently ambiguous, incoherent and inconsistent. That is, people can hold two mutually incompatible or contradictory ideas or beliefs at the same time and not be particularly troubled by that inconsistency" (Furnham 1988: 3). There is a tremendous variation in the quantity and quality of theories that people hold—teachers, as a group, are likely to hold more elaborate lay theories about media effects on children because of their many opportunities to observe large numbers of children and their closeness to scholarly discourse. Adults working in other kinds of fields would, of course, be likely to have undeveloped or nonexistent lay theories about media effects on young children.

To some extent, these interviews testify to the diffusion of a theory of direct media effects—especially among the most professional caretakers. They also indicate, however, the presence of a more flexible, "forgiving" theory of media effects—the cultural studies version, if you will—which attributes greater agency to the children, and places more value on the pleasures of popular culture. The interviews also indicate the ways that theories can be challenged by direct experience, and by the intervention of other factors. As I will demonstrate, the media are deemed most powerful by those working and living in situations of relative privilege; in the poorest centre the media are seen as only one factor—less significant than the part played by poverty, by parental absence, and by violence. . . .

Television and Teachers ◆

In the case studies that follow, I will suggest the ways that some of the work of teachers relates to status production and is explicitly tied to the censorship of popular media materials in the classroom. I will also ask how rules about TV in childcare settings help produce status differences and work to stratify and segment the childcare market.

Babysitting young children is one of the things television does best. Television is undeniably handy for calming children down, confining them to one area, reducing noise in the classroom, and postponing demands for adult attention. But such uses of television are widely condemned by the vast majority of early childhood professionals—or ignored in the publications and research of such groups as the National Association for the Education of Young Children. Objections to television viewing in institutional settings reflect the ambiguous status of these childcare spaces as intermediaries between the home (where television viewing is usually frequent, acceptable) and the school (where explicit learning, rather than merely childcare, is supposed to be taking place). The quantity of television viewing in daycare settings is frequently used to evaluate the quality of centres. If too much television viewing is done, middle-class parents often complain to teachers or centre directors. Some day-care centres claim superiority over home-based daycare, based on their restrictions of TV watching. For this reason, the corporate daycare chain Kindercare, which now claims 1 percent of the entire market, has written policies limiting the amount of time videos may be viewed at school, and specifying what types of video may be watched (such as those with general exhibition [G] or parental guidance [PG] certification only).

Those who care for and teach young children interpret and enact their jobs differently, with the most highly paid and educated women emphasizing their role as teachers, and the lowest paid emphasizing the type of care associated with mothers: such as providing affection, nutrition, and training in personal hygiene (Wrigley 1990: 304-5). Upper-middle-class pre-schools also seem to accomplish some of the important work of inculcating tastes that was formerly reserved for the home, while schools with working-class students emphasize teaching of letters and numbers. . . .

My research suggests that status production is an important part of the work of professional pre-school teachers—as it is with many pink-collar occupations—and the aspect of their work that may be most valued by the women themselves.

Within these parameters of teaching and childcare and the culture of the school or centre, then, complex attitudes and beliefs about media effects evolve—with those most interested in status production and who deem their job to be the most professional also the most critical of the media. . . .

A Montessori Pre-school ◆

Sara Kitses has taught at the suburban Montessori school for twenty-three years. Her half-day classroom combines children between the ages of three and six. She has a total of fifty students in her morning and afternoon classes. Sara describes her students as representing "very little economic diversity," mostly white, with a number of "Oriental children," often faculty children. Tuition is about the highest in the community, nearly $400 per month for less than four hours a day. Sara is the highest paid teacher in the community. The Montessori school is attended largely by the children of attorneys, physicians, and university professors. Sara is about 50 years of age, and holds a bachelor's degree in addition to specialized Montessori training.

More than any other teacher in the study, Sara denied having any knowledge of popular children's programming (she asked, "Who's Barney?" during the interview). In her long experience in the classroom she has picked up a passing acquaintance with some of the names of programmes and characters she herself has never seen—usually to marshal forces to ban them from the classroom. She rigorously excludes videotapes from the classroom, even banning the widely accepted Disney feature films, *Disney Sing-Along* videos, and PBS programmes. Such videos are so widely accepted that they were included in the libraries of every other centre I visited. Disney films have achieved flabbergasting levels of market penetration—as well as acceptance by adults as unobjectionable material. During the interviews, teachers were asked to check off tapes from a list of fifty currently popular videos with which they were familiar or had shown at school. The only video from the list that Sara had ever shown was an animated version of *Dr. Seuss*.

Sara requires parents to attend a meeting before the school year begins (unlike many centres, where children come and go from month to month, Sara's school enrolls children only in the autumn). Sara advises parents that the best thing to do with television is keep it off, but the least they must do is monitor what the child is watching very carefully and remain with the child during viewing. Sara commands considerable respect from the parents in her school, and openly claims the status of an expert with regard to the children—one who knows more than the parent. She has a great deal invested in her identity as a professional teacher. The Montessori school is typical of that segment of the childcare market which promises preparation for entry into the competitive world of the grade school. Sara's status depends in part on the degree to which parents grant her the power to evaluate their children's social and academic skills. Television threatens both the children's cognitive development and her own professional standing—if children can learn from videos, and be entertained through their childhood years, why would they need a special theory of education? Sara's mind was made up a long time ago to the view that television is a very negative influence on everyone—for more than a decade of her married life and throughout her children's early years she had no television set.

Sara's disdain for television dictates her selection of classroom media. She prefers showing 16-mm films and film strips to the students (she estimates she uses film three or four times more often than video), nearly all of them adaptations from children's literature. Videotapes are restricted to programmes such as *National Geographic* specials. While Sara spoke about exhaustion in her job, she does not consider media screenings to be appropriate for teachers to use as a break to do other chores in the classroom (she has a large number of assistant teachers in her class). She monitors the screenings vigilantly, and operates the 16-mm projector herself. While Sara retreats behind the projector, her assistant is in charge of supervising the children during the screenings.

Children and parents bring videotapes to school, and occasionally Sara will show the tape if it is deemed by her to be educational, if she has prescreened it, or if the parent is someone she trusts. All her recent examples of videos she allowed were nonfiction: a computer-animated film with an exclusively musical soundtrack by Philip Glass, distributed by the upmarket Nature Company; *Road Construction Ahead*, an independent video for children (featuring no words, just music). Children can bring objects from home every day to set on a viewing table. The rule is that whatever is brought to school must be educational, a concept that, according to Sara, the children and parents have no trouble grasping.

Sara's complaints about television and children cluster around issues of fantasy and passivity. Primary is the objection that television comes from adults, it does not originate with the child:

> I really believe there's a lot in children, and if you give them a proper environment, they will act upon it and will be constantly learning. They're very eager to learn. And if what you give them is a lot of television and passive stuff, or it's all coming at them, they have to make no decisions whatsoever except to turn it off or on. I don't think that's . . . [what] we should be advocating.

Television, Sara believes, is commercial and makes children want to buy things they don't need; Sara is interested in environmentalism and reducing material wants. She thinks that television is frightening for children, and introduces them to material inappropriate for their age. She even dislikes *Sesame Street* for its "silliness" and its presumption that children's attention spans are very short. In addition, television is simplistic in its advocacy of violent solutions to problems, and Sara finds the sex-role stereotypes and focus on appearance and decoration offensive in the media targeted at girls. Most importantly, television isn't real.

Sara believes children have a very tenuous hold on reality at this age, and the proper role of teachers is to guide them towards reality—thus her heavy emphasis on nonfiction materials. Television pushes children into fantasy and leaves them "perpetually confused." Television stories, unlike some more naturally occurring kinds of role play, do not equate with creative play:

> Certainly, make-believe and role-playing are wonderful and important things. But I don't consider that a fantasy that's being perpetuated by adults. That's coming from within the child, and fantasy coming from within the child is a good thing, but when they are playing games, like Ninja Turtles, they start playing Ninja Turtles on the playground, that's not creative play. It's something that's been given them, so I make a distinction between those two things.

Sara backs up her feelings about television with some stiff rules: no talk about television on the playground, no television play, conversations with her about television programmes are discouraged, and clothing with media characters are not allowed because they distract children (parents are informed of this on the first day). Sara spoke of one boy who was obsessed with what she believed was Nintendo and would talk at great length to the other children about the story and the characters. Sara was annoyed: "It was very boring. The other kids didn't like it." When the boy turned to talking to the teachers, Sara became increasingly forceful in limiting such talk:

> I had decided that I had a limit to listening to him. So when he would come to school, I'd let him talk and then I'd say, "Let's focus on the environment and what you might. . . ." I didn't tell him not to talk about it, I just redirected his attention. "What would you like to choose today? Can I help you make a

choice?" Trying to focus him in the classroom. Finally it came to the point where we had to say to him after that initial time, "While you're at school, we want you to just be talking about school things," because he was throwing the other kids off.

Reading between the lines, I would suspect that the other students' reactions to such television talk may not have been solely boredom, but that some amount of imitation of this unwanted behaviour led Sara to lay down the law.

Curiously, these rules apply much more leniently to girls, who tend to play in groups separate from boys. Sara knows that the girls play games in secret based on *Aladdin* or *Beauty and the Beast* while they are out on the playground. But the girls only play these games out of her hearing, and, because it does not create disruptions, she does not intervene. Also, Sara does not enforce the no-characters rules with the girls' clothing, allowing Jasmine and others to make their way into the classroom on shoes, socks, and T-shirts. She does enforce a ban on jewelry, and encourages parents to dress girls in slacks and sensible shoes.

Sara explained that there is a costume area in the classroom, stocked with Greek, Indian, and Native American costumes that she supplied herself. When the children enact a play, the teacher generates the story, acts as the narrator, and assigns the parts to the children: *Three Little Pigs* or *The Billy Goats Gruff* or *The Little Engine That Could* are examples of stories she might use. I was wondering why Sara saw no contradiction between these guided forms of dramatic play and her position on outside influences. Does an interest in Greece come from within the child, for example, or is it Sara's? Is acting out parts in a pre-scripted story any more creative than acting out parts in a television play? When I first introduced myself to Sara, I explained that I believed TV effects were often misunderstood and overestimated, so that I could discuss what I perceived to be contradictory positions openly with teachers during the follow-up interview. In this exchange I was more openly and directly challenging than in any of the other interviews, in part because I disagreed with and had the least rapport with Sara, and in part because she seemed eager to stake an intellectual defence of her position.

Sara: I like to see them doing role-playing kinds of things that might put them in an adult model. House kinds of things or positive adult kinds of things that where they're enacting something good instead of something horrible. I don't like it when they get involved in fantasy that's created by the media, because it doesn't go anywhere, and it's not coming, again, from within the child. They're re-enacting something they've seen. Part of that's inevitable, part of it's how they learn. But—

Ellen: How could you explain the difference, then, if they're acting out something that's from a book, like you said that you do plays from books?

Sara: That's a fairly structured activity when we do these plays. You take on this role and you are that particular role in the play. You're supposed to follow the storyline. We do that at two levels. One is just informally, in the circle, and the other is this play that these older kids put on every year. And they understand that quite well.

Ellen: So you see this in a different category because that's a structured—

Sara: Exactly, the teacher is guiding the children into that, whereas the other is out on the playground.

Sara is very clear that her role in the classroom is to provide authority and to keep the children under control. Television—as a video shown in class or as references in play or on a T-shirt—symbolizes a loss of control for Sara. Not only is television a world she is almost completely unfamiliar with, but—without viewing it—she has an overwhelming feeling that it undermines everything that her own classroom stands for. Sara's complaints are not the more common ones about rowdy behaviour or aggression, although she mentioned these in passing. Instead, they are phrased in the language of child psychology: TV delays the achievement of the developmental stage when children can discern the difference between reality and fantasy. But her goals are embedded in the dispositions of the class to which she and her students belong. By emphasizing creativity as a spontaneously produced result of children's play, she legitimates her role as an educator in aesthetics as well as behaviour.

In Sara's scheme of value, books are basically good and television is basically bad; film falls somewhere in between. Unlike most of the other teachers, however, for whom any reading is viewed as positive, Sara is unwilling to accept just any books. She discourages the purchase of "grocery-store books" such as *The Berenstein Bears*, as well as any media-related books, such as Disney stories. While her principles emphasize the generation of fantasy from within the child, she approves of the enactment—on the playground or in the classroom—only of stories from canonical children's literature: these forms of imitation are not recognized as imitation per se. Sara prefers older classics. *The Little Engine That Could*, which she reads to the children and has them enact as a play, could be seen as a consumerist fantasy—the story concerns the obstacles to the delivery of a trainload of toys and goodies for children at Christmas. I suspect that the age of the book, and its lack of adaptation into a well-known film or television form, work to exempt it from criticism or scrutiny. Nonfiction is preferred to fiction in the choice of videos, and for computer software. The children are encouraged to write "research papers" on topics of interest to them: this, I would suggest, is the highest activity on Sara's scale of value, combining as it does writing skills, an ordered display of encyclopaedic knowledge, and the rehearsal of forms of work that will certainly be required in grade school.

If television is the school's bad screen, to be used sparingly and purposefully, computers are its good screens, and access is open throughout the school day, limited only by the number of terminals available. Sara spoke with pride about running "ahead of the pack" because her school budget allocates money for computers, which she referred to as "an absolutely critical moment of information right now for young children." The classroom has one computer with a CD-ROM, and another computer set up with WordPerfect and Logo, software that teaches computer programming. A sign-up sheet and two chairs are placed at each computer, but the children are allowed to work alone if they wish. Sara is "flabbergasted" by the speed at which children learn to operate the mouse, and she uses computers heavily for teaching alphabet and reading skills.

Sara says the computers are fun for her because they represent something new after so many years of teaching. She compares CD-ROM to video this way:

> They're interactive. They have to make some choices as to what they want to do. It's much more informational than videos, so they're learning a lot. And there are levels of difficulty, so I find that the 5- and 6-year-old is going to a higher level of difficulty, so he can read and . . . they'll choose things that are challenging to them and interact with them. They're much more popular with boys than girls, but it might be because . . . I don't have any programs on the CD-ROMs yet that are other than mammals and the San Diego Zoo . . . [and] the dinosaur program—the boys tend to dominate it. I think it's better than videos because it's much more interactive, but it can't be their entire life.

. . . Despite Sara's harsh judgement of contemporary children's television, she spoke fondly of her television viewing as a child. Her parents paid little attention to what she watched. Television was a novelty then, and her family was early in getting a set. She never watched cartoons, but she remembers *Ozzie and Harriet, My Friend Flicka, Lassie, The Ed Sullivan Show, Superman,* and *The Jack Benny Show. Lassie* was the show that she felt a strong affection for and she believed television had a positive effect on her:

> Actually I think that it had a positive effect, because I was seeing children in other families and parents that were relating in a very idealistic way. Things were wonderful, and everyone was looking up to a glorious future, so I feel good about the television that I watched, especially *Lassie* because I loved animals so much. This dog did all these wonderful things in relationship to this boy, and his relationship to the family.

Sara's image of television during its golden age is overwhelmingly positive, and, although she has so little experience viewing television over the past twenty years, she compares it negatively to contemporary television: "They addressed heroic kinds of things, solving problems, moral values, ethical values. I think a lot of that has gone.'

Sara's belief system about children and the media typifies that of those with the most training and investment in the professionalization of childcare. She subscribes to a developmental view that emphasizes cognitive deficits, and thus children's incomprehension of television and films (Anderson 1983: 395-400). She constantly interprets children's popular media through the "frame" of developmental psychology. Sara's unfamiliarity with TV and her refusal to listen to the children's talk about it, however, make for a very limited basis on which to formulate her judgements. In fact, Sara herself is somewhat incompetent as a TV viewer, and she uses this studied ignorance about television to signal her erudition—she fears being "just like everybody else." By completely discrediting knowledge about television in the classroom, and limiting media use to those forms—such as 16-mm films—that are more difficult to operate, Sara also maintains her authority over the children.

Hodge and Tripp (1986) construe television as a barrier between teachers and students; middle-class teachers understandably might wish to bar television from the classroom in part because they know less about it than their students do:

> Not only are they untrained to deal with it, but it so often challenges their own knowledge and experience of life and understanding in general. In comparison with most teachers, the average pupil watches a great deal more television and quite different television programmes. Whereas 20 years ago teachers could, in a very real way, safely assume that their pupils knew a great deal less about everything than they did, today the children often know a great deal more than their teachers, albeit about things such as Batman, Spiderman, Superheroes. (1986: 170)

Hodge and Tripp found that while teachers do not overtly punish pupils for bringing their television experience in the class, signals are nevertheless clear that television is not a legitimate topic for discussion at school.

Running underneath the discourse about children's incompetent distinctions between reality and fantasy, and the fragility of their comprehension of narrative, is Sara's belief in the need for adults to shelter children from all that is too intensely emotional, too dramatic, or too peer-oriented because of their moral deficiency, their easy corruptibility. Thus, an essentially romantic view of the innocence of children is masked by the discourse of Piagetian cognitive development.

Reinforcing these notions of deleterious media effects is an equally strong belief in the need for explicit teaching in the area of aesthetics. Systems of distinction extend to clothing (should not be too feminine, should not be too representational—not purchased in discount stores), to books (should not be bought at the grocery store or the mass market). Sara is heavily interested in both what is acquired and how it is acquired—a distinction that increases in importance with status. She confines herself to a very narrow range of media forms, those most closely allied with books. She prefers 16-mm film and CD-ROM as modes of delivery over videos, despite the greater ease and affordability of video. As Bourdieu points out, the more difficult the means of acquisition, the more distinguished the cultural goods. Sara risks the appearance of authoritarianism (with her dress code), arbitrariness (with her censorship rules), and severity (with her banning of toys from the classroom). But if her job is viewed as one of status production and the inculcation of taste, the strictness of her rules and her lack of involvement with nurturing behaviour begin to make sense.

Girls and boys mount different forms of rebellion, different susceptibilities to vulgarity. The girls gravitate towards things that violate the aesthetic code (Disney characters) and the ideology of gender neutrality (frilly dresses). The boys tend to violate the decorum of the classroom by moving in too close to others, being too loud, dominating conversation. The boys' attachment to the media is pathologized because boys more often require direct intervention by the teachers to bring them under control. The genres boys gravitate towards as media fans—science fiction, superheroes, action-adventure—are associated with the derring-do masculinity that is especially disapproved of. These boys are encouraged to develop intellectual, not physical, abilities. Girls simply receive less attention altogether— Sara is disappointed by their lack of curiosity about the computer, for example, but she also finds that the girls conform to her standards as good students more readily.

Within the upper-middle-class milieu of the Montessori school, enforcing the ban on television should not be viewed as a marginal part of Sara's job or a personal idiosyncrasy. The TV ban is—as Sara herself believes it to be—a crucial element of her work. Its justification in terms of theories of childhood development masks a more class-conscious motivation, that of distinguishing these children and their education from that of the common mass. As Randall Collins describes this type of work: "The higher classes . . . observing the cultural style of the classes below them, engage in reflexive role distancing, once again re-establishing their superiority to those who have a less sophisticated view of cultural symbols" (1992: 217). Sara's vigilance in enforcing these norms may pit her against some parents at the school (who are left with many more hours of the day in which to occupy the child while keeping them away from undesirable media, and who generally fail to hold to Sara's high standards), yet on the whole they acquiesce for the sake of securing a successful future in the education system. Television is a key symbol in the very explicit taste- and class-distancing that the school provides.

◆ *Gloria's Family Daycare*

Along with her 74-year-old mother, Gloria Williams owns and teaches in a centre called Gloria's Place, which operates in her own home in an older, integrated neighbourhood close to downtown. This centre is a federally funded provider that offers twenty-four-hour care for children from infancy upwards. In the interviews, Gloria relates with pride that she is the only licensed black childcare-giver in town. Her influence in the community extends well past the children into the lives of the parents, most of whom are divorced. All of her mothers and fathers work for pay outside the home—unlike the Montessori school, where the half-day programme necessitates having one parent at home (meaning, usually, that the father is receiving something that can serve as a "family wage").

A 43-year-old woman from New York with a degree in computer programming, Gloria switched from her office job to childcare at the age of 25. She is not college-educated in early childhood education, although she is well read on the subject and receives a lot of training in the form of workshops as a daycare provider eligible for federal subsidies under Title XX. Gloria's mother works with her and has taught her a great deal about child-rearing. Recalling her own childhood, Gloria mentioned that there always seemed to be children for whom her mother cared around the house. Gloria charges a sliding fee: "I can't see a person making $200 a week and then you're taking over half of that in day-care, you know, I can't, so I have a scale where I go with the person's income."

Gloria conceives of her work very broadly, combining the role of foster mother and teacher. She strives to prepare children for school by teaching them letters and numbers and encouraging them to be independent from adults. She emphasizes giving the children experiences such as trips to the library that their parents don't have time for. Gloria's interview took place during Black History Month, and that week the library books she read to the children clustered around that theme: *The Black Women's Poetry Book*, *The Drinking Gourd*, and biographies of Sojourner Truth and Dr. Martin Luther King. But she also emphasizes the work of providing nutritious food, a safe environment, and affection. She was more frank than any other teacher we spoke to about how trying this kind of work can be:

> Some days . . . I mean, if they had a bad day at home, they're going to try to carry it on through here. [*Mimicking the children's voices*] Don't look at me. Don't touch me. Leave me alone. He's looking cross-eyed at me. What's he staring at? He touched me. He's got my Crayola. I was playing with that block. I don't want this. I'm not hungry. I don't like this kind of juice. Why can't we have

chocolate milk? Stuff like that. Things like that [make] you want to just put their coats on and march them right back out. So some days it's not worth getting up, but you know you have to.

Gloria considers the local wages to be especially low and says that she made twice as much, with all the advantages of a regular schedule (such as weekends, evenings, and vacations free) in her old job. Typical of family childcare providers, Gloria is threatened by many of the hazards of this type of work: burnout, emotional attachment to children she lacks the authority to protect, frustrations stemming from low pay and inadequate funds to care properly for children (Nelson 1990). But it is clear that a primary incentive is her dedication to the children she cares for, both as a foster mother and as a daycare operator.

Gloria's approach to television viewing was keenly interested and unapologetic. She shows tapes frequently and lets children choose among television broadcast and cable channels. (Home-based daycare is much more likely to have cable hook-ups than public daycare centres, thus greatly increasing the options for television viewing.) Of all the teachers interviewed, Gloria was the biggest fan of *Sesame Street* (which she much prefers to *Barney and Friends*), and her children watch the PBS line-up (as well, they visit the local PBS station each year to appear on air during fund drives). They also watch commercial television and choose from her large selection of purchased videotapes (including every Disney movie ever released).

Throughout the interview, Gloria chatted freely about a very wide range of television programmes and films; she was full of information and opinions about them. She had strong preferences about children's TV: for *He-Man* over *Power Rangers; Captain Planet* over World Wrestling Federation characters. She does not impose her preferences, however, when the children select programmes to watch. Television is used in the mornings, when children are

arriving; at lunch time to "quieten them down"; and at pick-up time around 5:00 p.m. Sometimes they have special character days, when they dress in special clothes or colours and enact stories based on their favourite characters. There are no restrictions on clothing or on toys, and Gloria is familiar with the wide range of items—shoelaces to backpacks—with licensed characters, as well as the latest toys and what is available at stores in town. She lets children bring anything to the centre with the exception of toy guns and knives.

In discussing children and television, Gloria refuted the argument against fantasy as a developmentally dangerous activity. Gloria herself is familiar with a broad range of film and television genres and gave the most informed and sophisticated readings of popular culture—those closest to the opinions of media studies academics, in fact, of all the teachers we interviewed. In striking contrast to Sara's concerns that children become lost in television fantasy, Gloria described her students as easily able to understand when something is "nothing but make-believe."

Well, you've got to go on the cartoon thing that they know it's make-believe, in the first place. And I think they're cutting the kids really short if they don't think kids have it in their brain that this is make-believe, that you cannot do it. It's like *The Three Stooges*. We knew we couldn't do those things and still be alive with a normal brain. That's the way it is with the cartoons. And the parents should know that they do have some imagination. And that it's nothing but make-believe. There are some violent cartoons, but you know the person (cartoon character) always gets up and goes on about its business or you see it (alive and unhurt) in the next section. So I think the child knows that it's make-believe.

Gloria reported that children talked about television or movies every morning when they come to her place, and frequently described to her the plots of entire movies they have seen over the weekends. Gloria perceives her children to be much more sophisticated about their viewing and understanding of genre rules than Sara perceives the children at the Montessori school. One reason may be the relaxed atmosphere at the centre and Gloria's openness to listening to conversation about television.

Ellen: Do you find the kids are pretty good at telling the stories of things they've seen?

Gloria: Yeah. A lot of them are. Some of them just roll two stories into one. But I usually let it go like that if they're telling the story, they're telling it their way. If I'm reading a book I'll straighten out the story. But when it's their time to tell the story I let it go. But it depends on when they want to talk. It's just when they want to, it's right there. But if you ask them on command, forget it. They're not going to do anything. You know . . . or you can creep up on them and hear them telling the stories. But if you ask them to get up in front of their own peers to tell the same story—forget it.

Gloria's careful attention to children's play scenarios has also influenced her opinion of television's promotion of violence in children's play. She seemed to have a more accurate, more vivid memory of play—and of movies and television—than many of the other teachers we interviewed. Her childhood as one of seven children—with four brothers—may also have promoted a much higher tolerance for physically active play than other teachers we interviewed. She thinks of rowdy play as substantially similar to the kinds of play of her childhood. For example, she reported that Ninja Turtles, which seemed to be universally reviled among pre-school teachers (and which

Gloria also found uninteresting), was, on second take, nothing more than cowboys and Indians:

> Everything that's on television today is spun off of something that we've seen back in the '50s or the '60s. And it's just made it more vivid, more violent I think. But the basic message is the same, to me it is. You know, you see Roy Rogers hiding behind a tree or a mountain. Or you see the Ninja Turtles hiding behind a street car. They've got a tunnel instead of a mountain. They still hide. They're still waiting to surprise somebody when they come out. Or they're still defending their territory. So John Wayne and the cowboys were defending his ranch, well, they're defending their sewer or raft or wherever . . . I don't see the difference.

Gloria's house has lots of open space, broken-down furniture, or no furniture at all—one reason for her calm attitude towards physical play. She also has a smaller number of children and does not feel compelled by a decorum of having a classroom space. As long as they are not "throwing furniture across the room" or landing punches, she does not interfere. Gloria reported a much higher level of engagement in rowdy play by girls in her classroom:

> Oh yes. We've got kickbox and *Karate Kid*. *X-man* [sic]. What's that show I didn't like? *Power Rangers*. They play a lot of that. That's their karate. They really try to kick, action, do the flips like the Power Rangers. On the *G.I. Joe* they get down and try to hide in little places and spring out on you. Or try to do that *Karate Kid* move on one foot and all that stuff. Now I do have some girls that will get in there with them. They'll stick with them just like the boys do, you know. Try the karate stuff.

Gloria also described boys—pre-school and school age—playing with Barbies and baby dolls at her place after school (noting the boys would not do this at kindergarten or at their own homes: "Gotta be a macho male when you go home. Dad's not gonna let you play."). While all of the other teachers we interviewed felt that popular media increased gender stereotypes, and segregated boys and girls in play, the play that Gloria described was the least gender stereotyped or segregated. "A lot of the boys still play with dolls and get all the baby dolls dressed up . . . it's no big deal. And they can put that down, go watch *Power Rangers*, come back and pick up the baby doll."

Gloria herself reported in her media diary a wide range of choices: videos, books on tape, books, radio, music. Her selections were eclectic in range and she seemed to have relatively little interest in "women's genres" such as soap operas or made-for-TV movies. Her favourite movies feature Jean Claude van Damme and Steven Seagal; her favourite shows are news magazines; she watches all sports except golf. She spoke enthusiastically about the media and the ways in which they provide her with entertainment—TV is especially important to her because she is restricted to her home/workplace seven days a week, with little or no opportunities for vacation.

Gloria's assessments of media and consumer culture were by no means uncritical. She was keenly aware of the manipulative effect of marketing strategies (such as the need kids feel to collect *all* the Power Rangers in a set). She was matter-of-fact in describing the best strategy for dealing with children's material desires:

> If you set your child down—well, 2- and 3-year-olds you really can't reason with them—but 4-, 5-, and 6-year-olds, if they're giving you a hard time, you just tell them, "Hey, this is the budget. This is what we can have. You can pick two of them out of this. This is all. That's it."

She often lectures parents about the need to keep children away from adult films and graphic violence. She strenuously advocates keeping children away from the violent action movies she most enjoys; pulling the plug on the TV set on a regular basis; and directly teaching children the limitations on consumer spending. One of her greatest concerns is the ways parents substitute consumer goods for parental companionship. She advises parents to turn off the television set and play cards or board games with their children.

Gloria watches the media carefully for black characters: she was more perceptive and more accurate than other teachers interviewed in noting the various types of character on different shows. Gloria also noticed the changing demographics of action figures to include more black characters, even though they are rarely the main hero. She speculated that *Teenage Mutant Ninja Turtles* were popular with her children, most of whom are African American, because they seemed to remain outside of racial categories.

When asked to envision the kind of changes she would like to see in her job, she spoke about the broader contexts of children's lives. She was the only teacher we interviewed who imagined structural changes (in the legal system, in governmental support) as a means of bettering children's lives:

> I'd probably have the government pay for everything. At a nice rate—not a low rate. And have them take some of the burdens off the parents that couldn't afford it, you know, they wouldn't have to go through so much red tape. And since I'm a foster mother I'd probably, if I ever see, well I do have some kids that are abused, I would change that system, so the parents wouldn't have them anymore. One time, you're out. If it's a little thing, I'll give them two times, but that's it. I wouldn't give them on back. And make sure if the kids came not dressed right, if the parents couldn't afford it, I'd have some kind of funds just out there and get what they need. If parents didn't

take care of it, I'll just keep it here. If they go out they wouldn't look like second-class citizens. That's my idea. And everybody had enough to eat. A lot of my kids don't.

◆ *"No Forks in Jail, Either . . ."*

Jean DeWitt has worked for four years at the daycare facility attached to the local hospital. Jean is taking college courses one at a time towards her bachelor's degree, while being employed full-time at the centre and single-parenting for her three daughters, who are 4, 8, and 10 years of age. The hospital is a regional centre for medical care and one of the town's leading employers. The daycare centre is housed in a remodelled elementary school: solidly built, with a security entrance, large airy classrooms, and modern facilities. It is the largest facility in town with 138 children—a group large enough to require three staggered lunch times. The parents who use the facility include nurses, janitors, clerical staff, and physicians. Jean teaches a classroom of seven to twelve 4-year-olds, four of whom are girls.

At Jean's school, the teachers share a single monitor and video recorder on a cart and they are officially limited—by order of the school director—to two one-hour blocks of video screening per week. The centre receives cable television, making it possible to watch Nickelodeon's pre-school programming or *Sesame Street*, or cartoons, in addition to videos. This is a common practice in the "multipurpose" group room where breakfast is served and where children wait for their parents to pick them up late in the day. The TV being on at pick-up and drop-off times had given parents a bad impression, despite the fact that other "choices"—toys and art activities—are always available in the multipurpose room. Some parents had trouble dragging their children away from the set at pick-up time

before a show or video finished playing. Jean thought TV was an important way for sleepy kids in the morning to ease into the situation of being in institutional care, and she defended the practice.

Jean voiced many common complaints about children's television and its effects on children. For example, she told this wry story about the first time she saw an episode of *Power Rangers*:

I thought that the kids that are the Power Rangers—I thought that they set very good examples. It was like, they were upright good kids that were leaders of the school and helped out in the community and did various community-service projects. And then we were watching it here—the first time I saw it at the daycare in the morning—and we were watching it and then all of a sudden they changed into these Power Rangers and started kicking and fighting and had weapons and all the teachers just kind of looked at each other and said "Uh" [*laughs*]. We just kind of turned it off and the kids just groaned and we knew what would happen. That they would be kicking and fighting and sure enough, they were re-enacting *Power Rangers* out on the playground, kicking and picking up sticks and pointing fingers and—

As our conversations ensued, however, it became clear that Jean held a more nuanced view of the media's role in children's lives. She held, in fact, a rather ironic sense of the media's effects and an appreciation for some of the pleasures TV viewing offered children—something closer to the cultural studies version of the interaction of TV and audiences. An avid reader of periodicals that are devoted to early childhood education (provided by the centre's director), Jean was fully engaged with the professional literature on early childhood development, while struggling to work out her own position on the best way to engage such materials in the classroom—apparently a more permissive strand of the literature on pedagogy than Montessori's writings. She gave the following humorous anecdote about attempting to employ the recommended strategy of extending the child's interest to her students:

> I've read books—the very liberal child psychology books that say, "Follow the children's lead and extend it" and one day I sat and watched some little boys play to see what their interests were. And after an hour of killing, maiming, and destroying, I thought [*laughs*], "How do I take this a step further?" [*Laughs*] I don't think this is the direction we want to head [*laughs*].

Still, Jean has facilitated a great deal of popular culture-based play, in a manner that is reminiscent of Gloria's theme days at her family daycare centre. When a child brought in the tape of the animated film *Fievel Goes West*, some Wild West play started in the classroom. Jean made them sheriff's badges with gold glitter on them and brought in the discarded cardboard box from a washing machine to make a jail. (The box was soon appropriated by the girls for doll play.) Jean allowed the kids to see the *Power Rangers* episode "Food Fight," and tried to incorporate it into a lesson plan about good table manners. In an attempt to downplay the weaponry, the students did a papier mâché art project making Power Ranger helmets.

Like Gloria, Jean has been an attentive observer of gendered patterns of children's play. Jean also reported a greater flexibility in gender roles—with more girls joining in action-adventure play—than did Sara at the Montessori school. She observed that *Power Rangers* had brought about a qualitative shift in the kinds of superhero play going on in her classroom:

Jean: Well see, the girls can get in. The girls can get in. They can be more than just the victim in the *Power Rangers*, which I guess that comment lends to its credit, so to speak, as far as the females are not excluded from power. There's two female Power Rangers, so that is a switch.

Ellen: So do the girls in your class like to play it?

Jean: Oh yes. And they're not the victims anymore.

Ellen: Are they in there kickin' and—

Jean: Yeah. They've got the guns and they're right in there with them. Now when they play Ninja Turtles, they're the victim. And they'll sit in a chair and pretend that they're tied. [*Laughs*] Yeah. And they come and get rescued by the Turtles.

Ellen: Do they play this kind of action cartoon play indoors and outdoors?

Jean: Yes. They would play it all day long if we let them [*Ellen laughs*]. They would play it from morning—they play it in their sleep sometimes [*laughs*]. That's why it's like it's gonna come out so I just try and keep it positive. No contact [*laughs*]. And draw the line that when somebody's unhappy or somebody's getting hurt then we have to stop. It's kind of good 'cause I can hold it over their head for behaviors. Like "I will not allow this if you can't behave this way." So in a way it helps me modify their behavior.

Jean sees the imitative violence as a somewhat natural form of children's play rather than a long-term effect on their minds, and turns it into an opportunity for promoting classroom unity or harmony consensus. She does not worry about long-term effects of viewing media violence; she expresses a good-natured acceptance of such play as a normal phase children go through—in this, her position is quite similar to Gloria's. There is also a willingness to use overt forms of control over the children, to enact punishments or withdraw privileges. TV is useful for both Gloria and Jean as a reward that can be taken away. Neither Gloria nor Jean has any concern for the aesthetic education of the children, or for raising their level of taste to something resembling that of adults. . . .

Jean adopts a very liberal policy about bringing toys to the classroom, seeing the space of the school as an important bridge between home and school. Children are allowed to bring toys in at any time, but if they argue about a toy she places it in a special, brightly decorated box:

> And that box comes in handy, and it's real bright and pretty and just right there and they can see it and they know that's where all the toys go if they don't play nicely in any way really, I mean, if they don't share and take turns. So they pretty much learn as a natural consequence that "Hey if I bring too many I'm going to lose one. If I don't share, if it's a toy I can't share, it's going to end up in the box." They pretty much monitor their own toys and what I saw—it's happened more than once—they start bringing in two. Two motorcycles or two Ninja Turtles, two Power Rangers [*laughs*]. They'll have one for their friend, one for themselves, and they can play nicely. They do really well. I'm surprised that other teachers don't like toys from home, 'cause I think it's a very important bridge between home and school. I think you learn a lot about the kids and their home life by what toys [*laughs*] they bring in. It gives you a real clue as to why a certain child behaves the way he behaves or—we gather a lot of information from the toys. And—

. . . Jean related a story about a child who had been watching *Cops*, a "reality" show following police on arrests, and seemed to be behaving differently. On this rare occasion, she intervened, speaking to the mother about what the child had been watching on TV. The mother blamed it on the father,

and thanked the teacher for bringing it up so that she could use the teacher's authority to get the father to be more careful in his television selections.

The teachers and I did get into an interesting discussion on how kids . . . get to watch the television show *Cops*. And we were kind of debating why parents let their kids watch this show, when it's definitely a graphic show. It has a warning before it, and, you know, these kids are obviously traumatized by what they see. I mean, it bothers them. They're upset about it. That's why they come to us and talk to us about it. And we were trying to . . . you know, figure out why parents let their kids watch these shows. And whether it was okay if the parent was sitting there and explaining things to them. Even then, I think it's better to shelter them. I mean, they don't need to see it at a tender age like that. Maybe, I mean it's inevitable they'll run into it, but . . . to just sit there and let them watch it.

Jean's feelings about the need to protect children are linked to her keen memory of her own childhood fears of the TV. Her father was a travelling salesman, and on Friday nights, when he returned home, the family would settle down for "a fun TV night" in front of a programme of old horror films. Jean recalls her father laughing at her for being so scared of these "hokey, B, horror flicks":

> And I remember being terrified and running and hiding behind his chair at these poorly made films. So I can just imagine the really good ones, or supposedly the good ones, that kids see nowadays. I'm sure they're petrified. They have to be, terrified of these.

Despite her liberal attitudes toward children's popular media in the classroom, at home Jean is quite strict about monitoring the television. She "has read" that there is a direct correlation between grades achieved in school and amounts of television watching. She describes herself as constantly battling with her daughters over the TV set. . . .

> Yeah, they are constantly trying to turn it on and I'm constantly turning it off. . . . Saturday mornings I feel like I got to let them watch at least one. So I read while they're, I let them basically while I'm getting breakfast ready. And then it's like, "OK, now we got to go."

. . . Jean's essential philosophy has to do with involving the child in the life of the classroom, and thus preparing them for educational success. She was able to have a theory of weaker media effects because she was willing to allow that creative things can happen in these play scenarios.

◆ *Conclusion*

Gloria sees children as active users of television and this view is based on an acceptance of television as a normal influence on play routines. Her familiarity with genre rules on the screen and in children's play allows her to see violence as symbolic and conventional. She rates her children's cognitive skills more highly than Sara rates those of the Montessori children. Gloria expects children to be able to handle violent content on children's shows; she is confident that the children can distinguish between media fiction and reality. Her assessment is based on close observation of children's play and TV viewing and frequent casual conversations with them about the media, in the context of a warmly affectionate relationship. Gloria accepts the children's immersion in a separate peer culture and does not expect to share their predilections. She has nothing invested in improving the children's taste; she does not expect to interfere with children's play or dissuade them from their interest in popular culture. Gloria is also more comfortable with overt forms of control than Sara is:

rather than attempting to "redirect their attention," as Sara phrases it, Gloria just says "no." The boundaries between adulthood and childhood are clear at Gloria's Place.

Gloria's approach is in keeping with the recommendations of education scholar Anne Haas Dyson, who has studied the use of superhero stories (*X-Men, Power Rangers,* and the like) in literacy education at a racially integrated, third-grade classroom in Oakland, California. Dyson has articulated the position in favour of teachers' openness to popular materials in the classroom:

> Curriculum must be undergirded by a belief that meaning is found, not in artifacts themselves, but in the social events through which those artifacts are produced and used. Children have agency in the construction of their own imaginations—not unlimited, unstructured agency, but, nonetheless, agency: They appropriate cultural material to participate in and explore their worlds, especially through narrative play and story. Their attraction to particular media programs and films suggests that they find in that material compelling and powerful images. If official curricula make no space for his agency, then schools risk reinforcing societal divisions in children's orientation to each other, to cultural art forms, and to school itself. (Dyson 1997: 181)

Television is cheap, easy, plentiful, and children love to watch it. It is also pathologized—often unreasonably—by those with the most invested in status distinctions and the most at stake in professionalizing childcare. As Julia Wrigley warns, in her useful discussion of professional expertise in childcare:

> In the absence of a social movement demanding child care as a universal right, a segmented child care market will continue to provide one set of stigmatized services for the poor and other

services geared to preparing middle-class children for entry into the competitive world of schooling. With such strong segregation of the children being served, caregivers can develop narrow ideologies that exacerbate the educational anxieties of one part of the population and emphasize the parental inadequacies of another. (1990: 305)

The Montessori school employs a notion of official curricula diametrically opposed to Dyson's and typical of the kind of narrow ideologies Wrigley criticized. Sara is at once completely unfamiliar with TV and absolutely certain that TV has a detrimental effect on children. Yet her classroom rules and avoidance of TV during her leisure time make her a poor observer of the phenomenon of television's effects. Sara's classroom is a place where children are supposed to get on with the work of adulthood, and this does not include the idle pleasures of television viewing. In some ways the boundaries between childhood and adulthood are more blurred at this school. "Work" is valued over play; books and computers are valued over television and toys. Children are taught to work quietly, alone at intellectual tasks. Bothering other children with talking or gregariousness is not permitted. When 16-mm films are shown, the students are expected to hold still and remain quiet, thus a passive viewing posture is enforced. Sara's classroom is a microcosm of the environments the children can expect to experience throughout their school and adult lives as middle-class professionals. Sara openly defines her role in terms of educating tastes, monitoring and pre-selecting cultural goods. One of the most important features of her work, then, is to sharpen the distinction between children's mass culture and educational materials. Banishing television as a subject of conversation or as an activity is a linchpin of Sara's strategy for enforcing cultural distinctions. . . .

For adults as well as children, holding a lay theory of deleterious media effects, and the alarmism that accompanies it, may be linked to the closeting of popular culture tastes, and to the suppression of talk about television. Ironically, middle-class adults— exceedingly anxious about the collapse of the public schools, and the diminished opportunities for upward mobility through education—may be the harshest and least empathetic about children's interest in popular culture, while those with less money and fewer chances of advancement may have the luxury of being empathetic to children's interest and enthusiasm for popular toys and television shows. . . .

References

Anderson, J. A. (1983). "Television Literacy and the Critical Viewer," in J. Bryant and J. A. Anderson (eds.), *Children's Understanding of Television: Research on Attention and Comprehension*. New York: Academic Press, 297-330.

Bourdieu, P. (1984). *Distinction: A Social Critique of the Judgement of Taste*. Trans. R. Nice. Cambridge, MA: Harvard University Press.

Collins, R. (1992). "Women and the Production of Status Cultures," in M. Lamont and M. Fournier, *Cultivating Differences*, 213-31.

Dyson, A. H. (1997). *Writing Superheroes: Contemporary Childhood, Popular Culture, and Classroom Literacy*. New York: Teachers College Press.

Furnham, A. (1988). *Lay Theories: Everyday Understandings of Problems in the Social Sciences*. Oxford, UK: Pergamon.

Hodge, B., and Tripp, D. (1986). *Children and Television: A Semiotic Approach*. Palo Alto, CA: Stanford University Press.

Lewis, L. (ed.) (1992). *The Adoring Audience: Fan Culture and Popular Media*. London and New York: Routledge.

Nelson, M. K. (1990). "Mothering Others' Children: The Experiences of Family Day Care Providers," in E. K. Abel and M. K. Nelson (eds.), *Circles of Care: Work and Identity in Women's Lives.* Albany, NY: State University of New York Press, 210-33.

Nelson, M. K. (1993). *Sold Separately: Children and Parents in Consumer Culture.* New Brunswick, NJ: Rutgers University Press.

Wrigley, J. (1990). "Children's Caregivers and Ideologies of Parental Inadequacy," in E. K. Abel and M. K. Nelson (eds.), *Circles of Care: Work and Identity in Women's Lives.* Albany, NY: State University of New York Press, 283-308.

37

LESSONS FROM LITTLETON

What Congress Doesn't Want to Hear About Youth and Media

◆ Henry Jenkins

◆ *Profile of Moral Panic*

In *Risk and Blame*, anthropologist Mary Douglas describes the cultural basis for witch hunts in traditional societies. "Whether the witch is able to do harm or not, the attribution of a hidden power to hurt is a weapon of attack against them. . . . A successful accusation is one that has enough credibility for a public outcry to remove the opportunity of repeating the damage."[1] A moral panic starts with an unspeakable tragedy that sparks an attempt to ascribe blame and responsibility. Initially, accusations flow freely but focus on those targets who are already the subject of anxiety. Douglas notes, "Though anyone can accuse, not all accusations will be accepted. To be successful an accusation must be directed against victims hated by the populace. The cause of harm must be vague, unspecific, difficult to prove or disprove." Once one accusation sticks, it becomes easier to pile on charges. Our rush to judgment overwhelms our ability to rationally assess the evidence. Our need to take action supersedes our ability to

NOTE: From Independent Schools/*Journal of National Association of Independent Schools*.

anticipate consequences. Moral panic shuts down self-examination at the very moment when real problems demand careful consideration.

Several weeks after the shootings at Columbine High School in Littleton, Colorado, the U.S. Senate Commerce Committee launched a series of hearings, chaired by Sen. Sam Brownback (R-Ark.), on the "marketing of violent entertainment to children." Introducing the investigation, Brownback explained, "We are not here to point fingers but to identify the causes of cultural pollution and seek solutions." The phrase "cultural pollution," of course, already presumed a consensus that popular culture was a worthless irritant responsible for various social harms. Brownback was prepared to sweep aside constitutional protections: "We are having endless debates about First and Second Amendment rights while our children are being killed and traumatized." Brownback focused his ire on forms of popular culture that met youth rather than adult tastes: "I am willing to bet that there aren't many adults who are huge fans of teen slasher movies or the music of Cannibal Corpse and Marilyn Manson." Sen. Orin Hatch (R-Utah) declared Manson's music tremendously "offensive to everyone in America who thinks," a category that seemingly does not include a significant number of high school and college students. William Bennett, former Secretary of Education and self-proclaimed guardian of American virtue, called on Congress to make "meaningful distinctions" between works that used violence to tell "a larger story" such as *Braveheart*, *Saving Private Ryan*, or *Clear and Present Danger*, and works that "gratuitously" exploited violence, such as *The Basketball Diaries*, *Cruel Intentions*, or *Scream*. His "commonsense" distinction was at heart an ideological one, separating works that offered adult perspectives from those that expressed youth concerns.[2]

Though they understood the hearings as a "ritual humiliation" of the entertainment industries, the senators were feeding a "cultural war" that was more and more focused on teenagers. As GOP operative Mike Murphy explained, "We need Goth control, not gun control."[3] Hatch engaged in homophobic banter about whether Manson was "a he or a she" while Brownback accused members of the Goth subculture of giving themselves over to "the dark side." Such comments reinforced bigotry and fear. Adult fears about popular culture were being transferred toward those people who consumed it. The Goths were a relatively small subculture whose members drew inspiration from Romantic literature and constructed their personal identity by borrowing from the iconography of the horror film and S/M pornography. The group could claim a twenty-year history without much public attention because it had previously not been associated with violent crime. However, the Columbine shooters had been mistakenly identified in some early news reports as Goths and as a result, this group had been singled out in the post-Littleton backlash.

From the outset, Congress was unlikely to set federal policies to regulate media content, which would not have sustained constitutional scrutiny. They counted on public pressure to intimidate the entertainment industry into voluntarily withdrawing controversial works from circulation. Manson canceled some concerts. MGM stopped selling *The Basketball Diaries*. The Warner Brothers Network withheld the airing of the season finale of *Buffy the Vampire Slayer* until midsummer.

The biggest impact of the moral panic, however, would be felt in the schools—both public and private—as teachers and administrators increasingly saw their students as "threats" to public safety and suspected popular culture of turning good kids into brutal "monsters." Online journalist Jon Katz's remarkable series, "Voices From the Hellmouth," circulated hundreds of first-person accounts of how American schools were reacting to the shootings. As Katz reported, "Many of these kids saw themselves as targets of a new hunt for oddballs—suspects in a bizarre, systematic search for the strange and the alienated. Suddenly, in this tyranny of the normal, to be different wasn't just to feel unhappy, it was to be dangerous."[4]

Many schools took away Web and Net access. Many kids were placed into therapy based on their subcultural identifications or interests in computer games or certain kinds of music. Students were punished for taking controversial positions in class discussions or on essay assignments. In one case, a student was suspended for wearing a Star of David to school because his teacher thought it was a gang insignia. Another was sent home for wearing a black coat that was officially part of his ROTC uniform. One school district banned heavy coats. Knowing little or nothing about the popular culture consumed by teens, teachers, principals, and parents were striking out blindly.

Other educators took risks, challenging the crackdowns on "Goths" in their schools and bringing the materials that Katz had gathered back into their classrooms for dialogue with their students. Local journalists investigated Katz's reports and found them accurate. Civil rights organizations were confronting a record number of complaints from students who felt their constitutional rights were being infringed. Then-presidential candidate Dan Quayle added fuel to the fires with a speech attacking the concept of "students rights" as an unjustified interference with classroom discipline, insisting, "Our children cannot learn in an environment of chaos. . . . If we're going to make an error, err on the side of school safety."[5]

◆ *What's Missing*
From This Picture?

Speaking before the Senate Commerce Committee, Lt. Col. David Grossman, author of *On Killing*, asserted, "The real media critic isn't Siskel and Ebert. It's the American Medical Association and it's time to place them in charge of the FCC and other such organizations." Grossman argued that current scientific and medical understandings of "media effects" supported his demands that government actively regulate media content. Grossman proposes expanding the current category of pornography to include violent entertainment. His language consistently pathologizes culture, depicting media products as "toxic substances" analogous to cigarettes in their damaging impact on children's mental and physical health.

With these hearings, the decades-old "culture war" rhetoric entered a third phase. In the first phase (during the Reagan years), the religious right refashioned itself as the "moral majority" in a belated backlash against the 1960s counterculture. This phase was largely ineffective, since Democrats directly challenged its overt effort to legally mandate religious doctrines and values. The phrase "culture war" was associated with political extremism. The second phase (the Bush years) was characterized by attacks on "political correctness" within higher education and had much more impact on public opinion, helping to decredentialize those in the humanities and social sciences who sought to better understand the complex nature of American culture. In the third phase, the rhetoric of morality is displaced by the language of medicine and science; doctors are assumed to speak an objective truth about media effects. The shift toward a language of scientific objectivity has made it possible for a significant number of liberal democrats, such as Sen. Joseph Lieberman (D-Conn.) or Sen. Max Cleland (D-Georgia), to align themselves with conservative Republicans in calling for the regulation of media content.

The Pseudo-Science of ◆
Media Effects

However, there are many problems with this "scientific" approach to culture. For starters, the American Medical Association has no specific cultural expertise. We can trace a long history of misdirected attacks by medical authorities against popular culture, dating at least as far back as the efforts in Shakespeare's England to close the theaters in the name of public hygiene. In most cases, the medical establishment promotes a fairly conservative agenda, suspicious of those cultural forms associated with the working class or ethnic and racial minorities, making recommendations that ratify their own tastes and quarantine works they dislike.[6]

Despite Grossman's claims, cultural works are not carcinogens. Cultural works are complex and contradictory, open to many different interpretations, subject to various unanticipated uses. Popular culture's complex relationship with its consumers cannot be reduced to simple variables or tested through lab experiments. Even if such rigor were possible, media activists exaggerate the body of scientific evidence supporting their claims. To date, relatively few studies have examined the impact of video and computer games on teens and nobody knows how relevant research on television is to our consumption of interactive media.[7]

The best media effects researchers qualify their findings and few argue for a direct link between consuming media images and performing real-world violence. If video game violence was an immediate catalyst, we would have difficulty explaining why none of the shootings involving teens have occurred in movie theaters or video arcades where the direct stimulus of game playing would be most acute. Instead, these murders have tended to occur in schools and we need to look at real-world factors to discover what triggers such violence. A more careful analysis would read video games as one cultural influence among many, as having different degrees of impact on different children, and as not sufficient in and of themselves to provoke an otherwise healthy and well-adjusted child to engage in acts of violence. Some children, especially those

who are antisocial and emotionally unbalanced, should be protected from exposure to the most extreme forms of media violence, but most children are not at risk from the media they consume. Parents, not governments, are in the best position to know what kinds of culture their children should consume. Media activists strip aside those careful qualifications, claiming that the computer games are "murder simulators" teaching our children to kill.

Our current legal definitions of obscenity insist that the work must be "taken as a whole," read according to prevailing community standards, and judged to be "utterly without redeeming . . . value." Media effects research, on the other hand, displays little or no interest in the work as a whole or in the work's meanings or values. It adopts a crude stimulus-response model of media consumption and focuses on localized "media images," not on their function within larger stories. In many cases, research subjects are forced to watch a rapid succession of violent images removed from any narrative context. Much of this research makes little or no distinction between different kinds of stories our culture might tell about violence.[8]

Much media effects research removes media consumption from real-world contexts and situates it in a laboratory. But media never functions in a vacuum. Playing a game in an arcade is a very different experience than playing it in one's own home or as part of a military training exercise. Media consumption gains its meaning through association with a range of other activities that constitute our everyday life. Media effects research shows limited interest in what those stories mean to the people who consume them.[9] The focus has been on measurable biological responses—neural stimulation, pulse, heart beat, pupil dilation. Such research essentially measures the adrenaline rush that occurs when we play an exciting video game. Yet neural stimulation is only part of the story. As current cognitive research into emotion suggests, the human body experiences remarkably similar degrees of neural stimulation riding a car off a bridge and riding a roller coaster, but one is experienced as terrifying and the other pleasurable. The difference has to do with our interpretations of those initial neural stimulations.[10]

Much media effects research assumes a causal connection between the physiological reactions or attitudinal shifts measured in the laboratory and subsequent real-world behavior. In a 1994 study, on the other hand, Ann Hagell and Tim Newburn noted that prisoners serving time for violent crimes had, on average, consumed far less media than the general population.[11]

Media effects research systematically deskills children, often assuming that they cannot separate fantasy from reality. Activists compound this problem by ignoring considerable developmental differences between small children and teens. Children at a relatively early age, around four or five, began to make basic distinctions between realistic and fantastic representations of violence, with documentary images (news reports of local crime, historical footage of war, nature footage of predators and prey) far more emotionally disturbing than cartoons or video games.[12] Primatologists note that many mammals make basic distinctions between play violence and actual violence.[13] The same two animals might jostle playfully in one context or fight to the death in another, depending on the presence or absence of "play faces" or reassuring noises. Surely, our children can make the same distinctions.

◆ A More Humanistic Perspective

Media effects research enjoys its current government support not because it is the best methodology for understanding the relationship between media consumption and real-world behavior but because its stimulus-response model offers simple solutions to complex problems. To really understand the place of violent entertainment in contemporary youth culture, we must broaden the conversation to include researchers of many different methodologies—anthropologists, criminologists, social and cultural historians, media scholars, experts on children's play and literature, and so forth. Rather than starting from the assumption that we are investigating what media content is doing to our children, we should ask what our children are doing with the media they consume. We are living through a period of profound media transition: the availability of new entertainment and information technologies impact all aspects of our social, cultural, political, economic, and educational experience. Children are often the first to embrace these new technologies and have discovered complex new ways to employ them in their social interactions with their friends, their recreational activities, their creative expression, their homework, and their political lives.[14] We trivialize these changes when we reduce the important conversations we should be having about future directions for technological development into a moralistic debate about violent video games. My field, comparative media studies, adopts humanistic and qualitative social science methodologies to better understand those changes and explain them to the general public. Humanistic research paints a very different picture of media consumption than found in the media effects literature.[15]

First, media consumption is assumed to be active (something we do) not passive (something that happens to us). Media technologies are tools and we can use them in a variety of ways—some constructive, some destructive.

Second, media consumption is assumed to be a process; we work on media content over a long period of time; our immediate emotional reactions are only part of what we need to understand if we want to predict real-world consequences of media consumption.

Third, different consumers react to the same media content in fundamentally different ways as it is fit into their larger understanding of the world, and so universalizing claims are fundamentally inadequate for accounting for media's social and cultural impact.

Fourth, consumer response to media is more often creative than imitative. All of us construct our own personal mythologies from the contents made available to us through the mass media and we are drawn toward images and stories that are personally meaningful to us because they match the way we see the world. We use them as vehicles to explore who we are, what we want, what we value, and how we relate to other people. Harris and Klebold were drawn toward darker and more violent images and invested those images with their most antisocial impulses. Another child might use those same images to emphasize the need for community and friendship in a world marked by violence and competition.

Finally, real life trumps media images every time. Media images are read against our perception of the world, which is built up through countless direct experiences. Real life has the power to exert material consequences. Harris and Klebold were legally required to go to school; they were subjected to real ridicule and abuse from their classmates and this real-world brutality helped to motivate their actions. Popular entertainment does not exert this same kind of coercive control over us. Media content is more likely to reinforce—rather than fundamentally alter—our existing prejudices and predispositions.

◆ The Meaningfulness of Violent Entertainment

Media effects research has had little to say about why children are drawn toward violent entertainment, except to ascribe a universalized blood lust. Humanistic research, on the other hand, offers useful tools for understanding why children find media violence attractive and meaningful. The

materials of popular culture are read as modern myths that reflect the values and desires of the people who produce and consume them. Although we need to spend much more time talking with teens about their relationship to popular culture before we can offer a full account, one can point to a number of possible explanations for the appeal of violent entertainment.

First, violent entertainment offers teens a fantasy of empowerment. The "Quake grrls," for example, are a subculture of young women who understand playing violent video games in explicitly feminist terms—as an opportunity to compete aggressively with boys without regard to biological differences and by doing so, to rehearse for later professional competitions.[16] But many boys come home from being bullied at school and also experience an enormous release in playing violent games. Blood-and-thunder imagery runs through the history of boyhood play and fantasy. Game images echo the pictures another generation of boys drew with crayons on their notebooks or had in their heads as they hurled pinecones on the playground.[17] The new technologies make these images more vivid and more open to adult scrutiny, but they do not fundamentally alter the contents of boys' imaginations.

Second, violent entertainment offers teens a fantasy of transgression, a chance to test the limits of their parent's culture.[18] Slasher films, for example, often depict a world where parents' attempts to protect teens from harsh realities place kids at risk and where adults dismiss youth efforts to explain monstrous events they have observed. Such films are often the only works that take seriously the experience of nonconformist teens who do not get the positive reinforcement received by football heroes and homecoming queens.

Third, violent entertainment offers teens an acknowledgment that the world is not all sweetness and light. The child psychologist Bruno Bettelheim argues that the violence and darkness of fairy tales is important for children to confront as a means of acknowledging the darker sides of their own nature.[19] Without such a depiction, a child might take his own transgressive impulses as evidence that he is a "monster," rather than learning how to recognize and control those aspects of himself. One Goth teen told me that he had been treated like a monster all of his life, by parents, teachers, and classmates, and so he had adopted a Goth persona because for the first time, it allowed him to decide what kind of monster he wanted to be and helped him to identify other teens who also felt stigmatized. Many teens come from broken homes, encounter domestic violence, confront poverty, and worry about crime in their own neighborhoods. Not surprisingly, they are drawn toward representations of the world that are dark and pessimistic and that acknowledge these troubling experiences.

Fourth, violent entertainment offers teens an intensification of emotional experience. Adolescence is a time of powerful, often overwhelming feelings. If teens are going to escape the intense feelings of rejection or damaged self-esteem they often experience, they require forms of popular culture that are loud and raucous, have pumped-up style, promise speed and spectacle, offer abrupt shifts between the comic and the violent. Their fascination with violent video games is as much a response to their aesthetic qualities as to their explicit content.

In short, teens aren't drawn to *Quake* or *Scream* because they are bloodthirsty or because they think violence is the best real-world response to their problems. These works offer them the best available vehicle for their fantasies of empowerment, take seriously what young people feel and think about the adult world, acknowledge the darker sides of the teenagers' everyday experiences, and offer an intense release from real-world tensions. If, for moral, political, or aesthetic reasons, we find such violent entertainment reprehensible, then we are going to have to offer new genres that satisfy those basic urges at least as well.

Proposals for the Future ◆

All of the above suggest a fairly simple conclusion: we should not let moral panic push us to abandon our commitment to free expression and to embrace increased government regulation of cultural content. We should take seriously our children's relationship to popular culture and create contexts where we can better understand what roles media play in their lives. The knee-jerk reactions to the Littleton shooting caused tremendous damage as adult authorities struck out blindly against non-conformist students, ensuring that we further alienated those already feeling alien and closed the door to meaningful adult-youth communication. As the one-year anniversary of the Littleton shootings approaches, we need to reassess how we engage with controversies over popular culture. Educators should adopt a basic ethical principle—above all, do no harm. The following are some aspects of a more constructive response to these issues:

1. SUPPORTIVE DIGITAL COMMUNITIES FOR YOUTH

Harris and Klebold weren't alienated because they went online. The online world offers many teens a new opportunity for social connections, for finding friends outside the often closed community of their own high schools. For example, online interventions are a powerful weapon for slowing the rate of gay and lesbian teen suicide at a time when many other institutions have failed to respond to the homophobia in their daily lives or offer basic information about their emerging sexuality.[20] For kids who are social pariahs, the online world offers a chance to find someone out there, anywhere on the planet, who doesn't think you are a hopeless geek. Some concerned adults responded to Littleton by constructing welcoming communities for teens who feel alienated from their classmates and school authorities. Projects, such as hsunderground.com, channel anti-social impulses into more constructive directions, offering a degree of free speech not found in even the most progressive private school, connecting angry kids to a larger social community.

2. THE DEMAND FOR K-12 MEDIA EDUCATION

Media education has historically been an occasional treat but not a central aspect of the curriculum. As media change influences all of our core institutions and practices, we need to acknowledge that media literacy is a basic skill, part of what it means to be a good researcher and writer, an intelligent citizen, or a shrewd consumer. Children already have a greater degree of media literacy than we imagine, but our refusal to mobilize those skills in the classroom, to value what teens have taught themselves about media, helps to build a wall between school teaching and real-world experience. Media education can take many forms, ranging from whole courses dealing with media and modern culture to more localized lessons on the ways communication technologies influenced the development of American democracy or on how to assess the reliability of different information sources.[21]

3. ADULT KNOWLEDGE AND RESPECT FOR POPULAR CULTURE

The "moral panic" embodied adult anxieties and ignorance about youth culture. Media education too often functions as an excuse for adults to impose their judgments, rather than as a means for mutual learning. Adults need to take the time to listen to what their children have to say about popular culture, just as we make time to listen to what children tell us about their little league games or band practices. We need to listen and learn because these forms of cultural consumption are an important part of children's lives. Schools can create opportunities for open dialogue about popular culture, but only if they lower the emotional temperature. Youths can't speak openly or honestly about their culture if the immediate adult response is to ban whatever comes to light. Adults need to enter into those conversations with open minds, ready to rethink their prejudices, but they also must be prepared to justify their own aesthetic choices and moral values.[22]

4. A MORE TOLERANT SCHOOL ENVIRONMENT

Talk to most high school students and they offer a similar explanation for the shootings: Harris and Klebold were cut off from their classmates because they were different; their isolation turned rancid inside them until they struck out blindly against their classmates. Many teens recognize those feelings within themselves, even if most of them have the self-control not to act on them. Kids whose cultural tastes are outside their school's mainstream feel at risk, ridiculed by their classmates, and held suspect by their teachers. Our schools need to invest at least as much effort into understanding and responding to the cultural differences introduced by contemporary youth cultures as we spend examining the historical differences between various races and ethnic groups. Every kid has the right to feel safe and welcome in his or her school.

5. PARENTAL DISCUSSION GROUPS ABOUT MEDIA CONTENT

If we are going to place the responsibility of policing culture onto parents, then we have to provide the resources they need to respond intelligently to a complex and changing cultural environment. A one-size-fits-all solution doesn't work because our children aren't the same size and don't mature at the same rate and our families come from many different backgrounds and don't have the same values. The Web enables parents to compare notes with other parents before purchasing a birthday or holiday gift. Such exchanges between parents about specific media content are much more valuable than ratings systems, because these ongoing interactions allow us to determine the values behind these assessments.[23]

6. CREATIVE RESPONSES FROM MEDIA PRODUCERS

Much popular culture isn't so much dangerous as it is banal and mind-numbing. Game designers and developers depend too heavily on formulas as a safe way of anticipating market demand. In doing so, they fall back on violent content as much out of laziness as from any desire to exploit bloodlust. For those reasons, we need to encourage the game industry to enter a phase of self-examination, to try to better understand what draws children to the existing games. The challenge is to broaden the range of available options, so that consumers find forms of culture that reflect their values and give expression to their fantasies. We probably can't tell stories without some element of conflict, but those conflicts can take various forms. We must explore other ways of representing and resolving conflict that supplement, even if they do not altogether replace, those currently on the market.[24]

◆ Notes

1. Mary Douglas, *Risk and Blame: Essays in Cultural Theory* (New York: Routledge, 1994), p. 87.

2. All quotes here taken from the transcript of "Marketing Violence to Youth," Hearing Before the Committee of Commerce, Science and Transportation, United States Senate, May 4, 1999.

3. Mike Murphy was quoted in "Verbatum," *Time*, December 3, 2001, as having made the remark on CNN's Crossfire, date unspecified.

4. Jon Katz, "Voices From the Hellmouth," and in subsequent issues. See also Jon Katz, *Geeks: How Two Lost Boys Rode the Internet Out of Idaho* (New York: Broadway, 2001) and Jon Katz, *Virtuous Reality: How America Surrendered Discussion of Moral Values to Opportunists, Nitwits, and Blockheads Like William Bennett* (New York: Random House, 1997). For an overview of the struggle over student and youth rights, see Marjorie Heins, *Not in Front of the Children: Indecency, Censorship, and the Innocence of Youth* (New York: Hill and Wang, 2001).

5. Dan Quayle, Speech to the Commonwealth Club of California, May 19, 1999.

6. For background on the role of medical authorities in regulating theater, see Jonas Barish, "The Antitheatrical Prejudice (Berkeley: University of California Press, 1981). Medical authorities have at other times argued that women were physically unfit for the rigors of higher education, that jazz put unnecessary strain on the human nervous system, that humans should watch their intake of jokes and comics because they might laugh themselves to death, that novel reading might lead to social isolation, and that comic book reading caused juvenile delinquency. See, for example, Carroll Smith-Rosenberg, *Disorderly Conduct: Vision of Gender in Victorian America* (Cambridge, UK: Oxford University Press, 1986); Henry Jenkins, *What Made Pistachio Nuts? Early Sound Comedy and the Vaudeville Aesthetic* (New York: Columbia University Press, 1990); Martin Barker, *The Haunt of Fears* (Jackson: University Press of Mississippi, 1992).

7. For critical assessments of the current state of media effects research, see Jeffrey Goldstein, "Does Playing Violent Video Games Cause Aggressive Behavior?" and Jonathon L. Freedman, "Evaluating the Research on Violent Video Games," presented at "Playing By the Rules: The Cultural Policy Challenges of Video Games," Center for Cultural Policy, University of Chicago, Oct. 16-27, 2001. See also David Gauntlett, "Ten Things Wrong With the Media

Effects Model," in Roger Dickinson, Ramaswani Harindranath, and Olga Linné, (Eds.), *Approaches to Audiences—A Reader* (London: Arnold, 1998).

8. For useful examples of how cultural studies scholars have critiqued media effects research, see Martin Barker and Julien Petley (Eds.), *Ill Effects: The Media/Violence Debate* (New York: Routledge, 2001); David Gauntlett, *Moving Experiences: Understanding Television's Influences and Effects* (London: John Libbey, 1995); David Buckingham, *After the Death of Childhood: Growing Up in the Age of Electronic Media* (London: Polity, 2000); Marsha Kinder, "Contextualizing Video Game Violence: From Teenage Mutant Ninja Turtles 1 to Mortal Kombat 2," in Patricia M. Greenfield and Rodney R. Cooking (Eds.), *Interacting With Video* (Norwood, NJ: Ablex, 1996).

9. For a book that addresses this question from a range of different methodological perspectives, see Jeffrey H. Goldstein (Ed.), *Why We Watch: The Attractions of Violent Entertainment* (Oxford, UK: Oxford University Press, 1998).

10. For a useful overview on how cognitive theory of affect might inform media studies, see Carl R. Plantinga and Greg M. Smith (Eds.), *Passionate Views: Film, Cognition and Emotion* (Baltimore: Johns Hopkins University Press, 1999).

11. Ann Hagell and Tim Newburn, *Young Offenders and the Media: Viewing Habits and Preferences* (London: Policy Studies Institute, 1994).

12. For a useful overview of this research, see David Hodge and Robert Tripp, *Children and Television: A Semiotic Approach* (Palo Alto, CA: Stanford University Press, 1986).

13. For an overview of current research on animals and play, see Marc Bekoff and John A. Byers (Eds.), *Animal Play: Evolutionary, Comparative, and Ecological Perspective* (Cambridge, UK: Cambridge University Press, 1998).

14. See, for example, Don Tappscott, *Growing Up Digital: The Rise of the Net Generation* (New York: McGraw-Hill, 1999) and Julian Sefton-Green (Ed.), *Digital Diversions: Youth Culture in the Age of Multimedia* (London: University College Press, 1998).

15. These ideas are more fully developed in Henry Jenkins, "Empowering Children in the Digital Age: Towards a Radical Media Pedagogy," *Radical Teacher*, Spring 1997, and Henry Jenkins (Ed.), *The Children's Culture Reader* (New York: New York University Press, 1998).

16. See, for example, Justine Cassell and Henry Jenkins, "Chess for Girls? Gender and Computer Games," and Henry Jenkins (Ed.), "Voices From the Combat Zone: Game Grrlz Talk Back" in Justine Cassell and Henry Jenkins (Eds.), *From Barbie to Mortal Kombat: Gender and Computer Games* (Cambridge, MA: MIT Press, 1998).

17. For a fuller development of this argument, see Henry Jenkins, "Complete Freedom of Movement: Computer Games as Gendered Playspaces," in Justine Cassell and Henry Jenkins (Eds.), *From Barbie to Mortal Kombat: Gender and Computer Games* (Cambridge, MA: MIT Press, 1998).

18. For a historical analysis that stresses the functions of resistant play, see E. Arthur Rotundo, *American Manhood: Transformations in Masculinity From the Revolution to the Modern Era* (New York: Basic Books, 1994). For a useful study of children's pleasures in transgressive fantasies, see Gerald Jones, *Killing Monsters: Why Children Need Superheroes, Fantasy Games, and Make-Believe Violence* (New York: Basic Books, 2002).

19. Bruno Bettelheim, *The Uses of Enchantment: The Meaning and Importance of Fairy Tales* (New York: Vintage Books, 1988).

20. See, for example, Steve Silberman, "We're Teen, We're Queer, and We've Got E-mail," in David Trend (Ed.), *Reading Digital Culture* (Oxford, UK: Basil Blackwell, 2001).

21. For a study guide that was used to conduct conversations about youth and media following Columbine, see Henry Jenkins, "Encouraging Conversations About Popular Culture and Media Convergence."

22. For an essay designed to model parent-child communications about popular culture, see Henry Jenkins III and Henry Jenkins IV, "The Monsters Next Door": A Father-Son Conversation About Buffy, Moral Panic, and Generational Differences," in Lisa Parks (Ed.),

Red Noise: Buffy the Vampire Slayer *and Critical Television Studies* (working title), Durham, NC: Duke University Press, forthcoming 2002.

23. I expand on this idea of rethinking the ratings system in Henry Jenkins, "Digital Renaissance: Ratings Are Dead; Long Live Ratings," *Technology Review*, November 2001.

24. For further reflections on the concept of "meaningful violence" in contemporary popular culture, see James Cain and Henry Jenkins, "I'm Gonna Git Medieval on Your Ass!": A Conversation About Violence and Culture," in Helaine Possner (Ed.), *The Culture of Violence* (Amherst: University of Massachusetts at Amherst, forthcoming).

38

HIDDEN POLITICS

Discursive and Institutional Policing of Rap Music

◆ Tricia Rose

. . . The way rap and rap-related violence are discussed in the popular media is fundamentally linked to the larger social discourse on the spatial control of black people. Formal policies that explicitly circumscribe housing, school, and job options for black people have been outlawed; however, informal, yet trenchant forms of institutional discrimination still exist in full force. Underwriting these de facto forms of social containment is the understanding that black people are a threat to social order. Inside of this, black urban teenagers are the most profound symbolic referent for internal threats to social order. Not surprisingly, then, young African Americans are in fundamentally antagonistic relationships to the institutions that most prominently frame and constrain their lives. The public school system, the police, and the popular media perceive and construct young African Americans as a dangerous internal element in urban America; an element that if allowed to roam freely, will threaten the social order; an element that must be policed. Since rap music is understood as the predominant symbolic voice of black urban males, it heightens this sense

NOTE: From *Black Noise: Rap Music and Black Culture in Contemporary America*, by Tricia Rose, 1994, Hanover, NH: Wesleyan University Press. Copyright © 1994. Reprinted by permission.

of threat and reinforces dominant white middle-class objections to urban black youths who do not aspire to (but are haunted by) white middle-class standards.

My experiences and observations while attending several large-venue rap concerts in major urban centers serve as disturbingly obvious cases of how black urban youth are stigmatized, vilified, and approached with hostility and suspicion by authority figures. I offer a description of my confrontation and related observations not simply to prove that such racially and class-motivated hostility exists but, instead, to use it as a case from which to tease out how the public space policing of black youth and rap music feeds into and interacts with other media, municipal, and corporate policies that determine who can publicly gather and how.

Thousands of young black people milled around waiting to get into the large arena. The big rap summer tour was in town, and it was a prime night to see and be seen. The "pre-show show" was in full effect. Folks were dressed in the latest fly-gear: bicycle shorts, high-top sneakers, chunk jewelry, baggie pants, and polka-dotted tops. Hair style was a fashion show in itself: high-top fade designs, dreads, corkscrews, and braids with gold and purple sparkles. Crews of young women were checking out the brothers; posses of brothers were scoping out the sisters, each comparing styles among themselves. Some wide-eyed pre-teenyboppers were soaking in the teenage energy, thrilled to be out with the older kids.

As the lines for entering the arena began to form, dozens of mostly white private security guards hired by the arena management (many of whom are off-duty cops making extra money), dressed in red polyester V-neck sweaters and gray work pants, began corralling the crowd through security checkpoints. The free-floating spirit began to sour, and in its place began to crystallize a sense of hostility mixed with humiliation. Men and women were lined up separately in preparation for the weapon search. Each of the concertgoers would go through a body patdown, pocketbook, knapsack, and

soul search. Co-ed groups dispersed, people moved toward their respective search lines. The search process was conducted in such a way that each person being searched was separated from the rest of the line. Those searched could not function as a group, and subtle interactions between the guard and person being searched could not be easily observed. As the concertgoers approached the guards, I noticed a distinct change in posture and attitude. From a distance, it seemed that the men were being treated with more hostility than the women in line. In the men's area, there was an almost palpable sense of hostility on behalf of the guards as well as the male patrons. Laughing and joking among men and women, which had been loud and buoyant up until this point, turned into virtual silence.

As I approached the female security guards, my own anxiety increased. What if they found something I was not allowed to bring inside? What was prohibited, anyway? I stopped and thought: All I have in my small purse is my wallet, eyeglasses, keys, and a notepad—nothing "dangerous." The security woman patted me down, scanned my body with an electronic scanner while she anxiously kept an eye on the other black women in line to make sure that no one slipped past her. She opened my purse and fumbled through it pulling out a nail file. She stared at me provocatively, as if to say "why did you bring this in here?" I didn't answer her right away and hoped that she would drop it back into my purse and let me go through. She continued to stare at me, sizing me up to see if I was "there to cause trouble." By now, my attitude had turned foul; my childlike enthusiasm to see my favorite rappers had all but fizzled out. I didn't know the file was in my purse, but the guard's accusatory posture rendered such excuses moot. I finally replied tensely, "It's a nail file, what's the problem?" She handed it back to me, satisfied, I suppose, that I was not intending to use it as a weapon, and I went in to the arena. As I passed her, I thought to myself, "This arena is a public place, and I am entitled to come here and bring a nail file if I want to." But these words rang empty in my head; the language of entitlement couldn't erase my sense of alienation. I felt harassed and unwanted. This arena wasn't mine, it was hostile, alien territory. The unspoken message hung in the air: "You're not wanted here, let's get this over with and send you all back to where you came from."

I recount this incident for two reasons. First, a hostile tenor, if not actual verbal abuse, is a regular part of rap fan contact with arena security and police. This is not an isolated or rare example, incidents similar to it continue to take place at many rap concerts.[1] Rap concertgoers were barely tolerated and regarded with heightened suspicion. Second, arena security forces, a critical facet in the political economy of rap and its related sociologically based crime discourse, contribute to the high level of anxiety and antagonism that confront young African Americans. Their military posture is a surface manifestation of a complex network of ideological and economic processes that "justify" the policing of rap music, black youths, and black people in general. Although my immediate sense of indignation in response to public humiliation may be related to a sense of entitlement that comes from my status as a cultural critic, thus separating me from many of the concertgoers, my status as a young African American woman is a critical factor in the way I was *treated* in this instance, as well as many others.[2]

Rap artists articulate a range of reactions to the scope of institutional policing faced by many young African Americans. However, the lyrics that address the police directly—what Ice Cube has called "revenge fantasies"—have caused the most extreme and unconstitutional reaction from law enforcement officials in metropolitan concert arena venues. The precedent-setting example took place in 1989 and involved Compton-based rap group NWA (Niggas with Attitude) that at that time featured Ice Cube as a lead rapper. Their album *Straight Outta Compton* contained a cinematic,

well-crafted, gritty, and vulgar rap entitled "___ the Police," which in the rap itself filled in the f.u.c.k. at every appropriate opportunity. This song and its apparent social resonance among rap fans and black youths in general provoked an unprecedented official FBI letter from Milt Ahlerich, an FBI assistant director, which expressed the FBI's concern over increasing violence (indirectly linking music to this increase) and stating that, as law enforcement officials "dedicate their lives to the protection of our citizens . . . recordings such as the one from NWA are both discouraging and degrading to the brave, dedicated officers." He justifies this targeting of NWA by suggesting that the song allegedly advocates violence against police officers. As far as Ahlerich knows, the FBI has never adopted an official position on a record, book, or artwork in the history of the agency.[3] NWA's "___ the Police" is what finally smoked them out. This official statement would be extraordinary enough, given its tenuous constitutionality, but what follows is even worse. According to Dave Marsh and Phyllis Pollack, nobody at the agency purchased the record, nor could Ahlerich explain how he had received these lyrics other than from "responsible fellow officers." Furthermore, Ahlerich's letter fueled an informal fax network among police agencies that urged cops to help cancel NWA's concerts. Marsh and Pollack summarize the effects of this campaign:

Since late spring (of 1989), their shows have been jeopardized or aborted in Detroit (where the group was briefly detained by cops), Washington, D.C., Chattanooga, Milwaukee, and Tyler, Texas. NWA played Cincinnati only after Bengal lineback and City Councilman Reggie Williams and several of his teammates spoke up for them. During the summer's tour, NWA prudently chose not to perform "____ the Police" (its best song), and just singing a few lines of it at Detroit's Joe Louis arena caused the Motor City police to rush the stage. While the cops scuffled with the security staff, NWA escaped to their hotel. Dozens of policemen were waiting for them there, and they detained the group for 15 minutes. "We just wanted to show the kids," an officer told the *Hollywood Reporter*, "that you can't say 'fuck the police' in Detroit."[4]

Unless, of course, you're a cop. Clearly, police forces have almost unchallengable entree in these arenas. If the police break through security to rush the stage, whom do security call to contain the police? Or as KRS-One might say, "Who Protects Us From You?" These large arenas are not only surveilled, but also they are, with the transmission of a police fax, subject to immediate occupation. What "justifies" this occupation? A symbolic challenge to the police in a song that, as Marsh and Pollack observe, "tells of a young man who loses his temper over brutal police sweeps based on appearance, not actions, like the ones frequently performed by the LAPD. In the end the young man threatens to smoke the next flatfoot who fucks with him." It is clearly not in the interests of business owners to challenge the police on these matters, they cannot afford to jeopardize their access to future police services, so that the artists, in this case, find themselves fleeing the stage after attempting to perform a song that is supposed to be constitutionally protected.

It is this ideological position on black youth that frames the media and institutional attacks on rap and separates resistance to rap from attacks sustained by rock 'n' roll artists. Rap music is by no means the only form of expression under attack. Popular white forms of expression, especially heavy metal, have recently been the target of increased sanctions and assaults by politically and economically powerful organizations, such as the Parent's Music Resource Center, The American Family Association, and Focus on the Family. These organizations are not fringe groups, they are supported by major corporations, national-level politicians, school associations, and local police and municipal officials.[5]

However, there are critical differences between the attacks made against black youth expression and white youth expression. The terms of the assault on rap music, for example, are part of a long-standing sociologically based discourse that considers black influences a cultural threat to American society.[6] Consequently, rappers, their fans, and black youths in general are constructed as coconspirators in the spread of black cultural influence. For the antirock organizations, heavy metal is a "threat to the fiber of American society," but the fans (e.g., "our children") are *victims* of its influence. Unlike heavy metal's victims, rap fans are the youngest representatives of a black presence whose cultural difference is perceived as an internal threat to America's cultural development. *They* victimize *us*. These differences in the ideological nature of the sanctions against rap and heavy metal are of critical importance, because they illuminate the ways in which racial discourses deeply inform public transcripts and social control efforts. This racial discourse is so profound that when Ice-T's speed metal band (*not rap group*) Body Count was forced to remove "Cop Killer" from its debut album because of attacks from politicians, these attacks consistently referred to it as a rap song (even though it in no way can be mistaken for rap) to build a negative head of steam in the public. As Ice-T describes it, "There is absolutely no way to listen to the song 'Cop Killer' and call it a rap record. It's so far from rap. But, politically, they know by saying the word *rap* they can get a lot of people who think, 'Rap-black-rap-black-ghetto,' and don't like it. You say the word *rock*, people say, 'Oh, but I like Jefferson Airplane, I like Fleetwood Mac—that's rock.' They don't want to use the word rock & roll to describe this song."[7] . . .

The social construction of "violence," that is, when and how particular acts are defined as violent, is part of a larger process of labeling social phenomena.[8] Rap-related violence is one facet of the contemporary "urban crisis" that consists of a "rampant drug culture" and "wilding gangs" of black and Hispanic youths. When the *Daily News* headline reads, "L.I. Rap-Slayers Sought" or a *Newsweek* story is dubbed "The Rap Attitude," these labels are important, because they assign a particular meaning to an event and locate that event in a larger context.[9] Labels are critical to the process of interpretation, because they provide a context and frame for social behavior. As Stuart Hall et al. point out in *Policing the Crisis,* once a label is assigned, "the use of the label is likely to mobilize this whole referential context, with all its associated meaning and connotations."[10] The question then, is not "is there really violence at rap concerts," but how are these crimes contextualized, labeled? . . . Whose interests do these interpretive strategies serve? What are the repercussions?

Venue owners have the final word on booking decisions, but they are not the only group of institutional gatekeepers. The other major powerbroker, the insurance industry, can refuse to insure an act approved by venue management. In order for any tour to gain access to a venue, the band or group hires a booking agent who negotiates the act's fee. The booking agent hires a concert promoter who "purchases" the band and then presents the band to both the insurance company and the venue managers. If an insurance company will not insure the act, because they decide it represents an unprofitable risk, then the venue owner will not book the act. Furthermore, the insurance company and the venue owner reserve the right to charge whatever insurance or permit fees they deem reasonable on a case-by-case basis. So, for example, Three Rivers Stadium in Pittsburgh, Pennsylvania, tripled its normal $20,000 permit fee for the Grateful Dead. The insurance companies who still insure rap concerts have raised their minimum coverage from about $500,000 to between $4 and 5 million worth of coverage per show.[11] Several major arenas make it almost impossible

to book a rap show, and others have refused outright to book rap acts at all.

These responses to rap music bear a striking resemblance to the New York City cabaret laws instituted in the 1920s in response to jazz music. A wide range of licensing and zoning laws, many of which remained in effect until the late 1980s, restricted the places where jazz could be played and how it could be played. These laws were attached to moral anxieties regarding black cultural effects and were in part intended to protect white patrons from jazz's "immoral influences." They defined and contained the kind of jazz that could be played by restricting the use of certain instruments (especially drums and horns) and established elaborate licensing policies that favored more established and mainstream jazz club owners and prevented a number of prominent musicians with minor criminal records from obtaining cabaret cards.[12]

During an interview with "Richard" from a major talent agency that books many prominent rap acts, I asked him if booking agents had responded to venue bans on rap music by leveling charges of racial discrimination against venue owners. His answer clearly illustrates the significance of the institutional power at stake:

> These facilities are privately owned, they can do anything they want. You say to them: "You won't let us in because you're discriminating against black kids." They say to you, "Fuck you, who cares. Do whatever you got to do, but you're not coming in here. You, I don't need you, I don't want you. Don't come, don't bother me. I will book hockey, ice shows, basketball, country music and graduations. I will do all kinds of things 360 days out of the year. But I don't need you. I don't need fighting, shootings and stabbings." Why do they care? They have their image to maintain.[13]

Richard's imaginary conversation with a venue owner is a pointed description of the scope of power these owners have over access to large public urban spaces and the racially exclusionary silent policy that governs booking policies. . . .

Because rap has an especially strong urban metropolitan following, freezing it out of these major metropolitan arenas has a dramatic impact on rappers' ability to reach their fan base in live performance. Public Enemy, Queen Latifah, and other rap groups use live performance settings to address current social issues, media miscoverage, and other problems that especially concern black America. For example, during a December 1988 concert in Providence, R.I., Chuck D from Public Enemy explained that the Boston arena refused to book the show and read from a *Boston Herald* article that depicted rap fans as a problematic element and that gave its approval of the banning of the show. To make up for this rejection, Chuck D called out to the "Roxbury crowd in the house," to make them feel at home in Providence. Each time Chuck mentioned Roxbury, sections of the arena erupted in especially exuberant shouts and screams.[14] Because black youths are constructed as a permanent threat to social order, large public gatherings will always be viewed as dangerous events. The larger arenas possess greater potential for mass access and unsanctioned behavior. And black youths, who are highly conscious of their alienated and marginalized lives, will continue to be hostile toward those institutions and environments that reaffirm this aspect of their reality.

The presence of a predominantly black audience in a 15,000 capacity arena, communicating with major black cultural icons whose music, lyrics, and attitude illuminate and affirm black fears and grievances, provokes a fear of the consolidation of black rage. Venue owner and insurance company anxiety over broken chairs, insurance claims, or fatalities are not important in and of themselves, they are important because they symbolize a loss of control that might involve challenges to the current social configuration. They suggest the possibility that

black rage can be directed at the people and institutions that support the containment and oppression of black people. As West Coast rapper Ice Cube points out in *The Nigga Ya Love to Hate*, "Just think if niggas decided to retaliate?"[15]

. . . Deconstructing the media's ideological perspective on black crime does not suggest that real acts of violence by and against black youths do not take place. However, real acts are not accessible to us without critical mediation by hegemonic discourses. Consequently, this "real" violence is always/already positioned as a part of images of black violence and within the larger discourse on the urban black threat. Although violence at rap concerts can be understood as a visible instance of crimes by and against blacks, because it takes place in a white safety zone, it is interpreted as a loss of control on home territory. The fact that rap-related concert violence takes place outside the invisible fence that surrounds black poor communities raises the threat factor. Rappers have rearticulated a longstanding awareness among African Americans that crimes against blacks (especially black-on-black crimes) do not carry equal moral weight or political imperative.

. . . The media's repetition of rap-related violence and the urban problematic that it conjures are not limited to the crime blotters, they also inform live performance critiques. In both contexts, the assumption is that what makes rap newsworthy is its spatial and cultural disruption, not its musical innovation and expressive capacity.[16] Consequently, dominant media critiques of rap's sounds and styles are necessarily conditioned by the omnipresent fears of black influence, fears of a black aesthetic planet.

In a particularly hostile *Los Angeles Times* review of the Public Enemy 1990 summer tour at the San Diego Sports Arena, John D'Agostino articulates a complex microcosm of social anxieties concerning black youths, black aesthetics, and rap music. D'Agostino's extended next-day rock review column entitled: "Rap Concert Fails to Sizzle in San Diego" features a prominent sidebar that reads: "Although it included a brawl, the Sports Arena concert seemed to lack steam and could not keep the under-sized capacity audience energized." In the opening sentence, he confesses that "rap is not a critics' music; it is a disciples' music," a confession that hints at his cultural illiteracy and should be enough to render his subsequent critique irrelevant. What music is for critics? To which critics is he referring? Evidently, critical reviews of rap music in *The Source* and the *Village Voice* are written by disciples. D'Agostino's opening paragraph presents the concert audience as mindless and dangerous religious followers, mesmerized by rap's rhythms:

> For almost five hours, devotees of the Afros, Queen Latifah, Kid 'N Play. Digital Underground, Big Daddy Kane and headliners Public Enemy were jerked into spasmodic movement by what seemed little more than intermittent segments of a single rhythmic continuum. It was hypnotic in the way of sensory deprivation, a mind- and body-numbing marathon of monotony whose deafening, prerecorded drum and bass tracks and roving klieg lights frequently turned the audience of 6,500 into a single-minded moveable beast. Funk meets Nuremberg Rally.[17]

Apparently, the music is completely unintelligible to him, and his inability to interpret the sounds frightens him. His reading, which makes explicit his fear and ignorance, condemns rap precisely on the grounds that make it compelling. For example, because he cannot explain why a series of bass or drum lines moves the crowd, the audience seems "jerked into spasmodic movement," clearly suggesting an "automatic" or "involuntary" response to the music. The coded familiarity of the rhythms and hooks that rap samples from other black music, especially funk and soul music, carries with it the power of black

collective memory. These sounds are cultural markers, and responses to them are not involuntary at all but in fact densely and actively intertextual; they immediately conjure collective black experience, past and present.[18] He senses the rhythmic continuum but interprets it as "monotonous and mind- and body-numbing." The very pulse that fortified the audience in San Diego, left him feeling "sensory deprived." The rhythms that empowered and stimulated the crowd, numbed his body and mind.

His description of the music as "numbing" and yet capable of moving the crowd as a "single-minded, moveable beast" captures his confusion and anxiety regarding the power and meaning of the drums. What appeared "monotonous" frightened him precisely because that same pulse energized and empowered the audience. Unable to negotiate the relationship between his fear of the audience and the wall of sound that supported black pleasure while it pushed him to the margins, D'Agostino interprets black pleasure as dangerous and automatic. As his representation of the concert aura regressed, mindless religious rap disciples no longer provided a sufficient metaphor. The hegemonic ideology to which D'Agostino's article subscribes was displaced by the sense of community facilitated by rap music as well as the black aesthetics the music privileged.[19] He ends his introduction by linking funk music to an actual Nazi rally to produce the ultimate depiction of black youths as an aggressive, dangerous, racist element whose behavior is sick, inexplicable, and orchestrated by rappers (that is, rally organizers). Rap, he ultimately suggests, is a disciples' soundtrack for the celebration of black fascist domination. The concert that "failed to sizzle" was in fact too hot to handle.

Once his construction of black fascism is in place, D'Agostino devotes the bulk of his review to the performances, describing them as "juvenile," "puerile," and, in the case of Public Enemy, one that "relies on controversy to maintain interest." Halfway through the review, he describes the "brawl" that followed Digital Underground's performance:

> After the house lights were brought up following DU's exit, a fight broke out in front of the stage. Security guards, members of various rappers' entourages, and fans joined in the fray that grew to mob size and then pushed into a corner of the floor at one side of the stage. People rushed the area from all parts of the arena, but the scrappers were so tightly balled together that few serious punches could be thrown, and, in a few minutes, a tussle that threatened to become a small scale riot instead lost steam.[20]

From my mezzanine-level stage side seat, which had a clear view of the stage, this "brawl" looked like nothing more than a small-scale scuffle. Fans did not rush from all areas to participate in the fight, which was easily contained, as he himself points out, in a few minutes. In fact, few people responded to the fight except by watching silently until the fracas fizzled out. He neglects to consider that the 20-plus minute waiting periods *between each act* and the overarching sense of disrespect with which young black fans are treated might have contributed to the frustration. Out of 6,500 people, a group of no more than 20, who were quickly surrounded by security guards, falls significantly short of a "mob" and "threatened to become a small scale riot" only in D'Agostino's colonial imagination.

D'Agostino's review closes by suggesting that rap is fizzling out, that juvenile antics and staged controversy no longer hold the audience's attention and therefore signify the death of rap music. What happened to the "single-minded moveable beast" that reared its ugly head in the introduction? How did black fascism dissolve into harmless puerility in less than five hours? D'Agostino had to make that move; his distaste for rap music, coupled with his fear of black youths, left him little alternative but to slay the single-minded beast by disconnecting its power source. His review sustains a fear of black energy and passion and at the same time allays these fears by suggesting that rap is dying. The imminent death of rap music is a dominant myth that deliberately misconstructs black rage as juvenile rebellion and at the same time retains the necessary specter of black violence, justifying the social repression of rap music and black youths. . . .

Rap music is fundamentally linked to larger social constructions of black culture as an internal threat to dominant American culture and social order. Rap's capacity as a form of testimony, as an articulation of a young black urban critical voice of social protest, has profound potential as a basis for a language of liberation.[21] Contestation over the meaning and significance of rap music and its ability to occupy public space and retain expressive freedom constitutes a central aspect of contemporary black cultural politics.

During the centuries-long period of Western slavery, there were elaborate rules and laws designed to control slave populations. Constraining the mobility of slaves, especially at night and in groups, was of special concern; slave masters reasoned that revolts could be organized by blacks who moved too freely and without surveillance.[22] Slave masters were rightfully confident that blacks had good reason to escape, revolt, and retaliate. Contemporary laws and practices curtailing and constraining black mobility in urban America function in much the same way and for similar reasons. Large groups of African Americans, especially teenagers, represent a threat to the social order of oppression. Albeit more sophisticated and more difficult to trace, contemporary policing of African Americans resonates with the legacy of slavery.

Rap's poetic voice is deeply political in content and spirit, but rap's hidden struggle, the struggle over access to public space, community resources, and the interpretation of black expression, constitutes rap's hidden politics.

◆ *Notes*

1. At a 1988 rap concert in New Haven, Connecticut, a young African American male protested the weapon search shouting, "Fuck it! I'm not going through the search." But after a short protest, realizing that he would have to forfeit his ticket, he entered the lines and proceeded through the search station. In the summer of 1990, outside the San Diego Sports Arena, a young woman wanted to go inside to see if her friend had already arrived and was waiting inside, but she said that she would rather wait outside a bit longer instead of having to go through the search twice if it turned out that her friend was not in fact inside.

2. Public space discrimination and the public injury to dignify it creates is not limited to black teenagers. Feagin's "Continuing Significance of Race" illustrates that in post-Civil Rights America, discriminatory practices against blacks of all ages and classes remain a significant part of public space interaction with whites. He points out a number of critical public spaces in which black men and women are likely to be humiliated and discriminated against. His findings are in keeping with my experiences and observations and the context within which they took place.

3. Dave Marsh and Phyllis Pollack, "Wanted for Attitude," *Village Voice*, 10 October 1989, pp. 33-37.

4. Ibid, pp. 33-37.

5. See Robert Walser, *Running With the Devil: Power, Gender and Madness in Heavy Metal Music* (Hanover, CT: University Press of New England, 1993). See also Marsh and Pollack, "Wanted," and *Rock and Roll Confidential (RRC)*, especially their special pamphlet "You've Got a Right to Rock: Don't Let Them Take It Away." This pamphlet is a detailed documentation of the censorship movements and their institutional bases and attacks. The *RRC* is edited by David Marsh and can be subscribed to by writing to *RRC*, Dept. 7, Box 341305, Los Angeles, CA 90034. See also Linda Martin and Kerry Seagrave, *Anti-Rock: The Opposition to Rock 'n' Roll* (Hamden, CT: Archon Books, 1988).

6. In fact, the attacks on earlier popular black expressions such as jazz and rock 'n' roll were grounded in fears that white youths were deriving too much pleasure from black expressions and that these primitive, alien expressions were dangerous to their moral development. See Steve Chapple and Reebee Garofalo, *Rock 'n' Roll Is Here to Pay* (Chicago: Nelson, 1979); Lewis A. Erenberg, *Steppin' Out*; Jones, *Blues People*; Ogren, *Jazz Revolution*; Lipsitz, *Time Passages*.

7. Cited in Light, "Ice-T."

8. See Messerschmidt, "*Capitalism*," especially Chapter 3, "Powerless Men and Street Crime." Messerschmidt notes that "public perception of what serious violent crime is—and who the violent criminals are—is determined first by what the state defines as violent and the types of violence it overlooks. . . . The criminal law defines only certain kinds of violence as criminal—namely, one-on-one forms of murder, assault, and robbery, which are the types of violence young marginalized minority males primarily engage in. The criminal law excludes certain types of avoidable killings, injuries, and thefts engaged in by powerful white males, such as maintaining hazardous working conditions or producing unsafe products" (p. 52).

9. Mark Kruggel and Jerry Roga, "L. I. Rap Slayer Sought," New York *Daily News,* 12 September 1988, p. 3; David Gates et al., "The Rap Attitude," *Newsweek*, 19 March 1990, pp. 56-63.

10. Stuart Hall et al., *Policing the Crisis* (London: Macmillan, 1977), p. 19.

11. Interview with "Richard," a talent agency representative from a major agency that represents dozens of major rap groups, October 1990.

12. Paul Chevigny, *Gigs: Jazz and the Cabaret Laws in New York City* (London: Routledge, 1991). See also Ogren, *Jazz Revolution*.

13. Rose interview with "Richard." I have decided not to reveal the identity of this talent agency representative, because it serves no particular purpose here and may have a detrimental effect on his employment.

14. Roxbury is a poor, predominantly black area in Boston.

15. Ice Cube, "The Nigga Ya Love to Hate," *AmeriKKKa's Most Wanted* (Priority Records, 1990).

16. See especially David Samuel, "The Real Face of Rap," *The New Republic*, 11 November 1991, and Gates et al., "The Rap Attitude." In contrast, Jon Parales and Peter Watrous, the primary popular music critics for the *New York Times*, have made noteworthy attempts to offer complex and interesting critiques of rap music. In many cases, a significant number of letters to the editor appeared in following weeks complaining about the appearance and content of their reviews and articles.

17. John D'Agostino, "Rap Concert Fails to Sizzle in San Diego," *Los Angeles Times* (San Diego edition), 28 August 1990, pp. F1, F5. This review is accompanied by subsequent short articles about charges brought against rappers for "obscene conduct" while on stage—fully clothed—during this concert and the massive coverage of the 2 Live Crew controversy regarding obscene lyrics. For example, Michael Granberry, "Digital Underground May Face Prosecution," *Los Angeles Times*, 17 November 1990, p. F9; "2 Rap Beat, Must Beat Rap," *New York Daily News*, 4 August 1990, p. 3. It is also quite important to point out how much D'Agostino's description of rap music is modeled after arguments made by T. W. Adorno regarding jazz music in the 1940s. In "On Popular Music," Adorno refers to rhythms in jazz as a sign of obedience to domination of the machine age: "The cult of the machine which is represented by unabating jazz beats involves a self-renunciation that cannot but take root in the form of a fluctuating uneasiness somewhere in the personality of the obedient." See Frith and Goodwin, eds., *On Record*, p. 313.

18. See Lipsitz, *Time Passages*, for an extended analysis of this process.

19. See Ray Pratt, "Popular Music, Free Space, and the Quest for Community," *Popular Music and Society*, vol. 13 no. 4, 59-76, 1989, on the question of public space moments of community experiences, and see Snead, "On Repetition."

20. D'Agostino, "Rap Concert," p. F5.

21. bell hooks, *Yearning: Race, Gender and Cultural Politics* (Boston: South End, 1990).

22. David Brion Davis, *The Problem of Slavery in Western Culture* (Ithaca, NY: Cornell University Press, 1966).

39

THE PORNOGRAPHY DEBATES

Beyond Cause and Effect

◆ Karen Boyle

C oncerns about media "effects"—and about the effects of violent and pornographic media in particular—have led to a massive research industry which has attracted considerable quantities of both funding and publicity over some 60 years. Yet, as has been well documented elsewhere, the results of this vast body of empirical work are both inconclusive and hotly contested.[1] As David Gauntlett (1997) notes in a recent article, there are two potential conclusions that can be drawn from any detailed analysis of this research. First, if, despite this plethora of research, direct effects of the media upon behaviour have not been identified, we may conclude that they are simply not there to be found.[2] Second, it can be argued that media effects research has consistently taken the wrong approach to the mass media, its audiences, and society in general (p. 120). It is this latter argument which should be of particular concern to feminists and will be the focus of this [chapter].

Feminist involvement in the effects debate has, not surprisingly, focused on the relationship between men's consumption of pornography and subsequent likelihood of violence against women. Although the scientific effects discourse is not a true reflection of anti-pornography feminists' theory

NOTE: Reprinted from *Women's Studies International Forum*, Vol. 23, No. 2, 2000, pp. 187-195, Boyle: "The Pornography Debates: Beyond Cause and Effect," with permission from Elsevier Science. Copyright © 2000 by Elsevier Science Ltd.

or epistemology, the findings of experimental studies have been used in feminist campaigns to convince policy makers about the harm of pornography (Hardy, 1998, pp. 10-13).[3] However, as I will demonstrate, linking the feminist case against pornography to flawed media effects research has significantly damaged the feminist anti-pornography movement. . . .

This [chapter] aims, first, to identify why traditional effects research, which attempts to establish a causal relationship between pornography and violent behaviour, is a dubious ally for anti-pornography feminism. Critical analysis of the complex and contradictory findings of effects research is beyond the scope of the current study and, in any case, has been thoroughly dealt with elsewhere.[4] Rather, in building on Gauntlett's (1997) claim that effects research has consistently taken the wrong approach to media, audiences, and society, the neglected issue of gender in effects research will be a central concern. This shall be explored with reference to the body of effects research rather than with specific reference to individual studies. Thus, the methodological complexities of different approaches to the question are contracted to enable an analysis of what I will call—following Gauntlett (1997)—the "effects model" (p. 120). Second, and developing out of this critique, I will explore the enduring implications of the effects model for feminist anti-pornography politics.

◆ Effects Research: A Dubious Ally

For readers unfamiliar with effects research, even a brief synopsis of the most commonly used research designs should be enough to set alarm bells ringing. The experimental work of U.S.-based effects researchers Edward Donnerstein, Daniel Linz, Neil Malamuth, and Dolf Zillmann is the most frequently cited by anti-pornography feminists (e.g., Dworkin & MacKinnon, 1988; Russell, 1993b, 1993c), yet this work has primarily been conducted in the artificial world of the laboratory. The basic procedure in such experiments is to perform an initial assessment on a selected sample of individuals, expose them, under laboratory conditions, to a specified category of "pornography" (e.g., nudity, non-violent sexual behaviour, violent sexual behaviour), and then conduct another assessment to measure the effects of the exposure. A number of controlled variables arise at each stage. At the first assessment, the sample may be classified by gender and/or predisposition to aggression, for example. The experimental stage may vary the category of pornography used, the degree of exposure, and the gender and interactive behaviour of the experimenter (Hardy, 1998, p. 32). The behavioural effects of exposure may be measured by asking respondents to administer electric shocks or aversive noise stimuli to one of the research team in the guise of a learning experiment. Attitudinal effects may be assessed through responses to a rape trial or to other reported sexual violence against women. Participants are not generally told the nature and purpose of the experiment, raising ethical concerns rarely considered in the literature.

There are a number of further problems with these studies that can be usefully summarised here. First, as Gauntlett (1997) notes, the effects model tackles social problems backwards:

To explain the problem of violence in society, researchers should begin with that social violence and seek to explain it with reference, quite obviously, to those who engage in it: their identity, background, character and so on. The "media effects" approach, in this sense, comes at the problem *backwards*, by starting with the media and then trying to lasso connections from there on to social beings, rather than the other way around . . . the "backwards" approach involves the mistake of looking at individuals, rather than society, in relation to the mass media. (pp. 120-121)

This should raise a number of concerns for feminists. To see pornography as the "*cause*" of yet-to-be-determined effects is to position pornography as the active agent and deny the agency, choice, and, crucially, the responsibility, of the individual men who use pornography in ways that are abusive to women. The effects model sees the media in isolation, divorced from society and as uniquely powerful. Further, theories of causality, by definition, cannot account for the cycle of abuse on which much audio-visual pornography depends and which, as I have suggested, has been central to anti-pornography feminists' analyses of pornography (Cole, 1989, p. 37). Thus the terms of the effects debate preclude a consideration of the harm done to women, men, and children in the *production* of pornography. If a woman is raped in order for a particular artefact to exist, then her reality is obscured if we ask simply whether the artefact is the cause of further violence.

However, although effects research begins with the artefact rather than the violence or its perpetrator, these studies have betrayed a startling lack of concern over those very artefacts. For example, effects studies have assumed that definitions of media material as "violent," "sexually explicit," or "sexually violent" reflect commonly held understandings. As a result, published accounts of such studies frequently provide little detailed information about the material shown to viewers in any of these categories. This makes replication of individual studies as well as cumulative analyses of the field difficult (Allen, D'Alessio, & Brezgel, 1995). More seriously for feminists, this also masks the ideological assumptions of the researcher. In relation to violence, for example, my own review of this literature found that effects research has been predominantly concerned with acts of male-on-male physical violence as both on-screen cause and off-screen effect (Boyle, 1999). In this way, researchers

perpetuate the "normality" of male violence whilst making much violence against women invisible. In terms of the experimental research used in the pornography debate, the terms *pornographic, erotic, obscene, sexually arousing*, and *sexually explicit* are used interchangeably to refer to a diverse range of materials, from nude photographs to sexual activity between consenting adults and scenes of sexualised mutilation (Senn, 1993, p. 180). Whether respondents share the researchers' perceptions of the material as "pornographic," "erotic," "obscene," "sexually" arousing," and/or "sexually explicit" is certainly debatable. The ideological implications of these terms—both for researchers and their respondents—are largely ignored.

The problem of defining pornography is one I will return to. However, it is useful to note here that the materials used in effects research are not necessarily "pornography" as the term is widely understood in Anglo-American culture (i.e., "material sold in pornography shops for the purposes of producing sexual arousal for mostly male consumers"; Dines & Jensen, 1998, p. 65). Nor is this material necessarily "pornography" as anti-pornography feminists have defined it, namely, as material which combines sex with violence, degradation, or humiliation (e.g., Dworkin & MacKinnon, 1988, T2c).

There is a further problem here in that effects research rarely differentiates between media. So, for example, evaluating the research evidence on the relationship between exposure to sexually explicit materials and acceptance of rape myths, both Linz (1989) and Allen, Emmers, Gebhardt, and Giery (1995) conflate the findings of studies using audio, written, visual, and audio-visual material. While the messages of these texts may be similar, are viewing, listening, and reading really equivalent experiences? The failure to differentiate between media tells us little about consumers' relationships to different forms of pornographic media and also serves to further obscure the varying conditions of production. In short, for filmed pornography to exist real women, men, and children have to perform sexual acts in front of a camera. In mainstream media, the sex and violence is simulated. In written pornography, the sex is only fantasy. This is not to say that filmed pornographic fiction mirrors actors' reality, but it is important to stress that such material is not *only* fantasy but also a re-presentation of sexual acts, authenticated by the signature shots of genitalia, penetration, and ejaculation. This is significant not only in view of the varying conditions of production but also in relation to the conventions of mainstream and pornographic sex and how these position consumers.[5]

With this in mind, do we really know what effects researchers are investigating the effects *of*? If their definitions of the "violent," "pornographic," "erotic," "sexually arousing," or "sexually explicit" are neither internally consistent nor compatible with a feminist politics, then to what extent are their findings, individually or cumulatively, useful to feminists?

Effects research is, by definition, interested in a limited range of individual physiological, behavioural, and attitudinal responses to media texts. Given that, as suggested above, pornography is widely defined by its on-screen act (sex) and off-screen reaction (arousal—masturbation—orgasm); this emphasis may not initially appear to be particularly problematic. Dyer (1985), for example, argues that the pornographic film is

> based on the effect that both producers and audiences know the film is supposed to have. It is not defined . . . like the Western, gangster film or musical, by such aesthetic, textual elements as iconography, structure, style and so on, but by what it produces in the spectator. It is like genres such as the weepie and the thriller, and also low or vulgar comedy. Like all of these, it is supposed to have an effect that is registered in the spectator's body—s/he weeps, gets goose

bumps, rolls about laughing, comes. (p. 27)

Although this is by no means a universal experience of pornography, it is a severe limitation of effects research that the very effect by which pornography is defined—masturbation to orgasm—is necessarily absent from analysis. While arousal can be physiologically measured in a laboratory, this tells us nothing about individual affective responses to that arousal (e.g., pleasure, fear, shame, guilt). Outside of the effects tradition, recent Swedish research has, for example, demonstrated that young women's experiences of being "turned on" by heterosexual pornography can be accompanied by a variety of contradictory emotions related to their perceptions of heterosexuality and gender roles (Berg, 1999). Men's accounts of their pornography consumption also reveal ambivalence and anxiety about sexuality, gender, and their relationships with partners and peers (Hardy, 1998; Jensen, 1998b). The effects model ignores affective responses and the artificiality—and formality—of the setting limits the ability to measure and evaluate effective responses.

This criticism applies not only to arousal and masturbation but equally to expressions of violence in the laboratory which bear a tangential relationship to real-world behaviours. For example, violent behaviour following exposure to sexually violent stimuli may be measured by administering electric shocks or aversive noise stimuli, hitting a doll, or being unflattering about the experimenter. Notably, respondents do not freely choose this behaviour from a range of possible options, and sexual aggression is, inevitably, excluded. This gives us little understanding of the processes whereby men may actively decide to use pornography in ways abusive to women and negates differences between sexual aggression and "general aggression" (Allen, D'Alessio, & Brezgel, 1995, p. 276). The emphasis on the violent or sexual *act*, both on- and off-screen, is also problematic. As Suzanne

Kappeler (1995) argues, "If we detach the act from the person acting and regard its consequences as an effect, personal responsibility is no longer an issue" (p. 17). Blaming pornography or the movies for real-world violence thus becomes a convenient means of dodging broader questions about society, culture, and individual responsibility.

Finally, effects research has been very limited in its populations of study, although this work is often used to make unfounded generalisations about *all* viewers. Unsurprisingly, male subjects have been the focus of a vast majority of the research in this field, although gender bias is frequently hidden behind gender-neutral terms like "college students" or "viewers."[6] This reflects the concern with behavioural effects, suggesting that men act, and are therefore worthy of study, while women are acted *upon*. . . .

In summary, there are five key areas of concern with effects research which make this work extremely problematic for feminist teachers, researchers, and activists. First, the key terms of the debate are poorly defined and the conservative ideological implications hidden behind the mask of scientific objectivity. The lack of information about the materials used in these studies and the failure to differentiate between media further mystify the research process and make the cumulation of findings difficult. More important, there is no consideration of how individual consumers use and understand pornographic media or an acknowledgement of their choice, responsibility, and accountability for their behaviours. The research is further limited by the focus on a limited range of behavioural effects with little consideration of how and why those behaviours are chosen by respondents in particular circumstances. Finally, the focus on men as the population worthy of study not only marginalises the experiences of women but also assumes an active/passive dynamic where men act and women are acted upon.

Given these limitations, traditional effects research is, at best, a dubious ally for anti-pornography feminism. More seriously, perhaps, the effects discourse appears to have permeated and distorted feminist debate so that whether pornography *causes* violence against women or not has arguably become the most contested issue and the starting point for any consideration of what can or should be done about pornography. In the remainder of this [chapter] I want to highlight why I believe this shift in emphasis has been damaging for anti-pornography feminism.

Anti-Pornography ◆ Feminism and the Effects Debate

It has become something of a cliché in writing on pornography to note the difficulty of definition, and I will not rehearse these arguments here. Within anti-pornography feminism the most commonly used definition is a variation on that used by Andrea Dworkin and Catharine MacKinnon which emphasises the violent, dehumanising, and subordinating nature of pornographic representation:

Pornography is the graphic sexually explicit subordination of women through pictures and/or words that also includes one or more of the following: (i) women are presented dehumanized as sexual objects, things or commodities; or (ii) women are presented as sexual objects who enjoy pain or humiliation; or (iii) women are presented as sexual objects who experience sexual pleasure in being raped; or (iv) women are presented as sexual objects tied up or cut up or mutilated or bruised or physically hurt; or (v) women are presented in postures or positions of sexual submission, servility or display; or (vi) women's body parts— including but not limited to vaginas, breasts, or buttocks—are exhibited such that women are reduced to those parts;

or (vii) women are presented as whores by nature; or (viii) women are presented being penetrated by objects or animals; or (ix) women are presented in scenarios of degradation, injury, torture, shown as filthy or inferior, bleeding, bruised, or hurt in a context that makes these conditions sexual.

The use of men, children or transsexuals in the place of women above is also pornography. (Dworkin & McKinnon, 1988, T2c)

Dworkin and MacKinnon (1988) argue that under this definition, "pornography *is* what pornography *does*" (T2c). However, while the commonly understood definitions of pornography outlined in the previous section focus on what pornography does *to male consumers*, Dworkin and MacKinnon emphasise what pornography does *to women*. Women—not men—are placed at the centre of analysis. Or are they? As we have seen in relation to effects research, to begin with the artefact (here, pornography) and then make connections to the behaviour of social beings accords the artefact a unique power and negates the importance of individual agency. So, in this formulation, pornography—not individual behaviour—causes violence against women.

It is important to distinguish here between "causality" and "evidence of harm" although, in attempts to influence policy makers, these terms are often used interchangeably in feminist anti-pornography discourse. A "cause" is "a person, thing, event, state or action that *produces* an effect" (*Collins Concise Dictionary*). As we have seen, a major problem with theories of causality is that, by definition, they cannot account for the cycle of abuse on which much audio-visual pornography depends, an issue I will return to. We can, however, demonstrate that a woman, man, or child was harmed in the production of pornography, through forced consumption of pornography, or by being forced to enact the scenarios of pornography (e.g., *Everywoman*, 1988; Lovelace [Marchiano] &

McGrady, 1980). In addition, work both with male perpetrators and female victims of violence has documented how pornography is used to motivate and instruct men to commit sexual violence against women and then to justify that behaviour (e.g., Jensen, 1998b; MacKinnon, 1993; Wyre, 1992). MacKinnon (1993) further documents how in the former Yugoslavia, the filming of actual rape for mass consumption makes the link between pornography and violence explicit—pornography becomes war propaganda. In such cases, the making of the pornography is part of the abuse, the film a permanent record of the abuse which is, in turn, used as propaganda for future abuse.

However, even in the cases documented by MacKinnon (1993), it is a mistake to see this as proof of a causal relationship rather than as evidence of how pornography is used by its producers and consumers in actual abuse. While pornography may be an influence it is not the abusive agent. The men who make and use pornography *choose* to accept its message, and to the extent that they have access to a different understanding of women than that presented in pornography they must be held accountable (Price, 1999). To hold individual perpetrators accountable for their actions while nevertheless examining the broader social and cultural conditions in which that violence is possible, it is necessary to move beyond the effects discourse. Such an approach has to begin—not, as effects research and much anti-pornography work does—with the pornographic text, but with the existence of real-world violence. This is a key difference that makes it far more difficult to negate the experiences of real women, men, and children and to dodge the issue of personal accountability. We are no longer asking whether pornography causes violence—or is, in *all* circumstances, a record of abuse—but examining how specific pornographic texts are made and used by producers and consumers in particular ways that are harmful to others.

For this to be achieved, we also need to question how useful the term *pornography* actually is as a category for analysis. As we have already seen, effects research rarely differentiates between pornographic media, their modes of production, and consumption, a pattern repeated in much feminist anti-pornography work. Tracing the etymology of "pornography" in *Pornography: Men Possessing Women*, Andrea Dworkin (1981) notes that the word derives from the ancient Greek, *porne*, meaning whore (specifically the cheapest kind of whore), and *graphos* meaning writing, etching, or drawing. Pornography is literally writing, etching, or drawing about whores (pp. 199-200). In a contemporary context, however, such a definition is hardly sufficient. Pornography is no longer restricted to writing, etching, or drawing but includes photography, film, video, the Internet, and cable television. Unlike written, etched, or drawn pornography, photography, film, television, and, to a lesser extent, Internet pornography require real women to exist. This is not an insignificant difference. The production of photographic and filmed pornography of adults is not *necessarily* abusive,[7] but the existence of such abuse is well documented (e.g., *Everywoman*, 1988; Lederer, 1980; Lovelace [Marchiano] & McGrady, 1980; MacKinnon, 1993; Russell, 1993a). Such claims cannot be made about written, etched, or drawn pornographies.

While feminists have provided useful analyses of pornography as a genre, this approach has serious limitations. Take, for example, the slide shows, which are frequently used by feminist anti-pornography campaigners to educate women about the content of pornography. As with effects research which uses clips or images taken from longer narratives, the slide show presents pornographic images and text out of context. The extent to which these examples are "representative" is questionable (Rubin, 1993), much of the material presented is very dated, and cartoons and written text are presented alongside pictorials (see Russell, 1993d). There is an implicit assumption here, as in the effects model, that the message of pornography transcends

the medium of its representation, is ahistorical and never changing. Such generalisations are incredibly problematic and easily challenged. More seriously still, if cartoons, written text, and photographs are seen as equivalent texts, then the actual woman whose body is re-presented in the pictorial is displaced from the centre of feminist anti-pornography politics.

If the effect of the undifferentiated pornographic text on the consumer becomes the central issue, then it is perfectly possible to discuss the "promise of pornography" as a genre, based on an analysis of *written* pornographic fiction alone (Ziv, 1999). Generalising about pornography based on an analysis of written texts (see also Hardy, 1998) avoids difficult questions about who the women in pornographic photographs and films actually are, how they got there, what our relationship to them is, and who profits from their sale (Cole, 1989, p. 137). Asking such questions does not preclude an analysis of the promise and pleasure different pornographic media hold for many male and female consumers but it forces us to look beyond individualised responses to the broader context of pornographic production, representation, and consumption.

In contrast, talking about the "effects" of pornography encourages a focus on *the individual*. Such an emphasis enables anti-anti-pornography feminists to challenge evidence of pornography-related harm by presenting the stories of individual women who exercise desire and control not only in the production but also in the consumption of pornography (e.g., Assiter & Carol, 1993; Gibson & Gibson, 1993; Segal & McIntosh, 1992). Pleasure, arousal, and sexual fantasy are emphasised in these accounts, factors which effects researchers and anti-pornography feminists alike have largely ignored. Thus, the pornography debate has been recast by some as a debate about sex in which anti-anti-pornography campaigners take up the pro-sex position while anti-pornography campaigners are labelled anti-sex (Assiter & Carol, 1993).

Looking at actual consumption patterns and practices could tell us the extent to which different pornographic media are really about sex, violence, and/or power for their consumers, whether and when they experience it as abuse, fantasy, inspiration, instruction, or something else entirely. Thinking beyond effects we must ask how pornograph*ies* are used in contemporary society and by whom.

◆ Conclusion

This [chapter] has highlighted the limitations of effects research for a feminist anti-pornography politics and demonstrated how the effects discourse, which has permeated feminist pornography debates and campaigns since the early 1980s, has shifted attention away from production practices, representational strategies, and, even, consumption patterns. To state—as I have done here—that the effects model has damaged the feminist campaign against pornography is not to suggest that there is no link between pornography and violence against women. The testimonies of women who have been harmed in the production and consumption of pornography demonstrate a strong link between pornography and violence. These testimonies are the foundation of feminist anti-pornography politics; they are, quite literally, about life and death (Dworkin, 1997). Yet, as I have argued, to talk about the relationship between pornography and violence as *causal* demands "science" (Jensen, 1998b, p. 101) which obscures these stories and negates the individual abuser's agency and accountability. While policy makers may be impressed by this pseudo-science, this cannot be a price that is worth paying for any feminist committed to challenging male violence.

In rethinking the terms of debate, we also need to ask to what extent "pornography" remains a meaningful category. This is not simply a question of the difficulty of defining pornography with any precision and, hence, of doing anything about it—what Jensen (1998a) dubs the "definitional dodge" (p. 3)—but, more fundamentally, about whether the term "pornography" is politically or practically useful. Certainly, when feminists first broke women's silence on pornography in the late 1970s and early 1980s, demonstrating the pervasiveness of the pornographic imagination was an important political strategy. Effects researchers were, and continue to be, similarly interested in the message—and not the medium—pornography. However, for feminists thinking beyond representation to the *harm* of pornography, failure to differentiate between media can obscure women's experiences. A *Playboy* pictorial, a *Black Lace* novel, and the filmed pornography made of women in Serbian rape camps may have much in common, but they are different in crucial and obvious respects. To call all three "pornography" may help us to understand these similarities but it obscures the fundamental differences.

It is impossible to prove that pornography—in any form—*causes* violence against women. As we enter the fourth decade of feminist teaching, research, and activism on pornography, we need to move beyond cause and effect to make new generations of students, pornography consumers, and policy makers aware of the very real harm in which some pornography is implicated. Moving beyond cause and effect will mean moving beyond the absolutes which have characterized much feminist anti-pornography work but this also opens up new opportunities for influencing policy and practice.

Notes ◆

1. Literally hundreds of studies have been published in this field with an emphasis on the effects of violent or sexually explicit media. Useful overviews of the field which give some sense of the diversity of opinion include Cumberbatch and Howitt (1989), Gauntlett (1995, 1997), and

Miller and Philo (1998). For an introduction to the effects literature on pornography, see Allen, Emmers, et al. (1995); Allen, D'Alessio, and Brezgel (1995); Donnerstein, Linz, and Penrod (1987); Linz (1989); Malamuth and Donnerstein (1984); Zillmann and Bryant (1989). Critical perspectives of this work are provided by Henry (1988); Howitt (1989); King (1993); Russell (1993b, 1993c); Segal (1993); Senn (1993).

2. This is, broadly speaking, the position Gauntlett (1995) takes in *Moving Experiences: Understanding Television's Influences and Effects.*

3. Examples are too numerous to mention, but one might note the selective use of effects studies in writings by Dworkin and MacKinnon (1988) and the use of effects researchers as "expert" witness in the Minneapolis Public Hearings on pornography and discrimination against women (*Everywoman*, 1988). Summaries of effects research have also been included in a number of feminist anti-pornography anthologies (Einsiedel, 1992; Russell, 1993b; Weaver, 1992.)

4. See note 1.

5. See Williams (1990) for an extended analysis of the conventions of hard-core pornographic film.

6. The abstracts collected in Signorielli and Gerbner's (1988) annotated bibliography of research on the effects of media violence provide ample evidence of this point.

7. Pornography involving children in its production is, by definition, abusive and illegal, a fact which can also become obscured in debates which generalize about *all* pornography.

◆ References

Allen, Mike, D'Alessio, Dave, & Brezgel, Keri. (1995). A meta-analysis summarizing the effects of pornography II. *Human Communication Research*, 22, 258-283.

Allen, Mike, Emmers, Tara, Gebhardt, Lisa, & Giery, Mary A. (1995). Exposure to pornography and acceptance of rape myths. *Journal of Communication 45*, 5-26.

Assiter, Alison, & Carol, Avedon. (Eds.). (1993). *Bad girls and dirty pictures: The challenge to reclaim feminism.* London: Pluto.

Berg, Lena. (1999). *Turned on by pornography: Still a good girl?* Paper presented to Women's Worlds: The 7th International Interdisciplinary Congress on Women, University of Tromsø, June 1999.

Boyle, Karen E. (1999). *Screening violence: A feminist critique of the screen violence debate.* Paper presented to Women's Worlds: The 7th International Interdisciplinary Congress on Women, University of Tromsø. June 1999.

Cole, Susan. (1989). *Pornography and the sex crisis.* Toronto: Amanita Press.

Cumberbatch, Guy, & Howitt, Dennis. (1989). *A measure of uncertainty: The effects of the mass media.* London: John Libbey.

Dines, Gail, & Jensen, Robert. (1998). The content of mass-marketed pornography. In Gail Dines, Robert Jensen, & Ann Russo (Eds.), *Pornography: The production and consumption of inequality* (pp. 65-100). London: Routledge.

Donnerstein, Edward, Linz, Daniel, & Penrod, Steven. (1987). *The question of pornography: Research findings and policy implications.* New York and London: Free Press.

Dworkin, Andrea. (1981). *Pornography: Men possessing women.* London: Women's Press.

Dworkin, Andrea. (1997). *Life and death: Unapologetic writings on the continuing war against women.* London: Virago.

Dworkin, Andrea, & MacKinnon, Catharine A. (1988). *Pornography and civil rights: A new day for women's equality* [Online]. Available: http://www.nostatus-quo.com/ ACLU/Porn/newday.htm.

Dyer, Richard. (1985). Male gay porn: Coming to terms. *Jump Cut, 30,* 27-29.

Einsiedel, Edna F. (1992). The experimental research evidence: Effects of pornography on the "average individual." In Catherine Itzin (Ed.), *Pornography: Women, violence and civil liberties—A radical new view* (pp. 248-283). Oxford, UK: Oxford University Press.

Everywoman. (1988). *Pornography and sexual violence: Evidence of the links.* London: Author.

Gauntlett, David. (1995). *Moving experiences: Understanding television's influences and effects.* London: John Libbey.

Gauntlett, David. (1997). Ten things wrong with the "effects model." In Roger Dickinson, Ramaswani Harindranath, & Olga Linné (Eds.), *Approaches to audiences: A reader* (pp. 120-130). London: Arnold.

Gibson, Pamela Church, & Gibson, Roma. (1993). *Dirty looks: Women, pornography, power.* London: BFI.

Hardy, Simon. (1998). *The reader, the author, his woman and her lover: Soft-core pornography and heterosexual men.* London: Cassell.

Henry, Alice. (1988). Does viewing pornography lead men to rape? In Gail Chester & Julienne Dickey (Eds.), *Feminism and censorship: The current debate* (pp. 96-104). Dorset: Prism.

Howitt, Dennis (1989). Pornography: The recent debate. In Guy Cumberbatch & Dennis Howitt (Eds.), *A measure of uncertainty: The effect of the mass media* (pp. 61-80). London: John Libbey.

Jensen, Robert. (1998a). Introduction: Pornographic dodges and distortions. In Gail Dines, Robert Jensen, & Ana Russo (Eds.), *Pornography: The production and consumption of inequality* (pp. 1-8). London: Routledge.

Jensen, Robert. (1998b). Using pornography. In Gail Dines, Robert Jensen, & Ann Russo (Eds.), *Pornography: The production and consumption of inequality* (pp. 101-146). London: Routledge.

Kappeler, Suzanne. (1995). *The will to violence: The politics of personal behaviour.* Cambridge, UK: Polity.

King, Alison. (1993). Mystery and imagination: The case of pornography effects studies. In Alison Assiter & Avedon Carol (Eds.), *Bad girls and dirty pictures: The challenge to reclaim feminism* (pp. 57-87). London: Pluto.

Lederer, Laura. (Ed.). (1980). *Take back the night: Women on pornography.* New York: William Morrow.

Linz, Daniel. (1989). Exposure to sexually explicit materials and attitudes toward rape: A comparison of study results. *Journal of Sex Research, 26,* 50-84.

Lovelace [Marchiano], Linda, & McGrady, Mike. (1980). *Ordeal.* New York: Berkley.

MacKinnon, Catharine A. (1993, July-August). Turning rape into pornography: Postmodern genocide. *Ms.,* pp. 24-30.

Malamuth, Neil, & Donnerstein, Edward. (Eds.). (1984). *Pornography and sexual aggression.* London: Academic Press.

Miller, David, & Philo, Greg. (1998). The effective media. In Greg Philo (Ed.), *Message received* (pp. 21-32). Harlow: Longman.

Price, Lisa S. (1999). *Understanding the man in the soldier-rapist: Some reflections on comprehension and accountability.* Paper presented to Women's Worlds: The 7th International Interdisciplinary Congress on Women, University of Tromsø, June 1999.

Rubin, Gayle. (1993). Misguided, dangerous and wrong: An analysis of anti-pornography politics. In Alison Assiter & Avedon Carol (Eds.), *Bad girls and dirty pictures: The challenge to reclaim feminism* (pp. 18-40). London: Pluto.

Russell, Diana E. H. (Ed.). (1993a). *Making violence sexy: Feminist views on pornography.* Buckingham: Open University Press.

Russell, Diana E. H. (1993b). Pornography and rape: A causal model. In Diana E. H. Russell (Ed.), *Making violence sexy: Feminist views on pornography* (pp. 120-150). Buckingham: Open University Press.

Russell, Diana E. H. (1993c). The experts cop out. In Diana E. H. Russell (Ed.), *Making violence sexy: Feminist views on pornography* (pp. 151-166). Buckingham: Open University Press.

Russell, Diana E. H. (1993d). *Against pornography: The evidence of harm.* Berkeley, CA: Russell Publications.

Segal, Lynne. (1993). Does pornography cause violence? The search for evidence. In Pamela Church Gibson & Roma Gibson (Eds.), *Dirty looks: Women, pornography, power* (pp. 5-12). London: British Film Institute.

Segal, Lynne, & McIntosh, Mary. (Eds.). (1992). *Sex exposed: Sexuality and the pornography debate.* London: Virago.

Senn, Charlene. (1993) The research on women and pornography: The many faces of harm. In Diana E. H. Russell (Ed.), *Making violence sexy: Feminist views on pornography* (pp. 179-193). Buckingham: Open University Press.

Signorielli, Nancy, & Gerbner, George. (1988). *Violence and terror in the mass media: An annotated bibliography.* New York: Greenwood.

Weaver, James. (1992). The social science and psychological research evidence: Perceptual and behavioural consequences of exposure to pornography. In Catherine Itzin (Ed.), *Pornography: Women, violence and civil liberties—A radical new view* (pp. 283-309). Oxford, UK: Oxford University Press.

Williams, Linda. (1990). *Hard core: Power, pleasure and the "frenzy of the visible."* London: Pandora.

Wyre, Ray. (1992). Pornography and sexual violence: Working with sex offenders. In Catherine Itzin (Ed.), *Pornography: Women, violence and civil liberties—A radical new view* (pp. 236-247). Oxford, UK: Oxford University Press.

Zillmann, Dolf, & Bryant, Jennings. (Eds.). (1989). *Pornography: Research advances and policy considerations.* Hillsdale, NJ: Lawrence Erlbaum.

Ziv, Amalia. (1999). *Girl meets boy: Cross-gender queer sex and the promise of pornography.* Paper presented to Women's Worlds: The 7th International Interdisciplinary Congress of Women, University of Tromsø, June 1999.

40

PORNOGRAPHY AND THE LIMITS OF EXPERIMENTAL RESEARCH

◆ Robert Jensen

We live in a culture that likes "science" answers provided by "experts," even when the questions are primarily about human values. Not surprisingly, experimental laboratory research has played an important role in the debate over pornography in the past three decades.[1] Advocates of regulation, both feminist and conservative, cite studies showing links between pornography and violence, whereas opponents of regulation point to other studies that show no link or that are inconclusive. One government commission read the evidence to support increased regulation (Attorney General's Commission, 1986); an earlier commission used the evidence available at that time to support lifting most regulation (Commission on Obscenity and Pornography, 1970).

Experimental research on pornography's effects looks at the perceptual and behavioral effects of viewing or reading sexually explicit material. A typical study might expose groups of subjects to different types or levels of sexually explicit material for comparison to a control group that views nonsexual material. Researchers look for significant differences between the groups on a measure of, for example, male attitudes toward rape. One such measure could be subjects' assessments of the suffering experienced by sexual assault victims or subjects' judgments of the appropriate prison sentence for a rapist. From such controlled testing—measuring the effect of an experimental stimulus (exposure to pornography) on a dependent variable (attitudes toward women or sex) in randomly selected groups—researchers make claims, usually tentative, about causal relationships.

Although there is disagreement among researchers about what has been "proved" by these studies (Linz, 1989; Zillmann, 1989), some themes emerge. I will be questioning the value of these studies, but I follow Weaver's (1992) assessment. He reads the evidence to support the sexual callousness model, which suggests that exposure to pornography activates sexually callous perceptions of women and promotes sexually aggressive behavior by men (Zillmann & Bryant, 1982; Zillmann & Weaver, 1989). This appears to be the result of both pornography's promotion of a loss of respect for female sexual autonomy and the disinhibition of men's expression of aggression against women (Weaver, 1992, p. 307).

After reviewing the experimental research, Russell (1988, 1993a) outlined four factors that link pornography to sexual violence. Pornography (a) predisposes some males to desire rape or intensifies this desire, (b) undermines some males' internal inhibitions against acting out rape desires, (c) undermines some males' social inhibitions against acting out rape desires, and (d) undermines some potential victims' abilities to avoid or resist rape.

Taking a different approach, Donnerstein, Linz, and Penrod (1987) argue that only pornography that combines violence and sex has been shown to be harmful, and then only in the sense of immediate effects; they hesitate to speculate on the long term. They conclude that there is not enough evidence to show that exposure to nonviolent pornography leads to increases in aggression against women under most circumstances, suggesting that "some forms of pornography, under some conditions, promote certain antisocial attitudes and behavior" (p. 171).

My work on pornography is grounded in a radical feminist critique that focuses on how male dominance and female submission is sexualized. Pornography is an expression and reinforcement of a male sexuality rooted in the subordination of women that endorses the sexual objectification of, and that can promote sexual violence against, women (Dworkin, 1981;

Itzin, 1992; MacKinnon, 1987; Russell, 1993b). Although much of the experimental work supports that position, I argue that we need to be skeptical of the value of such studies, no matter what the results; the limits of the experimental approach should lead us to look elsewhere for answers.

The Limits of ◆ Experimental Research

In addition to a number of specific technical complaints over methodology and research design (summarized and rejected by Donnerstein et al., 1987, pp. 12-22), most of the critics of these studies suggest that any connection between pornography and sexual violence found in the lab is probably overstated; they warn of overgeneralizing from experimental studies because the effects found might evaporate outside the lab:

> It is a considerable leap from the laboratory to the corner store where men rifle the pages of magazines kept on the top shelf. It is a long step from the laboratory exposure to such stimuli and subsequent aggression to real-world sexual and physical abuse. (Brannigan & Goldenberg, 1987, p. 277)

Although it is possible that the research overreaches, we should be at least as concerned that lab studies underestimate pornography's role in promoting misogynistic attitudes and behavior (see also Dines-Levy, 1988).

First, these studies may be incapable of measuring subtle effects that develop over time. If pornography works to develop attitudes and shape behavior after repeated exposure, there is no guarantee that studies exposing people to a small amount of pornography over a short time can accurately measure anything. For example, in one study, the group exposed to what the researchers called the "massive" category of pornography viewed six explicitly sexual 8-minute films per session for six sessions, or a total of 4 hours and 48 minutes of material (Zillmann & Bryant, 1982). The "intermediate" group saw half the number of sexual films. These categories are constructed, obviously, for comparative purposes, not to suggest that such an amount of viewing is massive. But even within the confines of a laboratory study, these amounts may be inadequate to test anything.

In addition, as Brannigan and Goldenberg (1987) suggest, no lab can reproduce the natural setting of the behavior being studied. They paint a rather harmless picture of men paging through magazines in the corner store, but what about the other common settings for the consumption of pornography? How is watching a pornographic movie in a university video lab (the experience of experimental subjects) different from being one of a dozen men in a dark movie theater, frightened but excited by the illicit nature of the setting? How is the lab different from the living room of a fraternity house where a group of young men might watch a pornographic videotape, drinking beer and urging each other to enjoy the tape? And how does the act of masturbating to pornography, a common male experience, influence the way in which men interpret and are affected by pornography?

The lab experience is unreal in terms of both the physical and the psychological environments. If experimental data seem to suggest, for example, that exposure to depictions in which women appear to enjoy being raped can increase men's acceptance of sexual violence against women and increase men's endorsement of that rape myth (Malamuth & Check, 1981), can we assume that those effects will be even more pronounced on a man who views that same sexual material in a real-world environment in which male aggression is often encouraged and sanctioned? Because it would be impossible, not to mention ethically unacceptable, to recreate such a situation in a lab, we must question the value of lab

data. Instead of assuming that the lab overstates the potential for aggression, we should consider how it could understate the effect.

These problems are compounded if one acknowledges that such studies can never be impartial and objective and always are value-laden. Researchers generally accept a mainstream definition of what is to be considered "normal" sexuality. Although the existence of sexual drive and interests is in some ways "natural," or biologically based, the form our sexual practices take is socially constructed, and that construction in this culture is rooted in the politics of gender. Relying on the majority view to determine what is erotic implicitly endorses the sexual status quo, which means accepting patriarchal definitions.

This point about values often is used by sexual libertarians, who contend that by labeling practices such as sadomasochism "deviant," research is biased. But the critique also has to come from a different angle; in patriarchal society, what has been considered normal sex generally has been what serves to enhance men's pleasure; the line between "normal" intercourse and "deviant" rape is a fine one. As Catharine MacKinnon (1989) puts it, "Compare victims' reports of rape with women's reports of sex. They look a lot alike"(p. 146).[2] Researchers must make value judgments about what is erotic, nonviolent, and normal, and those decisions define what is a deviant, unhealthy, callous, or socially undesirable response to the material. It is not that any specific researcher has blundered by letting value judgments in, but that such research always makes normative judgments about sexuality.

Listening to Stories ◆

He held up a porn magazine with a picture of a beaten woman and said, "I want you to look like that. I want you to hurt." He then began beating me. (*Public Hearings*, 1983, p. 48)

It would be simplistic and misleading to suggest that the magazine was the sole cause of the beating, and the vast majority of activists and scholars in the feminist antipornography movement do not make such a claim (Russell, 1988, 1993a). Still, for many people that lack of deterministic causality means that society cannot give the woman who was beaten any legal recourse against the creators and peddlers of the pornography. That simplistic view of causation is of little value in examining human behavior, which is always the product of complex factors and unpredictable contingencies. The important research question is not, What kind of experiment will tell us about causation? but rather, If we listen to people's accounts of the world, what do we learn?

Positivist social science considers the evidence that comes from such testimony to be merely "anecdotal" and warns that generalizing from personal experience is problematic. From that view, the fact that a woman was sexually assaulted by a man who modeled his attack on a pornographic work tells us nothing about how pornography generally influences male sexual behavior toward women. For proof of causation, social scientists look to the laboratory, not experience:

> Even if we were to observe a nearly one-to-one relationship between viewing violent pornography and committing a sexual assault or rape in the real world, this finding is not as compelling in a causal sense as is an experiment. (Donnerstein et al., 1987, p. 10)

Donnerstein et al. have faith in the possibilities of lab research to answer these questions, although other researchers who share their loyalty to experimental methods are far less optimistic about proving causation. Zillmann (1989), for example, warns that "research on pornography cannot be definitive. It cannot satisfy the demands for rigor and compellingness that have been placed on it" (p. 398). He believes that social science can, however, be of value in guiding policy and making final decisions. Although not definitive, this research is "far superior to hearsay, guessing, and unchecked common sense" (p. 399). But is guessing the only alternative to experimental research?

The work of feminist scholars who have challenged Western science's claims of objectivity and neutrality (e.g., Harding, 1991) and proposed alternatives to traditional methods of social science research (Reinharz, 1992) makes it clear that human behavior and social patterns can be understood through research that takes seriously the stories people tell about their lives. This kind of research, as Marilyn Frye (1990) points out, rests "on a most empirical base: staking your life on the trustworthiness of your own body as a source of knowledge" (p. 177). Instead of looking to science for answers to questions it cannot answer, we can look to each other.

What we learn from the testimony of women and men whose lives have been touched by pornography is how the material is *implicated* in violence against women and how it can perpetuate, reinforce, and be part of a wider system of woman hating. Rather than discussing simple causation, we think of how various factors "make something inviting."[3] In those terms, pornography does not cause rape, but rather helps make rape inviting. Research should examine people's stories about their experiences with pornography and sexual violence to help us determine how close is the relationship between the material and the actions, which can inform personal and collective decisions. This kind of examination will not produce certainty. The work of judging narratives can be difficult and sometimes messy; the process doesn't claim clear, objective standards that experimental research appears to offer. There are no experts to ask for authoritative answers; we all are responsible for building responsible and honest communal practices.

Although often drowned out in the policy debate, the stories that people tell about pornography have begun to be collected, both in public hearings and through research. Sources for the experiences of women include the following:

1. Silbert and Pines's (1984) study of prostitutes, in which 73% of the 200 women interviewed reported being raped, and 24% of those women mentioned that their assailants made reference to pornography.

2. Russell's (1980) survey of more than 900 women about experiences with sexual violence, which includes women's responses to the question "Have you ever been upset by anyone trying to get you to do what they'd seen in pornographic pictures, movies, or books?" Of the women, 10% reported at least one such experience.

3. Kelly's (1988) detailed interviews with 60 British women about how they experience sexual violence, during which women reported that pornography often is a part of the continuum of violence.

4. The Minneapolis hearings (*Public Hearings*, 1983) on a proposed anti-pornography civil rights ordinance, which included the testimony of a number of women about how pornography was used in acts of sexual violence against them.

5. The hearings of the Attorney General's Commission (1986), which gave women a forum to tell about their experiences with pornography.

There also is a small but growing body of work on men's experiences with pornography through autobiography and research (e.g., Kimmel, 1990; Marshall, 1988). I have conducted in-depth interviews with male pornography consumers and convicted sex offenders that illustrate the different ways in which pornography is an important factor in the sexually abusive acts of some men (Jensen, 1992). Those interviews provide specific examples of

how pornography can (a) be an important factor in shaping a male-dominant view of sexuality, (b) contribute to a user's difficulty in separating sexual fantasy and reality, (c) be used to initiate victims and break down resistance to sexual activity, and (d) provide a training manual for abuse. A quick tour through some of those stories follows.

Although some of the pornography consumers I interviewed reported positive effects in their lives from pornography consumption, some of the consumers and all of the sex offenders identified pornography as an unhealthy influence on their sexuality, hurting their intimate relationships with women. One sex offender, echoing a common experience, reported that heavy use of pornography beginning as a child contributed to his belief that women "were made for sex and that's all." The men's narratives make it clear that pornography was not the only source of such messages in their lives but was important in shaping their sexuality.

Another theme that emerged in some men's accounts was pornography's role in blurring the line between fantasy and reality. One man, who was convicted of molesting two 6-year-old girls and said he also had raped teenage girls, explained how he would masturbate at home to pornography while thinking of the young girls who rode the bus he drove and then watch the girls on the bus while fantasizing about the pornography.

Another man convicted of sexually abusing his teenage stepdaughter explained that he watched pornographic videotapes with her before and during sex. The tapes served both to break down the girl's initial resistance to his sexual overtures, showing her that such sex was "normal," and provide him with fantasy material that allowed him to pretend that he was having sex with the women on the screen, not with his stepdaughter.

Finally, although pornography may not independently create desire for a specific sexual act, pornographic scenarios shaped some men's sexual practices. One man—who detailed an extensive history of pornography use, visits to prostitutes, and rape and sexual abuse of women and girls—said he believed his obsession of having women perform oral sex on him was connected to the pornography he used. He explained how he would use "ways that would entice it in the movies" on his girlfriend, whose resistance often led to beatings. "I used a lot of force, a lot of direct demands, that in the movies women would just cooperate," he said. When women in his life didn't cooperate, he said he usually became violent.

None of the sex offenders avoided personal responsibility by contending that pornography caused them to rape; those who described themselves as heavy pornography users saw pornography as one of a number of factors that contributed to their abusive behavior.

◆ Conclusion

Three decades of experimental research on pornography's effects have not answered questions about sexually explicit material and sexual violence. Should we hold out hope that more experimental studies will provide answers? Should we privilege that research in the public policy debate over pornography? To do so marginalizes a type of knowledge that holds out much more promise for helping us understand pornography, sexuality, sexism, and violence.

Not taking steps to eliminate misogynist pornography is a political act that has consequences. Vulnerable individuals, mostly women and children, will continue to be hurt in the making and use of pornography, and the lack of definitive scientific proof of the connection between pornography and harm does not change that brutal reality. To postpone action until science gives us that definitive answer—which even scientists agree isn't possible—is simply a cover for unwillingness to confront the political

and moral questions. We know enough to act, and we should.

Notes ◆

1. In the courts, however, such studies are not necessary to defend obscenity laws. Chief Justice Warren Burger's decision in *Paris Adult Theatre v. Slaton*, 413 U.S. 49 (1973), stated that conclusive empirical evidence was not needed for states to exercise their "legitimate interest" in regulating obscenity in local commerce and public accommodations to safeguard the quality of life, protect the total community environment, and enhance public safety. The more recent attempts to confront pornography legally have focused on women's civil rights, not criminal obscenity law, but the courts have generally been unwilling to consider this new approach. For more on the differences between obscenity and the feminist antipornography critique, see MacKinnon (1987, 1989).

2. MacKinnon's assertion perhaps should be modified to say that *some* women's reports of sex look a lot like reports of rape. MacKinnon is often criticized for her "totalizing" theory that paves over the complexity of individual women's lives, and in this case that is a valid complaint. However, the essence of her point is well taken.

3. I borrow the phrase from feminist philosopher Marilyn Frye's remarks in an informal seminar at the University of Minnesota in 1991.

References ◆

Attorney General's Commission on Pornography. (1986). *Final report*. Washington, DC: U.S. Department of Justice.

Brannigan, A., & Goldenberg, S. (1987). The study of aggressive pornography: The vicissitudes of relevance. *Critical Studies in Mass Communication*, 4(3), 262-283.

Commission on Obscenity and Pornography. (1970). *Report*. New York: Bantam.

Dines-Levy, G. (1988). An analysis of pornography research. In A. W. Burgess (Ed.), *Rape and sexual assault II* (pp. 317-323). New York: Garland.

Donnerstein, E., Linz, D., & Penrod, S. (1987). *The question of pornography.* New York: Free Press.

Dworkin, A. (1981). *Pornography: Men possessing women.* New York: Perigee.

Frye, M. (1990). The possibility of feminist theory. In D. Rhode (Ed.), *Theoretical perspectives on sexual difference* (pp. 174-184). New Haven, CT: Yale University Press.

Harding, S. (1991). *Whose science? Whose knowledge?* Ithaca, NY: Cornell University Press.

Itzin, C. (Ed.). (1992). *Pornography: Women, violence and civil liberties.* Oxford, UK: Oxford University Press.

Jensen, R. (1992). *Knowing pornography.* Unpublished doctoral dissertation, University of Minnesota.

Kelly, L. (1988). *Surviving sexual violence.* Minneapolis: University of Minnesota Press.

Kimmel, M. S. (Ed.). (1990). *Men confront pornography.* New York: Crown.

Linz, D. (1989). Exposure to sexually explicit materials and attitudes toward rape: A comparison of study results. *Journal of Sex Research, 26*(1), 50-84.

MacKinnon, C. A. (1987). *Feminism unmodified: Discourses on life and law.* Cambridge, MA: Harvard University Press.

MacKinnon, C. A. (1989). *Toward a feminist theory of the state.* Cambridge, MA: Harvard University Press.

Malamuth, N., & Check, J. V. P. (1981). The effects of mass media exposure on acceptance of violence against women: A field experiment. *Journal of Research in Personality, 15*, 436-446.

Marshall, W. L. (1988). The use of sexually explicit stimuli by rapists, child molesters, and nonoffenders. *Journal of Sex Research, 25*(2), 267-288.

Public hearings on the proposed Minneapolis civil rights anti-pornography ordinance. (1983). Minneapolis: Organizing Against Pornography.

Reinharz, S. (1992). *Feminist methods in social research.* New York: Oxford University Press.

Russell, D. E. H. (1980). Pornography and violence: What does the new research say? In L. Lederer (Ed.), *Take back the night: Women on pornography* (pp. 218-238). New York: William Morrow.

Russell, D. E. H. (1988). Pornography and rape: A causal model. *Political Psychology, 9*(1), 41-73.

Russell, D. E. H. (1993a). *Against pornography: Evidence of harm.* Berkeley, CA: Russell.

Russell, D. E. H. (Ed.). (1993b). *Making violence sexy: Feminist views on pornography.* New York: Teachers College Press.

Silbert, M. H., & Pines, A. M. (1984). Pornography and sexual abuse of women. *Sex Roles, 10*(11/12), 857-869.

Weaver, J. (1992). The social science and psychological research evidence: Perceptual and behavioural consequences of exposure to pornography. In C. Itzin (Ed.), *Pornography: Women, violence and civil liberties* (pp. 284-309). Oxford, UK: Oxford University Press.

Zillmann, D. (1989). Pornography research and public policy. In D. Zillmann & J. Bryant (Eds.), *Pornography: Research advances and policy considerations* (pp. 387-403). Hillsdale, NJ: Lawrence Erlbaum.

Zillmann, D., & Bryant, J. (1982). Pornography, sexual callousness, and the trivialization of rape. *Journal of Communication, 32*(4), 10-21.

Zillmann, D., & Weaver, J. B. (1989). Pornography and men's sexual callousness toward women. In D. Zillmann & J. Bryant (Eds.), *Pornography: Research advances and policy considerations* (pp. 95-125). Hillsdale, NJ: Lawrence Erlbaum.

41

MASS MARKET ROMANCE
Pornography for Women Is Different

◆ Ann Barr Snitow

. . . What is the Harlequin romance formula? The novels have no plot in the usual sense. All tension and problems arise from the fact that the Harlequin world is inhabited by two species incapable of communicating with each other, male and female. In this sense these Pollyanna books have their own dream-like truth: our culture produces a pathological experience of sex difference. The sexes have different needs and interests, certainly different experiences. They find each other utterly mystifying.

Since all action in the novels is described from the female point of view, the reader identifies with the heroine's efforts to decode the erratic gestures of "dark, tall and gravely handsome"[1] men, all mysterious strangers or powerful bosses. In a sense the usual relationship is reversed: woman is subject, man, object. There are more descriptions of his body than of hers ("Dark trousers fitted closely to lean hips and long muscular legs . . .") though her clothes are always minutely observed. He is the unknowable other, a sexual icon whose magic is maleness. The books are permeated by phallic worship. Male is good, male is exciting, without further points of reference. Cruelty, callousness, coldness, menace, etc. are all equated with maleness and treated as a necessary part of the package: "It was an arrogant remark, but Sara had long since admitted his arrogance as part of his

NOTE: Excerpts reprinted from *Radical History Review* (Summer 1979), by permission of Cambridge University Press and Ann Barr Snitow.

attraction."[2] She, on the other hand, is the subject, the one whose thoughts the reader knows, whose constant re-evaluation of male moods and actions make up the story line.

The heroine is not involved in any overt adventure beyond trying to respond appropriately to male energy without losing her virginity. Virginity is a given here; sex means marriage and marriage, promised at the end, means, finally, there can be sex.

While the heroine waits for the hero's next move, her time is filled by tourism and by descriptions of consumer items: furniture, clothes, and gourmet foods. In *Writers Market* (1977) Harlequin Enterprises stipulate: "Emphasis on travel." (The exception is the occasional hospital novel. Like foreign places, hospitals offer removal from the household, heightened emotional states, and a supply of strangers.) Several of the books have passages that probably come straight out of guide books, but the *particular* setting is not the point, only that it is exotic, a place elsewhere.[3]

More space is filled by the question of what to wear. "She rummaged in her cases, discarding item after item, and eventually brought out a pair of purple cotton jeans and a matching shift. They were not new. She had bought them a couple of years ago. But fortunately her figure had changed little, and apart from a slight shrinkage in the pants which made them rather tighter than she would have liked, they looked serviceable."[4] Several things are going on here: the effort to find the right clothes for the occasion, the problem of staying thin, the problem of piecing together outfits from things that are not new. Finally, there is that shrinkage, a signal to the experienced Harlequin reader that the heroine, innocent as her intent may be in putting on jeans that are a little too tight, is wearing something revealing and will certainly be seen and noted by the hero in this vulnerable, passive act of self-exposure. (More about the pornographic aspects later. In any other titillating novel one would suspect a pun when tight pants are "serviceable" but in the context of the absolutely flat Harlequin

style one might well be wrong. More, too, about this style later on.)

Though clothes are the number one filler in Harlequins, food and furniture are also important and usually described in the language of women's magazines:[5] croissants are served hot and crispy and are "crusty brown,"[6] while snapper is "filleted, crumbed and fried in butter" and tomato soup is "topped with grated cheese and parsley"[7] (this last a useful, practical suggestion anyone could try).

Harlequins revitalize daily routines by insisting that a woman combing her hair, a woman reaching up to put a plate on a high shelf (so that her knees show beneath the hem, if only there were a viewer), a woman doing what women do all day, is in a constant state of potential sexuality. You never can tell when you may be seen and being seen is a precious opportunity. Harlequin romances alternate between scenes of the hero and heroine together in which she does a lot of social lying to save face, pretending to be unaffected by the hero's presence while her body melts or shivers, and scenes in which the heroine is essentially alone, living in a cloud of absorption, preparing mentally and physically for the next contact.

The heroine is alone. Sometimes there is another woman, a competitor who is often more overtly aware of her sexuality than the heroine, but she is a shadow on the horizon. Sometimes there are potentially friendly females living in the next bungalow or working with the patient in the next bed, but they, too, are shadowy, not important to the real story which consists entirely of an emotionally isolated woman trying to keep her virginity and her head when the only person she ever really talks to is the hero, whose motives and feelings are unclear: "She saw his words as a warning and would have liked to know whether he meant [them] to be."[8]

The heroine gets her man at the end, first, because she is an old-fashioned girl (this is a code for no premarital sex) and, second, because the hero gets ample opportunity to see her perform well in a number of female helping roles. In the course of a Harlequin romance, most heroines demonstrate passionate motherliness, good cooking, patience in adversity, efficient planning, and a good clothes sense, though these are skills and emotional capacities produced in emergencies, and are not, as in real life, a part of an invisible, glamourless work routine.

Though the heroines are pliable (they are rarely given particularized character traits; they are all Everywoman and can fit in comfortably with the lifestyle of the strong-willed heroes be they doctors, lawyers, or marine biologists doing experiments on tropical islands), it is still amazing that these novels end in marriage. After one hundred and fifty pages of mystification, unreadable looks, "hints of cruelty,"[9] and wordless coldness, the thirty-page denouement is powerless to dispel the earlier impression of menace. Why should this heroine marry this man? And, one can ask with equal reason, why should this hero marry this woman? These endings do not ring true, but no doubt this is precisely their strength. A taste for psychological or social realism is unlikely to provide a Harlequin reader with a sustaining fantasy of rescue, of glamour, or of change. The Harlequin ending offers the impossible. It is pleasing to think that appearances are deceptive, that male coldness, absence, boredom, etc. are not what they seem. The hero *seems* to be a horrible roué; he *seems* to be a hopeless, moody cripple; he *seems* to be cruel and unkind; or he *seems* to be indifferent to the heroine and interested only in his work; but always, at the end, a rational explanation of all this appears. In spite of his coldness or preoccupation, the hero really loves the heroine and wants to marry her.

In fact, the Harlequin formula glorifies the distance between the sexes. Distance becomes titillating. The heroine's sexual inexperience adds to this excitement. What is this thing that awaits her on the other side of distance and mystery? Not knowing may be more sexy than finding out. Or perhaps the heroes are really fathers—obscure, forbidden objects of desire. Whatever they are, it is more exciting to wonder about them than to know them. In romanticized sexuality the pleasure lies in the distance itself. Waiting, anticipation, anxiety—these represent the high point of sexual experience.

Perhaps there is pleasure, too, in returning again and again to that breathless, ambivalent, nervous state *before* certainty or satiety. Insofar as women's great adventure, the one they are socially sanctioned to seek, is romance, adventurousness takes women always back to the first phase in love. Unlike work, which holds out the possible pleasures of development, of the exercise of faculties, sometimes even of advancement, the Harlequin form of romance depends on the heroine's being in a state of passivity, of not knowing. Once the heroine knows the hero loves her, the story is over. Nothing interesting remains. Harlequin statements in *Writers Market* stress "upbeat ending essential here" (1977). Here at least is a reliable product that reproduces for women the most interesting phase in the love/marriage cycle and knows just when to stop. . . .

Are Harlequin Romances ◆ Pornography?

She had never felt so helpless or so completely at the mercy of another human being . . . a being who could snap the slender column of her body with one squeeze of a steel clad arm.

No trace of tenderness softened the harsh pressure of his mouth on hers . . . there was only a savagely punishing intentness of purpose that cut off her breath until her senses reeled and her body sagged against the granite hardness of his. He released her wrists, seeming to know that they would hang helplessly at her sides, and his hand moved to the small of her back to exert a pressure that crushed her soft outlines to the unyielding dominance of his and left her in no doubt as to the force of his masculinity.[10]

In an unpublished talk,[11] critic Peter Parisi has hypothesized that Harlequin romances are essentially pornography for people ashamed to read pornography. In his view, sex is these novels' real raison d'être, while the romance and the promised marriage are primarily salves to the conscience of readers brought up to believe that sex without love and marriage is wrong. Like me, Parisi sees the books as having some active allure. They are not just escape; they also offer release, as he sees it, specifically sexual release.

This is part of the reason why Harlequins, so utterly denatured in most respects, can powerfully command such a large audience. I want to elaborate here on Parisi's definition of *how* the books are pornography and, finally, to modify his definition of what women are looking for in a sex book.

Parisi sees Harlequins as a sort of poor woman's D. H. Lawrence. The body of the heroine is alive and singing in every fiber; she is overrun by a sexuality that wells up inside her and that she cannot control. ("The warmth of his body close to hers was like a charge of electricity, a stunning masculine assault on her senses that she was powerless to do anything about."[12]) The issue of control arises because, in Parisi's view, the reader's qualms are allayed when the novels invoke morals, then affirm a force, sexual feeling, strong enough to override those morals. He argues further that morals in a Harlequin are secular; what the heroine risks is a loss of social face, of reputation. The books uphold the values of their readers who share this fear of breaking social codes, but behind these reassuringly familiar restraints they celebrate a wild, eager sexuality which flourishes and is finally affirmed in "marriage," which Parisi sees as mainly a code word for "fuck."

Parisi is right: *every* contact in a Harlequin romance is sexualized:

Sara feared he was going to refuse the invitation and simply walk off. It seemed like an eternity before he inclined his head in a brief, abrupt acknowledgement of acceptance, then drew out her chair for her, his hard fingers brushing her arm for a second, and bringing an urgent flutter of reaction from her pulse.[13]

Those "hard fingers" are the penis; a glance is penetration; a voice can slide along the heroine's spine "like a sliver of ice." The heroine keeps struggling for control but is constantly swept away on a tide of feeling. Always, though, some intruder or some "nagging reminder" of the need to maintain appearances stops her. "His mouth parted her lips with bruising urgency and for a few delirious moments she yielded to her own wanton instincts." But the heroine insists on seeing these moments as out of character: She "had never thought herself capable of wantonness, but in Carlo's arms she seemed to have no inhibitions."[14] Parisi argues that the books' sexual formula allows both heroine and reader to feel wanton again and again while maintaining their sense of themselves as not that sort of women.

I agree with Parisi that the sexually charged atmosphere that bathes the Harlequin heroine is essentially pornographic (I use the word pornographic as neutrally as possible here, not as an automatic pejorative). But do Harlequins actually contain an affirmation of female sexuality? The heroine's condition of passive receptivity to male ego and male sexuality is exciting to readers, but this is not necessarily a free or deep expression of the female potential for sexual feeling. Parisi says the heroine is always trying to humanize the contact between herself and the apparently undersocialized hero, "trying to convert rape into love-making." If this is so, then she is engaged on a social as well as a sexual odyssey. Indeed, in women, these two are often joined. Is the project of humanizing and domesticating male sexual feeling an erotic one? What is it about this situation that arouses the excitement of the anxiously vigilant heroine and of the readers who identify with her?

In the misogynistic culture in which we live, where violence towards women is a common motif, it is hard to say a neutral word about pornography either as a legitimate literary form or as a legitimate source of pleasure. Women are naturally overwhelmed by the woman-hating theme so that the more universal human expression sometimes contained by pornography tends to be obscured for them.

In recent debates, sex books that emphasize both male and female sexual feelings as a sensuality that can exist without violence are being called "erotica" to distinguish them from "pornography."[15] This distinction blurs more than it clarifies the complex mixture of elements that make up sexuality. "Erotica" is soft core, soft focus; it is gentler and tenderer sex than that depicted in pornography. Does this mean true sexuality is diffuse while only perverse sexuality is driven, power hungry, intense, and selfish? I cannot accept this particular dichotomy. It leaves out too much of what is infantile in sex—the reenactment of early feelings, the boundlessness and omnipotence of infant desire and its furious gusto. In pornography all things tend in one direction, a total immersion in one's own sense experience, for which one paradigm must certainly be infancy. For adults this totality, the total sexualization of everything, can only be a fantasy. But does the fact that it cannot be actually lived mean this fantasy must be discarded? It is a memory, a legitimate element in the human lexicon of feelings.

In pornography, the joys of passivity, of helpless abandonment, of response without responsibility are all endlessly repeated, savored, minutely described. Again this is a fantasy often dismissed with the pejorative "masochistic" as if passivity were in no way a pleasant or a natural condition.

Yet another criticism of pornography is that it presents no recognizable, delineated characters. In a culture where women are routinely objectified it is natural and

progressive to see as threatening any literary form that calls dehumanization sexual. Once again, however, there is a more universally human side to this aspect of pornography. Like a lot of far more respectable twentieth-century art, pornography is not about personality but about the explosion of the boundaries of the self. It is a fantasy of an extreme state in which all social constraints are overwhelmed by a flood of sexual energy. Think, for example, of all the pornography about servants fucking mistresses, old men fucking young girls, guardians fucking wards. Class, age, custom—all are deliciously sacrificed, dissolved by sex.

Though pornography's critics are right—pornography *is* exploitation—it is exploitation of *everything*. Promiscuity by definition is a breakdown of barriers. Pornography is not only a reflector of social power imbalances, sexual pathologies, etc., but it is also all those imbalances run riot, run to excess, sometimes explored *ad absurdum*, exploded. Misogyny is one content of pornography; another content is a universal infant desire for complete, immediate gratification, to rule the world out of the very core of passive helplessness.

In a less sexist society, there might be a pornography that is exciting, expressive, interesting, even, perhaps, significant as a form of social rebellion, all traits which, in a sexist society, are obscured by pornography's present role as escape valve for hostility towards women, or as metaphor for fiercely guarded power hierarchies, etc. Instead, in a sexist society, we have two pornographies, one for men, one for women. They both have, hiding within them, those basic human expressions of abandonment I have described. The pornography for men enacts this abandonment on women as objects. How different is the pornography for women, in which sex is bathed in romance, diffused, always implied rather than enacted at all! This pornography is the Harlequin romance.

I described above the oddly narrowed down, denatured world presented in

Harlequins. Looking at them as pornography obviously offers a number of alternative explanations for these same traits: the heroine's passivity becomes sexual receptivity and, though I complained earlier about her vapidity, in pornography no one need have a personality. Joanna Russ observed about the heroines of gothic romances something true of Harlequin heroines as well: they are loved as babies are loved, simply because they exist.[16] They have no particular qualities, but pornography bypasses this limitation and reaches straight down to the infant layer where we all imagine ourselves the center of everything by birthright and are sexual beings without shame or need for excuse.

Seeing Harlequins as pornography modifies one's criticism of their selectivity, their know-nothing narrowness. Insofar as they are essentially pornographic in intent, their characters have no past, no context; they live only in the eternal present of sexual feeling, the absorbing interest in the erotic sex object. Insofar as the books are written to elicit sexual excitation, they can be completely closed, repetitive circuits always returning to the moment of arousal when the hero's voice sends "a velvet finger"[17] along the spine of the heroine. In pornography, sex is the whole content; there need be no serious other.

Read this way, Harlequins are benign if banal sex books, but sex books for women have several special characteristics not included in the usual definitions of the genre pornography. In fact, a suggestive, sexual atmosphere is not so easy to establish for women as it is for men. A number of conditions must be right.

In *The Mermaid and the Minotaur*, an extraordinary study of the asymmetry of male and female relationships in all societies where children are primarily raised by women, Dorothy Dinnerstein discusses the reasons why women are so much more dependent than men on deep personal feeling as an ingredient, sometimes a precondition, for sex. Beyond the obvious reasons, the seriousness of sex for the partner who

can get pregnant, the seriousness of sex for the partner who is economically and socially dependent on her lover, Dinnerstein adds another, psychological reason for women's tendency to emotionalize sex. She argues that the double standard (male sexual freedom, female loyalty to one sexual tie) comes from the asymmetry in the way the sexes are raised in infancy. Her argument is too complex to be entirely recapitulated here but her conclusion seems crucial to our understanding of the mixture of sexual excitement and anti-erotic restraint that characterizes sexual feeling in Harlequin romances:

> Anatomically, coitus offers a far less reliable guarantee of orgasm—or indeed of any intense direct local genital pleasure—to woman than to man. The first-hand coital pleasure of which she is capable more often requires conditions that must be purposefully sought out. Yet it is woman who has less liberty to conduct this kind of search: . . . societal and psychological constraints . . . leave her less free than man to explore the erotic resources of a variety of partners, or even to affirm erotic impulse with any one partner. These constraints also make her less able to give way to simple physical delight without a sense of total self-surrender—a disability that further narrows her choice of partners, and makes her still more afraid of disrupting her rapport with any one partner by acting to intensify the delight, that is, by asserting her own sexual wishes. . . .

> What the double standard hurts in women (to the extent that they genuinely, inwardly, bow to it) is the animal center of self-respect: the brute sense of bodily prerogative, of having a right to one's bodily feelings. Fromm made this point very clearly when he argued, in *Man for Himself*, that socially imposed shame about the body serves the function of keeping people submissive to societal authority by weakening in them some inner core of individual authority. . . .

On the whole . . . the female burden of genital deprivation is carried meekly, invisibly. Sometimes it cripples real interest in sexual interaction, but often it does not: indeed, it can deepen a woman's need for the emotional rewards of carnal contact. What it most reliably cripples is human pride.[18]

This passage gives us the theoretical skeleton on which the titillations of the Harlequin formula are built. In fact, the Harlequin heroine cannot afford to be only a mass of responsive nerve endings. In order for her sexuality, and the sexuality of the novels' readers, to be released, a number of things must happen that have little to do directly with sex at all. Since she cannot seek out or instruct the man she wants, she must be in a state of constant passive readiness. Since only one man will do, she has the anxiety of deciding, "Is this *the* one?" Since an enormous amount of psychic energy is going to be mobilized in the direction of the man she loves, the man she sleeps with, she must feel sure of him. A one-night stand won't work; she's only just beginning to get her emotional generators going when he's already gone. And orgasm? It probably hasn't happened. She couldn't tell him she wanted it and couldn't tell him *how* she wanted it. If he's already gone, there is no way for her erotic feeling for him to take form, no way for her training of him as a satisfying lover to take place.

Hence the Harlequin heroine has a lot of things to worry about if she wants sexual satisfaction. Parisi has said that these worries are restraints there merely to be deliciously overridden, but they are so constant an accompaniment to the heroine's erotic feelings as to be, under present conditions, inseparable from them. She feels an urge towards deep emotion; she feels anxiety about the serious intentions of the hero; she role plays constantly, presenting herself as a nurturant, passive, receptive figure; and all of this is part of sex to her. Certain social configurations feel safe and right and

are real sexual cues for women. The romantic intensity of Harlequins—the waiting, fearing, speculating—are as much a part of their functionings as pornography for women as are the more overtly sexual scenes.

Nor is this just a neutral difference between men and women. In fact, as Dinnerstein suggests, the muting of spontaneous sexual feeling, the necessity which is socially forced on women of channeling their sexual desire, is in fact a great deprivation. In *The Mermaid and the Minotaur* Dinnerstein argues that men have a number of reasons, social and psychological, for discomfort when confronted by the romantic feeling and the demand for security that so often accompany female sexuality. For them growing up and being male both mean cutting off the passionate attachment and dependence on woman, on mother. Women, potential mother figures themselves, have less need to make this absolute break. Men also need to pull away from that inferior category, Woman. Women are stuck in it and naturally romanticize the powerful creatures they can only come close to through emotional and physical ties.

The Harlequin formula perfectly reproduces these differences, these tensions, between the sexes. It depicts a heroine struggling, against the hero's resistance, to get the right combination of elements together so that, for her, orgasmic sex can at last take place. The shape of the Harlequin sexual fantasy is designed to deal women the winning hand they cannot hold in life: a man who is romantically interesting—hence, distant, even frightening—while at the same time he is willing to capitulate to her needs just enough so that she can sleep with him not once but often. His intractability is exciting to her, a proof of his membership in a superior class of beings but, finally, he must relent to some extent if her breathless anticipation, the foreplay of romance, is to lead to orgasm.

Clearly, getting romantic tension, domestic security, and sexual excitement together in the same fantasy in the right proportions is a delicate balancing act.

Harlequins lack excellence by any other measure, but they are masterly in this one respect. In fact, the Harlequin heroine is in a constant fever of anti-erotic anxiety, trying to control the flow of sexual passion between herself and the hero until her surrender can be on her own terms. If the heroine's task is "converting rape into love-making," she must somehow teach the hero to take time, to pay attention, to feel, while herself remaining passive, undemanding, unthreatening. This is yet another delicate miracle of balance which Harlequin romances manage quite well. How do they do it?

The underlying structure of the sexual story goes something like this:

1. The man is hard (a walking phallus).

2. The woman likes this hardness.

3. But, at the outset, this hardness is *too hard*. The man has an ideology that is anti-romantic, anti-marriage. In other words, he will not stay around long enough for her to come, too.

4. Her final release of sexual feeling depends on his changing his mind, but *not too much*. He must become softer (safer, less likely to leave altogether) but not too soft. For good sex, he must be hard, but this hardness must be *at the service of the woman*.

The following passage from Anne Mather's *Born Out of Love* is an example:

His skin was smooth, more roughly textured than hers, but sleek and flexible beneath her palms, his warmth and maleness enveloping her and making her overwhelmingly aware that only the thin material of the culotte suit separated them. He held her face between his hands, and his hardening mouth was echoed throughout the length and breadth of his body. She felt herself yielding weakly beneath him, and his hand slid from her shoulder, across her throat to find the zipper at the front of her suit, impelling it steadily downward.

"No, Logan," she breathed, but he pulled the hands with which she might have resisted him around him, arching her body so that he could observe her reaction to the thrusting aggression of his with sensual satisfaction.

"No?" he probed with gentle mockery, his mouth seeking the pointed fullness of her breasts now exposed to his gaze. "Why not? It's what we both want, don't deny it." . . .

Somehow Charlotte struggled up from the depth of a sexually-induced lethargy. It wasn't easy, when her whole body threatened to betray her, but his words were too similar to the words he had used to her once before, and she remembered only too well what had happened next. . . .

She sat up quickly, her fingers fumbling with the zipper, conscious all the while of Logan lying beside her, and the potent attraction of his lean body. God, she thought unsteadily, what am I doing here? And then, more wildly: Why am I leaving him? *I want him!* But not on his terms, the still small voice of sanity reminded her, and she struggled to her feet.[19]

In these romantic love stories, sex on a woman's terms is romanticized sex. Romantic sexual fantasies are contradictory. They include both the desire to be blindly ravished, to melt, and the desire to be spiritually adored, saved from the humiliation of dependence and sexual passivity through the agency of a protective male who will somehow make reparation to the woman he loves for her powerlessness.

Harlequins reveal and pander to this impossible fantasy life. Female sexuality, a rare subject in all but the most recent writing, is not doomed to be what the Harlequins describe. Nevertheless, some of the barriers that hold back female sexual feelings are acknowledged and finally circumvented quite sympathetically in these novels. They are sex books for people who have plenty of good reasons for worrying about sex.

While there is something wonderful in the heroine's insistence that sex is more exciting and more momentous when it includes deep feeling, she is fighting a losing battle as long as she can only define deep feeling as a mystified romantic longing, on the one hand, and as marriage, on the other. In Harlequins the price for needing emotional intimacy is that she must passively wait, must anxiously calculate. Without spontaneity and aggression, a whole set of sexual possibilities is lost to her just as, without emotional depth, a whole set of sexual possibilities is lost to men.

Though one may dislike the circuitous form of sexual expression in Harlequin heroines, a strength of the books is that they insist that good sex for women requires an emotional and social context that can free them from constraint. If one dislikes the kind of social norms the heroine seeks as her sexual preconditions, it is still interesting to see sex treated not primarily as a physical event at all but as a social drama, as a carefully modulated set of psychological possibilities between people. This is a mirror image of much writing more commonly labeled pornography. In fact one can't resist speculating that equality between the sexes as child rearers and workers might well bring personal feeling and abandoned physicality together in wonderful combinations undreamed of in either male or female pornography as we know it.

The ubiquity of the books indicates a central truth: romance is a primary category of the female imagination. The women's movement has left this fact of female consciousness largely untouched. While most serious women *novelists* treat romance with irony and cynicism, most women do not. Harlequins may well be closer to describing women's hopes for love than the work of fine women novelists. Harlequins eschew irony; they take love straight. Harlequins eschew realism; they are serious about fantasy and escape. In spite of all the audience manipulations inherent in the Harlequin formula, the connection between writer and reader is tonally seamless; Harlequins are respectful, tactful, friendly towards their audience. The letters that pour in to their publishers speak above all of involvement, warmth, human values. The world that can make Harlequin romances appear warm is indeed a cold, cold place.

Notes ◆

1. Lindsay (1977, p. 10).
2. Stratton (1977, pp. 56, 147).
3. Here is an example of this sort of travelogue prose: "There was something to appeal to all age groups in the thousand-acre park in the heart of the city—golf for the energetic, lawn bowling for the more sedate, a zoo for the children's pleasure, and even secluded walks through giant cedars for lovers—but Cori thought of none of these things as Greg drove to a parking place bordering the Inlet" (Graham, 1976, p. 25).
4. Mather (1977, p. 42).
5. See Russ (1973).
6. Mather (1977, p. 42).
7. Clair (1978, p. 118).
8. Lindsay (1977, p. 13.
9. Stratton (1977, p. 66). The adjectives "cruel" and "satanic" are commonly used for heroes.
10. Graham (1976, p. 63).
11. Delivered, April 6, 1978, Livingston College, Rutgers University.
12. Stratton (1977, p. 132).
13. Stratton (1977, p. 112).
14. Stratton (1977, pp. 99, 102, 139).
15. See Gloria Steinem (1978) and other articles in the November 1978 issue of *Ms.* An unpublished piece by Brigitte Frase, "From Pornography to Mind-Blowing," MLA talk, 1978, strongly presents my own view that this debate is specious. See also Susan Sontag's "The Pornographic Imagination," in *Styles of Radical Will* and the Jean Paulhan preface to *Story of O*, "Happiness in Slavery."
16. Russ (1973, p. 679).

17. Stratton (1977, p. 115).
18. Dinnerstein (1976, pp. 73-75).
19. Mather (1977, pp. 70-72).

◆ *References*

Clair, C. (1978). *A streak of gold*. Toronto: Harlequin.

Dinnerstein, D. (1976). *The mermaid and the minotaur: Sexual arrangements and human malaise*. New York: Harper & Row.

Graham, E. (1976). *Mason's ridge*. Toronto: Harlequin.

Lindsay, R. (1977). *Prescription for love*. Toronto: Harlequin.

Mather, A. (1977). *Born out of love*. Toronto: Harlequin.

Russ, J. (1973). Somebody's trying to kill me and I think it's my husband: The modern gothic. *Journal of Popular Culture, 6*(4), 666-691.

Sontag, S. (1991). The pornographic imagination. In S. Sontag, *Styles of radical will*. New York: Doubleday.

Steinem, G. (1978, November). Erotica and pornography: A clear and present difference. *Ms.*

Stratton, R. (1977). *The sign of the ram*. Toronto: Harlequin.

42

EVERYDAY PORNOGRAPHY

◆ Jane Caputi

As my title indicates, this chapter is not about X-rated porn. Rather, it is about advertising images that we encounter every day, in magazines such as *TV Guide*, *Vibe*, *Vogue*, *Seventeen*, *Time*, *Esquire*, and *Sports Illustrated*.[1] Influenced by a feminist perspective, I think of these types of images as everyday pornography. By pornography I do not mean simply sexually explicit materials. Rather, as I use it, pornography is material developed around exploitation, objectification, and "denigration of women and a fear and hatred of the female body" (Kaplan, 1991, p. 322). Catharine MacKinnon and Andrea Dworkin (Dworkin, 1989, pp. 253-275) define pornography as the "sexually explicit subordination of women." Pornography and everyday pornography construct feminine and masculine subjectivities based in gender inequality, conditioning us to eroticize domination, subordination, violence, and objectification, even when, as in some contexts, a woman takes the masculine role or a man the feminine.

Feminist criticism of pornography is not the same thing as moralistic postures, based in ridiculous notions of sex as sinful and "dirty"—unless it is confined to marital heterosexual intercourse. Let me be very clear. I think that we need and deserve resistant sexual images and pictures to both instruct us and arouse us, ones that represents nonphallocentric sexualities, ones that challenge the definition of sex *as* intercourse, ones that describe and shape "eroticism in ways that repudiate phallocentrism" and recognize women as desiring subjects (hooks, 1994, p. 112). Such erotic imagery and narratives represent sexualities, whether lifelong and committed, brief and recreational, same sex or not, monogamous or not, that are based in respect, and recognition of the other and the self as beings and not objects.

Pornography supports the sexual politics of the status quo. It capitalizes, literally, on the ignorance and shame induced in us through sexual repression and colonizes what Audre Lorde (1984) calls the "erotic"—the force of freedom, ecstasy, exuberance and creativity, the potency that enables us to act and create, to grow and transform, and to resist oppression. Many defenders of pornography argue that porn, which is sexually explicit and often a turn-on, is therefore automatically liberating and "sex positive." Yet pornography is no real alternative; it emerges from the same sex-negative worldview and reinforces many of the most fundamental precepts of mainstream morality, for example, a split between spirit and sex, mind and body.

Morality demands the transcendence of the sexual body, which is conceptualized, variously, as dumb, dirty, the gateway to the devil, and the antithesis of mind, spirit, and "god." Pornography does not challenge this but exploits it. This is abundantly clear in a 1977 poster for the New York Erotic Film Festival: the bare outline of a woman's body is shown. Her genital area, though, is highly detailed. It is the face of the devil, replete with protruding tongue and horns. Of course, the more sex becomes linked with evil, the more "the forbidden" beckons with erotic allure. The more "the good" is rendered asexual, the more "evil" (a vast rubric in this absurd moral system, including not only murder but also sex outside of marriage) is charged with sexual dynamism. Think *Natural Born Killers* (Caputi, 1999b).

On November 19, 1994, unknown vandals defaced bound volumes of women, gay, and gender studies journals at the library of the University of New Mexico. Some journals had "bitch propaganda" scrawled on them. The cover of an issue of *Lesbian Ethics* had the name crossed out and replaced with "God's Ethics." Underneath that was a swastika and the pronouncement: "God made women for men." Both pornography and godly morality ordain women (and indeed all of creation) to have been created for men—as objects of service, whether nurturant or sexual. Both endorse sexualities based in dominance and submission, whether found in marriages where women are promised not only greater saintliness but also hotter sex if they will just shut up, graciously submit, and surrender (Doyle, 2000) or in sadomasochistic pornography where women are literally bound and gagged before they are fucked.

In a pornographic culture, images of extreme domination and violence— Nazism, torture, nuclear weaponry, imperial conquest—are laden with sexual subtexts (Caputi, 1993; Dworkin, 2000; Griffin, 1981; Sontag, 1980). Pornography sexualizes, variously, the humiliation, capture, possession, occupation, objectification, and destruction of another human being, of animals, of the land, and even of the planet (Collard, 1988). Thus, such forms of masculinized aggression against feminized targets, such as enslavement of "primitive" peoples, imperialist conquest of a "virgin land," scientific penetration of the "mysteries" of the universe, and technological assaults against (Mother) Earth, acquire an undeniably sexual component. The worldview of what I term "everyday pornography" underlies not only the oppression of women and sex negativity, but infuses practices of consumerism, racism, homophobia, abuse of animals, militarism, and environmental devastations.

It is not always so easy to recognize the oppressive character of pornography and its popular culture manifestations precisely because it is so normal. These notions have exerted enormous pressure in shaping our sense of ourselves as women or men, teaching us to become aroused in and by oppressive situations: for example, men who use women as disposable objects and are terrified by intimacy; women attracted only to "bad boys." Pornography depends on very conventional notions of masculinity and femininity. Male and female are defined as inevitably oppositional and inherently unequal, yet ineluctably attracted to each other. The male partner is supposed to be taller, stronger, richer, older, and colder—in short, more powerful. The female partner is supposed to be shorter, weaker, better looking, vulnerable, younger, and warmer—in short, socially powerless (if privately a goddess of nurture, support, and sexual prowess (Think *Pretty Woman*; Caputi, 1991). I will begin my tour of everyday porn by looking at these very ordinary understandings of gender roles.

◆ Gender Porn

Over and over, we are told not simply that men and women are biologically different but that we are different in ways that ordain and justify social inequality. The headline of the January 20, 1992, cover of *Time* magazine reads: "Why Are Men and Women Different? It isn't just upbringing. New studies show they are born that way." The cover image is of a (probably) Latino boy and a girl, about 8 years old, standing in front of a brick wall. The boy, wearing the pants, takes up most of the frame. Pulling up his sleeve, flexing his right bicep, and admiring his small swollen muscle, he turns away from the skirted girl and focuses entirely on his performance. She gazes indulgently on him and places one hand under his elbow, offering support. We learn, visually, that males and females are utterly different, with self-absorbed males defined primarily by superior upper-body strength. His placement in the bulk of the available space connotes dominance, both physical and social. The girl is subordinated, yet acquiescent. Viewers might come away thinking she is the superior one; after all, her expression suggests she sees through the foolishness of his display. Nonetheless, she props him up and directs all her energy into the boy. Perhaps it is more worth it to her that he be strong/potent, than that she

have a life. Finally, there is that brick wall they are up against. As this image has it, there is no way out; our biological destiny is male dominance and female subordination, male self-centeredness and female acquiescence and self-denial.

A grown-up version of this pornographic couple appears in a Calvin Klein underwear ad from 1992. The ad is spread out over two pages. On the first page, Markie Mark appears clad only in his underpants, with a threatening look on his face and grabbing his penis in a bullying gesture. On the next page, Markie is relaxed and sitting on the floor; he faces front; turning toward him, and wrapping a supportive arm around his waist, is the notoriously slender "waif" Kate Moss (also dressed only in her Calvins).

A fashion spread in *Today's Black Woman* (October 2000) features a man and a woman—well, their bodies anyway because the figures are cut off at the head. He wears a jacket (unzipped to show his naked chest), pants, and sensible walking boots. She wears only an unzipped jacket, leather bikini underwear, one stocking, and high-heeled boots. His hand is tensed, held away from his body, and ready for action. Hers is limp, closed, and rests on her thigh. The man's other arm is wrapped around her naked waist and she leans into him.

The primal couple appears again in a 1999 ad for L'Oréal "straight up" hair straightener: A white woman with long hair gazes up, sweetly and trustingly, at her stern-faced boyfriend who towers over her. He is literally "in her face," visually dominating her. The ad commands them to "play it straight." Certainly, that command refers as much to conformity to male-over-seer/female underling heterosexuality as it does to chemically altered locks.

Sexual, gender, and racial projections abound in all of these depictions. In the first, Latino children are used to illustrate the alleged biological determinism of unequal gender characteristics.[2] Racist/sexist ideology has it that people of color, like children and women, are "closer to nature" and more subject to instinctual drives than the "civilized," and, hence, better able to illustrate those purportedly mindless biological drives. The white people keep their heads; the black people are pure body. The females wear fetish garb and are positioned to suggest vulnerability, stasis, and service. The males are active, incipiently violent, and in control. The eroticism exuded by the adult couples is clearly based in their inequality. These gender-porn images point to domination, violence, and control of space as intrinsic and defining components of masculinity: Not only hard male musculature but also the penis is graphically associated with violence and power. Femininity, on the other hand, is represented as contained, sidelined, insubstantial, intrinsically supportive, controlled, and fundamentally powerless. Moreover, as this one-way power dynamic implies, the feminine counterpart might well soon find herself at the other end of hardened muscle or hostile penis.

Violence Objects ◆

The sexualization of conquest, and indeed, apocalyptic devastation, is a common theme both in pornography and the pornography of everyday life. A 1987 porn feature, *Mr. MX*, features a man with a monstrously long penis: "Take a long look at the real weapon of the '80s. . . . See his 16 1/2-inch missile." How different is this overtly pornographic notion of male sexuality from everyday notions. Support for the notion of men as violence objects and the Freudian understanding of the penis as lethal weapon, driving machine, space rocket, and so on is found everywhere in popular culture (Caputi, 1987, 1993), suggesting a huge investment of male sexual self-esteem in these products. An ad for the Nissan Patrol GR in British *Esquire* (June 1995) sells itself by promising a rapist thrill. A stick-on replica of the SUV is provided as well as a panorama of "unspoiled" mountain wilderness. The caption reads: "Stick it where the hell you

like." A 2000 ad for Candies fragrances positions a man in front of a computer monitor. His fingers manipulate the keys, but he turns to smirk at the viewer. On the screen, we see the Space Shuttle zooming upward. A woman with spread legs sits atop the monitor. Is she even aware of the rocket that is aiming directly into her vagina?

Popular conceptions of masculinity suggest that men, like machines, must always be ready and "hard" (they even have to "die hard"). At the same time, this masculinity can always be called into question. Real men must have no trace of femininity. It's far better to be a nuclear missile than a pussy. When boys and men sexually harass other boys and men with words, they call them *woman, whore, candy-ass, weak sister, faggot, pussy, bitch*. A cartoon in the *New Yorker* by P. Byrnes (2000) shows a white man about to receive a rectal exam. He asks his doctor, another white man: "Does this make me your bitch?" Here the slur is both sexist and racist; in contemporary black slang, *bitch* and *ho* are misogynist slurs. The patient gets to entertain a pornographic fantasy of the twin degradations of being a black woman and being penetrated. According to gender conventions, being receptive, sexually or otherwise, is connoted as feminine and as deeply shameful for men. This includes practices of homophobic homosexuality, when the man who plays the "masculine" inserter role in anal sex considers himself "straight" but his partner gay. We might also ask what does this contempt for the feminine role simultaneously reveal about common male attitudes toward intercourse with women? *Fucking, screwing, banging, having, taking, possessing, scoring, nailing*: all these terms indicate an association of penetrative sex with violence, humiliation, conquest, and domination. Andrea Dworkin (1987) argues that, to the pornographic mindset, intercourse itself becomes a ritual of domination.

The ideal of permanently hard, penetrative, and purely masculine manhood is, of course, an impossible one. Men never rest secure in their masculinity, but must prove it over and over (Beneke, 1997). And, not surprisingly, violence, both physical and psychological, is the most basic and universal method of proving manhood. An ad for "Bitch Skateboards" appeared in 1994 in the teenage-boy magazine *Big Brother*. It depicts the public-bathroom stick figures for a man and a woman. The "man" holds his right arm outstretched, pointing a gun at the head of the "woman." Surely, this ad is about hating girls and women, but it is also about hating the "feminine" within the male self. To successfully attain patriarchal manhood, the teenage boy must execute his "inner bitch."

Instructive here is another *Time* magazine cover (April 24, 2000). A pumped-up white man is photographed from the top of his nose to midthigh. (The absence of his eyes suggests a dearth of those feminine-marked traits of empathy and soul.) He clenches his fists and bares crooked and dangerous looking teeth. Across his pumped up chest is the word *Testosterone*. Most men, of course, no matter how much testosterone they have, look nothing like this model and never will. Ironically, the dangerous pursuit of hypermasculinity (often through abusing artificial testosterone and other steroids) is spurred by fear of being perceived as feminine and/or gay.

James Gilligan (1996) suggests that most male violence is caused not because men are hormonally driven to aggression, but because perpetrators are shamed, most commonly by an insult to their "manhood." Because violence is so definitive to patriarchal manhood, many respond to this threat to their self-esteem with some form of violence, particularly if they have no other social resources (education, money, position) to assert dominance. With this in mind, I want to go back to the same cover of *Time*. In the top left-hand corner, a blurb announces an inside story: "Columbine a Year Later: Can You Spot a Killer Kid?" Probably not. But I can spot a killer notion of manhood: The very one embodied by "Testosterone Man" on *Time*'s cover. The

two mass murderers at Columbine were not hormonally driven to kill. Rather, they had been bullied and mocked as "faggots" and "wimps" by boys who, no doubt, were trying to prove their own manhood by projecting the feared femininity onto designated scapegoats. The scapegoats then responded with mass violence, ironically, to prove *their* manhood.

Anti-Bitch Propaganda ◆

Standard images of masculine power suggest that men oppress women because men are naturally stronger and smarter. Nawal El Saadawi (1977), the Egyptian novelist and political theorist, suggests that actually it is male insecurity and terror in the face of "the innate resilience and strength of the woman" that first led men to oppress and subjugate women, trying to "conquer the indomitable vitality and strength that lay within women, ready to burst out at any moment" (p. 100). Understanding men's fear of female potency helps us to identify the common denominator among such superficially diverse practices as the pornographic capture and display of female bodies; sexual bondage; corseting (encouraged in the August 2000 issue of *Vogue*); veiling; fashion-mandated thinness; feminizing makeup; crippling footwear; depilation of the legs, face, underarms, and genitals; cosmetic surgery (including laser surgery to tighten the vagina and diminish the size of the labia); and clitoridectomy and other forms of genital mutilation. All such practices (and the imagery that promotes them) represent the fear-based masculine project to contain, control, infantilize, and defeat female potency, what I call *cunctipotence*.[3] In the pornographic view, whenever there is a strong woman, there is a weak and castrated man—male potency veritably requires female impotence. Bob Guccione, editor of the glossy porn magazine *Penthouse*, admits as much in a comment on Viagra when he whines: "Feminism has emasculated the American male, and that emasculation has led to physical problems" (quoted in Roof, 1999, p. 5). Yet many women and men reject this equation and yearn for recognitions of female power, social as well as sacred, historical as well as mythic.

Barbara Walker (1983, p. 109) reveals that *Bitch* was "one of the most sacred titles of the Goddess Artemis-Diana," who often appeared as a dog herself, or in the company of hounds. Indeed, around the world, the Lady of the Beasts assumed the full or partial form of an animal; for example, she appeared with horns or carrying horns, or appeared with characteristic animals—birds, fish, pigs, snakes (Neumann, 1963, p. 268). This ancient, powerful Bitch is the sacred archetype behind the contemporary profanity, reflecting fear of the "bitch goddess" (as well as the sexually sovereign, creative, autonomous woman). In patriarchal religions, the Bitch is demonized. In the secular world, she is turned into pornography.

Arguably, modern pornography is a genre devoted to profaning and containing female potency. This function is evidenced in pornography's appropriation of imagery that previously signified female sacred power: sexual exuberance and activity; the honorific association of a goddess, or "Lady of the Beasts," with animals and with the Earth; nakedness to indicate potency (Marinatos, 2000); the naked dance to invoke power (Vogel, 1997, p. 59); the spread legs—a sign of yoni worship (Marglin, 1987, p. 330); the ritual revelation of the vulva to signify ultimate truth (Hurston, 1938/1983, p. 137).[4] Pornography takes all of these signs and reworks them to signify degradation. Similarly, ancient goddess imagery is demonized, subsumed into those familiar representations of the Christian devil. The horns, protruding tongue, and serpentine nature are some of the attributes of, for example, the Greek Medusa, the Aztec Coatlicue, and the Yoruban First Ancestor (Anzaldúa, 1987; Baring & Cashford, 1991; Graham, 1997; Sjöö & Mor, 1991).

In *Goddess: Myths of the Female Divine*, David Leeming and Jake Page (1994) trace an ancient history of goddess worship followed by systematic denigrations during the patriarchal era. Nevertheless, they note the continuing presence of goddess imagery, albeit abused and degraded, in the persistence of such popular figures as the *femme fatale*. Pam Keesey (1997) also finds a background of goddess worship animating contemporary images of the *femme fatale*, the vamp, vampire, and dominatrix. One image that she reproduces is a cover from the fetish magazine *Bizarre*. Here we find a contemporary version of the "Lady of the Beasts": a dark-haired seductress, her eyes lined with kohl, clad in a corset-like teddy, long black gloves, perilously high stiletto heels, and wielding a snake-like whip. A stuffed tiger sits at her feet. The message is a mixed one, of course. Female power is invoked, but immediately contained for, as her outfit and shoes indicate, she too is bound; her tiger is only a toy.

In a 1999 ad for Vassarette lingerie, we again encounter a Lady of the Beasts. Wearing a gray bra and panties, the dark-haired, kohl-eyed seductress stands under a headline reading: "Color: Shark. Note: Man eater." The *femme fatale* is a sexist and colonialist stereotype based in woman's alleged "basic instinct" for "evil"—which we can read, of course, as *resistance*. What lies beneath these stereotypes is a social recognition that *cunctipotence*, unleashed from misogynist definition, mutilation, and constraints, is a force that could not so much "castrate" men as radically upend the "man's world."

Gracious Submission ◆

In *Genesis* 4:16, God curses the rebellious Eve: "Your desire shall be for your husband and he shall rule over you." It sounds a lot like a sadomasochistic scenario, and indeed, imagery of Adam and Eve, the devil, the serpent, and the apple figure not only in religious stories but appear prominently in advertisements for pornographic entertainment. This is really not so surprising. Through patriarchal interpretations of this influential story, sex becomes synonymous with sin and active female desire is transmogrified into masochism. Pornography and the pornography of everyday life enthusiastically affirm these same messages. The dominatrix or *femme fatale* is the unchastened Eve before the "fall." The punished submissive is the "after" shot. Regularly, fashion images display women in poses and situations that suggest bondage and eroticize submission. In an ad for Natori (2000), a young white woman is decked out in black fetish lingerie and seated in a straight-backed chair. Her eyes are demurely downcast as she offers herself to the viewer.

Pornography sexualizes hierarchy, not only between the sexes under male supremacy but also between socially unequal—and sexually fetishized, enslaved, and colonized—races. Possession of women by conquering men, celebrated in such venues as the colonial or tourist postcard, serves as a symbolic facilitator of political, ideological, and military conquest (Alloula, 1986). In such fantasies, women are either fetishized—as passive, accessible, welcoming maidens—or feared as *femmes fatales*, voracious cannibals who must be annihilated. The first part of this fantasy is epitomized in a layout featuring Naomi Campbell, a darkskinned woman of African, Chinese, and European ancestry (*Harper's Bazaar*, April 1994). The layout uses fashion images, set off by quotes from French painter Paul Gauguin ("I had been seduced . . . by this land and by its simple and primitive people"). The first image is of an offered, cut-open tropical fruit, glistening with moisture. The second is of Campbell also offered and open—naked and face down on a bed!

In a 1999 ad for Skyy Vodka, a young, blonde white woman takes the dominant role. She lies, stomach down, on a mat, naked except for a towel over her buttocks. She props her head up, and extends one arm with a glass needing to be filled with vodka. An Asian woman is there to do the serving. She kneels alongside, her knees touching the woman's other outstretched arm. Sexual subordination is coded into her posture and downcast eyes. She is heavily made-up, elaborately coiffed, and wears a tight, red silk dress, slit up to her buttocks. The joys of sexualized/racialized domination, what bell hooks (1992) calls "eating the other" (pp. 21-39), are here offered to elite women.

Similar imagery frequently can be found in ads using men of color. An ad for Nike workout clothes (*GQ*, August 2000) uses a two-page spread. On the left, a darkskinned black man, wearing only the longtailed shirt, crouches awkwardly, legs apart. On the right, he stands, this time naked above the waist so that his prominent muscles are displayed. His arms are behind his back, as if he were handcuffed, and his head is so deeply lowered that we cannot even see his face. The body language connotes shame and submission, and invokes slavery; the black man is constructed as the submissive sex object.[5] Cultural theorist Ann duCille (1997) suggests that this "feminization" of black men is a product of white men's masked desire for black male bodies, a desire commonly denied by extreme manifestations of racism and homophobia. She recognizes a pornographic dynamic infusing such institutions as slavery, organized sports, and law enforcement, where white men discipline, gaze at, and control the bodies of dark men. In law enforcement, the black male body is disproportionately incarcerated as well as "frisked, patted down, probed, cuffed, spread and ordered to 'assume the position,' which after all, is the stance of anal intercourse" (duCille, 1997, p. 308).

Everyday Child ◆ Pornography

Kaplan (1991, p. 350) argues that when women demand and express our intellectual, sexual, and emotional freedom, society responds with both overtly woman-hating pornography and the increased sexualization of children. In pornographic videos, women are marked with clothing and hairstyles to suggest that they are children or teenagers (Jensen & Dines, 1998, p. 87). In everyday pornography, sexually objectified women are shown in poses and clothing that suggests that they are little girls, and actual girls are made-up and dressed as if they are adult seductresses—as in a recent series of ads for Chanel perfume. The now iconic JonBenet Ramsey haunting our culture demands that we recognize the pornographic object behind the "little beauty queen."

An ad from 1975 unforgettably illuminates the pornographic dynamic. It is a pitch for Love's Baby Soft Fragrance and depicts a heavily made-up child, about 5 or 6 years old. The headline reads: "Love's Baby Soft. Because innocence is sexier than you think." Pornographic sexuality is based in the notion that sex is "dirty," that sex defiles purity. Sexual gratification then becomes linked with defilement as well as transgression and conquest. Charles Stember (1976) describes standard notions of sexual pleasure: "The gratification in sexual conquest derives from the experience of defilement—of reducing the elevated woman to the 'dirty' sexual level, of polluting that which is seen as pure, sexualizing that which is seen as unsexual, animalizing that which is seen as 'spiritual'" (p. 49). The construction of childhood "innocence" does not necessarily protect children. Rather, in the pornographic paradigm, innocence *is* sexy precisely because violation itself is understood as synonymous with sex.

This notion of childhood innocence, suggesting that children's nudity has no sexual meaning to them or anyone else, also deflects our critical attention. In a 1996 pitch for funds for the Breast Cancer Research Foundation, a moppet with tousled curls is pictured from the waist up. She is naked and stands with her hands folded beneath her exposed nipples; her mouth is open and puckered, reminiscent of the mouth of a sex doll. In pornography, nakedness and an open mouth signifies accessibility. What purpose, if not that, do they serve here? The copy, written across her undeveloped breasts, reads: "Mommy, when I grow up will I get breast cancer?" In a culture where a woman' self- and socially perceived worth is all too often linked to her status as a sex object and breast size, dealing with breast cancer is particularly painful. To see this little girl sexually objectified in this context is most telling.

Specialized pornographic genres graphically focus on incest themes and pictorials (Russell, 1998). In 1979, *Playboy* too exploited incest for sexual thrills. A sequence, playfully titled "Father Knows Best," again features a young woman posing naked, but this time she is being photographed by her father. Underneath the headline, and before we get to the adult shots, is a full nude portrait of the daughter when she was three. Her backside is in view as she turns to look at her father. The accompanying copy reveals that the father would shoot nude models at home and that the little girl would take her clothes off, mimic the model's poses, and beg her daddy to photograph her too. He just had to comply for "She had the cutest little tush." Lots of parents photograph their young children naked with no harmful intent or effect. Yet photographing a child in the context of pornography shoots strikes me as a form of sexual abuse. The tongue-in-cheek title, "Father Knows Best," ironically enough, recognizes an underlying connection between family values and pornography. Patriarchal family values idealize a father's godlike authority in his home/castle, where wives and children, his dependents and, in classical form, his property, submit to his benevolent dominion. Incest and domestic abuse constitute the underside of that fundamentally unequal arrangement.

Child abuse generally is perpetrated not by strangers but by someone known to the child—a family member, priest, friend, neighbor—someone whom the child has been led to trust. An ad, in both print and television format (airing during the 2000 World Series) from the St. Paul Insurance Company, vividly promotes child sexual abuse.[6] A little tousled-haired white girl, utterly alone and utterly beautiful, stands in a field. In the distance we something long and hard rise up in the tall grass. It turns out to be the horn of a rhinoceros and the camera alternates between the child's face as she stands frozen, the charging rhino, and captions, which read: "Trust/Is not being afraid/even if you're vulnerable." As the rhino reaches her, a cloud of dust covers them. When it clears, we see the little girl reach out her hand and stroke the horn as she plants a kiss on it. The girl's vulnerability only enhances her erotic appeal. The child sexual abuser seems ugly even to himself. But, this ad assures him, he really is loveable and desired by his victim.

◆ Battery

As in the *Playboy* spread discussed above, one of the most common deceptions spread in support of sexual abuse is that women and girls invite it. A 1999 ad for Spree candies (*Seventeen*) shows a female mouth open and with her tongue sticking out. A Post-it on the tongue reads: "Kick me." Ads frequently include scenarios of men striking women, or of beaten women (Caputi, 1999a). In November 2000, a student gave me two pages torn from an unidentified fashion magazine. An Asian woman sits bereft and forlorn on a bench. Red makeup is applied around one eye to suggest that she has been beaten. On the next page, she wears a backless dress and is posed to suggest that she is utterly spineless. She stands with her back to us, her arms dangling, and bending to the side. Splotches of green make-up imply that she has bruises on her back and along her arm.

Battery is a long-term process of torture and intimidation meant to break the will of the victim. This is accomplished not only by physical assault but also through repeated humiliations, death threats, and psychological attacks on the victim's sense of self (Jones, 1994). Robert Jensen and Gail Dines (1998) note that a common scenario in pornographic novels involves women who at first do not understand their need to submit. As a man forces sex on her and humiliates her, she learns "to crave sex and domination" (p. 94). The same message is conveyed by a 1994 ad for boots that appeared in *Details*, a men's magazine. In this a woman is positioned on hands and knees with her buttocks high in the air and her face down; she is licking the floor. The copy reads: "An acquired taste." The pornographic message here is that if an abuser humiliates his partner long enough, she will learn to love it. Another ad for Candies fragrances (1999) conveys a similar message. The actress, Alyssa Milano, is bending over slightly; a man bends into her from behind. The copy encourages the man: "Anywhere you dare." And he takes the dare, pulling down her T-shirt to spray the fragrance on her now partially exposed breasts. Milano's smile belies the implicit assault. The implied anal sex in these ads does not suggest that this might be consensual activity, but promotes it as a way to demean women.

Rape ◆

A 1996 ad in *Seventeen* for Bonne Bell "no shine" cosmetic products mocks the feminist insistence on a woman's right to refuse sexual relations. The ad headlines the emblazoned words "*No means NO.*" It tells its teenage readers that, when they were little, "no" meant things like "no cookie before dinner." Now, they proclaim, "NO takes on a whole new meaning." It now means: "No more greasy makeup." One 1992 study found that girls younger than 18 accounted for 62% of rape victims (Johnston, 1992, p. A9). The well-known feminist retort "no means no" counters the pornographic insistence that a woman's *no* to sexual contact actually means *yes*. In this ad, antirape activism is grossly trivialized for the age group most susceptible to rape.

The excessive use of alcohol greatly increases the likelihood of acquaintance rape. In numerous ads aimed at men, it is suggested that drinking facilitates sex for men, whether the woman consents or not. A 1995 ad for Bacardi rum that appeared on the back cover of *Vibe* shows three men and one woman. At first glance, because her pants are the same color as one of the boys, it appears as if she is standing firmly on the ground. But, if you look closely, you clearly can see that the men are lifting her up in the air. Her legs are spread and a huge bottle of Bacardi rum is aimed into her crotch. All parties are smiling. Advertised here are the joys of (gang) rape and the uses to which alcohol can be put in facilitating it. A 2001 ad in *ESPN Magazine* for the "mudslide," a drink made with Kahlua, shows a screaming, provocatively dressed woman backed up against a pile of sandbags. The bottle, again, is poised to enter between her legs. The copy advises the reader of the ad: "Don't hold back."

◆ Snuff

An extreme form of violent pornography is the snuff film or photograph, images of someone actually being murdered: the killing is understood as the climactic part of the sex. A "virtual snuff" sensibility informs countless fashionable images that have appeared in advertising and fashion tableaux since the 1970s. Models (e.g., Linda Evangelista and Madonna) are showcased in positions suggesting that they are dead: suffocated under plastic bags; laid out in gift-box coffins; their heads and torsos buried under concrete; sprawled brokenly on stairs and boutique floors. Symbolic dismemberments have long been the norm in fashion photography (decapitated heads to

sell us perfume, amputated legs to push pantyhose, even crowds of disembodied eyes to sell us eye shadow) (Caputi, 1987). These dismemberments usually are not recognized as such, so habituated are we to them. We might notice them if they were being done to male bodies, but they are not in any comparable way.

An ad for the Voodoo computer card (2000) shows a woman whose Medusa-like head has been blown off due to the intensity of the charge in her hair dryer. One for Diamond.com (2000) shows an unconscious or dead woman, naked save for strategic strands of diamonds; she is caught in a pseudo-spider web of similar strands. The mythic Atlantis is evoked in an ad for Finlandia Vodka (1998). It shows a drowned woman, whose see-through dress clings to her voluptuous buttocks, evoking a necrophilic voyeurism. A series of ads for Perry Ellis fashions in late 2000 through 2001 are all set in a green-tiled room (obviously like the execution chamber for Timothy McVeigh shown regularly in the news during this period). One of these (*Vanity Fair*, September 2000) shows a naked man leaning over an elegantly dressed woman, who is stretched out on the floor. Her eyes are glassy and her arms extend awkwardly over her head. A few months later, another elegantly dressed body, this time a man's, lies on the floor of the same green-tiled room. A pair of unclad, shaven legs stand over him. Is it a woman who has killed him? Whatever the sex of the fashionable killers and corpses, the fact remains: murder, including state-sponsored murder, is linked to glamour and sexual situations.

The "pornographic murder" (Durgnat, 1978, p. 499) first was sensationalized in *Psycho* (Alfred Hitchcock, 1960) in the infamous shower scene. Such murder presents the subjectivity, desires, and point of view of the sex killer. An ad for *Law & Order* appeared in *TV Guide* (October 11, 1995). Under the headline "Coed Killer" is a drawing of a prostrate female corpse with plunging neckline and prominent breasts. When murder is so blatantly sexualized and exploited, we might have to realize that the sex killer is not a deviant, an incomprehensible monster, but rather the logical product of a pornographic culture that ubiquitously eroticizes violence (Caputi, 1987).

◆ *Silencing Women*

Hostility to female speech is a recurring preoccupation of sexist systems, enforced through such means as religious proscriptions, codes of modesty, and the exclusion of women from powerful arenas. A comic selection from *Hustler* is unforgettably overt in its hostility. Under a caption reading "Lip Service," we view a photograph of a woman's face; her mouth has been replaced by a vulva. The text below the picture reads:

> There are those who say that illogic is the native tongue of anything with tits. . . . It comes natural to many broads; just like rolling in shit is natural for dogs. . . . They speak not from the heart but from the gash, and chances are that at least once a month your chick will stop you dead in your tracks with a masterpiece of cunt rhetoric. . . . The one surefire way to stop those feminine lips from driving you crazy is to put something between them—like your cock, for instance. (cited in Russell, 1998, p. 65)

In other words, men can shut the offending "mouth" via rape—oral and vaginal.

The pornography of everyday life is more subtle but the message is the same. Frequently, women are mocked as silent, stupid, and inconsequential by being decapitated in ads, their very heads replaced by products or simply left out of the frame. An ad for Shredded Wheat (*Esquire*, March 2001) shows only the torso of a "babe" in a bikini. Written over her midsection are the words "8% substantial." The cereal is then lauded as "100% substantial." Many visuals suggest that a woman is gagged. A 2000 ad for Lexus shows a naked white woman bound in hot pink wrappings, though with plenty of her flesh showing. Her face is wrapped; only her eyes, looking glassy and stunned, show completely. A single strip effectively gags her mouth. A vicious ad for Miller appeared on the back cover of *Sports Illustrated* (2000). It shows a man's hand resting a beer on top of an ordinary looking middle-aged white woman's head—she must be on the floor. She is grimacing, her eyes almost closed (although, if you give it just a quick glance it might seem that she is smiling). She holds the label of the beer, in the manner of a gag, over her mouth. One woman, Viviana Cintolesi, told me this ad visually transmitted a common sexist saying in her country, Chile: The perfect woman has a flat head (on which a man can place a beer), big ears (so that he can hold her tight), and a toothless mouth (so that he can orally rape her with no danger to himself).

Sex Objects ◆

> Sexuality is socially organized to require sex inequality for excitement and satisfaction. The least extreme expression of gender inequality, and the prerequisite for all of it, is dehumanization and objectification. (MacKinnon, 1989, p. 243)

An ad for Nike "air" sports shoes appeared in *Sports Illustrated* in 1999. It shows the shoe as well as an uninflated sex doll. The caption reads: "Air is what makes it good." Although pornography is rumored to be all about lust and sexual excitement, in the long run pornography is about desensitization, disconnection, the constriction of the sexual imagination, and the increasing appeal of control and sadism to the numbed sensorium (Jensen, 1998, p. 139). Pornographic objectification is a process whereby a sentient being is dehumanized, someone turned into something that can be exchanged, owned, shown off, abused, disposed of, and used as a means to someone else's ends. And, the truth is, if you dehumanize others, you unavoidably do it to yourself as well. An article in *Men's Health* (Gutfield, 1999) warns readers that use of Internet pornography can cause men to become addicted to its engineered fix and lose their desire for real intimate interactions.

Women learn our status as objects through not only the harassment and surveillance we encounter regularly on the streets and at work but also through art, pornography, prostitution, fashion, cheesecake, beauty contests, tourist advertising, and so on. Drawing on the history of the female nude in European art, John Berger (1972, pp. 46-47) notes that such work served a pornographic function for their collectors. Moreover, in a sexist system "men act and women appear." The one who does the looking is in a position of power. Indeed those who are positioned as spectacle are reduced to slave, animal, and/or commodity status.

Patricia Hill Collins (1990, p. 168) argues persuasively that African American women are not included in pornography as an afterthought but that the history of racist enslavement and sexual exploitation of African American women forms a "key pillar on which contemporary pornography rests." Because of slavery, black women's bodies were continual objects of display on the auction block, were reduced to commodities for purchase, and forced sexually and reproductively. Collins (1990) writes: "The process illustrated by the pornographic treatment of the bodies of enslaved African women . . . has developed into a full-scale industry encompassing all women objectified differently by racial/ethnic pornography" (p. 169). Consider an ad for Moschino apparel that appeared in 1999 in *Elle* magazine. A dark-skinned black woman, with a big Afro and garbed in leopard-skin pants and halter top and high heels, stands with legs spread wide and arms flung out against the wall. Looking closely, we that she is literally stapled to

fabric on that wall. She registers no resistance; her eyes are half-closed and her mouth is open. It is hard to read her expression: she could be making bedroom eyes or she could be drugged. In her critique of pornography, the novelist Alice Walker (1980) writes: "Where white women are depicted in pornography as 'objects,' black women are depicted as animals" (p. 103). In a culture where animals are considered a lower species, this marks black women not only as sex objects but as subhumans. Walker continues: "Where white women are depicted as human bodies if not beings, black women are depicted as shit" (p. 103).

Dirty Pictures ◆

A cartoon in *Hustler* shows a black man wiping himself after defecating. Where the tissue wipes clean, his skin turns white. A mainstream version of this "joke" can be found in a 2000 ad for Calvin Klein "Dirty Denim" jeans. Lisa "Left Eye" Lopes, of the music group TLC, wearing short-short "dirty denims," is posed against a chain-link fence. It is nighttime and this doesn't look like a very safe place to be. She is standing, but bending forward so her buttocks protrude.

The moralistic/pornographic association of sex with "the dirty" is based in a mind/body split. Racist and sexist "civilization" define progress by how far a culture makes it known that it is removed from body functions, sexuality, and the animal and elemental world, which is understood as inferior and feminine. All women, to a greater or lesser degree depending on factors of race, class, and sexual experience; men of color; gay men; and Jews have been figured as "dirtier" than those who conveniently define themselves as cleaner, purer, more moral, civilized, and superior (Dijkstra, 1996). Within this pornographic dichotomy, some women are denounced as particularly sexual, animalistic, and dirty—women of color, prostitutes, poor women.

Other women are designated as impossibly "pure"—for example, upper- and middle-class white woman who are installed as the closely guarded symbol of "white purity, white culture, of whiteness itself" (Doane, 1991, p. 41).

This pattern is enacted with great visual charge in two disparate magazine ads from 1994. One, appearing in *Cosmopolitan*, is for Neutrogena soap, although you could easily think you are looking at a poster for a white supremacist group. A young, blonde, smiling woman, wearing faded blue jeans and a white blouse, stands against a white background. The boldfaced word—*Pure*—obviously refers equally to the woman and the soap. We should remember that in "honor crimes," "pure" woman must bear the honor of her male relatives and community. If she transgresses against what they believe to be proper behavior, and gets "dirtied," they can righteously kill or rape her (Baker, Gregware, & Cassidy, 1999).

Just as the elite woman is constructed as "pure," others (women of color, "white trash," and colonials, poor women, prostituted women) are said to be "dirty." In a 1994 ad for Diesel jeans, appearing in *Details*, a brown-skinned woman lies on a bed covered with zebra-striped sheets. She wears a black bra, unbuttoned jeans, and a crucifix (symbolizing colonization as well as theological notions of sexual filth/evil). Obviously, this woman is available for invasion and conquest. The headline reads: "How to control wild animals." In smaller print, this advice is given:

> We all want a safer world. So, come on, let's build more zoos. 1000s of them! Right now, there are far too many dangerous animals running around, wasting space, wasting time, using the planet as a toilet! Take our advice. Don't be fooled by "natural" beauty, stick em in practical, easy-to-clean metal cages.

By stigmatizing this woman, and those she represents, as a dangerous and filthy animal, the conditions are laid for any type of abuse to be done to her with impunity.

This moralistic understanding of sex as defilement and hence "dirty" is deeply ingrained. The mind/body split ordains that the body is divided into pure (head and face) and impure (sexual and elimination) zones. Following again on this split, whole peoples can be classified as inferior (dark, savage, bestial, dirty, sexual, "shitty," dangerous) and subjected to rape, lynching, colonization, genocide, or "ethnic cleansing" (Bauman, 1989). Moreover, under this model, animals (hairy, uncivilized, sexually unashamed) are figured as inferior creatures for use, and the Earth itself, the source of humanity (*human*, from the Latin *humus*, earth or dirt), becomes our enemy.

Crimes Against Nature ◆

> The definition and use of the female body is the paradigm for the definition and use of all things; if the autonomy of the female body is defined as sacred, then so will be the autonomy of all things. (Sjöö & Mor, 1991, p. 384)

The phrase "crimes against nature" usually means "perversions," such as homosexuality. Of course, it might be more apt to recognize the true crimes against nature as the denial of our own nature, abuse of animals, and environmental pollutions. Sometimes metaphoric language implicitly recognizes the connection. The cover of *Time* magazine (September 4, 1995) depicts a gray "polluted and plundered" wasteland. The headline reads: "The Rape of Siberia." Henry Kissinger once remarked that power is the ultimate aphrodisiac. A political cartoon by David Levine in *The Nation* (February 25, 1984) visualizes Kissinger's power by showing him "fucking" the Earth (a woman's body with the Earth as her head). We have no trouble getting the joke. Rena Swentzell (1993, p. 167), a Native American scholar from

Santa Clara Pueblo in New Mexico, scoffs at the normative/pornographic belief in "power as an integral part of sexuality." She demands that we recognize the historical implications of that belief: "That is what the inquisition was all about. That is what the whole conquest of the Southwest was about—power and control by males."

In popular imagery, the conquest continues. Both the land and the female body are shown as conquered, rendered into property that can be owned and mapped. A 1999 ad for car stereo speakers shows a naked, curvy, and inert, perhaps dead, young white woman lying on the ground. Inscribed over every inch of her body are roadmaps. The headline reads: "Feel the raw, naked power of the road." Here men are invited to experience driving as a form of sexual conquest over the Earth. Sometimes a woman's body represents the land; other times, the image of the Earth itself is used. As I have detailed elsewhere, in all manner of advertising imagery, paralleling the pornographic treatment of women's bodies, the Earth is shown stabbed, halved, rendered partially artificial, dominated, and "snuffed" (Caputi, 1993).

An everyday image of technological snuff using (part of) a woman's body can be found in a 1993 ad for Eclipse Fax machines. The headline reads: "Eclipse Fax: If It Were Any Faster, You'd Have to Send and Receive Your Faxes Internally." We see the decapitated head of a woman, again very Medusa-like, whose snaky hair fans out around her head. Two electrodes are attached to her forehead. Jammed into her eyes, ears, and mouth are cruel-looking metal pipes with wires going in multiple directions. Every visible opening is penetrated. The last line sneers: "to fax any faster, you'd have to break a few laws. Of physics." Of course, this image flaunts that familiar pornographic delight in taboo violation by symbolically visualizing the ongoing mutilation, rape, and murder of nature (*physics* is from the Greek *phusis*, nature).

Almost everyone has heard of the movie *The Stepford Wives* (and its made-for-TV sequels). In the mythic town of Stepford, husbands kill their spouses so that they can replace them with voluptuous and acquiescent robots. The artificial sex object is a recurring symbol in pornography and popular culture. In 1951, cultural theorist Marshall McLuhan claimed that this symbol, what he called "the mechanical bride," indicated that necrophilic sexual desires were being invested into technology and bespoke a numbed sensibility that experienced sensation only through sadism, by "pluck[ing] the heart out of the mystery" (p. 101). Like the "Stepford wife," the mechanical bride is the uncanny shell that remains when life/presence has been destroyed.

The mechanical bride points to the core connection between cultural degradation of women and an overall assault on the feminine principle in nature, what Vandana Shiva (1988, p. 40) defines as the active and creative principle in which both women and men participate. That animosity, as documented by Caroline Merchant (1980), Evelyn Fox Keller (1985), and others, riddles scientific language and metaphor that regularly refers to "mastery" over nature, "penetrating" the mysteries of the universe, and so on (Caputi, 1993). When the "heart" of the mystery—the erotic—is thus plucked, we are left in a soulless, still, and deeply sterile place, veritably a Stepford World.

The images I have described here are not just selling us the individual products or fashions that they promote. Nor is their subject matter some uncomplicated notion of "sex." Rather, we are being asked, forcefully and every day, to buy into an ideology and an attendant sexuality that normalizes and promotes an interlocking series of oppressions and violences. The pornographic worldview is perhaps best epitomized by a 1985 promo from the Canned Food Information Council in both print and video versions (the latter premiered during the Super Bowl). The setting is supposedly the year 3000. The future is represented by a shiny, supine, leg-spread, open-mouthed fembot (Daly, 1987, p. 98) replete with stiletto heels and sculpted uplift breasts. This pornographic "sex goddess" symbolizes a supposedly desirable future, one in which "dirty," that is, fertile, active, and exuberant, Nature is finally defeated and replaced by a shiny, man-made, and utterly controlled object. This vision celebrates a supposed triumph of mind over body, of men over women, of civilization over nature. Yet what it really bespeaks is a cosmic sterility (Caputi, 1998).

These visions do not remain unchallenged. A vital movement of art, literature, and ecological/feminist philosophy challenges the pornographic worldview and reclaims the erotic energies that have been appropriated (e.g., Anzaldúa, 2000; Caputi, 1998, 2001; Cisneros, 1996; Conner, 1993; Daly, 1984; Ensler, 1998; Gadon, 1989; Walker, 1983). That movement begins with the refusal of everyday pornography and a reclamation of the erotic. At its core is a recognition that the powers of mind are akin to, not opposed to, the powers of sex. I take heart from the response of a 6-year-old girl interviewed by Eve Ensler and included in the *Vagina Monologues*. When Ensler (1998) asked her, "What's special about your vagina?" she replied: "Somewhere deep inside I know it has a really really smart brain" (pp. 88-89).

◆ Notes

1. I want to thank friends and students who have brought some of these ads to my attention: Valentina Bruno, J. D. Checkit, Heather Stewart, Natalia Gago, Augusta Walden, and Ann Scales.

2. The ethnicity of the children is ambiguous. It was Latinos who told me that they recognized the children as Latino. This ambiguity leaves the racist message intact, but renders it with more subtlety.

3. *Cunctipotent* is a currently obsolete English word meaning "all powerful." I first encountered it in Barbara Walker's *Women's Encyclopedia of Myths and Secrets* (1983) while perusing the entry *cunt*. Until the 14th century, *cunt* was Standard English for the vulva and only became obscene in the 17th century. Eric Partridge (1961) writes that the word dropped out of Standard English due to its "powerful sexuality." Walker asserts that *cunt* is derivative of the Asian Great Goddess as Cunti, or Kunda, the Yoni of the Universe. Following Michael Dames, she associates *cunt* with the words *country*, *kin*, *kind*, *cunning*, and *ken*, as well as *cunctipotent*. Most linguists do not support this etymology. Nevertheless, we can accept it as a folk etymology and reclaim *cunctipotence* as a word meaning female potency, possibility, and potential—a concept sorely needed in the English language.

4. Two examples will have to suffice here of the associations of sacred power with the vulva. Among the Baule people of the Ivory Coast, the most powerful *amuin* (a power or supernatural spirit) is the *amuin bla*, the women's deities, notably Adyanun. An image of a spirit wife presents a naked woman with legs spread, signifying that she is especially close to the powers of Adyanun. In Baule culture, as in the story of Baubo, we find an association between females' naked dance and the averting of calamity: "The women dance Adyanun as a last recourse in times of impending calamity—epidemics, war, drought, a president's death—because it is more potent than all the other amuin. Adyanun may be danced after the men's *bo nun amuin* have failed, or if they are not considered strong enough. The women's *amuin* is danced naked because its locus of power is every woman's sexual organs" (Vogel, 1997, p. 59). Zora Neale Hurston (1938/1983) relates this conversation with her guide in her study of Haitian voodoo: "'What is the truth?' Dr. Holly asked me, and knowing that I could not answer him he answered himself through a Voodoo ceremony in which the Mambo, that is the priestess, richly dressed, is asked this question ritualistically. She replies by throwing back her veil and revealing her sex organs. The ceremony means that this is the infinite, the ultimate truth. There is no mystery beyond the mysterious source of life" (p. 137).

5. Thanks to Heather Stewart for pointing out this connection.

6. Thanks to Fran Chelland for alerting me to this ad and its implications.

◆ References

Alloula, M. (1986). *The colonial harem* (M. Godzich & W. Godzich, Trans.). Minneapolis: University of Minnesota Press.

Anzaldúa, G. (1987). *Borderlands/la frontera*. San Francisco: Spinsters/Aunt Lute Press.

Anzaldúa, G. (2000). *Interview/entrevistas* (A. Keating, Ed.). New York: Routledge.

Baker, N., Gregware, P., & Cassidy, M. (1999). Family killing fields: Honor rationales in the murder of women. *Violence Against Women, 5*(2), 164-184.

Baring, A., & Cashford, J. (1991). *The myth of the goddess: Evolution of an image*. New York: Arkana, Penguin.

Bauman, Z. (1989). *Modernity and the Holocaust*. Ithaca, NY: Cornell University Press.

Beneke, T. (1997). *Proving manhood*. Berkeley: University of California Press.

Berger, J. (1972). *Ways of seeing*. London: The BBC and Penguin Books.

Caputi, J. (1987). *The age of sex crime*. Bowling Green, OH: Bowling Green State University Press.

Caputi, J. (1991). "Sleeping with the enemy" as "Pretty woman Part II." *Journal of Popular Film and Television, 19*(2), 2-8.

Caputi, J. (1993). *Gossips, gorgons, and crones: The fates of the Earth*. Santa Fe, NM: Bear.

Caputi, J. (1998). The 21st century sex, love, and death goddess. *Blue Mesa Review, 10*, 3-14.

Caputi, J. (1999a). The pornography of everyday life. In M. Meyers (Ed.), *Mediated women: Representations in popular culture* (pp. 57-80). Cresskill, NJ: Hampton.

Caputi, J. (1999b). Small ceremonies: Ritual in *Forrest Gump, Natural Born Killers, Seven*, and *Follow Me Home*. In C. Sharret (Ed.), *Mythologies of violence in postmodern America*. Detroit, MI: Wayne State University Press.

Caputi, J. (2001). On the lap of necessity: A mythic interpretation of Teresa Brennan's energetics philosophy. *Hypatia: A Journal of Women and Philosophy, 16*(2), 1-26.

Cisneros, S. (1996). Guadalupe the sex goddess. In A. Castillo (Ed.), *Goddess of the Americas [La diosa de las Américas]: Writings on the Virgin of Guadalupe*. New York: Riverhead Books.

Collard, A., with Contrucci, J. (1988). *Rape of the wild: Man's violence against animals and the Earth*. Bloomington: Indiana University Press.

Collins, P. (1990). *Black feminist thought: Knowledge, consciousness, and the politics of empowerment*. New York: Routledge.

Conner, R. P. (1993). *Blossom of bone*. San Francisco: HarperSanFrancisco.

Daly, M. (1984). *Pure lust: Elemental feminist philosophy*. Boston: Beacon.

Daly, M., with Caputi, J. (1987). *Webster's first new intergalactic wickedary of the English language*. Boston: Beacon.

Dijkstra, B. (1996). *Evil sisters: The threat of female sexuality and the cult of manhood*. New York: Knopf.

Doane, M. (1991). *Femmes fatales: Feminism, film theory, psychoanalysis*. New York: Routledge.

Doyle, L. (2000). *The surrendered wife: A practical guide to finding intimacy, passion, and peace with a man*. New York: Simon & Schuster.

duCille, A. (1997). The unbearable darkness of being: "Fresh" thoughts on race, sex, and *The Simpsons*. In T. Morrison & C. Brodsky Lacour (Eds.), *Birth of a nation'hood: Gaze, script, and spectacle in the O. J. Simpson case* (pp. 293-338). New York: Pantheon.

Durgnat. R. (1978). Inside Norman Bates. In L. Braudy & M. Dickstein (Eds.), *Great film directors: A critical anthology* (pp. 496-506). New York: Oxford University Press.

Dworkin, A. (1987). *Intercourse*. New York: Free Press.

Dworkin, A. (1989). *Letters from a war zone*. New York: E. P. Dutton.

Dworkin, A. (2000). *Scapegoat: The Jews, Israel, and women's liberation*. New York: Free Press.

El Saadawi, N. (1977). *The hidden face of Eve*. New York: Zed Books

Ensler, E. (1998). *The vagina monologues*. New York: Villard.

Gadon, E. (1989). *The once and future goddess*. San Francisco: HarperSanFrancisco.

Gilligan, J. (1996). *Violence: Reflections on a national epidemic*. New York: Random House.

Graham, L. (1997). *Goddesses in art*. New York: Abbeville.

Griffin, S. (1981). *Pornography and silence: Culture's revenge against nature*. New York: HarperColophon.

Gutfield, G. (1999). The sex drive: Men who are hooked on cyberpornography. *Men's Health, 14*(8), 116-121.

hooks, b. (1992). *Black looks: Race and representation*. Boston: South End.

hooks, b. (1994). *Outlaw culture: Resisting representations*. New York: Routledge.

Hurston, Z. (1983). *Tell my horse*. Berkeley, CA: Turtle Island. (Original work published 1938)

Jensen, R. (1998). Using pornography. In G. Dines, R. Jensen, & A. Russo (Eds.), *Pornography: The production and consumption of inequality* (pp. 101-146). New York: Routledge.

Jensen, R., & Dines, G. (1998). The content of mass-marketed pornography. In G. Dines, R. Jensen, & A. Russo (Eds.), *Pornography: The production and consumption of inequality* (pp. 65-100). New York: Routledge.

Johnston, D. (1992, April 24). Survey shows number of rapes far higher than official figures. *New York Times*, national edition, p. A9.

Jones, A. (1994). *Next time, she'll be dead: Battering and how to stop it*. Boston: Beacon.

Kaplan, L. J. (1991). *Female perversions: The temptations of Emma Bovary*. New York: Doubleday.

Keesey, P. (1997). *Vamps*. San Francisco: Cleis.

Keller, E. F. (1985). *Reflections on gender and science*. New Haven, CT: Yale University Press.

Leeming, D., & Page, J. (1994). *Goddess: Myths of the female divine*. New York: Oxford University Press.

Lorde, A. (1984). Uses of the erotic: The erotic as power. In *Sister outsider* (pp. 53-59). Trumansburg, NY: The Crossing Press.

MacKinnon, C. (1989). *Toward a feminist theory of the state*. Cambridge, MA: Harvard University Press.

Marglin, F. (1987). Yoni. In *The encyclopedia of religion* (M. Eliade, Ed., Vol. 15, pp. 530-535). New York: Macmillan.

Marinatos, N. (2000). *The goddess and the warrior: The naked goddess and mistress of animals in early Greek religion*. New York: Routledge.

McLuhan, M. (1951). *The mechanical bride: Folklore of industrial man*. Boston: Beacon.

Merchant, C. (1980). *The death of nature: Women, ecology, and the scientific revolution*. San Francisco: Harper and Row.

Neumann, E. (1963). *The great mother: An analysis of the archetype*. Princeton, NJ: Princeton University Press.

Partridge, E. (1961). *A dictionary of slang and unconventional English*. London: Routledge and Kegan Paul.

Roof, J. (1999, Winter). We want Viagra, *Post Identity, 2*(1), 5-23.

Russell, D. E. H. (1998). *Dangerous relationships: Pornography, misogyny, and rape*. Thousand Oaks, CA: Sage.

Shiva, V. (1988). *Staying alive: Women, ecology and survival in India*. London: Zed Books.

Sjöö, M., & Mor, B. (1991). *The great cosmic mother: Rediscovering the religion of the Earth*. San Francisco: HarperSanFrancisco.

Sontag, S. (1980). Fascinating fascism. In *Under the sign of Saturn* (pp. 73-108) New York: Farrar, Straus and Giroux.

Stember, C. (1976). *Sexual racism*. New York: Elsevier, HarperColophon.

Swentzell, R. (1993). Commentaries on *When Jesus came the Corn Mothers went away: Marriage, sex, and power in New Mexico, 1500-1846*, by Ramón Gutiérrez. Compiled by Native American Studies Center, University of New Mexico. *American Indian Culture and Research Journal, 17*(3), 141-177.

Vogel, S. M. (1997). *Baule: African Art Western eyes*. New Haven, CT: Yale University Press.

Walker, A. (1980). Coming apart. In L. Lederer (Ed.), *Take back the night: Women on pornography* (pp. 95-104). New York: Bantam Books.

Walker, A. (1982). *The color purple*. New York: Washington Square.

Walker, B. (1983). *Women's encyclopedia of myths and secrets*. San Francisco: HarperSanFrancisco.

43

KING KONG AND
THE WHITE WOMAN

Hustler *Magazine and the Demonization of Black Masculinity*

◆   Gail Dines

From the box office success of *The Birth of a Nation* in 1915 to the national obsession with O. J. Simpson, the image of the Black man as the spoiler of White womanhood has been a staple of media representation in this country. The demonization by the media of Black men as rapists and murderers has been well documented by scholars interested in film (Carby, 1993; Guerrero, 1993; Mercer, 1994; Snead, 1994; Wiegman, 1993; Winston, 1982), news (Entman, 1990; Gray, 1989), and rap music (Dyson, 1993; Rose, 1994). Although this image stands in sharp contrast to the feminized Uncle Tom that was popular in early Hollywood films, both images serve to define Black men as outside the normal realm of (White) masculinity by constructing them as "other" (Wiegman, 1993). Although both the Uncle Tom and the sexual monster continue to define the limits of Black male representation in mainstream media, the latter image dominates and, according to Mercer (1994), serves to legitimize

NOTE: From *Violence Against Women*, Vol. 4, No. 3, June 1998, pp. 291-307. Copyright © 1998 by Sage Publications, Inc. Reprinted by permission of Sage Publications, Inc.

racist practices, such as mass incarceration of Black men, police brutality, and right-wing government policy.

Recently, scholars have turned their attention to pornography (Cowan & Campbell, 1994; Forna, 1992; Mayall & Russell, 1993; Mercer, 1994) and specifically how the codes and conventions of this genre (re)construct the Black male body, especially the penis, as dangerous and as a threat to White male power. The focus of this research tends to be poorly produced, hard-core pornography movies that are relegated to the shelves of adult-only stores because of their close-up shots of erect penises, ejaculation, and vaginal, anal, and oral penetration. What tends to be ignored in these studies is the content of the mass-produced, mass-circulated pornography magazines that, because they can be purchased in bookstores, newsstands, and airport terminals, have a much larger audience.

Of the hundreds of mass-produced, mass-distributed pornography magazines, the three best sellers are *Playboy*, *Penthouse*, and *Hustler* (Osanka, 1989).[1] Although these three magazines are often lumped together, they differ markedly in the type of world that they construct. *Playboy* and *Penthouse*, in their pictorials, cartoons, advertisements, and editorials, depict a Whites-only world, a world so affluent and privileged that Blacks are excluded by invisible market forces. Indeed, even the White working class is invisible in the *Playboy* world of expensive clothes, gourmet restaurants, and well-appointed homes. *Hustler*, however, in its pictorials, "beaver hunts" (explicit snapshots of readers' wives and girlfriends), advertisements, and editorials, constructs a world populated by working-class Whites who live in trailer homes, eat in fast-food restaurants, and wear ill-fitting clothes. Although Blacks are absent from most sections of the magazine, they appear regularly in caricatured form in the cartoons, where they are depicted as competing with White men for the few sexually available White women. *Hustler* cartoons depict a world filled with seething racial tensions brought about by the Black man's alleged insatiable appetite for White women. The competition between Black and White men and the ultimate victory of the Black man is the source of much humor in *Hustler* cartoons and serves to visually illustrate to the mainly White, working-class male readership what happens if Black masculinity is allowed to go uncontained. *Hustler* is by no means the first mass-distributed medium to visually depict the ultimate White fear; indeed, *The Birth of a Nation* and *King Kong* (1933) played similar roles. Only in *Hustler*, it is the White man who loses, as evidenced in his failure to win back the girl. This [chapter] will examine how *Hustler* draws from past regimes of racial representation and articulates a more contemporary myth of Black masculinity that, having been allowed to run amok because of liberal policies, has finally rendered White men impotent, both sexually and economically.

From The Birth of a ◆ Nation to Black Studs

Theorists such as Wiegman (1993) and Snead (1994) have traced back to the late 19th century the beginnings of the image of the Black man as a sexual monster, as the product of a White supremacist ideology that saw the end of slavery as bringing about an unleashing of animalistic, brute violence inherent in African American men. D. W. Griffith's *The Birth of a Nation* (1915) was, without question, the first major mass circulation of this image in film and was to become the blueprint for how contemporary mass media depict Black men.

The notion of the Black man as a sexual monster has been linked to the economic vulnerability that White working-class men feel in the face of a capitalist economy over which they have little power. Guerrero (1993), in his discussion of the emergence of this new stereotype in the novels of Thomas Dixon, suggests that the economic turmoil of the postbellum South served to

> undermine the white southern man's role as provider for his family; thus he sought to inflate his depreciated sense of manhood by taking up the honorific task of protecting White Womanhood against the newly constructed specter of the "brute Negro." (p. 12)

This encoding of the economic threat in a sexual context is, according to Snead (1994), the principal mechanism of cinematic racism and is one of the subplots of the enormously successful *King Kong* movie (renamed *King Kong and the White Woman* in Germany). Arguing that "in all Hollywood film portrayals of blacks . . . the political is never far from the sexual" (p. 8), Snead links the image of King Kong rampaging through the streets of Manhattan with a defenseless White woman clutched to his body to the increasing economic emasculation of White men in the Depression years and the growing fear that Black migration from the South had reduced the number of jobs available to working-class Whites. King Kong's death at the end of the movie remasculinizes the White man, not only through his conquest of the Black menace but also through regaining the woman. In this way, representations of Black men and White men are not isolated images working independently, but rather "correlate . . . in a larger scheme of semiotic valuation" (Snead, 1994, p. 4). Thus, the image of the Black man as a sexual savage serves to construct White male sexuality as the protector of White womanhood, as contained, and, importantly, as capable of intimacy and humanity.

In her analysis of Black and White masculinity in Hollywood movies, Jones (1993) argues that although Black and White actors are increasingly portrayed in terms of a violent masculinity, for White actors this violence is tempered by his sexually intimate scenes with a White woman. These scenes assure the audience that for all his violence, the White man is still capable of bonding with another human being and of forming relationships. For Black actors, however, this humanizing quality is absent, and thus he can be defined only in terms of his violence. The problem with these types of representations is that, according to Jones, "they suggest that there are fundamental differences in the sexual behavior of Black men and White men and are ultimately indicative of the psychic inferiority of the Black man" (p. 250) and the superiority of White masculinity.

Hard-core pornography similarly depicts Black men as more sexually dehumanized than White men. This seems surprising because in pornography, all participants, men and women, are reduced to a series of body parts and orifices. However, studies that compare the representation of White men and Black men in pornography (Cowan & Campbell, 1994; Mayall & Russell, 1993) have found that it is Black male characters who are granted the least humanity and are most lacking in the ability to be intimate. Moreover, in movies and magazines that feature Black men, the focus of the camera and plot is often on the size of his penis and his alleged insatiable sexual appetite for White women. Movies with titles such as *Big Bad Black Dicks*, *Black Stallions on Top*, *Black Pricks/White Pussy*, and *Black Studs* draw attention to the Black male body and in particular the penis, a rare occurrence in pornography targeted at heterosexual men. Movies such as *The Adventures of Mr. Tootsie Pole* (Bo Entertainment Groups) feature a Black man and a White woman on the cover. The text beneath the picture says, "He's puttin his prodigious pole to the test in tight white pussy." In *Black Studs* (Glitz Entertainment), three White women are shown having sex with three Black men. Above the pictures, the text reads, "These girls can't get enough of that long Black dick." The penis becomes the defining feature of the Black man, and his wholeness as a human being is thus rendered invisible.

The image of the Black man as sexually aggressive is a regular cartoon feature in *Hustler*, one of the best-selling hard-core porn magazines in the world (Osanka, 1989). Cartoons that have as their theme the sexual abuse of White women by Black men began appearing in the late 1970s, and by the mid-1980s, *Hustler* was running an average of two to three such cartoons an issue. *Hustler* was by no means the first to produce such an image, but it is probably the first mass-distributed cultural product (albeit in caricatured form) to visually depict an enormous Black penis actually doing severe physical damage to the vagina of a small White woman.

That these types of images have been marginalized in the debate on pornography is problematic, especially in light of the international success of *Hustler* magazine. Much of the analysis of pornography has focused on the ways the text works as a regime of representation to construct femininity and masculinity as binary opposites. This type of theorizing assumes a gender system that is race-neutral, an assumption that cannot be sustained in a country where "gender has proven to be a powerful means through which racial difference has historically been defined and coded" (Wiegman, 1993, p. 170). From the image of the Black woman as Jezebel to the Black man as savage, mainstream White representations of Blacks have coded Black sexuality as deviant, excessive, and a threat to the White social order. In *Hustler* sex cartoons, this threat is articulated par excellence in caricatured form and serves to reaffirm the racist myth that failure to contain Black masculinity results in a breakdown of the economic and social fabric of White society.

◆ "F*** You If You Can't Take a Joke": Marketing the Hustler Cartoon

In the history of American mass media, cartoons have been a major forum for the production and reproduction of racist myths. From the prestigious *Harper's Weekly* of the late 1900s to contemporary Disney cartoons, Blacks have been caricatured as savages, animals, and lazy servants. Cartoons, with their claim to humor, have been especially useful vehicles for the expression of racist sentiments that might otherwise be considered unacceptable in a more serious form. Indeed, in his award-winning documentary *Ethnic Notions* (1987), Marlon Riggs shows how the cartoon image of Blacks has changed little from the beginning of the century to the more contemporary versions, whereas other media forms were forced, in the post-civil rights era, to encode the racist myths in a more subtle manner.

The *Hustler* cartoons that have as their theme the Black man as the spoiler of White womanhood are an outgrowth of the portrait caricatures that originated in Italy at the end of the 16th century. These portrait caricatures, with their distinctive technique of "the deliberate distortion of the features of a person for the purpose of mockery" (Gombrich, 1963, p. 189), became very popular across Europe and were adapted in the middle of the 19th century by cartoonists who used similar methods of distortion against anonymous members of recognizable social groups, rather than well-known individuals. Gombrich, in his celebrated essay on caricatures, argues that the power of this visual technique is that the distorted features come to stand as symbols of the group and are thought to say something about the essential nature of the group as a whole. The Black male cartoon character in *Hustler* is caricatured to the point that his penis becomes the symbol of Black masculinity and his body the carrier of the essential nature of Black inferiority.

It is not surprising, therefore, that the only place where Blacks appear with any regularity in *Hustler* is the cartoon. To depict Black men as reducible to their penis in the more serious sections of the magazine might open *Hustler* up to charges of racism as well as the regular criticisms it receives from women's groups regarding the openly misogynist content. Indeed, the cartoon has become the only place where *Hustler*'s claim to being the most outrageous and provocative sex and satire magazine on the shelves is realized. Although Larry Flynt (publisher and editor of *Hustler*) regularly criticizes *Playboy* and *Penthouse* for being too soft and for "masquerading the pornography as art" (Flynt, 1983, p. 5), *Hustler*'s own pictorials tend to adopt the more soft-core codes and conventions (young, big-breasted women bending over to give the presumed male spectator a clear view of her genitals and breasts), rather than the hard-core ones that specialize in rape, torture, bondage, bestiality, defecation, and incest. However, these hard-core themes regularly appear in the cartoons, together with cartoons that focus on leaking and bad-smelling vaginas, exploding penises, impotent penises, disembodied corpses, bloody body parts being used as masturbation tools, and depictions of Black men raping, mutilating, and pimping White women.

One of the main reasons for the hardcore content of the cartoons is that *Hustler* has to be careful not to alienate its mainstream distributors with pictorials or articles that might be classed as too hard-core, thus relegating the magazine to the porn shops, a move that would severely limit its sales. (*Hustler*'s success is mainly due to its ability to gain access to mass distribution outlets in the United States and Europe.) On the other hand, *Hustler* also has to keep its promise to its readers to be more hard-core or else it would lose its readership to the more glossy, expensively produced softcore *Playboy* and *Penthouse*. Toward this end, *Hustler* relies on its cartoons to make good on its promise to its readers to be "bolder in every direction than other publications" (Flynt, 1988, p. 7) while keeping the pictorials within the limits of the soft-core genre.

Flynt regularly stresses that the cartoons' boldness is not limited to sexual themes, but extends to their political content. Indeed, in his editorials, Flynt (1983) regularly stresses that "we are a political journal as well as a sex publication" (p. 5). In an editorial responding to critics of *Hustler* cartoons titled "Fuck You If You Can't Take a Joke," Flynt (1988) tells his readers that his critics are not upset with the sexual content of the magazine, but rather, with his satire that carries "the sting of truth itself" (p. 7). Flynt continues by arguing that he will not allow his critics to censor what is, in effect, the political content of his magazine, because "satire, both written and visual, has . . . been the only alternative to express political dissent" (p. 7).

A strategy that Flynt has used to promote the cartoons to the readers is to elevate the long-standing cartoon editor of *Hustler*, Dwaine Tinsley, to a present-day major satirist. The creator of the "Chester the Molester" cartoon (a White, middle-aged pedophile who appeared monthly until Tinsley was arrested on child sexual abuse charges in 1989) and some of the most racist cartoons, Tinsley is described by *Hustler* editors as producing "some of the most controversial and thought-provoking humor to appear in any magazine" ("Show and Tell," 1983, p. 7) and, in some cases, cartoons that are "so tasteless that even Larry Flynt has had to think twice before running them" ("Tinsley in Review," 1983, p. 65). We are, however, reassured by *Hustler* that the tastelessness will continue, as "Larry is determined not to sell out and censor his creative artists" (p. 65) because satire "is a necessary tool in an uptight world where people are afraid to discuss their prejudices" ("Show and Tell," 1984, p. 9).

Thus, *Hustler* does not position itself simply as a sex magazine, but also as a magazine that is not afraid to tell the truth about politics. This linking of the sexual with the political makes *Hustler* cartoons a particularly powerful cultural means for the production and reproduction of racist ideology, for, as Snead (1994) argues, "It is both as a political and as a sexual threat that Black skin appears on screen" (p. 8). On the surface, these cartoons seem to be one more example of *Hustler*'s outrageous sexual humor, the Black man with the huge penis being equivalent to the other sexually deviant (White) cartoon characters. However, *Hustler*'s depictions of Black men are actually part of a much larger regime of racial representation, beginning with *The Birth of a Nation* and continuing with Willie Horton, which makes the Black man's supposed sexual misconduct a metaphor for the inferior nature of the Black "race" as a whole.

◆ Black Men and White Women: The White Man Under Siege

During the 1980s, *Hustler* featured the work of four cartoonists: Collins, Decetin, Tinsley, and Trosley. Surprisingly, although these cartoonists had very distinct styles, they all used a similar caricatured image of a Black man with an enormous muscular body, an undersized head (signifying retardation), very dark skin, and caricatured lips. The striking feature of this caricature is that the man is drawn to resemble an ape, an image that, according to Snead (1994), has historical and literary currency in this country. Pointing to *King Kong* as a prime example of this representation, Snead argued that "a willed misreading of Linnaean classification and Darwinian evolution helped buttress an older European conception . . . that blacks and apes, kindred denizens of the 'jungle,' are phylogenetically closer and sexually more compatible than blacks and whites" (p. 20). Black film critics have long argued that the *King Kong* movie and its sequels played a major role in the sexual demonization of Black masculinity because the ape—the carrier of blackness—was depicted as out of White control, resulting in the stalking and capturing of a White woman.

Whereas the original Kong lacked a penis, the *Hustler* version has, as his main characteristic, a huge black penis that is often wrapped around the "man's" neck or sticking out of his trouser leg. The penis, whether erect or limp, visually dominates the cartoon and is the focus of humor. This huge penis is depicted as a source of great pride and as a feature that distinguishes Black men from White men. For example, in one cartoon, a Black man and a White man are walking next to a fence. The White man makes a noise by dragging a stick along the fence, while the Black man does the same using his large penis, which is much bigger than the stick. The Black man, who is walking behind the White man, is snickering at the White man's stick (*Hustler*, February 1989, p. 95).

Black men are depicted as being obsessed by the size of their penises, one more example of how the dominant regime of racist representation constructs Blacks as "having bodies but not minds" (Mercer, 1994, p. 138). In one cartoon, a large Black man with an undersized head is looking at his newborn son and screaming at the White nurse, "Never mind how much he weighs, bitch! How long's my boy's dick?" (*Hustler*, December 1988, p. 32). Not only is the Black man depicted as verbally abusive, but also as lacking care and interest in his son's health and well-being. This image fits in with the dominant representation of Black men as either abusive or absent fathers who take advantage of the welfare system developed by misguided liberals (see below).

Whereas the *King Kong* movies left to the imagination what would happen to the White woman if Kong had his way, *Hustler* provides the mainly White readership with detailed images of the violence Black men are seen as capable of doing to White women's bodies. In many of the cartoons, the theme of the joke is the severely traumatized vagina of the White sexual partner. In one cartoon, a naked White woman is sitting on a bed, legs open, and her vagina has red stars around it, suggesting pain. Sitting on the end of the bed is a naked, very dark, apelike man, his huge, erect penis dominating the image. He is on the phone asking room service to send in a shoehorn.

The White woman looks terrified (*Hustler*, November 1988, p. 100). In another cartoon, a similar-looking couple are walking down the street. The Black man has his arm around the White woman and on his shirt is written "Fucker" and on hers, "Fuckee" (*Hustler*, May 1987, p. 79). Although the man is clothed, the outline of his huge penis can be seen. The woman's vagina, on the other hand, is clearly visible because it is hanging below her knees and is again red and sore, a marker of what Black men can and will do to White women if not stopped by the White male protector of White womanhood.

In *Hustler* cartoons, the White man is constructed as anything but the protector of White womanhood. He is a lower-working-class, middle-aged man whose flabby body is no match for the muscular, enormous Black body. In stark contrast to the big Black penis is the small-to-average White penis that is rarely erect and never threatening to White women. On the contrary, the size of the White man's penis is a source of ridicule or frustration to his sex partner (who is always White). Rather than showing empathy, the woman is constantly poking fun at his manhood by searching for it with magnifying glasses or binoculars. One cartoon, for example, has a White couple in bed, with the woman under the covers gleefully shouting, "Oh, I found it" (*Hustler*, May 1992, p. 10). The man is clearly embarrassed and is covering up his penis. Other cartoons show the White man endlessly searching pornography shops for penis enlargers (presumably the same enlargers that can be mail-ordered from the ads in the back of *Hustler*). A cartoon that speaks to the racial differences constructed in the cartoons depicts a Black man with a small penis. The joke is focused on the size, as a Black preacher is praying for his penis to grow. The caption reads, "Sweet Jesus—heal this poor brother! Rid him of his honkie pecker" (*Hustler*, March 1984, p. 15).

The size of the Black penis is the theme of a full-page interview between *Hustler* editors and "The Biggest, Blackest Cock Ever!" (1983). The page is in the same format as Hustler interviews, only in place of a person is a picture of a large Black penis. The subtitle reads: "A candid, explosive man-to-dick conversation with the most sought after piece of meat in the world." Hustler editors ask, "Why do women love big, black cocks?" The answer given by the cock (written, of course, by the *Hustler* editors) is, "They love the size. . . . You know any White guys hung like this?" The editors continue by framing the discussion in clearly political terms through their answer to the question of why Black men prefer White women: "I likes [*sic*] white pussy best. It's my way of gettin back at you honkies by tearin up all that tight white pussy. . . . I fuck those bitches blind." Indeed, the cartoons surrounding this interview provide visual testimony of how much damage the Black penis can do to White women.

The small penis would seem to be one of the reasons why White male cartoon characters, in contrast to Black male cartoon characters, have trouble finding willing sex partners. His sexual frustration leads him to seek female surrogates in the form of dolls, bowling balls, children, chickens, and skulls. The Black man, however, appears to have no problem attracting a bevy of young, White women. When the White man does find a willing sex partner, she tends to be middle-aged, overweight, and very hairy. The Black man's White sexual partner is, however, usually thin, attractive, and lacks body hair. This is a very unusual female image in *Hustler* cartoons and suggests that the Black man is siphoning off the few sexually available, attractive women, leaving the White man with rejects.

The message that White women prefer Black men is the theme of a spoof on Barbie, a doll that represents the all-American woman with her blonde hair, tiny waist, and silicone-like breasts. The picture is of Barbie dressed in black underwear, on her knees with ejaculate around her mouth. Standing next to her is a Black male doll pulling a very large penis out of her mouth.

The caption reads, "In an attempt to capture the market the manufacturer has been testing some new designs. . . . We're not sure, but perhaps this Slut Barbie (with her hard nipples, a permanently wet, open pussy and sperm dripping from her mouth) goes a bit too far" (*Hustler*, July 1984, p. 23). The obvious choice for Barbie's sex partner would have been Ken, her long-term boyfriend, but the suggestion here is that Ken, with his White penis, would not have been enough to entice an all-American girl to give up her virginal status.

Because of the lack of willing sex partners, the White man is often reduced to paying for sex. However, once again, Black men have the upper hand because almost all the pimps in *Hustler* cartoons are Black. These Black men have, however, traded in their large penises for big Cadillacs, heavy gold jewelry, and fur coats, riches no doubt obtained from White johns. The prostitutes are both Black and White, but the johns are almost always depicted as White. Many of the cartoons have as their theme the White man trying to barter down the Black pimp, with the Black pimp refusing to change the price. The power of the Black man is now absolute—not only can he get his pick of attractive White women, he also controls White prostitutes, leaving the White man having to negotiate to buy what he once got for free.

Not only is the Black man draining the White man's access to women, he is also draining his pocket in the form of welfare. The Black man is shown as deserting his family and numerous unkempt, diseased children, leaving the welfare system to pick up the tab. One cartoon features a Black woman surrounded by children and saying to a White interviewer, "Yes, we does [sic] believe in Welfare" (*Hustler*, December 1992, p. 47). Another example is a cartoon advertising different dolls. The first doll, called "Beach Darbie," is a Barbie look-alike in a bathing costume. The second doll, also Darbie, is dressed in a white jacket and is called "Ski Darbie." The third doll is an overweight White woman with bedroom slippers and a cigarette hanging out of her mouth; she is called "Knocked-Up Inner-City Welfare Darbie." In each hand she has a Black baby (*Hustler*, December 1992, p. 107).

In *Hustler* cartoons, Black men have precisely the two status symbols that White men lack: big penises and money. The White man's poor sexual performance is matched by his poor economic performance. Reduced to living in trailer homes, poorly furnished apartments, or tract houses, the *Hustler* White male cartoon character is clearly depicted as lower working class. His beer gut, stubble, bad teeth, and workingman's clothes signify his economic status and stand in sharp contrast to the signifiers of power attached to the image of the Black man.

A New Ending to ◆ an Old Story

The coding of Black men as sexual and economic threats takes on a contemporary twist in *Hustler*, as this threat cannot be easily murdered as in *King Kong*, but rather is now uncontainable and returns month after month to wreak havoc on White women's bodies and the White men's paychecks. This new ending changes the relationship between the binary representations of Black and White masculinity. In his analysis of the racial coding of masculinity in cinema, Snead (1994) argues that "American films . . . have always featured . . . implicit or explicit correlations between the debasement of Blacks and the elevation and mythification of Whites" (p. 142). In *Hustler* cartoons, both Black and White men are debased, the former for being hypermasculine and the latter for not being masculine enough.

As the target audience of *Hustler* is White men, it seems surprising that the cartoons regularly ridicule White men for being sexually and economically impotent and for failing to contain the Black menace. However, when class is factored into the analysis, it becomes apparent that it is not White men as a group who are being ridiculed. The debasement of White masculinity in *Hustler* cartoons is played out on the caricatured flabby, unkempt body of the lower-working-class White man, a class that few Whites see themselves as belonging to, irrespective of their income. Thus, in between the hypermasculinity of the Black man and the undermasculinized White lower-working-class man is the reader inscribed in the text who can feel superior to both types of "deviants." The reader is invited to identify with what is absent in the cartoons, a "real man" (*Hustler*'s first issue ran an editorial that introduced the magazine as one for "real men") who turns to *Hustler* because it is, according to its editors, "truly the only magazine that deals with the concerns and interests of the average American."

The reader, constructed as the average American, is, as *Hustler* is careful about pointing out, not the same as the cartoon characters. In an editorial praising Tinsley, the editors wrote, "Dwaine Tinsley is not a black, a Jew, a wino, a child molester, or a bigot. But the characters in his cartoon are. They are everything you have nightmares about, everything you despise" (p. 6). Thus, in coded terms, *Hustler* provides distance between the reader and the cartoon characters, who are either lower class (Black, wino, child molester, bigot) or the elite (Jew), by leaving open the middle class, the category in which most White Americans situate themselves (Jhally & Lewis, 1992).

The lower-class, sexually impotent White man in *Hustler* cartoons is, thus, not an object of identification, but rather of ridicule, and serves as a pitiful example of what could happen if White men fail to assert their masculinity and allow the Black man to roam the streets and bedrooms of White society. The *Hustler* White male cartoon character thus stands as a symbol of the devastation that Blacks can cause, a devastation brought about by bleeding-heart liberals who mistakenly allowed Blacks too much freedom. Just as Gus (the Black, would-be rapist) in *The Birth of a Nation* is an example of what might happen when Blacks are given their freedom from slavery (a dead White woman being the end result), the *Hustler* Black man is an example of what could happen if Black men are not contained by White institutional forces, such as the police and the courts. Whereas *The Birth of a Nation* and *King Kong* were, according to Snead (1994), the past's nightmare visions of the future, *Hustler*'s representation of Black men can be seen as the current nightmare vision of the future, because it "re-enacts what never happened, but does so in an attempt to keep it from ever happening" (p. 148).

By making the White man the loser, *Hustler* departs from the traditional racial coding of masculinity and provides a different ending to the nightmare vision of Black men taking over. This ending is, however, not simply restricted to the pages of *Hustler*; rather, it is articulated in the numerous news stories on welfare cheats, inner-city violence, and reverse discrimination. The White man is, according to the media, fast becoming the new minority who has to support Black families in the inner city and give up his job to an unqualified Black person because of past oppression. The White man is under siege and unless he fights back, he will lose his masculine status as breadwinner. The absence in *Hustler* cartoons of elite Whites as exploiters of poor Whites firmly positions the Black man as the other who is the source of White male discontent. Given the current economic conditions, which include falling wages, downsizing, and off-shore production, the average White man (along with everyone else who is not a member of the economic elite) is experiencing increasing levels of discontent and, as in previous periods of economic decline, it is the Black population that is demonized and scapegoated as the cause of the economic woes.

Although the racial codings of masculinity may shift, depending on the socioeconomic conditions, from the feminized Uncle

Tom to the hypermasculinized "buck," Black masculinity continues to be represented as deviant. It is this constructed, deviant status that continues to legitimize the oppression and brutality that condemns young Black men to a life on the margins of society and makes them the convenient scapegoat for the economic and social upheaval brought about by global capitalism and right-wing government policies. Although this [chapter] has foregrounded *Hustler* cartoons, the regime of racial representation discussed continues to inform most mainstream media content and contributes to the commonsense notion that Black culture, not White supremacy, is the source of racial strife in America.

◆ Note

1. Pornography is defined here as any product that is produced for the primary purpose of facilitating arousal and masturbation. Although the product may have other uses (for example, *Playboy* as a magazine to teach men how to live a playboy lifestyle), its main selling feature for the producer, distributor, and consumer (whether overtly or covertly) is sexual arousal.

◆ References

The biggest, Blackest cock ever. (1983, November). *Hustler*, p. 6.

Carby, H. (1993). Encoding White resentment: "Grand Canyon"—A narrative. In C. McCarthy & W. Crichlow (Eds.), *Race, identity and representation in education* (pp. 236- 247). New York: Routledge.

Cowan, G., & Campbell, R. (1994). Racism and sexism in interracial pornography: A content analysis. *Psychology of Women Quarterly, 18*, 323-338.

Dyson, M. (1993). *Reflecting Black: African-American cultural criticism.* Minneapolis: University of Minnesota Press.

Entman, R. (1990). Modern racism and the image of Blacks. *Critical Studies in Mass Communication, 7*, 332-345.

Flynt, L. (1983, November). The politics of porn. *Hustler*, p. 5.

Flynt, L. (1988, July). Fuck you if you can't take a joke. *Hustler*, p. 7.

Forna, A. (1992). Pornography and racism: Sexualizing oppression and inciting hatred. In C. Itzin (Ed.), *Women, violence and civil liberties: A radical new view* (pp. 102-112). Oxford, UK: Oxford University Press.

Gombrich, E. (1963). *Meditations on a hobby horse.* London: Phaidon.

Gray, H. (1989). Television, Black Americans and the American dream. *Critical Studies in Mass Communication, 6*, 376-385.

Guerrero, E. (1993). *Framing blackness: The African American image in film.* Philadelphia: Temple University Press.

Jhally, S., & Lewis, J. (1992). *Enlightened racism: The Cosby Show, audiences, and the myth of the American dream.* Boulder, CO: Westview.

Jones, J. (1993). The construction of Black sexuality: Towards normalizing the Black cinematic experience. In M. Diawara (Ed.), *Black American cinema* (pp. 247-256). New York: Routledge.

Mayall, A., & Russell, D. (1993). Racism in pornography. In D. Russell (Ed.), *Making violence sexy: Feminist views on pornography* (pp. 167-177). New York: Teachers College Press.

Mercer, K. (1994). *Welcome to the jungle: New positions in Black cultural studies.* New York: Routledge.

Osanka, F. (1989). *Sourcebook on pornography.* Lexington, MA: Lexington Books.

Riggs, M. (Producer & director). (1987). *Ethnic notions* [Documentary]. San Francisco: California Newsreel.

Rose, T. (1994). *Black noise: Rap music and Black culture in contemporary America.* Hanover, NH: University of New England Press.

Show and tell. (1983, November). *Hustler*, p. 7.

Show and tell. (1984, July). *Hustler*, p. 9.

Snead, J. (1994). *White screen, Black images: Hollywood from the dark side.* New York: Routledge.

Tinsley in review. (1983, November). *Hustler*, p. 65.

Wiegman, R. (1993) Feminism, "The Boyz," and other matters regarding the male. In S. Cohan & I. R. Hark (Eds.), *Screening the male: Exploring masculinities in Hollywood cinema* (pp. 173-193). New York: Routledge.

Winston, M. (1982). Racial consciousness and the evolution of mass communication in the United States. *Daedalus, 4,* 171-182.

PART V

TV BY DAY

The traditional categorization of television programming into daytime and nighttime formats and genres has eroded somewhat, as program distribution through cable, satellite dish, and Internet technologies has vastly increased the menu of choices available at any given moment, and technologies such as the VCR and digital recording for later viewing have given audiences far greater control over consumption practices. Yet for the moment, at least—whatever changes future technologies may bring to the industry—the *gendered* TV *genres* that evolved during the heyday of network broadcasting, when most daytime viewers were assumed to be housewives, still exercise a pervasive influence on contemporary media culture in the United States.

Despite its current relentless emphasis on the visual, television's immediate ancestor is not film, but radio. Like radio and unlike film, television technology had a "domestic" location and was sold to American consumers as a home technology, right from the beginning. Karen Altman (1989) has shown that whereas two-way radio technology was originally associated with the masculine realm, with peripheral spaces of the home, such as the attic or basement, where men and boys could indulge in mechanical and electronic tinkering, radio was re-gendered by marketing practices in the 1920s that assumed women or the family as the target audience for the new, reception-only sets. When television technology was commercialized in the late 1940s, it was also marketed through advertising imagery that linked it primarily with the home, women, and "femininity."

Early commercial TV developed in the postwar period when women war workers ("Rosie the Riveter") were being targeted with messages urging their "return to the home" to manage not only family life but also the consumption of newly available consumer goods. Thus, the industry developed scheduling and programming practices that reflected (and even magnified) the gendered division of labor and the ideology of separation between domestic/feminine and public/masculine spheres of competence. Women were assumed to be the daytime audience, whereas families, at least nominally dominated by fathers, were assumed to be the audience at night. These assumptions were key to the gendering of daytime and prime-time television programming.

As entertainment genres developed and evolved on TV, variety shows giving way to comic and dramatic series, many of the new genres and subgenres were clearly gendered—such as Westerns, police dramas, and spy adventures, which featured male protagonists and addressed a (presumed) masculine viewer. Others, such as the situation comedy (sitcom), were less overtly gendered because they assumed a family viewing as a group. Very few genres, however, were targeted exclusively at women—and those that were developed in the low-budgeted daytime slots that helped pay (in larger quantities of advertising time) for the more expensive productions of the more prestigious nighttime TV genres (Williams, 1992, p. 4).

One of the most intensively explored genres of daytime TV is the soap opera—a despised but resilient serialized, multiplotted story form centering on female characters that began as a 15-minute daily offering on radio in the 1930s, made the transition to television in the 1950s and early 1960s, and by the 1970s was drawing audiences of about 20 million (Williams, 1992, p. 3). Historically aimed at women at home, the soap opera form first drew the attention of social science researchers concerned about its negative social impact on wives and mothers (Allen, 1985).

The soap opera form has generated enormous interest among feminist cultural critics who agree that although the audience based has broadened, and overall viewing figures are down from the 1970s, the soap opera is still a major part of many women's cultural lives. Feminist critics of soap opera disagree, however, on the extent to which the text itself has subversive properties, and on the way real audiences read the text.

The earliest feminist critiques of soap opera contrasted the images of working women on these serials with the actual situations of women workers (Robinson, 1978) or analyzed the conservative underlying messages about home, family, and sexuality, which were built into the stories for the housewife (Lopate, 1976). A more sophisticated approach to the narrative using a psychoanalytic perspective was Tania Modleski's *Loving With a Vengeance* (1982). Modleski emphasized the way in which the text of this particular kind of narrative positions its viewer, causing us while we view to take on a particular "subject position" or temporary identity. According to her influential theory, because of soap opera's multiple characters and constantly shifting perspectives, we viewers are offered no single central character or protagonist to identify with, and therefore

> the subject/spectator of soap operas . . . is constituted as a sort of ideal mother: a person who possesses greater wisdom than all her children, whose sympathy is large enough to encompass the conflicting claims of her family (she identifies with them all). (p. 92)

Drawing on Modleski's approach to narrative analysis, John Fiske argues in "Gendered Television: Femininity" (Chapter 44) that the endless storyline itself embodies "feminine values" that are potentially subversive of patriarchal ideology: "The emphasis on the process rather than the product, on pleasure as ongoing and cyclical rather than climactic and final, is constitutive of a feminine subjectivity insofar as it opposes masculine pleasures and rewards."

Similarly, he argues, by employing multiple plots woven together so that each storyline is constantly interrupted by another, "soap operas offer their subordinated women viewers the pleasure of seeing [the] status quo in a constant state of disruption." Thus, the narrative form itself may be read as undermining or "subverting" the overt messages in the individual plotlines (at least in the older, traditional soaps) that seem to make marriage the be-all and end-all for women.

This idea that soap opera narrative itself undermined patriarchal ideology was later critiqued by scholars using actual audience responses. For example, Deborah Rogers, in "Daze of Our Lives" (Chapter 45), argues that although sophisticated textual critics of daytime (and prime-time) soaps are able to take advantage of the form's "openness" to construct subversive readings, actual viewers (including a group she studied through interviews) may "simply fail to recognize latent discourses." Indeed, other ethnographic studies of soap audiences do show a mixed picture of the reading situation. For example, a 1986 study by Ellen Seiter and associates of 64 white Oregon soap watchers found that

> female anger was far less repressed than ... Modleski's textual position allows for. In their interaction with the fictional world of the soap opera, women openly and enthusiastically admitted their delight in following soap operas as stories of female transgressions which destroy the ideological nucleus of the text—the sacredness of the family. (Seiter, Borchers, Kreutzner, & Warth, 1989, pp. 234-241)

In one of the few ethnographic studies so far to go beyond white viewership, Minu Lee and Chong Heup Cho (Chapter 46) studied a Korean community in the United States, in which the wives braved their student husbands' displeasure with their choice of "trash" entertainment (in this case, videotaped Korean soap operas rented for replay on the VCR). The wives used the Korean soaps' antipatriarchal stories about a husband's marital infidelity to raise questions among themselves and with their husbands about the sexual double standard legitimated by Confucianism. Lee and Cho found that the viewers "challenge[d] the traditional patriarchy within limits," by forming a video club that functioned "as a kind of forum to evaluate and criticize the husband's behavior." This study suggests that the social situation of women viewing such TV material entertainment together can lead to a kind of feminist consciousness-raising under the right circumstances.

More recent ethnographic studies of soap opera fandom have made use of the online discussion groups devoted to soap opera interpretation to examine more closely the process of bonding such discussion facilitates among the still primarily female audience. But the debate still goes on among these scholars about whether the interpretative activities of soap opera fans should be understood as potentially liberatory or as aligned with conventional patriarchal constructions of gender. In "'I Think of Them as Friends': Interpersonal Relationships in the Online Community" (Chapter 47), Nancy Baym takes a relatively optimistic view in her study of the ways online soap fans manage disagreement. She sees the creation of "an ethic friendliness" in this online community as a "communicative accomplishment" related to gendered communication styles in face-to-face interaction, as well as to "the gendered nature of the form" (soap opera) around which these fans "rally."

A less sanguine view is argued by Christine Scodari, in "'No Politics Here': Age and Gender in Soap Opera 'Cyberfandom'" (Chapter 48). Like Baym, Scodari explores such mechanisms for avoiding conflict and creating community as the common Internet *netiquette* that forbids "flaming." In her view, the behavioral norms that Baym sees as creating the "ethic of friendliness" have the effect of silencing and marginalizing minority and dissenting voices, including those of older fans or nonwhite fans wishing to discuss the politics of representation in the texts or in the production process.

In a sophisticated recent study that integrates analysis of material production conditions, text analysis, and audience reception, Jennifer Hayward views soap opera as "strongly marked by contradiction": It is both "generated by the imperatives of a patriarchal and capitalist entertainment industry" and an example of "women's fiction"—"primarily generated not only for but by women, a still marginalized subgroup within that industry" (Chapter 49). She is concerned with showing how "the development of soap opera is inextricably intertwined with the actual workings of the economy in which it is produced: its setting, characters, format, even subject matter are determined by economic imperatives." Showing us how the distinctively televisual aesthetics "unplug us from voyeurism," Hayward argues that "soaps' value as catalysts for discussion" of social issues "is increased." Examining in some detail the divided reaction of online soap opera fans to a "redeemed rapist" storyline on *One Life to Live* in the early 1990s, Hayward proposes that "soaps are ground breaking most of all in the community of viewers they produce."

Another denigrated daytime TV form originally aimed primarily at women is the morning/afternoon talk show, pioneered by Phil Donahue in the 1970s, shaped as even more distinctively "women's TV" by Oprah Winfrey in the 1980s, and then recast for a younger and more working-class and ethnic audience by Ricki Lake and Jerry Springer in the 1990s. As with soap opera, feminist critics have been drawn to TV talk shows as "women's TV," a place where hopes are raised for the discussion of social and political issues either trivialized or silenced elsewhere, and in particular in mainstream news media. Several recent studies help us see both the potential and the limits of this genre. For example, in "Cathartic Confessions or Emancipatory Texts?" (Chapter 50) Sujata Moorti suggests ways in which women's testimonials about sexual violence on the *Oprah Winfrey Show* can sometimes "move beyond a discussion of individual cases to create a protofeminist discursive space." In this textual *discourse analysis* building on the influential work of French historian of sexuality Michel Foucault, Moorti points out how Oprah Winfrey's role is akin to the role of the priest in the confessional in Foucault's analysis, helping to shape the way "the transformation of sex and sexual violence into discourse." Acknowledging that "there were other elements within this episodes that reframed sexual violence as spectacle," she concludes that the episodes she analyzes are only partially successful in promoting a kind of alternative or "counter" public sphere "independent from state interests" in which a democratic discussion of vital social issues (such as sexual violence) could take place.

In a similar vein, Janice Peck (Chapter 51) analyzes the limitations of talk shows as a cultural arena in which social issues can be productively explored. Looking specifically at two popular shows "hosted by women, oriented to women's concerns through 'feminine narrative' conventions, and directed at a primarily female audience," the *Oprah Winfrey* and *Sally Jessy Raphael* shows, Peck points to several important mechanisms by which these shows seek to control or "contain" the political implications of the problems they explore. Peck draws out attention in particular to the language of psychology employed both by the "experts" and the hosts, reminding us that "implicit in psychology is the assumption that societal changes are organic or natural processes to which individuals must learn to adapt." Giving this type of talk show credit for making "public many problems that once were deemed private—especially women's concerns that have historically been relegated to the private sphere"—Peck shows that "their narrative form . . . undermines the ability to take these problems seriously in the service of making them entertaining."

Our two final chapters in this section look at how class, race, and sexuality interact in the debate over the meaning of the contemporary talk show—especially the newer sensationalistic genre frankly aimed at a younger, urban, multiethnic demographic. Jo Tavener, in "The Case Against Sleaze TV" (Chapter 52), offers historical perspective on "the daytime talk show as a site around which moral panics circulate." Tavener likens the attack by the "respectable" news media on the new talk shows as "trash TV" to other "moral panics" over youth culture (discussed in more detail in Part IV, The Violence Debates). In her analysis, the "leader-class attacks on the popular media . . . mystify the class character of cultural conflict."

Joshua Gamson, in "Sitting Ducks and Forbidden Fruits" (Chapter 53), focuses in particular on the "moral discussions" of nonnormative sexuality that take place on talk shows as "one important piece of a public conversation over sexual moralities taking place in multiple, interacting sites." He relates the apparent "tolerance" of homosexuality embedded in such shows to the "ideology of liberal pluralism" that helps such shows make money ("the shows depend financially on the constant display of difference, which in a variety of ways makes the entertainment possible"), and "freedom of expression, which justifies the high-drama, channel-surf-resistant social conflict also so prevalent." Given this ideology, talk shows frequently cast "guests from the antigay right (religious or not)" as the "freaks." Yet as Gamson points out, this apparently progay stance is highly unstable: "When there is no one playing the 'bigot' role on the panel . . . audience members pick up the slack," frequently in a spectacle that pits "conservative religious African Americans" against "white bisexual, gay, lesbian, and transgender guests."

Inadvertently, talk show producers have stumbled onto an easy, inexpensive way to get the heat of moral condemnation, laced with an also-hot undertone of racial tension, and spiked with the exciting sight of less powerful people challenging the privileged, without ever directing endorsing an antigay conservative agenda.

References ◆

Allen, R. C. (1985). *Speaking of soap operas.* Chapel Hill: University of North Carolina Press.

Altman, K. (1989, Summer). Television as gendered technology: Advertising the American television set. *Journal of Popular Film and Television, 17,* 46-56.

Lopate, C. (1976). Day-time television: You'll never want to leave home. *Feminist Studies, 4*(6), 70-82.

Modleski, T. (1982). *Loving with a vengeance.* Hamden, CT: Shoe String Press.

Robinson, L. (1978). What's my line: Telefiction and women's work. In L. Robinson, *Sex, class and culture* (pp. 310-342). Bloomington: Indiana University Press.

Seiter, E., Borchers, H., Kreutzner, G., & Warth, E.-M. (1989). "Don't treat us like we're so stupid and naive": Toward an ethnography of soap opera viewers. In E. Seiter, H. Borchers, G. Kreutzner, & E.-M. Warth (Eds.), *Remote control: Television audiences and cultural power* (pp. 233-247). London: Routledge.

Williams, C. T. (1992). *It's time for my story: Soap opera sources, structure, and response.* Westport, CT: Praeger.

GENDERED TELEVISION

Femininity

◆   John Fiske

. . . I wish to explore some of the strategies by which television copes with, and helps to produce, a crucial categorization of its viewers into masculine and feminine subjects. Mellencamp (1985) traces this back to the 1950s, where she finds the origin of "the 'gender base' of television, with sport and news shows for men, cooking and fashion shows for women, and 'kid-vid' for children" (p. 31). Television's techniques for gendering its audience have grown more sophisticated, and nowhere more so than in its development of gender-specific narrative forms. I propose to look at soap opera as a feminine narrative. . . .

◆ *Soap Opera Form*

Brown (1987) lists eight generic characteristics of soap operas:

1. serial form which resists narrative closure

2. multiple characters and plots

NOTE: From *Television Culture*, by John Fiske, 1987, London: Routledge. Reprinted by permission of Taylor & Francis, Inc.

3. use of time which parallels actual time and implies that the action continues to take place whether we watch it or not

4. abrupt segmentation between parts

5. emphasis on dialogue, problem solving, and intimate conversation

6. male characters who are "sensitive men"

7. female characters who are often professional and otherwise powerful in the world outside the home

8. the home, or some other place which functions as a home, as the setting for the show. (p. 4)

Each of these characteristics merits considerable discussion, particularly if and why they constitute a feminine aesthetic. I wish to concentrate on the first two characteristics, that is, soap opera's ongoing, serial form with its consequent lack of narrative closure, and the multiplicity of its plots. . . . Traditional realist narratives are constructed to have a beginning, a middle, and an end, but soap opera realism works through an infinitely extended middle. Traditional narrative begins with a state of equilibrium which is disturbed: the plot traces the effects of this disturbance through to the final resolution, which restores a new and possibly different equilibrium. Comparing the states of equilibrium with which it begins and ends and specifying the nature of the threat of disturbance is a good way of identifying the ideological thrust of a story. The end of such a narrative is the point of both narrative closure and ideological closure. The narrative resolves the questions it posed, makes good its lacks and deficiencies, and defuses its threats. The resolutions of these disturbances prefer a particular ideological reading of its events, settings, and characters. For the aim of realist narrative is to make sense of the world, and the pleasure it offers derives from the apparent comprehensiveness of this sense. This comprehensiveness is evaluated according to relation to the ideologies of the reader, and through them, to the dominant ideology of

the culture. So a narrative with no ending lacks one of the formal points at which ideological closure is most powerfully exerted. Of course, individual plotlines can end, often with the departure or death of the characters central to them, but such endings have none of the sense of finality of novel or film endings. Departed characters can, and do, return, and even apparently dead characters can return to life and the program— four did so within two years on *Days of Our Lives*! But even without physical presence, the departed characters live on in the memory and gossip both of those that remain, and of their viewers.

Disruption   ◆

This infinitely extended middle means that soap operas are never in a state of equilibrium, but their world is one of perpetual disturbance and threat. The equilibrium of a happy, stable family is constantly there in the background, but is never achieved. Even a soap opera marriage, and marriages are ritual high points to be greatly savored, is not the same as a marriage in a traditional romance in which the couple are expected to live happily ever after. All soap opera marriages have within them the seeds of their own destruction. On one level the fans know that this is because a happy, unthreatened marriage is boring and incapable of producing good plotlines. But these generic conventions have not grown from some formalist ideal world of "good plotlines"; they have a social base. Marriage is not a point of narrative and ideological closure because soap operas interrogate it as they celebrate it. Building the threat into the celebration opens marriage up to readings other than those preferred by patriarchy. This double evaluation is generic to soap opera, and is part of the reason for its openness. A wife's extramarital sex, for instance is evaluated both patriarchally as unfaithfulness, but also, more resistingly, as a woman's independence and right to her own sexuality. Such affairs often spring from the man's, or the marriage's, inability to satisfy her. A wife's "unfaithfulness," then, is capable of being read by both masculine and feminine value systems simultaneously.

As Seiter et al. (1987) found in their study of soap opera fans,

> women openly and enthusiastically admitted their delight in following soap operas as stories of female transgressions which destroy the ideological nucleus of the text: the priority and sacredness of the family. (p. 27)

Two of the women to whom they talked expressed their pleasure in seeing marriage disrupted, and one went so far as to use this in a playful, but actual challenge to the power of her husband as it is inscribed in the conventions of marriage:

SW: But there's lots of times when you want the person to dump the husband and go on with this. . . .

JS: Oh Bruce [her husband] gets so angry with me when I'm watching the show and they're married and I'm all for the affair. [*Laughter.*] It's like it's like [*voice changed*] "I don't like this. I don't know about you." [*Laughter.*] Dump him. (p. 27)

The dominant ideology is inscribed in the status quo, and soap operas offer their subordinated women viewers the pleasure of seeing this status quo in a constant state of disruption. Disruption without resolution produces openness in the text. It can be read dominantly (patriarchally): such readings would produce fans who return to their more "normal" marriages with a sense of relief. But disruption can also serve to interrogate the status quo. As we shall see in our discussion of soap opera characters, the powerful women who disrupt men's power are both loved and hated, their actions praised and condemned.

The marital relationship is not the only one being simultaneously affirmed and questioned. One of the commonest plot themes is that of family ties and relationships. This concern to clarify relationships within the disrupted and unstable family may be seen as "women's matters," that is, as a domain where patriarchy grants women a position of some power. But if it is, its representation and the pleasure it offers overspill these ideological constraints. The ability to understand, facilitate, and control relationships is often shown as a source of women's power, used disruptively by the bitches and more constructively by the matriarchs. Men are often shown as deficient in these abilities and knowledges, and cause many problems by this masculine lack. This set of abilities and knowledges, normally devalued by patriarchy, is given a high valuation and legitimation in soap operas and can serve as a source of self-esteem for the fans and as an assertion of women's values against the place assigned to them in patriarchy. . . .

Deferment and Process ◆

Disruption is not the only effect of the infinitely extended "middle"; deferment is an equally important characteristic. As Modleski (1982, p. 88) puts it, a soap opera "by placing ever more complex obstacles between desire and fulfillment, makes anticipation of an end an end in itself." A soap opera narrative strand has no climax to close it off, no point at which it is seen to have finished: indeed, the outcome of most plotlines is relatively unimportant, and often not really in doubt. What matters is the process that people have to go through to achieve it. As Brunsdon (1984) argues, the pleasure in soap opera lies in seeing how the events occur rather than in the events themselves. Indeed, the soap opera press often summarizes future plotlines: the reader knows the events before they occur, [the reader's] interest lies in how the characters behave and feel as they react to the events. Each event always has consequences, final outcomes are indefinitely deferred, and narrative climax is rarely reached. Instead there is a succession of obstacles and problems to be overcome, and the narrative interest centers on people's feelings and reactions as they live through a constant series of disruptions and difficulties. No solutions are final; smooth patches are never free from the sense of impending disasters. The triumphs are small scale and temporary, but frequent.... These minor pleasures "buy" the viewers and win their apparently willing consent to the system that subordinates them. Women, this argument runs, harm themselves as a class by their pleasure as individuals.

But this endless deferment need not be seen simply as a textual transformation of women's powerlessness in patriarchy. It can be seen more positively as an articulation of a specific feminine definition of desire and pleasure that is contrasted with the masculine pleasure of the final success.... The emphasis on the process rather than the product, on pleasure as ongoing and cyclical rather than climactic and final, is constitutive of a feminine subjectivity insofar as it opposes masculine pleasures and rewards. This feminine subjectivity and the pleasures which reward and legitimate it are not bound to be understood according to their dominant construction as inferior to their masculine counterparts. Indeed, soap opera narratives consistently validate these feminine principles as a source of legitimate pleasure within and against patriarchy.

Deferment and process are enacted in talk and facial expression. The sound track of soap operas is full of words, and the screen is full of close-ups of faces. The camera lingers on the telling expression, giving the viewers time not just to experience the emotion of the character but to imagine what constitutes that emotion. Porter (1977, p. 786) suggests that "a face in close-up is what before the age of film only a lover or a mother saw."

Close-ups are, according to Modleski (1982, pp. 99-100), an important mode of representation in feminine culture for a number of reasons. They provide training in the feminine skills of "reading people" and are the means of exercising the feminine ability to understand the gap between what is meant and what is said. Language is used by men to exert control over the meanings of the world, but women question its effectivity in this, and find pleasure in the knowledges that escape it. Close-ups also encourage women's desire to be implicated with the lives of the characters on the screen, a desire that is also satisfied by the comparatively slow movement of soap opera plots which allow reactions and feelings to be savored and dwelt on. As Brown (1987) says, "Soaps allow us to linger, like the pleasure of a long conversation with an old friend." Feuer (1984) suggests that the acting style of soaps is excessive and exaggerates the hyperintensity of each emotional confrontation. Editing conventions work in the same way:

> Following and exaggerating a convention of daytime soaps, *Dallas* and *Dynasty* typically hold a shot on screen for at least a "beat" after the dialogue has ended.... [This] leaves a residue of emotional intensity just prior to a scene change or commercial break. (pp. 10-11)

An event, however momentous or climactic, is never significant for itself, but rather for the reactions it will cause and the effects it will have. Events originate or reactivate plots instead of closing them.

Sexuality and ◆ Empowerment

As Davies (1984) argues, soap opera sexuality is concerned with seduction and emotion rather than, as masculine sexuality is, with achievement and climax. If a woman's body and sexuality are all that patriarchy allows her, then, according to Davies, soaps show her how to use them as a weapon against men. It has been pointed out (e.g., by Geraghty, 1981) that soaps show and celebrate the sexuality of the middle-aged woman, and thus articulate what is repressed elsewhere on television as in the culture generally. In the prime-time soaps the sexual power of the middle-aged woman goes hand in hand with her economic power in a significant reversal of conventional gender ascription. . . . The powerful women in soap opera never achieve a settled state of power, but are in a continual process of struggle to exercise control over themselves and others. . . .

The "good" male in the daytime soaps is caring, nurturing, and verbal. He is prone to making comments like "I don't care about material wealth or professional success, all I care about is us and our relationship." He will talk about feelings and people and rarely expresses his masculinity in direct action. Of course, he is still decisive, he still has masculine power, but that power is given a "feminine" inflection. This produces different gender roles and relationships:

> Women and men in the soap operas are probably more equal than in any other form of art or drama or in any area of real life. By playing down men's domination over women (and children) the soaps and the game shows make the family palatable. On daytime TV the family is not a hierarchy, starting with the father and ending with the youngest girl, but an intimate group of people, connected to each other intimately through ties of love and kinship. (Lopate, 1977, pp. 50-51, in Hartley, 1985, p. 23)

The "macho" characteristics of goal centeredness, assertiveness, and the morality of the strongest that identify the hero in masculine television tend here to be characteristics of the villain. It is not surprising that, in women's culture, feminized men should be seen positively while the masculine men are more associated with villainy, but the reversal is not a simple one. The villains are typically very good-looking and are often featured in the press as desirable "hunks"; they are loved and hated, admired and despised. Similarly, the good, feminized men, particularly the younger ones, typically have the strong good looks associated with conventional heterosexual masculinity. It is rare to find sensitive, feminized looks (with their possible threat of homosexuality) going with the sensitivity of the character. . . .

Brown (1987), on the other hand, argues that soaps are positive and empowering in the way they handle sexuality and sexual pleasure:

> Thus the image of the body as sexual currency is absent, but the spoken discourse of the power of the female body to create is given crucial importance. There is no need to reiterate here the number of pregnancies, the importance attached to paternity and sometimes to maternity or the large number of sexual liaisons between characters in soap operas. However, contrary to the discourse which places the pregnant woman as powerless over natural events, often women in soaps use pregnancy as power over the father of the unborn child. The father will usually marry the mother of his child, whether or not he loves her (or whether or not the pregnancy is real), thereby achieving the woman's felt need to be taken care of in the only way that is available to her in the dominant system. Women characters, then, use their bodies to achieve their own ends. (pp. 19-20)

A woman's sexuality does not, in soap opera, result in her objectification for the male. Rather, it is a positive source of pleasure in a relationship, or a means of her empowerment in a patriarchal world. The woman's power to influence and control the male can never be finally achieved but is constantly in process. It is a form of power not legitimated by the dominant ideology and can thus exist only in the continuous struggle to exercise it. . . .

Modleski's (1982) account of the soap opera villainess reveals ... contradictions. She argues that the villainess is a negative image of the viewer's ideal self, which is constructed by the soaps as the ideal mother, able to sympathize with and understand all the members of her (and the soap opera's) extended family. Such a mother role is, of course, specific to the patriarchal family, for it denies the mother any claims on herself and requires her to find her satisfaction in helping her children to come to terms with and resolve their multiple difficulties. She is other-directed and decentered. ...

Seiter et al. (1987) found that many of their subjects explicitly rejected this textually constructed role:

> While this position [the Ideal Mother] was partially taken up by some of our middle-class, educated informants, it was also consciously resisted and vehemently rejected by most of the women we interviewed, especially by working-class women. (p. 24)

The villainess turns traditional feminine characteristics (which are often seen as weaknesses ensuring her subordination) into a source of strength. She uses pregnancy (real or alleged) as a weapon, she uses her insight into people to manipulate them, and she uses her sexuality for her own ends, not for masculine pleasure. She reverses male and female roles (which probably explains why Alexis in *Dynasty* is popular with the gay community) and, above all, she embodies the female desire for power which is both produced and frustrated by the social relations of patriarchy. The final control that the villainess strives for is, Modleski argues (1982, p. 97), control not over men, but over feminine passivity.

Seiter et al. (1987) found clear evidence of the appeal of the strong villainess for women chafing against their subjection in patriarchy:

All of these women commented on their preference of strong villainesses: the younger respondents expressed their pleasure in and admiration for the powerful female characters which were also discussed in terms of transgressing the boundaries of a traditional pattern of resistance for women within patriarchy:

LD: Yeah, they can be very vicious [*laughs*] the females can be very vicious.

JS: Seems like females have more of an impact than the males and they have such a mm ... conniving ...

SW: brain! Yeah! [*Laughter.*]

LD: They're sneaky!!! Yeah!

SW: They use their brain more [*laughter*] instead of their body! They manipulate, you know! (pp. 25-26)

But there was little evidence of any hatred for the villainess; rather, the respondents despised the woman who suffered despite her middle-class privileges, a character type they called the "whiner," or "the wimpy woman" (pp. 24-25).

But, in the portrayal of the villainess, soap operas set these "positive" feminine characteristics in a framework of moral disapproval, and follow them at work through a repeated narrative structure that denies their ultimate success. The woman viewer loves and hates the villainess, sides with her, and desires her downfall. The contradictions in the text and its reading position reflect the contradictions inherent in the attempt to assert feminine values within and against a patriarchal society. ...

References ◆

Brown, M. E. (1987). The politics of soaps: Pleasure and feminine empowerment. *Australian Journal of Cultural Studies, 4*(2), 1-25.

Brunsdon, C. (1984). Writing about soap opera. In L. Masterman (Ed.), *Television mythologies: Stars, shows, and signs* (pp. 82-87). London: Comedia/MK Media Press.

Davies, J. (1984). Soap and other operas. *Metro, 65*, 31-33.

Feuer, J. (1984). Melodrama, serial form and television today. *Screen, 25*(1), 4-16.

Geraghty, C. (1981). The continuous serial—A definition. In R. Dyer, C. Geraghty, M. Jordan, T. Lovell, R. Paterson, & J. Stewart (Eds.), *Coronation street* (pp. 9 26). London: British Film Institute.

Hartley, J. (1985). *Invisible fictions, television audiences and regimes of pleasure.* Unpublished manuscript, Murdoch University, Perth, WA.

Lopate, C. (1977). Daytime television: You'll never want to leave home. *Radical America, 2*, 3-51.

Mellencamp, P. (1985). Situation and simulation: An introduction to "I Love Lucy." *Screen, 26*(2), 30-40.

Modleski, T. (1982). *Loving with a vengeance: Mass produced fantasies for women.* London: Methuen.

Porter, D. (1977). Soap time: Thoughts on a commodity art form. *College English, 38*, 783.

Seiter, E., Kreutzner, G., Warth, E. M., & Borchers, H. (1987, February). *"Don't treat us like we're so stupid and naive": Towards an ethnography of soap opera viewers.* Paper presented at the seminar Rethinking the Audience, University of Tübingen, Germany.

45

DAZE OF OUR LIVES
The Soap Opera as Feminine Text

◆ Deborah D. Rogers

Soap operas are the only fiction on television, that most popular of mass cultural media, specifically created for women. This genre can therefore provide us with a valuable opportunity to examine the complexities of feminine cultural codes the more easily as they are writ large in feminine popular culture.... I argue that the fragmentation of soap narrative form reinforces the status quo with respect to the nature of sex roles and of interpersonal relationships in a patriarchal culture. Although the mixed messages of soap operas may allow scholars to construct subversive readings, actual viewers fail to respond in this manner....

Since they appeal to so many women, soap operas have naturally attracted the attention of feminists.... One major problem in dealing with soap operas is the historical denigration not only of television but also of forms of feminine popular culture. Indeed, the very term "soap opera" has become so pejorative that it is applied condescendingly to a variety of genres and situations to indicate bathetic superficiality and kitsch. This is so

NOTE: Excerpts reprinted from *Journal of American Culture*, Vol. 14 (Winter 1991), by permission of the editor, *Journal of American Culture*, Bowling Green University Popular Press.

much the case that one of the respondents to a recent survey I conducted attempted to justify her enthusiasm for *Days of Our Lives* by denial, insisting, "I really don't consider this show a soap opera."[1] Many feminists are similarly ambivalent about the genre: We desperately *want* to like a form that is popular with so many women but are repulsed by the conservative ideology. This ambivalence manifests itself when the same scholars who criticize soaps for promoting patriarchal stereotypes praise them for being "in the vanguard . . . of all popular narrative art" (Modleski, 1984, p. 13). In countering the denigration of feminine forms, however, we must be wary of going in the opposite direction, celebrating them just because they are female genres—especially when they might be potentially harmful. . . .

The cumulative effect of introducing in a fragmented text messages that reconcile women to traditional feminine roles and relationships is to reinforce patriarchal cultural behavior in a way that is difficult to identify during a typical—that is, casual—viewing experience. Perhaps the easiest way to demonstrate this process is by isolating soap tenets, abstracting them from the disjointed context in which they are embedded.

If soaps are featuring more career women, their romances and families take precedence over jobs, which may simply provide sites for gossip and personal relationships. The same could, of course, be said of the portrayal of male professionals. (Victor Newman, CEO of the multi-million-dollar Newman business empire, recently announced, "Generally I don't discuss business matters over the phone"—and generally he does not, and neither does anyone else.) Although soap jobs are hardly portrayed realistically, male professionals are depicted as superior beings who often transcend specialties. The same male doctor who handles AIDS patients, trauma victims, and neonatal care also delivers babies. Male corporate lawyers handle homicides. When we do see women engaged in professional activities, they are usually subordinate to men. For example, on one soap a young female lawyer is solely responsible for a murder case until shortly before it goes to trial, when she feels compelled to hire a more seasoned (male) co-counsel.

Women who devote too much time to jobs at the expense of their relationships and families are usually punished. For example, the son of one career woman who spent little time with him turns out to be a rapist. Another strong, aggressive, competent, and well-meaning career woman, *All My Children*'s Barbara Montgomery, glanced away while she was babysitting for a friend whose child was consequently hit by a car and killed. Is it pure coincidence that this accident occurred even as Barbara was composing an updated resume? Here we can ask of the soaps what Rosenblum (1986) asks concerning the "careerless career women" of other media who make a mess of their personal lives: "Is there a hidden message here, namely, that women had better stay out of the corner office or they'll get what's coming to them?"[2]

All this should not be surprising since in the soap world pregnancy within a marriage has always been the supreme state and children the ultimate "achievement" for women (Rogers, 1988). . . .

Mother Moran, a character in a radio soap, early elaborated the soaps' endorsement of patriarchal marriage and parenting ideas: "A cake ta bake, and a floor ta sweep. And a tired little babe ta sing ta sleep. What does a woman want more than this—A home, a man, and a child ta kiss" (quoted in Allen, 1985, p. 194). Similarly, on contemporary soaps, if childbearing is necessary for completeness, having both a child (or children) and a "good marriage" constitutes true bliss. (This sentiment may present some problems for women in the audience who, while they have their husbands and their babies, are still miserable.) For example, on *The Young and the Restless* Nikki tells her husband, Victor, "I am so lucky. I have everything a woman could want. . . . I have a beautiful daughter and a loving husband, and a wonderful marriage. . . ."

. . . In the fictionalized representation of motherhood on daytime soap operas, the myth of maternal omnipotence conceals the subordination and marginalization of women.

Employing the rhetoric of female apotheosis, soaps define having a baby as "the single most important thing in a woman's life." As one soap character remarked on the day she discovered she was pregnant: "This is what I've wanted all of my life, and now it's all coming true. . . . This is the most important day of my life." Male dominance is ideologically reinforced by the belief that women are gloriously suited for child care because they are by nature cheerfully domestic, nurturing, and self-sacrificing. This "innate" selflessness, essential to fulfilling their roles as wives and mothers, allows for the happiness of women to reside in being constantly attentive to the needs of other family members. For example, after being told sarcastically, "Lucky you—you get to listen to everybody's problems," one soap mother responded in all seriousness, "That's part of being a mother. You'll find out about it some day." Other soap mothers have recently made statements like "I'm here whenever you want to talk" and "I only want what's best for him" and have been asked such rhetorical questions as "what kind of mother are you, to put your feelings before the feelings of your child?" . . .

Without offspring, women are incomplete. Take, for example, the case of *General Hospital*'s Bobbie Meyer, who acknowledges the terrible emptiness of her barren state: "I'm thinking about the babies that I'm never going to have. . . . I just feel empty. . . . [My husband] is a man who *deserves* to have a child." Since failure to comply with moral norms is usually punished on soaps, and Bobbie is a former prostitute, her sterility may be no accident.

On another soap a new father extends this baby ethic to men:

Having a child of my own was one dream I just could never turn loose of. And when [my wife] became pregnant, I thought . . . the gods are smiling on me. And there was nothing left for me to ask for because there was nothing else I wanted. Ya know, I was—complete.

If such sentiments of completeness imply more male sensitivity, they never seem to extend to beliefs about shared parenting. It is therefore likely that these expressions may simply be a variation of the traditional male fantasy of procreation as immortality. This myth is stressed repeatedly on the soaps, where men "deserve" to have children and, as one character puts it, "any man . . . would just go crazy to have a son that would carry on your name and follow in your footsteps."

. . . Although women are overtly respected for bearing children and for being mothers, ironically, men treat them like children. For example, one soap husband tells his wife she should go "sleepy-bye," while another calls his baby daughter his "other little good girl," equating his wife and his infant. On *One Life to Live*, at the very moment she tells her husband, Cord, the results of her pregnancy test, Tina is infantilized:

Tina: Well, aren't you the least bit interested in whether you and I made a baby?—we didn't. What are you smiling for?

Cord: Well, to tell you the truth, I kinda' didn't think we did, but I tell ya—I think it's real cute you being so excited about it.

Another soap wife gets worked up because she has tried to serve "the most important dinner of my life—and I blow it. . . . I spill the appetizers. . . . I burn the dinner. . . ." Her husband predictably responds, "I think you're cute."

Although it is difficult to see how women can be taken seriously as long as they are being treated like children, their subordination may be obfuscated, as they collude in this pattern, decoding it in terms of "cuteness" and male protection. Soap women are repeatedly imaged as children: like children, they frequently "flood out," losing control in gales of laughter or in tears. They are playfully fed by men and are the objects of mock-assault games (of the food- or pillow-fight variety) that are usually reserved for children. Although on the soaps these "attacks" usually collapse into lovemaking, sociologist Erving Goffman (1979) has pointed out in another context that such "games" suggest what men could potentially do, should they ever get serious about it.

Unsurprisingly, on the soaps men give more orders and advice than women. This often extends to female topics (Turow, 1974). Women have no relief from this ubiquitous male instructor—a de facto role of authority that demands subordination—even during commercial "breaks," when they are subject to predominantly male voice-overs.[3] Not only do male voice-overs dominate the commercials themselves, in what Robert Allen (1985, pp. 154-170) considers to be a vestige of the omnipotent male announcers of radio soaps, today's announcers—all of whom are male—seem to control the networks' programming. They point to commercials, promise that the soap will resume after interruptions, signal the end of the commercial segments, and urge us to continue watching or to tune in tomorrow. While all these little expressions of male dominance and female submission may seem insignificant in and of themselves, they add up to create an effect that is overwhelming. Unfortunately, typical viewers do not seem to regard this behavior as suspect. . . .

Applying reader-response theories specifically to soaps, Jane Feuer (1984) finds *Dallas* and *Dynasty* "potentially progressive" because their serial form with its multiplicity of plot lines admits to unchallenged ideological stances: "Since no action is irreversible, every ideological position may be countered by its opposite" (p. 15). John Fiske (1987, pp. 179-197) argues that such a variety of reading positions allows for

an interrogation of patriarchy. Ellen Seiter (1982) is hopeful about the progressive potential of the soaps for similar reasons:

> The importance of small discontinuous narrative units which are never organized by a single patriarchal discourse or main narrative line, which do not build towards an ending or closure of meaning, which in their very complexity cannot give a final ideological word on anything, makes soap opera uniquely "open" to feminist readings. (p. 4)

Although I find that the dominant ideology of the soap is patriarchal and that any challenges implicit in contradictory readings are regularly trounced on as patriarchy continually rears its ugly head, the potential that Feuer, Fiske, and Seiter posit for constructing feminist interpretations of soaps from their inconsistencies certainly exists. But let me raise a crucial question: What if viewers fail to identify the subtext? . . . For example, most of the respondents to my survey are partially attentive viewers likely to gossip about soap characters for fun but unlikely to read or analyze soap operas as texts, watching with the rapt attention of the critic. . . .

When asked whether soaps contain messages, most of my respondents said yes and pointed to blatant messages about issues like sex and alcoholism. Many remarked that soaps teach about relationships and practical matters. One respondent, who credits the soaps with helping her get pregnant, first heard of ovulation prediction kits on *All My Children*, where they were mentioned obliquely—"It's blue. Let's get into bed"—when Brooke was trying to conceive. Some even mentioned worldview and distinguished between the obvious and the subtle. For example, an especially thoughtful respondent wrote:

> A "say no to sex before you are ready" (married was the suggested time to be "ready") campaign was written into one story line in hopes of preventing teenage

pregnancies and the spread of sexually transmitted diseases. I also see the message that being rich and powerful is not synonymous with happiness. There are both obvious and subliminal messages. The subliminal messages are male dominated and family oriented, but the blatant messages may have in some cases redeeming social value.

Now consider one of the messages widely praised in the press and by respondents as having this "redeeming social value." An astonishing number of respondents mentioned the rape story on *Santa Barbara*, recognizing the obvious moral: report rapes to the authorities. They were totally oblivious to the subtext which undercut this message, insidiously destroying the social value of this plot. On the soap Eden Castillo is raped. While this story line is developed, daily after the program we see the constructedness of the fiction, which is rare in the soap world (usually reserved for occasions like the death of an actor). At the end of each episode, Marcy Walker steps out of the frame, announcing that she is the actress who plays Eden and advising victims to report rapes. Perhaps part of the reason for this strategy is that the rape sequences are so gripping the audience needs to be reassured that this is a fiction. The ostensible reason—to promote the message—is, however, vitiated. In the story Eden does indeed report the rape and undergoes a pelvic examination. Our perspective is of her raised knees covered with a sheet. In the end we discover that the rapist is the very same gynecologist who performed the examination.

Unfortunately, the subtext here—the authorities we should report rapes to are equivalent to the rapists themselves—went unnoticed, even as it subverted the blatant message. This could create considerable anxiety for viewers who may find themselves unwilling to report male violence and brutality. The whole misogynistic plot may speak to women's fear of trusting male authority. . . .

Another familiar soap plot with a subtext that often goes unrecognized concerns the reformed rake. In perhaps the most famous example, *General Hospital*'s Luke raped—and later married—Laura, who subsequently referred to the event as "the first time we made love," perpetuating the fiction that women really want to be raped. (*General Hospital* producer Gloria Monty described the rape as "choreographed seduction"; Dullea, 1986). Luke and Laura became a romantic super-couple, as Luke underwent a transformation, eventually becoming not only mayor of Port Charles, but heartthrob to countless teenage girls. As Janice Radway (1984) found in her study of romances, in a society where male violence against women is a constant, women may deal with their fears by decoding male brutality as love. Such a strategy, however, fails to remedy the problem. In a cartoon in *Soap Opera Digest*, a woman tells a man, as they watch a male image on the screen, "For your information, he's now a sweet, sensitive person. You're not supposed to remember he used a chain saw on his sixth wife in 1982" (July 11, 1989, p. 59). Such transformations of soap villains are obviously recognized. Unfortunately, however, most viewers are oblivious of the fact that reinterpreting soap rapes and brutality as romance denies—if not legitimates and glorifies—male violence by reading it as love. Instead of constructing subversive readings of soaps, many viewers simply fail to recognize latent discourses. . . .

Notes

1. This ongoing survey, which is composed of seventy-one multiple-choice questions and eleven additional questions requiring a written response, has been completed by over 100 viewers.

2. Rosenblum (1986) argues that if movies, theatre, and prime time are now featuring women professionals, their careers are like

"touches of trendy window dressing to spruce them up for the late 80s." From Glenn Close's Alex in *Fatal Attraction* to Heidi in Wendy Wasserstein's *Heidi Chronicles*, the portrayal of professional women of the eighties with their "toy careers" is far removed from the depiction of 1940s career women like Katharine Hepburn in *Woman of the Year* and Rosalind Russell in *His Girl Friday*. Although the message of such movies is that what a woman really needs is a good man, the women were consummate professionals.

3. According to Butler and Paisley, 90% of voice-overs in television commercials are male (cited in Cantor & Pingree, 1983, p. 202).

◆ References

Allen, R. C. (1985). *Speaking of soap operas*. Chapel Hill: University of North Carolina Press.

Cantor, M., & Pingree, S. (1983). *The soap opera*. Beverly Hills, CA: Sage.

Dullea, G. (1986, July 11). As Gloria Monty's world turns. *New York Times*, p. Y19.

Feuer, J. (1984). Melodrama, serial form, and television today. *Screen*, 25(1), 4-16.

Fiske, J. (1987). *Television culture*. New York: Methuen.

Goffman, E. (1979). *Gender advertisements*. New York: Harper.

Modleski, T. (1984). *Loving with a vengeance: Mass-produced fantasies for women*. New York: Methuen.

Radway, J. (1984). *Reading the romance*. Chapel Hill: University of North Carolina Press.

Rogers, D. D. (1988, September 23). The soaps: Do they support or undermine the family? *Christian Science Monitor*, p. 21.

Rosenblum, C. (1986, February 26). Drop-dead clothes make the working woman. *New York Times*, p. 1H.

Seiter, E. (1982). Eco's TV guide—The soaps. *Tabloid*, 5.

Turow, J. (1974). Advising and ordering: Daytime, prime time. *Journal of Communication*, 24, 138-141.

46

WOMEN WATCHING TOGETHER

An Ethnographic Study of
Korean Soap Opera Fans in the United States

◆ Minu Lee and Chong Heup Cho

U nderstanding the audience watching programs on videotape is never
a simple task. It becomes a more complicated matter and requires
new theorization and empirical support if the audience is from another
country but consumes rather its own cultural products in a foreign country where more program choices are seemingly available. More specifically, this [chapter] concerns a question of "why is it that some Korean
housewives in America prefer Korean soap operas to American ones?" The
Korean programs were rented on tape from a local store, and watched by
women in a group.

    ... In order to collect the audience responses, twelve in-depth inter-
views were conducted with Korean student families residing in Madison,
Wisconsin, in November 1988. Subjects were all college graduates and
they were middle or upper-middle class.

    Ann Gray's study on the VCR in the home is one of the few examples
of researches in which the use of VCRs is addressed in the context of

NOTE: Excerpts reprinted from *Cultural Studies*, Vol. 4, No. 1 (1990), by
permission of the publisher, Routledge, Chapman and Hall.

gender relations within the family. She found in her study that, for many women, viewing choices are often negotiated and the programs which "women enjoy are rarely, if ever, hired by their male partners for viewing together because they consider such films to be 'trivial' and 'silly' and women are laughed at for enjoying them" (Gray, 1987, pp. 49-50). This observation is confirmed in the statements of most of the women we talked to:

S1: Fridays are my favorite day of the week. That's when we go to supermarkets together and rent some videos for the weekend. I usually let him choose his tape first and select mine later to avoid any nasty comments on my selection. If he is still sarcastic about my tape, he has to wait one more week to have his favorite dish on the dinner table.

S2: I think men consider whatever involves infidelities, incests, and complicated love stories as trash. But I don't see much quality in the martial art films either. Just as they need them to be excited, I need soap operas.

While some women insist on their own cultural tastes or viewing choices, most women feel shame when they enjoy soap operas. This underlying sense of denigration has influenced their viewing habit in such a way that they either watch alone late in the evening after the husband and children have gone to bed or together with friends during the day. But both viewing habits are not mutually exclusive as women often watch the same program twice.

S3: I know it's disappointing to indulge myself in the "low quality" soap operas, but I have nothing else to do to release my stress. I like to watch the tapes together with my friends when the big kid (husband) has gone to school. But when we get together, we just turn on the video and talk about something else such as cooking

recipes, big sales, scandals. . . . So, I watch the program again late in the evening.

S4: My husband just hates to see me watch the video. Once I stopped renting the videotapes for a while and read novels instead. But he complained again and asked me to do more constructive things. And that really hurt my feelings and pride, but I still asked him nicely, "What's more constructive than reading a book?" His answer was just incredible; "Do you call that a book? You are reading trashes!" . . . . After that incident, I watch the tape late in the evening when I am all alone.

The common strategy for the husband to discourage his wife from watching soap operas is to compare her viewing choice to that of a housemaid. The usual comment (that's something the housemaid watches) makes the women feel shame as they violate the natural law of the Confucian notion of family which specifies the role and the status of each family member based on gender and age. The Confucian code of behavior prescribes what constitutes appropriate women's behavior and what does not. The woman must not only respect her husband and elders but also must not damage the family image and honor. She must not begrudge her subjection, but must learn to be obedient to her husband. The superior status of the husband within the family is more than common sense. Woman's everyday life and her pleasures exist only within the realm of the Confucian worldview. While she is subjected to the family structure, however, her status may be ranked as superior to that of housemaid according to this "natural law." By equating the act of viewing with that of those who are at the bottom of the social order and thus generating the feeling of shame, something undesirable for family image, men try to regulate the wife's viewing choice. It is not surprising then that many women tend to denigrate their cultural taste as in the statement of the above subjects.

The testimonies also show that women often negotiate their program choices. Many women rarely do what they want to do for themselves and this is most evident in television watching. It is because the home is not considered as a sphere of leisure, but rather a work place, which constantly interrupts their television viewing. In other words, they have to negotiate the pleasures of television watching with their domestic responsibilities. Within this context, it would be difficult for them to concentrate on and enjoy television. As for men, however, home is the place for their leisure activities. What complicates the matter is the persistent social demand for the traditional work ethics in Asian societies where leisure is considered largely as "evil conduct" or "a waste of time." This social norm is so prevalent that women may feel shame when they watch television. These conflicting situations may also make women rearrange their viewing time and prefer to watch the video when they are alone.

It should be noted, however, that the very same women consciously challenge the traditional patriarchy within limits, using the skills they know best. It took various forms in the case of women we talked to: using her husband's favorite dish as a weapon against him (S1), enjoying gossip and thus releasing emotional strains (S3), or just women's refusal to view the video in company (S4)—all seem to indicate women's continuous struggle to expand their own social space although the power this cultural struggle gives is limited. The seemingly rigid patriarchal control then never guarantees its dominant ideology as it is faced with various cultural forms of resistive power possessed only by women. Social practice is the site on which the dominant ideology is constructed, but, at the same time, it is also the site of resistance to that ideology. The fact that men have to work hard to determine women's viewing taste indicates the difficulty of ideological control: "control," as Fiske (1987, p. 184) argues, "is a process that needs constant struggle to exercise it, it is ongoing, never finally achievable."

The difficulty of ideological control is most evident in the example of the video club operated by the women. In order to share the video rental fees, they have formed a video club. It is the secondary function, however, that is far more significant in terms of its potential as a means of resistance. As in the statement of S3, the program is sometimes not so important as the opportunities the video club creates to talk about scandals or problems common to their everyday lives. The topics range from a bargain sale at a local department store to the love life of famous television stars. But the social gathering usually ends up with talking about husbands' behavior in the family. Women are curious about other people's lives and compare them with their own. As such the video club operates as a kind of forum to evaluate and criticize the husband's behavior.

S1: Time passes really fast when we get together. What I hate most is that I have to prepare dinner before my husband gets home. This is especially true when I hear from my friend that her husband has just bought her a nice birthday present—My husband always forgets my birthday.

S3: I always promise to myself I would never talk about my husband. But if somebody starts talking about last night's fight with her husband, I cannot help joining her and complaining about my husband—and it makes me feel a hundred times better.

S7: If you talked to other people, you will be amazed how similar problems we all have. You learn a lot of things how to get your husbands by just chatting with more experienced wives.

It is clear from these examples that oral culture plays an important role in making meanings and pleasures from the routines of everyday life. More important, oral culture can be resistant and television is made into oral culture by gossip. And its meanings are recirculated in everyday life. Thus, the pleasure women find comes not from absorbing the dominant ideology but from their conscious resistance to the political power their husbands exercise. As we saw, this politics of family between husband's power and wife's resistance has little to do with the program itself. This struggle for meanings and pleasures already exists even before women watch the program. As Fiske (1987, p. 77) notes, "Television, with its already politicized pictures of the world, enters a context that is formed by, and subjected to, similar political lines of power and resistance. The intersection of its textual politics and the politics of its reception is a crucial point in its effectiveness and functions in our culture." For this reason, we now turn to the text and the process of viewing.

. . . Television entertainment programs have, then, played an important role, in developing countries, by providing a forum for the most progressive ideas to bear witness to the grim realities of everyday life.

A good example of the point is the Korean television mini-series *The Sand Castle*, which consists of eight episodes and depicts the family crisis of a middle-aged couple. The story is a typical love triangle story of a husband's extramarital affair. The wife's preoccupation with her feeling of rejection by the husband and his irresolute attitude toward both his wife and lover make the marriage unsuccessful and eventually lead the wife to decide to divorce him. The traumatic state of her emotions is much emphasized, if not exaggerated, as compared to the rational approach the husband takes to cope with the problem. Much of the subplot deals with the mistress, who is also depicted as a victim. What is unusual about this story is its feminist approach in representing sympathetically the female characters' points of view in a country where the Confucian notion of family prevails and a husband's extramarital affairs are considered as a norm rather than an exception. . . .

The controversy surrounding the program was enormous in Korea. Male audiences complained about the way the program dealt with the extramarital affair and were furious about the station's decision to broadcast such a feminist program. The complaints centered on female audiences' supposed inability to distinguish between reality and fiction. . . .

. . . The program had different appeals to different people. Women mobilized the meanings and pleasures differently from the same program, and the popularity of it depended in part on the way the text was recognized by the audience. One subject, for example, citing the case of her sister, told us how remarkably similar the program was to her sister's case. Thus her pleasure of reading the program was increased as she brought her own intertexual experience and attitudes. For her, the pleasure she found lay in the way the wife was portrayed. She was depicted as strong and resolute as contrasted to her real sister who forgave her husband after an affair.

S9: When my friend recommended it to me, she was trying to tell me the plot. At first, I thought it was just another typical story about a husband's affair. But as it was revealed, I was stunned. It was about my sister! So, I told her to stop telling me the story. I wanted to know exactly how it would end and how it would be different from my sister's real-life story. . . . I loved the way she treated her husband at the end.

In many cases, subjects rejected the dominant ideology and expressed sympathy for the wife and dislike for the mistress and the husband. The husband was most criticized for his arrogance and ambivalent attitude toward both women. It is interesting to note that many expressed dislike for the mistress although they agreed that "she was a victim of the system.". . .

. . . The operation of the video club made it possible for [the women] to feel comfortable to talk about the program and share their experiences together. Moreover, the inevitable consequence of this mode of watching was that the program became an important social issue, and women took advantage of the occasion to evaluate their husbands' behavior at home by positing the topic as a real problem they faced. After watching the program together with their friends, two subjects rented it again and tried to show it to their husbands. One had a similar experience to the woman reported in the magazine:

S7: After we watched the program together, no, he did not actually pay attention to the program much. I asked him a question anyway. I first asked him whether or not he would have an affair if he returned to Korea and I was shocked and disappointed to hear him saying, "Men can have an affair." I was upset because he took it as a matter of truth. I thought it was other men, not my husband who can actually say that! I felt cheated and asked myself, "Is this the man I dedicate myself to?" But I was still curious to know how he would handle the situation if he had the same problem. He then refused to answer the question because he knew I was upset by then. I did not talk to him for two days after that.

The other, too, aroused male resistance:

S3: We talked about the program until one o'clock in the morning. I did not understand why he sympathized with the husband. . . . We then changed the topic and ended up with talking about my career when we returned to Korea. I said to him, "Women too should have a career to avoid that problem." He said no and I said yes . . . we had a terrible fight that night.

. . . The operation of the video club can be seen as a form of oral culture, and it has been an important forum for women to participate in the discussion of their social experiences. . . .

. . . Our research leads us to . . . argue that Third World audiences are not simply exposed to the television texts, but are active meaning-producers themselves, selecting, rejecting, and transforming the text based on their cultures and experiences.

The following remarks are based on some of the descriptions by our subjects on the generic conventions of indigenous soap opera text as compared to those of American programs. In most cases, "realness" was the reason for selecting the Korean programs instead of American alternatives.

S1: I don't think any Korean audience understands one hundred percent of American programs. It's not the problem of language but the problem of culture. No matter how fluently you speak English, you never get the feeling of their culture. They don't look real as compared to the Korean programs.

While this subject describes the differences broadly, one woman explained the cultural differences in more concrete terms.

S2: I like to watch American programs. Actors and actresses are glamorous and the pictures are sleek. But the ideas are still American. How many Korean women are that independent? And how many men commit incest? I think American programs are about American people. They are not the same as watching the Korean programs. But I watch them for fun. And I learn the American way of living by watching them. I like the Korean programs because I get the sense of what's going on in my country. That helps me to catch up with the changes in my country I have forgotten while I am in America.

There is an obvious contradiction in this subject between the subject position produced by the consumption of American programs and her social subject position offered by the norms of Confucian morality. . . .

Despite cultural imperialism arguments, Third World audiences like to watch their own cultural products. Even when they are exposed to foreign programs, they don't necessarily soak up the dominant ideology transparently. . . . If the television text becomes meaningful to the audiences, it becomes meaningful in the sense that the text is transformed into the existing cultural context of the audiences. . . .

References ◆

Fiske, J. (1987). *Television culture*. London: Methuen.

Gray, A. (1987). Behind closed doors. In H. Baehr & G. Dyer (Eds.), *Boxed in: Women and television*. London: Methuen.

47

"I THINK OF THEM AS FRIENDS"

*Interpersonal Relationships
in the Online Community*

◆ Nancy K. Baym

People start to read online discussion groups because they are interested in the topics of discussion. When people first start reading rec.arts.tv.soaps (r.a.t.s.), they are attracted primarily to the wealth of information, the diversity of perspectives, and the refreshing sophistication of the soap opera discussion. Soon, however, the group reveals itself as an interpersonally complex social world, and this becomes an important appeal in its own right. For many, fellow r.a.t.s. participants come to feel like friends. . . .

When I asked them to compare r.a.t.s. to other groups on Usenet and other networks, nearly all of my survey respondents spoke in terms of the greater friendliness of r.a.t.s., indicating how this set the group apart:

> As to other newsgroups, it doesn't compare to the other technical groups that I read. Not the same camaraderie. (Erin, 1991 survey)

> People interact in this group. It is like having a conversation. Other groups have more caustic discussions. The people I have met from this

group have been really nice. It's the first group I read, and it is pleasant. (Linda, 1991 survey)

The creation of friendliness in r.a.t.s. is not a given but rather a communicative accomplishment. . . .

◆ Managing Disagreement

People in r.a.t.s. are particularly aware that their sense of friendliness is demonstrated largely through a behavior they avoid. The computer often has been accused of encouraging hostile and competitive discourse. The widely noted phenomenon of *flaming* (i.e., attacking others) has been hypothesized to result from "a lack of shared etiquette by computer culture norms or by the impersonal and text-only form of communication" (Kiesler, Siegel, & McGuire, 1984, p. 1130). These scholars argue that rather than being mitigated, as often is the case in face-to-face disagreements (Pomerantz, 1984), online disagreements are exaggerated. . . .

Although flaming is common online, it generally is considered bad manners. Mabry (1997) analyzed 3,000 messages collected from many forms of computer-mediated communication (CMC) and found that more "tense, antagonistic, or hostile argumentative statements" tended to be accompanied by more intense conciliatory behavior. McLaughlin, Osborne, and Smith (1995), analyzing a large corpus of messages chastising others' behavior, argue that Usenet standards discourage the wanton insulting or flaming of others. Despite this, flaming remains common in many groups. The r.a.t.s. newsgroup is not one of them, and this is inseparable from its friendliness:

I find this to be one of the most friendly and chatty groups on Usenet. Flames are very uncommon, particularly compared to rec.arts.startrek and rec.arts.tv. (Laurie, 1991 survey)

Comparing [r.a.t.s.] to other newsgroups: [It is] one of the nicer ones (less flame wars for the most part). (Lisa, 1991 survey)

The group in which I find the most flame wars (thus the least friendly and supportive, in my opinion) is a local group. . . . I would put rec.arts.tv.soaps right under rec.pets.dogs for friendliness, support, warm[th], lack of flame wars (in Y&R [*The Young and the Restless*] anyway, which is the only soap I watch and read about), in general, overall enjoyment. (Teresa, 1991 survey)

This tendency to explain friendliness in terms of flaming indicates that it is easy to be friendly so long as everyone is in apparent agreement; it is in the points of disagreement that friendliness is most challenged. However, at the same time as r.a.t.s. does not want disagreement, the group is, first and foremost, in the business of maximizing interpretations, a process that inevitably leads to disagreement, especially considering how overcoded the soap operas are. Rather than considering friendliness as accomplished through behaviors that r.a.t.s. participants avoid, I look in this section to the behaviors they use to construct disagreements that attend to the ethic of friendliness.

The potential for disagreement to damage the group's sense of solidarity was enhanced in the Carter Jones discussion. This (extremely friendly) post to r.a.t.s. from Anne indicates the problem that participants faced with this story line:

You know I realize that whenever AMC [*All My Children*] does a "heated" storyline, we all get "heated" too! We all agree tho, it's all the writers faults! :-)

Man . . . I'm really p*ssed at those writers. This is too important a topic for them to give it the cosmetic-kissy-kiss treatment.

Oh and the cosmetics dept. too :-) I am truly sorry to those of you that have been in an "abused" relationship. My heart goes out to you. I am very glad that you were smart enough to get out of it. Applause!

I won't say what I think of men who do it. The lowest of the low. This is just too deep a subject to even talk about on a computer. Carter is scum! But I guess John Wesley Shipp is ok :-) I hope to see him a "good guy" sometime. (October 20, 1992)

Anne's comments that the group participants all get "heated" discussing a story line concerning subjects too deep "to even talk about on a computer" suggests that discussing this story line brought out emotions difficult to discuss even when in agreement. Such difficulty could only be enhanced when participants did not see eye-to-eye on the story line. Thus, the disagreements concerning this story line offer a revealing window into the discourse strategies that create and maintain friendliness in r.a.t.s.

MITIGATING OFFENSE

Most disagreements contained verbal components, or message features, that functioned to lessen their negative impact. Just over 40% of the disagreements used qualifiers that framed disagreements as resulting from differences in subjective opinion. Qualification leaves room for the poster to turn out to be wrong and the other right, reducing the threat to the other's position. In this example, the poster places qualifiers prior to and following the point of disagreement (the qualifications are in boldface):

Tell me, why did Brooke give Carter Jones an invite to Weirdwind, & if
    She didn't INVITE him. They showed him at the door and the butler
    I may be wrong, but **I thought** Brooke did invite Carter Jones. **I actually thought** he **may** be covering the event as a reporter. Seeing as how Brooke started the homeless shelter, **I would think** that would give her some say in who may attend a fund raiser. I do know she had a guest list and showed it to Carter. That's how he knew

Galen would be there. Anyway, at the door, he wasn't named as an invited guest, but he identified himself as being with Tempo magazine. (July 23, 1992)

From time to time, but not often, people apologize for disagreeing. This example demonstrates the apology:

I'm sorry, Anne my buddy, but I have to disagree with both you and Liz. . . . (October 19, 1992)

A few participants lessened the potential offense of their disagreements by explicitly framing their messages as nonoffensive. This technique, used four times, is when the poster explicitly keyed her activity as something other than confrontational.[1] In one case, this involved prefacing a contradictory assessment with "I think this is so funny." In another case, someone wrote "no offense to *Knot's Landing*" just before suggesting that *Cape Fear* had been a greater influence on the story line.

BUILDING AFFILIATION

As if it were not enough to actively lessen the negative force of one's words by showing respect and backing off one's claims, as these strategies do, many disagreers articulated their disagreements in ways that actively built social alignment between the participants. For example, they frequently prefaced disagreements with partial agreements, a strategy that has been noted in face-to-face and epistolary interaction as well (Mulkay, 1985, 1986; Pomerantz, 1984). Fully 29% of the disagreements in r.a.t.s. were prefaced by partial agreements. Partial agreements generally were followed by words such as "but" and "though" or phrases such as "at the same time" that positioned what followed as disagreement. . . .

A second affiliative strategy in disagreement was the use of the other's name (used in 18% of the disagreements), as can be seen in this excerpt in which the poster makes explicit the affiliative quality of naming with the phrase "my buddy":

> I'm sorry, **Anne** my buddy, but I have to disagree with both you and **Liz**. . . .

Participants also explicitly acknowledged the perspective of the other in 12% of the disagreements. . . .

The single most common message feature of disagreements was elaboration, which occurred in 69% of them. . . . Offering reasoning to support the writer's perspective also was more common than any of the offense mitigators or social alignment strategies.[2] Reasoning was given in 61% of the disagreements. . . .

To summarize, instead of flaming, participants in r.a.t.s. attended to an ethic of friendliness by playing down the disagreement with qualifications, apologies, and reframings. They built social alignment with partial agreements, naming, and acknowledgments of the others' perspectives. They moved conversation rapidly away from the disagreement itself and back to the group's primary purpose of collaboratively interpreting the soap opera. It also is worth noting that there were relatively few disagreements over the story line—just under 10%—suggesting that one common disagreement strategy was to stay silent. The norms that protect interpretation seem to actively diffuse the force of disagreements and perhaps lead to their being voiced less often. . . .

◆ *Ritualized Space for Friendliness*

TANGENTS

To this point, I have considered how the ethic of friendliness is attended to throughout the messages discussing the soap opera. Although sticking to the topic of the soap opera has obvious benefits for a group organized to discuss soaps, it does pose some problems for friendship, which rarely (if ever)

is so topically constrained. Talking only about soaps impedes the group's ability to become a bunch of friends. During the early years of r.a.t.s., when the amount of message traffic was more manageable, participants handled this by simply digressing, a practice that generally was tolerated. However, in the fall of 1991, when traffic began to expand dramatically, people who barely had time to read the posts pertaining to the soap operas began to voice irritation with having to weed through messages that did not even relate to the soaps. Someone proposed that the convention of marking a subject line with "TAN" (for tangent) used in other Usenet newsgroups be imported, a suggestion that was adopted almost simultaneously and with little further discussion.[3]

TANs can cover any number of topics. They often begin with the soap opera and then turn personal:

> I like how story threads on the soap bring out story threads in people's lives that they then share on RATS (for example, stuff about children and pets in the various TANs). It's mostly light and fun. Even when it gets serious, it's still engaging. (Doreen, 1993 survey)

In other cases, the TANs share personal news. This post from one poster about another is typical:

> Hi everybody—Just wanted to let you know that Cindy Dold and the BH [better half] have a new little baby boy! . . . Congratulations to Cindy and Norman, and welcome Charles! (October 16, 1992)

A post like this one is likely to result in a flurry of congratulatory e-mail for Cindy:

> When something big happens (wedding, birth) that's made known to the Net, we do send each other e-mail. It's nice to get it, too. (Jane, 1991 survey)

The big "somethings" that people share in TANs are not always as happy as weddings or births, but the group provides social support through darker times as well. One longtime poster's surprise birth announcement told us that she had lost the baby to sudden infant death syndrome within days of her birth. When she shared her tragedy with the group in a post inspiring in its grace and strength, I was not the only one in tears. Many of us were deeply moved[4]:

> I like the personal tone of this newsgroup with people (mainly women) freely giving support and expressing care for one another. Recently, for example, Lisa's personal tragedy has touched my life most profoundly. (Doreen, 1993 survey)

Many people responded to Lisa, and it mattered to her:

> I had really looked forward to telling everyone about my baby and getting their surprised and pleased reactions, for example, and it helped to know so many people cared when she died. :-(Lisa, 1993 survey)

As another participant puts it, "We've developed a kind of family, and when good things and bad things happen, there's a lot of support out there on the Net" (Judy, 1993 survey).

Although I did not ask specifically about TANs, many people who responded to my survey explicitly pointed out their important role in personalizing the r.a.t.s. environment: "I also like the *AMC* TANs because it gives you a chance to get to know the poster and then people who post don't seem like faceless people on the other side of the country, they seem like a real person!" (Kelly, 1991 survey). Another parti-cipant's comment on the TAN offers a good sampling of the topics:

> I find the subjects brought up as tangents almost as interesting as the soaps . . . for example, the cross section of r.a.t.s. who are cat lovers, Star Trekkers, etc. Some

of us have shared our birthdays, our taste in beer, and our butt size. . . . We know who has read GWTW [*Gone With the Wind*]. . . . We know who has PMS [premenstrual syndrome]. (Debbie, 1991 survey)

As the mentions of "butt size" and "PMS" suggest, the tangents often are used as a forum for discussing issues of particular concern to women including experiences with violence against women, worst dates, and whether or not to change names when marrying. Less gender-bound topics might include how early participants put up their Christmas trees, other television shows, and notorious court cases. TANs offer participants a space in which to broaden their discussion and, when it is called for, to provide one another with social support. The marking and maintenance of this space can be seen as an institutional acknowledgment of the group's commitment to friendliness. At the same time, the indication that the post is tangential in the subject line lets those participants who are not interested in the group's social dimension to avoid these broader interactions.

UNLURKINGS

The last of the marked genres in r.a.t.s.[5] also is social in nature. Unlurkings, informally marked by the use of the terms *unlurking*, *unlurk*, and *lurker* in the subject lines, are posts in which new or rare posters introduce themselves to the group. These posts usually specify the poster's name, how long the poster has been lurking in r.a.t.s., the poster's occupation, the species and names of pets (especially cats, which are taken to be a common link among *AMC* participants), and almost always general opinions about *AMC*. This unlurking is typical:

> It's me again. I wanted to introduce myself. My name is Kari Barnes. I am a PhD student at Carnegie Mellon University in Pittsburgh. I have

been watching AMC for several years. At first, it was during the summers in the mid to late 70's—back when Erica was involved with Nick and her marriage to Tom (this was while I was in high school). Then I watched during my lunch hour. With the help of my faithful VCR, I have not missed an episode in about 4 years. My husband likes to watch it with me sometimes, but he is not a big fan. I like to read the updates and the posts, but I do not always have the time to read them all. My husband and I do like to know what other AMC fans think of the story-lines. That's it for now. (September 29, 1992)

Unlurkings are regular but not common. Unlurkings are introductions, flagging the entry of new members into the community and providing the others with the opportunity to welcome them. Responses to unlurkings work as a welcoming committee, encouraging new or returning participants to remain active voices by letting them know that they have an interested audience:

By the way, this is my second time unlurking. The first was yesterday when I sent a test message which actually made it. I don't have time to give you any background info on me at the moment—duty and deadlines call, but I wanted to alert everyone about the opportunity to see Jenny. Enjoy!! :)
Any time you have some to tell us more about yourself, Andrea, we wel-come it. (October 14, 1992)

For at least some posters, it was the welcoming responses they received to their first posts that made them into regular participants:

I stopped on r.a.t.s. to check out what was happening on *AMC* since I never get to watch it, and the rest is history. I was hooked. I posted, and it was great getting responses from people welcoming me to the group. I'm more interested in the Net than in the show. The members are more like friends. (Monica, 1993 survey)

Like TANs, unlurkings have become institutionalized through being labeled. That the

only two identified genres that are not informational are interpersonal indicates this group's ongoing orientation toward fostering a group environment of friendliness.

Dyadic Friendships ◆

The friendly nature of r.a.t.s. is further buttressed by a private but sometimes visible world of one-on-one friendships that have formed as participants move from public discussions to e-mail. A number of people who responded to my surveys indicated that they had formed a small number of close one-on-one friendships through the group:

I have met [two] friends, and I have met others who I consider [acquaintances], having not formed much more than that. (Anne, 1991 survey)

I e-mail daily with two other r.a.t.s. participants, and I consider them both close friends. Our relationships have expanded far beyond the discussion of *AMC*. I consider others on the Net-at-large to be friendly acquaintances whom I would enjoy getting to know better in a personal sense. (Carrie, 1991 survey)

Friendship pairs often develop out of Usenet groups. Parks and Floyd (1996) conducted a randomized e-mail survey of Usenet posters and found that 60.7% of them had established personal relationships through Usenet. Most had moved their interactions to e-mail and in some cases met face-to-face, as these two *Days of Our Lives (DOOL)* r.a.t.s. participants explain:

I've become good friends with several people I've met on the Net. One is now my housemate; another got me into square dancing; a third loaned me a car when I visited Portland recently. I'm sending Christmas presents to one r.a.t.s.'er in New Zealand for the second year. I do a large amount of Net-related e-mail each day. None [has] become [a lover]. Yet. B-) (John, 1991 survey)

I tell them it's a place where a group of us from all over the world sit and discuss soaps online. They look at me funny, and I try to explain, but it's not easy! I also tell them that I found all my long-lost sisters here (the Peels from *DOOL*) and that we get together all over the country. Then they REALLY look at me strangely and say "You drive to meet people that you've never met to talk about a soap opera!!" And I say "Heck yeah!" (Lynn, 1993 survey)

. . . Although these friendships often are conducted below the surface, they are referred to in the public discussion. For example, when one r.a.t.s. participant meets another from a different location, one (if not both) will post a report for the others to read. In smaller ways, posters might demonstrate a dyadic friendship by referring to another by name in one's message. Thus, these private pairs of more individualized friendships bubble up into the group's environment. . . .

Friendliness in r.a.t.s. is just one example of the general tendency of ongoing computer-mediated groups to develop behavioral norms. Some online norms span wide groupings of CMC users. For example, Myers (1987a) writes, "There is widespread acknowledgment of a national BBS [bulletin board system] community—with both positive and negative norms of behavior" (p. 264). . . . Users continually reinforce the norms of their groups by creating structural and social sanctions against those who abuse the groups' systems of meaning (Mnookin, 1996; E. M. Reid, 1991). Groups have differing norms about sanctioning themselves. Smith, McLaughlin, and Osborne (1997) found considerable variation across groups in the tone of reproaches for *netiquette* violations. In r.a.t.s., not surprisingly, violators are given what one respondent calls "gentle reminders."

Face-to-face experience and the medium are two influences on the norms that come to be important in organizing practice in r.a.t.s. and, I would suggest, in other computer-mediated groups. Two other important influences on emergent norms in online groups are the characteristics of the participants and the purpose of the group's interaction. . . . At this point, it is illustrative to consider how the fact that most participants are women may influence the group's adherence to an ethic of friendliness.

Usenet, like most CMC, is populated by many more men than women, a fact that stems in part from men's greater access to the medium. Because men have greater access, computer-mediated groups, including Usenet, are likely to exhibit male styles of communication, so that even when women have access, they might not be comfortable or interested in participating. Ebben (1993), Herring (1994, 1996), Selfe and Meyer (1991), and Sutton (1994) are among those who have shown that many of the gender inequities of face-to-face interaction are perpetuated online, where women speak less, are less likely to have their topics pursued, and are seen as dominating when they gain any voice at all.

Savicki, Lingenfelter, and Kelley (1996) found, in a large random sampling from many Usenet groups, that the gender balance of newsgroups has a modest correlation with language patterns within them (although they stress that there clearly were many other factors at play). Groups with more men used slightly more fact-oriented language and calls for actions, whereas those with fewer men were more likely to self-disclose and try to prevent or reduce tension. Herring (1994, 1996) describes an online female style she calls *supportive/attenuated*, which "idealizes harmonious interpersonal interaction" (Herring, 1996, p. 137). In this style, "views are presented in a hedged fashion, often with appeals for ratification from the group" (p. 119). Herring's description matches well the disagreement styles of r.a.t.s. participants, suggesting that the language practices in this group likely are influenced by participant gender. Given the concerns about gender inequities online, it is notable that r.a.t.s. is not only a place in which female language styles prevail but also a place in which there is considerable self-disclosure and support on the very types of female issues that provoke flame wars (if raised at all) in so many other groups.

The fact that so many women would come to this group in the first place stems from the gendered nature of the form around which they rally. Many aspects of the normative structure of r.a.t.s. come right back to the soap opera. Interpreting soaps is, after all, the group's primary purpose. It is hard to underestimate the influence of this purpose on the normative structures of r.a.t.s. For example, if one looks to the disagreements and compares the disagreements over interpretations to those over facts, one finds that all of the message features that lessen the threat of a disagreement and enhance friendliness are more likely to occur in disagreements over interpretations. . . . Disagreements over facts—what did or did not occur—challenge the participant's memories on truly minor issues. Disagreements on interpretations challenge the others' socioemotional standards and reasoning, a far greater threat. Loading such disagreements with protective wording demonstrates the group's orientation toward making it safe to voice interpretations.

One would not necessarily need safety to voice interpretations, but soaps . . . rely on their audiences to interpret them through reference to their own feelings and relationships. The discussion they stimulate often is quite personal. . . . There is a good deal of private and sometimes painful self-disclosure in the course of interpreting the soap opera. The richness that those disclosures provide is necessary for the soap's fullest collaborative interpretations. Thus, the group is invested in supporting these disclosures. This helps to explain how this group developed its social support function. That

social support has grown into tangents indicates the seriousness with which the personal is honored in r.a.t.s. as well as the pleasure that shared personalizing offers. . . .

Notes ◆

1. In using the term *keying*, I draw on Goffman (1974).

2. Reasoning and elaboration often were difficult to differentiate. For coding purposes, *reasoning* was defined as something that fit into the sentence form "I disagree because ____." More important than the division of examples into one category or the other is that they serve similar functions in the group's disagreement practices.

3. This is a nice example of how interactive and easy the creation of ongoing group traditions can be.

4. Indeed, 5 years later, knowing that she has since had two healthy children, I still get choked up writing this.

References ◆

Ebben. M. (1993). *Women on the Net: An exploratory study of gender dynamics on the soc.women computer network*. Paper presented at the annual meeting of the Organization for the Study of Communication, Language, and Gender, Tempe, AZ.

Goffman, E. (1974). *Frame analysis: An essay on the organization of experience*. Cambridge, MA: Harvard University Press.

Herring, S. (1994). Politeness in computer culture: Why women thank and men flame. In M. Bucholtz, A. C. Liang, L. Sutton, & C. Hines (Eds.), *Cultural performances: Proceedings of the Third Berkeley Women and Language Conference* (pp. 278-293). Berkeley, CA: Women and Language Group.

Herring, S. (1996). Posting in a different voice: Gender and ethics in computer-mediated communication. In C. Ess (Ed.), *Philosophical approaches to computer-mediated communication* (pp. 115-145). Albany: State University of New York Press.

Kiesler, S., Siegel, J., & McGuire, T. W. (1984). Social psychological aspect of computer-mediated communication. *American Psychologist, 39*, 1123-1134.

Mabry, E. (1997). Framing flames: The structure of argumentative messages on the Net. *Journal of Computer-Mediated Communication, 2*(4). Available on Internet: http://207.201.161.120/jcmc/vol12/issue4/mabry/html.

McLaughlin, M. L., Osborne, K. K., & Smith, C. B. (1995). Standards of conduct on Usenet. In S. G. Jones (Ed.), *Cybersociety: Computer-mediated communication and community* (pp. 90-111). Thousand Oaks, CA: Sage.

Mnookin, J. L. (1998). Virtual(ly) law: The emergence of law in LambdaMOO. *Journal of Computer-Mediated Communication, 2*(1). Available on Internet: http://207.201.161.120/jcmc/vo12/issue1/lambda.html.

Mulkay, M. (1985). Agreement and disagreement in conversations and letters. *Text, 5*, 201-227.

Mulkay, M. (1986). Conversations and texts. *Human Studies, 9*, 303-321.

Myers, D. (1987a). "Anonymity is part of the magic": Individual manipulation of computer-mediated communication contexts. *Qualitative Sociology, 19*, 251-266.

Parks, M. R., & Floyd, K. (1996). Making friends in cyberspace. *Journal of Communication, 46*(1), 80-97.

Pomerantz, A. (1984). Agreeing and disagreeing with assessments: Some features of preferred/dispreferred turn shapes. In J. M. Atkinson & J. Heritage (Eds.), *Structures of social action: Studies in conversation analysis* (pp. 57-101). Cambridge, UK: Cambridge University Press.

Reid, E. M. (1991). *Electropolis: Communication and community on Internet relay chat.* Unpublished thesis, University of Melbourne.

Savicki, V., Lingenfelter, D., & Kelley, M. (1996). Gender language style in group composition in Internet discussion groups. *Journal of Computer-Mediated Communication, 2*(3), Available on Internet: http://207.201.161.120/jcmc/vo12/issue3/savicki.html.

Selfe, C., & Meyer, P. (1991). Testing claims for on-line conferences. *Written Communication, 8*, 163-192.

Smith, C. B., McLaughlin, M. L., & Osborne, K. K. (1997). Conduct control on Usenet. *Journal of Computer-Mediated Communication, 2*(4). Available on Internet: http://207.201.161.120/jcmc/vo12/issue4/smith.html.

Sutton, L., (1994). Using Usenet: Gender, power, and silence in electronic discourse. In S. Gahl, A. Dolbey, & C. Johnsons (Eds.), *Proceedings of the Twentieth Annual Meeting of the Berkeley Linguistics Society* (pp. 506-520). Berkeley, CA: Berkeley Linguistics Society.

48

"NO POLITICS HERE"

Age and Gender in
Soap Opera "Cyberfandom"

◆ Christine Scodari

Critical/cultural media scholars debate the extent to which audiences interpret and use hegemonic texts in resistive ways. Political economists examine the issue macroscopically, arguing that the structures, processes, and commercial imperatives of capitalist media institutions determine a range of available content, restrict access and ownership, and, inevitably, reproduce hegemonies that help to maintain unequal power relations. Many cultural studies scholars shift the focus to the microscopic, localized consumption of media audiences, with some contending that a repertoire of appropriative strategies regularly confounds these forces of domination, particularly in the hands of those whose marginal status cultivates interpretive ingenuity. Some scrutinize fan subcultures, arguing that collective audience engagement facilitates resistive activity. Such claims emanate from ethnographic audience study, generally via focus groups, interviews, and observation.[1] . . .

This [chapter] examines soap opera "cyberfandom"—computer-mediated communication (CMC) and culture in cyberspace discussion groups devoted to television serials—to assess the ways in which these

NOTE: From *Women's Studies in Communication*, Vol. 21, No. 2, Fall 1998, pp. 168-187. Reprinted by permission.

forums welcome and/or inhibit the voices of traditionally marginalized viewers. The study was conducted through "virtual" ethnography entailing participant observation by this researcher over a four-year period in discussion groups on Usenet and information services such as CompuServe and America Online (AOL).[2] This [chapter] will endeavor to interrelate analyses of the contextual/institutional imperatives of soap opera production with the interactions and interpretations of cyberfans and the conditions and structures under which these interactions occur. Ultimately, the investigation refutes claims of resistive public space, finding that industry infiltration, "netiquette," and other factors construct these forums as sites of "escape" rather than "politics." Moreover, matters significant to older women and minorities are slighted, reproducing the "divide and flatter" demographics strategy of the advertisers and their media cohorts.

◆ Cyberspace and Empowerment

... The social, collaborative contexts of soap opera reception and interpretation have been theorized for more than a decade, since a trend toward public viewing was observed (see Allen, 1985, p. 81). More recently, Brown (1994, pp. 37, 79-84) studied soap opera fan "friendship networks" in which oral "gossip" allows women to "negotiate their positions in society" and derive pleasure through the construction of collective meanings and insights which acknowledge their subordinated role. The importance of such "collectivized" appreciation is stressed by Condit (1989, p. 117) in arguing that private pleasures are fleeting and largely inconsequential in their potential for social impact.

With the advent of the soap opera cyberfan, the opportunities for collaborative negotiation have proliferated. Discussion groups are merely one type of outlet, allowing fans to publicly post instantaneous and/or reflective negotiations with the primary text(s) as well as meta-textual material, such as magazines. They can also respond to initial posts or simply "lurk," perusing the sentiments of others and, perhaps, considering those views in light of their own negotiations.

Baym's (1993, p. 148) study of the soap opera newsgroup on Usenet identifies it as a site populated primarily by women, whereas more than seventy percent of Internet users overall are male (see Interrogate the Internet, 1996, p. 127). Baym sees within this "primarily female subculture" (1995, p. 142) opportunities and strategies for critical resistance and appropriation (pp. 149-151; 1993, pp. 159-173). Moreover, she argues that a certain egalitarianism prevails because "gender, race, rank . . . and other features of cultural identity are not immediately evident" (1995, p. 140). . . .

While this investigation, and the larger project from which it comes, concur that kibitzing on Net bulletin boards can be an empowering pleasure in and of itself, these analyses go beyond the above-mentioned audience studies to address these neglected issues and to examine cyberspace deliberations in conjunction with the ideologies inherent in the producers' commercial imperatives. . . .

It has been the potential for individuals (as opposed to commercial organizations) to address large numbers of people through CMC that has been most praised as an egalitarian and empowering potential of the technology. Accordingly, it is all the more crucial to determine the extent to which the de-politicization of the soap opera text—its insinuation that the personal transcends the political—is reproduced in discussion groups devoted to the genre.

Toward that end, the economic imperatives of soap opera production and their attendant political meanings require illumination. Since women hold the "power of the purse" when it comes to foodstuffs, clothing, cleaning products, health and hygiene products, and cosmetics, soap operas were designed and are still intended to sell commodity audiences of women to those who advertise such items. And, since women spend more on these products when they are first establishing their households, forming brand loyalties, and having and raising children, the most lucrative target audience has been women between the ages of 18 and 49 (Intintoli, 1984, p. 63). This tendency is further complicated by the fact that most fans begin watching soaps in their teens and gradually become "hooked," allowing producers to take them for granted (up to a point) and to continue skewing content and representation in favor of the younger audience they hope to entice and secure for the future (p. 70).

As baby boomers have begun to creep past that "magic 49," the soaps have attempted to lure viewers at increasingly younger ages. A relatively new daytime drama, Aaron Spelling's *Sunset Beach* (NBC), was expressly created to feature Generation Xers largely unrelated by blood, eschewing the traditional soap opera focus on multi-generational families (Baldwin, 1997, p. 31). Just as patriarchy perpetuates a double standard of aging, valuing women primarily for their youthful appearance and reproductivity rather than for qualities honed by age and experience (see Stoddard, 1983, pp. 3-11), the imperatives of commercial television favor women whose life stage and cultural understandings determine or foster the need for disposable diapers and tampons as well as, according to the advertisers' market research, more generous quantities of cold remedies and mascara ("Youthful products," 1995, p. 31). Conveniently, though not coincidentally, capitalism and boardroom politics facilitate patriarchy and bedroom politics—and vice versa.

Research on the interactions of soap opera viewers, both on- and offline, applauds the feminine subculture created out of the primary text. However, there is little attention paid to what vested interests connected to soap opera consider to be the most crucial marker of identity in addition to gender—age. If women may find solace as women within a "community" of soap opera enthusiasts, it should not be assumed that these women are not at cross purposes, both within and beyond this subculture, in terms of age and other aspects of identity.

In fact, it is more than conventional wisdom that an advertising strategy for seducing the young adult market is to compliment it at the expense of older, less desirable consumers (see Bowen, 1994). This "divide and flatter" tactic can have even more efficacy for women, since the double standard of aging is an entrenched but, often, invisible hegemony. . . .

So, when young Matt Cory sweetly reassured his older fiancée that "it doesn't matter how old you are, it matters how much you love" and counseled her to "trust in the universe" just before their two-year-long romance unraveled irretrievably on the NBC soap *Another World*, the de-politicization of the private realm and of soap opera generally was evident and acquiesced to by most cyberfans. Even for many who embraced the story, if an older woman/younger man romance couldn't survive into marriage it was merely a function of destiny and the strength of their love. It had little to do with the soap's well-publicized ultimatum to get "demographics up" or be canceled, the fact that a minority of fans thought that this kind of couple was "nauseating," or even that the writers had stated that they were concerned about snubbing young female viewers by keeping this "hunk" with an older woman (Cukor, 1994, p. 69).[3] The relative acceptance of this narrative turn as an artistic decision made in the service of "true love" rather than one expressly designed to flatter some fans and marginalize others in the service of profit reveals a key impediment to meaningful empowerment. With this example in mind, let us now turn to a broader consideration of soap opera discussion groups and their possibilities for inclusion, politics, and resistance.

◆ Hegemony: Reproduce or Resist?

. . . Network etiquette, or "netiquette," evolved out of early cyberculture (see McLaughlin, Osborne, & Smith, 1995), ostensibly to compensate for the lack of nonverbal cues and to preserve open and respectful communication (MacKinnon, 1995, p. 115). Yet rules of netiquette have the potential to reproduce the larger culture's hegemonic inhibitions (see MacKinnon, 1995; McLaughlin, Osborne, & Smith, 1995). They can be particularized within a given newsgroup (see McLaughlin, Osborne, & Smith, 1995) and according to individualized notions of proper social behavior.

While policies prohibiting explicit advertising and the posting of private e-mail correspondence are *de rigueur* on Usenet, sanctions against "flaming" have received the greatest scholarly attention.[4] Thompsen (1995, p. 299) lists more than a dozen publicized meanings of this term, all dancing around the notion of intentionally heated, incessant, or rude communication. Still, he observes distinctions based on whether one is sending or responding and/or being hostile or merely emotional (pp. 299-300).

Since we are considering soap opera forums, it is useful to localize our notions of flaming to the Usenet soap opera newsgroup(s), where Baym (1995, p. 158) noted that the activity is strongly discouraged. Curiously, the "Frequently Asked Questions" advisory on "Inappropriate Posts" (Gibbs, 1996) periodically disseminated on these newsgroups does not explicitly define or prohibit flaming. Instead, participants are warned against responding to "trolls" whose only purpose is to "start trouble even if the troll him/herself gets immolated

in flames." Trolling, then, can be understood as a hostile, provocative post that is intended to invite flames—thereby conceived as belligerent replies—and to "challenge the long-standing traditions of the group." A poster who declares that "soap operas suck" is clearly a troll, the advisory explains, before admonishing participants to resist the bait.

Such interpretations are liquid, however, and this can be appreciated when posts dealing with representational issues are scrutinized. For instance, a poster who blatantly announced his/her "Asian American rage" in the subject heading went on to lambaste soaps for their treatment of Asians. Those who responded did so primarily to designate the poster as a troll, thereby short-circuiting any serious discussion of minority inclusion. But, was this poster only trying to make trouble and invite flames?

Similarly, on AOL bulletin boards, an African American fan who repeatedly censured *Another World* for its underrepresentation of blacks was automatically castigated and labeled a racist herself. While her language was uncompromising, she appeared to be sincere in her opinions and not merely "baiting." But, even the most courteous responses warned her that unless an overtly discriminatory message was purveyed on the show, racism was an unfair charge. And, because this viewer posted on no other topic, she was considered a traitor among true fans and told to cease and desist. Occasional, carefully worded posts of this ilk are tolerated, as long as the poster is clearly interested in, if not favorable towards, other facets of the soap. Even so, they are few and rarely generate extensive deliberation compared to those tackling "lighter" topics.

In terms of age and similar issues, this loose interpretation of trolling can be even more problematic. On the Usenet soap opera newsgroup, *Days of Our Lives* fans were serious when implying, in one case, that a forty-something character was too old to "play the young couple in love" and, in another case, that the sight of two midlifers in bed was "gross," and some did politely challenge their assumptions. Yet, when an *Another World* fan on AOL proclaimed that she was "going to be sick" just thinking about how "adorable young Matt" once preferred a woman "old enough to be his mother" when he is "cute enough to be with any woman he wanted." Only one or two very gentle, self-effacing reproaches followed. The result is that hegemony-reinforcing messages are aired without sufficient rebuttal and their underlying politics remain unexplored. The assumption that such viewpoints are aberrations and not taken to heart can play right into the hands of those who reproduce them in the culture. Clearly, in the case of the intergenerational love story, the attitude expressed by this fan was taken seriously by the powers that be, who catered to it by ending the story, disgracing and back-burnering the older woman, and placing the young man in a featured romance with an unsullied heroine considerably younger than he. And, gradually, many of the names and Internet "handles" of those who had been vocal devotees of the unconventional couple became less visible on several of the bulletin boards. Some retreated to e-mailing groups and conversed primarily with one another while their viewpoints faded from public display.

Age and related matters emerge in other ways. Many *Another World* cyberfans rallied after discovering, late in 1995, that the network was threatening to cancel the show if it didn't boost demographics by emulating its highly rated, youth- and fantasy-oriented companion soap, *Days of Our Lives* (see Logan, 1996, p. 46). *Days of Our Lives* was immediately disparaged for preferring models to actors, victimizing women, and for storylines involving demon possession and premature burial. However, the fact that *Days of Our Lives* also tends to relegate its older cast to its most bizarre plots and/or to pigeonhole them as over-the-top villains or sanitized, story-less "listening posts" was not discussed in this context. An unhappy *Another World* fan on Usenet directed her ire at *Days of Our Lives* fans and their postings, saying that she feels "insulted and ashamed" to weed through subject headings such as "Sami is a big fat whore. . . ." She was ignored, and the text's role in setting its audience's conversational agenda was not examined. Later, when a troll labeled an actress who returned to *Another World* after her maternity leave a "planetoid," those who seized the opportunity to begin a dialogue on the politics of appearance and gender were scolded for taking the bait. "This newsgroup is about *Another World*," a poster responded vehemently. "It is not about weight, it is not about gender, it is not about race. . . ."

On AOL, the assumption that politics and soap opera are mutually exclusive was echoed when some posters began discussing feminism in connection to an *Another World* couple. "If you want to post something political go to a political folder," they were warned. "Soaps have offered an escape from everyday life and when these issues are raised I want to scream." Although a few begged to differ, the topic was soon dropped and the use of words such as "politics" or "feminism" continued to be regarded with suspicion. . . .

Although Baym (1995, p. 147) argues that sensitive personal issues are addressed on the Usenet soap opera newsgroups, this study observes pressure to avoid linking these issues to larger political contexts. This pressure mimics that which is exerted upon soap opera creators who are often sanctioned against dealing with "socially conscious topics" to avoid offending segments of viewers (Intintoli, 1984, p. 102). . . .

Antagonism is a more conspicuous manifestation of age-related biases transferred from the balance sheets of the networks and advertisers into cyberspace. With the demise of the older hero in the spring of 1998, *Another World* had effectively reduced its number of baby boom characters to three, and only one middle-aged woman remained as part of an ongoing romance. This fifty-something duo, Carl and Rachel, had its share of enthusiasts—one of whom had been attracted to the show for what she described as the "passionate love between two people in my age group." Others took exception, however. "Personally it disgusts me to watch them," stated one of several outspoken dissenters. "Carl reminds me of the dirty old man down the street." "Nauseous is the word that comes to mind," echoed a second. The wishes of these naysayers were soon granted when the actor who portrayed Carl was fired, leaving the program potentially bereft of love stories featuring older women.

Age-discriminatory sentiments are not limited to this couple or to *Another World*. "I have absolutely no interest in watching John or Marlena get passionate," remarked a poster about the sole midlife romance on *Days of Our Lives*. "[It] reminds me too much of my parents." Of diva Erica Kane on *All My Children*, one fan bristled: "She makes me want to puke, she has to be almost 50." Another chimed in: "I'm sick of all the stories and men revolving around her dried up behind." Middle-aged mavens Stephanie and Sally from *The Bold and the Beautiful* fared even worse, being dismissed by one discriminating viewer as "flaccid, shriveled monsters."

Additional signs of this generational divide can be seen in responses to the Matt and Vanessa romance on *Guiding Light*. Although similar to the scuttled older woman/younger man love story on *Another World*, this relationship had endured into marriage, perhaps owing to the vigilance of its mostly older fans. Still, there were persistent protests from primarily younger viewers who found the idea of such a marriage "ridiculous" and who hoped for Vanessa's scheming daughter, Dinah, to steal the heart of her stepfather. When Vanessa underwent a near death experience after the birth of her child, one detractor began a bulletin board subject heading entitled, "Vanessa, go toward the light." Added

a likeminded fan: "I agree, send Vanessa into the light. Then let Dinah and Matt raise the baby." These remarks were in direct conflict with the delighted reactions of Matt/Vanessa followers happy to see some attention paid their favorite couple after a long dry spell. Their marginal pleasures were, in this instance and at this juncture, consecrated by creators but not by the derisive judgments of other fans. In smaller, face-to-face fan groups such as those studied by Brown (1994), affirmation of these pleasures might be possible. But, amidst the larger, more diverse collective inhabiting cyberspace, cohesion and validation are constantly threatened.

If the pressures of netiquette and the gradual silencing of marginalized audiences can neutralize or discourage political debate and foster the goals of the powers that be, so, too, can the interventions of those very powers. Obviously, "official" network websites constitute one type of forum for these interests, but their visibility elsewhere has also escalated. *Soap Opera Digest*, for instance, instituted its own forum on AOL which includes message boards that soon exceeded the unsponsored AOL boards in traffic and gradually led to an integrated Internet website. The forum and website also provide interviews, polls, and tidbits linked with its current issue, the cover of which is prominently displayed.

Accordingly, the agenda of the magazine helps to set that of the message boards. And, as Fiske (1987, p. 118) observes, the magazines are not independent of the larger soap opera enterprise since they "rely on studio press releases and cooperation for their material and access to their players for interviews." The networks' sites on AOL and Microsoft Network also house soap opera bulletin boards subject to the same spillover. So, the soaps' desire to promote younger stars and their stories registers on these sites and filters into the content of message boards.

One article in *Soap Opera Digest* fueled a scant, shortlived, but angry outcry on the magazine's AOL site and illustrates how soap opera publications embrace the imperatives of the industry upon which they depend. In a critique of *One Life to Live* ("Thumbs up," 1997, pp. 74-75), the magazine argued that the program was "wasting" too much story on its aging cast members when the younger audience would not be enticed:

What were they thinking by showcasing so many graphic scenes of, shall we say, "mature" people having sex? . . . fans are "treated" to Carlotta's fantasies of Hank, which has us thinking 9 1/2 Eeks. . . . As for Dorian, it's nice that post-menopausal women can still rip up the sheets with the best of them.

If the previously recounted slights against older women and couples on the soaps are any indication, the sentiments of this piece concur with the preferences of the favored audience and may contribute to the marginalization of older viewers and their identifications.

Additionally, media-sponsored forums provide an expanded means by which diverse groups of viewers can, however fleetingly, experience an illusion of empowerment, when any actual audience influence proceeds primarily from market research keyed to the producers' demographic goals. As Intintoli (1984, p. 183) concluded from the comments of an insider in his exhaustive, backstage analysis of *Guiding Light*: "Whereas the degree to which the story could be changed by mail was limited, suppliers liked the audience to *feel* it can affect the show." Despite the privileging of youthful stories, characters, and sentiments, soap opera cyberfan sites still offer equal access and participants may overestimate their impact accordingly.

But, what about industry encroachment on the presumably independent Usenet soap opera newsgroups? The evolutionary structure of these newsgroups is relevant. When a single soap opera newsgroup became too unwieldy, the solution was to divide it into three separate newsgroups

according to network. So, like many of the commercial bulletin boards, these newsgroups now reproduce and assist the networks' efforts to create a "flow" which carries the same audience from one of their soaps to another. It becomes necessary for someone who watches soaps on two or more networks to subscribe to and manage more than one newsgroup—a disincentive to channel surfing.

Other examples of indirect influences emerged when *Another World* was under the axe. Those who protested content changes linked to the push for demographics were consistently chastised by other fans and accused of endangering the soap's status. Fans who had endeavored to keep the show on the air through letter-writing campaigns, etc., had taken a leadership role and determined that such negative commentary was counter-productive to the goal of keeping the show afloat at all costs, even if it was becoming *Another World* in name only. Though well-intended, these leaders were instructing fans to do exactly what the powers that be hoped—that is, to continue watching even if the "new *Another World*" didn't suit them and thereby allow themselves to be taken for granted while other audience segments were courted.

Those in the industry have also exerted some influence through their participation in discussion groups. During *Another World's* cancellation hubbub on Usenet, an insider began providing insightful information on decision making behind the scenes. While he didn't reveal his official position, his input was highly valued, with much of it eventually confirmed in magazine articles and interviews. Quick to toe the party line, he defended a controversial executive producer who had improved the show's demographics and scolded fans who did not appreciate the changes that preceded this: "Why the sniping at *Another World*? If bottom line—motivated NBC sees reason to give the show a chance and continued support based on the numbers, why can't the people here?" And, amazingly, nobody (except this researcher) contested the notion that NBC's profit motivated criteria should also be their own. The act of (politely) challenging this insider's recommendation seemed to border on heresy and was dismissed by some as flaming. . . .

◆ Conclusion

. . . After feminist scholars initiated a justifiable defense of female audiences who had been summarily dismissed for their devotion to soap opera and other "feminine" texts (see Brundson, 1995, pp. 60-62), many of them neglected to adequately deliberate the limits of the pleasure and resistance they chronicled. This researcher acknowledges that many soap opera fans are able to intuit the reasons their enjoyment is belittled by the larger culture. Consider this letter to a magazine addressing the issue of why soaps "get no respect" ("Why soaps," 1997, p. 37):

> The answer is simple: because it's a woman thing. . . . Powerful women in leading roles don't appeal to most men. . . . I will not buy a . . . soap magazine if a man is behind me in the checkout . . . as quite a few times men have made comments like, "Do you really read that garbage?" I shrug, "No, I just look at the pictures. I read *Playboy* for the really informative stuff."

Although a haven from such external disapproval, soap opera discussion groups on the Net provide new spaces for the disparagement of marginal women's pleasures more so than for the "collectivized" celebration of such pleasures. As Interrogate the Internet (1995, p. 127) contends, "The structure of the technology and the content" are intimately entwined with the "broader cultural context" and commercial imperatives of media filter into these groups and privilege the pleasures of the producers' "preferred" segment of the audience.

This occurs when the more marginal segments—nonwhite and, especially, older women—are compelled to incessantly defend their interests amidst the diminishing options and returns offered by soap opera creators or else fall silent. As Condit (1989, p. 109) argues, there is a "greater work load imposed on oppositionally situated audience groups," and the effect of such burdensome labor may be to muffle their voices. . . .

Just because many soap opera fans are savvy, critical consumers of the text and, in certain instances, the economic imperatives behind it does not mean that their views are typical or part of some large-scale, resistive impulse. And, just because the Internet has been touted as a place where marginal voices can be heard does not mean that existing cultural and economic arrangements have no bearing on the disposition of these voices and perspectives. Additional study must continue to focus on the push-pull of hegemony vs. resistance on the Internet as elsewhere.

As this research indicates, however, the advertisers' strategy of "divide and flatter" subjects the "feminine subculture" of soap opera fandom to rupture along other lines of identity. Minorities and their concerns are underrepresented; older characters, viewers, and themes are slighted; the private is divorced from the public; and cultural hegemonies—such as the double standard of aging—persist and even flourish. Just because the age, race, gender, or class of cybersurfers might not be immediately obvious, it does not follow that there is equality of participation or that such traits are not central to the commercial goals of the powers that be or to politics generally. Pretending otherwise does not change this; it can, in fact, play into the hands of those who help to reproduce hegemony while insisting, as *Another World's* writers did, that "it doesn't matter how old [or what color, or what gender, or how wealthy, etc.] you are." At this juncture, Mumford's (1995, p. 66) judgment lingers: "There are no politics—and there is therefore no feminism—in the soap opera community." And, the cyberfan community appears to be no exception.

◆ *Notes*

1. For an overview of the tension between political economic and cultural stances in critical media studies, see Harms and Dickens (1996), Garnham (1995), and Grossberg (1995). For ethnography of and negotiation within marginalized fan subcultures, see Jenkins (1995a, 1995b).

2. Data collection for this article transpired between June of 1994 and February of 1997. The Usenet soap opera newsgroup, RATS (rec.arts.tv.soaps), began as a single group and then split into three: RATS-CBS (CBS soaps), RATS-ABC (ABC soaps), and RATS-Misc. (all others). Bulletin boards on America Online include those linked to the *Soap Opera Digest* (SOD) site, ABC Online, and unsponsored areas. CompuServe has harbored two sponsored forums devoted to soap opera. Participation included observation (lurking) and occasional posting on various topics, with a periodic statement that I was engaging in research in addition to participating as a fan. The NBC soap *Another World* was the focus of my attention, since it is the soap with which I am most familiar and was undergoing changes linked to demographics and other production imperatives during the research period.

3. On the other hand, when a romance involving a white woman and an African American man was abruptly ended, cyberfans did conclude that the decision was due to a racist backlash. While many were disappointed and wrote the show, the issue was soon dropped.

4. What, also, might be the impact of prohibitions against "spamming"—in this usage, the posting of "long and verbose" messages (see Strate, Jacobson, & Gibson, 1995, p. 12)? Is the inclination to communicate a cogent, well-supported argument squelched by such sanctions?

◆ *References*

Allen, R. (1985). *Speaking of soap operas.* Chapel Hill: University of North Carolina Press.

Ang, I. (1996). *Living room wars: Rethinking media audiences in a postmodern world.* New York: Routledge.

Baldwin, K. (1997, January 10). A new spin on soaps. *Entertainment Weekly*, p. 31.

Baym, N. K. (1993). Interpreting soap operas and creating community inside a computer-mediated fan culture. *Journal of Folklore Research, 30*(2/3), 143-176.

Baym, N. K. (1995). The emergence of community in computer-mediated communication. In S. G. Jones (Ed.), *Cybersociety: Computer-mediated communication and community* (pp. 138-163). Thousand Oaks, CA: Sage.

Bowen, W. (1994). *Divide and flatter: TV's stealth attack on the Woodstock generation.* Citizens for Media Literacy: http://interact. uoregon.edu/MediaLit/FA/MLArticle-Folder/Divide

Brown, M. E. (1994). *Soap opera and women's talk: The pleasure of resistance.* Newbury Park, CA: Sage.

Brundson, C. (1995). The role of soap opera in the development of feminist television scholarship. In R. Allen (Ed.), *To be continued . . . Soap operas around the world* (pp. 49-65). New York: Routledge.

Condit, C. (1989). The rhetorical limits of polysemy. *Critical Studies in Mass Communication, 6*(2), 103-122.

Cukor, M. (1994, Feb. 8). Sleepless in Bay City. *Soap Opera Update*, pp. 68-69.

Fiske, J. (1987). *Television culture.* New York: Methuen.

Garnham, N. (1995). Political economy and cultural studies: Reconciliation or divorce? *Critical Studies in Mass Communication, 12*(1), 62-71.

Gibbs, M. (1996). Inappropriate Posts mini-FAQ. http://rtfm.mit.edu/usenet/news.answers/to/suaps/faq/port/thru4

Grossberg, L. (1995). Cultural studies vs. political economy: Is anyone else bored with this debate? *Critical Studies in Mass Communication, 12*(1), 72-81.

Harms, J., & Dickens, D. (1996). Postmodern media studies: Analysis or symptom? *Critical Studies in Mass Communication, 13*(3), 210-227.

Interrogate the Internet. (1996). Contradictions in cyberspace: Collective response. In R. Shields (Ed.), *Cultures of Internet: Virtual spaces, real histories, living bodies* (pp. 125-132). Thousand Oaks, CA: Sage.

Intintoli, M. J. (1984). *Taking soaps seriously: The world of "Guiding Light."* New York: Praeger.

Jenkins, H. (1995a). "At other times like females": Gender and *Star Trek* fan fiction. In J. Tulloch & H. Jenkins (Eds.), *Science fiction audiences: Watching "Dr. Who" and "Star Trek"* (pp. 196-212). New York: Routledge.

Jenkins, H. (1995b). Out of the closet and into the universe: Queers and *Star Trek*." In J. Tulloch & H. Jenkins (Eds.) *Science fiction audiences: Watching "Dr. Who" and "Star Trek"* (pp. 237-265). New York: Routledge.

Logan, M. (1996, July 27). Days-ed and confused, *TV Guide*, p. 46.

MacKinnon, R. C. (1995). Searching for Leviathan in Usenet. In S. G. Jones (Ed.), *Cybersociety: Computer-mediated communication and community* (pp. 112-137). Thousand Oaks, CA: Sage.

McLaughlin, M. L., Osborne, K. K., & Smith, C. B. (1995). Standards of conduct on Usenet. In S. G. Jones (Ed.), *Cybersociety: Computer-mediated communication and community* (pp. 90-111). Thousand Oaks, CA: Sage.

Mumford, L. S. (1995). *Love and ideology in the afternoon: Soap opera, women and television genre.* Bloomington: University of Indiana Press.

Stoddard, K. (1983). *Saints and shrews: Women and aging in American popular film.* Westport, CT: Greenwood.

Strate, L., Jacobson, R., & Gibson, S. (1995). Surveying the electronic landscape: An introduction to communication and cyberspace. In L. Strate, R. Jacobson, & S. Gibson (Eds.), *Communication and cyberspace: Social interaction in an electronic environment* (pp. 1-22). Cresskill, NJ: Hampton.

Thompsen, P. A. (1995). What's fueling the flames in cyberspace? A social influence model. In L. Strate, R. Jacobson, & S. Gibson (Eds.), *Communication and cyberspace: Social interaction in an electronic environment* (pp. 298-315). Cresskill, NJ: Hampton.

Thumbs up/thumbs down. (1996, September 2). *Soap Opera Digest*, pp. 74-75.

Why soaps get no respect. (1997, August 26). *Soap Opera Weekly*, p. 37.

Youthful products. (1995, May). *American Demographics*, p. 31.

49

CONSUMING PLEASURES
Active Audiences and Soap Opera

◆ Jennifer Hayward

. . . The first soap opera (defined in that era as a serial aimed at a female audience and marked by a domestic setting, emphasis on emotional and interpersonal concerns, and continuing narrative) is credited as Irna Phillips's *Painted Dreams* (1931), which followed the activities of a strong, courageous woman, Mrs. Moynihan, and her daughters. Immensely successful, the show inspired a plethora of continued radio dramas, which quickly proved themselves the most powerful advertising vehicles yet developed. . . .

In 1951, *Search for Tomorrow* made the transition to television, and other serials followed its example. In 1960, all remaining radio soaps ended abruptly in mid-narrative (in America, that is; the British pattern of development was very different, and in fact *The Archers* still airs on the radio and has a devoted following). Television's added visual dimension introduced complications, among them the need for a greatly expanded cast since viewers could now identify characters by appearance as well as voice. Larger casts required more involved plots, which in turn demanded lengthened segments, and this development eventually worked to encourage

---

multiple subplots and to complicate plots even further. The initial fifteen-minute episodes were extended to a half hour in 1956 and to a full hour for most soaps by the late seventies.

Then came the VCR. On January 9, 1990, the editor of *Soap Opera Digest* opened the new year with these remarks: "To my mind, the most significant change of the 1980s was the advent of the VCR. This little machine, which is now in half of all American households, changed viewing habits forever. . . . The videocassette recorder forced soaps to be faster-paced and to appeal to a broader audience." Time, shifting. No longer are soap audiences at the mercy of the networks' scheduling decisions. The *TV Guide* becomes a timetable for the week's recording, rather than a dictate for scheduling leisure.[1] Like the remote control, VCRs increase audiences' power over the televisual text. Viewers have the technology to "channel-surf"—catching the wave of one show, skipping to another, jumping over the trough of advertisements—and watch one show while taping another to be viewed later as they skim efficiently through commercial breaks. Advertisers are understandably unhappy about these new technologies, and the shifts in viewing habits they have produced have already effected changes in soap narrative construction and production values. For example, VCR technology has changed demographics since working viewers can catch up on shows in the evening, and the fact that viewers can now record shows means increased pressure to compete for overall viewer hours against prime-time shows and cable as well as other soaps. Therefore soaps try to keep ratings up by incorporating MTV and prime-time conventions into the shows, with apparent success: according to the network, *All My Children* is the most taped show on television. Also, since dedicated viewers can now watch every episode, sharply decrease viewing time by fast-forwarding through commercials and less interesting subplots, and save and rewatch favorite episodes,

soaps have had to quicken their pace. They now include faster moving storylines, less repeated dialogue and scenes, high-action mystery and adventure subplots, and location shoots.[2] Really crucial scenes in Friday's cliff-hanger may still be "rewound" or repeated on Monday, and the day's teaser (the first segment of the show) may still repeat a locating phrase from the previous day (or reair especially expensive special effects—producers like to get the most for their money), but overall there is much less explicit repetition in present-day soaps.

In addition to transforming narrative aspects of serial fiction, the translation to a new medium produced essential changes in the economic exigencies of serial production. Unlike both serial novels and comic strips, radio and television segments are free. Once the initial investment in a set has been made, there is no direct cost per episode; profits depend upon advertising revenues. Of course, part-issue novels and periodicals also relied on paid advertising, but in both cases a per-unit cost reinforced the link between the consumer exercising "free choice" and the commodity he or she chose to consume. The airwaves elide this direct economic relationship. The text is no longer the commodity: it is the reader of that text who generates profit when packaged in units of a thousand and sold, or "delivered," to advertisers. Networks, the middlemen in this transaction, seek to acquire as many units of the listener/viewer commodity as possible. A complex network of ratings systems attempts to convince both current and potential advertisers of the effectiveness of their investment in terms of viewers reached and influence obtained. Obviously, networks have an enormous stake in maintaining high ratings day after day, week after week. This compulsion directly inflected soap structure in its extension of the long-standing serial tendency of deferred and problematized closure into a *refusal* of closure. In other words, the narrative structure so often seen as determined by a female audience actually has more to do with the material conditions of the genre's development. Tune in tomorrow, same time, same place—the soap slogan makes visible its economic imperative. . . .

Although the demonstrable links between early soap opera and women's rhythms of work, for example, are certainly worthy of notice, it is actually the content and themes of this particular incarnation of serial fiction, rather than its narrative structure, that mark it as a form developed by and for women. . . .

In the early days of television, women seeking to break into the business could often find jobs only on the soaps, while men were reluctant to work on a form seen even at its inception as trash. The shows therefore quickly became female-dominated by default, reinforcing their reputation as women's shows, satisfying either essential or socially constructed desires of women. . . .

Now, forty years later, the women who produced soaps when men would not are in control of an enormously valuable commodity, and one no longer associated with an exclusively female audience. Although the portrayal of soap opera men has become much more complex in the last twenty years as women acquire more real power in the external world, and the form now claims many male fans (30 percent of the audience, according to some Nielsen statistics), soaps remain unique both in positively portraying strong women and in being a form still produced primarily *by* women. Female soap producers have begun to redress gender imbalances by tending to hire and train other women, who then move up through the network and continue the legacy. Agnes Nixon, who created many of the most popular soaps (including *All My Children* and *One Life to Live*), is often dubbed "the mother of Daytime." Despite the condescension implicit in this title, she is an enormously powerful woman who steps in when she sees her shows going off track and generally manages to save them.[3] And women play an active part in soap production all the way down the line. In 1992, for example, the creator, producer, associate producer, head writer,

and all but one of the "stable" of outliners and dialoguers who write the actual scripts of *All My Children* were women. One of the show's production assistants described an apparently unique television production experience: being in the editing room when putting an episode together and realizing that all the people involved, from head writer to technical crew, were female.

Given this history, it is not surprising that soap opera is strongly marked by contradiction. As mass entertainment, it is generated by the imperatives of a patriarchal and capitalist entertainment industry; as "women's fiction," it is primarily generated not only for but *by* women, a still marginalized subgroup within that industry. In the last decade, though, daytime drama has become slightly more prestigious and infinitely more profitable. As a consequence, men are increasingly involved in soap production. In contrast to the primarily female production team of ABC's *All My Children*, in 1994 the same network's *One Life to Live* had two male head writers and a stable of six male and three female scriptwriters.[4] This shift toward male representation in both production and consumption raises an important question: is soap opera also shifting in response to the increasing percentages of male viewers, producers, creators, and writers? I will discuss the handling of an ongoing rape storyline on *One Life to Live*, asking whether the departure from earlier rape plots indicates the perspective of a male writing team, the producers' acknowledgment of an increasingly male audience, a shifting cultural climate, or simply the normal variations in recycled storylines as writers seek to tell the same story differently.

Audiences and Soap ◆ Opera Production

. . . Unlike many critics, all networks are forced to acknowledge, at least to some extent, the actual viewing practices of soap audiences as well as their active involvement in the interpretation, uses, and even creation of the shows they watch. In the soap world, all aspects (creation, production, advertising, consumption) interact. To produce a profitable show, networks must increase advertising revenues; increasing revenues requires keeping ratings up; high ratings imply satisfied viewers; and viewer satisfaction demands a compelling show, which means networks must keep close tabs on what viewers consider compelling. And audiences are more than willing to inform networks of their desires. Phenomenal in emotional investment as well as in sheer numbers, soap fans cluster outside the studios from early morning till evening, waiting for the actors to emerge; write letters praising particular performers and storylines, condemning others, and suggesting possible developments or romantic pairings for the future; and threaten to stop watching if their suggestions are ignored. They play an active role in interpreting the narrative and televisual codes that soap producers have developed, and soaps, thoroughly enmeshed in the social and economic network, respond—in some of their manifestations and in limited ways—to the desires of audiences.

. . . Like all serials, the development of soap opera is inextricably intertwined with the actual workings of the economy in which it is produced: its setting, characters, format, even subject matter are determined by economic imperatives. For example, soap scenes usually center on a dyad or triad because intimate conversation is infinitely cheaper to tape than group or action scenes and can be set in any one of a number of small, reusable sets that fit easily into the studio. Although clearly economically determined, this interiority enhances daytime's "women-centered" atmosphere since its dyadic structure and familiar setting necessitate a primarily emotional and interactive, rather than action-oriented, narrative. Paralleling women's entry into the work force and their consequent escape from the confines of the home, increasing soap profits led to larger production budgets, which in turn enabled soaps' escape from the ubiquitous kitchen, living room, and hospital waiting room sets to explore the narrative possibilities of restaurants, hotels, health clubs, nightclubs, and outdoor sets. Still, the sets are not hermeneutically crucial in themselves, as they are in cinema. Soaps focus on what characters say to one another, not where they say it.

Since they are taped in cramped studios with limited budgets and extremely limited production time, soaps must *mean* as economically as possible, restricting visuals to one or two camera positions and one small set per scene. Camerawork is highly coded, delivering well-established cues to viewers trained to read them. As Bernard Timberg argues in "The Rhetoric of the Camera in Television Soap Opera," "Like the visibility of the purloined letter in Poe's short story, the very obviousness of the cinematic codes of soap opera keeps people from thinking about them and thus makes them more effective in doing their job: to shape and direct the audience's point of view" (p. 166). Soaps rely almost exclusively on a long shot to set the scene, tracking in to alternate between the standard two-shot and a modified shot-reverse shot and ending each scene with a close-up to catch every nuance of character reaction to the usual cliff-hanger. An intensification of classic cinema's reaction shot, this close-up becomes temporally extended to a sometimes disconcerting extent at the end of each "act," or group of three or four scenes between commercial breaks. This much mocked soap "freeze" is actually highly functional in creating soap meaning. Like the cinematic close-up, it invites viewers to attend to an actor's reaction, to imagine his or her thoughts. As Timberg expresses it, the camera's slow truck-ins and "elegiac movement" toward a character's face have "the effect of bringing the viewer closer and closer to the hidden emotional secrets soap opera explores: stylized expressions of pity, jealousy, rage, self-doubt" (p. 166). We are so close, this shot tells us, that we *must* be almost inside the character's mind and therefore must know what is happening there.

However, while actors do occasionally manifest the emotions Timberg describes . . . in most cases they are actually trained to keep the expression intense but neutral: projecting strong, concentrated, *impenetrable* emotion.[5] What fascinates about the soap version of reaction shots is their strategic purpose. Since it is so difficult to read—and thus impossible to predict—exactly what a character will do or say next, the freeze's intense neutrality fosters doubt and suspense, which in turn ensures that viewers stay tuned through the commercial break. So the shot has a dual and seemingly contradictory purpose, functioning both to pull us into empathy by zooming, as Timberg elegantly describes it, almost into the actor's thoughts and to push us into objectivity by making strange the contours of a face so minutely scanned, forcing the realization that in fact we cannot possibly enter this Other's thoughts.

This paradoxical function signals a larger ambivalence reverberating across soap televisuals and echoing within soap narrative. . . . On one level, soap techniques work to create intimacy with the characters. The camera literally pulls us into each scene, positions us at eye level with the actors, situates us inside living rooms, kitchens, and bedrooms, enables us to share with certain characters knowledge unavailable to others. We hear the most intimate details of characters' lives, individuals who have become familiar over years or even decades, to the extent that viewer letters claim to have known them longer than many friends or even family members.

On another level, this familiarity is paired with estrangement. Though pulling us into the action, soap televisual techniques have the peculiar effect not of establishing viewer identification with one character (as cinematic point-of-view shots do) or of effectively inserting the viewer into the scene as *voyeur*, but of maintaining a certain distance between viewer and text. We remain a little outside every scene, quite literally: the shot/countershot or glance/object editing that works in Hollywood cinema to suture viewers into one point of view is practically unavailable to the soap director, since it requires too many camera positions and too many takes. Most soaps are shot from the fourth wall of a long row of three-sided sets packed into an urban studio. Like a theater audience, then, we remain cut off from the action and cannot be sutured into it by the ability to see exactly what any one character would see. Glance/object editing is rare because it is technically difficult and expensive. Even the standard shot/reverse shots used to establish conversation between two people have to be carefully angled, their width kept well under the cinematic 180 percent. This method leaves a large gap of absent space in which we as viewers are positioned, but crucially we are rarely assigned a specific, voyeuristic perspective.

And soap narrative follows the restrictions imposed by production exigencies; thus we see all sides of every story. In the summer of 1993, for example, the ratings-sweep storyline of *One Life to Live* was the gang rape trial of three fraternity brothers: Todd Manning, Zachary Rosen, and Powell Lord III. All characters involved in the trial know part of the story: Marty Saybrooke knows she was raped and by whom, the perpetrators know they are guilty as well as where they hid the evidence, the Llanview community knows these are "fine boys" from good families whereas Marty is a notorious liar and "bad girl." However, we—represented by the camera—see all these sides and more. For example, we watch the increasingly guilt-ridden Powell try to convince his "brothers" to admit what they have done, and later see him telephone his attorney Nora Gannon to confess and then hang up the phone; we cut to Nora, puzzled, staring at the silent receiver. So far, so *The Accused*, but the difference is that many of these are characters we ourselves have "known" for years. We are familiar with the histories and interrelations of all participants in the rape and in the trial, and the multiple points of view thus encourage us to weigh motivations and personal agendas as well as facts, arriving at a more complex interpretation of the case than would be possible without this sense of history and perspective. While each character involved understands only a small part of the total whirlpool of events, "we," represented by the camera, see all—and what is more, we *know* that we alone are privileged. Like the freeze that ends most "acts," these technically dictated techniques create an interesting interpretive confusion. We are privileged to see and hear the most private moments, a voyeurism even more intimate because more familial/familiar than that of cinema. At the same time, we see more than any character and are thus distanced from them. Soap camera work parallels the form's multiple and intertwined narratives in that both enable the viewer alone to understand all sides of the story. Thus while Marty was seeking evidence to support her claim of rape, many episodes ended with a tight shot of the sweatband used to gag her and now hidden in the woods behind the frat house; this clue was "seen" and fetishized by the camera but remained unseen by any of the characters.

Soap directors occasionally depart from these conventions, and when they do it is worthy of notice. For example, while most of the rape storyline is shot using traditional soap camera work, scenes of the rape itself depart in significant ways from the conventional. First, our spectator positioning changes. As we have seen, soap point of view virtually never positions us with any one character; instead, we see all action from the fourth wall of a three-sided set. During the rape, however, the director made the highly unusual decision to position us with Marty. We saw, through a hand-held camera's jumpy eye, the rapists approaching, weaving in and out of focus, and pinning us/her down. Next we saw each rapist's face distorted through a fishbowl lens, looking down into the camera

and victimizing us, the hapless spectators, just as each victimized Marty. . . . Clearly, and for obvious reasons, these visuals refuse the distance that generally works to encourage empathy with all points of view. After the rape, however, the camera's view of Marty reverted back to the objective in order to carry out one of soaps' most valuable functions: forcing public attention to and debate about difficult but important social issues while educating viewers about these issues. Marty's post-rape visit to the hospital was carefully chronicled, using traditional camerawork so as not to distract from the information presented. Her choices were clearly explained and each stage of the physical examination, collection of evidence, and police report was carefully followed.

In this context, it is important to emphasize the very different feel of televisual, as opposed to cinematic, spectatorship. First, the camera positioning, production values, scene construction, even acting style are much "smaller" and more intimate in television. Second, the viewing context is very different. Dominated by the vast screen above, surrounded by darkness and strange bodies, the cinemagoer's viewing experience is both spectacular and specular. Glancing at a small screen, surrounded by familiar objects and people, the television watcher's viewing experience is both intimate and distracted. She or he virtually exchanges glances with the smaller than lifesized actors, placed at eye level, watching them within the private space of the home rather than in a public theater. If others are present, they may or may not be watching (but in either case will probably be talking over, wandering in front of, and otherwise distracting attention from) the television, a small, familiar piece of household furniture. Perhaps most important, the viewer has power over the images. . . .

John Ellis, in his *Visible Fictions*, discusses the distinction between cinema and television. Citing differences in both visual qualities and viewing contexts, Ellis points out that television "engages the look and the glance rather than the gaze, and thus has a different relation to voyeurism from the cinema's" (p. 128). In the close-up, for example, cinema iconicizes vast, godlike actors; by contrast, television close-ups explore a face scaled to approximately normal size and located close to the viewers' own eye level, producing equality—even intimacy—as opposed to the "distance and unattainability" imposed by the size and positioning of the cinema screen (pp. 130-131). The cost of this intimacy is that "the voyeuristic mode cannot operate as intensely as in cinema," the advantage that the physical presence of the television set pushes us into awareness of the activity of watching, thus defusing the rapt voyeurism that films can produce (pp. 137-138). TV watching is a conscious activity, a fact enforced by commercial breaks as well as by the freedom most viewers feel to talk during or comment on shows, a practice that is firmly hushed in movie theaters. . . .

In July 1992, ABC's *One Life to Live* tackled an exploration of homosexuality and AIDS. Having spent weeks building the teen storyline most soaps develop over school holidays to attract students, the show plunged viewers into the problems faced by one of the most popular characters, sixteen-year-old Billy, as he "comes out" to his closest friends, to a local minister, Andrew Carpenter, and indirectly to us. As usual, we have been prepared for increased objectivity by following all sides of the story as they develop: Billy's vexed relation to his snobbish and dictatorial parents; their terror of homosexuality and well-meant though misguided overprotection of their only child; Billy's friends' reactions, both positive and negative, public and private. We simultaneously track troublemaker Marty, following her to various covert vantage points as she spies on Andrew and plots against him; the camera then pulls back to allow us to catch *her* reaction. And finally, we watch Andrew as he prepares and delivers a funeral service for a parishioner who died of AIDS. He urges the importance of AIDS education in schools, lashes into the upper classes who ignore the epidemic because of class- and race-based imaginary immunity, announces the fact that his own brother died of complications resulting from the disease, and publicly pins the red badge of HIV awareness onto his surplice. These independent subplots begin to converge when Billy's parents, already falsely "warned" that Andrew is gay by jealous Marty, spot the minister (who has been counseling Billy) holding the boy's shoulders and looking into his eyes and—

At this point in the narrative, a witch-hunt seemed imminent, but all was ultimately resolved when the NAMES project memorial quilt came to Llanview, its names intoned in a reconciliatory ritual that united previously antagonistic characters. Although using the quilt, sacred to so many people, to resolve a soap storyline might seem cynical, it also gave millions of viewers the chance to experience, albeit vicariously, the power of the quilt as a symbol and source of communal mourning. When Andrew and others added a square they had made for Andrew's brother William, their act drove home the fact that each square is a narrative in itself, an iconic representation of an individual life.

Citing the dynamics of television watching—its familial give-and-take, the distraction inherent in the activity, and the "flow" of televisual life—Ellis and Feuer underline the crucial role viewers play in creating the meaning of a television text. As with the rape storyline discussed earlier, in following the Billy Douglas saga viewers can choose to respond on any one of a number of levels, including fury at the violence of homophobia (which positions us with Billy himself as well as with Andrew Carpenter, Viki Buchanan, and a number of other characters who are both open-minded and safely "straight"), disgust at the idea of homosexuality (which positions us with Andrew's father, Sloan Carpenter, Billy's father, and Viki's husband, Clint Buchanan), or simply desire to find out *what happens next.* Perhaps most important, most viewers discuss their reactions to this controversial plot with others, thus allowing a more open exchange of ideas than might be possible if discussing actual people rather than television characters. Like Andrew's and Billy's fathers, we may learn to overcome prejudice through emotional involvement with characters we have grown to "know" and respect. . . .

As a women's narrative form, soap opera initially restructured gender relations by focusing on women's emotions and relationships and figuring men as peripheral in many ways to the bonds between women. In its present incarnation on television, some of the most interesting soap storylines remain female-centered in a stereotypical but perhaps still useful sense in that they seek to produce empathy and even identification with characters. The real force of storylines like that of Billy fighting for acceptance, Marty surviving the aftereffects of rape, or the black *All My Children* character Terrence struggling to understand racism after his house is bombed by a white supremacist group comes as we experience such characters' anguished lack of control, rejection of even long-standing (straight, male, or white) friends who prove unable to understand that anguish, and (of course) the community's eventual ability to at least partially heal itself through increased tolerance and understanding. Despite the often facile resolutions of these stories, their sheer duration, our longstanding history with the characters involved, and above all the collaborative viewing practices favored by soap fans mean that these stories can have enormous impact in impelling open debate about underlying issues. And this impact is heightened by televisual dynamics. Because the physical qualities of the TV set itself unplug us from voyeurism, soaps' value as catalysts for discussion is increased. It is not surprising, therefore, that audiences find their greatest pleasure in the collaborative viewing practices they engage in and the degree of power they are increasingly able to wield over "their stories."

Audiences and Power ◆

I want to thank, most of all, the fans—because without you none of this would be happening. And we all know that. (actor David Canary, accepting *Soap Digest*'s Outstanding Lead Actor award)[6]

. . . Networks acknowledge audience involvement in the interpretation, uses, and even creation of "their" shows, and facilitate this by holding "forums" in which they invite panels of fans to view an upcoming episode and discuss their reactions to characters and storylines while producers and writers note responses, which are then brought into weekly planning sessions. Each show also has a fan mail department where letters are analyzed quantitatively and qualitatively. Producers and writers study a monthly report detailing the number of letters each actor received, the number of letters the show received, an abstract of particular suggestions regarding each storyline and couple, and a synopsis of attitudes toward the show. If strong reaction occurs in favor of or in opposition to a storyline, couple, or character, writers may alter planned scripts accordingly. . . .

All My Children fan letters attest to the confidence of these viewers that their voices will be heard.[7] Letters discuss characters as distinct from actors, revealing their considerable knowledge of offscreen relations between actors and how these may affect onscreen chemistry. Not incidentally, such letters also prove that fans do not in fact confuse character and actor. Letters harangue the show's producers, suggesting that they get the wheels rolling and give devoted and very disappointed fans what they want. . . .

Almost all those viewers who bother writing to the show (admittedly a small percentage of the total audience, though the minimum number of letters received, twelve hundred per month, is not inconsiderable) are both articulate and sophisticated, demonstrating awareness of the role of production factors in determining storylines. They have a strong stake in articulating opinions about "their" show; many apparently expect to have a voice in its creation. The only correspondence that did not demonstrate some degree of awareness of the production process and the economic factors underlying soap fictions was brief notes requesting autographed pictures.[8] Letters often close with thanks for the interest they feel the show takes in their opinions, an expression of confidence that soap fans' voices are heard and heeded.

A more collaborative forum for soap discussion is the Internet. The Usenet discussion group r.a.t.s., for example, is a powerful testimonial to the alternative uses to which mass culture can be put. A loosely linked collection of "net friends" and "lurkers" who collaborate to increase their enjoyment of soap watching, group members volunteer to write daily updates of the show's events so that others who missed the show can find out what happened. These updates go far beyond a simple blow-by-blow recounting of the episode to include clear awareness of the narrative structure of soap opera, as well as ironic commentary on the text, past history to clarify plot twists, and other insider knowledge. . . .

◆ *Case Study: Redeeming the Rapist*

When you look in Todd's eyes, you can see that there's no heart or soul in there anymore. He's made a pact with the devil, sold his soul to the devil. He can find a way out when there's no way to be found, he keeps going on, he keeps coming back, and there's *nothing* we can do about it. (Marty, *One Life to Live*)

Sorry, babe, but this door's locked—and you know what happens with you and me when we're behind locked doors. (Todd, *One Life to Live*)

To explore r.a.t.s.ers' interaction with a specific text, I will draw on the debate surrounding a storyline already discussed here, *One Life to Live*'s three-year portrayal of the consequences of the gang rape of Marty Saybrooke by three fraternity boys. To summarize the story so far: in 1992, Marty Saybrooke showed up in Llanview as a "poor little rich girl" orphaned by a car crash and abandoned to the tender mercies of her socialite Aunt Kiki. On soaps, most rich girls are also bad girls, and Marty was no exception; she drank, did drugs, and tried to seduce the local minister. But in the spring of 1993, she began to settle down. A few weeks later, Todd—with whom she had had sex once, though she had refused more recently—took his revenge when he found her drunk at Spring Fling. He raped her and incited two of his friends to rape her as well. As in the stories of Billy, the homosexual teen trying to come out to his friends and family, and Terrence, whose house was bombed by white thugs, we focus on Marty's terrifying powerlessness in that situation and her consequent need to prove that "I can't go on being a victim. I am going to take back control over my own life." Terrence and Marty's storylines were initially flawed in that the racist thugs and two of the rapists were demonized, their subjectivity denied in ways that tended to oversimplify the situations and thereby failed to capture the complex power relations underlying racism or violence toward women. The perpetrators of these crimes were simply evil or out of control and therefore could be rejected along with the mindsets they represent.

Marty's was a gang rape, so the figure of the rapist was split into three: the evil instigator, the good resister, and the mediator between these polarized figures. The instigator, Todd Manning, was transformed in the process of raping Marty from a crude but still human character to a dehumanized embodiment of rage. Set over against the absolute evil of Todd Manning was the relative "good" of Powell Lord—like Dickens, soap writers sometimes choose names dripping with symbolism—who initially resisted the rape, urging his friends to let Marty go, but ultimately gave in to peer pressure. As mediator we had Zach Rosen, who never acquired much of an identity beyond his function as go-between.

As we have seen, serials are fascinated by the instability of identity—hence the recurrence of radical character transformations, returns from the dead, evil twins, and so on—and the splitting in this storyline enhances interrogation of the identity of the rapist. What becomes especially clear is that for these characters the act of rape is not about sex, about women, or even about Marty. It is about what takes place, as Eve Sedgwick would put it, *between men* and hence marks a departure in soap treatment of rape. As in the case of the Bradley Headstone/Eugene Wrayburn rivalry, the polarization this splitting produces marks a transition from realism to melodrama. Soap opera rapes draw on powerful archetypes, most dramatically the fight between good and evil, weak and strong; soaps tend to configure these archetypes in ways that resemble their use in nineteenth-century melodrama to critique power relations, especially the oppression of the poor by the rich and of women by men. This particular storyline, though, polarizes not only the gap between rapist and raped but also the figure of the rapist himself. The show also departs from the rape paradigm not only by insisting on the essential "goodness" of Powell Lord—which many viewers have found hard to accept, considering that he *did* commit rape, a crime for which "peer pressure made me do it" is hardly an adequate (or even a physiologically possible) excuse—but even more startlingly by redeeming the evil Todd.

Initially, Todd was unequivocally bad: sullen, remorseless, charmless. Writers clearly had a terrific time camping up Todd as the embodiment of evil. Just before his incarceration, for example, he attempted to rape Marty again to punish her for "winning" the trial, and her friend Luna stopped him by whacking him with a crowbar, thus marking him with a nasty scar zigzagging across his right cheek. The camera loved to fetishize that scar as the symbol of his villainy, zooming in to linger on it at every opportunity. . . . The character seemed headed for a killing spree and then a quick end, but the actor playing Todd, Roger Howarth, is highly skilled and managed against all odds to add depth to a one-dimensional character. His popularity grew as a result, so the show's producers faced a conundrum. Todd had become the devil, but Howarth was boosting ratings. Executive producer Susan Bedsow Horgan and head writer Michael Malone chose a solution that proved highly controversial: they set out to complicate their one-dimensional rapist.

After Powell Lord (who finally confessed, attempted suicide, and was publicly forgiven by Marty herself) was sentenced to only three months in jail while Todd and Zach each received eight-year sentences, Todd, as furious as many viewers about Powell's light sentence, vowed he would be out in three months also.[9] His character veered increasingly toward the demonic, and he succeeded in making good his threat to escape by drugging himself, waking from a coma to leap from a speeding ambulance, and then reviving himself again by stabbing a knife through his hand while rolling his eyes heavenward and exulting, "Pain. Pain is good." By this point in the narrative, such excess had become characteristic, with Howarth camping up the villainy for all he was worth and many fans responding enthusiastically. After escaping, Todd returned to Llanview to stalk Nora Gannon, the attorney who had refused to defend him once she learned that he was guilty. He then attempted to rape Marty for the third time, killed Marty's boyfriend Suede, kidnapped an ingenue named Rebecca, went on the lam with her, stole a car, was found by police and shot in the chest, fell off a bridge into a freezing river in far upstate New York, was washed downstream among the ice floes, crawled out again, lay on the bank for a few episodes while the camera panned slowly up his apparently lifeless body, regained consciousness, began walking, and immediately saw a sign saying, "Llanview, PA, 50 miles."

After Todd's third or fourth miraculous escape and recovery, fans began calling him the Terminator or alternatively the Energizer Bunny, nicknames reflecting fan recognition of the fact that Todd had clearly crossed the border separating realistic soap character from the villain appropriated from nineteenth-century melodrama and Gothic traditions. In apparent contradiction but in clear response to the actor's growing popularity, writers simultaneously began to "deepen" the character by, for example, emphasizing his tenderness toward the innocent Rebecca and including flashbacks and testimony of his father's brutality toward him. We were therefore encouraged to read a causal narrative— "abusive father produces abusive child"— into the scenario. However, as many fans noted, this reading does not historicize the problem but simply removes the cause of violence one step. In the absence of any analysis of social, political, and economic factors, "my abusive father made me do it" just demonizes the father rather than the son.

In the spring of 1994, one year after the rape, Todd began to be "redeemed" (soap fan parlance for the process of turning a "bad" character into a "good" one, thus allowing that character to become incorporated into the community). Since Todd had crossed so far into absolute villainy, this transformation has required a whole arsenal of heavy symbolic weaponry. As far as I know, it is unprecedented for a rapist to be redeemed in exactly this way. Traditional soap narrative treatment of rapists must be seen in relation to soap's initially female writers and viewers and their early constructions of masculinity, the "wheelchair syndrome" for example. Generally, soap men commit rape as a result of a long-standing rage and/or need to control. The

rape does not function as a turning point in character development, then, but as a culmination, an act after which the character slides quickly into irredeemable villainy. Rape has been the one unforgivable crime. Thus, the rapist often wreaks havoc on the entire soap community for the duration of a ratings sweep and is then either committed to life imprisonment and/or sent away (like Ross Chandler, *All My Children*) or very often killed off by one of the characters he has hurt (like Will Cortlandt, also *All My Children*). In either case, the rapist is shunted off the show, never to return.

There are precedents for redemption of actors considered too popular to be written off the show, the most famous of which is the Luke and Laura storyline on *General Hospital*.[10] Luke Spencer stalked Laura and then raped her, but since the couple proved overwhelmingly popular, writers rewrote past history to the extent that as far as Luke and Laura themselves are concerned, the rape was "semi-consensual" (whatever that means). Interestingly, though, the treatment of this exception actually underscores the strength of the rule: the fact that the rape had to be erased from collective memory indicates that in the minds of the writers, a rapist *could not* become a good character and therefore the rape itself had to be denied and dissolved. What is more, viewers so vehemently and publicly expressed their horror at the thought that *One Life to Live* might be heading in such a direction that the executive producer issued a statement (published in *Soap Opera Digest*) to the effect that a Luke/Laura style romance—explicitly so labeled—between Todd and Marty was "absolutely, categorically out of the question."[11]

The writers who redeemed Todd included an unusually high number of male writers (eight men and three women were on the team during much of this storyline) and were led by head writer and novelist Michael Malone (since replaced by Jean Passanante), known for his "Dickensian" plots. Malone's nineteenth-century influences are overt and conscious in the redemption of Todd; for example, in a *Village Voice* article he compared Rebecca's decision to marry Powell rather than Todd to Cathy's decision to marry Edgar Linton rather than Heathcliff (Aug. 16, 1994). More disturbingly, in a *TV Guide* article focusing on the recent pattern of rapists redeemed (June 1994), he claims: "The bond between the woman and the violator is a great, historical tradition in fiction and in films. . . . Rudolph Valentino, Humphrey Bogart, Kirk Douglas, and Clark Gable all began as totally irredeemable villains. . . . You certainly don't want to say that these women want to be raped or that they are drawn to violence, because that's not true. But they *are* responding to the intensity of passion and an actor who lets you inside the torment. Some [women] believe they can be swept up in that passion and still turn it good. They think, 'With *me*, he'd be different.'"[12] The article's author, Michael Logan, pushes home the subtext here by stating, "Let's call a spade a spade: There is a very large contingent of American female soap viewers who find something very attractive about rapists." It is hardly necessary to mention that actual "female soap viewers" were furious at being so categorized. The response of one woman to her r.a.t.s. group will stand for many. "This is such a stupid statement," she says, in response to Logan's generalization. "Speaking only for myself, I don't like Todd because he's a rapist. I like Todd because Roger Howarth is a great actor. Powell and Zach raped Marty too, and I'm not a bit fond of either one of them."[13]

In working to recuperate Todd for the purpose of future storylines and ratings, the team used four techniques drawn from the conventions of Victorian sentimental fiction. First, we learn about Todd's unhappy childhood and specifically about his love for his mother and the cruelty of his wealthy, domineering, abusive father. Second, Todd repents and begins visiting a church to confess both past misdeeds and present impulses (to murder Powell, for example—something also high on many

fans' agenda). Third, we see his "pure" love for an innocent and highly religious virgin, Rebecca, who by "believing in him" helps him to express his rage against his father. This relationship is one that many viewers found particularly hard to swallow, given both Todd's earlier predilection for raping any woman who ran across his path and Rebecca's open-mouthed passivity. With her pre-Raphaelite curls, "drooping head," and inarticulate cries, Rebecca is almost a caricature of Dickens's more sentimental and less felicitous heroines. Visually, the scenes between Todd and Rebecca are heavily iconic: symbolic representations include the Virgin, the Mother, and also the feminization (with heavy homage to Freud) of Todd himself as, for example, he opens Rebecca purse, reminisces about his mother's purse, and then attempts to use women's makeup to hide the scar of a violent masculinity.

A fourth and crucial weapon used in Todd's redemption is his friendship with two children, Sarah and C. J., who find him hiding in their garden shed. This subplot bears an uncanny (and almost certainly deliberate, given Malone's affection for nineteenth-century literature) resemblance to the monster's narrative in Mary Shelley's *Frankenstein*. Shelley's monster describes his rescue of a drowning young girl, which is misunderstood as an attack on her; he also tells of sadly watching, from his hideout in an outbuilding, two happy, innocent children going about their lives. Similarly, from his post in the toolshed Todd rescues the children's teenage cousin Jessica, who is being accosted by an older boy; he also mournfully watches the family's activities, longs to be part of them, and spends his time carving toys for the two children. After the children accidentally discover him, Todd convinces them to keep his secret and to bring him food by telling them that he is a genie on the run from an evil master. The stories he tells them function as clear metaphors for his feelings about his father. For example, one day when C. J. asks him why he looks sad, he replies, "Every genie wants the same thing, you know? We all want our masters to smile, and care about us. We all want to grow up to be just like our masters. But some masters, C. J., some masters they don't deserve genies. They hit them, and they punish them, and they send them away . . . and they tell them that they're stupid, and worthless. And after a while, the genies start to think that they *are* stupid. And maybe they are . . . 'cause they just want the masters to care about them. They never will." Interestingly, even while constructing such consciously touching scenes the directors seem aware that viewers may be disturbed by watching small children in contact with a character who has so successfully been established as evil. These scenes make extensive use of unusual visual techniques, shooting from the children's perspective down on a crouching Todd to diminish the threat he poses when he is with them and using shots from the ground up as well as zooming in on the scar to increase the threat when he is alone. For many viewers, the final, damningly obvious blow in this battle to redeem Todd was the writer's choice to have Todd save the life of the woman he'd raped, Marty, by rescuing her and one of the children he'd befriended after a car accident.

Does the unprecedented handling of this rape storyline simply reflect a need to recycle an old story in a new way, or does it reflect important shifts in soap narrative as a result of the newly male-dominated writing team on *One Life to Live*? A partial answer can be found in viewer reaction. Responses were violently split along lines reflecting attitudes toward gender relations as well as soaps' own split between narrative realism and fantasy. Some viewers loathed Todd and were furious that the writers seem to be intending to keep him on the show. For example, one r.a.t.s.er writes, "I think it would be a real kick in the head to anyone who's ever been raped to have them show something like [Rebecca falling in love with Todd, and Todd staying on the show to be involved with her] . . . I know that's been done in the past, but hopefully things

have changed since Luke and Laura"[14] (Jan. 28, 1994). This writer clearly values soaps' long-standing respect for independent, strong women. In addition, she prefers a realistic treatment of rape storylines and privileges soaps' social realism over their fantasy. Conversely, a male fan who seems to prefer fantasy says, "I don't care where [Todd] goes . . . just as long as he keeps coming back. One of soapdom's greatest tricks is to keep bringing villains back from the dead. . . . a few years back, *One Life to Live* ran the same route with Jamie whatshisname. That guy was even more evil than Todd" (Feb. 11, 1994).

Clarifying the underlying issues involved in Todd's redemption, another fan points out:

> The writers are sort of playing mind games on us with this character. He's been talking a lot about his mom lately, and it looks like they might try to redeem him rather than kill him. I *might* be able to go along with that, even though he raped Marty. BUT, he tried to rape her again—twice! That's pretty hard to forgive, and pretty hard for a character to overcome, I think. But I still think Todd is one of the most interesting and well-acted characters I've seen in a long time, and I really enjoy his scenes. Maybe they'll wound him, he'll be taken to the hospital, and they'll find out a brain tumor was causing all of his aggression. Then they can remove it . . . and he'll be Mr. Nice Guy. Hey, anything could happen! [Jan. 22, 1994]

These last two writers clearly appreciate the fantastic conventions of serial fiction, chief among them the interrogation of identity that over the years has produced tropes such as radical character changes. . . . However, the last commentator is both conflicted and disturbed by the too easy leap from narrative realism to fantasy: she appreciates Roger Howarth's skill as well as the complexity of the character but does not want past violence to be forgotten.

My own response to this storyline is equally ambivalent. On the one hand, Todd's redemption certainly conveys one of the most important lessons of soapdom: never leap to conclusions about people based on race, class, appearance, rumor, or even fact, because it is impossible to understand the Other without understanding the history that has shaped him or her. On the other hand, using powerful narrative and visual techniques to mobilize sympathy for a man who has raped at least three women, attempted to rape several others, killed a man, and so on seems dubious at best. The narrative weight placed on Rebecca's role in Todd's redemption, for example, seems to encourage both female and male fantasies about the power of a "good woman" to save a man from his own violent impulses.

Given actor Howarth's popularity—a result not of his onscreen persona but of his undeniable acting ability, praised even by Todd haters—it seemed doubtful that producers would respond to the minority of fans who wanted Todd off the show. But a combination of fan response and the actor himself impelled producers to add a new twist to the storyline. Roger Howarth, who works with his wife in a rape crisis center, was disgusted by his redemption. In published interviews he stated that he had been hired to play an evil rapist, was horrified when the redemption process began, and decided to quit when the writers would not listen to his protests. A contract dispute followed, only resolved by Howarth's promise not to appear on a competing soap for two years. He remained on the show while writers worked to write him out, finally achieved by the old ploy of sending him off a cliff in a car. In the spring of 1996, we saw him lying on the coast of Ireland, fingers twitching to tell fans (in a less than subtle manner) that Todd would return when all the furor had died down. Tune in tomorrow. . . .

All such controversial storylines spur active debate over the issues involved, the realism of the writers' depiction, and possible resolutions to the story. These televisual explorations of power relations are, then, valuable as they promote discussion, and even more valuable if they do respond to viewers. Countering the traditional view of soaps as pernicious, mindless entertainment, Nochimson, Allen, and others have argued that they have enormous potential to effect social change. Supporters of soap operas cite their socially relevant storylines as well as their creation of that rare mass-cultural entity, a female-dominated narrative that refuses to privilege teleology or closure, does privilege interpersonal relations and communication, and allows even female protagonists space to develop newly defined identities. In addition to these factors, I would argue that soaps are ground breaking most of all in the community of viewers they produce. . . .

Notes

1. Reinforcing VCR domination of the soap experience, the Jan. 23 issue of *Soap Digest* featured a full-page ad for pink-labeled videocassettes with matching cases reading "All My Soaps . . . Your special tape for recording soap operas." The *Soap Digest* table of contents also reflects the new primacy of video, including as it does a weekly feature called the "VCR alert," which keeps viewers informed about upcoming soap highlights (weddings, deaths, location shoots) that viewers will want to tape and save for repeated viewing.

2. However, it is important to emphasize that the essential structure of the soap opera, developed under earlier conditions of production, at least so far maintains its peculiar relation to narrative time. VCR-addicted viewers wishing to save those special soap moments have difficulty doing so because of the sheer volume of output: the storage space required for even a month's worth of episodes is considerable, as is the cost of videotapes. Most viewers have a single tape on which they record each day's episode, taping over it after viewing.

3. Michael Malone, head writer of *One Life to Live*, unwittingly epitomized this condescension

toward Nixon when accepting the 1994 Daytime Emmy Award for "best writing team." He thanked Nixon for "creat[ing] the world that we live in" and then added, "If Charles Dickens is the father of daytime, she's his daughter, and we're very proud to be among her children."

4. These figures were true at the time of analysis (spring 1994); however, writing teams change constantly.

5. Classes for new or would-be soap stars teach the "freeze" technique, among other soap-specific skills.

6. January 10, 1992. David Canary plays twin brothers Adam and Stuart Chandler on *All My Children*.

7. Many thanks to the anonymous former viewer mail department employee who volunteered to waylay a number of letters (after quantitative and qualitative analysis by the department) and forward them to me in 1989.

8. To determine letter-writers' awareness of *All My Children* as constructed text, I looked for references to the distinction between the actor and the character he/she portrays; the importance of actors' contract negotiations, soap opera conventions, and competition with other soaps in determining story lines; and awareness of viewer power—as rulers of the ratings—over *AMC* writers and producers.

9. As mentioned earlier, soon after the rape the character Powell Lord was depicted as unproblematically "good": he apologized for his role in the rape, was forgiven, and had apparently put the whole thing behind him. Viewers were appalled by this facile dismissal of Powell's part in the crime. They complained to each other on the net, wrote individual letters to the show, and finally (July 1994) collaborated on a letter to producers; they began, diplomatically, by praising the show's earlier handling of the story line, but then argued that Powell's overnight redemption was both offensive and untenable. A month later, Powell and his friends suddenly "realized" that he had repressed his role in the rape too quickly, and he began participating in therapy. Fan complaints continued, however, and Powell eventually took over the "monster" role in the story line, as what he had repressed consumed

his personality. He became a serial rapist and was written off the show in short order.

10. Other redeemed rapists include Jack Deveraux and Lawrence Alamain on *Days of Our Lives*, and Roger Thorpe on *Guiding Light*.

11. *Soap Opera Digest*, Aug. 2, 1994; quoted from a r.a.t.s. post, July 17, 1994.

12. Michael Logan, "Rapists: Unlikely Heartthrobs." *TV Guide*, June 18, 1994.

13. r.a.t.s. post, June 20, 1994.

14. These and all other fan comments have been quoted, with permission when contact could be made with their authors, from posts to the Usenet rec.arts.tv.soaps bulletin board.

References ◆

Allen, Robert. 1992. "Audience-Oriented Criticism and Television." In *Channels of Discourse, Reassembled*, ed. Robert C. Allen. Chapel Hill: University of North Carolina Press.

Allen, Robert C. 1985. *Speaking of Soap Operas*. Chapel Hill: University of North Carolina Press.

Allen, Robert C. 1989. "Bursting Bubbles: 'Soap Opera,' Audiences, and the Limits of Genre." In *Remote Control: Television, Audiences, and Cultural Power*, ed. Ellen Seiter et al. New York: Routledge.

Ellis, John. 1982. *Visible Fictions*. London: Routledge & Kegan Paul.

Feuer, Jane. 1986. "Narrative Form in American Network Television." In *High Theory/Low Culture: Analyzing Popular Television and Film*, ed. Colin MacCabe. Manchester: Manchester University Press.

Nochimson, Martha. 1992. *No End to Her: Soap Opera and the Female Subject*. Berkeley: University of California Press.

Timberg, Bernard. 1984. "The Rhetoric of the Camera in Television Soap Opera." In *Television: The Critical View*, ed. Horace Newcomb. New York: Oxford University Press.

50

CATHARTIC CONFESSIONS OR EMANCIPATORY TEXTS?

Rape Narratives on The Oprah Winfrey Show

◆ Sujata Moorti

Entertainment is the last thing I am looking for. . . . My goal is to try to uplift, encourage, and enlighten you in some way. I'm looking for the moment that makes you say, "Ah ha, I didn't know that."

—Oprah Winfrey

Over the last twenty years, daytime talk shows have become an integral part of the television programming lineup in the United States. In 1995, more than 15 million people tuned in daily to watch *Oprah: The Oprah Winfrey Show*; it attracted a greater number of female viewers than news programs, nighttime talk shows, morning network programs, and any sing.le daytime soap opera. Although cultural critics, politicians, and journalists have been harsh in condemning the form and content of talk shows, their popularity among daytime audiences combined with the economics of production have ensured this genre a stable place in the television schedule.[1] Criticisms of talk shows invariably point out the sensational nature of the topics discussed; critics argue that the programs appeal to the prurient interests of the largely female audience and do not serve the "public good." Contradicting these criticisms, in this [chapter] I argue that daytime talk shows, where guests and audience members bare intimate details of their lives for public debate, should be integrated in discussions about the role of television in democratic society. Examining *Oprah* episodes on rape and acquaintance rape that aired between 1989 and 1991, I argue that these programs help us reconceptualize the public spheres constituted by the media.[2] Partially endorsing Winfrey's statement in the epigraph, I suggest that in the area of sexual violence these daytime programs are useful as sites of information because they make available a plurality of positions reflecting different social understandings of the issue. This analysis reveals that these *Oprah* episodes on rape often move beyond a discussion of individual cases to create a protofeminist discursive space: they foreground the pain and violence that result from sexual violence, not the legal and police procedures involved in naming an act as rape. The act of giving voice to pain contains the potential to transform these television programs into cathartic events for the participants. Simultaneously, the multiplicity of perspectives offered and the emphasis on discussion make it possible to conceptualize daytime talk shows as sites of an emancipated public sphere that highlights marginalized women's voices.

While I point out the textual potential contained in daytime talk shows, I would caution against celebrating them as the primary site of the public sphere, since economic concerns over audience ratings sharply limit the nature and scope of their discussions. The topics addressed by this genre are sharply defined by producers' perceptions of what appeals to its predominantly female audience.[3] All topics are placed in a domestic or personal context and presented within a dramatic structure that invariably plays out as a confrontation between individuals. Discussions on talk shows, therefore, fail to deal with structural issues, focusing instead on individual solutions. Notwithstanding *Oprah*'s ability to give voice to marginalized groups, it is necessary to remember that the subversive or emancipatory potential of these discussions is sharply curtailed by the host and experts. Unlike in the ideal public sphere, where everybody could participate as equals, talk show discourses are structured around the moral authority and knowledge of the host and experts. Together they shape what is spoken and how stories are told.

"Report Card Problems"; "Should Handguns Be Banned?"; "Cholesterol Cures"; "Tightwads and Pack Rats"; "Wives Meet the Other Women": these are the titles for a week of *Oprah* shows in 1989. This range of topics is customary for talk shows that oscillate between "serious" topics such as gun control and "typically female" issues such as the "other woman."[4] Focusing on these "female" topics, scholars have tended to dismiss the talk show genre as sensational, lurid, and shallow. Todd Gitlin, for instance, contends that talk shows employ individual pain voyeuristically "to get an audience" and that "nothing is served but selling products."[5] Similarly, Walter Goodman of the *New York Times* describes a discussion of acquaintance rape as "a peep show in the interests of sensitivity training."[6] Examining the changing nature of talk shows, Jane Shattuc argues persuasively against such readings. She contends that these programs are predicated on an active and vociferous studio audience and not the anonymous and silent audience of peep shows or of voyeurism; the technological apparatus of television visually identifies audiences while the narrative structure of talk shows give them voice.[7] Other studies have provided a nuanced understanding of why audiences find these programs compelling and why they derive pleasure from them. Several scholars have pointed out that by focusing on individual storytelling and by privileging oral histories over traditional forms of debate these programs open new avenues for knowledge building and discussion.[8] Others have tried to assess how the "public articulation of sexual difference and gender conflict"[9] allows talk shows to thematize feminist concerns. The analysis in this [chapter] is informed by these readings.

Daytime talk shows have been in existence since the 1950s but were strikingly different from their contemporary counterparts. The early talk show format consisted primarily of "celebrity" guests sitting around a coffee table and sharing recipes and other "secrets" relating to the domestic sphere of activities.[10] The issue-oriented talk show format analyzed in this [chapter] originated in the early 1970s, with *Donahue*. Phil Donahue organized his hourlong show around topics that focused on "ordinary" people rather than on celebrities. More important, Donahue was the first television host to abandon his place on the stage and to position himself with the predominantly female audience, whose comments and questions were actively incorporated into the program. *Donahue* also altered the content of talk shows. No longer was the focus on recipes, dress patterns, or so-called girl talk. Instead, his show, which has been characterized as an "exercise in sociopolitical discourse," tackled a range of issues dealing with both the profound and the profane—he has dealt with serious national issues such as presidential elections, war, poverty, and AIDS, as well as titillating topics such as female impersonators and lesbian mud wrestlers.[11] According to Linda Haag, *Donahue* was the "first talk show to market 'serious' girl-talk and to concede the importance of the female voice."[12] This new talk show gained fame not for its discussion of serious topics, however, but for discussing private issues that were considered taboo. Several scholars have argued that the low production costs of daytime talk shows ($25,000 to $50,000

for each half hour), their high profit margins, their daytime placement, and their nonnetwork status have enabled a focus on "silenced" and controversial issues, such as rape. Furthermore, the talk show's degraded status as a "female" genre allows these programs to tackle taboo topics in a manner rarely seen on network television.[13]

Like Donahue, Oprah Winfrey gave up a career in the newsroom to become a nationally syndicated talk show host in 1986. Her show soon overlook *Donahue* in the ratings war; in its first five months *Oprah* became the leading daytime talk show and the third-highest-rated syndicated show behind *Wheel of Fortune* and *Jeopardy!*.[14] By 1988 Winfrey's salary and the profits she accrued from *Oprah* allowed her to buy the production rights for the program. She created Harpo Production, Inc.—the first African American-owned film and television production studio—to produce her show. *Oprah* is currently distributed to 204 markets in the United States and 120 other countries through King World Productions, a syndication company.[15] In 1996, *Oprah* represented about half of King World's profits; the show had generated $180 million in revenues, and *Forbes* magazine named Winfrey as the highest paid entertainer in the United States.[16] Following Winfrey's success, the daytime talk show arena became very crowded; in 1997 there were seventeen nationally syndicated talk shows, although few have been able to replicate her achievements.[17] Like other television genres, talk shows operate within a limited repertoire of narrating devices, with discussions dictated by ritualized codes and conventions. . . .

Oprah tends to follow a problem/solution narrative structure. In the first quarter-hour, Winfrey and her guests identify the problem, establishing the parameters for the ensuing conversation; the guests present their experiences of sexual assault individually, often following a repetitive and fragmented narrative structure. In the second quarter-hour, the audience begins to address and confront guests' inconsistencies as the host plays moderator; at this stage the personal experience of sexual assault is generalized to a larger social issue of collective gendered identity. In the final half-hour, the "experts" are drawn into the conversation, and together with the audience they start to offer solutions. Through the problem/solution format we are led to believe that Winfrey, her guests, and her audience are engaging in conversation, while what we watch is an interview, a "genre of public speaking in which an individual, under cross-examination, produces certain forms of speech which are appropriate for public circulation."[18] . . .

As a genre, daytime talk shows obscure the distinctions between experts and laypersons, privileging the storytelling of personal struggles over the knowledge provided by experts. Often, the studio audience members challenge the experts and position their individual experiences as possessing greater validity and moral authority. In these programs, the real expert is considered to be the storytelling voice of the layperson. This focus on individual stories allows talk shows to highlight the familiar and the domestic over characteristics traditionally associated with the rational critical debate of the public sphere. Additionally, the experts, who are predominantly women, are expected to exhibit their knowledge through the "feminine" characteristics of nurturance, interpersonal skills, and the ability to solve dilemmas with commonsensical solutions.[19]

Through the studio setup, daytime talk shows also confound definitions of the studio audience and the host. Typically, Winfrey is not seated with the guests but instead wanders between the guests and the studio audience, thrusting her microphone at audience members. According to Robert Allen, this gesture collapses the categories of host, studio audience, and home audience into television's fictive "we," thereby creating a space "where intimacy itself can be both the form and substance of programming."[20] The *Oprah* show adds a further twist since the host often participates in emotional self-confessions of childhood sexual abuse, weight loss, and other personal details. As Gloria Masciarotte contends, Winfrey is always one of her own guests.[21]

Above all, daytime talk shows are associated with intimacy primarily because of their degraded status as a "female" genre. *Oprah* marks its "feminine" nature through a battery of intentional and unintentional devices. Program topics, scheduling, advertised products, and guest choices are all directed to appeal to the middle-American female viewer. Janice Peck has pointed out that talk shows traditionally cast their topics in everyday, albeit provocative, language.[22] They attempt to make their programs seem open and accessible even when the issues are complex. Through the script and set design, the topics debated, and the everyday "plain folks" language employed, which the producers believe appeal to women, daytime talk shows have reconstituted the public/private divide. *Oprah*, like many other daytime talk shows, tends to present private acts as socially relevant and the social as personal. The program focuses on topics that emanate from current social problems but highlights only individual narratives. Thus, in the various *Oprah* segments devoted to rape, which I discuss in this [chapter], Winfrey strikingly eschewed any discussion of the "celebrity rapes" that were in the news between 1989 and 1991. While Donahue conducted shows dealing with the Central Park jogger's case, as well as the William Kennedy Smith and Mike Tyson rape trials, *Oprah* episodes instead focused on individual experiences of rape, highlighting a collective gendered identity.

Performing Pain ◆

Oprah promotes a "feminine" mode of discussion: it emphasizes the emotional over the rational and fragmented and repetitive dialogue over narrative closure, and it foregrounds individual experience and interpersonal dimensions of issues.[23] The voices of rape victims and other women in the studio audience trying to articulate ill-defined, ongoing struggles dominated the discussions of rape on *Oprah*. The episodes focused on social understandings about sexual violence rather than on legal processes about rape trials. Winfrey began each show with individual women's detailed accounts of their rapes. During the course of the hourlong show we encountered rape victims who repeatedly articulated their experiences of sexual assault; the guests and women in the audience narrated their life stories, their understandings of sexual violence, and their bewilderment. Many of the rape victims were emotional and defiant as they justified their behavior preceding the sexual assault. The victims explained how they were affected by the rape, the trauma they suffered, and the guilt and shame they experienced. "What did I do to provoke this?" one woman asked; another explained, "I just could not go on with my life. I just wasn't concentrating. I gained a large amount of weight." Overall, each of these individual narratives shattered the myth of "real" rape.[24] These women explained that they were raped by friends, ex-husbands, acquaintances, and so on. They also revealed that they were attacked in "safe" spaces and that they rarely bore the physical marks of resistance and nonconsent.

These storied voices of rape victims called into question prevailing stereotypes of rape and female sexuality and clarified a woman-centered understanding of sexual assault. Here, we have the possibility of a feminist narrative where women speak for themselves and where the unrepresentable, rape, is finally voiced and no longer "unspeakable." Masciarotte argues that daytime talk shows have borrowed elements from the women's movement to valorize the female voice, adopting many techniques of consciousness raising that were integral to the identity politics of the late 1960s and early 1970s. Both the format of talk shows and the consciousness-raising

strategies of the women's movement rely on personal testimony, speaking out experiences at random, relating and generalizing individual testimonies, and "starting to stop," that is, overcoming repressions and delusions.[25] This trend is predominant on *Oprah*, where many of the panelists revealed that they did not immediately define their assaults as rape; however, by the time they were on the show they were able to speak for themselves and name the act. This loquacious narration of pain and the act of naming provide the cathartic element to talk shows.[26] Examining black women writers' marginalized location in the United States, bell hooks argues that racism, sexism, and class exploitation suppress and silence their voices. Citing her experience as a scholar, she argues that the act of talking back, to speak as an equal to an authority figure, is an empowering gesture. Other feminist theorists agree that to have a voice that is heard marks the "movement from object to subject" and protects women from dehumanization and despair.[27] Through speaking about their experiences of rape these guests move from object to subject position, at least for the duration of the show. The presence of feminist scholars, rape counselors, and other "experts" makes it possible for these rape victims to translate this temporary moment of empowerment into a more permanent subject status, one marked by connection with women's groups. The individual solutions offered by the programs, however, mitigate against the possibility that these talking subjects will be transformed into agents in their social lives. In the shows analyzed here, Winfrey repeatedly draws our attention to rape prevention mechanisms that would move these women out of their victim status. There is little evidence, though, that the discussions on these shows enable guests to reconfigure their relationships with their acquaintance rapists or gain agency in their quotidian lives.

Notwithstanding these limitations, the discussions of sexual violence draw our attention to the subjective pain of the women. By allowing women to speak about their experiences of pain and victimization, *Oprah* focuses on the unspeakable reality of pain and its investment in the individual body. Elaine Scarry has pointed out the difficulties involved in expressing physical pain and its resistance to objectification in language.[28] *Oprah*, with its insistence on detailed descriptions of sexual assaults, transports the issue of individual, private pain into the area of shared public discourse. By narrating sexual violence, the discussions on *Oprah* affirm a female experience that has often been repressed and rendered invisible. The debate engendered by these individual experiences transmutes the personal into the collective. . . .

The guests and panelists on shows discussing rape and acquaintance rape shattered monolithic definitions of sexual violence by offering a plurality of understandings. This polysemy is evident even at the level of production practices, which are most noticeable in the labels attached to the various participants. For instance, on the show titled "Date Rape," the panelists were described as "Raped by Acquaintances," "Raped by a Friend," "Raped by a Date." Thus, *Oprah* took the singular definition of rape victim and provided us with multiple ways of defining this individual. In addition, through their participation in the discussion the various audience members elaborated on these multiple definitions of a rape victim, some of them reproducing existing understandings while others broadened them. Through this plurality of storied voices, *Oprah* circulated discourses that were already in currency and opened them for debate. While all the voices heard on *Oprah* uniformly depicted rape as a deplorable phenomenon, the show provided a forum for the expression of multiple perspectives in dealing with particular instances of sexual violence.

In the various episodes, Winfrey repeatedly asserted that her program was primarily educational and that by providing a plurality of voices she hoped to activate people into taking steps against rape. But even though these discussions make available a significant discursive space to situate the issue of rape, these conversations are not emblematic of democratic debate and discussion. Many of the limitations in these discussions are dictated by the show's need to maintain a large viewing audience. The voicing of feminist understandings of women's oppression in society is thus tempered by the need to not alienate viewers. The following section of this [chapter] suggests the limits of talking about sexual violence on *Oprah*, where differences are allowed as long as the articulation of difference remains at the level of identity and does not imply political activism against the system that produces sexual violence.

Loquacious ◆ Narration of Sex

Many feminist scholars have found Michel Foucault's theories useful frameworks to understand the elaborate and ritualized discussions of sex and sexuality facilitated by contemporary television. In *The History of Sexuality*, Foucault argues that contrary to common perceptions the Victorian era did not silence talk about sex. Rather, there was a "veritable discursive explosion" around and apropos of sex. Foucault contends that during this period it was only possible to talk about sex in specific places and in specific ways. Conversations about sex were relegated to the church confessional, and sex was essentially transformed into a discourse. The confessional, Foucault contends, became "an apparatus for producing an ever greater quantity of discourse about sex" and determined the distinctions between licit and illicit behavior.[29] The power relationships governing the ritual were, however, marginalized, and the confession was seen instead as a liberatory process where people expressed "with the greatest precision, whatever is most difficult to tell."[30]

The narrative structure of *Oprah* constructs an analogous situation; it enables the transformation of sex and sexual violence into discourse. However, here individual identity is not constructed in secrecy or in the privacy of the confessional. . . .

In the shows examined here, Winfrey functions in a manner akin to the priest in the confessional that Foucault describes.[31] She is the "authority who requires the confession, prescribes and appreciates it and intervenes in order to judge, punish, forgive, console, and reconcile"; through the confession the guest is liberated and transformed.[32] Winfrey prods her guests for more detailed descriptions about sexual violence and the "sense of confusion" they felt. "Were you screaming? Did you think he was going to kill you?" "In the week before you told your best friend, what were you going through? What kind of stuff were you feeling, thinking, doing?" One of the women responded to these questions by explaining, "I stopped going to parties. I stopped going out on dates." This rape victim also admitted to a loss of confidence and an inability to trust her judgment about people. Winfrey's role as the interlocutor allowed rape victims to articulate their pain and confusion.

Is this act of confession a liberating step for these women? Does this new knowledge liberate them from their sense of confusion? Does it offer them a transformed sense of female identity? Do the discussions uncover the political dimensions of their experiences of sexual assault, help them confront the contradictions of existing gender roles, and lead to a sense of female solidarity? Or do they constitute a soul searching that uncritically privileges personal feeling and self-awareness? . . .

With their focus on the individual and the particular, the confessional discourses of *Oprah* are partially successful in identifying the problem of sexual violence and presenting it as a threat that could forge a collective gendered identity. In their discussions about rape, both Winfrey and her guests often tried to make connections between incidents of sexual violence and systemic problems such as gender-role socialization. Winfrey invariably juxtaposed individual women's narratives with statistics revealing the prevalence of this crime. "Acquaintance and date rape is more common than being left-handed," she clarified during one show. Commercial breaks on the show were punctuated by statistics on the prevalence of rape in the United States. Often Winfrey would enumerate the more sensational statistics. For instance, she highlighted the results of a survey conducted on junior high school students as follows:

Twenty-five percent of the boys said that a man has a right to rape a woman if he's spent money on her during a date, and 16 percent of the girls agreed with that. Sixty-five percent of the boys felt it's okay to force sex on a woman if the couple has been dating for at least six months. Forty-seven percent of the girls agreed with that.

This use of statistics, combined with her choice of rape counselors and feminist scholars as guests, was intended to illustrate how women are socialized to believe that sexual violence is, as she put it during one show, "just part of what happens." The majority of the experts enumerated the different and subtle ways in which gender-role socialization is effected. "We imprint our children with these kinds of messages, that women somehow cause rapes to happen, that women are responsible for men's sexuality, that women make men do these things," Robin Warshaw, author of a *Ms.* survey on date rape, explained. Similarly, Myriam Miedzian, who was identified on the show as the author of *Boys Will Be Boys*, elaborated on the cultural scripts of masculinity and femininity that enable a rape culture. Winfrey, too, contributed to this discourse with the suggestion that society views women as objects and men as uncontrollable and that this attitude leads to rape.

In all of these episodes, Winfrey framed the programs as educational endeavors that would help "women to understand that any time you are having sex against your will and sex is forced upon you, it is considered rape." She included lessons for women on how to prevent rape and cope with sexual assaults, and she repeatedly encouraged women to take self-defense courses. Winfrey thus enabled the formation of narratives that moved beyond exploring women's status as always-already victims and allowed women to see themselves as potential agents in their liberation from a shared threat. Through the experts' voices, the shows called for a change in female attitudes. These statements affirmed a collective gendered identity and identified a shared sense of oppression, something Felski points out is an essential step in the formation of a feminist counter public sphere.[33]

Even as *Oprah* allowed for the possibility of a protofeminist discursive space, there were other elements within these episodes that reframed sexual violence as spectacle. In "Date Rape," which aired on 7 December 1989, the first guest was a convicted rapist who had been invited, Winfrey clarified, to "tell women how his mind worked when he was out with a woman on a date, which women he decided to rape." The rapist's storied voice provided a commonsensical understanding of gender-role socialization. He explained that men are socialized differently from women and that as a rapist he exploited these differences. He looked for women who could be manipulated; further, he pointed out that he refused to take "no" for an answer. The rapist reiterated the critique of social practices that was a common thread in these episodes and hinted at the systemic roots of sexual assault. By giving precedence to this rapist's voice over those of the three rape victims, however, *Oprah* negated the emancipatory impulse of the show. The convicted rapist who talked about his crimes, rather than the rape victims, remained the focus of the show. The show presented the convicted rapist as

a freak, undoing the earlier discussions that identified gender-role socialization as creating a rape-enabling culture.

Additionally, although the guests, the experts, and Winfrey enunciated for the most part a woman's, and often a feminist, perspective of sexual violence, Winfrey would set up controversy by showcasing dominant stereotypes of rape. Winfrey occupied an awkward and contradictory position: she both espoused and disavowed feminist perspectives on rape. Every time feminist definitions of rape predominated on the show, Winfrey introduced patriarchal definitions of female sexuality that invariably stimulated an agitated conversation. For instance, on the show entitled "'She Asked for It' . . . The Rape Decision," which aired on 17 October 1989, Winfrey clarified that a woman's dress is not a "signal that she might be interested in sex or a signal to a jury that … she somehow asked for it." Yet, when many among the audience concurred with her she repeatedly held up the clothes of the woman whose rape trial was dismissed because the jury believed her dress was "advertising for sex." Throughout the episode Winfrey, not the audience members, returned to the idea that the alleged rape victim wore a "halter top that showed her midriff," and the discussion recentered on the woman's "seductive" apparel when she was attacked. Not only did this extended discussion of the woman's clothing merely whet people's prurient interests, the tone of the discussion between Winfrey and her guests seemed to negate the feminist redefinitions of rape and female sexuality the show tended to promote otherwise. It should come as no surprise that audience members on these shows were emboldened to assert that men only "want" what they see and that sex is the underlying theme of all male-female interactions. In effect, *Oprah* aired paradoxical definitions of rape: some privileged feminist understandings and others rewrote nonconsensual, violent sex into consensual sex.

Winfrey also used her panelists and experts as confrontational devices to incite heated debate. For instance, Winfrey identified one of her experts, a defense attorney, as someone who believed that "it's become too easy for women to cry rape." Winfrey was not alone in vocalizing patriarchal understandings of female sexuality; several audience members reiterated these beliefs. They essentialized gender difference and argued that men are biologically equipped to see women only in terms of their sexual availability. One argued that "women are innately coy while men are innately the aggressors." Another contended that men are aggressive because "they are intimidated by the aggressiveness that women have today. They are intimidated by the independence that women have today." A defense lawyer (for an alleged rapist) argued that a woman's clothes "advertised her as a prostitute" and therefore as willing to have sexual intercourse with men. Effectively, each of these positions asked women to share the responsibility for the rape and blamed feminism for the prevalence of rape. When antifeminist sentiments predominated, Winfrey espoused the contrary position, often physically distancing herself from audience members whose opinions she disliked. She resorted to sarcasm, calling one audience member "Mr. Profound Thinker," while telling another one, "You're in the hole. You are digging yourself deeper in the hole." . . .

Winfrey and several of her panelists reiterated that a central problem with sexual violence was poor communication skills, if not the complete breakdown of communications, between men and women. For instance, the convicted rapist who appeared on "Date Rape" argued that the primary problem was a communication breakdown. "We're not clear with each other," he said. Similarly, all of the rape victims on the show admitted that they had sent out "mixed signals" and believed this was the central cause for their assaults. Winfrey also forwarded the view that the only solution was "to keep talking and keep talking," affirming the Foucauldian theory of the confession as a means to overcome

repression. In a manner akin to the Victorian era described by Foucault, in which talk about sexuality did not disappear but reappeared in particular locations and through the use of specific rhetorical strategies, *Oprah* becomes a site where women (and men) talk obsessively about a taboo subject. It does not offer solutions, but, like the confessional, the act of speaking is seen as important. Winfrey emphasized as well that many of the rape victims who appeared on her shows were once unable to identify or name their assaults as rape. Thus *Oprah* appears to tell us that these women are testimony to the power of communication. Where once they were unable to define their assaults as rape, now through the act of voicing their experiences these women are intrinsically modified. They are able to give a name to their trauma. By overcoming their guilt and shame, they are able to discuss it in a "public" arena.

Somehow, the problem and solution this argument forwards correspond with the general tendency of talk shows to locate all solutions within the individual's grasp—that communication and individual resolve together can solve most social problems. These shows suggest that even in the absence of a final solution, the very act of communication offers a partial solution. These episodes reduce the complex operations of social and political questions to self-awareness and self-expression. The experts and audience rarely offered systemic solutions; instead, the programs repeatedly presented short-term, depoliticized answers to structural problems. . . .

Fragmented ◆ Oppositional Discourses

Jürgen Habermas's conceptualization of democracy as a discursive process and the central role of the public sphere within it is a primary concern in this analysis of *Oprah*. In *The Structural Transformation of the Bourgeois Public Sphere*, Habermas formulates an enabling model of democratic society that inscribes an autonomous arena of debate and discussion, the public sphere.[34] He defines it as an autonomous forum where people meet as equals and debate issues of common concern in a rational-critical manner; it is a public domain independent from state interests and potentially enables the circulation of discourses that are critical of the state.[35] Political participation and citizen control of society are enacted through the medium of talk in the public sphere. Tracing the sociohistorical formation of the bourgeois public sphere, Habermas identifies tea shops and literary salons, and later newspapers, as the originary sites of rational-critical debate. With the growth of capitalism and the rise of industrialized society, however, the relations between state and society became intertwined and the distinctions between civil society and state became blurred. With the loss of this critical boundary marker, the public sphere as an autonomous forum has become untenable. Tracing the decline of the bourgeois public sphere and the colonization of the media by marketplace interests, Habermas calls for a new arena that could facilitate the formation of informed and critical public opinion. . . .

Within Habermas's definition, the fragmented, emotional, and repetitive discussions of rape on *Oprah* would not be considered as constituting rational critical debate. *Oprah*, thus, cannot be conceived as constituting a public sphere even though it enables a debate about the definitions of sexual assault, its effects, and its causes. Feminist theories provide a different understanding for these public articulations of female sexuality on *Oprah*. Many feminist scholars, and in particular black feminist theorizers, have pointed out that oral histories and emotional narratives constitute an engendered form of knowledge building; they are alternative sites of self-definition for marginalized communities. Further, they argue that dialogues are central to the construction of an empowered community.[36]

Thus, one could argue that the active participation of panelists, experts, and audience members in the *Oprah* episodes on rape allow for testing of ideas about the phenomenon of rape and do constitute a woman-centered public sphere. . . .

Felski and Fraser, however, have pointed out that if public opinion formation and participatory parity are central elements to a democracy, a multiplicity of public spheres would be a more appropriate model than the unitary model, Habermas proposed. In stratified societies, they argue, there would exist several counter public spheres that stand in a contestatory relationship to dominant publics. If one were to examine talk shows as promoting a counter public sphere, the *Oprah* episodes analyzed here simultaneously succeed and fail at the task. A feminist counter public sphere should be "structured around an ideal of a communal gendered identity," Felski points out.[37] The *Oprah* episodes critique cultural practices from the standpoint of women as an oppressed group in society. They generate a female-specific identity grounded in a consciousness of the fear of rape and seek to convince society of the validity of women's claims and assertions. The show enables a counter public sphere that affirms and critiques the construction of female identity as always-already victims.

At the same time, *Oprah* fails at the task of enabling a counter public sphere because the focus on individual solutions has co-opted the real changes feminists have sought. As a genre, daytime talk shows reject radical structural changes and work only within existing structures. In the shows analyzed in this [chapter], although feminist definitions of rape were aired, Winfrey tended to go out of her way to "balance" conversation. This resulted in a majority or consensus discussion that ensured that the terms of the debate never strayed toward the "extremes." These programs do not create a counter public sphere as much as they provide a forum in which we can discuss issues, one that is sharply regulated by the concerns of audience ratings.

Daytime talk shows have broadened the nature of debate enabled by other television programs and they provide a plurality of positions from which one can approach the issues of rape, gender, and sexuality. They enable a discursive space in which nonhegemonic definitions can be articulated. They also point out a way in which the concept of the public sphere could accommodate bodily and affective aspects of human existence within the realm of debate and discussion. Simultaneously, the central problem Habermas identified, that the demands of the marketplace shape media debates, is particularly valid in this area. Daytime talk shows render into spectacles issues of rape; titillatory tendencies that objectify women reside alongside the multiplicity of views that offer women agency.

◆ Notes

1. Jane Shattuc, *The Talking Cure: TV Talk Shows and Women* (New York: Routledge, 1997), 7; Wayne Munson, *All Talk: The Talk-show in Media Culture* (Philadelphia: Temple University Press, 1993), 4.

2. In this [chapter] I do not elaborate on the possibility of counter public spheres outside the media as eloquently suggested by the various articles in *The Phantom Public Sphere* (Minneapolis: University of Minnesota Press, 1993). Instead, I argue here that even the mainstream media offer us opportunities to pluralize the concept of the public sphere.

3. Marilyn Matleski points out that broadcasting executives target most of their daytime programming to eighteen- to forty-nine-year-old women because they constitute the largest percentage of habitual viewers and they still are the primary purchasers of household items. See Matleski, *Daytime Television Programming* (Boston: Focal, 1991). An *Oprah* publicist provided Jane Shattuc (*Talking Cure*, 47) with the profile of a typical audience member: she is in the "Roseanne Connor" mold, a stay-at-home,

non-white-collar woman with about a ninth-grade education.

4. Although women continued to constitute 80 percent of her audience, in 1996 Winfrey abandoned the single-issue format, shifting her focus away from so-called female topics. In an effort to distance herself from her now numerous competitors, who often encouraged more confrontational and violent interaction among guests, Winfrey adopted a format that resembles the daytime talk shows of the 1950s with less audience participation. Now, Winfrey and her guests sit separated from the studio audience, whose role has been reduced to applauding celebrities and occasionally voicing appreciation of guests' achievements. In another effort to distinguish her show from those of her competitors, Winfrey has introduced an on-air book club to discuss fictional works with authors. This allows *Oprah* to appeal to an audience broader than the stay-at-home female viewer and recasts the host as a popular intellectual, which is in striking contrast to the image of her competitors. In this [chapter], however, I focus on the earlier, single-issue, participatory-audience format, and all further references are to the early, pre-1996 Oprah.

5. Quoted in "Dark Secrets? Tell 16 Million of Your Closest Friends," *San Francisco Chronicle*, 19 June 1990, B3, B5.

6. Walter Goodman, "Three Queens of Talk Who Rule the Day," *New York Times*, 29 July 1991, C11.

7. Shattuc, *Talking Cure*, 7-8.

8. See Janice Peck, "Talk About Racism: Framing a Popular Discourse of Race on *Oprah Winfrey*," *Cultural Critique* 27 (spring 1994): 89-126; Gloria Masciarotte, "C'mon Girl: Oprah Winfrey and the Discourse of Feminine Talk," *Genders* 11 (fall 1991): 81-110; Sonia Livingstone and Peter Lunt, *Talk on Television: Audience Participation and Public Debate* (New York: Routledge, 1994).

9. Tania Modleski, "Femininity as Masquerade," in *High Theory/Low Culture*, ed. Colin McCabe (New York: St. Martin's, 1984), 39.

10. Virginia Graham's *Girl Talk* is considered to be the predecessor of the contemporary daytime talk show. *Girl Talk* was an early-1960s show that brought together women in public life—movie stars, TV stars, and so on—to

chat about things. Graham's show was closely modeled on women's magazines and featured celebrities to define notions of femininity.

11. Denis McDougal, "Donahue's Dilemma: Balancing Truth, Trash," *Los Angeles Times*, 28 January 1990, 8.

12. Linda Haag, "Oprah Winfrey: The Construction of Intimacy in the Talk Show," *Journal of Popular Culture* 26 (spring 1993): 116.

13. See Patricia Priest, *Public Intimacies: Talk Show Participants and Tell-All TV* (Cresskill, NJ: Hampton, 1995), 11; and Shattuc, *Talking Cure*, 66.

14. Shattuc, *Talking Cure*, 39.

15. http://www.mrshowbiz.com/starbios/oprahwinfrey/a.html.

16. http://www.southam.com/nmc/waves/depth/yearend/forbes.html.

17. *Ricki Lake*, which appeals to a younger audience, is considered the closest rival to *Oprah*. See Shattuc, *Talking Cure*, 148.

18. Robert C. Allen, "Audience-Oriented Criticism and Television," in *Channels of Discourse Reassembled*, ed. Robert Allen (Chapel Hill: University of North Carolina Press, 1992), 122.

19. Shattuc, *Talking Cure*, 124.

20. Allen, "Audience-Oriented Criticism and Television," 122.

21. Gloria Masciarotte, "C'mon Girl," 94.

22. Peck, "TV Talk Shows as Therapeutic Discourse," 63.

23. Mary Ellen Brown (*Television and Women's Culture* [Newbury Park, CA: Sage, 1990]) and John Fiske (*Television Culture* [New York: Routledge, 1987]) characterize programs that lack closure; emphasize process, dialogue, and intimate conversation; and focus on relational issues as constructing a "feminine" discursive space.

24. *Real rape* refers to the dominant stereotype that the rapist is an armed stranger in a ski mask who attacks unaware women in dark, public spaces. There is a vast literature on this subject. See, in particular, Helen Benedict, *Virgin or Vamp: How the Press Covers Sex Crimes* (New York: Oxford University Press, 1993); Susan Brownmiller, *Against Our Will: Men, Women, and Rape* (New York: Bantam, 1976); Susan Estrich, *Real Rape* (Cambridge, MA: Harvard University Press, 1987); and Susan Griffin, *Rape, The Politics of Consciousness*, 3d ed. (San Francisco: Harper and Row, 1986).

25. For a discussion of these and other features of consciousness-raising sessions, see Robin Morgan, *Sisterhood Is Powerful* (New York: Random House, 1970).

26. Patricia Priest (*Public Intimacies* [Cresskill, NJ: Hampton, 1995]) argues that talk show participants find the act of public disclosure an empowering experience.

27. bell hooks, "Talking Back," in *Talking Back: Thinking Feminist, Thinking Black* (Boston: South End, 1989), 9.

28. Elaine Scarry, *The Body in Pain: The Making and Unmaking of the World* (New York: Oxford University Press, 1985), 8.

29. Michel Foucault, *The History of Sexuality*, vol. 1, trans. Robert Hurley (New York: Vintage, 1980), 23.

30. Ibid., 59.

31. Reggie Nadelson ("The Importance of Being Oprah," *Independent* [London], 13 March 1990, 20) quotes Winfrey as describing her show as "my ministry."

32. Foucault, *History of Sexuality*, 61-62.

33. Rita Felski, *Beyond Feminist Aesthetics* (Cambridge, MA: Harvard University Press, 1989), 121.

34. Jürgen Habermas, *The Structural Transformation of the Bourgeois Public Sphere* (Cambridge, MA: Harvard University Press, 1989).

35. See James Curran, "Rethinking the Media as a Public Sphere," in *Communication and Citizenship*, ed. Peter Dahlgren (New York: Routledge, 1991), 27-57.

36. See Patricia Hill Collins, *Black Feminist Thought* (New York: Routledge, 1990); and hooks, *Talking Back*.

37. Felski, *Beyond Feminist Aesthetics*, 167-68.

51

THE MEDIATED TALKING CURE

Therapeutic Framing of
Autobiography in TV Talk Shows

◆ Janice Peck

Autobiography—the relating of everyday stories—is central to daytime television talk shows. Hosts, "expert" and "ordinary" guests, and studio audience members produce/narrate their lives and comment on those of others; home viewers consume/interpret these narratives in light of their own biographies. Part of the appeal of these programs is that they appear to let people speak for themselves and tell their own stories. At the same time, these interwoven narratives are located within institutional, political-economic, and sociohistorical structures that determine what can be spoken, by whom, and to what ends. In this [chapter], I examine the process through which the telling of "personal" stories in daytime talk television is shaped by these structural constraints. In particular, I ask how these shows' incorporation of therapeutic language and assumptions works to frame the lives narrated within them.[1]

I focus here on two of the most popular talk shows—*The Oprah Winfrey Show* and *Sally Jessy Raphael*—programs hosted by women, oriented to women's concerns through "feminine narrative" conventions,

NOTE: From *Getting a Life: Everyday Uses of Autobiography*, edited by Sidonie Smith and Julia Watson, 1996, Minneapolis: University of Minnesota Press. First published in *Communication Theory*, 1995. Reprinted by permission of Oxford University Press.

and directed at a primarily female audience.[2] I suggest that these shows are fueled by social tensions that originate "outside" the shows but are imported "inside," where they become the object of the talk and the site of ideological labor. This sets in motion the programs' internal contradiction: they address social conflicts that can never be fully resolved on television while holding out the possibility that talking will lead to, or is itself a form of, resolution. The belief that communication can guide people out of their dilemmas makes these shows compatible with therapeutic discourse; their relational focus, confessional mode, and therapeutic orientation make them appealing to female viewers. The ongoing pursuit and deferral of final solutions—which helps sustain viewers' interest and commitment and generates ratings and advertising revenue—also makes this format attractive to the TV industry.[3] If producers of the programs recognize that conflict and controversy attract viewers in the first place, they must also find ways to depict these tensions without jeopardizing advertising support or violating the industry's economic priorities. In this [chapter], I look at how the programs negotiate those demands by mediating and managing the social conflicts from which their appeal arises.

◆ Gendered Dimensions of Therapeutic Discourse

Grounded in psychology—which takes the individual psyche as its object of study—therapy is intended to remedy individual "dysfunction" through perceptual or behavioral change.[4] Explanations of the growth of therapy, however, tend to cite social causes: modernization, the growth of bureaucracy and increasing complexity of society, technological innovation, and the erosion of community are said to result in individual isolation and anomie.[5] Such forces have supposedly created a void in contemporary experience that must be remedied with therapeutic intervention. Implicit in psychology is the assumption that societal changes are organic or natural processes to which individuals must learn to adapt.[6]

Therapeutic discourse, formulated around intimate, revelatory conversation, emotional expression, and reliance on (traditionally) male expertise and guidance, resonates for many women because of their socially constructed "feminine" subject position and discursive orientation. Because women are typically socialized to attend to interpersonal processes and needs, they are encouraged to develop communicative practices that foster relatedness. . . .

White argues that confession and therapy have become "privileged and prominent discourses in contemporary television" and that these discourses are "implicitly associated with a specific gendered [female] audience" (1992, 36). Daytime talk shows have incorporated therapeutic, confessional discourse as a narrative strategy related to their female viewership. Programs aimed at women exhibit features that both Brown and Fiske have identified as constituting "feminine narratives": lack of closure, an emphasis on process and intimate dialogue, a correspondence to "real time," and a focus on relational issues.[7] These qualities are similarly associated with therapeutic settings and interactions. Given the target audience of *The Oprah Winfrey Show* and *Sally Jessy Raphael*, it is not surprising to find in them a feminine style of talk, feminine narrative conventions, and reliance on therapeutic discourse.

The TV Personality ◆ System, Para-Sociality, and Mediated Intimacy

In the mid-1970s, Phil Donahue pioneered what has been called the "new" talk show organized around topics, focusing on "ordinary" (rather than famous) people, and featuring hosts who have abandoned their place on stage to encourage audience questions and comments. Carpignano and his colleagues argue that turning the studio audience into "a major player" is the key innovation of "new" talk shows like *The Oprah Winfrey Show* and *Sally Jessy Raphael*.[8] But if these changes have given the "ordinary public" (as guests and studio audience members) a more central role on television, the para-sociality of the talk show form and its use of personalization strategies and therapeutic discourse constrain the content, relationships, and identities in the programs.

The "television personality system," argues Langer, is most prominent in "factual" program forms (e.g., news, game and talk shows), where TV personalities "play themselves," are presented as "part of [daily] life," are accessible on a regular basis, and work to "construct intimacy and immediacy."[9] Because talk shows focus on the realm of the "personal," they create a space "where intimacy itself can be both the form and substance of the programming" (p. 360). This mediated intimacy has both practical and formal bases. The fact that TV viewing usually occurs in "the intimate and familiar terrain" of the home encourages us to respond to "television's own 'intimacies' and 'familiarities' brought to us through its personalities" (p. 356). Repeated contact with such personalities contributes to what Horton and Wohl call a "para-social relationship," where viewers come to feel they know TV personalities "in somewhat the same way they know their chosen friends: through direct observation and interpretation of appearance, gestures and voice, conversation and conduct in a variety of situations." Viewers are thus invited to feel that "they are involved in a face-to-face exchange rather than a passive observation."[10] "New" talk shows further enhance this sense of immediacy because studio audience members, who stand in for viewers, actively participate in the programs.

Although we refer to TV personalities by their first names and are privy to some aspects of their private lives, what we know are their "television selves," narratively constructed public personas. Viewers' pleasure in a given talk show is based on identification with the host's public personality/biography, develops over time, and permits them to make personal judgments about, for instance, Winfrey or Raphael.[11] A woman who watches these shows regularly confidently told me that "Oprah really cares about people," whereas "Sally is too cold." Her assessment is based partly on Winfrey's televisual manner—crying easily, hugging guests and audience members—which is part of her TV self and a means of constructing intimacy and eliciting emotion on the show. The gap between the TV persona and the actual person behind it, however, ensures that viewers' relationship with talk show hosts remains bounded by para-sociality: "The interaction, characteristically, is one-sided, non-dialectical, controlled by the performer, and not susceptible to mutual development" (Horton and Wohl 1976, p. 212). This lack of reciprocity is what distinguishes para-social from interpersonal relationships. "This form of communication is highly institutionalized and control is not in the hands of either the sender or receiver, but is preplanned by media specialists who design and orchestrate the interaction."[12] Para-social interaction is an integral part of the talk show locale and provides hosts, guests, and audience members with "already mapped-out subject [narrator] positions."[13] The successful TV persona is one capable of "initiating an intimacy which [her] audience can believe in" (Horton and Wohl 1976, p. 216). This "intimacy at a distance" is enhanced with technical and representational codes. Sets are designed to look like casual living spaces, speech is informal, interaction is on a first-name basis, the host is physically involved with the studio audience, and television's abundant facial close-ups provide "maximal opportunity for disclosure of subjective manifestations" (Langer 1981, p. 361). These elements help blur the distance between the private space of the viewer and the institutional space of the studio.[14] Direct address intended to engage viewers in "a potentially intimate, interactive scene" is particularly important in inviting viewers to identify with the people and emotions on the screen. Through such address, TV personalities "appear actively to be taking their viewers 'into account'" so that the "spectator is positioned to engage with the television personality with equivalent directness and immediacy" (Langer 1981, p. 362).

The fact that these shows focus on guests' private lives enhances the formally constructed intimacy. Episodes are organized around topics cast in everyday, if provocative, language: "Couples Who Fight About Money," "Women Who Love Abusive Men," "Violent Teens," and so on. A typical episode opens with the host introducing the topic and the first guest(s). Each guest (or family unit) is usually given a brief segment alone before engaging with other participants. Experts generally appear later to comment on the stories already presented. The host's job is to draw out the "ordinary" guests' stories, encourage and regulate feedback from the audience, solicit advice from the experts, and make sure advertisers get their allotted time. . . .

Television's reliance on "mythic images" works to erase social divisions, "deny social cleavage," and "formulate a collective identity for a fragmented society."[15] Talk show hosts help construct such unity for the diverse issues tackled on their programs. Their relatively stable television personas become the programs' "anchoring points" that counterbalance the chaotic world represented by the guests' endless problems (Langer 1981, p. 357). The ethos that informs *Sally Jessy Raphael* and *The Oprah Winfrey Show*, and to which their personas are anchored, is a therapeutic one. This therapeutic ethos gives coherence to the topical issues, becomes the field of intelligibility for making sense of guests' narratives, and reinforces the code of intimacy that structures the shows' meanings. . . .

Synthetic Personalization ◆ and Strategic Discourse

Fairclough suggests that the same forces that produced the need for therapy also produced therapeutic discourse as an answer to that need. In contemporary capitalist society, our lives have come increasingly under the control of large, complex, and impersonal systems—the economy, the state, and myriad public and private institutions—that exert great influence over all aspects of experience. This control is exercised through the mechanisms of the economy and commodity market, through various forms of bureaucracy, and through the media. Drawing on Habermas, Fairclough refers to the extension of these webs of power as a "colonization of people's lives by systems" that is carried out, in part, within the "societal order of discourse." He cites the emergence of three distinctly modern discourses—consumerism/advertising, bureaucracy, and therapy—all of which are "strategic" in that they are "oriented to instrumental goals, or getting results" (1989, pp. 97, 197-98).[16] The ascendance of these strategic discourses reflects the extension of methods of social control specific to capitalism's historical development—the instrumental use of discourse/communication for purposes of social management in line with the priorities of capitalist expansion and its corresponding need for cooperative subjectivities.[17] Such discourses help manage the inevitable tensions of a stratified social order with unequal access to political-economic wealth and power. On *Sally Jessy Raphael* and *The Oprah Winfrey Show*, bureaucratic and therapeutic discourses are central to the framing of the topics and personal narratives about them.

Health workers, counselors, personnel managers, and so on are trained in the use of bureaucratic "discourse technologies" based on the assumption that the client/patient is less competent in essential social skills the expert has acquired by virtue of her or his training. . . . This bureaucratic discourse masks the actual inequity of encounters where neither power nor disclosure is equally distributed.

The most explicit use of bureaucratic discourse in talk shows occurs between invited experts and "ordinary" guests whose equality is formally constructed even as it is substantially denied. The former ask questions of, make comments about, and offer advice to the latter; the reverse is almost never true. Nor are the experts required to reveal their own problems and personal lives (when they do, it is typically in the past tense—evidence of having conquered their troubles and the basis of their current expertise). The problems on the shows are the property of the ordinary guests, who need some kind of external (e.g., professional) help in understanding their predicaments and altering their behavior. Commonly, what they lack are "good communication skills," which the experts, as trained communicators, are in a privilege position to provide. . . .

Talk show hosts also exercise power through strategic discourse. Unspoken rules of the talk show form allow the host to cut off and dismiss some speakers and to invite and draw out others. Winfrey and Raphael have different styles of exercising this power (Winfrey tends to use humor and explicit body language; Raphael is more clinical and efficient), but both clearly assert control on their shows. They also have different ways of creating "rapport." Winfrey relies more on empathic identification and direct confrontation, whereas Raphael uses simple restatement, analytic interpretation, and overt guidance. Raphael comes across, more so than Winfrey, as a social services provider—authoritative, somewhat detached, consciously employing "caring skills." Both women, however, rely on managing and evoking the emotions of their guests and audiences. Winfrey elicits emotional response through the projection of her own feelings, whereas Raphael draws out emotions with probes and acts as a blank screen upon which the feelings of others are projected. In both cases, the evocation of emotional response is central to the shows' entertainment function, to their appeal to women viewers, and to the simulated intimacy essential to their success.

Therapeutic discourse is similarly strategic. . . . Fairclough argues that the proliferation of this discourse is both an effect of and an attempt to manage the subordination of persons to systems. That subordination "has resulted in problems and crises of social identity for many people," a significant number of whom "now seek some form of 'help' with their 'personal problems,' be it in the casual form of 'problem' columns or articles in magazines, or through various forms of therapy or counseling" (1989, p. 198).

The media have become an increasingly important site of such help-seeking activity; it is no accident that a proliferation of self-help books, support groups, state and private treatment agencies, and the ever-expanding Twelve-Step "recovery movement" has accompanied a rapid growth in mediated forms of therapy.[18] Daytime talk shows' incorporation of therapeutic discourse is part of this trend and is related to the expansion of such discourse into an array of social institutions (education, workplace management, social work, medicine, occupational guidance). Although therapy may be personally beneficial, it can also be seen as a further subordination of persons to systems. Fairclough proposes that therapy is a "technology of discipline" through which we are taught to blame ourselves (or our relationships) for our problems and to seek solutions by adapting to or acquiescing in the social structures responsible for those problems in the first place. Therapeutic discourse thus becomes a form of intrapersonal coercion that "places the onus on the individual to discipline herself" (1989, p. 226; see also Illouz 1991, p. 242).

It is in this emphasis on the self as the source of one's suffering and the logical site of solutions that the TV personality system, synthetic personalization, and therapeutic discourse come together in the service of legitimating the existing social order. At the heart of this complex synthesis is the concept of the "free individual" as author and agent of her actions and destiny. This mythic individual is also the cornerstone of "bourgeoise-liberal formal democracy" that posits society as a collection of sovereign individuals organized as a "freely-given and 'natural' coming together into a *consensus* which legitimates the exercise of power" (Hall 1979, p. 339). Talk shows participate in this construction of consensus through their individualization of social conflict effected through therapeutic discourse.

◆ Ideological Containment Strategies in Talk Shows

Talk shows cannot guarantee solutions to the problems they present, but their appeal is based on the *possibility* of resolution, and in particular on the premise that talking is itself a solution. . . . This is also a grounding assumption of therapy—that communication can ameliorate or is a necessary condition for resolving intra- and interpersonal problems. As White notes, "The therapeutic ethos is an incitement to talk, to talk constantly, of oneself to others. It regenerates conversation" (1992, p. 23).

Talk shows are premised on this idealization of communication; how could it be otherwise in a cultural form whose substance and purpose is the production of talk? The programs are sites for the popularized display of the "talking cure" where the act of communicating is intended to lead to new information, insights, behavior, and identities. . . .

A key containment strategy is the relentless personalization of issues and experiences through topical frames. The ideological character of topicality becomes apparent if we consider alternative ways of framing a particular episode. For example, an episode of *The Oprah Winfrey Show*

titled "Couples Who Fight About Money" would take on a quite different meaning if it were recast as "Money, Power, and Gender" or "Gendered Inequality Within the Economy." Granted, these latter titles wouldn't make for catchy promo teasers, but they would provide a definition of the "problem" at odds with the function and values of the programs and of TV in general.

The topics set the parameters for who appears on the programs, what they are entitled to talk about, and their relationship to each other and to the host and audience. Guests are initially solicited through the mechanism of the topic, their stories are inserted into this frame, their connection to other guests is mediated by their shared link to the topic, and they are guided back to it if the conversation strays. The host has primary responsibility for keeping guests "on topic," and most guests (and studio audience members) accept this framing device and use it to keep themselves and fellow panelists in line. I have often witnessed a host or guest remark, "That's not the topic of the show," usually to keep someone from pursuing a line of talk that is troubling in some way. I will return to this point in discussing transgressions of the shows' narrative boundaries.

Another personalizing strategy is labeling guests according to their relationship to the topic. Talk show guests are given on-screen tags: "Jean—wants her husband to get a job," "John—cheated on his wife," "Kathy—says her husband is a mama's boy." The tags help fuse guests and topic and personify the day's problem; they also make the problem a distinct property of that particular individual, objectifying the guest *as* her problem and nothing else. The effect is to abstract these people and their troubles from the larger social world in which their everyday lives, their struggles, and the structural determinants of those problems exist. . . .

I turn now to examples of containment strategies. "I Caught My Father Cheating on My Mother" (*Sally Jessy Raphael*) features four adult children, the unfaithful parent of two of them, and a psychotherapist. Among the family pairs are a young woman (Suzanne) and her professional father (Milt), and a woman from a poor background and her 35-year-old daughter (Sue and Sandy). Milt says he left his family because he and his wife had "grown apart." His affair with another woman was based on shared work interests. Sue left her family for another man when she discovered she was pregnant by him. Because her husband had received a vasectomy ten years earlier, Sue feared his anger at her infidelity even though she *and* her daughter acknowledge that he was repeatedly unfaithful throughout the marriage. Mother and daughter describe a chaotic home with few financial resources and a husband/father who was illiterate, abusive, and frequently absent. Sue says she left her five children because she had no way to support them and feared her lover would abandon her if she brought her kids along.

These family stories are united through the topic frame ("cheating parents") and focus on the anger and pain of the children who suffered their parents' abandonment. The therapeutic intent, promoted by Raphael and the psychotherapist, involves encouraging the adult children to express their feelings, getting the parents to apologize for their actions, and helping both generations achieve new insight and improved relationships by communicating openly. The effect of this orchestration is to construct a meaning for these families' troubles that sidesteps analysis of the social forces that create problems for people and that create structural differences in the options and resources available for solving them for people differently positioned within society. In the program, Sue and Milt are the same—people who cheated on their spouses and left their children. The disparity between their experiences, their socioeconomic classes, and their genders—that is, the difference in their actual social power—is insignificant within the confines of the frame. Suzanne and Sandy are also the same. The fact that Suzanne's father is a

successful upper-middle-class professional and Sandy's is an illiterate laborer does not count.

"Couples Who Fight About Money" (*Oprah Winfrey*) includes three couples—two white, one black—and a psychologist. In the white marriages, conflict centers on husbands who control their wives by controlling (and withholding) the family finances. One of these couples is apparently working class; the husband of the other is described as "a millionaire," though it is obvious he and his wife are nouveau riche rather than "old money." Conflict for the black couple arises between the wife, an employed professional, and the husband, who floats between low-paying, unsatisfying jobs while being supported by his spouse. All three couples are encouraged to fight openly on the air according to the dictates of the topical script. Several questions from Winfrey and the studio audience and comments by the guest expert make links between gender issues and money conflicts, but the racial and class dimensions of the different couples' conflicts remain submerged and unarticulated. For example, the audience does not sympathize equally with the white wives; comments suggest that the working-class woman has been unfairly denied life's ordinary pleasures by her skinflint husband, whereas the millionaire's wife is seen as greedy, irresponsible with money, and deserving of her husband's ire. In the case of the black couple, audience comments favor the wife while implicitly endorsing both the "naturalness" of the male as primary breadwinner and the racist view of blacks as gender deviant (e.g., "strong" women and "shiftless" men). Because the different intersections of race, class, and gender for blacks and whites cannot be accommodated within the topic frame, the narrative of marital discord permits an acknowledgment of gender issues only—a logical solution given the target audience. The result is a displacement of class and race issues onto gender—a phenomenon also noted by Jhally and Lewis in a study of audience responses to *The Cosby*

Show (where viewers substituted racial categories for class categories) and in Aronowitz's study of popular representations of the working class (where class discourse is displaced onto gender/sex relations).[19] The problem perpetually "unproblematized" in these talk shows is that of social class. The near absence of public discussion of class issues in the media, as Jhally and Lewis argue, suggests that "American society does not have a way of talking about one of its central organizing features" (1992, p. 70).

"Secrets From the Past" (*Oprah Winfrey*) features three guests whose secrets have inadvertently come to light and a psychotherapist who offers strategies for coping with this exposure. Bryan's ("past caught up with him") secret, that as a young man he had prostituted himself with men and was convicted, was revealed when he was subpoenaed years later to testify in a murder case. He explains his past actions as economic necessity. The oldest of six children, Bryan describes a childhood of poverty, abuse, and abandonment. His father was imprisoned for raping one of Bryan's sisters; the children were shuttled between foster homes before being returned to a mother ill equipped to support them. Bryan says he was obsessed as a boy with keeping his family together and turned to shoplifting, petty theft, selling blood, and ultimately prostitution to help out financially. He eventually put this past behind him, moved to another state, married, and got a job in a small town, but still "lived in fear" that his "secret" would destroy his new life.

Bryan's story presents an opportunity to explore the desperation that poverty breeds and its impact on children, who now constitute one of the largest segments of poor Americans. The topic and therapeutic intent of the show preclude that exploration, however. Winfrey and the psychotherapist focus on the "toxicity" of secrets, the "loss of self" they result in, and the "healing" to be gained from revealing them. Most of the studio audience members

appear to accept this framing and are supportive of Bryan's desire to "come clean" and overcome his "toxic shame." One man in the audience, however, is hostile to Bryan's statement that he had done "what was necessary at the time."

Audience member: He chose it. No one forced him to do that. If we all did that where would we be?

Bryan: Have you never done anything you regret? Of course I've made mistakes. . . .

Audience member: When you steal a piece of candy from the 5 and 10 you're ashamed, when you're a kid. I mean, c'mon, there are other ways he could have lived.

This exchange points to a struggle between structural and individual explanations of behavior, but one that cannot be resolved, or even adequately explored, within the show's narrative boundaries. Not only does the talk show form discourage that examination, the participants themselves inhibit it. Both Bryan and his accuser frame their comments within the code of individual responsibility and choice. The audience member rejects the notion of social determinants on behavior and the therapeutic emphasis on motives over deeds and emotional healing over moral atonement. Bryan, too, is caught between these two positions, simultaneously describing his youthful behavior as the result of social necessity and as a personal moral failure. Immediately following the exchange, an older woman in the audience stands and commends Bryan's efforts to "admit his mistakes." The audience, which has been silent during the man's critique, breaks into applause. The psychotherapist then asserts that "the issue is not that anything goes," but how shame forces people to keep secrets. Winfrey echoes this position before cutting to a commercial.

Such occasions of competing stories—when social conflicts beneath the topics surface—occur fairly often in these programs and provide the moments of tension that can make talk shows so compelling. But such clashes are rarely sustained, and almost never explicitly discussed, because topicality, personalization, and therapeutic discourse are such effective framing devices. Thus, Bryan's problem is the shame that plagues people with secrets, not the social conditions that limited his horizons as a child. The solution is individual (how he deals with his shame), rather than social (why there were *not* "other ways he could have lived" and why this might also be true for millions of other young people in similar circumstances). The man in the audience's inability, or unwillingness, to imagine that people's ranges of choices are determined by anything outside their personal control, and Bryan's own ambivalence on this point, reflects what DeMott calls Americans' inability to "think straight about class": "Several hallowed concepts—independence, individualism, choice—are woven into this web of illusion and self-deception. But presiding over the whole stands the icon of *classlessness*."[20]

◆ *Ideological Breakdown in the Talking Cure*

If the transmutation of social conflict into individual problems is an underlying object of these programs, the fact that they address these conflicts at all means they always run the risk of failing to contain them within the boundaries of therapeutic narrative. I turn now to such a transgression and its management. "Don't Tell Me How to Raise My Kids" (*Sally Jessy Raphael*) features guests who have been "victimized" by child abuse laws, including Sandra, a black woman from southern California who had been jailed for beating her eleven-year-old son with a belt. (The boy had called the police himself.) Although

Sandra ("says it's OK to beat her children with a belt") is presented as an individual example of the generic topic, she refuses to submit passively to the narrow identity it imposes. She does assert that how she raises her children is her own business, thereby affirming the ideology of individual rights, but her argument is also referenced through her belonging to a particular racial/class grouping (blacks at or near the lower end of the socioeconomic ladder). Her narrative is articulated around her experience as a member of a specific social group that she believes authorizes parenting methods at odds with those advocated as universal by Raphael and a white expert. Sandra had beaten her son when he came home after dark in direct violation of the family rules. She justifies her actions in terms of her specific autobiographical experience as a black woman living in a state "where a man can be handcuffed and beat by ten policemen, and taxpayers pay for their defense."

Sandra: If he was out in the street and the police seen him doing something wrong and they beat him in the head, that is justifiable force. But when I beat him, as his mother, a loving mother, concerned and loving my child, then I go to jail, my child goes to foster care. Now what kind of sense does that make? That don't make no kind of sense.

Later in the show, white pediatrician Dorothy Greenbaum states that physical punishment of children is unnecessary, a parental failure. A second white expert, Dr. Don Boys, head of the conservative Christian organization Common Sense, retorts, "That's your opinion," to which Greenbaum replies, "That is my educated, medical, pediatric opinion." At this point Sandra interrupts and speaks passionately to the pediatrician; their exchange illustrates the multilayered tensions that the show must negotiate.

Sandra: Excuse me ... excuse me. You know what? ... You are a white mother. I'm a black mother. It's a totally different situation. When my kids walk out in the street. ...

Greenbaum: I can't believe you're going to say that.

Sandra: I don't care what you can believe. That's the truth. That's the way it is. And as long as we deny it, as black people, that it ain't no difference when our sons walk out on the street, that's why they keep getting killed. That's why they keep selling dope. That's why our kids are always victims. Now you're a doctor. You're a Ph.D. I'm a loving, Christian mother. That's what I am.

Greenbaum: I'm a loving mother too.

Here Sandra raises the issue of race and questions the universality of Greenbaum's expertise, and in so doing pushes at the boundaries of the topical frame; she pulls in the world outside the studio to argue that the identities and actions of herself and the pediatrician are differently situated in society. The doctor resists this assertion of difference by identifying herself and Sandra equally as "mothers." Raphael joins the exchange to clarify the basis of Greenbaum's expertise—"Isn't it M.D.?" (rather than Ph.D.), thereby displaying Sandra's lack of familiarity with such distinctions. Raphael then gives the floor to Greenbaum ("Would you like to respond?"), who returns to the troubling issue of race. (During this exchange, Sandra shouts while Greenbaum remains calm and clinical.)

Greenbaum: What I would like to say is, it would be devastating to think that we are actually going to say that there's a different way to raise a child based upon race. I cannot believe you're going to say that.

Sandra: It *is*. You know what? You know what? You can't believe it—You can't believe it because your child is not black. You're not raising a black child in this society. That's why you can't believe it. I can believe it because I live it.

Greenbaum: I have to tell you that our training, the way I look at the world, the way all of us who are pediatricians—

Sandra: You look at it through blue eyes, I've got brown eyes. That's how you look at it. I'm looking at it the way I look at it, through brown eyes and black kinky hair and brown skin.

Greenbaum: Every child is a human being.

Sandra: That's right. That's right.

Greenbaum: You don't whip an animal and you don't whip a child.

At this point the conversation has clearly violated the parameters of the topical frame, and Raphael moves in to derail that detour and repersonalize Sandra's problem.

Raphael: Okay, I have a little problem here. I thought we were going to discuss children. We got into race relations. And I'm not quite sure how these things happen to me. [She looks at Greenbaum, who nods and smiles in agreement.]

Greenbaum: I don't know how that happened either.

The two women's shared confusion here reflects a key element of white privilege—the luxury of being able to ignore race when it is convenient to do so.[21] Sandra makes a final attempt to resist Raphael's control through the mechanism of the topic by comparing a man in California who had been jailed for kicking a dog to a woman who killed a fifteen-year-old black girl and went free: "So don't tell me nothing about whupping no dog and whupping no human being."[22] At this point Don Boys remarks: "There's no doubt there's a lot of inequities." This gives Raphael a chance to terminate the transgression; she formally recognizes Boys, who quickly shifts gears from the specificity of those "inequities" to the "problem with Dr. Spock."

This episode illustrates the conflictual terrain upon which talk shows engage in their ideological work. That work is ongoing because television operates in a social world fraught with tensions, hierarchies of power, competing interests, perspectives, and experiences. The talk show form may seek to manage those tensions—to resolve symbolically what is denied in reality—but it cannot ultimately eliminate them. Raphael may end a particular line of talk or silence a problematic guest (indeed, Sandra never uttered another word on the show), but the social tensions that generate conversations like this one live on in the world inside and outside the studio. Television is "an inherently conflictual medium" precisely because of its centrality in producing and circulating public meanings, including the meaning of social and cultural identities. If the talk show form encourages narrators such as Sandra to take up "already mapped-out subject positions," it also provides them occasions to tell stories that have been deemed "culturally unspeakable," and in so doing, to exercise agency and become "subjects of narrative" (Smith and Watson, "Introduction," p. 14). Here we see the irreconcilable contradiction of TV talk shows: in order to carry out the ideological work of containing and organizing the meaning of social conflicts, they also give voice to those who live those conflicts.

The Repression ◆ of the Social

Talk shows are particularly resonant for female viewers both because women's efforts to achieve social equality have involved getting their so-called private concerns recognized as legitimate *public* issues and because the narrative form corresponds to women's experience, learned discursive style, and relational orientation. *The Oprah Winfrey Show* and *Sally Jessy Raphael* are compelling, as are therapeutic explanations generally, because the structural conflicts they present are lived and felt at a personal level. The pain and anger are real, as is our desire to find ways of understanding and overcoming them. As the major consumers of therapy,[23] and the gender assigned primary responsibility for emotional work, women appear to be especially susceptible to this way of framing problems—one that helps obscure other possible interpretive frameworks and solutions.

Although social tensions generate the personal problems in TV talk shows, the way they are narrated discourages our full recognition of those problems *as social*. The TV personality system, the para-sociality and simulated intimacy of the talk show form, the synthetic personalization common in the media, and the therapeutic discourse of the programs strive to confine social conflict within narratives of individual and interpersonal dysfunction. Within those confines, all problems seem to yield to therapeutic intervention—to treatment through the "talking cure." Therapeutic discourse proposes that we change ourselves, our attitudes and behavior, without also recognizing that our identities and actions are determined by and respond to social conditions that will not change simply because we decide to interpret and handle them differently on an individual basis. Operating at the level of intra- and interpersonal relations, therapeutic discourse translates the political into the psychological. Problems are personal (or familial) and have no origin or target outside the individual's own psychic processes.[24] Because the topics addressed by these shows are at root political problems that require organized political action, they cannot be finally resolved through therapeutic intervention. There is a radical difference between saying, "I'm ill, I've been abused, I need recovery," and saying, "I'm angry, I'm oppressed, my oppression is based on structural inequities that I share with others, with whom I must work to change society." This difference has also been criticized by feminists who question the move to redefine women's problems as individual emotional illness (e.g., "codependency") rather than as a consequence of gender oppression, and many women's own embrace of that redefinition.[25]

Although therapeutic communication might be personally beneficial, it may be so by helping us adapt to a social order that requires analysis itself. . . . These talk shows do make public many problems that once were deemed private—especially women's concerns that have historically been relegated to the private sphere; they give voice to people who have historically been silenced (women, people of color, working-class people); and they dramatize the embodiment of selected public issues in personal experience. At the same time, their narrative form discourages the adoption of critical engagement with and reflection on those problems in favor of immediate identification and catharsis, and undermines the ability to take these problems seriously in the service of making them entertaining. The televised talking cure manages conflict and crisis by relegating them to the domain of "personal" stories that can then be folded into a disciplinary, therapeutic narrative. In so doing, the talk show form drives a wedge between the personal and the political—encouraging us to forget that

autobiographical narratives are also always stories about our shared social world.

Notes

1. The use of the individual psyche to explain social phenomena and the belief that social problems can be resolved with psychological management are reflections of what critics have identified as a "therapeutic ethos" in contemporary American culture. See T. J. Jackson Lears, "From Salvation to Self-Realization: Advertising and the Therapeutic Roots of Consumer Culture, 1880-1830," in R. W. Fox and T. J. Jackson Lears, eds., *The Culture of Consumption: Critical Essays in American History, 1880-1980* (New York: Pantheon, 1980), 1-38; Robert N. Bellah, Richard Madsen, William L. Sullivan, Ann Swidler, and Steven M. Tipton, *Habits of the Heart: Individualism and Commitment in American Life* (Berkeley: University of California Press, 1985); Eva Illouz, "Reason Within Passion: Love in Women's Magazines," *Critical Studies in Mass Communication* 8 (1991): 231-48 (page references for all subsequent citations of this work are included in the text in parentheses); Debra Grodin, "The Interpreting Audience: The Therapeutics of Self-Help Book Reading," *Critical Studies in Mass Communication* 8 (1991): 404-20; Mimi White, *Tele-Advising: Therapeutic Discourse in American Television* (Chapel Hill: University of North Carolina Press, 1992) (page references for all subsequent citations of this work are included in the text in parentheses); Wendy Simonds, *Women and Self-Help Culture: Reading Between the Lines* (New Brunswick, NJ: Rutgers University Press, 1992) (page references for all subsequent citations of this work are included in the text in parentheses).

2. *The Oprah Winfrey Show* is the top-rated daytime talk show in the United States, with a daily audience of fourteen million, 76 percent of whom are women eighteen years of age and older, according to its syndicator, King World Productions. The audience for *Sally Jessy Raphael* is eight million, according to the show's publicity department; a spokesperson said

"most of our viewers are women," but gave no concrete figures (personal correspondence, November 1993).

3. Relatively inexpensive to produce, talk shows are one of the fastest-growing formats in television. Besides the networks' morning and late-night talk programs, there were more than thirty syndicated talk shows in the 1993-94 lineup. See Monte Williams, "Voices of 30-plus Exclaim: Can We Talk?" *Advertising Age* (March 8, 1993): S-6. Their proliferation also reflects the industry's conscious decision to target women eighteen to forty-nine years old as "the most desirable television audience (because of their consumer roles)." Douglas Kellner, *Television and the Crisis of Democracy* (Boulder, CO: Westview, 1990), 120.

4. Miriam Greenspan, *A New Approach to Women and Therapy* (New York: McGraw-Hill, 1983), 11.

5. Dean Barnlund, "Introduction to Therapeutic Communication," in D. C. Barnlund, ed., *Interpersonal Communication: Survey and Studies* (New York: Houghton Mifflin, 1968); Gary Kreps, "The Nature of Therapeutic Communication," in Gary Gumpert and Sandra Fish, eds., *Talking to Strangers: Mediated Therapeutic Communication* (Norwood, NJ: Ablex, 1990).

6. Edward E. Sampson, *Justice and the Critique of Pure Psychology* (New York: Plenum, 1983).

7. Mary-Ellen Brown, "The Politics of Soaps: Pleasure and Feminine Empowerment," *Australian Journal of Cultural Studies* 4, no. 2 (1987): 1-25; John Fiske, *Television Culture* (London: Methuen, 1987).

8. Paolo Carpignano et al., "Chatter in the Age of Electronic Reproduction: Talk Television and the 'Public Mind,'" *Social Text* 26 (1991): 48. Page references for all subsequent citations of this work are included in the text in parentheses.

9. John Langer, "Television's Personality System," *Media, Culture & Society* 4 (1981): 352-53 (page references for all subsequent citations of this work are included in the text in parentheses).

10. Donald Horton and R. Richard Wohl, "Mass Communication as Para-social Interaction: Observations on Intimacy at a Distance," in James E. Combs and Michael Mansfield, eds.,

Drama in Life: The Uses of Communication in Society (New York: Hastings House, 1976), 213 (page references for all subsequent citations of this work are included in the text in parentheses).

11. A prime example of this familiarity was displayed on a May 1992 episode of *The Oprah Winfrey Show* devoted to letters from viewers.

12. Robert Cathcart and Gary Gumpert, "Mediated Interpersonal Communication: Toward a New Typology," in Gary Gumpert and Sandra Fish, eds., *Talking to Strangers: Mediated Therapeutic Communication* (Norwood, NJ: Ablex, 1990), 46.

13. Sidonie Smith and Julia Watson, "Introduction," in Sidonie Smith and Julia Watson, eds., *Getting a Life: Everyday Uses of Autobiography* (Minneapolis: University of Minnesota Press, 1996), 11.

14. John Corner," The Interview as Social Encounter," in Paddy Scannell, ed., *Broadcast Talk* (London: Sage, 1991), 32.

15. Todd Gitlin, "Television's Screens: Hegemony in Transition," in Michael Apple, ed., *Cultural and Economic Reproduction in Education* (London: Routledge, 1982), 211.

16. See also Anthony Giddens, *Modernity and Identity: Self and Society in the Late Modern Age* (Stanford, CA: Stanford University Press, 1991).

17. See Ma'sud Zavarzadeh, *Seeing Films Politically* (Albany: State University of New York Press, 1991); Walter Davis, *Inwardness and Existence: Subjectivity in/and Hegel, Heidegger, Marx, and Freud* (Madison: University of Wisconsin Press, 1989).

18. Wendy Kaminer, *I'm Dysfunctional, You're Dysfunctional: The Recovery Movement and Other Self-Help Fashions* (Reading, PA: Addison-Wesley, 1992); see also Gary Gumpert and Sandra Fish, eds., *Talking to Strangers: Mediated Therapeutic Communication* (Norwood, NJ: Ablex, 1990); and Simonds, *Women and Self Help Culture*.

19. Sut Jhally and Justin Lewis, *Enlightened Racism: The Cosby Show, Audiences, and the Myth of the American Dream* (Boulder, CO: Westview, 1992) (page references for all subsequent citations of this work are included in the text in parentheses); Stanley Aronowitz, "Working Class Culture in the Age of Electronic

Reproduction," in Ian Angus and Sut Jhally, eds., *Cultural Politics in Contemporary America* (New York: Routledge, 1989), 135-50.

20. Benjamin DeMott, *The Imperial Middle: Why Americans Can't Think Straight About Class* (New Haven, CT: Yale University Press, 1992), 9.

21. Peggy McIntosh, "Understanding Correspondences Between White Privilege and Male Privilege Through Women's Studies Work," paper presented at the National Women's Studies Association annual meeting, Atlanta, 1987.

22. Significantly, Sandra supports her arguments about race by referring to the cases of Rodney King and Latasha Harlins (the teenager murdered by a Korean grocer in 1991)—both of which were central sources of black anger in the L.A. riots a few months later. See Mike Davis, "Urban America Sees Its Future: In L.A., Burning All Illusions," *Nation* (June 1, 1992): 743-46.

23. Women make up nearly two-thirds of the adult population of community mental health centers, psychiatric hospitals, and outpatient clinics, and an estimated 84 percent of all private psychotherapy patients are female; Greenspan, *A New Approach,* 5. More than two-thirds of prescriptions written each year for psychotropic drugs are for women. See Nancy Russo, *A Women's Mental Health Agenda* (Washington, DC: American Psychological Association, 1985), 0-21.

24. The ascendant paradigm in psychology—that of reducing emotional problems to genetic, chemical, or neurological causes—is an even more vivid attempt to naturalize (and desocialize) people's problems.

25. Harriet Goldhor Lerner, "Problems for Profit?" *Women's Review of Books* (April 1990): 15; Betty Tallen, "Co-dependency: A Feminist Critique," *Sojourner: The Women's Forum* (January 1990): 20-21; Susan Faludi, *Backlash: The Undeclared War Against American Women* (New York: Crown, 1991).

52

THE CASE AGAINST SLEAZE TV

◆   Jo Tavener

From their inception issue-oriented daytime talk shows have provoked criticism from the mainstream press. Though such criticism arises from their transgression of the accepted boundaries of public decorum, the immediate cause is more often than not a rise in their ratings.[1] When *The Phil Donahue Show* topped the ratings of *The Tonight Show* in 1979, an article appeared in *Newsweek* (29 October 1979) that expressed the dismay and distaste of the dominant culture: "One sometimes suspects that Donahue's idea of a perfect guest is an interracial lesbian couple who have a child by artificial insemination. Sure enough, that couple appeared last March" (p. 77).

In the February 1998 sweeps *The Jerry Springer Show* received a 9.4 rating/22 share and in March the show topped *Oprah Winfrey* with an 8.1 national rating, compared to her 6.8 (*Broadcasting & Cable*, 6 April 1998, p. 16). Why had Springer's ratings risen 183% in only one year? How had he managed to top the Queen of daytime? Such were the questions addressed by the media as talk shows once again provoked moral panic. *Time* (30 March 1998) quoted a farmer from Oregon, "It's white trailer trash! I love it!" and an 81-year-old grandmother (who had driven from Indiana with her granddaughter); "I hope they fight. They

NOTE: From "Media, Morality, and Madness: The Case Against Sleaze TV," in *Critical Studies in Media Communication*, Vol. 17, No. 1, March 2000 (pp. 63-85). Copyright © 2000. Used by permission of the National Communication Association.

better fight." Though such audience responses point to the show's broad appeal, the media was more alarmed by *Springer's* popularity among the coveted 18-to-34 and 18-to-49 demographic brackets. A special on "E!" network, *Jerry Springer: Behind the Scenes* (7 June 1998), focused on this audience segment. Its findings were underwhelming. As the show's promo goes, "Everyone's talkin' Jerry" because Jerry delivers. What the studio audience enjoyed most were the obscenity-laced yelling matches and the bar room brawls. Guests who were interviewed stated that they appeared on the show because of its lack of public decorum. One guest said she went on the show to humiliate an ex-boyfriend; another stated that she wanted to have it out no holds barred.

More upsetting still, though not for "E!" whose *Talk Soup* plays ironically off talk show excessiveness, was the implication of *Springer's* success. As noted in *Time* (p. 63), the "era of niceness" was over. To explain the rise of *Jerry Springer*, the *Time* article glossed the recent history of the genre. The success of *Ricki Lake* and her more confrontational style had led to a "clutch of imitators and a new round of fretting about trash television" (p. 63). "Encouraged" by a drop in ratings, brought on by such competition, and "encouraged" by the Jenny Jones scandal and the success of *The Rosie O'Donnell Show*, Rivera and Lake opted for Oprah's more high-minded style.[2] A "nastiness vacuum [was] created and Springer was there to fill it" (p. 63).

From 1979 to 1998 daytime talk shows have been uniformly denigrated as "trash TV" by cultural critics and the mainstream press. Each transgression of civility, accompanied by a rise in ratings, has repeatedly provoked moral panic. In 1995 William Bennett launched a campaign against what he described as "the giant popular culture sleaze machine" claiming that talk shows and other offensive forms of popular culture were polluting the "human environment, a kind of tropism toward the sordid." "[What] the nation desperately need[ed]," he claimed, was "more opportunities for moral uplift. . . . Progress [could] be made through moral suasion and justifiable public discontent" (in Shattuc, 1997, p. 144). A similar critique was expressed on the left. In *The Nation* (1995, 5 June p. 801) Jill Nelson wrote that though she found the Jenny Jones murder "frightening," what was more "terrifying" was "the daily killing off of any sense of understanding, connectedness, collective responsibility and the potential for redemption that these shows foster." While Nelson and Bennett disagree about the causes of cultural pollution and public incivility, they agree about the dangers that talk shows present for the health of the body politic. They both assume that cultural objects could and should be evaluated in terms of their moral value and their ability to inculcate the proper beliefs and norms of behavior for the nation at large.

This [chapter] will explore the daytime talk show as a site around which moral panics circulate. Such panics are ideologically key to the re-establishment of a moral center and the formation of a national consensus. . . . Taking the sensational talk show as a prime example, what is at stake in the controversy over popular culture is nothing less than the ongoing struggle over who will represent the nation. In contrast to both Bennett and Nelson, the threat to the nation that such shows represent arises from their ability to destabilize the articulation between "high" culture and the nation. . . . Whether moral panics touch down around talk shows, gangsta rap, or cartoon characters, their goal is to disarticulate "the people" from "the popular" in order to re-establish the moral authority of the middle-class moral order and its version of "America." . . .

Culture as the ◆ Republic's Moral Realm

Implicit in the construction of popular culture/media moral panics is the high/low distinction that evolved during the Gilded Age as culture was afforded a new and central role in relation to the nation. Colonial Americans had placed their faith in republican virtue as the necessary ingredient for a just and egalitarian society. Such virtue, they believed, arose from a nation of freehold property owners whose economic independence enabled a freedom of mind for the contemplation of a disinterested common good. With the advent of what Michael Schudson (1978, p. 58) calls "the democratic market society" of the Jacksonian era, culture was asked to provide a similar ground for the creation of a similar virtue.[3] Its separation from marketplace aggressions and its emphasis on self-cultivation as the basis for individual and societal regeneration would provide the Republic once again with its moral center (Trachtenberg, 1982). Culture would create its requisite national character. By the 1870s, the mid-Victorian notion of culture was more narrowly defined by the established and "educated" Yankee elites as religion, the high arts, and formal education, and as "polite cultivation and manners" as well as "genteel styles of speech and dress" (Trachtenberg, p. 143). Understood as "high culture," it was opposed to the plebeian or "low" culture of the masses, the saloons of "sporting-male culture" and the Bowery of popular pleasures. While "high" culture was perceived as positive and morally uplifting, "low" culture was denigrated as negative and immoral. As Alan Trachtenberg (1982, p. 143) notes in his study of the Gilded Age, high culture was conceived as "the official middle-class image of America" and celebrated as a "democratizing influence, accessible to all those willing to raise themselves to the status of American. . . . Culture and refinement conveyed a political message, a vision of a harmonious body politic under the rule of reason, light, and sweet, cheerful emotion."

During the Gilded Age the conflation of "high culture" with the nation masked the class conflicts through which such a notion of culture was formed as today it masks the class inflection of contemporary "official" culture. While such a conflation gives the appearance of consensus between the ruling class factions and the nation, it actually signals the presence of social conflict. As noted by Trachtenberg (1982) and theorized by Antonio Gramsci (1971), symbolic struggles over the meaning of the nation represent very real struggles over who will lead the state in the name of "the people." They are intimately connected, in terms of legitimacy, to political struggles over who will control the economic and social resources of the nation and the purposes to which such resources are put.

For more than a hundred years, the high/low distinction has been used not only to denigrate "low" or "popular culture" but also to authenticate (what I call) "the middle-class moral order" and legitimate the cultural and moral leadership of its ruling class factions. The current panic over television violence and the media's negative effects is only the latest incarnation of such legitimation struggles. The "new" moral panic over incivility in public life is a very old story. So too is the "new" moral panic over popular culture. The two have been connected for much of their history perceived as creating a powerful threat to the moral health of the body politic. Clinton's strategic use of Sista Soljah during the 1992 presidential campaign is one example of this rhetorical deployment. Another is William Bennett's call (in *Newsweek*, 1995, 6 November, p. 46) for "constructive hypocrisy." "Civilization depends," he argues, "on keeping most perversions under wraps" (p. 46). Talk shows, gangsta rap, such cultural "heroes" as Madonna and "bad boy" Dennis Rodman—these are the "nightmares of depravity" that "pollute youthful minds" and incite the passions of the "popular classes" (p. 46). . . .

The following year Benjamin Demott noted in *The Nation* (1996, 9 December) that civility had become the catchword of public life, the "new" standard of propriety for "the national conversation" taking place in the media as well as on Capitol

Hill. Feeding on the hysteria over media violence, the call for a national code of civility generalized the fear among certain factions of the "leader class," and its allies, that American society was being undermined by a host of malcontents: by the drug, women-hating, and cop-baiting rap culture of the degenerative "underclass"; by talk show sensationalism broadcasting the perversity of American life; and by talk-radio hosts who fan the fires of white, male, working-class discontent similar to that of the militia movement. According to Demott, the leader-class call for civility was an attempt to rein in such voices and demand a style of speech and address for the democratic polity that distinguished between reasonable and responsible talk and a violent, disruptive "hate" speech. Rather than acknowledge such incivility as the expression of an "impotent fury at corroded leader-class values and standards" and a "flat-out rejection of leader-class claims of respect," as Demott (p. 14) argued, the "leader class define[d] public discontent as incivility and identifie[d] such incivility as the cause of the national distemper."

. . . Moral panics displace complex social issues of political importance onto the cultural terrain and attempt to resolve them through a discourse that attributes a moral dimension to culture. . . . Though such panics ebb and flow from one historical conjuncture to another, there has been an unrelenting antagonism between dominant values and those embraced by popular culture. That they have routinely involved the media in their construction arises from the media's production of a mass culture national in scope and popular in taste.

The leader-class attacks on the popular media have been strategic here, for they divert attention away from the meaning of sociocultural conflict by blaming the messenger. They mystify the class character of cultural conflict and deploy a nationalistic rhetoric that defines the stakes in terms of the "common good, civic trust (and) communal participation" (Demott, p. 12).

The nation is perceived as under threat, not from its ruling-class factions, but from those who refuse to defer to their "better" judgment and respect their higher moral purpose. In effect, the current hysteria over talk shows and other forms of popular culture is a means of creating, circulating, and legitimating a broader set of panics that enables the formation of alliances between groups that would otherwise oppose one another. This is why critiques from the left, like that of Jill Nelson's, are so worrisome. Embracing culture as a moral realm, they help forge a national consensus that denigrates the very people and silences the very voices they otherwise support. The creation of moral panic around public incivility has enabled the leader class to justify its call for greater governmental surveillance of fringe groups, the "underclass," and the popular mass media. By so doing, it has bolstered its claim to leader-class status, reasserting its moral authority and national leadership in the regeneration of public life and the revitalization of American culture.

Media Moral Panics ◆

. . . According to Stuart Hall et al. (1978), moral panics are ideological frameworks that prescribe the meaning and moral significance of concrete events and behaviors. Furthermore, those who identify and define such panics are the very ones who provide the official response—the politicians and other government officials such as the police and the judiciary, as well as editorial page columnists, television pundits, and other "public" intellectuals whom the media designates as authoritative sources and appropriate molders of public opinion (p. 30). . . .

Though panics are identified and defined in the media by sources that it considers appropriate and authoritative, these are the very sources that criticize the media for its negative effects—its misrepresentation of reality, its misinformation, and its sensationalism (pp. 53-76). The media is seen as either instigating or intensifying the very social ills around which panics form. It is not surprising then that whatever the panic—whether it be around family values, drugs, or crime—it is always linked to the media and its negative effects on society. Here, then, is the dilemma. For moral panics to occur, they need the collusion of the media; at the same time, the media is perceived as part of the problem.

The dilemma is partially resolved by the high/low distinction that separates the "respectable" media of *Nightline* and *60 Minutes* from the "disreputable" media of television sensationalism, from *A Current Affair* to *Geraldo* to *Ricki Lake* and the like. . . . The high/low distinction provides a means for cultural critics and media effects scholars to stand outside mass culture with a slide rule that not only masks the class inflection of the "official" moral discourse but also legitimizes its use.[4] . . .

◆ **Notes**

1. See Jane Shattuc, *The Talking Cure: TV Talk Shows and Women*, for an excellent analysis of the relationship between talk show demographics, the economics of syndication, and the industrial construction of femininity. Also see Jane Feuer, *Seeing Through the Eighties*, for an illuminating look at the relationship between television, most notably prime time soaps and politics during the Reagan era. For a more extended bibliography, consult the one provided in *The Talking Cure*.

2. By 1995 the confrontational style of Ricki Lake had been rationalized. With the routine staging of "ambush disclosures" talk shows could count on guests to perform on cue. The strategy backfired on *Jenny Jones* when Jonathan Schmitz

was confronted with the disclosure of a secret crush by his gay friend Scott Armedure. Three days later Schmitz killed Armedure apparently for humiliating him on national television.

3. Schudson uses the phrase to signal the articulation of liberal capitalism with specific Jacksonian political reforms, not to infer that the market was a friend of the working man.

4. My use of the term "popular culture" does not signal a disagreement with Richard Ohmann's (1996) description of mass culture. I find the term useful to refer to those "mass" forms of culture that are denigrated by middle-class "official" (formerly "high") culture.

◆ *References* ◆

Demott, B. (1996, December 9). Seduced by civility: Political manners and the crisis of democratic values. *The Nation*, pp. 11-19.

Feur, J. (1995). *Seeing through the eighties: Television and Reaganism.* Durham, NC: Duke University Press.

Gramsci, A. (1971). *Selections from the Prison Notebooks.* Q. Hoare & G. Nowell Smith (Eds.). New York: International.

Hall, S., et al. (1978). *Policing the crisis: Mugging, the state and law and order.* London: Macmillan. 1978.

Nelson, J. (1995, June 5). Talk is cheap. *The Nation*, pp. 800-02.

Ohmann, R. (1996). *Selling culture.* London: Verso.

Schudson, M. (1978). *Discovering the news: The social history of American newspapers.* New York: Basic Books.

Shattuc, J. (1997). *The talking cure: TV talk shows and women.* New York and London: Routledge.

Trachtenberg, A. (1982). *The incorporation of America: Culture and society in the Gilded Age.* New York: Hill and Wang.

53

SITTING DUCKS AND FORBIDDEN FRUITS

◆ Joshua Gamson

. . . On nearly every talk show in which homosexuality makes a showing, some audience member stands up and mocks a guy named Steve. He is spoken of in dismissive, derisive tones, since he apparently receives no mention whatsoever in the Bible. "God made Adam and Eve," the mantra goes, "not Adam and Steve." No one seems to tire of saying or hearing this line; in fact, people seem to be competing to be the one to say it, disappointed when someone else gets to it first, since its rhyme gets a response every time. Applied to women, the saying is a bit more awkward and goofy. "It was Adam and Eve," I watched a woman tell a panel of femme lesbians on *Sally*, "not Jane and Eve." But the meaning is the same: you are not right, you are not loved, you were not created, you do not even really exist. . . .

Moral discussions [about sexual nonconformity] on talk shows take their place in a crucial hearts-and-minds battle for public opinion. They are one important piece of a public conversation over sexual moralities taking place in multiple, interacting sites—educational institutions and electoral politics, most obviously—which sets paths for sexual freedoms or their denial.

NOTE: From *Freaks Talk Back: Tabloid Talk Shows and Sexual Nonconformity*, 1998, pp. 106-137, 254-257, Chicago: University of Chicago Press. Copyright © 1998. Reprinted by permission of The University of Chicago Press.

◆ 553

On talk shows, these moral disputes are especially significant because they are especially constant. A recent Michigan State University study, for instance, found that the theme of sexual propriety was prominent in half the programs sampled;[1] although a concern with propriety is not the same as moral condemnation, the two often go together. A few rough percentages from my own sample of talk show transcripts begin to tell the story. We collected all of the available transcripts from national, daytime, topic-oriented talk shows in which gays, lesbians, cross-dressers, bisexuals, and transgendered or transsexual people were central, for the years 1984-86 and 1994-95. Among other things, we coded the shows for ten different primary themes (topics of sustained discussion, often but not always loosely defined by the producers' frame) such as promiscuity, honesty, the morality of unconventional sexualities and genders, tolerance, telling the difference between male and female or gay and straight, rights and discrimination, mental health and therapy, and so forth. The results offer an interesting snapshot of the talk show field: sex and gender nonconformists sit against a backdrop of extensive, if rarely high-level, moral and political discussion—despite the image of talk shows as hotbeds of amorality and depoliticized pap. Moral themes remain the most common ones to emerge on TV talk shows about sex and gender nonconformity; like political themes, which operate more or less as counterpoints to the moral ones, moral discussions dominate on nearly a fifth of the programs in my sample. While several themes hover at around 10 percent of the programming and a few others at around 5 percent or below, moral discussions were prominent on 17 percent of these shows, and political discussions on 18 percent. Whether or not the shows always have it in mind, and whether they are screaming matches or reasoned arguments, many TV talk shows on homosexuality, bisexuality, or transgenderism turn out to focus on the morality and politics of these statuses. Not all sexual dissidents get

the same kind of treatment, we will soon see, and that fact carries a morality and politics of its own, but the breadth of both moral and political discussion on these programs as a whole is undeniable.

Knowing that moral (and political) talk remains commonplace on daytime television does not, however, tell us much about how such talk works. Like everything else on talk shows, they are certainly messy; propositions fly around without much priority, hosts say one thing and then immediately contradict themselves, conversations are nonlinear and sometimes nearly incoherent. Viewed as a whole strip of activity—that is, seen the way viewers encounter them—talk shows are filled with inconsistent moral assertions, which compete without much pressure toward resolution. Yet the shows themselves clearly structure the sorts of discussions that emerge, encouraging certain themes and ignoring others, loosely scripting the program, as we have seen, in an attempt at managed spontaneity. The discussions of the morality of sex and gender nonconformity are a particularly interesting illustration of how the mix of sloppiness and control turns the tables on the antigay right, producing an unusual acceptance of gay and lesbian, and some bisexual and transgendered, people—a tenuous, easily undermined, conditional acceptance, but a rare Band-Aid on the wounds of the past.

The Bigot as Freak ◆

. . . The religious opposition to nontraditional sex and gender populations is very familiar, from so many years of repetition in this culture: God made things this way, and told us how things should be. Men have penises, women have vaginas; they are meant to come together to procreate and raise children, which also requires monogamous, committed relationships. Other versions—men with vaginas, women and women together, and so on—are perversions of God's plan, wrong and twisted and devilish. They must be turned around, or at least stopped. As a young white man in a tie summarized it from *Sally*'s audience, "How come there are two kinds of people, man and woman? Why wasn't the world created with just one kind of body? There's a reason. God has a balance in everything that He does. We have nuts and bolts. They can't go together, these two, there are nuts and bolts for that."[2] Although it is hard to keep it fresh, this position is also often terrific for television, with its familiarity and simplicity, its resistance to proof but not to counterargument, and the fire-and-brimstone, accusatory, hate-filled words with which it is typically delivered. Along with antigay allies from the world of "research," such as the members of the Family Research Council, right-wing religious guests can wake up the crowd, both in the studio and at home. "In particular shows, a producer says we have to have this element of controversy, we have to have somebody like [radical-right psychologist] Paul Cameron," says an associate producer for one of the more moderate shows. "The producer is going to come to you and say, 'This is all fine, but we have to have some kind of rabble-rousing figure, or something that's going to generate the heat.'" Given the programs' reliance on controversy and conflict, the notion that homosexuality is a moral abomination gets tremendous play on talk shows. The rabble-rousers get the mike for the simple reason that they can rouse the rabble.

So we find a white pastor on *Donahue* saying that God teaches that sodomy is "a deviant, vile affections *[sic]* and it's wrong and it's worthy of death" and that "God hates fags," and a black preacher on another *Donahue* explaining why he would march with the KKK against gays, making the argument that homosexuality cannot be a black thing, since slaves with limp wrists would not be bought, and pointing out that "you don't see no drunkards that are asking for special rights." A radio commentator on *Rolonda* decries the "dangers that lurk inside the homosexual lifestyle" and a 15-year-old boy on another *Rolonda* tells "fags" to "turn or burn, you're going to hell for eternity" while his mother Shirley adds, "When they die and they split hell wide open, that won't comfort them any." A young man on *Oprah* ("opposed to Hannah being gay," reads his identifying caption) argues that "it goes against the Bible and it goes against nature"; bearded Christian John Lofton scolds Oprah on another show for wrinkling her nose and saying she knew she was going to hear "what God thought about this and that," since God, Lofton reports, "says this is a vile sin."[3]

. . . Talk shows make a little room for even the most retro of arguments, as long as they promise to get some backs up. Thus, although talk radio and news are the right wing's media of choice, daytime TV talk makes a great deal of space for such voices of antigay Christian conservatives and their scientific and political allies. And what they have to say, over and over, is consistent: you are not right, you are not loved, you do not even really exist.

Yet daytime TV is not the most welcoming spot for such views. Talk shows are among the few places where right wing paranoia about the liberal media is not so far off. ("Gay and lesbian is about tolerance. It's about acceptance," says one executive producer, a line shared by many other producers with whom I spoke.) For one thing, post-*Ricki* talk shows have often simply gone about the business of accepting lesbian, gay, and bisexual people as members of the tribe, integrating them into shows on nongay topics, such as *Jerry Springer*'s "I Love Someone I Can't Have," "Confess, You Liar!" and "I Can't Stand My Sibling"; *Ricki*'s "Today I'm Going to Break Up My Ex and His New Chick" and "Surprise! I'm Hooking You Up"; *Geraldo*'s "I Saw You on Geraldo and Just Had to Meet You"; *Donahue*'s "Is There Life After a Career in Porn?" *Dennis Prager*'s "Comedians Against Prejudice"; or *Sally*'s "Why I Was Fired."[4] Here it is another identity that defines lesbian, gay, bisexual, or transgendered guests—comic, porn star, vengeful ex, sibling, liar, unrequited lover. There is little room in these shows for complaints that homosexuals are sinners, violators of family values, or sick; these shows are *about* something else, and gay people on them just *are*.

On the many shows that are directly focused on sex and gender nonconformity, moreover, the voices of moral condemnation of homosexuality are almost never endorsed by the show itself, through its host or its overall framing. In general, talk shows fit into four different program types: what I think of as "testimonial" programs, in which a number of people are brought on primarily to tell their interesting stories in what amounts to an interview by the host and audience (what it is like to be a gay teenager, for instance), make up about a quarter of the shows; about another fifth of the shows are organized as "issues" programs, in which guests, host, and audience discuss the political aspects of personal experience, or debate public policy directly (workplace discrimination of sexual minorities, for instance); roughly another fifth of the sample consists of "family conflict" shows, in which relatives, usually of different generations, battle it out for the cameras (for example, parents who don't accept their sons' cross-dressing), and a final fifth concerns "relationship troubles" (men whose wives have cheated on them with other women, for example). Claims that homosexuality is an abnormality and abomination in the eyes of God are made within these program types, usually on programs constructed as political or interpersonal disputes. Morality is always the response, but never quite the question asked by the show.

The *Rolonda* show with the mother and son, for instance, was set up as a discussion of whether teenagers should be allowed school credit for "bashing gays." The *Oprah* show evaluating Hannah's disputed "lifestyle" was arranged as an issue of what sort of schooling gay teens should have, and included progay testimonial statements from lesbian celebrities Melissa Etheridge and Amanda Bearse; the *Oprah* featuring John Lofton was a discussion of gay marriage, and included married bodybuilding sweater guys Bob and Rod Jackson-Paris ("marriage comes from the heart," they say, and "we just got a new puppy, and we have a bird").[5] The God-hates-fags *Donahue* show was an examination of antigay violence, and the black-preacher-against-homosexuals show was a referendum on gay rights, and included black bisexual minister and religion professor Elias Farajaje-Jones ("the problem is that when lesbian, gay, bisexual, transgender people in the African American community have to deal with racism in the dominant culture, as well as with homophobia at home, you know, that makes it all the more painful") and PoMo Afro Homos, an African American gay performance trio ("Brothers, join the struggle. Let's put an end to these demeaning depictions of black gay men as snap-happy sissies perched above the masses. We demand an end, I said an end, to mainstream misappropriation of Negro faggotry!").[6] These are topics seldom drawn from the agenda of the radical right, but instead from, dare I say it, the gay agenda.

Especially since the recent "younging" of talk shows, right-wing antigay voices emerge even more commonly through programs formatted as interpersonal conflicts. As one executive producer explains, it used to always be "right, wrong, Bible thumping," but "that's the old days."

We don't treat it as a controversial issue. It's not enough anymore. It's like, "Okay, I know there's two sides of an issue." These people are going to repeat the same thing, that if God wanted to create Adam and Adam he would have, blah blah blah. It's all been said and done before, so how are we going to advance it? You never get anywhere. You're never going to change the Bible thumpers. Never. No matter what you do. So why make that the issue of an hour show? It is one of those issues that people are so entrenched religiously, emotionally. How are we going to maybe change some of their minds? How are we going to maybe create tolerance? The only way you do it is not inherently make that the focus of the hour, not making it a right or wrong issue. It's not like it's right or wrong, it's more like, "Can this mother accept her son's gay lover?" It's like we're taking the assumption that the mother is accepting the son is gay. What you do is take real people that have real family concerns and they in particular want to try to get over it. Or they themselves within the two of them, the son and the mother, want to have some sort of peace. Like, "My mom kicked me out because I'm gay," okay. We're talking about individuals now. We're not talking about the issue of gayness. We're talking about an issue where a son wants to be able to go back into the house because he loves his mother. The mother can't accept the fact that he's gay. That goes beyond saying is gay right or wrong. We have a family in a crisis.

Even for companies less geared toward conflict (such as NBC's *Leeza*, one of the few programs bought by a network, which always wanted a show they could feel was "respectable"), the interpersonal or family framework is useful. "The thing we constantly ask ourselves is, 'Is this something our audience can relate to?'" says *Leeza*'s executive producer, Nancy Alspaugh. For shows on homosexuality that women at home can "relate to," the show typically places the issue in a family context, with families that look like the middle-class, white viewers—hosting Martina Navratilova's ex-lover Judy Nelson and her "all American" sons, for example.

So whereas lesbian issues aren't something that maybe middle America, you know, maybe the housewife with three kids who's in Kansas City isn't that

related to, but yet she can understand a mother-son relationship. I think that people can kind of relate to what it must be like to be going through something like that and have to deal with your children. Or like coming out to your parents and friends. It's not necessary that everyone can relate to being homosexual, but people can relate to having to reveal something to your parents, reveal something to your friends, that's going to potentially cause problems.

These production maneuvers, while not necessarily rooted in any vision of a gay-loving world, put moral objections to sexual nonconformity at a bit of a disadvantage, since they are somewhat out of their element. In the playing fields of rights (be they "equal" or "special") and interpersonal difficulties, the issues near and dear to the radical right are not the central ones: at the hub is "Is discrimination against gay people acceptable?" or "How can a mother deal with a cross-dressing son?" not "Is homosexual desire and behavior right?" Moral evaluations of homosexual status are pushed to the sidelines. Members of the religious-political right, in these kinds of shows, are a bit like people who have shown up at the wrong party but jump right into the fun. Indeed, those audience members who are not commenting about Adam and Steve often begin their challenges to antigay guests by asking them where they are from. "Where are you from? Are you a Mormon?" a Latina woman on *Ricki*, to laughter and applause, asks a guest who has said she will raise her children to believe that homosexuality is wrong. "No," the woman replies, smiling as though she has been asked if she is from another planet.[7] Mormons and people who believe that homosexuality is wrong do not quite make sense on the talk show planet.

How can such a planet exist, we should wonder, in a system that is widely known to be so risk-averse, money-driven, and ideologically timid? After all, years of studies of the television industry have documented that commercial and occupational commitments tend to dominate all others.[8] If talk shows are, as many critics contend, the triumph of the bottom line, why do they so often seem to let particular ideological leanings guide them? In part, given that they are so inexpensive to produce and so profitable, Jane Shattuc points out, talk shows are allowed "an ideological latitude or a certain open political bias" not allowed in prime time.[9] In part, it is simply because, as many producers report, many of the current and former hosts, especially Donahue and the women—Oprah Winfrey, Ricki Lake, Jane Whitney, Sally Jessy Raphael, Jenny Jones—are "gay-friendly," both politically and personally, and because of the high proportion of gay male production staff. Yet it is also clear that those individual leanings alone are not enough to explain the fate of antigay morality on talk shows. As *Leeza*'s Alspaugh explains, it is mostly just luck if your personal views coincide with the commercial approach of a show.

> I feel very fortunate that I'm in a position that my personal feelings can be reflected in what I do, and I work with somebody who very much is on the same wavelength as I am. At the same time, if I were a producer of *Hard Copy*, would I make it the best tabloid show it could be? Yes. I mean, these companies have goals with their programs. They identify a niche. They identify a market, and you have to produce into that. If you're going to do it, revel in it and do the best you can. Just do it and say, "This is entertainment. We're not here to change the world." We wouldn't do what a lot of the other shows do, because of Leeza and because of what she wants to do with the show, and because of the network. But if that was the directive of the company, I would. I'm just incredibly fortunate.

There is something more at work here than progay staffers doing their bit for the cause by squeezing religious objections to homosexuality into uncomfortable niches. With television, ideology has to be consonant with commercial and institutional needs. Ideology has to be entertaining.

More general ideological commitments crucial to their commercial niche, not just the personal inclinations of those putting them together, are what make talk shows not terribly warm homes for religious conservatives. Talk shows work not so much with an explicitly progay agenda, but with an ideology of liberal pluralism: we are all different, live and let live, tolerate and respect the rights of others to be who they are. "My view is that everybody should be able to tolerate everything," says host Jerry Springer. "It's only the First Amendment, it's only free speech. The show is crazy and it is outrageous, but this is a forum for that to happen." Whether or not one sees this as a heartfelt commitment, it reveals the match between talk shows and the we're-all-different ideology: the shows depend financially on the constant display of difference, which in a variety of ways makes the entertainment possible. Add to that what host Rolonda Watts calls "that American thing," freedom of expression, which justifies the high-drama, channel-surf-resistant social conflict also so prevalent. "I mean," says Ro, misattributing the words of Voltaire, "as Patrick Henry said, 'I may not agree with what you say, but I'll defend to the death your right to say it.'" Looking at one of her guests, the bitter, hatred-filled Shirley, she adds, "May we also learn understanding and tolerance and let each person speak one at a time."[10] For TV talk to work, everyone must be allowed to speak, or yell, regardless of their position; appeals in the name of tolerance, understanding, and Patrick Henry/Voltaire give this talk at least the appearance of a purpose.

This pluralist tone gets wedded, moreover, to the therapeutic values which give an extra push toward tolerance. "What we are trying to tackle in this one hour," Oprah Winfrey once said, "is what I think is the root of all the problems in the world—lack of self-esteem is what causes war, because people who really love themselves don't go out and try to fight other people."[11] This emphasis on individual self-knowledge, self-determination, self-love, and self-improvement allows talk shows to claim a "service" function, to push for money shots of self-revelation, and to pursue postfeminist female audiences with little patience for men who tell them what to do and be. That focus on the individual self is tightly linked to an "essentialist" faith, an assumption that what is inside has always been there, given by nature, and needs to be treated with care and respect; the search is for the true self, whatever it turns out to be. These are important ideological support beams for talk shows' show-and-tell entertainment: we are just uncovering what is there, promoting understanding and self-understanding, which are good, if emotionally difficult, things.

Two-faced as it is, this therapeutic-pluralism-turned-entertainment is much more sympathetic to liberal approaches to sexual nonconformity than to conservative condemnations of it—not only to coming out as a positive act of self-empowerment, but to tolerance, and to the protection from arbitrary prejudices of individuals who are just being who they are.

The result, often, is that the bigot becomes the freak. A 1994 *Jerry Springer* show, for instance, pitted a lesbian couple running a feminist center in Mississippi against townsfolk saying that "we don't want these people being role models," "anyone who is homosexual or lesbian is against what God teaches and has—they have a sick mind," "they have gone against nature," and "they know the judgment of God, and those who do that are worthy of death." The lesbians' daughter argues that "we're governed by the laws of the Constitution of the United States, not by the Bible and not by bigotry," and Springer agrees in his daily "final thought" commentary, which as it always does, conflicts drastically with the outrageousness that came before. Typically, Springer, having

hosted a show filled with ridicule, talks about how sexual and gender identities are innate and therefore should not be subject to ridicule. On this day, however, he instead appeals to the American thing, distinguishing himself from the backwoods bigots of Ovett, Mississippi.

> We've spent considerable time today talking about homosexuality: whether it's godly or not; whether one chooses to be homosexual, or by birth simply is; whether it threatens the values of the majority community. And yet in this case none of that may be relevant. Clearly, most folks in Ovett, Mississippi, don't want the camp there, don't want the lesbian lifestyle anywhere near them. And yet, this is America. And though it is the business of each of us to instill a value system in our children, it is the business of none of us to impose such lifestyle, value system, religion, politics, or sex-ier—sexual orientation on our neighbors. We may have the right to say, "I don't want a Catholic or a Baptist or a Jew or a Black in my neighborhood." But we don't have the right to enforce it. It's really very fundamental. If you can stop someone from living in your town because of what they are, then one day they can stop you from living where you want because of what you are. There are places in the world where that is the case. But they are not called America.[12]

When the ideology of living the "truth" of the self fades, the rhetoric of tolerance often renders it irrelevant, and homosexuality is stirred into the mix of protected differences that make talk shows' bread and butter. Springer makes explicit the position generally taken by daytime talk shows themselves: it is those guests who impose antigay morality who are sick, ungodly, bigoted, un-American freaks.

When guests from the antigay right (religious or not) are prominent, in fact, the audience, and often the host, tend to turn against them. In 1993, for instance,

Geraldo hosted two same-sex couples who had caused controversies by attending their high school proms. In the front row sits dough-faced Paul Cameron, chairman of the Family Research Institute, whose credibility as a psychologist has already been widely discredited outside of the talk show circuit; a few people down the row sits one of the founders of Parents and Friends of Lesbians and Gays, a somewhat frail middle-aged white woman in glasses who had lost her son to AIDS two weeks earlier. When Cameron begins to talk about how "depressing" it is that we are encouraging such mistakes in children, how "irresponsible" it is of the school system to allow them to enter a "lifestyle that will kill them," and so on, the show becomes almost a ritualized bashing of Cameron and his views. One after another, audience members and panelists denounce Cameron, to cheering and applause. Eventually, he begins to talk about AIDS, using the other guest's son as an example. "This poor woman," he begins, and she stands up to scream at him. "I am not a poor woman," she shouts to immediate and long-lasting cheers and applause. "I can hold my head up high," she continues, the rest of her sentence drowned out by prolonged clapping. This denunciation of Cameron continues, but he pushes ahead, until Geraldo, riding the explosive anti-Cameron audience energy, simply says, "Shut up, I don't want to hear your story."[13]

Or take *Rolonda*'s Shirley, who is roundly demolished over the course of the hour by members of the studio audience, who stand up and make a series of statements: "God loves everybody in the world no matter if they're gay or what," says one; "What right do you have to tell anybody about their sexuality?" another asks; "If anybody should burn in hell," another tells Shirley, "I think it should be you," while still another declares her "an ugly woman, God does not love ugly, and the statements that comes out of your mouth and the nonsense you're teaching these children is wrong." Shirley becomes the ugly one,

unloved by God himself, while the audience continually preaches a liberal, individualist politic in which lesbian and gay people are included: "I think in my opinion," as one sums it up to audience applause, "it doesn't matter what sexual orientation, race, creed, or color, you should judge a person, but you should judge a person by what their heart and what their personality is." In the meantime, the screen flashes statistics from the FBI, the National Gay and Lesbian Task Force, and Yankelovich Partners on hate crimes against lesbians and gays, gay teen suicide rates, and gay population percentages.[14] Here, as in many programs in which public attitudes toward homosexuality are central, the claim that homosexuality is immoral, that heterosexuality is the exclusive law of either nature or the Bible, cuts against the show's assumptions and triggers audience hostility. Lesbians and gays are not only victims of bigotry, but also more similar to the audience—more normal, one might say—than those guests seeking to enforce antigay sexual morality. Indeed, the presence of the religious-political right, brought on in the interest of heating things up, creates a narrative in which the need for protection is even more obvious: they are the attackers.

The Ricki Lake Show, often credited with triggering the lowering of talk show standards, has produced some of the most explicitly and unrelentingly progay television via this same programming strategy: arranging bigots like ducks in a row. One 1994 show called "White Men Fight Back" paraded a series of put-upon white men ("African blacks are more violent than white people" and "white men are the minority," they assert) in front of its almost entirely nonwhite, and entirely unsympathetic, audience. In the role of the opposition, with the enthusiastic support of the audience, is Donald Suggs—black, openly gay, and then the public affairs director of the Gay and Lesbian Alliance Against Defamation. Suggs recalls "sitting next to this guest who at one point said, 'I think what you sodomites do is disgusting.' And

I said exactly what went through my head at the time. I turned to him and said, 'You know what, it would be disgusting if I was doing it with you.' The audience howled and howled. The audience loved it. I would never say that on a news show, but at this particular setting, it was really the perfect thing to say." Here is the unusual, orchestrated spectacle of an articulate, outspoken, gay man of color leading the charge against white men espousing racial superiority along with complaints about "sodomites," wildly championed by a mob of urban teenagers.[15]

Suggs is not the only gay activist to be brought onto *Ricki* as an expert. Writer, outing-promoter, and ACT UP veteran Michelangelo Signorile, for instance, took the role usually given to a therapist, holding forth from a thronelike chair on a show whose title, "I'm Gay . . . Get Over It!" even recalls Queer Nation's "We're here, we're queer, get used to it!" Various family members denounce their gay relatives, refusing, in Lake's terms, "to accept you for who you are": Tammy tells her sister Pam, a butch lift-truck operator from Georgia, that she doesn't know what she's missing ("I know what I'm missin', but I know what I'm a-gittin', too," Pam responds); a cute, bleach-blond gay white 14-year-old's grandmother says she knew there was something wrong with her grandson when he was born ("Not wrong, just different," corrects Lake). "Michelangelo, can you educate her?" Lake says, turning to Signorile. "Michelangelo, enlighten us," which he does, telling this one to love her child and that one that there's nothing she can do about it.[16] Signorile, who had appeared on many shows as an advocate, now with a book to promote, was here the authority. . . .

On another 1995 show in which antigay family members confront their gay relatives, Ricki Lake, as always, is openly sympathetic to the gay guests. DJ and Tamarra, a large, many-chinned white couple, both in blue, quickly explain how they moved to another state when they found out her father was gay ("his boyfriend was lower

class, really rude"); Jim, the ponytailed, earringed, Birkenstocked father, enters to applause and cheering, and explains how after thirty-five years, he decided to stop hiding from himself. "I praise you for being able to be true to yourself and to live your life the way you want to live it," Lake says, backed by shots of the applauding young audience, "but I can't imagine how it must feel after doing that to have your daughter reject you." If your dad was such a good influence on you, she asks Tamarra, who has expressed concerns for her children ("it would really confuse them"), why wouldn't he be a good influence on your children? "I guess the situation scares me," Tamarra says, to which Lake responds with an impatient whine. "But what's *wrong* with being gay?" . . .

Several minutes later, a black woman in big earrings and a big white sweater adds religion back into the mix, but reverses the usual Adam and Steve logic. "Who told you that homosexuals are going to hell?" she says, pointing directly at the skinny white Bible thumper on stage. "What Bible? How can you get up on television—no, my Bible doesn't tell me that homosexuals are going to hell. *Bigots and people that judge are going to hell.*" Ricki Lake's final word, after a straight woman comes on to praise her gay babysitter, is in keeping with the show's set-up-the-bigots strategy. "Remember," she says to the camera, sitting casually on the steps of the stage as if on a Brooklyn stoop, "children are not born to hate and fear, they are *taught* to hate and fear." Or, as Tempestt says simply to the audience of her own "Get Used to It" show, after a series of young gay people of all colors have told off their friends, "You *have* to learn tolerance."[17]

Although it is not entirely controllable, neither is this kind of show accidental. After all, producers select the cast and write the script, even if unpredictability is written in. One openly gay producer tells of seeing a newspaper story about a small-town mayor who had come out of the closet and then returned from a trip to find "Fag, get out" painted all over his house.

So what we did was we booked him, and we booked a couple from the town who is dead set against him as the mayor. Like, "We don't want a fag in our town as the mayor," that kind of thing. And we booked people from the town who were very much in support of him. He's a great guy, a great mayor. And then in researching, we found a transsexual who's running for mayor of her town, and we booked her and other people. And that was a great show. It presented these gay people—and you know, this man who was the mayor of this small town was just a nice guy, an upstanding citizen, a normal, very positive gay role model. We also had a transsexual on the show who's like, if you didn't know she was a transsexual, you might think she is just the funniest, neatest, funny lady, classy lady. Just classy, just fun. Part of me feels like, you know, I'd love that everybody in America could see those two role models. And then they saw these people from this town who were so bigoted, who were missing their teeth, who were bigoted. And I thought, to me this was a good show.

The upstanding gay and transsexual citizens are set against the small-town bigots; in a cross-fertilization of gay, lesbian, bisexual, and transgender mainstreaming and talk show class representations, the bigots fare badly not just because of their prejudice, but because of their toothless announcement of small-town poverty in the face of the "classy" people they hate. "We didn't set them up," the producer says. "We didn't go looking for them or anything." But of course the fact that the bigots really have bad teeth and really hate queers does not mean they have not, in a more general sense, been set up to, as the producer puts it, "show America 'don't be so bigoted.'"

The order and presentation of guests, although it is no guarantee of an outcome, can shape audience reaction significantly. I asked another openly gay supervising producer of a similar bigot-bashing program if he had explicitly set up homophobic guests as audience targets. "In a word," he answered quickly, "absolutely." Driven by their own commitments, and even more by the confidence that their young, urban, largely African American and Latino studio audience would, given a structure that moves from strong-willed bigots to we're-not-going-to-take-it victims, rise up against bigotry, the show's producers arranged the story with a clear movement from "bad guys" to "good guys." . . .

By the time the gay voices emerge, audience sympathy is firmly set against the homo-haters. The moral chorus is conducted, by the show's structure, to sing loud and strong against antigay prejudice, drowning it out with an ethic, sometimes biblical and often not, of love, honesty, and suspension of judgment.

The Nice Thing About ◆ White Supremacist Sexist Homophobic Men

Despite a baseline ideology that is sympathetic to self-determination and sexual freedom, it does not take much for a show's tune to change dramatically, so that antigay moralizing is celebrated rather than stigmatized. Ironically, a shift in the way panels are put together, often sought by gay media activists, goes a long way: shows programmed *without* Bible-thumping, moralizing guests often wind up legitimizing Bible-thumping moralizing. When there is no one playing the "bigot" role on the panel—which is increasingly the case, as relationship programs displace issues programs, and as lesbian, gay, bisexual, and transgender guests appear simply to tell their stories unopposed—audience members pick up the slack, inevitably making the "Adam and Eve, not Adam and Steve" and "keep it in the closet" arguments. These audience members meet with much less hostility than "extremist" panelists, and in fact more often meet with strong audience support. In the absence of hateful embodiments of intolerance, audience hatred and intolerance are often fired up.

On a 1993 show on bisexuality, to take just one example among very many, the guests are all openly bisexual people and their families, along with one expert. The usual range of questions and objections is raised by audience members along the way: a young black man wants to know if they are going to make their children gay, a white woman complains of being followed around by two bisexual women at a party who "ruined my evening," a middle-aged white guy smugly suggests that the "young ladies" might "resolve your dilemma" by "dating men who like to dress like women." There are questions about friends' and parents' reactions, pressure from the gay and lesbian community, how early the awakening to sexual difference took place, religious beliefs. The latter question, like most of them, is simply asked and answered: "God is Love," says activist Lani Ka'ahumanu, "and we're talking about loving other human beings here." But it is not until late in the show, when a young black woman in a white shirt and black vest responds to Ka'ahumanu's comment from half an hour earlier, that the show really picks up steam. "God is Love," the woman says, "but God does not condone what you're doing. If he did, Moses and Sarah wouldn't have gotten married, and Jesus himself would have married John the Baptist." The audience explodes into applause, as if their leader has finally spoken. "You are confused," she says, pointing, "yes you are."

The host, Bertice Berry, tries to move the show in other directions, initiating a sort of rap session between the psychologist and the panel, and then interviewing a bisexual-man-heterosexual-woman couple in the audience, but the show has bogged down and the audience is not finished. A light-skinned, middle-aged African American woman (deep red dress, done hair) stands up and tells a young African American woman named Terri (brown vest, backward baseball cap) that she applauds the mother who, having kicked Terri out of the house, prays for her; she talks about "spirit" and "lust of the flesh" and "the truth and the light," while the cameras catch the reaction of the white mothers on the panel. "You have been deceived!" she cries, a charge enthusiastically received by much of the studio audience.[18] The arguments are no different from those made by (typically white) Christian or pseudoscientific right-wing panelists, but the dynamic is nearly turned around; what looks extreme in one case looks mainstream in the other. Ironically, the absence of panelists articulating religious-right rhetoric, combined with the talk show's celebration of the common-sense authority of "ordinary" people, opens up space for the regular folks in the studio to make the moral and political argument that gay, lesbian, and bisexual people are abominable.

And often it is not just *any* ordinary person who stands up to Adam-and-Steve the show. Since talk shows draw on an association of elite authority with whiteness (and everyday authority with darker skin), they often wind up staging encounters between a white moral voice and a moral voice carried by audience members of color. Conservative religious African Americans, often with a good deal of support from the rest of the largely African American and Latino studio audience, issue moral condemnations of white bisexual, gay, lesbian, and transgender guests. This racialized spectacle is quite common, especially now that the *Donahue*-derived format, in which white gay activists face off against white religious denouncers, has been used up. The picture shifts, of course, on those increasingly frequent occasions when there are gay people of color on the panel, and we get what is rarely seen in mainstream media culture: an internal African American cultural dialogue (sometimes including black host, black audience members, and black guests) about sexual morality. But more often than not, on programs directly focused on homosexuality, bisexuality, or transgenderism as *political* issues, a predominantly white panel speaks humanist liberalese while many audience members of color speak traditional conservatese.

In fact, on shows where moral disputes erupt, the racial dynamics can sharply alter the bigot-as-freak phenomenon. As a general rule, when white speakers are bigoted, their racial privilege (and sometimes class privilege as well) undercuts their authority to a large degree; when people of color speak, they speak with the talk show authority of everyday, less powerful folks, less susceptible to the hostility aroused by those who seem to think they're better than everybody else. This has something to do, for sure, with the strength of gender conservatism and homophobia in African American and Latino cultures; yet that homophobia is easily exaggerated, and many shows with similar audiences and similar topics activate love-and-compassion responses rather than you're-going-to-hell responses, so there is no simple transmission of attitudes going on here. These racialized encounters over sex and gender norms are *structured* by talk shows—unintentionally, really, through the accidents and habits of talk show producing. Inadvertently, talk show producers have stumbled onto an easy, inexpensive way to get the heat of moral condemnation, laced with an also-hot undertone of racial tension, and spiked with the exciting sight of less powerful people challenging the privileged, without ever directly endorsing an antigay conservative agenda.

◆ The Helen Factor

It is not just the absence of white bigots that can turn a show's tenor, regardless of the intentions of producers, from accepting and celebratory of sexual freedoms to critical and belittling. The personalizing push of both the television medium and the talk show genre—the emphasis on personality above all else, most centrally—means that a gay person who comes across as *unlikable* can manage to turn a sympathetic studio audience into a nasty one, and that a character demonized in one instance can, paired with the right opposing figures, gain support in another. Television's personality-über-alles tendency has been pointed out by critics for decades now,[19] and many repeat guests report the discovery that likability, not the particularities of what they had to say, seemed to be the key to getting audience support. Longtime activist Ann Northrop, who had worked as a producer on the *CBS Morning News* and as a writer for *Good Morning, America*, sized up an early *Donahue* appearance as "much too strident and argumentative and angry." Over time, appearing on *Donahue, Geraldo, Rolonda*, and other programs, she came to follow the rules she knew well as a producer.

> Don't let yourself get angry and out of control because the whole thing is the people want to like you as a person. I can get angry at the drop of a hat, and I don't think that's a winning strategy. What you want to do is ingratiate yourself with an audience, smile a lot, be very lovable, and then you can say anything and they'll go along with it. Smile a lot. Try to stay very calm. Sit up straight. Put the small of your back against the seat because the tendency is to slump and you'll look terrible doing that. Speak very calmly. The people in the audience really don't care what you're saying. They are going to judge you as a person and whether you are a good person or a bad person. What stays with you is the sense of whether you liked someone or didn't like someone.

> . . . As anyone who has watched a talk show knows, many people do not come across as charming, calm, sensible, smiley, and lovable. This may be what experienced talk show guests learn to be, but most guests are not experienced; it may be what strategically oriented guests want to be, but

producers are certainly encouraging most of them to be otherwise. Besides, as most talk show guests attest, there is not much time to be self-conscious: the studio lights are on, the camera is on, everybody's talking, the situation has a life of its own. And when they are not likable—likability and sexual identity are not, these shows amply demonstrate, necessarily linked—or when they make a move toward a particular talk show no-no such as selfishness or bad parenting, they can easily fire up displays of antigay sentiment. . . .

[From a *Ricki Lake* show,] Karen, a 15-year-old heterosexual African American student from Illinois, is there to tell her mother, Helen . . . that she thinks "being gay or lesbian is disgusting." Helen, who has seven kids, quickly crosses her arms and speaks angrily about how this is "something Karen has to deal with" and how "her opinion doesn't matter to me." . . . The sympathy, not surprisingly, quickly moves toward the daughter, . . . and Helen becomes a lightning rod for audience hostility the rest of the program. . . .

Given the genre's emphasis on individual character, an unsympathetic homosexual can undermine a show's sympathy for homosexuals in general. The show's structuring mechanisms—a bunch of conflict, a touch of chaos, good guys who can just as easily function as bad guys—make for a very unstable acceptance of gay people.

◆ The Partitioned Garden

. . . It is quite clear that producers for the most part program shows on homosexuality with an emphasis on tolerance and acceptance of nontraditional attachments. They habitually sketch within the lines of a be-true-to-yourself-and-let-others-be-themselves credo. But this framework is quite shaky, despite the habit of stringing up bigots like so many punching bags. It is, moreover, conditional. Producers' interest is certainly not in effecting social change—although that can be a happy by-product of their work—but in attracting audiences. The trick is to simultaneously challenge and affirm the audience's beliefs and experiences; the challenge is engaging, the affirmation comforting. Talk show sexual morality thus becomes a murky brew of political liberalism and cultural conservatism. Nowhere does this become clearer than in a comparison of the fate of homosexuality with that of bisexuality and gender-crossing.

The treatment of same-sex relationships as morally acceptable in fact takes place on the condition that two other norms remain conserved and supported: of gender conformity (men should look and act like "men" and women like "women") and monogamy (people should only couple in exclusive pairs). Some of this setup shows up in a certain division of labor into which sex and gender nonconformists are fed on talk shows, the formats into which, say, transsexuals appear most often as compared to those most common for homosexuals. If same-sex desire is so often morally acceptable in the talk show world, that is partly because it is *not* bisexuality or gender-crossing; put simply, bisexuality is commonly equated with promiscuity and becomes morally suspect, while transsexuality and cross-dressing are routinely placed outside the audience's moral universe.[20] . . .

Some kinds of sexual nonconformity barely qualify as even eligible for political and moral disputes. Gay men and lesbians are much more likely than bisexuals, transsexuals, or cross-dressers, for instance, to appear on shows that treat the political issues affecting their lives; while moral questions remain a constant for all kinds of populations, for gay people the controversy and conflict are often exactly over the political consequences of moral disapprobation. In my sample as a whole, about a fifth of the shows are produced in political-issue formats (discrimination, military policy, law, and so on); when we look at the homosexuality-themed shows alone, more than two-fifths are formatted as political issues.

Taking another cut, when we look at the shows programmed around political issues, we find the near total elimination of transsexuals, cross-dressers, and bisexuals from the picture; 96 percent of these sorts of shows in my sample involve gay or lesbian topics and guests. Lesbians and gay men, much more often than their bisexual and transgendered colleagues, fit into formats in which theirs is a political status, in which the question of their sameness to or difference from heterosexuals is on the table, in which they are asked to speak up against those who damn them. Moral condemnation takes a place in those shows, but it competes with political support.

Cross-dressers and transsexuals, however, get a program niche that almost entirely shuts down any question of their similarity to those who never "cross" traditional gender lines. First of all, they appear in formats that are largely displays, often sandwiched between conversation, such as pageants or performances. Except for the occasional gay comedians show, display programs exclusively involve gendercrossers, be they transvestites, drag queens, or transsexuals; while only about 7 percent of the sample as a whole involves performances, a full third of the shows on crossdressing involve these display-yourself formats. At its most extreme, such a show might involve a contest, as when a *Richard Bey* show pitted drag queens against "real women" in such stunts as "Feminine Family Feud" (categories: hair removal, PMS symptoms), nail pounding, and sawing a board in half; more often, it will involve a bit of lip-synching or stripping or a parade of transgendered women in bikinis, as in *Sally*'s transsexual versus nontranssexual women's bikini contest, or the ubiquitous female-impersonator shows.[21]

On the one hand, gender-crossers fare quite well in these display formats, which more or less preclude moral condemnations. But more significantly, they escape such disapproval simply because they are not taken seriously enough to be subject to evaluation one way or the other. Why

bother condemning a harmless jester? "I have made at least thirty talk show appearances," says drag queen Miss Understood, whom I met in his boy persona, Alex. "Twenty-three *Richard Beys*, three *Geraldos*, two *Rolondas*, *Gordon Elliott*, *Mark Walberg*, *Tempestt*. And I've never actually got to talk about anything." As he tells it, this is just the deal he is offered. "We're there to make it look colorful." That may work for drag queen performers, but for the transsexuals and transvestites reeled into the same format, for example, it means agreeing to be a showthing rather than a person.

Gender-crossers also appear disproportionately in family-conflict formats—kids and parents and siblings arguing with one another. For instance, while transsexualism is a primary topic in roughly 23 percent of my overall sample of gay, lesbian, bisexual, and transgender programming, it is the primary topic in around 36 percent of the family-conflict shows in the sample; similarly, cross-dressing is twice as common a topic in family-conflict formats as it is when all formats are taken together. When they are not called upon to dance or show off, then, gender-crossers and their family members are confronting one another, as on *Maury Povich*, when Stephanie, formerly Roger, Sr., confronted his ex-wife Dixie ("until he has his penis taken off, he'll always be Roger"), and his sons Thomas ("he's not my father, really, because he's like a woman and he has breasts") and Joshua ("there's not much to do at his house").[22] Gendercrossers may not always be freaks, but programming strategies tend to channel them into nooks that exclude political discussion, and emphasize either their laughable difference from other humans or their conflict-causing difference from their families of origin. A nonconforming gender status largely puts transgendered people outside the moral and political realms, implying that gender conformity is a condition for *entry* to a place where freedom and acceptance might, on a good day, even be possible.

Bisexuality and bisexuals get a somewhat different program niche. Political issues shows, compared to the field for homosexuals, are relatively rare when it comes to discussions of bisexuality; in their place, on the one hand, is more testimonial programming, in which the general topic of "what is bisexuality and what's it like to be bisexual" structures a show. (The simple phenomenon and experience of bisexuality, at least for the moment, is still exotic enough to be a stand-alone topic, as homosexuality was in the early days of talk shows.) On the other hand, bisexuality is also more often formatted in terms of the problems it creates in intimate relationships, and especially in terms of a tie to sexual nonmonogamy. While relationship-trouble formats account for about a fifth of the overall sample, for instance, they account for about a third of the shows focused on bisexuality: bisexuals are disproportionate relationship troublers, in the talk show world.... Again, this niching of bisexuality, while it has many more openings for supportive moral and political voices, also suggests a condition for approval: a renunciation of anything but monogamous pairings.

What goes for gay people, then, does not go for the rest of the crowd of sex and gender nonconformists, who are disproportionately programmed as either amoral outsiders or immoral sexpots. In many ways, bisexuals and transgendered people pay the price for daytime television's pro-gay moral cheerleading. The moral defense of homosexuality, in fact, is shaped by the frequent dismissal of transgendered and bisexual people on TV talk. When same-sex desire is linked to nonmonogamy (as it so often is on programs dealing with bisexuality), or when it is closely associated with gender crossing (as it consistently is, especially on *Jerry Springer, Richard Bey*, and the other outrageousness-is-our-business shows), we hit a brick wall in the drive toward a morality of love, freedom, and acceptance. The morality that the talk show seems structured to protect is not so much the denunciation of Adam and Steve and

Jane and Eve, not so much the moral superiority of heterosexuality, but the moral inferiority of unconventional gender presentation and sexual nonmonogamy: Adams with more than one partner, butch Eves, Janes with a wandering eye, Steves who might be a little bit on the Eve side of things. A step across the wrong line, and the morality of tolerance so strenuously pushed by talk shows is withdrawn.

Conditional Love ◆

Like most of what we have been seeing, the conditions under which sex and gender dissidents are subject to moral condemnation and moral defense on daytime television are, above all, *production* conditions, which themselves most often derive from economic ones, as our lives are used to make money in an industry whose morality is profit. The representations emerge through producers' intentions, but even more so through the requirements of the daily production of these kinds of nonfiction dramas.

Sometimes, too, they are shaped by forces above and beyond producers and their everyday routines, since corporate executives have the first and last words. Toward the end of her run, for example, when her show was moved to daytime on NBC, Jane Whitney's special interest in gay and lesbian topics had to be toned down. "Too controversial. 'We don't do abortions, we don't do gay and lesbian rights. Don't want to alienate anybody.' It's a whole lot safer to go with 'two kids who slept on a department store bed' than it is with 'a couple in New York fighting for adoption rights for gays and lesbians.'" Despite her resistance, discussion of homosexuality as a political topic was, at the behest of the network, edged out by discussions of heterosexuality as a purely personal one. The fear that certain kinds of topics would be perceived by advertisers as potentially alienating to viewers was well recognized by William Bennett and others participating in the brief mobilization to "clean up" talk shows. "When you realize that [Jenny] Jones and [Ricki] Lake are two of the leading 'cultural assassins' of trash talk TV," the American Family Association's Donald Wildmon wrote to his troops, "you can see why it's so important for you to write Procter & Gamble today."[23] For some shows—the more outrageous ones such as *Jerry Springer*, for instance, whose advertisers already knew they were sponsoring wrestling-style mania—the chill never came, and for most others, at least those that survived cancellation, the advertiser vigilance wore off after the public attention faded. But for a period, on programs like the one for which Martin Calder was a producer, the word from above was cut back on anything that looked "unclean." Instructively, this list included gay people, black people, drag queens, and risqué dressers.

> All the William Bennett stuff came out and advertisers started paying attention to that. So after advertisers started paying attention to that, we were told no more gay guests. "No gay guests." It wasn't just gay guests. It was also certain things about, you know, you can't put them out in low-cut tops. Like you had to watch how they were dressed. If somebody stripped, you know, if somebody got up and started a gyrating dance, edit it out. It was editing out anything that was at all like sex, like dirty. No more drag queens. I did a show that had a Madonna impersonator that was a guy, and that was okay, but no drag queen issues, no more, "I'm a drag queen." It was never written down on paper, but it was clear. It was also like, "Scale back on the number of black shows." We're going to be rerunning a lot of shows. No shows that have openly gay guests will rerun. It sickened me and made me furious, but it's not like I'm in a position of power. I have to pay the bills.

The message from the executive-gods at Paramount, Warner Brothers, Multimedia, and the like demonstrates the ultimate condition of love: give them voice, and do it however you want, unless they threaten profits, in which case, please shut them up.

Such conditions are obvious enough, and as we have seen they are nowhere near the whole story, since talk show producers manage for the most part to routinely use their loose ideologies of self-esteem, truth-telling, tolerance, and personalized authority to make profitable entertainment. There are many people with genuine political commitments here, even in the television industry, and often, when they are consonant with the overriding ideologies of TV talk, their allegiances translate into an active attempt to stage the demolition of religiously and politically driven hatred. But advertisers pay the bills, and major media corporations run the ship—and besides, even when those parties are satisfied or looking the other way a slight change in talk show casting can shift the tide. In a genre so dependent on individual personality and unpredictability, waves of hatred often sweep over the television screen, as audiences join in the bashing, antagonized by a lousy presentational style, or apparent selfishness, or a violation of the ethics of discernible genders and monogamy, or boredom. These waves are a reminder to many of us watching, a repetition of the message many of us, the luckier ones actually, have received elsewhere in our lives: you may be both gay and loved, but it is not the kind of love you want or need. *There are always conditions*. We may take the opportunity to yell back at bigots or to smile calmly as others do it for us, just as we sometimes accept scraps of acceptance because we are so starved. But that does not do nearly enough to heal the wounds of knowing that you are accepted and loved, once again, here again, here where you at least sometimes rule, conditionally.

◆ *Notes*

1. The Michigan State University study of talk show content, conducted somewhat differently from my own on a more general sample (transcripts of eighty different episodes of June-July 1995, videotapes from ten episodes of the eleven top Nielsen-rated shows of July-August 1995), provides interesting results for comparison. The study found that family relations and sexual activity were the major topics of discussion, that sexual propriety was the most common "proposition" under consideration, at issue in 50 percent of their sample, and that sexual orientation was a discussion topic on 11 percent of their sample. On average, they also found, sixteen personal disclosures are made per episode (42 percent by the guest about him- or herself, 30 percent about another guest, and 28 percent by the host about a guest), with one of them disclosure of sexual orientation. See Bradley Greenberg et al., *The Content of Television Talk Shows: Topics, Guests, and Interactions* (Lansing: Michigan State University, November 1995).

2. Multimedia Entertainment, *Sally Jessy Raphael* ("Former Homosexuals"), date unavailable.

3. Multimedia Entertainment, *Donahue* ("When Hatred Against Gays Turns Deadly"), February 21, 1995; Multimedia Entertainment, *Donahue* ("Black Preacher Says I'll March With the KKK Against Gays"), November 4, 1994; King World, *Rolonda* ("No Gays in My Town"), January 18, 1994; King World, *Rolonda* ("Bashing Gays for School Credit"), January 10, 1995; King World, *Oprah* ("School for Gay Teens"), October 24, 1994; King World, *Oprah* ("Gay Marriages"), December 19, 1989.

4. Multimedia Entertainment, *The Jerry Springer Show* ("I Love Someone I Can't Have"), October 18, 1995; Multimedia Entertainment, *The Jerry Springer Show* ("Confess, You Liar!"), December 7, 1995; Multimedia Entertainment, *The Jerry Springer Show* ("I Can't Stand My Sibling"), December 19, 1995; Paramount Pictures, *Ricki Lake* ("Watch Me! Today I'm Going to Break Up My Ex and His New Chick"), July 29, 1996; Paramount

Pictures, *Ricki Lake* ("You Both Have No Clue Why You're Here . . . Surprise! I'm Hooking You Up"), September 15, 1995; Investigative News Group, *Geraldo* ("I Saw You on Geraldo and Just Had to Meet You"), October 10, 1995; Multimedia Entertainment, *Donahue* ("Is There Life After a Career in Porn?"), March 1, 1995; Multimedia Entertainment, *The Dennis Prager Show* ("Comedians Against Prejudice"), August 11, 1995; Multimedia Entertainment, *Sally Jessy Raphael* ("Why I Was Fired"), April 13, 1994.

5. King World, *Oprah* ("Gay Marriages").

6. Multimedia Entertainment, *Donahue* ("Black Preacher Says I'll March With the KKK Against Gays").

7. Paramount Pictures, *Ricki Lake* ("Get It Straight: I Don't Want Gays Around My Kids"), June 15, 1995.

8. See, for example, Todd Gitlin, *Inside Prime Time* (New York: Pantheon, 1983); Robin Andersen, *Consumer Culture and TV Programming* (Boulder, CO: Westview, 1995); Herbert Gans, *Deciding What's News* (New York: Vintage, 1979).

9. Jane Shattuc, *The Talking Cure: TV Talk Shows and Women* (New York: Routledge, 1997), 66.

10. King World, *Rolonda* ("Bashing Gays for School Credit").

11. In Barbara Grizzuti Harrison, "The Importance of Being Oprah," *New York Times Magazine*, June 11, 1989, 130.

12. Multimedia Entertainment, *The Jerry Springer Show* ("Mississippi Violence Over Lesbian Camp"), February 14, 1994.

13. Investigative News Group, *Geraldo* ("Gay Teenagers at the High School Prom"), June 25, 1993.

14. King World, *Rolonda* ("Bashing Gays for School Credit").

15. Paramount Pictures, *Ricki Lake* ("White Men Fight Back: I'm Sick of Being Discriminated Against"), February 23, 1994.

16. Paramount Pictures, *Ricki Lake* ("Listen, Family, I'm Gay . . . It's Not a Phase . . . Get Over It!"), November 20, 1995.

17. Paramount Pictures, *Ricki Lake* ("Get It Straight: I Don't Want Gays Around My Kids"); Columbia-Tristar Television, *Tempestt* ("I'm Gay, Get Used to It!"), July 31, 1996.

18. Bertice Berry Show, *The Bertice Berry Show* ("Parents and Their Bisexual Kids"), November 16, 1993.

19. See Richard Schickel, *Intimate Strangers: The Culture of Celebrity* (New York: Fromm International, 1985); Andersen.

20. At issue here are the *formats* into which certain populations tend to appear—testimonials, which are more or less group interviews and storytelling, or family conflicts, or political issues, or relationship troubles, or displays such as pageants and makeovers. The way producers format a show does not always mean that *conversation* sticks within these particular boundaries, of course.

21. All American Television, *Richard Bey* ("Drag Queens vs. Real Women"), August 24, 1995; Multimedia Entertainment, *Sally Jessy Raphael* ("Women Who Are Really Men"), April 17, 1995.

22. Paramount Pictures, *Maury Povich* ("Dad Wants to Be a Woman"), May 3, 1994.

23. American Family Association, *Action! Page*, January 1996, newsletter.

PART VI

TV BY NIGHT

Entertainment programming on television at night includes a wide variety of standardized types or *genres*, including situation comedies set in homes or homelike workplaces; action and adventure dramas, such as police shows; newer hybrids, such as prime-time soaps or melodrama-influenced dramatic series; late-night talk shows; made-for-TV social issue movies; sports spectacle programming; and so-called reality-based shows (such as *Survivor*).

TV critics have traditionally used a genre-based analysis to help them sort out the televisual codes and conventions governing the sheer quantity of entertainment material appearing on television at night. Such codes and conventions also influence viewers' expectations and satisfactions. Experienced viewers, including relatively young children, have acquired sophisticated cultural competence that allows us to *decode* or interpret characters, actions, and speech in very distinct ways, depending on whether the generic context is comic, melodramatic, or "realistic." As one critic puts it,

> Audiences' different potential pleasures are channeled and disciplined by genres, which operate by producing recognition of the already known set of responses and rules of engagement. Audiences aren't supposed to judge a western for not being musical enough, a musical for not being very horrific, or a sitcom for not being sufficiently erotic. (Hartley, 1985, quoted in Fiske, 1987, p. 114)

TV formulas can be very tenacious, as Richard Butsch shows us in an overview of four decades of representations of working-class males in TV sitcoms and drama (Chapter 54). Once having established a "winning formula," such as the Ralph Kramden "buffoon" of the 1950s *Honeymooners* sitcom, the television industry tend to replicate the formula endlessly, despite dramatic changes in the social world outside TV. Going behind the texts we see on the screen to investigate the production conditions of the network dramatic series, he demonstrates that the creative personnel (television producers and writers) unwittingly reproduce their own class privilege in part because of the way the industry is set up to avoid financial risk. "New shows are chosen by network executives, and these purchasers have always been few in number and averse to new ideas. . . . When a sitcom producer has a secure contract with a network, there are few opportunities to avoid stereotypes."

Yet certain dramatic changes in the organization of the mass entertainment industries altered the TV programming pictures in the last decade of the 20th century, as it affected the representation of groups formerly invisible or denigrated. Chief among these changes was Fox network's challenge to what had long been a three-way monopoly of the major networks. Kristal Brent Zook argues in "The Fox Network and the Revolution in Black Television" (Chapter 55) that this new network, launched by Rupert Murdoch in 1986, targeted a young, urban, and specifically black viewership, an audience largely ignored by the three major networks, and in so doing inadvertently "fostered a space for black authorship in television." Fox offered prominent African American entertainers such as Keenen Ivory Wayans, Charles Dutton, Martin Lawrence, and Sinbad the opportunity to act as executive producers of their own shows, and as a result, According to Zook, "by 1993, the fourth network was airing the largest single crop of black-produced shows in television history." But the authorial control did not endure. Looking to become more "mainstream" after Fox committed $1.6 billion to the rights to NFL Sunday games, Fox canceled four of its six African American-targeted shows in 1994.

The Fox channel's programming also made a contribution to significant shifts in the representation of gay men on TV. Kylo-Patrick Hart points out (Chapter 56) that the Fox network's willingness to "offer greater creative freedom" to producers, as well as "the opportunity to be far more daring in language use and overall content," led to some important representational "victories" in several shows targeting the 18- to 34-year-old demographic. (Hart also alerts us to continuing problems in such representations, however, such as "outdated, stereotypical representations of AIDS that . . . link the disease almost exclusively with gay men" and "the inclusion of gay story lines only when their outcomes will be negative.")

One important taboo still operating in television's representations of gays and lesbians (especially on commercial TV stations supported by advertising) regards openly erotic expression. The famous lesbian kiss on the *Roseanne* show in the 1980s did not lead to relaxation of the taboo. For example, on *Ellen*, the first show to have an out lesbian (Ellen DeGeneres) in the leading role, we find a somewhat asexual character. Missing from the famous coming-out episode was, according to Susan Hubert (Chapter 57), "any intimations of same-sex activity." Like Hart, Hubert points out that the show was aimed at a heterosexual audience who might be unsettled by same-sex sex activity. Indeed, the producers at Disney were cautious to the point that "the script had to be approved, and the first script was rejected, reportedly because it focused too much on the reaction of Ellen's friends." Hubert also criticizes the show for its depoliticization of lesbianism and for "making fun of lesbians who do care about politics." By avoiding any discussion of the politics of lesbianism and homophobia, the show reduces the political to the personal and becomes just another sitcom about people trying to form relationships. This in itself would not be problematic were it not for the antihomosexual ideology that both Hart and Hubert clearly illustrate still exists in society.

In another analysis of how economic and industrial shifts have reshaped programming, Jackie Byars and Eileen Meehan (Chapter 58) explore the historical changes that gave birth to the Lifetime channel, a cable network that specifically targets upscale "working women." In its quest to attract and retain these viewers, Lifetime movies and series offer an updated version of "feminine" TV. The movies often treat topics defined as "women issues," which include rape, battery, problems with children, and adultery, and they tend to feature a strong female protagonist. Although many of the women are seen as overcoming adversity, they do so in a way that foregrounds individual rather than collective solutions that rely on structural changes. As Byars and Meehan point out, "The pattern throughout emphasizes the personal as individuals right individual wrongs through individual actions." In this way, they argue, Lifetime television avoids an explicitly feminist agenda by avoiding issues such as the segmented labor force, patriarchal violence against women, and equality in the home.

Karen Lindsey provides a less qualified enthusiasm for the "new women's TV" dramatic series at night (Chapter 59), as well as some of Lifetime's recent original prime-time drama. Writing from the perspective of a long-time feminist and antiracist TV viewer, Lindsey points to early-21st-century "strong women" network shows such as *Judging Amy* and *Family Law*, and the Lifetime series *Strong Medicine*, as shows that combine "strong women, antiracism, class awareness, good writing, and good acting." Pointing out the complexity of these shows' treatments of social issues in workplace and family settings, Lindsey asserts that "they prove that the medium can provide both entertainment and social responsibility."

Hour-long urban workplace dramas on network TV in the 1990s similarly allowed their audiences, including "older, more educated African American viewers," an unprecedented television opportunity to engage with serious, complex African American characters. Police dramas such as *N.Y.P.D. Blue* and *Law & Order* and hospital dramas such as *ER* and *Chicago Hope* were critically acclaimed, and Donald

Bogle (Chapter 60) concedes that "for the most part, these were well-written, well-directed, and tensely acted programs in which issues of race were sometimes examined." Enriching his textual analysis with behind-the-scenes information on producers' and writers' decisions, as derived from interviews with some of the actors from such shows, Bogle examines the limits that still apply to the treatment of African American characters and the topic of race in integrated ensemble dramatic programming targeting the "quality" (mainstream) viewer.

"Reality-based" crime shows such as *LAPD: Life on the Beat, America's Most Wanted*, and *Cops* may seem at first to be similar to several of the workplace dramas Bogle discusses, in their emphasis on the work of fighting crime and enforcing the law. However, Fred Turner, in "This Is for Fighting, This Is for Fun" (Chapter 61), provides us with a provocative analysis of this relatively new genre's distinctive ideological work through its distinctive televisual techniques (such as positioning the camera so that the viewer looks from the perspective of the gun). Setting this genre within the political context of the Reagan-Bush administrations of the 1980s, and in particular the escalation of the "war on drugs" of that era, Turner points to a "propaganda function":

> the America of today, like the Vietnam of yesterday and the Wild West before it, becomes a landscape in which to act out a national drama of justice. In this landscape, the gun symbolizes the link between past and present, and with it the link between the righteousness of American laws and the masculinity of their enforcers. By means of its conflation with the camera, the gun offers viewers a chance to walk alongside the bounty hunters, to undertake a mission on behalf of the nation, a mission to penetrate the dank, dark regions of American society, to "see" the suspect there, to "know" his crimes and thereby to humiliate him.

So far, our discussion of images of people of color on television has been confined to African Americans. In "Here Comes the Judge: The Dancing Itos and the Televisual Construction of the Enemy Asian Male" (Chapter 62), Brian Locke warns us that "the polarized black-and-white structure of racial discourse renders the status of any position that is neither 'black' nor 'white' more uncertain, or at times even invisible." For Locke, it is this polarized notion of race that allowed *The Tonight Show* to "deploy a racist parody"—a chorus line of dancers costumed to resemble Judge Lance Ito (presiding magistrate at the O. J. Simpson trial)—"without . . . provoking charges of racism." At first glance, the Dancing Itos appeared to obscure the markers of "Asianness" because "the costuming hides a key facial detail, for the viewer cannot see the shape of the dancers' eyes. . . . The costuming gives the overall impression that the Itos hide themselves deliberately, make themselves inscrutable: the eyeglasses, the thick black mustache and beard look like a mask." However, as Locke points out, it is this inscrutability itself that should be read as a racial signifier (symbolic element) because "Asians have been coded in U.S. popular culture as a threat, a people who keep their motives and means well hidden."

Chyng Feng Sun also directs our attention to the 20th-century history of representation of Asian Americans in U.S. popular culture (Chapter 63)—a background knowledge essential to our understanding of race and gender in nighttime TV in the early 21st century. Sun analyzes Lucy Liu's character Ling Woo (on the *Ally McBeal* show) against this backdrop. Sun points out that although Liu disrupts the "China doll" stereotype, an image that has been the staple of numerous movies, she exhibits characteristics that are like a "dragon lady" in that she is "tough, rude, candid, aggressive, sharp-tongued, and manipulative." The relationship between Woo and her boyfriend, Richard Fish (played by Greg Germann, a white man), includes a sexuality that is constructed as (comically) deviant. And though she restrains herself from having sex with him, the reason she gives is "all the more tantalizing: once men have had sex with her, they cannot have enough."

American Jews face representational dilemmas on TV sitcoms and dramas that are similar (though not identical) to those of Asian Americans. Joyce Antler's reading of *The Nanny* (Chapter 64) highlights how television images of Jewish women are rare but when depicted they "are usually overblown caricatures and pejorative stereotypes that misrepresent the lifestyles and attitudes of real women." Although Fran Fine (played by Fran Dresher) is supposed to be from a blue-collar background, she is depicted within the limited range of stereotypes that constitute the anti-Semitic, sexist image of the Jewish American Princess. She is overly concerned with money, looks, designer labels, and catching a man. She is loud and vulgar and interferes in the lives of those around her. She is in fact "the kind of coarse, greedy, and selfish Jew that any anti-Semite might envision." Although there have been more images of Jewish men on television in the 1990s (*Seinfeld, Mad About You,* and *Northern Exposure* to name just a few), they tend to be shown as assimilated with few markers of their Jewishness. Interestingly, most of the Jewish male characters marry non-Jewish women, suggesting that they are more desirable than Jewish women. Given the image of Jewish women on television, it is not surprising that Jewish male characters opt to stay away from women of their own ethnic group. When Antler argues that "the limited range of the Jewish female characters on television reflects a failure of imagination," she could well be talking about the image of women in general and women of color specifically.

◆ Reference

Fiske, J. (1987). *Television culture.* New York: Methuen.

54

RALPH, FRED, ARCHIE, AND HOMER

Why Television Keeps Re-creating the White Male Working-Class Buffoon

◆ Richard Butsch

Strewn across our mass media are portrayals of class that justify class relations of modern capitalism. Studies of 50 years of comic strips, radio serials, television drama, movies, and popular fiction reveal a very persistent pattern, an underrepresentation of working-class occupations and an overrepresentation of professional and managerial occupations among characters.[1]

My own studies of class in prime-time network television family series from 1946 to 1990 (Butsch, 1992; Butsch & Glennon, 1983; Glennon & Butsch, 1982) indicate that this pattern is persistent over four decades of television, in 262 domestic situation comedies, such as *I Love Lucy*, *The Brady Bunch*, *All in the Family*, and *The Simpsons*. In only 11% of the series were heads of house portrayed as working-class, that is, holding occupations as blue-collar, clerical, or unskilled or semiskilled service workers. Blue-collar families were most underrepresented: only 4% (11 series) compared with 45% of American families in 1970.

NOTE: Copyright © 2003 by Richard Butsch.

Widespread affluence was exaggerated as well. More lucrative, glamorous, or prestigious professions predominated over more mundane ones: 9 doctors to 1 nurse, 19 lawyers to 2 accountants, 7 college professors to 2 schoolteachers. Working wives were almost exclusively middle class and in pursuit of a career. Working-class wives, such as in *Roseanne*, who have to work to help support the family, were very rare. Particularly notable was the prevalence of servants: one of every five series had a maid or butler.

The working class is not only underrepresented; the few men who are portrayed are buffoons. They are dumb, immature, irresponsible, or lacking in common sense. This is the character of the husbands in almost every sitcom depicting a blue-collar (white) male head of house, *The Honeymooners*, *The Flintstones*, *All in the Family*, and *The Simpsons* being the most famous examples. He is typically well-intentioned, even lovable, but no one to respect or emulate. These men are played against more mature, sensible wives, such as Ralph against Alice in *The Honeymooners*.

In most middle-class series, there is no buffoon. More typically, both parents are wise and work cooperatively to raise their children in practically perfect families, as in *Father Knows Best*, *The Brady Bunch*, and *The Cosby Show*. In the few middle-class series featuring a buffoon, it is the dizzy wife, such as Lucy. The professional/managerial husband is the sensible, mature partner. Inverting gender status in working-class but not middle-class sitcoms is a statement about class.

◆ How Does It Happen?

The prevalence of such views of working-class men well illustrates ideological hegemony, the dominance of values in mainstream culture that justify and help to maintain the status quo. Blue-collar workers are portrayed as requiring supervision, and

managers and professionals as intelligent and mature enough to provide it. But do viewers, and particularly the working class, accept these views? Only a handful of scattered, incidental observations (Blum, 1969; Gans, 1962; Jhally & Lewis, 1992; Vidmar & Rokeach, 1974) consider how people have responded to portrayals of class.

And why does television keep reproducing these caricatures? How does it happen? Seldom have studies of television industries pinpointed how specific content arises. Studies of production have not been linked to studies of content any more than audience studies have. What follows is an effort to make that link between existing production studies and persistent images of working-class men in domestic sitcoms. In the words of Connell (1978), "No evil-minded capitalistic plotters need be assumed because the production of ideology is seen as the more or less automatic outcome of the normal, regular processes by which commercial mass communications work in a capitalist system" (p. 195). The simple need to make a profit is a structural constraint that affects content (see also Ryan, 1992).

Let us then examine how the organization of the industry and television drama production may explain class content in television series. I will look at three levels of organization: (a) network domination of the industry, (b) the organization of decisions within the networks and on the production line, and (c) the work community and culture of the creative personnel. I will trace how these may explain the consistency and persistence of the portrayals, the underrepresentation of the working class, and the choice of the particular stereotypes of working-class men in prime-time domestic sitcoms.

NETWORK DOMINATION AND PERSISTENT IMAGES

For four decades ABC, CBS, and NBC dominated the television industry. Of television audiences, 90% watched network programs. The networks accounted for over half of all television advertising revenues in the 1960s and 1970s and just under half by the late 1980s (Owen & Wildman, 1992). They therefore had the money and the audience to dominate as almost the sole buyers of drama programming from Hollywood producers and studios.[2]

During the 1980s, the three-network share of the audience dropped from about 90% to 60%; network share of television ad revenues declined from 60% to 47% (Owen & Wildman, 1992). These dramatic changes have generated many news stories of the demise of the big three. Cable networks and multistation owners (companies that own several local broadcast stations) began to challenge the dominance of the big three. They became alternative markets for producers as they began purchasing their own programs.

But program development is costly; even major Hollywood studios are unwilling to produce drama programs without subsidies from buyers. Nine networks have sufficient funds in the 1990s to qualify as buyers of drama programming: the four broadcast networks (ABC, CBS, Fox, and NBC) and five cable networks (Disney, HBO, Showtime, TNT, and USA Network) (Blumler & Spicer, 1990). But ABC, CBS, and NBC still account for the development of the overwhelming majority of new drama series, the programming that presents the same characters week after week—and year after year in reruns.

This is the case in part because the broadcast networks still deliver by far the largest audiences. Even in 1993, the combined ratings for the 20 largest cable audiences would still only rank 48th in ratings for broadcast network shows. The highest rated cable network, USA Network, reached only 1.5% of the audience, compared to an average of 20% for ABC, NBC, and CBS. The larger audiences translate into more dollars for program development.

And producers still prefer to work for the broadcast networks. When sold to broadcast networks, their work receives much broader exposure, which enhances their subsequent profits from syndication after the network run and increases the likelihood for future purchases and employment.

Moreover, whether or not dominance by the big three has slipped, many of the same factors that shaped their programming decisions shape the decisions of their competitors as well. The increased number of outlets has not resulted in the innovation and diversity in program development once expected. Jay Blumler and Carolyn Spicer (1990) interviewed more than 150 industry personnel concerned with program decision making and found that the promise of more openness to innovation and creativity was short-lived. The cost of drama programming limits buyers to only a handful of large corporations and dictates that programs attract a large audience and avoid risk. How has this affected content?

Using their market power, the networks have maintained sweeping control over production decisions of even highly successful producers from initial idea for a new program to final film or tape (Bryant, 1969, pp. 624-626; Gitlin, 1983; Pekurny, 1977, 1982; Winick, 1961). Their first concern affecting program decisions is risk avoidance. Popular culture success is notoriously unpredictable, making decisions risky. The music recording industry spreads investment over many records so that any single decision is less significant (Peterson & Berger, 1971). Spreading risk is not a strategy available to networks (neither broadcast nor cable), because only a few programming decisions fill the prime-time hours that account for most income. Networks are constrained further from expanding the number of their decisions by their use of the series as the basic unit of programming. The series format increases ratings predictability from week to week. Each decision, then, represents a considerable financial risk, not simply in production costs but in advertising income. For example, ABC increased profits from $35 million in 1975 to $185 million in 1978 by raising its average prime-time ratings from 16.6 to 20.7 (personal communication, W. Behanna, A. C. Nielsen Company, June 1980).

Because programming decisions are risky and costly and network executives' careers rest on their ability to make the right decisions, they are constrained, in their own interest, to avoid innovation and novelty. They stick to tried-and-true formulas and to producers with a track record of success (Brown, 1971; Wakshlag & Adams, 1985). The result is a small, closed community of proven creative personnel (about 500 producers, writers, directors) closely tied to and dependent on the networks (Gitlin, 1983, pp. 115, 135; Pekurny, 1982; Tunstall & Walker, 1981, pp. 77-79). This proven talent then self-censor their work on the basis of a product image their previous experience tells them the networks will tolerate (Cantor, 1971; Pekurny, 1982; Ravage, 1978) creating an "imaginary feedback loop" (DiMaggio & Hirsch, 1976) between producers and network executives.

These same conditions continue to characterize program development in the late 1980s (Blumler & Spicer, 1990), as the new buyers of programming, cable networks, operate under the same constraints as broadcast networks.

To avoid risk, network executives have chosen programs that repeat the same images of class decade after decade. More diverse programming has appeared only in the early days of an industry when there were no past successes to copy—broadcast television in the early 1950s and cable in the early 1980s—or when declining ratings made it clear that past successes no longer worked (Blumler & Spicer, 1990; Turow, 1982b, p. 124). Dominick (1976) found that the lower the profits of the networks, the more variation in program types could be discerned from season to season and the less network schedules resembled each other. For example, in the late 1950s, ABC introduced hour-long western series to prime time to become competitive with NBC and CBS (Federal Communications Commission [FCC], Office of Network Study, 1965, pp. 373, 742). Again, in 1970, CBS purchased Norman Lear's then controversial *All in the Family* (other networks turned it down) to counteract a drift to an audience of undesirable demographics (rural and over 50). Acceptance by networks of innovative programs takes much longer than conventional programs and requires backing by the most successful producers (Turow, 1982b, p. 126). *Roseanne* was introduced by Carsey-Werner, producers of the top-rated *Cosby Show*, when ABC was trying to counter ratings losses (Reeves, 1990, pp. 153-154). Hugh Wilson, the creator of *WKRP* and *Frank's Place*, described CBS in 1987 as desperate about slipping ratings; "Consequently they were the best people to work for from a creative standpoint" (Campbell & Reeves, 1990, p. 8).

NETWORK DECISION MAKING— PROGRAM DEVELOPMENT

The second factor affecting network decisions on content is the need to produce programming suited to advertising. What the audience wants—or what network executives imagine they want—is secondary to ad revenue. (Subscriber-supported, pay cable networks, which do not sell advertising, also do not program weekly drama series.) In matters of content, networks avoid that which will offend or dissatisfy advertisers (Bryant, 1969). For example, ABC contracts with producers in 1977 stipulated that

> no program or pilot shall contain . . . anything . . . which does not conform with the then current business or advertising policies of any such sponsor; or which is detrimental to the good will or the products or services of . . . any such sponsor. (FCC, Network Inquiry, 1980, Appendix C, p. A-2)

Garry Marshall, producer of several highly successful series, stated that ABC rejected a story line for *Mork & Mindy*, the top rated show for 1978, in which

Mork takes TV ads literally, buys everything, and creates havoc. Despite the series' and Marshall's proven success, the network feared advertisers' reactions to such a story line.

An advertiser's preferred program is one that allows full use of the products being advertised. The program should be a complimentary context for the ad. In the 1950s, an ad agency, rejecting a play about working-class life, stated, "It is the general policy of advertisers to glamourize their products, the people who buy them, and the whole American social and economic scene" (Barnouw, 1970, p. 32). Advertisers in 1961 considered it "of key importance" to avoid "irritating, controversial, depressive, or downbeat material" (FCC, Office of Network Study, 1965, p. 373). This requires dramas built around affluent characters for whom consuming is not problematic. Thus, affluent characters predominate, and occupational groups with higher levels of consumer expenditure are overrepresented.

A third factor in program decisions is whether it will attract the right audience. Network executives construct a product image of what they *imagine* the audience wants, which surprisingly is not based on actual research of audiences in their homes (Blumler & Spicer, 1990; Pekurny, 1982). For example, Michael Dann, a CBS executive, was "concerned the public might not accept a program about a blue collar worker" when offered the pilot script for *Arnie* in 1969 (before *All in the Family* proved that wrong and after a decade in which the only working-class family appearing in prime time was *The Flintstones*). On the other hand, in 1979 an NBC executive expressed the concern that a couple in a pilot was too wealthy to appeal to most viewers (Turow, 1982b, p. 123).

With the exception of the few anecdotes I have mentioned, almost no research has examined program development or production decisions about class content of programs. My research found no significant differences between characters in sitcom pilots and series from 1973 to 1982,

indicating that class biases in content begin very early in the decision-making process, when the first pilot episode is being developed (Butsch, 1984). I therefore conducted a mail survey of the producers, writers, or directors of the pilots from 1973 to 1982. I specifically asked how the decisions were made about the occupation of the characters in their pilot. I was able to contact 40 persons concerning 50 pilots. I received responses from 6 persons concerning 12 pilots.

Although this represents only a small portion of the original sample, their responses are strikingly similar. Decisions on occupations of main characters were made by the creators and made early in program development, as part of the program idea. In no case did the occupation become a matter of debate or disagreement with the networks. Moreover, the choice of occupation was incidental to the situation or other aspect of the program idea; thus, it was embedded in the creator's conception of the situation. For example, according to one writer, a character was conceived of as an architect "to take advantage of the Century City" location for shooting the series; the father in another pilot was cast as owner of a bakery after the decision was made to do a series about an extended Italian family; in another pilot, the creator thought the actor "looked like your average businessman." The particular occupations and even the classes are not necessitated by the situations that creators offered as explanations. But they do not seem to be hiding the truth; their responses were open and unguarded. It appears they did not think through themselves why this *particular* class or occupation; rather, the occupations seem to them an obvious derivative of the situation or location or actors they choose. The choice of class is thus diffuse, embedded in their culture.

This absence of any awareness of decisions about class is confirmed by Gitlin's (1983) interviews with industry personnel about social issues. Thus, the process of class construction seems difficult to document given the unspoken guidelines, the indirect manner in which they suggest class, and the absence of overt decisions about class. Class or occupation is not typically an issue for discussion, as are obscenity or race. To examine it further, we need to look at the organization of the production process and the culture of creative personnel.

THE HOLLYWOOD INPUT— PROGRAM PRODUCTION

Within the production process in Hollywood studios and associated organizations, and in the work culture of creative personnel, we find factors that contribute to the use of simple and repetitive stereotypes of working-class men.

An important factor in television drama production is the severe time constraints (Lynch, 1973; Ravage, 1978; Reeves, 1990, p. 150). The production schedule for series requires that a finished program be delivered to the networks each week. Even if the production company had the entire year over which to complete the season's 22 to 24 episodes, an episode would have to be produced on the average every 2 weeks, including script writing, casting, staging, filming, and editing. This is achieved through an assembly line process in which several episodes are in various stages of production and being worked on by the same team of producer, writers, director, and actors, simultaneously (Lynch, 1973; Ravage, 1978; Reeves, 1990).

Such a schedule puts great pressure on the production team to simplify the amount of work and decisions to be made as much as possible. The series format is advantageous for this reason: When the general story line and main characters are set, the script can be written following a simple formula. For situation comedy, even the sets and the cast do not change from episode to episode.

The time pressures contribute in several ways to the dependence on stereotypes for characterization. First, if ideas for new series are to be noticed, they cannot be "subtle ideas and feelings of depth," but rather, "have to be attention getters—loud farts," in the words of a successful director (Ravage, 1978, p. 92).

Also, time pressure encourages type-casting to obtain casts quickly. The script is sent to a "breakdown" agency, which reads the script and extracts the description of characters that need to be cast. One such agency, employing six persons, provided this service for the majority of series (Turow, 1978). These brief character descriptions, not the script, are used by the casting agency to recommend actors, particularly for minor characters. Not surprisingly, the descriptions are highly stereotyped (Turow, 1980). Occupation—and by inference, class—was an important part of these descriptions, being identified for 84% of male characters.

Producers, casting directors, and casting agencies freely admit the stereotyping but argue its necessity on the basis of time and dramatic constraints. Type-casting is much quicker. They also argue that to diverge from stereotypes would draw attention away from the action, the story line, or other characters and destroy dramatic effect. Thus, unless the contradiction of the stereotype is the basic story idea—as in *Arnie*, a blue-collar worker suddenly appointed corporate executive—there is a very strong pressure, for purposes of dramatic effect, to reproduce existing stereotypes.

The time pressures also make it more likely that the creators will stick to what is familiar to them whenever possible. Two of the most frequent occupations of main characters in family series were in entertainment and writing, that is, modeled on the creators' own lives (Butsch & Glennon, 1983). The vast majority of producers grew up in middle-class homes, with little direct experience of working-class life (Cantor, 1971; Gitlin, 1983; Stein, 1979; Thompson & Burns, 1990). Moreover, the tight schedules and deadlines of series production leave no time for becoming familiar enough with a working-class lifestyle to be able to capture it realistically. Those who have done so— for example, Jackie Gleason, Norman Lear—had childhood memories of working-class neighborhoods to draw on.

Thus, the time pressure encourages creative personnel to rely heavily on a shared and consistent product image—including diffuse and undifferentiated images of class—embedded in what Elliott (1972) called "the media culture." The small, closed community of those engaged in television production, including Hollywood creators and network executives (Blumler & Spicer, 1990; Gitlin, 1983; Stein, 1979; Tunstall & Walker, 1981; Turow, 1982a) shares a culture that includes certain conceptions of what life is like and what the audience finds interesting. According to Norman Lear, the production community draws its ideas from what filters into it from the mass media (Gitlin, 1983, p. 204). From this, they try to guess what "the public" would like and formulate images of class they think are compatible (Gitlin, 1983, pp. 225-226).

Although the consistency of image, the underrepresentation of the working class, and the use of stereotypes can be explained by structural constraints, the particular stereotypes grow from a rather diffuse set of cultural images, constrained and framed by the structure of the industry. Any further specification will require a close examination of the construction of the consciousness of the program creators and network executives from, among other things, their exposure to the same media they create—a closed circle of cultural reproduction. Whether one can indeed extract the process of class image making from the totality of this occupational culture remains a challenge to researchers.

◆ *Industry and Image in the 1990s: A Postscript*

Although by 2000 cable networks began to purchase new drama and comedy series ("B'cast, Cable," 2000), commercial broadcast networks still accounted for the development of the overwhelming majority of new drama and sitcom series. At the same time, competition from cable and other media forms began to take their toll on broadcast network television, the patrons of sitcom production.

From the mid-1970s to the mid-1980s, the average household's television use increased from 6 to 7 hours per day, due to increased numbers of cable channels and independent broadcast stations, and to the growth of VCRs and video rental. The increase in television use leveled off around 1984, as VCR and cable growth plateaued. Television viewing remained at 7 hours per day through the 1990s (Butsch, 2000, p. 269).

The increased television viewing, however, did not benefit the broadcast networks. Rather, broadcast networks' television ratings, the percentage of television households with the television turned on and tuned to a broadcast network, continued to decline as people turned to cable, VCR, and the Internet. In 1990, the big four commercial broadcast networks (ABC, CBS, NBC, Fox) had shrunk to a combined rating of 39.7% from 56.5% in 1980, about when the decline began (Butsch, 2000, p. 269). By mid-1999, the big four combined rating had slipped to 28.6% ("Upscale Auds," 1999). Advertising-supported cable had grown from 9.6% in 1990 to 23.9% in mid-1999 to become substantial competitors of the broadcast networks. A Nielsen study of their ratings concluded that among 18- to 34-year-olds, television use overall declined about 5 rating points from 1991 to 1997 ("Young Auds," 1999).

This decline of broadcast network hegemony began to influence domestic sitcoms. The networks even began to fear that people might not only leave the networks but desert television altogether for other entertainments, especially the young turning to the Internet and computer games, the first time in television history that household television use would not have been increasing. In response, the networks reduced the number of sitcoms scheduled for prime time. The fall schedules, where new shows are traditionally debuted, now included fewer domestic sitcoms; new sitcoms were more youth- and single- rather than family-oriented. Also, the industry replaced sitcoms with less expensive formats such as "reality" shows, even though they drew a less desirable (for advertisers) lower-income audience ("Genre-ation Gap," 1999; "TV Tosses," 1999; "Webs' Final," 1999).

Broadcast networks began to seek a downscale audience on the premise that they had already lost the upscale audience to pay-cable. Because ratings had been declining, network executives were more willing to try innovations, including sitcoms that differed from the usual formulas. They tried animated, singles, and other "situations" instead of the family situation. Domestic sitcoms that did make it to prime time featured different families than they had in the past, especially downscale families more frequently than ever before. Of 53 new domestic sitcoms from 1990 to 1999, 16 featured working-class families; 11 series featured black families. Other shows for which the occupation was not blue collar or was not specified were set in working-class locales.

Nevertheless, even in this new environment, the Hollywood culture's image of working-class men persisted. The 1998 series *King of Queens* was called a Ralph Kramden remake, with a wife that was a little too bright for her husband. *Bless This House* (1995) featured a macho postal worker and feisty wife and also was described as *The Honeymooners* with kids. In 1991, *Roc* featured a not-too-bright black garbageman with a stereotypic macho attitude and a more educated nurse as his wife. *King of the Hill* (1998) caricatures southern working-class men as beer drinking, gun toting, pickup truck driving, narrow-minded, and uncommunicative. In *Grace Under Fire* (1993), the father was an unreliable drunken "good for nothing" who abandoned the family. In the new

Cosby show (1996), the husband was an unemployed airport worker while his wife co-owned a flower shop and his daughter was a lawyer. Even mainstream reviewers criticized *Costello* (1998) for its crude stereotypes of working-class men. In many cases, wives and mothers overshadowed the men. In addition to the brighter wives mentioned above, Jesse, Thea, and Grace presented single mothers who exhibited strength and good character that put their men to shame.

Many 1990s shows featured dysfunctional families, but the more serious dysfunctions were blue collar. Alcoholism, spouse abuse, and children abandoned or put up for adoption appeared in working-class shows. Divorce and quirky personalities were typical "dysfunctions" for middle-class shows (James, 1995). So, although there were more shows featuring working-class people in the 1990s, the men continued to be stereotyped as not too bright, immature, and contrasted to their more capable and responsible wives or adult female relatives. Plus ça change, plus c'est la même chose.

It would seem that the great changes in industry structure have not changed the outcome when it came to issues of class. One thing has not changed in the industry. The market for sitcoms has always been oligopsonistic, that is, few buyers and many more sellers. Sitcom series have had only one market, network television. New shows are chosen by network executives, and these purchasers have always been few in number and averse to new ideas. When the FCC's financial interest and syndication rules in 1970 forced the networks out of producing their own shows, they still remained the only purchasers of such shows from movie studios and independent producers, and thus still represented a conservative force against innovation and risk. Also, they still were financed by advertisers who were risk-averse. The re-creation of vertical integration and the horizontal integration across broadcast, cable, and movie studios in the 1990s likewise did not change the fundamental fact of oligopsony (Gomery, 1999). The only thing that has motivated innovation or change, from the 1950s through the 1990s, has been declining ratings and profits for established networks and the need for new networks such as Fox to break into the market. Once rating rebounded or new networks established themselves, they shied away from innovation. (e.g., see Zook, 1999, pp. 102-104, on Fox).

Remarkably, even these pressures to try something new have not deterred stereotyping of working-class men. The unchanged nature of sitcom production, where these ideas are created and put on tape, is the source of continuity in this respect. When a sitcom producer has a secure contract with a network, there are few opportunities to abandon stereotypes. The production schedule's time pressures eliminate opportunities to explore new character types. These have not changed from the days of Lucy and Ozzie in the 1950s to Archie in the 1970s, and *Mad About You* in the 1990s (Meisler, 1997).

◆ Notes

1. Subordinate statuses, generally, race and gender as well as class, are underrepresented and/or presented negatively.

2. The sellers, the production companies, on the other hand, are not an oligopoly. Market concentration is low compared to the buyers (broadcast and cable networks); there was high turnover in the ranks of suppliers and great year-to-year fluctuation in market share; and collusion between suppliers is very difficult (FCC Network Inquiry Special Staff, 1980; Owen & Wildman, 1990).

◆ References

Barnouw, E. (1970). *The image empire: A history of broadcasting in the U.S. from 1953.* New York: Oxford University Press.

B'cast, cable: Trading places. (2000, April 24). *Variety*, p. 61.

Blum, A. (1969). Lower class Negro television spectators. In A. Shostak (Ed.), *Blue collar world* (pp. 429-435). New York: Random House.

Blumler, J., & Spicer, C. (1990). Prospects for creativity in the new television marketplace. *Journal of Communication, 40*(4), 78-101.

Brown, L. (1971). *Television: The business behind the box.* New York: Harcourt Brace Jovanovich.

Bryant, A. (1969). Historical and social aspects of concentration of program control in television. *Law and Contemporary Problems, 34,* 610-635.

Butsch, R. (1984, August). *Minorities from pilot to series: Network selection of character statuses and traits.* Paper presented at the annual meeting of the Society for the Study of Social Problems, Washington, DC.

Butsch, R. (1992). Class and gender in four decades of television situation comedy. *Critical Studies in Mass Communication, 9,* 387-399.

Butsch, R. (2000). *The making of American audiences.* Cambridge, UK: Cambridge University Press.

Butsch, R., & Glennon, L. M. (1983). Social class: Frequency trends in domestic situation comedy, 1946-1978. *Journal of Broadcasting, 27*(1), 77-81.

Campbell, R., & Reeves, J. (1990). Television authors: The case of Hugh Wilson. In R. Thompson & G. Burns (Eds.), *Making television: Authorship and the production process* (pp. 3-18). New York: Praeger.

Cantor, M. (1971). *The Hollywood TV producer.* New York: Basic Books.

Connell, B. (1978). *Ruling class, ruling culture.* London: Cambridge University Press.

DiMaggio, P., & Hirsch, P. (1976). Production organization in the arts. *American Behavioral Scientist, 19,* 735-752.

Dominick, J. (1976, Winter). Trends in network prime time, 1953-1974. *Journal of Broadcasting, 26,* 70-80.

Elliott, P. (1972). *The making of a television series: A case study in the sociology of culture.* New York: Hastings.

Federal Communications Commission, Network Inquiry Special Staff. (1980). *Preliminary reports*. Washington, DC: Government Printing Office.

Federal Communications Commission, Office of Network Study. (1965). *Second interim report: Television network program procurement* (Part 2). Washington, DC: Government Printing Office.

Gans, H. (1962). *The urban villagers*. New York: Free Press.

Genre-ation gap hits sitcoms. (1999, April 26). *Variety*, p. 25.

Gitlin, T. (1983). *Inside prime time*. New York: Pantheon.

Glennon, L. M., & Butsch, R. (1982). The family as portrayed on television, 1946-78. In National Institute of Mental Health, *Television and social behavior: Ten years of scientific progress and implications for the eighties* (Vol. 2, Technical Review, pp. 264-271). Washington, DC: Government Printing Office.

Gomery, D. (1999). The television industry. In B. Compaine & D. Gomery, *Who owns the media?* Mahwah, NJ: Lawrence Erlbaum.

James, C. (1995, December 3). Dysfunctional wears out its welcome. *New York Times*, p. H1.

Jhally, S., & Lewis, J. (1992). *Enlightened racism*: The Cosby Show, *audiences and the myth of the American dream*. Boulder, CO: Westview.

Lynch, J. (1973). Seven days with *All in the Family*: A case study of the taped TV drama. *Journal of Broadcasting*, 17(3), 259-274.

Meisler, A. (1997, February 2). Paul Reiser's balancing act. *New York Times*, p. H42.

Owen, B., & Wildman, S. (1992). *Video economics*. Cambridge, MA: Harvard University Press.

Pekurny, R. (1977). *Broadcast self-regulation: A participant observation study of NBC's broadcast standards department*. Unpublished doctoral dissertation, University of Minnesota.

Pekurny, R. (1982). Coping with television production. In J. S. Ettema & D. C. Whitney (Eds.), *Individuals in mass media organizations*. Beverly Hills, CA: Sage.

Peterson, R. A., & Berger, D. (1971). Entrepreneurship in organizations: Evidence from the popular music industry. *Administrative Science Quarterly*, 16, 97-107.

Ravage, J. (1978). *Television: The director's viewpoint*. New York: Praeger.

Reeves, J. (1990). Rewriting culture: A dialogic view of television authorship. In R. Thompson & G. Burns (Eds.), *Making television: Authorship and the production process* (pp. 147-160). New York: Praeger.

Ryan, B. (1992). *Making capital from culture: The corporate form of capitalist cultural production*. New York: Walter de Gruyter.

Stein, B. (1979). *The view from Sunset Boulevard*. New York: Basic Books.

Thompson, R., & Burns, G. (Eds.). (1990). *Making television: Authorship and the production process*. New York: Praeger.

Tunstall, J., & Walker, D. (1981). *Media made in California*. New York: Oxford University Press.

Turow, J. (1978). Casting for TV parts: The anatomy of social typing. *Journal of Communication*, 28(4), 18-24.

Turow, J. (1980). Occupation and personality in television dramas. *Communication Research*, 7(3), 295-318.

Turow, J. (1982a). Producing TV's world: How important is community? *Journal of Communication*, 32(2), 186-193.

Turow, J. (1982b). Unconventional programs on commercial television. In J. S. Ettema & D. C. Whitney (Eds.), *Individuals in mass media organizations*. Beverly Hills, CA: Sage.

TV tosses kiddie litter. (1999, December 6). *Variety*, p. 1.

Upscale auds ease b'casters. (1999, August 23). *Variety*, p. 34.

Vidmar, N., & Rokeach, M. (1974). Archie Bunker's bigotry: A study in selective perception and exposure. *Journal of Communication*, 24, 36-47.

Wakshlag, J., & Adams, W. J. (1985). Trends in program variety and prime time access rules. *Journal of Broadcasting and Electronic Media*, 29(1), 23-34.

Webs' final answer: Reality. (1999, November 8). *Variety*, p. 27.

Winick, C. (1961). Censor and sensibility: A content analysis of the television censor's comments. *Journal of Broadcasting*, 5(2), 117-135.

Young auds seek Web, not webs. (1999, January 4). *Variety*, p. 65.

Zook, K. B. (1999). *Color by Fox: The Fox network and the revolution in black television*. New York: Oxford University Press.

55

THE FOX NETWORK AND THE REVOLUTION IN BLACK TELEVISION

◆ Kristal Brent Zook

. . .Black productions of the 1990s were individual autobiographies as well as communal outpourings of group desire—collective rememberings not unlike slave narratives. During this period, black producers and consumers engaged in awkward modes of resistance and representation. It seemed that we wanted both capitalism and communalism; feminism as well as a singular, authentic self; patriarchy plus liberation; Africa the motherland *and* the American dream. These yearnings were explored, celebrated, and contested in black-produced shows of the 90s. . . .

In the 1980s middle-class white audiences began to replace standard network viewing with cable subscriptions and videocassette recorders. Since working-class African American and Latino audiences in general did not yet have access to these new technologies, they continued to rely on the "free" networks—NBC, CBS, and ABC. Consequently, "urban" audiences suddenly became a key demographic in the overall network viewership. During this period, black audiences watched 44 percent more network television than nonblacks. What's more, they clearly preferred black shows.[1]

These shifts had a profound effect on television programming. In the mid-1980s good pitches, or show ideas presented to producers, began to be defined as those appealing to both "urban" and "mainstream" audiences. NBC, in particular, boasted crossover hits such as *The Cosby Show* (the nation's number one program for five seasons), *A Different World*, and *The Fresh Prince of Bel Air*. In fact, NBC could even be considered something of a prototype for Fox's urban network, given that it had always carried more "ethnic" shows than either CBS or ABC.[2] (When Fox owner Rupert Murdoch assembled his programming department, he even brought Garth Ancier, Kevin Wendle, and other former NBC employees on board.)

The new network launched in 1986. By "narrowcasting" or targeting a specific black viewership (what Pam Veasey referred to cynically as the "Nike and Doritos audience"), and "counter-programming" against other shows to suit that audience's taste, Fox was able to capture large numbers of young, urban viewers. By 1993, the fourth network was airing the largest single crop of black-produced shows in television history. And by 1995, black Americans (some 12 percent of the total U.S. population) were a striking 25 percent of Fox's market.

The Fox network was unique, then, in that it inadvertently fostered a space for black authorship in television. It did this to capitalize on an underrepresented market, of course. But the fact that entertainers such as Keenen Ivory Wayans, Charles Dutton, Martin Lawrence, and Sinbad were made executive producers of their own shows was no small feat. Such titles increased (to varying degrees) their decision-making power and enabled them to hire writers, producers, and directors who shared their visions.

After Keenen Ivory Wayans's 1988 $3 million film *I'm Gonna Git You Sucka* made $20 million at the box office, the director-comedian held a private screening for Fox film executives, hoping to get financial backing and distribution for his next project. Although no film executives showed up at the screening, Fox's TV people did, offering Wayans a weekly half-hour series in which he could do "whatever he wanted." So it was that Wayans became the creator, director, executive producer, and star of *In Living Color*, an unprecedented arrangement for a black entertainer in 1990.

Fox was "completely different" from traditional networks in its early days, recalled Wayans.[3] "Barry Diller, who had been responsible for bringing Eddie Murphy to Paramount, was there. And there were a lot of other young, cutting-edge executives. They wanted to be the rebel network." In fact, had Wayans's idea for a sketch variety show like *In Living Color* come along in the 1980s, noted Twentieth Television president Harris Katleman, it would have been considered "too ethnic." Fox aired the irreverent series when it did because it needed "an intriguing spin" to distinguish it from the more traditional networks.[4]

It was in this same spirit that Fox programmer Garth Ancier had approached the comedy writing team of Ron Leavitt and Michael Moye (who are white and black, respectively) three years earlier. "Do anything you want," said Ancier, "but make sure it's different . . . Fox is here to give you the chance to do things you can't do anywhere else."[5] While Leavitt and Moye had written for shows like *The Jeffersons* in the past, it was extremely rare, in 1987, for a black writer to create his (and certainly never her) own series. *Married . . . With Children*, Leavitt and Moye's invention, went on to become the longest-running sitcom in network history.

We should look more closely, then, at what I see as four key elements of black-produced television. Based on over a decade of researching shows that have black casts and involve a significant degree of black creative control, I have found that four common traits reappear consistently. These can be summarized as: autobiography, meaning a tendency toward collective and individual authorship of black experience; improvisation, the practice of inventing and ad-libbing unscripted dialogue or action; aesthetics, a certain pride in visual signifiers of blackness; and drama, a marked desire for complex characterizations and emotionally challenging subject matter. . . .

To talk about autobiography, or authorship, in television is tricky, given that there can never be a single "author" of any particular show. As Tim Reid put it, there's "always somebody else you've got to answer to in network television . . . There's this guy and this guy's boss. Then that division and that division's boss. Then the network. Then the advertisers. They're like lawyers," said Reid. "They stand in front of you five and six deep, and they all have a say in the quality of what you're doing." In short, television production is a collective process, and black television in particular reveals group memories as well as individual ones.

For example, writer-producer Rob Edwards (*A Different World*) notes that he has often run "into trouble" by making in-group references while working on white shows. "I would start pitching stuff from a specifically black childhood," he recalls. "Like parents combing your hair. [But] you can't pitch a nap joke on *Full House*."[6] Writer-producer Susan Fales (*A Different World*) agrees. "There's a certain gift of the gab . . . a tendency to riff," she notes, "that has been a part of our survival and is absolutely more common on black-produced shows." This penchant for improvisation, says Fales, "can also lead to problems . . . like when actors refer to 'ashy skin.' You can't do that unless you're a very big hit."

Not only are black-produced scripts full of such collective autobiographical references, but these allusions also appear, as Fales indicates, in unscripted forms such as slips of the tongue, bloopers, and ad-libbed dialogue. This leads us to the second characteristic of black television: improvisation.

Historically, the improvisational practices of "cuttin' up" and "playing the dozens" have enabled black Americans to communicate with one another, often under hostile conditions. . . . Cultural theorists have also described this private discourse as "bivocality," "in-jokes," and "minor discourse."[7] Whatever we may call it, such in-group referencing is certainly a dialogic process in black television.

During a taping of Fox's *The Show*, for example, the predominantly African American and Latino studio audience failed to respond when comedian Mystro Clark followed his script closely in a scene with white co-star Sam Seder. In scenes with other black actors however, Clark spontaneously broke into improvisation, which the audience loved. From that point on, network executives routinely instructed black performers on the series to "play the dozens" during tapings.

Autobiography and collective memory are also revealed "extratextually," or outside a given narrative. While I have discussed briefly how autobiography and collective memory appear in the narratives of TV show scripts and unscripted dialogue, David Marc argues that television personalities relate to audiences in three ways: through a "frankly fictional" character; through a "presentational" character, in which the actor appears as her- or himself within a theatrical space such as a commercial; and through a "documentary" persona, in which the actor's real-life activities, opinions, and lifestyle are revealed through outside media.[8] Viewers register presentational and documentary associations linked to an actor as well as the fictional character he or she plays. (One may think of how this assemblage works in the case of someone like Bill Cosby, whose fictional Cliff Huxtable of *The Cosby Show* combines with the presentational image of the wholesome spokesperson for Jell-O pudding and the documentary persona of the real-life family man and philanthropist found in Cosby's autobiographical bestseller *Fatherhood*.)[9] Often, it is by examining fictional, presentational, and documentary personas together that we begin to recognize the most dynamic and intriguing patterns in our own reception practices.

The third characteristic of black television is culturally specific aesthetics. While rap music and graffiti-like graphics were common on white shows of this era as well, Afrocentric clothing, hairstyles, and artifacts performed specific functions in black shows. Frequent references to Malcolm X in *The Fresh Prince of Bel Air, Martin*, and *Roc*, for instance, in the form of posters, photographs, and T-shirts, invoked romanticized spaces of mythical unity and nationalist desire.[10]

Characters on *A Different World* displayed images of Yannick Noah, a world-renowned black French tennis player, and Angela Davis on their dormitory walls. Sportswear carrying the names of black colleges such as Howard and Spelman were common sights on *The Cosby Show, A Different World, Roc, The Sinbad Show*, and *Living Single*, as were black-owned publications like *Emerge, Ebony*, and *Essence*. The paintings of Varnette Honeywood featured in the Huxtable home even led some viewers and producers to invest in her work.[11]

Like the 1960s *The Bill Cosby Show*, which included frequent references to H. Rap Brown, dashikis, and soul food, such aesthetic markings did more than construct imagined community: They proposed a politics.[12] In his highly successful sitcom of the 1980s, Cosby even went to battle with NBC (and won) over an "Abolish Apartheid" sticker on Theo Huxtable's bedroom door.[13]

The fourth trait of black television is the struggle for drama. Whereas traditional sitcom formats demanded a "joke per page," many black productions of the 1980s and 90s resisted such norms by consciously and unconsciously crafting dramatic episodes. With less explicit story lines, unresolved endings, and increasingly complex characters, these "dramedies" allowed for exploration of painful in-group memories and experiences.[14]

While dramedies were often praised on white sitcoms (for example, in *Home Improvement*'s treatment of leukemia), such moves on black shows were rarely welcomed by networks, as was made clear with the cancellation of *Frank's Place*, a hard-hitting dramedy that looked at intraracial class and color differences among other issues. "There have been sparks of renewed hope in television," noted Tim Reid, who starred in and produced the show. "[But] the attempt to redefine the black sitcom formula is still a goal."[15]

Another example of network resistance to black drama was NBC's premature cancellation of *A Different World*. In its first season, the show was set in "a black college with a lot of white faces," said former staff writer Calvin Brown Jr. (Viewers may recall Marisa Tomei's early appearances.) "Although they had Thad Mumford and Susan Fales," said Brown, "the first season was not black-produced." That changed by season three, however, when Bill Cosby hired director-producer Debbie Allen to revamp the series.

Because Allen encouraged her largely African American staff to explore serious issues, the sitcom began to evolve around dramatic story lines: a woman physically abused by her boyfriend, a student with AIDS, white racism toward black shoppers in a posh jewelry store. One episode even addressed intraracial color prejudice and the fact that some light-skinned southerners had owned slaves. As Susan Fales recalled, this was a particularly explosive episode. "Discussion went on for three hours after that first table reading," said Fales. "The actors and writers had such painful memories . . . and we got so many calls and letters. People connected with the show on a very profound level."

"Debbie Allen came on and saved us," recalled former cast member Sinbad, as the show became, in the words of J. Fred MacDonald, "a vehicle for exploring social problems as disparate as date rape and the high percentage of blacks in the U.S.

military."[16] But while *A Different World* remained among the top five of all shows according to Nielsen (and even, at one point, outranked *Cosby* among black viewers in particular), the series was oddly canceled in 1991.

"Advertisers started requesting scripts of the show beforehand," recalled Debbie Allen. "This was new. But I had been given orders by Bill Cosby himself to go in and clean house, and to make it a show about intelligent young black people." Indeed, Allen had been given a rare opportunity; one that would not come again anytime soon. . . .

Three years later the Fox network also canceled *The Sinbad Show, Roc, South Central*, and *In Living Color*—four of its six black productions—in one fell swoop. Reverend Jesse Jackson initiated boycott threats and letter-writing campaigns; Ralph Farquhar and Tina Lifford (producer and star of *South Central*, respectively) traveled to Washington, D.C., to enlist the support of the Congressional Black Caucus; and Representative Ed Towns (D-NY) lambasted what he called the network's "plantation programming." "Fox-TV created its niche based upon racy, black, and youth-oriented programming," said a press release from the congressman's office. "Apparently, as the network moves to become more mainstream, its attitude to positive black programs is, we don't need, nor want them anymore. . . . I can assure you, the CBC [Congressional Black Caucus] and the black community is not going to allow [Rupert Murdoch] to blatantly treat us with disrespect and apparent contempt."

And yet it did. Fox cited poor ratings in canceling the shows, but it wasn't black faces or producers that did the programs in: It was black *complexity*. After Murdoch spent $1.6 billion on the rights to the National Football League's Sunday games, the network began to seek white "legitimacy." As Calvin Brown Jr. explained, only black folks and teenagers were watching Fox in its early days, "so they could get away with a little more. But now with

football, baseball, and hockey, that's over. We won't ever have another space in network television like that again."[17] . . .

"Did you ask Keenen," inquired director Bill Duke when I interviewed him in his Pacific Palisades home, "who has the rights to all those *In Living Color* reruns in Asia, and all over the world?" It was a good question, one I had not asked. Which brings us to the problem of media ownership.

In 1997, the Reverend Jesse Jackson was again on the heels of the media monsters, noting in his keynote address to the National Association of Minorities in Communication that minority media ownership had fallen by 15 percent over the past year alone.[18] At this rate, continued Jackson, there might be no remaining minority-owned stations by the year 2004. Without delving too far into the legalese of the Federal Communications Commission (FCC), I think it worthwhile to highlight some key events in recent telecommunications history—events that slipped past us while we debated the pros and cons of "positive" versus "negative" imagery.

Twenty years ago, President Nixon initiated a tax certification policy to help minority entrepreneurs buy fairer shares of the broadcast media pie. The incentive allowed for station owners and cable system operators to defer taxes on capital gains should they sell to minority buyers. As a result of the initiative, more than three hundred broadcast properties were sold to minorities over the next seventeen years, raising the percentage of minority ownership from 0.5 percent to a far grander 3 percent.

In 1995, however, something strange happened: An "especially slick" congressional bill generated "almost overnight" by Texas Republican Bill Archer called for an end to the tax incentive.[19] To ensure the bill's speedy passage, it was tucked inside an initiative to provide significant health care deductions for self-employed taxpayers—legislation that Republicans knew President Clinton wanted to see passed.

Why the sudden urge to end such a long-standing provision (barring the simple possibility of anti-civil rights backlash, of course)? The answer had everything to do with Rupert Murdoch, who sought to destroy a pending deal between his competitor, Viacom, and minority investor Frank Washington. The cancellation of the tax incentive did just that.[20] (Fox, on the other hand, managed to squeeze through its own minority investment deal: the $150 million sale of an Atlanta station to Qwest, a minority-controlled venture founded by Quincy Jones, Don Cornelius, Geraldo Rivera, and former pro football star Willie Davis.)

The irony in these events is that throughout the late 1980s and early 1990s, Rupert Murdoch not only found ways to profit from the cultural production and consumption practices of African Americans, but he also manipulated, to the collective detriment of black people, governmental infrastructures designed to balance the racially distorted playing field of media ownership. When such infrastructures threatened to limit Murdoch's monopolistic domination, in other words, he simply had them removed.

In 1994, for example, Fox took advantage of tax breaks for minority-owned enterprises by sinking $20 million into Blackstar Communications so that the minority venture could expand from three to fourteen stations (of which Fox would own a 20 percent interest). No act of goodwill, this was a move designed to circumvent FCC ownership limits. At the time, broadcast groups were limited to owning no more than twelve stations, covering no more than 25 percent of the nation's homes. In contrast, the limit for minority-controlled groups was fourteen stations and 30 percent coverage. Perhaps Jason Elkins, CEO of New Vision Television, put it most succinctly: "Those of us in broadcasting would [all] like to own twenty stations. It may be that Fox has found a way to do it through minority ownership."[21]

I've provided these brief musings on ownership so that we might keep in mind the larger contexts of global capitalism, even as we interrogate specific shows. In an environment in which government and market forces are actively hostile to non-white media ownership, the possibilities for black authorship are tentative at best. In fact, any potential for intraracial dialogue and collective autobiography in television is clearly mediated, sporadic, and forever subject to market-driven goals.[22]

Having said this, I'd like to close with a look at the changing landscape of black programming since 1994—the year that Fox canceled four of its six black shows. In 1993, Rupert Murdoch purchased the broadcast rights to Sunday afternoon football for $1.58 billion. This was followed by a $500 million deal with New World Communications that allowed Fox to expand from six to twenty-two stations, and to reach some 40 percent of U.S. households by 1997. Both transactions signaled the dawning of a new era for the fourth network, which was no longer content with its own "ghettoization" (or what was referred to in kinder days as "narrowcasting"). Because the fourth network now set out to be a legitimate contender alongside ABC, CBS, and NBC, it needed more white viewers.[23]

But the programming designed to entice Fox's newfound white male audience—shows such as *Fortune Hunter*, *Hardball*, and *Wild Oats*—was a dismal failure with the imagined beer-guzzling sports audience. Sunday's post-NFL schedule was gutted twice before Fox executives decided to backtrack, adding more of *The Simpsons* to its Sunday lineup, plus new episodes of the Latino-oriented *House of Buggin'*, starring John Leguizamo.

But then came a surprise. Both Warner Brothers (WB) and United Paramount (UPN) launched the "fifth" and "sixth" networks in 1996, consciously replicating Fox's early strategies in order to cash in on what now appeared to be an abandoned market. As Fox's president of sales noted, "[The new networks] are trying to outfox Fox, using our success in going for the young [black] audience."[24]

Just as Fox employees were once recruited from the then blackest network, NBC, new WB employees were snatched up from Fox. Suzanne Daniels, who helped to develop *Living Single*, became head of prime-time development at WB; Jaime Kellner became chief executive; Garth Ancier was again programming chief; and Bob Bibb and Louis Goldstein, who promoted Fox during its first two years, became marketing heads. "We are basically targeting the same old Fox demos," noted Bibb and Goldstein. "We want to convey the same attitude of hip."[25]

For their respective 1996-97 seasons, both WB and UPN aired a string of black-cast comedies. On WB, these included: *The Wayans Brothers*, *The Parent 'Hood* (starring *Hollywood Shuffle* director Robert Townsend), *The Jamie Foxx Show*, and *Lush Life*, a pilot from Yvette Lee Bowser, which was quickly canceled. In addition, WB picked up both *The Steve Harvey Show* and *Sister, Sister* following their cancellations on ABC.

Encouraged by the success of its *Moesha*, UPN also immersed itself in programming starring African Americans and Latinos. Among its new pilots were *Working Guy*, a sitcom about a black veteran adjusting to life on Wall Street; *American Family*, which tracked the goings on of an upwardly mobile Latino family; *Goode Behavior*, starring Sherman Helmsley as a con-artist father who moves in with his university dean son; *Sparks*, with Robin Givens; *Malcolm and Eddie*; and *Homeboys From Outer Space*. UPN also picked up the L. L. Cool J vehicle, *In the House*, following its cancellation on NBC.

Although it could be argued that black stars and producers also exercised significant creative control on each of these shows, the later productions never explored intraracial issues with the same seriousness of purpose as earlier shows discussed above. In contrast, African American decision makers such as Townsend, Shawn and Marlon Wayans, Jamie Foxx, Steve Harvey, and Suzanne de Passe almost never ventured beyond standard sitcom formats and mainstream, aracial themes. It is important to understand then, that while there were some twenty-one shows with black lead characters in 1997 (as compared to eight in 1990), these new series carefully avoided in-group dialogue around issues of color, class, gender, and sexuality. Network executives, it seems, now realized that they could have black-looking shows without the hassle of black complexity.

In fact, when ABC canceled its "black" lineup in 1995—shows like *On Our Own*, *Me and the Boys*, and *Sister, Sister*—*Los Angeles Times* television writer Rick DuBrow asked an important question: Why were these cancellations any different from Fox's axing of African American shows two years earlier? Why was there no protest over the cancellation of such "positive" black comedies? I would argue that black viewers did not complain—or even notice—because we had never invested the same degree of hope in these productions. These were black-*cast* shows as opposed to black *productions*. The shows that black audiences have been most passionate about, historically, are those presenting African American characters as multilayered, historical subjects who are ever-conscious of the collective.[26] . . .

While viewers aren't likely to see the Fox of the early 1990s again, racial narrowcasting remains an essential strategy for broadcast outlets such as Fox, WB, and UPN, as well as for cable stations such as Black Entertainment Television (BET), which purchased the rights to *Roc* and *Frank's Place* following their respective cancellations on network TV.[27] The growing Latino audience has also inspired Spanish-language premium services such as GEMS Television (the equivalent of Lifetime for Latinas), HBO en Espanol, and the Fox Latin American Network.

In short, the wave of the future for in-house, culturally specific dialogue will not necessarily be in network television. More and more, it will probably be found in cable or online services. As *Entertainment*

Weekly speculated, "The bigger UPN and the WB get, the whiter they'll become."[28] Whatever possibilities the new technologies may present, authorship will continue to be mediated by increasingly consolidated, transnational media conglomerates. . . .

I'm not particularly optimistic about the future of African American cultural representation. As Wayans reminded me, "Fox changed the course of black television *unintentionally*. They didn't go out to make black shows. They went out to make alternative programming. And when I came along with *In Living Color*, they were actually very fearful of what I was doing. But they knew that it was something different. And that's what they have to get credit for. By allowing that voice to be expressed, they discovered a whole new audience." Like an unfaithful lover, Fox continues to need black viewers—but on its own terms.

"The only reason Fox, WB, and UPN get involved in black programming," added a network vice president who did not wish to be named, "is so that they can temporarily sustain themselves. The minute they can, they pull out. The last thing these executives want to do is go to parties and talk about *Sparks, Sparks,* and more *Sparks*. It's something they want nothing to do with." "They build themselves up with black audiences," agreed former *New York Undercover* producer Judith McCreary. "Then once they're established, they dump us."

This [chapter] bears witness to the internal contradictions of African American producers and consumers. While our collective yearning for the mythical American dream is apparent in virtually every episode of every black-produced show, black Americans are stepping into a new century largely removed from the benefits of a global capitalist economy. Our challenge remains one of critical engagement. Because visual media colonize our imaginations, we must continue to strive for vigilant and sophisticated readings of television culture. We must continue to create transformative psychic—and physical—spaces in which to live fuller, more just lives.

Television, like the larger society it reflects, is at a crossroads. Shall we live and work and play together, or not? Integration, or niche markets? Fox, more than any other network, could provide a representational bridge to the future. Neither blatantly homeboyish like its successors, nor as Wonder Breadish as the original three networks, the fourth network has now set its sights on an "organic" multiculturalism. . . .

In the meantime, it would serve us well to remember that where integration fails, African Americans will always find ways to talk to one another, to dream and desire collectively. The Fox network of the early 1990s was one such place. Almost by accident, the fourth network nurtured dramatic episodes of *The Fresh Prince of Bel Air*, *The Sinbad Show*, and *South Central* that addressed intraracial classism and colorism; episodes of *Martin* and *Living Single* that looked at issues of black sexuality, gender, and romance; *Roc* that asked us to define a contemporary model of social responsibility and collective action; and *New York Undercover* that wrestled with shared yearnings among African Americans and Latinos.

Like a blast of fresh air after rain, African American productions of the early 1990s allowed us to inhale just a bit deeper, to reflect a fraction of a dramatic minute longer. Such shows helped us to know that our fears, desires, and memories are often collective, not individual. We may have been watching alone in our homes, but black shows of the 1990s were not unlike those conversations our grandparents used to have on front porches, in segregated cities, so far away from home.

Notes

1. See Nielsen 1987 and Alligood.

2. See David Atkin for a summary of NBC and black programming. By the early 1990s, ABC's lineup also included black-cast comedies such as *Family Matters, Hangin' With*

Mr. Cooper, and *Sister, Sister*. However, these were not black productions in that they were not headed by majority-black production staffs.

3. Unless otherwise noted, all quotes are from interviews with the author.

4. Feinberg, 3.

5. Block, 275.

6. Harris, 39.

7. See John Tulloch and Manuel Alvarado, Norma Schulman, Tricia Rose. Schulman borrows Deleuze and Guattari's notion of a "minor discourse" to talk specifically about black sitcoms. I find her reading problematic, however, as it categorically labels *Roc, The Fresh Prince of Bel Air, South Central*, and *The Sinbad Show* "assimilationist" narratives. My overriding point . . . is that such shows reveal, more accurately, a desire for that which is both African and American.

8. Also see Alperstein, who describes "imaginary social relationships" between viewers and actors based on gossip and prior media exposure.

9. Also see Gray 1989.

10. As Fredric Jameson makes clear in his classic study *The Political Unconscious*: "[Art] constitutes a symbolic act, whereby real social contradictions, insurmountable in their own terms, find a purely formal resolution in the aesthetic realm. . . . From this perspective, ideology is not something which informs or invests symbolic production; rather the aesthetic act is . . . to be seen as an ideological act in its own right" (70).

11. From a phone conversation with Eric Hanks, owner of M. Hanks Art Gallery and brother to Camille Cosby. Further extratextual ties may be seen in Bill Cosby's best-selling children's book, *Money Troubles*, which contains illustrations by Varnette Honeywood.

12. This description of *The Bill Cosby Show* is J. Fred MacDonald's, 1990, 118.

13. I thank Reebee Garofolo for alerting me to this point.

14. This is largely Ella Taylor's definition of a dramedy, 154.

15. Reid, 5. In fact Reid went on to create and co-executive produce, together with Susan Fales, yet another dramedy in 1998 called

Linc's. Debuting to rave reviews on Showtime, the series (directed by Debbie Allen) again addressed intraracial class issues as well as what Reid called "black homophobia." And yet having an executive producer credit does not always guarantee creative freedom, as Reid reminded me in 1994. "I had control on *Snoops*," he noted. "I had a certain amount of shared control on *Frank's Place*. Anything you see my name on, I'm gonna exercise control. However, in doing so you can antagonize the system. You can cause yourself to be in contention with the structure of network television that can create an atmosphere in which you don't get the proper enthusiasm for your project, especially if you're African American."

16. MacDonald 1990, 286.

17. A word on the ratings excuse: Warner Brothers (parent company of HBO/HIP) research confirms that *Roc*'s average ratings for 1991-92 were 13-14, about right for Fox. In 1993, the show was moved from Sunday to Thursday, and ratings predictably dropped. *Martin*, meanwhile, was placed in *Roc*'s former Sunday slot, where it garnered an average of 14. As these figures suggest, *Roc*'s ratings were less an indication of audience rejection than of network scheduling practices. In fact, black audiences preferred *Roc* (number 2) to *Martin* (number 4). The problem was that Fox was now interested in white audiences, which preferred *Martin*. See also Zook, "Dismantling *M.A.N.T.I.S.*," for a description of how one show was rewritten to reflect the network's shift from an Afrocentric aesthetic to one more suitable for white audiences.

18. Hettrick.

19. Holsendolph 1995.

20. President Clinton, meanwhile, expressed regret that he had not been better able to "deal with the Murdoch situation" as he might have done had he possessed the power of line-item veto.

21. Stern. Murdoch has also avoided paying his fair share of taxes. Whereas most large corporations—be they American, British, or Australian—pay between 20 percent and 40 percent of their taxable income, Murdoch's global empire paid less than 7 percent in 1995, by

using a system of "intra-company loans." Cowe.

22. Even a powerhouse such as Quincy Jones—who shares control of Quincy Jones-David Salzman Entertainment (QDE), Qwest Broadcasting, and *Vibe* magazine with Time Warner, Warner, and Time Ventures, respectively—does not participate in a single venture in which black ownership exceeds 50 percent. Another case in point is that of Black Entertainment Television (BET). Although commonly perceived as black-owned, due to its highly visible African American shareholder Robert Johnson, the subscription service was founded with Johnson's borrowed $15,000 and $500,000 invested by John Malone's TCI. See Trescott, *Emerge* 1995: 66.

23. As former president of network distribution for Fox Broadcasting, Preston Padden noted, "The NFL . . . marked the point in time when Rupert Murdoch decided he was not content to be the fourth network. He wanted to be number one." See Don West, 18.

24. Cerone, January 2, 1995.

25. Tobenkin.

26. 1994 NBC dramas such as *The Cosby Mysteries* and *Sweet Justice* were equally disappointing. Although they starred Bill Cosby and Cicely Tyson as "positive" professionals (a detective and an attorney, respectively), these shows were essentially white productions that situated African American viewers in uncomplicated, non-race specific ways.

27. Other possibilities for black authorship and collective autobiography might resemble ventures such as the African Heritage Network, a minority syndicator owned by Frank Mercado-Valdes and Baruch Entertainment. A similar enterprise was the now-defunct World African Network headed by Phyllis and Eugene Jackson, with backing from Clarence Avant, Percy Sutton, and Sidney Small. Although this premium channel "dedicated to the cultural uplift of African descendants" never materialized, it was a fascinating study in self-representation. Its founders planned to use what they called an "Africanity index" to rate the "cultural correctness" of its programming.

28. Jacobs, 15.

References ◆

WORKS CONSULTED

Alligood, Doug. "Monday Memo." *Broadcasting & Cable*, April 26, 1993: 74.

Alperstein, Neil M. "Imaginary Social Relationships With Celebrities Appearing in Television Commercials." *Journal of Broadcasting and Electronic Media* 35, no. 1 (Winter 1991): 43-58.

Atkin, David. "An Analysis of Television Series with Minority-Lead Characters." *Critical Studies in Mass Communication* 9, no. 4 (December 1992): 337-49.

Block, Alex Ben. *Outfoxed: Marvin Davis, Barry Diller, Rupert Murdoch, Joan Rivers, and the Inside Story of America's Fourth Television Network*. New York: St. Martin's, 1990.

Cerone, Daniel Howard. "A More Grown Up Look for Fox." *Los Angeles Times*, July 4, 1995: F1-F16.

Cosby, Bill. *Fatherhood*. Garden City, NY: Doubleday, 1986.

____. *Money Troubles*. Illustrated by Varnette P. Honeywood. New York: Scholastic Inc., 1998.

Cowe, Roger, and Lisa Buckingham. "Murdoch and His Small Tax Secret." *The Guardian Weekly*, July 28, 1996: 14.

Feinberg, Andrew. "TV Test-Drives New-Wave Comedy" Jerry, Carol and Keenen Go for Post-Sitcom Laughs." *TV Guide*, June 2, 1990: 3-6.

Gray, Herman. "Television, Black Americans, and the American Dream." *Critical Studies in Mass Communication* 6, no. 4, December 1989: 376-86.

Harris, Joanne. "Why Not Just Laugh? Making Fun of Ourselves on Television." *American Visions*, April-May 1993: 38-41.

Hettrick, Scott. "Jackson: Minority Media Off 15% on Tax Shift." *The Hollywood Reporter*, March 19, 1997: 6.

Holsendolph, Ernest. "Eroding Support for Minority Broadcasters." *Emerge*, May 1995: 21-22.

Jacobs, A. J. "Black to the Future: UPN and the WB's Focus on Black Shows Reignites Old Issues About TV's Color Barrier." *Entertainment Weekly*, June 14, 1996: 15-16.

Jameson, Fredric. *The Political Unconscious: Narrative as a Socially Symbolic Act.* Ithaca, NY: Cornell University Press, 1981.

MacDonald, J. Fred. *One Nation Under Television: The Rise and Decline of Network TV.* New York: Pantheon, 1990.

A. C. Nielsen Co. *Television Viewing Among Blacks: January-February 1987.* Northbrook, IL: A. C. Nielsen, 1987.

Reid, Tim. "A Tale of Two Cultures: An Actor-Producer's Perspective During Black History Month." *Los Angeles Times*, TV Times section, February 20-26, 1994: 1, 5.

Rose, Tricia. *Black Noise: Rap Music and Black Culture in Contemporary America.* Middletown, CT: Wesleyan University Press; Hanover, NH: University Press of New England, 1994.

____. *Never Trust a Big Butt and a Smile.* New York: Oxford University Press, forthcoming.

Schulman, Norma Miriam. "Laughing Across the Color Line: *In Living Color.*" *Journal of Popular Film and Television* 20, no. 1 (Spring 1992): 2-7.

Stern, Christopher. "Small Investments Yield Big Benefits: Networks Use Minority Interest in Stations to Lock in Affiliations." *Broadcasting & Cable*, October 17, 1994: 26, 28.

Taylor, Ella. *Prime-Time Families: Television Culture in Postwar America.* Berkeley: University of California Press, 1989.

Tobenkin, David. "Plotting WB-ification." *Broadcasting & Cable*, July 25, 1994: 15.

Trescott, Jacqueline. "Fifteen Years and Rising for BET's Star." *Emerge*, September 1995: 66-67.

Tulloch, John, and Manuel Alvarado. "Sendup: Authorship and Organization." In *Popular Fiction: Technology, Ideology, Production, Reading*, edited by Tony Bennett. London: Routledge, 1990.

West, Don. "Preston Padden: Strategizing to Move Fox From Underdog to Head of the Pack." *Broadcasting & Cable*, October 17, 1994: 18-26.

Zook, Kristal Brent. "Dismantling *M.A.N.T.I.S.*" *L.A. Weekly*, September 2, 1994: 41-42.

PERSONAL INTERVIEWS AND TELEVISION PROGRAMS

[EDITORS' NOTE: See *Color by Fox*, pp. 137ff, for a full list of personal interviews and television programs.]

56

REPRESENTING GAY MEN ON AMERICAN TELEVISION

◆ Kylo-Patrick R. Hart

At the start of the 1998-99 television season, NBC made television history with the premiere of *Will & Grace*, its new situation comedy featuring prime-time television's first gay male lead character. The show pairs Will Truman (Eric McCormack), a successful gay Manhattan lawyer, and Grace Adler (Debra Messing), an interior designer, as soulmates who support each other through happy times and sadder ones, such as the process of nursing broken hearts. Nielsen ratings reveal that audience members have responded favorably to this pairing as well as to Will's gay friend, Jack, played by Sean Hayes ("Culture," 1999). What is perhaps most noteworthy about the portrayal of these two gay male characters to date, however, is the striking contrast between the two: Will remains so low-key about his sexual orientation that it has become almost inconsequential to the show, while Jack is consistently presented as the stereotypical flamboyant queen. In other words, Will and Jack are extreme opposites on the spectrum of possible media representations of gay men. Is it true, as many critics claim, that Jack is too gay and Will is not

NOTE: Originally published in the *Journal of Men's Studies*, Vol. 9, No. 1, 59-79 (Fall 2000). Reprinted by permission of Men's Studies Press.

gay enough ("Culture," 1999)? Is it more accurate to argue, as others have, that these two characters simply represent the diversity of personality types that exist within the gay community?

◆ What Is Media Representation?

. . . The phenomenon of symbolic annihilation pertains to the historical nonrepresentation or underrepresentation of specific groups by the media—and/or to the trivialization of those groups when and if they infrequently appear—as a result of decisions by the powers-that-be at media outlets regarding what sorts of groups will and will not be represented in American media offerings and how they will be represented.

Clark (1969) identified four chronological stages of media representation of social groups. During the first stage, nonrecognition, the group simply does not appear at all in media offerings. Viewers from other cultures, therefore, would never know that members of that group exist in American culture if they receive all of their information about the United States through mass media channels. Once a specific group begins to be represented in media offerings, it enters the second stage: ridicule. During this stage of representation, the group is stereotyped and its members are frequently presented as being "buffoons," as were African Americans in the early television program *Amos 'n' Andy* or, more recently, with the character J. J. on *Good Times*. During the third stage of representation, regulation, members of the social group are presented as protectors of the existing social order, such as police officers and detectives. Finally, during the fourth and final stage of representation as identified by Clark—respect—members of the social group are presented in the complete range of roles, both positive and negative, that their members actually occupy in real life. Stereotypical characters may still appear during this stage, but they are part of a wide range of other characters from the same social group; as such, they are not considered to be as harmful to the process of social constructionism as are stereotypical characters when only a handful of characters representing the social group are present in the media overall.

Media representation matters because every media user can identify components of his or her "knowledge" of the social world that derive either wholly or partially from media representations, fictional or otherwise (Gross, 1994). This reality is especially relevant in the case of media representations of gay men on American television, since many heterosexual Americans do not (knowingly) interact with gay men on a regular basis and may, therefore, rely heavily on the mass media for their knowledge of gay men and the gay lifestyle. . . .

Representational ◆ Overview of Gay Men on American Television

The representation of gay men on American television from the late 1960s to the present has undoubtedly influenced the way the American public thinks about and responds, both socially and politically, to gay men and the issues of greatest relevance and concern to them. Media representations have shaped the way Americans come to understand the phenomenon of homosexuality and, ultimately, they have had a direct bearing on the already complex relationships within and between various social groups in American society (Estrada & Quintero, 1999). As these media representations have become part of the American social agenda, they have contributed significantly to the commonly accepted ways of discussing and considering the status of gay men and their lived realities. Media representations of gay men in recent decades have provided ideological guidance to

American audience members, since the codes, conventions, symbols, and visuals they have offered have contributed significantly to the social construction of gay men and to the resulting social ramifications of that construction.

Gay men remained in the nonrecognition stage of representation on American television until the late 1960s, when the nation regularly was being confronted with a host of social issues ranging from racial tensions and race riots to concerns about free love, drug abuse, and abortion. The masses received their first exposure to gay men and the gay lifestyle on national television on March 7, 1967, with the airing of the *CBS Reports* documentary "The Homosexuals" (Alwood, 1996). The goal of this documentary series was to "delve into social issues that were too controversial for most [other] programs" (Alwood, 1996, p. 69), and an installment about homosexuality promised to catch the public's attention. To represent the diversity of gay men in America, the producers arranged interviews with a variety of men, such as a sailor, a rodeo rider, a truck driver, and a female impersonator; despite this reality, during the production phase of this documentary, a prominent CBS correspondent referred to the project as the "pity a poor homosexual" show (Alwood, 1996, p. 70). Perhaps that is because some of the interview subjects were shown lying on an analyst's couch and many others were presented with their faces hidden in the leafy shadows of potted plants, as if they were filled with shame; perhaps it is because the program featured assessments from psychiatrists such as "The fact that somebody's homosexual . . . automatically rules out the possibility that he will remain happy for long," or uncomplimentary self-assessments by gay men such as "I know that inside now I'm sick—I'm not sick just sexually; I'm sick in a lot of ways" (Alwood, 1996, pp. 72-73). A final memorable aspect of the documentary was the stereotypical description of homosexuality offered by CBS correspondent Mike Wallace:

The average homosexual, if there be such, is promiscuous. He is not interested in nor capable of a lasting relationship like that of a heterosexual marriage. His sex life—his "love life"—consists of chance encounters at the clubs and bars he inhabits, and even on the streets of the city. The pickup—the one-night stand— these are characteristic of the homosexual relationship. And the homosexual prostitute has become a fixture on the downtown streets at night. (quoted in Rothenberg, 1981, p. 7)

With those words, gay men emerged from the nonrecognition stage on American television and entered Clark's (1969) second stage: ridicule. They remained primarily as objects of ridicule for several years, until the impact of the gay liberation movement increased the visibility of gay men in various social positions nationwide and produced increased levels of social tolerance. . . .

Alwood (1996) points out that NBC's *Rowan and Martin's Laugh-In* was the first network television show to approach the subject of gay men and their lifestyles with some regularity by creating in 1970 the stereotypically effeminate character named Bruce, who was subjected to long strings of antigay jokes; within a few years, the show was averaging one joke per program about gay men and gay liberation. . . .

Gay men entered the regulation stage of media representation, as defined by Clark (1969), in the late 1970s with the introduction of a positive gay male character on the police-precinct-based situation comedy *Barney Miller*; other positive gay characters appeared during this period in the short-lived series *The Nancy Walker Show* and the longer-running sitcom *Alice* (Alwood, 1996). By then, the gay liberation movement had revealed the range of positions gay men hold in American society, and "the term 'gay' [had been] wrenched away from the older pejorative discourse of 'homosexuality'" (Watney, 1996, p. 18). Such positive portrayals continued into the 1980s when NBC introduced the situation comedy *Love, Sidney*, starring Tony Randall. This series, based on a made-for-television movie about a man who had recently broken up with his male lover, almost provided American prime-time television with its first gay male lead character. The network, however, backed away from the character's homosexuality and deleted all references to it, going so far as to say that the series was not directly related to the movie. Although the character of Sidney was quite a sympathetic one, the series was soon canceled as a result of low ratings.

The positive representational strides achieved by gay men in the late 1970s and early 1980s suffered a series of setbacks in the mid- to late 1980s, as acquired immune deficiency syndrome (AIDS) emerged as a health threat in American society and became representationally linked to gay males. Early on, the condition was referred to as GRID, which stood for "gay-related immunodeficiency" and linked the disease directly with the gay male lifestyle from the earliest days of media coverage (Piontek, 1992). The term AIDS was adopted by the Centers for Disease Control in Atlanta in 1982, but by then the stage had already solidly been set for media representations of AIDS as "a gay plague," "the price paid for anal intercourse," "a fascist ploy to destroy homosexuals," and "a disease that turns fruits into vegetables," among similar others (Treichler, 1988, pp. 32-33). Such representations persisted even as other risk groups—including intravenous drug users and Haitians who had emigrated to the United States—were added to the list of infected individuals, along with hemophiliacs, the first "innocent victims" (Gross, 1994; Hart, 1999). Gay men who were already stigmatized as "deviant" were further stigmatized as "lethally contagious" and were represented to be a significant health threat to "innocent" individuals in the population at large (Cadwell, 1991, p. 237). . . .

In the late 1980s, several prime-time television shows—including *21 Jump Street, Designing Women, The Equalizer, Houston Knights, Leg Work, Midnight Caller, Mr. Belvedere,* and *A Year in the Life*—represented AIDS in individual episodes, and virtually all of them served to solidify the link between gay men and AIDS either explicitly or implicitly (Netzhammer & Shamp, 1994). . . .

In the AIDS episode of *21 Jump Street,* Officer Tom Hanson (Johnny Depp) is assigned to guard a male teen with AIDS from harassment by his peers. Although the teen's father claims that his son is a hemophiliac and contracted HIV/AIDS as a result of a blood transfusion, Hanson eventually learns that the father has lied because he is ashamed of the true cause of his son's condition. Instead, the teen reveals that he is gay and that he has never had a blood transfusion nor injected drugs of any kind. This revelation, concealed until the episode's end, intensifies the inseparability of AIDS and gay males by "accepting the logic of religious fundamentalists—unspeakable acts have brought forth this disease" (Netzhammer & Shamp, 1994, p. 96).

American television programs in the 1990s continued to represent AIDS. Although a few shows have occasionally strived intentionally to break the representational link between gay men and AIDS (such as the AIDS story line on *ER*), many others (including *Beverly Hills, 90210,* as discussed at length in the next section of this [chapter]) have continued to perpetuate this harmful pattern of media representation. This persistent representational approach has become especially suspect as the decade of the 1990s has progressed and the demographics of Americans being diagnosed with AIDS have undergone dramatic change. Today, reported cases of AIDS resulting from heterosexual transmission of HIV are rising steadily, with heterosexual women, heterosexual African American men, and heterosexual adolescents now comprising sizable high-risk groups for HIV transmission and AIDS (Tewksbury & Moore, 1997; Wright, 1997). Unfortunately, because the earliest reported cases of AIDS were exclusively among gay men, the representation of AIDS in so many prime-time television offerings since the late 1980s has either explicitly or implicitly linked homosexuality and AIDS, framing AIDS as "a universal problem perpetuated by gays" (Altman, 1986; Netzhammer & Shamp, 1994, p. 92).

Despite such persistent representations of gay men in relation to AIDS, gay men ultimately entered the respect stage of representation on American television, as defined by Clark (1969), in the 1990s. The conservative Reagan-Bush era was drawing to a close, and President Bill Clinton was soon elected to office after actively seeking the support of gay men and lesbians for the first time in the history of presidential politics (McKinney & Pepper, 1999). Gay men achieved wider recognition and greater levels of social tolerance than in the past, and the major network prime-time shows began to increasingly represent diverse and inclusive gay male characters that cumulatively reflect the wide range of roles that gay men occupy in American society. In 1990, for example, the drama series *thirtysomething* introduced two recurring gay male characters who ended up sleeping together and were shown together in bed. In 1992, the daytime soap opera *One Life to Live* featured a summer story line about a gay teen's self-discovery of his sexual orientation that culminated in an onscreen scene between the teen and his boyfriend ("Gay and Lesbian Suds," 1997). In the mid-1990s, the sitcom *Roseanne* introduced two recurring gay male characters—Roseanne's business partner Leon (Martin Mull) and his lover Scott (Fred Willard)—who ultimately participated in a wedding ceremony on the show. Beginning in 1995, producers of the daytime soap opera *All My Children* introduced several gay characters—high school history teacher, Michael Delaney (Chris Bruno); high school student, Kevin Sheffield (Ben Jorgensen); television station stage manager, Rudy (Lance Baldwin); and orthopedic specialist, Dr. Brad Phillips (Daniel McDonald)—and went on to feature them in groundbreaking story lines, including the burgeoning romantic relationship between Michael and Brad that included a New Year's Eve proposal and the men establishing a joint life and home together (Kent, 1997).

By the time the ABC sitcom *Ellen* made television history in 1997 by introducing the first lesbian lead character on a prime-time series, regular and recurring gay male characters were present on a variety of prime-time shows, including *Chicago Hope, Cybill, Frasier, Melrose Place, Party of Five, Profiler, Roseanne, The Simpsons, Spin City,* and *Unhappily Ever After* ("GLAAD Scorecard," 1997). With the launch of the 1998-99 television season, there were more gay characters of color on American television than ever before, and *Will & Grace* introduced prime-time television's first gay male lead character ("TV," 1999). . . . The following discussion of the representation of gay men on Fox prime time highlights both the representational strides that have been made with regard to gay men over the past decade and the representational shortcomings that need yet to be more fully addressed.

Representation of ◆ Gay Men on Fox Prime Time

. . . From its very beginning, the Fox network has owed a great deal of its success as an entrant into the television marketplace to its creative programming choices and strategies. The management at Fox believed that if the network was to compete effectively with the big three American television networks, they would need to draw from the same talent pool in order to provide appealing prime-time programs. As a result, to attract several of the top television producers who were constantly in demand, Fox made an implicit promise to offer greater creative freedom than was possible at the big three networks, the opportunity to be far more daring in language use and overall content, and minimal network interference in day-to-day production processes of the shows it broadcasts (Block, 1990). Fox soon became a creative magnet for television producers seeking to experiment and to push the content boundaries of the medium to new levels, which resulted in the creation and widespread popularity of such unique hits as *The Tracey Ullman Show*, *In Living Color*, and *Married . . . With Children* (Grover & Duffy, 1990).

Fox executives strived to ensure that their programs would always be less subject to mass-audience pressures than the offerings of the big three networks. "If we've got a good male action series," explained Fox network president Jamie Kellner in 1986, "we won't add children, dogs and females to make it appeal to other demographics" (Zoglin, 1986, p. 98). Further, as part of a conscious desire to appeal to a highly profitable, younger demographic target audience, the network remained more willing over time to test the boundaries of permissible content, as evident in various episodes of the oft-tasteless situation comedy *Married . . . With Children* and the half-hour comedy-skit program *In Living Color*, which featured a number of eyebrow-raising and sometimes controversial sketches such as "Riding Miss Daisy," a parody of the movie in which the chauffeur and his employer go at it in the back seat (Zoglin, 1990). This is the same program that offered one of the most pervasive early representations of gay men on the Fox network, in the form of a pair of flaming gay entertainment critics who dress stereotypically in delicate, brightly colored fabrics and snicker over sexually suggestive movie titles such as "Dick Tracy" and "Moby Dick" (Gray, 1995; Zoglin, 1990).

In the 1990s, Fox continued to provide a variety of popular programming geared primarily toward viewers between the ages of 18 and 34. Three of the network's most popular programs during this decade have been *Beverly Hills, 90210*, *Melrose Place*, and *Party of Five*, and each of these programs has represented gay men in various ways over the years. . . .

Representing Gay Men ◆ on Beverly Hills, 90210

Having recently completed its tenth and final season, *Beverly Hills, 90210* appeared in the Fox prime-time lineup during the 1990-91 television season. Although early reviews of the show were mixed, this series about a Midwestern family transplanted to Beverly Hills, California, and its twin children, Brandon and Brenda Walsh, who began attending high school there emerged as a keeper while two other, more critically embraced high-school-based shows—NBC's *Hull High* and *Ferris Bueller*—vanished quickly without a trace (Littwin, 1991).

By the end of its first season, *Beverly Hills, 90210* had established itself as a demographic magnet for teenage and young-adult viewers, and only recently has the show's appeal begun to fade. A major goal of this series from its inception, as series creator Darren Star has explained, has been to provide a truthful, sophisticated show that would speak to younger television viewers the same way that the series *thirtysomething* spoke to members of its generation (Littwin, 1991). As the series has progressed over the years and the characters have graduated from both high school and college and entered the working world, the show's commitment to representing noteworthy social problems and conditions has persisted (Hart, 1999). Thus, because so many episodes of the show have dealt in candid, prosocial ways with issues ranging from substance abuse by teens and adults to clinical depression and homelessness, viewers likely expected to encounter a similar same sort of prosocial treatment regarding the topic of gay men. They have not usually received this sort of treatment, however.

Beverly Hills, 90210 first represented the issue of gay male sexuality early in the show's second season, in the form of the "confused" teen. During a series of summer days at the beach, regular character Kelly Taylor (Jennie Garth) could not figure out why an attractive male teen did not seem interested in her sexually, even though he seemed to like her. When the sense of rejection Kelly was feeling began to endanger her self-esteem, she finally confronted the object of her affections about his sexual orientation. "Are you gay?" she asked him directly. "No—I don't know," he responded, before the two agreed to remain friends. From an ideological standpoint, this treatment of homosexuality enabled the series to take up the issue of homosexuality without actually taking up the issue at all, since the "confused" teen represents "potential" homosexuality rather than "actual" homosexuality. . . .

The series represented gay men next near the end of its fourth season, when the car in which regular characters Brandon Walsh (Jason Priestley) and Steve Sanders (Ian Ziering) were riding broke down near a gay coffee house. Once inside to use a pay telephone, Steve glimpsed the president of his fraternity, Mike Ryan, surrounded by gay patrons. Panicked by what he saw, Steve thereafter feared the moment when Mike might make "one move on [him], one gesture, one look," and, after another fraternity brother jokingly questioned Steve's own heterosexuality, Steve shared the information of Mike's "deviant" sexual orientation. By episode's end, distressed at his own homophobia (as pointed out by his friends) and the likely implications of his actions, Steve convinced the other fraternity brothers to allow Mike to remain in the fraternity and as its president. To some extent, therefore, the representation of gay men in this episode was a positive one, since Mike—the attractive fraternity president and skilled athlete—was presented sympathetically and defied stereotypes of gay men. At the same time, however, this episode treated homosexuality as a problem to be dealt with, after which this gay character disappeared from visibility entirely.

Three seasons later, near the start of the 1996-97 television season, *90210* introduced a third gay character as part of a three-week story line about AIDS. This time around, character Kelly Taylor began working at an AIDS hospice in exchange for college credit, where she met an aspiring gay magician named Jimmy (Michael Stoyanov). As the first AIDS episode unfolded, Kelly and Jimmy began to converse frequently and think of each other as friends, which suggested that the entire AIDS story line would be one about caring for others in times of need, despite individual differences (including those of sexual orientation). The second AIDS episode, however, revealed that this was not what the story line was ultimately going to be about after all. In that episode, Kelly disappeared from Jimmy's life, despite what appeared to be their burgeoning friendship, after he cut his hand while preparing dinner and she got some of his blood on her own hands. Despite Jimmy's assurances that her odds of contracting HIV that way were one in a million, subsequent scenes in the episode presented Kelly relentlessly washing her hands and making excuses as to why she could not revisit Jimmy at the hospice. It was only after Kelly's doctor assured her that unbroken skin posed a barrier to the virus contained in Jimmy's blood and an HIV test revealed that she was HIV-negative that Kelly renewed her relationship with Jimmy. At that moment, however, despite looking and acting as if he were in remarkably good health, Jimmy informed Kelly that the end was near. He was right. The content of the third and final AIDS episode wrapped up the story line quite efficiently, as Jimmy's health took a sudden downturn and he died. With the exception of a brief replay clip featuring Jimmy on his deathbed at the start of the following week's episode, neither Jimmy nor the risk of HIV/AIDS was mentioned again in the weeks and months that followed.

Although *90210* did a somewhat admirable job of portraying Jimmy as an articulate, well-adjusted, sympathetic character who defied traditional stereotypes, there is simply no denying that the reinforcement of the representational link between gay men and AIDS was completely unnecessary in this instance. . . . Had the decision instead been made to feature a central character with AIDS who was not a gay male, the series would have made a significant representational stride toward undermining the conceptualization of AIDS as a "gay disease," rather than reinforcing this stereotypical notion. Although it appeared that *90210* was preparing to explore the issue of HIV/AIDS and heterosexual women at the start of the show's ninth season—after regular character Valerie Malone (Tiffani-Amber Thiessen) had unprotected sex with an intravenous drug user and was awaiting the results of her HIV test during the final episode of the eighth season—the series backed away from that promising story line entirely by giving Valerie a clean bill of health less than five minutes into the start of the next season.

During the show's eighth season, *Beverly Hills, 90210* introduced a handful of other gay male characters in brief story lines pertaining to a gay teen who became estranged from his parents after revealing his sexual orientation, as well as a gay couple who had faced several years' worth of difficulty attempting to adopt a child. Although the show presented all three of these gay men as likable, sympathetic characters, the primary function they served was to enable the show's regular characters to confront their own homophobic impulses and then to resurface as the gay characters' heroes—much as the character Steve did in his interactions with the fraternity president in the fourth season—rather than to motivate a thorough exploration of issues of significance to gay men in American society. . . .

Representing Gay Men ◆ *on* Melrose Place

Having spun off from *Beverly Hills, 90210* in 1992, *Melrose Place* presents the daily adventures of a group of young adults with ties to the same Los Angeles apartment complex. In contrast to the representation of gay men on *90210*, however, this series included a regular gay male character, Matt Fielding (Doug Savant), from its inception and until the start of its sixth season in 1997. By featuring a gay male character each week who was consistently likable, well-adjusted, and civic-minded, *Melrose Place* took a major step forward in the representational right direction. Unfortunately, the primary shortcoming of the resulting representation of gay men on this show stems from the reality that Matt has alternatively qualified as the "most straight" gay male character in modern television offerings (during the show's first two seasons) as well as the poster boy for dysfunctional gay relationships (during the character's final three seasons on the show). . . .

Matt left Los Angeles on the first episode of the show's sixth season to complete his residency at an AIDS research facility in San Francisco. He disappeared without a trace, taking the visibility of gay characters with him as he departed. Then, in a surprising move early in the show's seventh (and final) season, Matt (never shown on screen) was killed in a Los Angeles automobile accident while supposedly on his way to a reunion dinner organized by Amanda (Heather Locklear). As such, the gay male character who had been gone for more than one season was symbolically reintroduced only to be sacrificed, eradicating his "deviance" once and for all. In all, although the regular presence of Matt Fielding challenged mediated heterosexism to some extent each week through the ongoing representation of a gay man on screen, Matt's character ultimately proved to be a "groundbreaking" one primarily only in the sense that he consistently pushed the limits of dysfunctional gay relationships to newer and greater extremes.

◆ Representing Gay Men on Party of Five

Fox's *Party of Five* follows the lives of the Salingers, five siblings who remain determined to stay together as a family unit following the unexpected death of their parents. This one-hour drama series, winner of the 1996 Golden Globe Award for Best Drama Series, has featured the recurring gay male character Ross (Mitchell Anderson) from its inception, who serves as the music instructor to teen violinist Claudia Salinger (Lacey Chabert).

During *Party of Five*'s first season in 1994-95, Claudia and her siblings wrestled with issues of homophobia and acceptance of others despite individual differences after Ross came out to his student, and the Salinger clan came to Ross's assistance months later when Ross encountered obstacles resulting from his sexual orientation in his attempt to adopt a baby. Both of these episodes were thoughtfully presented, and the reality that Ross, as a single gay male, successfully adopted a beautiful baby girl and served as a wonderful parent to her was a representational victory for gay men in American society. During the rest of this first season and throughout the second season, Ross was consistently presented as a likable, well-adjusted, sincere, caring gay man and father who helped Claudia to expand her range of musical talents and the Salinger family to deal with the emotional situations they regularly encountered.

During the show's third season, in contrast, Ross was rarely presented on screen, and the only episode that featured his character in any significant way involved his burgeoning romantic relationship with an English teacher, Mr. Archer, at Claudia's school. Like Matt on *Melrose Place*, Ross believed that he had finally met the man of his dreams, and all went well initially. Soon, however, Ross learned that the teacher was not secure with his sexual orientation and that he felt the need to keep his relationship with Ross completely under wraps, concealing it even from his mother and close others. Although Ross decided to end this romantic relationship immediately rather than remain involved with someone who appeared to be ashamed of him—which from a representational standpoint was a positive decision, challenging the stereotype that gay men must simply settle for whatever relationships they can find—this story line nevertheless reinforced the view persistent in Fox prime time that romantic happiness is not to be found by gay men living in the modern age.

Again during the fourth season of *Party of Five*, Ross's visibility decreased to the point of no return. In what initially appeared to be the character's last appearance on the show (and only his second brief appearance that season), Ross attended the wedding ceremony of Julia (Neve Campbell) and Griffin (Jeremy London) alone, at which he stereotypically sang show tunes to calm a young girl who got locked in a bathroom. On that note, the most promising (from the standpoint of prosocial media representation) gay male character in Fox prime time disappeared (almost) without a trace. He resurfaced only for a few minutes late in the show's fifth season to commiserate with Claudia about how it feels to love somebody one cannot have, and then again for a few minutes during the show's sixth and final season to help Claudia refocus her attention on her musical abilities. . . .

Concluding Remarks ◆

. . . The examples presented in this [chapter] reveal not only how much progress has been made regarding the representation of gay men on American television in recent decades but also how much progress has yet to be made.

Certainly, including gay male characters as recurring, regular, and lead characters in American television programs is a crucial first step toward enhancing the overall representation of gay men on American television. What the producers and writers of such programs opt to do with those characters once they exist, however, is equally important. Care must be devoted to consciously avoiding outdated, stereotypical representations of AIDS that thoughtlessly link the disease almost exclusively with gay men, the inclusion of gay story lines only when their outcomes will be negative, and the reduction of diverse gay communities to a singular, stereotypical "lifestyle" or presumed way of life.

◆ References

Altman, D. (1986). *AIDS in the mind of America*. Garden City, NY: Anchor.

Alwood, E. (1996). *Straight news: Gays, lesbians, and the news media*. New York: Columbia University Press.

Block, A. B. (1990). *Outfoxed: The inside story of America's fourth television network*. New York: St. Martin's.

Cadwell, S. (1991). Twice removed: The stigma suffered by gay men with AIDS. *Smith College Studies in Social Work*, *61*(3), 236-246.

Clark, C. (1969). Television and social controls: Some observation of the portrayal of ethnic minorities. *Television Quarterly*, *9*(2), 18-22.

Culture: But "Will" he kiss? (1999, March 10). *Out Post*, p. 10.

Estrada, A., & Quintero, G. A. (1999). Redefining categories of risk and identity: The appropriation of AIDS prevention information and constructions of risk. In W. N. Elwood (Ed.), *Power in the blood: A handbook on AIDS, politics, and communication*

(pp. 133-147). Mahwah, NJ: Lawrence Erlbaum.

Gay and lesbian suds. (1997, Spring). *GLAAD Images*, *2*(1), 21.

GLAAD scorecard (1997, April). Available: http://www.glaad.org/glaad/scoreboard.html

Gray, H. (1995). *Watching race: Television and the struggle for "blackness."* Minneapolis: University of Minnesota Press.

Gross, L. (1994). What is wrong with this picture? Lesbian women and gay men on television. In R. J. Ringer (Ed.), *Queer words, queer images: Communication and the construction of homosexuality* (pp. 143-156). New York: New York University Press.

Hart, K. (1999). Retrograde representation: The lone gay white male dying of AIDS on *Beverly Hills, 90210*. *The Journal of Men's Studies*, *7*, 201-213.

Kent, S. (1997, Spring). Will there be love, will there be sex? *GLAAD Images*, *2*(1), 18-20.

Littwin, S. (1991, July 13). *Beverly Hills, 90210* has struck a nerve with young people. *TV Guide*, *39*(28), 11-12.

McKinney, M. S., & Pepper, B. G. (1999). From hope to heartbreak: Bill Clinton and the rhetoric of AIDS. In W. N. Elwood (Ed.), *Power in the blood: A handbook on AIDS, politics, and communication* (pp. 77-92). Mahwah, NJ: Lawrence Erlbaum.

Netzhammer, E. C., & Shamp, S. A. (1994). Guilt by association: Homosexuality and AIDS on prime-time television. In R. J. Ringer (Ed.), *Queer words, queer images: Communication and the construction of homosexuality* (pp. 91-106). New York: New York University Press.

Piontek, T. (1992). Unsafe representations: Cultural criticism in the age of AIDS. *Journal for Theoretical Studies in Media and Culture*, *15*(1), 128-153.

Rothenberg, D. (1981, June 15). Media watch. *New York Native*, pp. 7-9.

Tewksbury, R., & Moore, D. K. (1997). Men's sexual risk factors of HIV infection: Racial differences in behavior, knowledge, and self-perceptions. *The Journal of Men's Studies*, *6*, 91-102.

Treichler, P. A. (1988). AIDS, homophobia, and biomedical discourse: An epidemic of signi-fication. In D. Crimp (Ed.), *AIDS: Cultural analysis, cultural activism* (pp. 31-70). Cambridge, MA: MIT Press.

TV: 1998 in review. (1999, January 6). *Out Post*, p. 12.

Watney, S. (1996). *Policing desire: Pornography, AIDS and the media*. Minneapolis: University of Minnesota Press.

"Will & Grace" to move to Thursdays. (1999, March 10). *Out Post*, p. 12.

Wright, E. R. (1997). The social construction of AIDS. In E. R. Wright & M. Polgar (Eds.), *Teaching the sociology of HIV/AIDS* (pp. 69-88). Washington, DC: ASA Teaching Resources Center.

Zoglin, R. (1986, May 19). The Joan vs. Johnny show. *Time*, p. 98.

Zoglin, R. (1990, August 27). The Fox trots faster. *Time*, pp. 64-66.

57

WHAT'S WRONG WITH THIS PICTURE?

The Politics of Ellen's Coming Out Party

◆ Susan J. Hubert

The controversy over Ellen's coming out episode was largely a media-created event. Josh Ozersky called it "one of the most publicized pseudo-events in TV history" (Ozersky 80). And it worked. The audience was the third largest for a single series episode in the history of television (Steyn 80), even though the show's popularity had been declining. The advertising spots went for premium rates, some for as much as 20% more than *Ellen*'s usual $170,000 fee for a thirty-second commercial (Grover 6). Gay and lesbian organizations throughout the country organized "Come Out With Ellen" parties on the night of the episode, and the *Miami Herald* called Ellen DeGeneres "a gay Jackie Robinson" (Steyn 49). Not everyone was taken in by the hype, however. Lesbian comedian Kate Clinton pointed out the overblown quality of the controversy by writing about a supposed friend who had come to believe that "Ellen's coming out will usher in not only the end of homophobia but also the end of racism, sexism, and ageism" (Clinton 46). On the contrary, Ellen's supposedly

NOTE: From *Journal of Popular Culture*, Vol. 32, No. 2 (Fall 1999). Copyright © 1999 by Bowling Green State University. Reprinted by permission.

controversial attempt to push the limits of acceptability actually reinscribes conventional sexual politics.

Yet, the controversy over Ellen's coming out reveals a lot about homophobia in the United States. Organizations associated with the Religious Right took out a full-page ad in *Variety*, calling the show "a slap in the face to American families" (Steyn 80). The Reverend Jerry Falwell referred to Ellen DeGeneres as "Ellen Degenerate" (quoted in Handy, "Roll Over" 83). "Falwell . . . wrote to *Ellen* advertisers warning of Moral Majority retaliation" (Grover 6), and "the Rev. Donald E. Wildmon's American Family Association also issued barely veiled threats to boycott Ellen's advertisers" (Handy, "Roll Over" 83). Two major advertisers, Chrysler and J. C. Penney, cancelled their sponsorship of the show, and an ABC affiliate in Birmingham, Alabama, refused to broadcast the controversial episode (Steyn 49). The taping of the final segment of the show was disrupted by a bomb threat (Handy, "Roll Over" 81), and, months after the episode was broadcast, DeGeneres was harassed at a concert by a man who called her "an embarrassment to Jesus" (De Vries 29). These incidents reveal the level of hostility directed toward gays and lesbians in American society today.

However, homophobia was also apparent from the "inside." Disney Television, the producer of *Ellen*, wanted to be cautious. The script had to be approved, and the first script was rejected, reportedly because it focused too much on the reaction of Ellen's friends (Martin and Miller 66). Plans to have the show open with Melissa Etheridge singing a serious song about coming out were changed. As one of the writers remarked, "There were so many fences to walk. If we go one way, someone will get offended" (Rice 41). The episode was geared to the entertainment and political tastes of American moderates and distanced itself from both conservatives and progressives. Several popular figures made cameo appearances to sanctify the episode for

television viewers, and the program excluded anything that might alienate its intended audience. Ellen DeGeneres did the talk-show circuit to publicize the show and to test audience reaction. "It was depressing, that song and dance she did on the talk shows," said Camille Paglia. "She was asking America, 'Is it O.K.? Will you still like me if . . . ?' It was wimpy. It robbed the act of any courage" (quoted in Bellafante 91). DeGeneres has also made a few unfortunate remarks, such as saying that she uses the word *gay* more often than *lesbian* because *lesbian* "sound[s] like somebody with some kind of disease" (Handy, "Roll Over" 79).

A major component behind the complexity of the show is DeGeneres herself. Perhaps it's easy for her to reject the claims of conservatives and progressives, because she appears to have no political commitments at all. Despite the enthusiasm of gay and lesbian activists, DeGeneres's motivation was not political. "I didn't do it to make a political statement," she said. "I did it selfishly for myself and because I thought it was a great thing for the show, which desperately needed a point of view" (Handy, "Ellen Degenerate" 86). At the same time, DeGeneres had other reasons for coming out. One of her aims is to counter media stereotypes of gays and lesbians. "Unfortunately," DeGeneres says, "the people who get the most attention on the news [are] dykes on bikes or these men dressed as women" (Handy, "Ellen Degenerate" 86). She claims that "the whole point of what I'm doing is acceptance of everybody's differences" (Handy, "Ellen Degenerate" 86). Although it is important to portray the diversity among gay and lesbian communities, the problem with Ellen's approach is that oppression is not merely the result of a lack of tolerance. Heterosexism is deeply imbedded in American culture, and the structures of social injustice must be confronted.

In addition, it can be just as harmful to ignore differences between people as it is to focus on them. *Ellen* tries to ignore the differences. The coming out episode portrays an apolitical gay woman who is "just like" heterosexuals and fits right into mainstream American society. Ellen's sexual orientation turns out to be practically inconsequential. As Ozersky writes, "Throughout the episode, the point is made over and over: why should anyone care about Ellen's sexual orientation?" (Ozersky 80). The show also avoided any association with gay and lesbians politics. The scene at a women's coffeehouse, for instance, parodies performances by lesbian-feminist singers. k.d. Lang closes a song about lesbian sisterhood by making a fist, and, after Audrey gets the men to participate in a rousing chorus, one of them says, "You should have been here for 'Sister, Sister, O My Sister.'" Dean Valentine, president of Disney television, said, "I told Ellen, I'm not interested in standing on political soapboxes" (Martin and Miller 66). Apparently, there was no problem with making fun of lesbians who do care about politics.

Another problem with the politics of the episode is the way the show tries to make parallels between homophobia and racism. In a session with her African American therapist, played by Oprah Winfrey, Ellen asks, "You mean I have to drink from a separate fountain?" There are other echoes of racist rhetoric. For instance, in the coffeehouse scene, one of Ellen's friends asks, "What do you people drink?" Although such lines bring to mind the African American struggle against societal injustice and individual prejudice—a struggle that continues to this day—the association between racism and heterosexism doesn't succeed in a depoliticized television show. Moreover, there is a racist edge to such careless parallels between racial oppression and heterosexism. When an interviewer remarked that "it must be odd having your sexuality a subject of national debate," DeGeneres responded affirmatively and said, "That's why I want to get beyond this . . . let's get beyond this, and let me get back to what I do. Maybe I'll find something even bigger to do later on. Maybe I'll become black" (Handy, "Ellen Degenerate" 86).

Even with all the publicity and a large television audience, Ellen Morgan's sexuality is divorced from the public realm of political activity. At the same time, though, the blurring of the lives of Ellen Morgan and Ellen DeGeneres also mixes the private and public spheres. The coming out scene at the airport mimics the dual meaning of the event. Ellen inadvertently steps in front of a public address microphone just as she says to Susan, "I'm gay." Ellen DeGeneres's mother plays one of the airline customers who are present when Ellen comes out not only to Susan but also to the entire airport. In addition, ABC followed the show with a special segment on Ellen DeGeneres, in which she and her parents talked about her sexual orientation and the struggles they'd had over it. Try as she might to claim that sexuality is a private affair, the personal begs to become the political.

Despite all these factors, Ellen doesn't really allow the personal to become political. The two Ellens are supposed to be in different places. One magazine finds it significant that DeGeneres's character isn't comfortable with her sexuality, claiming that "her show's new direction will be groundbreaking not only for having a gay lead character, but for having a gay lead character who is not yet entirely comfortable with her sexuality—a departure from the normal run of things in the '90s, when gay characters on TV tend to be proud, assertive and more or less uplifting" (Handy, "Roll Over" 85). DeGeneres herself says that "Ellen Morgan and I are in very different places in our lives: She has just discovered she's gay, but I've known this for a long time, and believe me, I can go a whole day without having a single gay reference" (De Vries 24). Ellen Morgan might not be comfortable with her sexuality, but Ellen DeGeneres doesn't appear to be comfortable with the political aspects of being openly lesbian.

The confusion between the public and private spheres also placed the audience in a voyeuristic position. However, despite the curiosity of some viewers about gay and lesbian sexuality, the show did not contain any intimations of same-sex activity. In fact, the most sexually explicit scene involves Ellen's unsuccessful encounter with an old boyfriend. As Ellen recounts the incident, she is encouraged to embellish the tale for her heterosexual friends' voyeuristic pleasure. Her friends even allow her to revise her description of the incident without questioning the credibility of the story. (Ellen tells about enjoying a post-sex cigarette, but changes her story when it is pointed out to her that she doesn't smoke.) The fantasized sex scene is dramatized on the set as Ellen's voice-over tells the story.

That the most explicit sex scene involves heterosexuality is a jab at the Religious Right, which is so concerned to keep "immorality" off television. The scene is typical of sitcoms, which often present sexual situations, and these portray heterosexuals and not same-sex couples. The toaster oven joke also pokes fun of the fears of the Religious Right. The gag consists of Susan winning a toaster oven for her role in Ellen's coming out and makes fun of the idea that gays and lesbians recruit heterosexuals by trying to convert them to the so-called homosexual lifestyle. At the end of the episode, Melissa Etheridge awards the toaster oven to Susan as Ellen once again proclaims her sexual orientation.

However, the blatant asexuality of the relationship does follow the unspoken rule that gay and lesbian sexuality must remain in the closet. In some ways, the two women seem as innocent as the children Falwell wants to protect. The failed sexual encounter between Ellen and her old boyfriend is juxtaposed with Susan's faithfulness to a committed, monogamous relationship. Susan's relationship with her partner, and her faithfulness to that relationship—despite her apparent attraction to Ellen—reflects an element of so-called family values. Despite her sexual orientation, Susan's relationship could be described in terms of such "traditional" values as fidelity, commitment, and responsibility.

Indeed, the two lesbians aren't so different from the heterosexuals on the show. Ellen's heterosexual friends are, for the most part, supportive, and the point is made that she is, after all, the same person. The jokes bring home this point through the superfluous use of the word *gay*. When Ellen learns that Susan is not available, her friends talk about the situation by saying, "Susan dropped her like a gay hot potato." And, when Ellen misinterprets an interaction at the women's coffeehouse, Audrey calls it Ellen's "first gay faux pas." The superfluous use of "gay" in these lines points out that such incidents are not "gay" at all but the kind of situations that happen regardless of sexual orientation. As co-writer Jonathan Stark said, "We didn't want it to be so much of a gay story as a human story. She meets someone she cares about and it doesn't work out" (Rice 41).

Ellen's coming out episode provides a good measure of what the entertainment industry considers to be both within limits and off-limits for prime-time television portrayals of gays and lesbians. Political statements, expressions of sexual attraction between members of the same sex, and anything that might acknowledge that human sexuality encompasses far more than romance and sexual activity are off-limits. Television shows about gays and lesbians try to be consistent with the perceived consensus of moderate Americans. To return to Kate Clinton's joke that "all will be well" after Ellen comes out, it's important to take a close look at the episode before joining the party. Instead of challenging homophobia and racism, the episode and its rhetoric might even contribute to homophobic and racist attitudes in American society. Despite the media hype, Ellen's party has a limited guest list, and the celebration might have had more to do with the show's ratings than anything else.

◆ *References*

Bellafante, Ginia. "Looking for an Out." *Time* 7 Oct. 1996: 90-91.

Clinton, Kate. "Life After Ellen." *The Progressive* Feb. 1997: 46.

De Vries, Hilary. "Out and About." *TV Guide* 11 Oct. 1997: 20-27.

Grover, Ron. "An Opening Closet Spooks Chrysler." *Business Week* 14 Apr. 1997: 6.

Handy, Bruce. "He Called Me Ellen Degenerate?" *Time* 14 Apr. 1997: 86.

____. "Roll Over, Ward Cleaver." *Time* 14 Apr. 1997: 78-85.

Martin, Rick, and Sue Miller. "Ellen Steps Out." *Newsweek* 14 Apr. 1997: 65-67.

Ozersky, Josh. "'Coming Out' in the Middle of the Road." *Tikkun* July-Aug. 1997: 89+.

Rice, Lynette. "'Ellen': From Controversy to Emmy Nominee." *Broadcasting & Cable* 4 Aug. 1997: 41.

Steyn, Mark. "Everybody Out!" *The American Spectator* June 1997: 48-50.

ONCE IN A LIFETIME

Constructing "The Working Woman" Through Cable Narrowcasting

◆ Jackie Byars and Eileen R. Meehan

We feared people would see us as "The Feminism Channel" or the "Betty Crocker Channel."

—Marge Sandwick, Senior Vice President for Marketing and Communication (1989), Lifetime[1]

While denying that it is "feminist," Lifetime lays claim to the "feminine" side of television and in its advertising defines "feminine" television as strong-willed, smart, funny, compassionate, passionate—and only on cable. . . .

What leads a single media entity, one cable channel—Lifetime—to call itself *the* feminine side of television? What exactly *is* feminine television? What is Lifetime's construction of "the feminine"? How does

NOTE: From Jackie Byars and Eileen R. Meehan, "Once in a Lifetime: Constructing 'The Working Woman' Through Cable Narrowcasting," *Camera Obscura*, Vols. 33-34, Nos. 1-2, 1994-1995, pp. 13-41. Copyright © 1995 by Camera Obscura. All rights reserved. Reprinted by permission of Duke University Press.

Lifetime's attempt at gendered narrowcasting actually affect its programming? Is its programming different from other cable channels and from broadcast networks? In exploring the implications of these questions, we outline the history of the category "women's television" and the development of a new and valuable commodity audience, "working women," that Lifetime explicitly targets; analyze Lifetime's policies regarding its programs; and examine the effect of its corporate philosophical assumptions on actual content, focusing primarily on that programming explicitly designed for "working women." . . .

◆ What Was—and Is— "Women's Television"?

From the inception of commercial broadcasting, advertisers, networks, and the ratings monopolists[2] have had a strong interest in the "ladies of the house," as they once called women working in the home. Such women were perceived as comprising a daytime audience of domestic purchasing agents—agents who bought for the entire family.[3] Every standard history of broadcasting notes that the innovation of radio's daily domestic melodrama can be traced to the willingness of soap manufacturers to buy time from the networks and scripts from Irna Phillips (or her imitators) in order to mount an inexpensive but continuing story in which their products were frequently featured.[4] Such soap operas were structured around the rhythm of housework, with enough repetition to allow the stereotypical housewife to perform her noisy chores without missing anything important.[5] Although highly profitable, soaps were generally treated as second-class entertainment by those in the broadcasting industry and in the news media. . . .

During radio's hegemony, then, broadcasting for women meant daytime serial dramas and talk shows. When evening fell, broadcasters assumed that the family, with father as its focus, gathered around the radio. Networks shifted genres to match this shift in audience, offering genres targeted to the entire family in the early evening (situation comedies, variety shows) and, as the evening wore on, moving to more adult genres that tended to be male identified (Westerns, cop shows, private detective shows, adventure programs, and so forth).[6]

The technological move by CBS and NBC from radio to television meant a similar move in genres and programs from radio to television. . . . Soap operas still dominate the networks' programming during the heart of the house worker's day, when the (presumably male) primary wage earner and older children are expected to be away from the house. Today's soaps follow the classic formula of the serial, domestic melodrama. All emphasize personal relations, familial ties, and emotional crises, which are generally worked out in domestic space or in a domesticated work place. The multiple story lines are woven together to generate the complex and fabulous plots that distinguish the form. Powerful matriarchs, scheming vixens, clever businesswomen, and sincere beauties still populate the soaps, along with their male counterparts—powerful patriarchs, scheming gigolos, clever businessmen, and sincere hunks. However, in the struggle to win ratings, current soaps also include more location shooting, physical action, fashionable costuming, elaborate sets, sexual play, and discussion of social issues than were previously incorporated in the genre. But if soaps are the jewels in the crown of network daytime television, those jewels are still surrounded by talk shows. . . . The daytime talk show has absorbed some of the melodramatic elements of the soap opera to produce a highly volatile hybrid that attracts large and loyal audiences of women.

This emphasis on melodrama has meant a shift from social controversies to domestic controversies. Hosts like Ricki Lake,

Richard Bey, Jenny Jones, and Jerry Springer have further revolutionized the talk show; they engage their guests and their audience in highly charged arguments about the guests' personal lives, focusing mainly on sexual relations, familial ties, and emotional crises. These newer talk shows have dispensed with professional therapists, allowing the audience this role as hosts arrange often melodramatic confrontations between would-be lovers, ex-lovers, adulterous spouses, birth mothers, lost siblings, absentee fathers, and so on.[7] Called "ambushes" in the trade, such confrontations trigger on-camera reactions ranging from embarrassment to fist fights. This focus on the melodramatic—on personal issues and personal confrontations—imports the essence of soap opera into the talk show format.

But where the soap opera is fiction, melodramatic talk shows are "reality television" in which the outcomes of confrontations between real people are always unpredictable. The success of this melding is suggested by the strong female audiences that view both the new talk shows and the old soap operas as well as by the proliferation of new melodramatic talk shows that increasingly dominate the syndication market. . . .

Where melodramatic talk shows have been profitable and unrespectable, soaps have retained their profitability and gained new respectability within the television industry. Selections from the Daytime Emmys are even broadcast on evening television. Melodrama, whether packaged as fiction or reality, clearly draws a strong female audience and remains the vital force in women's television. When packaged as fiction, daytime melodrama seems to enjoy a higher status . . . than previously; packaged as reality, melodrama attracts large audiences of women, especially the 18- to 34-year-old females that advertisers prize highly. This new respectability accorded to soaps matched with the new profitability of melodramatic talk shows suggests that the overall industrial status of women's television may be changing.

Traditionally treated as second-class television, women's television now figures in prime time. Networks commission series that interweave elements of the soap opera into traditionally male genres (*Hill Street Blues, N.Y.P.D. Blue*). Affiliates move melodramatic talk shows and tabloid news shows (*A Current Affair, American Journal, Hard Copy*) into the time slots leading up to local news. And networks utilize "reality" series that intermix personal confrontation, threats to domesticity, and unpredictability (*Rescue 911, America's Most Wanted, Sightings*) to fill out their schedules. Overall, this embrace of melodrama suggests a rise in the industrial status of women's television and female audiences. But this rise is not a function of changes in television programming alone.

Television and the ◆ "Working Woman"

The new status is due, at least in part, to the economic impact of second wave feminism in the 1970s, multiple recessions starting in 1975, changes in the working life of middle-class women, changes in the television industry itself, and changes in technology. In this section, we explore these five forces, forces that combined not only to raise the status of women's television but also to make possible the creation of a cable channel targeted to women.

The histories of second wave feminism are many, and we will only sketch some of the effects of that multifaceted, highly variegated movement. Suffice to say that the women's movement, rising out of the civil rights struggle and the anti-war movement of the 1960s, addressed the significant disparities in social, economic, political, sexual, and cultural power that existed between the genders and that still persist to the present day. In terms of employment, pay, and working conditions, the movement won considerable legal changes, including the publication of job advertisements by employers engaged in governmental contracts, gender desegregation of job advertisements, equal pay for equal work, and criminalization of sexual harassment.

All this might have been in vain had the movement not addressed sexist ideologies that linked women's self-worth to dependency, both economic and emotional, on males. The combination of consciousness-raising and legal access to careers was an especially potent force for those women who turned college educations into a career. Spurning the chance to earn her "MRS" or to prepare for employment in traditional pink-collar jobs, these "new women" sought careers as business executives, financial officers, lawyers, professors, research scientists, physicians, and so forth. The potential spending of such women attracted considerable attention from advertisers seeking to intertwine feminist notions with product consumption. Perhaps the best remembered slogan from the period was that used to promote Virginia Slims cigarettes. Noting that "you've come a long way, baby," the ad campaign humorously suggested that the right to smoke cigarettes in public was the ultimate goal of the women's movement. In retrospect, this equal right to addiction and lung disease holds little humor. At the time, however, it marked the recognition of a new market: females with considerable disposable income who maintained control over that income. With manufacturers targeting advertisements at these women, it is little wonder that, in 1976, the A. C. Nielsen Company added a new category to its demographic measurements of the television audience: working women. This category measured the viewing of women who worked outside the home for a minimum of 30 hours per week and then divided those working women into "upscale," meaning white collar, and "downscale," meaning blue collar. Advertisers expressed considerable interest in reaching those upscale working women.

But if the early 1970s presented college-educated women with greater economic opportunities, that largesse came under pressure by mid-decade as the U.S. economy began to suffer recurrent recessions that persist to this day. The early recessionary waves had the greatest impact on blue-collar workers as corporations in the manufacturing sector downsized operations through massive lay-offs, plant closings, de-unionization campaigns, decreases in wages or benefits, and exportation of operations to Third World countries. By the 1980s, the cooperative relationship that had been forged among big business, big labor, and big government to counteract the "Communist threat" was thoroughly undermined.[8] This destabilization has worked against the interests of labor, regardless of "collar," resulting in periodic increases in unemployment and underemployment as well as declines in real wages, job benefits, and buying power. These problems were exacerbated by Reaganist economic policies fostering deregulation, financial speculation, militarization, privatization, and further de-industrialization. Such monetarist policies fostered the transfer of real wealth from the middle and working classes to the capitalist elite, resulting in a significant loss of income for most Americans.

For the middle class, this loss placed considerable pressure on the familial division of labor. Now many households required two incomes to achieve the spending power that one had previously ensured. In order to help their families remain in the middle class, many homemakers joined the flood of women that deluged the paid labor force. Furthermore, marketing studies not only demonstrated that women in dual-income households retained some control over their own wages, but also that they continued to fulfill the traditional female role as domestic purchasing agent for the household. The significance of this phenomenon was not lost on advertisers, on the media corporations that sell advertisers access to consumers, or on the companies that measure the quality and quantity of audiences drawn to the media.

For television's advertisers and networks, these economic shifts effectively narrowed the consumerist caste. That is, a smaller proportion of the population had sufficient disposable income to regularly purchase a broad array of goods and services according to brand rather than price, as well as to frequently purchase items on the basis of impulse. More people had less money to spend, and those who suffered the greatest cut in disposable incomes—now termed "downscale viewers"[9]—were the least attractive to advertisers regardless of gender. Advertisers responded to these economic changes by targeting their commercials to "upscale viewers" who comprised the consumerist caste. With advertisers exerting a demand for upscale viewers, networks responded by targeting their programming to such viewers. With upscale working women specifically measured by the ratings, advertisers could and did demand access to this attractive target audience, and networks began to program for both upscale men *and* women.

This provides one explanation for network experiments in so-called hybrid series. Such prime-time series blended elements of serial melodrama into traditionally male genres. An early example of a hybridized series is *Cagney and Lacey* (1981-1988) that introduced personal issues and continuing stories into the buddy cop genre.[10] In later hybrids, characters were connected variously by professional status (*St. Elsewhere, L.A. Law*), workplace (*Hill Street Blues*), intergalactic missions (*Star Trek: The Next Generation*), generational status (*thirtysomething*), and even geography (*Northern Exposure*). As *Northern Exposure* demonstrates, the generic hybrid can secure high ratings that the television industry interprets as wide acceptance by viewers. For the networks, trying to attract both upscale males and females, hybrid series may well be more cost-efficient than series that stick to a specific, gendered genre. This emerging practice falls nicely within the networks' traditional formula for manufacturing broadcast series: every show is completely new and totally familiar; every show provides something for everybody. Increasingly, the "new" relies on a mix of generic elements while the "familiar" relies on the genres themselves. And "everybody" excludes downscale men and women but includes upscale women, with particular attention paid to upscale working women.

The impact of second wave feminism and economic recession gradually changed the way that television networks competed for advertisers' dollars. The competition for television viewers narrowed to a competition for upscale viewers as measured by the Nielsen ratings. But, since 1977, the Nielsen sample was no longer limited to network television viewers or to "real time" viewing. Nielsen's ratings increasingly sampled cable subscribers thereby expanding the overall competition in the marketplace. They also included those programs that were recorded on videocassette recorders (VCRs) for (presumably) later viewing by both broadcast and cable audiences. In essence, the business of television became larger than the business of broadcasting.

As measured by the Nielsen ratings since the late 1970s, audiences for broadcast television were gradually being eroded by increased access to and use of cable television. The quantity of the audience for broadcast television was shrinking as the quantity of audience for cable expanded. But this was not the only bad news for networks: Nielsen also found that the audience for broadcast television mixed together upscale and downscale viewers, while cable television attracted more upscale viewers who watched significant amounts of television. Apparently, having paid the toll to get access to cable, subscribers organized much of their leisure time around the consumption of its channels. So, although these channels had relatively small audiences, those viewers were of high quality. Nielsen ratings, then, confirmed the cable industry's promotional materials: cable's total audience was comprised by large numbers of the consumerist caste, of those upscale men and women targeted by advertisers.

Further, marketing studies suggested that cable subscribers were high-quality consumers: they bought more advertised products than users of other media. For advertisers and the Nielsen Company, this made cable subscribers a high-quality audience, despite the fact that they were still a low-quantity one compared to that for broadcast television.

Advertisers interpreted these indicators as signs that cable television was becoming viable as a commercial medium for national distribution of advertising. . . . Cable system operators separated communities into those that had sufficient profit potential for the firm to incur costs of installing the cable infrastructure and those deemed lacking in profit potential. Within those favored communities, cable's subscription fees separated households into subscribers and nonsubscribers. In the current recessionary cycle, subscription has proven that a household is comprised by bona fide consumers who want to consume television, who can afford fees for such consumption, and who subsequently organize their domestic lives around TV viewing. This makes cable a particularly attractive buy: it can sift the consumerist wheat from the nonconsumerist chaff.

One effect of Reaganist deregulation was the networks' invasion of the cable industry. Networks themselves started cable channels ranging from CBS's ambitious attempt to deliver very upscale audiences via its high-culture Arts channel (an offer that advertisers easily refused) to channels started by ABC and NBC that targeted more traditional demographic groups. ABC's A&E targeted the PBS crowd, its ESPN targeted sports fans, and its Daytime targeted women. NBC's recent soft-news channel CNBC targets upscale men and women interested in news features and informational programming. Other cable channels targeted some slice of the consumerist caste with formats based on programming practices developed by networks to target demographic segments. For example, Nickelodeon targeted all children just as local after-school programming and

networks' Saturday cartoons had; MTV turned *American Bandstand, Dance Party,* and similar teen rock shows into a 24-hour format that replaced lip-synching live performers with videotaped performances, and so on.[11] . . .

Pundits editorialized over the loss of a cohesive television experience, suggesting that targeted channels functionally destroyed the unified American culture created by network television.[12] Less often discussed was cable's ability to divide the audience into people who can afford to pay a monthly fee and people who cannot. Cable subscription's ability to thus presort the audience into bona fide consumers and mere viewers was enhanced during Reaganist deregulation, as cable operators doubled and even tripled the cost of basic subscription while lowering the prices for extra services on pay channels. Such a division of the audience, in conjunction with economic downturns and Reaganism, piqued advertisers' interest in cable, perhaps especially in the new category of upscale working women.

That interest was not limited to programs such women watched in real time. VCRs allowed that audience to record programs for viewing at more convenient times or, depending on the technology of their cable system, to watch one program while recording another. By 1987, almost half of U.S. households (48.7% or 43 million) reported owning a VCR; those numbers climbed to 77.1% and 72 million by 1993, making the VCR one of the most quickly adopted technologies to hit the consumer market.[13] This created a measurement problem for the Nielsen ratings: although the Nielsen meters could identify what channel was being taped, they could not subsequently determine if the taped program was ever played for viewing. Nielsen's decision that taping was the equivalent of viewing seems generous given research that suggests that shows taped may well be shows never viewed.[14] However, the impact of this decision was significant indeed, especially in light of the fact that many upscale working women taped their soaps. If such upscale women could be persuaded to master VCR technology in order to tape serial melodramas, perhaps they could be attracted to programs that incorporated elements of the soaps into the slicker, more expensive programs that filled prime time. Here we find another impetus to hybridize prime-time programs.

The road to women's cable television, then, was paved by social, economic, technological, and industrial changes. Upscale women gained the opportunity for economic independence through the feminist movement of the 1970s, only to find that long-term recessions required them to remain employed in order to secure their household's class position. Even upscale women who eschewed feminism reaped the benefits of feminism in terms of employment opportunities when the recessions hit. As upscale women left the house for daywork, their VCRs allowed them to record daytime programming and the Nielsen sample duly noted their time shifting. Attracting upscale audiences, and specifically upscale women, became increasingly important as advertisers reacted to the recessions' narrowing of the consumerist caste, as cable fees guaranteed that their subscribers were bona fide consumers, and as the Nielsen ratings increasingly reported cable subscribers as *the* television audience. Networks identified "female" programming as the key to securing gender integration of upscale audiences through the hybridization of male-identified genres ranging from buddy cop shows to news. Taken together, these events not only raised the industrial status of women's television but also made possible the creation of a cable channel targeted to women.

◆ From Women's Television to Women's Cable Television

Changing conditions, then, opened a market niche into which Lifetime firmly settled in 1984. The result of a merger between Viacom's Cable Health Channel and Hearst/ABC's Daytime, Lifetime's original schedule combined exercise programs, cooking shows, talk shows based on Hearst's magazines for women, and medical in-service programming. This thematically confused line-up still managed to attract an upscale, female audience that Lifetime set about cultivating as it developed a more coherent mix of programming.[15]

Like Daytime, Lifetime consistently identified itself to affiliates and to advertisers as a channel that especially targeted women, but Lifetime did not "come out" to its viewers as "Television for Women" until February of 1995.[16] Lifetime had announced its audience orientation in the trades via campaigns in 1986 and 1988; in 1988, its print ads in the trades described the channel as a "unique environment designed to attract an elusive audience" comprised by "high spending women" who were "highly selective about the programming they watch and the ads they buy,"[17] thereby reiterating a consistent metaphor in capitalist cultures where ideas as well as products are bought. In fact, women's role as domestic purchasing agent matched with cable's ability to assemble an audience of bona fide consumers gave Lifetime tremendous commercial potential.

How, then, to attract those upscale, female homemakers? Lifetime's daytime programming drew from the programming models used by the networks and independent stations, mixing talk shows, game shows, old movies, and melodramatic series. Early morning series such as *Everyday Workout, Old MacDonald's Sing-Along Farm*, and *Your Baby & Child* addressed homemakers and their young children. Mid-day has variously been programmed with game shows *(Supermarket Sweep, Shop Til You Drop)*, talk shows *(Barbara Walters Interviews of a Lifetime, Live From Queens)*, syndicated "reality" shows *(Unsolved Mysteries)*, programs on domestic arts *(Our Home, The Frugal Gourmet)*, movies, or syndicated series *(Sisters, thirtysomething)*. Late afternoon has also featured movies, syndicated shows, and game shows. This programming mix has been focused on concerns traditionally identified as feminine: exercise, food, decorating, children, family, celebrities, and melodrama.

But if daytime was women's time, prime time was for upscale men and women. Lifetime may conceptualize its working women as economically independent, but not as emotionally independent from men. The channel thus programmed its prime-time hours for upscale women *and* men who would spend their evening "cocooning" in front of the television set—hence the stress on Lifetime as feminine but never feminist. Such a practice has positioned the channel as a consistent buyer of hybrid programs after their network runs, including the series *Cagney and Lacey, Spenser: For Hire, The Days and Nights of Molly Dodd, thirtysomething, China Beach*, and *L.A. Law*. Similarly, Lifetime acquired series that often placed strong female characters in traditionally male roles, including private detectives *(Partners in Crime)*, physicians *(Kay O'Brien)*, and police officers *(Lady Blue)*. The channel continued this practice in its original series *(Confessions of Crime, The Hidden Room, Veronica Clare)* as well as in the movies that it purchased *(The Burning Bed, Runaway Father, Deadly Deception)*, made *(Stop at Nothing, Stolen Babies, Shame)*, or remade *(Notorious)*. This move into originating series and movies allowed Lifetime to exercise considerable control over content, topics, and casting, and thereby to enact its own vision of women's television.

◆ Made for Lifetime: Male-Friendly Women's Television

Lifetime's basic formula for its World Premier Movies (made specifically for Lifetime) revolves around a strong, competent woman who overcomes adversity. Generally, the films involve a social issue believed to be of particular concern to women: domestic violence, sexual harassment, adoption, AIDS, or rape. Female protagonists generally work within the system to correct some injury, often in a professional capacity. Most of the actresses cast in these original movies are white and middle-aged. Actresses like Blair Brown, Stephanie Zimbalist, Christine Lahti, and Cathy Lee Crosby typify Lifetime's vision of female protagonists as fully adult women with weaknesses, soft edges, and strong emotions. This emphasis on emotions inflects Lifetime's productions with a distinctly melodramatic edge, regardless of genre. Lifetime consistently focuses on the personal and the familial, even when the setting is institutional. Systemic challenge is rare; solutions are generally personal, as the following sketch of some typical movies indicates.

In *Stolen Babies* (1992), Lea Thompson's social worker exposes Mary Tyler Moore's misuse of the courts to take babies from poor families and sell the infants to wealthy, childless couples.[18] In *The Good Fight* (1992), a lawyer (Christine Lahti) sues a giant tobacco company after one of her children's friends dies from cancer. The case reunites her with her estranged husband. In *Shame* (1992), another lawyer (Amanda Donohoe) obtains justice for a young girl raped in a small town. In *Wildflower* (1992), a girl with epilepsy (Patricia Arquette) is imprisoned in a shed by her brutish father. She is saved by a young girl who, with the aid of her brother, helps the girl with epilepsy find a better life. In *And Then There Was One* (1994), a comedy-writing couple discover, after the birth of a daughter, that the entire family is HIV positive. In *Other Women's Children* (1993), a pediatrician (Melanie Mayron) struggles to balance work and family. The pattern throughout emphasizes the personal as individuals right individual wrongs through individual actions. Even in one of the few Lifetime movies that suggests that a major institution can be flawed, *Stop at*

Nothing (1991), solutions are ultimately personal: Veronica Hamel solves the problem of abusive ex-husbands having visitation rights or custody by helping their ex-wives hide their children.

Of course, not all Lifetime movies directly address social issues. But, given the channel's commitment to a strong female protagonist as an essential part of its formula, even the "pure entertainment" movies indirectly raise social concerns. For example, in the gothic thriller *Night Owl* (1993), a woman (Jennifer Beals) defeats the ghost that has endangered her husband. In the costume drama *Guinevere* (1994), Camelot's queen (Sheryl Lee) gives up Lancelot as well as her goddess to steer Arthur and England toward a glorious future under his masculine and male-dominated Christian religion. By transforming such male-identified characters as crusading lawyers, overworked physicians, and ghost chasers into women, Lifetime ruptures gender stereotypes. By emphasizing the emotional, personal, and domestic concerns of such characters, Lifetime sutures that rupture. The result is "male friendly" but feminine movies—movies that attract upscale working women without alienating either upscale homemakers or upscale men. . . .

◆ *The Lifetime Woman and Feminine Television*

. . . Lifetime's daytime schedule approximates network programming with its line-up of talk shows, game shows, and domestic arts programs. As a substitute for soap operas, Lifetime runs syndicated series and movies. The films are generally melodramatic examinations of personal lives. By stripping the series, that is, by running the shows every weekday in the same time slot, Lifetime heightens their similarity to the daily unfolding of the soap opera. This similarity is strengthened by the use of hybrid series that incorporate continuing plots that are explicitly melodramatic. In these practices, Lifetime agrees with the major networks that women prefer melodramas and hybrid shows heavily inflected with melodrama.

However, for Lifetime, there is more to feminine television than melodrama. In the major networks' hybrid series, the male genre generally dominates; melodrama is typically subordinated and functions as a way to develop the main characters by giving them lives beyond what is strictly necessary in terms of the dominant genre. The assumption seems to be that women presumably filter out any story elements that are supposed to appeal to men but not women. The three most obvious "masculine" story elements are the absence of strong, female protagonists; fairly explicit violence, often against women; and the objectification of women. At this writing, Lifetime has been reluctant to acquire rights to syndicated series and movies that simply overlay such story elements with a bit of domesticity. As its World Premier Movies suggest, Lifetime is committed to the notion that upscale audiences of working women, homemakers, and men will watch melodramas in which strong women overcome adversity, particularly if that triumphant struggle involves the love of a good man. . . .

In Lifetime's enactment, feminine television offers viewers a complex, contradictory vision: women act in the public domain, work in the "real" world, and earn their independence—but ultimately rely on heterosexual relationships to round out their lives. For advertisers, this replicated their commercials' vision of the new woman who could (as a character in one commercial put it) "bring home the bacon/fry it up in a pan/and never let you forget you're a man/'cause I'm a *woman*."[19] For upscale working women, Lifetime's vision would seem to reiterate the emerging ideology of "having it all"—working outside the home as a professional, marrying and having children, and shouldering responsibility for domestic labor in the household. In this way, Lifetime's formula addresses lived experience in its frustrations and rewards, but only in terms of the personal, the emotional, the domestic. By not challenging the assumptions about labor, sexuality, and power that underlie the model of "having it all," Lifetime remains commercially viable, presenting television that provides role models for a way of life made possible by second wave feminism, but which Lifetime defines as feminine, never feminist.

◆ Notes

1. Quoted in Michael Burgi, "If at First You Don't Succeed . . . " *Channels* September 1989: 66. Research for the project from which this [chapter] comes has been funded by the Office of the Vice President for Research and Sponsored Projects and the Graduate School and from the Humanities Center at Wayne State University and from the Office of the Vice President for Research and the Office of the Dean of Fine Arts at the University of Arizona.

2. Historically, the ratings industry has been controlled by a single entity, ranging from the initial monopolist, the Cooperative Analysis of Broadcasting (founded by the Association of National Advertisers in 1930), which was replaced by the C. E. Hooper company in the early 1930s, to the current monopolist, the A. C. Nielsen Company, which achieved an effective monopoly over television and radio ratings in the 1950s. In 1963, political pressure was brought to bear on the Nielsen monopoly, and the firm relinquished control over radio ratings while tolerating the appearance of competition in television ratings. For details, see E. R. Meehan, "Why We Don't Count," in Patricia Mellencamp, ed. *Logics of Television* (Bloomington: Indiana University Press and London: British Film Institute, 1990) 117-137.

3. E. R. Meehan, "Heads of Households and Ladies of the House: Gender, Genre, and Broadcast Ratings, 1929-1990," in William S. Solomon and Robert W. McChesney, eds.

Ruthless Criticism: New Perspectives in U.S. Communication History (Minneapolis: University of Minnesota Press, 1993) 204-221; Karen S. Buzzard, *Chains of Gold: Marketing the Ratings and Rating the Markets* (Metuchen, NJ: Scarecrow, 1990). Also see Erik Barnouw, *Tube of Plenty: The Evolution of American Television*, 2nd rev. ed. (New York and Oxford: Oxford University Press, 1990) 471, for a CBS brochure entitled "Where the Girls Are" that was designed to assist advertisers in matching the demographics of product purchasers. The use of demographics is discussed from pp. 469-474. While the title of the brochure may strike one as indicative of "the bad old days," the brochure was issued in the early 1970s.

4. Standard histories include Erik Barnouw, *Tube of Plenty*, 1970, and the second revised edition, 1990; the three-volume set includes *A Tower of Babel: A History of Broadcasting in the United States to 1933*; *The Golden Web: A History of Broadcasting in the United States, 1933-1953*; and *The Image Makers: A History of Broadcasting in the United States from 1953* (all New York and Oxford, UK: Oxford University Press). See also Muriel Cantor, *Prime-Time Television: Content and Control* (Beverly Hills, CA: Sage, 1980) and J. Fred MacDonald, *Don't Touch That Dial: Radio Programming in American Life From 1920 to 1960* (Chicago: Nelson-Hall, 1979). For book-length analyses of soap operas, see Muriel Cantor and Suzanne Pingree, *The Soap Opera* (Beverly Hills, CA: Sage, 1983); R. W. Steadman, *The Serials: Suspense and Drama in Installments* (Norman: University of Oklahoma Press, 1977); R. W. Steadman "A History of the Broadcasting of Daytime Serial Drama in the United States," University of Southern California diss., 1959; and Robert C. Allen, *Speaking of Soap Operas* (Chapel Hill: University of North Carolina Press, 1985).

5. Tania Modleski has illustrated how this rhythmic pattern translates into daytime television programming on the major networks and their affiliates, which concentrates on game shows and soap operas, program types characterized by segmentation and repetition; see her "Rhythms of Reception: Daytime Television and Women's Work," in E. Ann Kaplan ed.

Regarding Television (American Film Institute/ University Publications of America, 1983) 67-75.

6. For accounts of the evolution of the flow of evening programming, see Erik Barnouw, *Tube of Plenty*; Laurence Bergreen, *Look Now, Pay Later: The Rise of Network Broadcasting* (Garden City, NY: Doubleday, 1980); and E. R Meehan, "Heads of the Household and Ladies of the House."

7. For a full-blown analysis of the talk show phenomenon, see Jane Shattuc, *The Talking Cure: TV Talk Shows and Women* (Routledge, 1997).

8. Barry Bluestone and Bennett Harrison, *The Deindustrialization of America* (New York: Basic Books, 1992).

9. Throughout the advertising, broadcasting, and cable industries, the terms "upscale" and "downscale" have been adopted as designations of consumers' economic status. This rhetoric of scales avoids issues of class structure, class differentiation, and economic exploitation. The terminology also manages to disparage those who are "downscale"—that is, people in the working class—and to subtly reinforce class-based prejudices. Although important in terms of capitalist ideology, such prejudices are irrational in economic terms when advertising products that are inexpensive, ubiquitous, and socially necessary (e.g., hand soap, tampons, toothpaste).

10. Julie D'Acci, *Defining Women: Television and the Case of "Cagney & Lacey"* (Chapel Hill and London: University of North Carolina Press, 1994).

11. The pattern of developing channels based on programming strategies used in network television and by local stations in programming off-network times has been noted by E. R. Meehan in "Technical Capability vs. Corporate Imperatives: Toward a Political Economy of Cable Television," in Janet Wasko and Vincent Mosco, eds. *The Political Economy of Information* (Madison: University of Wisconsin Press, 1988): 167-187. Where Meehan argues that cable television means "more of the same for slightly fewer," Oscar H. Gandy argues in *Beyond Agenda Setting: Targeting Information Subsidies and Public Policy* (Norwood, NJ: Ablex, 1983) that media

corporations will use "new" technologies like cable television to target narrower audiences with carefully drawn messages that have been crafted for highly specified demographics and psychographics. Suffice to say, that debate continues as such cable channels as Nickelodeon target children in a manner similar to the networks' Saturday "kid video" or stations' after-school mix of reruns and cartoon shows; or as religious channels like the old Christian Broadcasting Network (now the Family Channel) or Eternal Word Network or the Inspiration Channel target Christians a la the Sunday morning religious ghetto on networks and independent television stations. Similarly, networked or syndicated "teen shows" like *American Bandstand, Dance Party*, or *Lloyd Thaxton* are spun into entire channels that are differentiated in the same manner as radio stations: MTV for hard rockers, VH-1 for soft rockers, MTV-Latino for Spanish-language rockers. One finds dozens of examples: ESPN 1 & 2, as well as regional sports channels, for sports fans; the Science Fiction Channel for fans of old SF movies, serials, and series; the Country Music Channel for fans of country music and westernalia; The Learning Channel and Arts & Entertainment for fans of PBS programming.

12. Gandy, *Beyond Agenda Setting*.

13. United States Bureau of the Census, *Statistical Abstract of the United States* (Washington, DC: GPO, 1994): 567.

14. Mark R. Levy, "Home Video Recorders: A User Survey," *Journal of Communication* 30.4 (Autumn 1980): 23-27; Mark R. Levy, "Program Playback Preferences in VCR Households," *Journal of Broadcasting* (1980): 327-336; and Mark R. Levy, "Home Video Recorders and Timeshifting," *Journalism Quarterly* 58 (1981): 401-405. Levy found that people tape programs that they often don't get around to watching, unless there's some compelling reason to watch the tape—like it's a soap.

15. Douglas W. McCormick, Lifetime's President and Chief Executive Officer, personal interview, 3 March 1995.

16. Meredith Wagner, Senior Vice President for Public Affairs for Lifetime, described Lifetime's policy as quite conscious. In about 1992, Lifetime executives began to feel

that they could go public as a women's network, and in July of 1994 they began to refer to the network as television for women, but it was not until February of 1995 that the promotional campaign "Lifetime: Television for Women" was launched in women's magazines, in press kits, and finally, in on-air promotions (personal interviews, 14 January 1995 and 24 May 1995).

17. *Ad Age* 11 April 1988: S8-9.

18. Although Lifetime runs many made-for-TV movies originally broadcast on network television, it is rare for a Lifetime movie to be picked up by a network. *Stop at Nothing* and *Stolen Babies* are notable exceptions, probably because they star extremely well-known actresses who have starred in major network series.

19. In the commercial, for a perfume called Enjoli, a tall, thin woman wearing a body-tight evening gown removes her jacket, swings it over her shoulder and walks toward the camera singing these words, words that naturalize the construction of the working woman who has "everything," who works outside the home in a "job" and inside the home in every room of the house, especially the kitchen and the bedroom.

59

IN THEIR PRIME
Women in Nighttime Drama

◆ Karen Lindsey

I love television. I don't like going to the movies. They give me headaches, and they make a demand of me that I resent: their largeness, and the darkness that surrounds the screen—a quality many film fans love—annoys me. Why should I be forced to be wholly engaged with the screen?

TV, on the other hand, has to earn my wholehearted attention. If I want—if the show gives me the motivation—I can shut everything else out of my mind, just as I could at a movie theater. If I don't want that much focus, I can give it most of my attention, or half of my attention, or a fraction of my attention. I can turn it off if I'm bored, and not lose a penny. If I'm watching with other people, I don't have to put up with a dull film or be the spoilsport who ruins everyone's fun—I can just go into another room and read a book. If I want to watch a movie, I watch it on TV.

But mostly, I don't want to watch movies. I love the forms of television, as well as its convenience. Series television is satisfying in a way no one-shot story can be. I don't get attached to these people, only to be deserted when the show is done, or at best hope I'll meet them again in a few years in a sequel. I know I'm leaving them only for a week and that I'll have them in my life for at least a year, and often several years. It's cozy, curling up on my couch and inviting these friends to join me on a regular basis, to watch them evolve over time, to meet their new friends and say goodbye to the characters that are leaving—sad, perhaps, at the individual loss, but secure in the knowledge that I still have the rest of my fictional community.

At the same time, I'm a leftist, an antiracist, and above all a feminist. Which means that there aren't all that many fictional communities I can feel at home with. For someone with my values, the "vast wasteland" that Federal Communications Commission (FCC) chair Newton Minow complained of half a century ago remains a disturbing reality.

Oh, things have gotten better over the years. There are more African–American, Asian American, and Hispanic American characters than there used to be. Once in a while, there's even an intelligent Native American character. And there are more female characters with careers and families, with sex lives, with at least the trappings of feminist lives. Most of the ensemble shows—*Law & Order*, *The Practice*, *ER*, etc.—have black characters and female professionals, even if the real authority, like that of the real world, is uncritically in the hands of men. And there are some terrific female characters in these shows: Ellenor, played by the comfortably chunky Camryn Mannheim in the law firm of *The Practice*, S. Epatha Merkerson's no-nonsense police captain in *Law & Order*. (Captain Van Buren is also African American, in a predominantly white cast.)

But since the 1980s gave us the gritty, compassionate, role-challenging policewomen of *Cagney and Lacey*, I had been longing in vain for a drama series that combined strong women, antiracism, class awareness, good writing, and good acting. And the gods answered my prayers at the turn of the century, with five shows that are almost all I could want.

Two of these shows are on the broadcast network CBS, and the three others are on the Lifetime ("television for women") cable channel.

Judging Amy ◆

Judging Amy premiered on CBS in the 1999 fall season. Its heroine is a lawyer in her 30s, recently appointed judge, who has left a promising career in New York and moved back with her daughter to the family home in Hartford, Connecticut. She is trying to pull her life together in the wake of a shattering divorce, and now lives with her widowed mother, Maxine. Amy is an excellent character, but Maxine is a splendid one. When women over 50 appear on television, rarely enough, they tend to be loveable granny types, or, worse, loveably feisty. Maxine is neither. Played by one of America's best actors, Tyne Daly, Maxine is an unpretentiously vital woman in her 60s who is a full-time and passionate social worker. She has already raised her kids, and, although willing to help her daughter with a bit of baby-sitting when it's needed, has no time to be a loveable old granny. Like her daughter, she's busy with a job whose limits she struggles with, and unlike her daughter, she is ready to bend rules to help a desperate client, creating occasional illuminating conflict between the women.

As a newly appointed judge, Amy is assigned to the juvenile court, the lowest rung of the ladder. She accepts this grudgingly, till she can get her promotion to the more prestigious criminal law court. But as she does this work, she sees how important these cases are to ordinary people who are dealing with issues of child custody, abuse, and other life-wrenching situations. When, midway through the first season, she is offered the prize of criminal law, she turns it down to remain where she is.

Her work often parallels, and sometimes clashes with, Maxine's. Maxine is dedicated to caring for her clients, despite an overload of work. She struggles when her concern for protecting women and children clashes with her determination not to impose American values on third-world people (as in an episode in which an

Arab teenager has been clearly stabbed by someone in her family, and denies it. Maxine refuses to simply take the girl from her family, and instead painstakingly investigates to learn what has happened and why.). Maxine meets an attractive man and has an affair with him—a real affair, in bed, not chaste hand-holding between two cute codgers, which is what we usually get on those rare occasions when nighttime TV allows older characters any romance at all.

Both women's jobs expose them—and thus us—to poverty, racism, drug addiction, and profound family suffering. We see racism in every stratum of society. Amy's legal assistant, Bruce, is a handsome black man who in the beginning strenuously avoids anything like a friendship with her because he knows, and she discovers, that a friendship will be perceived as sexual and that the perception can destroy both their careers. They have grown into a friendship during the show's three seasons, and it too is one of the glories of this program. In one second-season series of episodes, their very camaraderie has the effect Bruce feared, and they are, quite falsely, accused and penalized for improper conduct in the courthouse. In the process, Amy has to deal with her own unexplored racism, as she earnestly and disastrously makes unilateral decisions for herself and Bruce about fighting the injustice of it. In the 2000-2001 season, we saw much more of Bruce's own life, including his struggles as a single father, his complicated relationship with his family, and his strong religious faith.

Interestingly, the star, Amy Brenneman, is also one of its executive producers, and the show is based on Brenneman's own mother, a superior court judge in juvenile matters.[1] Since Brenneman is also one of the show's executive producers, this may account for some of its believability.

Over its two seasons, the show has taken on many important social and political issues, giving them the complexity they deserve. When Maxine takes on the case of a 5-year-old rape victim, the obvious culprit is her new stepfather. But the girl (using dolls provided by psychologists since she's too traumatized to speak) indicates instead that it's her older brother. Realizing that the adolescent boy himself has been sexually abused, Maxine again suspects the stepfather—then realizes, to her horror, that it's the children's mother.

In another episode, Amy is able to find a legal way to allow lesbian parents to keep their daughter, in spite of the lack of same-sex partnership laws in Connecticut. She is committed to the law, more than some of us (and her mother) might like, but the glow on her face when she realizes that she can honor both the law and her sympathies is superb. (The women had both wanted biological involvement with their child, and so one conceived the child and the embryo was implanted in the other. Amy rules that this then is not a case of same-sex partnerships, but of two biological parents.)

A later episode takes on a more controversial and daring gender issue. Inspired, perhaps, by the 1997 French film *Ma Vie en Rose*, the plot focuses on the expulsion from school of an 8-year-old boy who dresses as a girl. The mockery and hostility of the children, says the principal, constantly disrupts the school. The father testifies, awkwardly and painfully. The boy has wanted to be a girl since he was 3; they've been to therapists and counselors, they've harassed him themselves, and finally, seeing his misery, have let him have his way. They don't like it; they don't understand it, but, as the father says, tearfully and defiantly, "he's smiling again." Amy questions the child himself; very lucidly, he explains that he doesn't like being a boy and never has, but now "I'm a girl!" And so he is—pretty, sweet, classically feminine. Amy goes, as his parents have, from disbelief (can a child know from the age of 3 that he doesn't like his gender?) to acceptance. For the sake of the school and "Sasha's" education, she makes a deal with him. He will "pretend" to be a boy in school, and be what he really is at home. In one astounding sentence, she turns the traditional concepts on their heads. Whatever Sasha's genitals or chromosomes may say, she's a girl—a girl who must pretend, for part of the day, to be something else because of society's narrow restrictions. This is important stuff—the sort of thing we expect to see on an occasional PBS documentary, perhaps, but not on a prime-time network drama.

Equally important in *Judging Amy* are the portrayals of domestic life. Too often dramas about "strong women" confine their plots to the workplace, and occasionally the romantic arena. Domesticity becomes relegated to sitcoms: like traditional women, domesticity is implicitly seen as necessary but uninteresting. But life plays out in several arenas, and the lives of women, and men, at home are as important and dramatic as they are at work. *Judging Amy* honors that reality.

Amy and Maxine support each other, and they clash—both personally and professionally. Both struggle with the boundaries of their relationship: how much should a mother interfere with an adult child's life, especially when they're living under the same roof? There is a wonderful, complex texture in the relationship of these two women and, to a lesser degree, in both their relationships to Amy's two brothers. Even Amy's motherhood is placed firmly in context. When her daughter, Lauren, complains in one episode that Amy's job keeps them from having as much time together as one of her friend's has with her stay-at-home mom, Amy starts to recite a clearly familiar litany of reasons why it's best for Lauren that Amy works. Then she stops, and adds that it's also better for Amy herself—she loves her work, she helps people and helps herself, and that this too is important.

And yes, Amy longs for romance. She has a few bad near relationships, and finds herself attracted her daughter's much younger karate teacher. Amy likes this guy, and loves sex with him, but she's not in love and knows it. She knows that that gap between them is more than just age: he's intelligent and thoughtful, but Amy confesses to her brother, "he has an empty bookcase in his apartment How can anyone be an adult and

have an empty bookcase?" And Amy allows this relationship to be what it is—honest, tender, sexy, and temporary.

◆ Family Law

A similar, and even more realistic show is CBS's *Family Law*. Its heroine, Lynn, is a suddenly abandoned lawyer whose philandering husband has also been her law-firm partner. When he leaves the marriage, he takes the firm and all its clients with him. She starts over again, building a new firm with a team of partners and associates with widely disparate lifestyles and values. Danny, a friend who worked with her old firm, is a younger woman—cynical, emotional, tough, and sometimes confused. Randi is an elegant, middle-aged lawyer of conservative politics and a dramatic background: she got her law degree in prison while serving several years for the murder of her abusive husband. Though these three want to specialize in cases they believe in, Lynn realizes that such cases won't pay the bills, and she hires Rex, a womanizing, sleazy, corrupt lawyer who will bring in rich clients. In the second season, the show brought on sitcom star Tony Danza as the newest partner, and at first glance, I wondered if this was meant to dilute the show's feminist, progressive bent with a heftier dose of testosterone. But Danza's character soon reassured me. Joe may be macho, but he's also a Communist, and his only concern is fighting against the establishment (including any law firm he works with) and for the rights of his working-class and poor constituents. Throughout many episodes, he stubbornly insists on taking too many pro bono cases, alarming the rest of the firm and infuriating Rex. His clashes with judges come close to losing him clients, and he respects the law only to the extent that he can use it to thwart the system he abhors.

Equally challenging a character is Randi, the ex-convict (played by Dixie Carter).

She's in her 50s, and a fascinating contrast to Tyne Daly's Maxine in *Judging Amy*: slim, stylish, elegant, and ladylike. But like Maxine, she's tough—with the "steel magnolia" touch that Carter does so well.

There are moments of dark comedy, and more of the painful realism of no-win cases, compromises that are sometimes more painful for the partners than defeat. Here again, issues of age, class, race, are addressed, and rarely simplistically. In a first-season episode, parents of a mentally retarded child sue the doctor who performed amniocentesis and told them, knowing otherwise, that the child would be fine, because he opposed abortion. Against their wishes, Lynn does the only thing that will win her case: she puts the child on the stand. They win, but the mother confronts Lynn, accusing her of doing what the doctor had done, of taking away her right to make her own decisions. We're not left with an easy answer, or indeed any answer, but only with a hard, excruciating question.

One second-season episode was so disturbing the network held back on rerunning it during its scheduled airing in mid-summer because Procter & Gamble threatened to withdraw its sponsorship. (It ran in early September with other sponsors.) The issue was gun control—controversial, indeed, but it's been dealt with before on network television, without sponsorship withdrawal. But then, TV tends to want good guys and bad guys, and this show refused to deliver. A child has been shot, and his 8-year-old brother admits to the killing. Lynn is able to save the boy from criminal conviction. Then the children's father, recently divorced from his wife, sues for custody. Lynn's client, the children's mother, has turned her gun over to the police, but bought another one.

Lynn is horrified, even after her friend explains. She bought the gun soon after the divorce, when a man broke into the house and raped her, vowing to kill the children if she made any effort to stop him. Even with one child dead, she fears her other son's safety if she doesn't have a gun.

Assuming that everyone in the office shares her position on gun control, Lynn brings it to a staff meeting, only to have Rex go to his office and return defiantly with the gun he keeps in his desk. The staff's emotional debate about the case reinforces the complexity of the issue. Lynn's argument for her client, passionately delivered and against all her deepest beliefs, is electrifying. She wins her case.

In the episode's last scene we see Lynn lock up her house, nervously looking for prowlers as she does so. The camera switches to Rex, turning in his gun to the police and walking away with an agonized face. There's no right or wrong offered us, only pain and hard decisions in a hard world. While this might be less satisfying than a pro-gun-control conclusion, it demands of us that we think through the difficulties of the issue rather than handing us an emotionally easy answer.

My major complaint about *Family Law* had been the fact that all its women were beautiful in a standard American way, in spite of their age range. The 2001 season has brought a startling and significant exception to that. To replace the character of Danni in the wake of actor Julie Warner's departure, two new female lawyers were introduced in the season's first episode. One is a thirtyish, pretty Irish woman. The other is a pretty, thirtyish dwarf. As Lynn and Rex stare in surprise, and Rex only barely smothers a smirk, Emily pushes past the stammering secretary, sits down, shoots out her impressive qualifications, and calmly threatens to sue them for discrimination if they don't hire her. I had a moment of nervousness watching the episode: was this going to be a one-shot display of liberalism? But as the firm discusses Emily's application, Randi points out that Emily has them all running scared. The rest of the season to date has seen her as a strong, very active member of the law firm.

On November 12, 2001, *Family Law* aired what is probably its most important episode ever. Unusually, the show confined itself to one storyline—a very controversial one, in which the firm takes on the case of an Arab American held by the federal government on suspicion of passing classified information to terrorists. There is enough evidence to make it possible, but nowhere near enough to make him certain. Yet he is held without bail, without visitors, forbidden to receive drawings from his young son, for fear they are really messages from terrorists. He is not allowed to see his court-appointed lawyer, who seems willing to accept this.

Lynn, contacted by the suspect's wife, is not willing to accept it, and she and Joe take on the case. Their decision causes a furor at the firm, and the meeting of the partners, in spite of Lynn's effort to keep the discussion focused on the case itself, becomes an outpouring of emotions. Those who want to take the case have slightly different reasons. Lynn is concerned with the violation a prisoner's of civil rights. Emily identifies with anyone discriminated against for the way they look. Joe agrees with both, but also has a larger political concern. He blames the September 11, 2001, attack on the World Trade Center and the Pentagon in part on U.S. policy over the years. Of course Arab countries are angry, he yells. The sanctions on Iraq alone, he says, have left thousands of people starving and dying. This latter is particularly impressive, because it's a point of the view the network news rarely if ever mentions. Ironically, CBS's fiction here offers more fact than its newscasts do.

But others are opposed, just as vehemently. A refrain throughout the program—as indeed throughout America—is echoed: "Things are different since September 11." Brandi's granddaughter had to leave her kindergarten early because someone found a box with something strange in it. She and the others want Americans at peace again, even if it means risking the imprisonment of innocent people. The people in the hijacked planes and the attacked buildings, she says, were also innocent.

As the case moves on, we see the prosecuting attorney, government representatives, and others justify the draconian measures taken against the suspect. We also see the ugly attacks on Arab Americans and even those who support them: as one of the lawyers comes out of the suspect's home, a man beats her up for supporting "turban heads." But as always, we are left with no firm conclusion—only one of TV's better explorations of the complexity September 11th has thrown at us.

The Lifetime ◆ Cable Channel

Like CBS, at least one cable channel seems committed to depicting strong women and progressive political concerns. *Family Law* and *Judging Amy* bear a strong resemblance to the recent lineup of Lifetime's original prime-time dramas, run on Sunday nights from 8 through 11 p.m. Lifetime has had an interesting evolution from its beginnings in 1984, when it tried to attract a female viewership with a "thematically confused lineup" of cooking shows, medical-information shows, exercise workout programs, and reruns of old network programs.[2] Originally the targeted audience was less feminist than traditional— "upscale, female homemakers."[3] Evening programming focused on reruns of shows women would watch with their husbands, such as *Spenser: For Hire*, *L.A. Law*, and, significantly, the controversially 1980s feminist hit *Cagney and Lacey*. There were a few original series, but they faded out in a few years.

In 1998, Lifetime once again ventured into an original series with *Any Day Now*, the story of two women, one black and one white, in Alabama. Best friends as children, then separated, they come across each other as adults and become again best friends. As the adults deal with issues of the turn of this century, we get flashbacks to their childhood days in the late 1960s, fighting a racism far more overt than the subtle forms they face in the present. The show has been very successful, partly because of the wonderful acting of stars Lorraine Toussaint and Annie Potts. Toussaint's Rene is a lawyer, following in the footsteps of her adored father, a civil rights judge. Her focus, like that of the women in *Family Law*, is on fighting discrimination, and, like those lawyers, she sometimes has to deal with wealthier clients to keep the firm going. Potts's character, Mary Elizabeth, is a housewife and aspiring writer, whose commitment to fighting racism has remained staunch, and over several moving episodes, has threatened her marriage. The flashbacks to the past are as much a part of the show as the present, and do a fairly good job of showing both the progress and the failures of four decades in which white America has largely refused to deal with its continuing racism. The friendship of the women remains central, and crucial.

In 2000, Lifetime added another Sunday night series, *Strong Medicine*, a harder-hitting and wider-ranging show that, like *Family Law*, adds class to its list of concerns. Its executive producer is Whoopi Goldberg, who got the idea for the show during the birth of her grandchild.[4] Goldberg has proven as fine a producer as she is an actor and comedian. In the first episode, white, upscale, Harvard educated Dr. Dana Stowe is working to keep her new women's health center at the prestigious Rittenhouse Hospital. Dr. Luisa Delgado runs an inner-city clinic for women, with a tiny staff and even tinier budget—and the clinic is about to be closed down because they can't pay their bills. The women clash on first meeting, mirroring some of the real-life clashes between career-oriented feminists and social-justice-oriented feminists. But they are forced to work together when the funding both need will be supplied only if the clinic merges into the hospital. No one is happy with the compromise: Lu fears her poor clients won't be able to get to

Rittenhouse, which is in an upper-middle-class neighborhood far away from the old clinic. Dana and the hospital's (male, of course) chief of staff are dismayed at the visible presence of drug addicts, homeless people, and the badly dressed poor—as well as Lu's receptionist, a tough black ex-stripper, and her New Age-y male nurse-midwife.

The hostility between Lu and Dana, once established, recedes, emerging only when they clash professionally. They have a sometimes affectionate, though grudging, respect for each other that verges on friendship. But the clashes are frequent, since class struggle is always an underpinning of the show. In fact, I've never seen television deal with class so well, and so consistently. *Family Law* has Joe, the Communist, who fights for the poor. But Lu, a Latina who grew up in the neighborhood where she built her clinic, is much more intimately connected to poverty. Every episode begins with a meeting in her "chat room," in which low-income women have an hour's discussion of health issues with Lu or one of the staff. The contrast between rich and poor, working class and professional class is always visible, in the very setting of the program. Often, the episodes deal directly with the effects of class—as when Lu discovers that one of her patients, a 17-year-old, has been persuaded by Dana to become an egg donor for Dana's childless, well-to-do patients. For Dana, it's a win-win situation: the girl will get money for college and the couple will get their child. For Lu, it's a rip-off of a poor girl's future fertility in the service of the wealthy. "What does Our Lady of the High Heels want with one of my patients?" she mumbles when she sees the girl going into Dana's office. In another episode, a patient of Lu's dies of breast cancer, having been previously misdiagnosed by doctors uninterested in the symptoms of poor black patents.

The relationship between Lu and Dana remains intriguing: they like each other, finally, and support each other, since both are concerned with women. But the barrier of class is always present, and in each episode we are, at the very least, presented with one story that reflects Lu's world and one that reflects Dana's. And when their worlds come together—as in the episode in which Terri Garr plays a middle-class woman in a wheelchair who is dying of cervical cancer because doctors have refused to give her pap smears, assuming that a disabled woman isn't sexually active and not wanting to take the extra time to get her on an examining table—it's especially powerful.

The most recent of the Lifetime drama series, debuting in 2000, is *The Division*. This is also the closest to a contemporary *Cagney and Lacey*—a standard cop drama with a major twist. Here the captain of the San Francisco Police Department's Central Station is a woman. Captain McCafferty, played by Bonnie Bedelia, is a "seasoned, politically savvy career officer who survived the early days when women on the police force were few and unwanted."[5] She is tough and laconic and tries to promote the solidarity among her female officers that she had no access to in her own early days.

These women are diverse in class and ethnicity. Jinni comes from a tough, white working-class family, all of whom, including herself, have alcohol problems. Angela is the black daughter of a general in the army, highly ambitious. Magdalena comes from a poor Latina family and is a single mother, struggling to raise her son and worried that her job will deprive him of his mother. Her toughness matches Jinni's, and they are close personal friends as well as, eventually, partners. C. D. is white and, like Angela, middle class; they have been partners and have grown into friendship. It's a good, suspenseful cop show, and the evolving relationships among the women doing work that forces them to see the most brutal aspects of human behavior are compelling.

How stable these shows are remains to be seen. The 2001 season saw three woman-centered new programs that might threaten them. The quality of the shows might be gauged by the cover of *TV Guide*'s fall-preview issue: each is about one woman, not a community of women, and each woman is young and sexy. On the cover, they're dressed alike, in clingy tank tops and low-hanging jeans, staring provocatively at the camera: the caption reads: "Tough Women Rule, As If You Wanted It Any Other Way." *Crossing Jordan* is a crime show about a State Coroner's medical examiner who tries to solve the murders of the cadavers she dissects. NBC has shrewdly placed it opposite *Family Law*. The first episode was good enough—Quincy as a sexy young woman—but certainly showed no hint of the social conscience that drives its rival. ABC's *Philly* is clearly meant to draw viewers away from *Judging Amy*—it's on at the same time and is about a tough (and sexy and young) DA. Finally, Lifetime's *The Division* faces competition from *Alias*, in which a gorgeous grad student is also a CIA agent. It's another sexy show—a mildly entertaining cross between *Ally McBeal* and *Mission Impossible*.

I like TV fluff, in its place. But I also like series dramas that bring, along with the comforting continuity that is one of the form's joys, reminders of the less entertaining realities that are part of our culture and indeed of human life. We get enough fluff on TV, and certainly enough evasion, even in the news. These five series prove that the medium can provide both entertainment and social responsibility.

◆ *Notes*

1. From CBS's press packet for *Judging Amy*.

2. Byars, J., and E. R. Meehan, "Once in a Lifetime: Constructing 'The Working Woman' Through Cable Narrowcasting," *Camera Obscura*, Vols. 33-34, Nos. 1-2, 1994-1995.

3. Ibid.

4. From Lifetime's press packet for *Strong Medicine*.

5. From Lifetime's press packet for *The Division*.

60

WORKPLACE DRAMAS, ENSEMBLE CASTS, 1990s STYLE

◆ Donald Bogle

M ore serious African American characters and situations—which indeed appealed to older, more educated African American viewers—turned up on the hour-long dramatic series of the 1990s: such programs as *N.Y.P.D. Blue*, *Law & Order*, *Homicide: Life on the Streets*, *ER*, *New York Undercover*, *Chicago Hope*, *Brooklyn South*, *Third Watch*, and *The Practice*. (Or HBO's *Oz*.) For the most part, these were well-written, well-directed, and tensely acted programs in which issues of race were sometimes examined. Yet good as the programs were, Black viewers often yearned to know more about the Black characters. In a series like David Kelley's *The Practice*, the Black lawyers Eugene and Rebecca often appeared deracialized; the series rarely commented on race as a factor in their lives. In fact, it dramatized little about their personal lives. Viewers knew that Eugene had a son. But episodes were not developed around Eugene's personal situation until well into the run of the series. At that time, his teenage son Kendall was arrested on a drug charge. Afterward Eugene's ex-wife took him to court, seeking full custody of the boy. The actors on Kelley's series—Steve Harris, Lisa Gay Hamilton, as well as Lisa Nicole

NOTE: From "The 1990s: Free-For-Alls," in *Primetime Blues: African Americans on Network Television*, by Donald Bogle. Copyright © 2001 by Donald Bogle. Reprinted by permission of Farrar, Straus and Giroux.

Carson and Jesse Martin on *Ally McBeal*—were strong enough to create credible characters. But where these characters came from culturally was anybody's guess.

On such series as *Law & Order* and *N.Y.P.D. Blue*, the African American characters were too often confined to the sidelines. The long-running *Law & Order* included Black actor Richard Brooks as assistant district attorney Paul Robinette in its original cast. But only after Brooks, having left the series, returned for a guest appearance did viewers get to see Robinette actually try a case. Apparently in an attempt to appeal more to female viewers, the Robinette character was replaced by a female assistant district attorney in the series' fourth season. Also brought in to play police lieutenant Anita Van Buren was S. Epatha Merkerson, a stage-trained African American actress who had appeared on Broadway in *The Piano Lesson* and in Spike Lee's film *She's Gotta Have It*. Brisk, intelligent, and sensitive, she quickly emerged as one of the more intriguing Black female characters on episodic television.

Many viewers probably waited for "special" episodes that would focus on her. On the episode *Black Tie*, Van Buren had to deal with Detective Mike Logan's discomfort at having a woman in charge. On another, *Competence*, Van Buren briefly moved center stage. While at an ATM machine, she was held up by two teens. Pulling out her revolver, she ended up killing another teen, a mentally handicapped boy. As the case was investigated, her professionalism was questioned within the department. She also had to face the dead boy's mother: one African American woman trying to explain her tragic mistake to another. Merkerson and Black actress Lisa Louise Langfold played the scene beautifully, subtly shading it without overdrawn histrionics. But usually Merkerson seemed underused.

"Why am I in a position of authority yet you rarely see me on-screen?" actress Merkerson once complained.[1] "You can write stories for me without them necessarily being about a Black issue, but it never happens that way." Aware that her Van Buren could always be counted on for counseling and common sense, Merkerson was also conscious of the character's earth mother qualities. "I think that's why Van Buren has been made Black and female," she said, adding that the earth mother was "another role we tend to find ourselves in: 'Come and tell me the problems and I'll help you out.' You know, 'Come sit on Mammy's knee.'"

With its minimalist scripts (sticking mainly to the story at hand with few diversions) and with its use of handheld cameras (early episodes were shot by cinematographer Ernest Dickerson), *Law & Order* had a documentary feel that lifted it above the ranks of general episodic television. To its credit, *Law & Order* was willing to focus on complex racial issues. One episode that examined a case of sexual harassment seemed drawn from the Anita Hill/Clarence Thomas headlines. Yet it was dramatized in an unexpected way. Regina Taylor guest-starred as a woman who accused her former boss, now a prominent liberal white city councilman, of having demanded sex in return for a partnership at his law firm. In her courtroom testimony, Taylor's character spoke chillingly of her humiliation. But then the script shrewdly moved from a comment on gender issues in the workplace to racial ones. Still another episode drew on the riots in Brooklyn's Crown Heights. A Black adolescent was killed in a hit-and-run accident. But the Jewish driver of the car was not indicted. Afterward a Black minister (no doubt inspired by New York's Reverend Al Sharpton) led a protest. A riot ensued in which an Italian man, mistaken for the Jewish driver, was killed by a young Black man. The African American lawyer Shambala Green (a recurring character played by Lorraine Toussaint) defended the youth. Ultimately, the episode commented on the once bonded, now strained, relations between the African American and Jewish communities. Another episode, which focused on the assassination of an African American leader, possibly by an organization fighting for the rights of African Americans, called to mind the assassination of Malcolm X—and the past rumors of the Nation of Islam's involvement. Later in its run, *Law & Order* added African American actor Jesse L. Martin to its cast.

Among the characters on Steven Bochco's *N.Y.P.D. Blue* was the African American police lieutenant Arthur Fancy (James McDaniel). Though the series explored the troubled private lives of its cop heroes, usually little of Fancy's life was dramatized. Generally, Fancy was depicted as a taciturn, exacting, strictly-by-the-book officer who once fired a detective who had an affair with an informant. Co-creator David Milch felt that Fancy was a character "who, by his own account, says he has trained himself not to want things he can't have, which in a way is one of the strategies of Blacks in America."[2] But Milch was also aware of the limitations of the role. "We knew it would be a feat of acting to sustain such a character over the first episodes, [but] Jimmy is like a Zen actor," said Milch. "He accomplishes an enormous amount with a minimal amount of effort." "[Fancy] has a certain type of sanity the others don't," said actor McDaniel.[3] "I can provide exposition the others can't. To a certain extent it's boring stuff, but it's challenging for me as an actor."

But on some sequences, he was featured more prominently as the series sought to examine the feelings of a Black man in a profession considered hostile and unjust to African American men. At one point, a Black character berated Fancy, saying, "You ain't nothing but an Uncle Tom." Fancy himself questioned his role as a Black cop in the police department, especially when he was faced with Officer Andy Sipowicz's racism.

N.Y.P.D. Blue was rather bold in depicting Sipowicz—one of its central characters—as a man who struggled not only with his alcoholism but with his racial attitudes as well. This was best dramatized in an

episode when Sipowicz has a heated confrontation with another Black character. The angry Black man yells at Sipowicz, "I don't have to go anywhere with you. You're dealing with that one nigger in a thousand who knows what you can and cannot do." Sipowicz responds, without thinking, we assume: "I'm dealing with the nigger whose big mouth is responsible for this mess." The scene was written in such a way that many viewers may have felt Sipowicz was provoked into using the word.

Nonetheless, the episode reveals—in a rather self-congratulatory way—the more acceptable responses of other characters. Sipowicz's partner, Bobby Simone (Jimmy Smits), tells him, "I was not comfortable with those words. I am not comfortable with the thoughts behind it. I just want you to understand that." At home, Sipowicz discusses the racial incident that *provoked* him into using the N-word. He asks his wife if she's ever heard him say it. She answers that she hasn't. But she has seen him use certain gestures when talking about African Americans. "It's code," he tells her. "So you don't have to say it." "Don't ever show it to our child," she then says. "Don't teach him to think in that way." Viewers may have felt that Sipowicz was too likable and vulnerable to be a Mark Fuhrman. But upon closer examination, Sipowicz may have more of an affinity to Fuhrman than we'd like to admit.

But for African American viewers, it was more intriguing to watch Fancy's response to Sipowicz. Often without uttering a word of dialogue, McDaniel looked as if he were wearied by the daily accretion of racism he must deal with—or ignore—to get his job done. When he gets into an argument with Sipowicz, he lets it be known that should Sipowicz be removed from the precinct, "They'll send me another like you. Only worse." Then he says, "Maybe you can't handle a Black man being your boss."

On another episode, Sipowicz arrests an innocent African American man in a murder case. Though the man eventually gets off, Sipowicz is blind to his own bigotry. The episode ended with Fancy taking him to a restaurant in Harlem where Sipowicz is the only white man. When the two talk, Sipowicz says "it doesn't matter" whether or not he is a racist as long as he is fair when he does his job. Fancy says to him, "You're uncomfortable in this restaurant, but imagine how you'd feel if these waiters had badges and guns." Not only does Fancy refute Sipowicz's point of view but he makes him consider how his life would be if he were African American and on the other side of the law. Still, effective as this scene was, it said more about Sipowicz than about Fancy. Though *N.Y.P.D. Blue* frequently featured Black guest stars, it didn't add another Black character—Baldwin Jones, played by Henry Simmons—until its seventh season.

Among *N.Y.P.D. Blue*'s strongest assets was African American director Paris Barclay, who won Emmys two years in a row for his work on the series. So, too, was African American writer Kevin Arkadie.

Based on the book *Homicide: A Year on the Killing Streets* by Baltimore *Sun* crime reporter David Simon and executive-produced by Barry Levinson and Tom Fontana, the gritty police show *Homicide* was set in Baltimore. Known for its quirky look and sound—the handheld camera shots, the jump cuts, and the blues or rock music pulsating on the soundtrack—it was a drama less interested in highly developed story lines than in its idiosyncratic characters. The detectives did not so much solve cases as close them. Sometimes a case went from one week to the next. Often justice was ambiguous. On some occasions, the cast of *Law & Order* was brought on as the characters of the two series joined forces to resolve a case. Always the detectives had short fuses, ready to explode not only with the criminals that they sometimes could not bring to justice but with one another as well.

Homicide could boast of three important African American characters, played by actors Yaphet Kotto, Clark Johnson, and Andre Braugher. Later Giancarlo Esposito and Michael Michele joined the cast. Such African American actors as Erik Todd Dellums, Clayton LeBoeuf, and Al Freeman Jr. also appeared on some episodes in supporting roles. Like *The Defenders* and *N.Y.P.D. Blue, Homicide* also featured a number of African Americans in guest roles: James Earl Jones, Lynn Thigpen, Alfre Woodard, Chris Rock, Gloria Reuben, and Melvin Van Peebles. So many African American faces appeared that some critics mistakenly considered *Homicide* a Black show. Never was it situated enough in an African American cultural context to be *that*. But its Black protagonists as well as some of its story lines were startlingly new for television.

Most of the attention was focused on Andre Braugher—"one of television's most thoughtful, deeply realized characters," wrote Caryn James[4]—as the lapsed Catholic detective Frank Pembleton. Critic John Leonard called Braugher "the best actor on series television."[5] Other critics agreed. Earlier in his career, Braugher had played a cop on *Kojak* during the 1989-90 season. But he had hated the producers' conception of his character as a bed-hopping womanizer. On *Homicide*, Pembleton is a family man who struggles with himself to remain that. Hot-tempered and moody yet philosophical, he's keenly aware of the toll his job has taken on his home life. He's a man who's wound up so tight that we can feel the knot in his stomach. Yet as gifted an actor as Braugher was, he could also overplay his hand. His use of language and his delivery, his movements and his moods themselves, sometimes became almost archly stylized. Even when he uttered intentionally mundane dialogue, Braugher aimed for bravura effects. In turn, he occasionally became a lot of hot brilliant flash; an actor who seemed to enjoy hearing the sound of his own voice; savoring his own dulcet tones. Yet all of those effects, ironically, made him compellingly watchable. Later, Braugher starred in the series *Gideon's Crossing*.

Often overlooked was the sturdy presence of Yaphet Kotto as Lieutenant Al "Gee" Giardello, the half African American, half Italian lieutenant who gave the men their orders and who also understood their weaknesses and their frustrations. Having worked in theater, movies, and television for years, Kotto brought an assured maturity to the part and the series itself; his was the perceptive intelligence in the squad room that held everything together. Kotto also wrote for the series. Clark Johnson as the streetwise Meldrick Lewis contrasted effectively with both Kotto and Braugher.

Homicide's real surprise came in its sixth season with the arrival of actress Michael Michele. Almost everyone wondered how this stunner would make it in the gritty testosterone world of *Homicide*. Previously, Michele had played a pampered rich girl in the glossy nighttime series *Central Park West*. As she gossiped or partied or commiserated with her white friends on that earlier show, as she became involved with the wealthy father of a friend, her character was one of television's most culturally unanchored heroines. Nothing explained how this young Black woman became so entangled in this world of wealth and privilege. (The character didn't even have the basic cultural demarcations of *Dynasty's* Dominique.) Michele seemed as if she had never experienced any crisis more serious than not being able to find the right lip gloss. She also appeared for a season on *New York Undercover*.

When she showed up in *Homicide*, she was still a stunner: tall, angular, and haughty, although not as glamorous. Wisely, the series didn't try to camouflage her looks. It was explained that she was a former beauty queen who has to prove herself to the guys in the homicide unit. Somehow Michele pared herself down to essentials, emerging as a tough, resilient heroine.

Despite its innovations and unusual characters, *Homicide* never had high ratings. It was always more of a critic's favorite than an audience's.

Of these dramatic shows, *New York Undercover* and *ER* had a greater impact with African American viewers. A cop show with a healthy dose of weekly action, *New York Undercover*—created by Dick Wolf and Kevin Arkadie—was one of the rare dramatic series that Fox pitched at African American viewers. Within its traditional formula, its younger hip cop detective heroes, the African American J. C. (Malik Yoba) and the Latino Eddie (Michael DeLorenzo), appealed to a young audience. So too did its use of music (jazz, rap, rhythm and blues), its sexy, fast-paced New York setting, and its cinema verité style. Later joining the cast were Lauren Velez and Tommy Ford (showing off his acting skills in a way that *Martin* didn't permit).

ER's Benton and Boulet: ◆ Making the Most Out of Marginalized Lives

Created by best-selling author Michael Crichton, *ER* was an innovative doctor's series that shot to the top of the ratings, emerging at the end of its first season as the highest-rated new drama in television history. Set in the emergency unit of Chicago's County General Hospital, the series dramatized the experiences of a group of (relatively) young doctors who struggle not only to save lives but to work out their own personal dilemmas. Among the group was the African American surgeon Peter Benton (Eriq La Salle). For Black viewers, Benton quickly became both an exciting and frustrating hero. On the one hand, you had to respect the skills of this hardworking professional, demanding the best of himself and those around him. Seeing Benton (like seeing his predecessor played by Denzel Washington on *St. Elsewhere*), you realized that television images of African American men indeed had inched forward. Yet in an unexpected way, Peter Benton sometimes appeared to embody a familiar 1960s-style media type: the angry young Black man. Benton was a man with a scowl; a surly sourpuss if ever there was one.

For too long, the series did not explain Benton's tensions and anger; or put them into a context that gave them meaning. As was true of most of these nighttime dramas, *ER* was eager to comment on the lives of the major white characters: the heartthrob Dr. Ross (George Clooney), the sensitive Dr. Greene (Anthony Edwards), the emotionally fragile nurse Hathaway (Julianna Margulies), the young, eager-to-please resident John Carter (Noah Wyle), the earnest physician Dr. Lewis (Sherry Stringfield). Viewers learned about Dr. Ross's relationships with various women, Greene's problems with his lawyer wife, and Hathaway's shaky romance with a physician as well as her once devastating relationship with Dr. Ross. Those characters also frequently befriended each other. Yet except for his relationship with the resident under his supervision, Carter, who idolized him and was almost desperate to please him, Benton was left isolated. With Benton and Carter, *ER* wisely refused to go the bonding route. It was altogether realistic that the Black Benton might not care to develop a personal relationship with a white colleague. But there was no one at the hospital that he seemed close to. When African American actresses like C. C. H. Pounder and the striking Tyra Ferrell made guest appearances as physicians, you hoped Benton might express his feelings about being the only African American doctor on the ER team; perhaps then we'd understand the source of his anger or alienation. But no such thing happened. He remained as removed from them as from everyone else. Where did this man go after he left the hospital?

A semblance of a home life was created for Benton when that great marvel of an actress Beah Richards appeared in various episodes as his elderly mother. As the warm and even-tempered mother, who was revealed to be suffering from Alzheimer's disease, Richards created a stunning portrait of a woman fearful of losing control over not only her life but her very sense of identity. Together, Benton and his sister (Khandi Alexander) were faced with the painful decision to put their mother into a nursing home. At the end of that episode, Benton was seen massaging his mother's feet while looking over a family photo album. "Your talent is God's gift to you," Richards tells him. "What you do with it is your gift back to God." It was a beautiful moment. But the scene said more about the mother than the son. Ving Rhames also appeared as Benton's brother-in-law Walter. Yet even with his family Benton was still a cipher.

Eventually, *ER* gave Benton a love life. He first became involved with his mother's caretaker, a married woman, Jeanie Boulet (Gloria Reuben). In his intimate scenes with Boulet, La Salle's Benton remained remote, frustrating viewers all the more. Whereas the sadness and disillusionment in actor George Clooney's eyes had lifted his Dr. Ross womanizer character out of a one-dimensional cad category (the writers seemed to write with Clooney, the man, in mind to create a fully dimensional, engaging hero), La Salle appeared unable to infuse a flat character with some personal warmth or idiosyncrasies. "Benton is probably the most misunderstood [character]," wrote *Jet*, "as he rarely allows his wall of defense to come down."[6]

Later the writers created two other romances for Benton: first with Carla (Lisa Nicole Carson), with whom he has a son, Reese, but to whom he cannot commit; then an interracial affair with a British doctor, Elizabeth Corday (Alex Kingston). Significantly, Corday pursues him, trying her best to get him to let his guard down. But he's still a stiff. His most spontaneous moment came on a Halloween episode. During the closing segment, viewers saw Benton dressed as movie hero Shaft (with Isaac Hayes's music in the background). It provided the Benton character with a great cultural reference (which otherwise was usually missing).

In the third season, an episode of *ER* finally commented on the subject that many African American viewers were most curious about: Benton's feelings about race. A young African American intern at the hospital, Dennis Gant (Omar Epps), wants very much to connect to Benton. But Benton is always tough on him (as much so as he was with Carter). Finally, in a telling sequence, when the two are alone, Gant confronts Benton. Benton asks if Gant checked "Black" on his medical school application. When Gant replies yes, Benton informs him that everyone will assume Gant is there because of a quota system, not because of merit. Therefore Gant must work harder and be better to prove them wrong. It was one of the rare times when viewers felt they had been given some concrete comment on Benton's feelings of (racial) isolation as the only African American doctor on the ER staff. In time, Benton's one-note remoteness became, to put it politely, uninteresting.

Later the writers tried softening the Benton character as he struggled to accept his young son's deafness. But it wasn't a particularly engrossing plot development. In the fifth season, an entire episode of *ER* was devoted to Benton. When asked during an appearance on *The Today Show* why it had taken so long for a special episode on Benton, actor La Salle answered, "I don't know. You'd have to ask the producers. They've done it with every original member of the cast. They've actually done it multiple times. For five years, I said, 'Okay, guys, I'm on the show as well.'" La Salle admitted he had to put his foot down. "I think it was a bit unfortunate that it gets to that level. But I think it's really about that this is an ensemble show. And the word 'ensemble' implies fair treatment and equality. I think we're here. And it's a great challenge. I'm definitely glad and pleased with the show. But it was a struggle."

To his credit, La Salle also voiced his other concerns about *ER*. "As an African American man, it becomes a bit offensive if the negative things are all you're showing,"[7]

he said. "Because in real life we romance and get on each other's nerves and laugh and do all the things that any other race of people do." He urged the writers to drop the romantic story line between Benton and the white Corday. "So if the only time you show a balanced relationship is in an interracial relationship whether it's conscious or subconscious, it sends a message I'm not comfortable with. [The writers] were sending a message that I didn't want to be a part of, which was the only time that this man becomes human and tender and vulnerable and open is when he falls in love with a white woman." He added that his relationships with African American women on the series had been dysfunctional. "One was an adulterous relationship with Jeanie Boulet and then the next relationship I got into was with Carla. And unfortunately the writing there was, every time you see them they're either fighting or [having sex]." The writers dropped the Benton/Corday story line. Later a romance was developed for Benton and a new character, Dr. Cleo Finch, played by African American actress Michael Michele.

Like *Hill Street Blues*, *ER* sometimes fell back on familiar, even stock characterizations of urban African Americans. On one episode, two young Black men were brought into the emergency room, each with gunshot wounds. Two young Black women—who visit the men—argue and get into a shoving match. They are asked to leave the room. But in the hospital corridor they begin to fight and are told to get out of the hospital or the police and security will be called. Later one of the women is brought back to the hospital with stab wounds, apparently having been attacked by the other woman. On another episode, Carter ends up in the inner city, where he stumbles across two Black children sitting on a doorstep outside a doorway. He walks inside the house to find their tubercular mother breathing heavily. As he attempts to help, a Black man suddenly appears, demanding to know what Carter is doing in his home. Though Carter says he only wants to help the woman get medical treatment, the man—irrationally—insists that he leave.

During the fifth season, new cast members Djimon Hounsou and Akosua Busia played a married West African couple who are political refugees from Nigeria, where Hounsou was tortured. He's a janitor at the hospital; she works in the cafeteria's food service. One day she confides in the nurse Hathaway that she was raped while in Nigeria but thus far she has been unable to tell her husband. She fears his reaction. Later she ends up with a knife wound to the chest and wheeled into the emergency room on a gurney. We learn that her husband "freaked out" and we assume he attacked her. Though this story line later had a surprising twist, you wonder why all these episodes relied on a continuing depiction of a world of crime or violence for these Black characters.

Despite its shortcomings, *ER* reached a segment of the African American community. Part of the appeal was that *ER* also developed a fine lineup of Black supporting players: Yvette Freeman as nurse Haleh Adams; Deezer D. as nurse Malik McGrath; Conni Marie Brazelton as nurse Conni Oligario; guest star C. C. H. Pounder as Dr. Angela Hicks. Freeman with her short Afro, Brazelton with her dreads, Pounder with her traditional coif all provided the workplace with an interesting visual comment on the various styles and looks of African American women.

Certainly, the most moving story line for an African American woman centered on Jeanie Boulet. Married to a man who has cheated on her, she ends up briefly in the arms of Benton. Later working as a physician's assistant, Jeanie solemnly walks through the corridors, hallways, and elevators of the hospital, always ready to help others. Jeanie's story attained a distinct emotional power when she learned that she was HIV-positive. Fearful of losing her job, she keeps her condition a secret. There was some grumbling that *ER*'s depiction of an HIV-positive Black character was a negative comment on the African American community, especially since she contracted the disease from her husband, a promiscuous Black man. But the Black characters on *ER*, like the white ones, had to have problems, great and small. AIDS was a real problem within the African American and Latino communities, and *ER* neither sensationalized nor exploited the subject. Yet television's one prime-time weekly African American heroine—who was mature, sophisticated, *and* sexual—looked as if she might disappear.

Though Gloria Reuben was not an especially expressive actress (with her flat voice, she spoke almost in a monotone), her passivity and melancholic air worked beautifully for the character. Some of the most affecting moments of the television season were those when the camera came in close to record Reuben/Jeanie's despair. You felt you were losing something special, right before your eyes. You dreaded seeing her die. Then the writers did an unexpected thing. They let the character live with her disease. Eventually, little was said about her condition. Then, without much fanfare, the character married and was written out of the series. But no viewer ever forgot Boulet.

Despite the limitations of the hour-long dramatic ensemble series, these remained the only weekly programs that African Americans could turn to for serious, mature Black characters. Such dramatic Black series as *Under One Roof*, Thomas Carter's multigenerational family story, and *413 Hope Street*, executive-produced by Damon Wayans, disappeared quickly from the prime-time schedule. Set in a crisis center with a mixed but predominantly Black cast, *413 Hope Street* had promise. It scored well with Black viewers, becoming their third most watched show. But when *413 Hope Street* failed to bring in the big ratings, Fox, rather than giving the series time to find a broader audience, dropped it. Black dramatic series still could not survive on the prime-time schedule.

◆ *Notes*

1. Why am I in: Kevin Courrier and Susan Green, *Law & Order: The Unofficial Companion* (Los Angeles: Renaissance Books, 1998).

2. who, by his own: Verne Gay, "A Patient 'Blues' Man," New York *Newsday*, April 5, 1994.

3. [Fancy] has a certain: Ibid.

4. one of television's most: Caryn James, "Critic's Choice/Television: Officer's Last Harangue," *The New York Times*, May 8, 1998.

5. the best actor on: John Leonard, "Television: Swept Away," *New York*, June 10, 1996.

6. Benton is probably the: "Eriq La Salle and Gloria Reuben Help Make 'ER' a Top-Rated TV Series," *Jet*, February 17, 1997.

7. As an African American: Michael Starr, "Why the Romance Went Out of 'ER,'" *New York Post*, April 14, 1999.

61

THIS IS FOR FIGHTING, THIS IS FOR FUN

Camerawork and Gunplay in Reality-Based Crime Shows

◆ Fred Turner

Several years ago, I interviewed a Vietnam veteran named Brian Winhover. He had survived three tours of combat duty, but when he tried to tell me how he felt when he was under fire, it took him a while to find the words. Eventually he said, "[you could] call me a piece of ice. . . . You couldn't impregnate me with anything."[1] At first I was taken aback— I hadn't expected a word like "impregnate" to crop up in a war story—but the more we talked, the clearer the psychology of his combat experience became. Winhover had lived out all the confusions embedded in the ubiquitous boot camp chant, "This is my rifle, this [penis] is my gun. One is for killing, one is for fun."[2] Killing could be sex, the chant implied, and sex of a very particular kind. For Winhover, as for generations of soldiers before and since, to be a man, to belong to the unit, was to penetrate; to fail at those tasks, to be an enemy to the unit, was to be penetrated like a woman or a homosexual "bottom." The battlefield was a site of sexualized conflict, one at which it was Winhover's duty to assert his difference from the enemy by proving it "feminine." This Winhover did with aplomb: by his own description, he became a mechanical, rifle-like creature in Vietnam, hard and numb. He dedicated his days in the field to killing, to trying to penetrate the bodies of enemy soldiers, to trying to "impregnate" the enemy with his weapon. In short, he became the perfect soldier.

Winhover came home in 1969, yet the psychosexual dynamics that characterized his combat experiences remain very much alive. In fact, they are a defining feature of the now ten-year-old American television genre of "reality-based" crime programs. In these highly popular and resilient shows, viewers encounter a world much like the one Winhover saw in Vietnam, a world in which heavily armed, uniformed men move among impoverished civilians, trying to sort guerrilla-like criminals from the population. They also encounter the psychosexual economy of that realm. In boot camp, Winhover's drill sergeants trained him to confuse his penis and his rifle and thus to take a physical pleasure in being a soldier. In the far less coercive world of television, and toward a similar end, reality-based crime programs urge viewers to confuse the guns of the police with the cameras through which they see events. Just as military training has long sought to break down the psychic barriers between killing and sex in the minds of its soldiers, so the visual styles of these programs work to intermingle the processes of seeing and shooting, of knowing and arresting, and of consuming goods and upholding the law. As the producers of reality-based crime programming acknowledge, these shows aim not to be *watched*, but to be *experienced*.[3] With the full support and cooperation of the police themselves, the cameramen of reality-based crime programs invite viewers—both male and female—to feel the highly sexualized,

hyper-masculine power of the State within their sedentary bodies.[4]

They extend this invitation by carefully equating their own cameras with the guns of the policemen and bounty hunters the cameras depict. After watching ten episodes of each of four of the most popular reality-based crime shows in the United States— *Cops* (1989), *Bounty Hunters* (1996), *America's Most Wanted* (1988), and *LAPD: Life on the Beat* (1995)—I've noticed that guns most frequently appear onscreen in three contexts: as weapons aimed at suspects, as holstered emblems of police authority, and, in advertising trailers especially, as explicit echoes of the cinematic six-shooter. These three incarnations correspond to three televisual devices common to the real-life crime genre: handheld camera work, computer graphics, and intertextuality. Like aimed pistols, handheld video cameras grant the viewer a policeman's power to pursue and arrest the suspect, albeit visually. Like holstered weapons, computer graphics make visible an omnipresent power—in this case, the power of TV producers, cooperating state authorities, and the viewer to embed potentially disruptive criminal activity in a body of knowledge. Finally, as symbols manipulated by TV producers, guns link the local realm of the arrest scene to the mythology of the American frontier. In these ways, guns and cameras work together to transform real-life crime programs into a sort of visual boot camp for the TV audience, one in which viewers are subtly coerced into taking pleasure in the feminization and domination of the poor and of people of color by a well-armed, fun-craving masculinized State.

The link between cameras and guns naturally precedes the advent of real-life crime programming (consider the phrase "shooting a movie"), just as the link between weapons and penises preceded the Vietnam War. Yet, in the four programs I will focus on, producers put extraordinary effort into maintaining and naturalizing the gun-camera analogy.

This is true despite the fact that each show features its own unique aesthetics. *Cops* and *Bounty Hunters*, for instance, offer seemingly raw (though in fact heavily edited) video-*verité* accounts of pursuit and capture. Each half-hour episode of *Cops* follows the exploits of police in a single American city, and includes between three and five sequences of police officers in action.[5] These are preceded by a video-montage title sequence which depicts some of the most dramatic moments from footage already gathered in that city, accompanied by the show's now-infamous reggae theme song ("*Bad boys, bad boys—What'cha gonna do when they come for you?*"). Each action sequence opens with a shot of the policeman centrally involved—a shot in which the officer frequently describes his motives for joining the force—and proceeds to show him responding to a radio call.[6] It then depicts the officer pursuing and usually capturing a suspect and concludes with that officer or one of his colleagues commenting laconically on the events that have just unfolded. *Bounty Hunters* follows a similar pattern. Each half-hour episode focuses on the work of one or two teams of bail enforcement agents and includes two to four sequences in which they discuss how to find and capture a particular bail jumper, pursue that person, arrest him, and bring him to jail.[7]

LAPD and *America's Most Wanted* feature a more varied menu of police activities and a correspondingly wider range of televisual devices. As its name suggests, *LAPD* attends exclusively to the activities of the Los Angeles Police Department. In addition to depicting pursuits and arrests, this half-hour show focuses considerable attention on the gathering of evidence. It also often has detectives recount the circumstances of unsolved crimes and ask the viewer for leads. At the end of many episodes, Los Angeles Mayor Richard Riordan appears on screen to encourage those with an interest in law enforcement to sign up for the force.

America's Most Wanted similarly encourages viewer participation. Hosted by John Walsh, an actor whose son Adam was murdered, the program's hour-long episodes tend to eschew capture sequences in order to introduce an average of three to five unsolved crimes or missing criminals, sometimes through re-enactments, and then ask viewers to assist in bringing the "bad guys" to justice. If they should spot one of these fugitives among their neighbors or can offer other leads, viewers are instructed to call "1-800-CRIMETV." Periodically, the program's producers present updates in which they show viewers how their calls have led to the arrest of fugitives from previous episodes.

With the exception of *America's Most Wanted*, then, each of these programs regularly features several sequences in which law enforcement officials pursue and capture suspects. These pursuits normally culminate in an arrest vignette. In one common form, this vignette depicts a group of policemen or bounty hunters bursting into a house, guns drawn, tackling an often half-naked suspect, and throwing him to the ground. In another form, it consists of a group of officers pointing their pistols at a suspect some feet away, forcing him or her to lie on the ground, face down, and then creeping closer until they loom over the suspect's prone figure. In a third, the arrest vignette features officers fingering their weapons while forcing a suspect to bend forward over the hood of a police cruiser, legs spread in preparation for an imminent frisking (itself often depicted as well).

Monotonously styled and frequently repeated, these vignettes are the equivalents of the "money shot" or "cum shot" in a porn movie: they are moments at which the full masculine potency of the leading character is revealed. These moments differ slightly from their pornographic equivalents, though, in the forms of pleasure they offer. In the conventional, heterosexual cum shot, the camera closes in strategically on the hard body and erect penis of the male performer. It thus offers the viewer at least two possible pleasures: of watching a powerful male control a female and of imagining himself as that male. The cameras of reality-based crime shows, on the other hand, go several steps further in enforcing an identification between the viewer and the protagonist (in this case, a police officer). Repeatedly, cameramen seek out not just the point of view of the officers, but points of view suggested by their *weapons*. In police cars on the way to crime scenes, camera operators record the dashboard and radio from the waist-level vantage point of a gun belt. At the moment of capture, they point their lenses down at prone suspects like pistols. When those lenses zoom in on key parts of a suspect's body—a pocket, a scarred chest, and, especially often, the buttocks (a place where a weapon or drugs might be hidden and where the suspect might be penetrated sexually)—they draw the viewer toward the suspect along the trajectory of an imaginary bullet. Unlike their counterparts in heterosexual pornography, the cameramen of reality-based crime shows will not simply let their viewers watch. Rather, by conflating camera and pistol, they demand that the viewer personally experience the power of penetration embodied in the weapons of the officers of the State.[8]

This power is highly sexualized, but only in a limited sense. As in much heterosexual pornography, the twinned phallic weapons of camera and gun are used here in order to humiliate and subjugate rather than excite a feminized Other. The pleasure on offer is not a fantasy of congress, but a fantasy of control. And what needs to be controlled is the sexualized agency of the "enemy"—in this case, the poor and people of color. Sometimes, this agency is represented by a weapon, or at least the possibility of one. Virtually every arrest vignette features a police pat-down of a suspect for knives and guns, a search conducted as though the almost-always impoverished suspect could actually have the same access to weapons that the police themselves have. In this way, reality-based crime shows imply that the agency of the "enemy" may be masculine—that is, that it may be able to "penetrate"

the bodies of the police on the screen (and by impltaition, of police and viewers in the off-screen world as well).

More often though (and sometimes simultaneously), these programs suggest that the agency of suspects and their friends and families is symbolically female. When police arrive at a crime scene, cameras quickly record any signs of difference between the police and the citizenry. They peer over the uniformed shoulders of the police and zoom in on unkempt hair, scars and bruises, and tattoos. Likewise, when cameramen follow officers into a home, they focus on disorder, on piles of dishes, unwashed children, unmade beds. In contrast to the officers—who stand erect and uniformed, their bodies often hard with muscles or body armor—the suspects are depicted as unruly, messy, corpulent, and disorderly. They are "soft" where the officers are "hard." Often upset, they appear "hysterical" where the officers appear commanding and "rational." In these ways, producers imply that the poor are not only undisciplined individuals but stereotypically feminine as well. Producers here do much the same psychological work as Army drill sergeants: faced with the symbolically masculine potential of those whom they've defined as antagonists to assault policemen and viewers alike, to "penetrate" them so to speak, they assist viewers in labeling these antagonists not as "men," but as "women" who must themselves be symbolically penetrated by the forces of the State. Like Army recruits, viewers are invited to join the masculine community of these forces and to take pleasure in the domination of a feminized enemy.

That feminized enemy, however, constantly threatens to devour its masculine counterpart. Even weaponless, the poor are dangerous: in episode after episode, the sexualized entropy of their lives threatens to overwhelm the orderly police. And while this is true for all such suspects, it is especially so for people of color. In keeping with centuries-old American stereotypes, both male and female African Americans are often depicted as having uncontrollable libidos. In an episode of *Cops* set in Kansas City, Kansas, for instance, several white officers pull up to a disturbance in the middle of the night. At the edges of the light cast by the camera team, we can see black figures running here and there, like escaped slaves in some nineteenth-century plantation owner's nightmare. Then, a large African American woman rushes to the center of the frame, wielding a pipe. She points out a young black man and accuses him of lifting up her teenage daughter's shirt in front of her. The policemen chase, tackle, and arrest the young man, who is clearly intoxicated. Later, a policeman explains: "A lot of the people we deal with out here are on what we call 'water'—that's marijuana dipped in formaldehyde. That gentleman obviously was trying to have sex with a young girl in front of the child's mother. Now it's time to do a lot of paperwork and move on to the next one."[9] The implied alignment of forces is clear: young black men run wild in the streets looking for sex; young white men work to preserve a chaste world of order and reason. White men work with their minds on "paper work," whereas young black men are out of their minds on "water."

This episode of *Cops* presents a fairly extreme example, but the principles at work within it run throughout reality-based crime programming. By depicting the poor and people of color as symbolically female, producers of real-life crime programs remind viewers of the pleasures of aligning themselves with a dominant and symbolically male State. Nor are these pleasures merely intellectual: when producers force viewers to look down (and sometimes, seemingly, *out of*) the barrels of police guns, they invite viewers to feel those weapons as extensions of their own bodies.

Alongside this form of camerawork, however, these programs also feature an abundance of computer-generated graphics. At the outset of each arrest sequence on *LAPD*, for instance, an icon appears on the screen, looking much as it might in a Windows computer interface, giving the title of the segment. Subsequent icons introduce the officers involved, describe the type of crime under consideration, and even present a map of the area the officers routinely patrol. *America's Most Wanted* regularly features a graphic drawing of a target zone into which the images of criminals are drawn as if dragged and clicked by a mouse across a screen. It also presents surveillance photographs from stores and banks, photographs which producers manipulate on screen as if they were digitized images on a home computer. Even the comparatively low-tech *Cops* and *Bounty Hunters* present onscreen tags at the start of each segment identifying the time, city, crime at hand, and officer in pursuit.

On one hand, these graphics are the products of a larger change in television style. As television critic John Caldwell has noted, the 1980s saw a shift across the medium "from programs based on rhetorical discourse to ones structured around the concepts of pictorial and stylistic embellishment."[10] Having come into being at the end of the decade, the reality-based crime genre reflects this shift. On the other hand, however, I think we can read the uses of computer graphics as an extension of an already-established conflation of gun, camera, and masculine agency. In much the way that holstered pistols signal an omnipresent power to contain a given situation, so too do computer graphics seem to surround and neutralize dangerous individuals without necessarily assaulting them directly. When the computer *does* assault a suspect, it acts as a pistol might: by tearing apart the body. With the click of an off-screen mouse, producers reduce people to mug shots; that is, they eliminate their bodies and surround the faces that remain with statistics and icons. They take all that is dangerous and original in the criminal and embed it in the seemingly safe, rational world of information. In other words, they dam the flow of "water" with "paperwork."[11]

Computer graphics thus extend the camera/gun analogy in two ways: first, by fragmenting the bodies of suspects, they recall the pistol's ability to violate the boundaries of a human body; secondly, by surrounding the suspect with information, they suggest the power of the police to surround and arrest any individual—a power assured on the scene by weapons. These same visual techniques also work to normalize police activities by linking them to other, seemingly unrelated practices. Drag-and-click graphics, for instance, suggest a link between the pursuit of criminals on television and the pursuit of information on home computers. The penetrating style of camerawork that offers viewers a chance to look through the eyes of a weapon echoes the point of view available in many video and computer games and in broadcast news accounts of contemporary military actions (most notably the 1991 Gulf War, in which Americans delighted in being able to see through the eyes of "smart" bombs).

Extensive use of statistics and of overhead helicopter shots even suggests a resemblance between the televised monitoring of crime and the televised monitoring of sports such as baseball. This is not to say that viewers confuse crime, war, and baseball in any conscious sense, but rather to note that to the extent that real-life crime programs share a visual style with other activities, they may also be able to borrow the perceived legitimacy of those activities. That is, to the extent that the viewer watches war or crime on TV as he watches baseball—from high above, from the heights reserved for the owners of luxury boxes, or, in the case of war, from the aerial vantage points usually reserved for government authorities— he may well be inclined to feel that war and the pursuit of criminals are naturally right and rule-bound in the manner of a sport.

Nor are such linkages confined to the predominantly masculine domains of the battlefield, the baseball diamond, or the video game. Real-life crime programs are shown in a highly commercial context and for the purpose of selling ad time, and in many ways, the structure of pursuit and arrest—a structure controlled in the material field through the use of weapons and in the televisual field through the use of cameras and computer graphics—mirrors that of the pursuit and acquisition of consumer goods. With each new crime, the viewer joins the police or the bounty hunters in a process of revealing a need to make an acquisition (in this case, of a suspect), of identifying the target for acquisition, of capturing that target, and finally, of taking that target "home" to jail. In real-life crime programming, the sexualized landscape of crime and its containment soon overlaps the commercial landscape of desire and its satisfaction, and producers know this.

To take one particularly glaring example, the Sam Adams Brewing Company advertises its beer (in California, at least) on *Bounty Hunters*. Their ad features a man drinking a beer who sees another man steal a woman's purse. The beer drinker flicks a bottle cap at the suspect's head and knocks him out cold, thus saving the day—and thus suggesting that the buying of beer and the capturing of suspects might each represent the exercise of a masculine agency.

That agency does not belong to the viewer alone, however, nor even to the law enforcement officials on the TV screen; it belongs to the American nation. In the same way that boot camp taught Brian Winhover not only to be a killer, but to be an American soldier, reality-based crime programs teach their viewers to feel not only the power of individual men within themselves, but the masculine power of the State itself. They do this by referring constantly to the Old West of American myth. The opening of *Bounty Hunters*, for instance, features four men wearing black vests or long range coats with silver badges on their chests. Scruffy, macho, they carry pistols and a rifle. "When the West was won," explains the voice-over, "bounty hunters helped to create law and order. In 1873, federal law gave them the power to enter residences and cross state lines in pursuit of bail jumpers. Today, modern bounty hunters continue to use that power to return fugitives to justice. Their motto: *You can run, but you can't hide.*"

With such references, the America of today, like the Vietnam of yesterday and the Wild West before it, becomes a landscape in which to act out a national drama of justice. In this landscape, the gun symbolizes the link between past and present, and with it the link between the righteousness of American laws and the masculinity of their enforcers. By means of its conflation with the camera, the gun offers viewers a chance to walk alongside the bounty hunters, to undertake a mission on behalf of the nation, a mission to penetrate the dank, dark regions of American society, to "see" the suspect there, to "know" his crimes and thereby to humiliate him. In the slums of the twentieth century, as on the prairies of the nineteenth, those whom the government has identified as wanton and uncivilized "can run, but they can't hide."

But why should Americans and Canadians want to "see" criminals in the first place? And how is it that enough Americans and Canadians want to watch these shows that they should appear, in first-run and serialized episodes, twice a day, every day of the week, in a number of major North American media markets?

In part, the answer is economic: reality-based crime programs typically cost between $150,000 and $250,000 per episode to produce, while a typical news magazine program might cost between $250,000 and $400,000.[12] Prime-time dramas and action adventure programs usually run between $900,000 and $1 million per episode.[13] Thus, even before they take the often substantial revenues from syndication into account, producers know that they need not attract either huge audiences or high-budget advertisements to turn a profit. Moreover, because viewers often perceive these shows as resembling news, programmers see them as effective programs with which to lead into and out of the local evening news or with which to counter-program against other genres, such as sitcoms.[14]

Yet I think these shows remain popular for more historical reasons as well. The first reality-based crime programs, *America's Most Wanted* and *Cops*, emerged in 1988 and 1989 respectively. These years fall toward the end of a nearly decade-long period in which first the Reagan administration and then the Bush administration sought to marginalize the poor and people of color. Under Reagan, this process took the form of cuts in aid to the poor, including $6.8 billion from the food stamp budget and $5.2 billion from child nutritional services between 1981 and 1987.[15] During the Bush administration, this process gained particular momentum as part of the "War on Drugs"—a war started under Reagan. In 1989, for instance, drug czar William Bennett implemented the National Drug Control Strategy. Even as it acknowledged that "the typical cocaine user is white, male, a high school graduate employed full time and living in a small metropolitan area or suburb," the Bennett plan devoted some 70% of its resources to law enforcement and focused most of its attention on the inner cities—areas inhabited predominantly by people of color and areas in which full-time employment outside the drug trade can often be hard to find.[16] As Michael Omi and Howard Winant have pointed out, these policies have been accompanied by "a regressive redistribution of income and a decline in real wages [across the country], a significant shift to the ideological right in terms of public discourse, and an increase in the use of coercion on the part of the state."[17] This broader process in turn, they argue, has resulted in the creation of an impoverished, disproportionately dark-skinned Third World inside the United States.

In that sense, then, reality-based crime shows represent the propaganda arm of a multi-tiered American State. Produced with the active assistance of local police departments (and at times national forces such as the FBI), they serve as an ideological reservoir from which politicians and citizens alike can draw justifications of oppressive actions. This is particularly true of *LAPD: Life on the Beat*, a program first aired in 1995, two years after the Los Angeles Riots. As historian Mike Davis has pointed out, the Los Angeles Police Department considered South Central Los Angeles an internal Vietnam throughout the late 1980s. It thought of African American housing projects as "strategic hamlets" and regularly launched "search-and-destroy" missions in the area.[18] The 1992 riots exposed this process on live television. It should be no surprise, then, that the Los Angeles Police Department was eager to join MGM Television in producing a new series about its activities. As Chief of Police Willie L. Williams told a reporter in 1994, "For some time, the Los Angeles Police Department has been searching for a forum that would allow the public to see firsthand the dedication and selfless efforts of the men and women of the L.A.P.D. as they go about serving our community. The reality-based television series *L.A.P.D.* is a window through which the viewer will be able to see the truth of department activities."[19]

Yet despite their obvious propaganda function, we must be careful not to read reality-based crime programs only in the light of the services they provide to the State or to the television industry. We need to acknowledge the ways in which these programs deliberately confuse and intermingle several struggles, including the struggle of the State to justify its policies, the struggle of men and women at times to affirm and at times to tear down systems of racial and sexual distinction, and the struggle of people throughout our society to manage their economic and social anxieties.

We should also continue to examine the ways in which visual technologies and styles translate these sometimes abstract struggles into felt experiences of the body. As Kevin Robins and Les Levidow have written, "War converts fear and anxiety into perceptions of external threat; it then mobilizes defenses against alien and thing-like enemies. In this process, new image and vision technologies can play a central role."[20] Over the last two decades, the American government has fought a low-intensity war on the poor. For generations, American society has been plagued by persistent conflicts over racial and gender boundaries. By equating guns and cameras and by sexualizing the work of each, reality-based crime shows not only define the poor and people of color as external threats to their viewers but engage viewers in a process of defining the poor and people of color as alien and thing-like. As in the military, the "good guys" are "men like us," men who take pleasure in being well-equipped, so to speak, and "hard." The "bad guys" are (symbolically) women or perhaps homosexual males, creatures who deserve to be penetrated and who indeed *must be penetrated* if their threat to the heterosexual male social order is to be contained. In the world of reality-based crime programs, as formerly on the battlefields of Southeast Asia, to be a good American is to be impregnable.

Notes ◆

1. Fred Turner, *Echoes of Combat: The Vietnam War in American Memory* (New York: Anchor Books, 1996), 76. Brian Winhover is a pseudonym for a veteran who requested anonymity.

2. Ibid.

3. As John Langley, co-creator of *Cops*, puts it, "What we try to do is capture the experience of being a cop. We put the viewers as close to being a cop as possible, to let them experience what a cop experiences. My ideal segment would have no cuts. We have very few cuts as it is. We try to be as pure as possible and take viewers through the experience from beginning to end." (Quoted in Cynthia Littleton, "True Blue: John Langley helped set the tone for the reality genre with 'Cops'," *Broadcasting & Cable* [May 20, 1996], 26.)

4. Ratings have consistently shown that men and women watch reality-based crime programs in similar numbers. For example, a summary of the February 1997 Nielsen ratings for *LAPD: Life on the Beat* broadcast on KUSI, San Diego, California,

shows that in the Monday-Friday 5:30-6:00 PM time slot, an average of 9,000 females and 15,000 males between the ages of 25 and 54 watched the show. Another local station, KNSD, reports similar figures for February 1996: an average of 7,000 females and 9,000 males watched the show when it was broadcast Monday through Friday from 3:00 to 3:30 PM (Source: Tapscan, Inc.) The broad appeal of these programs is widely recognized by both producers and advertisers. As Cynthia Littleton has noted, the "broad-based demographics" of these shows have made them very popular with merchants selling such staples as frozen foods (Cynthia Littleton, "Reality Television: Keeping the heat on," *Broadcasting & Cable* [May 20, 1996], 25.) For a discussion of the economics of reality-based crime programs, see "Special Report: Reality's Widening Role in the Real World of TV," *Broadcasting & Cable* (April 12, 1993), 24-38.

5. With one glaring exception: In 1989, *Cops* broadcast a one-hour special on Russian police.

6. And it is almost always a "him"—female police officers appear rarely in these programs.

7. Bail jumpers do include women of course, but on *Bounty Hunters*, males outnumber females approximately 2 to 1.

8. We need to note that the stimulation on offer brings violence and power together in a highly structured way: the viewer is never allowed to see through the "enemy's" weapons and is never allowed to look back at the officers at work. Much as boot camp limits the range of relationships open to a new recruit, and thus makes it easier and more pleasurable for him to give himself over to membership in the platoon, so the camerawork in these shows limits the range of identifications open to the viewer and makes it easier for him to enjoy an imaginary allegiance with the police.

9. *Cops*, Kansas City, KS; Broadcast XETV, Ch. 6, January 17, 1998.

10. John Caldwell, *Televisuality: Style, Crisis, and Authority in American Television* (New Brunswick, NJ: Rutgers University Press, 1995), 233.

11. I'm drawing here on concepts outlined by Klaus Theweleit in *Male Fantasies, Volume 1: Women, Floods, Bodies, History* (Minneapolis: University of Minnesota Press, 1987). For the Freikorps soldiers Theweleit studied, as I believe for the policemen here, the labeling of an enemy as feminine and the generation of masculinized response to that enemy occur simultaneously. One metaphor which participants have used to describe this process, Theweleit notes, is one of damming a flood.

12. Mike Freeman, "The economics of first-run reality," *Broadcasting & Cable* (April 12, 1993), 35.

13. Caldwell, *Televisuality*, 289.

14. According to Greg Meidel, president of syndication for Twentieth Television, "All our research says that viewers closely identify *Cops* content with that of similar sorts of law enforcement coverage on newscasts locally. That's why [*Cops*] has been so compatible as a lead-in or lead-out from local news programming. It looks, feels and tastes like a first-run news program." (Quoted in Mike Freeman, "Ratings are reality for off-net," *Broadcasting & Cable* [April 12, 1993], 32.) For a lengthy discussion of reality-based crime shows and programming tactics, see Cynthia Littleton, "Reality matures into 'utility' player," *Broadcasting & Cable* (May 20, 1996).

15. Michael Z. Letwin, "Report from the Front Line—The Bennett Plan: Street-Level Drug Enforcement in New York City and the Legalization Debate," *Hofstra Law Review*, Vol. 18, No. 4 (Spring), 810; cited in Robin Andersen, *Consumer Culture and TV Programming* (Boulder, CO: Westview, 1995), 184.

16. Office of National Drug Control Policy 1989, 4; Quoted in Andersen, *Consumer Culture*, 182.

17. Michael Omi and Howard Winant, "The L.A. Race Riot and U.S. Politics" in Robert Gooding-Williams, ed., *Reading Rodney King/Reading Urban Uprising* (New York and London: Routledge, 1993), 108.

18. Mike Davis, *City of Quartz* (New York: Vintage, 1990), 268 and 244; quoted in Caldwell, *Televisuality*, 311.

19. Quoted in David Tobenkin, "MGM Television follows 'LAPD' into syndication," *Broadcasting & Cable* (August 19, 1994), 20.

20. Kevin Robins and Les Levidow, "Soldier, Cyborg, Citizen," in James Brook and Iain A. Boal, eds., *Resisting The Virtual Life: The Culture and Politics of Information* (San Francisco: City Lights Books, 1995), 106.

HERE COMES THE JUDGE

The Dancing Itos and the Televisual Construction of the Enemy Asian Male

◆ Brian Locke

If for nothing else, Lance Ito will be remembered as the presiding judge in the 1995 O. J. Simpson murder trial. This third-generation Japanese American son of WWII internees directed the proceedings of the most extensively covered criminal trial in U.S. history. Consequently, Ito seemed to be everywhere on television during the trial. Court TV and CNN devoted several hours of programming a day to its ongoing coverage. In addition, his figure, a stern face behind his glasses, mustache, and beard, surfaced in the program lineups of both news and entertainment television.

Like any celebrity in the news, Ito became the butt of countless topical jokes, especially on late-night talk shows. This humor suggested vaguely that Ito may have been hiding something beneath his robes; the jokes of guests and hosts expressed a desire to investigate and expose what hid underneath the black judicial wrapper. On one episode of NBC's *The Tonight Show With Jay Leno*, the host asked the African American comedian George Wallace to voice his opinion about Ito, and he responded with the punchline, "You know, he's really naked under there." *The Tonight Show*'s late-night CBS rival, *The Late Show With David Letterman*, also participated. A "Top Ten List" from early February 1995, "Ways to Annoy Judge Ito," included the following two entries: "Pull robe over head. Spin. Push into street," and "Ask permission to have a television camera in his pants."

During the spring of 1995, *The Tonight Show* repeatedly televised its own fantasy of Ito, providing ample opportunity to peek underneath the judge's robes. In these skits, the show presented the Dancing Itos, a troupe of a half-dozen smiling men performing standard chorus-line routines. The dancers were marked as Judge Ito by their long black judicial robes, straight black hair parted on the side, glasses with thick lenses, and exaggerated black mustache and beard. In addition to these costumes, the Dancing Itos also impersonated well-known dancing groups such as the 1970s gay disco band, the Village People, and Parisienne can-can dancers.

Both of these impersonations relied on exposure for their comedic power. In their routine, "The Village Itos" lip-synch and dance to the tune of the band's signature pop song, "YMCA," here rewritten as "OJ LA." They begin the dance in a single-file line, then move into wedge formation with the lead dancer at the apex, nearest to the camera and the audience. At the climactic moment, the lead dancer reaches down to the hem of his robe and pulls it up over his head to reveal his crotch, gyrating his hips wildly. On a subsequent episode, "The Can-Can Itos" cartwheel onto the stage, then move into a single-file line, shoulder to shoulder. Their costumes resemble those of French chorus-line dancers except that their skirts are judicial-robe black. After doing the splits and rolling backwards *ensemble*, they bend over, flip up their skirts, and expose their rear ends to the audience.[1]

The Dancing Ito skits proved to be very popular. During the introductions to most performances, Leno mentioned the unusually high home audience response, once stating,

"We've gotten thousands of letters asking when they'd be back!" And in the studio, the audience response was clearly ecstatic. As the band played lively music, the cameras panned an audience clapping in rhythm. The finales of each routine pushed the audience to scream with satisfaction. Usually Leno appeared unable to contain his own laughter, hopping and twisting his body as he announced the night's guest and cut to commercials. During one appearance, the camera focused upon a young Asian man amidst the gaiety who, laughing and clapping with the rest of the audience, smiled and waved to the home viewer.

This [chapter] will analyze these and other representations of Lance Ito from several episodes of *The Tonight Show*. In doing so, it seeks to disrupt the black-and-white binary of contemporary racial discourse in the United States by showing how visual markers of "Asianness" play a central role in these representations. . . .

A visit by a *Tonight Show* guest in early April 1995 reveals the presumptions about race upon which the show relies. After a Dancing Itos routine, stand-up comedian Jack Cohen appears and tells a series of jokes dealing with sensitive topics: gun control, treatment of the elderly, the misogyny of divorced husbands, the Jeffrey Dahmer murder trial. The white comedian's material also explores issues of race in general and the Simpson trial in particular: black solidarity with Simpson, black people and criminality, racism in the Los Angeles Police Department and in the criminal justice system.

Despite the topicality of the material, neither Leno's monologue nor Cohen's routine included the biggest news at that time regarding race and the trial. Only a day before, the media had been abuzz with a story concerning Ito and Alphonse D'Amato, a Republican senator from New York and the chair of the Whitewater hearings. Two days prior to Cohen's appearance, D'Amato was interviewed by nationally syndicated radio talk show host Don Imus. During the live broadcast,

D'Amato had complained about the duration of the Simpson trial and its potentially disruptive impact on the hearings; he called Ito an egomaniac, dubbed his performance "a disgrace," and blamed him for dragging out the trial unnecessarily.[2] Whereas these comments were not particularly remarkable, the stereotypical "Oriental" accent he used to imitate the judge was. . . . The story of the senator's racial slur surfaced on the front pages of major newspapers the next morning.

Although it is not unusual that Cohen's practiced routine would fail to mention D'Amato's slur, it seems very unusual that Leno would fail to mention the day's hot political story. Prior to coming to *The Tonight Show*, Leno had made a name for himself as a political comedian. Furthermore, the show relies consistently on topical news like the Simpson trial for much of its comedic content, especially for the introductory monologue. This particular episode was no exception; nearly half of the jokes in a nine-minute monologue revolved around the trial, including several about Ito. Clearly, D'Amato's slur was somehow too fraught for the show.

In Leno's postperformance chat with Cohen, the reason behind this structuring absence becomes clear. When Leno asks his first question, "Do you ever worry about hurting anybody's feelings?" Cohen responds, "I don't worry about it much because we're comics. . . . It's not like we're . . . senators." Immediately, Cohen's brief reference to D'Amato's racial slur disrupts the show. As Leno leans back in his chair and replies monosyllabically, Cohen retorts, "How stupid! Did you see that?" pushing Leno to explain the reference to the audience. Leno improvises awkwardly, "Oh . . . D'Amato . . . He did his . . . Alphonse D'Amato, he did his . . . impression of Judge Ito . . . the most racist thing."

Cohen's unexpected reference to D'Amato and Leno's shaky response illuminate an insoluble contradiction. The show wants to include the popular Dancing Itos, yet the naked racial aggression of D'Amato's recent slur makes such an inclusion a very tricky matter. Had Leno mentioned the slur, the juxtaposition of the slur and the Dancing Itos skit would have threatened to expose *The Tonight Show*'s own televisual "impression of Judge Ito" as equivalent to D'Amato's "most racist thing"—a point not lost on Cohen. Laughing at Leno's efforts to contain the damage, Cohen responds, "Yeah. Too bad he didn't have a robe and was dancing. He would have been all right." Once again, Leno flounders; the band plays its punchline tag; the audience starts to clap and hoot. . . .

Cohen's surprise jokes about D'Amato question the innocence of the Dancing Itos and translate the show's discourse into terms that are explicitly racial. This translation, in turn, provides insights into the structure of contemporary racial discourse of which the D'Amato event and *The Tonight Show* are symptomatic. In the political atmosphere of the mid-1990s, D'Amato would surely not have characterized an African American on national radio in such terms. Such a slur would have hailed our commonsense notion of what counts as race, and therefore as racism, in a much more familiar way. In turn, the polarized black-and-white structure of racial discourse renders the status of any position that is neither "black" nor "white" more uncertain, or at times even invisible, as a racial position. The structure of racial discourse thus creates a space in which *The Tonight Show* can deploy a racist parody without invoking the vexing issue of race or provoking charges of racism. . . .

When forced to describe the racial aspects of the Dancing Itos, . . . one runs into a paradox. If the figures somehow convey Ito's status as a person of Japanese ancestry, then one would expect to find scrutable markers of Asianness. But at first glance, one is hard-pressed to find any; it is not immediately clear how the representations deploy race. Nearly every part of the body is covered, most notably the face. Indeed, the costuming hides a key facial detail, for the viewer cannot see the shape of the dancers' eyes. Because the glasses reflect the glare of the stage lights, two bouncing circles of brightness usually fill the spaces where the eyes should be. The eyewear overshadows the one physiognomic aspect that most typically serves as a foundation for the stereotypical visual establishment of Asianness: eyes with epicanthic folds.

The costuming gives the overall impression that the Itos hide themselves deliberately, make themselves inscrutable: the eyeglasses, the thick black mustache, and beard look like a mask. This easily recognizable mask corresponds to the show's interest in exposing. The Dancing Itos become flashers, lifting their robes to wild applause. But what is the link between Ito's representation, inscrutability, and the fascination with exposure? Initially, it is difficult to make the case that race plays a significant role in *The Tonight Show*'s representation of Ito because the Dancing Itos' costumes tend to obscure visual markers of race. But, as John Fiske explains, in a culture that purports to be color-blind, racial signifieds are often expressed through signifiers that, at first glance, seem to have no connection to issues of race.[3] . . . Rather than accepting Ito's inscrutability as a marker of the impossibility of reading race into the representations, we must instead *read* that inscrutability as a racial signifier.

In fact, the signifier has a long history. Asians have been coded in U.S. popular culture as a threat, a people who keep their motives and means well hidden. Bret Harte's 1870 poem "That Heathen Chinee" represents an earlier version of this view.[4] Characterizing "Chinese cheap labor" as possessing "dark ways" that hide "vain tricks," the poem is a thinly veiled warning to Americans about a Yellow Peril overwhelming the nation via our western shores. Similarly, the figure of Dr. Fu Manchu, the evil genius and namesake of Sax Rohmer's popular series of dime-store novels of the 1930s, evokes the inscrutable Asian; the difficulty of fighting the doctor

stems from the inability of any Westerner to fathom his brilliant, but twisted, Chinese mind.

When China became an ally of the United States with the advent of WWII, anti-Japanese sentiment blossomed and required a reconsideration of the signifiers of Asianness. Shortly after Pearl Harbor, federal authorities began drawing up plans to intern every person of Japanese ancestry living on the West Coast, regardless of the specifics of citizenship, nativity, or status as resident aliens prohibited by law from U.S. naturalization. Despite the fact that the Axis alliance included other countries, persons with ancestral ties to Germany and Italy were never seriously considered for federal relocation, forced or not. America feared sabotage by the loyal subjects of the Emperor of Japan. Even if U.S. citizens of Japanese ancestry behaved as if they were loyal to the United States, many assumed that such loyalty was merely a cover for sinister motives.[5]

The new political culture dictated a rehabilitation of the Chinese character. Two weeks after Pearl Harbor in December 1941, stories appeared in two national newsmagazines, *Time* and *Life*, about the need to distinguish between Chinese and Japanese people, between friend and enemy Asians. These articles reveal that the signs of Japaneseness, the connection between certain visual signifiers and the signifieds of inscrutability and threat, have remained remarkably stable over the years, despite vastly different historical contexts. Both articles conflate nationality and race, and they rely on physical anthropology's central premise that different national/racial groups can be distinguished by examining the body for unique physical signifiers. The articles state that precise knowledge of these signifiers equips one to distinguish between individual foes and allies.

Both articles deploy physiognomy as a key strategy for finding the truth of national/racial identity.[6] *Time*'s "How to Tell Your Friends From the Japs" asserts that "those who know them best often rely on facial expression to tell them apart" and tells us exactly what to look for: "the Chinese expression is likely to be more . . . open" than the Japanese, implying that the latter hide their intentions by hiding their faces. Facial hair figures prominently as well. The *Time* article holds that the "Chinese, not as hairy as the Japanese, seldom grow an impressive mustache."[7] The *Life* article asserts that Chinese exhibit a "scant beard," whereas a "heavy beard" marks one as Japanese.[8]

Finally, the articles emphasize the eyes. If one can examine only the face, *Time* states, then the only scrutable marker for Japanese identity is the "almond-eye[s]."[9] The article notes their importance: "some aristocratic Japanese have thin, aquiline noses, narrow faces and, except for their eyes, look like Caucasians." Furthermore, *Time* claims that "most Chinese avoid horn-rimmed glasses."[10] To reinforce this point, the *Life* article includes a photograph of the Japanese premier and general Hideki Tojo wearing horn-rimmed glasses, whereas the Chinese man in the photo directly above does not.[11]

Taken together, the articles warn that the enemy Japanese will try to hide their racial otherness and identity by hiding their eyes. Indeed, were it not for the eyes, these "aristocratic Japanese," posing as U.S. citizens, would be racially indistinguishable from whites. They would be able to infiltrate the United States without detection—an invisible, inscrutable enemy within.

Growing out of this history, the masks in the Dancing Itos skits signify the inscrutability of Japanese men. The Dancing Itos seem to have no scrutable racial signifiers due to their costumes. They prevent the possibility of examining the person behind them and thus of making a "racial" determination, the eyes hidden by the glare of the television lights. Furthermore, there are no buck teeth, Orientalized accents, Charlie Chan fortune cookie syntax. Yet the history of representations of Japanese men makes it clear that such inscrutability, coupled with a lack of direct racial markers, constitutes

a hidden racial threat. In a manner that recalls the WWII-era articles, the show codes the Dancing Itos as Japanese figures who hide their own unique racial signifier and thus render themselves inscrutable. . . .

Notes ◆

1. I leave much unsaid here. The staging of the Dancing Itos as the Village People and French can-can dancers requires analysis about how drag and camp figure into these representations. I hope this [chapter] will serve as an aid to such a critique, especially one that addresses how issues of gender and sexuality articulate with racial construction.

2. Lawrence Van Gelder, "D'Amato Mocks Ito and Sets Off Furor," *New York Times,* 6 April 1995, B1.

3. John Fiske, *Media Matters: Everyday Culture and Political Change* (Minneapolis: University of Minnesota Press, 1994), 37-38.

4. Bret Harte, *Selected Western Stories and Poems* (New York: Walter J. Black, 1932), 255-257.

5. For a concise historical account of the Japanese American community in Seattle, Washington, and the Pacific Northwest throughout the WWII years, see David Takami, *Executive Order 9066: Fifty Years Before and Fifty Years After* (Seattle: Wing Luke Asian Museum, 1992). Along more literary lines, see John Okada, *No No Boy* (Seattle: University of Washington Press, 1979). For a video account, see Lise Yasui, *A Family Gathering* (Alexandria, VA: PBS Video, 1990).

6. Elaine H. Kim, *Asian American Literature: An Introduction to the Writings and Their Social Context* (Philadelphia: Temple University Press, 1982), 281, n. 1.

7. "How to Tell Your Friends From the Japs," *Time,* 22 December 1941, 33.

8. "How to Tell Japs From the Chinese," *Life,* 22 December 1941, 81.

9. "How to Tell Your Friends," 33.

10. Ibid.

11. "How to Tell Japs," 81.

LING WOO IN HISTORICAL CONTEXT

The New Face of Asian American Stereotypes on Television

◆ Chyng Feng Sun

In contemporary mass media, representations of Asian Americans are still rare. Although they comprise 3.6% of the U.S. population (Census 2000), only 0.8% of TV characters in the period 1991-1992 and 1.3% of TV characters in 1994-1997 were Asian Americans, and the majority of the roles were minor (Gerbner, 1998). According to *Fall Colors 2000-2001*, Asian Pacific American characters comprise 3% of the prime-time characters; however, if one focuses on primary recurring characters, the percentage drops to 2%. (Children Now, 2001, p. 15). Although the presentation of Asian American characters has increased in recent years, the underrepresentation and stereotyping of Asian Americans persists. One Asian American high school student stated, "[When you watch TV] you want to think I could do that. I could be there. That could be me in five or six years. But you don't see anything of yourself" (Children Now, 2001, p. 21)

It is against this historical backdrop of invisibility that Lucy Liu seized public attention and became the most visible Asian American female star

NOTE: The author wants to acknowledge Nancy Inouye's crucial collaboration in research and Karen Cardozo's and Nancy Rothschild's editorial assistance.

on TV with her role as Chinese American lawyer Ling Woo on the hit show *Ally McBeal*. Her presence also spreads out onto the big screen, and her latest role as one of the lead characters in *Charlie's Angels* was a step up to her stardom. If we examine Lucy Liu's representations in movies such as *Payback* and *Charlie's Angels*, we can trace the origins of her characterization of Ling Woo. Ling Woo is strong, outspoken, secure in her opinions, and open about her sexuality. Unlike the more common fresh-off-the-boat refugee Asian American character who speaks little or no English, Ling is an articulate, high-powered, and acculturated attorney. Very importantly, she breaks the "China doll" stereotype of Asian American women as submissive, frail, and quiet. Being an Asian beauty, Ling Woo also counters the blond-haired, blue-eyed white beauty standard. (Not only do men lust over her, but even Ally McBeal says that Ling has a "perfect, perfect" face.) As the most visible Asian American role on TV, Ling Woo's character raises the question: Is she breaking the stereotypes or actually reinforcing them? To answer this question, Elaine Kim has emphasized, "You have to place Ling in the context of at least a 100-year history of sexualization of Asian women (Lee, 1999, para. 10).

◆ **Asian American "Controlled Images" in the Media**

Ideological constructs very often reflect material conditions, and therefore it is important to understand the historical circumstances that led to the development of stereotypical perceptions. From the 1840s to the 1930s, a million men immigrated from China, Japan, Korea, the Philippines, and India to the United States and Hawaii to work as cheap laborers; U.S. immigration law treated those workers as temporary, disposable, and exploitable labor and prohibited the entry of their families and Asian American women, fearing the permanent presence and growth of Asian Americans (Espiritu, 2000). During the late 19th century, the economic recession stirred up the Nativist movement against Asian immigrants. Congress passed the Chinese Exclusion Act in 1882, and eventually in 1924 barred all Asians from immigrating to the United States (Mansfield-Richardson, 1996).

This immigration history helps explain why Asian American males are seen to this day as sexually deviant, paradoxically either asexual or as a rape threat to white women. In the pre-World War II era, Asian American males were forced to establish "bachelor societies" because of the unavailability of the women of their race. Anti-miscegenation laws prohibiting them from marrying white women. Chinese were posted as rape threats to the white woman and considered to have an "undisciplined and dangerous libido"; for example, in 1912, Saskatchewan law prohibited white women from being employed by Chinese-owned business (Fung, 1996, p. 82). At the same time, they were excluded from working at higher paying jobs in the growing metallurgical, chemical, and electrical industries, and were confined instead to low-paid, dead-end jobs as laborers, or doing "women's work" as laundrymen, cooks, and domestic servants (Ling, 1990, p. 145).

Because media are important "ideological state apparatuses" that reinforce hegemony (Althussur, 1971), the dissemination and perpetuation of the desexualized Asian American male stereotype obscure the history that prevented many Asian Americans from establishing conjugal families in pre-World War II United States (Espiritu, 2000, p. 91). Alfred Wang observed that between 1868 and 1952, "No other racial groups have been subjected to worse legalized . . . sexual deprivation than the Chinese male immigrants (Wang, 1988, p. 18, quoted in Espiritu, 2000, p. 19). In presenting Asian American males as "eunuchs," the media have helped render the social and cultural oppression invisible. These emasculated stereotypes are embodied by Charlie Chan and Fu Manchu, the most far-reaching symbols for almost a half century.

The detective character Charlie Chan, developed by novelist Earl Derr Biggers in 1925 to 1932 and used in movies and television as recently as 1981, is a yellow-faced "house nigger" (Xing, 1998, p. 61) who walks with "the light dainty step of a woman" (Chin, Chan, Inada, & Wong, 1974, p. xvi) and speaks in fortune-cookie English (Cao & Novas, 1996). He represents "the helpless heathens to be saved by Anglo heroes or the loyal and lovable allies, sidekicks, and servants" (Kim, 1982, p. 4) and is "in essence an effeminate, wimpy, nerdy, inscrutable Asian male" (Cao & Novas, 1996, p. 60).

In contrast to Charlie's passivity, Dr. Fu Manchu is a cruel, cunning, diabolical representative of the "yellow peril" (Xing, 1998, p. 57) who threatens to destroy Western civilization. Although Fu Manchu is powerful, he still lacks "masculine heterosexual prowess" and is an emasculated character

> wearing a long dress, batting his eyelashes, surrounded by muscular black servants in loin cloths, and with his habit of caressingly touching white men on the leg, wrist, and face with his long fingernails is not so much a threat as he is a frivolous offense to white manhood. (Chin & Chan, 1972, p. 60, quoted in Espiritu, 2000, p. 91)

The emasculation of Asian American males continues today in the form of "nerdy Asian American adolescent math geniuses and brainy Asian American scientists who speak fortune-cookie English" (Cao & Novas, 1996, p. xvi.) Kung Fu masters, mostly played by Chinese actors but not Chinese Americans such as Jet Lee and Jackie Chan, can kick butt, but almost never play romantic and loving roles.

The hypersexualization of Asian American women stands in contrast to this portrayal of Asian American men as asexual, but this stereotype also has its root in immigration practice. When Asian American men were not allowed to establish conjugal families, they sought sexual outlets in prostitution. It was estimated that in 1870, 61% of the 3,536 Chinese women in California were prostitutes. In 1875, the Page Law prohibited the importation of Chinese prostitutes, but all Chinese women nevertheless continued to be suspected of being prostitutes, and regardless of their social status, were subject to harassment (Cao & Novas, 1996, p. 29; Chan, 1991, p. 132; Espiritu, 2000, p. 18).

The hypersexualization of Asian women in popular culture was also reinforced by U.S. military involvement in Asian in the 20th century when troops fought battles or were stationed in Korea, the Philippines, Taiwan, Japan, and the counties of Southeast Asia. These soldiers "often developed strong perceptions of Asian women as prostitutes, bargirls and geishas"; these images are also prevalent in Asian war movies of this period (Villapando, 1989, p. 324). Thus, Asian American male asexuality and Asian American female hypersexuality serve to "confirm the white man's virility and superiority" (Espiritu, 2000, p. 13).

Although America's popular culture is generally male centered and male dominant, Asian American women are currently more visible than Asian American men, as Feng (1993) stresses:

> Novelist Amy Tan is more widely read than novelist Shawn Wong; comedian/ actor Margaret Cho got a shot at network television series, while Russell Wong had to settle for starring in the syndicated *Vanishing Son* and Asian American women anchor local news broadcasts across the country, while Asian American men occupy less visible positions as field reporters. (p. 27)

Though more visible, Asian American female actors still play very narrow roles. Tajima (1989) summarizes the Asian American female archetypes:

> There are two basic types: the Lotus Blossom Baby (a.k.a. China Doll, Geisha Girl, shy Polynesian beauty) and the Dragon Lady (Fu Manchu's various female relations, prostitutes, devious madams). . . . Asian women in film are, for the most part, passive figures who exist to serve men—as love interests for white men (Lotus Blossoms) or as partners in crime of men of their own kind (Dragon Ladies). (p. 309)

Lotus Blossom is "a sexual-romantic object"; characters of her vein are the "utterly feminine, delicate and welcome respites from their often loud, independent American counterparts"(p. 309). Dragon Lady is her opposite—cunning, manipulative and evil; Anna May Wong immortalized that role in *Thief of Baghdad* (1924) where her character uses treachery to help an evil Mongol prince attempt to win the Princess of Baghdad. Both Lotus Blossom and Dragon Lady are hypersexualized, but the former is passive and subservient while the latter is aggressive and "exudes exotic danger" (Chihara, 2000, p. 26).

Tajima (1989) also points out the two very different kinds of relationships that Asian American women characters in popular culture have with white men and with men of their own race. She further suggests that "noticeably lacking is the portrayal of love relationships between Asian women and Asian men, particularly as lead characters" (p. 312) On-screen romance between Asian American men and white women is even more scarce because it ruptures white male hegemony (Hamamoto, 1994, p. 39). When sexuality is involved, an Asian American male is more likely to be portrayed as a "yellow peril" who presents a rape threat to white women, as is well documented by Marchetti (1993). She states that "rape narratives pose the danger

that the 'pure' but hopelessly fragile and childlike white woman will be 'ruined' by contact with the dark villain" (p. 8) and mainly uses examples from movies in the early part of the 20th century to demonstrate her points, movies such as Cecil B. DeMille's *The Cheat* (1915), D. W. Griffith's *Broken Blossoms* (1919), and *The Bitter Tea of General Yen* (1933). In contemporary American popular culture, Xing (1998) observed that the yellow peril narrative may be less blatant but did not stop haunting the silver screen. He states that TV programs such as *Girls of the White Orchid* (1985) (a made-for-television program about white slavery in Tokyo), or movies such as the *Karate Kid* series (1980s) all have the subplots of "threat of rape" (p. 58).

On the other hand, the pairing of a white male and Oriental female is naturalized and has its colonialist root, manifested in the "rescue" narrative. Ella Shohat (1997) points out:

> Not only has the Western imaginary metaphorically rendered the colonized land as a female to be saved from her environmental disorder, it has also projected rather more literal narratives of rescue, especially of Western and non-Western women—from African, Asian, Arab, or Native American men. (p. 39)

Buescher and Ono (1996), in their critique of Disney's *Pocahontas*, state that "in the name of saving women, colonialism presented itself as a necessary and benevolent force" (p. 132). It is important to note that the rescue is not only physical but also psychological. *The World of Suzie Wong* (1960), *The Year of Dragon* (1985), *Good Morning, Vietnam* (1987), *Karate Kid II* (1986), and *The Red Corner* (1998) are just some obvious examples.

The West's dominance is secured through narratives of romance and sexuality that justify white men's possession of the bodies of the women of color (Marchetti, 1993, p. 6). The romantic relationship between a white male and an Asian female is always unequal and demands her total devotion and submission, body and soul. *Madame Butterfly*, the ultimate symbol of Oriental femininity, was first written as a short story by John Luther Long in 1898. It was adapted by Giacomo Puccini as an opera, premiered in 1904 in Milan, and in a very short time became popular and was widely performed (Xing 1998, p. 59). It is a story about Pinkerton, a U.S. naval officer stationed in Nagasaki, who had a love affair with a local prostitute Cho-Cho-San. After Pinkerton goes back to United States, devoted Cho-Cho-San gives birth to his son and awaits his return. Betraying Cho-Cho-San's love, Pinkerton gets married and several years later, he comes back to Japan with his American wife to claim his son, indifferent to Cho-Cho-San's suffering. Heartbroken, she commits suicide. Cho-Cho-San is reincarnated again and again in the public imagination as a Japanese Takarazuka performer in *Sayonara* (1957), and a Vietnamese prostitute in Miss Saigon (1991). Wilkinson (1990) states:

> In recent centuries the rich tradition of Oriental exoticism took a new form as colonial conquest and rule provided the opportunity in the form of readily available girls, and encouraged Europeans and Americans to think of the West as active and masculine and the East as passive and feminine. (p. 13)

Madame Butterfly symbolizes and justifies the Orient's submission to the West's patriarchal domination in that the creators naturalized her inferiority, selfless dedication, and ultimate self-sacrifice.

◆ Ally McBeal

Launched in the fall of 1998, within months, *Ally McBeal* won the Golden Globe award for best comedy, and Calista Flockhart, who plays the title character,

won the best actress award (Leafe, 1998). Both critically and commercially acclaimed, this show even placed Flockhart's face on a *Time* magazine cover as the poster child for postfeminism with the title: "Is Feminism Dead?" (Bellafante, 2000). The show is centered around Ally McBeal, a young female lawyer in a law firm where partners are lovers with their associates and colleagues discuss sex more than work.

In its first season, this show drew 12 million viewers, half of them men and half women, and in 1998, the audience reached 14.8 million (Cooper, 1999). This show is often described by critics as either loved or hated by its viewers. Bellafante (1998) states that Ally McBeal represents an "It's all about me" type of feminism. "If feminism of the '60s and '70s was steeped in research and obsessed with social change, feminism today is wed to the culture of celebrity and self-obsession" (para. 7). Shalit (1998) calls Ally McBeal a "do-me feminist" who is

> plucky, confident, upwardly mobile, and extremely horny. She is alert to the wounds of race and class and gender, but she knows that feminism is safe for women who love men and bubble baths and kittenish outfits; that the right ideology and the best sex are not mutually exclusive. She knows that she is as smart and as ambitious as a guy, but she's proud to be a girl and girlish. (para. 6)

Shalit (1998) condemned the show as "a slap in the face of the real-life working girl, a weekly insult to the woman who wants sexual freedom and gender equality, who can date and litigate in the same week without collapsing in a Vagisil heap" (p. 27). But Chambers (1998) thinks the show

> has clearly struck a nerve with twenty-something women who feel both excited and confused by the choices bestowed upon them by the feminist movement. They understand Ally's big question: "If I have it all, can I be happy?"... It

captures the sense of anxious expectation that people feel in their 20s, when most of life's important decisions still lie ahead. (para. 3)

And Chambers's interviewees seemed to confirm her observations with comments such as "Emotionally, I've been through a lot of similar feelings to Ally," and "This isn't exactly the way [putting long hours at the office] I saw my life playing out. If all this is being put off, then I want a great marriage. I want him to knock my socks off. I want him to blow me away." Cooper (1999) argues that the show constantly pokes fun of male chauvinism and asserts female sexuality and freedom. (p. 3). Cooper draws from Laura Mulvey's concept of the "male gaze" in film studies, which proposes that classic Hollywood films force the viewers to look at women characters from a masculine viewer's perspective, regardless of the real gender of the viewer, but applies Arbuthnot and Seneca's reading of *Gentlemen Prefer Blondes* to *Ally McBeal*, stating that the characters refuse to yield to the male gaze but become active; they gaze back and expose the gazer (p. 7). Lewis (1998), a dedicated male fan, fiercely defends the show and can't understand why feminist critics were unable to differentiate comedies from reality and believes "people who are aghast . . . should have their medication checked" (para. 4). Overall, the critics have been concerned about the gender issues in the show, but have largely overlooked its racial dimensions. Lucy Liu's character Ling Woo stands out among the mostly blond beauties, not only for her looks but also for the way she evokes a longstanding symbolic history of Orientalism in a new way.

◆ Ling Woo

Ling Woo is tough, rude, candid, aggressive, sharp-tongued, and manipulative. She certainly breaks the "China doll" stereotype,

and she is neither submissive nor selfless. However, she is suspiciously like a "dragon lady" when she growls like an animal, breathing fire at Ally, walking into the office with the music of Wicked Witch of the West in *The Wizard of Oz*. But what really makes Ling Woo stand out is how the producer David Kelley has built an ultra sexualized aura around her. In fact, Kelley created the character especially for Lucy Liu after she originally auditioned unsuccessfully for the role of Nell (Mendoza, 1999). When Ling was first introduced to the show, she was suing a Howard Stern-like disc jockey, Wick, because his programs contributed to sexual harassment in her workplace. He said that the reason why Ling brought suit was that she had a "slutty little Asian thing going." And Ling said, in a pretty twisted logic, that part of her wanted to sleep with him because if she did, she would kill him.

Ling also sexualizes and objectifies herself. In another show, Ling sued a nurse for pretending to have breast implants, a trick that led to Ling's sister's plastic surgery. Ling recalled that the nurse "unveils. She's full. Soft. Without a hint of a blemish. I almost signed up and my breasts are beyond reproach." Ling also has owned a mud-wrestling club as well as an escort service marketed to underage boys.

Although almost all the women in the show are sex-hungry, Ling still stands out for her kinky sexual preferences and techniques. Her talk on sex is explicit and graphic ("What I really want out of a relationship at the end of the day . . . is a penis." Or she has a polyp in her throat because her boyfriend "didn't want her to scream.") She used to tape hundred-dollar bills to her privates to "smell like money." She asks her boyfriend, Richard Fish (played by Greg Germann, a white man), not to call her by her name but to call her "fruit" or anything related to food. She performs "hair jobs" (brushing her long hair on his bare chest to arouse him), sucks his finger, and becomes a sex kitten when he caresses her knee-pit. At the beginning of their relationship, she restrains herself from having sex with Richard and her reason is all the more tantalizing: once men have had sex with her, they cannot have enough. Later, when their relationship has a problem, the first thing she says is that she is faking her orgasm.

In an episode aired on November 1, 1999, during the sweeps period when ratings are used to set local station's advertising rates, Ling kisses Ally. Although it seems to be producer David Kelley's ratings-boosting technique to use tantalizing lesbian kissing scenes (all the while affirming those kissers' heterosexuality), Ling's role is particularly seductive when compared to the other heterosexual situations. Ally once kissed her office assistant Elaine and another time her co-worker Georgia, but both times are out of unpleasant necessity: getting rid of a man she is not interested in dating. But for her third lesbian-ish kiss, she is definitely seduced by Ling. Scott Seomin from the Gay & Lesbian Alliance Against Defamation explained that the reason why Ling was chosen to be the seducer was because she is "the exotic, erotic experimenter of the group" (Lee, 1999, para. 3).

Consistent with a history of representation that scarcely ever shows Asian men as sexually desirable, Ling has romantic involvements with both white men (primarily with the law firm partner Richard Fish) and a black man (a lawyer Jackson Duper, played by Taye Diggs), but no "yellow" man. One episode that had visible Asian American men in the show included a waiter in a Chinese restaurant (played by Alex Shen) who barely spoke English, misunderstood the order, and cooked Ling's colleague's pet frog. Although frog leg is also a delicacy in French cuisine, Kelley may have had his conscious or unconscious reasons to set the storyline in a Chinese restaurant because it resonates with the common myth that Chinese "eat everything" including their pet dogs and cats. Thus, Hollywood's history of emasculating Asian American men and hypersexualizing Asian American women is alive and well in *Ally McBeal*.

Ling's character is controversial in Asian American communities. She is popular among Asian American female college students who cheer how that character breaks the stereotypes of submissive and quiet Asian American females. Their opinions can be summed up by the author who wrote "Lucy Liu ... My Girl From *Ally McBeal*" in a college publication for Asian American students:

> Strong Asian female role models are few and far between in the media today. Typically, Asian women are seen as "fresh off the boat," non-English speaking, small, naïve, sex objects, or in denial about their culture. ... Ling is not the soft spoken, passive, quiet Asian woman that society has stereotyped us as. She is tough, aggressive, and worldly ... she is ... a beautiful, sexy woman with a mind that is both cunning and slick ... she is not the typical Asian "geisha" girl. Let her be a model for us to be strong, smart, sexy, and aggressive. (Tolenino, 1999, p. 16)

At the same time, Darrell Hamamoto, whose *Monitored Peril* is so far the most comprehensive study of Asian American characters on TV, calls Ling "a neo-Orientalist masturbatory fantasy figure" who is "concocted by a white man whose job it is to satisfy the blocked needs of other white men who seek temporary escape from their banal and deadening lives by indulging themselves in a bit of visual cunnilingus while relaxing on the sofa" (Lee, 1999, para. 7). Helen Liu, a media consultant about Asian American issues, states that people are drawn to Ling not because she was central or powerful but because of her stereotypical qualities (Chihara, 2000, p. 26). Although Ling is problematic, there is a common sentiment that "it is better than nothing": as Chun (2000) said in *Asian Week*, "It is pretty cool that there's an all-American Asian Angel—that would never have happened in the 70s" (p. 31).

These different and opposed readings of Ling's character demonstrate the polysemic nature of the media text (Fiske, 1986) as well as how differing levels of knowledge about the historic context of Asian American representations affect the reading. It is also true that the message of the character "depends largely on what the viewer brings to the sofa" (Zahra, 1999, p. 20) and that audiences do make resistive or oppositional readings even if they are dedicated fans (Jenkins, 1995). Research that can bridge an examination of Asian American representations with an analysis of how those representations actually affect both Asian Americans and other racial groups is urgently needed. Ethnographic interviews and small groups would be particularly helpful in investigating the tension between media hegemony and the individual viewer's autonomy. We should also examine how the media's political economy affects Asian American's media representations and agitate for regulatory and systematic change.

◆ **References**

Althusser, L. (1971). Ideology and ideological state apparatuses. In *Lenin and philosophy and other essays*. London: New Left Books.

Bellafante, G. (1998, June 29). Feminism: It's all about me! [Electronic version] *Time*, 151 (25), p. 54 (7).

Buescher, D. T., & Ono, K. A. (1996). Civilized colonialism: Pocahontas as neocolonial rhetoric. *Women's Studies in Communication*, 19(2), 229-249.

Cao, L., & Novas, H. (1996). *Everything you need to know about Asian-American history*. New York: Plume.

Chambers, V. (1998, March 2). How would Ally do it? *Newsweek*.

Chan, S. (1991). *Asian Americans: An interpretive history*. New York: Twayne.

Chihara, M. (2000, February 25). Casting a cold eye on the rise of Asian starlets. *The Boston Phoenix*, p. 26 (3).

Children Now. (2001). *Fall colors 2000-2001: Prime time diversity report*. Oakland, CA.

Chin, F., Chan, J., Inada, L., & Wong S. (1974). *Aiiieeeee!: An anthology of Asian American writers*. New York: Mentor.

Cooper, B. (1999). *Ally McBeal vs. Hollywood's male gaze—Round One*. National Convention of the Association of Educators in Journalism and Mass Communication, New Orleans, LA.

Chun, K. (2000, November 9). Charlie's Angels fly high: Lucy Liu gets her big-screen wings with action-hero chops. *Asian Week*, 22(11), 31.

Espiritu, Y. L. (2000). *Asian American women and men*. New York: AltaMira.

Feng, P. (1993). Redefining Asian American masculinity: Steven Okazaki's American sons. *Cineaste*, 22(3), 27 (3).

Fiske, J. (1986). Television: Polysemy and popularity. *Critical Studies in Mass Communication*, 3, 391-408.

Fung, R. (1996). Looking for my penis: The eroticized Asian in gay video porn. In R. Leong (Ed.), *Asian American sexualities: Dimensions of the gay and lesbian experience*. New York: Routledge.

Gerbner, G. (1998). *Casting and fate in '98. Fairness and diversity in television: An update and trends since the 1993 SAG report* (A Cultural Indicators Project report to the Screen Actors Guild). Philadelphia: Temple University.

Jenkins, H. (1995). Out of the closet and into the universe. In J. Tulloch & H. Jenkins, *Science fiction audiences* (pp. 239-265). London and New York: Routledge.

Kim, E. H. (1982). *Asian American literature: An introduction to the writings and their social context*. Philadelphia: Temple University Press.

Leafe, A. S. (1998, August). *Blurring the lines: Postfeminism, sanity and Ally McBeal*. Paper presented at the annual meeting of the Association for Education in Journalism and Mass Communication, Baltimore.

Lee, C. (1999). Ling Woo below: Admirably "free" or "neo-Orientalist masturbatory fantasy figure"? [Electronic version]. *Village Voice*, 44(48), 65 (1).

Lee, R. (1999). *Orientals: Asian Americans in popular culture*. Philadelphia: Temple University Press.

Lewis, G. (1998). Ally's no.1 ally. [Electronic version]. *MediaWeek, 8*(7), 38 (1).

Ling, A. (1990). *Between worlds: Women writers of Chinese ancestry*. New York: Pergamon.

Mansfield-Richardson, V. D. (1996). *Asian-Americans and the mass media: A content analysis of twenty United States newspapers and a survey of Asian-American journalists*. Unpublished doctoral dissertation, Ohio University.

Marchetti, G. (1993). *Romance and the "Yellow Peril": Race, sex, and discursive strategies in Hollywood fiction*. Berkeley: University of California Press.

Mendoza, N. F. (1999). Lucy Alexis Liu. *UltimateTV News*. www.ultimatetv.com/news/w/a/99/03/10liu.html.

Shalit, R. (1998). Canny and lacy [Electronic version]. *The New Republic, 218*(14), 27 (6).

Shohat, E. (1997). Gender and culture of empire: Toward a feminist ethnography of the cinema. In M. Bernstein & G. Studlar (Eds.), *Visions of the East: Orientalism in film*. New Brunswick, NJ: Rutgers University Press.

Tajima, R. E. (1989). Lotus Blossoms don't bleed: Images of Asian women. In Asian Women United of California (Ed.), *Making waves: An anthology of writings by and about Asian American women* (pp. 308-317). Boston: Beacon.

Tolenino, K. (1999). Lucy Liu . . . My girl from *Ally McBeal. RealizAsian: Journal of Umass AASA, 5*(3), 16 (1).

Villapando, B. (1989). The business of selling mail-order brides. In Asian Women United of California (Ed.), *Making waves: An anthology of writings by and about Asian American women* (pp. 318-326). Boston: Beacon.

Wang, A. (1988). Maxine Hog Kingston's reclaiming of America: The birthright of the Chinese American male. *South Dakota Review*, 26, 18-29.

Wilkinson, E. (1990). *Japan versus the West: Image and reality*. London: Penguin.

Xing, J. (1998). *Asian America though the lens: History, representations an identity*. Walnut Creek, CA: AltaMira.

Zahra, T. (1999, January-February). The feminism gap. *The American Prospect*, p. 20.

JEWISH WOMEN ON TELEVISION
Too Jewish or Not Enough?

♦ Joyce Antler

... In the almost fifty-year history of television, images of Jewish women, especially in leading roles, have been all too rare. When they are present, they are usually overblown caricatures and pejorative stereotypes that misrepresent the lifestyles and attitudes of real women.

With the departure of *The Goldbergs* from television in 1955 after a six-year run, Jewish women virtually disappeared from the small screen for almost twenty years. Then came Rhoda Morgenstern, the wisecracking best friend and sidekick of the character Mary Richards in *The Mary Tyler Moore Show*. Sassy and self-deprecating, Rhoda constantly fought against the constraints of her situation—whether her self-perceived unattractiveness, her envy of Mary's perkiness, or the meddling of her parents, who wanted her married off. Played by the non-Jewish Valerie Harper, *Rhoda* premiered in 1974 as a spin-off from Moore's show. Although it was up against popular Monday night football, *Rhoda* won its time slot. In a mere eight weeks, Rhoda was married off to a non-Jew, played by David Groh (fifty million viewers were said to have watched the wedding). Although the program continued to showcase Rhoda's Jewishness and that of her

NOTE: From *Talking Back: Images of Jewish Women in American Popular Culture*, edited by Joyce Antler. Copyright © 1998 by the Trustees of Brandeis University. Reprinted by permission of the University Press of New England.

♦ 665

very ethnic Jewish sister, Brenda (played by Julie Kavner), Rhoda somehow seemed less appealing as a married woman than as a feisty, angst-ridden single one. Soon the show was canceled.[1]

With the demise of *Rhoda* came another long absence for Jewish women on the TV screen. With the exception of occasional characters—for example, the mother and grandmother on the critically acclaimed but short-lived *Brooklyn Bridge*—there were few women characters who were identifiably Jewish and none in a leading role for almost another two decades. Compare this to the male Jewish characters on television series in recent years, both comedies and drama: Paul Buchman (Paul Reiser) in *Mad About You*, Jerry Seinfeld in *Seinfeld*, Miles Silverberg (Grant Shaud) in *Murphy Brown*, Richard Lewis in *Anything but Love*, Jackie Mason in *Chicken Soup*, Michael Steadman (Ken Olin) in *thirtysomething*, Stuart Markowitz (Michael Tucker) in *L.A. Law*, Joel Fleischman (Rob Morrow) in *Northern Exposure*, Marshall Brightman (Joshua Rifkind) in *Marshall Chronicles*, and Jim Eisenberg (Alan Arkin), in *A Year in the Life*.

Then, in 1993, came *The Nanny*, a show about a thirty-something, Queens-born former salesgirl who finds a position as a nanny to three children of a British theatrical producer. Written and produced by Fran Drescher, who plays the title character, and her husband, Peter Marc Jacobson, the show has become an unexpected hit. Often at the top of the Nielsen charts, it has attracted a national and even international following (many Israelis are fans); Drescher was nominated for an Emmy for her performance, and there are "Nanny" dolls, "Nanny" fashions, and "Nanny" home pages. Drescher's autobiography, *Enter Whining*, which aptly describes her TV character, has become a best-seller as well.[2]

The show's success is predicated on the premise of culture clash; it pits blueblood English against blue-collar Jewish. The upper-class Maxwell Sheffield, the debonair, widowed theatrical producer; his three children; the butler, Niles; and uppity female associate, C. C. Babcock, face off against Fran Fine, the nanny from Queens. Although Fran's Jewishness is not essential to the plot, which requires only that the uneducated, lower-class lass wind up teaching her social betters, aspects of the character's Jewish background are featured in most episodes. From the nasal whine, to Yiddish words, to the nanny's Jewish female desires—like getting married, preferably to a nice Jewish doctor—and certainly, shopping ("My first words," says the nanny, were "Can I take it back if I wore it?"), mannerisms that are identified as Jewish along with Jewish Princess stereotypes fill the air. The contrast—the key to the show's slim plot device—is between the nanny's authenticity, which, however coarse and ostentatious, is a product of her ethnic, supposedly lowerclass origins, and the sterility of the British upper class and their hangers-on.

This is not, however, a Pygmalion story. Mr. Sheffield does not try to improve the nanny, nor is she interested in making herself over. Satisfied with herself as is, the nanny lacks only a man: her crush on her boss and his never fully acknowledged attraction for her drives the show. After Mr. Sheffield, in fact, any husband would do, though a Jewish one is clearly preferred.

Neither is the show an updated *Upstairs, Downstairs*, for there is little that divides the so-called servants—the butler and the nanny—from the Sheffields and C. C., except perhaps the servants' greater capacity for humor. And although Fran's family and her Jewish milieu serve as a foil to the Sheffield's posh world, they are never presented as morally superior.

Jewishness is, then, an attitude, a phrase, even a set of clothes—glitzy, gaudy, and ornate. It is a shtick, a framing device that sets the heroine apart from the others in the cast. But it is an artificial, exaggerated Jewishness, drawn from anomalous images and negative stereotypes—Jewish women's self-centered and encompassing desires for money, men, and food—that are long out of date and mainly fictional in origin.

How an exaggerated Jewishness provides the central image and dramatic device of the show is exemplified in an episode aired in April 1996, in which the nanny is dating the young cantor of her mother's synagogue. When the star of Mr. Sheffield's forthcoming Broadway musical falls ill, he taps the cantor to play the lead. "God has sent us a nice Jewish boy," Mr. Sheffield intones. But Fran's mother, Sylvia (played by Renee Taylor), is deeply agitated that no one in her temple will talk to her because they blame her for the loss of their cantor. Sylvia threatens her daughter that she will get even: "Our God is not a merciful God," she warns. With that, locusts appear and there is lightning and thunder. Overlooking the disturbances, Fran's eye falls on an advertising circular on the hallway table. "Oh my God, I missed the Loehmann's yearly clearance," she wails. "God, why are you doing this to me?"

In the final scene of the episode, Fran, dressed in a hot pink miniskirted suit, and her mother, in a loud yellow one, enter their temple and take seats in the last row. "We've been exiled to Siberia," Fran moans as her mother takes out a bacon-lettuce-and-tomato sandwich. "At temple?" Fran asks incredulously. "Nobody can see us here," Sylvia replies. "I can [even] throw a luau."

Fran's discomfort increases when she sees her friend Debby, proudly sporting an engagement ring, seated a few rows ahead. Envious, she asks what she ever did to God to deserve such neglect. Remembering that she scammed five hundred dollars from an airline, Fran goes up to the rabbi to contribute the airline's check to the temple. Immediately, her luck changes. Debby is overhead in a dispute with her fiancé and returns the ring, while another congregant tells Sylvia that she can be first for the front-row seats she no longer needs for the High Holidays. Thankful, Fran and her mother bow their heads: "Find her a doctor," the mother prays. "Find me a doctor," Fran says simultaneously.

Here, not only Jewishness but Judaism as a religion is portrayed stereotypically and negatively. The Jewish God is vengeful, the synagogue is a place for lavish and competitive display, and prayer itself is merely a means for special pleading regarding dating and marriage. The violation of religious norms apparent in eating a sandwich during a service (the running joke has Mrs. Fine an out-of-control eater at all times) is exaggerated by having the sandwich be bacon, lettuce, and tomato; even Reform Jews, which presumably the Fines are, might well balk at taking pork into the sanctuary.

In using Jewishness as the setting for humor, few episodes have gone as far as this one in their disregard for the ethical and moral seriousness of the Jewish religion. Sometimes, as in "The Kibbutz," first aired in December 1995, a Jewish environment is presented as attractive and appealing. In this show, Fran wants Mr. Sheffield to permit his sixteen-year-old daughter, Maggie, to go to a kibbutz in Israel for her school break, but Mr. Sheffield does not want to send her alone. In a flashback, Fran recalls losing her virginity to a handsome sabra on the same kibbutz when she was younger. The show ends with Maggie, accompanied by her father and the nanny, picking fruit on the kibbutz, where she too meets a handsome stranger. Although exotic and foreign, the kibbutz is cleverly used as a plot device, and viewers are at least introduced, although rather haphazardly, to the notion of Jewish collective farming.

Episodes with Jewish settings are exceptions, however. For the most part, the nanny's Jewishness lies in her inflection, her whine, her Yiddishisms, her mania for shopping and for men, and her Jewish family. Like Fran, they are authentics, whether her gaudily overdressed, canasta-playing mother or her chain-smoking Grandma Yetta. But, like Fran, these relatives are without taste and refinement, even without manners, as in "A Fine Family Feud," shown in October 1995, when Fran's Aunt Freta (played by Lainie Kazan) and her sister, Fran's mother, carry on a long-standing feud by throwing cream pies down each other's bare bosoms at a Sweet Sixteen party in a nightclub. It is a vulgar display.

Yet *The Nanny* has called forth admiration and approval, as well as disgust: One critic cites Drescher as the "only reigning Jewish actress on television with the chutzpah to celebrate her ethnic 'otherness.'"[3] What many find likeable in the show are the nanny's cleverness, honesty, sense of pride, and warmth. Not infrequently resorting to manipulation (like her model, Lucille Ball in *I Love Lucy*), Fran Drescher as the nanny always outsmarts her dramatic antagonists, whoever they may be, because of her innate shrewdness, a genuine concern for others, and the folk wisdom apparently imparted from her heritage. This is perhaps the most accurate aspect of her Jewish characterization. Historically, relatively few Jewish women, whether adolescents or thirty-year-olds, consciously chose to become nannies or other live-in domestics; those who moved up from the lower to middle classes more likely worked in garment factories, retail stores, and classrooms. While the nanny's unabashed materialism may not have been foreign to young Jewish women throughout the twentieth century, it was often combined with concerns about the conditions of daily life and a collective consciousness unusual among both ethnic and native-born workers for its depth and inclusiveness.

The incongruity of the Jewish nanny provides a large part of the show's appeal. Much as Gertrude Berg as immigrant matriarch in a 1950s suburb had become anachronistic, so the premise of *The Nanny* does not fit its time—if indeed the characters fit any era. Viewers' recognition not only of the cultural dissonance between the nanny and the Sheffields but the nanny's employment in such an occupation to begin with enhances the show's humor.

Other aspects of the show are decidedly less funny. The nanny's grasping materialism, her limited interests and anti-intellectualism, her family's and her own vulgar dress and manners—all of these denigrate women

and Jews. Despite the nanny's warmth, wit, and honesty, including the breezy sexuality she openly flaunts, she remains the kind of coarse, greedy, and selfish Jew that any anti-Semite might envision. Like Woody Allen's Hasidic rabbi that he conjures in the imagination of the character he plays in *Annie Hall*, the exaggerated qualities of Drescher's Nanny Fine make her a Jewish nightmare, not a dream about which Jews or women may be proud.

Television also has embraced the image of the exaggerated, stereotypical Jewish mother. In a recent article, *New York Times* television critic John J. O'Connor noted that in contrast to warm and nurturing Black mothers and other ethnic types, television seemed "curiously partial to neurotically overprotective, brash and often garish mothers of the unmistakably Jewish persuasion." "Sure, caricature is endemic to prime time," he acknowledges. "But why do Jewish mothers seem to have a monopoly on its more extreme forms? . . . Too many Jewish mothers, it seems to this puzzled goy, become props for humor that often teeters on outright ridicule or even occasional cruelty."[4]

As examples, O'Connor cites Paul Reiser's "take-charge" mother in *Mad About You* and the "growling" mother of the character George Costanza (played by Jason Alexander) in *Seinfeld*. (O'Connor assumes the Costanzas are Jewish, presumably because of their patterns of speech and mannerisms, although their name suggests Italian origins. In fact, the ethnicity of the family is never clarified.) He observes that the obnoxious, "loud-and-brassy" Jewish mother is as likely to appear on Tracey Ullman comedy hours and other special programming as on network TV. . . .

Television does not know what to make of Jewish women. In the absence of wellworn stereotypes, depictions of Jewish women fade to gray. Melissa, Michael Steadman's cousin in the now defunct *thirtysomething*, as played by Melanie Mayron retained a modicum of Jewishness, although at the cost of being shown as too neurotic and unstable to have viable relationships. Another exception was the half-Jewish character Andrea Zuckerman in *Beverly Hills 90210*; Jewish-looking, although played by a non-Jewish actress, the somewhat nerdy Andrea, while often peripheral to the group, is respected for her intelligence. In one episode, when she pledges for a sorority that doesn't admit Jews and is warned by the president to take off her Jewish star and hide her ethnicity, Andrea withdraws in disgust, moving the president, who has denied her own Jewishness, to own up to who she really is. Eventually, Andrea marries a Chicano and has a baby; she accompanies him when he goes East to Yale, and what will become of Andrea's ambitions is unclear.

. . . *Friends* does feature two unambiguously Jewish female characters. The first is Chandler's sometime girlfriend Janice, nasal, crass, and overdressed. Janice may look and sound like Fran Fine, but she lacks the nanny's integrity; after stealing Chandler's heart, she betrays him by returning to her former husband, the mattress salesman. And if Janice is a nanny manqué, Mrs. Geller belongs in the pantheon of overbearing Jewish mothers, whose chief occupation is worrying about why their daughters aren't married. At least Fran Fine and her mother get along (most of the time); Mrs. Geller and [her daughter] Monica are like oil and water.

A more positive image is that of Debbie Buchman, Paul's sister on *Mad About You*. Yet Debbie's proud lesbianism is more openly flaunted than her Jewishness. Like Monica Geller, Debbie is Jewish primarily in relation to the demeanor and manners of the main star rather than her own inherent characteristics. Mrs. Buchman in particular is concerned about her daughter's lesbianism, but her anxieties are somewhat allayed by the fact that Debbie's girlfriend is a doctor! Neither [parent] shows much concern about Paul's decidedly non-Jewish wife, Jamie, played by Helen Hunt.[5]

Not only in *Mad About You* but in such shows as *Northern Exposure, L.A. Law, thirtysomething, Murphy Brown*, and *Seinfeld*, Jewish men date or marry non-Jewish women; only rarely is a specifically Jewish woman portrayed romantically on such shows. Consider Elaine, the former girlfriend of Dr. Joel Fleischman on *Northern Exposure*, who appears in one episode to free Fleischman from the constraints of his New York past (his Jewishness?), enabling him to bond with the down-to-earth, Catholic-school-educated pilot Maggie.

Another aspect to this Jewish woman disappearing act is the use of Jewish actresses for non-Jewish roles: Roseanne as a working-class woman in *Roseanne*; Rhea Pearlman's Italian waitresses, first in *Cheers*, more recently in *Pearl*; Bea Arthur's Irish Maude Finlay in the 1970s hit series, *Maude*. Such casting raises fascinating questions involving the seeming universalism of Jewish looks if not Jewish traits (is it true, as Mel Brooks once suggested, that everyone, including Native Americans, is really Jewish?) but also speaks to the lack of specifically Jewish roles for Jewish actresses. If she had waited for a role as a Jewish woman, Bea Arthur once commented, she would have remained unemployed.

As this survey suggests, Jewish women characters on television rarely demonstrate the full range of human characteristics—intelligence, generosity, ambition, striving, achievement, conflict—that truly represent contemporary Jewish women's lives; these qualities are more likely to be present in dramas and comedies with non-Jewish heroines. And relatively few Jewish women appear on television as they do in real life—as writers, journalists, teachers, doctors, lawyers, mayors, senators, and judges. Yet the writers, producers, and directors of these shows are often Jewish; indeed, they sometimes are Jewish women. Marketplace considerations play a vital role in the fact that despite their own high profiles in the media, they have collaborated to erase or exaggerate the more varied activities of Jewish women in the real world.

Yet it is noteworthy that in the world of contemporary television, creative and marketing teams apparently find Jewish men's personas more appealing to popular audiences than those of Jewish women. While there were relatively few Jewish characters in television's first forty years—most scripts were "de-Jewishized" or "midwestized," as one executive put it—Jewish male characters have been a fixture of prime time in recent years.[6] The presence of such Jewishly identified characters differs from earlier television shows, in which the star's background was deliberately left hazy—for example, George Burns's and Jack Benny's comedy hours; *Taxi*, with Judd Hirsch; *Barney Miller*, with Hal Linden; and *Quincy, M.E.*, with Jack Klugman. (Recall, too, that *The Dick Van Dyke Show*, written and directed by Carl Reiner, starred Dick Van Dyke because Reiner was "too Jewish" to play himself on the air. Instead, he played the comedian Alan Brady—an Irishman!)

The emergence of the newer crop of unmistakably Jewish (male) characters may be a product of the success of many recent Black shows and perhaps, too, of the growing self-confidence of Jews in top positions in the networks and production companies. While television still remains a vehicle for the "great drama of American assimilation," as cultural critic Todd Gitlin puts it, these executives may be more willing to imagine that characters like themselves are of interest to mass audiences and less defensive about real or perceived charges that Jews are too powerful in the media, which once led them to shy away from presenting Jewish plots or characters.[7]

The same considerations apparently do not hold for Jewish female characters, who appear primarily as stereotypes—like Nanny Fine or Mike Myers's *Saturday Night Live* character, Linda Richman, certain conduits to easy laughs—or who are so universalized that their ethnicity, like that of the new sugar-coated mass-marketed bagel, is unrecognizable. These characters and the shows they are in often *are* funny. Yet in their negative aspects they approximate the kind of anti-Semitic and misogynist characteristics of much Jewish Princess/Jewish mother humor. Audiences who accept the characterizations as truthful, although exaggerated, will have a warped sense of the potentialities of Jewish women; such false perspectives are most dangerous for young Jewish women who may also confuse the stereotypes with reality, engendering negative self-images and even self-hatred.[8] The limited range of the Jewish female characters on television reflects a failure of imagination. There is no reason that mainstream audiences cannot respond to images of Jewish women as both ethnic and American, distinctive yet representative, intelligent and caring, as easily as they do to other smart and sassy female characters or to Jewish men onscreen. There are models from the media, like Izzy in *Crossing Delancey*, as well as many real-life professionals—teachers, lawyers, doctors, and activists of all kinds—who can point the way.

Ethnicity need not be subsumed by distinctions that are egregiously false and absurd, nor need it be erased in the drive to present characters who are racially, religiously, and ethnically indistinct. In homogenizing or exaggerating the portrayal of Jewish women, television silences the diverse voices of real women and renders their authentic experiences invisible. Moreover, in portraying Jewish men almost invariably in relationships with non-Jewish women, TV shows foster the notions that Jewish women are undesirable and unattractive and that Jews only rarely, if ever, become romantically involved with each other.

The inclusion of viable characters and situations that provide a fair range of the multiple ethnicities of American life without resorting to simplistic exaggeration is the challenge of the future, both for creative artists, writers, and executives and for all of us, the audiences who by their responses can encourage image makers to take greater risks.[9]

◆ *Notes*

1. I am indebted to Marlene Adler Marks for this discussion of *Rhoda*. Also see Risa Whitney Gordon, "On Television, Jewish Women Get the Short End of the Script," *Jewish Exponent*, May 7, 1993; Susan Kaplan, "From 'Seinfeld' to 'Chicago Hope': Jewish Men Are Everywhere, but the Few Jewish Women on Television Perpetuate Negative Stereotypes," *Forward*, November 29, 1996; and Michael Medved, "Is Hollywood Too Jewish?" in *Moment* 21 (August 31, 1996), p. 36.

2. Fran Drescher, *Enter Whining* (New York: HarperCollins, 1996). Also see Drescher, *The Wit and Wisdom of "The Nanny": Fran's Guide to Life, Love, and Shopping* (New York: Avon, 1995). Drescher also did a cartoon Christmas special, "Oy to the World."

3. Drescher claims that she insisted on a Jewish nanny despite CBS executives' preference for an Italian character. Robin Cembalist, "Big Hair, Short Skirts—and High Culture," *Forward*, February 14, 1997.

4. John J. O'Connor, "This Jewish Mom Dominates TV, Too," *New York Times*, October 14, 1993.

5. *Relativity*, which debuted during the 1997 season, also featured an explicitly Jewish female character, Rhonda (Lisa Epstein), the older sister of the male lead (whose girlfriend is Gentile).

6. Todd Gitlin, *Inside Prime Time*, cited in John J. O'Connor, "TV View," *New York Times*, July 15, 1990.

7. Ibid.

8. Among the many wide-ranging accounts on negative images of Jews, see Linda Nochlin and Tamar Garb, eds., *The Jew in the Text: Modernity and the Construction of Identity* (London: Thames and Hudson, 1995) and Sander L. Gilman, *Jewish Self-Hatred: Anti-Semitism and the Hidden Language of the Jews* (Baltimore: Johns Hopkins University Press, 1986).

9. I would like to thank Lauren and Rachel Antler, Phyllis Deutsch, Marlene Adler Marks, Jonathan Sarna, and Mara Fein for their helpful comments on this [chapter].

PART VII

THE INTERNET

One of the most discussed (and hotly debated) questions in media studies in recent years has been about the potential impact of the global computer network called the Internet (and its graphical version, the World Wide Web). How will this new technology transform the communication industries; the material, social, and psychological lives of individuals and communities that use computer-facilitated communications; and cultural representation in general?

Early theorists of *cyberspace* have argued optimistically that the kinds of electronic communication made possible by Internet technology can revolutionize in positive ways many aspects of our social, political, and psychological worlds. It has been claimed, for example, that the Internet "de-emphasizes hierarchical political associations, degrading gender roles and ethnic designations, and rigid categories of class relationships found in traditional, visually based and geographically bound communities" (Ebo, 1998, quoted in Arnold and Plymire, Chapter 70). Moreover, computer-facilitated communication is promoted as empowering to the user and therefore potentially a technology that will help "democratize" our society and the world. Such a view helps sell computers to parents anxious about the impact on children of the older technology of television:

> The computer is often defined against, and pitched as an improvement on the television set: where television viewing is passive, computer use is interactive; where television programmes are entertaining in a stale, commercialized, violent way, computer software and the Internet are educational, virtuous, new. (Seiter, Chapter 67)

The chapters in this last section explore both the enthusiastic "utopian" claims made for Internet (and Web) communication technology and the perspectives of less enthralled critics. Many of the latter view excessive expectations for the Internet as playing into the hands of corporations such as Microsoft, as they reposition themselves to control and commercialize the content of the Internet and to contain its revolutionary potential within familiar parameters.

Robert McChesney's "The *Titanic* Sails On" (Chapter 65) alerts us to the way in which the media giants are likely to contain the threat of a democratic Internet. Although acknowledging that the Net has had an enormous impact on the media landscape, McChesney argues that "the evidence so far strongly suggests that, left to the market, the Internet . . . will not free us from a world where Wall Street and Madison Avenue have control over journalism and culture." Contrary to popular opinion, McChesney claims that the Internet is encouraging greater media concentration because large companies are using the Internet "to stimulate interest in their traditional fare—a relatively inexpensive way to expand sales." Moreover, it is only the large corporations that can afford to absorb losses that are common to many Internet companies.

Similarly, in "Where Do You Want to Go Today?" (Chapter 66), Lisa Nakamura challenges the idea that computer-aided communication can produce a cyberspace in which social relations are magically transformed, as the text of a recent commercial from MCI would have it: "There is no race. There is no gender. There is no age. There are no infirmities. There are only minds. Utopia? No, Internet" ("Anthem," quoted in Nakamura).

Examining several print and television advertisements for high-tech products and services, Nakamura shows that such ads cast the viewer in the role of the tourist in the reassuringly static third world.

Networking ads that promise the viewer control and mastery over technology and communications discursively and visually link this power to a vision of the other which, in contrast to the mobile and networked tourist/user, isn't going anywhere.

Ellen Seiter also expresses skepticism about "claims that the Internet will revolutionize communications (as well as education, work life, and domestic leisure)." In "Television and the Internet" (Chapter 67), Seiter argues that although the Internet can indeed be a tool for political organizing (on the left or the right and anywhere on the political spectrum in between), "It seems increasingly likely . . . that commercialization of the Web will discourage activism in favour of consumerism and the duplication of familiar forms of popular mass media, such as magazines, newspapers, and television programmes." As she points out, reminding ourselves of the history of television as a "domestic object" may help us predict how the Internet may evolve as a purveyor of entertainment genres. Reminding us that television, "for all of its failings—has been cheap, easy to watch at home, enjoyable to talk about with others, and reasonably successful as an educational tool," Seiter urges feminist media researchers in particular to "understand the ways in which such social features of broadcast technologies are missing or modified in the new technologies."

One much discussed potentially utopian impact of cyberspace has been in the realm of gender identity and sexual relationships. Sherry Turkel, an influential early analyst of the social and psychological ramifications of Internet communication, studied the electronic messages exchanged on MUDs (multiuser domains, a kind of specialized electronic "chat room" for fantasy role-playing games). She found that many users experimented with gender-swapping and virtual sexual activity (dubbed

TinySex) when interacting in the bodiless textual world of the Internet. Although such playful escape from one's socially imposed gendered behavior could have a liberating effect for some, Turkel's (1995) analysis reminds us that "the technology changes us as people, changes our relationships and sense of ourselves" and warns against the temptation "to believe that simple fixes can solve complicated problems" (p. 232).

Inspired by a similar interest in the social impact of Internet use, as part of a larger concern with "the role of media technologies in the domestic context of the household," Lynn Schofield Clark studied how teenage dating was influenced by the new medium, in "Dating on the Net: Teens and the Rise of 'Pure' Relationships" (Chapter 68). Clark's is an ethnographic study that combines an analysis of the texts of messages in chat rooms with information derived from interviews with her target audience. Clark looks at the ways teenage girls in particular may find Internet dating (text-based communication in chat rooms) "liberating" to some extent because it frees them from excessive concern with looks. But as Clark emphasizes, "Teen dating relationships in chat rooms mirror the relationships of 'real life' in their adherence to norms of heterosexism and sexism."

We end with two chapters that suggest the important real-world activism and community organizing facilitated by the Internet in its noncommercial infancy—a kind of activism that needs to be maintained as the Internet is increasingly brought under corporate control. Rhona O. Bautista gives us a brief history of a women's organization that developed ways of supporting grassroots organizations in many different Asian countries in the 1990s (Chapter 69). Her description of the pilot Web site project Asian Women's Resource Exchange offers one model for using the Internet to increase the access of nonelite women to information resources. Bautista concludes optimistically,

Despite the many obstacles and unfavourable conditions that restrict their access to electronic media, women have shown themselves to be excellent networkers, extending solidarity across national and global boundaries via electronic mail, print, and real face-to-face encounters. One can only imagine the unleashing of the creative energies of women in the service of communication and progress when the barriers to women's full participation in the new information technologies are dismantled.

Ellen Arnold and Darcy Plymire, in "The Cherokee Indians and the Internet" (Chapter 70), are similarly hopeful. Their study of the Web sites of the Eastern Band Cherokees and the Cherokee Nation of Oklahoma provides support for the more "utopian" view of the potential role of electronic communication in creating new bases for community. They conclude that "tribal websites can be powerful agents for community development and cultural continuity within change." Pointing in particular to the links with an elementary school homepage, where "a visitor can click on a 'culture' option to hear a Native story-teller recite Cherokee legends in English with Cherokee translations," Arnold and Plymire interpret this electronic text as "a symbol of the Eastern Band's commitment to education and technology as tools for self-determination."

Reference ◆

Turkel, S. (1995). *Life on the screen: Identity in the age of the Internet.* New York: Simon & Schuster.

65

THE *TITANIC* SAILS ON

Why the Internet
Won't Sink the Media Giants

◆ Robert McChesney

The January [2000] announcement of the proposed merger of AOL and Time Warner—the largest deal in history—crystallizes one trend, and may trigger another, more ominous one.

It can be seen as yet another of the colossal media deals that has dotted the past decade, such that only a handful of conglomerates now own almost all the film studios, TV networks, music studios, cable TV channels, and much, much, more. But more than that, the deal represents what may be the first great move toward convergence, where the handful of giants who dominate computer software, the Internet, and media begin to formally merge with each other.

This all makes sense, because as everything switches to digital language, the technical distinctions between these categories recede and are ultimately nonexistent. The end result of this process—five, 10, or 15 years down the line—may be an integrated global communication market dominated by no more than a dozen (often closely linked) firms of unfathomable size and economic and political power. By any known standard of a free press in a democratic society, these developments should provoke intense concern, if not outrage.

NOTE: From *Extra!* Reprinted by permission of FAIR.

In the wake of the AOL-Time Warner announcement, their executives and defenders pooh-poohed the idea that, in the Age of the Internet, we have any grounds for concern that our media and communication systems are in too few hands. The Internet, we are told, has blasted open the communication system and increased exponentially the ability of consumers to choose from the widest imaginable array of choices. If everything is in the process of becoming digital, if anyone can produce a website at minimal cost, and if it can be accessed worldwide via the World Wide Web, it is only a matter of time (e.g., expansion of bandwidth, improvement of software) before the media giants find themselves swamped by countless high-quality competitors. Their monopolies will be crushed.

The Electronic Frontier Foundation's John Perry Barlow, in a memorable comment from 1995, dismissed concerns about media mergers and concentration. The big media firms, Barlow noted, are "merely rearranging deck chairs on the Titanic" (*New York Times*, 9/24/95). The "iceberg," he submitted, would be the Internet with its 500 million channels.

Clearly, the Internet is changing the nature of our media landscape radically. As Barry Diller, builder of the Fox TV network and a legendary corporate media seer, put it (*Electronic Media*, 12/15/97), "We're at the very early stages of the most radical transformation of everything we hear, see, know."

But will these changes pave the way for a qualitatively different and better media culture and society? Or will the corporate, commercial system merely don a new set of clothing? The evidence so far strongly suggests that, left to the market, the Internet is going in a very different direction from that suggested by the Internet utopians. The Internet as a technology, in short, will not free us from a world where Wall Street and Madison Avenue have control over our journalism and culture.

Big Media Go Online ◆

The main argument made by defenders of the AOL-Time Warner deal, and by defenders of the media status quo, is that the Internet is going to launch innumerable new commercially viable competitors, such that any concerns about concentrated corporate control are unfounded. If anything, the AOL-Time Warner deal should have hammered the last nail in the coffin of that argument. It is now clear that the Internet will probably not spawn any new commercially viable media entities; the media giants will rule the roost. Indeed, the Internet is encouraging even greater media concentration, not to mention convergence.

This might seem a bizarre assertion, since the big media firms have seemed to approach the Internet in such a bewildered and clumsy manner. Time Warner's Pathfinder website, for example, began in 1994 with visions of conquering the Internet, only to produce a "black hole" for the firm's balance sheet (*Advertising Age*, 6/8/98). Likewise, the New Century Network, a website consisting of 140 newspapers run by nine of the largest newspaper chains, was such a fiasco that it was shut down in 1998.

Far from being visionary, the initial motivation for media firms to dominate the Internet is as much fear as it is the prospects of mega-profits. "For traditional media companies," the *New York Times* correctly noted (1/11/98), "the digital age poses genuine danger." "The entertainment companies are terrified of being blindsided by the Internet," a business consultant said (*The Economist*, 11/21/98), "as the broadcasting networks were blindsided by cable in the 1980s."

In fact, it remains unclear exactly how the Internet will become a commercially viable media content enterprise. It is clear that there is a huge market for internet service providers (ISPs) (e.g., AOL) and for electronic commerce (e.g., Amazon.com), but profits for online ventures that operate more like traditional media outlets are less assured. As Time Warner CEO Gerald Levin put it (*New York Times*, 1/11/98), it is "not clear where you make money on it." But even if the Internet takes a long time to develop as a commercial medium, it is already taking up some of the time that people used to devote to traditional media. An A. C. Nielsen study conducted late in 1998 determined that Internet homes watched 15 percent less television overall than unwired homes.

In the past two years, all major media have made the Internet "mission critical," as Disney CEO Michael Eisner put it, and have launched significant Web activities. The media firms use their websites, at the very least, to stimulate interest in their traditional fare—a relatively inexpensive way to expand sales. Some media firms duplicate their traditional publications or even broadcast their radio and television signals over the net (with commercials included, of course). The newspaper industry has rebounded from the New Century Network debacle and has a number of sites to capture classified advertising dollars as they go online.

But most media giants are going beyond this on the Web. Viacom has extensive websites for its CBS Sports, MTV, and Nickelodeon cable TV channels, the point of which is to produce "online synergies." These synergies can be produced by providing an interactive component and additional editorial dimensions to what is found in the traditional fare, but the main way websites produce synergies is by offering electronic commerce options for products related to the site. Several other commercial websites have incorporated Internet shopping directly into their editorial fare. As one media executive notes (*Advertising Age*, 2/9/98), Web publishers "have to think like merchandisers." Electronic commerce is now seen as a significant revenue stream for media websites.

In conjunction with this upsurge in media giant Internet activity, the possibility of new Internet content providers emerging

to slay the traditional media appears farfetched. In 1998, there was a massive shakeout in the online media industry, as smaller players could not remain afloat. Forrester Research estimated that the cost of an "average-content" website increased threefold to $3.1 million by 1998, and would double again by 2000 (*Financial Times*, 3/12/98). "While the big names are establishing themselves on the Internet," *The Economist* wrote (3/21/98), "the content sites that have grown organically out of the new medium are suffering." Even a firm with the resources of Microsoft flopped in its attempt to become an online content provider, abolishing much of its operation in 1998. "It's a fair comment to say that entertainment on the Internet did not pan out as expected," said a Microsoft executive (*Variety*, 5/4/98).

By 1998, the current pattern was established: more than three-quarters of the 31 most visited news and entertainment websites were affiliated with large media firms, and most of the rest were connected to outfits like AOL and Microsoft (*Broadcasting and Cable*, 6/22/98).

Why the ◆ *Iceberg Didn't Hit*

We can see now that those who forecast that the media giants would smash into the Internet "iceberg" exaggerated the power of technology and failed to grasp the manner in which markets actually work. There are six reasons why the media giants have blown any prospective competitors out of the Internet waters.

1. The giant media firms are willing to take losses on the Internet that would be absurd for any other investor to assume. For a Disney or Time Warner or Viacom to lose $200-$300 million annually on the Internet is a drop in the bucket, if it means their core activities worth tens of billions of dollars are

protected down the road. As one media executive put it (*Advertising Age*, 6/8/98), Internet "losses appear to be the key to the future." The media giants have to try to cover all their online bases until they can see how the Internet develops as a commercial medium. For any other investor, who is not protecting media assets worth $50-$100 billion, assuming such annual losses would be absurd and irrational. The same money could be spent pursuing some other aspect of the Internet (or economy writ large) and generate much larger returns with less risk.

2. The media giants have digital programming from their other ventures that they can plug into the Web at little extra cost. This, in itself, is a huge advantage over firms that have to create original content from scratch.

3. To generate an audience, the media giants can and do promote their websites incessantly on their traditional media holdings, to bring their audiences to their online outlets. By 1998, it was argued that the only way an Internet content provider could generate users was by buying advertising in the media giants' traditional media. Otherwise, an Internet website would get lost among the millions of other Web locations. As the editor-in-chief of MSNBC on the Internet put it (*Electronic Media*, 1/19/98), linking the website to the existing media activity "is the crux of what we are talking about; it will help set us apart in a crowded market." Indeed, much of the TV advertising boom of the past year is attributed to Internet firms spending wildly to draw attention to their Web activities. The media giants can do at nominal expense what any other Internet firm would have to pay hundreds of millions of dollars to accomplish.

4. As the possessors of the hottest "brands," the media firms have the leverage to get premier locations from browser software makers, ISPs, search engines, and portals. Microsoft Internet Explorer 4.0 offers 250 highlighted channels, and the "plum positions" belong to Disney and Time Warner. Similar arrangements are taking place with Netscape and Pointcast. Indeed, the portals are eager to promote "Hollywoodesque programming" in the competition for users.

5. With their deep pockets, the media giants are aggressive investors in start-up Internet media companies. Some estimates have as much as one-half the venture capital for Internet content start-up companies coming from established media firms (*Global Media*, Herman and McChesney). The Tribune Company, for example, owns stakes in 15 Internet companies, including the portals AOL, Excite, and iVillage, which targets women.

Some media giants, like Bertelsmann and Sony, have seemingly bypassed new acquisitions of traditional media to put nearly all their resources into expanding their Internet presence. GE's NBC arguably has taken this strategy the furthest. To cover all the bases, GE has invested over $2 billion in more than 20 Internet companies, in addition to NBC's own Web activities. "It wants to be wherever this thing takes off," an industry analyst said (*Electronic Media*, 8/10/98). In sum, if some new company shows commercial promise, the media giants will be poised to capitalize upon, not be buried by, it.

6. To the extent that advertising develops on the Web, the media giants are positioned to seize most of these revenues. Online advertising amounted to $900 million in 1997, and some expect it to reach $5 billion by 2000 (*Electronic Media*, 3/23/98; 4/6/98). The media giants have long and close relationships with the advertising industry, and can

and do get major advertisers to sponsor their online ventures as a package deal when the advertisers buy spots on the media giants' traditional media.

◆ *More Hamburger*

This corporate media domination of the Internet has distinct implications for the nature of Web media content. "The expansion in channel capacity seems to promise a sumptuous groaning board," TV critic Les Brown wrote (*Television Business International*, 4/98), "but in reality it's just going to be a lot more of the same hamburger."

The most striking feature of corporate Internet fare is that it increases, rather than reduces, the hypercommercialism of our media culture. This may seem ironic, since one might think that on the Internet consumers have so many choices they will avoid excessive commercialism. But the fact is that the media giants are desperate to bring advertisers aboard their sites to generate revenue. Traditional TV-style advertising, where people basically are forced to sit through an ad, won't work. To get advertisers' dollars, websites increasingly have to permit a commercial intermingling with editorial content that has traditionally been frowned upon on the media. The rise of electronic commerce increases the commercialization of media sites that much more.

The most popular areas for Web content are similar to those of the traditional commercial media, and, for the reasons just listed, they are dominated by the usual corporate suspects.

Music. Viacom's MTV is squaring off with GE's NBC, AT&T's TCI, and *Rolling Stone* to, as one of them put it, "own the mind share for music." Each of the companies' websites is "slavishly reporting recording industry news and gossip," all to become the, or one of the, "default destinations for people interested in music on the Web" (*Wall Street Journal*, 4/15/98). The stakes

are high: Forrester Research estimates that online music sales, concert ticket sales, and music-related merchandise sales could reach $2.8 billion by 2002.

Sports. The greatest war for market share is with regard to sports websites, where Disney's ESPN, News Corp.'s Fox, GE and Microsoft's MSNBC, Time Warner's CNNSI, and Viacom/CBS's SportsLine are in pitched battle. Sports is seen as the key to media growth on the Web; advertisers, for one, understand the market and want to reach it. Plus sport websites are beginning to generate the huge audiences that advertisers like.

To compete for the Internet sports market, it is mandatory to have a major television network that can constantly promote the website. One Forrester Research survey found that 50 percent of respondents visited a sport website as a direct result of its being mentioned during a sport broadcast. Indeed, 33 percent said they visited a Web sport site while watching a sports event on TV (*Advertising Age*, 5/11/98).

News. The most visited websites for news and information are those associated with the corporate TV news operations and the largest newspaper chains (*Wall Street Journal*, 11/16/98). At present, the trend for online journalism is to accentuate the worst synergistic and profit-hungry attributes of commercial journalism, with its emphasis on trivia, celebrities, and consumer news. Columnist Norman Solomon (6/11/98) characterized the news offerings on AOL, drawn from all the commercial media giants, as less a "marketplace of ideas" than "a shopping mall of notions."

The increasingly seamless relationship on the Web between advertising and editorial fare is pronounced in its journalism too. "On the Web," the West Coast editor of *Editor & Publisher* wrote, advertising and journalism "often overlap in ways that make it difficult for even journalists and editors to differentiate between the two." (M. L. Stein, www.mediainfo.com, 6/12/98).

◆ *Time Warner: A Case Study*

Taking Back Cyberspace ◆

The Internet activities of Time Warner, before the AOL deal, are a good indication of how the media giants are approaching cyberspace. In addition to its activities as a cable company, Time Warner produces nearly 200 websites, all of which are designed to provide what it terms an "advertiser-friendly environment," and it aggressively promotes to its audiences through its existing media (*Advertising Age*, 1/19/98). Time Warner uses its websites to go after the youth market, to attract sports fans, and to provide entertainment content similar to that of its "old" media.

Time Warner is bringing advertisers aboard with long-term contracts, and giving them equity interest in some projects (*IQ*, 8/18/97). Its most developed relationship with advertisers is the ParentTime website joint venture it has with Procter & Gamble (*Advertising Age*, 8/18/97).

Establishing hegemony over any new media rivals on the Web, of course, does not mean that cyberspace will prove particularly lucrative; one could argue it proves the opposite. Time Warner was exultant that it had sold enough online advertising to cover nearly 50 percent of its online unit's budget for 1998 (*Advertising Age*, 1/19/98). For a small start-up venture, this would spell death.

However it develops, the comment of the president of Time, Inc. (*Financial Times*, 6/9/97) seems fairly accurate: "I believe the electronic revolution is simply one new form of communications that will find its place in the food chain of communications and will not displace or replace anything that already exists, just as television did not replace radio, just as cable did not replace network television, just as the VCR did not replace the movie theatres." The evidence so far suggests the media giants will be able to draw the Internet into their existing empires.

While the Internet is in many ways revolutionizing the way we lead our lives, it is a revolution that does not appear to include changing the identity and nature of those in power. Those who think the technology can produce a viable democratic public sphere by itself where policy has failed to do so are deluding themselves.

This does not mean that there will not be a vibrant, exciting, and important noncommercial citizen's sector in cyberspace, open to all who veer far off the beaten path. For activists of all political stripes, the Web increasingly plays a central role in organizing and educational activities. But from its once lofty perch, this nonprofit and civic sector has been relegated to the distant margins of cyberspace; it is nowhere near the heart of the dominant commercial sector. And we should be careful not to extrapolate from the experience of activists what the Internet experience will look like for the bulk of the population.

In fact, as the corporate media domination of Internet "content" crystallizes, the claims of the Internet utopians are beginning to get downsized. We are probably going to hear less about how the Internet will invigorate media competition and more about how since anyone can start a website, we should all just shut up and be happy consumers. But, in the big scheme of things, having the ability to launch a website at a nominal expense is only slightly more compelling than saying we have no grounds of concern about monopoly newspapers because anyone can write up a newsletter and wave it in their front window or hand it out to their neighbors.

Viable websites for journalism and entertainment need resources and people who earn a living at producing them, precisely what the market has eliminated any chance of developing. Moreover, just having a zillion amateur websites may not be all that impressive. One expert estimates that over 80 percent of all websites fail to show up on any search engines, making them virtually impossible to find, and the situation may only get worse.

The moral of the story is clear: If we want a vibrant noncommercial and non-profit sector on the Internet, in the near term it will require existing institutions like labor and progressive funders to subsidize such activities. In the long run, the key to democratizing the Internet as a medium will be to structurally change our media system to lower the power of Wall Street and Madison Avenue, and to increase the power of Main Street and every other street.

A media system chock full of new nonprofit, noncommercial, and even small commercial entities would go a long way toward improving the Internet as a medium. This is something the American people have every right to do. The federal government created and subsidized the Internet for three decades before it was effectively privatized and opened to commercial domination—with zero public debate or press coverage—in the early 1990s. It is time to take it back.

66

"WHERE DO YOU WANT TO GO TODAY?"

Cybernetic Tourism,
the Internet, and Transnationality

◆ Lisa Nakamura

There is no race. There is no gender. There is no age.
There are no infirmities. There are only minds. Utopia?
No, Internet.

—"Anthem," television commercial for MCI

The television commercial "Anthem" claims that on the Internet, there are no infirmities, no gender, no age, that there are only minds. This pure, democratic, cerebral form of communication is touted as a utopia, a pure no-place where human interaction can occur, as the voice-over says, "uninfluenced by the rest of it." Yet can the "rest of it" be written out as easily as the word *race* is crossed out on the chalkboard by the hand of an Indian girl in this commercial? . . .

The ironies in "Anthem" exist on several levels. For one, the advertisement positions MCI's commodity—"the largest Internet network in the world"—as a solution to social problems. The advertisement claims to produce a radical form of democracy that refers to and extends an "American" model of social equality and equal access. This patriotic anthem, however, is a paradoxical one: the visual images of diversity (old, young, black, white, deaf, etc.) are displayed and celebrated as spectacles of difference that the narrative simultaneously attempts to erase by claiming that MCI's product will reduce the different bodies that we see to "just minds." . . .

The supposedly liberal and progressive tone of the ad camouflages its depiction of race as something to be eliminated, or made "not to count," through technology. If computers and networks can help us to communicate without "the rest of it," that residue of difference with its power to disturb, disrupt, and challenge, then we can all exist in a world "without boundaries."

Another television commercial, this one by AT&T, that aired during the 1996 Olympics asks the viewer to "imagine a world without limits—AT&T believes communication can make it happen." Like "Anthem," this narrative posits a connection between networking and a democratic ethos in which differences will be elided. In addition, it resorts to a similar visual strategy—it depicts a black man in track shorts leaping over the Grand Canyon.

Like many of the ads by high-tech and communications companies that aired during the Olympics, this one has an "international" or multicultural flavor that seems to celebrate national and ethnic identities. This world without limits is represented by vivid and often sublime images of displayed ethnic and racial difference in order to bracket them off as exotic and irremediably other. Images of this other as primitive, anachronistic, and picturesque decorate the landscape of these ads.

Microsoft's recent television and print media campaign markets access to personal computing and Internet connectivity by describing these activities as a form of travel. Travel and tourism, like networking technology, are commodities that define the privileged, industrialized first-world subject, and they situate him in the position of the one who looks, the one who has access, the one who communicates. Microsoft's omnipresent slogan "Where do you want to go today?" rhetorically places this consumer in the position of the user with unlimited choice; access to Microsoft's technology and networks promises the consumer a "world without limits" where he can possess an idealized mobility. Microsoft's promise to transport the user to new (cyber)spaces where desire can be fulfilled is enticing in its very vagueness, offering a seemingly open-ended invitation for travel and new experiences. A sort of technologically enabled transnationality is evoked here, but one that directly addresses the first-world user, whose position on the network will allow him to metaphorically go wherever he likes.

This dream or fantasy of ideal travel common to networking advertisements constructs a destination that can look like an African safari, a trip to the Amazonian rain forest, or a camel caravan in the Egyptian desert. The iconography of the travelogue or tourist attraction in these ads places the viewer in the position of the tourist who, in Dean MacCannell's words, "simply collects experiences of difference (different people, different places)" and "emerges as a miniature clone of the old Western philosophical subject, thinking itself unified, central, in control, etc., mastering Otherness and profiting from it" (xv). Networking ads that promise the viewer control and mastery over technology and communications discursively and visually link this power to a vision of the other which, in contrast to the mobile and networked tourist/user, isn't going anywhere. The continued presence of stable signifiers of otherness in telecommunications advertising guarantees the Western subject that his position, wherever he may choose to go today, remains privileged.

An ad from Compaq . . . that appeared in the *Chronicle of Higher Education* reads, "Introducing a world where the words 'you can't get there from here' are never heard." It depicts a "sandstone mesa" with the inset image of a monitor from which two school-children gaze curiously at the sight. The ad is selling "Compaq networked multimedia. With it, the classroom is no longer a desti-nation, it's a starting point." Like the Microsoft and AT&T slogans, it links net-works with privileged forms of travel, and reinforces the metaphor by visually depict-ing sights that viewers associate with tourism. The networked classroom is envi-sioned as a glass window from which net-worked users can consume the sights of travel as if they were tourists.

Another ad from the Compaq series . . . shows the same children admiring the net-worked rain forest from their places inside the networked classroom, signified by the frame of the monitor. The tiny box on the upper-right-hand side of the image evokes the distinctive menu bar of a Windows product, and frames the whole ad for its viewer as a window onto an "other" world.

The sublime beauty of the mesa and the lush pastoral images of the rain forest are nostalgically quoted here in order to assuage an anxiety about the environmental effects of cybertechnology. In a world where sandstone mesas and rain forest are becoming increasingly rare, partly as a result of industrialization, these ads posi-tion networking as a benign, "green" type of product that will preserve the beauty of nature, at least as an image on the screen. As John Macgregor Wise puts it, this is part of the modernist discourse that envisioned electricity as "transcendent, pure and clean," unlike mechanical technology. The same structures of metaphor that allow this ad to dub the experience of using net-worked communications "travel" also enables it to equate an image of a rain for-est in Nature (with a capital N). The enrap-tured American schoolchildren, with their backpacks and French braids, are framed as user-travelers. With the assistance of Compaq, they have found their way to a world that seems to be without limits, one in which the images of nature are as good as or better than reality. . . .

This virtual field trip frames Nature as a tourist sight and figures Compaq as the educational tour guide. In this post-Internet culture of simulation in which we live, it is increasingly necessary for stable, iconic images of Nature and the Other to be evoked in the world of technology advertis-ing. These images guarantee and gesture toward the unthreatened and unproblem-atic existence of a destination for travel, a place whose beauty and exoticism will somehow remain intact and attractive. If technology will indeed make everyone, everything, and every place the same, as "Anthem" claims in its ambivalent way, then where is there left to go? What is there left to see? What is the use of being asked where you want to go today if every place is just like here? Difference, in the form of exotic places or exotic people, must be demonstrated iconographically in order to shore up the Western user's identity as himself. . . .

Since the conflicts in Mogadishu, Sarajevo, and Zaire (images of which are found elsewhere in the magazines from which these ads came), ethnic difference in the world of Internet advertising is visually "cleansed" of its divisive, problematic, tragic connotations. The ads function as corrective texts for readers deluged with images of racial conflicts and bloodshed both at home and abroad. These advertise-ments put the world right; their claims for better living (and better boundaries) through technology are graphically acted out in idealized images of Others who miraculously speak like "us" but still look like "them." . . .

The notion of the computer-enabled "global village" envisioned by Marshall McLuhan also participates in this rhetoric that links exotic travel and tourism with technology. . . .

It is part of the business of advertising to depict utopias: ideal depictions of being that correctively reenvision the world and prescribe a solution to its ills in the form of a commodity of some sort. And like tourist pamphlets, they often propose that their products will produce, in Dean MacCannell's phrase, a "utopia of difference," such as has been pictured in many Benetton and Coca-Cola advertising campaigns.

Coca-Cola's slogan from the seventies and eighties, "I'd like to teach the world to sing," both predates and prefigures these ads by IBM, Compaq, Origin, and MCI. The Coca-Cola ads picture black, white, young, old, and so on holding hands and forming a veritable Rainbow Coalition of human diversity. These singers are united by their shared song and, most important, their consumption of bottles of Coke. The viewer, meant to infer that the beverage was the direct cause of these diverse Coke drinkers overcoming their ethnic and racial differences, was given the same message then that many Internet-related advertisements give us today. The message is that cybertechnology, like Coke, will magically strip users down to "just minds," all singing the same corporate anthem.

References ◆

Hollinger, David. *Postethnic America: Beyond Multiculturalism.* New York: Basic Books, 1995.

MacCannell, Dean. *The Tourist: A New Theory of the Leisure Class.* New York: Schocken Books, 1989.

McLuhan, Marshall. *Understanding Media: The Extensions of Man.* Cambridge: MIT Press, 1994.

Rushdie, Salman. "Damme, This Is the Oriental Scene for You!" *New Yorker*, 23 and 30 June 1997, 50-61.

Trinh Minh-ha. *Woman, Native, Other: Writing Postcoloniality and Feminism.* Bloomington: University of Indiana Press, 1989.

Wise, John Macgregor. "The Virtual Community: Politics and Affect in Cyberspace." Paper delivered at the American Studies Association Conference, Washington, DC, 1997.

67

TELEVISION AND THE INTERNET

◆ Ellen Seiter

C laims that the Internet will revolutionize communications (as well as education, work life, and domestic leisure) are now commonplace. Yet there is a danger that computer communications—and by this I mean their uses, the discourses surrounding computers and the Internet, and research about them—will substantially buttress hierarchies of class, race, and gender. One healthy corrective is to recognize the many parallels between television and the Internet, and incorporate the insights of television audience research into the uses of technologies in the domestic sphere, the articulation of gender identities through popular genres, the complexity of individuals" motivations to seek out media, and the variety of possible interpretations of media technologies and media forms. Ethnography can offer a rich context of understanding the motivations and disincentives to using computers: an important research topic in a world in which non-users are likely to be labelled recalcitrants, technophobes, or slackers. . . .

◆ Television on Computers

As the number of personal computers increases in middle-class homes, the boundaries between leisure and work time, public and private space, promise to become increasingly blurred (Kling 1996). As the Internet develops from a research-oriented tool of elites to a commercial mass medium, resemblances between Web sites and television programming will increase.

The Internet can be used to organize users around political matters in ways unimaginable through broadcast television or small format video—and fundamentalist Christians are one group that has already proven this potential. It seems increasingly likely, however, that commercialization of the Web will discourage activism in favour of consumerism and the duplication of familiar forms of popular mass media, such as magazines, newspapers, and television programmes (Morris and Ogan 1996). The World Wide Web reproduces some popular genres from television (and radio) broadcasting: sports, science fiction, home shopping clubs, news magazines, even cyber-soap operas with daily postings of the serialized lives of its characters. In fact, the most popular Web sites represent the same genres—science fiction, soap operas, and "talk" shows—that form the topic of some of the best television audience research, by, for example, Press (1991), Jenkins (1992), Gillespie (1995), and Shattuc (1997). The much-publicized presence of pornography on the Internet also parallels the spectacular success of that genre on home video.

The prevalence of television material on the Web confirms the insight provided by media ethnographers of the importance of conversation about television in everyday life, and suggests that television plays a central role as common currency, a *lingua franca*. Television fans are a formidable presence on the Internet: in chatrooms, where fans can discuss their favourite programmes or television stars; on Web sites, where fan fiction can be posted; and as the presumed market for sales of television tie-in merchandise. The dissemination of knowledge of the programming language for the creation of Web sites (or home pages) unleashed countless die-hard television fans eager to display their television knowledge—and provide free publicity for television producers. Hundreds of painstakingly crafted home pages have been devoted to old television shows. For example, one site devoted to the 1964-5 Hanna-Barbera cartoon *Jonny Quest* provides plot summaries and still frames of every episode ever made. In fact, the Web is a jamboree of television material, with thousands of official and unofficial sites constituting television publicity, histories, cable and broadcast schedules, and promotional contests. Search engines turn up roughly three times as many references to television as they do for topics such as architecture, chemistry, or feminism. Apparently, television was one of the first topics people turned to when trying to think of something to interest a large and anonymous group of potential readers—other Internet users.

It would be a mistake, however, to see the rise of television material on the Internet exclusively from a fan or amateur perspective, because the connections between television and computer firms are proliferating. The association between television and the Internet has been heavily promoted at the corporate level by access providers eager to lure as sponsors companies that invest heavily in television advertising, and by others seeking sources and inspiration for the new Internet "programming" (Schiller 1997). The software giant Microsoft corporation has acquired stakes in media entertainment companies, developed an interactive television network, and looked to television and film for the basis for entertainment "software" with a more "universal," that is, mass-market, appeal. Microsoft's partnership with NBC to form the twenty-four-hour news cable network and online news and information service MSNBC is the most obvious example. Microsoft also has joint-venture deals with the cable network Black Entertainment Television; with Stephen Spielberg, Jeffrey Katzenberg, and David Geffen's company Dream Works SKG; and with Paramount Television Group—all of which is leading to speculation that Microsoft is "morphing into a media company for the new millennium" (Caruso 1996). Disney, now the owner of the television network ABC, is also one of the biggest interactive media producers in the world. America Online, the commercial Internet and e-mail access provider, has followed a vigorous commercial strategy, which includes extensive coverage of television in all its familiar publicity aspects as well as encouragement of fan activity, to build a broad base of subscribers and to court advertisers. The A. C. Nielsen company, the television industry leader in audience ratings, produces reports on Internet users. Worldgate Communications is offering a set-top box and hand-held remote control device that allows a viewer to access Web sites tied to television programmes currently being watched.

In 1996, Microsoft made its intention to break into broadcasting explicit when it released a revised version of its online service, whose browser interface sends users straight to an "On Stage" section with six different channels, each hosting "shows" (Helm 1996). The goal was to give users a better idea of what to expect from each programme by standardizing its offerings, a strategy strikingly familiar from the history of early radio and television (Boddy 1990; McChesney 1996). Video-streaming, already a commonplace on the World Wide Web, has been implemented on Web sites such as Cable News Network's to replay the "News Story of the Week." Advertising industry analysts predict that animated advertisements on the Web will dominate in the years ahead. . . .

The relatively high penetration rates of home computers among the professional classes (including writers about computer issues) often give the false impression that everyone has a computer. The majority of homes do not have a PC, but they do have a television. Therefore, the computer industry continues to eye television greedily as a future market. Microsoft has entered the cable television business, exploring set-top boxes and television programming, and vigorously campaigning to thwart the

success of high definition television (HDTV) in favour of "digital TV," which would use computer monitors. Television set manufacturers are gambling on a variety of designs that integrate Web access with television viewing through cable boxes, double windows, wireless keyboards, and television remote controls with data entry features. Digital TV sets are being designed to maximize flexibility for future uses with satellite receivers, Internet navigators, digital video disc-players, and set-top boxes. . . .

For its part, television plays a crucial role as publicizer of the Web and computer use. Television programmes are already filled with references to computers and the Internet that both dramatize the importance of the new technologies and attempt to play a major role in educating the public about new media. Television's appetite for novelty, as well as its fears about losing viewers to computer screens, makes computers one of its predictable obsessions. Silverstone and Hirsch are right to point to the dual nature of communication technologies such as television sets and computers "as quintessentially novel objects, and therefore as the embodiment of our desires for the new," which simultaneously act as "transmitters of all the images and information that fuel those desires" (1992: 3). . . .

Online communications have been used both to support and to attack television shows and their sponsors. Television networks are exploiting e-mail and Internet communications with audiences to gain feedback on script or character changes, to compile mailing lists for licensed products relating to shows, and to publicize tie-in merchandise. The creation of an Internet home page for the *X-Files* was credited with saving the show from cancellation after its first season. The *X-Files* producers recognized the perfect synergy of its high demographic fans and the Internet, and targeted its audience through the World Wide Web, a move that helped both to prove its audience share to executives contemplating axing the show and to generate more publicity for the programme. Protests against television animate the online communications as well: Christian Right organizations such as The American Family Association use the Internet to organize protests against television sponsors of objectionable material (a list it calls "The Dirty Dozen") and "filth" *(N.Y.P.D. Blue)*. . . .

For its target market of the professional upper-middle class, advertisers are promoting the installation of the computer as a domestic object in a process similar to the guidelines for installing the television set in the home in the 1950s studied by Lynn Spigel (1992). Computers are advertised on utopian claims to enrich family life, enhance communications, strengthen friendship and kin networks, and, perhaps most important, make children smarter and give them a competitive advantage in the educational sphere. In advertising, in news broadcasts, in education journals, the computer is often defined against, and pitched as an improvement on the television set: where television viewing is passive, computer use is interactive; where television programmes are entertaining in a stale, commercialized, violent way, computer software and the Internet are educational, virtuous, new.

. . . Comparisons between television viewing and use of the World Wide Web are inevitable. Like television programming, computer media—software, Web sites, etc.—serve as topics of conversation, but the latter hold more legitimacy among the educated middle classes. Among middle-class professionals, the group best positioned to parlay computer use into improved earning power, discussing a new Web site holds more cachet than talking over last night's sitcom. The negative associations of being a computer nerd, or even a hacker, have abated considerably in the last decade (Turkle 1995), while computer magazines such as *Wired* have promoted fashionable postmodern associations with computer use. While some sanctions are

associated with being a nerd, this stereotype has a higher gender, class, and intellectual standing than the couch potato. On the other hand, those with less disposable income and less familiarity with computers may reject computers for the values they represent (such as dehumanization), their emphasis on written rather than oral culture, their associations with white male culture (hackers and hobbyists), and their solitary, antisocial nature.

Gendered Uses ◆ of Computers at Home

Television sets and computers introduce highly similar issues in terms of placement in domestic space, conflicts among family members over usage and control, and value in the household budget. We can expect these conflicts to be articulated within gender roles in the family. Some research on gendered conflicts over computers (Haddon 1992; Murdock et al. 1992; Giacquinta et al. 1993) reproduces themes of family-based studies about control of the television set. Already, researchers have noted a strong tendency for men and boys to have more access to computers in the home. Television studies such as those carried out by Ann Gray (1992), David Morley (1986), and myself (Seiter et al. 1989) suggest that women in nuclear families have difficulty watching a favourite television show (because of competition for control of the set from other family members, and because of shouldering the majority of childcare, housework, and cooking). If male family members gravitate towards the computer as hobbyists, the load of chores relegated to female family members will only increase, and make it more difficult for female members to get time on the home computer. Computers require hours of trial-and-error experimentation, a kind of extended play demanding excess leisure time. Fully exploring the Internet demands time for lengthy downloading, and patience with connections that are busy, so much so that some have dubbed the World Wide Web the World Wide Wait.

In the family, computers can create anxiety, too: young children must be kept away from the keyboard because of potential damage to the machine. Mothers, who have traditionally been charged with securing the academic success of their children, would have a strong incentive to relinquish computer time to older children, who are thought to benefit greatly from all contact with the technology. When anxieties increase and moral panics are publicized about children's encounters with pornography through the computer, or the unhealthy effects of prolonged computer use, the brunt of responsibility for enforcing restrictions on computer use will fall to mothers and teachers.

Some qualitative research has already explored these areas. . . . Most of these studies are somewhat dated, and do not provide any information about the use of electronic mail and the World Wide Web. These two uses of the computer, in their facilitation of personal communications, most closely resemble the telephone, a communications technology particularly valued by women (Rakow 1988; Livingstone 1992; Spender 1995). Reliable information about Web users is hard to come by, and most research relies upon self-selection of its sample, that is, people responding to various postings asking for Internet users to fill out a survey form. Some of this recent survey information suggests that the Internet may be attracting women, especially younger, white, middle-class women under 35, at surprising rates. In 1995, the Georgia Tech World Wide Web users survey reported that 29 percent of their respondents are female—a number that has increased significantly over the last three years. There has been a substantial increase in female Web users between the ages of sixteen and twenty, and an increase in female users who teach kindergarten through twelfth grade—there was a 10 percent increase in female users in this category observed in one year, 1994-5. The importance of access through public education institutions for women is significant: 39 percent of women responding gained Internet access that way, compared to 28 percent of men. Yet there are clear signs that women are less likely to use computers intensively in their free time. At the weekends—an indication of hobbyist users—the gap widens to 75 percent male and only 25 percent female: thus, three times as many men are weekend users of computers compared to women. Women users were less likely than men to spend time doing "fun computing" or to use a computer for more than thirty-one hours a week. Although the Web is attracting men over the age of 46 in increasing numbers—many of them as a retirement hobby—the relative numbers of women of that age who use the Internet are declining.

Much has been written about the ways in which the Internet can be used to explore personality and identity (for example, Turkle 1995; Star 1995). But women and the poor are going to be less advantageously positioned to engage in such activities for a complex set of reasons (Star 1995). As Roger Silverstone has explained:

> The ability to use information and communication technology as a kind of extension of the personality in time and space . . . is also a matter of resources. The number of rooms in a household relative to the number of people, the amount of money that an individual can claim for his or her own personal use, the amount of control of his or her own time in the often intense atmosphere of family life, all these things are obviously of great relevance. (1991: 12)

Computerized Work ◆

Are women more likely to use the Internet if they use computers on the job? Working on a computer can mean very different things: if we are to understand the differential desire to use computers during leisure time, it is essential to make distinctions between kinds of computerized work. For example, huge numbers of female employees occupy clerical jobs that use computers for processing payroll, word-processing, conducting inventory, sales, and airline reservations—more than 16 million women held such positions in the USA in 1993 (Kling 1996). Women overwhelmingly outnumber men in the kinds of job where telephones and computers are used simultaneously: airline reservations, catalogue sales, telephone operators. In contrast, fewer than half a million women work as computer programmers or systems analysts.

The type of employment using a computer that is likely to be familiar to the largest number of women, then, is a kind of work where keystrokes might be counted, where supervisors may listen in on phone calls, where productivity is scrutinized on a daily and hourly basis, where conversation with co-workers is forbidden (Clement 1994; Iacono and Kling 1996). The stressful and unpleasant circumstances under which this kind of work is performed might explain women's alienation from computer technology and their tendency to stay away from it during their leisure time. . . .

Telecommuting, working from the home through a modem or Internet access to the office, is a different category of computerized work which is supposed to hold special appeal to women. Telecommuting is now officially sanctioned by the U.S. government, according to Rob Kling:

A recent report developed under the auspices of the Clinton administration included a key section, "Promoting Telecommuting," that lists numerous advantages for telecommuting. These include major improvements in air quality from reduced travel; increased organizational productivity when people can be more alert during working hours;

faster commercial transit times when few cars are on the roads; and improvements in quality of worklife. The benefits identified in this report seem so overwhelming that it may appear remarkable that most organizations have not already allowed all of their workers the options to work at home. (1996: 212)

While there are growing numbers of women doing pink-collar jobs such as clerical and sales work at home—that is, using their home computers at jobs such as credit-card verification and telephone solicitations—this form of telecommuting is also largely invisible in the mass media. Instead, we see images of female professionals using computers to work from home, perhaps while their one and only child conveniently naps in the next room. As Lynn Spigel has noted, computer publications suggest "a hybrid site of home and work, where it is possible to make tele-deals while sitting in your kitchen" (1996: 11). In her discussion of a *Mac Home* magazine cover, Spigel suggests that "the computer and Net offer women a way to do two jobs at once—reproduce and produce, be a mother and hold down a high powered job. Even while the home work model of domestic space finds a place for women, it does not really break down the traditional distinctions between male and female" (1996: 12). . . .

The role of feminist researchers will include tempering enthusiasm for these new technologies, as Kramarae and Kramer argue:

The so-called popular media treat the new electronic systems as sexy, but the media fail to deal seriously with most of the gender-related issues. As those who are working closely with its developments know, the Internet will not, contrary to what the media tout, ride the world of hostility, ignorance, racism, sexism, greed and undemocratic governments. The Internet has the potential for creating a cooperative collective international web; but, as with all technologies, the Internet system will be shaped by prevailing communication behaviors, economic policy, and legal decisions. (1995: 15)

One of the most important functions of ethnography, then, may be as an antidote to the hype about computers. Ethnography can describe, for example, the full context in which barriers to entrance onto the information highway exist—especially among people still worrying about keeping a car running on the real highway, much less having the extra time and money to maintain a computer at home.

When turning to the Internet, it will be especially important to treat computer communications as deeply cultural, as employing fiction and fantasy as well as information, and as open to variable interpretations based on gender, race, and ethnicity. As the Internet is championed as the ultimate in "interactive" media use, it will be extremely important for media researchers to put forward appropriate scepticism about the laudatory uses of the term "active" in discussions of media use, and to problematize the complex factors involved in attracting both television viewers and computer users to particular contents and genres.

Ethnography can offer an appreciation of some of television's advantages over computers (such as its accessibility by more than one person at a time, and its visual and aural modes of communication) and guard against the unnecessary pathologization of television viewing, which almost always acts to stigmatize the already socially powerless. It will be important to look at the reasons why and the contexts in which television might be more appealing than the Internet. We know that television—for all of its failings—has been cheap, easy to watch at home, enjoyable to talk about with others, and reasonably successful as an educational tool. It will be important to understand the ways in which such social features of broadcast technologies are missing or modified in new technologies.

Finally, scholars should work to change the media and the structures of access to communication technologies, while politicizing the public discussion of media in ways that make explicit the gains and the losses at stake in promoting different representations of TV audiences and computer users.

References ◆

Boddy, W. (1990). *Fifties Television: The Industry and Its Critics*. Urbana: University of Illinois Press.

Caruso, D. (1996). "Microsoft Morphs Into a Media Company." *Wired* 4/6: 126-9.

Clement, A. (1994). "Computing at Work: Empowering Action by 'Low-level Users.'" *Communications of the ACM* 37/1:52-65. Also reprinted in R. Kling, *Computerization and Controversy* (1996).

Giacquinta, J. B., Bauer, J. A., and Levin, J. E. (1993). *Beyond Technology's Promise: An Examination of Children's Educational Computing at Home*. Cambridge and New York: Cambridge University Press.

Gillespie, M. (1995). *Television, Ethnicity and Cultural Change*. London and New York: Routledge.

Gray, A. (1992). *Video Playtime: The Gendering of a Leisure Technology*. London and New York: Routledge.

Haddon, L. (1992). "Explaining ICT Consumption: The Case of the Home Computer," in R. Silverstone and E. Hirsch, *Consuming Technologies*, 82-96.

Helm, L. (1996). "Microsoft Unveils Revamped Online Service." *Los Angeles Times*, 11 October: D2.

Iacono, S., and Kling, R. (1996). "Computerization Movements and Tales of Technological Utopianism," in R. Kling, *Computerization and Controversy*, 85-107.

Jenkins, H. (1992). *Textual Poachers: Television Fans and Participatory Culture*. London and New York: Routledge.

Kling, R. (ed.). (1996). *Computerization and Controversy: Value Conflicts and Social*

Choices, 2nd ed. San Diego, CA: Academic Press.

Kramarae, C., and Kramer, J. (1995). "Legal Snarls for Women in Cyberspace," *Internet Research: Electronic Networking Applications and Policy* 5:14-24.

Livingstone, S. M. (1992). "The Meaning of Domestic Technologies: A Personal Construct Analysis of Familial Gender Relations," in R. Silverstone and F. Hirsch, *Consuming Technologies*, 113-30.

McChesney, R. W. (1996). "The Internet and U.S. Communication Policy-Making in Historical and Critical Perspective." *Journal of Communication* 46/1:98-124.

Morley, D. (1986). *Family Television*. London: Comedia/Routledge.

Morris, M., and Ogan, C. (1996). "The Internet as a Mass Medium." *Journal of Communication* 46/1:39-50.

Murdock, G., Hartmann, P., and Gray, P. (1992). "Contextualizing Home Computing Resources and Practices," in R. Silverstone and E. Hirsch, *Consuming Technologies*, 146-60.

Press, A. (1991). *Women Watching Television*. Philadelphia: University of Pennsylvania.

Rakow, L. (1988). "Women and the Telephone: The Gendering of a Communications Technology,'" in C. Kramarae (ed.), *Technology and Women's Voices: Keeping in Touch*. New York: Routledge and Kegan Paul, 207-28.

Schiller, D. (1997). "Les marchands à l'assaut de l'Internet" (Cornering the Market in Cyberspace). *Le Monde Diplomatique* 516/March: 1,24,25.

Seiter, E., Borchers, H., Kreutzner, G., and Warth, E. (eds.). (1989). *Remote Control: Television, Audiences and Cultural Power*. London: Routledge.

Shattuc, J. (1997). *The Talking Cure: TV Talk Shows and Women*. New York: Routledge.

Silverstone, R. (1991). "Beneath the Bottom Line: Households and Information and Communication Technologies in an Age of the Consumer." London: PICT (Programme in Information and Communication Technologies), Policy Research Papers No. 17.

Silverstone, R., and Hirsch, E. (eds.). (1992). *Consuming Technologies: Media and Information in Domestic Spaces*. London: Routledge.

Spender, D. (1995). *Nattering on the Net: Women, Power and Cyberspace*. North Melbourne, Australia: Spinifex Press.

Spigel, L. (1992). *Make Room for TV: Television and the Family Ideal in Postwar America*. Chicago, IL: University of Chicago Press.

Spigel, L. (1996). "Portable TV: Studies in Domestic Space Travel," paper delivered at Console-Ing Passions: The Annual Conference on Television, Video, and Feminism.

Star, S. L. (1995). "Introduction," *The Cultures of Computing*. Oxford, UK: Blackwell, 1-28.

Turkle, S. (1995). *Life on the Screen*. New York: Simon & Schuster.

68

DATING ON THE NET

Teens and the Rise
of "Pure" Relationships

◆ Lynn Schofield Clark

◆ Studying Teens and the Internet

... This study on dating and the Internet emerged out of a broader qualitative study on the role of media technologies in the domestic context of the household.[1] Over the course of a year, I conducted a series of interviews and observations with 15 families and two focus groups, devoting between 4 and much more than 30 hours of conversation, observation, or both to each family. A total of 47 teens and 26 of their family members were included in the interviews, groups, and observations. An additional six families (14 teens) were interviewed by an associate researcher on the project, who has corroborated my findings.

From the families interviewed, three teenagers were selected for the further study of Internet use: Elizabeth, a 15-year-old white female from a lower-income single-parent household; Jake, a 17-year-old white male from a middle-income blended (two-parent, second marriage) household; and Michael, a 15-year-old African American male from a lower-income single-parent household. These individuals were chosen because they represented "information-rich cases," in that I expected that they would yield findings that would contrast from expectations and from each other due to their differing social, economic, and political positions within the wider culture (Yin, 1994, pp. 45-46). . . . I also selected them for their ability to be thoughtful, articulate, and responsible, as I wanted to train them to serve as leaders of what I have called *peer-led discussion groups*, focus groups that were led and participated in solely by teens. This format was adopted as a means to more closely observe how teenagers "really" talk about these issues when an adult is not present. . . .

Whereas my research primarily is based on these interviews and observations in "real life," I supplemented the knowledge gained through these methods by "lurking" in teen chat rooms. Elizabeth also allowed me to read many of the e-mail exchanges she had had with her online male friends.

Although many of the teens discussed using the Net for school-related research, the teens in my study primarily used the Net to communicate with other young people in the teen chat rooms of Microsoft Network, America Online, and the teen lobby of Yahoo! These "socially produced spaces" constitute a form of "synchronistic communication," in that the posts are ephemeral and immediate (Baym, 1995; Jones, 1995). They are seen by all those in the chat room at the same time, and answers to various queries posted to the chat room often overlap, creating a cacophony of conversation. Most of the teens with whom I spoke had experienced similar periods of intense experimentation in the chat rooms, sometimes devoting more than 4 hours a day to online chats for a period of several weeks or even months. In most cases, however, this period was followed by parent sanctioning, which either severely limited or discontinued the teen's chat room participation altogether. Despite the frequent warnings concerning the dangers facing teens on the Internet, parents were largely unaware of the content of the chat rooms; the limits were set based on what in some cases were alarmingly high bills from their service providers.[2]

Much like the adults on the Net discussed by Rheingold (1991) and others, teens seemed to be drawn to Internet chat rooms by the promise of fantasy and fun. As Kramarae (1995) noted in her critique of the overwhelmingly male population in cyberspace, the males far outnumbered the females in teen chat rooms as well. Yet there were also differences between the communications between teens and those I witnessed on the adult chat lines. Perhaps most obvious was the "age and sex check," the frequent request that resulted in the sharing of ages and genders among participants, often serving as a precursor for those of similar ages to break off into a separate chat room of only two persons, which the girls, at least, agreed constituted an "Internet 'date.'" . . . Sometimes these initial conversations between two teens would last for several hours. The topics of conversation mirrored those one might hear at a teen party. Internet dating, much like the practice's counterpart in "real life," exists within a specific environment that in many ways, not surprisingly, shares similarities with the other social contexts in which teens find themselves. Thus, we turn to a discussion of the environment of teen chat rooms within which (or out of which) Internet dating occurs, beginning with a review of the practice in its historical context.

Teenagers and Dating: ◆ A Brief History

Teenage "dating"—the casual romantic interactions between males and females (or, even more recently, between persons of the same gender)—is a relatively recent phenomenon. Historians argue that it emerged among middle-class teens in the 1920s during a time of gender role upheaval (Bailey, 1988). With the rise of both compulsory education and restrictive child labor laws during this era, teens of immigrant and farm families who once had been expected to work, as well as teens from more privileged classes, were now sent to school. Education was cemented into the American teen experience, affording increased public opportunities for young people to interact with one another under minimal supervision by their parents.

The rise of the "dance craze" in the 1920s also has been linked to the emergence of the practice of "dating" (Modell, 1989). Whereas some teens in the decade before had attended community dances that were sponsored by neighborhoods or other social clubs (and hence had fairly strict social restraints that limited the "tendency to overstep moral rules"), it was the opening of a dance "palace" in New York City in 1911 that ushered in new practices surrounding dancing and dating (Modell, 1989, p. 71). The large dance halls that subsequently sprang up in urban areas made dancing with relative strangers an accessible and intriguing new option for teens. The dance style of the period, as it moved away from formal steps and toward increased free expression and physical contact, encouraged the establishment of casual heterosexual relationships in a way not previously seen.

During the same era, film houses multiplied throughout urban as well as rural areas, and weekly attendance at motion pictures increased dramatically. The darkened theater and the heightened emotions film evoked offered further opportunities for physical closeness. Whereas films often were attended by groups of teens, they quickly became vehicles for the exploration of exclusive intergender relations as well (Blumer, 1933).

Modell (1989) credited middle-class girls of this era with actually initiating the practice of dating, as they had the most to gain

from the establishment of the practice. He wrote, "Before dating, parents had tended to construe strictly girls' obligation to enter marriage untainted by even a hint of scandal, and they supervised courting accordingly, limiting both its occasion and the set of eligibles." As parents were more concerned with their daughters' reputations than their sons', "girls were far more constrained by parental oversight" (Modell, 1989, p. 95). Whereas dating in the early part of the [last] century still required the male to take initiative, it shifted control over the girls' interactions—and by extension, her sexuality—from her parents to her peers. It thus served as a potent aspect of youth rebellion against parents and their traditional ways. Whereas girls of this generation would not be considered sexually liberated by today's standards, dating enabled girls to play a more active role in constructing and maintaining heterosexual interaction through informal rules of conduct. Dating required teen boys to negotiate with teen girls and their peers directly, rather than through their families. To a significant extent, dating shifted the approval and sanctioning of romantic relationships from parents to peers.

Dating then, as now, consisted of going to movies, dances, or restaurants. As such, dating, and by extension romance, quickly came to be linked with leisure and consumption, as Illouz (1997) argued. Moreover, as the rising consumerism of this era encouraged immediate gratification, young people began to think of self-denial for its own sake as old-fashioned, seeking in dancing and dating some fulfillment of the sexual tensions of adolescence (Fass, 1977). Whereas chaperoning and "calling" were steadily replaced among middle-class teens by the practice of dating, however, those teens of all races with less means were less likely to date. Part of this is due to the fact that these teens were usually encouraged to lighten the family's financial obligations either by seeking employment or marrying. By the middle of the century, however, in part due to the popular romanticized narratives of the practice in film, television, and magazines, "dating" became an integral part of the teen experience in the United States.

Since the cultural shifts and sexual revolutions of the 1960s, however, dating as a teenage institution has been in decline. Ironically, as Modell (1989) pointed out, dating, which originally caught on as a form of rebellion from establishment and traditional values, "had moved from a 'thrill'-based innovation half a century before to a somewhat fading bastion of essentially 'traditional' marriage values" by the 1960s (p. 303). Today, teens use the term "dating" in a somewhat bemused way, often with self-conscious ironic reference to the 1950s version of the practice. Whereas they still go out on dates, these occasions are less fraught with specific expectations. They are less frequently planned in advance, for example, and there is also less compulsion to report on the experience to one's peers. "Dating" has become much more idiosyncratic, with less reference to the external peer group and more relation to the self-gratifications and pleasures of the individuals involved. This is part of a larger turn toward issues of self-reflexivity and identity as central aspects of relationships, as I will show.

◆ *Cyberdating Relationship as Emancipatory*

Cyberdating's potential to limit emotional pain in relationships seems particularly appealing for teen girls. Indeed, the girls in my study were, on the whole, much more enthusiastic about the possibilities afforded to Net dating than the boys of the same age. "I'm not too popular with the guys," 15-year-old Elizabeth explained to me, noting that Net relationships held less potential for the pain of rejection. On the Internet, employing her excellent skills in verbal articulation and humor, she seemed to have no difficulty meeting and developing rela-

tionships with boys and was even "dating four guys at once." "Usually I act a lot more aggressive when I'm on the Internet," she stated. "I just express my feelings a lot more in the chat rooms and stuff, so if somebody talks about something that I don't like, then I'll say it. And I would probably never do that in class, in school and everything." As Reid has written of the Net experience in general, "Users are able to express and experiment with aspects of their personality that social inhibition would generally encourage them to suppress" (Reid, 1991, cited in Baym, 1995, p. 143). This suggests that girls may use the verbal skills they might otherwise suppress to parlay themselves into a stronger position in relationship to their male counterparts, thereby assuming more authority in the construction of the heterosexual relationship. This was illustrated in one of the peer-led discussion group's conversations about sexual behaviors on the Net:

Elizabeth: The only thing I didn't like about those guys [two "brothers" she was dating simultaneously] was that they liked sex just a little bit too much.

Vickie: Cybersex?

Lisa: Kinky?

Elizabeth: They liked sex, it was scary. They e-mailed me a message that like, had a lot to do with sex, and you know, we didn't—I didn't have my own screen name or e-mail address, so it was like, oh my God! [Either her mother or brother, who share her account, could have read it] So I like deleted it before I even read it. And when I was talking with them later, they're all, "did you get my message?" And I'm all, "uh, no. Yes, I did, but I didn't have a chance to read it. My brother tried to read it, so I deleted it before I could read it, I'm sorry." Yeah—right! [the girls all laugh]. But you know I never even told those guys I was getting off the Internet when I did. So I just kinda like, disappeared.

Betsi: How long do you think they were talking, thinking you were there?

Vickie: They're like, sitting there writing all these messages to you, and you're gone.

Elizabeth: Well, I got off the Internet, my mom canceled the thing [the AOL account], and I never told them that I was gonna cancel.

In this situation, unwanted sexual advances were not only rebuffed but resulted in Elizabeth's creation of a potentially embarrassing situation for the boys as they may have found themselves talking (or masturbating?) without an audience. Further, the boys were objectified as the story became a shared experience of female triumph among the girlfriends.

To further strengthen their position in the dating interaction, several teen girls reported that they adopt new physical personae, describing their looks in such a way as to appear more attractive to the males. This not only fulfills the function of avoiding potential pain and rejection but also neutralizes some of the power aspects of the heterosexist system in which beautiful girls are given more attention and more social opportunities (Brown & Gilligan, 1992). If everyone constructs their appearance in accord with the imagined "ideal," after all, no one can be judged more or less desirable based solely on appearances. Thus in effect, boys lose some of their power as one of the primary tools of the evaluation of desirability is removed from the equation. It would appear that in these relationships, it is no longer wholly a matter of the men as consumers and women as consumed, as has been argued in less interactive contexts (see, e.g., Kramarae, 1995). Girls feel

empowered through the power of self-presentation.

Interestingly, both Michael and Jake state that they dislike it when girls lie about their looks in the chat rooms. As Jake said,

Jake: You can kinda like tell [if they're lying, because of] how they're putting it and all. Sometimes they get too extreme with their lying. You're like, "whatever."

Interviewer: So that's kind of a turnoff, then, when you can tell that they're lying?

Jake: Yeah. "Bye." And then go back into the chat room.

Michael noted that looks are less important on the Net than they are in real life.

Interviewer: So what is the difference, do you think, between meeting someone in the chat room and dating somebody in person?

Michael: Well, when you're dating somebody and it seems like, you're more looking at them, but when you're like, chatting to them, you can't see them, but you can get that trust going with the person, and you can really get to know them before you see them. And if you know 'em before you see them, you'll like, even if they don't look physically attractive to you, you'll still like them because you know them and you have a lot in common.

When he learned that one of the girls with whom he was chatting had lied about her looks, Michael noted that he did not abandon the relationship because he had not entered it with romantic intent based on looks:

Michael: Okay, I ask them [girls he's met in chat rooms] to describe themselves, and some of them, they lie. Like one girl, she said she was 5'5", 130 some pounds, I forgot, and I went on her Web page, and she was pretty big. [laughs.] So I asked her why she lied, she was like, "I was scared you wouldn't like me." But I talk to her still, though . . .

Interviewer: Have you ever, when people have said what they looked like, decided that you didn't like them?

Michael: No. Mostly, when I go on the Web, I'm looking for friends, so it really doesn't matter what they look like.

Thus, even though boys may dislike the changing of looks, they are still able to find online relationships with girls satisfying. Instead of being under pressure by their peers to pair with the "right" girls whose looks approximate the ideal, the Internet allows for more egalitarian exchange freed from most of the restraint of peer approval. Indeed, several of the teens noted that what begins as somewhat romantic or titillating Internet exchanges often grows into positive, ongoing relationships with members of the opposite sex. This suggests some hope for the Net's ability to contribute to positive teen communities both in cyberspace and beyond. Also, because physical contact is (usually) impossible in a Net relationship, young people may find that they are able to communicate with one another free from the social and peer pressures toward expressed sexuality.

Yet, whereas this might suggest a depth of relationship is possible, my research actually affirmed that the opposite is much more common. This is not surprising, as the environment of teen chat rooms in many ways mirrors the social restraints teens experience in "real life." For example, let us return to the consideration of the fact that girls change their appearances to achieve more social power. In this action, teen girls are not redefining standards of acceptability based on beauty but are using the Net to actively construct what they believe is a more socially acceptable version of themselves. Each of the teen discussion groups expressed agreement in the fact that "on the Internet, they [persons of the opposite sex] cannot see you." Whereas the lack of physical presence undoubtedly lowers inhibitions as Kiesler and colleagues argued, the fact that each group mentioned this when contrasting dating on the Internet to dating in "real life" demonstrates the importance of visual appearance in the currency of popularity and hence one's desirability as a "date" (Kiesler, Siegel, & McGuire, 1984). Not surprisingly, given the opportunities afforded on the Net, girls are very conscious of the online presentations of themselves. Elizabeth notes, for example, "Usually I describe myself skinnier or taller. Skinnier and taller, with longer hair, and a lighter color blond, usually." In this way, Elizabeth's employment of the technology is in keeping with social conventions concerning gender roles. She was not interested in meeting the boys with whom she conversed, as this might undermine her attractive and aggressive online persona. In fact, when one of the male friends suggested that they talk on the phone, she deliberately kept her phone line busy during the appointed time so that he would not be able to get through. She said that they did not "talk" again online after that, something she seemed to have no regrets about, even though she reported that the relationship had been fairly intimate before that time. She also noted that although she had never "met" anyone online from her own school, she had decided to terminate one relationship owing to the fact that the boy attended a neighboring school:

We started comparing notes about who we knew in each other's schools. But I didn't want to meet him, or someone from my own school, because then what if I knew who he was in person and he said something mean about me, I'd be like, hurt.

"Dates" with faceless and voiceless boys from faraway places held no such possible consequences. The fact that Elizabeth avoided rejection in "real" relationships and still sensed a need to censure her ideas when not online further demonstrates that the power afforded through self-construction on the Net does not translate into changed gender roles and expectations in the social world beyond cyberspace. Consistent with the findings of Rakow and Navarro in their study of the introduction of cellular phones, therefore, we must conclude that the possibility that new communication technologies might subvert social systems is limited (Rakow & Navarro, 1993; see also Rakow, 1988). Indeed, there is evidence of much more that is socially reproduced into the chat rooms from the environment of "real life."

◆ Border Patrol: The Policing of Gender and Taboo Relationships

The content of teen chat rooms on the whole appears to be much tamer than many of the adult chat rooms.[3] Whereas adults are explicit about their desires, as Seabrook (1997) has illustrated, teens are much more reserved and, not surprisingly, less creative verbally. Much like the furtive illicit activities of the proverbial backseat, teens were reluctant to speak of their sexual experimentation, and what happened in the "private" two-person chat sessions was not up for discussion in the more public chat rooms.

Sex was an exciting but also heavily policed topic in the teen chat rooms. On several occasions in teen chat rooms, in fact, persons who issued explicit invitations

for cybersex were sanctioned through prolonged "silences" (in which the on-screen dialogue was halted) followed by statements such as, "Whoa" or even "watch the language." There were also comments of mockery directed at the overzealous pursuer, such as the comment following an age and sex check: "ha ha RYAN, all 2 young 4 you!" On the whole, the teens seemed much less comfortable expressing their sexual desires and fantasies in the larger group of a teen chat room than the adults did in their counterpart rooms, although there were suggestive screen names adopted by the teens, such as "Tigerlover," or the more explicit "Rydher69her."

Just as in "real life," teens in chat rooms seem to be more vocal than their adult counterparts in policing the boundaries of race and sex. . . .Teens are more overtly critical of homosexuality and use derogatory terms to police the boundaries of heterosexuality and to place themselves safely within its realm. In his analysis of the heterosexist culture of adolescent schooling, Friend (1993) has observed, "a systematic set of institutional and cultural arrangements exist that reward and privilege people for being or appearing to be heterosexual, and establish potential punishments or lack of privilege for being or appearing to be homosexual" (p. 210). Friend pointed to textbooks that assume a heterosexual norm and teachers reluctant to discuss homosexuality altogether as ways in which heterosexism is reinforced through silencing. Heterosexist ideas extend beyond the classroom to the adolescents' homes and are reinforced in the media through texts that assume the norm of heterosexuality. Being labeled a homosexual or lesbian by one's peers, regardless of the reason, then, has real material consequences: Loss of friendships, marginalization, and physical violence may result. Thus teens, both heterosexual and homosexual, have a great investment in maintaining a "straight" identity in the context of public schools and constantly seek to assert their heterosexuality. Teen chat rooms, along with other locations in which teen discussions occur, serve as platforms on which young people may assert their alignment with the dominant ideology of heterosexuality as a means of affirming that they are accepted and acceptable among their peers. One can therefore imagine the therapeutic and liberating potential of gay and lesbian teen chat rooms for young persons. I have not analyzed these chat rooms here because among the teens in my study, experiences in these locations were not discussed except in instances in which the speaker was asserting his or her own heterosexuality. For instance, mention of gay and lesbian chat rooms surfaced in the discussion groups when the peer leaders asked them, "which is the worst chat room to meet boys or girls?" In each group someone answered, "The gay [or lesbian] lounge," followed by raucous laughter. . .

The norm of interaction in teen chat rooms, therefore, to extend the earlier argument, is of heterosexual dyads between two persons of the opposite sex and approximately the same age who did not know one another in other contexts. This of course echoes the norms of romantic interaction occurring in the high school. Yet chat room and follow-up e-mail experiences have afforded teen participants an opportunity to experiment with heterosexual relationships in ways that are rather different from, and in certain ways less risky than, those occurring in their junior high and high schools. Even with their limits in terms of overturning gendered hierarchies, therefore, these relationships suggest changes that are occurring in the adolescent interactions and expectations between males and females.

◆ Dating and the "Pure Relationship" in a "Risk" Society

Much like the dance halls 70 years earlier, today's cyberculture affords teenagers new opportunities to experiment with gender relations, with results potentially as far-reaching as those initiated during that time period. I would like to suggest that the relationships online are characteristically different along both physical and emotional lines. The *physical* hazards of relationships, at least in terms of consensual premarital sex, were limited more than 30 years ago with the introduction of "the pill" and the consequent rise in acceptability of other forms of birth control to avoid pregnancy and sexually transmitted diseases. It is almost too obvious to state that the Net introduces disembodied relations, thereby limiting physical contact between most teens. After all, even if they had wanted to meet their Net romance in person, the challenges of distance and a lack of transportation or resources limit this to a significant degree among teens. Net relationships, therefore, operate in tandem with or as verbal "practice" for the actual events in "real life" rather than eliminating or restructuring the sexual mores that preceded them. Yet in the contemporary situation, "Internet dating" emerges as an alluring option for intimate hetero- and homosexual experimentation that holds the possibility of decreasing the potential *emotional* hazards of intimate relations.

Someone from an older generation might wonder why teens would feel that dating is an emotional minefield to be navigated carefully. After all, those older than teens might look back on the youthful dating scene as carefree. Yet dating, like other cultural institutions, must be considered in context. Borrowing the term from Ulrich Beck, Giddens referred to the current situation as a "risk society" (Beck, 1986, cited in Giddens, 1991). Giddens noted that this implies more than the increased exposure to new forms of danger:

> To accept risk as risk, an orientation which is more or less forced on us by the abstract systems of modernity, is to acknowledge that no aspects of our activities follow a predestined course, and all are open to contingent happenings. . . .

Living in the "risk society" means living with a calculative attitude to the open possibilities of action, positive and negative, with which, as individuals and globally, we are confronted in a continuous way in our contemporary social existence. (p. 28)

As a part of their developmental process, therefore, teens must garner the skills necessary to envision various possible outcomes to their actions. Even as this has occurred, the decline of the authority of adult institutions throughout culture in general has left young people with more autonomy and hence more authority over their own behavior. Moreover, with the rise of part-time employment hours, young people themselves now have greater control over resources (financial and educational) that allow them to choose the timing of the events in their own life course to a greater extent than in previous generations. This combination of factors results in a strikingly different approach to the future than the concept of one's "fate," which teens of earlier generations had been taught to accept, even if implicitly. Perhaps in the past teens felt that society held a specific place for them and their task was simply to find out what that was by undergoing an "identity crisis" of some kind, as Erickson (1968) postulated. Instead, with the rise of a plethora of potential courses of action, teens learn that they will, throughout their lives, continually be called on to choose between "possible worlds." They have witnessed their parents and other adults in their lives changing their minds about mates, careers, and home locations, after all. Teens therefore have come to expect that while intimate relationships may offer fulfillment, such satisfaction may be ephemeral. Relationships are pursued as a part of a self-reflexive process in this context and may be understood in terms of what Giddens (1991) characterized as a "pure relationship":

[Pure relationships] offer the opportunity for the development of trust based on voluntary commitments and an intensified intimacy. Where achieved and relatively secure, such trust is psychologically stabilizing, because of the strong connections between basic trust and the reliability of the caretaking figures. (p. 186)

. . . The "pure" relationship, Giddens argued, is justified not in reference to one's kinship or other social ties but in reference to romantic love. Indeed, it is considered "pure" because it is no longer constituted within the social context of kin and community. Persons are no longer constrained in their selection of romantic partners by the social mores of their families or communities. Instead, relationships are sought out and maintained solely for the gratifications they provide to the persons involved. Therefore, these relationships of modernity, Giddens argued, are always organized in relation to the reflexive self who asks, "how is this relationship fulfilling to *me*?" With the lowering of sexual inhibitions through the social transformations of the last four decades, sex has come to be more closely aligned with contemporary concepts of intimacy and even identity and thus is a key aspect of the "pure" relationship. . . .

The participants in the relations experience a satisfaction in relationships that have no reference to their peer group or social status and may be considered more individualistic as a result. Moreover, it is not a complete lack of commitment but a tenuous and ephemeral commitment that links the participants in the Internet date and provides satisfaction for its participants. In this context, it is perhaps not surprising that it does not matter whether or not the participant in the relationship is accessible in "real life," and why in some cases such connection is studiously avoided, as was illustrated in Elizabeth's avoidance of the male Net friend who wanted to speak with her on the telephone. The lack of accessibility fulfills a function in keeping such individualized expressions of intimacy and self-gratification from impinging on one's local, lived experience. In essence, the relationship has many of the benefits of the "pure" relationship but without the restraints of a commitment of time or emotional resources. In this sense it might be said to be a postmodern "pure" relationship: one comprised of self-reflexivity in which experimentation and self-construction are central. Unlike adult participants in chat rooms, teens are limited in their ability to parlay an emotional tie forged on the Net into something that would have material consequences in the local context. Thus, the relationships that emerge transcend time and space to deliver satisfaction through the medium of a disembodied, "surface" communication, allowing the teen to feel connected to others while allowing them to experience affirmation in an environment that does not risk their current social position.

◆ *Conclusion*

What, then, might be the implications for a teen community on the Internet in this environment? I have argued that whereas teen dating relationships in chat rooms mirror the relationships of "real life" in their adherence to norms of heterosexism and sexism, we also see a difference in the role of trust and intimacy in these relations when compared with those of the past and in "real life." Internet dating, despite its possibilities for verbal intimacy and egalitarian relationships, is in actuality more frequently employed for fleeting, "fun" relationships that hold little consequence in the "real" lives of the teens who engage in them beyond self-gratification. Further, the emphasis on "fun" and inconsequentiality suggests that the norms of conduct for teens online may be localized to such an extent that teens feel no need to consider how their own participation might influence others. Because the focus in the Internet date is on

individual gratification, teens experience no sense of obligations to the person with whom they are ephemerally committed; as Elizabeth noted, if a person fails to show up at the preappointed time, there are no consequences. Of course, this assumes that both parties agree to the lack of seriousness with which such relations are entered into. Denial of a more intimate connection is not out of maliciousness; those who believe that they are experiencing more than simply a "fun," ephemeral connection are assumed to be not "playing by the rules," as it were.

Teens participating in Internet dating also seem to feel no need to justify their actions among their "real-life" peers, as they might for other, more widely observable actions. In the Net environment, teens are unmoored from local peer groups in which so much of identity is constituted among this age group. Peers are only involved when the participant chooses to involve them, either by conversing about one's individual experiences online or, on frequent occasions, watching over one's shoulder as a friend converses with others online. Most frequently, however, teens online experience themselves as individuals removed, to some extent, from their local social context. As autonomous persons in interaction, teens are like the adult counterparts to Giddens's (1991) "pure" relationship in their search for connection yet are very different in that trust is not a factor in the relationships achieved, nor must they risk "authentic" self-revelation to achieve gratification.

It is also worth noting that much like the teen dating experiences of the midcentury, there is a noticeable absence of other classes and races beyond the Caucasian, middle-class norm of the Net. Participation in teen chat rooms is increasingly forbidden in school and community center contexts, and thus young people with limited means are less likely than their middle-class counterparts to have access to the technology.

This research, therefore, leaves us with several more questions regarding the future of the Internet as a possible site for community building, particularly among teens. If these postmodern "pure" relationships might be considered a youthful precursor to the more serious, "pure" relationships its participants will presumably enter on adulthood, one wonders: will authenticity in the lived environment appear less—or perhaps more—important as a characteristic of these meaningful relationships as a result? I think the fact that the "other" in the relationship is hardly considered, or is assumed to share one's level of commitment and self-gratification, is telling. Teens in chat rooms, after all, experience themselves as a gathering of unconnected individuals, seeking others (or usually one other) with whom to converse and thereby achieve gratification. Perhaps these individualistic relationships underscore the increased localization of caring, thus implying the increased lack of any communal sense of identity. Teen chat rooms become a space outside the stream of everyday life, a space for the development of the ideal "pure" relationship of the contemporary age: one with imagined intimacy but no need for trust or commitment; thus one that is fulfilling and liberating, ultimately and primarily, to the self. In this sense, then, the self-gratification of dating on the Net can be seen as a natural outgrowth of current cultural conditions. The technology does not enable a wide-scale social change toward greater self-reflexivity but allows this already occurring practice to find a new avenue for its expression and development.

◆ Notes

1. I serve as Associate Researcher on the Lilly Endowment funded project, "Media, Meaning, and the Lifecourse," which is under the direction of Stewart M. Hoover at the Center for Mass Media Research, University of Colorado. I gratefully acknowledge the funding for the research in this chapter, which has been provided by the Lilly Endowment and by a dissertation fellowship from the Louisville Institute.

2. For an illustration of warnings in the popular press, see, for example, Rozen, L. (1997, November). Undercover on the Internet. *Good Housekeeping*, pp. 76-78, 82.

3. It should be noted, however, that while the teens in my study by and large noted preferences for the teen chat rooms, many of them had experimented with the more racy adult chat rooms, as well.

References ◆

Bailey, B. (1988). *From front porch to back seat*. Baltimore: Johns Hopkins University Press.

Baym, N. K. (1995). The emergence of community in computer-mediated communication. In S. G. Jones (Ed.), *Cybersociety: Computer-mediated communication and community* (pp. 138-163). Thousand Oaks, CA: Sage.

Blumer, H. (1933). *The movies and conduct*. New York: Macmillan.

Brown, L., & Gilligan, C. (1992). *Meeting at the crossroads: Women's psychology and girls' development*. Cambridge, MA: Harvard University Press.

Erickson, E. (1968). *Identity: Youth and crisis*. New York: Norton.

Fass, P. (1977). *The damned and the beautiful: American youth in the 1920s*. New York: Oxford University Press.

Friend, R. (1993). Choices, not closets: Heterosexism and homophobia in schools. In L. Weis & M. Fine (Eds.), *Beyond silenced voices: Class, race, and gender in United States schools* (pp. 209-235). Albany: State University of New York Press.

Giddens, A. (1991). *Modernity and self-identity: Self and society in the late modern age*. Palo Alto, CA: Stanford University Press.

Illouz, E. (1997). *Consuming the romantic Utopia: Love and cultural contradictions of capitalism*. Berkeley: University of California Press.

Jones, S. (1995). Understanding community in the information age. In S. G. Jones (Ed.),

Cybersociety: Computer-mediated communication and community (pp. 10-35). Thousand Oaks, CA: Sage.

Kiesler, S., Siegel, J., & McGuire, T. (1984). Social psychological aspect of computer-mediated communication. *American Psychologist, 39*(10), 1123-1134.

Kramarae, C. (1995). A backstage critique of virtual reality. In S. G. Jones (Ed.), *Cybersociety: Computer-mediated communication and community* (pp. 36-56). Thousand Oaks, CA: Sage.

Modell, J. (1989). *Into one's own: From youth to adulthood in the United States 1920-1975.* Berkeley: University of California Press.

Rakow, L. (1988). Gendered technology, gendered practice. *Critical Studies in Mass Communication, 5*(1), 57-70.

Rakow, L., & Navarro, V. (1993, June). Remote mothering and the parallel shift: Women meet the cellular telephone. *Critical Studies in Mass Communication, 10*(2), 144-157.

Rheingold, H. (1991). *The virtual community: Homesteading on the electronic frontier.* Reading, MA: Addison-Wesley.

Rozen, L. (1997, November). Undercover on the Internet. *Good Housekeeping, 225*(10), 76-78, 82.

Seabrook, J. (1997). *Deeper: My two-year odyssey in cyberspace.* New York: Simon & Schuster.

Yin, R. (1994). *Case study research: Design and methods* (2nd ed.). Thousand Oaks, CA: Sage.

69

STAKING THEIR CLAIM
Women, Electronic Networking, and Training in Asia

◆ Rhona O. Bautista

◆ Do Women Have Access?

The new information technology industry is one of the fastest growing industries in Asia. Information technologies do indeed pave the way for people to exchange everything from recipes to summaries of the Human Development Report swiftly and without the use of intermediaries. The crucial question for us here, however, is how women are benefiting from such a revolutionary technology as the Internet. In this chapter we ask what are women's experiences with this technology, and what are the impediments to women's access and training in Asia?

◆ Women, Poverty, and Access to the Internet in Asia

In the last quarter of 1997 and the beginning of 1998, the tide of growth and economic aggression in Asia completely ebbed away, resulting in a deep

NOTE: From *Women @ Internet*, 2nd ed., edited by Wendy Harcourt, 1999, London: Zed Books. Reprinted by permission.

financial crisis in the region extending to the "tiger" economies of Singapore, Hong Kong, Taiwan, South Korea, and Japan. This has led to a general worsening of living conditions for women in the region.

Most people in South Asia are affected by human poverty. The Asian region has the largest number of people in economic poverty: 515 million. Together, South Asia, East Asia, South-East Asia, and the Pacific have more than 950 million of the 1.3 billion economic poor worldwide, of which 70 percent are women. According to the United Nations Development Programme (UNDP), in Asia "poverty has a woman's face." Women are too often disempowered and burdened by the strains of productive work, the birth and care of children, and other household and community responsibilities (UNDP, 1997). In the last 20 years, the number of rural women living in absolute poverty has risen by nearly 50 percent.

Despite this, or precisely because of this, women in Asia continue to work for social reforms and for the promotion of women's economic, political, and cultural status. Women's groups are organized around issues of resource access, property rights, inheritance laws, and expansion of public and private rights—particularly reproductive rights. For women in Asia, recognizing the value of new access to resources also means access to new information technology (IT).

The economic and social potentials of IT are also now being recognized by governments across Asia. In Singapore, during the Fourth ASEAN Forum in 1996, government ministers responsible for information agreed that ASEAN should seize the opportunities presented by the new media, the Internet in particular.

This enthusiasm, however, has not led to access for the greater part of the population. Usage of IT in Asia is limited to private individuals from the higher income bracket working in colleges and universities, government agencies, telecommunication companies, banks or financial institutions, and business firms (*Philippine Daily Inquirer*, 15 May 1996).

Access to the Internet is particularly difficult for women. Potentially the Internet may be the most powerful tool for accessing and communicating information, but it can also be alienating for women who have neither equipment nor proper training. As it is, the majority of Asia's women still do not have the resources to connect with other women using the old technology such as the telephone. The gap in access to IT is even wider between countries with infrastructural deficiencies. The problem is not only access to technology but also involves factors related to widespread poverty, organization, training in different aspects of information, financial support, and language accessibility.

Fighting for Space ◆ on the Internet

In 1996, only 3.4 percent of the worldwide number of computers connected to the Internet were in Asia. It has been estimated that there are approximately 45 million users worldwide but most of these are in developed countries where communication infrastructure makes new types of communication readily available even in the household. In contrast, 80 percent of the world still lacks basic telecommunications facilities, and two-thirds of the world's population have never made a phone call. Internet access is twelve times more expensive in Indonesia than it is in Italy, and 95 percent of all Internet users are in Europe and North America (Sandhya and Natesan, 1996).

When women enter cyberspace, their participation and articulation are also hindered by the dominant form of interaction and debate used on the Internet and in e-mail. On the Internet, male perspectives and voices dominate over women's, who have neither been taught nor trained to use this medium (Paterson, 1996; Spender, 1995).

Even in a rich and technologically advanced Asian country like Japan, women are far behind when it comes to Internet access. According to the Asia-Japan Network (AJN), an e-mail network founded by women activists who were inspired by the success of the women's electronic networking initiatives during the Fourth U.N. World Conference on Women, very few women's groups and nongovernmental organizations (NGOs) in Japan have e-mail, much less Internet connection. Lack of computers, high cost of hook-up and maintenance, the predominant use of English on e-mail, and the lack of resources and a workforce for translation were cited as the primary reasons for this situation. According to AJN, Internet hook-up in Japan costs US$3,000 and the monthly fee is US$2,000. Lack of training and know-how for the use of electronic mail and the Internet also contributes to their problems.[1]

In Pakistan, computers are being used for desktop publishing in the worlds of high finance, advertising, and education. Former Prime Minister Benazir Bhutto, as part of her literacy programme, opened computer learning centres in the country and many private urban schools have computer classes from the primary levels. Access to databases is rapidly increasing and the electronic newspaper has made its appearance, but Internet and e-mail are still very much a tool for the elite, and very few women's groups have access to it.

In India, all electronic media, ranging from satellite television to e-mail and the Internet, are accessible only to the privileged classes and cater almost exclusively to their predominantly male information and entertainment needs and desires. In Bangladesh, the cost of hooking up to the Internet could feed a family for a year.

In the Philippines, despite the much-touted economic gains in the last five years, access to a telephone line is still prohibitively expensive. Given a mandated minimum daily wage of US$6.36, a telephone line costing US$200 or an Internet hook-up amounting to US$200 is beyond the reach of even the middle class. For the average two-income Filipino household, the computer is still too expensive. It is a luxury item for most families and access to it is work-related. The Philippine computer density is one computer for every 50 individuals (1:50) while other economically developed Asian countries have a ratio of one computer for every 10 persons (1:10).

What all these figures and statistics reveal is that the 'Infobahn's' traffic flow is heavier on its North-to-South lane. In the South, access to the Internet is primarily available to the traditional elite who are educated, urban-based, and largely male.

The Isis IT Experience ◆

Even given these difficulties, information plays a vital role in the struggle to promote and enhance women's status in society (Villanueva, 1997). Such a role will become even more important as Asia faces the reality of new computer technologies and their impact on people's lives. But how have women in the region actually utilized these technological advancements in their works?

The experiences and examples of women's engagement in new technologies in the region are steadily increasing (Bautista, 1996). For women globally, new technologies have become an important element in the women's movement. Our own experience in Isis International[2] mirrors most women's organizations' experience in using these new technologies. Isis was introduced to e-mail in 1992. Then, our use of this potentially dynamic and powerful tool was mainly as electronic "postwoman." After six years, we have developed projects and campaigns around new technologies (Bautista, 1995).[3]

Isis further strengthened its electronic communication capability in 1993 in its effort to provide service for the various programmes and women's groups with more efficiency and speed. Since then we have participated in training and workshops on e-mail, the first of these organized by the South-East Asia Forum for Development Alternatives (SEAFDA) in Kuala Lumpur. This was followed by the Asian Women's Policy and Technical Workshop, organized by the APC's Women's Networking Support Program (WNSP) in January 1994 in New Delhi.[4] . . .

◆ *Electronic Conferencing and Resourcing*

. . . In Isis International-Manila, together with the E-mail Centre, a communication service provider in Manila and a member of the APC, we established the Asia-Women list serve in February 1996. Asia-Women is used for disseminating information on current issues affecting women in Asia and the Pacific region. It has about 60 subscribers to date, mostly women's organizations and documentation centres in Asia and the Pacific region. It also features the Isis monthly bulletin, *Women Envision*.

We also facilitate an electronic forum called Asia gendermedia, set up as a virtual link to the Gender and Media Policy Conference held in Antipolo, Philippines, in July 1997.[5] Asia-gendermedia now provides about 65 other media, information, and communication organizations worldwide, the majority coming from the region, with a summary of the conference discussions and subsequent resolutions and actions. Using this experience as a model, we are opening other electronic conferences along our advocacy themes of food security, globalization, and violence against women.

Our website, opened in January 1998, contains original feature articles by women; news of issues, campaigns, action alerts, post-Beijing updates and announcements; a listing of books published by Isis; and links to women's resources on the Internet with an Asia and Pacific focus.

Isis is also active in advocating the use of electronic technology and training women's groups in the Philippines. In 1997, we organized three forums and a training workshop with the support of Woman-Health Philippines, E-mail Centre, and the APC's WNSP. The forums focused on Emerging Information Economies and Women's Responses, while the training was on e-mail, surfing the Internet, and basic webpage construction.

In April 1998, Isis organized a workshop in Manila, Philippines, on Electronic Networking and Resourcing: Strategies for Women's Information Centres. The exchange is geared towards developing the capacity of women's information centres for electronic resource sharing and networking using new information and communication technologies such as e-mail and the Internet. At the end of the workshop, the participants agreed to set up a pilot website project called Asian Women's Resource Exchange (AWORC).

AWORC will be a collaborative project geared towards building sustainable electronic resource sharing among women's information centres in Asia and promoting Internet literacy and activism among individual women and women's organizations. It will be a source of information on women's issues and the women's movements in Asia. AWORC will highlight contemporary and critical issues for women in the region and pay special attention to areas where there is a dearth of information about women. It will be proactive, providing information that may be valuable for women in the future. It will also serve as a communication channel among women's organizations in this region and support their advocacies. The group identified some key contemporary issues for women in Asia:

◆ Violence against women;

◆ Status of women;

◆ Globalization;

◆ Women's access to information, focusing on gaps among different sectors;

◆ Women's health and reproductive rights;

◆ Issues related to the Council of the Status of Women (CSW);

◆ Female children;

◆ Elderly women;

◆ Women and the environment;

◆ Vision of the women's movement in Asia.

AWORC's main feature will be a multilingual search system of databases and other resources which are housed in individual centres. Other features include a description of participating women's information centres and agencies; a bulletin board where activities, conferences, and other announcements can be posted; electronic hosting of campaigns by Asian women's organizations; and networks and links to sites, list serves, and other resources relevant to women in Asia. Another feature that may be developed in the future is a directory of women's organizations in the region.

The six organizations from Japan, Korea, Malaysia, and the Philippines that participated in the Manila workshop will collaborate during the initial stage of website development. They comprise two Women's Regional Information Centres (WRICs), two national WRICs, one academic library, and one online communications NGO that volunteered the host site. The number of participating organizations will be expanded in accordance with stages of development agreed on at the workshop.

Other activities envisaged around the development of the AWORC website include a skill-sharing workshop for online information access by women's groups, information experts in women's groups, and technical support by women.

Asian Women ◆ Staking Their Claim

Recognizing the potential of the new information technologies, Asian NGOs and women's organizations in particular continue to explore ways to tap these technologies to enhance their organizing, information, and advocacy work. Moreover, across the development of these technologies "cyberfeminist" theorists are emerging, speaking, and gathering. They reshape, redefine, and reclaim the new electronic technologies for women.

In Thailand, a group of NGOs—including women's organizations—formed a cooperative to share an e-mail box with assistance from Computer Communication Access. This cooperative is now using a bulletin board system that supports Thai and English for communication.

In Japan, the group Women's On-line Media (WOM)[6] has a home page which provides information not typically available in official publications and government announcements on the current status of Japanese women, as well as assisting in creating a network among different women's groups scattered throughout Japan.[7] WOM also provided information on the Fourth World Conference on Women, and publicized its activities on the NetNews and via its WWW home page.

In Singapore, there is Women-Connect-Asia, an electronic network created by four women's organizations to help businesswomen living and working in Asia. Women-Connect-Asia's website features a directory through which women in the region and beyond can offer their products and services to one another.[8]

Most women's groups in Asia enjoy the services provided by the networks of the APC. APC disseminates substantial information through its conferences and Gopher relating to development, environment, women's rights, violence against women, and other issues. APC's networks are venues for women's groups and individuals, spaces for sharing information, activities related to U.N. conferences, and activities and their work in general.

◆ *The Way Forward*

The way forward for women in the region is to address the lack of access and training. Access to information, and to the tools to define and broadcast information, are critical issues for women in Asia. Some of the ways being proposed to help women gain wider access to information and information technologies include increasing support for local training initiatives that are gender-sensitive and "hands-on"; developing user-friendly motivational training and educational manuals in appropriate languages; and providing local user support for women. This approach is based on the fact that only a minority of women are online, and these are mostly middle-class, educated, and city-based women. Providing adequate information and public access to the Internet (through personal mailboxes, for example) will help to bridge the gap between women who have access and those who do not.

The Isis Resource Centre can play a crucial role in providing individuals, women's groups, and other organizations with access to electronic and print information globally and regionally. We are working to make our resource accessible by Internet with e-mail boxes available for resource centre members and users. In response to the diverse ways in which women in the region access and move information, in the next three years Isis is expanding its use of ICTs. We see this as complementary to our main communication medium of print and our advocacy of women's issues. As well as offering public access, Isis will continue a programme for developing the capacity of women to organize in the field of electronic communication through training and research.

Despite the many obstacles and unfavourable conditions that restrict their access to electronic media, women have shown themselves to be excellent networkers, extending solidarity across national and global boundaries via electronic mail, print, and real face-to-face encounters. One can only imagine the unleashing of the creative energies of women in the service of communication and progress when the barriers to women's full participation in the new information technologies are dismantled.

Notes ◆

1. These were cited by participants in a forum organized by the Asia-Japan Network and the Asia-Japan Women's Resource Centre on 27 October 1996, to which two Isis staff were invited as speakers.

2. A feminist organization that promotes communication, cooperation, and networking among women and groups working with women, and has a vision of developing information and resourcing among women in our region.

3. Isis International-Manila is an international nongovernmental women's organization founded in 1974 to promote the empowerment of women through information sharing communication and networking. Isis's network includes individuals and organizations in 150 countries.

4. Thirty-one representatives of women's NGOs and several other organizations representing eight countries passed a resolution for the Beijing conference in September 1995. The participants agreed to promote e-mail as a tool in intervention during the conference. The group also recommended the need for technical resources, including service providers that will organize training programmes. This will enable more women to use e-mail technology.

5. Twenty-five media practitioners and activists gathered in Antipolo, Philippines, from 30 July to 2 August 1997 to discuss policy recommendations at the Regional Conference on Gender and Communication Policy. The conference coordinators, World Association for

Christian Communication (WACC) and Isis International-Manila, extended their welcome to delegates from Australia, Canada, China, India, Indonesia, Japan, Korea, Malaysia, Philippines, Sri Lanka, and Thailand. Each country presented an overview of their women and media situation.

6. WOM is a nonprofit, independent organization founded in August 1995 by seven creative Japanese women. It counts among its diverse membership company employees, homemakers, and students.

7. http://www.suehiro.nakano,tokyo.ip/WOM/English/WOM/index.html.

8. http://www.women-connect-asia.

◆ *References*

Bautista, R. (1995). "Linking Women Worldwide," *Annual Report of Isis International*. Isis International, Manila.

Bautista, R. (1996). "Global Information Through Computer Networking Technology Workshop," paper presented at the U.N. Conference on Global Information Through Computer Networking Technology, New York, 26-28 June 1996.

Paterson, N. (1996). "Cyberfeminism," *Fireweed*, No. 54.

Sandhya R. and N. Ch. Natesan (1996). "Internet: Threat or Opportunity for India?" *Media Asia*, Vol. 23, No. 2.

Spender, D. (1995). *Nattering on the Net: Women, Power and Cyberspace*. Spinifex, Melbourne.

United Nations Development Programme (UNDP) (1997). *Human Development Report*. Oxford University Press, New York.

Villanueva, P. (1997). "Wielding New Technologies." *Women Envision*, No. 45 (May).

70

THE CHEROKEE INDIANS AND THE INTERNET

◆ Ellen L. Arnold and Darcy C. Plymire

Current use of the internet by the Cherokee Indians reflects many aspects of the historical situation of the Cherokees since the early 1800s. The Cherokee people, who called themselves *Ani '-Yun 'wiya*, or the "Principal People," originally occupied approximately 135,000 square miles in parts of what are now eight southeastern states. By the early 1800s, their territory had been drastically reduced through treaties and other actions by the U.S. government. One of the so-called Five Civilized Tribes of the Southeast, the Cherokees were quick to adopt many of the ways of the Europeans. In 1821, Sequoyah created the Cherokee Syllabary, which enabled their language to be written, and the Cherokee people quickly gained a greater degree of literacy than their Euro-American contemporaries. They drafted their own constitution, published the first Indian newspaper (the *Cherokee Phoenix*), and established the town of New Echota in Georgia, which served as both a seat of government and an economic centre for a thriving independent nation.

Under pressure from Euro-American settlers seeking gold and land, the U.S. Congress made plans to remove the Cherokee people from their land.

NOTE: From *Web Studies: Rewriting Media Studies for the Digital Age*, edited by David Gauntlett, 2000, New York: Oxford University Press. Copyright © 2000. Reprinted by permission of Edward Arnold Ltd..

Progressive Cherokees, proponents of Americanization, fought in the American courts to force the U.S. government to honour its treaties with the Cherokee Nation, arguing its sovereign status. Many traditionals opposed assimilation into American society, yet the Cherokee Memorials—eloquent documents arguing against removal—demonstrated that even the progressive leaders who drafted them wished to preserve a distinct cultural identity as well as their newly acquired status as "civilized." When the Cherokees lost their battle in the courts, 16,000 of them were forced by the U.S. Army to relocate 1,000 miles to the west to Indian Territory. On this infamous Trail of Tears, called *Nunadautsun't* ("the trail where we cried") in the Cherokee language, more than 4,000 Cherokees died.

Several hundred Cherokee people, mostly traditionals, remained in the east, hiding from settlers and soldiers. Eventually they re-established themselves and, in 1848, were formally recognized by the U.S. government as the Eastern Band of Cherokee Indians. The Eastern Band now numbers about 12,000 enrolled members, the majority of whom live on the Qualla Boundary in western North Carolina, a 56,000-square-acre portion of their original homeland which has its seat in the town of Cherokee. This land, purchased by Will Thomas, the adopted White son of a Cherokee leader, and presented to the Cherokees in the late nineteenth century, is now held in trust for the Cherokee people by the U.S. government and is administered as a reservation. Like other reservations, Qualla Boundary has a complex status as a semi-sovereign nation, exempt from the jurisdiction of state governments in most matters, yet subject to a great deal of control by federal government. The Western Band of Cherokees, known officially as the Cherokee Nation of Oklahoma, now occupies a jurisdictional service area of 4,480,000 square acres with a capital at Tahlequah, and has 170,000 enrolled members. Together Cherokees form one of the two largest tribal groups in the USA.

The question of assimilation remains relevant to Cherokee Indians today. The construction and use of the official websites of the Eastern Band (www.Cherokee-nc.com) and the Cherokee Nation of Oklahoma (www.Cherokee.org) reflect many elements of the historical relationship of the Cherokee Nation to the nation and government of the USA. The Oklahoma site primarily serves its community by providing links to human services, political news and organizations, and cultural and historical information. The Eastern Band site provides access to cultural and historical information as well, but because of its proximity to the popular Smoky Mountains National Park and the Blue Ridge Parkway, the Eastern Band has also been able to use its website to help build a thriving tourist economy. Observing the websites as outsiders, we suggest that they are skillfully designed aspects of increasingly successful political and economic efforts to use the dominant paradigm and its technologies to protect and preserve the unique cultural heritage and identity of the Cherokee people, and at the same time to expand the nation's control over its own affairs and its influence on American culture.

The Debates ◆

Cherokee use of the internet must be considered in the light of wider debates about whether computer technology and the internet medium help to preserve or tend to destroy indigenous cultures and traditions. Mark Trahant (1996), a professional scholar and member of the Shoshone-Bannock tribe of Idaho, speculates that the internet might be a medium particularly well suited to teaching in Indian communities, because it is more like traditional oral and pictographic forms of communication than are the typical written forms of the dominant culture. The imagery and fluidity of the Web, like pictographs, allows users to enter where they like and continue in whatever direction they choose; like the story-telling tradition, in which both teller and audience participate in the exchange of stories and their meaning, the Web undermines both the power of the individual author and the presumed linearity of history. The stories told on the Web, like the stories told in pictographs or oral narration, change according to the teller, listener, or user.

According to Trahant, internet use by Native Americans is on the rise. He speculates that growing use of the internet by tribal groups will have several beneficial consequences. Since the medium requires less capital outlay than does print media, Native groups might get their perspectives on political and social issues into circulation more easily. Second, tribes might use the sites to teach language and history, as do the Navajos and the Cherokees. Third, Trahant states that "one of the oldest battles in the Native American press is over who controls information" (19). Print media may give tribal governments or federal agencies the power of censorship, while the internet grants individuals a greater voice. Finally, individuals might use the net to communicate with one another, through newsgroups and e-mail discussion lists, to build the bonds of community across time and space.

Trahant's high hopes for the new medium mirror the utopian tenor of much mainstream scholarship on the internet. For example, Paul Levinson (1997) contends that "telecommunication of text via computer is . . . a revolution in writing or authorship" (126), since anyone with access to a computer and modem is potentially an author, publisher, and distributor of texts. Though the cost of personal computers may still be high for many individuals or groups, the technology is far more accessible than is the publishing industry. That accessibility virtually eliminates gatekeepers, such as editors and publishers, and allows a far greater diversity of ideas to enter circulation. Based on these characteristics of the internet, many have come to

view the medium as a virtual democratic utopia. We agree that the implications of online publishing do seem to have revolutionary potential. If Michel Foucault (1980) is correct in stating that the producers of knowledge have power over those who are the subjects of knowledge, then the established media will typically produce relationships of power that privilege those who already hold positions of social power in capitalist societies. The internet, which opens the publishing field to groups who lack capital and power, can in theory allow marginalized individuals and groups to produce their own knowledge, put it into circulation and, as a result, gain a greater measure of social power.

In addition, proponents such as Sherry Turkle (1997) claim that "on the Internet . . . people [may] recast their identity in terms of multiple windows and parallel lives" (72). Theoretically, one may produce an online identity that does not correspond to one's real-life race, class, or gender, or one may produce multiple identities, all of which may be in circulation concurrently. This may make the internet a particularly effective medium for negotiating the complex, and often conflicting, demands of both American and tribal cultural identities. According to the cybertopian worldview, "the Internet de-emphasizes hierarchical political associations, degrading gender roles and ethnic designations, and rigid categories of class relationships found in traditional, visually based and geographically bound communities" (Ebo, 1998: 3). Communities online, therefore, have the potential to create meaningful social groups that do not merely reproduce inequalities among real-life social groups. If that is the case, then the medium might be a force for building more egalitarian communities by breaking down race, gender, and class barriers.

The idea of virtual community has been subjected to necessary scrutiny, however. Laura Gurak (1997) argues that while online aggregations are not the same as communities bounded by time and place, the internet can foster rhetorical communities united by a common ethos. Others, like Shawn Wilbur (1997), are more sceptical. He contends that, at worst, virtual community is "the illusion of a community where there are no real people and no real communication" (14). Likewise, Derek Foster (1997) asserts that the medium "allows each individual user an equal voice, or at least an equal opportunity to speak" (23). Yet, he wonders if the ease of communication in cyberspace actually translates into a sense of community—"a set of voluntary, social and reciprocal relations that are bound together by an immutable 'we-feeling'" (25).

For Indians, many objections are more specifically cultural. *New York Times* writer Elizabeth Cohen (1997) summarizes the concerns of Native spokespeople she interviewed that "websites may not always represent the people and tribes they say they do, and that certain sacred and guarded cultural knowledge could be misunderstood or misused if it ends up on the Web" (2); she especially decries "'cyber-shamans' [who] feign tribal affiliation to sell various so-called native goods and services" (3). Lakota scholar Craig Howe (1999) maintains that, because land and geographic location are fundamental to specific tribal identities, "the pervasive universalism and individualism of the World Wide Web is antithetical to the particular localities, societies, moralities, and experiences that constitute tribalism" (7). Or, as Dakota/Salish novelist Philip Red Eagle (1999) put it in an online discussion of the subject, "Community is about responsibility to a specific group of people who practice culture with one another." Jerry Mander (1991), a non-Native writer, insists that the computer destroys ways of thinking and acting that are fundamental to oral cultures, and inculcates values counter to Indian traditions. Because computers rely on an information exchange model of communication, they contribute to a worldview that reduces the natural world to resources to be managed and controlled, at the expense of an embodied interrelationship with the world that is characteristic of traditional indigenous lifeways.

The internet also may reproduce rather than challenge social inequalities. Though users cannot see each other, they may not have abandoned all judgements on the basis of race, class, gender, and ethnicity. If members of socially marginalized groups appear equal on the internet, it may simply be that they can successfully masquerade as white and/or male. Second, while individuals and minority groups may more easily "publish" on the internet, readership is limited at best. Thus knowledge and ideas that challenge the status quo may remain marginalized. Third, access to the internet is not equally distributed along lines of race, class, gender, and ethnicity. Demographic statistics show that the majority of internet users are college educated, affluent, white, and male (though the balances are slowly changing— see www.newmediastudies.com/stats.htm). Thus the democratic potential of the internet has hardly been realized.

Wolf (1998) notes that studies she surveyed on internet usage by minority groups make no note of use by Native Americans. As in many other disciplines, research and critical attention to Indian use of the internet is ghettoized, limited primarily to studies specifically about Native Americans; such a practice reproduces what many have called "the vanishing Indian syndrome" by implying that Indians no longer exist as a vital and influential part of the American population. In addition, start-up costs of internet use (i.e., a computer and a modem) are still prohibitively high for many Native Americans. Native Americans remain the poorest minority in the USA, and many do not even have access to the telephone service (Yawakie, 1997). Yet, internet sites for and about Indians abound. An Indian Circle webring (www.indiancircle.com) provided by the Western Band site lists the more than 550 federally recognized Indian tribes of the continental USA and Alaska, 100 of whom have active websites. Searching for "Cherokee Indians" in a search engine such as AltaVista yields thousands of pages.

◆ *The Websites*

The sheer number of sites pertaining to Cherokee Indians makes a general survey impractical, so we chose to limit our study to the official homepages of the Eastern and Western Bands. Both homepages are works in progress; while we were studying them, design and content changed, and we assume that those changes will continue. In addition, there are many "unofficial" sites for and about the Cherokees. Many of them are interesting and informative, but some appropriate the trappings of Cherokee identity while spreading unreliable information. Thus our study does not represent a comprehensive survey of information on the Cherokees.

Both homepages are produced by outside organizations under the direction of tribal members, but the two pages offer striking contrasts. The Oklahoma page (www.cherokee.org) is designed primarily for Cherokee users and sympathetic outsiders. Entitled "The Official Site of the Cherokee Nation," it offers access to tribal government pages with links to educational and human services, information on community development, finance, and genealogy, as well as news, politics, culture, and history. News comes in the form of press releases issued by tribal government and items from current and past issues of the *Cherokee Advocate,* the modern descendant of the *Cherokee Phoenix.* The Western Band offers links to sites as diverse as the Alpha Bet Jewish Day School and the Department of the Interior but, surprisingly, this Cherokee Nation homepage does not mention the Eastern Band.

The Eastern Band's homepage, called simply *Cherokee* (www.cherokee-nc.com), with a line at the bottom of the page identifying it as "The official homepage of the Cherokee Nation," links the user directly to information on tourism and gaming (casino gambling) on the Cherokee Reservation and in the Great Smoky Mountains National Park. Attractions on the reservation mirror those in the surrounding park—fishing, hiking, and camping—but the town of Cherokee also offers visitors shopping, museums, and a chance to gamble at Harrah's Cherokee Casino. Like the Western Band, the Eastern Cherokee site provides a link to press releases, but those documents, too, offer a contrast.

Whereas the Western Cherokees' press releases provide information on politics and current events, the Eastern Band's press releases inform the reader about coming attractions. While the Western Band homepage makes no mention of the Eastern Band, the Eastern Band site now links to the Western Band, although for a number of years it did not, reflecting the geographical and historical division of the nation. However, the addition of this link in late 1999 suggests that the Web may indeed have the potential to bring these two communities closer together.

The contrast between the press releases raises an interesting point about the internet and freedom of the press. Trahant (1996) argues that the internet can help Indians avoid censorship by corrupt tribal governments. Recent press releases from Oklahoma reveal that the tribal government in Tahlequah is in disarray. Information on corruption at the highest levels of government is freely available on the internet through the tribe's own newspapers. On the other hand, the North Carolina press releases are prosaic, and no part of this site offers the exchange of hard news or information on politics. The site functions, in effect, as an agent of impression management. The primarily non-Native visitors to the *Cherokee-NC* site will see a limited view of the Cherokee people and their community.

Tribal member Dave Redman, who created the North Carolina website in 1997, confirms that this homepage is intended for use by tourists, and that tourists are indeed the primary users (personal communication,

1999). Its goal is to expand tourism and advance economic growth on the reservation. Gaming is the lynchpin of the Cherokees' development strategy, as it has been on other reservations. Like other tribes, many Cherokees view gaming as "simply a profitable business, upon which economically dormant Indian nations can regain long lost territory, cultural prerogatives and community structures built on respect" (Johnson, 1995: 18). Capital acquisition, however, is not an end in itself for the Cherokee Nation in North Carolina. The proceeds of gaming are reinvested in the community. Projects funded by gaming revenues include a new youth centre, which provides access to computers and the internet, and a community computer centre. Other beneficiaries include a new Cultural Resources Division, a newly redesigned museum, a language preservation programme (which records native speakers of Cherokee language on CD-ROM), and the Cherokee school system. A link from the Eastern Band's homepage brings the user to a Cherokee elementary school site and the homepages of Cherokee fifth graders. Each child's page contains his or her picture, their name in Cherokee, and a short autobiographical description.

The elementary school homepage is interesting on several levels. The children's homepages might be viewed as a marketing ploy. If the Cherokee use their Web pages to sell themselves to tourists, then why not use the words and faces of their children to enhance the appeal? Yet there seems to be much more to the school pages than marketing. The Nation's homepage and most of the pages to which it is linked consist of text with a few pictures. They offer convenient access to information that could be provided in brochures and other print formats. The elementary school's homepage is far more complex, a multimedia page with exciting graphics, moving pictures, and sound. For example, a visitor can click on a "culture" option to hear a Native storyteller recite Cherokee legends in English with Cherokee translations.

The elementary school homepage reflects a process of building physical relationships among Cherokee children and the elders of the community through a restoration of the story-telling tradition and the Cherokee language. Thus links are reforged between children who are just beginning to learn the language and their few remaining elders for whom Cherokee is their first language, a connection broken by decades of Indian boarding school experience which forbade the use of Native languages. At the same time, parents and extended family are drawn to take advantage of internet access at the local public library and the planned community computer centre in order to experience the results of the children's efforts. The oral tradition and language translation reproduced on the internet thus becomes a mode of translation between Cherokee and English, and a translation across the generations—a literal re-linking of community members who have been separated by the destruction of their language and culture, and by the introduction of outside educational models.

The elementary school's homepage may also be viewed as a symbol of the Eastern Band's commitment to education and technology as tools for self-determination. The fifth-grade students were not merely learning skills for success in education or work when they created their Web pages. They were learning skills that will ultimately allow the Cherokee to be less reliant on outside businesses and organizations to develop their technological capacities. And, as Trahant points out, "images are likely to evolve into the Internet's most powerful element," and Indians have an opportunity to be at "the cutting edge" of this new technology (1996: 18). The Eastern Band website and its links also both reflect and contribute to increasingly successful efforts by Cherokee leaders to recover and retain profitable participation in the capitalist economy of the larger nation. Profits are not only channelled into community services and cultural preservation, they have also expanded the actual land base of the community by funding the purchase of an ancient burial site, and they support business ventures such as the Nation's new bottled water industry and small business loans. Redman hopes the website will increasingly be used to link to websites for local businesses.

Thus the Eastern Band website actively alters the way Qualla interfaces with surrounding cultures. The website draws non-Natives from around the world (Redman reports that a large percentage of site visitors are German, French, Japanese, and of other nationalities) to contribute to economic recovery and cultural preservation. The website creates a balance of welcome and invitation with subtle suggestions of responsibility. The site design encourages visitors to recognize connections between historical removal and destruction, and the current living situations of real people, and thus potentially to perceive their consumption of Cherokee attractions and products as participation in recovery. The site also clearly builds connections with other indigenous peoples, not only by creating links to resources, like the *NativeWeb* link (www.nativeweb.org) available on the genealogy pages, but also by connecting groups and individuals. On the day of our last conversation (October 1999), Dave Redman reported that he had just received a request from a child of a tribal group in Scandinavia for a pen pal in Cherokee.

◆ Conclusion

In our examination of the two websites, we attempted to address the question: Does use of this potent western technology necessarily lead to the degeneration of Native groups, or can Indians use the medium to further the goal of "reindigenization"—the process of strengthening tribal ties while asserting sovereign rights and fostering self-determination? We conclude from our study that tribal websites can be powerful agents for community development and

cultural continuity within change. The Cherokee Nation of Oklahoma site offers the possibility of developing a sense of community by linking people to services and organizations, and to each other through free e-mail accounts and discussion lists; both bands' sites literally enlarge community by providing information about genealogy and enrolment that will help people with Cherokee ancestry become members of the tribe, while screening out non-Native wannabes or those merely interested in gaming profits. While the internet may not have yet "earned the name Great Equalizer" (Wolf, 1998: 18), the Eastern Band website in particular suggests that some communities are already realizing the internet's potential for democratic and material equalization. For the Eastern Band, the internet helps to control access by the dominant culture to Cherokee culture and its representations; it also appears to be a significant part of a stunning recovery of its success in the early 1800s as a thriving community in the intersections of Euro-American and tribal cultures.

Useful Websites ◆

Cherokee (Eastern Band): www.cherokee-nc.com. The official site of the Cherokee Nation (Western Band): www.cherokee.org. The sites discussed in this chapter.

NativeWeb: www.nativeweb.org. Resources for indigenous cultures around the world.

The Cherokee Messenger: http://www.powersource.com/cherokee. Produced by the Cherokee Cultural Society of Houston.

First Nations site index: www.dickshovel.com. Lists many internet Native American resources.

Indian Country Today: www.indiancountry.com. Website of America's largest Indian newspaper, offering news, archives, editorial features, and more.

Virtual Library—American Indians: www. hanksville.org/NAresources. An index of Native American resources on the internet.

NativeNet: http://cs.fdl.cc.mn.us/natnet/index.html. Website dedicated to "protecting and defending Mother Earth and the rights of indigenous people worldwide."

◆ References

Cohen, E., 1997: "For Native Americans, the net offers both promise and threat," *The New York Times on the Web.* www. nytimes. com/library/cyber/week/041697natives. html.

Ebo, B., 1998: "Internet or outernet?" in Ebo, B. (ed.), *Cyberghetto or Cybertopia? Race, Class, and Gender on the Internet.* Westport, CT: Praeger, 1-12.

Foster, D., 1997: "Community and identity in the electronic village," in Porter, D. (ed.), *Internet Culture.* New York: Routledge, 23-37.

Foucault, M., 1980: *Power/Knowledge: Selected Interviews and Other Writings, 1972-77.* Gordon, C. (ed. and trans.), New York: Pantheon.

Gurak, L., 1997: *Persuasion and Privacy in Cyberspace: The Online Protests Over Lotus Marketplace and the Clipper Chip.* New Haven, CT: Yale University Press.

Howe, C., 1999: "Cyberspace is no place for tribalism," rptd from *Wicazo-Sa Review* 13:2. www.ualberta.ca/~pimohte/howe.html.

Johnson, T., 1995: "The dealer's edge: Gaming in the path of Native America," *Native Americas* 12, 16-24.

Levinson, P., 1997: *The Soft Edge: A Natural History and Future of the Information Revolution.* New York: Routledge.

Mander, J., 1991: *In the Absence of the Sacred: The Failure of Technology and the Survival of the Indian Nations.* San Francisco: Sierra Club Books.

Red Eagle, P., 1999: Online discussion. NativeLit-L@raven.cc.ukans.edu.

Trahant, M. N., 1996: "The power of stories: Native words and images on the internet," *Native Americas* 13:1, 15-21.

Turkle, S., 1997: "Multiple subjectivity and virtual community at the end of the Freudian century," *Sociological Inquiry* 67, 72-84.

Wilbur, S. P., 1997: "An archaeology of cyberspaces: Virtuality, community, identity," in Porter, D. (ed.), *Internet Culture.* New York: Routledge, 5-22.

Wolf, A., 1998: "Exposing the great equalizer: Demythologizing internet equity," in Ebo, B. (ed.), *Cyberghetto or Cybertopia? Race, Class, and Gender on the Internet.* Westport: CT: Praeger, 15-32.

Yawakie, M. P., 1997: "Building telecommunication capacity in Indian country," *Winds of Change* 12, 44-46.

A LIST OF MEDIA ACTIVIST ORGANIZATIONS

The following organizations have Web pages and links.

About-Face

About-Face is a media literacy organization focused on the impact mass media has on the physical, mental, and emotional well-being of women and girls. About-Face works to engender positive body-esteem in girls and women of all ages, sizes, races, and backgrounds.

Adbusters Media Foundation (AMF)

AMF publishes *Adbusters* magazine, operates a Web site, and offers its creative services through PowerShift, its advocacy advertising agency. Based in Vancouver, British Columbia, Canada, *Adbusters* is a not-for-profit, reader-supported, 85,000-circulation magazine concerned about the erosion of our physical and cultural environments by commercial forces.

AlterNet

AlterNet.org is a project of the Independent Media Institute, a non-profit organization dedicated to strengthening and supporting independent and alternative media. The AlterNet article database includes more than 7,000 stories from over 200 sources.

American Center for Children's Television

The goals of the American Center for Children's Television are to strengthen the capabilities, insights, and motivation of children's programming professionals; to facilitate collaboration among TV, new media, education, research, and child development experts; to evolve guidelines and standards for recognizing outstanding work; and to increase public awareness and understanding of quality television.

American Society of Educators (ASE)

This multifaceted professional organization serves the nation's teachers by providing information and evaluation of media resources and technologies for effective classroom use.

Association for Media Literacy (AML)

The AML is an organization made up of teachers, librarians, consultants, parents, cultural workers, and media professionals concerned about the impact of the mass media in the creation of contemporary culture.

Black Film Center Archives— Indiana University

The Black Film Center Archives is repository of films and related materials by and about African Americans. Its holdings list more than 700 films and videocassettes, as well as archival photographs. It also provides information about its *Black Camera* newsletter, as well as contact information, collections use policy, and pointers to other film sites of interest.

Center for the Analysis of Commercialism in Education

This organization investigates the use of advertising and product promotion in schools.

Center for Media Literacy

The center maintains a national organization of supporters of media literacy and develops and distributes, via a printed and online catalog, media literacy educational materials to teachers, schools, parents, youth and community leaders, and others. It also designs, develops, and conducts media literacy workshops, teacher trainings, seminars, and special events.

Center for a New American Dream

The center is a nonprofit organization dedicated to helping Americans change the way they consume to improve quality of life, protect the environment, and promote social justice.

Citizens for Media Literacy (CML)

CML is a nonprofit, public interest organization linking media literacy with the concepts and practices of citizenship.

Fairness and Accuracy in Reporting (FAIR)

FAIR, the national media watch group, has been offering well-documented criticism of media bias and censorship since 1986. FAIR publishes *Extra!*, the award-winning magazine of media criticism, and produces the weekly radio program *CounterSpin*, the show that brings you the news behind the headlines.

HYPE

HYPE is a Web site that monitors the black image in the media. It covers all channels, including film, books, television, newspapers and magazines, video, cable, wire services, books, and the Internet.

The Just Think Foundation

Established to promote critical thinking about popular media, the foundation addresses the fundamental issues behind how traditional and interactive media influence the behavior of young people.

Media Awareness Network

The Media Awareness Network offers practical support for media education in the home, school, and community. It is also a place where educators, parents, students, and community workers can share resources and explore ways to make media a more positive force in children's lives.

Media Education Foundation

This foundation is a nonprofit educational organization devoted to media research and production of resources to aid educators and others in fostering analytical media literacy.

Media Literacy Clearinghouse

The Media Literacy Clearinghouse contains links to numerous articles, background, and lesson plans designed to help teachers integrate media literacy into classroom instruction.

Media Literacy Review (MLR)

The *MLR* provides links to active media education sites around the world. There are also extensive article databases and a directory of international organizations. In addition, each edition of the *MLR* offers a special features page focused around a specific topic or theme.

Media Watch

An activist organization working to educate about how women and children are victimized by the media, Media Watch produces a newsletter and educational material.

Media Watch Dog

Media Watch Dog is a collection of online media watch resources, including specific media criticism articles and information about media watch groups. The emphasis is on critiquing the accuracy and exposing the biases of the mainstream media.

National Alliance for Media Arts and Culture

This nonprofit organization is dedicated to increasing public understanding of and support for the field of media arts in the United States.

Project LOOK SHARP

This initiative's goals are to promote and support the integration of media literacy into classroom curricula at all grade levels and instructional areas, as well as to evaluate the effectiveness of media literacy education in the schools.

GLOSSARY

Active audiences. See **Reception theory.**

Address, Subject address. See **Subject position.**

Agency. See **Resistance.**

Appropriation. This term can refer, in a neutral sense, to how we make sense of the meanings encoded into cultural texts, and incorporate these into our daily lives. It is frequently used by cultural critics to highlight power relations in an unequal society. Thus, appropriation can refer to the process whereby members of relatively privileged groups "raid" the culture of marginalized groups, abstracting cultural practices or artifacts from their historically specific contexts. Frequently, this involves *co-optation*, by which a cultural item's resistant or counterhegemonic potential is lost through its translation into the dominant cultural context. Adding insult to injury, appropriation frequently means profit for the appropriator.

Artifact. Cultural artifact. These terms are borrowed by cultural studies from anthropological usage, where they refer to any human-created object. Cultural studies scholars use these terms as a way of broadening the definition of what aspects of culture in modern societies are worthy of serious study. As used in relation to media culture, they refer not only to tangible objects such as photographs in magazines but also to intangible verbal, visual, and auditory expressions, such as those in a rock music video.

Audience reception. See **Reception theory.**

Binary. In critical race and gender studies, this refers to the "either-or" conceptualization of "race" as black/white, or gender as masculinity/femininity, in contrast to a system allowing for multiple racial or gender identities.

Black feminist perspective. See **Feminist studies.**

Capitalism. This is an economic system based on private (rather than public or collective) ownership of the means of production, the market exchange of goods and services, and wage labor. This book tends to adopt the Marxist critique of capitalism, which sees it as a system based on oppression and coercion, rather than consensus.

Class. Social class. These are much-debated terms in both sociology and economics. They tend to be used by sociologists to refer to a social stratum whose members share certain social, economic, and cultural characteristics. However, critical sociologists use a modified version of the classic Marxist usage, which defined class as a group of people occupying a similar position within the social relations of economic production. Whereas Marx argued that there are only two major classes under capitalism, the bourgeoisie (owner class) and the proletariat (worker class), critical sociologists five: the ruling class, the professional/managerial class, small business owners, the working class, and the poor.

Codes. Semiotic codes. Media codes. These terms are used in *semiotics*-influenced media studies to refer to rules and conventions that structure representations on a number of levels—some are specific to certain media such as narrative film or advertising photographs, whereas others are shared with other modes of communication. Audiences learn to "read" the conventional verbal, visual, and auditory features that make up the "languages" or "sign systems" of media and other cultural forms in much the same way children learn the complex, often arbitrary systems of meaning in natural languages. See **Semiotics** and **Encoding/decoding.**

Commodity. This is any object or service that can be bought and sold in the marketplace. Marxists argue that capitalism reduces all aspects of life to commodities.

Content analysis. This is a social-scientific method of describing and analyzing the "content" of a range of media texts, either in qualitative or quantitative terms. Quantitative content analysis (counting the number of times certain types of material appear) is especially useful for describing the broad contours of a large quantity of texts, but it tends to miss the more subtle and complex ways in which texts construct meaning.

Counterhegemonic. Antihegemonic. See **Hegemony.**

Critical race theory. In contrast to older approaches to "race" that assumed "white" or Euro-American norms and focused on "nonwhite" identities as "the problem," critical race studies are based on the assumption that the proper object of study is the construction of hierarchical racial categories by which "white privilege" came to seem "natural." Critical race theorists are particularly concerned with challenging the black/white *binary* that has dominated U.S. academic discourse on "race," rendering invisible anyone who cannot be made to exemplify one of these two artificially constructed categories. In general, critical race theorists view "race" as a purely historical construct in the service of political goals.

Critical theory. Critical media theory. Critical media pedagogy. Also see **Marxism.** This is an approach to the analysis of social and cultural phenomena that highlights the dominant role of a capitalist economic system, and the resulting economic and social inequalities. See Kellner's chapter in Part I for an extensive discussion of critical cultural studies.

Cultural studies. This is an approach to the study of communication in society that is drawn from a number of sources, including Marxism, semiotics, literary and film analysis, psychoanalysis, feminism, and critical race and postcolonial theory. As used in this book, it locates the production, textual construction, and consumption of media texts in a society characterized by multiple systems of inequality. Of key importance is the study of the role media forms play in the production and reproduction of these systems of inequality. See Kellner's chapter in this reader for an extended discussion of this approach and also **Culture.**

Culture. This term has many different meanings, depending on the school of thought in which it occurs. In anthropology, it refers to everything created by humans, including artifacts or objects, ideas, institutions, and expressive practices. In traditional humanities fields such as art history and literature, culture has tended to be conceptualized as the highest-status arts of the wealthy and socially dominant, such as oil paintings, opera, or poetry. *Cultural studies* rejects this view of culture as elitist, replacing it with the more anthropological usage. In particular, cultural studies takes as its area of study all of the expressive, meaningful, interactive aspects of everyday life in an industrial society.

Cyberspace. Cyber fandom. Cyberspace is a cover term referring to the world of Internet-facilitated communication and pop cultural phenomena. Among the types of new interactive communities made possible by widespread use of the Internet are multiuser domains (MUDs), newsgroups or chat rooms where many computer users who are physically remote can experience simulated real-time conversation and disembodied social interaction. See Part VII, The Internet, for several discussions of the possible social impacts of such technologically assisted new communication forms.

Decode. See **Encoding/decoding.**

Difference. This term is used in critical race (and gender) studies to indicate how distinctions between racial (and gender) categories are conceptualized.

Discourse(s). Discourse analysis. Discursive. This is an approach within cultural studies that emphasizes how power relations in societies are sustained by and reflected in a variety of specialized ways of speaking and writing, such as those of elite institutions and groups such as medical professionals, religious institutions, and academics, as influentially articulated in the work of the French historian Michel Foucault in *The History of Sexuality*. The view that social and cultural power operates through competing and often clashing discourses (including media discourses) was highly influential in U.S. cultural studies in the 1990s, and characterizes many of the chapters in this volume.

Effects research. Media effects research. This refers to an older, social-scientific approach to the study of the possible impacts of media texts on social realities, an approach now regarded by most media scholars as based on an overly simple cause-and-effect model. For several discussions of the shortcomings of media effects research and theory, see Part IV, The Violence Debates.

Encoding/decoding. "Encoding/Decoding" is the title of an influential article by British cultural studies writer Stuart Hall. It proposes that meaning does not simply reside in a *media text's codes*, but is the result of a complex *negotiation* between specific audiences and texts. In contrast to former critical media theorists who assumed that audiences had very little control over meaning and were vulnerable to being "brainwashed" by the media, Hall proposed three possible audience responses to the dominant ideology contained in the media text's codes, or three distinct reading positions, corresponding to audiences' different social situations: *dominant reading* (accepting the preferred meaning), *negotiated reading* (accepting aspects of the preferred meaning, but rejecting others); and *oppositional reading* (rejecting the preferred meaning) (see Fiske, 1987a, p. 260).

Ethnography. This is a social research method first used by anthropologists and now adopted by some cultural studies scholars for understanding the role of media audiences in the production of meaning. It can involve participant observation, which requires that the researcher becomes a part of the group studied for a specified period. For an example of an ethnographic media study, see Radway's chapter in this reader. Also see **Reception theory.**

Fandom. Fan subcultures. Ethnographic media audience studies sometimes focus on specialized groups of audiences, the enthusiasts, or fans, who seem to exemplify the "active audience" phenomenon in a particularly intensive way. As Henry Jenkins showed in his study of Star Trek fans, a fan community can be based on collective borrowing ("poaching") from, and creative "rewriting" of, commercial media texts. Fans often engage in heated discussions over the meaning of the text, using passionate and interactive revision as one basis for community.

Feminist studies. This is a multidisciplinary approach to social analysis, rooted in the contemporary women's movement(s) and the gay/lesbian liberation movement. Emphasizing gender as a major organizing feature of power relations in society, feminists argue that the role of the media is crucial in the construction and dissemination of gender ideology, and thus in gender socialization. Feminists of color have critiqued the tendency in some feminist theory to privilege gender over other categories of experience; in particular, cultural analysts with a *black feminist* (sometimes called "womanist") *perspective* have brought to the foreground the ways in which gender is "inflected" or modified by race and class factors.

Feminist film theory. This influential strand of cultural studies combines a feminist view of the centrality of gender in cultural analysis with a generally psychoanalytic orientation to the study of audience reception of film. Feminist film theorists working through textual analysis have explored such issues as *gendered spectatorship*, the ways in which the film text through its formal codes "addresses" the hypothetical or ideal viewer as either male or female. An early formulation asserted that any viewer of classic Hollywood narrative film was encouraged by both plot and camera work and editing to adopt a "masculine subject position," and share in the *male gaze* of both protagonist and camera at a female object of desire. Some feminist film theorists have questioned the universal applicability of a Freudian-based psychoanalytic account of the development of gender differences; others have worked to explore how real audiences actually (consciously) experience film spectatorship.

Fetish. Fetishism. These are derogatory terms borrowed from psychoanalysis and used by some cultural critics to indicate fixation on, excessive attention to, or reverence for a particular idea.

Formal analysis. Formalism. Formal analysis in a neutral sense refers to studying the way in which the aesthetic properties (narrative structure, style, tone, color, etc.) of a cultural artifact influence the range of meanings it may have for audiences or readers. (*Formalist* or *formalistic* is sometimes used in a negative sense to refer to an analysis that is preoccupied with form, and loses sight of other important considerations, such as the social and economic context in which the artifact is created and consumed.)

Gay and lesbian studies. Gay/lesbian/bisexual/transgender studies (GLBT). See **Queer theory.**

Gaze. Male gaze. See **Feminist film theory.**

Gender. Gendering. Gendered. Whereas sex differences (anatomical and hormonal) between genetic males and genetic females are biological in nature, *gender* is a social concept, by which a society defines as "masculine" or "feminine" one particular set of characteristics and behaviors, and then socializes children accordingly. Just which characteristics belong to which gender (and even how many gender categories there are) can vary tremendously over time and between cultures and even different social groups within cultures. Some contemporary scholars argue that both gender and sexuality (sexual identity, sexual preference, sexual object choice) are more accurately understood as continuums, rather than in binary (only two, either-or) categories.

Gendered subjectivity. Sexual subjectivities. See **Gender** and **Subject position.**

Genre. Generic. Genre criticism. Originally a term used by literary and art critics to refer to categories of works marked by distinctive styles, form, or content, *genre* is also used to group together into categories related types of film, television shows, and popular music forms. In cultural studies genre criticism, which is influenced by *semiotics*, genres "are not neutral categories, but rather, they are ideological constructs that provide and enforce a pre-reading," acting as a contract between producer and consumer that "serves to limit the free play of signification" (Feuer, 1987, p. 118). In an effort to bring the experiences and perspectives of women to the foreground in cultural studies, feminist critics of popular literature and film have explored the distinctive aspects of *women's genres*—forms targeting predominantly female audiences.

Hegemony. Hegemonic. The term *hegemony* was developed by Italian Marxist theorist Antonio Gramsci to refer to the process by which those in power secure the consent of the socially subordinated to the system that oppresses or subordinates them. Rather than requiring overt force (as represented by the military or police), the elite, through their control of religious, educational, and media institutions, attempt to persuade the populace that the hierarchical social and economic system is fixed and "natural," and therefore unchangeable. According to Gramsci, however, such consent is never secured once and for all, but must continually be sought, and there is always some room for *resistance* through subversive (*counterhegemonic*) cultural work.

Heterocentrism. Heteronormativity. These terms were coined recently to refer to the placing of heterosexual experience at the center of one's attention, or the routine assumption that heterosexuality is "normal" and any other sexuality is "deviant."

Heterosexism. This term was coined by analogy with *sexism*. The dictionary defines it as "discrimination or prejudice against gay or homosexual people by heterosexual people." As with *racism* and *sexism*, this book takes the view that it is structural or institutional forces that underpin social inequalities, rather than individual prejudiced attitudes. Thus, heterosexism would refer to the heterosexual ideology that is encoded into and characteristic of the major social, cultural, and economic institutions of our society. See **Racism** and **Sexism.**

Homophobia. This is a psychological concept, referring to deep-seated fear of homosexuality, in others or in oneself. Also see **Heterosexism** and **Heterocentrism.**

Ideology. Traditionally, this term was used by Marxists to refer to ideas imposed on the proletariat (working class) by the bourgeoisie (owners of the means of production), to get the subservient classes to consent to their own oppression. Today, critical theorists tend to use a broader concept of ideology, for example, "the complex of ideas in society and their expression in social institutions, whether the military or the arts or the courts, which in turn dominate the way we live and how we understand the world around us" (Downing, 1990, p. 366). For a definition of ideology, see Hall's chapter in this reader.

Intertextuality. John Fiske has explicated a theory of *intertextuality* to help explain the way audiences experience a wide variety of media texts as interrelated, allowing their knowledge of one to influence their reading of another. "The theory of intertextuality proposes that any one text is necessarily read in relationship to others and that a range of textual knowledges is brought to bear upon it" (Fiske, 1987b, p. 108). Fiske also distinguishes "horizontal textuality" (relationships that exist among texts of a similar kind) from "vertical textuality"(the relations of one kind of texts with others "of a different type that refer explicitly to it"). For example, if a *primary media text* is a specific book, film, television show; then *a secondary text* might be "studio publicity, journalistic features, or criticism" about the primary text, and *tertiary texts* might include viewers' letters, gossip, and conversation about the primary text (Fiske, 1987b, pp. 108-109). Also see **Text.**

Image. Media image. This term has two distinct meanings for media critics. (1) any *representation* of social reality, as in "images of women in media." (This use of *image* suggests, as in "mirror image," a closer, less constructed relationship with "reality" than is now proposed for media representations, by those scholars working with more complex theoretical paradigms.) See **Representation.** (2) a specifically *visual representation*. See Jhally's chapter in this volume.

Internet studies. See **Cyberspace.**

Lesbigay, GLBT. See **Queer theory.**

Liberatory. Like *emancipatory,* or *progressive*, this term is used in critical cultural studies to indicate a positive political impact, a tendency toward a socially subordinate group's greater power or freedom (liberation or emancipation).

Liminal. Liminality. These terms are used by some cultural studies scholars to mean an area of ambiguity or mixture, at the border between two different conditions.

Marxism. Marxist. Marxian. Marxism is a general theory of historical change originally developed by 19th-century German philosopher Karl Marx. Marx argued for the centrality of economics in social history, and he developed a critique of capitalism that has had a major influence on political theory and on social revolutions in the 19th and 20th centuries. In the realm of cultural studies, classic Marxism argued that the economic structure of society (the "base") shapes major cultural institutions (the "superstructure") including the military, legal system, educational system, arts, and media. This is because, according to Marx, "the class which has the means of material production at its disposal has control over the means of mental production" (Marx & Engels, 1938). For a modification of classic Marxist ideas of this relationship, see **Hegemony.**

Masculinities. See **Men's studies.**

Media. Mass media. Mass communication media. Mediated. The term *media* is originally the plural of *medium* (communication medium). It has become a shorthand way of referring to the whole range of technologically assisted means by which images and messages can be created and distributed by producers for later consumption by "the masses," vast numbers of people. Older "mass media" included printed texts such as books, newspapers, and magazines; and newer graphical and audiovisual media such as still and film photography, radio and television broadcasting, cablecasting, satellite transmissions, and now computer-facilitated digital forms such as recordings on compact discs (CDs) or "streaming video." To say that communication is "mediated" is to draw attention to its highly second-hand character (as opposed to real-time, face-to-face traditional cultural forms such as storytelling, live theater, acoustic musical performances for live audiences, etc.).

Men's studies. An approach to the study of the social impacts of male gender roles, men's studies has been influenced by feminist analysis and in the United States is conducted independently largely by male feminist scholars. (Male gender roles are called *masculinities* in the plural to emphasize the view that ideals of manhood are multiple and have varied by race and class and across time and cultural contexts.)

Misogyny. Literally, this term means "hatred of women." Feminist cultural critics analyze ways in which misogyny or sexism is embedded in culture, often in ways that are made to seem "natural" rather than historically specific constructions social arrangements in which males are allocated social and cultural supremacy.

Multicultural. Multiculturalism. As used in this book, multiculturalism refers to a movement affecting curricula, teaching methods, and scholarship in a variety of fields, within universities and colleges in the United States. The broad objectives of activists in this educational movement include democratizing knowledge and education, by bringing to the foreground and validating the experiences and perspectives of all those groups formerly marginalized or culturally and socially dominated in our society.

Multidisciplinary. Interdisciplinary. This is an approach that encourages students and teachers to cross the boundaries between traditional academic disciplines or areas of knowledge (such as history, sociology, philosophy, economics, or political science), to be able better to capture the complexity of the subject studied.

Negotiated reading. See **Encoding/decoding.**

Netiquette. This is a term for the behavioral rules evolving to govern social interaction on the Internet, to control the negative effects of such antisocial behavior as "flaming" (angry or verbally abusive messages sent to newsgroups or e-mail distribution lists).

Newsgroups. These are Internet-facilitated communication communities consisting of Internet users who share common interests.

Objectify. Objectification. Objectifying. Literally, this means "to make into an object"; more figuratively, to depersonalize someone. In the context of feminist theory, objectification of women is implied by excessive emphasis on body parts and external appearances, especially in media representations designed to be erotic. The Dworkin/MacKinnon legal definition of *pornography* depended in part on this interpretation of the function of certain types of graphic sexual imagery.

Objectivist. This term is used to imply that "all reality is objective and external to the mind and that knowledge is reliably based on observed objects and events" (*American Heritage Dictionary of the English Language*, third ed.). Cultural studies generally takes a critical perspective toward this view, emphasizing instead the importance of language to thought and subjectivity to knowledge. Also see **Positivist.**

Oppositional reading. See **Encoding/decoding.**

Orientalism. Orientalist. These terms derived from the influential book *Orientalism*, by Edward Said, which examines critically the "exotic" stereotypes historically associated with what Europeans viewed (with a condescending Eurocentric perspective) as "the Orient."

Patriarchal. Patriarchy. This literally means "rule by the father," and refers to family (and clan) systems in which one older man had absolute power over all members of the group, including women, children, and younger male relatives and servants. As used by contemporary feminists, it is a concept developed to examine and critique continuing male domination of social institutions such as the family and the state, the educational system, and the media.

Political economy. In critical theory, this is a perspective that "sets out to show how different ways of financing and organizing cultural production have traceable consequences for the range of discourses and representations in the public domain, and for audiences' access to them" (Golding & Murdoch, 1991, p. 15). This often involves studying who owns the media industries and analyzing how ownership influences media content. (See, in particular, Butsch's chapter in this reader.)

Polysemic text. A polysemic text is one that is "open" to various readings or has multiple meanings. Cultural studies scholars currently disagree among themselves about how "open" texts are. See **Encoding/decoding.**

Positivist. This refers to the philosophical view that knowledge must be based only on what can be perceived by the senses, and therefore measured precisely. Although it provides the basis of empirical natural scientific research methods, this approach as applied to social research is frequently criticized as narrow and reductionist. See **Effects research.**

Postmodernism. Originally "postmodern" referred, in literary and art criticism, to "art, architecture or literature that reacts against earlier modernist principles." ("Modernism" was itself "the deliberate departure from tradition and the use of innovative forms of expression," in many styles of European art and literature in the early 20th century.) Those who use the term postmodern frequently acknowledge that it has now been used in so many different ways as to be virtually impossible to define clearly. In John Fiske's (1987b) formulation, "postmodernism emphasizes the fragmentary nature of images, their resistance to sense, the way that the images are more imperative than the real and have displaced it in our experience" (p. 254).

Pornography. Most broadly, this refers to sexually explicit graphic and/or written texts designed to produce sexual arousal in consumers. (Depending on one's political perspective and view of the social impact of the production and consumption of such materials, the same texts could be seen merely as *erotica*—a more neutral term—or as *pornography*—a term implying community disapproval.) The definition has been politicized and was strenuously contested during the 1980s, when feminists proposed city ordinances by which the production and distribution of certain classes of pornography could be prosecuted as civil rights violations, rather than under traditional anti-vice criminal law. Anti-pornography feminists argued that certain classes of pornography embodied and helped reproduce *misogyny*. See Part IV, The Violence Debates, for several chapters discussing pornography texts and the pornography industry.

Postcolonial theory. This is an approach that has been heavily influenced by the Indian feminist Gayatri Spivak, who points out the continuing impact of imperialist thinking on Western cultural studies scholarship, including some interpretations by Western feminists.

Preferred reading. This concept was developed by Stuart Hall to circumscribe the degree of "openness" (*polysemy*) of media texts. According to Hall, the structure of mainstream media texts always "prefers" or strongly suggests a single "correct" meaning that tends to promote the dominant ideology. Within cultural studies, there continues to be a lively debate over whether a preferred meaning can be said to be a property of the text; some would argue that the making of meaning ultimately resides with audiences. Also see **Encoding/decoding.**

Psychoanalysis. According to feminist film and TV analyst Sandy Flitterman-Lewis (1987), "Psychoanalysis, as a theory of human psychology, describes the ways in which the human being comes to develop a specific personality and sexual identity within the larger network of social relations called culture. It takes as its object the mechanisms of the unconscious—resistance, repression, sexuality, and the Oedipal complex—and seeks to analyze the fundamental structures of desire that underlie all human activity." The French psychoanalytic philosopher Lacan, "by reinterpreting Freud in linguistic terms," had a major impact on one strand of cultural studies—especially film studies. He built on the Freudian theory of how a sense of self as distinct from the mother, as well as a firm gender identity, is established in children through the Oedipal stage (which works differently for boys and girls). "Because of his emphasis on language, Lacan rereads the Oedipal complex," giving the childhood acquisition of language a central role in moving the child "out of the pre-Oedipal unity with the mother," but leaving aspects of our relationship to language unconscious. Later film theorists such as Christian Metz and Laura Mulvey drew on the Lacanian theory of the unconscious in developing the idea of *gendered spectatorship* (Flitterman-Lewis, 1987, p. 173). See **Feminist film theory.**

Public sphere. Jürgen Habermas, in *The Structural Transformation of the Bourgeois Public Sphere* (1989), conceptualized "democracy as a discursive process" that once took place in a "public sphere," a "domain independent from state interests," until the rise of capitalism and the industrialization of societies brought on "the decline of the bourgeois public sphere and the colonization of the media by marketplace interests" (Moorti, in this volume). Although Habermas's view of the public sphere emphasized a particular kind of rational debate among male citizens, contemporary feminist cultural critics have sought to apply an expanded version of the concept to the analysis of such mass media genres as the talk show.

Queer theory. Queer studies. This is a relatively new, interdisciplinary, and politically radical approach to cultural studies that emphasizes the instability and fluidity of gender and sexuality categories, in contrast to the view of gay and lesbian studies and some gay and lesbian activists that sexual identity is a fixed, permanent "essence." The term *queer* is adopted in order to reclaim it from derogatory usage, as well as to create a more inclusive vision of the areas of study. See Raymond's chapter in this volume.

Race. Many people tend to think of race as a fixed entity linked to biological realities. However, in this book as in critical theory generally, "the effort must be made to understand race as an unstable complex of social meanings constantly being transformed by political struggle" (Omit & Winant, 1987).

Racism. In everyday usage, racism can be used to mean holding or displaying prejudiced or bigoted attitudes or indulging in discriminatory behavior toward someone else (usually people of color, but sometimes whites as well), on the basis of that person's apparent race, ethnicity, or color. However, in critical theory, and in this book, the term refers to the white-supremacist ideology encoded into and characteristic of the major social, cultural, and economic institutions of this society.

Reception theory. According to Robert C. Allen (1987), "'reader-response criticism,' 'reception theory,' and 'reader-oriented criticism' are all names given to the variety of recent works in literary [and media] studies that foreground the role of the reader in understanding and deriving pleasure from . . . texts." Those who take this approach believe "that . . . meaning should no longer be viewed as an immutable property of a text but must be considered as the result of the confrontation between reading act and textual structure" (p. 75).

Representation. Cultural representation. Media representation. These terms refer to "the creation of a convincing illusion of reality," through such media as painting, drawing, graphic prints, still photographs, films, recorded sound, live acting on stage, television technology, computer graphics, or the like. "Representations" include all kinds of media imagery that, no matter how convincing their likeness to everyday social reality, are always to be recognized as "constructions taken from a specific social and physical viewpoint, selecting one activity or instant out of vast choices to represent, and materially made out of and formed by the technical processes of the medium and its conventions" (King, 1992, p. 131).

Resistance. In critical cultural studies, this can refer to the refusal of the reader, viewer, or audience to take up or accept the *preferred reading* and/or the *subject position* encoded into the media text. There is a general debate among cultural studies scholars on how much opportunity to resist is offered by the text (how "open" or *polysemic* it is). Some have criticized the tendency to "romanticize" the idea of interpretive community's resistance (Scholle, 1990, p. 8). Others question the notion that *resistance* is in and by itself positive, citing the resistance of those with conservative social ideologies to texts whose preferred meaning is politically "progressive" (see Kellner's chapter in Part I). Finally, many point out that "resistive readings" may or may not translate into political resistance to cultural *hegemony*. (A related term, *agency*, refers to the degree to which a consumer of culture can be understood to be a free agent whose choices must be respected by the cultural critic, as opposed to merely being a passive victim of cultural brainwashing.)

Secondary text. See **Intertextuality.**

Semiotics. Semiology. Semiotics is a linguistics-based field of study that has had an important influence on the way cultural studies scholars discuss the "codes" in media texts. It is concerned with the study of "signification," or the ways in which both languages and nonlinguistic symbolic systems operate to associate meanings with arbitrary "signs" such as words, visual images, colors, or objects. Signs actually consist of two elements—that which is *signified* (the meaning) and that which signifies (the *signifier* or symbol itself). See **Encoding/decoding.**

Serial fiction. These are long and sometimes "endless" narratives or stories that are delivered to consumers in many installments in a series, such as soap operas, or comic books.

Sexism. Coined by the women's movement in an analogy with *racism,* sexism is used several ways. In common usage, it can refer to prejudicial or disrespectful attitudes or discriminatory behavior on the part of individuals toward others (usually women, but sometimes men as well), on the basis of gender. In this book, it is used to refer to male-supremacist ("patriarchal") ideology encoded into and characteristic of the major social, cultural, and economic institutions of this society.

Signifier. Signified. See **Semiotics.**

Spectatorship. See **Feminist film theory.**

Stereotype. This popular term was much used in 1970s media criticism and activism to describe and critique reductive, much-repeated social imagery (as in "Uncle Tom and Aunt Jemima are racist stereotypes"; "Aunt Jemima and the Playboy Bunny are sexist stereotypes"). For a more nuanced concept of the relationship between cultural artifacts and social reality, see **Representation.**

Subject position. This concept was developed within psychoanalytically oriented media theory, particularly literary and film criticism, that claims that narrative texts themselves produce through their codes an ideal "viewing position" or "subject position" from which the narrative is experienced by any viewer/reader. A male viewer could be invited to experience a particular text from a "female subject position," for example, just as a heterosexual reader might temporarily occupy a "queer subject position" through adopting the perspective offered by a particular media text. The text "addresses" the reader as someone with a presumed or hypothetical social identity, regardless of the social identity of the "real" reader. A related term for this process is *interpellation*, which means that the text can be seen as "hailing" or calling a particular type of reader. See **Feminist film theory** and **Reception theory.**

Subjectivity. Subjectivities. *Subjectivity* is a term used to describe the consciousness of self within the mind. Sexual subjectivities refers to distinct senses of sexual identity one might bring to the reading of a media text.

Symbolic annihilation. This term was coined in the 1970s to describe and critique the way mass media either ignored or misrepresented certain marginalized social groups. See Gross's chapter in this volume.

Televisual apparatus. By analogy with a similar concept in film studies, the televisual apparatus is everything distinctive about television as a business, a cultural institution, and a communication medium. This would include its distinctive complex of technological characteristics and text forms, its sites of consumption (the living room at home and other locations), and its system of production, distribution, and finance.

Text. Media text. Originally referring to a verbal/written cultural artifact (such as a story, play, or song lyrics), text is now used much more broadly by cultural critics. It can refer to any communicative or expressive artifact produced by the media industries. *Textual analysis*, or a close examination of how particular media texts generate meaning, is one of the key activities of contemporary cultural studies. However, Kellner argues in his chapter in this volume that *audience reception* and *political economy* approaches are also needed to locate texts in their social and political contexts.

Textual analysis. See **Text.**

Transgender. Transgendered. This is a relatively recent umbrella term covering a wide variety of nontraditional or "nonnormative" gender statuses. It includes transsexual people in the United States and other high-technology societies, who have elected to change anatomical sex through surgical and hormonal technologies; those who occupy a "middle" or "third gender" status that is recognized by a particular culture; and gender "nonconformists,"those who flout the rigid behavioral and appearance norms established for their biological sex (such as those who occasionally or permanently cross-dress), as well as feminine men and manly women, some of whom may also identify as gay or lesbian.

Transgressive. This term is often used positively in cultural criticism to indicate the writer's approval of an act that challenges traditional (oppressive) rules or social or cultural hierarchies.

Tropes. These are figures of speech, such as metaphors, or other literary or narrative elements identified in text analysis.

Usenet. Usenet is an Internet-facilitated network for interactive online discussion. "Although less famous than the World Wide Web, America Online's chat rooms and folders, or the interactive real-time conversation spaces known as multiuser domains (MUDs) and multiuser domains object oriented (MOOs), Usenet is arguably the oldest, largest, most widely accessible, and most widely used network for interactive online discussion" (Baym, 2000, p. 5).

Whiteness studies. See **Critical race theory.**

Womanism. This term was coined by novelist and essayist Alice Walker to refer to black feminism. See **Feminist studies.**

Women's film. Women's genres. See **Genre.**

◆ References

Allen, R. C. (1987). Reader-oriented criticism and television. In R. C. Allen (Ed.), *Channels of discourse* (pp. 74-112). Chapel Hill: University of North Carolina Press.

Baym, N. K. (2000). *Tune in, log on: Soaps, fandom, and online community.* Thousand Oaks, CA: Sage.

Downing, J., Mohammadi, A., & Sreberny-Mohammadi, A. (1990). *Questioning the media.* Newbury Park, CA: Sage.

Dworkin, A., & MacKinnon, C. A. (1988). *Pornography and civil rights: A new day for women's equality.* Minneapolis, MN: Organizing Against Pornography.

Feuer, J. (1987). Genre study and television. In R. C. Allen (Ed.), *Channels of discourse* (pp. 113-133). Chapel Hill: University of North Carolina Press.

Fiske, J. (1987a). British cultural studies and television. In R. C. Allen (Ed.), *Channels of discourse* (pp. 254-289). Chapel Hill: University of North Carolina Press.

Fiske, J. (1987b). *Television culture.* London: Methuen.

Flitterman-Lewis, S. (1987). Psychoanalysis, film and television. In R. C. Allen (Ed.), *Channels of discourse* (pp. 172-210). Chapel Hill: University of North Carolina Press.

Golding, P., & Murdoch, G. (1991). Culture, communication and political economy. In J. Curran & M. Gurevitch (Eds.), *Mass media and society.* London: Edward Arnold.

King, C. (1991). On representation. In F. Bonner et al. (Eds.), *Imagining women* (pp. 131-139). Cambridge, UK: Open University Press.

Marx, K., & Engels, F. (1938). *German ideology* (R. Pascal, Trans.). London: Lawrence and Wishart.

Omi, M., & Winant, H. (1993). On the theoretical concept of race. In S. M. James & A. P. A. Busia (Eds.), *Theorizing black feminisms: The visionary pragmatism of black women.* New York: Routledge.

Sholle, D. (1990). Resistance: Pinning down a wandering concept in cultural studies discourse. *Journal of Urban and Cultural Studies, 1*(1), 87-105.

BIBLIOGRAPHY

◆ *Media Theory*

Abercrombie, N., & Longhurst, B. (1998). *Audiences*. Thousand Oaks, CA: Sage.

Andersen, R., & Strate, L (Eds.). (2000). *Critical studies in media commercialism*. New York: Oxford University Press.

Bagdikian, B. (1997). *The media monopoly* (5th ed.). Boston: Beacon.

Barker, C. (2000). *Cultural studies: Theory and practice*. London: Sage.

Barker, C. (2002). *Making sense of cultural studies: Central problems and critical debates*. Thousand Oaks, CA: Sage.

Best, S., & Kellner, D. (2001). *The postmodern adventure: Science, technology, and cultural studies at the third millennium*. New York: Guilford.

Briggs, A., & Cobley, P. (Eds.). (1998). *The media: An introduction*. Harlow, UK: Longman.

Campbell, N., & Kean, K. (1998). *Cultural studies: An introduction to American culture*. New York: Routledge.

Cobley, P. (1996). *The communication theory reader*. New York: Routledge.

Croteau, D., & Hoynes, W. (1994). *By invitation only: How the media limit political debate*. Monroe, ME: Common Courage.

Croteau, D., & Hoynes, W. (2000). *Media/society: Industries, images and audiences*. Thousand Oaks, CA: Pine Forge.

Croteau, D., & Hoynes, W. (2001). *The business of media: Corporate media and the public interest*. Thousand Oaks, CA: Pine Forge.

Curran, J., & Park, M. (Eds.). (2000). *De-Westernizing media studies*. London and New York: Routledge.

Cvetkovich, A., & Kellner, D. (Eds.). (1997). *Articulating the global and the local: Globalization and cultural studies*. Boulder, CO: Westview.

DeFleur, M. (1998). *Understanding mass communication: A liberal arts perspective*. Boston: Houghton Mifflin.

Downing, J., Mohammadi, A., & Sreberny-Mohammadi, A. (Eds.). (1995). *Questioning the media: A critical introduction*. Thousand Oaks, CA: Sage.

Durham, G., & Kellner, D. (Eds.). (2001). *Media and cultural studies: Keyworks*. Malden, MA: Blackwell.

During, S. (Ed.). (1993). *The cultural studies reader*. London and New York: Routledge.

Dyer, R. (1993). *The matter of images: Essays on representations*. New York: Routledge.

Fiske, J. (1996). *Media matters: Everyday culture and political change*. Minneapolis: University of Minnesota Press.

Fox, R., & Van Sickel, R. (2001). *Tabloid justice: Criminal justice in an age of media frenzy*. Boulder, CO: Lynne Rienner.

Frith, S., & Goodwin, A. (1995). *On record: Rock, pop and the written word*. New York: Pantheon.

Giroux, H. (1994). *Disturbing pleasures: Learning popular culture*. New York: Routledge.

Giroux, H. (1999). *The mouse that roared: Disney and the end of innocence*. Lanham, MD: Rowman & Littlefield.

Grossberg, L., & Radway, J. (1997). *Controversies in cultural studies*. New York: Routledge.

Hagen, I., & Wasko, J. (Eds.). (2000). *Production and reception in media research*. Cresskill, NJ: Hampton.

Hartley, J., & Pearson, R. (Eds.). (2000). *American cultural studies: A reader*. Oxford, UK, and New York: Oxford University Press.

Harris, C., & Alexander, A. (Eds.). (1998). *Theorizing fandom: Fans, subculture, and identity*. Cresskill, NJ: Hampton.

Hiebert, R. (Ed.). (1999). *Impact of mass media: Current issues*. New York: Longman.

Hoover, S. M., & Lundby, K. (1997). *Rethinking media, religion & culture*. Thousand Oaks, CA: Sage.

Lewis, J. (2002). *Cultural studies—The basics*. Thousand Oaks, CA: Sage.

Lewis, L. (1992). *The adoring audience: Fan culture and popular media*. New York: Routledge.

Livingstone, S., & Bovill, M. (Eds.). (2001). *Children and their changing media environment: A European comparative study*. Mahwah, NJ: Lawrence Erlbaum.

Lull, J. (1995). *Media, communication, culture: A global approach*. New York: Columbia University Press.

Mackay, H., & O'Sullivan, T. (Eds.). (1999). *The media reader: Continuity and transformation*. Thousand Oaks, CA: Sage.

McChesney, R. (1999). *Rich media, poor democracy: Communication politics in dubious times*. Urbana: University of Illinois Press.

McDonagh, G., Gregg, R., & Hing-Yuk Wong, C. (Eds.). (2001). *Encyclopedia of contemporary American culture*. New York: Routledge.

McRobbie, A. (Ed.). (1997). *Back to reality: Social experience and cultural studies*. Manchester, UK: Manchester University Press.

Morris, N., & Waisbord, S. (Eds.). (2001). *Media and globalization: Why the state matters*. Lanham, MD: Rowman & Littlefield.

Mosco, V. (1996). *The political economy of communication: Rethinking and renewal*. London and Thousand Oaks, CA: Sage.

Negus, K. (1999). *Music genres and corporate cultures*. New York: Routledge.

Rayner, P., Kruger, S., & Wall, P. (2001). *Media studies: The essential introduction*. New York: Routledge.

Ryan, J. (1999). *Media and society: The production of culture in the mass media*. Boston: Allyn & Bacon.

Sedgewick, P., & Edgar, A. (1999). *Key concepts in cultural theory*. New York: Routledge.

Shea, D. (Ed.). (1999). *Mass politics: The politics of popular culture*. New York: St. Martin's.

Turner, B. (1996). *British cultural studies: An introduction*. New York: Routledge.

Turow, J. (1999). *Media today: An introduction to mass communication*. Boston: Houghton Mifflin.

Phillips, M., Wasko, J., & Meehan, E. (Eds.). (2001). *Dazzled by Disney? The global Disney Audiences Project*. London and New York: Leicester University Press.

◆ *Gender, Race, and Class*

Andrews, D. (Ed.). (2001). *Michael Jordan, Inc.: Corporate sport, media culture, and late modern America*. Albany: State University of New York Press.

Baehr, H., & Gray, A. (Eds.). (1996). *Turning it on: A reader in women & media*. London: Arnold.

Berger, M., Wallis, B., & Watson, S. (Eds.). (1995). *Constructing masculinity*. New York and London: Routledge.

Biagi, S., & Kern-Foxworth, M. (1997). *Facing difference: Race, gender, and mass media*. Thousand Oaks, CA: Pine Forge.

Blount, M., & Cunningham, G. (Eds.). (1995). *Representing black men*. New York: Routledge.

Bobo, J. (1995). *Black women as cultural readers*. New York: Columbia University Press.

Bogle, D. (2001). *Primetime blues: African Americans on network television*. New York: Farrar, Straus and Giroux.

Bordo, S. (1999). *The male body: A new look at men in public and in private*. New York: Farrar, Straus and Giroux.

Brown, A. (1998). *Fanatics: Power, identity and fandom in football*. New York: Routledge.

Brunsdon, C., D'Acci, J., & Spigel, L. (Eds.). (1997). *Feminist television criticism: A reader*. Oxford, UK: Clarendon.

Buchbinder, D. (1994). *Masculinities and identities*. Melbourne: University Press.

Buchbinder, D. (1998). *Performance anxieties: Re-producing masculinity*. Sydney, Australia: Allen and Unwin.

Burston, P., & Richardson, C. (Eds.). (1995). *A queer romance: Lesbians, gay men and popular culture*. London: Routledge.

Cashmore, E. (1997). *The black culture industry*. New York: Routledge.

Coleman, R. M. (1998). *African American viewers and the black situation comedy: Situating racial humor*. New York: Garland.

Coleman, R. M. (Ed.). (2001). *Say it loud! African American audiences, media, and identity*. New York: Routledge.

Dates, J., & Barlow, W. (Eds.). 1993). *Split image: African Americans in the mass media*. Washington, DC: Howard University Press.

Davis, L. (1997). *The swimsuit issue and sport: Hegemonic masculinity in* Sports Illustrated. New York: State University of New York Press.

Dimitriadis, G. (2001). *Performing identity/performing culture: Hip hop as text, pedagogy, and lived practice*. New York: P. Lang.

Douglas, S. (1995). *Where the girls are: Growing up female with the mass media*. New York: Times Books.

Dyson, M. (1993). *Reflecting black: African-American cultural criticism*. Minneapolis: University of Minnesota Press.

Dyson, M. (2001). *Holler if you hear me: Searching for Tupac Shakur*. New York: Basic Civitas Books.

Edwards, T. (1997). *Men in the mirror: Men's fashion, masculinity and consumer society*. London: Cassell.

Entman, R., & Rojecki, A. (2000). *The black image in the white mind: Media and race in America*. Chicago: University of Chicago Press.

Ferguson, R. (1998). *Representing "race": Ideology, identity, and the media*. London and New York: Arnold.

Gandy, O. (1998). *Communication and race: A structural perspective*. London: Arnold.

Gabriel, J. (1998). *Whitewash: Racialized politics and the media*. New York: Routledge.

Giroux, H. (1996). *Fugitive cultures: Race, violence, and youth*. New York: Routledge.

Giroux, H. (1997). *Channel surfing: Race talk and the destruction of today's youth*. New York: St. Martin's.

Golden, T. (1995). *Black male: Representations of masculinity in contemporary American art*. New York: Whitney Museum of Art.

Gray, H. (1995). *Watching race: Television and the struggle for "blackness."* Minneapolis: University of Minnesota Press.

Griffin, S. (2000). *Tinker belles and evil queens: The Walt Disney Company from the inside out*. New York: New York University Press.

Gross, L. (Ed.). (1999). *The Columbia reader on lesbians and gay men in media, society, and politics*. New York: Columbia University Press.

Holmberg, C. B. (1998). *Sexualities and popular culture*. Thousand Oaks, CA: Sage.

Holtzman, L. (2000). *Media messages: What film, television, and popular music teach us about race, class, gender and sexual orientation*. New York: M. E. Sharpe.

Hunt, D. M. (1999). *O. J. Simpson facts and fictions: News rituals in the construction of reality*. Cambridge, UK: Cambridge University Press.

Ingraham, C. (1999). *White weddings: Romancing heterosexuality in popular culture*. New York: Routledge.

Jacobs, R. N. (2000). *Race, media, and the crisis of civil society: From Watts to Rodney King*. New York: Cambridge University Press.

Jhally, S., & Lewis, J. (1992). *Enlightened racism*: The Cosby Show, *audiences, and the myth of the American dream*. Boulder, CO: Westview.

Kilbourne, J. (1999). *Can't buy my love How advertising changes the way we think and feel*. New York: Simon & Schuster

Kirkham, P. (Ed.). (1996). *The gendered object*. Manchester and New York: Manchester University Press.

Krims, A. (2000). *Rap music and the poetics of identity*. Cambridge: Cambridge University Press.

Lhamon, W. (1998). *Raising Cain: Blackface performance from Jim Crow to hip hop*. Cambridge, MA: Harvard University Press.

Lont, C. (1995). *Women and media: Content, careers, criticism*. Belmont, CA: Wadsworth.

Mayne, J. (2000). *Framed: Lesbians, feminists, and media culture*. Minneapolis: University of Minnesota Press.

Meyers, M. (Ed.). (1999). *Mediated women: Representations in popular culture*. Cresskill, NJ: Hampton.

Morrison, T., & Lacour, C. B. (Eds.). (1997). *Birth of a nation'hood: Gaze, script, and spectacle in the O. J. Simpson case*. New York: Pantheon.

Nelson, G. (1998). *Hip hop America*. New York: Viking.

Nixon, S. (1996). *Hard looks: Masculinities, spectatorship and contemporary consumption*. London: UCL Press.

Perchuk, A., & Posner, H. (Eds.). (1995). *The masculine masquerade: Masculinity and representation*. Cambridge, MA: MIT Press.

Perkins, W. (Ed.). (1996). *Droppin' science: Critical essays on rap music and hip hop culture*. Philadelphia: Temple University Press.

Pfeil, F. (1995). *White guys: Studies in postmodern domination and difference*. London and New York: Verso.

Pieterse, J. N. (1992). *White on black: Images of blacks in Western popular culture*. Amsterdam, The Netherlands: KIT Publishers.

Rodríguez, C. E. (Ed.). (1997). *Latin looks: Images of Latinas and Latinos in the U.S. media*. Boulder, CO: Westview.

Rogers, M. F. (1999). *Barbie culture*. London: Sage.

Rose, T. (1994). *Black noise: Rap music and black culture in contemporary America*. Hanover, NH: Wesleyan University Press.

Ross, K. (1996). *Black and white media: Black images in popular film and television*. Cambridge, UK: Polity.

Spigel, L. (2001). *Welcome to the dreamhouse: Popular media and postwar suburbs*. Durham, NC: Duke University Press.

Sreberny, A., & Zoonen, L. (Eds.). (2000). *Gender, politics and communication*. Cresskill, NJ: Hampton.

Valdivia, A. (Ed.). (1995). *Feminism, multiculturalism, and the media: Global diversities*. Thousand Oaks, CA: Sage

Walters, S. (2001). *All the rage: The story of gay visibility in America*. Chicago: University of Chicago Press.

Williams, L. (2001). *Playing the race card: Melodramas of black and white from Uncle Tom to O. J. Simpson*. Princeton, NJ: Princeton University Press.

Wilson, C. C., II, & Gutiérrez, F. (1995). *Race, multiculturalism, and the media: From* mass to class communication. Thousand Oaks, CA: Sage.

Valdivia, A. (2000). *A Latina in the land of Hollywood and other essays on media culture.* Tucson: University of Arizona Press.

Zook, K. B. (1999). *Color by Fox: The Fox network and the revolution in black television.* New York: Oxford University Press.

◆ *Consumerism and Culture*

Angus, I. (2000). *Primal scenes of communication: Communication, consumerism, and social movements.* Albany: State University of New York Press.

Barnouw, E. (1978). *The sponsor.* New York: Oxford University Press.

Barthel, D. (1988). *Putting on appearances: Gender and advertising.* Philadelphia: Temple University Press.

Berger, J. (1972). *Ways of seeing.* New York: Penguin.

Bianchi, M. (Ed.). (1998). *The active consumer: Novelty and surprise in consumer choice.* New York: Routledge.

Brumberg, J. (1997). *The body project: An intimate history of American girls.* New York: Random House.

Chapkis, W. (1987). *Beauty secrets: Women and the politics of appearance.* Boston: South End.

Cook, G. (2001). *The discourse of advertising.* New York: Routledge.

Crane, D. (2000). *Fashion and its social agendas: Class, gender, and identity in clothing.* Chicago: University of Chicago Press.

Du Gay, P. (Ed.). (1997). *Production of culture/cultures of production.* London: Open University Press.

Entwistle, J. (2000). *The fashioned body: Fashion, dress and modern social theory.* Cambridge, UK: Polity.

Ewen, S. (1976). *Captains of consciousness: Advertising and the social roots of the consumer culture.* New York: McGraw-Hill.

Ewen, S. (1988). *All consuming images.* New York: Basic Books.

Ewen, S., & Ewen, E. (1982). *Channels of desire: Mass image and the shaping of American consciousness.* New York: McGraw-Hill.

Fox, R. W., & Lears, T. J. J. (Eds.). (1983). *The culture of consumption: Critical essays in American history, 1880-1980.* New York: Pantheon.

Gibson, P. C., & Bruzzi, S. (Eds.). (2000). *Fashion cultures: Theories, explorations, and analysis.* New York: Routledge.

Goldman, R. (1992). *Reading ads socially.* New York: Routledge.

Goldman, R., & Papson, S. (1999). *Nike culture: The sign of the swoosh.* Thousand Oaks, CA: Sage.

Harris, D. (2000). *Cute, quaint, hungry, and romantic: The aesthetics of consumerism.* New York: Basic Books.

Jameson, F., & Miyoshi, M. (1998). *The cultures of globalization.* Durham, NC: Duke University Press.

Jamieson, K. H., & Campbell, K. K. (2000). *The interplay of influence: News, advertising, politics, and the mass media.* Belmont, CA: Wadsworth.

Jhally S. (1987). *The codes of advertising: Fetishism and the political economy of meaning in the consumer society.* New York: St. Martin's.

Kitch, C. (2001). *The girl on the magazine cover: The origins of visual stereotypes in American mass media.* Chapel Hill: University of North Carolina Press.

Klein, N. (1999). *No logo: Taking aim at the brand bullies.* New York: Picador.

Kondo, D. K (1997). *About face: Performing race in fashion and theater.* New York: Routledge.

Lears, J. (1994). *Fables of abundance: A cultural history of advertising.* New York: Basic Books.

Lee, M. (1993). *Consumer culture reborn: The cultural politics of consumption.* New York: Routledge.

Malcolm, B. (1996). *Fashion as communication.* New York: Routledge.

McRobbie, A. (1999). *In the culture society: Art, fashion, and popular music.* London and New York: Routledge.

Meinhof, U., & Smith, J. (Eds.). (2000). *Intertextuality and the media: From genre to everyday life*. Manchester and New York: Manchester University Press.

Miles, S. (1998). *Consumerism: As a way of life*. Thousand Oaks, CA: Sage.

Nava, M. (1992). *Changing cultures: Feminism, youth and consumerism*. London and Newbury Park, CA: Sage.

Nava, M., Blake, A., MacRury, I., & Richards, B. (1997). *Buy this book: Studies in advertising and consumption*. New York: Routledge.

Schor, J. (1998). *The overspent American: Upscaling, downshifting, and the new consumer*. New York: Basic Books.

Schor, J. B., & Holt, D. B. (Eds.). (2000). *The consumer society reader*. New York: New Press.

Scranton, P. (Ed.). (2001). *Beauty and business: Commerce, gender, and culture in modern America*. New York: Routledge.

◆ The Violence Debates

Barker, M., & Petley, J. (Eds.). (1997). *Ill effects: The media violence debate*. New York: Routledge.

Berkeley, K. (1995). *Pornography and difference*. Bloomington: Indiana University Press.

Bishop, R., & Robinson, L. (1998). *Night market: Sexual cultures and the Thai economic miracle*. New York: Routledge.

Chancer, L. (1998). *Reconcileable differences: Confronting beauty, pornography, and the future of feminism*. Berkeley: University of California Press.

Cornell, D. (1995). *The imaginary domain: Abortion, pornography and sexual harassment*. New York: Routledge.

Cornell, D. (Ed.). (2000). *Feminism & pornography*. Oxford, UK: Oxford University Press.

Dines, G., Jensen, R., & Russo, A. (1998). *Pornography: The production and consumption of inequality*. New York: Routledge.

Duggan, L., & Hunter, N. (Eds.). (1995). *Sex wars: Sexual dissent and political culture*. New York: Routledge.

Dworkin, A. (1989). *Pornography: Men possessing women*. New York: Plume.

Dyson, R. (2000). *Mind abuse: Media violence in an information age*. Montreal: Black Rose Books.

Egendorf, L. (2001). *Violence: Opposing viewpoints*. San Diego, CA: Greenhaven.

Gibson, P., & Gibson, R. (Eds.). (1993). *Dirty looks: Women, pornography, power*. London: BFI Publishing.

Goldstein, J. (Ed.). (1998). *Why we watch: The attractions of violent entertainment*. New York: Oxford University Press.

Grossman, D., & DeGaetano, G. (1999). *Stop teaching our kids to kill: A call to action against TV, movie & video game violence*. New York: Crown.

Hamilton, J. (1998). *Channeling violence: The economic market for violent television programming*. Princeton, NJ: Princeton University Press.

Hunt, L. (Ed.). (1993). *The invention of pornography: Obscenity and the origins of modernity 1500-1800*. New York: Zone Books.

Itzin, C. (Ed.). (1993). *Pornography: Women, violence, and civil liberties*. New York: Oxford University Press.

Juffer, J. (1998). *At home with pornography: Women, sexuality, and everyday life*. New York: New York University Press.

Kelly, P. (Ed.). (1999). *Television violence: A guide to the literature*. Commack, NY: Nova Science Publishers.

Kipnis, L. (1996). *Bound and gagged: Pornography and the politics of fantasy in America*. New York: Grove.

Lane, F. (2000). *Obscene profits: The entrepreneurs of pornography in the cyber age*. New York: Routledge.

Lederer, L., & Delgado, R. (Eds.). (1995). *The price we pay: The case against racist speech, hate propaganda, and pornography*. New York: Hill and Wang.

Levin, D. (1998). *Remote control childhood? Combating the hazards of media culture*. Washington, DC: National Association for the Education of Young Children.

MacKinnon, C., & Dworkin, A. (Eds.). (1997). *In harm's way: The pornography civil rights hearings*. Cambridge, MA: Harvard University Press.

Maschke, K. (Ed.). (1997). *Pornography, sex work, and hate speech*. New York: Garland.

O'Toole, L. (1998). *Pornocopia: Porn, sex, technology and desire*. London: Serpent's Tail.

Potter, J. (1999). *On media violence*. Thousand Oaks, CA: Sage.

Prince, S. (Ed.). (2000). *Screening violence*. New Brunswick, NJ: Rutgers University Press.

Russell, D. (Ed.). (1993). *Making violence sexy*. New York: Teachers College Press.

Russell, D. (1998). *Dangerous relationships: Pornography, misogyny, and rape*. Thousand Oaks, CA: Sage.

Seiter, E. (1999). *Television and new media audiences*. Oxford and New York: Clarendon.

Thompson, K. (1999). *Moral panics*. New York: Routledge.

Torr, J. (Ed.). (2001). *Violence in the media*. San Diego, CA: Greenhaven.

Wekesser, C. (Ed.). (1997). *Pornography: Opposing viewpoints*. San Diego, CA: Greenhaven.

Zillmann, D., & Vorderer, P. (Eds.). (2000). *Media entertainment: The psychology of its appeal*. Mahwah, NJ: Lawrence Erlbaum.

◆ TV by Day

Allen, R. (1985). *Speaking of soap operas*. Chapel Hill: University of North Carolina Press.

Allen, R. (Ed.). (1995). *To be continued: Soap operas around the world*. London and New York: Routledge.

Ang, I. (1985). *Watching Dallas*. London: Methuen.

Baym, N. K. (2000). *Tune in, log on: Soaps, fandom, and online community*. Thousand Oaks, CA: Sage.

Blumenthal, D. (1997). *Women and soap opera: A cultural feminist perspective*. Westport, CT: Praeger.

Brown, M. (1994). *Soap opera and women's talk: The pleasure of resistance*. Thousand Oaks, CA: Sage.

Brunsdon, C. (2000). *The feminist, the housewife, and the soap opera*. New York: Oxford University Press.

Frentz, S. (Ed.). (1992). *Staying tuned: Contemporary soap opera criticism*. Bowling Green, OH: Bowling Green State University Popular Press.

Gamson, J. (1998). *Freaks talk back: Tabloid talk shows and sexual nonconformity*. Chicago: University of Chicago Press.

Glynn, K. (2000). *Tabloid culture: Trash taste, popular power, and the transformation of American television*. Durham, NC: Duke University Press.

Gripsrud, J. (1995). *The dynasty years: Hollywood television and critical media studies*. London and New York: Routledge.

Harrington, L., & Bielby, D. (1995). *Soap fans: Pursuing pleasure and making meaning in everyday life*. Philadelphia: Temple University Press.

Hayward, J. (1997). *Consuming pleasures: Active audiences and serial fictions from Dickens to soap opera*. Lexington: University of Kentucky Press.

Matelski, M. (1999). *Soap operas worldwide: Cultural and serial realities*. Jefferson, NC: McFarland & Co.

Modleski, T. (1982). *Loving with a vengeance: Mass-produced fantasies for women*. New York: Methuen.

Mumford, L. (1995). *Love and ideology in the afternoon: Soap opera, women, and television genre*. Bloomington: Indiana University Press.

Nochimson, M. (1992). *No end to her: Soap opera and the female subject*. Berkeley: University of California Press.

Shattuc, J. (1997). *The talking cure: TV talk shows and women*. New York: Routledge.

Tolson, A. (Ed.). (2001). *Television talk shows: Discourse, performance, spectacle*. Mahwah, NJ: Lawrence Erlbaum.

TV by Night ◆

Antler, J. (Ed.). (1998). *Talking back: Images of Jewish women in American popular culture*. Hanover, NH: University Press of New England.

Barrett, M., & Barrett, D. (2001). Star Trek: *The human frontier.* New York: Routledge.

Bettig, R., V. (1993). *Who owns prime time? The political economy of television program and broadcast rights.* New York: Routledge.

Bonann, G., & Lewis, B. (2000). Baywatch: *Rescued from prime time.* Beverly Hills, CA: Millennium.

Budd, M., & Steinman, C. (1999). *Consuming environments: Television and commercial culture.* New Brunswick, NJ: Rutgers University Press.

Butler, J. (2002). *Television: Critical methods and applications.* Mahwah, NJ: Lawrence Erlbaum.

Cantor, M. (1991). *Prime-time television: Content and control.* Newbury Park, CA: Sage.

Cantor, P. (2001). *Gilligan unbound: Popular culture in the age of globalization.* Lanham, MD: Rowman & Littlefield.

Cuklanz, L. M. (2000). *Rape on prime time: Television, masculinity, and sexual violence.* Philadelphia: University of Pennsylvania Press.

D'Acci, J. (1994). *Defining women: Television and the case of* Cagney & Lacey. Chapel Hill: University of North Carolina Press.

Dow, B. (1996). *Prime-time feminism: Television, media culture, and the women's movement since 1970.* Philadelphia: University of Pennsylvania Press.

Geraghty, C. (1991). *Women and soap opera: A study of prime time soaps.* Cambridge, UK: Polity.

Gitlin, T. (2000). *Inside prime time.* Berkeley: University of California Press.

Gray, H. (1995). *Watching race: Television and the struggle for blackness.* Minneapolis: University of Minnesota Press.

Inness, S. (1999). *Tough girls: Women warriors and wonder women in popular culture.* Philadelphia: University of Pennsylvania Press.

Irwin, W., Conard, M., & Skoble, A. (Eds.). (2001). The Simpsons *and philosophy: The D'oh! of Homer.* Chicago: Open Court.

Jarvis, R., & Joseph, P. (Eds.). (1998). *Prime time law: Fictional television as legal narrative.* Durham, NC: Carolina Academic Press.

McKinley, G., (1997). Beverly Hills, 90210: *Television, gender, and identity.* Philadelphia: University of Pennsylvania Press.

Miller, M. C. (1988). *Boxed in: The culture of TV.* Evanston, IL: Northwestern University Press.

Moorti, S. (2001). *Color of rape: Gender and race in television's public sphere.* New York: State University of New York Press.

Osgerby, B., & Gough-Yates, A. (2001). *Action TV, tough guys, smooth operators and foxy chicks.* New York: Routledge.

Parenti, M. (1992). *Make-believe media: The politics of entertainment.* New York: St. Martin's.

Pomerance, M., & Sakeris, J. (Eds.). (1998). *Bang BANG, shoot SHOOT! Essays on guns and popular culture.* New York: Simon & Schuster.

Projansky, S. (2001). *Watching rape: Film and television in postfeminist culture.* New York: New York University Press.

Sander, M., & Rock, M. (1994). *Waiting for prime time: The women of television news.* Urbana: University of Illinois Press.

Scheuer, J., (2001). *The sound bite society: How television helps the right and hurts the left.* New York: Routledge.

Shanahan, J., & Morgan, M. (1999). *Television and its viewers: Cultivation theory and research.* Cambridge, UK: Cambridge University Press.

Shubik, I. (2000). *Play for today: The evolution of television drama.* Manchester, UK: Manchester University Press.

Stark, S. (1997). *Glued to the set: The 60 television shows that made us who we are today.* New York: Delta Books.

Suman, M. (Ed.). (1997). *Religion and prime time television.* Westport, CT: Praeger.

Taylor, E. (1989). *Prime-time families: Television culture in postwar America.* Berkeley: University of California Press.

Torres, S. (Ed.). (1998). *Living color: Race and television in the United States.* Durham, NC: Duke University Press.

Treichler, A., Grossberg, L., & Fiske, J. (Eds.). (1987). *Intersections of power:*

Criticism-television-gender. New York: Gordon and Breach.

Zillmann, D., & Vorderer, P. (Eds.). (2000). *Media entertainment: The psychology of its appeal.* Mahwah, NJ: Lawrence Erlbaum.

◆ *The Internet*

Baym, N. K. (2000). *Tune in, log on: Soaps, fandom, and online community.* Thousand Oaks, CA: Sage.

Bell, D. (2001). *An introduction to cybercultures.* New York: Routledge.

Bell, D., & Kennedy, B. (2000). *The cybercultures reader.* London: Routledge.

Bolter, J., & Grusin, R. (1999). *Remediation: Understanding new media.* Cambridge, MA: MIT Press.

Dodge, M., & Kitchin, R., (2000). *Mapping cyberspace.* New York: Routledge.

Dutton, W., Ellison, N., Loader, D., & Pleace, N. (Eds.). (2002). *Cyberculture: The key concepts.* New York: Routledge.

Featherstone, M., & Burrows, R. (Eds.). (1996). *Cyberspace/cyberbodies/cyberpunk: Cultures of technological embodiment.* London: Sage.

Gauntlett, D. (Ed.). (2000). *Web.studies: Rewiring media studies for the digital age.* London: Arnold.

Green, L. (2002). *Communication, technology, and society.* Thousand Oaks, CA: Sage.

Hague, B., & Loader, B. (Eds.). (1999). *Digital democracy: Discourse and decision Making in the information age.* London: Routledge.

Hakkem, D. (1999). *Cybergs @ cyberspace: An ethnographer looks to the future.* New York: Routledge.

Harcourt, W. (Ed.). (1999). *Women @ Internet: Creating new cultures in cyberspace.* London: Zed Books.

Hawisher, G., & Selfe, C. (Eds.). (2000). *Global literacies and the World-Wide Web.* London: Routledge.

Herman, A., & Swiss, T. (Eds.). (2000). *The World Wide Web and contemporary cultural theory.* London: Routledge.

Jones, S. G. (Ed.). (1998). *Cybersociety 2.0: Revisiting computer-mediated communication and community.* Thousand Oaks, CA: Sage.

Jones, S. G. (Ed.). (1999). *Doing Internet research: Critical issues and methods for examining the Net.* London: Sage.

Kolko, B., Nakamura, L., & Rodman, G. (Eds.). (2000). *Race in cyberspace.* London: Routledge.

Lievrouw, L. A., & Livingstone, S. (Eds.). (2002). *Handbook of new media: Social shaping and consequences of ICTs.* London: Sage.

Livingstone, S. (2002). *Young people and new media.* London: Sage.

Loader, B. (1997). *The governance of cyberspace: Politics, technology and global restructuring.* New York: Routledge.

Loader, B. (Ed.). (1998). *Cyberspace divide: Equality, agency and policy in the information society.* London: Routledge.

Ludlow, P. (Ed.). (1999). *High noon on the electronic frontier: Conceptual issues in cyberspace.* Cambridge, MA: MIT Press.

Ludlow, P. (Ed.). (2001). *Crypto anarchy, cyberstates, and pirate utopias.* Cambridge, MA: MIT Press.

Mackay, H., & O'Sullivan, T. (Eds.). (1999). *The media reader: Continuity and transformation.* Thousand Oaks, CA: Sage.

Mosco, V., & Schiller, D. (Eds.). (2001). *Continental order? Integrating North America for cybercapitalism.* Lanham, MD: Rowman & Littlefield.

Porter, D. (Ed.). (1997). *Internet culture.* New York: Routledge.

Samoriski, J. (2001). *Issues in cyberspace: Communication, technology, law, and society on the Internet frontiers.* Boston: Allyn & Bacon.

Shields, R. (Ed.). (1996). *Cultures of the Internet: Virtual spaces, real histories, living bodies.* London: Sage.

Slevin, J. (2000). *The Internet and society.* Cambridge, UK: Polity.

Smith, M., & Kollock, P. (Eds.). (1999). *Communities in cyberspace*. New York: Routledge.

Swiss, T. (Ed.). (2000). *Unspun: Key concepts for understanding the World Wide Web*. New York: New York University Press.

Toulouse, C., & Luke, T. (1998). *The politics of cyberspace*. New York: Routledge.

Turkle, S. (1995). *Life on the screen: Identity in the age of the Internet*. New York: Simon & Schuster.

AUTHOR INDEX

Fahey, P., 125
Faison, S., 197
Faludi, S., 240
Farnall, O., 300
Fass, P., 698
Faust, B., 72
Fejes, F., 215, 216, 303, 304
Feng, P., 658
Fennick, J., 96
Feuer, J., 472, 479, 731
Firestone, S., 121
Fisher, K., 125
Fiske, J., 16, 17, 117, 305, 479, 484,
    485, 502, 663, 729, 732, 734
Flatt, V., 217
Floyd, K., 493
Flynt, L., 455
Forna, A., 452
Foster, D., 718
Foucault, M., 104, 275, 527, 717
Frederick, C., 231
Freedman, E., 5
Freitas, A., 316, 330
Friend, R., 702
Fritsch, J., 197
Frye, M., 420
Fung, R., 657
Furnham, A., 368
Fuss, D., 104, 105

Gabor, M., 235
Gadon, E., 448
Gagnon, J. H., 216
Gans, H., 576
Garbarino, J., 360
Gates, H. L., Jr., 80
Gauntlett, D., 406, 407
Gebhardt, L., 408
Geng, V., 122
Geraghty, C., 473
Gerbner, G., 340, 343, 345, 364, 656
Giacquinta, J. B., 691
Gibbs, M., 500
Gibson, D. P., 288
Gibson, P. C., 412
Gibson, R., 412
Giddens, A., 703, 704, 705
Giery, M. A., 408
Gillespie, M., 689
Gilligan, C., 700
Gilligan, J., 438
Gingrich, A., 231, 235
Gitlin, T., 62, 577, 578, 579, 580, 581
Gladwell, M., 163
Glennon, L. M., 575, 580

Gluckman, A., 304
Goerne, C., 296
Goffman, E., 265, 302, 315, 317, 479
Goldberg, C., 163
Goldenberg, S., 418, 419
Golding, P., 734
Goldman, K., 296
Goldman, R., 316
Gombrich, E., 454
Gomery, D., 583
Goodman, E., 262
Goss, J., 164, 165
Gottdeiner, M., 164
Gragg, R., 160, 161
Graham, L., 439
Gramsci, A., 11, 62, 550
Gray, A., 483, 691
Gray, H., 451, 602
Gray, P., 691
Greenberg, B. S., 101
Greenberg, J., 363
Gregware, P., 446
Griffin, S., 435
Gross, L., 101, 340, 343, 345, 598, 600
Grover, R., 608, 609
Gubernick, L., 166
Guernica, A., 289
Guerrero, E., 451, 452
Gurak, L., 717
Gutfield, G., 445
Guy, R., 121

Habermas, J., 530, 531, 532
Haddon, L., 691
Hahn, H., 296, 297
Haineault, D. L., 304
Hall, C., 316, 330
Hall, S., 15, 17, 61, 62, 64, 65, 126, 200,
    305, 551, 729
Hammidi, T., 316, 330
Handy, B., 609, 610
Hanke, R., 350
Harding, S., 420
Hardy, S., 407, 409, 412
Harrington, S., 119
Hart, K., 600, 602
Hartley, J., 473
Hartmann, P., 691
Hartnett, M., 160, 161
Haytko, D. L., 329
Healy, E., 320
Heath, D., 316
Helm, L., 690
Hendrix, K., 363
Henley, N. M., 315, 320, 322, 323, 327

SUBJECT INDEX

ABOUT THE EDITORS

Gail Dines is Associate Professor of Sociology and Women's Studies at Wheelock College and chair of the American Studies Department. She lectures on pornography and violence at colleges and community groups throughout the United States, and she is coauthor of *Pornography: The Production and Consumption of Inequality* (1998).

Jean M. Humez is Professor of Women's Studies at the University of Massachusetts, Boston, and teaches both women's studies and American studies courses. She has published books and articles on African American women's spiritual and secular autobiographies, and on women and gender in Shaker religion. She is currently at work on a documentary biography of Harriet Tubman.

ABOUT THE CONTRIBUTORS

Joyce Antler is Chair of the American Studies Department at Brandeis University, where she is also Samuel Lane Professor of American Jewish History and Culture. She is author of *The Journey Home: How Jewish Women Shaped Modern America* (1997).

Ellen R. Arnold is Assistant Professor of English at East Carolina University. She is author of *Conversations With Leslie Marmon Silko* (2000).

Rhona O. Bautista is the Resource Centre Administrator of Isis International, a feminist nongovernmental organization (NGO) dedicated to women's information and communication needs by creating and strengthening alternative networks and channels for women's advocacy. She is also a member of the Women's Networking Support Program of the Association for Progressive Communications (APCWNSP).

Nancy K. Baym is Assistant Professor of Communication Studies at the University of Kansas. She is author of *Tune In, Log On: Soaps, Fandom, and Online Community* (2000) and editor of a special issue of the *Electronic Journal of Communication* on the topic of interpersonal relationships and the Internet.

Chris Berry is Associate Professor of Film Studies and Dramatic Art at the University of California, Berkeley, and coeditor *of The Filmmaker and the Prostitute: Dennis O'Rourke's "The Good Woman of Bangkok."*

◆ 771

Donald Bogle teaches at the University of Pennsylvania and New York University. He is author of five books about representations of blacks in popular media. He has also published *Dorothy Dandridge: A Biography* (1997).

Karen Boyle is Lecturer in Women's Studies at the University of Wolverhampton and author of *Feminist Perspectives on Media Violence* (forthcoming, 2003).

Kenon Breazeale is Professor of Art at California State University, Northridge, and author of "The Female Nude in Public Art: Constructing Women's Sexual Identity in the Visual Arts" (1986).

Richard Butsch is Professor of Sociology at Rider University, Lawrenceville, New Jersey. He is author of *The Making of American Audiences* (2000) and editor of *For Fun and Profit: The Transformation of Leisure Into Consumption*.

Jackie Byars is Associate Professor of Communication and Codirector of Film Studies at Wayne State University. With Eileen Meehan, she is author of the forthcoming book *Telefeminism: The Lifetime Cable Channel*.

Jane Caputi is Professor of Women's Studies at Florida Atlantic University. She is author of *The Age of Sex Crime* (1987) and *Gossips, Gorgons, and Crones* (1993). Her current book project is *Cuncti-potence: On Female Potency and Possibility*.

Nancy Carlsson-Paige is Professor at Lesley University and a cofounder of Lesley's master's degree program in conflict resolution and peaceable schools. She has coauthored four books and many articles with Diane Levin on topics that relate to how young children learn violent attitudes and behaviors and how they learn the skills of peacemaking and conflict resolution.

Chong Heup Cho did his doctoral work in the Department of Communication Arts at the University of Wisconsin–Madison. His research included a study of the cultural

politics and dependent economy of an authoritarian state.

Lynn Schofield Clark is a postdoctoral fellow at the Center for Mass Media Research at the University of Colorado at Boulder. She is coeditor of *Practicing Religion in the Age of the Media* (2001).

Robin R. Means Coleman is Assistant Professor of Media Ecology at New York University and editor of *Say It Loud! African American Audiences, Media, and Identity* (2001).

Diana Crane is Professor of Sociology at the University of Pennsylvania. She is author, most recently, of *Production of Culture: Media and the Urban Arts* (1992) and *Fashion and Its Social Agendas: Class, Gender and Identity in Clothing* (2000).

David Croteau is Associate Professor of Sociology and Anthropology at Virginia Commonwealth University. He is coauthor, with William Hoynes, of *The Business of Media: Corporate Media and the Public Interest* (2001).

Susan G. Davis is Division Administration of Humanities and Social Sciences at Caltech and author of *Spectacular Nature: Corporate Culture and the Sea World Experience*.

Fred Fejes is Professor of Communication at Florida Atlantic University. He is author of "Murder, Perversion and Moral Panic: The 1954 Media Campaign Against Miami's Homosexuals and the Discourse of Civic Betterment."

John Fiske, now retired, was Professor of Communication Arts at the University of Wisconsin–Madison. He has written widely on popular culture and is author of *Media Matters: Everyday Culture and Political Change* (1996).

Joshua Gamson is Associate Professor of Sociology at Yale University. He is author of *Claims to Fame: Celebrity in Contemporary America* (1994) as well as *Freaks Talk Back: Tabloid Talk Shows and Sexual Nonconformity* (1998).

George Gerbner is Bell Atlantic Professor of Telecommunications at Temple University and Dean Emeritus of the Annenberg School for Communication at the University of Pennsylvania. He is the author of numerous articles and books on the media.

Sanjukta Ghosh is Professor in the Department of Communication at Castleton State College in Vermont, where she teaches cultural studies. Interested particularly in race, class, and gender issues, she has also written on postcolonial cinema. Currently, she is finishing a book-length manuscript on representations of South Asians in U.S. media.

Henry A. Giroux holds the Waterbury Chair Professorship at Penn State University. His latest books are *Public Spaces, Private Lives: Beyond the Culture of Cynicism* (2001) and *Breaking Into the Movies: Film and the Politics of Culture* (2002).

Sean Griffin is Assistant Professor in Cinema-Television at Meadows School of the Arts, Southern Methodist University. He is author of *Tinker Belles and Evil Queens: The Walt Disney Company From the Inside Out* (2000), as well as articles on animation, soap operas, Internet fan culture, and musicals.

Félix Gutiérrez is Senior Vice President of Newseum and former Executive Director of the Freedom Forum Pacific Coast Center.

Stuart Hall is Professor of Sociology at the Open University in England and is one of the founders of the Centre for Contemporary Cultural Studies at the University of Birmingham in England. He has published widely and is coeditor of *Questions of Cultural Identity* (1997).

Beth A. Haller is Associate Professor in the Department of Mass Communication and Communication Studies at Towson University. Her research has been published in journals such as the *Journal of Magazine and New Media Research, Journalism Studies, Disability & Society,* and the *Journal of Popular Film and Television.*

Kylo-Patrick R. Hart is Assistant Professor of Mass Communication at the University of Virginia's College at Wise. He is author of *The AIDS Movie: Representing a Pandemic in Film and Television* (2000).

Jennifer Hayward is Assistant Professor of English at the College of Wooster. Her book *Consuming Pleasures: Active Audiences and Serial Fictions From Dickens to Soap Opera* was named an Outstanding Academic Book for 1998 by *Choice* magazine.

William Hoynes is Associate Professor of Sociology at Vassar. He is coauthor with David Croteau of *The Business of Media: Corporate Media and the Public Interest* (2001).

Susan J. Hubert teaches English and women's studies at Western Michigan University. She is author of *Questions of Power: The Politics of Women's Madness Narratives* (2002).

Henry Jenkins is Director of the Comparative Media Studies Program at Massachusetts Institute of Technology and author of six books and more than 50 essays on popular culture. He is coeditor, with Justine Cassell, of *From Barbie to Mortal Kombat: Gender and Computer Games* (1998) and author of *Textual Poachers: Television Fans and Participatory Culture* (1992).

Robert Jensen is Associate Professor in the Department of Journalism at the University of Texas at Austin. He is coeditor of the collection of essays *Freeing the First Amendment: Critical Perspectives on Freedom of Expression* (1995).

Sut Jhally is Professor of Communications at the University of Massachusetts, Amherst. He is author of the forthcoming book *Advertising and the End of the World.* Jhally is also founder of the Media Education Foundation that has produced films for classroom use such as *Dream-Worlds* and *Slim Hopes*.

Jackson Katz is the creator of the educational video *Tough Guise: Violence, Media and the Crisis in Masculinity*. He is also founder of the Mentors in Violence Prevention (MVP) model for gender violence and bullying prevention.

Douglas Kellner is George Kneller Chair in the Philosophy of Education at the University of California, Los Angeles, and is author of many books on social theory, politics, history, and culture, including *Media Spectacle and the Theft of an Election* (2001) and *The Postmodern Adventure. Science, Technology, and Cultural Studies at the Third Millennium*, coauthored with Steve Best (2001).

Jean Kilbourne is an independent scholar and lecturer internationally recognized for her pioneering critical work on alcohol and tobacco advertising and the image of women in advertising. Her latest documentary film is *Killing Us Softly 3*.

Pat Kirkham is Professor at the Bard Graduate Center. She is editor *of Women Designers in the USA, 1900-2000: Diversity and Difference* (2000).

Minu Lee is a former broadcaster in Seoul, Korea. At the time her chapter was published, she was at the University of Wisconsin–Madison, working on research on soap operas and the politics of domestic leisure in Korea.

Diane E. Levin is Professor of Education at Wheelock College, where she teaches courses on children's play, media, and violence and a summer institute on media education in a violent society. She is author of six books including *Remote Control Childhood? Combating the Hazards of Media Culture,* and *Teaching Young Children in Violent Times: Building a Peaceable Classroom* and the cofounder of TRUCE (Teachers Resisting Unhealthy Children's Entertainment), an advocacy group that works to promote positive media and play.

Karen Lindsey is a Boston-based teacher, writer, poet, soap opera fan, and media analyst with many books to her credit, including *Divorced, Beheaded, Survived: A Feminist Reinterpretation of the Wives of Henry VIII* (1995). She has also collaborated with Susan Love on books on the breast and menopause.

George Lipsitz is Professor of Ethnic Studies at the University of California, San Diego. He is author of *The Possessive Investment in Whiteness: How White People Profit From Identity Politics* (1998).

Brain Locke is Assistant Professor of English at the University of Utah. His publications include "'Top Dog,' 'Black Threat,' and 'Japanese Cats': The Impact of the White-Black Binary on Asian American Identity" in *Radical Philosophy Review* (1998).

James Lull is Professor of Communication Studies at San Jose State University. He is author of *Culture in the Communication Age* (2001).

Fran Martin currently lectures in the Cultural Studies Program at the University of Melbourne. She is coediting with Chris Berry and Audrey Yue a collection of essays called *Mobile Cultures: New Media and Queer Asia*.

Robert McChesney is Research Associate Professor at the University of Illinois at Urbana-Champaign. He is author of *Rich Media, Poor Democracy: Communication Politics in Dubious Times* (1999).

Eileen R. Meehan is Professor of Communications at the University of Arizona. She and Jackie Byars collaborated on the forthcoming book *Telefeminism: The Lifetime Cable Channel*.

Sujata Moorti is Assistant Professor of Women's Studies at Old Dominion University. She is author of *The Color of Rape: Gender & Race in Television's Public Sphere* (2001).

Lisa Nakamura is Assistant Professor of English at Sonoma State University, where she teaches postcolonial literature and critical theory. She is author of *Cybertypes: Race, Ethnicity, and Identity on the Internet* (2002).

Laurie Ouellette is Assistant Professor of Media Studies at Queens College, City University of New York. Her forthcoming book is on cultural studies and public broadcasting.

Janice Peck is Associate Professor of Journalism at the University of Colorado. She is author of *The Gods of Televangelism* (1993).

Imani Perry is Research Fellow and Adjunct Professor at Georgetown University Law Center. She has completed a forthcoming book called *Prophets of the Hood: Politics and Poetics in Hip Hop*.

Jan Nederveen Pieterse has taught at universities in the Netherlands, Ghana, and the United States and is presently Associate Professor of Sociology at the Institute of Social Studies in The Hague. He is editor of *World Orders in the Making: Humanitarian Intervention and Beyond* (1998).

Darcy C. Plymire is Adjunct Instructor in the Department of Interdisciplinary Studies and Women's Studies at Appalachian State University.

Janice A. Radway is Francis Fox Professor of Literature at Duke University. Most recently, she is author of *A Feeling for Books: The Book-of-the-Month Club, Literary Taste, and Middle-Class Desire* (1997).

Sue Ralph is Senior Lecturer in Education and the Mass Media, School of Education, University of Manchester (UK). Her research has been published in journals such as *Journalism Studies*, *Research in Social Science and Disability*, *Journal of the Multi-Handicapped Person*, *Australian Disability Review*, and *British Journal of Special Education*.

Diane Raymond is Professor of Philosophy and Women's Studies and Associate Dean at Simmons College in Boston. She is author of *Existentialism and the Philosophical Tradition* and editor of *Sexual Politics and Popular Culture* as well as numerous articles in the fields of applied ethics and feminist/queer theory. She is currently working on a book-length project on feminist conceptions of autonomy and community.

Frank Rich is an op ed columnist for the *New York Times* and a senior writer for the magazine.

Deborah D. Rogers is Professor of English at the University of Maine. Her publications include *The Critical Response to Ann Radcliffe* (1994).

Mary F. Rogers is Professor of Sociology at the University of West Florida, Pensacola. She is author of *Barbie Culture* (1999) and coeditor, with Susan E. Chase, of *Mothers and Children: Feminist Analyses and Personal Narratives* (2001).

Tricia Rose is Assistant Professor of History and Africana Studies at New York University. She is author of *Black Noise: Rap Music and Black Culture in Contemporary America* (1994).

Juliet Schor is Professor of Sociology at Boston College. She is author *of The Overspent American: Upscaling, Downshifting, and the New Consumer* (1998).

Christine Scodari is Associate Professor of Communication at Florida Atlantic University. She is coauthor of *Creating a Pocket Universe: 'Shippers,' Fan Fiction, and* The X-Files *Online*.

Ellen Seiter is Professor of Communications at the University of San Diego. She has written widely on children and the media. Her many books include *Sold Separately: Children and Parents in Consumer Culture* (1993).

Katherine Sender is Assistant Professor at the Annenberg School for Communication at the University of Pennsylvania. She has produced, directed, edited, and written documentary programs, including *Off the*

Straight and Narrow: Lesbians, Gays, Bisexuals, and Television (Media Education Foundation).

Ann Barr Snitow teaches gender studies at the New School University. She is coeditor of *The Feminist Memoir Project: Voices From Women's Liberation* (1998).

Carol A. Stabile is Associate Professor of Communications and Director of Women's Studies at the University of Pittsburgh. She is coeditor of *Turning the Century: Essays in Media and Cultural Studies* (2000).

Gloria Steinem was founding editor of *Ms.* magazine—the first national women's magazine run by women. She is author of many articles and books including *Revolution From Within: A Book of Self Esteem* (1994).

Chyng Feng Sun is the producer of *Mickey Mouse Monopoly: Disney, Childhood and Corporate Power*. A children's book author in Chinese and English, she is currently a Ph.D. candidate in communication at the University of Massachusetts, Amherst.

Jo Tavener has taught in the Department of Communication at the University of Pittsburgh and is author of "Media, Morality, and Madness: The Case Against Sleaze TV," in *Critical Studies in Media Communication* (2000).

Fred Turner is author of *Echoes of Combat: The Vietnam War in American Memory* (1996).

Alex Weller is at the youth and lifestyle agency Third Planet International, specializing in freesports marketing.

Clint C. Wilson II is Associate Professor of Print Journalism at Howard University. He is coauthor of *A History of the Black Press* (1997).

Kristal Brent Zook is a journalist and Assistant Professor of Pan African Studies at California State University, Northridge. She is author of *Color by Fox: The Fox Network and the Revolution in Black Television* (1999).